T0255424

Lecture Notes in Computer Science   11125

Commenced Publication in 1973
Founding and Former Series Editors:
Gerhard Goos, Juris Hartmanis, and Jan van Leeuwen

Editorial Board

More information about this series at http://www.springer.com/series/7410

Chunhua Su · Hiroaki Kikuchi (Eds.)

Information Security Practice and Experience

14th International Conference, ISPEC 2018
Tokyo, Japan, September 25–27, 2018
Proceedings

 Springer

Editors
Chunhua Su
University of Aizu
Aizuwakamatsu
Japan

Hiroaki Kikuchi
Meiji University
Tokyo
Japan

ISSN 0302-9743   ISSN 1611-3349   (electronic)
Lecture Notes in Computer Science
ISBN 978-3-319-99806-0   ISBN 978-3-319-99807-7   (eBook)
https://doi.org/10.1007/978-3-319-99807-7

Library of Congress Control Number: 2018952672

LNCS Sublibrary: SL4 – Security and Cryptology

This Springer imprint is published by the registered company Springer Nature Switzerland AG
The registered company address is: Gewerbestrasse 11, 6330 Cham, Switzerland

Preface

This volume contains the papers presented at ISPEC 2018: the 14th International Conference on Information Security Practice and Experience held during September 25–27, 2018, in Tokyo.

The ISPEC conference series is an established forum that brings together researchers and practitioners to provide a confluence of new information security technologies, including their applications and their integration with IT systems in various vertical sectors. Previously, ISPEC took place in Singapore (2005), Hangzhou, China (2006), Hong Kong, SAR China (2007), Sydney, Australia (2008), Xi'an, China (2009), Seoul, Korea (2010), Guangzhou, China (2011), Hangzhou, China (2012), Lanzhou, China (2013), Fuzhou, China (2014), Beijing, China (2015), Zhangjiajie, China (2016) and Melbourne, Australia (2017).

In this year, there were 73 submissions in total. Each submission was reviewed by an average of 2.8 Program Committee (PC) members. The committee decided to accept two invited papers, 25 full papers, and 12 short papers, with an acceptance ratio of 34.2%. ISPEC 2018 was made possible by the joint effort of numerous people and organizations worldwide. There is a long list of people who volunteered their time and energy to put together the conference and who deserve special thanks. First and foremost, we are deeply grateful to all the PC members for their great effort in reading, commenting on, debating, and finally selecting the papers. We also thank all the external reviewers for assisting the PC in their particular areas of expertise.

We would like to emphasize our gratitude to the general chairs, Prof. Kazuamsa Omote and Prof. Jiageng Chen, for their generous support and leadership that ensured the success of the conference. Thanks also go to the liaison chair, Dr. Naoto Yanai, the local organizing chair, Dr. Keita Emura, the publication chairs, Dr. Weizhi Meng and Prof. Takeshi Okamoto, the publicity chair, Prof. Atsuo Inomata, and the registration chair, Prof. Masaki Fujikawa.

We sincerely thank the authors of all submitted papers and all the conference attendees. Thanks are also due to the staff at Springer for their help in producing the proceedings and to the developers and maintainers of the EasyChair software, which greatly helped simplify the submission and review process. Last but certainly not least, our thanks go to the Japanese Research Society ISEC of IEICE and CSEC of IPSJ for supporting the conference, as well as Hitachi, Ltd., Mitsubishi Electric Corporation, TOSHIBA Corporation, Huawei Technologies Co., Ltd., and ANDISEC, Ltd. for sponsoring the conference.

July 2018

Chunhua Su
Hiroaki Kikuchi

Organization

Honorary Chair

Eiji Okamoto   University of Tsukuba, Japan

General Co-chairs

Kazumasa Omote   University of Tsukuba, Japan
Jiageng Chen   Central China Normal University, China

Program Co-chairs

Chunhua Su   University of Aizu, Japan
Hiroaki Kikuchi   Meiji University, Japan

Liaison Chair

Naoto Yanai   Osaka University, Japan

Local Organizing Chair

Keita Emura   NICT, Japan

Publication Co-chairs

Weizhi Meng   Technical University of Denmark, Denmark
Takeshi Okamoto   Tsukuba University of Technology, Japan

Publicity Co-chairs

Debiao He   Wuhan University, China
Atsuo Inomata   Tokyo Denki University/NAIST, Japan

Registration Chair

Masaki Fujikawa   Kogakuin University, Japan

Web Chair

Kaitai Liang   University of Surrey, UK

Program Committee

Man Ho Au	The Hong Kong Polytechnic University, SAR China
Joonsang Baek	University of Wollongong, Australia
Aniello Castiglione	University of Salerno, Italy
David Chadwick	University of Kent, UK
Xiaofeng Chen	Xidian University, China
Chen-Mou Cheng	Osaka University, Japan
K. Raymond Choo	The University of Texas at San Antonio, USA
Mauro Conti	University of Padua, Italy
Robert Deng	Singapore Management University, Singapore
Dieter Gollmann	Hamburg University of Technology, Germany
Stefanos Gritzalis	University of the Aegean, Greece
Jinguang Han	University of Surrey, UK
Gerhard Hancke	ISG Smart Card Centre, Royal Holloway, University of London, UK
Shoichi Hirose	University of Fukui, Japan
Xinyi Huang	Fujian Normal University, China
Julian Jang-Jaccard	Massey University, New Zealand
Hiroaki Kikuchi	Meiji University, Japan
Kwangjo Kim	Korea Advanced Institute of Science and Technology, South Korea
Noboru Kunihiro	The University of Tokyo, Japan
Miroslaw Kutylowski	Wroclaw University of Technology, Poland
Costas Lambrinoudakis	University of Piraeus, Greece
Albert Levi	Sabanci University, Turkey
Shujun Li	University of Kent, UK
Yingjiu Li	Singapore Management University, Singapore
Joseph Liu	Monash University, Australia
Zhe Liu	Nanjing University of Aeronautics and Astronautics, Singapore
Giovanni Livraga	University of Milan, Italy
Javier Lopez	NICS Lab
Rongxing Lu	University of New Brunswick, Canada
Di Ma	University of Michigan, USA
Weizhi Meng	Technical University of Denmark
Chris Mitchell	Royal Holloway, University of London, UK
David Naccache	École normale supérieure, France
Günther Pernul	Universität Regensburg, Germany
Josef Pieprzyk	CSIRO/Data61, Australia
C. Pandu Rangan	Indian Institute of Technology Madras, India
Indrajit Ray	Colorado State University, USA
Na Ruan	Shanghai Jiao Tong University, China
Sushmita Ruj	Indian Statistical Institute, India
Pierangela Samarati	University of Milan, Italy
Jun Shao	Zhejiang Gongshang University, China

Willy Susilo	University of Wollongong, Australia
Qiang Tang	Cornell University, USA
Cong Wang	City University of Hong Kong, SAR China
Ding Wang	Peking University, China
Yu Wang	Guangzhou University, China
Qianhong Wu	Beihang University, China
Shouhuai Xu	University of Texas at San Antonio, USA
Toshihiro Yamauchi	Okayama University, Japan
Wun-She Yap	Universiti Tunku Abdul Rahman, Malaysia
Kuo-Hui Yeh	National Dong Hwa University, Taiwan
Xun Yi	RMIT University, Australia
Siu Ming Yiu	The University of Hong Kong, SAR China
Yong Yu	Shaanxi Normal University, China
Tsz Hon Yuen	Huawei, Singapore

Additional Reviewers

Ah, Hyunhcheol
Ahn, Hyunhcheol
Chakraborthy, Suvradip
Dietz, Marietheres
Gochhayat, Sarada Prasad
Guo, Jiale
Han, Shangbin
Huang, Hui
Jiang, Tao
Li, Yalan
Li, Zengpeng
Lin, Cheng-Han
Lin, Chengjun
Menges, Florian

Nieto, Ana
Pan, Jing
Paul, Arinjita
Poh, Geong Sen
Shen, Limin
Song, Yongcheng
Tang, Wenyi
Tian, Yangguang
Vielberth, Manfred
Wang, Chenyu
Wang, Jian
Yang, Xu
Zhang, Yuexin

Contents

(Post-quantum) Signature Schemes

Security Protocols

Network Security

Security in Mobile Environment

Secure Computation and Data Privacy

Cryptographic Protocols

System Security

Macros Finder: Do You Remember LOVELETTER?

Hiroya Miura$^{(\boxtimes)}$, Mamoru Mimura, and Hidema Tanaka

National Defense Academy, Yokosuka, Japan
{em56030,mim,hidema}@nda.ac.jp

Abstract. In recent years, the number of targeted email attacks which use Microsoft (MS) document files has been increasing. In particular, damage by malicious macros has spread in many organizations. Relevant work has proposed a method of malicious MS document files detection. To the best of our knowledge, however, no method of detecting malicious macros exists. Hence, we proposed a method which detects malicious macros themselves using machine learning. First, the proposed method creates corpuses from macros. Our method removes trivial words in the corpus. It becomes easy for the corpuses to classify malicious macros exactly. Second, Doc2Vec represents feature vectors from the corpuses. Malicious macros contain the context. Therefore, the feature vectors of Doc2Vec are classified with high accuracy. Machine learning models (Support Vector Machine, Random Forest and Multi Layer Perceptron) are trained, inputting the feature vectors and the labels. Finally, the trained models predict test feature vectors as malicious macros or benign macros. Evaluations show that the proposed method can obtain a high F-measure (0.93).

Keywords: Macro · Machine learning
Natural language processing technique · Bag-of-Words · Doc2Vec

1 Introduction

In recent years, email has become one of the most popular communication tools. In this situation, targeted email attacks have become a big threat to society. A targeted email attack is a specific attack in which the attacker attempts to persuade a victim to run specific action. Depending on the specific action, there are two types of targeted email attacks. One is to open malicious links and to download a malware, and the other is to open malicious attachments. Attackers attempt to earn credibility with their victims through an eloquent mail text. Moreover, the attackers convince victims to unknowingly download a malicious file attachment or click-through to a malicious site. According to a report published by Sophos [1], most targeted email attacks are the attachment type. Moreover, the report shows that 85% of the attached files are Microsoft Office documents (MS documents) files. The report shows that most malicious

© Springer Nature Switzerland AG 2018
C. Su and H. Kikuchi (Eds.): ISPEC 2018, LNCS 11125, pp. 3–18, 2018.
https://doi.org/10.1007/978-3-319-99807-7_1

MS document files have malicious macros. Malicious macros have a long history. For example, the LOVELETTER worm of malicious macro infected more than 45 million computers, and some organizations suffered serious damage in 2000. After that, the occurrence of malicious macros gradually slacked off. However, they were enlivened again from 2014 onwards.

Next, we show the importance of detecting malicious macros themselves. Relevant work [5] analyzes the structure of docx files, and detects malicious docx files. The work does not, however, discriminate between malicious macros and benign macros. If the dataset contains benign macros and malicious macros, the work probably cannot detect malicious docx files. If malicious docx files are camouflaged with a structure of benign docx files, attackers can probably evade the detection model. Detecting malicious macros themselves can overcome these weaknesses. Hence, detecting malicious macros is an effective and important method.

We will introduce an outline of the proposed method. The proposed method detects malicious macros themselves using machine learning. First, the proposed method creates corpuses from macros. Our method reduces trivial words in the corpus. It becomes easy for the corpuses to classify malicious macros exactly. We use Term Frequency (TF) or Term Frequency-Inverse Document Frequency (TFIDF) in the reducing words process. TF is a method which weights value corresponding to frequency of words in a corpus. TFIDF is a method which weights a representative word in a corpus. Second, Doc2Vec (D2V) or Bag-of-Words represents feature vectors from the corpuses. D2V is a model that represents vectors from the context of the documents. Bow is a method that represents vectors corresponding to the frequency of the words.

Next, Support Vector Machine (SVM), Random Forest (RF) and Multi Layer Perceptron (MLP) are trained, inputting the feature vectors and the labels. Finally, the trained models predict test feature vectors as malicious macros or benign macros.

Next, we will show three viewpoints of verification experiments in this paper.

(1) Which is more effective, TF or TFIDF?
(2) Which is more effective, D2V or Bow?
(3) What is the best combination of these methods and classifiers?

In order to answer these questions, we conducted verification experiments. Based on the results of these verification experiments, this paper makes the following contributions:

(1) we confirmed that D2V was effective in classifying malicious macros.
(2) we confirmed that reducing words using TF was effective in classifying malicious macros.
(3) we confirmed that classifiers in which the strong point was to solve the problem of linear separability, were effective in classifying malicious macros.

We will introduce the structure of this paper. Section 2 introduces relevant work and reveals the differences between this paper other and relevant study.

Section 3 presents an overview of the background. Section 4 presents the proposed method. Section 5 describes experiments. Section 6 discusses the results of the experiments. Finally, we conclude this paper.

2   Related Work

In targeted email attacks, attackers use document files in which are embedded malicious source codes, or executable files. Most malicious executable files are camouflaged with a change of document icon and the file extension. Methods of detecting these malicious files can be categorized into static analysis and dynamic analysis. Dynamic analysis is the testing and evaluation of a program by executing data in real-time. Static analysis is a method of program debugging that is done by examining the code without executing the program.

Malicious document files are roughly categorized into MS document files and PDF files [1]. This section presents the relevant work in two parts (MS document files detection and malicious PDF files detection). Since our method does not execute specimens for detecting malicious macros, our method is the static analysis. Therefore, we present the relevant work within the static analysis range, in this section.

We will show representative work for malicious executable files detection using the dynamic analysis, as a reference. Rieck et al. [2] proposed a framework for the dynamic analysis of malicious executable binaries behavior using machine learning. Bayer et al. [3] proposed a tool which monitors the behavior of Windows API, to classify malicious executable files. Next, we will show representative work for malicious executable files detection using the static analysis. Perdisci et al. [4] proposed a framework which detects malicious executable files using the static analysis. The framework classifies malicious executable codes using n-gram analysis. Even if executable files are packed, the framework is able to classify.

MS Document File. This section presents relevant work on the detection of malicious MS document files. Nissim et al. [5] proposed a framework (ALDOCX) that classifies malicious docx files using various machine learning classifiers. ALDOCX created feature vectors from the path structure of docx files. This is a practical method, because ALDOCX framework has updatability and incorporates new unseen malicious docx files created daily. Naser et al. [6] proposed a method to detect malicious docx files. The method parses structure of docx files, and analyzes suspicious keywords. These works do not support the classification of Excel files and Power Point files. Our method, however, can be applied to malicious MS document files which are Word files, Excel files and Power Point files.

Otsubo et al. [7] proposed a tool (O-checker) to detect malicious document files (e.g. rtf, doc, xls, pps, jtd, pdf). O-checker detects malicious document files which contain executable files, using deviation of file format specifications. O-checker focuses on embedded executable files however, and cannot classify macros themselves. Even if the malicious documents do not contain executable files, our proposed method can detect malicious macros.

Boldewin implemented a tool (OfficeMalScanner) [8] to detect MS document files which contain malicious shellcodes or executable files. The tool scans entirely malicious files, and detects features of strings of Windows API, shellcode patterns and embedded OLE data [9]. The tool scores each document corresponding to each of the features. If the scores are more than a certain threshold, the tool judges the file as a malicious file.

Mimura et al. [10] de-obfuscate embedded executable files in a malicious document file (e.g. doc, rtf, xls, pdf) and detect them. The detection rate was verified in the work, and it was confirmed that the detection rate was higher than the detection rate of OfficeMalScanner. [7,8,10] focused on embedded malicious executable files or shellcodes, but not, however, on detecting malicious macros themselves.

PDF File. Next, this section presents related work which deals with the detection of malicious PDF files. Igino Corona et al. [11] proposed a method that refers to the frequency of suspicious reference APIs, to classify malicious PDF files. Liu et al. [12] proposed a method that analyzes obfuscated scripts to classify malicious PDF files. This method uses the characteristics of obfuscation, which is common to our method. However, these methods classify only malicious PDF files, and are fundamentally different from our method, which classifies malicious macros.

3   Relevant Techniques

3.1   Malicious Macros

This section describes the behavior of malicious macros, and reveals their features. There are two types of malicious macros, Downloader and Dropper.

Downloader is a malicious macro which enforces download malware upon a victim. An attacker uses a slick text of the type that the victim expects, and induces the victim to open an attachment. When the victim opens the attachment, the computer is forced into connecting to a malicious server. When Downloader connects to the server, it tends to uses external applications (Internet Explorer, etc.). Finally, the computer downloads and installs a malware from the server.

With Dropper, malicious codes (a binary of EXE files, etc.) are embedded in Dropper itself. When a victim opens the attachment of a phishing email, Dropper executes the codes contained in it as an executable file. The difference between Dropper and Downloader is that Dropper itself is able to fraudulently operate upon victim computers. Unlike Downloader, Dropper can infect victims without communicating an external resource (server or database, etc.).

Table 1. Typical obfuscation methods

#	summary
1	Obfuscation of replacing statement name, etc.
2	Obfuscation of encoding and decoding ASCII code
3	Obfuscation of character string by encoding conversion using exclusive OR
4	Splitting characters
5	Using reflection function

3.2   Obfuscation of Malicious Macros

The source codes of most malicious macro tend to be obfuscated. Therefore, capturing the characteristics of obfuscation can effectively predict malicious macros. We will show some obfuscation methods of the source codes.

Table 1 shows typical obfuscation methods in the source codes. Method 1 replaces class names, function names, etc with random strings. The random strings tend to be more than 20 characters. Method 2 encodes and decodes strings to ASCII codes. Macros provide AscB function and ChrB function. AscB function encodes character strings to ASCII codes. ChrB function encodes ASCII codes to character strings. Using AscB functions, attackers can conceal strings to encode the hexadecimal of ASCII codes. Moreover, ChrB function can convert ASCII codes to readable character strings. Method 3 performs using exclusive-OR any strings with a key. Many of the keys are intricately calculated and perform logic operations. Method 4 subdivides strings. Subdivided character strings are assigned to variables. By adding together those variables, the original strings are restored. Method 5 uses reflection functions which execute strings as instructions. For example, the strings are function names, class names and method names. CallByName function is a reflection function in the source codes. Using the CallByName function, attackers can hide the executing function.

3.3   Bag-of-Words

Words and documents need to be represented by feature vectors so that computers can interpret a natural language. Bow is the most basic natural language processing technique. Bow is a method of representing the frequency of a token in a sentence to an element of a vector corresponding to the token. Bow does not consider word order or meaning of tokens. In Bow, the number of unique tokens and the number of elements are the same. When the number of unique tokens diverges, the number of elements likewise diverges. Therefore, when Bow represents feature vectors, it may be necessary to adjust the number of dimensions.

3.4   Doc2Vec

D2V is a natural language processing technique. D2V is a model that is improved Word2Vec (W2V). First of all, we will introduce W2V. W2V is a model that is used to represent word embeddings. W2V is a two-layer neural network that is trained to reconstruct the linguistic context of words. W2V has a hidden layer and an output layer. The input of W2V is a large corpus of documents, and W2V represents the input in feature vectors. The number of dimensions of the feature vector is typically several hundred. Each unique token in the corpus is assigned a corresponding element of the feature vector. Word vectors are positioned in the vector space such that common contexts in the corpus are positioned in close proximity to one another in the space. This is based on the probability of words co-occurrence around a word. W2V has two algorithms, which are Continuous Bag-of-Words (CBow) and Skip-Gram. CBow is an algorithm which predicts a centric word from surrounding words. Skip-Gram is an algorithm which predicts surrounding words from a centric word. Using these algorithms, W2V can obtain similarity of words, and also predict equivalent words.

D2V has two algorithms which are Distributed Memory (DM) and Distributed Bag-of-Words (DBow). DM is an algorithm that is improved CBow. In addition to a large corpus of documents, those document-IDs input into DM. DBow is an algorithm which improves Skip-Gram. The input of DBow is not the words of documents but document-IDs. Using these algorithms, D2V can obtain similarity of documents, and also vectorize the documents.

3.5   Term Frequency-Inverse Document Frequency

Term Frequency-Inverse Document Frequency ($TFIDF$) is a numerical value that determines the importance of the words in the corpus. We will introduce how $TFIDF$ value is calculated.

$$TFIDF = frequency_{i,j} \times \log_2 \frac{D}{document\_freq_i}$$

The $frequency_{i,j}$ is the frequency of a token i in a document j. The $document\_freq_i$ is the frequency of documents in which the token i appears. The TF is the $frequency_{i,j}$. The IDF is the logarithm of a value in which D (the number of total documents) is divided by the $document\_freq_i$. $TFIDF$ value is a value which is the multiplication of TF and IDF. Finally, $TFIDF$ value is normalized.

When a word appears rarely in an entire corpus and appears frequently in a document, the $TFIDF$ value increases the priority of the word.

4   Proposed Method

This section proposes our method. Figure 1 shows an outline of the proposed method. The purpose of the proposed method is to detect unseen malicious macros with high classification accuracy. Step 1 extracts macros from MS document files. Step 2 separates words in the macros to create corpuses. Step 3 replaces words with characteristics of the same types of obfuscation (such as

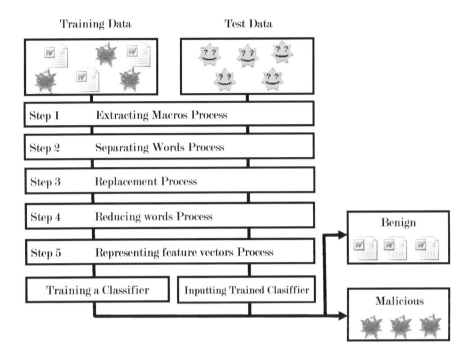

Fig. 1. Process procedure of unseen malicious macros detection

hexadecimal ASCII codes), with a word. Step 4 reduces trivial words in the corpuses using TF or TFIDF. Step 5 represents feature vectors from the corpus using Bow or D2V. The proposed method inputs the training feature vectors and the labels into classifiers (SVM, RF and MLP). Finally, we input the test feature vectors into trained classifiers, and obtain the labels.

4.1 Extract Source Code Process

The proposed method extracts macros from MS document files using Olevba [13]. Olevba is open source software that can extract macros from MS document files. Olevba can extract regardless of the platform.

4.2 Separating Words Process

The purpose of the separating words process is to create corpuses of the macros. The process replaces special characters that are shown in Table 2 with a blank. The source codes of malicious macros are intricately written, with many special characters. Therefore, the separating words process creates simple corpuses which are only alphabets and numbers.

Table 2. Replaced special characters

Special character	Name	Special character	Name
"	double quote	+	plus
'	single quote	/	slash
{	quare bracket	&	and
(	round bracket	%	percentage
,	comma		yen sign
.	period	$	dollar sign
*	asterisk	#	sharp
-	haihun	@	at mark

Table 3. Replacing specific strings

Methods	Characters pattern	Replaced strings
1	Hexadecimal (Type of 0xXX)	0xhex
2	Hexadecimal (Type of &HXX)	andhex
3	Asc, AscB, AscW	asc
4	A string of 20 or more characters	longchr
5	A number of 20 digits or more	longnum
6	Element of array	Elementofarray

4.3   Replement Process

This section discusses the replacement process. The purpose of the process is to collect words into each obfuscation. The process replaces words with characteristics of same type of obfuscation, with one token. Generally, malicious macros are obfuscated. The process can convert the corpuses to improve classification accuracy.

We will show an example of the process. The process replaces the hexadecimal values with one token as follows.

Before the process: 0xFF 0x14 0xA2

After the process: 0xhex 0xhex 0xhex

In this example, each hexadecimal value is treated as a different token before the process replacing the tokens. However, after the process of replacing characteristics, they are treated as the same token. The process replaces words regarded as different features with one word. Therefore, the replacement process improves the classification accuracy. Table 3 shows string patterns and replaced strings. These string patterns frequently appear in malicious macros.

4.4   Reducing Words Process

The purpose of the reducing words process is to reduce trivial words for improving classification accuracy. The frequency of words in macros is biased. A feature vectors of D2V and Bow are affected by the frequency of words. Thus, each word in a corpus has the some worth for the classification of malicious macros.

The process prioritizes words in the corpuses with TF or TFIDF. First, the process calculates the TF or $TFIDF$ of each word in all the corpuses. Next, we define a threshold. Finally, the process replaces words in which the TF or TFIDF value is less than the threshold, with "NONE". Through the process, the words which are bigger than the threshold remain in the corpuses.

4.5   Representing Feature Vectors Process and Classification of Macros

In the representing feature vectors process, D2V or Bow represents feature vectors by processed corpuses. Next, we input training feature vectors and the labels into classifiers (SVM, RF and MLP) in order to train the classifier. Test feature vectors are input into the trained classifier, and our method detects malicious macros.

5   Experiment

This section describes the verification experiments. The objective is to verify the next four factors.

1 Investigating the most effective corpus for improving F-measure
2 Comparing D2V and Bow
3 Comparing TF and TFIDF
4 Investigating the best combination of the above factors and classifiers (SVM, RF and MLP).

Verification Experiment 1 investigates effective corpuses which classify malicious macros. Bow represents feature vectors from malicious corpuses, benign corpuses and corpuses which are both. Next, SVM classifies each the feature vector, and obtains each classification accuracy.

The classification accuracy of D2V and Bow is compared in Verification Experiment 2. Each method represents feature vectors from corpuses. The best corpuses in Verification Experiment 1 are used in Verification Experiment 2. The feature vectors are classified using SVM, RF and MLP.

The classification accuracy of TF and TFIDF is compared in Verification Experiment 3. The best corpuses in Verification Experiment 1 are used in Verification Experiment 3. Feature vectors are represented using the best method (D2V or Bow) in Verification Experiment 2.

5.1   Experiment Environment

We implemented our proposed method with Python2.7 in the environment as shown in Table 4. We used gensim-2.0.0 [14] to implement Bow and D2V. Gensim has many functions related to natural language processing techniques. We used scikit-learn-0.18.1 [15] to implement SVM, RF and MLP. Scikit learn is a machine learning library and has many classification algorithms.

Table 4. Experiment environment

CPU	IntelCorei7 (3.30 GHz)
Memory	32 GB
OS	Windows8.1Pro

Table 5. Breakdown of The dataset

Specimens of 2015		Specimens of 2016	
Benign files	Malicious files	Benign files	Malicious files
622	515	1200	641

5.2   DataSet

This section presents the dataset of the experiments. Table 5 shows the breakdown of the dataset. This dataset was collected and provided by Virus Total [16]. We selected specimens which had been uploaded to Virus Total for the first time between 2015 and 2016. We collected macros whose file extensions have doc, docx, xls, xlsx, ppt and pptx. We treat the specimens which more than 29 out of 58 anti-virus vendors judged as malicious, as malicious specimens. We treated the specimens which all anti-virus vendors judged as benign, as benign specimens. There was no overlap in these specimens.

5.3   Evaluation Measure

This section presents the evaluation measures in the experiments. Malicious macros is treated as true label and benign macros is treated as false labels in the experiments. Table 6 shows the confusion matrix. We used Precision (P), Recall (R) and F-measure (F) as evaluation metrics. We will indicate the definition of each evaluation metric.

$$Precision = \frac{TP}{TP + FP}$$

$$Recall = \frac{TP}{TP + FN}$$

$$F - measure = \frac{2Recall \times Precision}{Recall + Precision}$$

Table 6. Confusion matrix

		Actual value	
		True	False
Predicted result	Positive	*TP*	*FP*
	False	*FN*	*TN*

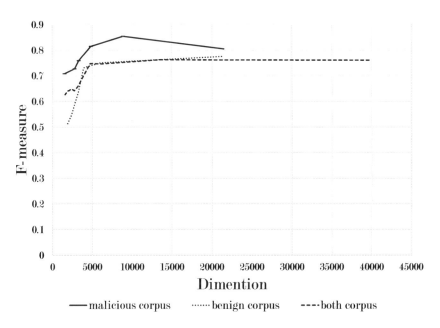

Fig. 2. The classification accuracy of each corpus in each dimension using TF and Bow

5.4   Verification Experiment 1

Experimental Approach. The objective is to investigate the most effective corpus for improving F-measure in Verification Experiment 1. The experiment selects from malicious corpuses, benign corpuses and corpuses which are both. The procedure of the experiment is shown next. The corpuses are created using Step 1 to Step 3 in Fig. 1. In the reducing process, we reduce the words in the corpus using the TF threshold. When the TF of a word is less than the TF threshold, the word is replaced with one word. Next, Bow represents three feature vectors from malicious corpuses, benign corpuses and corpuses which are both. Training feature vectors and the labels are input into an SVM classifier for training. Test feature vectors are input into the trained classifier to obtain predicted labels. The parameter of SVM is the default. Training data are specimens from 2015. Test data are specimens from 2016.

Result of Verification Experiment 1. Figure 2 shows the classification accuracy of each feature vector. The horizontal axis is the dimensions, and the vertical axis is the F-measure. When we represent feature vectors from malicious corpuses, the classification accuracy is higher than the classification accuracy of benign corpuses and corpuses which are both. Therefore, we conclude that the malicious feature vectors are effective in classifying malicious macros.

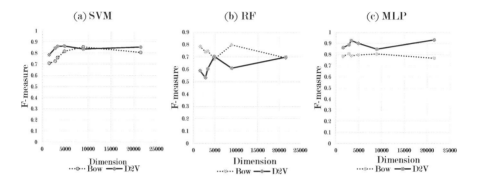

Fig. 3. The classification accuracy of each classifier using TF

5.5   Verification Experiment 2

Experimental Approach. The objective is to compare the classification accuracy of D2V and Bow in Verification Experiment 2. The procedure of the experiment is shown next. The corpuses are created using Step 1 to Step 3 in Fig. 1. In the reducing words process, we reduce the words in the corpus using TF. The feature vectors of two patterns are represented from malicious macros using D2V and Bow. D2V is set up such that the number of dimensions is 100, the number of epochs is 30 and the algorithm is DBow. Each of the feature vectors and the labels are input into three classifiers (SVM, RF and MLP) for training. The parameters of SVM and RF are default values. Verification Experiment 2 sets up MLP such that the input layer size is the number of unique tokens, the hidden layer size is 500, and the activation function is ReLU (Rectified Linear Unit). The classifier is input into the test feature vectors to predict malicious macros and benign macros. Finally, we obtain the F-measure of each of the feature vectors. Training data and test data are the same as for Verification Experiment 1.

Result of Verification Experiment 2. (a), (b) and (c) in Fig. 3 show the result of Verification Experiment 2 in each classifier. The horizontal axis is the dimensions, and the vertical axis is the F-measure. The F-measure of D2V is higher than Bow in (a) and (c). In contrast, the F-measure of Bow is higher than D2V in (b). In (c), when the number of dimensions is 21506 using D2V, the F-measure is the best (0.93). Moreover, the F-measure of a combination of MLP and D2V is stable.

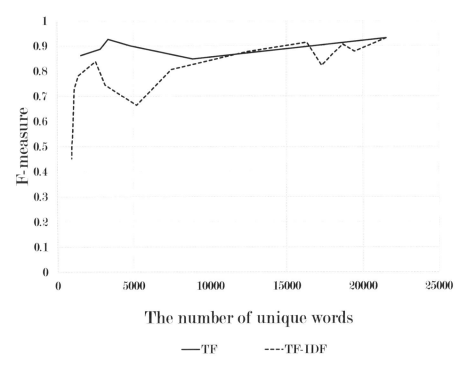

Fig. 4. The classification accuracy of each dimension using TF and TFIDF

5.6   Verification Experiment 3

Experimental Approach. The objective is to compare the F-measure of the TF and the TFIDF in Verification Experiment 3. The corpuses are created using Step 1 to Step 3 in Fig. 1. In the reducing process, we reduce the words in the corpus using two methods, which are TF and TFIDF. The feature vectors are represented using D2V. The settings of D2V are the same as in Verification Experiment 2. Each of the training feature vectors and the labels are input into MLP for training. MLP is input into the test feature vectors to predict malicious macros and benign macros. Finally, we obtain the F-measure of each of the feature vectors. The training data and the test data are the same as for Verification Experiment 1.

Result of Verification Experiment 3. Figure 4 shows the result of Verification Experiment 3. The horizontal axis is the number of unique tokens, and the vertical axis is the F-measure. Generally, the classification accuracy of the $TFIDF$ threshold is decreased. However, the classification accuracy of the TF threshold is stable and high. The highest F-measure is 0.93.

6   Discussion

6.1   Efficient Corpus

In Verification Experiment 1, we confirmed high classification accuracy using malicious corpuses. Benign macros are used for various purposes. Therefore, benign macros contain various tokens. In contrast, the purpose of malicious macros is simple. The purpose of malicious macros is to infect the victim's computer with malware. The source codes of the malicious macros contain many tokens which communicate to external servers, and are obfuscated. The source codes of the malicious macros frequently contain these characteristic tokens. Therefore, the replacement process can capture the characteristic, and the proposed method obtains high classification accuracy. In Bow, an element of the feature vectors is the frequency of a token. Therefore, malicious corpuses do better than other corpuses in Verification Experiment 1.

Table 7. Characteristic tokens

Token	Appearance ratio of malicious macro	Token	Appearance ratio of benign macro
Elementofarray	99%	Elementofarray	43%
Andchr	93.9%	Andchr	28%
Next	90.9%	Next	27.9%
Function	85.1%	Function	18.3%
String	83.3%	String	25.7%
Len	79%	Len	14.7%
Public	77.5%	Public	17.7%
Longchr	73.7%	Longchr	19.7%
Createobject	73%	Createobject	6.6%
Error	73%	Error	20.7%
Byte	56.1%	Byte	1.5%
Callbyname	51.3%	Callbyname	0.1%

6.2   Effectiveness of Bow and D2V

In Verification Experiment 2, we verified an efficient method of representing feature vectors. As a result, we concluded that D2V is better than Bow. As the *TF* threshold is high, low frequently-tokens are reduced and high frequently-tokens remain. In (c) of Fig. 3 using D2V, even if the dimension is the smallest (concretely, the dimension is 1515), the classification accuracy remains high. D2V represents word embedding. Therefore, we consider that the high-frequency token contains the context.

6.3   Efficient Classifier

In Verification Experiment 2, we confirmed that the classification accuracy of MLP and SVM was high. However, the classification accuracy of the RF classifier was low. Generally, the strong point of MLP and SVM is in solving the problem of linear separability. However, the strong point of RF is in solving the problem of linear inseparability. Therefore, we consider that the feature vectors of D2V can be separated linearly. In (a) and (c) of Fig. 3, the classification accuracy of D2V is higher than Bow. As a reason for this, we conclude that D2V tends to suit SVM and MLP in the classification of malicious macros.

6.4   Effectiveness of TFIDF

When the number of tokens is small, the classification accuracy decreased in Fig. 4 using TFIDF. Many words which are replaced in the replacement process, exist in the malicious corpus. Therefore, the TFIDF values of replaced words are small. While the $TFIDF$ threshold is high, replaced words are reduced. We indicate the representative tokens in Table 7. We define the appearance ratio as "Number of the files which contain the token / Number of files". Therefore, we consider that the classification accuracy decreased using the $TFIDF$ threshold.

In Fig. 4 using a TF threshold, the classification accuracy is more stable and we higher than TFIDF. As the TF threshold is high, the characteristic words of malicious macros remained and low frequently-word are reduced. Therefore, TF is more effective than TFIDF.

7   Conclusion

In this paper, we discussed effective methods of detecting unseen malicious macros. The proposed method reduces trivial words in corpuses. Next, the corpuses are converted to feature vectors using a linguistic approach. The training feature vectors and labels are input into a classifier. Finally, the test feature vectors are input into the trained classifier, and we obtain predicted labels. This paper investigated effective methods of reducing trivial words (TF and TFIDF), vectorizing methods (D2V and Bow) and classifiers (SVM, RF and MLP). As a result, it was seen that the combination of TF, D2V and MLP is effective for the detection of unseen malicious macros in our method. The highest F-measure is 0.93. We discussed effectiveness of the proposed method in this paper. We concluded that the feature vectors of D2V are effective in classifying unseen malicious macros. Our future work is to implement a tool which can detect malicious macros in real-time.

References

1. Wolf in sheep's clothing: a SophosLabs investigation into delivering malware via VBA. https://nakedsecurity.sophos.com/2017/05/31/wolf-in-sheeps-clothing-a-sophoslabs-investigation-into-delivering-malware-via-vba/
2. Rieck, K., Trinius, P., Willems, C., Holz, T.: Automatic analysis of malware behavior using machine learning. J. Comput. Secur. **19**(4), 639–668 (2011)
3. Bayer, U., Moser, A., Kruegel, C., Kirda, E.: Dynamic analysis of malicious code. J. Comput. Virol. **2**, 67–77 (2006). https://doi.org/10.1007/s11416-006-0012-2
4. Perdisci, R., Lanzi, A., Lee, W.: McBoost: boosting scalability in malware collection and analysis using statical classification of executables. In: Computer Security Applications Conference (2008). https://doi.org/10.1109/ACSAC.2006.53
5. Nissim, N., Cohen, A., Elovici, Y.: ALDOCX: detection of unknown malicious microsoft office documents using designated active learning methods based on new structural feature extraction methodology. IEEE Trans. Inf. Forensics Secur. **12**(3), 631–646 (2017)
6. Naser, A., Hadi, A.: Analyzing and detecting malicious content: DOCX files. Int. J. Comput. Sci. Inf. Secur. (IJCSIS) **14**(8), 404–412 (2016)
7. Otsubo, Y., Mimura, M., Tanaka, H.: O-checker: detection of malicious documents through deviation from file format specification. In: Black Hat USA (2016)
8. Boldewin, F.: Analyzing MSOffice malware with OfficeMalScanner. https://ja.scribd.com/document/21143233/Analyzing-MSOffice-Malware-With-OfficeMalScanner
9. OLE Background. https://msdn.microsoft.com/en-us/library/19z074ky.aspx
10. Mimura, M., Otsubo, Y., Tanaka, H.: Evaluation of a brute forcing tool that extracts the RAT from a malicious document file. In: 2016 11th Asia Joint Conference on Information Security (Asia JCIS) (2016). https://doi.org/10.1109/AsiaJCIS.2016.10
11. Corona, I., Maiorca, D., Giacinto, G.: Lux0R: detection of malicious PDF-embedded JavaScript code through discriminant analysis of API references (2014)
12. Liu, D., Wang, H., Stavrou, A.: Detecting malicious Javascript in PDF through document instrumentation. In: 2014 44th Annual IEEE/IFIP International Conference Dependable Systems and Networks (DSN), pp. 100–111, ISBN 978-1-4799-2233-8 (2014)
13. olevba. https://github.com/decalage2/oletools/wiki/olevba
14. python package index gensim 0.10.1. https://pypi.python.org/pypi/gensim/0.10.1
15. python package index scikit learn 0.19.0. https://pypi.python.org/pypi/scikit-learn/0.19.0
16. Virus Toral. https://www.virustotal.com/

Time Series Analysis: Unsupervised Anomaly Detection Beyond Outlier Detection

Max Landauer[1]([⊠]), Markus Wurzenberger[1], Florian Skopik[1],
Giuseppe Settanni[1], and Peter Filzmoser[2]

[1] Austrian Institute of Technology, Vienna, Austria
{max.landauer,markus.wurzenberger,florian.skopik,
giuseppe.settanni}@ait.ac.at
[2] Vienna University of Technology, Vienna, Austria
peter.filzmoser@tuwien.ac.at

Abstract. Anomaly detection on log data is an important security mechanism that allows the detection of unknown attacks. Self-learning algorithms capture the behavior of a system over time and are able to identify deviations from the learned normal behavior online. The introduction of clustering techniques enabled outlier detection on log lines independent from their syntax, thereby removing the need for parsers. However, clustering methods only produce static collections of clusters. Therefore, such approaches frequently require a reformation of the clusters in dynamic environments due to changes in technical infrastructure. Moreover, clustering alone is not able to detect anomalies that do not manifest themselves as outliers but rather as log lines with spurious frequencies or incorrect periodicity. In order to overcome these deficiencies, in this paper we introduce a dynamic anomaly detection approach that generates multiple consecutive cluster maps and connects them by deploying cluster evolution techniques. For this, we design a novel clustering model that allows tracking clusters and determining their transitions. We detect anomalous system behavior by applying time-series analysis to relevant metrics computed from the evolving clusters. Finally, we evaluate our solution on an illustrative scenario and validate the achieved quality of the retrieved anomalies with respect to the runtime.

Keywords: Log data · Cluster evolution · Anomaly detection

1 Introduction

Recent technological advancements have led to an increase of network communication between computer systems. Unfortunately, this also causes the appearance of novel attack vectors and other previously unimaginable threats. Potential entry points allowing intrusions thereby include legacy systems that are not updated regularly or products that loose vendor support and are insufficiently protected because of outdated security measures.

© Springer Nature Switzerland AG 2018
C. Su and H. Kikuchi (Eds.): ISPEC 2018, LNCS 11125, pp. 19–36, 2018.
https://doi.org/10.1007/978-3-319-99807-7_2

It is therefore necessary to deploy Intrusion Detection Systems (IDS) that are differentiated between three forms: (i) signature-based detection, a blacklisting approach that compares events with a known set of patterns, (ii) anomaly-based detection, which is able to detect deviations from learned normal system behavior, and (iii) stateful protocol analysis, a whitelisting approach that requires expert knowledge to build a model of allowed system behavior [13]. However, complex computer systems generally require too much effort to be appropriately modeled and blacklisting approaches are not protecting against unknown forms of attacks. Thus, we argue that anomaly detection offers a feasible alternative while being able to flexibly adapt to changing system environments.

Many anomaly detection techniques base on machine learning algorithms that operate in three different settings: (i) supervised, where a training set that contains labeled events both for normal and malicious behavior is analyzed to classify future events, (ii) semi-supervised, where only normal system behavior is provided as training input, and (iii) unsupervised, where no training set is required and learning happens on-the-fly during detection [4]. We recommend an unsupervised approach for several reasons. First, creating a comprehensive labeled data set for supervised algorithms that considers all types of attacks is a difficult task that requires time-consuming manual work and expert knowledge. Second, capturing normal system behavior for semi-supervised algorithms requires anomaly-free environments that can hardly be guaranteed in practice. Finally, dynamic networks that exhibit changing system behavior over time frequently require regenerations of the training data even in anomaly-free settings.

Attacks are usually planned to only show minor visible effects on the system. Fortunately, even very subtle intrusions manifest themselves in log files that record all events taking place in a system. Moreover, it is possible to trace a detected attack to its origin by analyzing the corresponding log lines. Such an investigation on historic data that detects anomalies in hindsight is known as forensic analysis. Contrary to that, online anomaly detection processes the lines as they are generated and identifies anomalies that do not comply with the learned behavior, thereby identifying attacks close to the time when they occur.

There exist norms on what characters are allowed in log data (e.g., RFC3164) and standards that define the syntax of log messages for specific services (e.g., syslog for UDP). However, log files often accumulate logs from multiple services and thus several standards may be mixed together, each of which requiring its own parser. Therefore, a more general approach that employs string metrics for grouping similar log lines independent from their structure is beneficial. Methods that form such cluster maps, i.e., sets of grouped log lines, successfully detected anomalous lines in [17], however provide only a static view on the data. Such existing solutions do not focus their attention on the following challenges:

- Log data is inherently dynamic and thus insufficiently analyzed by static cluster maps. Cluster Evolution (CE) techniques solve this problem by identifying connections between clusters from different maps.
- Anomalous log lines not only differ in their similarity but also relate to sudden changes in frequency, correlation or interruptions of temporal patterns.

- Cluster features, i.e., metrics retrieved from CE, require time-series analysis (TSA) methods for detecting anomalies in their continuous developments.
- Parsers cannot be defined for text-based log lines without known syntaxes and thus string metrics are required for similarity-based clustering.

Therefore, there is a need for dynamic log file anomaly detection that does not only retrieve lines that stand out due to their dissimilarity with other lines, but also identifies spurious line frequencies and alterations of long-term periodic behavior. We therefore introduce an anomaly detection framework containing the following novel features:

- An algorithm for consolidating the evolution of clusters from a continuous and potentially endless series of static cluster maps,
- the computation of metrics based on the temporal cluster developments,
- time-series modeling and one-step ahead prediction for anomaly detection,
- linear scalability on the number of log lines allowing real-time analysis,
- detection of contextual anomalies, i.e., outliers within their neighborhood,
- a realistic scenario evaluating the efficiency and effectiveness of our method.

The paper is structured as follows: Sect. 2 summarizes the field of CE for anomaly detection. Section 3 gives an overview about the concept of our approach. Sections 4 and 5 explore the theoretical background of CE and TSA respectively. Section 6 contains the evaluation and Sect. 7 concludes the paper.

2   Related Work

A large amount of research in the field of Cluster Evolution (CE) focuses on graphs (e.g., [3]). With its well-founded theoretical basis that covers both static and dynamic techniques, graph theory is a powerful tool for analyzing many kinds of network structures. For example, social networks conveniently represent graphs and are therefore frequently the target of so-called community evolution analyses. Similarly, the network connections between users within a computer system are often represented as a graph that allows the derivation of several relevant metrics that facilitate reasoning over the current state and behavior of the system. This idea has successfully been extended to anomaly detection by approximating and examining the dynamic development of metrics with time-series models [12]. However, most graph-based algorithms are not designed for a direct application of text-based CE.

When observing clusters over time it is important to identify any occurring changes of individual clusters or the overall cluster structure. Spiliopoulou et al. [15] introduces an algorithm on detecting these changes. Potentially applicable metrics derived from cluster interdependencies are given in [16].

He et al. [8] generate an event count matrix as a template for storing the frequencies of log lines. They then employ machine learning on fixed time windows, sliding time windows and session identifiers in order to identify deviations from the template. Applications that require tracking clusters over time also exist in research areas other than security, such as GPS tracking [9] where groups of points move across a plane. The clusters are described by relevant properties such as size, location and direction of movement, all of which are incrementally updated in every time step. Zhou et al. [19] introduce a similar dynamic collection of cluster features called Exponential Histogram of Cluster Features. Lughofer and Sayed-Mouchaweh [11] discuss an incremental method that supports adding and removing elements from clusters as well as merges and splits that can occur when clusters collide into or move through each other.

Chi et al. [5] suggest to smooth the time-series for retrieving more robust insights into the cluster developments and introduce two frameworks that focus on preserving the cluster quality and cluster memberships respectively. Xu et al. [18] extend these techniques by an evolutionary clustering algorithm. Chakrabarti et al. [2] outline the importance of alignment with snapshots of historical clusterings and propose an adapted hierarchical and K-Means algorithm as a solution.

3   Concept

This section uses an illustrative example to describe the concept of the anomaly detection approach that employs Cluster Evolution (CE) and time-series analysis (TSA). For this, consider log lines that correspond to three types of events, marked with $\bigcirc$, $\triangle$ and $\square$. The bottom of Fig. 1 shows the occurrence of these lines on the continuous time scale that is split up by t_0, t_1, t_2, t_3 into three time windows. The center of the figure shows the resulting sequence of cluster maps $\mathcal{C}, \mathcal{C}', \mathcal{C}''$ generated for each window. Note that in this example the clusters are marked for clarity. Due to the isolated generation of each map it is usually not possible to draw this connection and reason over the developments of clusters beyond one time window. The cluster transitions shown in the top of the figure, including changes in position ($C_\triangle$ in $[t_1, t_2]$), spread ($C_\triangle$ in $[t_2, t_3]$), frequency ($C_\square$ in $[t_2, t_3]$) as well as splits ($C_\bigcirc$ in $[t_2, t_3]$), are thus overseen.

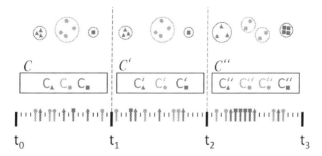

Fig. 1. Bottom: log lines occurring within time windows. Center: static cluster maps for every window. Top: schematic clusters undergoing transitions.

We therefore introduce an approach for dynamic log file analysis that involves CE and TSA in order to overcome these problems (Fig. 2). In step (1), the algorithm iteratively reads the log lines either from a file or receives them as a stream. Our approach is able to handle any log format, however, preprocessing may be necessary depending on the log standard at hand. In our case, we use the preprocessing step (2) to remove any non-displayable special characters that do not comply to the standard syslog format defined in RFC3164. Moreover, this step extracts the time stamps associated with each log line as they are not relevant for the clustering. This is due to the fact that the online handling of lines ensures that each line is processed almost instantaneously after it is generated.

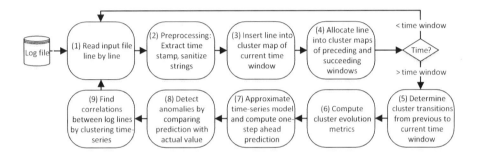

Fig. 2. Flowchart of the dynamic clustering and anomaly detection procedure.

Step (3) involves grouping log lines within each time window according to their similarity, resulting in a sequence of cluster maps. It is non-trivial to determine how clusters from one map relate to clusters from the maps created during their preceding or succeeding time windows. Clustering the lines constituting each map into the neighboring maps (4) establishes this connection across multiple time windows and allows the determination of transitions (5). A cluster from one time window evolves to another cluster from the following time window if they share a high fraction of common lines. More sophisticated case analysis is also able to differentiate advanced transitions such as splits or merges.

Several features of the clusters are computed (6) and used for metrics that indicate anomalous behavior. As the computations of these metrics follow the regular intervals of the time windows, we use TSA models (7) to approximate the development of the features over time. The models are then used to forecast a future value and a prediction interval lying one step ahead. If the actual recorded value occurring one time step later does not lie within these limits (8), an anomaly is detected. Figure 3 shows how the prediction limits (dashed lines) form "tubes" around the measured cluster sizes. Anomalies appear in points where the actual cluster size lies outside of that tube.

Finally, the time-series of the cluster properties are also grouped according to their pairwise correlations. An incremental algorithm groups the time-series similarly to the clustering of log lines. Carrying out this correlation analysis in

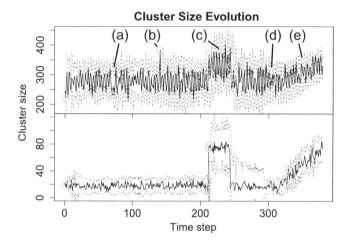

Fig. 3. Time-series representing the sizes of two evolving clusters (black solid lines) with prediction intervals (blue dashed lines) and detected anomalies (red circles). Top: a cluster affected by all anomalies. Bottom: a cluster not affected by periodic events. Anomalies are caused by (a) incorrect periodicity, (b) sudden frequency increase, (c) long-term frequency increase, (e) slow frequency increase. (d) is a false positive. (Color figure online)

regular intervals allows determining whether time-series that used to correlate with each other over a long time suddenly stop or whether new correlations between clusters appear, which are indicators of anomalous events (9).

4   Cluster Evolution

This section describes in detail how online CE is performed on log lines. The approach is introduced stepwise, starting with a novel clustering model that establishes connections between cluster maps. Subsequently, we explain the process of tracking individual clusters and determining their transitions.

4.1   Clustering Model

Considering only the lines of a single time window, we employ our incremental clustering approach introduced in [17]. The procedure is as follows: The first line always generates a new cluster with itself as the cluster representative, a surrogate line for the cluster contents. For every other incoming line the most similar currently existing cluster is identified by comparing the Levenshtein distances between all cluster representatives and the line at hand. The processed line is then either allocated to the best fitting cluster or forms a new cluster with itself as the representative if the similarity does not exceed a predefined threshold t.

This clustering procedure is repeated for the log lines of every time window. The result is an ordered sequence of independent cluster maps $\mathcal{C}, \mathcal{C}', \mathcal{C}'', \ldots$.

While the sequence itself represents a dynamic view of the data, every cluster map created in a single time window only shows static information about the lines that occurred within that window. The sequence of these static snapshots is a time-series that only provides information about the development of the cluster maps as a whole, e.g., the total number of clusters in each map. However, no dynamic features of individual clusters can be derived. It is not trivial to determine whether a cluster $C \in \mathcal{C}$ transformed into another cluster $C' \in \mathcal{C}'$ due to the fact that a set of log lines from a different time window was used to generate the resulting cluster. This is due to the nature of log lines that are only observed once in a specific point of time, while other applications employing CE may not face this problem as they are able to observe features of the same element over several consecutive time windows.

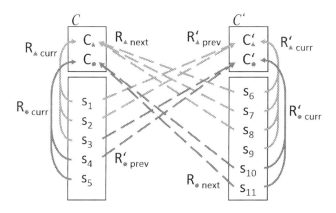

Fig. 4. Solid lines: construction of cluster map. Dashed lines: log lines allocated to neighboring map.

In order to overcome the problem of a missing link between the cluster maps, we propose the following model: Every log line is not only clustered once to establish the cluster map in the time window in which it occurred, but is also allocated to the cluster maps created in the preceding and succeeding time windows. These two cases are called construction and allocation phase respectively. The construction phase establishes the cluster map as previously described and each cluster stores the references to the lines that it contains. The allocation phase allocates the lines to their most similar clusters from the neighboring cluster maps. This is also carried out using the incremental clustering algorithm, with the difference that no new clusters are generated and no existing clusters are changed, but only additional references to the allocated lines are stored.

Figure 4 shows the phases for two consecutive cluster maps. The solid lines represent the construction of the cluster maps $\mathcal{C}$ and $\mathcal{C}'$ by the log lines $s_1, \ldots, s_{11}$ that occurred in the respective time window, e.g., clusters $C_\triangle$ and $C_\bigcirc$ store references to the lines in $R_{\triangle curr}$ and $R_{\bigcirc curr}$ respectively, and $C'_\triangle$ and $C'_\bigcirc$

store their references in $R'_{\triangle curr}$ and $R'_{\bigcirc curr}$. The dashed lines represent the allocation of the lines into the neighboring cluster maps. Clusters in $\mathcal{C}$ store references to allocated log lines from the succeeding time window in $R_{\triangle next}$ and $R_{\bigcirc next}$. Analogously, clusters in $\mathcal{C}'$ store references to allocated log lines from the preceding time window in $R'_{\triangle prev}$ and $R'_{\bigcirc prev}$. Note that in the displayed example, s_3 was allocated to $C_\triangle$ in $\mathcal{C}$ but to $C_\bigcirc$ in $\mathcal{C}'$. Further, s_5 and s_9 are not allocated at all. The following section describes how this model is used for tracking individual clusters over multiple time windows.

4.2   Tracking

For any cluster $C \in \mathcal{C}$ and any other cluster $C' \in \mathcal{C}'$, a metric is required that measures whether it is likely that C transformed into C', i.e., whether both clusters contain logs from the same system process. An intuitive metric that describes the relatedness of C and C' is their fraction of shared members. As previously mentioned, it is not possible to determine which members of each cluster are identical and it is therefore necessary to make use of the previously introduced clustering model that contains references to the neighboring lines. There exists an overlap metric based on the Jaccard coefficient for binary sets introduced in [7] that was adapted for our model by formulating it in the following way:

$$overlap(C, C') = \frac{\left| (R_{curr} \cap R'_{prev}) \cup (R_{next} \cap R'_{curr}) \right|}{\left| R'_{curr} \cup R'_{prev} \cup R_{next} \cup R_{curr} \right|} \tag{1}$$

Note that the sets of references R_{curr} and R'_{prev} both correspond to log lines that were used to create cluster map $\mathcal{C}$ and can thus be reasonably intersected, while R_{next} and R'_{curr} both reference log lines from cluster map $\mathcal{C}'$. The overlap lies in the interval $[0, 1]$, where 1 indicates a perfect match, i.e., all log lines from one cluster were allocated into the other cluster, and 0 indicates a total mismatch.

Clusters can also be tracked over multiple time windows by applying the same idea to C' and C'', C'' and C''', and so on. In a simplistic setting where clusters remain very stable over time, this is sufficient for tracking all log line clusters separately. However, in realistic scenarios with changing environments clusters frequently undergo transitions such as splits or merges which negatively influence the overlap and may indicate anomalies. In the following chapter, the tracking of clusters is therefore extended with a mechanism for handling transitions.

4.3   Transitions

Clusters are subject to change over time. There exist internal transitions that only influence individual clusters within single time windows, and external transitions that affect other clusters as well [15]. We consider the cluster size denoted by $|C|$ as the most important internal feature as it directly corresponds to the frequency of log lines allocated to cluster C. Formally, a cluster C grows in size from one time step to another if $|C'| > |C|$, shrinks if $|C'| < |C|$ and remains of constant size otherwise. Alternative internal features derived from the distribution of the cluster members are their compactness measured by the standard deviation, their relative position as well as their asymmetry, i.e., their skewness.

Clusters from different time windows are affected by external transitions. In the following, θ is a minimum threshold for the overlap defined in Eq. (1) and θ_{part} is a minimum threshold for partial overlaps that is relevant for splits and merges. In general, partially overlapping clusters yield smaller overlap scores, thus $\theta_{part} < \theta$. We take the following external transitions into account:

1. Survival: A cluster C survives and transforms into C' if $overlap(C, C') > \theta$ and there exists no other cluster $B \in \mathcal{C}$ or $B' \in \mathcal{C}'$ so that $overlap(B, C') > \theta_{part}$ or $overlap(C, B') > \theta_{part}$.
2. Split: A cluster C splits into the parts $C'_1, C'_2, \ldots, C'_p$ if all individual parts share a minimum amount of similarity with the original cluster, i.e., $overlap(C, C'_i) > \theta_{part}, \forall i$, and the union of all parts matches the original cluster, i.e., $overlap(C, \bigcup C'_i) > \theta$. There must not exist any other cluster that yields an overlap larger than θ_{part} with any of the clusters involved.
3. Absorption: The group of clusters $C_1, C_2, \ldots, C_p$ merge into a larger cluster C' if all individual parts share a minimum amount of similarity with the resulting cluster, i.e., $overlap(C_i, C') > \theta_{part}, \forall i$, and the union of all parts matches the resulting cluster, i.e., $overlap(\bigcup C_i, C') > \theta$. Again, there must not exist any other cluster that yields an overlap larger than θ_{part} with any of the clusters involved.
4. Disappearance or Emergence: A cluster C disappears or a cluster C' emerges if none of the above cases holds true.

By this reasoning it is not possible that a connection between two clusters is established if their overlap does not exceed θ_{part}, which prevents partial clusters that do not exceed this threshold from contributing to the aggregated cluster in the case of a split or merge. In order to track single clusters it is often necessary to follow a specific "path" when a split or merge occurs. We suggest to prefer paths to clusters based on the highest achieved overlap, largest cluster size, longest time that the cluster exists or combinations of these.

4.4 Evolution Metrics

Knowing all the interdependencies and evolutionary relationships between the clusters from at least two consecutive time windows, it is possible to derive in-depth information about individual clusters and the interactions between clusters. Definite features such as the cluster size that directly corresponds to the frequency of the log lines within a time window are relevant metrics for anomaly detection, however do not necessarily indicate anomalies regarding changes of cluster members.

A more in-depth anomaly detection therefore requires the computation of additional metrics that also take the effects of cluster transitions into account. Toyoda and Kitsuregawa [16] applied several inter-cluster metrics in CE analysis that were adapted for our purposes. For example, we compute the stability of a cluster by $s = |R'_{prev}| + |R_{curr}| - 2 \cdot |R'_{prev} \cap R_{curr}|$, where low scores indicate small changes of the cluster and vice versa. For a better comparison with other clusters, a relative version of the metric is computed by dividing the result by $|R'_{prev}| + |R_{curr}|$. There exist numerous other metrics that each take specific types of migrations of cluster members into account.

A simple anomaly detection tool could use any of the desired metrics, compare them with some predefined thresholds and raising alarms if one or more of them exceeds this threshold. Even more effectively, these metrics conveniently form time-series and can thus be analyzed with TSA methods.

5   Time-Series Analysis

The time-series derived from metrics such as the cluster size are the foundation for analytical anomaly detection. This section therefore describes how TSA methods are used to model the cluster developments and perform anomaly detection by predicting future values of the time-series.

Model. Time-series are sequences of values associated with specific time points. For our purposes, a time step therefore describes the status of the internal and external transitions and their corresponding metrics of each cluster at the end of a time window. These sequences are modeled using appropriate methods such as autoregressive integrated moving-average (ARIMA) processes. ARIMA is a well-researched modeling technique for TSA that is able to include the effects of trends and seasonal behavior in its approximations [6].

Clearly, the length of the time-series is ever increasing due to the constant stream of log messages and at one point will become problematic either by lack of memory or by the fact that fitting an ARIMA model requires too much runtime. As a solution, only a certain amount of the most recent values are stored and used for the model as older values are of less relevance.

Forecast. With appropriate estimations for the parameters, an extrapolation of the model into the future allows the computation of a forecast for the value directly following the last known value. In our experiments an ARIMA model is fitted in every time step and we are interested only in predictions one time step ahead rather than long-term forecasts.

The smoothness of the path that a time-series follows can be highly different. Therefore, neither a threshold for the absolute nor the relative deviation between a prediction and the actual value is an appropriate choice for anomaly detection. Assuming independent and normally distributed errors, the measured variance of previous values is therefore used to generate a prediction interval which contains the future value with a given probability. Using the ARIMA estimate $\hat{y}_t$, this interval is computed by

$$I_t = \left[\hat{y}_t - \mathcal{Z}_{1-\frac{\alpha}{2}} s_e, \hat{y}_t + \mathcal{Z}_{1-\frac{\alpha}{2}} s_e\right] \tag{2}$$

where $\mathcal{Z}_{1-\frac{\alpha}{2}}$ is the quantile $1 - \frac{\alpha}{2}$ of the standard normal distribution and s_e is the standard deviation of the error, $s_e = \sqrt{\frac{1}{n-1} \sum (y_t - \bar{y}_t)^2}$.

Correlation. Some types of log lines appear with almost identical frequencies during certain intervals, either because the processes that generate them are linked in a technical way so that a log line always has to be followed by another line, or the processes just happen to overlap in their periodical cycles. In any way, the time-series of these clusters follow a similar pattern and they are expected to continue this consistent behavior in the future. The relationship between two time-series y_t, z_t is expressed by the cross-correlation function [6], which can be estimated for any lag k as

$$CCF_k = \begin{cases} \frac{\sum_{t=k+1}^{N}(y_t - \bar{y}) \cdot (z_{t-k} - \bar{z})}{\sqrt{\sum_{t=1}^{N}(y_t - \bar{y})^2}\sqrt{\sum_{t=1}^{N}(z_t - \bar{z})^2}} & \text{if } k \geq 0 \\ \frac{\sum_{t=1}^{N+k}(y_t - \bar{y}) \cdot (z_{t-k} - \bar{z})}{\sqrt{\sum_{t=1}^{N}(y_t - \bar{y})^2}\sqrt{\sum_{t=1}^{N}(z_t - \bar{z})^2}} & \text{if } k < 0 \end{cases} \tag{3}$$

where $\bar{y}$ and $\bar{z}$ are the arithmetic means of y_t and z_t, respectively. Using the correlation as a measure of similarity allows grouping related time-series together.

Detection. For every evolving cluster, the anomaly detection algorithm checks whether the actual retrieved value lies within the boundaries of the forecasted prediction limits calculated according to Eq. 2. An anomaly is detected if the actual values falls outside of that prediction interval, i.e., $y_t \notin I_t$. Figure 3 shows the iteratively constructed prediction intervals forming "tubes" around the time-series. The large numbers of clusters, time steps and the statistical chance of random fluctuations causing false alarms often make it difficult to pay attention to all detected anomalies. We therefore suggest to combine the anomalies identified for each cluster development into a single score. At first, we mirror anomalous points that lie below the tube on the upper side by

$$s_t = \begin{cases} y_t & \text{if } y_t > \hat{y}_t + \mathcal{Z}_{1-\frac{\alpha}{2}} s_e \\ 2\hat{y}_t - y_t & \text{if } y_t < \hat{y}_t - \mathcal{Z}_{1-\frac{\alpha}{2}} s_e \end{cases} \tag{4}$$

With the time period τ_t describing the number of time steps a cluster is already existing we define $\mathcal{C}_{A,t}$ as the set of clusters that contain anomalies at time step t and exist for at least 2 time steps, i.e., $\tau_t \geq 2$. We then define the anomaly score a_t for every time step by

$$a_t = 1 - \frac{\sum_{C_t \in \mathcal{C}_{A,t}} \left((\hat{y}_t + \mathcal{Z}_{1-\frac{\alpha}{2}} s_e) \cdot log(\tau_t) \right)}{|\mathcal{C}_{A,t}| \sum_{C_t \in \mathcal{C}_{A,t}} (s_t \cdot log(\tau_t))} \tag{5}$$

When there is no anomaly occurring in any cluster at a specific time step, the anomaly score is set to 0. The upper prediction limit in the numerator and the actual value in the denominator ensure that $a_t \in [0, 1]$, with 0 meaning that no anomaly occurred and scores close to 1 indicating a strong anomaly. Dividing by $|\mathcal{C}_{A,t}|$ and incorporating the cluster existence time τ_t ensures that anomalies detected in multiple clusters and clusters that have been existing for a longer time yield higher anomaly scores. The logarithm is used to dampen the influence of clusters with comparatively large τ_t.

Finally, we detect anomalies based on changes in correlation. Clusters which correlate with each other over a long time during normal system operation should continue to do so in the future. In the case that some of these cluster permanently stop correlating, an incident causing this change must have occurred and should thus be reported as an anomaly. The same reasoning can be applied to clusters which did not share any relationship but suddenly start correlating. Therefore, after the correlation analysis has been carried out sufficiently many times to ensure stable sets of correlating clusters, such anomalies are detected by comparing which members joined and left these sets.

6   Evaluation

This section describes the evaluation of the introduced anomaly detection methodology. At first, the attack scenario and evaluation method are outlined. Then the detection capabilities of our method with different values for the similarity threshold and time window size are assessed and discussed.

6.1   Attack Scenario

In order to identify many clusters, we pursue high log data diversity. For this, we propose the following evaluation scenario that adapts an approach introduced in [14]: A MANTIS Bug Tracker System[1] is deployed on an Apache Web Server. Several users frequently perform normal actions on the hosted website, e.g., reporting and editing bugs. At some point, an unauthorized person gains access to the system with user credentials stolen in a social engineering attack. The person then continues to browse on the website, however following a different scheme, e.g., searching more frequently for open issues which simulates suspicious espionage activities. Such actions do not cohere with the behavior of the other users and we therefore expect to observe corresponding alterations in the developments of the log clusters. Due to the fact that only the probabilities for clicking on certain buttons are changed, we expect that the log lines produced by the attacker will be clustered together with the log lines describing normal behavior and that this causes an increase in the measured cluster size. In addition, an automatized program that checks for updates in regular intervals is compromised by the attacker and changes its periodic behavior. In this case, we expect that the changes of the periodic cycles are also reported as anomalies. The injected attacks include one missing periodic pulse, two sudden increases of cluster size with different length and one slowly increasing cluster size.

---

[1] https://www.mantisbt.org/.

6.2   Evaluation Environment

The log data was generated on a general purpose workstation, with an Intel Xeon CPU E5-1620 v2 at 3.70 GHz 8 cores and 16 GB memory, running Ubuntu 16.04 LTS operating system. The workstation runs a virtual Apache Web server hosting the MANTIS Bug Tracker System, a MySQL database and a reverse proxy. The log messages are aggregated with syslog. The anomaly detection algorithm was implemented in Java version 1.8.0.141 and runs on a 64-bit Windows 7 machine, with an Intel i7-3770 CPU at 3.4 GHz and 8 GB memory.

6.3   Method

The log data was collected for 96 h from the previously mentioned Bug Tracker System. Furthermore, sample log lines that correspond to the injected system changes were extracted. These lines were aggregated with their respective occurrence time points in a ground truth table. One of these entries is counted as a true positive (TP) if the algorithm detects an anomalous log cluster with a representative similar to the log line specified in the ground truth table, i.e., the computed string similarity is not smaller than the similarity threshold t used during clustering, and additionally the detection time is not earlier than 30 min or later than 60 min of the time specified in the ground truth table. If one of these requirements is not met, the entry is counted as a false negative (FN). Detected anomalies that do not correspond to any entries are counted as false positives (FP). True negatives (TN) are determined computationally.

With this setting, statistically relevant characteristics regarding the quality of the resulting classification were measured. These include the true positive rate $(TPR = \frac{TP}{TP+FN})$, false positive rate $(FPR = \frac{FP}{FP+TN})$, precision $(P = \frac{TP}{TP+FP})$ and recall $(R = TPR)$. Plotting the latter two against each other leads to the Receiver Operating Characteristic (ROC) curve, a common evaluation and comparison method for classification systems. Curves are created by running the anomaly detection algorithm with different parameter settings, with well-performing classifiers being located in the top-left corner of the ROC diagram (high TPR, low FPR). We also added the first median as it describes the performance of a random guesser and every reasonable classifier has to lie above this line. Finally, also the well-known $F_1\text{-}score = \frac{2 \cdot P \cdot R}{P+R}$ is computed.

6.4   Results

Figure 3 shows the cluster size developments of two log line clusters, the one-step ahead prediction limits forming tubes around the curves and the anomalies that are detected whenever the actual size falls outside of this tube. The present types of anomalies in the plot are: (a) a periodic process skipping one of its peaks, (b) a spike formed by a rapid short-term increase in line frequency, (c) a plateau formed by a long-term frequency increase, (d) a false positive and (e) a slowly increasing trend. The curve in the top part of the figure corresponds to a cluster affected by all injected anomalies. While anomalies (a)-(c) are appropriately detected, anomaly (e) is not detected in this cluster because the model adapts to the slow increase of frequency that occurs within the prediction boundaries, thereby learning the anomalous behavior without triggering an alarm. We intentionally injected (e) in order to show these problems that occur with most self-learning models. These issues can be solved by employing change point analysis methods that detect long-term changes in trends [10]. The bottom part of the figure corresponds to a cluster containing only log lines that are specifically affected by anomalies (c) and (e). Accordingly, the anomalies manifest themselves more clearly and the high deviations from the normal behavior makes their detection easier. The fact that each of the numerous evolving clusters are specific to certain log line types is a major advantage of our method. In particular, more than 300 evolving clusters representing more than 90% of the total amount of log lines were identified.

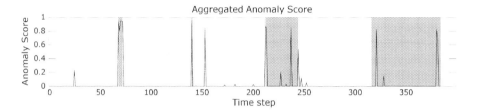

Fig. 5. The aggregated anomaly score displayed as a time-series and correctly increasing when the system behavior changes (red shaded intervals). (Color figure online)

The anomaly score aggregated over all evolving clusters that exist for at least 20 time steps is displayed in Fig. 5. The figure clearly shows that the anomaly score increases at the beginning and end of every attack interval. This corresponds to the fact that our algorithm detects changes of system behavior, but almost immediately adapts to the new state. Only returning from this anomalous state to the normal behavior is again detected as an anomaly.

Different parameters were used to create the ROC curves displayed in Fig. 6. In the left plot, the similarity threshold $t \in [0, 1]$ from the incremental clustering procedure was varied. A high similarity threshold causes that only highly similar lines are allocated to the same cluster, i.e., the total number of clusters per time window increases. A low similarity threshold causes the opposite. We discovered that low similarity thresholds ($t < 0.5$) cause too many different log line types being grouped into the same clusters and the cluster representatives therefore not appropriately describing their content. This in turn leads to mismatching clusters between the time windows that do not reach the minimum required threshold for establishing a connection.

The curves were created by changing the prediction level $(1 - \alpha)$, i.e., the width of the prediction interval, with narrow tubes leading to higher TPR and FPR and broad tubes leading to lower TPR and FPR. Favorable values (high

TPR, low FPR) are located close to the top-left corner of the plot. The figure shows that a moderate width is superior to the extremes as they suffer from either low TPR or high FPR. All threshold values yield reasonably good performances in the ROC plot because our injected anomalies always manifest themselves in multiple clusters, but there is a preference towards thresholds around 0.85 achieving $TPR = 61.8\%$ with only $FPR = 0.7\%$. In general, higher thresholds enable an increased granularity and should therefore be preferred for detecting anomalies that only affect a single or few log line types.

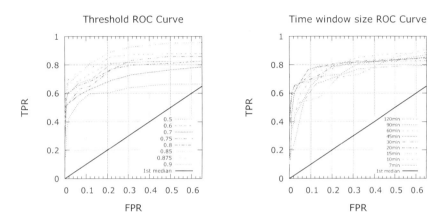

Fig. 6. Left: ROC curves for different threshold values. Right: ROC curves for different time window sizes.

The top left part of Fig. 7 shows the runtime with respect to different threshold values. Moderate threshold values yield lower runtimes then values closer to 0 or 1. The top right part of the figure shows that the runtime scales linearly with the number of log lines, which is important for processing continuous streams.

In addition to the threshold, the influence of the time window size was investigated. The right side of Fig. 6 shows ROC curves where the same data set was analyzed with a similarity threshold of 0.9 and varying time window sizes. The curves indicate that good results are achieved with time window sizes similar to the attack durations (10–30 min). In general, very large time windows are not sufficiently fine-grained and therefore easily miss anomalies that only occur during very short intervals. Clearly, smaller time windows yield finer granularities (i.e., more time steps in any given period) and also reduce the average reaction time, i.e., the average amount of time that passes between an anomaly occurring and being detected ($\frac{time\ window}{2}$). On the other hand, time windows smaller than the appearance frequency of certain log line types may result in incomplete cluster maps that do not contain evolving clusters of these logs. Thus, the correct choice for the time window size largely depends on the log frequencies.

Finally, the measurements regarding the runtime are shown in the bottom part of Fig. 7. Time window sizes that performed well in the ROC analysis also

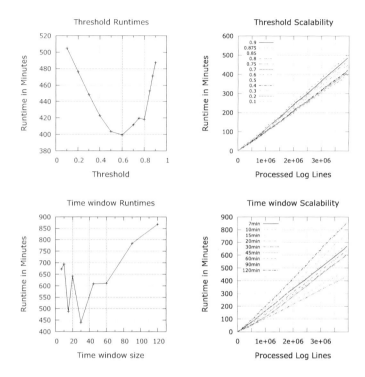

Fig. 7. Left: runtime comparison for different parameter settings. Right: runtime measured with respect to the number of processed log line shows linear scalability. Top: threshold as changed parameter. Bottom: time window size as changed parameter.

showed low runtimes, because generating the time-series model is easier when the time window is aligned to the period. Again, the runtimes scaled linearly with the number of log lines independent from the size of the time window.

For brevity, we only discuss the results of the evaluation centered around the F_1-score but omit the plots. The results showed that the recall increases for a higher threshold almost up to 1. Moreover, the size of the prediction interval had a clear influence on the recall for any given threshold level, with smaller sizes increasing the achieved recall score. This is due to the fact that actual anomalies fall outside of the tube more easily and thus improve the recall. While the precision also improves with a higher threshold, the results showed just the opposite characteristic regarding the prediction interval size, with large tubes increasing the precision. This is due to the fact that from all the detected anomalies, only highly diverging points that are likely to be actual anomalies exceeded the limits of the tube. For high similarity thresholds, precision scores between 0.2 and 0.3 are reached. Only when precision and recall are combined in the F_1-score the superiority of moderate tube sizes over the extremes becomes apparent. These observations emphasize the importance of the tube size and confirm the superiority of higher similarity thresholds already ascertained in the ROC analysis.

7   Conclusion and Future Work

In this work we introduced a dynamic anomaly detection algorithm for log data. By deploying an incremental clustering algorithm on multiple time windows rather than the whole data, we were able to establish a sequence of static cluster maps that collectively represent dynamic system behavior. We used cluster evolution techniques in order to identify developments of single clusters and employed time-series analysis for detecting anomalous deviations of relevant metrics.

The evaluation showed that clusters formed by groups of log lines belonging to a certain event are successfully tracked over time. Furthermore, the results showed that injected anomalies manifested themselves as sudden changes in the generated time-series and were appropriately detected by our algorithm.

We computed the overlap between cluster maps from two neighboring time windows. However, the quality of the connections between clusters could be enhanced by taking more distanced time windows into account. Moreover, there exist other time-series models able to predict future values, some of which may show a higher precision or runtime enhancements compared to ARIMA models.

As most unsupervised self-learners, our model suffers from poisoning of the data, i.e., anomalous behavior affecting future detections [1]. For example, regularly occurring log lines from malicious processes are learned after some time. An attacker is able to exploit this vulnerability by carefully injecting log lines that slowly adapt the learner to the changed system behavior. We are planning to investigate methods for change point analysis in order to solve these issues.

Acknowledgment. This work was partly funded by the FFG project synERGY (855457).

References

1. Biggio, B., et al.: Poisoning behavioral malware clustering. In: Proceedings of the 2014 Workshop on Artificial Intelligent and Security Workshop, pp. 27–36. ACM (2014)
2. Chakrabarti, D., Kumar, R., Tomkins, A.: Evolutionary clustering. In: Proceedings of the 12th ACM SIGKDD International Conference on Knowledge Discovery and Data Mining, pp. 554–560. ACM (2006)
3. Chan, J., Bailey, J., Leckie, C.: Discovering correlated spatio-temporal changes in evolving graphs. Knowl. Inf. Syst. **16**(1), 53–96 (2008)
4. Chandola, V., Banerjee, A., Kumar, V.: Anomaly detection: a survey. ACM Comput. Surv. (CSUR) **41**(3), 15 (2009)
5. Chi, Y., Song, X., Zhou, D., Hino, K., Tseng, B.L.: On evolutionary spectral clustering. ACM Trans. Knowl. Discov. Data (TKDD) **3**(4), 17 p. (2009)
6. Cryer, J., Chan, K.: Time Series Analysis: With Applications in R. Springer Texts in Statistics. Springer, Heidelberg (2008). https://doi.org/10.1007/978-0-387-75959-3. https://books.google.at/books?id=MrNY3s2difIC
7. Greene, D., Doyle, D., Cunningham, P.: Tracking the evolution of communities in dynamic social networks. In: Advances in Social Networks Analysis and Mining (ASONAM), pp. 176–183. IEEE (2010)

8. He, S., Zhu, J., He, P., Lyu, M.R.: Experience report: system log analysis for anomaly detection. In: 2016 IEEE 27th International Symposium on Software Reliability Engineering (ISSRE), pp. 207–218. IEEE (2016)
9. Jensen, C.S., Lin, D., Ooi, B.C.: Continuous clustering of moving objects. IEEE Trans. Knowl. Data Eng. **19**(9), 1161–1174 (2007)
10. Killick, R., Fearnhead, P., Eckley, I.A.: Optimal detection of changepoints with a linear computational cost. J. Am. Stat. Assoc. **107**(500), 1590–1598 (2012)
11. Lughofer, E., Sayed-Mouchaweh, M.: Autonomous data stream clustering implementing split-and-merge concepts-towards a plug-and-play approach. Inf. Sci. **304**, 54–79 (2015)
12. Pincombe, B.: Anomaly detection in time series of graphs using arma processes. Asor Bull. **24**(4), 2 (2005)
13. Scarfone, K., Mell, P.: Guide to intrusion detection and prevention systems (IDPS). NIST Special Publication 800-94 (2007)
14. Skopik, F., Settanni, G., Fiedler, R., Friedberg, I.: Semi-synthetic data set generation for security software evaluation. In: 2014 Twelfth Annual International Conference on Privacy, Security and Trust (PST), pp. 156–163. IEEE (2014)
15. Spiliopoulou, M., Ntoutsi, I., Theodoridis, Y., Schult, R.: MONIC: modeling and monitoring cluster transitions. In: Proceedings of the 12th ACM SIGKDD International Conference on Knowledge Discovery and Data Mining, pp. 706–711. ACM (2006)
16. Toyoda, M., Kitsuregawa, M.: Extracting evolution of web communities from a series of web archives. In: Proceedings of the Fourteenth ACM Conference on Hypertext and Hypermedia, pp. 28–37. ACM (2003)
17. Wurzenberger, M., Skopik, F., Landauer, M., Greitbauer, P., Fiedler, R., Kastner, W.: Incremental clustering for semi-supervised anomaly detection applied on log data. In: Proceedings of the 12th International Conference on Availability, Reliability and Security, p. 31. ACM (2017)
18. Xu, K.S., Kliger, M., Hero III, A.O.: Adaptive evolutionary clustering. Data Min. Knowl. Discov. **28**(2), 304–336 (2014)
19. Zhou, A., Cao, F., Qian, W., Jin, C.: Tracking clusters in evolving data streams over sliding windows. Knowl. Inf. Syst. **15**(2), 181–214 (2008)

Universal Wavelet Relative Distortion: A New Counter–Forensic Attack on Photo Response Non-Uniformity Based Source Camera Identification

Venkata Udaya Sameer[✉] and Ruchira Naskar

Department of Computer Science and Engineering,
National Institute of Technology, Rourkela 769008, Orissa, India
{515CS1003,naskarr}@nitrkl.ac.in

Abstract. *Photo Response Non–Uniformity (PRNU)* is one of the most effective fingerprints used to detect the source camera of an image. *Image Anonymization* on the other hand, is a task of fooling the source camera identification, in order to protect the user's anonymity in sensitive situations involving whistleblowers, social activists etc. To protect the privacy of users especially over the web, image anonymization is of huge importance. Counter–Forensic attacks on source camera identification try to make an image anonymous by nullifying the detection techniques. For almost every counter–forensic source camera identification attack, anti–counter attacks are being designed and hence there is a need to either strengthen the previous counter–forensic attacks or design a new attack altogether. In this work, we propose a new counter–forensic attack to source camera identification, using the *Universal Wavelet Relative Distortion* function designed for steganography. The main principle behind Universal Wavelet Relative Distortion is to embed changes in an image in regions such as textures or noisy parts which are crucial to source camera identification. We show through our experiments, when a random bit–string is inserted recursively in an image, the correlation strength of the noise residual based source camera identification gets significantly weak and such methods fail to map the source camera of the image under question. In the proposed method, the visual quality of the modified image is not changed, which makes our method a strong solution to image anonymization.

Keywords: Cybercrime · Counter forensics · Digital forensics
Fingerprint · PCE · PSNR · SSIM · Steganography
Source camera identification

1   Introduction

Multimedia forensics is an emerging field which investigates the evidence in the form of digital materials from a crime scene. Image forensics deals with providing evidence in a court of law or to help the investigative agencies regarding the

© Springer Nature Switzerland AG 2018
C. Su and H. Kikuchi (Eds.): ISPEC 2018, LNCS 11125, pp. 37–49, 2018.
https://doi.org/10.1007/978-3-319-99807-7_3

images found with a suspect. *Source Camera Identification* is a crucial task of identifying the source camera of an image under question. By mapping an image under question back to its source, important evidence can be gathered against any culprits with malicious intentions such as child pornographers. Now, with a great success in source camera identification, images found in a crime scene can be produced in a court of law as evidences. But, it rises an important debate on the privacy and secrecy aspects in certain situations such as whistleblowers and social/human activists who wish to share/send sensitive images and want to remain anonymous. *User Anonymization* [1–3] is a field of science that deals with making users remain anonymous while being able to share multimedia information over the Internet. It is necessary for certain online users to be not concerned about their privacy when using Internet and not worried about being tracked online. Especially for social activists and whistleblowers, spreading their information while maintaining anonymity is highly essential. It has been successfully established [4–7] that the noise residual content in an image is a strong fingerprint which determines the source camera of the test image. The noise pattern in an image is added by the underlying camera sensor while capturing a scene. It is possible to map an image to its camera sensor by matching the noise residual in the image against the Sensor Pattern Noise (SPN) of the camera. As a counter-attack to Photo Response Non Uniformity (PRNU) based source camera identification, image anonymization technqiues either suppress the PRNU content in an image or follow some other transformation on the image to make the underlying source detection process fail.

The main principle involved in PRNU based source identification is to find a correlation between the noise residual (PRNU) in an image and the sensor pattern noise (SPN) of each camera in hand. The correlation is either in the form of Normalized Cross Correlation (NCC) [4] or Peak–to–Correlation–Energy ratio (PCE) [5]. The source camera is mapped to an image based on a decision threshold against the correlation value. When a test image is manipulated through the image anonymization techniques, the correct source mapping is not possible. At present, *Image anonymization* techniques [8–12] w.r.t source camera identification are successful in deceiving the PRNU based source camera identification techniques. These techniques are also known as the *counter–forensic* attacks on source camera identification. In case of anonymization techniques such as Seam Carving [12] and Adaptive PRNU Denoising (APD) [10], the correlation value of the manipulated test image with its source camera falls below the threshold value, making it difficult to make any decision about the source of the image. In case of Fingerprint Copy [11] anonymization technique, the noise residual in the test image is removed and a fingerprint of another camera is added to the test image, thus making the correlation value falsely point to the other camera but not the original source. Though the present image anonymization techniques are successful, recent advances [13–16] in source camera identification are able to combat the geometrical manipulations as well the image anonymization techniques. In this paper we follow the approach of suppressing the PRNU content in an image, because several common geometrical transformations such as rotation, scaling etc. could not effect the PRNU based methods of source detection [17].

Our major contribution in this paper is a new image anonymization counter-forensic attack on PRNU based Source Camera Identification (SCI). In this paper, we adopt a recent steganographic technique to embed a random bit–string into the test images. The distortion used in this paper, ultimately suppresses the PRNU content in the test image to very low levels such that the correlation between the PRNU of the image and that of the camera becomes very weak to positively identify the source of the test image. The embedding mechanism of the distortion function makes the PRNU based source camera identification task insignificant.

The rest of the paper is organised as follows. Section 2 describes the background about PRNU based source camera identification and the other counter–forensic attacks in brief. In Sect. 3, we detail our proposed counter–forensic attack using the universal wavelet relative distortion. In Sect. 4, we show our experimental findings and conclude in Sect. 5 with a direction towards future work.

2   Background

Ever since the breakthrough about the usage of noise residual as a unique fingerprint of camera in [4], there have been multitude of works to address Source Camera Identification (SCI). For each camera at hand, a reference noise pattern is estimated as the unique camera fingerprint and the test image's noise residual is used to map against the reference pattern. The PRNU based schemes also found to be robust to many manipulations such as JPEG compression, gamma correction, resizing and rotation [18]. Various enhancements [6] have been carried out to improve the PRNU based methods, by making the schemes more adaptive to any scene content. More recently, the use of sensor pattern noise in SCI is strengthened by including a locally adaptive DCT filtering [7]. In this paper we target the PRNU based SCI techniques for image anonymization. We describe the methodologies of PRNU based SCI in Sect. 2.1.

2.1   PRNU Based Source Camera Identification

An image is formed in a camera sensor as per the reaction to the reflected light from the object. While forming the final digital image, the sensor pattern noise (K) of the camera is added along with other noise components such as dark current, shot noise etc. The sensor pattern noise of the camera being a multiplicative noise, is specific to each camera device [18] and thus the final image formed can be represented as follows:

$$P_x = P_0 + (P_0 K + \phi_1) \tag{1}$$

where P_x is the final digital image formed, P_0 is the amount of incident light on the sensor from the object, K is the PRNU factor of the sensor and ϕ_1 is the collection of other noises.

Through the application of a de–noise filter, majority of the other noise components are eliminated. Thus, the Noise Residual or the PRNU component of a single (i^{th}) image I_i can be calculated as:

$$PRNU_{I_i} = P_x^{(i)} - DF(P_x^{(i)}) \qquad (2)$$

where, DF is a de–noise filter (we use Weiner filter in the wavelet domain). The de–noised image is then subtracted from the original image to generate the noise residual $PRNU_{I_i}$.

The camera fingerprint K can be approximated from the noise residuals of N number of images taken from the same camera (N should be sufficiently large for example greater than 50).

Camera fingerprint or the Sensor Pattern Noise (SPN) of a camera C_j can then be calculated as:

$$SPN_{C_j} = \frac{\sum_{i=1}^{N} PRNU_{I_i} \cdot P_x^{(i)}}{\sum_{i=1}^{N} \left(P_x^{(i)}\right)^2} \qquad (3)$$

To map an image under question, I_{test} to one of the sensor pattern noises available with the forensic analyst, a correlation mechanism is employed such as Normalized Cross Correlation (NCC) [4] or the Peak–to–Correlation–Energy ratio (PCE) [5]. The NCC between the noise residual (NR) of I_{test} and SPN of a camera C_j is calculated as:

$$\rho_j(I_{test}) = \frac{(NR(I_{test}) - \overline{NR(I_{test})}).(SPN(C_j) - \overline{SPN(C_j)})}{\left\|NR(I_{test}) - \overline{NR(I_{test})}\right\| \left\|SPN(C_j) - \overline{SPN(C_j)}\right\|} \qquad (4)$$

where,$'.'$ is the dot product, $\|\|$ is L_2 norm, bar represents the mean value.

The similarity between an image PRNU and a camera SPN is computed in terms of Peak–to–Correlation–Energy ratio (PCE) as,

$$PCE(I_i, C_j) = \frac{\rho_{peak}^2}{\frac{1}{|r|-|\epsilon|} \sum_{r \notin \epsilon} \rho_r^2} \qquad (5)$$

where, ρ represents the normalized cross correlation between $PRNU_{I_{test}}$ and SPN_{C_j}. ρ_{peak} is the largest cross correlation value specific to (I_{test}, C_j) by shifting the image k possible times, r represents the set of all cross correlation values for (I_{test}, C_j) and ϵ represents a small area near the cross correlation peak which is removed in order to calculate the PCE ratio, ρ_r represents the cross correlation values corresponding to the entries in r, but not belonging to ϵ.

As discussed in [5], PCE is a much stable test statistic than the NCC, for the simple reason that PCE can perform well for any image size. In this paper, we use the PCE as the correlation test statistic and target to minimize the PCE value. Without any loss of generality, we state that PCE value between the noise residual of I_{test} and SPN of camera C_j is HIGH when the test image actually belongs to C_j, else it will be LOW. PCE is a better correlation metric, because, the threshold selection for NCC has to be changed every–time the cameras in hand changes. For the case of PCE, a fixed decision threshold can be applied [12]. Our goal in this paper is to make the PCE value of the noise residual of *modified* test image and the sensor patter noise of the source camera to be less than the fixed threshold, while maintaining the same image quality.

3 Proposed Image Anonymization

Image anonymization against PRNU based Source Camera Identification (SCI) majorly involve disturbing the correlation process and hence making the source attribution fail. We propose a technique to attack PRNU based SCI by formulating a distortion function which is used in steganography as a means to disturb the correlation process in SCI [19,20]. In this section, we provide a detailed description of the proposed image anonymization technique.

3.1 The Counter–Forensic Attack Model

In this section, we propose an image anonymization technique to counter PRNU based source camera identification. We use the Universal Wavelet Relative Distortion (UNIWARD) distortion technique [20] to perform image anonymization here. The key functionality in the distortion function is to embed a random bit–string into noisy/textured regions of the image. On doing so, the image noise characteristics are disturbed, so that source camera identification based on PRNU of those images (as discussed in Sect. 2.1), fails.

The proposed image anonymization technique using UNIWARD is shown in Algorithm 1. The technique can be broadly summarized into the following steps:

- First, the Sensor Pattern Noise (SPN) of the camera C is calculated by averaging the PRNU noise residuals of N (= 100 in our experiments) images.
- Then, image $\overline{I_{test}}$ is generated from the input image I_{test}, by repeatedly embedding random bit–strings into the image, until the PCE correlation between $PRNU_{\overline{I_{test}}}$ and SPN_C is less than a pre–defined *decision threshold*. When the PCE falls below the threshold, the image is considered to be sufficiently anonymized so as to prevent its source attribution.

Different authors have adopted PCE ≈ 50 as the decision threshold [5,12], but to further strengthen the proposed attack, we use a much lesser threshold value of 10. In the proposed attack, we perform the embedding continuously till PCE reaches 0 or less.

Unlike the other steganographic algorithms which does the embedding in *clean edges* of the image, UNIWARD finds the regions with *textured and/or noisy regions* for embedding. A distortion function is applied in the form of a sum of relative changes between the embedded image and original in wavelet domain. The distortion function is constructed using the directional filter banks that find possible directions of *texture and/or noisy regions* for embedding [20].

Algorithm 1. Generation of manipulated image for counter–forensic attack on SCI

Input: An image I_{test} taken by camera C to be anonymized, Set of 100 images taken by C for SPN calculation.

Output: Source anonymized image $\overline{I_{test}}$.

1   $Numerator = 0$; //Initialization
2   $Denominator = 0$; //Initialization
3   $SPN_C = 0$; //Initialization
4   **for** *each image I taken by camera C* **do**
5      $PRNU(I) = I - DF(I)$;
6      $Numerator = Numerator + PRNU(I).I$; /* '.' is the dot product operator*/
7      $Denominator = Denominator + I^2$;
8   **end**
9   $SPN_C = \frac{Numerator}{Denominator}$; // SPN computation for Camera C
10   $\overline{I_{test}} = I_{test}$;
11   $PCE_{Prev} = PCE(PRNU(\overline{I_{test}}), SPN_C)$;
12   $PCE_{Current} = PCE_{Prev}$;
13   **repeat**
14      $PCE_{Prev} = PCE_{Current}$;
15      $I_{temp} = \overline{I_{test}}$;
16      $Payload = GeneratePayload(N_P)$;
17   **repeat**
18   /*Find the best region to embed the payload by computing the distortion cost from Eq. 6 */
19        $X = I_{temp}$
20        $Y = X \rightarrow (X + 1)$
21   /* K is the kernel built from 1-D low pass wavelet decomposition filters*/
22   **for** $k = 1\ to\ 3$ **do**
23          $W^k(X) = K^k \star X$
24          $W^k(Y) = K^k \star Y$
25   **end**
26   /* Each W is of size $n_1 \times n_2$ */
27        $(n1, n2) = size(W^1(X))$
28   /* $C \approx 10^{-5}$ is a very small number to avoid division by zero */
29        $MinCost = \infty$
30   **for** $i = 1\ to\ 3$ **do**
31   **for** $j = 1\ to\ n_1$ **do**
32   **for** $k = 1\ to\ n_2$ **do**
33            $D(X, Y) = D(X, Y) + \frac{\left| W^i_{jk}(X) - W^i_{jk}(Y) \right|}{C + W^i_{jk}(X)}$
34   **end**
35   **end**
36   **end**
37   **if** $D(X, Y) < MinCost$ **then**
38          $MinCost = D(X, Y)$
39          $J = j$
40          $K = k$
41   **end**
42   **until** *All the regions are covered*;
43      $\overline{I_{test}} = Embed(I_{temp}, payload, J, K)$;
44      $PCE_{Current} = PCE(PRNU(\overline{I_{test}}), SPN_C)$;
45   /* Exit criteria to ensure finiteness of the algorithm */
46   **if** $PCE_{Current} - PCE_{Prev} < \epsilon$ **then**
47   **return** $PCE_{Current}$;
48   **end**
49   **until** $PCE_{Current} < 0$;

As described in [19], smoothness of the image is found in multiple directions using Daubechies 8-tap Wavelet Directional Filter Bank. Direction residuals are calculated in horizontal, vertical and diagonal directions to detect smoothness. The directional residual for an image I is given as $W^{(k)} = K^{(k)} \star I$, $\star$ is the mirror padded convolution operation, $k \in 1, 2, 3$ denotes various directions, K denotes the kernels in each specific direction.

Impact of embedding is pre–computed on the wavelet coefficients when a JPEG coefficient is changed by 1. The pixels are chosen for embedding where the impact is minimum i.e. sum of relative changes is minimum. The impact between a pair of images (X, Y) where X is the input cover image, Y is the output stego image, is called as the distortion function defined as follows:

$$D(X, Y) = \sum_{i=1}^{3} \sum_{j,k} \frac{\left| W_{jk}^i(X) - W_{jk}^i(Y) \right|}{\epsilon + W_{jk}^i(X)} \tag{6}$$

where W denotes the wavelet coefficients of an image, i denotes the decomposition levels in wavelet domain, (j, k) denote the corresponding wavelet coefficients, ϵ is a very small number used to avoid division by zero. In case of JPEG images, the distortion is calculated by decompressing the images into spatial domain and using the above equation. When one JPEG coefficient is changed, it impacts 8×8 pixels which in turn affect $(8 + (s - 1)) \times (8 + (s - 1))$ wavelet coefficients (where $s \times s$ is the size of 2-D wavelet support). The payload is of no significance for image anonymization, but serves purely to perform the distortion (through UNIWARD) and disturb the PRNU content of the image by embedding in noisy regions.

To ensure the finiteness of the algorithm, we set an exit criteria by checking if there is only a negligible change (we used $\epsilon = 10^{-2}$, in step 49, in Algorithm 1) in the PCE value between two successive iterations.

3.2   Attack Analysis

For PRNU based source camera identification to fail, there should not be any block in the test image, whose noise residual matches with the SPN of the corresponding camera. In this section, we analyse the proposed image anonymization technique, so as to find out whether there is any block in the final output image, whose SPN matches with the source camera. Our claim is as follows:

Claim: *There is no block in the final anonymized image, $\overline{I}$, that matches with the SPN of camera C.*

Proof: *Let P be the statement that there is a block in the final anonymized image, $\overline{I}$, that matches with the SPN its source camera C. We use the technique of proof by contradiction to prove that P is true. Let us assume P is false, i.e., there are L blocks in $\overline{I}$ that match the SPN of camera C (denoted as SPN_C). For all of these L blocks that match SPN_C, the NCC values (ρ in Eq. 4) will be high. This causes the PCE value to be high as there will be a ρ_{peak} (as in*

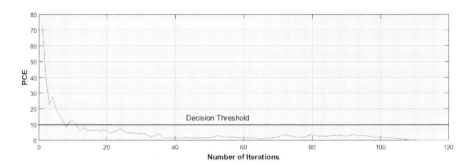

Fig. 1. Performance evaluation of PCE value variation over 113 iterations for one test image from camera C4 (Panasonic DMC FZ50).

Eq. 5) associated with these L matched blocks. But, according to Algorithm 1, the PCE between the final image and camera C, is bound to be less than 0, which contradicts our assumption. Hence, it is proved that there is no block in the final images, which matches with the SPN of its source.

The UNIWARD distortion discussed, finds a noisy region in one of the blocks B_l for which the cost is least, $(l \in 1, 2, 3...L)$ and embeds the dummy payload there. By the definition of NCC discussed, the ρ value corresponding to that block B_l where the embedding happened, would be low (which means it is not a match). In the next iteration, the same process is repeated and now $l \in 1, 2, 3...L - 1$. Ultimately when the PCE value becomes less than 0, it signifies that there are no more noisy regions to embed. When there are no noisy regions to embed, the PRNU based SCI techniques fail to map the source camera.

4   Experimental Results and Discussion

In this section, the performance of the proposed anonymization technique is evaluated. The benchmarks for evaluation are as follows: (I) PCE of the anonymized image, to judge the strength of the attack, and (II) PSNR and SSIM for evaluating image quality degradation. In our experiments, we use Dresden Image

Table 1. List of cameras used in our experiments from dresden database

Camera make	Model	Resolution	Format	Alias
KODAK	M1063	3664×2748	JPEG	C1
NIKON	D70	3008×2000	JPEG	C2
OLYMPUS	MJU	3648×2736	JPEG	C3
PANASONIC	DMC-FZ50	3648×2736	JPEG	C4
PRAKTICA	DCZ5.9	2560×1920	JPEG	C5
SAMSUNG	L74	3072×2304	JPEG	C6
SONY	H50	3456×2592	JPEG	C7

Table 2. Average PCE obtained by different counter–forensic attacks, for seven camera models, and ten images from each.

Camera	PCE value of counter–forensic attack				
	Original	Seam carving [12]	APD [10]	FP Copy [22]	Proposed attack
C1	6528.16	0.221	0.65	1.69	−0.59
C2	1018.43	0.85	0.71	−0.13	−1.005
C3	333.31	−0.26	0.22	0.431	−0.94
C4	172.4	0.51	0.58	2.73	−0.86
C5	285.27	1.16	0.803	0.527	−0.72
C6	390.55	1.241	0.697	0.96	−0.64
C7	1778.5	−0.95	−0.23	−0.29	−1.32

Database [21], which is a benchmark dataset for Image Source Identification and related forensic researches. We experiment with a set of 7 cameras of different makes and models, the list of which is provided in Table 1. We use 100 images from each camera, for calculating the Sensor Pattern Noise (SPN) of each camera. We test the proposed image anonymization technique with 10 images taken from each camera (total 70 images). A pre–defined decision threshold is adopted in our experiments for source camera identification. If PCE of the anonymized image is greater than the threshold, only then it is possible to attribute the image to its corresponding source camera. In earlier works, a decision threshold of 50 was used [5,12], but to further strengthen the proposed attack, we use a much lesser threshold value of 10. Hence, if the proposed attack is strong enough for a threshold of 10, it is definitely strong for any threshold higher than 10.

4.1   PCE Results and Analysis

The objective of the proposed image anonymization technique is to minimise the PCE correlation between the sensor pattern noise (SPN) of the camera and the PRNU noise residual of the test image. We construct the SPN of the reference cameras with 100 test images. The PRNU extraction is performed for the test image, as explained in Sect. 2. The PCE correlation is found considering the entire images (no cropping). In the proposed approach, we repeatedly embed random bit–strings into the image until the PCE of the anonymized image is less than 0. This can be clearly observed from Table 2, which presents the average PCE results of different counter–forensic schemes. Specifically, in Table 2, we present the performance evaluation results of the following state–of–the–art counter–forensic attacks: Seam Carving [12], Adaptive PRNU Denoising [10], Fingerprint Copy [22], in terms of anonymized image PCE, for the camera models listed in Table 1. Total 10 images, which were not used in calculating the sensor pattern noise, are used for testing here.

For a counter–forensic technique to be considered as a successful attack on PRNU based source camera identification, the PCE correlation values must

A) Original Image
PCE: 73.98

B) Final Anonymized Image
PCE: 0.26

Fig. 2. Image Qualities (a) Before anonymization, and (b) After anonymization using the proposed technique.

be sufficiently low, so as to prevent mapping of the image to its source. In effect, the PCE values must be lower than the decision threshold. The average PCE values of different counter–forensic attacks are shown in Table 2. The PCE values of the anonymized images using the proposed technique, fall below 0. For the other attacks, the PCE values are not mandatorily negative. This is achieved by pre–defining the desired PCE range (<0, in Algorithm 1) of the counter–forensically modified image, and controlling the number of iterations of the algorithm, accordingly. PCE is the primary statistic to measure the strength of image anonymity brought about by a counter–forensic attack. Since, for every counter–forensic attack mentioned in Table 2, the obtained PCE value falls below the decision threshold of 10, all of them qualify as successful counter–forensic attacks. The proposed anonymization technique constitutes a new form of counter–forensic attack, which would help to further strengthen existing PRNU based source camera identification models.

The proposed anonymization technique is iterative, i.e., in each iteration a random bit–string is embedded and the PCE value between the noise residual and the SPN of the camera is measured. If the PCE value in i^{th} iteration is above the decision threshold then the iterations are repeated until the desired threshold is reached. In Fig. 1, we show the plot between the number of iterations and the corresponding PCE values of one test image from camera C4 (Panasonic DMC FZ50). The decision threshold is PCE $= 10$, and the PCE value can be observed to gradually decrease over the subsequent iterations. After the tenth iteration, it reaches below the threshold. However, we can further reduce the PCE by conducting additional iterations, as evident from Fig. 1.

4.2   Image Quality Analysis

The proposed anonymization technique as well as all the compared methods (namely APD, FP Copy and Seam Carving) are successful in defeating the PRNU based source camera identification schemes (as discussed in Sect. 4.1).

Table 3. Average PSNR of the anonymized images with respect to the originals

Camera	Average PSNR [db]			
	APD [10]	FP copy [22]	Proposed	Seam carving [12]
C1	38.76	38.56	32.45	28.75
C2	36.52	39.91	31.2	29.84
C3	37.41	37.81	33.16	31.46
C4	34.68	41.59	28.97	32.67
C5	35.28	38.64	29.53	28.79
C6	32.69	33.63	31.25	30.28
C7	32.28	39.71	30.18	29.16

Table 4. Average SSIM of the anonymized images with respect to the originals

Camera	Average SSIM [db]			
	APD [10]	FP Copy [22]	Proposed	Seam Carving [12]
C1	0.994	0.987	0.911	0.910
C2	0.991	0.976	0.964	0.925
C3	0.983	0.995	0.932	0.928
C4	0.982	0.979	0.922	0.915
C5	0.992	0.988	0.907	0.917
C6	0.999	0.991	0.929	0.911
C7	0.997	0.982	0.936	0.928

In this section, we perform an analysis on the image quality generated from different schemes. In Fig. 2, we present a comparison of a test image captured by Panasonic DMC-FZ50 (camera C4), with its anonymized form (using the proposed technique), in terms of image quality. There are no visually evident artefacts in the anonymized image, shown in Fig. 2(b), as compared to the original image in Fig. 2(a). In this paper, we use Peak Signal to Noise Ratio (PSNR) and Structural Similarity Index (SSIM), as the evaluation metrics to measure the quality of the final anonymized image. The PSNR and SSIM results for different camera models, averaged over 10 test images from each, are shown in Tables 3 and 4 respectively. Out of all the compared methods, the Adaptive PRNU Denoising (APD) method works best for preserving the image quality while removing the noise residual in an image. The Fingerprint Copy (FP Copy) method also fairs well in preserving the image quality to a great extent. The quality of the images anonymized by the proposed technique is better than that of Seam Carved images both in terms of PSNR and SSIM.

The reduction in PSNR/SSIM is nothing but the cost to be incurred to achieve considerably low PCE value. If we accept a higher PCE value (for e.g. 2), then the PSNR and SSIM results would be close to APD and FP Copy. This can be controlled in our attack model in step 49 of Algorithm 1. The results presented in Tables 3 and 4, prove that the proposed image anonymization technique, preserves the image quality considerably, while reducing the PCE value which is less than all other anonymization techniques.

5   Conclusion

The current counter–forensic image anonymization methods are being studied carefully and anti measures are in place to overcome image anonymization. In this scenario, every possibility of new image anonymization attacks, are very crucial to be known to forensic experts. In this paper, we introduce a new counter–forensic attack on PRNU based source camera identification. We showed through our experiments that, the UNIWARD distortion function which is famously used in steganography, can be a very efficient attack on the PRNU based source attribution techniques. The embedding of random bit–strings may also serve as a distraction apart from serving as a counter–forensic attack.

In future, we would like to extend this work and try to improve the output image quality. We would like to experiment the robustness of the attack under various image manipulations such as JPEG compression, image resizing etc.

References

1. Kobsa, A., Schreck, J.: Privacy through pseudonymity in user-adaptive systems. ACM Trans. Internet Technol. (TOIT) **3**(2), 149–183 (2003)
2. Zhu, Y., Xiong, L., Verdery, C.: Anonymizing user profiles for personalized web search. In: Proceedings of the 19th International Conference on World Wide Web, pp. 1225–1226. ACM (2010)
3. DeLeeuw, W.C., Smith, N.M.: Techniques and architecture for anonymizing user data. US Patent 9,589,151, 7 March 2017
4. Lukas, J., Fridrich, J., Goljan, M.: Digital camera identification from sensor pattern noise. IEEE Trans. Inf. Forensics Secur. **1**(2), 205–214 (2006)
5. Goljan, M., Fridrich, J., Filler, T.: Large scale test of sensor fingerprint camera identification. In: Media Forensics and Security, vol. 7254, p. 72540I. International Society for Optics and Photonics (2009)
6. Li, C.-T.: Source camera identification using enhanced sensor pattern noise. IEEE Trans. Inf. Forensics Secur. **5**(2), 280–287 (2010)
7. Lawgaly, A., Khelifi, F.: Sensor pattern noise estimation based on improved locally adaptive dct filtering and weighted averaging for source camera identification and verification. IEEE Trans. Inf. Forensics Secur. **12**(2), 392–404 (2017)
8. Goljan, M., Fridrich, J., Chen, M.: Defending against fingerprint-copy attack in sensor-based camera identification. IEEE Trans. Inf. Forensics Secur. **6**(1), 227–236 (2011)
9. Dirik, A.E., Karaküçük, A.: Forensic use of photo response non-uniformity of imaging sensors and a counter method. Optics Express **22**(1), 470–482 (2014)
10. Karaküçük, A., Dirik, A.E.: Adaptive photo-response non-uniformity noise removal against image source attribution. Digital Invest. **12**, 66–76 (2015)

11. Quiring, E., Kirchner, M.: Fragile sensor fingerprint camera identification. In: 2015 IEEE International Workshop on Information Forensics and Security (WIFS), pp. 1–6. IEEE (2015)
12. Dirik, A.E., Sencar, H.T., Memon, N.: Analysis of seam-carving-based anonymization of images against prnu noise pattern-based source attribution. IEEE Trans. Inf. Forensics Secur. **9**(12), 2277–2290 (2014)
13. Zeng, H.: Rebuilding the credibility of sensor-based camera source identification. Multimed. Tools Appl. **75**(21), 13871–13882 (2016)
14. Taspinar, S., Mohanty, M., Memon, N.: PRNU based source attribution with a collection of seam-carved images. In: 2016 IEEE International Conference on Image Processing (ICIP), pp. 156–160. IEEE (2016)
15. Taspinar, S., Mohanty, M., Memon, N.: PRNU-based camera attribution from multiple seam-carved images. IEEE Trans. Inf. Forensics Secur. **12**(12), 3065–3080 (2017)
16. Li, H., Luo, W., Rao, Q., Huang, J.: Anti-forensics of camera identification and the triangle test by improved fingerprint-copy attack. arXiv preprint arXiv:1707.07795 (2017)
17. Goljan, M., Fridrich, J.J.: Sensor fingerprint digests for fast camera identification from geometrically distorted images. In: Media Watermarking, Security, and Forensics, p. 86650B (2013)
18. Chen, M., Fridrich, J., Goljan, M., Lukás, J.: Determining image origin and integrity using sensor noise. IEEE Trans. Inf. Forensics Secur. **3**(1), 74–90 (2008)
19. Holub, V., Fridrich, J.: Digital image steganography using universal distortion. In: Proceedings of the First ACM Workshop on Information Hiding and Multimedia Security, pp. 59–68. ACM (2013)
20. Holub, V., Fridrich, J., Denemark, T.: Universal distortion function for steganography in an arbitrary domain. EURASIP J. Inf. Secur. **2014**(1), 1 (2014)
21. Gloe, T., Böhme, R.: The dresden image database for benchmarking digital image forensics. J. Digit. Forensic Pract. **3**(2–4), 150–159 (2010)
22. Caldelli, R., Amerini, I., Novi, A.: An analysis on attacker actions in fingerprint-copy attack in source camera identification. In: 2011 IEEE International Workshop on Information Forensics and Security (WIFS), pp. 1–6. IEEE (2011)

Compact Ring Signature in the Standard Model for Blockchain

Hao Ren[1], Peng Zhang[1(✉)], Qingchun Shentu[1], Joseph K. Liu[2],
and Tsz Hon Yuen[3]

[1] College of Information Engineering, Shenzhen University, Shenzhen, China
renhao2016@email.szu.edu.cn, zhangp@szu.edu.cn, shentuqc@bankledger.com
[2] Faculty of Information Technology, Monash University, Melbourne, Australia
joseph.liu@monash.edu
[3] Huawei, Singapore, Singapore
YUEN.TSZ.HON@huawei.com

Abstract. Ring signature is a variant of digital signature, which makes any member in a group generate signatures representing this group with anonymity and unforgeability. In recent years, ring signatures have been employed as a kind of anonymity technology in the blockchain-based cryptocurrency such as Monero. Recently Malavolta et al. introduced a novel ring signature protocol that has anonymity and unforgeability in the standard model [33]. Their construction paradigm is based on non-interactive zero-knowledge (NIZK) arguments of knowledge and re-randomizable keys.

In this work, for the purpose of lower bandwidth cost in blockchain, we improve their ring signature by proposing a compact NIZK argument of knowledge. We show our NIZK holds under a new complexity assumption *Compact Linear Knowledge of Exponent Assumption*. Without the expense of security, our proposed ring signature scheme is anonymous and unforgeable in the standard model. It saves almost half of storage space of signature, and reduces almost half of pairing computations in verification process. When the ring size is large, the effect of our improvements is obvious.

Keywords: Blockchain · Ring signature · NIZK
Argument of knowledge

1 Introduction

In 2008, Satoshi Nakamoto first proposed the blockchain to build cryptocurrency bitcoin as a public transaction ledger [34]. With the decentralization of blockchain, cryptocurrency bitcoin first solves double-spending problem without a central server. The blockchain and bitcoin have also provided inspirations for various applications offering value or trust [41]. In recent years, ring signature was deployed to build transaction protocols for blockchain-based cryptocurrencies. Monero is one of the popular cryptocurrencies that mainly focuses on

© Springer Nature Switzerland AG 2018
C. Su and H. Kikuchi (Eds.): ISPEC 2018, LNCS 11125, pp. 50–65, 2018.
https://doi.org/10.1007/978-3-319-99807-7_4

anonymity, and its underlying CryptoNote protocol deploys ring signature as core cryptographic tools to provide anonymity [36].

The notion of ring signature was first proposed to leak secrets, by Rivest, Shamir and Tauman [35] with many extensions after that such as using different mathematical assumptions [16], based on different cryptosystems [2,4,5], with linkability and/or revocability [1,3,20,22,23,25,27,40], with blinding feature [8], in a threshold setting [24,39,42,44,45], security enhancement [10,18,26,28,30–32] and efficiency improvement [21,29,43]. This cryptographic tool has ability to leak the endorsement of any messages signed by one member in a group, but does not reveal his identification. Compared with the group in group signatures [9], a ring is not managed by a group manager. Actually, ring members can be included in the ring completely unawarely. Since rings are ad-hoc, which means that the signing process cannot be controlled by any centralized authority after original setup.

In the past years, the security of most ring signature constructions holds in ROM (Random Oracle Model) [11] or CRS (Common Reference String) model [19]. In ASIACRYPT 2017, Malavolta et al. presented a generic ring signature construction that has anonymity and unforgeability in the standard model [33]. In their scheme, a ring signature protocol can be divided into two components: the re-randomizable key and the NIZK (Non-Interactive Zero-Knowledge) system. A novel feature of this scheme is that one can modify its NIZK system independently to obtain variants of the original scheme.

Bandwidth usage is one of the main targets for blockchain benchmarks, which influences transaction processing performance of blockchain significantly. To reduce bandwidth in blockchain, Groth et al. proposed a logarithmic-size ring signature for blockchain cryptocurrency [15]. Sun et al. proposed an accumulator-based transaction protocol for Monero to reduce transaction size [38]. These two works are both in the ROM. In this work, to improve the efficiency, we design a new assumption CL-KEA (*Compact Linear Knowledge of Exponent Assumption*), then a compact NIZK argument of knowledge under this assumption is proposed. With the remarkable properties of our compact NIZK, we build a compact ring signature scheme in standard model. Compared with Malavolta et al.'s scheme [33], the signature size of our scheme is smaller, and the verification computation is more efficient.

2   Preliminaries

In this work, we use λ to denote a security parameter, use $\mathsf{negl}(\lambda)$ to denote a negligible function in a security parameter λ, and use $[n]$ to denote a set $\{1, ..., n\}$ for a positive integer $n \in \mathbb{N}$. We define $y \leftarrow S$ for sampling y from a set S randomly.

2.1 Bilinear Maps

Let g_1 and g_2 be generators of two cyclic groups $(\mathbb{G}_1, \mathbb{G}_2)$ of large prime order p, respectively. There exits a homomorphism function $\phi : \mathbb{G}_2 \to \mathbb{G}_1$ and a bilinear map function $e : \mathbb{G}_1 \times \mathbb{G}_2 \to \mathbb{G}_T$ which holds:

- Non-degeneracy. $e(g_1, g_2) \neq 1$.
- Computability. All group operations in $(\mathbb{G}_1, \mathbb{G}_2, \mathbb{G}_T)$, the homomorphism ϕ and the map e are efficiently computable.
- Bilinearity. For all $(a, b) \in \mathbb{Z}_p^2$ and $(C, D) \in \mathbb{G}_1 \times \mathbb{G}_2$, $e(C^a, D^b) = e(C, D)^{a \cdot b}$.
- Homomorphism. For all $(D, E) \in \mathbb{G}_2^2$, $\phi(D \cdot E) = \phi(D) \cdot \phi(E)$.

2.2 NIZK Arguments of Knowledge

Definition 1 (NIZK Arguments of Knowledge [14]). *Let $\mathcal{R}$ be a relation corresponding to a NP language $\mathcal{L}$. NIZK arguments of knowledge have following* PPT *algorithms:*

$(\alpha, \theta) \leftarrow \mathcal{G}(1^\lambda)$: *On input the security parameter λ, this algorithm outputs a trapdoor α and a common reference string θ.*

$\pi \leftarrow \mathcal{P}(\theta, w, s)$: *On input a θ, a witness w and a statement s, where $(w, s) \in \mathcal{R}$, this algorithm outputs a argument π.*

$1/0 \leftarrow \mathcal{V}(\theta, \pi, s)$: *On input a θ, a proof π and a statement s, this algorithm outputs a bit b, which is 1 or 0.*

$\pi \leftarrow \mathcal{S}(\theta, \alpha, s)$: *On input a θ, a trapdoor α and a statement s, this algorithm outputs an argument π.*

$(s, \pi, w) \leftarrow \mathcal{E}(\alpha, \theta)$: *On input a trapdoor α and a θ, this algorithm outputs a statement s, a argument π and a witness w.*

Definition 2 (Perfect Completeness). *For all $\lambda \in \mathbb{N}$, $(\alpha, \theta) \leftarrow \mathcal{G}(1^\lambda)$ and $(w, s) \in \mathcal{R}$ such that*

$$\Pr[(\alpha, \theta) \leftarrow \mathcal{G}(1^\lambda), \pi \leftarrow \mathcal{P}(\theta, w, s) : 1 \leftarrow \mathcal{V}(\theta, \pi, s)] = 1.$$

Definition 3 (Perfect Zero-Knowledge). *For all $\lambda \in \mathbb{N}$, $(\alpha, \theta) \leftarrow \mathcal{G}(1^\lambda)$ and $(w, s) \in \mathcal{R}$, there exists a simulator $\mathcal{S}$ such that*

$$\Pr[\mathcal{P}(\theta, w, s) = \mathcal{S}(\theta, \alpha, s)] = 1.$$

Definition 4 (Computational Knowledge Soundness). *For all $\lambda \in \mathbb{N}$, $(\alpha, \theta) \leftarrow \mathcal{G}(1^\lambda)$, $(w, s) \in \mathcal{R}$ and any* PPT *adversary $\mathcal{A}$, there is an extractor $\mathcal{E}$ that has full access to the adversary it holds that*

$$\Pr\left[\begin{matrix} (\pi, s) \leftarrow \mathcal{A}(\theta), (s, \pi, w) \leftarrow \mathcal{E}_\mathcal{A}(\alpha, \theta) \\ : (w, s) \in \mathcal{R} \end{matrix} \middle| 1 \leftarrow \mathcal{V}(\theta, \pi, s) \right] \geq 1 - \mathsf{negl}(\lambda).$$

2.3   Ring Signature

Definition 5 (Ring Signature [6]). *A ring signature protocol includes a triple of* PPT *algorithms* RSig = (Gen, Sig, Ver) *as follows:*

$(vk, sk) \leftarrow$ Gen(1^λ): *On input the security parameter λ, this algorithm outputs a verification key vk and a signing key sk. Define the ring $R = \{vk_i\}_{i \in [n]}$.*

$\sigma \leftarrow$ Sig(R, sk, m): *On input a ring R, a signing key sk and a message m, this algorithm outputs a signature σ.*

$1/0 \leftarrow$ Ver(R, m, σ): *On input a ring R, a message m and a signature σ, this algorithm outputs a bit 1 which means the ring signature passes the verification. Otherwise, output a bit 0.*

*A ring signature must satisfies **Anonymity** and **Unforgeability** as defined in [6].*

2.4   Programmable Hash Function

Definition 6 (Programmable Hash Function [17]). *There are two algorithms* H = (HGen,HEval) *in the programmable hash function as follows:*

$k \leftarrow$ HGen(1^λ): *On input the security parameter λ, this algorithm generates a public key k.*

$c \leftarrow$ HEval(k, m): *On input a public key k and a message $m \in \{0,1\}^*$, this algorithm outputs a hash value c.*

3   Overview of Malavolta et al.'s Scheme

In this section, we show an overview of Malavolta et al.'s scheme [33].

3.1   NIZK

Firstly, we recall the language $\mathcal{L}$ corresponding to disjunction of discrete logarithm defined in [33] as follows:

$$\mathcal{L} = \{\{A_i\}_{i \in [n]} \in \mathbb{G}_1^n : \exists(a, i) : g_1^a = A_i\}.$$

Then we recall the NIZK system of [33] as Fig. 1.

As we can see, this NIZK argument doesn't need random oracles and the security is mainly based on L-KEA (*Linear Knowledge of Exponent Assumption*). We note that although there exists a common reference string in their NIZK, it doesn't mean their ring signatures need the CRS, we talk about it later.

$$
\begin{array}{lll}
\mathcal{G}(1^\lambda) & \mathcal{P}(\theta, w, s) & \mathcal{V}(\theta, \pi, s) \\[4pt]
\hline
\\
\alpha \leftarrow \mathbb{Z}_p & \text{parse } \theta = T \in \mathbb{G}_2 & \text{parse } \theta = T \in \mathbb{G}_2 \\
\theta \leftarrow g_2^\alpha & w = (a, j) & \pi = \{T_i\}_{i \in [n]} \in \mathbb{G}_2^n \\
\text{output } (\alpha, \theta) & s = \{A_i\}_{i \in [n]} \in \mathbb{G}_1^n & \{Q_i\}_{i \in [n]} \in \mathbb{G}_1^n \\
& \forall i \in [n]\backslash j : & s = \{A_i\}_{i \in [n]} \in \mathbb{G}_1^n \\
& \quad t_i \leftarrow \mathbb{Z}_p & \text{output 1 iff} \\
& \quad T_i \leftarrow g_2^{t_i} & \prod_{i \in [n]} T_i = T \wedge \\
& \quad Q_i \leftarrow (A_i)^{t_i} & \forall i \in [n] : \\
& \quad T_j \leftarrow T \cdot \left(\prod_{i \in [n]\backslash j} g_2^{t_i} \right)^{-1} & \quad e(Q_i, g_2) = e(A_i, T_i) \\
& \quad Q_j \leftarrow \phi(T_j^a) & \\
& \text{output } \pi = \{(T_i, Q_i)\}_{i \in [n]} &
\end{array}
$$

Fig. 1. NIZK for disjunctive statements in Malavolta et al.'s scheme [33]

3.2 Ring Signature

Then we show the generic ring signature constructions introduced by Malavolta et al. as Fig. 2. Their novel work is based on re-randomizable keys [12] and the above NIZK arguments of knowledge. To make their ring signature scheme independent with the CRS, they divide the CRS of NIZK into a part of each verification key, achieving that the CRS of NIZK is not the CRS of ring signature. A potential feature of their ring signature is that the NIZK argument of knowledge is a independent component, thus it can be modified with other valid NIZK systems, such as [13,14].

An obvious deficiency of their ring signature scheme is the signature size. In their scheme, a signature includes two proofs of NIZK arguments of knowledge and each proof consists of $2n$ group points for a n-sized ring. Consequently, their signature consists of $(4n + 3)$ group points and an integer.

4   Our NIZK Arguments of Knowledge

We propose a new NIZK argument of knowledge to improve efficiencies of [33]. Our main idea is to compress the size of NIZK argument without changing degrees of the polynomials in the security proof of assumption, thus the security of new NIZK arguments of knowledge holds as before. We note that our NIZK is secure based on CL-KEA, which is a variant of L-KEA.

4.1 Complexity Assumptions

Assumption 1 (Compact Linear Knowledge of Exponent (CL-KEA)).
For all $\lambda \in \mathbb{N}$, $n \in \mathsf{poly}(\lambda)$ and PPT adversaries $\mathcal{A}$ there is a PPT algorithm $\mathcal{E}_\mathcal{A}$ with full access to $\mathcal{A}$ it holds that

$\mathsf{Gen}(1^\lambda)$	$\mathsf{Sig}(R, sk, m)$	$\mathsf{Ver}(R, m, \sigma)$
$(\alpha, x) \leftarrow \mathbb{Z}_p^2$	parse $R = \{vk_i\}_{i\in[n]}$	parse $R = \{vk_i\}_{i\in[n]}$
$C \leftarrow g_2^\alpha$	if $\nexists i : vk = vk_i$	$vk_i = (z_i, C_i, k_i)$
$k \leftarrow \mathsf{HGen}(1^\lambda)$	$\quad$ output $\bot$	$\sigma = (\sigma', \pi, z')$
output $(x, (g_2^x, C, k))$	parse $vk = (z, C, k)$	$\sigma' = (s, y, c)$
	$\qquad vk_i = (z_i, C_i, k_i)$	$x := R\|z'\|c\|(m, R)$
	$(s, \rho, \delta) \leftarrow \mathbb{Z}_p^3$	$b \leftarrow \mathcal{V}\left(\prod_i C_i, x, \pi\right)$
	$z' \leftarrow z \cdot g_2^\rho$	
	$x' \leftarrow sk + \rho$	$b' = 1$ if
	$c \leftarrow \mathsf{HEval}(k, m\|R)^\delta$	$\quad e(y, vk' \cdot g_2^s) = e(c, g_2)$
	$x := R\|z'\|c\|(m, R)$	output $(b = b' = 1)$
	$\pi \leftarrow \mathcal{P}\left(\prod_i C_i, (\rho, \delta, i), x\right)$	
	$y \leftarrow c^{\frac{1}{x'+s}}$	
	$\sigma = (s, y, c)$	
	output (σ, π, z')	

Fig. 2. Ring signature scheme in Malavolta et al.'s scheme [33]

$$\Pr\left[\begin{array}{l} (Q, \{T_i, A_i\}_{i\in[n]}) \leftarrow \mathcal{A}(p, e, g_1, g_2, g_2^x), \\ (a, P, \{T_i, A_i\}_{i\in[n]}) \leftarrow \mathcal{E}_\mathcal{A}(p, e, g_1, g_2, g_2^x) \end{array} \middle| \begin{array}{l} \sum_{i\in[n]} \mathsf{Dlog}_{g_2}(T_i) \cdot \mathsf{Dlog}_{g_1}(A_i) \\ = \mathsf{Dlog}_{g_1}(Q) \\ \wedge \prod_{i\in[n]} T_i = g_2^x \\ \wedge \forall i \in [n] : g_1^a \neq A_i \end{array} \right]$$

$$\leq \mathsf{negl}(\lambda).$$

W.l.o.g., we use $\mathcal{O}$ to represent the set of five oracles with the generic group model from [7] and we randomly pick encoding functions $(\gamma_1, \gamma_2, \gamma_T)$ corresponding to groups $(\mathbb{G}_1, \mathbb{G}_2, \mathbb{G}_T)$ in the following.

Theorem 1. *For all* $\lambda \in \mathbb{N}$, $n \in \mathsf{poly}(\lambda)$ *and* PPT *adversaries* $\mathcal{A}$ *with oracle access to* $\mathcal{O}$ *there is a* PPT *extractor* $\mathcal{E}_A$ *with full access to* $\mathcal{A}$ *such that*

$$\Pr\left[\begin{array}{l} (\gamma_1(q), \{\gamma_2(t_i), \gamma_1(a_i)\}_{i\in[n]}) \leftarrow \mathcal{A}(p, \gamma_1(1), \gamma_2(1), \gamma_2(x)), \\ (a, \gamma_1(q), \{\gamma_2(t_i), \gamma_1(a_i)\}_{i\in[n]}) \leftarrow \mathcal{E}_\mathcal{A}(p, \gamma_1(1), \gamma_2(1), \gamma_2(x)) \end{array} \middle| \begin{array}{l} \sum_{i\in[n]} t_i \cdot a_i \\ = q \\ \wedge \sum_{i\in[n]} t_i \\ = x \\ \wedge \forall i \in [n] : \\ a \neq a_i \end{array} \right]$$

$$\leq \mathsf{negl}(\lambda).$$

Proof. We construct an extractor $\mathcal{E}$ as follows.

1. $\mathcal{E}$ initializes 3 lists $(\mathcal{W}_1, \mathcal{W}_2, \mathcal{W}_T)$.
2. $\mathcal{E}$ randomly picks $s_1 \leftarrow \{0,1\}^*$, $s_2 \leftarrow \{0,1\}^*$ and $s_x \leftarrow \{0,1\}^*$, then it adds $(1, s_1)$ to $\mathcal{W}_1$, adds $(1, s_2)$ to $\mathcal{W}_2$ and adds (x, s_x) to $\mathcal{W}_1$. We note that the entries of the lists can be denoted by (F, s), where F is a generic polynomial and s is a randomly picked string.
3. $\mathcal{E}$ simulates the queries of $\mathcal{A}$ to the oracle set $\mathcal{O}$:
   – On input 2 strings (s_i, s_j), $\mathcal{E}$ first retrieves F_i and F_j from lists $\mathcal{W}_1$, $\mathcal{W}_2$ or $\mathcal{W}_T$. Next it calculates $F_k = F_i \pm F_j$ and outputs s_k if $(F_k, s_k) \in \mathcal{W}_*$.
   – On input 2 strings (s_i, s_j), $\mathcal{E}$ first retrieves F_i and F_j from lists $\mathcal{W}_1$ or $\mathcal{W}_2$. Next it calculates $F_k = F_i \cdot F_j$ and outputs s_k if $(F_k, s_k) \in \mathcal{W}_T$.
   – On input a string s_k, $\mathcal{E}$ first retrieves F_k from list $\mathcal{W}_2$. Next it outputs s_i if $(F_k, s_i) \in \mathcal{W}_1$.
   Whenever $(F_k, s_*) \notin \mathcal{W}_*$, $\mathcal{E}$ randomly picks $s'_k \leftarrow \{0,1\}^*$, adds (F_k, s'_k) to the corresponding list $\mathcal{W}_*$ and outputs s'_k.
4. At some time, $\mathcal{E}$ receives a tuple $(q, \{a_i, t_i\}_{i \in [n]})$ from $\mathcal{A}$.
5. For all $i \in [n]$, $\mathcal{E}$ retrieves F_{a_i} from list $\mathcal{W}_1$, which corresponds to a_i.
6. If some F_{a_i} is a constant ($\deg_x(F_{a_i}) = 0$), $\mathcal{E}$ returns F_{a_i}. Otherwise it aborts.

Whenever $\mathcal{E}$ doesn't abort, we denote the element that $\mathcal{E}$ outputs by o, thus $\gamma_1(o) = a_i$. Then we prove this happens with negligible probability.

Our prove includes three lemmas, first we recall the lemma in [37]:

Lemma 1. *Let $F(\{x_i\}_{i \in [m]})$ be a polynomial and $\deg(F) \leq d$, p be the largest prime dividing a integer n' and we randomly generate $\{x_i\}_{i \in [m]} \leftarrow \mathbb{Z}_{n'}^m$ it holds that:*

$$\Pr[F(\{x_i\}_{i \in [m]}) = 0 \mod n'] \leq \frac{d}{p}$$

Lemma 1 provides any polynomials $F = 0$ with deterministic maximum probability. As our extractor described above, we note that $\deg_x(F_i) \leq 1$ and $\deg_x(F_j) \leq 1$, then $\deg_x(F_k) \leq 2$, where $(F_i, s_i) \in \mathcal{W}_1$, $(F_j, s_j) \in \mathcal{W}_2$ and $(F_k, s_k) \in \mathcal{W}_T$.

Lemma 2. *For all $(F_{a_i}, s_{a_i}) \in \mathcal{W}_1$ and $(F_{t_i}, s_{t_i}) \in \mathcal{W}_2$ it holds that:*

$$\Pr[\deg_x(F_{t_i}) = 1 \wedge \deg_x(F_{a_i}) = 1] \leq \mathsf{negl}(\lambda).$$

Proof. Let F_q be a polynomial such that $(F_q, s_q) \in \mathcal{W}_1$, thus $\deg_x(F_q) \leq 1$. If we assume $F_q = \sum_{i \in [n]} F_{t_i} \cdot F_{a_i}$, it is obvious that for all $i \in [n]$ either F_{t_i} or F_{a_i} must be a constant. For some random $x \leftarrow \mathbb{Z}_p$, it is required that $F_q(x) = \sum_{i \in [n]} F_{t_i}(x) \cdot F_{a_i}(x)$.

By Lemma 1 we know that:

$$\Pr[F_q(x) - \sum_{i \in [n]} F_{t_i}(x) \cdot F_{a_i}(x) = 0] \leq \frac{1}{p}$$

where $\frac{1}{p}$ is negligible. It follows that

$$\Pr[F_q - \sum_{i \in [n]} F_{t_i} \cdot F_{a_i} \neq 0] \leq \frac{1}{p}.$$

Then we conclude that

$$\Pr[\deg_x(F_{t_i}) = 0 \vee \deg_x(F_{a_i}) = 0] \geq \epsilon(\lambda)$$

where ϵ is a non-negligible function.   □

Here we note that $\deg_x(F_{t_i}) = \deg_x(F_{a_i}) = 0$ doesn't contradict our theorem.

Lemma 3. *For all* $(F_{t_i}, s_{t_i}) \in \mathcal{W}_2$:

$$\Pr[\forall i \in [n] : \deg_x(F_{t_i}) = 0] \leq \mathsf{negl}(\lambda).$$

Proof. We assume that for all $i \in [n]$:

$$\Pr[\forall i \in [n] : \deg_x(F_{t_i}) = 0] \geq \epsilon(\lambda).$$

As we argued that $\sum_{i \in [n]} F_{t_i}(x) = x$, it is required that

$$\Pr[\sum_{i \in [n]} F_{t_i}(x) - x = 0] \geq \epsilon(\lambda)$$

where $\sum_{i \in [n]} F_{t_i}(x)$ is some random constant. Obviously this contradicts Lemma 1. Thus we conclude that there exits at least one i such that $\deg_x(F_{t_i}) = 0$.

□

By Lemmas 2 and 3 we show that there exits an i:

$$\Pr[\deg_x(F_{t_i}) = 1 \wedge \deg_x(F_{a_i}) = 0] \leq \mathsf{negl}(\lambda)$$

which follows that the extractor $\mathcal{E}$ returns o with negligible probability.   □

4.2   Our Construction

Then we propose a new NIZK argument of knowledge. Our scheme is described in Fig. 3. The biggest improvement we make is to sum all Q_i to obtain one element Q in the process of proving, and then we replace Q_i with Q to reduce the size of argument. At the same time, the smaller argument size yields less pairing computations in the verification process. Thus our construction saves almost half of storage space of signature and reduces almost half of pairing computations. When n is large, the effect of this improvement is obvious.

Theorem 2. *The scheme in Fig. 3 has perfect zero-knowledge.*

Proof. We construct a simulator $\mathcal{S}(\theta, \alpha, s)$ to prove perfect zero-knowledge as follows:

$\mathcal{G}(1^\lambda)$	$\mathcal{P}(\theta, w, s)$	$\mathcal{V}(\theta, \pi, s)$
$\alpha \leftarrow \mathbb{Z}_p$	parse $\theta = T \in \mathbb{G}_2$	parse $\theta = T \in \mathbb{G}_2$
$\theta \leftarrow g_2^\alpha$	$w = (a, j)$	$\pi = \{T_i\}_{i\in[n]} \in \mathbb{G}_2^n$
output (θ, α)	$s = \{A_i\}_{i\in[n]} \in \mathbb{G}_1^n$	$Q \in \mathbb{G}_1$
	$\forall i \in [n]\backslash j:$	$s = \{A_i\}_{i\in[n]} \in \mathbb{G}_1^n$
	$\quad t_i \leftarrow \mathbb{Z}_p$	output 1 iff
	$\quad T_i \leftarrow g_2^{t_i}$	$\displaystyle\prod_{i\in[n]} T_i = T \wedge$
	$\quad Q_i \leftarrow (A_i)^{t_i}$	
	$T_j \leftarrow T \cdot (\displaystyle\prod_{i\in[n]\backslash j} g_2^{t_i})^{-1}$	$\displaystyle\prod_{i\in[n]} e(A_i, T_i) = e(Q, g_2)$
	$Q_j \leftarrow \phi(T_j^a)$	
	$Q = \displaystyle\prod_{i\in[n]} Q_i$	
	output $\pi = (Q, \{T_i\}_{i\in[n]})$	

Fig. 3. NIZK for disjunctive statements.

1. $\mathcal{S}$ parses the common reference string θ as $T \in \mathbb{G}_2$ and parses a statement s as $\{A_i\}_{i\in[n]} \in \mathbb{G}_1^n$.
2. $\mathcal{S}$ randomly picks a $j \leftarrow [n]$ and $\{t_i\}_{i\in[n]\backslash j} \leftarrow \mathbb{Z}_p^{n-1}$, it computes $\{T_i = (g_2)^{t_i}\}_{i\in[n]\backslash j}$ and $\{Q_i = (A_i)^{t_i}\}_{i\in[n]\backslash j}$.
3. $\mathcal{S}$ computes

$$T_j = \frac{T}{\prod_{i\in[n]\backslash j} g_2^{t_i}}$$

$$Q_j = A_j^{\alpha - \sum_{i\in[n]\backslash j} t_i}$$

$$Q = \prod_{i\in[n]} Q_i.$$

4. $\mathcal{S}$ outputs $(Q, \{T_i\}_{i\in[n]})$.

As this simulation is efficient, we note that $\{T_i\}_{i\in[n]}$ is picked identically to $\mathcal{P}$ and $Q = \prod_{i\in[n]} A_i^{\mathsf{Dlog}_{g_1}(T_i)}$. It shows that the scheme has perfect zero-knowledge.
□

Theorem 3. *The scheme in Fig. 3 has computational knowledge soundness.*

Proof. We construct an extractor $\mathcal{E}$ to prove computational knowledge soundness as follows:

$\mathcal{E}(\alpha, \theta)$. This extractor runs the adversaries $\mathcal{A}$ on the θ and receives $(s = \{A_i\}_{i\in[n]}, \pi = (Q, \{T_i\}))$. As we defined above, $\mathcal{E}$ has full access to $\mathcal{A}$ to obtain (s, π, w). For all $i \in [n]$, it outputs (a, i) when $A_i = g_1^a$.

We note that if $\prod_{i\in[n]} T_i = T = g_2^\alpha$ and $\mathsf{Dlog}_{g_1}(Q) = \sum_{i\in[n]} \mathsf{Dlog}_{g_2}(T_i) \cdot \mathsf{Dlog}_{g_1}(A_i)$, the extraction is successful. As CL-KEA we described above, it happens with $\epsilon(\lambda)$.   □

5 Compact Ring Signature

In this section, we present a compact ring signature scheme based on our proposed NIZK arguments of knowledge. Before introducing our ring signature scheme, we first recall the corresponding language described in [33].

$$\mathcal{L} = \left\{ \begin{array}{c} (\{k_i\}_{i\in[n]}, c, \{z_i\}_{i\in[n]}, z', m) \in \mathbb{G}_1^{\lambda\cdot n+1} \times \mathbb{G}_2^{n+1} \times \{0,1\}^* : \\ \exists(\rho, \delta, i) : \dfrac{z'}{z_i} = g_2^\rho \wedge c = \mathsf{HEval}(k_i, m)^\delta \end{array} \right\}.$$

This language can be separated into two sub-languages as follows:

$$\mathcal{L}_1 = \left\{ \begin{array}{c} (\{z_i\}_{i\in[n]}, z') \in \mathbb{G}_2^{n+1} : \\ \exists(\rho, i) : \dfrac{z'}{z_i} = g_2^\rho \end{array} \right\}.$$

$$\mathcal{L}_2 = \left\{ \begin{array}{c} (\{k_i\}_{i\in[n]}, c, m) \in \mathbb{G}_1^{\lambda\cdot n+1} \times \{0,1\}^* : \\ \exists(\delta, i) : c = \mathsf{HEval}(k_i, m)^\delta \end{array} \right\}.$$

We note that $\mathcal{L}$ essentially includes two NIZK arguments of knowledge for disjunctive discrete logarithms $(\frac{z'}{z_i}, \rho)$ and (c, δ) as above. It is easy to see the first language $\mathcal{L}_1$ works well with their NIZK arguments of knowledge. However we have no idea for the second one, in their scheme the set $\{\mathsf{HEval}(k_i, m)^\delta\}_{i\in[n]\setminus j}$ is not public to all and not generated. To make it compatible we make some small changes such that:

$$\mathcal{L}_2' = \left\{ \begin{array}{c} (\{k_i\}_{i\in[n]}, c, m) \in \mathbb{G}_1^{\lambda\cdot n} \times \mathbb{G}_2 \times \{0,1\}^* : \\ \exists(\dfrac{1}{\delta}, i) : \mathsf{HEval}(k_i, m) = c^{\frac{1}{\delta}} \end{array} \right\}.$$

First we change the witness from (δ, i) to $(\frac{1}{\delta}, i)$, thus the corresponding disjunctive discrete logarithm becomes $(\mathsf{HEval}(k_i, m), \frac{1}{\delta})$. Then we change the range of hash function from $\mathbb{G}_1$ to $\mathbb{G}_2$. From these two changes, it is easy to show that both $\mathcal{L}_1$ and $\mathcal{L}_2'$ can work well with their NIZK arguments of knowledge, same to ours. More details about this feature are shown in Figs. 4 and 5.

Formally, we combine $\mathcal{L}_1$ and $\mathcal{L}_2'$ as follows:

$$\mathcal{L}' = \left\{ \begin{array}{c} (\{k_i\}_{i\in[n]}, \{z_i\}_{i\in[n]}, z', c, m) \in \mathbb{G}_1^{\lambda\cdot n} \times \mathbb{G}_2^{n+2} \times \{0,1\}^* : \\ \exists(\rho, \dfrac{1}{\delta}, i) : \dfrac{z'}{z_i} = g_2^\rho \wedge \mathsf{HEval}(k_i, m) = c^{\frac{1}{\delta}} \end{array} \right\}.$$

5.1 Scheme Description

Based on primitives, our ring signature $\mathsf{RSig} = (\mathsf{Gen},\mathsf{Sig},\mathsf{Ver})$ includes three algorithms as follows:

$\mathsf{Gen}(1^\lambda)$: on input a security parameter λ, this algorithm randomly picks $x \leftarrow \mathbb{Z}_p$, $\beta \leftarrow \mathbb{Z}_p$ and generates k by calling $\mathsf{HGen}(1^\lambda)$. It calculates $z = g_1^x$ and $C = g_2^\beta$, outputs (sk, vk), where $vk = (z, k, C)$ is a verification key and $sk = x$ is a signing key.

$\mathsf{Sig}(R, sk_j, m)$: on input $R = \{vk_i\}_{i \in [n]}$, a signing key sk_j and a message m, this algorithm randomly picks $(s, \rho, \delta) \leftarrow \mathbb{Z}_p^3$, generates a re-randomizable signing key $sk_j' = sk_j + \rho$ and corresponding re-randomizable verification key $z_j' = z_j \cdot g_1^\rho$, computes $c_i = \phi(\mathsf{HEval}(k_i, m||R)) \in \mathbb{G}_1$, $c = \mathsf{HEval}(k_j, m||R)^\delta \in \mathbb{G}_2$ and $y = c^{\frac{1}{x'+s}}$. This algorithm proves two statements as follows:

- Prove a statement (R, z') by calling $\mathcal{P}\left(\prod_{i \in [n]} C_i, (R, z'), (\rho, j)\right)$ as Fig. 4 and outputs π_1.
- Call $\mathcal{P}\left(\prod_{i \in [n]} C_i, (R, c_i, c), (\frac{1}{\delta}, j)\right)$ to prove a statement (R, c_i) as Fig. 4 and outputs π_2.

As a result, this algorithm outputs $\sigma = (\pi_1, \pi_2, c, y, s, z')$.

$\mathsf{Verify}(R, m, \sigma)$: on input a ring $R = \{vk_i\}_{i \in [n]}$, a message m and a signature σ, compute $c_i = \phi(\mathsf{HEval}(k_i, m||R)) \in \mathbb{G}_1$. First this algorithm verifies two statements as follows:

- Verify a statement (R, z') by calling $\mathcal{V}\left(\prod_{i \in [n]} C_i, (R, z'), \pi_1\right)$ as Fig. 5 and outputs b_1.

$\mathcal{P}\left(\prod_{i \in [n]} C_i, (R, z'), (\rho, j)\right)$	$\mathcal{P}\left(\prod_{i \in [n]} C_i, (R, c_i, c), (\frac{1}{\delta}, j)\right)$
$T = \prod\limits_{i \in [n]} C_i \in \mathbb{G}_2$	$T = \prod\limits_{i \in [n]} C_i \in \mathbb{G}_2$
$\forall i \in [n] \backslash j :$	$\forall i \in [n] \backslash j :$
$\quad t_i \leftarrow \mathbb{Z}_p$	$\quad t_i \leftarrow \mathbb{Z}_p$
$\quad T_i \leftarrow g_2^{t_i}$	$\quad T_i \leftarrow c^{t_i}$
$\quad Q_i \leftarrow (\frac{z'}{z_i})^{t_i}$	$\quad Q_i \leftarrow (c_i)^{t_i}$
$T_j \leftarrow T \cdot (\prod\limits_{i \in [n] \backslash j} T_i)^{-1}$	$T_j \leftarrow T \cdot (\prod\limits_{i \in [n] \backslash j} T_i)^{-1}$
$Q_j \leftarrow \phi(T_j^\rho)$	$Q_j \leftarrow \phi(T_j^{\frac{1}{\delta}})$
$Q = \prod\limits_{i \in [n]} Q_i$	$Q = \prod\limits_{i \in [n]} Q_i$
output $\pi_1 = (Q, \{T_i\}_{i \in [n]})$	output $\pi_2 = (Q, \{T_i\}_{i \in [n]})$

Fig. 4. Proving of NIZK arguments of knowledge.

$$\mathcal{V}\left(\prod_{i\in[n]} C_i, (R, z'), \pi_1\right) \qquad\qquad \mathcal{V}\left(\prod_{i\in[n]} C_i, (R, c_i, c), \pi_2\right)$$

output 1 iff

$$\prod_{i\in[n]} T_i = \prod_{i\in[n]} C_i \wedge$$

$$\prod_{i\in[n]} e(\frac{z'}{z_i}, T_i) = e(Q, g_2)$$

where

$$\prod_{i\in[n]} e(\frac{z'}{z_i}, T_i)$$

$$= \prod_{i\in[n]} e(g_1, T_i)^{sk'-sk_i}$$

$$= \prod_{i\in[n]\setminus j} e(g_1, g_2)^{(sk'-sk_i)\cdot t_i} \cdot e(g_1^{sk'-sk_j}, T_j)$$

$$= \prod_{i\in[n]\setminus j} e(g_1, g_2)^{(sk'-sk_i)\cdot t_i} \cdot e(g_1, T_j^{sk'-sk_j})$$

$$= \prod_{i\in[n]\setminus j} e(Q_i, g_2) \cdot e(Q_j, g_2)$$

$$= \prod_{i\in[n]} e(Q_i, g_2)$$

$$= e(Q, g_2)$$

output 1 iff

$$\prod_{i\in[n]} T_i = \prod_{i\in[n]} C_i \wedge$$

$$\prod_{i\in[n]} e(c_i, T_i) = e(Q, c)$$

where

$$\prod_{i\in[n]} e(c_i, T_i)$$

$$= \prod_{i\in[n]\setminus j} e(c_i, c)^{t_i} \cdot e(c_j, T_j)$$

$$= \prod_{i\in[n]\setminus j} e(c_i, c)^{t_i} \cdot e(c_j^{\delta}, T_j^{\frac{1}{\delta}})$$

$$= \prod_{i\in[n]\setminus j} e(c_i^{t_i}, c) \cdot e(Q_j, c)$$

$$= \prod_{i\in[n]\setminus j} e(Q_i, c) \cdot e(Q_j, c)$$

$$= e(Q, c)$$

Fig. 5. Verification of NIZK arguments of knowledge.

– Verify a statement (R, c_i) by calling $\mathcal{V}\left(\prod_{i\in[n]} C_i, (R, c_i, c), \pi_2\right)$ as Fig. 5 and outputs b_2.

Then if $e(z' \cdot g_1^s, y) = e(g_1, c) \wedge b_1 = 1 \wedge b_2 = 1$ it returns 1. Otherwise it returns 0.

5.2 Scheme Analysis

The **Anonymity** and **Unforgeability** of this kind of ring signature have been proven in [33], we don't show details again. We compare Malavolta et al.'s scheme and ours in Table 1.

As shown in the table, both L-KEA and CL-KEA are secure in the generic group model, thus the improvements are not at the expense of security. On the other hand, we do not change the sizes of signing key and verification key. Our main contribution is that we reduce almost half of the signature size and half of pairing computations in verification, when n is large.

Table 1. Comparisons between Malavolta et al.'s scheme[33] and ours

Ring signature	[33]	Ours
Model	Standard	Standard
Anonymity	✓	✓
Unforgeability	✓	✓
Assumption	q-SDH + L-KEA	q-SDH + CL-KEA
Ring size	$\mathsf{poly}(\lambda)$	$\mathsf{poly}(\lambda)$
Signing key size	$\mathbb{Z}_p$	$\mathbb{Z}_p$
Verification key size	$(\lambda + 2)\mathbb{G}$	$(\lambda + 2)\mathbb{G}$
Signature size	$(4 \cdot n + 3)\mathbb{G} + \mathbb{Z}_p$	$(2 \cdot n + 5)\mathbb{G} + \mathbb{Z}_p$
Signing computations	$(4 \cdot n + 3)\mathrm{E} + n\mathrm{H}$	$(4 \cdot n + 3)\mathrm{E} + n\mathrm{H}$
Verification computations	$(4 \cdot n + 2)\mathrm{P} + \mathrm{E} + n\mathrm{H}$	$(2 \cdot n + 4)\mathrm{P} + \mathrm{E} + n\mathrm{H}$

Here we denote an exponentiation computation by E, a bilinear pairing computation by P and a hash function computation by H.

6   Conclusion

In this work, first we propose a new NIZK argument of knowledge. With its good properties, a compact ring signature scheme is constructed in the standard model. Compared with the Malavolta et al.'s scheme [33], our construction reduces the signature size and pairing computations in verification process. We believe this improvement will reduce bandwidth cost in blockchain in the future.

Acknowledgement. This work was supported by the National Natural Science Foundation of China (61702342), the Science and Technology Innovation Projects of Shenzhen (GJHZ 20160226202520268, JCYJ 20170302151321095, JCYJ 20170302145623566) and Tencent "Rhinoceros Birds" -Scientific Research Foundation for Young Teachers of Shenzhen University.

References

1. Au, M.H., Liu, J.K., Susilo, W., Yuen, T.H.: Constant-size ID-based linkable and revocable-iff-linked ring signature. In: Barua, R., Lange, T. (eds.) INDOCRYPT 2006. LNCS, vol. 4329, pp. 364–378. Springer, Heidelberg (2006). https://doi.org/10.1007/11941378_26

2. Au, M.H., Liu, J.K., Susilo, W., Yuen, T.H.: Certificate based (linkable) ring signature. In: Dawson, E., Wong, D.S. (eds.) ISPEC 2007. LNCS, vol. 4464, pp. 79–92. Springer, Heidelberg (2007). https://doi.org/10.1007/978-3-540-72163-5_8

3. Au, M.H., Liu, J.K., Susilo, W., Yuen, T.H.: Secure ID-based linkable and revocable-iff-linked ring signature with constant-size construction. Theor. Comput. Sci. **469**, 1–14 (2013)

4. Au, M.H., Liu, J.K., Susilo, W., Zhou, J.: Realizing fully secure unrestricted ID-based ring signature in the standard model based on HIBE. IEEE Trans. Inf. Forensics Secur. **8**(12), 1909–1922 (2013)

5. Au, M.H., Liu, J.K., Yuen, T.H., Wong, D.S.: ID-based ring signature scheme secure in the standard model. In: Yoshiura, H., Sakurai, K., Rannenberg, K., Murayama, Y., Kawamura, S. (eds.) IWSEC 2006. LNCS, vol. 4266, pp. 1–16. Springer, Heidelberg (2006). https://doi.org/10.1007/11908739_1

6. Bender, A., Katz, J., Morselli, R.: Ring signatures: stronger definitions, and constructions without random oracles. In: Halevi, S., Rabin, T. (eds.) TCC 2006. LNCS, vol. 3876, pp. 60–79. Springer, Heidelberg (2006). https://doi.org/10.1007/11681878_4

7. Boneh, D., Boyen, X., Shacham, H.: Short group signatures. In: Franklin, M. (ed.) CRYPTO 2004. LNCS, vol. 3152, pp. 41–55. Springer, Heidelberg (2004). https://doi.org/10.1007/978-3-540-28628-8_3

8. Chan, T.K., Fung, K., Liu, J.K., Wei, V.K.: Blind spontaneous anonymous group signatures for Ad Hoc groups. In: Castelluccia, C., Hartenstein, H., Paar, C., Westhoff, D. (eds.) ESAS 2004. LNCS, vol. 3313, pp. 82–94. Springer, Heidelberg (2005). https://doi.org/10.1007/978-3-540-30496-8_8

9. Chaum, D., van Heyst, E.: Group signatures. In: Davies, D.W. (ed.) EUROCRYPT 1991. LNCS, vol. 547, pp. 257–265. Springer, Heidelberg (1991). https://doi.org/10.1007/3-540-46416-6_22

10. Chow, S.S.M., Wei, V.K., Liu, J.K., Yuen, T.H.: Ring signatures without random oracles. In: ASIACCS 2006, pp. 297–302. ACM (2006)

11. Dodis, Y., Kiayias, A., Nicolosi, A., Shoup, V.: Anonymous identification in *Ad Hoc* groups. In: Cachin, C., Camenisch, J.L. (eds.) EUROCRYPT 2004. LNCS, vol. 3027, pp. 609–626. Springer, Heidelberg (2004). https://doi.org/10.1007/978-3-540-24676-3_36

12. Fleischhacker, N., Krupp, J., Malavolta, G., Schneider, J., Schröder, D., Simkin, M.: Efficient unlinkable sanitizable signatures from signatures with re-randomizable keys. In: Cheng, C.-M., Chung, K.-M., Persiano, G., Yang, B.-Y. (eds.) PKC 2016. LNCS, vol. 9614, pp. 301–330. Springer, Heidelberg (2016). https://doi.org/10.1007/978-3-662-49384-7_12

13. Groth, J.: Simulation-sound NIZK proofs for a practical language and constant size group signatures. In: Lai, X., Chen, K. (eds.) ASIACRYPT 2006. LNCS, vol. 4284, pp. 444–459. Springer, Heidelberg (2006). https://doi.org/10.1007/11935230_29

14. Groth, J.: On the size of pairing-based non-interactive arguments. In: Fischlin, M., Coron, J.-S. (eds.) EUROCRYPT 2016. LNCS, vol. 9666, pp. 305–326. Springer, Heidelberg (2016). https://doi.org/10.1007/978-3-662-49896-5_11

15. Groth, J., Kohlweiss, M.: One-out-of-many proofs: or how to leak a secret and spend a coin. In: Oswald, E., Fischlin, M. (eds.) EUROCRYPT 2015. LNCS, vol. 9057, pp. 253–280. Springer, Heidelberg (2015). https://doi.org/10.1007/978-3-662-46803-6_9

16. Herranz, J., Sáez, G.: Forking lemmas for ring signature schemes. In: Johansson, T., Maitra, S. (eds.) INDOCRYPT 2003. LNCS, vol. 2904, pp. 266–279. Springer, Heidelberg (2003). https://doi.org/10.1007/978-3-540-24582-7_20

17. Hofheinz, D., Kiltz, E.: Programmable hash functions and their applications. J. Cryptol. **25**(3), 484–527 (2012)

18. Huang, X., et al.: Cost-effective authentic and anonymous data sharing with forward security. IEEE Trans. Comput. **64**(4), 971–983 (2015)

19. Lai, R.W.F., Zhang, T., Chow, S.S.M., Schröder, D.: Efficient sanitizable signatures without random oracles. In: Askoxylakis, I., Ioannidis, S., Katsikas, S., Meadows, C. (eds.) ESORICS 2016. LNCS, vol. 9878, pp. 363–380. Springer, Cham (2016). https://doi.org/10.1007/978-3-319-45744-4_18

20. Liu, D.Y.W., Liu, J.K., Mu, Y., Susilo, W., Wong, D.S.: Revocable ring signature. J. Comput. Sci. Technol. **22**(6), 785–794 (2007)
21. Liu, J.K., Au, M.H., Susilo, W., Zhou, J.: Online/offline ring signature scheme. In: Qing, S., Mitchell, C.J., Wang, G. (eds.) ICICS 2009. LNCS, vol. 5927, pp. 80–90. Springer, Heidelberg (2009). https://doi.org/10.1007/978-3-642-11145-7_8
22. Liu, J.K., Au, M.H., Susilo, W., Zhou, J.: Linkable ring signature with unconditional anonymity. IEEE Trans. Knowl. Data Eng. **26**(1), 157–165 (2014)
23. Liu, J.K., Susilo, W., Wong, D.S.: Ring signature with designated linkability. In: Yoshiura, H., Sakurai, K., Rannenberg, K., Murayama, Y., Kawamura, S. (eds.) IWSEC 2006. LNCS, vol. 4266, pp. 104–119. Springer, Heidelberg (2006). https://doi.org/10.1007/11908739_8
24. Liu, J.K., Wei, V.K., Wong, D.S.: A separable threshold ring signature scheme. In: Lim, J.-I., Lee, D.-H. (eds.) ICISC 2003. LNCS, vol. 2971, pp. 12–26. Springer, Heidelberg (2004). https://doi.org/10.1007/978-3-540-24691-6_2
25. Liu, J.K., Wei, V.K., Wong, D.S.: Linkable spontaneous anonymous group signature for Ad Hoc groups. In: Wang, H., Pieprzyk, J., Varadharajan, V. (eds.) ACISP 2004. LNCS, vol. 3108, pp. 325–335. Springer, Heidelberg (2004). https://doi.org/10.1007/978-3-540-27800-9_28
26. Liu, J.K., Wong, D.S.: On the security models of (threshold) ring signature schemes. In: Park, C., Chee, S. (eds.) ICISC 2004. LNCS, vol. 3506, pp. 204–217. Springer, Heidelberg (2005). https://doi.org/10.1007/11496618_16
27. Liu, J.K., Wong, D.S.: Linkable ring signatures: security models and new schemes. In: Gervasi, O., et al. (eds.) ICCSA 2005. LNCS, vol. 3481, pp. 614–623. Springer, Heidelberg (2005). https://doi.org/10.1007/11424826_65
28. Liu, J.K., Wong, D.S.: Enhanced security models and a generic construction approach for linkable ring signature. Int. J. Found. Comput. Sci. **17**(6), 1403–1422 (2006). https://doi.org/10.1142/S0129054106004480
29. Liu, J.K., Wong, D.S.: A more efficient instantiation of witness-indistinguishable signature. I. J. Netw. Secur. **5**(2), 199–204 (2007)
30. Liu, J.K., Wong, D.S.: Solutions to key exposure problem in ring signature. I. J. Netw. Secur. **6**(2), 170–180 (2008)
31. Liu, J.K., Yeo, S.L., Yap, W., Chow, S.S.M., Wong, D.S., Susilo, W.: Faulty instantiations of threshold ring signature from threshold proof-of-knowledge protocol. Comput. J. **59**(7), 945–954 (2016)
32. Liu, J.K., Yuen, T.H., Zhou, J.: Forward secure ring signature without random oracles. In: Qing, S., Susilo, W., Wang, G., Liu, D. (eds.) ICICS 2011. LNCS, vol. 7043, pp. 1–14. Springer, Heidelberg (2011). https://doi.org/10.1007/978-3-642-25243-3_1
33. Malavolta, G., Schröder, D.: Efficient ring signatures in the standard model. In: Takagi, T., Peyrin, T. (eds.) ASIACRYPT 2017. LNCS, vol. 10625, pp. 128–157. Springer, Cham (2017). https://doi.org/10.1007/978-3-319-70697-9_5
34. Nakamoto, S.: Bitcoin: a peer-to-peer electronic cash system (2008). https://bitcoin.org/bitcoin.pdf
35. Rivest, R.L., Shamir, A., Tauman, Y.: How to leak a secret. In: Boyd, C. (ed.) ASIACRYPT 2001. LNCS, vol. 2248, pp. 552–565. Springer, Heidelberg (2001). https://doi.org/10.1007/3-540-45682-1_32
36. van Saberhagen, N.: Cryptonote v 2.0 (2013). https://cryptonote.org/whitepaper.pdf
37. Schwartz, J.T.: Fast probabilistic algorithms for verification of polynomial identities. J. ACM **27**(4), 701–717 (1980)

38. Sun, S.-F., Au, M.H., Liu, J.K., Yuen, T.H.: RingCT 2.0: a compact accumulator-based (linkable ring signature) protocol for blockchain cryptocurrency monero. In: Foley, S.N., Gollmann, D., Snekkenes, E. (eds.) ESORICS 2017. LNCS, vol. 10493, pp. 456–474. Springer, Cham (2017). https://doi.org/10.1007/978-3-319-66399-9_25

39. Tsang, P.P., Au, M.H., Liu, J.K., Susilo, W., Wong, D.S.: A suite of non-pairing ID-based threshold ring signature schemes with different levels of anonymity (extended abstract). In: Heng, S.-H., Kurosawa, K. (eds.) ProvSec 2010. LNCS, vol. 6402, pp. 166–183. Springer, Heidelberg (2010). https://doi.org/10.1007/978-3-642-16280-0_11

40. Tsang, P.P., Wei, V.K., Chan, T.K., Au, M.H., Liu, J.K., Wong, D.S.: Separable linkable threshold ring signatures. In: Canteaut, A., Viswanathan, K. (eds.) INDOCRYPT 2004. LNCS, vol. 3348, pp. 384–398. Springer, Heidelberg (2004). https://doi.org/10.1007/978-3-540-30556-9_30

41. Wijaya, D.A., Liu, J.K., Suwarsono, D.A., Zhang, P.: A new blockchain-based value-added tax system. In: Okamoto, T., Yu, Y., Au, M.H., Li, Y. (eds.) ProvSec 2017. LNCS, vol. 10592, pp. 471–486. Springer, Cham (2017). https://doi.org/10.1007/978-3-319-68637-0_28

42. Wong, D.S., Fung, K., Liu, J.K., Wei, V.K.: On the RS-code construction of ring signature schemes and a threshold setting of RST. In: Qing, S., Gollmann, D., Zhou, J. (eds.) ICICS 2003. LNCS, vol. 2836, pp. 34–46. Springer, Heidelberg (2003). https://doi.org/10.1007/978-3-540-39927-8_4

43. Yang, X., Wu, W., Liu, J.K., Chen, X.: Lightweight anonymous authentication for Ad Hoc group: a ring signature approach. In: Au, M.-H., Miyaji, A. (eds.) ProvSec 2015. LNCS, vol. 9451, pp. 215–226. Springer, Cham (2015). https://doi.org/10.1007/978-3-319-26059-4_12

44. Yuen, T.H., Liu, J.K., Au, M.H., Susilo, W., Zhou, J.: Threshold ring signature without random oracles. In: ASIACCS 2011, pp. 261–267. ACM (2011)

45. Yuen, T.H., Liu, J.K., Au, M.H., Susilo, W., Zhou, J.: Efficient linkable and/or threshold ring signature without random oracles. Comput. J. **56**(4), 407–421 (2013)

Public Key Cryptography

A Generic Construction of Integrated Secure-Channel Free PEKS and PKE

Tatsuya Suzuki[1($\boxtimes$)], Keita Emura[2], and Toshihiro Ohigashi[1]

[1] Tokai University, 2-3-23, Takanawa, Minato-ku, Tokyo 108-8619, Japan
t-suzuki@star.tokai-u.jp, ohigashi@tsc.u-tokai.ac.jp
[2] National Institute of Information and Communications Technology, 4-2-1,
Nukui-Kitamachi, Koganei, Tokyo 184-8795, Japan
k-emura@nict.go.jp

Abstract. To provide a search functionality for encrypted data, public key encryption with keyword search (PEKS) has been widely recognized. In actual usage, a PEKS scheme should be employed with a PKE scheme since PEKS itself does not support the decryption of data. Since a naive composition of a PEKS ciphertext and a PKE ciphertext does not provide CCA security, several attempts have been made to integrate PEKS and PKE in a joint CCA manner (PEKS/PKE for short). In this paper, we further extend these works by integrating secure-channel free PEKS (SCF-PEKS) and PKE, which we call SCF-PEKS/PKE, where no secure channel is required to send trapdoors. We give a formal security definition of SCF-PEKS/PKE in a joint CCA manner, and propose a generic construction of SCF-PEKS/PKE based on anonymous identity-based encryption, tag-based encryption, and one-time signature. We also strengthen the current consistency definition according to the secure-channel free property, and show that our construction is strongly consistent if the underlying IBE provides unrestricted strong collision-freeness which is defined in this paper. Finally, we show that such an IBE scheme can be constructed by employing the Abdalla et al. transformations (TCC 2010/JoC 2018).

Keywords: PEKS · Integration of PEKS and PKE
Secure-channel free · Joint CCA security

1 Introduction

Integration of Searchable Encryption and Public Key Encryption:
Public key encryption with keyword search (PEKS) [6] has been widely recognized as a cryptographic primitive providing a search functionality for encrypted data. Briefly, a trapdoor t_ω is generated with respect to a keyword ω, and one can search a ciphertext of ω by using t_ω. As defined by Abdalla et al. [1], PEKS should provide (wrong keyword) consistency and keyword privacy. Briefly, the former guarantees that for two distinct keywords ω and ω', a ciphertext of ω

© Springer Nature Switzerland AG 2018
C. Su and H. Kikuchi (Eds.): ISPEC 2018, LNCS 11125, pp. 69–86, 2018.
https://doi.org/10.1007/978-3-319-99807-7_5

is not searched by $t_{\omega'}$. The latter guarantees that no information of keyword is revealed from the ciphertext. Abdalla et al. [1] gave a generic construction of PEKS from anonymous identity-based encryption (IBE), e.g., [7,11,23].

In actual usage, PEKS should be employed with a PKE scheme since PEKS itself does not support the decryption of data. For example, assume that an e-mail is required to be encrypted. Then, a sender encrypts the mail header or title using a PEKS scheme, and encrypts the mail body using a PKE scheme whose public key is managed by the receiver. Then, a mail gateway can forward the encrypted e-mail by using PEKS, and the receiver can decrypt the ciphertext using their own secret key of the PKE scheme. From now on, we denote the integrated PEKS and PKE as PEKS/PKE as in [30]. As a naive composition, for a PEKS ciphertext C_{PEKS} and a PKE ciphertext C_{PKE}, a ciphertext of PEKS/PKE is described as its concatenation $C_{\mathsf{PEKS}}||C_{\mathsf{PKE}}$.

Although indistinguishability against chosen ciphertext attack (IND-CCA) is widely recognized as a standard security definition of PKE, obviously, the naive composition does not provide CCA security even if the underlying PKE scheme is CCA secure. For example, the challenge ciphertext $C_{\mathsf{PEKS}}^*||C_{\mathsf{PKE}}^*$ can be modified such as $C_{\mathsf{PEKS}}||C_{\mathsf{PKE}}^*$ where $C_{\mathsf{PEKS}} \neq C_{\mathsf{PEKS}}^*$, and one can send it to the decryption oracle. This was pointed out by Baek et al. [4] who gave a definition of joint CCA security for PEKS/PKE. Later, Zhang and Imai [30] pointed out that Baek et al.'s definition does not consider keyword privacy. They gave a formal definition of PEKS/PKE that captures both data privacy and keyword privacy, and proposed a generic construction of PEKS/PKE. Abdalla et al. [2,3] further pointed out that there is a room for improvement in the Zhang-Imai model since an adversary is not allowed to access the test oracle in the model. Chen et al. [12] further considered the trapdoor oracle, and proposed a generic construction of PEKS/PKE from (hierarchical) IBE schemes. As concrete constructions, Buccafurri et al. [9] and Saraswat and Sahu [27] proposed PEKS/PKE schemes from (asymmetric) pairings.[1]

Secure-Channel Free PEKS: In typical usage of PEKS, a receiver generates a trapdoor, and sends it to a server (e.g., mail gateway). Then, since anyone can run the test algorithm when they obtain a trapdoor, the trapdoor must be sent to the server via a secure channel. To remove the secure channel, secure-channel free PEKS (SCF-PEKS), which is also called designated tester PEKS, has been proposed [13–15,20,26,28]. Unlike the case of employing SSL/TLS in a naive way, only the designated server can run the test algorithm even if trapdoors are exposed. In SCF-PEKS, the server also has a public key and a secret key, and a keyword is encrypted by using the server pubic key in addition to the receiver pubic key. The test algorithm is run by using the server secret key in addition to a trapdoor.

---

[1] As a similar primitive, decryptable searchable encryption has been proposed [18,21] where keywords can be recovered from ciphertexts via the decryption procedure. One main difference from PEKS/PKE is that no plaintext space is defined.

Our Contribution: As in PEKS, all PEKS/PKE have assumed that trapdoors are sent to the server via a secure channel. In this paper, to remove this limitation we propose PEKS/PKE supporting secure-channel free property, which we call SCF-PEKS/PKE.

First we give a formal security definition of SCF-PEKS/PKE in a joint CCA manner. Basically, we extend the security definition of SCF-PEKS given by Fang et al. [16].[2] We strengthen their consistency definition as follows. First, an adversary is allowed to access the trapdoor oracle in our model. Owing to the secure-channel free property, this setting is natural since trapdoors are sent via a public channel. Moreover, we give the server secret key to the adversary to guarantee that the server has no way of producing inconsistent ciphertexts. We call this weak consistency. We further strengthen the consistency, which we call strong consistency, where (1) an adversary can obtain trapdoors even for challenge keywords, and (2) an adversary is allowed to produce the challenge ciphertext. The first extension is the same as that of unrestricted strong robustness [17], and the second extension is the same as those of strong robustness [2,3] and strong collision-freeness [25]. For keyword privacy, as in Fang et al., we consider two situations where either an adversary is modeled as the server (then the server secret key is given to the adversary), or an adversary is modeled as a receiver (then the receiver secret key is given to the adversary). In the former, the adversary is allowed to access the trapdoor oracle and the test oracle, and in the latter, the adversary is allowed to access the test oracle. We additionally consider the decryption oracle to integrate SCF-PEKS and PKE in our joint CCA security. We further define data privacy. To guarantee that the server does not obtain information of data via the test procedure, we give the server secret key to the adversary. Moreover, the adversary is allowed to access the decryption oracle.

Second, we propose a generic construction of SCF-PEKS/PKE with weak consistency from anonymous IBE, tag-based encryption (TBE) [24], and a one-time signature (OTS). We also show that our construction is strongly consistent if the underlying anonymous IBE provides unrestricted strong collision-freeness which is implied by unrestricted strong robustness [17]. We will show how to construct these ingredients in Sect. 5. Our construction can be seen as an extension of a generic construction of SCF-PEKS from the same ingredients as above, proposed by Emura et al. [14], by considering an observation given by Abdalla et al. [2,3]. Namely, Abdalla et al. mentioned that if PEKS and PKE support tags, then these can be combined via the Canetti-Halevi-Katz (CHK) transformation [10], leading to a PEKS/PKE scheme secure in the joint CCA manner. That is, by introducing an OTS scheme, a verification key is regarded as a tag of both ciphertexts, and a signature is produced on them. We point out that the Emura et al. construction yields a "tag-based" SCF-PEKS scheme. By introducing a TBE scheme as the underlying PKE scheme supporting tags, we can construct SCF-PEKS/PKE secure in the joint CCA manner. We further modify the construction to protect against re-encryption attacks (See Sect. 4: High-level

---

[2] Remark that we do not consider security against keyword guessing attacks which is considered by Fang et al. [16], and leave it as a future work of this paper.

Description of Our Construction for details) by preparing an IBE plaintext to be correlated to a verification key.

2   Preliminaries

We denote that $x \overset{\$}{\leftarrow} S$ when x is chosen uniformly from a set S. $y \leftarrow A(x)$ means that y is an output of an algorithm A under an input x. We denote $State$ as the state information transmitted by the adversary to himself across stages of the attack in experiments.

First, we introduce the definition of TBE [24] as follows. Let $\mathcal{TAG}$ and $\mathcal{M}_{\mathsf{TBE}}$ be a tag space of TBE and a plaintext space of TBE, respectively.

Definition 1 (Syntax of TBE). *A TBE scheme* TBE *consists of the following three algorithms,* TBE.KeyGen, TBE.Enc *and* TBE.Dec:

TBE.KeyGen(1^κ): *This key generation algorithm takes as an input the security parameter $\kappa \in \mathrm{N}$, and return a public key pk_{TBE} and a secret key sk_{TBE}.*
TBE.Enc(pk_{TBE}, t, M): *This encryption algorithm takes as input pk_{TBE}, a message $M \in \mathcal{M}_{\mathsf{TBE}}$ with a tag $t \in \mathcal{TAG}$, and returns a ciphertext C_{TBE}.*
TBE.Dec(sk_{TBE}, t, C_{TBE}): *This decryption algorithm takes as inputs sk_{TBE}, t, and C_{TBE}, and returns a message M or a reject symbol $\bot$.*

Correctness is defined as follow: For all $(pk_{\mathsf{TBE}}, sk_{\mathsf{TBE}}) \leftarrow$ TBE.KeyGen(1^κ), all $M \in \mathcal{M}_{TBE}$, and all $t \in \mathcal{TAG}$, TBE.Dec(sk_{TBE}, t, C_{TBE}) $= M$ holds, where $C_{\mathsf{TBE}} \leftarrow$ TBE.Enc(pk_{TBE}, t, M).

Next, we define selective-tag weakly secure against chosen ciphertext attack (IND-stag-CCA) as follows.

Definition 2 (IND-stag-CCA). *For any probabilistic polynomial-time (PPT) adversary $\mathcal{A}$ and the security parameter $\kappa \in \mathrm{N}$, we define the experiment* $\mathrm{Exp}_{\mathsf{TBE},\mathcal{A}}^{\mathrm{IND\text{-}stag\text{-}CCA}}(\kappa)$ *as follows.*

$\mathrm{Exp}_{\mathsf{TBE},\mathcal{A}}^{\mathrm{IND\text{-}stag\text{-}CCA}}(\kappa)$:

$\quad (t^*, State) \leftarrow \mathcal{A}(1^\kappa); \ (pk_{\mathsf{TBE}}, sk_{\mathsf{TBE}}) \leftarrow$ TBE.KeyGen(1^κ)

$\quad (M_0^*, M_1^*, State) \leftarrow \mathcal{A}^{\mathcal{O}_{\mathsf{TBE.DEC}}}(\mathsf{find}, pk_{\mathsf{TBE}}); \ \mu \overset{\$}{\leftarrow} \{0,1\}$

$\quad C_{\mathsf{TBE}}^* \leftarrow$ TBE.Enc($pk_{\mathsf{TBE}}, t^*, M_\mu^*$); $\ \mu' \leftarrow \mathcal{A}^{\mathcal{O}_{\mathsf{TBE.DEC}}}(\mathsf{guess}, C_{\mathsf{TBE}}^*, State)$

$\quad$ *If $\mu = \mu'$ then output 1, and 0 otherwise*

– $\mathcal{O}_{\mathsf{TBE.DEC}}$: *This decryption oracle takes as input a tag and a ciphertext $(t, C_{\mathsf{TBE}}) \neq (t^*, C_{\mathsf{TBE}}^*)$ and returns the result of* TBE.Dec($sk_{\mathsf{TBE}}, t, C_{\mathsf{TBE}}$).

We say that TBE *is IND-stag-CCA secure if the advantage*

$$\mathrm{Adv}_{\mathsf{TBE},\mathcal{A}}^{\mathrm{IND\text{-}stag\text{-}CCA}}(\kappa) := | \ \mathrm{Pr}[\mathrm{Exp}_{\mathsf{TBE},\mathcal{A}}^{\mathrm{IND\text{-}stag\text{-}CCA}}(\kappa) = 1] - 1/2 \ |$$

is negligible for any PPT adversary $\mathcal{A}$.

Next, we introduce definition of anonymous IBE with CCA security [19] as follows. Let $\mathcal{ID}$ and $\mathcal{M}_{\mathsf{IBE}}$ be an identity space and a plaintext space of IBE, respectively.

Definition 3 (Syntax of IBE). *An IBE scheme* IBE *consists of the following four algorithms,* IBE.Setup, IBE.Extract, IBE.Enc *and* IBE.Dec*:*

IBE.Setup(1^κ): *This setup algorithm takes as an input the security parameter* $\kappa \in \mathrm{N}$, *and return a public key params and a master key mk.*

IBE.Extract$(params, mk, ID)$: *This extract algorithm takes as input an identity* $ID \in \mathcal{ID}$ *and mk, and returns a secret key* sk_{ID} *corresponding to* ID.

IBE.Enc$(params, ID, M)$: *This encryption algorithm takes as input params,* ID $\in \mathcal{ID}$, *a message* $M \in \mathcal{M}_{\mathsf{IBE}}$, *and returns a ciphertext* C_{IBE}.

IBE.Dec$(params, sk_{ID}, C_{\mathsf{IBE}})$: *This decryption algorithm takes as inputs* sk_{ID} *and* C_{IBE}, *and returns a message* M *or a reject symbol* $\perp$.

Correctness is defined as follows: For all $(params, mk) \leftarrow$ IBE.Setup(1^κ), all $M \in \mathcal{M}_{\mathsf{IBE}}$, and all $ID \in \mathcal{ID}$, IBE.Dec$(params, sk_{ID}, C_{\mathsf{IBE}}) = M$ holds, where $C_{\mathsf{IBE}} \leftarrow$ IBE.Enc$(params, ID, M)$ and $sk_{ID} \leftarrow$ IBE.Extract$(params, mk, ID)$.

Next, we define indistinguishability against chosen ciphertext attack (IBE-IND-CCA) as follows.

Definition 4 (IBE-IND-CCA). *For any PPT adversary* $\mathcal{A}$ *and the security parameter* $\kappa \in \mathrm{N}$, *we define the experiment* $\mathrm{Exp}_{\mathsf{IBE},\mathcal{A}}^{\mathrm{IBE\text{-}IND\text{-}CCA}}(\kappa)$ *as follows.*

$\mathrm{Exp}_{\mathsf{IBE},\mathcal{A}}^{\mathrm{IBE\text{-}IND\text{-}CCA}}(\kappa)$:

   $(params, mk) \leftarrow$ IBE.Setup(1^κ)

   $(M_0^*, M_1^*, ID^*, State) \leftarrow \mathcal{A}^{\mathcal{O}_{\mathsf{IBE.DEC}}, \mathcal{O}_{\mathsf{IBE.EXTRACT}}}(\mathsf{find}, params)$; $\mu \xleftarrow{\$} \{0, 1\}$

   $C_{\mathsf{IBE}}^* \leftarrow$ IBE.Enc$(params, ID^*, M_\mu^*)$

   $\mu' \leftarrow \mathcal{A}^{\mathcal{O}_{\mathsf{IBE.DEC}}, \mathcal{O}_{\mathsf{IBE.EXTRACT}}}(\mathsf{guess}, C_{\mathsf{IBE}}^*, State)$

   If $\mu = \mu'$ *then output* 1, *and* 0 *otherwise*

- $\mathcal{O}_{\mathsf{IBE.DEC}}$: *This decryption oracle takes as input* $(ID, C_{\mathsf{IBE}}) \neq (ID^*, C_{\mathsf{IBE}}^*)$ *and returns the result of* IBE.Dec$(params, sk_{ID}, C_{\mathsf{IBE}})$ *where* $sk_{ID} \leftarrow$ IBE.Extract$(params, mk, ID)$.
- $\mathcal{O}_{\mathsf{IBE.EXTRACT}}$: *This extract oracle takes as input an identity* $ID \neq ID^*$ *and returns the corresponding secret key* $sk_{ID} \leftarrow$ IBE.Extract$(params, mk, ID)$.

We say that IBE *is IBE-IND-CCA secure if the advantage*

$$\mathrm{Adv}_{\mathsf{IBE},\mathcal{A}}^{\mathrm{IBE\text{-}IND\text{-}CCA}}(\kappa) := \mid \mathrm{Pr}[\mathrm{Exp}_{\mathsf{IBE},\mathcal{A}}^{\mathrm{IBE\text{-}IND\text{-}CCA}}(\kappa) = 1] - 1/2 \mid$$

is negligible for any PPT adversary.

Next, we define anonymity against chosen-ciphertext attack (IBE-ANO-CCA).

Definition 5 (IBE-ANO-CCA). *For any PPT adversary $\mathcal{A}$ and the security parameter $\kappa \in \mathbb{N}$, we define the experiment $\mathrm{Exp}_{\mathsf{IBE},\mathcal{A}}^{\mathrm{IBE\text{-}ANO\text{-}CCA}}(\kappa)$ as follows.*

> $\mathrm{Exp}_{\mathsf{IBE},\mathcal{A}}^{\mathrm{IBE\text{-}ANO\text{-}CCA}}(\kappa)$:
>
> > $(params, mk) \leftarrow \mathsf{IBE.Setup}(1^\kappa)$
> >
> > $(ID_0^*, ID_1^*, M^*, State) \leftarrow \mathcal{A}^{\mathcal{O}_{\mathsf{IBE.DEC}}, \mathcal{O}_{\mathsf{IBE.EXTRACT}}}(\mathsf{find}, params);\ \mu \xleftarrow{\$} \{0, 1\}$
> >
> > $C_{\mathsf{IBE}}^* \leftarrow \mathsf{IBE.Enc}(params, ID_\mu^*, M^*)$
> >
> > $\mu' \leftarrow \mathcal{A}^{\mathcal{O}_{\mathsf{IBE.DEC}}, \mathcal{O}_{\mathsf{IBE.EXTRACT}}}(\mathsf{guess}, C_{\mathsf{IBE}}^*, State)$
> >
> > *If $\mu = \mu'$ then output 1, and 0 otherwise*

- $\mathcal{O}_{\mathsf{IBE.DEC}}$: *This decryption oracle takes as input $(ID, C_{\mathsf{IBE}}) \notin \{(ID_0^*, C_{\mathsf{IBE}}^*), (ID_1^*, C_{\mathsf{IBE}}^*)\}$ and returns the result of $\mathsf{IBE.Dec}(params, sk_{ID}, C_{\mathsf{IBE}})$ where $sk_{ID} \leftarrow \mathsf{IBE.Extract}(params, mk, ID)$.*
- $\mathcal{O}_{\mathsf{IBE.EXTRACT}}$: *This extract oracle takes as input $ID \notin \{ID_0^*, ID_1^*\}$ and returns the corresponding secret key $sk_{ID} \leftarrow \mathsf{IBE.Extract}(params, mk, ID)$.*

We say that IBE is IBE-ANO-CCA secure if the advantage

$$\mathrm{Adv}_{\mathsf{IBE},\mathcal{A}}^{\mathrm{IBE\text{-}ANO\text{-}CCA}}(\kappa) := |\Pr[\mathrm{Exp}_{\mathsf{IBE},\mathcal{A}}^{\mathrm{IBE\text{-}ANO\text{-}CCA}}(\kappa) = 1] - 1/2\,|$$

is negligible for any PPT adversary.

Next, we define unrestricted strong collision-freeness where strong means that an adversary is allowed to produce the challenge ciphertext C_{IBE}^*. This is an extension of strong collision-freeness [25]. Informally, strong collision-freeness guarantees that no adversary can produce a ciphertext whose decryption result for two decryption keys are the same, i.e., $M_0^* = M_1^*$. In addition, in our unrestricted strong collision-freeness definition, the trapdoor oracle has no restriction as in unrestricted strong robustness [17]. Informally, unrestricted strong robustness guarantees that no adversary can produce a ciphertext whose decryption result for two decryption keys are both non-$\perp$. Since the condition $M_0^* = M_1^*$ is not required, our unrestricted strong collision-freeness is an intermediate notion where it is weaker than unrestricted strong robustness and is stronger than strong collision-freeness. How to construct an IBE scheme with unrestricted strong collision-freeness is explained in Sect. 5.

Definition 6 (Unrestricted Strong Collision-Freeness). *For any PPT adversary $\mathcal{A}$ and the security parameter $\kappa \in \mathbb{N}$, we define the experiment $\mathrm{Exp}_{\mathsf{IBE},\mathcal{A}}^{\mathrm{IBE\text{-}usCF}}(\kappa)$ as follows.*

> $\mathrm{Exp}_{\mathsf{IBE},\mathcal{A}}^{\mathrm{IBE\text{-}usCF}}(\kappa)$:
>
> > $(params, mk) \leftarrow \mathsf{IBE.Setup}(1^\kappa)$
> >
> > $(C_{\mathsf{IBE}}^*, ID_0^*, ID_1^*) \leftarrow \mathcal{A}^{\mathcal{O}_{\mathsf{IBE.EXTRACT}}}(\mathsf{find}, params)$
> >
> > $sk_{ID_0^*} \leftarrow \mathsf{IBE.Extract}(params, mk, ID_0^*);\ sk_{ID_1^*} \leftarrow \mathsf{IBE.Extract}(params, mk, ID_1^*)$
> >
> > $M_0^* \leftarrow \mathsf{IBE.Dec}(params, sk_{ID_0^*}, C_{\mathsf{IBE}}^*);\ M_1^* \leftarrow \mathsf{IBE.Dec}(params, sk_{ID_1^*}, C_{\mathsf{IBE}}^*)$
> >
> > *If $M_0^* \neq \perp \wedge M_1^* \neq \perp \wedge M_0^* = M_1^*$ then output 1, and 0 otherwise*

– $\mathcal{O}_{\mathsf{IBE.EXTRACT}}$: *This extract oracle takes as input ID with no restriction, and returns the corresponding secret key $sk_{ID} \leftarrow \mathsf{IBE.Extract}(params, mk, ID)$.*

We say that IBE is unrestricted strongly collision-free if the advantage

$$\mathrm{Adv}_{\mathsf{IBE},\mathcal{A}}^{\mathrm{IBE\text{-}usCF}}(\kappa) := \Pr[\mathrm{Exp}_{\mathsf{IBE},\mathcal{A}}^{\mathrm{IBE\text{-}usCF}}(\kappa) = 1]$$

is negligible for any PPT adversary $\mathcal{A}$.

Next, we introduce OTS [5] as follows. Let $\mathcal{M}_{\mathsf{Sig}}$ be a message space.

Definition 7 (Syntax of OTS). *A OTS scheme OTS consists of the following three algorithms, $\mathsf{Sig.KeyGen}$, Sign and Verify:*

$\mathsf{Sig.KeyGen}(1^\kappa)$: *This key generation algorithm takes as an input the security parameter $\kappa \in \mathrm{N}$, and returns signing/verification key pair (K_s, K_v).*
$\mathsf{Sign}(K_s, M)$: *This signing algorithm takes as inputs K_s and a message $M \in \mathcal{M}_{\mathsf{Sig}}$, and returns a signature σ.*
$\mathsf{Verify}(K_v, M, \sigma)$: *This verification algorithm takes as input K_v, M, and σ, and returns 1 (valid) or 0 (invalid).*

Correctness is defined as follows: For all $(K_s, K_v) \leftarrow \mathsf{Sig.KeyGen}(1^\kappa)$ and all $M \in \mathcal{M}_{\mathsf{Sig}}$, $\mathsf{Verify}(K_v, M, \sigma) = 1$ holds, where $\sigma \leftarrow \mathsf{Sign}(K_s, M)$.

Next, we define strong existential unforgeability against chosen message attack (sEUF-CMA) of OTS as follows.

Definition 8 (one-time sEUF-CMA). *For any PPT adversary $\mathcal{A}$ and the security parameter $\kappa \in \mathrm{N}$, we define the experiment $\mathrm{Exp}_{\mathsf{OTS},\mathcal{A}}^{\mathrm{one\text{-}timesEUF\text{-}CMA}}(\kappa)$ as follows.*

$\mathrm{Exp}_{\mathsf{OTS},\mathcal{A}}^{\mathrm{one\text{-}time\ sEUF\text{-}CMA}}(\kappa)$:

$\quad (K_s, K_v) \leftarrow \mathsf{Sig.KeyGen}(1^\kappa); \ (M, State) \leftarrow \mathcal{A}(K_v); \ M \in \mathcal{M}_{\mathsf{Sig}}$

$\quad \sigma \leftarrow \mathsf{Sign}(K_s, M); \ (M^*, \sigma^*) \leftarrow \mathcal{A}(\sigma, State)$

$\quad$ *If $\mathsf{Verify}(K_v, M^*, \sigma^*) = 1$ and $(M^*, \sigma^*) \neq (M, \sigma)$ then output 1, and 0 otherwise*

We say that OTS is one-time sEUF-CMA secure if the advantage

$$\mathrm{Adv}_{\mathsf{OTS},\mathcal{A}}^{\mathrm{one\text{-}time\ sEUF\text{-}CMA}}(\kappa) := \Pr[\mathrm{Exp}_{\mathsf{OTS},\mathcal{A}}^{\mathrm{one\text{-}time\ sEUF\text{-}CMA}}(\kappa) = 1]$$

is negligible for any PPT adversary.

3 Definitions of SCF-PEKS/PKE

In this section, we define SCF-PEKS/PKE. As in SCF-PEKS, the server and a receiver manage keys separately. A keyword ω and a plaintext M are encrypted by the server public key, pk_{S}, and the receiver public key, pk_{R}. Although a secret key of the receiver, sk_{R}, plays the role of generating trapdoors in SCF-PEKS, we additionally require that sk_{R} plays a role of decrypting a ciphertext. To search for an encrypted keyword, the test algorithm requires both the server secret key, sk_{S}, and the corresponding trapdoor. Let $\mathcal{K}$ be the keyword space and $\mathcal{M}$ be the message space.

Definition 9 (Syntax of SCF-PEKS/PKE). *A SCF-PEKS/PKE scheme* SCF-PEKS/PKE *consists of the following six algorithms,* SCF-PEKS/PKE.KeyGen$_S$, SCF-PEKS/PKE.KeyGen$_R$, SCF-PEKS/PKE.Trapdoor, SCF-PEKS/PKE.Enc, SCF-PEKS/PKE.Dec *and* SCF-PEKS/PKE.Test:

SCF-PEKS/PKE.KeyGen$_S$(1^κ): *This server key generation algorithm takes as input the security parameter* 1^κ *($\kappa \in \mathrm{N}$), and returns a server public key* pk_S *and a server secret key* sk_S.

SCF-PEKS/PKE.KeyGen$_R$(1^κ): *This receiver key generation algorithm takes as input the security parameter* 1^κ *($\kappa \in \mathrm{N}$), and returns a receiver public key* pk_R *and a receiver secret key* sk_R.

SCF-PEKS/PKE.Trapdoor(pk_R, sk_R, ω): *This trapdoor generation algorithm takes as input* pk_R, sk_R, *and a keyword* $\omega \in \mathcal{K}$, *and returns a trapdoor* t_ω *corresponding to keyword* ω.

SCF-PEKS/PKE.Enc(pk_S, pk_R, ω, M): *This encryption algorithm takes as input* pk_R, pk_S, ω, *and a message* $M \in \mathcal{M}$, *and returns a ciphertext* λ.

SCF-PEKS/PKE.Dec(pk_R, sk_R, λ): *This decryption algorithm takes as input* pk_R, sk_R, *and* λ, *and returns a message* M *or a reject symbol* $\perp$.

SCF-PEKS/PKE.Test(pk_S, sk_S, pk_R, t_ω, λ): *This test algorithm takes as input* pk_S, sk_S, pk_R, t_ω, *and* λ, *and returns 1 if* $\omega = \omega'$, *where* ω' *is the keyword which was used for computing* λ, *and 0 otherwise.*

Correctness is defined as follows: For all $(pk_S, sk_S) \leftarrow$ SCF-PEKS/PKE.KeyGen$_S$ (1^κ), all $(pk_R, sk_R) \leftarrow$ SCF-PEKS/PKE.KeyGen$_R$(1^κ), all $\omega \in \mathcal{K}$ and all $M \in \mathcal{M}$, let $\lambda \leftarrow$ SCF-PEKS/PKE.Enc(pk_S, pk_R, ω, M) and $t_\omega \leftarrow$ SCF-PEKS/PKE. Trapdoor(pk_R, sk_R, ω). Then

$$\text{SCF-PEKS/PKE.Test}(pk_S, sk_S, pk_R, t_\omega, \lambda) = 1 \; and$$
$$\text{SCF-PEKS/PKE.Dec}(pk_R, sk_R, \lambda) = M \; holds.$$

Next, we define consistency. Basically, consistency guarantees that for two trapdoors t_{ω^*} and $t_{\hat{\omega}^*}$ where $\omega^* \neq \hat{\omega}^*$, a ciphertext of ω^* is not searched by $t_{\hat{\omega}^*}$. We give two definitions. The former case, which we call weak consistency, is essentially the same as that of Chen et al. [12] where the ciphertext λ^* is honestly generated. Due to the secure-channel free setting, we additionally consider the trapdoor oracle, and give sk_S to the adversary.

Definition 10 (Weak Consistency). *For any PPT adversary $\mathcal{A}$ and the security parameter $\kappa \in \mathrm{N}$, we define the experiment* $\mathrm{Exp}^{\text{WEAK-CONSIST}}_{\text{SCF-PEKS/PKE},\mathcal{A}}(\kappa)$ *as follows.*

$\mathrm{Exp}^{\text{WEAK-CONSIST}}_{\text{SCF-PEKS/PKE},\mathcal{A}}(\kappa)$:

   $(pk_S, sk_S) \leftarrow$ SCF-PEKS/PKE.KeyGen$_S$(1^κ)

   $(pk_R, sk_R) \leftarrow$ SCF-PEKS/PKE.KeyGen$_R$(1^κ)

   $(M^*, \omega^*, \hat{\omega}^*) \leftarrow \mathcal{A}^{\mathcal{O}_{\text{SCF-PEKS/PKE.TRAP}}}(pk_S, sk_S, pk_R)$

$M^* \in \mathcal{M}; \ \omega^*, \ \hat{\omega}^* \in \mathcal{K}; \ \omega^* \neq \hat{\omega}^*$

$\lambda^* \leftarrow \mathsf{SCF\text{-}PEKS/PKE.Enc}(pk_\mathrm{S}, pk_\mathrm{R}, \omega^*, M^*)$

$t_{\hat{\omega}^*} \leftarrow \mathsf{SCF\text{-}PEKS/PKE.Trapdoor}(pk_\mathrm{R}, sk_\mathrm{R}, \hat{\omega}^*)$

$If \ \mathsf{SCF\text{-}PEKS/PKE.Test}(pk_\mathrm{S}, sk_\mathrm{S}, pk_\mathrm{R}, t_{\hat{\omega}^*}, \lambda^*) = 1 \ then \ output \ 1, \ and \ 0 \ otherwise$

– $\mathcal{O}_{\mathsf{SCF\text{-}PEKS/PKE.TRAP}}$: *This trapdoor oracle takes as input* ω *where* $\omega \notin \{\omega^*, \hat{\omega}^*\}$ *and returns* $t_\omega \leftarrow \mathsf{SCF\text{-}PEKS/PKE.Trapdoor}(pk_\mathrm{R}, sk_\mathrm{R}, \omega)$.

We say that $\mathsf{SCF\text{-}PEKS/PKE}$ *is weakly consistent if the advantage*

$$\mathrm{Adv}_{\mathsf{SCF\text{-}PEKS/PKE},\mathcal{A}}^{\mathrm{WEAK\text{-}CONSIST}}(\kappa) := \Pr[\mathrm{Exp}_{\mathsf{SCF\text{-}PEKS/PKE},\mathcal{A}}^{\mathrm{WEAK\text{-}CONSIST}}(\kappa) = 1]$$

is negligible for any PPT adversary $\mathcal{A}$.

Next, we strengthen weak consistency, which we call strong consistency. Here, an adversary is allowed to produce the ciphertext λ^*. This situation is the same as those of strong robustness [2,3] and strong collision-freeness [25]. Note that, an adversary is not allowed to obtain decryption keys for challenge identities in these models. In our model, the trapdoor oracle has no restriction, i.e., an adversary can obtain trapdoors of challenge keywords. This situation is the same as that of unrestricted strong robustness [17]. Our strong consistency captures the following situation. Owing to the secure-channel free property, an adversary can observe trapdoors. Let the adversary obtain t_{ω^*} and $t_{\hat{\omega}^*}$. Moreover, assume that the adversary knows keywords ω^* and $\hat{\omega}^*$ associated with t_{ω^*} and $t_{\hat{\omega}^*}$, respectively.[3] Then, the adversary may produce a ciphertext where the test algorithm decides that the ciphertext is associated with both ω^* and $\hat{\omega}^*$. Strong consistency prevents this attack.

Definition 11 (Strong Consistency). *For any PPT adversary* $\mathcal{A}$ *and the security parameter* $\kappa \in \mathrm{N}$, *we define the experiment* $\mathrm{Exp}_{\mathsf{SCF\text{-}PEKS/PKE},\mathcal{A}}^{\mathrm{STRONG\text{-}CONSIST}}(\kappa)$ *as follows.*

$\mathrm{Exp}_{\mathsf{SCF\text{-}PEKS/PKE},\mathcal{A}}^{\mathrm{STRONG\text{-}CONSIST}}(\kappa)$:

    $(pk_\mathrm{S}, sk_\mathrm{S}) \leftarrow \mathsf{SCF\text{-}PEKS/PKE.KeyGen_S}(1^\kappa)$

    $(pk_\mathrm{R}, sk_\mathrm{R}) \leftarrow \mathsf{SCF\text{-}PEKS/PKE.KeyGen_R}(1^\kappa)$

    $(\lambda^*, \omega^*, \hat{\omega}^*) \leftarrow \mathcal{A}^{\mathcal{O}_{\mathsf{SCF\text{-}PEKS/PKE.TRAP}}}(pk_\mathrm{S}, sk_\mathrm{S}, pk_\mathrm{R}); \ \omega^*, \hat{\omega}^* \in \mathcal{K}; \ \omega^* \neq \hat{\omega}^*$

    $t_{\omega^*} \leftarrow \mathsf{SCF\text{-}PEKS/PKE.Trapdoor}(pk_\mathrm{R}, sk_\mathrm{R}, \omega^*)$

    $t_{\hat{\omega}^*} \leftarrow \mathsf{SCF\text{-}PEKS/PKE.Trapdoor}(pk_\mathrm{R}, sk_\mathrm{R}, \hat{\omega}^*)$

    $If \ \mathsf{SCF\text{-}PEKS/PKE.Test}(pk_\mathrm{S}, sk_\mathrm{S}, pk_\mathrm{R}, t_{\omega^*}, \lambda^*) = 1 \ and$

    $\mathsf{SCF\text{-}PEKS/PKE.Test}(pk_\mathrm{S}, sk_\mathrm{S}, pk_\mathrm{R}, t_{\hat{\omega}^*}, \lambda^*) = 1$

    then output 1, *and* 0 *otherwise*

– $\mathcal{O}_{\mathsf{SCF\text{-}PEKS/PKE.TRAP}}$: *This trapdoor oracle takes as input* ω *with no restriction, and returns* $t_\omega \leftarrow \mathsf{SCF\text{-}PEKS/PKE.Trapdoor}(pk_\mathrm{R}, sk_\mathrm{R}, \omega)$.

---

[3] This assumption is also natural since we do not consider keyword guessing attacks [16].

We say that SCF-PEKS/PKE *is strongly consistent if the advantage*

$$\mathrm{Adv}_{\mathsf{SCF\text{-}PEKS/PKE},\mathcal{A}}^{\mathrm{STRONG\text{-}CONSIST}}(\kappa) := \Pr[\mathrm{Exp}_{\mathsf{SCF\text{-}PEKS/PKE},\mathcal{A}}^{\mathrm{STRONG\text{-}CONSIST}}(\kappa) = 1]$$

is negligible for any PPT adversary $\mathcal{A}$.

Next, we define two security notions for keyword privacy, indistinguishability of keywords against chosen keyword attack with the server secret key (IND-CKA-SSK) and indistinguishability of keywords against chosen keyword attack with all trapdoors (IND-CKA-AT). In the IND-CKA-SSK definition, an adversary $\mathcal{A}$ is modeled as the server, and thus sk_S is given to $\mathcal{A}$. If $\mathcal{A}$ obtains trapdoors, then $\mathcal{A}$ can run the test algorithm by myself. Thus, trapdoors of challenge keywords (ω_0^*, ω_1^*) are not given to $\mathcal{A}$. Instead, $\mathcal{A}$ is allowed to access the test oracle for $(\lambda, \omega) \notin \{(\lambda^*, \omega_0^*), (\lambda^*, \omega_1^*)\}$. To guarantee that no information of keyword is revealed via the decryption procedure, $\mathcal{A}$ is allowed to access the decryption oracle with no restriction.

Definition 12 (IND-CKA-SSK). *For any PPT adversary* $\mathcal{A}$ *and the security parameter* $\kappa \in \mathrm{N}$, *we define the experiment* $\mathrm{Exp}_{\mathsf{SCF\text{-}PEKS/PKE},\mathcal{A}}^{\mathrm{IND\text{-}CKA\text{-}SSK}}(\kappa)$ *as follows.*

$\mathrm{Exp}_{\mathsf{SCF\text{-}PEKS/PKE},\mathcal{A}}^{\mathrm{IND\text{-}CKA\text{-}SSK}}(\kappa)$:

    $(pk_S, sk_S) \leftarrow \mathsf{SCF\text{-}PEKS/PKE.KeyGen}_S(1^\kappa)$

    $(pk_R, sk_R) \leftarrow \mathsf{SCF\text{-}PEKS/PKE.KeyGen}_R(1^\kappa)$

    $(\omega_0^*, \omega_1^*, M^*, State)$

    $\leftarrow \mathcal{A}^{\mathcal{O}_{\mathsf{SCF\text{-}PEKS/PKE.DEC}}, \mathcal{O}_{\mathsf{SCF\text{-}PEKS/PKE.TRAP}}, \mathcal{O}_{\mathsf{SCF\text{-}PEKS/PKE.TEST}}}(\mathsf{find}, pk_S, sk_S, pk_R)$

    $\mu \xleftarrow{\$} \{0,1\}; \ \lambda^* \leftarrow \mathsf{SCF\text{-}PEKS/PKE.Enc}(pk_S, pk_R, \omega_\mu^*, M^*)$

    $\mu' \leftarrow \mathcal{A}^{\mathcal{O}_{\mathsf{SCF\text{-}PEKS/PKE.DEC}}, \mathcal{O}_{\mathsf{SCF\text{-}PEKS/PKE.TRAP}}, \mathcal{O}_{\mathsf{SCF\text{-}PEKS/PKE.TEST}}}(\mathsf{guess}, \lambda^*, State)$

    If $\mu = \mu'$ *then output* 1, *and* 0 *otherwise*

– $\mathcal{O}_{\mathsf{SCF\text{-}PEKS/PKE.DEC}}$: *This decryption oracle takes as input* λ *with no restriction, and returns the result of* $\mathsf{SCF\text{-}PEKS/PKE.Dec}(pk_R, sk_R, \lambda)$. *Remark that* λ^* *is also allowed to input.*

– $\mathcal{O}_{\mathsf{SCF\text{-}PEKS/PKE.TRAP}}$: *This trapdoor oracle takes as input* ω *where* $\omega \notin \{\omega_0^*, \omega_1^*\}$ *and returns* $t_\omega \leftarrow \mathsf{SCF\text{-}PEKS/PKE.Trapdoor}(pk_R, sk_R, \omega)$.

– $\mathcal{O}_{\mathsf{SCF\text{-}PEKS/PKE.TEST}}$: *This test oracle takes as input* (λ, ω) *where* $(\lambda, \omega) \notin \{(\lambda^*, \omega_0^*), (\lambda^*, \omega_1^*)\}$, *compute* $t_\omega \leftarrow \mathsf{SCF\text{-}PEKS/PKE.Trapdoor}(pk_R, sk_R, \omega)$, *and returns result of* $\mathsf{SCF\text{-}PEKS/PKE.Test}(pk_S, sk_S, pk_R, t_\omega, \lambda)$.

We say that a SCF-PEKS/PKE scheme SCF-PEKS/PKE *is IND-CKA-SSK secure if the advantage*

$$\mathrm{Adv}_{\mathsf{SCF\text{-}PEKS/PKE},\mathcal{A}}^{\mathrm{IND\text{-}CKA\text{-}SSK}}(\kappa) := | \Pr[\mathrm{Exp}_{\mathsf{SCF\text{-}PEKS/PKE},\mathcal{A}}^{\mathrm{IND\text{-}CKA\text{-}SSK}}(\kappa) = 1] - 1/2 |$$

is negligible for any PPT adversary $\mathcal{A}$.

Next, we define IND-CKA-AT. In the IND-CKA-AT definition, an adversary $\mathcal{A}$ is modeled as a receiver. Thus, sk_R is given to $\mathcal{A}$. Then, $\mathcal{A}$ can generate trapdoors for all keywords. Since $\mathcal{A}$ does not have sk_S, $\mathcal{A}$ is not allowed to run the test algorithm. Thus, $\mathcal{A}$ is allowed to access the test oracle for $(\lambda, \omega) \notin \{(\lambda^*, \omega_0^*), (\lambda^*, \omega_1^*)\}$. To guarantee that no information of keyword is revealed via the decryption procedure, $\mathcal{A}$ is allowed to access the decryption oracle with no restriction.

Definition 13 (IND-CKA-AT). *For any PPT adversary $\mathcal{A}$ and the security parameter $\kappa \in \mathrm{N}$, we define the experiment $\mathrm{Exp}_{\mathsf{SCF\text{-}PEKS/PKE},\mathcal{A}}^{\mathrm{IND\text{-}CKA\text{-}AT}}(\kappa)$ as follows.*

$$\mathrm{Exp}_{\mathsf{SCF\text{-}PEKS/PKE},\mathcal{A}}^{\mathrm{IND\text{-}CKA\text{-}AT}}(\kappa):$$

$\qquad (pk_S, sk_S) \leftarrow \mathsf{SCF\text{-}PEKS/PKE.KeyGen}_S(1^\kappa)$

$\qquad (pk_R, sk_R) \leftarrow \mathsf{SCF\text{-}PEKS/PKE.KeyGen}_R(1^\kappa)$

$\qquad (\omega_0^*, \omega_1^*, M^*, State)$

$\qquad \leftarrow \mathcal{A}^{\mathcal{O}_{\mathsf{SCF\text{-}PEKS/PKE.DEC}}, \mathcal{O}_{\mathsf{SCF\text{-}PEKS/PKE.TEST}}}(\mathsf{find}, pk_S, pk_R, sk_R)$

$\qquad \mu \xleftarrow{\$} \{0,1\}; \ \lambda^* \leftarrow \mathsf{SCF\text{-}PEKS/PKE.Enc}(pk_S, pk_R, \omega_\mu^*, M^*)$

$\qquad \mu' \leftarrow \mathcal{A}^{\mathcal{O}_{\mathsf{SCF\text{-}PEKS/PKE.DEC}}, \mathcal{O}_{\mathsf{SCF\text{-}PEKS/PKE.TEST}}}(\mathsf{guess}, \lambda^*, State)$

$\qquad If \ \mu = \mu' \ then \ output \ 1, \ and \ 0 \ otherwise$

- $\mathcal{O}_{\mathsf{SCF\text{-}PEKS/PKE.DEC}}$: *This decryption oracle takes as input λ with no restriction, and returns the result of $\mathsf{SCF\text{-}PEKS/PKE.Dec}(pk_R, sk_R, \lambda)$. Remark that λ^* is also allowed to input.*
- $\mathcal{O}_{\mathsf{SCF\text{-}PEKS/PKE.TEST}}$: *This test oracle takes as input $(\lambda, \omega) \notin \{(\lambda^*, \omega_0^*), (\lambda^*, \omega_1^*)\}$, computes $t_\omega \leftarrow \mathsf{SCF\text{-}PEKS/PKE.Trapdoor}(pk_R, sk_R, \omega)$, and returns result of $\mathsf{SCF\text{-}PEKS/PKE.Test}(pk_S, sk_S, pk_R, t_\omega, \lambda)$.*

We say that a SCF-PEKS/PKE scheme $\mathsf{SCF\text{-}PEKS/PKE}$ is IND-CKA-AT security if the advantage

$$\mathrm{Adv}_{\mathsf{SCF\text{-}PEKS/PKE},\mathcal{A}}^{\mathrm{IND\text{-}CKA\text{-}AT}}(\kappa) := \mid \Pr[\mathrm{Exp}_{\mathsf{SCF\text{-}PEKS/PKE},\mathcal{A}}^{\mathrm{IND\text{-}CKA\text{-}AT}}(\kappa) = 1] - 1/2 \mid$$

is negligible for any PPT adversary $\mathcal{A}$.

Next, we define the data privacy for SCF-PEKS/PKE under chosen ciphertext attack with the server secret key and all trapdoors (IND-CCA-SSK/AT) as follows. To guarantee that the server does not obtain any information of plaintext, the adversary $\mathcal{A}$ is given to sk_S. Moreover, to guarantee that no information of plaintext is revealed via the text procedure, $\mathcal{A}$ is allowed to access the trapdoor oracle with no restriction.

Definition 14 (IND-CCA-SSK/AT). *For any PPT adversary $\mathcal{A}$ and the security parameter $\kappa \in \mathrm{N}$, we define the experiment $\mathrm{Exp}_{\mathsf{SCF\text{-}PEKS/PKE},\mathcal{A}}^{\mathrm{IND\text{-}CCA\text{-}SSK/AT}}(\kappa)$ as follows.*

$$\mathrm{Exp}_{\mathsf{SCF\text{-}PEKS/PKE},\mathcal{A}}^{\mathrm{IND\text{-}CCA\text{-}SSK/AT}}(\kappa):$$

$(pk_{\mathrm{S}}, sk_{\mathrm{S}}) \leftarrow \mathsf{SCF\text{-}PEKS/PKE.KeyGen}_{\mathrm{S}}(1^{\kappa})$

$(pk_{\mathrm{R}}, sk_{\mathrm{R}}) \leftarrow \mathsf{SCF\text{-}PEKS/PKE.KeyGen}_{\mathrm{R}}(1^{\kappa})$

$(\omega^*, M_0^*, M_1^*, State)$

$\leftarrow \mathcal{A}^{\mathcal{O}_{\mathsf{SCF\text{-}PEKS/PKE.DEC}}, \mathcal{O}_{\mathsf{SCF\text{-}PEKS/PKE.TRAP}}}(\mathsf{find}, pk_{\mathrm{S}}, sk_{\mathrm{S}}, pk_{\mathrm{R}})$

$\mu \xleftarrow{\$} \{0, 1\}; \quad \lambda^* \leftarrow \mathsf{SCF\text{-}PEKS/PKE.Enc}(pk_{\mathrm{S}}, pk_{\mathrm{R}}, \omega^*, M_\mu^*)$

$\mu' \leftarrow \mathcal{A}^{\mathcal{O}_{\mathsf{SCF\text{-}PEKS/PKE.DEC}}, \mathcal{O}_{\mathsf{SCF\text{-}PEKS/PKE.TRAP}}}(\mathsf{guess}, \lambda^*, State)$

If $\mu = \mu'$ then output 1, and 0 otherwise

- $\mathcal{O}_{\mathsf{SCF\text{-}PEKS/PKE.DEC}}$: *This decryption oracle takes as input a ciphertext $\lambda \neq \lambda^*$, and returns the result of* $\mathsf{SCF\text{-}PEKS/PKE.Dec}(pk_{\mathrm{R}}, sk_{\mathrm{R}}, \lambda)$.
- $\mathcal{O}_{\mathsf{SCF\text{-}PEKS/PKE.TRAP}}$: *This trapdoor oracle takes as input ω with no restriction, and returns $t_\omega \leftarrow \mathsf{SCF\text{-}PEKS/PKE.Trapdoor}(pk_{\mathrm{R}}, sk_{\mathrm{R}}, \omega)$. Remark that ω^* is also allowed to input.*

We say that a SCF-PEKS/PKE scheme $\mathsf{SCF\text{-}PEKS/PKE}$ *is IND-CCA-SSK/AT secure if the advantage*

$$\mathrm{Adv}_{\mathsf{SCF\text{-}PEKS/PKE},\mathcal{A}}^{\mathrm{IND\text{-}CCA\text{-}SSK/AT}}(\kappa) := \mid \Pr[\mathrm{Exp}_{\mathsf{SCF\text{-}PEKS/PKE},\mathcal{A}}^{\mathrm{IND\text{-}CCA\text{-}SSK/AT}}(\kappa) = 1] - 1/2 \mid$$

is negligible for any PPT adversary $\mathcal{A}$.

4   Generic Construction of SCF-PEKS/PKE

In this section, we propose a generic construction of SCF-PEKS/PKE. We construct SCF-PEKS/PKE from IBE = (IBE,Setup,IBE.Extract,IBE.Enc,IBE.Dec), TBE = (TBE.KeyGen,TBE.Enc,TBE.Dec), and OTS = (Sig.KeyGen,Sign,Verify). Our construction can be seen as an extension of a generic construction of PEKS (from anonymous IBE proposed by Abdalla et al. [1]) and a generic construction of SCF-PEKS (from anonymous IBE, TBE, and OTS proposed by Emura et al. [14]).

The Abdalla et al. construction is briefly explained as follows. A receiver has the master key mk as its secret key $sk_{\mathrm{R}}^{\mathsf{IBE}}$. A keyword ω is regarded as an identity, i.e., $\mathcal{K}$ is set to $\mathcal{ID}$, and is encrypted as follows. First, a random plaintext $R \in \mathcal{M}_{\mathsf{IBE}}$ is chosen, and next R is encrypted by IBE such that $C_{\mathsf{IBE}} \leftarrow \mathsf{IBE.Enc}(params, \omega, R)$. Then, the PEKS ciphertext is (C_{IBE}, R). A trapdoor t_ω is the decryption key $sk_\omega \leftarrow \mathsf{IBE.Extract}(params, sk_{\mathrm{R}}^{\mathsf{IBE}}, \omega)$. The test algorithm outputs 1 if $\mathsf{IBE.Dec}(params, t_\omega, C_{\mathsf{IBE}}) = R$ holds. Since the underlying IBE is required to be anonymous, no information of ω is revealed from C_{IBE}. By additionally employing TBE and OTS, Emura et al. [14] added the secure-channel property to the Abdalla et al. construction. In their construction, the server manages a key pair of TBE $(pk_{\mathrm{S}}^{\mathsf{TBE}}, sk_{\mathrm{S}}^{\mathsf{TBE}})$. A random plaintext $R \in \mathcal{M}_{\mathsf{IBE}}$ is encrypted by IBE, and the IBE ciphertext is encrypted by

TBE such that $C_{\mathsf{TBE}} \leftarrow \mathsf{TBE.Enc}(pk_{\mathrm{S}}^{\mathsf{TBE}}, H_{tag}(K_v), C_{\mathsf{IBE}})$, where the verification key K_v is regarded as the tag and $H_{tag} : \{0,1\}^* \rightarrow \mathcal{TAG}$ is a target collision-resistant (TCR) hash function. Finally, a signature is computed such that $\sigma \leftarrow \mathsf{Sign}(K_s, (C_{\mathsf{TBE}}, R))$. The SCF-PEKS ciphertext is $(C_{\mathsf{TBE}}, K_v, \sigma)$. The test algorithm first decrypts C_{TBE} using $sk_{\mathrm{S}}^{\mathsf{TBE}}$, next it decrypts its decryption result using a trapdoor, and then obtains R. The test algorithm outputs 1 if σ is valid on (C_{TBE}, R). Owing to the double encryption, both $sk_{\mathrm{S}}^{\mathsf{TBE}}$ and t_ω are required to run the test algorithm. It is particularly worth noting that the random plaintext R is NOT contained in the ciphertext. Emura et al. mentioned that even if R is contained in a ciphertext, it does not affect the security, and the reason for removing R is to reduce the ciphertext size.

High-Level Description of Our Construction: To integrate SCF-PEKS and PKE, the receiver additionally manages a key pair of TBE $(pk_{\mathrm{R}}^{\mathsf{TBE}}, sk_{\mathrm{R}}^{\mathsf{TBE}})$. Since the Emura et al. construction above can be seen as "tag-based" SCF-PEKS, a plaintext $M \in \mathcal{M}_{\mathsf{TBE}}$ is encrypted by $pk_{\mathrm{R}}^{\mathsf{TBE}}$ with the same tag $H_{tag}(K_v)$ such that

$$C_{\mathsf{TBE,S}} \leftarrow \mathsf{TBE.Enc}(pk_{\mathrm{S}}^{\mathsf{TBE}}, H_{tag}(K_v), C_{\mathsf{IBE}}) \ and$$
$$C_{\mathsf{TBE,R}} \leftarrow \mathsf{TBE.Enc}(pk_{\mathrm{R}}^{\mathsf{TBE}}, H_{tag}(K_v), M)$$

Here, for the sake of clarity, we use subscript S for ciphertexts encrypted by the server pubic key $pk_{\mathrm{S}}^{\mathsf{TBE}}$, and use subscript R for ciphertexts encrypted by the receiver pubic key $pk_{\mathrm{R}}^{\mathsf{TBE}}$. The sender computes the OTS σ on $(C_{\mathsf{TBE,S}}, C_{\mathsf{TBE,R}}, R)$. A SCF-PEKS/PKE ciphertext is described as $\lambda = (C_{\mathsf{TBE,S}}, C_{\mathsf{TBE,R}}, K_v, \sigma, R)$. It is particularly worth noting that the random plaintext R is contained in the ciphertext unlike in the Emura et al. construction. The ciphertext now provides public verifiability since anyone can verify σ. Since the decryption algorithm needs to verify σ, this public verifiability is necessary.

The construction basically works well since TBE+OTS yields CCA-secure PKE [24]. The main difficulty to be handled is explained as follows. Let $\lambda^* = (C_{\mathsf{TBE,S}}^*, C_{\mathsf{TBE,R}}^*, K_v^*, \sigma^*, R^*)$ be the challenge ciphertext in the IND-CKA-SSK game. Now we consider how to reduce the IND-CKA-SSK security to the IBE-ANO-CCA security. Since the adversary $\mathcal{A}$ has $sk_{\mathrm{S}}^{\mathsf{TBE}}$, $\mathcal{A}$ can decrypt $C_{\mathsf{TBE,S}}^*$. Let C_{IBE}^* be the decryption result. Then, $\mathcal{A}$ can compute a valid ciphertext $\lambda \neq \lambda^*$ such that (1) (K_s, K_v) is chosen by $\mathcal{A}$ with the condition $K_v \neq K_v^*$, (2) C_{IBE}^* is re-encrypted with the tag $H_{tag}(K_v)$ such that $C_{\mathsf{TBE,S}} \leftarrow \mathsf{TBE.Enc}(pk_{\mathrm{S}}^{\mathsf{TBE}}, H_{tag}(K_v), C_{\mathsf{IBE}}^*)$, (3) $C_{\mathsf{TBE,R}} \leftarrow \mathsf{TBE.Enc}(pk_{\mathrm{R}}^{\mathsf{TBE}}, H_{tag}(K_v), M)$ is computed with arbitrary M, (4) $\sigma \leftarrow \mathsf{Sign}(K_s, (C_{\mathsf{TBE,S}}, C_{\mathsf{TBE,R}}, R^*))$ is computed, and (5) $\lambda = (C_{\mathsf{TBE,S}}, C_{\mathsf{TBE,R}}, K_v, \sigma, R^*)$ is sent to the test oracle with $\omega \in \{\omega_0^*, \omega_1^*\}$. Although the reduction algorithm obtains C_{IBE}^*, the algorithm cannot send the challenge ciphertext C_{IBE}^* with either ω_0^* or ω_1^* to the decryption oracle of IBE. Thus, the security proof fails. To protect against this re-encryption attack, we modify the plaintext of C_{IBE} as

$$C_{\mathsf{IBE}} \leftarrow \mathsf{IBE.Enc}(params, \omega, R) \text{ with } R = H_{ibe}(K_v)$$

where $H_{ibe} : \{0,1\}^* \to \mathcal{M}_{\mathsf{IBE}}$ is a TCR hash function, and the test algorithm checks whether or not $R = H_{ibe}(K_v)$. This structure prevents the adversary from employing different K_v and thus, if C^*_{IBE} appears as above, then $K_v = K^*_v$ must hold unless the TCR property is broken. Since this situation contradicts sEUF-CMA security, our simulation works well. Since R can be computed from K_v, we can now remove R from λ without losing public verifiability, and an SCF-PEKS/PKE ciphertext is described as $\lambda = (C_{\mathsf{TBE,S}}, C_{\mathsf{TBE,R}}, K_v, \sigma)$.

We give our construction as follows. Assume that $\mathcal{C}_{\mathsf{IBE}} \subseteq \mathcal{M}_{\mathsf{TBE}}$ and $\mathcal{C}_{\mathsf{TBE}} \times \mathcal{C}_{\mathsf{TBE}} \times \mathcal{M}_{\mathsf{IBE}} \subseteq \mathcal{M}_{\mathsf{Sig}}$, where $\mathcal{C}_{\mathsf{IBE}}$ and $\mathcal{M}_{\mathsf{IBE}}$ are a ciphertext space and plaintext space of IBE respectively, $\mathcal{M}_{\mathsf{TBE}}$ is a plaintext space of TBE, and $\mathcal{M}_{\mathsf{Sig}}$ is a message space of OTS.

The Proposed Construction

SCF-PEKS/PKE.KeyGen$_\mathsf{S}(1^\kappa)$: Run $(pk^{\mathsf{TBE}}_\mathsf{S}, sk^{\mathsf{TBE}}_\mathsf{S}) \leftarrow \mathsf{TBE.KeyGen}(1^\kappa)$. Output $pk_\mathsf{S} = pk^{\mathsf{TBE}}_\mathsf{S}$ and $sk_\mathsf{S} = sk^{\mathsf{TBE}}_\mathsf{S}$.

SCF-PEKS/PKE.KeyGen$_\mathsf{R}(1^\kappa)$: Run $(pk^{\mathsf{IBE}}_\mathsf{R}, sk^{\mathsf{IBE}}_\mathsf{R}) \leftarrow \mathsf{IBE.Setup}(1^\kappa)$ and $(pk^{\mathsf{TBE}}_\mathsf{R}, sk^{\mathsf{TBE}}_\mathsf{R}) \leftarrow \mathsf{TBE.KeyGen}(1^\kappa)$. Output $pk_\mathsf{R} = (pk^{\mathsf{IBE}}_\mathsf{R}, pk^{\mathsf{TBE}}_\mathsf{R})$ and $sk_\mathsf{R} = (sk^{\mathsf{IBE}}_\mathsf{R}, sk^{\mathsf{TBE}}_\mathsf{R})$. We assume that TCR hash functions $H_{tag} : \{0,1\}^* \to \mathcal{TAG}$ and $H_{ibe} : \{0,1\}^* \to \mathcal{M}_{\mathsf{IBE}}$ are contained in pk_R.

SCF-PEKS/PKE.Trapdoor$(pk_\mathsf{R}, sk_\mathsf{R}, \omega)$: Parse $pk_\mathsf{R} = (pk^{\mathsf{IBE}}_\mathsf{R}, pk^{\mathsf{TBE}}_\mathsf{R})$ and $sk_\mathsf{R} = (sk^{\mathsf{IBE}}_\mathsf{R}, sk^{\mathsf{TBE}}_\mathsf{R})$. Run $sk_\omega \leftarrow \mathsf{IBE.Extract}(pk^{\mathsf{IBE}}_\mathsf{R}, sk^{\mathsf{IBE}}_\mathsf{R}, \omega)$ and output $t_\omega = sk_\omega$.

SCF-PEKS/PKE.Enc$(pk_\mathsf{S}, pk_\mathsf{R}, \omega, M)$: Parse $pk_\mathsf{S} = pk^{\mathsf{TBE}}_\mathsf{S}$ and $pk_\mathsf{R} = (pk^{\mathsf{IBE}}_\mathsf{R}, pk^{\mathsf{TBE}}_\mathsf{R})$. Run $(K_s, K_v) \leftarrow \mathsf{Sig.KeyGen}(1^\kappa)$ and compute $t = H_{tag}(K_v)$ and $R = H_{ibe}(K_v)$. Run $C_{\mathsf{IBE}} \leftarrow \mathsf{IBE.Enc}(pk^{\mathsf{IBE}}_\mathsf{R}, \omega, R)$. Compute $C_{\mathsf{TBE,S}} \leftarrow \mathsf{TBE.Enc}(pk^{\mathsf{TBE}}_\mathsf{S}, t, C_{\mathsf{IBE}})$, $C_{\mathsf{TBE,R}} \leftarrow \mathsf{TBE.Enc}(pk^{\mathsf{TBE}}_\mathsf{R}, t, M)$, and $\sigma \leftarrow \mathsf{Sign}(K_s, (C_{\mathsf{TBE,S}}, C_{\mathsf{TBE,R}}, R))$, and output $\lambda = (C_{\mathsf{TBE,S}}, C_{\mathsf{TBE,R}}, K_v, \sigma)$.

SCF-PEKS/PKE.Dec$(pk_\mathsf{R}, sk_\mathsf{R}, \lambda)$: Parse $pk_\mathsf{R} = (pk^{\mathsf{IBE}}_\mathsf{R}, pk^{\mathsf{TBE}}_\mathsf{R})$, $sk_\mathsf{R} = (sk^{\mathsf{IBE}}_\mathsf{R}, sk^{\mathsf{TBE}}_\mathsf{R})$ and $\lambda = (C_{\mathsf{TBE,S}}, C_{\mathsf{TBE,R}}, K_v, \sigma)$. Compute $R = H_{ibe}(K_v)$. If $\mathsf{Verify}(K_v, (C_{\mathsf{TBE,S}}, C_{\mathsf{TBE,R}}, R), \sigma) = 0$, then output $\bot$. Otherwise, compute $t = H_{tag}(K_v)$ and output $M \leftarrow \mathsf{TBE.Dec}(pk^{\mathsf{TBE}}_\mathsf{R}, sk^{\mathsf{TBE}}_\mathsf{R}, t, C_{\mathsf{TBE,R}})$.

SCF-PEKS/PKE.Test$(pk_\mathsf{S}, sk_\mathsf{S}, pk_\mathsf{R}, t_\omega, \lambda)$: Parse $pk_\mathsf{S} = pk^{\mathsf{TBE}}_\mathsf{S}$, $sk_\mathsf{S} = sk^{\mathsf{TBE}}_\mathsf{S}$, $pk_\mathsf{R} = (pk^{\mathsf{IBE}}_\mathsf{R}, pk^{\mathsf{TBE}}_\mathsf{R})$, and $\lambda = (C_{\mathsf{TBE,S}}, C_{\mathsf{TBE,R}}, K_v, \sigma)$. Compute $t = H_{tag}(K_v)$, and run $C'_{\mathsf{IBE}} \leftarrow \mathsf{TBE.Dec}(pk^{\mathsf{TBE}}_\mathsf{S}, sk^{\mathsf{TBE}}_\mathsf{S}, t, C_{\mathsf{TBE,S}})$ and $R' \leftarrow \mathsf{IBE.Dec}(pk^{\mathsf{IBE}}_\mathsf{R}, t_\omega, C'_{\mathsf{IBE}})$. Output 1 if $R' = H_{ibe}(K_v)$ and $\mathsf{Verify}(K_v, (C_{\mathsf{TBE,S}}, C_{\mathsf{TBE,R}}, R'), \sigma) = 1$ hold, and 0 otherwise.

Obviously, correctness holds if TBE, IBE, and OTS are correct. Due to the page limitation, we omit security proofs of following theorems. We will show the details of proofs in the full version of this paper.

Theorem 1. SCF-PEKS/PKE *is weakly consistent if* IBE *is IBE-IND-CPA secure.*

Theorem 2. SCF-PEKS/PKE *is strongly consistent if* IBE *is unrestricted strong collision-free.*

Theorem 3. SCF-PEKS/PKE *is IND-CKA-SSK secure if* IBE *is IBE-ANO-CCA secure,* OTS *is one-time sEUF-CMA secure, and* H_{ibe} *is a TCR hash function.*

Theorem 4. SCF-PEKS/PKE *is IND-CKA-AT secure if* TBE *is IND-stag-CCA secure,* OTS *is one-time sEUF-CMA secure, and* H_{tag} *is a TCR hash function.*

Theorem 5. SCF-PEKS/PKE *is IND-CCA-SSK/AT secure if* TBE *is IND-stag-CCA secure,* OTS *is one-time sUF-CMA secure, and* H_{tag} *is a TCR hash function.*

5   Instantiation of Our Generic Construction

For TBE, we can simply employ the Kiltz TBE scheme [24], and for the OTS, we can employ any sEUF-CMA secure OTS scheme, e.g., the Wee OTS scheme [29]. We explain how to construct an IBE scheme that matches our requirements, i.e., with unrestricted strong collision-freeness which defined in this paper, and with IBE-ANO-CCA security. To the best of our knowledge, the strongest notion among several robustnesses and collision-freenesses is complete robustness defined by Farshim et al. [17]. They showed that complete robustness implies unrestricted strong robustness. Since unrestricted strong collision-freeness is implied by unrestricted strong robustness, it is enough to construct an IBE scheme with complete robustness for our purpose. Farshim et al. also showed that the transformation from weakly robust IBE (and commitment with the standard hiding and binding properties) to strongly robust IBE, proposed by Abdalla et al. [2,3], is already powerful enough to construct completely robust IBE.[4] Moreover, Abdalla et al. also proposed a transformation from IBE to weakly robust IBE. Since these transformations preserve the anonymity and CCA security of the underlying IBE scheme, we can construct an IBE-ANO-CCA secure IBE scheme with unrestricted strong collision-freeness by applying the two Abdalla et al. transformations (from normal to weakly robust, and from weakly robust to strongly robust).

We have three candidates as the underlying IBE scheme.[5] One candidate is the Gentry IBE scheme [19] which is IBE-ANO-CCA secure in the standard model. As another standard model construction, we can employ a variant of the Boyen-Waters IBE scheme [8] that uses the CHK transform to achieve IBE-ANO-CCA security. Although Abdalla et al. [2,3] mentioned that these schemes

---

[4] Farshim et al. [17] showed that a transformation proposed by Mohassel [25] is also powerful enough to construct completely robust IBE,al though the transformation requires the random oracle.

[5] Although other anonymous IBE schemes without random oracles based on simple assumptions have been proposed, we cannot employ them. For example, the Chen et al. IBE scheme [11] and the Jutla-Roy IBE scheme [22,23] are IBE-ANO-CPA secure. Although Jutla and Roy gave a CCA version, the scheme is not anonymous due to its public verifiability where one can check whether or not a ciphertext is valid for an identity.

are not robust, we can add unrestricted strong collision-freeness property to them via the Abdalla et al. transformations. Other candidate is the CCA-version of the Boneh-Franklin IBE scheme [7] which is IBE-ANO-CCA secure in the random oracle model. The scheme is also known to provide strong robustness. However, it is not clear whether the scheme provides unrestricted strong collision-freeness. Thus, we need to properly employ the Abdalla et al. transformation.

Since unrestricted strong collision-freeness is weaker than complete robustness, employing the two Abdalla et al. transformations as above may be somewhat excessive. Thus, directly and simply constructing an IBE-ANO-CCA secure IBE scheme with unrestricted strong collision-freeness is left as an interesting open problem.

Acknowledgement. This work was supported in part by the JSPS KAKENHI Grant Number JP16H02808 and the MIC/SCOPE #162108102. We thank Dr. Yohei Watanabe for helpful discussion.

References

1. Abdalla, M., et al.: Searchable encryption revisited: consistency properties, relation to anonymous IBE, and extensions. J. Cryptol. **21**(3), 350–391 (2008)
2. Abdalla, M., Bellare, M., Neven, G.: Robust encryption. In: Micciancio, D. (ed.) TCC 2010. LNCS, vol. 5978, pp. 480–497. Springer, Heidelberg (2010). https://doi.org/10.1007/978-3-642-11799-2_28
3. Abdalla, M., Bellare, M., Neven, G.: Robust encryption. J. Cryptol. **31**(2), 307–350 (2018)
4. Baek, J., Safavi-Naini, R., Susilo, W.: On the integration of public key data encryption and public key encryption with keyword search. In: Katsikas, S.K., López, J., Backes, M., Gritzalis, S., Preneel, B. (eds.) ISC 2006. LNCS, vol. 4176, pp. 217–232. Springer, Heidelberg (2006). https://doi.org/10.1007/11836810_16
5. Bellare, M., Shoup, S.: Two-tier signatures, strongly unforgeable signatures, and Fiat-Shamir without random oracles. In: Okamoto, T., Wang, X. (eds.) PKC 2007. LNCS, vol. 4450, pp. 201–216. Springer, Heidelberg (2007). https://doi.org/10.1007/978-3-540-71677-8_14
6. Boneh, D., Di Crescenzo, G., Ostrovsky, R., Persiano, G.: Public key encryption with keyword search. In: Cachin, C., Camenisch, J.L. (eds.) EUROCRYPT 2004. LNCS, vol. 3027, pp. 506–522. Springer, Heidelberg (2004). https://doi.org/10.1007/978-3-540-24676-3_30
7. Boneh, D., Franklin, M.: Identity-based encryption from the Weil pairing. In: Kilian, J. (ed.) CRYPTO 2001. LNCS, vol. 2139, pp. 213–229. Springer, Heidelberg (2001). https://doi.org/10.1007/3-540-44647-8_13
8. Boyen, X., Waters, B.: Anonymous hierarchical identity-based encryption (without random oracles). In: Dwork, C. (ed.) CRYPTO 2006. LNCS, vol. 4117, pp. 290–307. Springer, Heidelberg (2006). https://doi.org/10.1007/11818175_17
9. Buccafurri, F., Lax, G., Sahu, R.A., Saraswat, V.: Practical and secure integrated PKE+PEKS with keyword privacy. In: SECRYPT, pp. 448–453 (2015)
10. Canetti, R., Halevi, S., Katz, J.: Chosen-ciphertext security from identity-based encryption. In: Cachin, C., Camenisch, J.L. (eds.) EUROCRYPT 2004. LNCS, vol. 3027, pp. 207–222. Springer, Heidelberg (2004). https://doi.org/10.1007/978-3-540-24676-3_13

11. Chen, J., Lim, H.W., Ling, S., Wang, H., Wee, H.: Shorter IBE and signatures via asymmetric pairings. In: Abdalla, M., Lange, T. (eds.) Pairing 2012. LNCS, vol. 7708, pp. 122–140. Springer, Heidelberg (2013). https://doi.org/10.1007/978-3-642-36334-4_8

12. Chen, Y., Zhang, J., Lin, D., Zhang, Z.: Generic constructions of integrated PKE and PEKS. Des. Codes Cryptogr. **78**(2), 493–526 (2016)

13. Emura, K.: A generic construction of secure-channel free searchable encryption with multiple keywords. In: Yan, Z., Molva, R., Mazurczyk, W., Kantola, R. (eds.) NSS 2017. LNCS, vol. 10394, pp. 3–18. Springer, Cham (2017). https://doi.org/10.1007/978-3-319-64701-2_1

14. Emura, K., Miyaji, A., Rahman, M.S., Omote, K.: Generic constructions of secure-channel free searchable encryption with adaptive security. Secur. Commun. Netw. **8**(8), 1547–1560 (2015)

15. Fang, L., Susilo, W., Ge, C., Wang, J.: A secure channel free public key encryption with keyword search scheme without random oracle. In: Garay, J.A., Miyaji, A., Otsuka, A. (eds.) CANS 2009. LNCS, vol. 5888, pp. 248–258. Springer, Heidelberg (2009). https://doi.org/10.1007/978-3-642-10433-6_16

16. Fang, L., Susilo, W., Ge, C., Wang, J.: Public key encryption with keyword search secure against keyword guessing attacks without random oracle. Inf. Sci. **238**, 221–241 (2013)

17. Farshim, P., Libert, B., Paterson, K.G., Quaglia, E.A.: Robust encryption, revisited. In: Kurosawa, K., Hanaoka, G. (eds.) PKC 2013. LNCS, vol. 7778, pp. 352–368. Springer, Heidelberg (2013). https://doi.org/10.1007/978-3-642-36362-7_22

18. Fuhr, T., Paillier, P.: Decryptable searchable encryption. In: Susilo, W., Liu, J.K., Mu, Y. (eds.) ProvSec 2007. LNCS, vol. 4784, pp. 228–236. Springer, Heidelberg (2007). https://doi.org/10.1007/978-3-540-75670-5_17

19. Gentry, C.: Practical identity-based encryption without random oracles. In: Vaudenay, S. (ed.) EUROCRYPT 2006. LNCS, vol. 4004, pp. 445–464. Springer, Heidelberg (2006). https://doi.org/10.1007/11761679_27

20. Guo, L., Yau, W.: Efficient secure-channel free public key encryption with keyword search for EMRs in cloud storage. J. Med. Syst. **39**(2), 11 (2015)

21. Hofheinz, D., Weinreb, E.: Searchable encryption with decryption in the standard model. IACR Cryptology ePrint Archive 2008:423 (2008)

22. Jutla, C.S., Roy, A.: Shorter quasi-adaptive NIZK proofs for linear subspaces. In: Sako, K., Sarkar, P. (eds.) ASIACRYPT 2013. LNCS, vol. 8269, pp. 1–20. Springer, Heidelberg (2013). https://doi.org/10.1007/978-3-642-42033-7_1

23. Jutla, C.S., Roy, A.: Shorter quasi-adaptive NIZK proofs for linear subspaces. J. Cryptol. **30**(4), 1116–1156 (2017)

24. Kiltz, E.: Chosen-ciphertext security from tag-based encryption. In: Halevi, S., Rabin, T. (eds.) TCC 2006. LNCS, vol. 3876, pp. 581–600. Springer, Heidelberg (2006). https://doi.org/10.1007/11681878_30

25. Mohassel, P.: A closer look at anonymity and robustness in encryption schemes. In: Abe, M. (ed.) ASIACRYPT 2010. LNCS, vol. 6477, pp. 501–518. Springer, Heidelberg (2010). https://doi.org/10.1007/978-3-642-17373-8_29

26. Rhee, H.S., Park, J.H., Lee, D.H.: Generic construction of designated tester public-key encryption with keyword search. Inf. Sci. **205**, 93–109 (2012)

27. Saraswat, V., Sahu, R.A.: Short integrated PKE+PEKS in standard model. In: Ali, S.S., Danger, J.-L., Eisenbarth, T. (eds.) SPACE 2017. LNCS, vol. 10662, pp. 226–246. Springer, Cham (2017). https://doi.org/10.1007/978-3-319-71501-8_13

28. Wang, T., Au, M.H., Wu, W.: An efficient secure channel free searchable encryption scheme with multiple keywords. In: Chen, J., Piuri, V., Su, C., Yung, M. (eds.) NSS 2016. LNCS, vol. 9955, pp. 251–265. Springer, Cham (2016). https://doi.org/10.1007/978-3-319-46298-1_17

29. Wee, H.: Public key encryption against related key attacks. In: Fischlin, M., Buchmann, J., Manulis, M. (eds.) PKC 2012. LNCS, vol. 7293, pp. 262–279. Springer, Heidelberg (2012). https://doi.org/10.1007/978-3-642-30057-8_16

30. Zhang, R., Imai, H.: Combining public key encryption with keyword search and public key encryption. IEICE Trans. **92**–**D**(5), 888–896 (2009)

An Almost Non-interactive Order Preserving Encryption Scheme

Jingjing Guo[1,2], Jianfeng Wang[1,3], Zhiwei Zhang[1], and Xiaofeng Chen[1(✉)]

[1] State Key Laboratory of Integrated Service Networks (ISN), Xidian University,
Xi'an 710071, People's Republic of China
jiaozuoguojing@163.com, {jfwang,zwzhang,xfchen}@xidian.edu.cn
[2] The State Key Laboratory of Cryptology,
PO Box 5159, Beijing 100878, People's Republic of China
[3] State Key Laboratory of Information Security, Institute of Information Engineering,
Chinese Academy of Sciences, Beijing 100093, People's Republic of China

Abstract. Order preserving encryption (OPE) is an encryption scheme that the ciphertexts retain the order of their underlying plaintexts. It could be used to perform the order comparison or the efficient range query over encrypted data. Recently, plenty of work has been proposed on the construction of OPE scheme. Nevertheless, many existing OPE schemes require multiple rounds ($O(\log n)$) of interaction. As a result, real-time online, network delay and communication transmission failure are the efficiency challenges for the order comparison or range query. In this paper, we propose an almost non-interactive OPE scheme called BF-OPE. The BF-OPE scheme works by integrating Bloom filter and prefix encoding. They enable the encrypted data items to be compared when a token is provided by the client. Furthermore, the padding technique has been used to hide the frequency information both in data items and query ranges on the ciphertexts. Finally, we prove that the proposed scheme is secure with respect to the leakage function $\mathcal{L}_I$.

Keywords: Range query · Order preserving encryption
Order revealing encryption · Ideal security

1 Introduction

Range query, a common query operation, is generally used to select contiguous elements according to a label such as a timestamp and index. In particular, it draws much attention in "Big Data" for its power of boosting the system to perform some analysis over the stored data. To support high efficiency and low cost, these databases are always stored on remote untrusted servers, which drives the need to secure outsource the database. It is well-known that the traditional encryption schemes provide a way to achieve data confidentiality, however, it also destroys the order information and makes query difficult without decryption, notably for range query.

© Springer Nature Switzerland AG 2018
C. Su and H. Kikuchi (Eds.): ISPEC 2018, LNCS 11125, pp. 87–100, 2018.
https://doi.org/10.1007/978-3-319-99807-7_6

OPE is a simple and efficient encryption scheme where the order of plaintexts remained in the ciphertexts, namely, $\text{Enc}(x) > \text{Enc}(y)$ if and only if $x > y$. It enables the cloud server to perform comparison and range query directly over encrypted database [9,11,13,31,32], thus makes it very suitable in the outsourcing [8,10,26,30] in cloud computing. Therefore, the study on designing a secure and efficient OPE scheme is of both theoretical and practical significance.

Agrawal et al. [1] firstly proposed the definition of OPE while gave no security analysis. Boldyreva et al. [4] provided a rigorous treatment about the security and proved that ideal security is infeasible for OPE under certain implicit assumptions. As a result, they proposed an OPE scheme named as BCLO, and it achieves random order preserving function (ROPF) security, a weaker security definition. The ROPF security was later shown to leak at least half of the plaintext bits [5]. Popa et al. [24] proposed the first ideal security OPE scheme which is a mutable order preserving encryption (mOPE) scheme. The mOPE ensures that it will not reveal no more information except the order of the plaintexts. The main idea of mOPE is to build a balanced tree containing the plaintexts encrypted by the traditional encryption scheme. In addition, the mOPE scheme is interactive and requires multiple rounds of communication between the client and the cloud server. When updating or querying, it requires $O(\log n)$ rounds of communication and $O(1)$ client storage, where n is the number of items in database. The multiple rounds of interaction bring the new challenge for the client real-time online and network communication.

Recently, different from the traditional OPE schemes, Boneh et al. [6] firstly formalized the notion of order revealing encryption (ORE) scheme, which reveals the order of the corresponding plaintexts and nothing else. It is a generalization of OPE scheme. However, based on multilinear maps, the scheme in [6] is too impractical for most applications and remains a theoretical result. Lewi et al. [19] proposed an efficient ORE scheme, which is secure with the leakage function $\mathcal{L}_I$. Due to the size of the ciphertext is linear to the plaintext space, it is limited to small message spaces.

1.1 Our Contributions

In this paper, we further study the problem on the construction of order preserving encryption scheme. The contributions of this paper are as follows:

- We present a new non-interactive OPE scheme named BF-OPE by integrating Bloom filter and prefix encoding. BF-OPE can achieve efficient comparison over encrypted data without requiring additional interactions between the client and the server.
- We introduce the padding technique [25] to randomize the data items and query ranges, which can hide the frequency information on both data items and ranges. Security analysis shows that the proposed scheme satisfies the desired security goal.

1.2   Related Work

The problem of range query [7, 21] is the most important query operation in "Big Data". The approach of range query can be divided into fully homomorphic encryption, searchable encryption [20, 27, 28] and order preserving encryption. OPE, as a practical approach for range query, has been studied in the past decades [1, 4, 14, 18, 24].

The concept of OPE was proposed by Agrawal et al.[1] in 2004. The basic idea is to take a target distribution which provided by a client and transform plaintext in such a way that the transformation preserves the order and follows target distribution. This scheme can only be used in a static system, and gave no security analysis. In [4], Boldyreva et al. introduced the ideal security definition and proposed the first provable OPE scheme, which we call BCLO scheme. They also proved that an OPE scheme is impossible to achieve ideal security unless its ciphertext space is extremely large exponential in the size of plaintext space. Therefore, the proposed BCLO scheme achieved a weaker security ROPF. Later, they showed that a ROPF scheme achieves security of window one-wayness. However, Boldyreva et al. [5] and Xiao et al. [29] proved that the BCLO scheme leaked at least half of plaintext bits. In [12], Dyer et al. designed an OPE scheme based on approximate integer common divisor problem. But scheme [12] only achieved window one-wayness security. There are other schemes [16, 22, 23, 29] provided weaker security guarantee by making some assumptions about the attack, which donot hold in practice.

Popa et al. [24] proposed the first ideally-secure order preserving encoding scheme based on a data structure, where this scheme revealed no more information besides the lexicographical order. The main idea of their scheme is mutable ciphertext, which means order preserving encodings for several plaintexts change with updating a value. They proved that it is impossible for a linear length encryption scheme to achieve ideal security even if the encryption is stateful, namely, the mutable ciphertext is the precondition for ideal security. Kerschbaum [17] pointed out every (deterministic) OPE scheme suffer a simple attack from the frequency information. Therefore, he proposed a stronger security definition, indistinguishability under frequency analyzing ordered chosen plaintext attack (IND-FAOCPA), and settled for an encryption scheme with this stronger security. The main idea of this scheme is to randomize ciphertext to hide frequency information. Inspired by the buffer tree [2], Roche et al. [25] proposed a construction technique of order preserving tree and designed the partial order preserving encoding (POPE) scheme. The POPE scheme supports insert-heavy database and leaks less order information. However, all these schemes need multiple rounds of interaction.

1.3   Organization

The rest of this paper is organized as follows. The preliminaries are given in Sect. 2. The construction of BF-OPE scheme is given in Sect. 3. The security and efficiency analysis of the proposed scheme are given in Sect. 4. Finally, we give the conclusions in Sect. 5.

2   Preliminaries

In this section, we present some cryptographic tools and techniques used in our scheme, and the general definition of OPE scheme.

2.1   Bloom Filter

In [3], Bloom proposed the concept of Bloom filter (BF), which can be used to test whether an element belongs to a set. A Bloom filter contains a bit array of m bits and r independent hash functions defined as follows: $h_i : \{0,1\}^* \rightarrow [1,m]; i \in [1,r]$. In the initial phase, all the positions of the bit array are set to 0. If an element is added to the set, put it into the r hash functions to get r array positions, and turn these positions to 1. If the value of this position is 1, the operation does not work.

Given an element, the BF can test whether the element belongs to the set. Given an element x, the BF computes the r hash functions to get r array positions. If a value of these positions is 0, the element does not belong to the set. On the contrary, if all the positions are 1, we cannot decide whether this element belongs to the set or not. This is because of the existence of false positive.

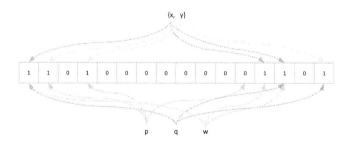

Fig. 1. A Bloom filter construction.

As shown in Fig. 1, it is easy to see that element p does not belong to the set and w belongs to. Although all the positions are 1, the element q does not belong to. That is called as false positive. The false positive satisfies $P_f = (1 - e^{-kn/m})^k$ and reaches its minimum value 2^{-r}, if $r = \ln 2 * (m/n)$, where n denotes the number of elements, r the number of hash functions, m the size of the Bloom filter.

2.2   Prefix Encoding

In [15], Gupta et al. utilized the prefix encoding to proceed range query over the plaintexts. The basic idea of prefix encoding is to convert the problem whether an element belongs to a range into the problem whether the intersection of two sets is empty.

Given an element x of w bits and its binary representation $x = b_1b_2\cdots b_w$, the prefix family of x is $F(x) = \{b_1b_2\cdots b_w, b_1\cdots b_{w-1}*, \cdots, b_1*\cdots*, **\cdots*\}$, which has the size of $w + 1$. Given a range $[a, b]$, we denoted the minimum cover set of prefixes as $S([a, b])$. Its size is at most $2w - 2$, where a and b are two elements of w bits. For example, given 3 of 5 bits, its prefix family is $F(3) = \{00011, 0001*, 000**, 00***, 0****, *****\}$ and the range prefix of $[0, 6]$ is $S([0, 6]) = \{000**, 0010*, 00110\}$. For a data item x and range $[a, b]$, x belongs to range $[a, b]$ if and only if there exists a prefix $P \in F(x)$ such that $P \in S([a, b])$, i.e., $F(x) \cap S([a, b]) \neq \phi$. From the above example, we can draw the conclusion that $3 \in [0, 6]$ because $F(3) \cap S([0, 6]) = \{000**\}$.

2.3 Order Preserving Encryption

An order preserving encryption scheme is a tuple of polynomial-time algorithms OPE=(**KeyGen, BuildTree, Enc, Search, Update, Dec**) defined over a database $\mathcal{D}$ with the following properties:

- **KeyGen**$(1^\lambda) \to SK$: On input the security parameter λ, the **KeyGen** algorithm is run by the client to generate a secret key SK, which is secretly stored by the client.
- **BuildTree**$(\mathcal{D}) \to \Gamma$: On input the database $\mathcal{D}$, the **BuildTree** algorithm is run by the client to build an OPE tree Γ, which is used to store and index the data items.
- **Enc**$(SK, \Gamma) \to \Gamma^*$: On input the secret key SK and the OPE tree Γ, the **Enc** algorithm is run by the client to produce the encrypted tree Γ^*.
- **Search**$(SK, \Gamma^*, R) \to I^*$: On input the secret key SK, encrypted OPE tree Γ^* and query range R, the **Search** algorithm is run to output the encrypted results for the client.
- **Update**$(\Gamma^*, SK, a) \to \Gamma^*$: On input the secret key SK and the data item a, the **Update** algorithm inserts the new data item into the OPE tree.
- **Dec**$(SK, I^*) \to I$: On input the secret key SK and the encrypted results I^*, the **Dec** algorithm is run by the client to obtain the results I.

Remark 1. In this paper, we use Γ^* and I^* to denote the ciphertexts of OPE tree Γ and result I, respectively.

Following, we also introduce some necessary definitions in our scheme. As described in [19], the correctness and security definitions were proposed as follows.

Definition 1 *(Correctness). We say that an OPE scheme over a well-domain $\mathcal{D}$ is correct if for $SK \leftarrow$ **KeyGen**(1^λ) such that, for $\forall m \in \mathcal{D}$ and range R, if $m \in R$, $I^* = $ **Search**(SK, Γ^*, R) then $m \in$ **Dec**(SK, I^*).*

Definition 2 *(Security). We say that an OPE scheme is secure with leakage function $\mathcal{L}_1$ if for all adversaries $\mathcal{A}$, the scheme reveals no more information* *besides the leakage function $\mathcal{L}_I$. In particular, we define leakage function $\mathcal{L}_I$ as follows:*

$$\mathcal{L}_I(m_i, m_j) = \{position_{diff}(m_i, m_j)\},$$

where $position_{diff}(m_i, m_j)$ gives the position of the first bit where m_i and m_j differ.

3   Main Construction of BF-OPE Scheme

In this work, we consider an OPE scheme used in the range query system in the outsourcing computing model, as illustrated in Fig. 2. The system model contains two entities: the client and the cloud server. The client is an entity who wants to outsource his own database to the cloud server, and the cloud server is an entity who provides the storage service and stores encrypted database on behave of the clients. We can view the cloud server as "honest-but-curious". That means, the cloud server follows the proposed protocol and returns the answers honestly, but tries to learn information about the encrypted data.

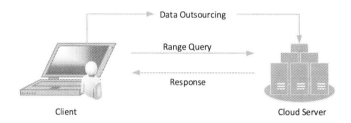

Fig. 2. Architecture of range query.

3.1   Main Idea

In this paper, we propose a new order preserving encryption scheme, BF-OPE scheme, for range query over encrypted database in cloud computing. The BF-OPE scheme can reduce the communication overhead between the client and the cloud server. Our main idea is that we insert an OPE index after the ciphertext of the data item. The OPE index can help the cloud server to decide the order information, therefore, the cloud server does not need to seek the order information by the interactions between him and the client.

We use the prefix encoding technique to change the problem on how to construct an OPE index to test whether the intersection of two sets is empty. Trivially, the problem can be solved by testing whether an element belongs to a set. In this condition, we use Bloom filter to test over the ciphertexts. However, the frequency information is revealed in the phase of **Update** and **Search**. This is because that the data item and range prefix is unique. To solve this problem, we use padding technique to hide the frequency information. Moreover, to protect the functionality of query, we take different padding techniques for the data item and query range. The detailed description is presented as follows.

3.2 The BF-OPE Scheme

A B-tree is a tree in which leaf node stores data items and internal node stores split points indicating the difference of subtrees. All data items in the left subtree of v are smaller than v and all data items in the right subtree are larger than v. The cloud server cannot obtain the order of two encrypted data in the same leaf node. In this paper, we build an OPE tree index which is inspired by the B-tree in the proposed scheme. For each node, we suppose that it has a storage limitation L, where L is the storage capacity of the client. Without loss of generality, we assume that all data items are w_1-bit and greater than 0. A detailed description of the proposed scheme is as follows.

- **KeyGen** (1^λ): Taking the security parameter λ as input, the client initializes the system parameters.
  1. By DET, we refer to an IND-CPA secure symmetric encryption scheme DET = (DET.Key, DET.Enc, DET.Dec). The client generates the secret key $sk_1 \leftarrow$ DET.Key(1^λ).
  2. A Bloom filter with r hash functions is initialized. At the same time, the client uses r secret keys $k_1, k_2, \cdots, k_r$ to compute r keyed hash functions.
  Therefore, the client has the secret key $SK = (sk_1, sk_2)$, where $sk_1 =$ DET.Key(1^λ), $sk_2 = (k_1, k_2, \cdots, k_r)$.
- **BuildTree**$(\mathcal{D})$: Taking the database $\mathcal{D}$ as input, a client stores the data items in a B-tree in plaintext.
  1. The client firstly randomizes the data items d through padding a w_1-bit random number r as $d||01||r$. For simplicity, we always use d to represent its randomization. Therefore, d is a w-bit data, where $w = 2w_1 + 2$.
  2. Afterwards, the client computes the data prefix $F(d)$ and range prefix $S([0, d])$ (only for internal node), and then inserts the prefixes in the corresponding node. The client builds the OPE tree as Γ, where $\Gamma = \{(d_1, F(d_1)), \cdots, (d_n, F(d_n)), (t_1, F(t_1), S([0, t_1])), \cdots, (t_m, F(t_m), S([0, t_m]))\}$, n is the number of data items in the database and m denotes the number of split points in the OPE tree. A toy example of OPE tree Γ is shown in Fig. 3.
- **Enc** (SK, Γ): Taking secret key SK and OPE tree Γ as input, the client encrypts data items, data prefix and rang prefix to protect the privacy of data items.
  1. The client firstly encrypts data items as

$$C_{d_i} = \text{DET.Enc}(sk_1, d_i), \ (1 \leq i \leq n)$$
$$C_{t_j} = \text{DET.Enc}(sk_1, t_j), \ (1 \leq j \leq m).$$

  2. The client computes the Bloom filter for the set of data prefix and range prefix. For leaf node d, the client computes its Bloom filter of set $F(d)$ as BF_{1d}. For split point t, namely internal node, the client computes Bloom filters of $F(t)$ and $S([0, t])$ as BF_{1t} and BF_{2t}, respectively.

The client uploads encrypted OPE tree $\Gamma^* = \{(C_{d_1}, BF_{1d_1}), \cdots, (C_{d_n}, BF_{1d_n}), (C_{t_1}, BF_{1t_1}, BF_{2t_1}), \cdots, (C_{t_m}, BF_{1t_m}, BF_{2t_m})\}$ to the cloud server.

- **Search** $(SK, \Gamma^*, [a, b])$: Taking secret key $SK = (sk_1, (k_1, k_2, \cdots, k_r))$ and query range $[a, b]$ as input, the client generates the search token TK for the range $[a, b]$. Subsequently, the cloud server searches over the encrypted tree Γ^*, achieves the encrypted results I^*, and returns it to the client.

  1. For a query range $[a, b]$, the client firstly randomizes the range through padding w_1-bit random numbers r_1, r_2 as $a||0||r_1$ and $b||11||r_2$. For simplicity, we always use a and b to represent its randomization, respectively.
  2. The client computes range prefix as $S([a, b]) = \{P_1, P_2, \cdots, P_l\}$ and outputs its search token as a matrix to the cloud server.

  $$M_{[a,b]} = \begin{pmatrix} H(k_1, P_1) & H(k_2, P_1) & \cdots & H(k_r, P_1) \\ \vdots & \vdots & \ddots & \vdots \\ H(k_1, P_l) & H(k_2, P_l) & \cdots & H(k_r, P_l) \end{pmatrix}$$

  3. After receiving the matrix $M_{[a,b]}$, the cloud server searches OPE tree from the root node to the leaf node. The cloud server could find the leftmost and rightmost leaf nodes that intersect with range. Subsequently, the cloud server outputs the ciphertexts in the leaf node between these two leaf nodes and tests the data items in these two leaf nodes whether belong to the range, if belongs to, outputs it. More concretely, the cloud server tests whether $S([a, b])$ intersects with data index $F(t)$, where t is a split point. If intersects, there exists a prefix $P_i \in S([a, b])$ such that $P_i \in F(t)$, namely, there exists a row i in matrix $M_{[a,b]}$ such that $BF_1(P_i) = 1$. The equation $BF_1(P_i) = 1$ means the values at the position $H(k_1, P_i), H(k_2, P_i), \cdots, H(k_r, P_i)$ of Bloom filter BF_1 are all equal to 1. After finding the leftmost and rightmost leaf nodes, the cloud server returns data in the leaf node between these two leaf nodes. The data items in these two nodes can be decided as above.

- **Update** (Γ^*, a): Taking encrypted OPE tree Γ^* and the new data item a, the client generates the ciphertext C_a and the token TK_a, and submits them to the cloud server. Afterwards, the cloud server uses the ciphertext C_a and the token TK_a to update the encrypted OPE tree Γ^*.

  1. The client computes ciphertext C_a, data index BF_1, and matrix $M_{F(a)}$, where

  $$M_{F(a)} = \begin{pmatrix} H(k_1, P_1) & H(k_2, P_1) & \cdots & H(k_r, P_1) \\ \vdots & \vdots & \ddots & \vdots \\ H(k_1, P_{w+1}) & H(k_2, P_{w+1}) & \cdots & H(k_r, P_{w+1}) \end{pmatrix}$$

  Then the client submits them to the cloud server.

  2. After receiving $(C_a, BF_{1a}, M_{F(a)})$, the cloud server searches the leaf node to insert new data through texting whether there exists a row i satisfies $BF_1(P_i) = 1$. Finally, the cloud server inserts data a into its corresponding leaf node. The test algorithm is similar to the range query.

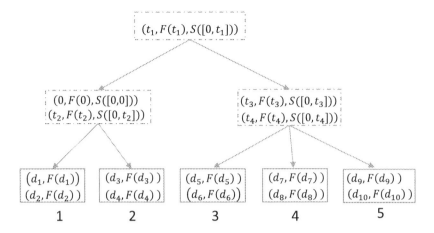

Fig. 3. The OPE tree construction.

When arriving at its storage limitation L, this leaf node splits into two leaf nodes and inserts a new split point into its parent node. The cloud server first returns left and right split point of this leaf node to the client, like C_{92}, C_{118}. If it is the rightmost leaf node, the cloud server only returns its left split point. After receiving these two split points, he decrypts them, selects a value a between these two split points, computes $(C_a, BF_1, BF_2, M_{[0,a]})$, and uploads it to cloud server. The cloud server splits the leaf node into two leaf nodes and inserts (C_a, BF_1, BF_2) as a new split point, as shown in Fig. 4. If the parent contains too many split points, the split propagates upward. Tree splitting is the only step which needs intersection in our scheme. The deletion operation is a little different from the insertion operation. In deletion, the client computes $M_{F(a)}$ and submits it to the cloud server. The cloud server finds the data items precisely. In the leaf node, the cloud server decides whether two elements are the same one. Namely, there is no row i in matrix $M_{F(a)}$ such that $BF_1(P_i) = 0$ (the Bloom filter of data in leaf node). In this paper, we divide modification into deletion and insertion. Thus, the proposed scheme can be used in a dynamic database. If we donot take data update into consideration, the range index BF_2 can be removed from split point.

- **Dec(SK, I^*):** Taking the secret key SK and encrypted results I^* as input, the client decrypts the encrypted results and obtains results I. Furthermore, the client removes the padding numbers and obtains the data item.

4   Analysis

In this section, we present the security and efficiency analysis of the proposed BF-OPE scheme.

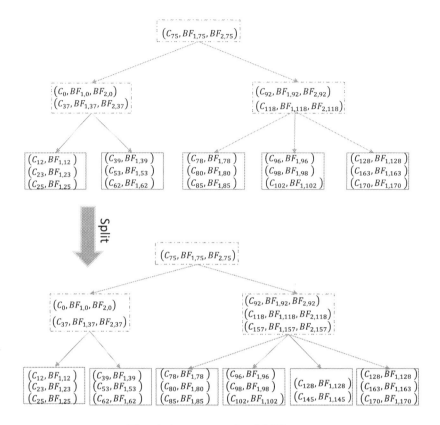

Fig. 4. A toy example of OPE tree.

4.1 Security Analysis

Theorem 1. *The proposed BF-OPE scheme over a well-domain $\mathcal{D}$ is correct.*

Proof. We suppose that data item $d \in \mathcal{D}$, range $\in [a, b]$ and their randomization $d||01||r, a||00||r_1, b||11||r_2$, where r, r_1, r_2 are three w_1-bit random numbers. If $d \in [a, b]$, then we have $d||01||r \in [a||00||r_1, b||11||r_2]$ holds.

If $d||01||r \in [a||00||r_1, b||11||r_2]$ holds, then $F(d||01||r) \cap S([a||00||r_1, b||11||r_2]) \neq \phi$. In this condition, data $d||01||r$ will be returned as the search result, namely, $C_{d||01||r} \in I^*$, where $I^* = \mathbf{Search}(SK, \Gamma^*, [a, b])$. After decryption, we have $d \in \mathbf{Dec}(SK, I^*)$.

Theorem 2. *The proposed BF-OPE scheme is secure with respect to leakage function $\mathcal{L}_I$.*

Proof. The ciphertexts were composed of C_a and index. The ciphertext C_a was produced through a plaintext-indistinguishable encryption scheme. In this case, the ciphertexts have the property that they are semantically-secure encryptions.

Furthermore, we consider the security of index, which has not been solved by padding technique. If $|F(a) \cap F(b)| = m$, then the first bit, where m_i and m_j differ, occurs at $m-$th, namely, $a_1 = b_1, \cdots, a_{m-1} = b_{m-1}$, and $a_m \neq b_m$. Since padding technique runs through padding randomness number r behind data d, it cannot solve the above problem. The basic reason is that an adversary has the ability to decide whether $P_1 = P_2$, where $P_1 \in F(a)$ and $P_2 \in F(b)$. In insertion phase, the client provides the matrix $M_{F(a)}$ and $M_{F(b)}$. In this condition, the cloud server decides the identical row in matrix $M_{F(a)}$ and $M_{F(b)}$. Therefore, the cloud server knows the leakage function $\mathcal{L}_I(m_i, m_j) = \{position_{diff}(m_i, m_j)\}$.

4.2   Efficiency Analysis

For the convenience of discussion, some marks are introduced. We denote by E an encryption, D a decryption, H an operation of Hash, r the number of Hash in Bloom filter, n the size of a database, and w the bits of our data item. We omit other operations such as comparison of plaintexts.

Table 1. Computation cost of our scheme

Schemes	Scheme [19]	Scheme [24]	BF-OPE
Security	IND-rOCPA	IND-OCPA	$\mathcal{L}_I(m_i, m_j)$
Interaction	0	$\log n$	0
Client (Insert)	$E + 2^w \cdot (D + H)$	$E + \log n \cdot D$	$E + (w+1) \cdot rH$
Client (Delete)	E	$\log n \cdot D$	$(w+1) \cdot rH$
Client (Search)	$2E$	$2 \log n \cdot D$	$(2w - 2) \cdot rH$
Cloud (Insert)	$\log n \cdot H$	0	0
Cloud (Delete)	$\log n \cdot H$	0	0
Cloud (Search)	$2 \log n \cdot H$	0	0

Table 1 presents the comparison among scheme [19], scheme [24] and BF-OPE scheme. It can be seen that scheme [24] achieves IND-OCPA security, which is the first scheme who achieved the ideal security. In scheme [19], the right components achieve IND-OCPA security denoted as IND-rOCPA security. The proposed BF-OPE scheme leaks the bit where the difference happens.

When inserting, deleting and querying, scheme [24] needs $\log n$ rounds of interaction. The client decrypts ciphertexts to help cloud server to decide the order of two ciphertexts in update and query phase. In scheme [24], the cloud server does nothing computation in update and query phase. In BF-OPE scheme, the cloud server checks whether the position of Bloom filter is equal to 1. Owing to the low computation overhead, both the computation of cloud server are denoted as 0.

5   Conclusions

In this paper, we propose an almost non-interactive order preserving encryption scheme for range query, which is a basic search operation in the outsourced database. Note that the state-of-the-art order preserving encryption scheme called mOPE needs multiple rounds of interaction between the clients and the cloud server. Therefore, the mOPE is easily influenced by the network failures and increases the communication burden. Based on these reasons, we designed a BF-OPE scheme, which is secure with respect to the leakage function $\mathcal{L}_I$ and can hide the frequency information of outsourced data. Furthermore, the proposed scheme leaks partial order information among the ciphertexts.

Acknowledgements. This work was supported by the National Cryptography Development Fund (No. MMJJ20180110).

References

1. Agrawal, R., Kiernan, J., Srikant, R., Xu, Y.: Order-preserving encryption for numeric data. In: Proceedings of the ACM International Conference on Management of Data (SIGMOD), Paris, France, pp. 563–574 (2004)
2. Arge, L.: The buffer tree: a technique for designing batched external data structures. Algorithmica **37**(1), 1–24 (2003)
3. Bloom, B.H.: Space/time trade-offs in hash coding with allowable errors. Commun. ACM **13**(7), 422–426 (1970)
4. Boldyreva, A., Chenette, N., Lee, Y., O'Neill, A.: Order-preserving symmetric encryption. In: Proceedings of the International Conference on the Theory and Applications of Cryptographic Techniques (EUROCRYPT), Sofia, Bulgaria, pp. 563–594 (2015)
5. Boldyreva, A., Chenette, N., O'Neill, A.: Order-preserving encryption revisited: improved security analysis and alternative solutions. In: Rogaway, P. (ed.) CRYPTO 2011. LNCS, vol. 6841, pp. 578–595. Springer, Heidelberg (2011). https://doi.org/10.1007/978-3-642-22792-9_33
6. Boneh, D., Lewi, K., Raykova, M., Sahai, A., Zhandry, M., Zimmerman, J.: Semantically secure order-revealing encryption: multi-input functional encryption without obfuscation. In: Oswald, E., Fischlin, M. (eds.) EUROCRYPT 2015. LNCS, vol. 9057, pp. 563–594. Springer, Heidelberg (2015). https://doi.org/10.1007/978-3-662-46803-6_19
7. Boneh, D., Waters, B.: Conjunctive, subset, and range queries on encrypted data. In: Vadhan, S.P. (ed.) TCC 2007. LNCS, vol. 4392, pp. 535–554. Springer, Heidelberg (2007). https://doi.org/10.1007/978-3-540-70936-7_29
8. Chen, X., Huang, X., Li, J., Ma, J., Lou, W., Wong, D.S.: New algorithms for secure outsourcing of large-scale systems of linear equations. IEEE Trans. Inf. Forensics Secur. **10**(1), 69–78 (2015)
9. Chen, X., Li, J., Huang, X., Ma, J., Lou, W.: New publicly verifiable databases with efficient updates. IEEE Trans. Dependable Secure Comput. **12**(5), 546–556 (2015)
10. Chen, X., Li, J., Ma, J., Tang, Q., Lou, W.: New algorithms for secure outsourcing of modular exponentiations. IEEE Trans. Parallel Distrib. Syst. **25**(9), 2386–2396 (2014)

11. Chen, X., Li, J., Weng, J., Ma, J., Lou, W.: Verifiable computation over large database with incremental updates. IEEE Trans. Comput. **65**(10), 3184–3195 (2016)
12. Dyer, J., Dyer, M., Xu, J.: Order-preserving encryption using approximate integer common divisors. In: Garcia-Alfaro, J., Navarro-Arribas, G., Hartenstein, H., Herrera-Joancomartí, J. (eds.) ESORICS/DPM/CBT -2017. LNCS, vol. 10436, pp. 257–274. Springer, Cham (2017). https://doi.org/10.1007/978-3-319-67816-0_15
13. B. Fuller, et al.: Sok: cryptographically protected database search. In: Proceedings of the IEEE Symposium on Security and Privacy (SP), San Jose, CA, USA, pp. 172–191 (2017)
14. Furukawa, J.: Request-based comparable encryption. In: Crampton, J., Jajodia, S., Mayes, K. (eds.) ESORICS 2013. LNCS, vol. 8134, pp. 129–146. Springer, Heidelberg (2013). https://doi.org/10.1007/978-3-642-40203-6_8
15. Gupta, P., McKeown, N.: Algorithms for packet classification. IEEE Netw. **15**(2), 24–32 (2001)
16. Kadhem, H., Amagasa, T., Kitagawa, H.: A secure and efficient order preserving encryption scheme for relational databases. In: Proceedings of the International Conference on Knowledge Management and Information Sharing (KMIS), Valencia, Spain, pp. 25–35 (2010)
17. Kerschbaum, F.: Frequency-hiding order-preserving encryption. In: Proceedings of the ACM Conference on Computer and Communications Security (CCS), Denver, CO, USA, pp. 656–667 (2015)
18. Lee, S., Park, T., Lee, D., Nam, T., Kim, S.: Chaotic order preserving encryption for efficient and secure queries on databases. IEICE Trans. Inf. Syst. **92**(11), 2207–2217 (2009)
19. Lewi, K., Wu, D.J.: Order-revealing encryption: new constructions, applications, and lower bounds. In: Proceedings of the ACM Conference on Computer and Communications Security (CCS), Vienna, Austria, pp. 1167–1178 (2016)
20. Li, J., Chen, X., Xhafa, F., Barolli, L.: Secure deduplication storage systems supporting keyword search. J. Comput. Syst. Sci. **81**(8), 1532–1541 (2015)
21. Li, Y., Lai, J., Wang, C., Zhang, J., Xiong, J.: Verifiable range query processing for cloud computing. In: Liu, J.K., Samarati, P. (eds.) ISPEC 2017. LNCS, vol. 10701, pp. 333–349. Springer, Cham (2017). https://doi.org/10.1007/978-3-319-72359-4_19
22. Liu, D., Wang, S.: Programmable order-preserving secure index for encrypted database query. In: Proceedings of the IEEE International Conference on Cloud Computing (CLOUD), Honolulu, HI, USA, pp. 502–509 (2012)
23. Liu, D., Wang, S.: Nonlinear order preserving index for encrypted database query in service cloud environments. Concurr. Comput.: Pract. Exp. **25**(13), 1967–1984 (2013)
24. Popa, R.A., Li, F.H., Zeldovich, N.: An ideal-security protocol for order-preserving encoding. In: Proceedings of the IEEE Symposium on Security and Privacy (SP), Berkeley, CA, USA, pp. 463–477 (2013)
25. Roche, D.S., Apon, D., Choi, S.G., Yerukhimovich, A.: POPE: partial order preserving encoding. In: Proceedings of the ACM Conference on Computer and Communications Security (CCS), Vienna, Austria, pp. 1131–1142 (2016)
26. Wang, J., Chen, X., Huang, X., You, I., Xiang, Y.: Verifiable auditing for outsourced database in cloud computing. IEEE Trans. Comput. **64**(11), 3293–3303 (2015)

27. Wang, J., Chen, X., Li, J., Zhao, J., Shen, J.: Towards achieving flexible and verifiable search for outsourced database in cloud computing. Future Gener. Comput. Syst. **67**, 266–275 (2017)
28. Wang, Y., Wang, J., Chen, X.: Secure searchable encryption: a survey. J. Commun. Inf. Netw. **1**(4), 52–65 (2016)
29. Xiao, L., Yen, I.: Security analysis for order preserving encryption schemes. In: Proceedings of the Conference on Information Sciences and Systems (CISS), Princeton, NJ, USA, pp. 1–6 (2012)
30. Zhang, X., Jiang, T., Li, K.-C., Castiglione, A., Chen, X.: New publicly verifiable computation for batch matrix multiplication. Inf. Sci. (2017). https://doi.org/10.1016/j.ins.2017.11.063
31. Zhang, Z., Chen, X., Li, J., Tao, X., Ma, J.: HVDB: a hierarchical verifiable database scheme with scalable updates. J. Ambient Intell. Humaniz. Comput. (2018). https://doi.org/10.1007/s12652-018-0757-8
32. Zhang, Z., Chen, X., Ma, J., Shen, J.: SLDS: secure and location-sensitive data sharing scheme for cloud-assisted cyber-physical systems. Future Gener. Comput. Syst. (2018). https://doi.org/10.1016/j.future.2018.01.025

Leveled Hierarchical Identity-Based Fully Homomorphic Encryption from Learning with Rounding

Fucai Luo[1,2(✉)], Kunpeng Wang[1,2], and Changlu Lin[3]

[1] School of Cyber Security, University of Chinese Academy of Sciences, Beijing, China
[2] State Key Laboratory of Information Security, Institute of Information Engineering, Chinese Academy of Sciences, Beijing, China
luofucai@iie.ac.cn, kpwang@sina.cn
[3] College of Mathematic and Informatics, Fujian Normal University, Fuzhou, China
cllin@fjnu.edu.cn

Abstract. Hierarchical identity-based fully homomorphic encryption (HIBFHE) aggregates the advantages of both fully homomorphic encryption (FHE) and hierarchical identity-based encryption (HIBE) that permits data encrypted by HIBE to be processed homomorphically. This paper mainly constructs a new leveled HIBFHE scheme based on Learning with Rounding (LWR) problem, which removes Gaussian noise sampling in encryption process. In more detail, we use the lattice basis delegation method proposed by Agrawal, Boneh and Boyen at CRYPTO 2010 to generate delegated basis, while cleverly exploit a scaled rounding function of LWR problem to hide plaintext rather than adding an auxiliary Gaussian noise matrix. Besides, Gentry, Sahai and Waters constructed the first leveled LWE-based HIBFHE schemes from identity-based encryption scheme at CRYPTO 2013, in this work, however, we also focus on improving their leveled HIBFHE scheme, using Alperin-Sheriff and Peikert's technically simpler method. We prove that our schemes are adaptively secure under classic lattice hardness assumptions.

Keywords: FHE · Hierarchical identity-based encryption
Learning with Rounding

1 Introduction

Fully Homomorphic Encryption (FHE) is a very attractive cryptographic primitive that allows computations of arbitrary programs on encrypted data without decrypting it first, and then is a powerful tool for handling many core problems in cloud computing, e.g., private outsourcing of computation, SQL query, private information retrieval, secure multi-party computation (MPC), etc. The first candidate lattice-based FHE scheme is based on ideal lattices proposed by Gentry [19] in 2009. In particular, he put forward a remarkable "bootstrapping"

© Springer Nature Switzerland AG 2018
C. Su and H. Kikuchi (Eds.): ISPEC 2018, LNCS 11125, pp. 101–115, 2018.
https://doi.org/10.1007/978-3-319-99807-7_7

theorem for the first time, which implies that if a scheme is capable of evaluating its own (augmented) decryption circuit (it needs an "encryption" of the secret key) and added with the "circular security" assumption made in [19], then one can transform it into a full fledged one which enables arbitrarily large homomorphic computations on encrypted data. However, his solution is complicated and involves relatively untested cryptographic assumptions.

The more attractive and implementable lattice-based FHEs (see [3,9,10,12, 21]) started with the work of Brakerski and Vaikuntanathan (BV11b) [12], who devised *relinearization* and *dimension-modulus reduction* techniques that play a key role in their construction. The optimized version of the scheme [10] proposed by Brakerski, Gentry and Vaikuntanathan (BGV) is Halevi and Shoup's scheme [23], which was recognized as one of the most efficient leveled FHE[1] schemes, using the *dimension reduction* and *modulus reduction* iteratively and gradually. It is worth mentioning that Gentry, Sahai and Waters [21] (GSW) used a novel technique of so-called *approximate eigenvector* method to construct a conceptually simpler leveled FHE scheme with simpler and more directly homomorphic operations. Moreover, this GSW needs no user's "evaluation key" and has an interesting property of asymmetric noise growth because of its GSW-style matrix operations. The GSW was subsequently improved by Alperin-Sheriff and Peikert [3] (GSW variant) who leveraged a "gadget matrix" $\mathbf{G}$ developed by Micciancio and Peikert [24].

In fact, the above lattice-based FHEs have been enjoying the intensive study for their faster implementation, stronger malleability and applicability; and more importantly, stronger security, since these schemes are based on Learning with Errors (LWE) problem [27] which was proved to be at least as hard as some worst-case lattice problems [11,27] (e.g., GapSVP, which was regarded to be secure even after the advance of quantum computers). Therefore, these lattice-based FHEs are very attractive and conductive for the studying of the post-quantum cryptography.

IBE and HIBE. Identity-Based Encryption (IBE) is a generalization of public key encryption (PKE) that allows a sender to encrypt a message using the recipient's identity – any arbitrary string such as an e-mail address – as a public key, which was first proposed by Shamir [28] in 1984. The ability to use identities as public keys avoids the need to distribute public key certificates, which is very useful in many applications such as email where the recipient is often off-line and unable to present a public-key certificate while the sender encrypts a message. The first construction of IBE is based on bilinear maps assumption [7] or quadratic residue assumption [17]. Since then, a series of schemes, which are based on bilinear maps assumption [31], quadratic residue assumption [8] and LWE assumption [1,2,14,20], have been proposed.

Hierarchical Identity-Based Encryption (HIBE) is an extension of IBE scheme where entities are arranged in a directed tree [22]. Specifically, each entity in the tree obtains a private key from its "parent" (higher-level) and then

---

[1] Leveled FHE is capable of evaluating arbitrary polynomial-depth circuits, without Gentry's bootstrapping procedure.

delegates private keys for its "children" (lower-level) so that a child entity can decrypt plaintext intended for it, or for its children, but cannot decrypt plaintext intended for any other nodes in the tree; this delegation process is one-way: a child node cannot use its private key to recover the key of its parent or its siblings. Based on this kind of framework, a few HIBEs based on LWE problem (see [1,2,14]) and (H)IBEs based on the LWR problem (see [18,32]) have been presented. We will give a formal introduction for LWR problem [5] in Sect. 2. As far as the efficiency of HIBEs is concerned, the lattice basis delegation problem is the main bottleneck, although the problems that existed in IBEs, e.g., the size of ciphertext and parameters, also affect the efficiency.

HIBFHE. Hierarchical Identity-Based FHE (HIBFHE) as an extension of HIBE, as a matter of fact, has captured researchers' attentions as it aggregates the advantages of both FHE and HIBE [21]. Roughly speaking, the data encrypted by HIBE support arbitrarily complex evaluations without being decrypted, and such properties of hierarchy and homomorphism are very useful in access control of encrypted data [15]. However, there are a few results. In fact, Gentry, Sahai and Waters [21] also used their "flatten" technique to compile all HIBEs [1,2,14], which thus results in leveled HIBFHE schemes. After that, Wang *et al.* [30] used the MP12-trapdoor for lattices [24] to improve the IBE scheme in [1], then compiled this improved IBE and obtained a leveled IBFHE. However, if we extend their leveled IBFHE to leveled HIBFHE, it is very easy to find that the dimension of lattice will expand when the delegation mechanism is used to generate delegated basis for the identity of lower-level; or more precisely, the dimension will increase linearly with the depth of hierarchy. Consequently, private keys and ciphertexts become longer and longer as one descends into the hierarchy. This problem also resides in Sun *et al.*' [29] RLWE-based leveled IBFHE (which is selective-ID secure). Actually, this RLWE-based leveled IBFHE is based on the structure of GSW and thus is impractical, because the GSW is not fully compatible with RLWE problem due to its asymmetric noise growth [21].

It is worth noting that all (H)IBFHEs aforementioned are leveled homomorphic, which means that they can only bear homomorphic computations of a priori polynomial-depth circuits, except the first non-leveled IBFHE scheme proposed by Clear and McGoldrick [16] under the existential hypothesis of indistinguishable obfuscator. This is because we cannot use bootstrapping theorem to transform a leveled (H)IBFHE scheme into "pure" one, for bootstrapping in the identity-based setting needs to non-interactively derive from the public parameters an "encryption" of the secret key for an arbitrary identity. But this "encryption" is user-specific and is not identity-based, in the sense that it only can be obtained interactively from user-specific. While obtaining this "encryption" interactively undermines the main appeal of IBE: its non-interactivity.

Our Contributions. We present two leveled HIBFHE schemes with fixed dimensions and short ciphertexts. Our first and main scheme, which is based on LWR problem [5] and is proved to be secure against adaptive chosen-identity attack, needs no Gaussian noise sampling in encryption process. In our

LWR-based leveled HIBFHE scheme, we use the basis delegation technique in [2] to generate identity-specific basis without increasing the dimension of the lattice in derive phase, and then use the preimage sampleable algorithm in [20] to yield the identity-specific secret key in extract phase. In encryption process, we cleverly use the scaled rounding function of LWR problem to hide plaintext rather than adding an auxiliary Gaussian noise matrix. The resulting ciphertexts have constant size and are not relevant to the depth of hierarchy. Our LWR-based leveled HIBFHE scheme gets rid of Gaussian noise sampling merely in encryption process, but this is enough for improving the efficiency. Because the generating processes of public keys and secret keys, which involve Gaussian sampling, are implemented only once in general case, while there are a large number of times for the encryption process. More importantly, removing the Gaussian noise sampling in encryption process will strengthen safety, due to some potential side-channel vulnerabilities (result in complete leakage of the secret key) incurred by Gaussian noise sampling in every encryption process [13,26]. Although it is possible to create good implementations which protect against side-channel attacks, these implementations are very complex. However, such improvements are obtained with a penalty: the size of the secret key, the public key and the ciphertext of the LWR-based leveled HIBFHE scheme are all slightly bigger than that of our improvement on the LWE-based leveled HIBFHE scheme [21] (up to a small polynomial in n), and the security reduction loss of our LWR-based leveled HIBFHE scheme is also bigger due to the reduction between LWE and LWR (up to a polynomial). These can be seen from the Table 1 in the full version of the paper.

We also present a more efficient leveled HIBFHE scheme based on LWE problem. In our LWE-based leveled HIBFHE scheme, we use a technically simpler variant method [3] of GSW to generate ciphertext with constant length, and then we obtain more compact parameters due to the simple and tight noise analysis technique when performing homomorphic evaluations. In fact, that we present this improved construction is meant to help us compare the LWE-based leveled HIBFHE scheme with our novel LWR-based leveled HIBFHE scheme more clearly.

Organization. In Sect. 2, we give the preliminaries including notations, hardness assumptions and some related algorithms to be used in this paper. The definition of hierarchical identity-based FHE, the lattices and discrete Gaussians can be found in the full version of the paper. In Sect. 3, we present our construction of LWR-based leveled HIBFHE scheme. Section 4 follows an improvement on the previous LWE-based leveled HIBFHE. Finally, we conclude the paper with future direction in Sect. 5.

2   Preliminaries

Notations. We say that a function $negl(n)$ is negligible if $negl(n)$ is smaller than all polynomial fractions for sufficiently large n. For a positive integer q, we define the set $\mathbb{Z}_q \triangleq [-q/2, q/2) \cap \mathbb{Z}$, and all logarithms on q are base 2. All arithmetics are performed over $\mathbb{Z}$ or $\mathbb{Q}$ when division is used, and for ease of use, we let $[n] \triangleq \{1, \cdots, n\}$. We denote vectors in bold lowercase (e.g., $\mathbf{x}$) and matrices in bold uppercase (e.g., $\mathbf{A}$); $\mathbf{x}^t$ (resp. $\mathbf{A}^t$) denotes the transpose of the vector $\mathbf{x}$ (resp. $\mathbf{A}$). For any $x \in \mathbb{Q}$, we denote by $\lfloor x \rfloor$, $\lceil x \rceil$, $\lceil x \rfloor$ the rounding of x down, up, or to the nearest integer; these notations also apply to vector and matrix. The multiplication between two vectors $\mathbf{x}$, $\mathbf{y}$ over $\mathbb{Z}_q$ is denoted by $<\mathbf{x}, \mathbf{y}>_q$ (i.e., $<\mathbf{x}, \mathbf{y}>$ mod q). In this paper, $\|\cdot\|$ denotes Euclidean norm unless otherwise stated, and for a n-dimensional vector $\mathbf{x} = \{x_1, \cdots, x_n\}$, we denote its magnitude by $|\mathbf{x}| \triangleq \max\{|x_i|\}_{i \in [n]}$ where $|x_i|$ refers to x_i' s magnitude, moreover, vectors (e.g., $\mathbf{a}$) are treated as columns. We let $x \xleftarrow{\$} \mathcal{D}$ denote that x is randomly sampled from a distribution $\mathcal{D}$ and $x \xleftarrow{\$} \mathcal{S}$ denote that x is uniform over a set $\mathcal{S}$. For any matrix $\mathbf{A} \in \mathbb{Z}_q^{n \times m}$, $\mathbf{A} \in \mathcal{X}^{n \times m}$ (resp. $\mathbf{A} \xleftarrow{\$} \mathcal{X}^{n \times m}$) denotes that for $i \in [n], j \in [m]$ its entry $\mathbf{A}[i][j] \in \mathcal{X}$ (resp. $\mathbf{A}[i][j] \xleftarrow{\$} \mathcal{X}$) where $\mathcal{X}$ is a set or distribution. This also applies to vector.

2.1 Hardness Assumptions

Learning with Errors (LWE). The well-known learning with errors (LWE) problem has been enjoying a fame for its versatility in the constructions of lattice-based schemes, and was conjectured to be secure in quantum setting ever since Regev [27] introduced it and gave a quantum reduction from some standard lattice problems to the LWE problem (subsequently followed by some classical reduction [11,25]). The binLWE problem is a specific form of LWE where the secret $\mathbf{s}$ is chosen uniformly from $\{0,1\}^n$, or generating the binLWE problem directly from $\mathsf{LWE}_{n,q,m,\chi}(\mathcal{D})$ by letting $\mathcal{D} = \{0,1\}^n$. As for the security of binLWE problem, Brakerski *et al.* [11] proved that the binLWE problem is at least as hard as the original LWE problem.

Definition 1 (*B*-Bounded Distributions [6,9]). *A distribution ensemble* $\{\chi_n\}_{n \in \mathbb{N}}$, *supported over the integers, is called B-bounded if* $Pr[e \xleftarrow{\$} \chi_n \mid \|e\| > B] = negl(n)$. *We say a B-bounded distribution* e *is balanced if* $Pr[e \geq 0] \geq \frac{1}{2}$ *and* $Pr[e \leq 0] \geq \frac{1}{2}$.

Learning with Rounding (LWR). As a deterministic variant of LWE problem, Learning with Rounding (LWR) problem, was firstly proposed by Banerjee, Peikert and Rosen [5] for improving the efficiency of pseudorandom generator (PRG) based on the LWE problem. Interestingly enough, the implicit noise in LWR is deterministic which derandomizes the random noise in LWE. Meanwhile, the single implicit noise in LWR is smaller than that in LWE. Specifically, the noise in LWE is B-bounded, while the implicit noise has magnitude less than $\frac{1}{2}$ in LWR.

For the positive integers n, m and $p < q$, we firstly recall the scaled rounding function [5] $\lceil \cdot \rfloor_p$ which will be used in encryption process in Sect. 3. It is defined as follows:

$$\lceil \cdot \rfloor_p \quad : \mathbb{Z}_q \quad \to \mathbb{Z}_p$$
$$a \quad \mapsto \left\lceil \tfrac{p}{q} \cdot a \right\rfloor.$$

The scaled rounding function $\lceil \cdot \rfloor_p$ denotes the component-wise rounding if the entry is a vector or matrix.

For a n-dimensional vector $\mathbf{s}$ sampled from a distribution $\mathcal{D} \subset \mathbb{Z}_q^n$, we define the LWR distribution $\mathsf{LWR}_{n,q,p}(\mathcal{D}) \triangleq \{(\mathbf{a}_i, \lceil \langle \mathbf{a}_i, \mathbf{s} \rangle \rfloor_p) \in \mathbb{Z}_q^n \times \mathbb{Z}_p | \mathbf{a}_i \xleftarrow{\$} \mathbb{Z}_q^n\}$ in which the pair $(\mathbf{a}_i, \lceil \langle \mathbf{a}_i, \mathbf{s} \rangle \rfloor_p)$ denotes a LWR sample (instance). As with the LWE problem, LWR problem can be also divided into two problems: the search and decision problems. The search LWR problem is defined as finding the secret $\mathbf{s}$ given m independent instances chosen from $\mathsf{LWR}_{n,q,p}(\mathcal{D})$. While the decision LWR problem, denoted by $\mathsf{DLWR}_{n,m,q,p}(\mathcal{D})$, is to distinguish (with non-negligible advantage) m samples $(\mathbf{a}_i, \lceil \langle \mathbf{a}_i, \mathbf{s} \rangle \rfloor_p)$ chosen from $\mathsf{LWR}_{n,q,p}(\mathcal{D})$, from m independent samples chosen according to the uniform distribution over $\mathbb{Z}_q^n \times \mathbb{Z}_p$. The $\mathsf{LWR}_{n,q,p}(\mathcal{D})$ assumption implies that the $\mathsf{DLWR}_{n,m,q,p}(\mathcal{D})$ problem is infeasible. As with the binLWE problem, we can also get binLWR problem from $\mathsf{LWR}_{n,q,p}(\mathcal{D})$ by letting $\mathcal{D} = \{0,1\}^n$.

As for the hardness of the LWR problem, Banerjee *et al.* [5] presented an efficient reduction from LWE problem to LWR problem for super-polynomial modulus q. Subsequently, Alwen *et al.* [4] gave a reduction that allows for a polynomial modulus q, but that restricts the number of samples and fails to apply to all values of the modulus q. In 2016, the reduction in [4] was extended by Bogdanov *et al.* [6] who eliminated the theoretic restriction on the modulus q, though the number of samples in [6] is required to be less than $O(q/Bp)$ (weaker than that in [4]). For completeness, we give the Theorem 1 that is adapted from [6]. Note that the reduction from LWE to binLWE was shown in [11], hence by combining the reduction with Theorem 1, we can safely reduce the hardness of binLWR problem to LWE problem.

Theorem 1 ([6]). *For every $\epsilon > 0$, positive integers n, m, $q > 2mpB$, $p|q$, and if there is an algorithm $\mathcal{A}$ such that*

$$\left| Pr_{\mathbf{A},\mathbf{s}}[\mathcal{A}(\mathbf{A}, \lceil \mathbf{As} \rfloor_p) = 1] - Pr_{\mathbf{A},\mathbf{v}}[\mathcal{A}(\mathbf{A}, \mathbf{v}) = 1] \right| \geq \epsilon,$$

where $\mathbf{A} \xleftarrow{\$} \mathbb{Z}_q^{m \times n}$, $\mathbf{s} \xleftarrow{\$} \{0,1\}^n$ and $\mathbf{v} \xleftarrow{\$} \mathbb{Z}_p^m$, then there exists another algorithm $\mathcal{B}$ that runs in time polynomial in n, m, the number of divisors of q, and the running time of $\mathcal{A}$ such that

$$Pr_{\mathbf{A},\mathbf{s}}[\mathcal{B}(\mathbf{A}, \mathbf{As} + \mathbf{e}) = \mathbf{s}] \geq \left(\frac{\epsilon}{4qm} - \frac{2^n}{p^m} \right)^2 \cdot \frac{1}{(1 + 2Bp/q)^m}$$

for noise distribution $\mathbf{e}$ that is B-bounded and balanced in each coordinate, where it requires that $B \geq 2\sqrt{n}$ due to the reduction (quantum or classical) from certain lattice problems to LWE problem [11,27].

Note that Theorem 1 concerns the search bin-LWE problem, which is not easier than its decision problem. Moreover, we remark that the term $Pr_{\mathbf{A},\mathbf{s}}[\mathcal{A}(\mathbf{A}, \lceil \mathbf{As} \rfloor_p) = 1] - Pr_{\mathbf{A},\mathbf{v}}[\mathcal{A}(\mathbf{A}, \mathbf{v}) = 1]$ in Theorem 1 can be interpreted as the decision $\mathsf{DLWR}_{n,m,q,p}(\mathcal{D})$ problem for the fixed $\mathbf{s} \xleftarrow{\$} \{0,1\}^n$ (set $\mathcal{D} = \{0,1\}^n$).

2.2 Gadget Matrices and Some Algorithms

In this subsection, we recall the gadget matrix [24] and four important algorithms that will be used in our constructions and security proofs. Roughly speaking, we generate the master public matrix together with a short basis by employing the trapdoor generation algorithm [24] and then use the lattice basis delegation algorithm [2] to generate delegated basis. At last, output the identity-specific secret key by utilizing the preimage sampleable algorithm [20].

For the integer q, we define the gadget matrix $\mathbf{G} := \mathbf{I}_{m+1} \otimes \mathbf{g}^t$, where $\mathbf{g}^t := (1, 2, \cdots, 2^{\lceil \log q \rceil - 1}) \in \mathbb{Z}_q^{\lceil \log q \rceil}$ and $\mathbf{I}_{m+1}$ denotes the $(m+1)$-dimensional identity matrix. Moreover, we define the deterministic inversion function $\mathbf{G}^{-1} : \mathbb{Z}_q^{(m+1) \times m'} \to \{0, 1\}^{m' \times m'}$ where $m' = (m+1) \cdot \lceil \log q \rceil$, which is equal to bit decomposition that decomposes x into its bit representation over $\mathbb{Z}_q$ and has the property that for any matrix $\mathbf{A} \in \mathbb{Z}_q^{(m+1) \times m'}$ it holds that $\mathbf{G} \cdot \mathbf{G}^{-1}(\mathbf{A}) = \mathbf{A}$. Since there are two moduli q, p in LWR problem, here we construct another gadget matrix $\widehat{\mathbf{G}}$ constructed as $\widehat{\mathbf{G}} := \mathbf{I}_{m+1} \otimes \widehat{\mathbf{g}}^t$ where $\widehat{\mathbf{g}}^t := (1, 2, \cdots, 2^{\lceil \log p \rceil - 1}) \in \mathbb{Z}_p^{\lceil \log p \rceil}$. The deterministic inversion function $\widehat{\mathbf{G}}^{-1}$ is defined by the same method as above.

Lemma 1 ([24]). *Let n, $q > 2$ and $m \approx 2n \log q$ be positive integers, there is a PPT algorithm $\mathsf{GenTrap}(1^n, 1^m, q)$ that outputs a parity-check matrix $\mathbf{A} \in \mathbb{Z}_q^{n \times m}$ and a trapdoor $\mathbf{X}$ with a tag $\mathbf{H}$ such that the distribution of $\mathbf{A}$ is statistically close to the uniform. Then one can use the trapdoor and any basis $\mathbf{S}$ for $\Lambda_q^\perp(\mathbf{G})$ to generate a short basis $\mathbf{T_A}$ for lattice $\Lambda_q^\perp(\mathbf{A})$, and the parameters satisfy $s_1(\mathbf{X}) \le 1.6\sqrt{n \log q}$ and $\|\widetilde{\mathbf{T}}_\mathbf{A}\| \le 3.8\sqrt{n \log q}$, where $s_1(\mathbf{X})$ is the largest singular value of $\mathbf{X}$.*

Remark 1. Note that it is easy to compute a basis $\mathbf{S}$ for $\Lambda_q^\perp(\mathbf{G})$, whenever the modulus q is power-of-two or not, since $\mathbf{G}$ is gadget matrix whose trapdoor is publicly known.

The following $\mathsf{SampleRwithBasis}$ lemma plays a key role in our security proofs, this is due to the fact that the simulator (challenger) calls the $\mathsf{SampleRwithBasis}$ algorithm to generate short basis, and then uses this basis to generate identity-specific secret key for answering the secret key query. While the Lattices Basis Delegation lemma is of crucial importance in the constructions of our schemes. In the lattices basis delegation mechanism, it is required that the matrix $\mathbf{R}$ is invertible mod q in $\mathbb{Z}_q^{m \times m}$ where all the columns of $\mathbf{R}$ are "low norm". Similarly with [2], we denote by $\mathcal{D}_{m \times m}$ the distribution $(\mathcal{D}_{\mathbb{Z}_q^m, \sigma_\mathbf{R}})^m$ conditioned on the matrix $\mathbf{R}$ being invertible mod q in $\mathbb{Z}_q^{m \times m}$, where $\sigma_\mathbf{R} = \sqrt{n \log q} \cdot \omega(\sqrt{\log m})$.

Lemma 2 ([2]). *Let $q > 2$ be a prime and $m \ge 2n \log q$. For all but at most a q^{-1} fraction of rank n matrices $\mathbf{A}$ in $\mathbb{Z}_q^{n \times m}$, there exists a PPT algorithm $\mathsf{SampleRwithBasis}(\mathbf{A})$ that outputs a matrix $\mathbf{R} \in \mathbb{Z}^{n \times m}$ sampled from a distribution statistically close to $\mathcal{D}_{m \times m}$ and a basis $\mathbf{T_B}$ for lattice $\Lambda_q^\perp(\mathbf{B})$ with the parameter $\sigma_\mathbf{R} \ge \|\widetilde{\mathbf{T}}_\mathbf{B}\| \cdot \omega(\sqrt{\log m})$ with overwhelming probability, where it holds that $\mathbf{B} = \mathbf{A} \cdot \mathbf{R}^{-1} \pmod q$.*

Lemma 3 ([2]). *Let $q > 2$ and let $\mathbf{A}$ be a matrix in $\mathbb{Z}_q^{n \times m}$ with $m \geq 2n \log q$. Let $\mathbf{T_A}$ be a basis for lattice $\Lambda_q^{\perp}(\mathbf{A})$. Given a matrix $\mathbf{R}$ sampled from the distribution $\mathcal{D}_{m \times m}$ and the parameter $\sigma > \|\widetilde{\mathbf{T}}_{\mathbf{A}}\| \cdot \sigma_{\mathbf{R}} \cdot \sqrt{m} \cdot \omega(\log^{3/2} m)$, there is a PPT algorithm BasisDel $(\mathbf{A}, \mathbf{T_A}, \mathbf{R}, \sigma)$ that outputs a basis $\mathbf{T_{AR^{-1}}}$ for the lattice $\Lambda_q^{\perp}(\mathbf{AR}^{-1})$ with overwhelming probability, where $\mathbf{T_{AR^{-1}}}$ satisfies $\|\mathbf{T_{AR^{-1}}}\| \leq \sigma \cdot \sqrt{m}$.*

One can generate identity-specific secret keys for all identities in hierarchy via the following preimage sampleable algorithm [20].

Lemma 4. *Let n and q be positive integers with $q \geq 2$, and let $m > n$. Let $\mathbf{T_A}$ be a short basis for lattice $\Lambda_q^{\perp}(\mathbf{A})$ and $\sigma \geq \|\widetilde{\mathbf{T}}_{\mathbf{A}}\| \cdot \omega(\sqrt{\log m})$. Then for $\mathbf{c} \in \mathbb{R}^m$ and $\mathbf{u} \in \mathbb{Z}_q^n$:*

1. *$Pr[\ \mathbf{x} \xleftarrow{\$} \mathcal{D}_{\Lambda_q^{\mathbf{u}}(\mathbf{A}), \sigma} \ \mid \ \|\mathbf{x}\| > \sqrt{m} \cdot \sigma\ ] \leq \text{negl}(n)$.*
2. *There is a PPT algorithm SamplePre$(\mathbf{A}, \mathbf{T_A}, \sigma, \mathbf{u})$ that outputs $\mathbf{x} \in \Lambda_q^{\mathbf{u}}(\mathbf{A})$ sampled from a distribution statistically close to $\mathcal{D}_{\Lambda_q^{\mathbf{u}}(\mathbf{A}), \sigma}$.*

3   Our LWR-Based Scheme

In this section, based on LWR problem, we use the three algorithms outlined in Sect. 2.2 to construct a leveled hierarchical identity-based FHE in the random oracle model. Similarly to [2], we also utilize a hash function $H : (\{0, 1\}^*)^{\leq d} \to \mathbb{Z}_q^{m \times m} \mid \mathbf{id} \mapsto H(\mathbf{id}) \sim \mathcal{D}_{m \times m}$ for mapping the identity $\mathbf{id}$ to a matrix in $\mathbb{Z}_q^{m \times m}$, where the requirement is that the $H(\mathbf{id})$ is distributed as $\mathcal{D}_{m \times m}$ over the choice of the random oracle H.

3.1   Leveled Hierarchical Identity-Based FHE from LWR

As what mentioned before, the leveled HIBFHEs have the properties of hierarchy and homomorphism, thus we assume the maximal depth of the hierarchy is d and the maximal homomorphically evaluable depth is L. Similarly to [2], we choose a Gaussian parameter $\sigma = (\sigma_1, \cdots, \sigma_d)$ needed in **Derive** and **Extract** processes, where it holds that

$$\begin{cases} \sigma_\ell > \sigma_{\ell-1} \cdot m^{3/2} \cdot \omega(\log^2 m) > \sigma_1 \cdot \left(m^{3/2} \cdot \omega(\log^2 m) \right)^{\ell-1} \\ \sigma_1 > \|\widetilde{\mathbf{T}}_{\mathbf{A}}\| \cdot \sigma_{\mathbf{R}} \cdot \sqrt{m} \cdot \omega(\log^{3/2} m). \end{cases}$$

Comparing to the LWE-based scheme, our LWR-based leveled HIBFHE scheme uses the scaled rounding function to hide plaintext instead of Gaussian noise sampled from a discrete Gaussian distribution, and therefore it doesn't need the Gaussian noise parameter $\alpha = (\alpha_1, \cdots, \alpha_d)$ any more.

- **Setup**$(1^\lambda, 1^d, 1^L)$. Choose a lattice dimension parameter $n = n(\lambda, d, L)$, moduli $q = q(\lambda, d, L)$ and $p = p(\lambda, d, L)$ that satisfies $p|q$. Also, choose parameter $m = m(\lambda, d, L) \geq 2n \log q$. Let $k = \lceil \log p \rceil$ and $N = (m + 1) \cdot k$. Then call the PPT algorithm $\mathsf{GenTrap}(1^n, 1^m, q)$ to generate a parity-check matrix $\mathbf{A} \in \mathbb{Z}_q^{n \times m}$ and a trapdoor $\mathbf{X}$ with a tag $\mathbf{H}$ such that the distribution of $\mathbf{A}$ is statistically close to the uniform. Based on Lemma 1, use the trapdoor $\mathbf{X}$ and a random basis $\mathbf{S}$ for $\Lambda_q^\perp(\mathbf{G})$ to generate a short basis $\mathbf{T_A}$ for $\Lambda_q^\perp(\mathbf{A})$. Choose uniformly at random a vector $\mathbf{u} \in \mathbb{Z}_q^n$. Finally, the master public parameters is $mpk := (\mathbf{A}, \mathbf{u})$, and the corresponding master secret key is $msk := (\mathbf{T_A})$.

- **Derive**$(mpk, \mathbf{T_{id|\ell}}, \mathbf{id})$. Take as input public parameters mpk, a private basis $\mathbf{T_{id|\ell}}$ corresponding to a "parent" identity $\mathbf{id}_{|\ell} = (\mathbf{id}_1, \cdots, \mathbf{id}_\ell)$ at level ℓ and a "child" identity $\mathbf{id} = (\mathbf{id}_1, \cdots, \mathbf{id}_\ell, \cdots, \mathbf{id}_k)$ of a lower level k where $k \leq d$, do the following processes:
  1. For $i \in [\ell]$, compute $H(\mathbf{id}_i)$, and set $\mathbf{R_{id|\ell}} = H(\mathbf{id}_\ell) \cdots H(\mathbf{id}_1) \in \mathbb{Z}^{m \times m}$. Then compute $\mathbf{B_{id|\ell}} = \mathbf{A} \cdot \mathbf{R_{id|\ell}^{-1}} \in \mathbb{Z}_q^{n \times m}$. Let $\mathbf{T_{id|\ell}}$ be the short basis for $\Lambda_q^\perp(\mathbf{B_{id|\ell}})$.
  2. Compute $\mathbf{R} = H(\mathbf{id}_k) \cdots H(\mathbf{id}_{\ell+1}) \in \mathbb{Z}^{m \times m}$ and set $\mathbf{B_{id}} = \mathbf{B_{id|\ell}} \cdot \mathbf{R}^{-1} \in \mathbb{Z}_q^{n \times m}$.
  3. Invoke $\mathbf{T}' \leftarrow \mathsf{BasisDel}(\mathbf{B_{id|\ell}}, \mathbf{T_{id|\ell}}, \mathbf{R}, \sigma_k)$ to obtain a short random basis for $\Lambda_q^\perp(\mathbf{B_{id}})$.
  4. Output the delegated basis $\mathbf{T_{id}} = \mathbf{T}'$.
- **Extract**$(mpk, \mathbf{B_{id}}, \mathbf{T_{id}}, \mathbf{id})$. Take as input public parameters mpk, and an identity $\mathbf{id}$ of depth $|\mathbf{id}| = \ell$. Run the PPT algorithm $\mathsf{SamplePre}(\mathbf{B_{id}}, \mathbf{T_{id}}, \sigma_\ell, \mathbf{u})$ to sample a short vector $\mathbf{x} \in \mathbb{Z}^m$ such that $\mathbf{B_{id}} \cdot \mathbf{x} = \mathbf{u} \pmod q$. Then output identity-specific public key $pk_{\mathbf{id}} : \mathbf{P} = \begin{bmatrix} \mathbf{B_{id}^t} \\ \mathbf{u}^t \end{bmatrix}$, and the identity-specific secret key $sk_{\mathbf{id}} : \mathbf{s} = (-\mathbf{x}, 1)$. Note that $\mathbf{s}^t \cdot \mathbf{P} = 0 \pmod q$.
- **Enc**$(pk_{\mathbf{id}}, \mathbf{id}, \mu)$. To encrypt a message $\mu \in \{0, 1\}$, sample a small matrix $\mathbf{M} \xleftarrow{\$} \{0, 1\}^{n \times N}$. Output a ciphertext

$$\mathbf{C} = \lceil \mathbf{P} \cdot \mathbf{M} \rfloor_p + \mu \widehat{\mathbf{G}} \in \mathbb{Z}_p^{(m+1) \times N}.$$

- **Dec**$(\mathbf{C}, sk_{\mathbf{id}})$. Choose the penultimate column vector $\mathbf{c}$ of ciphertext $\mathbf{C}$, and then compute

$$\mu = \left| \lceil \frac{2}{p} \cdot \langle \mathbf{s}, \mathbf{c} \rangle_p \rfloor \right|.$$

- **Add**$(\mathbf{C}_1, \mathbf{C}_2)$. For two ciphertext matrices $\mathbf{C}_1$ and $\mathbf{C}_2$ decrypting to plaintexts μ_1 and μ_2 under identical identity, output

$$\mathbf{C}_{\mathrm{Add}} \triangleq \mathbf{C}_1 + \mathbf{C}_2.$$

- **Mult**$(\mathbf{C}_1, \mathbf{C}_2)$. For two ciphertext matrices $\mathbf{C}_1$ and $\mathbf{C}_2$ decrypting to plaintexts μ_1 and μ_2 under identical identity, the multiplication is defined as

$$\mathbf{C}_{\mathrm{Mult}} \triangleq \mathbf{C}_1 \cdot \widehat{\mathbf{G}}^{-1}(\mathbf{C}_2).$$

3.2   Correctness and Parameters

Firstly, according to Lemma 4, $\mathbf{x} \in \Lambda_q^{\mathbf{u}}(\mathbf{A})$ is sampled from a distribution statistically close to $\mathcal{D}_{\Lambda_q^{\mathbf{u}}(\mathbf{A}),\sigma_\ell}$ that satisfies $||\mathbf{x}|| \leq \sqrt{m} \cdot \sigma_\ell$ with overwhelming probability. Combining Lemmas 1 and 3 with the parameters set in Sect. 3.1, we can set $\sigma_\ell = m^{\frac{3}{2}\ell} \cdot \omega(\log^{2\ell} m)$. Next, we analyze the correctness and the magnitude of noise. The penultimate column vector of $\widehat{\mathbf{G}}$ is $(0, 0, \cdots, v) \in \mathbb{Z}_p^{m+1}$ where $v \in (p/4, p/2]$. We write $\mathbf{E} = \lceil \mathbf{P} \cdot \mathbf{M} \rfloor_p - \frac{p}{q} \cdot \mathbf{P} \cdot \mathbf{M} \in [-1/2, 1/2]^{(m+1) \times N}$, and then its penultimate column vector is $\mathbf{e} \in [-1/2, 1/2]^{m+1}$. According to the **Dec** algorithm, we have

$$\mu = \Big|\Big\lceil \frac{2}{p} \cdot \langle \mathbf{s}, \mathbf{c} \rangle_p \Big\rfloor\Big| = \Big|\Big\lceil \frac{2}{p} \cdot \big(\langle \mathbf{s}, \mathbf{e} \rangle + \mu v\big)\Big\rfloor\Big|,$$

as long as

$$|e'| = |\langle \mathbf{s}, \mathbf{e} \rangle| \leq ||\mathbf{e}|| \cdot (||\mathbf{x}|| + 1) \leq m^{\frac{3}{2}\ell+1} \cdot \omega(\log^{2\ell} m) < p/4. \tag{1}$$

Since the homomorphic addition is obvious, we mainly analyze homomorphic multiplication.

Homomorphic Multiplication. To multiply two ciphertext matrices $\mathbf{C}_1, \mathbf{C}_2 \in \mathbb{Z}_p^{(m+1) \times N}$ designated for messages $\mu_1, \mu_2 \in \{0, 1\}$, we have

$$\begin{aligned}
\mathbf{s}^t \cdot \mathbf{Mult}(\mathbf{C}_1, \mathbf{C}_2) = \mathbf{s}^t \cdot \mathbf{C}_1 \cdot \widehat{\mathbf{G}}^{-1}(\mathbf{C}_2) &= (\mathbf{s}^t \cdot \mathbf{E}_1 + \mu_1 \mathbf{s}^t \cdot \widehat{\mathbf{G}}) \cdot \widehat{\mathbf{G}}^{-1}(\mathbf{C}_2) \\
&= (\mathbf{e}_1' \cdot \widehat{\mathbf{G}}^{-1}(\mathbf{C}_2) + \mu_1 \mathbf{e}_2') + \mu_1 \mu_2 \mathbf{s}^t \cdot \widehat{\mathbf{G}},
\end{aligned}$$

where $\widehat{\mathbf{G}}^{-1}(\mathbf{C}_2) \in \{0, 1\}^{N \times N}$. Then $\mathbf{e}_1' \cdot \widehat{\mathbf{G}}^{-1}(\mathbf{C}_2) + \mu_1 \mathbf{e}_2'$ is the total noise which is of magnitude

$$|\mathbf{e}_1' \cdot \widehat{\mathbf{G}}^{-1}(\mathbf{C}_2) + \mu_1 \mathbf{e}_2'| \leq m^{\frac{3}{2}\ell+1} \cdot \omega(\log^{2\ell} m) \cdot (N + 1)$$

by Eq. (1). It is clear that the noise growth factor is $N + 1$, and therefore after L levels of homomorphic multiplication, the noise grows from an initial magnitude of $m^{\frac{3}{2}\ell+1} \cdot \omega(\log^{2\ell} m)$, to $m^{\frac{3}{2}\ell+1} \cdot \omega(\log^{2\ell} m) \cdot (N + 1)^L$.

Our LWR-based scheme removes Gaussian noise sampling in encryption process, but there are two moduli p, q satisfying $q > 2mpB$ and $p|q$ where $B \geq 2\sqrt{n}$ (according to Theorem 1). In fact, it is sufficient to set $q = pn^{\frac{3}{2}}$ due to $m \geq 2n \log q$, and then we have $m \geq 2n \log q = 2n \log p + 3n \log n$. Therefore, we can get the the following theorem.

Theorem 2. *For the parameters λ, d, L, $n = n(\lambda, d, L)$ and $m = m(\lambda, d, L) \geq 2n \log q$, if the polynomial size moduli $p \geq (4n \log^2 p)^{\frac{3}{2}d+L+1} \cdot \omega\big((2 \log n)^{2d}\big)$ and $q = pn^{\frac{3}{2}}$, our LWR-based scheme is a correct L-leveled HIBFHE.*

Overall, the moduli p and q are both of polynomial size in parameter n, and then combining the Theorem 1 with the reductions between LWE problem and certain standard lattice problems (e.g., GapSVP), we can base the security of our LWR-based leveled HIBFHE scheme on these worst-case lattice problems with polynomial approximation factors.

3.3   Security

We prove that our LWR-based leveled HIBFHE scheme is INDr-ID-CPA secure. More precisely, the challenger in our simulated attack model can answer any type of query sent by the adaptive adversary. Comparing to the security proof in [2], the setup of simulated attack model and the random oracle hash H query are almost the same as theirs (for simplicity, we omit them in our security proof), but the challenger needs to run PPT algorithm SamplePre to obtain the secret key for answering the identity-specific secret key query in our security proof. The full proof of Theorem 3 is given in the full version of the paper.

Theorem 3. *Let $\mathcal{A}$ be a PPT adversary that attacks our LWR-based scheme, and Q_H be the number of hash H queries made by $\mathcal{A}$ and d be the maximal hierarchy depth, where H is a hash function modeled as a random oracle. Then there is a PPT algorithm $\mathcal{B}$ that solves the $\mathsf{DLWR}_{n,m,q,p}(\mathcal{D})$ problem with advantage ϵ, such that, if $\mathcal{A}$ is an adaptive adversary (INDr-ID-CPA) with advantage ϵ', then it holds that $\epsilon' \leq \epsilon \cdot (d \cdot Q_H^d) + \mathrm{negl}(n)$.*

4   Improvement on Previous LWE-Based Scheme

4.1   Our Leveled Hierarchical Identity-Based FHE from LWE

Here, we also assume the maximal depth of the hierarchy is d and the maximal homomorphically evaluable depth is L, and we choose a Gaussian parameter $\sigma = (\sigma_1, \cdots, \sigma_d)$ (the same as that in Sect. 3.1) and a Gaussian noise parameter $\alpha = (\alpha_1, \cdots, \alpha_d)$ needed in the encryption process. We omit the corresponding homomorphic addition and multiplication, since they are identical to that of LWR-based scheme presented in Sect. 3.

- **Setup**$(1^\lambda, 1^d, 1^L)$. Choose a lattice dimension parameter $n = n(\lambda, d, L)$, modulus $q = q(\lambda, d, L)$, also, choose parameter $m = m(\lambda, d, L) \geq 2n \log q$. Let $k = \lceil \log q \rceil$ and $N = (m + 1) \cdot k$. Call the PPT algorithm GenTrap$(1^n, 1^m, q)$ to generate a parity-check matrix $\mathbf{A} \in \mathbb{Z}_q^{n \times m}$ and a trapdoor $\mathbf{X}$ with a tag $\mathbf{H}$ such that the distribution of $\mathbf{A}$ is statistically close to the uniform. As per Lemma 1, use the trapdoor $\mathbf{X}$ and a random basis $\mathbf{S}$ for $\Lambda_q^\perp(\mathbf{G})$ to generate a short basis $\mathbf{T_A}$ for $\Lambda_q^\perp(\mathbf{A})$. Choose uniformly at random a vector $\mathbf{u} \in \mathbb{Z}_q^n$. Finally, the master public parameter is $mpk := (\mathbf{A}, \mathbf{u})$, and the corresponding master secret key is $msk := (\mathbf{T_A})$.
- **Derive**$(mpk, \mathbf{T_{id|\ell}}, \mathbf{id})$. Take as input public parameter mpk, a private basis $\mathbf{T_{id|\ell}}$ corresponding to a "parent" identity $\mathbf{id}_{|\ell} = (\mathbf{id}_1, \cdots, \mathbf{id}_\ell)$ of level ℓ and a "child" identity $\mathbf{id} = (\mathbf{id}_1, \cdots, \mathbf{id}_\ell, \cdots, \mathbf{id}_k)$ of lower level k where $k \leq d$, do the following processes:
  1. For $i \in [\ell]$, compute $\mathbf{H}(\mathbf{id}_i)$ and set $\mathbf{R_{id|\ell}} = \mathbf{H}(\mathbf{id}_\ell) \cdots \mathbf{H}(\mathbf{id}_1) \in \mathbb{Z}^{m \times m}$. Then compute $\mathbf{B_{id|\ell}} = \mathbf{A} \cdot \mathbf{R_{id|\ell}^{-1}} \in \mathbb{Z}_q^{n \times m}$. Let $\mathbf{T_{id|\ell}}$ be the short basis for $\Lambda_q^\perp(\mathbf{B_{id|\ell}})$.
  2. Compute $\mathbf{R} - \mathbf{II}(\mathbf{id}_k) \cdots \mathbf{H}(\mathbf{id}_{\ell+1}) \in \mathbb{Z}^{m \times m}$ and then set $\mathbf{B_{id}} = \mathbf{B_{id|\ell}} \cdot \mathbf{R}^{-1} \in \mathbb{Z}_q^{n \times m}$.

3. Invoke $\mathbf{T'} \leftarrow \mathsf{BasisDel}(\mathbf{B_{id}}_{|\ell}, \mathbf{T_{id}}_{|\ell}, \mathbf{R}, \sigma_k)$ to obtain a short random basis for $\Lambda_q^{\perp}(\mathbf{B_{id}})$.
4. Output the delegated basis $\mathbf{T_{id}} = \mathbf{T'}$.

- **Extract**$(mpk, \mathbf{B_{id}}, \mathbf{T_{id}}, \mathbf{id})$. Take as input public parameter mpk, and an identity $\mathbf{id}$ of depth $|\mathbf{id}| = \ell$. Run the PPT algorithm SamplePre$(\mathbf{B_{id}}, \mathbf{T_{id}}, \sigma_\ell, \mathbf{u})$ to sample a short vector $\mathbf{x} \in \mathbb{Z}^m$ such that $\mathbf{B_{id}} \cdot \mathbf{x} = \mathbf{u} \pmod q$. Then output identity-specific public key $pk_{\mathbf{id}} : \mathbf{P} = \begin{bmatrix} \mathbf{u}^t \\ \mathbf{B_{id}}^t \end{bmatrix}$, and the identity-specific secret key $sk_{\mathbf{id}} : \mathbf{s} = (1, -\mathbf{x})$. Note that $\mathbf{s}^t \cdot \mathbf{P} = 0 \pmod q$.
- **Enc**$(pk_{\mathbf{id}}, \mathbf{id}, \mu)$. To encrypt a message $\mu \in \{0,1\}$, sample a small matrix $\mathbf{M} \xleftarrow{\$} \{0,1\}^{n \times N}$ and a small noise matrix $\mathbf{E} \xleftarrow{\$} \mathcal{D}_{\mathbb{Z}, \alpha_\ell q}^{(m+1) \times N}$. Output a ciphertext $\mathbf{C} = \mathbf{P} \cdot \mathbf{M} + 2\mathbf{E} + \mu \mathbf{G} \in \mathbb{Z}_q^{(m+1) \times N}$.
- **Dec**$(sk_{\mathbf{id}}, \mathbf{C})$. Choose the first column vector $\mathbf{c}$ of ciphertext $\mathbf{C}$. Output $\mu = \langle \mathbf{s}, \mathbf{c} \rangle_q \pmod 2$.

4.2 Correctness, Parameters and Security

Performing the decryption procedure on ciphertext in the scheme, we have $\langle \mathbf{s}, \mathbf{c} \rangle \equiv \mu + 2\langle \mathbf{e}, \mathbf{s} \rangle \bmod q$. According to Lemma 4, the noise term $\mathbf{e}$ is the column vector of $\mathbf{E} \xleftarrow{\$} \mathcal{D}_{\mathbb{Z}, \alpha_\ell q}^{(m+1) \times N}$ that satisfies $||\mathbf{e}|| \leq \sqrt{m+1} \cdot \alpha_\ell q$ with overwhelming probability, while $\mathbf{x} \in \Lambda_q^{\mathbf{u}}(\mathbf{A})$ is sampled from a distribution statistically close to $\mathcal{D}_{\Lambda_q^{\mathbf{u}}(\mathbf{A}), \sigma_\ell}$ that satisfies $||\mathbf{x}|| \leq \sqrt{m} \cdot \sigma_\ell$ with overwhelming probability. As with that in Sect. 3.2, we can set $\sigma_\ell = m^{\frac{3}{2}\ell} \cdot \omega(\log^{2\ell} m)$ and then $\alpha_\ell = \left(m^{\frac{3}{2}\ell + 2L + 1} \cdot \omega(\log^{2\ell + 1} m) \right)^{-1}$. While according to Regev's reduction [27] which requires $\alpha_{\ell+1} q > 2\sqrt{n}$, we can choose q of polynomial size such that $\alpha_\ell q = O(\sqrt{n}) > 2\sqrt{n}$. It follows that

$$|2\langle \mathbf{e}, \mathbf{s} \rangle| \leq 2||\mathbf{e}|| \cdot (||\mathbf{x}|| + 1) = O(\sqrt{n}) \cdot m^{\frac{3}{2}\ell + 1} \cdot \omega(\log^{2\ell} m) < q/2.$$

Moreover, similarly with our LWR-based leveled HIBFHE and [3], after performing homomorphic evaluations on ciphertexts, the noise grows linearly in $N + 1$ and asymmetrically in the ciphertexts' respective noises. For simplicity, we just present the result by the following theorem.

Theorem 4. *For the parameters λ, d, L, $n = n(\lambda, d, L)$ and $m = m(\lambda, d, L) \geq 2n \log q$, if the polynomial size modulus $q \geq (3n \log^2 q)^{\frac{3}{2}d + L + 1} \cdot \omega\big((2 \log n)^{2d}\big)$, our construction based on* LWE *is a correct L-leveled HIBFHE.*

The modulus q is of polynomial size and the Gaussian noise rate α is of inverse-polynomial size in the parameter n, this allows the security to be based on certain worst-case lattice problems with polynomial approximation factors. As for the security, we note that the main difference between our LWR-based scheme and LWE-based scheme depends on **Enc** algorithm. The LWR-based scheme uses the scaled rounding function to hide plaintext contrast to the Gaussian noise used in the LWE-based scheme, therefore the security proofs for both are almost identical, except that they are based on different hard problems. For completeness, we give the following theorem.

Theorem 5. *Let $\mathcal{A}$ be a PPT adversary that attacks our LWE-based scheme, and Q_H be the number of hash H queries made by $\mathcal{A}$ and d be the maximal hierarchy depth, where H is a hash function modeled as a random oracle. Then there is a PPT algorithm $\mathcal{B}$ that solves the DLWE$_{n,q,m,\chi}(\mathcal{D})$ problem with advantage ϵ, such that, if $\mathcal{A}$ is an adaptive adversary (INDr-ID-CPA) with advantage ϵ', then it holds that $\epsilon' \leq \epsilon \cdot (d \cdot Q_H^d) + \mathrm{negl}(n)$.*

5   Conclusion and Future Direction

We presented two leveled HIBFHE schemes from LWR and LWE. Our LWE-based leveled HIBFHE scheme is an improvement on the previous LWE-based leveled HIBFHE scheme. Our novel leveled HIBFHE scheme is based on LWR problem, which is, to the best of our knowledge, the first LWR-based leveled HIBFHE scheme. Our proposed LWR-based leveled HIBFHE scheme has bigger parameters than the previous LWE-based leveled HIBFHE scheme and our improved scheme, but it does not need Gaussian noise sampling in encryption process. Thus, the LWR-based leveled HIBFHE scheme still has advantage and can be seen as an alternative one. Furthermore, in this work we proved that our two leveled HIBFHE schemes are both secure against adaptive chosen-identity attack. However, the bootstrapping method cannot be used to transform our leveled HIBFHE into non-leveled (pure) HIBFHE, due to IBE's property of non-interactivity. Therefore, a subject of our future work is to design a pure IBFHE without indistinguishable obfuscator.

Acknowledgments. The authors would like to thank the anonymous reviewers for their detailed reviews and helpful comments. This research is supported in part by the National Nature Science Foundation of China (Nos. 61672030, 61272040 and U1705264; Nos. 61572132 and U1705264).

References

1. Agrawal, S., Boneh, D., Boyen, X.: Efficient lattice (H)IBE in the standard model. In: Gilbert, H. (ed.) EUROCRYPT 2010. LNCS, vol. 6110, pp. 553–572. Springer, Heidelberg (2010). https://doi.org/10.1007/978-3-642-13190-5_28
2. Agrawal, S., Boneh, D., Boyen, X.: Lattice basis delegation in fixed dimension and shorter-ciphertext hierarchical IBE. In: Rabin, T. (ed.) CRYPTO 2010. LNCS, vol. 6223, pp. 98–115. Springer, Heidelberg (2010). https://doi.org/10.1007/978-3-642-14623-7_6
3. Alperin-Sheriff, J., Peikert, C.: Faster bootstrapping with polynomial error. In: Garay, J.A., Gennaro, R. (eds.) CRYPTO 2014. LNCS, vol. 8616, pp. 297–314. Springer, Heidelberg (2014). https://doi.org/10.1007/978-3-662-44371-2_17

4. Alwen, J., Krenn, S., Pietrzak, K., Wichs, D.: Learning with rounding, revisited. In: Canetti, R., Garay, J.A. (eds.) CRYPTO 2013. LNCS, vol. 8042, pp. 57–74. Springer, Heidelberg (2013). https://doi.org/10.1007/978-3-642-40041-4_4

5. Banerjee, A., Peikert, C., Rosen, A.: Pseudorandom functions and lattices. In: Pointcheval, D., Johansson, T. (eds.) EUROCRYPT 2012. LNCS, vol. 7237, pp. 719–737. Springer, Heidelberg (2012). https://doi.org/10.1007/978-3-642-29011-4_42

6. Bogdanov, A., Guo, S., Masny, D., Richelson, S., Rosen, A.: On the hardness of learning with rounding over small modulus. In: Kushilevitz, E., Malkin, T. (eds.) TCC 2016. LNCS, vol. 9562, pp. 209–224. Springer, Heidelberg (2016). https://doi.org/10.1007/978-3-662-49096-9_9

7. Boneh, D., Franklin, M.: Identity-based encryption from the weil pairing. In: Kilian, J. (ed.) CRYPTO 2001. LNCS, vol. 2139, pp. 213–229. Springer, Heidelberg (2001). https://doi.org/10.1007/3-540-44647-8_13

8. Boneh, D., Gentry, C., Hamburg, M.: Space-efficient identity based encryption without pairings. In: 48th Annual IEEE Symposium on Foundations of Computer Science 2007. FOCS 2007, pp. 647–657. IEEE (2007)

9. Brakerski, Z.: Fully homomorphic encryption without modulus switching from classical GapSVP. In: Safavi-Naini, R., Canetti, R. (eds.) CRYPTO 2012. LNCS, vol. 7417, pp. 868–886. Springer, Heidelberg (2012). https://doi.org/10.1007/978-3-642-32009-5_50

10. Brakerski, Z., Gentry, C., Vaikuntanathan, V.: (Leveled) fully homomorphic encryption without bootstrapping. In: Innovations in Theoretical Computer Science 2012, Cambridge, MA, USA, 8–10 January 2012, pp. 309–325 (2012)

11. Brakerski, Z., Langlois, A., Peikert, C., Regev, O., Stehlé, D.: Classical hardness of learning with errors. In: Proceedings of the Forty-Fifth Annual ACM Symposium on Theory of Computing, pp. 575–584. ACM (2013)

12. Brakerski, Z., Vaikuntanathan, V.: Efficient fully homomorphic encryption from (standard) LWE. In: IEEE 52nd Annual Symposium on Foundations of Computer Science. FOCS 2011, Palm Springs, CA, USA, 22–25 October 2011, pp. 97–106 (2011)

13. Groot Bruinderink, L., Hülsing, A., Lange, T., Yarom, Y.: Flush, gauss, and reload – a cache attack on the BLISS lattice-based signature scheme. In: Gierlichs, B., Poschmann, A.Y. (eds.) CHES 2016. LNCS, vol. 9813, pp. 323–345. Springer, Heidelberg (2016). https://doi.org/10.1007/978-3-662-53140-2_16

14. Cash, D., Hofheinz, D., Kiltz, E., Peikert, C.: Bonsai trees, or how to delegate a lattice basis. In: Gilbert, H. (ed.) EUROCRYPT 2010. LNCS, vol. 6110, pp. 523–552. Springer, Heidelberg (2010). https://doi.org/10.1007/978-3-642-13190-5_27

15. Clear, M., Hughes, A., Tewari, H.: Homomorphic encryption with access policies: characterization and new constructions. In: Youssef, A., Nitaj, A., Hassanien, A.E. (eds.) AFRICACRYPT 2013. LNCS, vol. 7918, pp. 61–87. Springer, Heidelberg (2013). https://doi.org/10.1007/978-3-642-38553-7_4

16. Clear, M., McGoldrick, C.: Bootstrappable identity-based fully homomorphic encryption. In: Gritzalis, D., Kiayias, A., Askoxylakis, I. (eds.) CANS 2014. LNCS, vol. 8813, pp. 1–19. Springer, Cham (2014). https://doi.org/10.1007/978-3-319-12280-9_1

17. Cocks, C.: An Identity based encryption scheme based on quadratic residues. In: Honary, B. (ed.) Cryptography and Coding 2001. LNCS, vol. 2260, pp. 360–363. Springer, Heidelberg (2001). https://doi.org/10.1007/3-540-45325-3_32

18. Fang, F., Li, B., Lu, X., Liu, Y., Jia, D., Xue, H.: (Deterministic) hierarchical identity-based encryption from learning with rounding over small modulus. In: Proceedings of the 11th ACM on Asia Conference on Computer and Communications Security, pp. 907–912. ACM (2016)

19. Gentry, C.: Fully homomorphic encryption using ideal lattices. In: Proceedings of the 41st Annual ACM Symposium on Theory of Computing. STOC 2009, Bethesda, MD, USA, 31 May–2 June 2009, pp. 169–178 (2009)

20. Gentry, C., Peikert, C., Vaikuntanathan, V.: Trapdoors for hard lattices and new cryptographic constructions. In: Proceedings of the Fortieth Annual ACM Symposium on Theory of Computing, pp. 197–206. ACM (2008)

21. Gentry, C., Sahai, A., Waters, B.: Homomorphic encryption from learning with errors: conceptually-simpler, asymptotically-faster, attribute-based. In: Canetti, R., Garay, J.A. (eds.) CRYPTO 2013. LNCS, vol. 8042, pp. 75–92. Springer, Heidelberg (2013). https://doi.org/10.1007/978-3-642-40041-4_5

22. Gentry, C., Silverberg, A.: Hierarchical ID-based cryptography. In: Zheng, Y. (ed.) ASIACRYPT 2002. LNCS, vol. 2501, pp. 548–566. Springer, Heidelberg (2002). https://doi.org/10.1007/3-540-36178-2_34

23. Halevi, S., Shoup, V.: Bootstrapping for HElib. In: Oswald, E., Fischlin, M. (eds.) EUROCRYPT 2015. LNCS, vol. 9056, pp. 641–670. Springer, Heidelberg (2015). https://doi.org/10.1007/978-3-662-46800-5_25

24. Micciancio, D., Peikert, C.: Trapdoors for lattices: simpler, tighter, faster, smaller. In: Pointcheval, D., Johansson, T. (eds.) EUROCRYPT 2012. LNCS, vol. 7237, pp. 700–718. Springer, Heidelberg (2012). https://doi.org/10.1007/978-3-642-29011-4_41

25. Peikert, C.: Public-key cryptosystems from the worst-case shortest vector problem. In: Proceedings of the Forty-First Annual ACM Symposium on Theory of Computing, pp. 333–342. ACM (2009)

26. Pessl, P.: Analyzing the shuffling side-channel countermeasure for lattice-based signatures. In: Dunkelman, O., Sanadhya, S.K. (eds.) INDOCRYPT 2016. LNCS, vol. 10095, pp. 153–170. Springer, Cham (2016). https://doi.org/10.1007/978-3-319-49890-4_9

27. Regev, O.: On lattices, learning with errors, random linear codes, and cryptography. J. ACM (JACM) **56**(6), 34 (2009)

28. Shamir, A.: Identity-based cryptosystems and signature schemes. In: Blakley, G.R., Chaum, D. (eds.) CRYPTO 1984. LNCS, vol. 196, pp. 47–53. Springer, Heidelberg (1985). https://doi.org/10.1007/3-540-39568-7_5

29. Sun, X., Yu, J., Wang, T., Sun, Z., Zhang, P.: Efficient identity-based leveled fully homomorphic encryption from RLWE. Secur. Commun. Netw. **9**(18), 5155–5165 (2016)

30. Wang, F., Wang, K., Li, B.: An efficient leveled identity-based FHE. Network and System Security. LNCS, vol. 9408, pp. 303–315. Springer, Cham (2015). https://doi.org/10.1007/978-3-319-25645-0_20

31. Waters, B.: Dual system encryption: realizing fully secure IBE and HIBE under simple assumptions. In: Halevi, S. (ed.) CRYPTO 2009. LNCS, vol. 5677, pp. 619–636. Springer, Heidelberg (2009). https://doi.org/10.1007/978-3-642-03356-8_36

32. Xie, X., Xue, R., Zhang, R.: Deterministic public key encryption and identity-based encryption from lattices in the auxiliary-input setting. In: Visconti, I., De Prisco, R. (eds.) SCN 2012. LNCS, vol. 7485, pp. 1–18. Springer, Heidelberg (2012). https://doi.org/10.1007/978-3-642-32928-9_1

Searchable and Functional Encryption

Leakage-Resilient Chosen-Ciphertext Secure Functional Encryption from Garbled Circuits

Huige Wang[1(⊠)], Kefei Chen[2,5], Joseph K. Liu[3], and Ziyuan Hu[4]

[1] Department of Computer, Anhui Science and Technology University,
Fengyang 233100, China
whgexf@163.com

[2] Department of Mathematics, Hangzhou Normal University,
Hangzhou 311121, China

[3] Faculty of Information Technology, Monash University, Melbourne 3800, Australia

[4] Department of Computer Science and Engineering, Shanghai Jiao Tong University,
Shanghai 200240, China

[5] Westone Cryptologic Research Center, Beijing 100070, China

Abstract. At Asiacrypt 2013, Qin and Liu showed a leakage-resilient chosen-ciphertext attacks (LR-CCA) secure public-key encryption (PKE) from one-time lossy filter (OT-LF) and hash proof system (HPS), from which, combining garbled circuits (GC), we present an LR-CCA secure generic construction for single-key and single-ciphertext functional encryption (FE) via hash proof system (HPS) and one-time lossy filter (OT-LF). We bypass known obstacles in realizing leakage-resilient using garbled circuits that make a non-black-box use of the underlying cryptographic primitives. Efficient instantiations of DDH-based and DCR-based HPS and OT-LF indicate that our approach is practical in realizing LR-CCA secure FE scheme under the standard assumptions. Moreover, our constructions from the DDH and DCR assumptions result in the same leakage rate as Qin and Liu's.

Keywords: Functional encryption
Leakage-resilient chosen-ciphertext · Garbled circuits

1 Introduction

As one of the most fundamental and widely used cryptographic primitives, traditional public-key encryption (PKE) is viewed as a method to encrypt point-to-point communication where encrypted data x is aimed at a known user in advance. This primitive guarantees that only the user that owns the (unique) secret key sk corresponding to the encryption key pk can decrypt ct_x (where ct_x encrypts x under pk) and obtains the plaintext x. Due to the single functionality on the secret key for PKE, any holder of the secret key has very limited control on the encrypted messages. To overcome this problem, functional encryption

© Springer Nature Switzerland AG 2018
C. Su and H. Kikuchi (Eds.): ISPEC 2018, LNCS 11125, pp. 119–140, 2018.
https://doi.org/10.1007/978-3-319-99807-7_8

(FE) [32], as one of the most advanced cryptographic primitives which enables a system having flexibility in controlling encrypted data, was proposed and got developed [13,14,26,29,32]. At a high level, in a functional encryption, an owner of a master secret key msk can generate a functional decryption key sk_f for a function f belonging to a family $\mathcal{F}$. By decrypting a ciphertext ct_x of a message x using sk_f except which no information about x is revealed from ct_x.

Due to the ability to generate functional decryption keys, functional encryption enables one to construct a cryptographic system with fine-grained access control. Informally, a secure functional encryption should resist the indistinguishability (IND) security in which the adversary tries to distinguish the encryptions of two messages even given some functional keys for functions that the adversary adaptively chooses. Formal security models for FE were developed in [13,14]. Later, many provably secure FEs were proposed, where the research mainly falls into two lines: the first line mainly focuses on the work in exploring different security models (such as indistinguishable chosen-plaintext attacks security (IND-CPA), indistinguishable chosen-ciphertext attacks security (IND-CCA), etc.) [2,3,9,10,13]; the second line aims to developing [5,7,8,15,20,23,24,34] different hardness assumptions (such as indistinguishable obfuscation (IO), multi-linear maps, etc.) that FEs base on.

Note that none of the above FEs can achieve leakage-resilient security. Leakage-resilient cryptography emerged as a theoretical foundation to address side-channel attacks, when a significantly fraction of the secret key is leaked to the adversary. Despite the great success in leakage-resilient cryptography in the past decade, little progress was made on functional encryptions (FEs) until the work of Zhang et al. [36] and Chow et al. [16]. Concretely, the work in [36] introduced an encoding mechanism and then used it to construct two leakage-resilient (LR) attribute-based encryption (ABE) schemes based on composite order bilinear groups assumption. While in [16], Chow et al. proposed three practical leakage-resilient identity-based encryptions (IBEs) from simple assumptions in the standard model by combining identity-based hash proof system (IB-HPS) with three IBE variants (i.e., Boneh-Boyen IBE, Waters IBE, and Lewko-Waters IBE). Before this, LR secure IBE [4,6] were not desirable because they were either provably secure in the random oracle model or based on non-static assumptions. Although progress in LR security in the above two types of schemes, there still exists some inherent problems: (1) the access structures seem specific to different constructions; (2) most of these constructions are not generic due to the use of concrete assumptions. Thus, we raise the following questions: *is it possible to construct leakage-resilient FE with more general functionalities supportting different access structures, and does there exist generic FE framework that can resist chosen-ciphertext attacks (CCA) without relying on concrete assumptions?*

1.1   Our Contribution

In this paper, we give a new generic FE framework (in the public key setting for deterministic functions) from garbled circuits (GC), hash proof system (HPS) and one-time lossy filter (LF), which achieves leakage-resilient chosen-ciphertext security (LR-CCA security) in the standard model. We mainly benefit from several useful features of the underlying primitives: (1) the HPS is perfectly universal, i.e., the hash value is completely uniform over the key space even given invalid ciphertexts and the projection key; (2) the OT-LF is $(\mathcal{K}, l_L)$-lossy which helps to achieve CCA-security, where l_{LF} is the allowable leakage on input $\mathcal{K}$; (3) the garbled circuits provide privacy for circuits, which helps to solve the key-leakage problem in private key queries (note that the circuit is constructed mainly based on the master secret key). By carefully employing the above features, we bypass several obstacles, e.g., the master secret key-leakage on the functional keys, to obtain a generic framework for FE with LR-CCA security (in the public-key settings for deterministic functions) in the standard model.

Note that, despite the leakage-resilient secure IBEs [16] and ABEs [36] may be viewed as two special examples of FE, the techniques in both schemes are still unable to apply to our scheme. The reason mainly focuses on the following points. First, in the IBE schemes [16], since the encryption algorithm only binds the identity with a plaintext-irrelevant component of the ciphertext (the ciphertext consists of three components), the functions used for generating functional keys will be independent of the decrypted plaintexts; second, since our scheme is generic and does not rely on any concrete assumptions, especially the composite order bilinear groups and the customized encoding mechanism, it is still unable to satisfy our requirement by using the techniques in [36]. We achieve our goal by first adapting the PKE scheme in [30] to the FE setting, and then combining the technique of garbled circuits with LF. Technically, the garbled circuits are needed for solving the key-leakage problem in the key queries and the LF is needed for verifying the well-formedness of the ciphertext. Besides, we also provide an instantiation for our scheme through the existing DDH-based HPS [30] and OT-LF [30] and obtain a same leakage rate $1/2 - o(1)$ as in [30].

1.2   Our Techniques

Our starting point is Qin and Liu's LR-CCA secure public-key encryption scheme [30] where the hash proof system (HPS) and one-time lossy filter (OT-LF) were used for the fundamental building blocks. Informally, in their scheme, the private key is just the secret key of the HPS, and the ciphertext ct consists of $(C, s, U = \mathsf{Ext}(K, s) \oplus x, \pi = \mathsf{LF}_{lpk,t}(K), t_c)$, where $K = \mathsf{HPS}.\mathsf{Pub}(pk, C, w)$, $C \leftarrow_\$ \mathcal{V}$, $s \leftarrow_\$ \{0, 1\}^d$, and $t_c \leftarrow_\$ \mathcal{T}_c$. The key K, with the random string s together as input of the extractor Ext, masks the message x and handles the key-leakage, and the function $\mathsf{LF}_{lpk,t}(K)$ is applied to verify the well-formedness of the ciphertext and thus guarantees that the scheme achieves CCA security. Just as its name suggests, the OT-LF only allows making one time lossy tag query to the oracle.

Since our scheme allows the adversary to make challenge query once, the OT-LF just satisfies our requirements. Moreover, to deal with the key-leakage from functional key queries, we apply a circuit garbling scheme GC which, introduced by Yao [35] to our scheme for computing functional keys, where the circuit garbling scheme allows computing a function f on an input x without leaking anything about f or x besides $f(x)$. In particular, the one-time property on LF and GC is employed to respond to the single-key and single-challenge of our scheme. Specifically, a garbling scheme has three related algorithms: garbling algorithm GC.Grl, evaluation algorithm GC.Eval and simulation algorithm Sim. The garbling algorithm taking as input a circuit $\mathcal{G}$ and outputting a pair of garbled circuit and labels $(\widetilde{\mathcal{G}}, \{\mathsf{L}_{w,b}\}_{w\in\mathsf{inp}(\mathcal{G}),b\in\{0,1\}})$ is used for computing our functional key $sk_f = (\widetilde{\mathcal{G}}, \{\mathsf{L}_{w,b}\}_{w\in\mathsf{inp}(\mathcal{G}),b\in\{0,1\}})$. The evaluation algorithm taking as input a garbled circuit $\widetilde{\mathcal{G}}$ and an input encoding $\{\mathsf{L}_{w,ct_w}\}_{w\in\mathsf{inp}(\mathcal{G})}$ and outputting $\mathcal{G}(ct)$ is used for decrypting. While the simulator Sim is used for simulating the functional key in the proof without knowing the circuit. The circuit privacy guarantees that the keys generated in both cases are computationally indistinguishable.

Roughly speaking, our scheme consists of the following key steps: (1) in the setup phase, the secret key sk of the HPS serves as the master secret key of our scheme; (2) the encryption algorithm encrypts a message x in the same way as [30], i.e.,

$$K \leftarrow \mathsf{HPS.Pub}(pk, C, w), \ U = \mathsf{Ext}(K, s) \oplus x, \ \pi = \mathsf{LF}_{lpk,t}(K);$$

(3) the functional key sk_f is computed via the garbling algorithm GC.Grl, i.e., $sk_f = (\widetilde{\mathcal{G}}, \{\mathsf{L}_{w,b}\}_{w\in\mathsf{inp}(\mathcal{G}),b\in\{0,1\}})$, where $(\widetilde{\mathcal{G}}, \{\mathsf{L}_{w,b}\}_{w\in\mathsf{inp}(\mathcal{G}),b\in\{0,1\}}) \leftarrow_{\$}$ GC.Grl$(1^\lambda, \mathcal{G}[mpk, msk, f])$ (see Fig. 2 for the circuit $\mathcal{G}[mpk, msk, f]$); (4) the decryption uses the evaluation algorithm GC.Eval$(\widetilde{\mathcal{G}}, \{\mathsf{L}_{w,ct_w}\}_{w\in\mathsf{inp}(\mathcal{G})})$ to decrypt by using labels $\{\mathsf{L}_{w,ct_w}\}_{w\in\mathsf{inp}(\mathcal{G})}$ in the private key. By the correctness of the schemes GC and HPS, we can get $f(x)$ with overwhelming probability.

Our LR-CCA secure FE scheme is immediate if the underlying hash proof system and lossy filter can be instantiated. Fortunately, DDH-based and DCR-based hash proof system (HPS) and one-time lossy filters (LF) can be found in [30]. In addition, [23] shows that a garbling scheme can be constructed from one-way function. Embedding these building blocks to the generic FE construction, we can obtain DDH-based and DCR-based FEs with LR-CCA security. Like ABEs in [1,36], in our scheme, the private key size, ciphertext size and leakage bound are $\Theta(\tilde{n})$ times larger than that of IBEs in [16]. Although the leakage rate, $1/2 - o(1)$, in our scheme is $1/2$ times less than that of ABEs in [1,36] (achieving $(1 - o(1))$), it is $1/6 - o(1)$ larger than that of IBEs in [16] (achieving at most $1/3 - o(1)$). Besides, our scheme also obtains CCA security and more general functionalities compared with the schemes in [1,16,36].

1.3   Other Related Works and Discussions

The leakage-resilient notion was proposed by Halderman et al. in [27] in order to solve side-channel attacks on hardware device where a significant fraction of the secret key is leaked to the adversary. Since that, leakage-resilient (LR) security got further developed via various methods [19,30,31]. Particularly, at Asiacrypt 2013, Qin and Liu proposed an LR-CCA secure public key encryption (PKE) from hash proof system and one-time lossy filter where the leakage rate was first raised to $1/2 - o(1)$ in practical PKE. Followed by their work, at Asiacrypt 2016, Faonio and Venturi [19] further promoted LR security in PKE by combining the technique of tamper resilience. Identity-based encryption (IBE) and attribute-based encryption (ABE), as two special examples of functional encryption (FE), also capture progress in LR security. The early-age LR IBEs [4,6] are designed based on regular IBE [12,21,22] which is efficient but only provable secure in the random oracle model or from "nonstatic" assumption in the standard model. Following the work in [4,6], Chow et al. [16] presented practical LR IBEs from simple assumptions in the standard model. In 2013, the LR security in ABE was first considered by Zhang et al. [36] where a customized encoding mechanism was used to construct access structure.

All the above schemes (including IBEs and ABEs) seem specific to access control structures which are either for identity functions (in IBEs) or from customized encoding mechanism (in ABEs). Up to now, realizing FEs with LR security for general functionalities, especially those with LR-CCA security under standard assumptions, is still not resolved. In this paper, we focus on this problem and solve it by presenting a generic construction of FE with LR-CCA security and giving an instantiation based on the DDH assumption.

1.4   Organizations

The rest of this paper consists of the following parts. In Sect. 2, we provide some preliminaries to help readers review some known notions. In Sect. 3, we give the definition and security model of functional encryption (FE). In Sect. 4, we present a generic construction of FE and prove its security. In Sect. 5, we provide an instantiation based on the DDH assumption and analyze its security. In Sect. 6, we show a comparison in efficiency and security with the existing related schemes. In Sect. 7, we give our conclusions and further open problems.

2   Preliminaries

In this section, we introduce some notations and present definitions for various cryptographic primitives that we shall use in our construction of functional encryption. We assume familiarity with standard secure chameleon hashing function and the reader can refer to Sect. 2.4 in [30] for the details. Below, we recall the notions of randomness extractor, garbled circuits, hash proof system and one-time lossy filter.

2.1   Notations

Throughout the paper, we let $\mathbb{N}$ denote the set of natural numbers, $\lambda \in \mathbb{N}$ denote the security parameter, and "PPT" denote probabilistic polynomial time. If x denotes a string, then $\bar{x}$ denotes its complement. Let $y \leftarrow A(x_1, \cdots ; R)$ denote the operation of running algorithm A on inputs $x_1, \cdots$ and coins R to output y. For simplicity, we write $y \leftarrow A(x_1, \cdots ; R)$ as $y \leftarrow_{\$} A(x_1, \cdots)$ with implied coins.

If $n \in \mathbb{N}$, we let $[n]$ denote the set $\{1, \cdots, n\}$. We call a function $negl$ negligible in λ if $negl(\lambda) \in \lambda^{-\omega(1)}$ and a function $poly$ a polynomial if $poly \in \lambda^{\mathcal{O}(1)}$. If X is a random variable over the set S, then we write $\max_{a \in S} \Pr[X = a]$ to denote the predictability of X and $-\log(\max_{a \in S} \Pr[X = a])$ denote the min-entropy $\mathsf{H}_\infty(X)$ of X. If C denotes circuit, then we use notation $\mathsf{C}[z]$ to emphasize the fact that the value z is hard-wired into C. If $\mathcal{D}$ denotes a distribution over a set S, then $x \leftarrow_\$ \mathcal{D}$ denotes uniformly and randomly choosing an element from set $\mathcal{S}$ according to distribution $\mathcal{D}$, and $x \leftarrow_\$ S$ denotes choosing an element randomly from set $\mathcal{S}$.

In this paper, for convenience, we apply a code-based game playing framework in [11,33] to our scheme. Roughly speaking, a game G has a main procedure, and possibly other procedure. G begins by executing the main procedure which runs an adversary $\mathcal{A}$ after some initialization. $\mathcal{A}$ can make oracle calls permitted by G. When $\mathcal{A}$ finishes execution, G continues to execute with $\mathcal{A}$'s output. By $\mathsf{G}^\mathcal{A} \Rightarrow y$, we denote the event that G executes with $\mathcal{A}$ to output y. Generally, we abbreviate $\mathsf{G}^\mathcal{A} \Rightarrow true$ or $\mathsf{G}^\mathcal{A} \Rightarrow 1$ as G. The boolean flag and set are initialized to false and $\emptyset$ respectively.

2.2   Randomness Extractor

In this section, we recall the definition of randomness extractor. First we recall some basic notions from [30]. Let $\mathsf{SD}(X, Y) = \frac{1}{2}\sum_{a \in \mathcal{D}}|\Pr[X = a] - \Pr[Y = a]|$ denote the statistical distance of random variables X and Y over set $\mathcal{D}$. If the min-entropy of X is defined as $\mathsf{H}_\infty(X) = -\log(\max_{a \in \mathcal{D}} \Pr[X = a])$, then the average min-entropy of X conditioned on Y is formalized as $\widetilde{\mathsf{H}}_\infty(X|Y) = -\log(E_{y \leftarrow Y}[2^{-\mathsf{H}_\infty(X|Y=y)}])$.

Lemma 1 [18]. *Let X, Y and Z be random variables. If Y has at most 2^l possible values, then $\widetilde{\mathsf{H}}_\infty(X|(Y, Z)) \geq \widetilde{\mathsf{H}}_\infty(X|Z) - l$.*

Definition 1 (Randomness Extractor). *An efficient function $\mathsf{Ext} : \mathcal{X} \times \mathcal{S} \to \mathcal{Y}$ is an average-case (ν, ϵ_2)-strong extractor if for all pairs of random variables (X, Z) such that $X \in \mathcal{X}$ and $\widetilde{\mathsf{H}}_\infty(X|Z) \geq \nu$, we have*

$$\mathsf{SD}((Z, s, \mathsf{Ext}(X, s)), (Z, s, U_\mathcal{Y})) \leq \epsilon_2.$$

Where $s \leftarrow_\$ \mathcal{S}$ and $U_\mathcal{Y}$ is uniform over $\mathcal{Y}$.

Applying the general Leftover Hash Lemma in [18], it is easy to conclude that a family of universal hash functions $\mathbb{H} = \{H_s\}_{s \in \mathcal{S}}$ can be viewed as an average-case $(\widetilde{\mathsf{H}}_\infty(X|Z), \epsilon_2)$-strong extractors when $\widetilde{\mathsf{H}}_\infty(X|Z) \geq \log|\mathcal{Y}| + 2\log(1/\epsilon_2)|$ holds.

2.3   Garbled Circuits [23]

In this section, we review the definition of circuit garbling scheme from [23]. A circuit garbling scheme GC consists of two PPT algorithms $\mathsf{GC} = (\mathsf{GC.Grl}, \mathsf{GC.Eval})$, where GC.Grl is a circuit garbling procedure and GC.Eval is the corresponding evaluation procedure. We give the formal description as follows.

Garbling. The garbling algorithm $\mathsf{GC}.\mathsf{Grl}(1^\lambda, \mathsf{C})$ takes as input a security parameter 1^λ and a circuit $\mathsf{C} \in C_\lambda$, where $C = \{C_\lambda\}_{\lambda \in \mathbb{N}}$ is a family of circuits. It outputs a garbled circuit $\widetilde{\mathsf{C}}$ and labels $\{\mathsf{L}_{w,\alpha}\}_{w \in \mathsf{inp}(\mathsf{C}), \alpha \in \{0,1\}}$ where each $\mathsf{L}_{w,\alpha} \in \{0,1\}^\lambda$.

Evaluation. The evaluation algorithm $\mathsf{GC}.\mathsf{Eval}(\widetilde{\mathsf{C}}, \{\mathsf{L}_{w,x_w}\}_{w \in \mathsf{inp}(\mathsf{C})})$ takes as input a garbled circuit $\widetilde{\mathsf{C}}$ and an input encoding $\{\mathsf{L}_{w,x_w}\}_{w \in \mathsf{inp}(\mathsf{C})}$ on $x \in \{0,1\}^{\mathsf{inp}(\mathsf{C})}$, where $\mathsf{inp}(\mathsf{C})$ denotes the input length of C. It outputs $y = \mathsf{C}(x)$.

Correctness. For correctness, we require that for any circuit C and input $x \in \{0,1\}^{\mathsf{inp}(\mathsf{C})}$, we have

$$\Pr[\mathsf{C}(x) = \mathsf{GC}.\mathsf{Eval}(\widetilde{\mathsf{C}}, \{\mathsf{L}_{w,x_w}\}_{w \in \mathsf{inp}(\mathsf{C})})] = 1,$$

where $(\widetilde{\mathsf{C}}, \{\mathsf{L}_{w,\alpha}\}_{w \in \mathsf{inp}(\mathsf{C}), \alpha \in \{0,1\}}) \leftarrow_\$ \mathsf{GC}.\mathsf{Grl}(1^\lambda, \mathsf{C})$.

Security. Let Sim be a PPT simulator. We define the game between a challenger $\mathcal{C}$ and a PPT adversary $\mathcal{A}$ as follows.

Initialization. First, the challenger $\mathcal{C}$ chooses a random bit $b \leftarrow_\$ \{0,1\}$ and sends 1^λ to the adversary $\mathcal{A}$. Then, $\mathcal{A}$ sends a circuit $\mathsf{C} \in C_\lambda$ and a message $x \in \{0,1\}^{\mathsf{inp}(\mathsf{C})}$ to $\mathcal{C}$. If $b = 0$, $\mathcal{C}$ computes $(\widetilde{\mathsf{C}}, \{\mathsf{L}_{w,\alpha}\}_{w \in \mathsf{inp}(\mathsf{C}), \alpha \in \{0,1\}}) \leftarrow_\$ \mathsf{GC}.\mathsf{Grl}(1^\lambda, \mathsf{C})$ and returns $(\widetilde{\mathsf{C}}, \{\mathsf{L}_{w,x_w}\}_{w \in \mathsf{inp}(\mathsf{C})})$; otherwise, it returns $(\widetilde{\mathsf{C}}, \{\mathsf{L}_{w,x_w}\}_{w \in \mathsf{inp}(\mathsf{C})}) \leftarrow_\$ \mathsf{Sim}(1^\lambda, |\mathsf{C}|, \mathsf{C}(x))$.

In this game, we define the advantage of the adversary $\mathcal{A}$ as

$$\mathsf{Adv}^{\mathsf{gc}}_{\mathsf{GC}, \mathsf{Sim}, \mathcal{A}}(\lambda) = |\Pr[b' = 1|b = 0] - \Pr[b' = 1|b = 1]|.$$

We say that GC is secure if there exists a PPT simulator Sim such that for any PPT $\mathcal{A}$, the advantage function $\mathsf{Adv}^{\mathsf{gc}}_{\mathsf{GC}, \mathsf{Sim}, \mathcal{A}}(\lambda)$ is negligible.

As noted in [23], a circuit garbling scheme GC can be constructed from one-way function. Any such construction is also suitable for our scheme. In particular, we stress that the circuit garbling scheme defined here is one-time, namely, we allow the adversary to obtain at most one input encoding.

2.4   Hash Proof System (HPS)

Here, we review the definition of hash proof system (HPS) introduced by Cramer et al. in [17]. First, we give the definition of projective hash function.

Definition 2 (Projective Hash Function). *Let $\mathcal{PK}$ be a public key set, $\mathcal{SK}$ a secret key set, $\mathcal{K}$ an encapsulated key set, $\mathcal{C}$ a ciphertext set and $\mathcal{V} \subset \mathcal{C}$ a valid ciphertext set and we assume that there exists efficient algorithms which can sample $sk \leftarrow_\$ \mathcal{SK}$, $(C, w) \leftarrow_\$ \mathcal{V}$ and $C \leftarrow_\$ \mathcal{C} \backslash \mathcal{V}$, where w is a witness showing $C \in \mathcal{V}$. Let Λ_{sk} be a hash function indexed with $sk \in \mathcal{SK}$ that maps the ciphertext set $\mathcal{C}$ to the encapsulated key set $\mathcal{K}$. The hash function Λ_{sk} is **projective** if there exists a projection function $\mu : \mathcal{SK} \to \mathcal{PK}$ such that $\mu(sk) \in \mathcal{PK}$ determines the behavior of Λ_{sk} over the subset $\mathcal{V}$ of valid ciphertexts. In addition, we also assume that both $\Lambda_{(\cdot)}$ and μ are efficiently computable.*

Definition 3 (Universal [17]**).** *A projective hash function Λ_{sk} is ϵ_1-universal, if for all $pk \in \mathcal{PK}$, $C \in \mathcal{C}\backslash\mathcal{V}$, and $K \in \mathcal{K}$, the probability $\Pr[\Lambda_{sk}(C) = K|(pk, C)] \leq \epsilon_1$ holds with $\mathsf{H}_\infty(\Lambda_{sk}(C)|(pk, C)) \geq \log(1/\epsilon_1)$, where the probability is over all $sk \in \mathcal{SK}$ such that $pk = \mu(sk)$.*

Definition 4 (Hash Proof System (HPS)). *A hash proof system consists of three PPT algorithms* (HPS.Gen, HPS.Pub, HPS.Priv)*. The parameter generation algorithm* HPS.Gen(1^λ) *takes as input 1^λ and outputs system public parameter $pp = ($Description$, \mathcal{PK}, \mathcal{SK}, \mathcal{K}, \mathcal{C}, \mathcal{V}, \Lambda_{(\cdot)} : \mathcal{C} \to \mathcal{K}, \mu : \mathcal{SK} \to \mathcal{PK})$, where* Description *contains some description information about pp. The public evaluation algorithm* HPS.Pub(pk, C, w) *takes as input a pubic key $pk = \mu(sk)$, a ciphertext $C \in \mathcal{V}$ and a witness w of C and outputs the encapsulated symmetric key $K = \Lambda_{sk}(C)$. The private evaluation algorithm* HPS.Priv(sk, C) *takes as input the secret key sk and a ciphertext $C \in \mathcal{V}$ and outputs the encapsulated symmetric key $K = \Lambda_{sk}(C)$. We call **a hash proof system HPS** is ϵ_1-**universal**, if*

1. *For all sufficiently large $\lambda \in \mathbb{N}$ and $pp \leftarrow$ HPS.Gen(1^λ), the underlying projective hash function is $\epsilon_1(\lambda)$-universal for negligible $\epsilon_1(\lambda)$.*
2. *The underlying subset membership problem defined below is hard. Furthermore, a hash proof system HPS is called perfectly universal if $\epsilon_1(\lambda) = 1/|\mathcal{K}|$.*

Definition 5 (Subset Membership Problem (SMP) [30]**).** *We say that the subset membership problem with respect to a hash proof system* HPS *holds if the ciphertexts $C_0 \leftarrow_\$ \mathcal{V}$ and $C_1 \leftarrow_\$ \mathcal{C}\backslash\mathcal{V}$ are computationally indistinguishable. Formally, if for all PPT adversary $\mathcal{A}$, the advantage function* $\mathsf{Adv}^{\mathsf{smp}}_{\mathsf{HPS},\mathcal{A}}$ *defined below*

$$\mathsf{Adv}^{\mathsf{smp}}_{\mathsf{HPS},\mathcal{A}}(\lambda) = |\Pr[\mathcal{A}(\mathcal{C}, \mathcal{V}, C_0) = 1|C_0 \leftarrow_\$ \mathcal{V}] - \Pr[\mathcal{A}(\mathcal{C}, \mathcal{V}, C_1) = 1|C_1 \leftarrow_\$ \mathcal{C}\backslash\mathcal{V}]|,$$

is negligible in the security parameter λ.

2.5   One-Time Lossy Filter (LF) [30]

We review the definition of one-time lossy filter from [30].

Definition 6 (One-Time Lossy Filter). *An* $(\mathsf{D}, l_{\mathsf{LF}})$ *one-time lossy filter (LF) consists of three PPT algorithms* LF $=$ (LF.KG, LF.Eval, LF.Ltag)*. Below, we describe the three algorithms, respectively.*

Key Generation. *The algorithm* LF.KG(1^λ) *takes as input 1^λ and outputs a key pair of (lpk, ltk). The public key lpk defines a tag space $\mathcal{T} = \{0, 1\}^* \times \mathcal{T}_c$ which consists of two disjoint subsets, the lossy tag subset $\mathcal{T}_{loss} \subset \mathcal{T}$ and the injective tag subset $\mathcal{T}_{inj} \subset \mathcal{T}$. A tag $t = (t_a, t_c)$ contains an auxiliary tag $t_a \in \{0, 1\}^*$ and a core tag $t_c \in \mathcal{T}_c$ which may be injective or lossy or neither. ltk is a trapdoor that helps to compute a lossy tag.*

Evaluation. *The algorithm* LF.Eval(lpk, t, X) *takes as input the public key lpk, a message $X \in \mathsf{D}$ and a tag $t = (t_a, t_c) \in \mathcal{T}$ and computes the value* LF$_{lpk,t}(X)$.

Lossy Tag Generation. *The algorithm* LF.Ltag(ltk, t_a) *takes as input a trapdoor* ltk *and an auxiliary tag* t_a *and returns a core tag* t_c *such that* $t = (t_a, t_c)$ *is lossy.*

Lossiness. *If* t *is injective, the function* LF$_{lpk,t}(X)$ *is injective and has image size of* $|\mathsf{D}|$. *If* t *is lossy, then* LF$_{lpk,t}(X)$ *is lossy and has image size at most* l_{LF}.

Indistinguishability. *Lossy tags are indistinguishable from random ones. Formally, for all PPT adversary* $\mathcal{A}$, *if the advantage function* $\mathsf{Adv}^{ind}_{\mathsf{LF},\mathcal{A}}(\lambda)$ *defined below*

$$\mathsf{Adv}^{ind}_{\mathsf{LF},\mathcal{A}}(\lambda) = \Pr[\mathcal{A}(1^\lambda, lpk)^{\mathsf{LF.Ltag}(ltk,\cdot)} = 1] - \Pr[\mathcal{A}(1^\lambda, lpk)^{\mathcal{O}_{T_c}(\cdot)} = 1],$$

is negligible in λ, *where* $(lpk, ltk) \leftarrow$ LF.KG(1^λ) *and* $\mathcal{O}_{T_c}(\cdot)$ *is the oracle that samples a random core tag* t_c.

Evasiveness. *Non-injective tags are hard to find, even if given multiple lossy tags. Formally, for all PPT adversary* $\mathcal{A}$, *the advantage function* $\mathsf{Adv}^{evs}_{\mathsf{LF},\mathcal{A}}$ *defined below*

$$\mathsf{Adv}^{evs}_{\mathsf{LF},\mathcal{A}}(\lambda) = \Pr[t \in \mathcal{T} \backslash \mathcal{T}_{inj} | t \leftarrow \mathcal{A}(1^\lambda, lpk)^{\mathsf{LF.Ltag}(ltk,\cdot)}],$$

is negligible in λ, *where* $(lpk, ltk) \leftarrow$ LF.KG(1^λ) *and* $t = (t_a, t_c)$ *is a non-injective tag such that* t_c *is not obtained via oracle* LF.Ltag$(ltk, \cdot)$.

Remark 1. *As remarks in* [30], *the term "one-time" in the above definition means that the adversary is allowed to query lossy tag generation oracle only once in both indistinguishability and evasiveness games which just is the need for our scheme constructed below.*

3 Public-Key Functional Encryption (PK-FE) for Deterministic Functions

In this section, we describe the definition of public-key functional encryption (PK-FE) for deterministic functions (hereafter, we abbreviate "public-key functional encryption for deterministic functions" as "FE"). Below, let $\mathcal{X} = \{\mathcal{X}_\lambda\}_{\lambda \in \mathbb{N}}$, $\mathcal{Y} = \{\mathcal{Y}_\lambda\}_{\lambda \in \mathbb{N}}$ and $\mathcal{F} = \{\mathcal{F}_\lambda\}_{\lambda \in \mathbb{N}}$ be the message space, image space and function space, respectively, where each function $f \in \mathcal{F}$ takes as input a string $x \in \mathcal{X}$ and outputs $f(x) \in \mathcal{Y}$.

3.1 Definition for PK-FE for Deterministic Functions [25]

An FE scheme FE consists of four PPT algorithms FE = (FE.Setup, FE.KG, FE.E, FE.D) over message space $\mathcal{X} = \{\mathcal{X}_\lambda\}_{\lambda \in \mathbb{N}}$ and function space $\mathcal{F} = \{\mathcal{F}_\lambda\}_{\lambda \in \mathbb{N}}$.

Setup. The setup algorithm FE.Setup(1^λ) takes as input 1^λ and outputs a key pair (mpk, msk), where mpk is the master public key and msk is the master secret key.

Key Generation. The key generation algorithm FE.KG(msk, f) takes as input a master secret key msk and a function $f \in \mathcal{F}_\lambda$ and outputs a private key sk_f.

Encryption. The encryption algorithm FE.E(mpk, x) takes as input a master public key mpk and a message $x \in \mathcal{X}_\lambda$ and outputs a ciphertext ct.

Decryption. The decryption algorithm FE.D(sk_f, ct) takes as input a private key sk_f and a ciphertext ct which encrypts a message x, outputs $f(x) \cup \{\bot\}$.

For correctness, we require that there exists a negligible function $negl(\lambda)$ such that for all sufficient large $\lambda \in \mathbb{N}$, for all $(mpk, msk) \leftarrow_\$ \mathsf{Setup}(1^\lambda)$, $f \in \mathcal{F}_\lambda$ and $x \in \mathcal{X}_\lambda$, it holds that

$$\Pr[\mathsf{FE.D}(\mathsf{FE.KeyGen}(msk, f), \mathsf{FE.E}(mpk, x)) = f(x)] \geq 1 - negl(\lambda).$$

3.2   Security Definitions

We now present leakage-resilient chosen-ciphertext (LR-CCA) security definitions for FE. We first observe that existing LR security definitions for FE (e.g., the LR security for ABE [36] and IBE [16]) only consider the malicious receiver and key-leakage settings, in that they intuitively guarantee that an adversary who owns a secret key sk_f corresponding to a deterministic access structure f cannot learn x from an encryption of x even a significantly fraction of the secret key is leaked to the adversary (imply the leakage to the master secret key). In this work, we are also interested in achieving security against both malicious senders and key-leakage for general access structure. In particular, we would like guarantee that the adversary cannot learn anymore than $f(x)$ for a general access structure f from a ciphertext even leaking a fraction of the master secret key to the adversary.

We consider a unified adversarial model that captures malicious receiver, malicious senders and key-leakage. Here we present a semi-adaptive security definitions, where the adversary may choose the challenge messages and function after the master public key. Note that our definition here is for single-key query and single-ciphertext FE, namely, in the security game, the adversary is only allowed to make key and challenge ciphertext only once. In order to formalize the intuition that an adversarial sender cannot force "incorrect" outputs on honest receivers, we allow the adversary to make arbitrary decryption queries (ct, g) such that $ct \neq ct^*$ to a decryption oracle, where ct^* is the challenge ciphertext. After receiving (ct, g), the challenger decrypts ct under the secret key sk_g which is generated using the master secret key msk and the function g.

Formally, we give a concrete description about the security via a game $\mathsf{INDLRCCA}^{\mathcal{A}}_{\mathsf{FE}, l_L, \mathcal{F}}(\lambda)$ (in Fig. 1) between a challenger $\mathcal{C}$ and an adversary $\mathcal{A} = (\mathcal{A}_1, \mathcal{A}_2)$, where the leakage bound l_L is predefined at the beginning of the game. We call an adversary $\mathcal{A}$ admissible if the tuple (x_0, x_1, f) chosen by the adversary satisfies $f(x_0) = f(x_1)$. We define the advantage of an admissible adversary $\mathcal{A}$ in the indistinguishable game $\mathsf{INDLRCCA}^{\mathcal{A}}_{\mathsf{FE}, l_L, \mathcal{F}}(\lambda)$ as $\mathsf{Adv}^{\mathsf{IND\text{-}LR\text{-}CCA}}_{\mathsf{FE}, l_L, \mathcal{F}, \mathcal{A}}(\lambda) = |\Pr[\mathsf{INDLRCCA}^{\mathcal{A}}_{\mathsf{FE}, l_L, \mathcal{F}}(\lambda) = 1] - \frac{1}{2}|$.

Game $\mathsf{INDLRCCA}^{\mathcal{A}}_{\mathsf{FE},l_L,\mathcal{F}}(\lambda)$	$\mathsf{DEC}(ct, g)$
$b \leftarrow_\$ \{0,1\};$	If $ct = ct^*$
$lk \leftarrow 0;$	return $\bot;$
$(mpk, msk) \leftarrow \mathsf{FE.Setup}(1^\lambda);$	$sk_g \leftarrow \mathsf{FE.KG}(msk, g);$
$(x_0, x_1, f, st) \leftarrow \mathcal{A}_1(1^\lambda);$	Return $y = \mathsf{FE.D}(sk_g, ct).$
$sk_f \leftarrow \mathsf{FE.KG}(msk, f);$	
$ct^* \leftarrow \mathsf{FE.E}(mpk, x_b);$	$\mathsf{LEAK}(f')$
$b' \leftarrow \mathcal{A}_2^{\mathsf{DEC},\mathsf{LEAK}}(st, mpk, sk_f, ct^*).$	$lk = lk + |f'(msk)|;$
If $b = b'$ return 1.	If $lk \leq l_L$
	Return $f'(msk).$

Fig. 1. INDLRCCA game for IND-LR-CCA security of FE.

Definition 7 (IND-LR-CCA). *We say that FE is indistinguishability-based l_L-leakage-resilient chosen-ciphertext secure (IND-based l_L-LR-CCA secure) if for any PPT admissible adversary $\mathcal{A}$, the advantage function $\mathsf{Adv}^{\mathsf{IND\text{-}LR\text{-}CCA}}_{\mathsf{FE},l_L,\mathcal{F},\mathcal{A}}(\lambda)$ is negligible.*

Note that, for convenience, we write "indistinguishability-based l_L-LR-CCA" as "IND-LR-CCA" or "l_L-LR-CCA" in the following sections.

4   The Construction

In this section, we give a construction of FE (public key functional encryption for deterministic functions). The scheme $\mathsf{FE} = (\mathsf{FE.Setup}, \mathsf{FE.KG}, \mathsf{FE.E}, \mathsf{FE.D})$ needs the following building blocks:

- A ϵ_1-universal hash proof system $\mathsf{HPS} = (\mathsf{HPS.Gen}, \mathsf{HPS.Pub}, \mathsf{HPS.Priv})$.
- A $(\mathcal{K}, l_{\mathsf{LF}})$ one-time lossy filter $\mathsf{LF} = (\mathsf{LF.KG}, \mathsf{LF.Eval}, \mathsf{LF.Ltag})$.
- An average-case $((\nu - l_{\mathsf{LF}} - l_L), \epsilon_2)$-strong extractor $\mathsf{Ext} : \mathcal{K} \times \{0,1\}^d \to \{0,1\}^m$.
- A secure circuit garbling scheme $\mathsf{GC} = (\mathsf{GC.Grl}, \mathsf{GC.Eval})$.

Setup. On input 1^λ, the setup algorithm $\mathsf{FE.Setup}(1^\lambda)$ first samples a public parameter $pp \leftarrow_\$ \mathsf{HPS.Gen}(1^\lambda)$ and a key-pair $(lpk, ltk) \leftarrow_\$ \mathsf{LF.KG}(1^\lambda)$. Next, it picks $sk \leftarrow_\$ \mathcal{SK}$ and sets $pk = \mu(sk)$, where $\mathcal{SK}$ is contained in pp. Finally, it outputs the master public key $mpk = (pp, lpk, pk)$ and master secret key $msk = sk$.

Encryption. On input the master public key mpk and a message $x \in \{0,1\}^m$, the encryption algorithm $\mathsf{FE.E}(mpk, x)$ first samples a seed $s \leftarrow_\$ \{0,1\}^d$, a core tag $t_c \leftarrow_\$ \mathcal{T}_c$, and a $C \leftarrow_\$ \mathcal{V}$ with witness w. Then, compute

$$K \leftarrow \mathsf{HPS.Pub}(pk, C, w), \quad U = \mathsf{Ext}(K, s) \oplus x, \quad \pi = \mathsf{LF}_{lpk,t}(K),$$

where $t = (t_a, t_c)$ with $t_a = (C, s, U)$. Finally, it outputs ciphertext $ct = (C, s, U, \pi, t_c)$.

Key Generation. On input the master secret key msk and a function $f \in \mathcal{F}_\lambda$, the key generation algorithm $\mathsf{FE.KG}(msk, f)$ first constructs a circuit $\mathcal{G}[mpk, msk, f](\cdot)$ (as in Fig. 2) with mpk, msk and f hardwired in. Then, it computes $(\widetilde{\mathcal{G}}, \{\mathsf{L}_{w,b}\}_{w \in \mathsf{inp}(\mathcal{G}), b \in \{0,1\}}) \leftarrow_\$ \mathsf{GC.Grl}(1^\lambda, \mathcal{G}[mpk, msk, f])$ and sets private key $sk_f = (\widetilde{\mathcal{G}}, \{\mathsf{L}_{w,b}\}_{w \in \mathsf{inp}(\mathcal{G}), b \in \{0,1\}})$. Finally, it outputs sk_f.

Decryption. On input a private key $sk_f = (\widetilde{\mathcal{G}}, \{\mathsf{L}_{w,b}\}_{w \in \mathsf{inp}(\mathcal{G}), b \in \{0,1\}})$ and a ciphertext ct, the decryption algorithm $\mathsf{FE.D}(sk_f, ct)$ computes $y = \mathsf{Eval}(\widetilde{\mathcal{G}}, \{\mathsf{L}_{w, ct_w}\}_{w \in \mathsf{inp}(\mathcal{G})})$ and outputs y.

Constants : mpk, msk, f
Input : ct

1. Parse ct into C, s, U, π, t_c, mpk into pp, lpk, pk, and msk into sk.
2. Compute $K = \mathsf{HPS.Priv}(sk, C)$.
3. Compute $\pi' = \mathsf{LF}_{lpk,t}(K)$, where $t = (t_a, t_c)$, $t_a = (C, s, U)$.
4. If $\pi' \neq \pi$, output $\bot$, else proceed the following steps.
5. Compute $x = \mathsf{Ext}(K, s) \oplus U$.
6. Compute $y = f(x)$ and output y.

Fig. 2. Circuit $\mathcal{G}_{[mpk, msk, f]}$

Correctness. The correctness of the above construction follows from the correctness of the underlying hash proof system HPS, the one-time lossy filter LF and the circuit garbling scheme GC.

Ideas. As in [30], a hash proof system HPS and a one-time lossy filter LF are employed separately to deal with the key-leakage in the ciphertext and the CCA security of the scheme. Specifically, the hash proof system HPS first generates an encapsulated key K, which is then converted to a shorter key to hide the plaintext x via an extractor. The lossy filter LF helps to verify the well-formedness of the ciphertext. Furthermore, to deal with the secret-key leakage in the functional key queries, a garbling scheme GC is used to compute the functional keys. Specifically, in the real scheme, we employ the garbling algorithm GC.Grl to compute the functional key, while in the security proof which is computed using a simulator Sim. This works well because the latter only reveals a function output of challenge plaintexts for a function with which the adversary makes a key query. Furthermore, by the security definitions of FE (the security definition of FE requires that the outputs of a function f on any two challenge messages (x_0, x_1) are equal, i.e., $f(x_0) = f(x_1)$), this leakage would not help the adversary in an attacking game. In the challenge ciphertexts, since the filter LF works in the lossy mode, it only leaks a little information about the key K. In particular, for an invalid ciphertext submitted by the adversary in the decryption queries, since the filter works in the injective mode with overwhelming probability, the ciphertext will be rejected by the decryption oracle with the same large probability.

Parameters, Leakage Rate and CCA-Security. As in [30], to make our construction tolerate leakage rate as much as possible, it is necessary to consider a perfectly ϵ_1-universal hash proof system, i.e., $\epsilon_1 \leq 1/|\mathcal{K}|$. In this way, $\nu = \log(1/\epsilon_1) \geq \log|\mathcal{K}| - 1$. Thus, when K is large enough, the leakage rate achieves $\log|\mathcal{K}|/|sk_f|$ asymptotically, where $|sk_f|$ is the bit size of individual functional key sk_f. In particular, we stress that the leakage on the private key in fact implies the leakage on the master secret key. In addition, if $l_L = 0$ and $1/\epsilon_1 \geq m + l_{\mathsf{LF}} + \omega(\log\lambda)$, the above construction is CCA-secure.

Security. The security of the construction follows the theorem below.

Theorem 1. *Assume the ϵ_1-universal hash proof system* HPS *exists,* LF *is an $(\mathcal{K}, l_{\mathsf{LF}})$ lossy filter,* $\mathsf{Ext} : \mathcal{K} \times \{0,1\}^d \rightarrow \{0,1\}^m$ *is an average-case $((\nu - l_{\mathsf{LF}} - l_L), \epsilon_2)$-strong extractor, the circuit garbling scheme* $\mathsf{GC} = (\mathsf{Grl}, \mathsf{Eval})$ *is secure, $\mathcal{A} = (\mathcal{A}_1, \mathcal{A}_2)$ is a PPT adversary, l_L is a bounded amount of leakage on the private key. Let $\nu - m - l_{\mathsf{LF}} - l_L \geq \omega(\log\lambda)$ and $\nu = \log(1/\epsilon_1)$. Then there exists four PPT adversaries $\mathcal{A}_{ind}, \mathcal{A}_{smp}, \mathcal{A}_{grl}$ and $\mathcal{A}_{evs}$ and a simulator* Sim *running in approximately the same time as $\mathcal{A}$ such that*

$$\mathsf{Adv}^{\mathsf{IND\text{-}LR\text{-}CCA}}_{\mathsf{FE}, l_L, \mathcal{F}, \mathcal{A}}(\lambda) \leq \mathsf{Adv}^{\mathsf{ind}}_{\mathsf{LF}, \mathcal{A}_{ind}}(\lambda) + \mathsf{Adv}^{\mathsf{smp}}_{\mathsf{HPS}, \mathcal{A}_{smp}}(\lambda) + 2\mathsf{Adv}^{\mathsf{gc}}_{\mathsf{GC}, \mathsf{Sim}, \mathcal{A}_{grl}}(\lambda)$$
$$+ q_d\mathsf{Adv}^{\mathsf{evs}}_{\mathsf{LF}, \mathcal{A}_{evs}}(\lambda) + q_d.2^{l_L + l_{\mathsf{LF}} + m}/(2^\nu - q_d) + 2\epsilon_2 \qquad (1)$$

where q_d is a polynomial in the security parameter λ.

Proof. We first define a sequence of games and then prove the output of every game is computationally indistinguishable from that of its adjacent game. In each game, we assume that the adversary $\mathcal{A}$ is admissible and makes at most q_d decryption queries.

Game Sequence. Our proof employs the following game sequence.

G_0: This is the original game where the challenge ciphertext encrypts the challenge message x_b. In this game, each decryption query (ct, g) is answered using a decryption key $sk_g = (\widetilde{\mathcal{G}}, \{\mathsf{L}_{w,b}\}_{w \in \mathsf{inp}(\mathcal{G}), b \in \{0,1\}}) \leftarrow_\$ \mathsf{GC.Grl}(1^\lambda, \mathcal{G}[mpk, msk, g])$, where $\mathcal{G}[mpk, msk, g]$ is the same as $\mathcal{G}[mpk, msk, f]$ (see Fig. 2), except that it has function g hardwired in it. For convenience, we write $\mathcal{G}[mpk, msk, g]$ as $\mathcal{G}_g$.

G_1: The same as G_0 except that the core tag t_c^* in challenge ciphertext ct^* is computed as $t_c^* = \mathsf{LF.Ltag}(ltd, t_a^*)$ instead of sampling $t_c^* \leftarrow_\$ \mathcal{T}_c$, where $t_a^* = (C^*, s^*, U^*)$.

G_2: The same as game G_1 except that the computation of K^* in challenge ciphertext ct^* is different. In this game, we compute $K^* = \mathsf{HPS.Priv}(sk^*, C^*)$ rather than $K^* = \mathsf{HPS.Pub}(pk^*, C^*, w^*)$.

G_3: The same as G_2 except the generation of C^* in challenge ciphertext ct^* is different. We sample $C^* \leftarrow_\$ \mathcal{C}\backslash\mathcal{V}$ instead of $C^* \leftarrow_\$ \mathcal{V}$.

$G_{3'}$: The same as G_3 except that the private key $sk_f = (\widetilde{\mathcal{G}}, \{\mathsf{L}_{w,b}\}_{w \in \mathsf{inp}(\mathcal{G}), b \in \{0,1\}})$ is replaced with $sk_f = (\widetilde{\mathcal{G}}, \{\mathsf{L}_{w,(x_b)_w}\}_{w \in \mathsf{inp}(\mathcal{G})} \cup \{\mathsf{L}'_{w,\overline{(x_b)}_w}\}_{w \in \mathsf{inp}(\mathcal{G})})$, where $(\widetilde{\mathcal{G}'}, \{\mathsf{L}'_{w,\overline{(x_b)}_w}\}_{w \in \mathsf{inp}(\mathcal{G})}) \leftarrow \mathsf{Sim}(1^\lambda, |\mathcal{G}|, f(\overline{x_b}))$.

G_4: The same as $G_{3'}$ except that the private key $sk_f = (\widetilde{\mathcal{G}}, \{L_{w,(x_b)_w}\}_{w\in\mathsf{inp}(\mathcal{G})} \cup \{L'_{w,\overline{(x_b)}_w}\}_{w\in\mathsf{inp}(\mathcal{G})})$ is replaced with $sk_f = (\widetilde{\mathcal{G}''}, \{L''_{w,(x_b)_w}\}_{w\in\mathsf{inp}(\mathcal{G})} \cup \{L'_{w,\overline{(x_b)}_w}\}_{w\in\mathsf{inp}(\mathcal{G})})$, where $(\widetilde{\mathcal{G}''}, \{L''_{w,(x_b)_w}\}_{w\in\mathsf{inp}(\mathcal{G})}) \leftarrow \mathsf{Sim}(1^\lambda, |\mathcal{G}|, f(x_b))$.

G_5: The same as G_4 except that when the adversary delivers a decryption query (ct, g) such that $ct = (C, s, U, \pi, t_c)$ with $C \in \mathcal{C}\backslash\mathcal{V}$, the decryption oracle outputs $\perp$.

G_6: The same as G_5 except that U^* in challenge ciphertext ct^* is computed as $U^* = \mathsf{Ext}(K^*, s^*) \oplus 0^{|x_b|}$ instead of $U^* = \mathsf{Ext}(K^*, s^*) \oplus x_b$.

The detail proofs about the indistinguishabilities between any two adjacent games are shown in the full version of this paper[1].

5   Instantiations

Since in [30], the authors have given concrete constructions for HPS and LF from the DDH and DCR assumptions. By using these building blocks, our scheme can also be instantiated from these assumptions. For simplicity, we only give the DDH-based instantiation for our FE scheme, while for DCR-based instantiation, please refer to Sects. 4.1 and 4.2, Appendix C and D in [30].

5.1   DDH-Based Instantiation

In this section, we first review DDH-based (Decisional Diffie-Hellman) hash proof system (HPS) and DDH-based one-time lossy filter (LF) respectively from [30]. Then we apply these building blocks to our generic construction (see Sect. 4) to obtain an efficient LR-CCA secure FE. Finally, we show a comparison of our scheme with existing related schemes.

DDH [28]. The Decisional Diffie-Hellman (DDH) assumption over a goup G of prime order q states that for every PPT adversary $\mathcal{A}$, the following advantage function is negligible:

$$\mathsf{Adv}^{\mathsf{DDH}}_{G,\mathcal{A}}(\lambda) = \Pr[\mathcal{A}(g, g^x, g^y, g^{xy}) = 1] - \Pr[\mathcal{A}(g, g^x, g^y, g^z)],$$

where g is a uniform generator of G, and x, y, $z \leftarrow_\$ Z_q$ are uniform.

5.2   A DDH-Based HPS [30]

Let G be a cyclic group of prime order q and let g be a uniform generator of G. Select $n \in \mathbb{N}$. Let $\mathsf{Map} : G \to \mathbb{Z}_q$ be an efficient injective mapping function. For any $u = (u_1, \cdots, u_n) \in G^n$, define $\widetilde{\mathsf{Map}}(u) = (\mathsf{Map}(u_1), \cdots, \mathsf{Map}(u_n)) \in \mathbb{Z}_q^n$. Then, we instantiate a hash proof system $\mathsf{HPS} = (\mathsf{HPS.Gen}, \mathsf{HPS.Pub}, \mathsf{HPS.Priv})$ below.

The public parameter $pp = (\mathsf{Description}, \mathcal{PK}, \mathcal{SK}, \mathcal{K}, \mathcal{C}, \mathcal{V}, \Lambda_{(\cdot)} : \mathcal{C} \to \mathcal{K}, \mu : \mathcal{SK} \to \mathcal{PK})$ is defined as follows.

---
[1] Please contact the authors for it.

– Description = group = $<q, G, g_1, g_2, n>$, $\mathcal{C} = (G \times G)$, $\mathcal{V} = \{(g_1^r, g_2^r) : r \in \mathbb{Z}_q\}$.
– $\mathcal{K} = \mathbb{Z}_q^n$, $\mathcal{SK} = (\mathbb{Z}_q \times \mathbb{Z}_q)^n$, $\mathcal{PK} = G^n$.
– $sk = (x_{i,1}, x_{i,2})_{i \in [n]} \in \mathcal{SK}$, define $pk = (pk_i)_{i \in [n]} = \mu(sk) = (g_1^{x_{i,1}} g_2^{x_{i,2}})_{i \in [n]}$.
– For all $C = (u_1, u_2) \in \mathcal{C}$, define $\Lambda_{sk}(C) = \widetilde{\mathsf{Map}}((u_1^{x_{i,1}} u_2^{x_{i,2}})_{i \in [n]})$.

The public evaluation and private evaluation algorithms are defined as follows:

– For all $C = (g_1^r, g_2^r) \in \mathcal{V}$ with witness $r \in \mathbb{Z}_q$, define $\mathsf{HPS.Pub}(pk, C, r) = \widetilde{\mathsf{Map}}(pk_1^r, \cdots, pk_n^r)$.
– For all $C = (u_1, u_2) \in \mathcal{C}$, define $\mathsf{HPS.Priv}(sk, C) = \Lambda_{sk}(C)$.

The correctness of HPS follows the definition of μ and Λ_{sk}. The subset membership problem (SMP) holds under the DDH assumption.

Theorem 2. *Assume the DDH assumption holds, then* HPS *is perfectly universal hash proof system with encapsulated key size* $|\mathcal{K}| = q^n$.

The proof follows that of Theorem 2 in [30].

5.3   A DDH-Based OT-LF [30]

Let $A = (A_{i,j})$ be a $n \times n$ matrix over $Z_{\widetilde{q}}$ and $\widetilde{g}$ be a generator of $\widetilde{q}$-order group $\widetilde{G}$. Define $\widetilde{g}^A$ as matrix $(\widetilde{g}^{A_{i,j}})$ over $\widetilde{G}^{n \times n}$. For a vector $X = (X_1, \cdots, X_n) \in \mathbb{Z}_{\widetilde{n}}^n$ and a matrix $E = (E_{i,j}) \in \widetilde{G}^{n \times n}$, we define $X \cdot E = (\prod_{i=1}^n E_{i,1}^{X_i}, \cdots, \prod_{i=1}^n E_{i,n}^{X_i})$. Let $\mathsf{CH} = (\mathsf{CH.KG}, \mathsf{CH.Eval}, \mathsf{CH.Equiv})$ denote a chameleon hashing function with image set $Z_{\widetilde{q}}$. The one-time lossy filter is constructed as follows.

Key Generation. The algorithm $\mathsf{LF.KG}(1^\lambda)$ generates $(\widetilde{q}, \widetilde{G}, \widetilde{g})$. Sample a key pair $(ek_{\mathsf{CH}}, td_{\mathsf{CH}})$ for a chameleon hash function $\mathsf{CH} : \{0,1\}^* \to \{0,1\}^\lambda$. Pick a random pair $(t_a^*, t_c^*) \leftarrow \{0,1\}^* \times \mathcal{R}_{\mathsf{CH}}$ and computes $b^* = \mathsf{CH.Eval}(ek_{\mathsf{CH}}, t_a^*; t_c^*)$. Sample $r_1, \ldots, r_n, s_1, \ldots, s_n \leftarrow \mathbb{Z}_{\widetilde{q}}$, and generate a matrix $A = (A_{i,j}) \in \mathbb{Z}_{\widetilde{q}}^{n \times n}$ with $A_{i,j} = r_i s_j$ for $i, j \in [n]$. Compute matrix $E = \widetilde{g}^{A - b^* \mathbf{I}} \in \widetilde{G}^{n \times n}$, where $\mathbf{I}$ is the identity matrix over $\mathbb{Z}_{\widetilde{q}}^{n \times n}$. Output $lpk = (\widetilde{q}, \widetilde{G}, \widetilde{g}, ek_{\mathsf{CH}}, E)$ and $ltd = (td_{\mathsf{CH}}, t_a^*, t_c^*)$. The tag space is defined as $\mathcal{T} = \{0,1\}^* \times \mathcal{R}_{\mathsf{CH}}$, where $\mathcal{T}_{loss} = \{(t_a, t_c) : (t_a, t_c) \in \mathcal{T} \wedge \mathsf{CH.Eval}(ek_{\mathsf{CH}}, t_a; t_c) = b^*\}$ and $\mathcal{T}_{inj} = \{(t_a, t_c) : (t_a, t_c) \in \mathcal{T} \wedge \mathsf{CH.Eval}(ek_{\mathsf{CH}}, t_a; t_c) \notin \{b^*, b^* - \mathbf{Tr}(A)\}\}$.

Evaluation. For a tag $t = (t_a, t_c) \in \{0,1\}^* \times \mathcal{R}_{\mathsf{CH}}$ and an input $X = (X_1, \ldots, X_n) \in \mathbb{Z}_{\widetilde{q}}^n$, $\mathsf{LF.Eval}(lpk, t, X)$ first computes $b = \mathsf{CH.Eval}(ek_{\mathsf{CH}}, t_a; t_c)$ and outputs

$$y = X \cdot (E \otimes \widetilde{g}^{b\mathbf{I}}),$$

where "$\otimes$" denotes the operation of entry-wise multiplication.

Lossy Tag Generation. For an auxiliary tag t_a, $\mathsf{LF.LTag}(ltd, t_a)$ computes a core tag $t_c = \mathsf{CH.Equiv}(td_{\mathsf{CH}}, t_a^*, t_c^*, t_a)$ with the trapdoor $ltd = (td_{\mathsf{CH}}, t_a^*, t_c^*)$.

Theorem 3. *One-time lossy filter constructed above is* $(Z_{\widetilde{q}}^n, \log \widetilde{q})$-*OT-LF if the DDH assumption holds.*

The proof follows that of Theorem 3 in [30].

5.4   The Instantiation for FE from DDH Assumption

Let $\mathbb{G} = <q, G, g>$, $\widetilde{\mathbb{G}} = <\widetilde{q}, \widetilde{G}, \widetilde{g}>$, be two group descriptions. Suppose $n \in \mathbb{N}$ satisfies $n \log q \geq m + \log \widetilde{q} + l_L + \omega(\log \lambda)$. Set $\widetilde{n} = \lceil n \log q / \log \widetilde{q} \rceil$. Let $(ek_{\mathsf{CH}}, td_{\mathsf{CH}}) \leftarrow \mathsf{CH.KG}(1^\lambda)$ be a chameleon hash function with image set $\mathbb{Z}_{\widetilde{q}}$. Let $\mathsf{Ext} : \mathbb{Z}_q^n \times \{0,1\}^d \rightarrow \{0,1\}^m$ be an average-case $(n \log q - \log \widetilde{q} - l_L, \epsilon_2)$-strong extractor. Applying the DDH-based HPS and LF to the generic construction in Sect. 4, we obtain a FE from the DDH assumption. The concrete construction is as follows.

Setup. The setup algorithm $\mathsf{FE.Setup}(1^\lambda)$ first chooses g_1, g_2 $\leftarrow_\$ G$, $(x_{i,1}, x_{i,1}) \leftarrow_\$ \mathbb{Z}_q^2$ for $i \in [n]$, $\widetilde{g} \leftarrow_\$ \widetilde{G}$. Set $pk_i = g_1^{x_{i.1}} g_2^{x_{i.2}}$ and $sk_i = (x_{i,1}, x_{i,1})$ for $i \in [n]$. Run $(ek_{\mathsf{CH}}, td_{\mathsf{CH}}) \leftarrow \mathsf{CH.KG}(1^\lambda)$. Choose $(t_a^*, t_c^*) \leftarrow \{0,1\}^* \times \mathcal{R}_{\mathsf{CH}}$ and computes $b^* = \mathsf{CH.Eval}(ek_{\mathsf{CH}}, t_a^*; t_c^*)$. Sample $r_1, \ldots, r_n, s_1, \ldots, s_n \leftarrow \mathbb{Z}_{\widetilde{q}}$, and compute $E = (E_{i,j})_{i,j\in[n]} \in \widetilde{G}^{n \times n}$ where $E_{i,j} = \widetilde{g}^{r_i, s_j}$ for $i, j \in [n]$ and $i \neq j$; $E_{i,i} = \widetilde{g}^{r_i, s_i} \widetilde{g}^{-b^*}$ for $i \in [n]$.
Set $pp = (\mathsf{group}, \mathcal{PK} = G^n, \mathcal{SK} = (\mathbb{Z}_q \times \mathbb{Z}_q)^n, \mathcal{K} = \mathbb{Z}_q^n, \mathcal{C} = (G \times G), \mathcal{V} = \{(g_1^r, g_2^r) : r \leftarrow_\$ \mathbb{Z}_q\}, \Lambda_{sk}, \mu)$, where $\mathsf{group} = <q, G, g_1, g_2, n>$.
Return $mpk = (pp, \widetilde{G}, \widetilde{q}, \widetilde{g}, \widetilde{n}, E, ek_{\mathsf{CH}}, (pk_i)_{i\in[n]})$ and $msk = (sk_i)_{i\in[n]}$.

Encryption. The algorithm $\mathsf{FE.E}(mpk, x)$ takes as input the master public key mpk and a message $x \in \{0,1\}^m$. It chooses $s \leftarrow_\$ \{0,1\}^d$, $t_c \leftarrow_\$ \mathcal{R}_{\mathsf{CH}}$, and $r \leftarrow_\$ \mathbb{Z}_q$, where $\mathcal{R}_{\mathsf{CH}}$ is the randomness space of the chameleon hash function CH. Then it computes

$$C = (g_1^r, g_2^r), \quad K = \widetilde{\mathsf{Map}}(pk_1^r, \cdots, pk_n^r) \in \mathbb{Z}_q^n, \quad U = \mathsf{Ext}(K, s) \oplus x, \quad (2)$$

$$\pi = K.(E \otimes \widetilde{g}^{b\mathbf{I}}) \quad (3)$$

where $b = \mathsf{CH.Eval}(ek_{\mathsf{CH}}, t_a; t_c)$, $t_a = (C, s, U)$. Note that in the computation of π, K is treated as a vector of dimension $\widetilde{n}$ over $\mathbb{Z}_{\widetilde{q}}$ (this is reasonable since we assume that $n \log q \leq \widetilde{n} \log \widetilde{q}$). Return $ct = (C, s, U, \pi, t_c) \in G^2 \times \{0,1\}^d \times \{0,1\}^m \times \widetilde{G}^{\widetilde{n}} \times \mathcal{R}_{\mathsf{CH}}$.

Key Generation. The algorithm $\mathsf{FE.KG}(msk, f)$ takes as input the master secret key msk and a function f. First it construct a circuit $\mathcal{G}[mpk, msk, f](\cdot)$ (see Fig. 2) with mpk, msk and f hardwired in and then computes $(\widetilde{\mathcal{G}}, \{L_{w,b}\}_{w\in\mathsf{inp}(\mathcal{G}), b\in\{0,1\}}) \leftarrow \mathsf{GC.Grl}(1^\lambda, \mathcal{G}[mpk, msk, f])$. Finally, it sets the private key $sk_f = (\widetilde{\mathcal{G}}, \{L_{w,b}\}_{w\in\mathsf{inp}(\mathcal{G}), b\in\{0,1\}})$ and outputs sk_f.

Decryption. The algorithm $\mathsf{FE.D}(sk_f, ct)$ takes as input a private key sk_f and a ciphertext ct. It computes $y = \mathsf{GC.Eval}(\widetilde{\mathcal{G}}, \{L_{w,ct_w}\}_{w\in\mathsf{inp}(\mathcal{G})})$ and outputs $y = f(x)$.

Note that, substituting the master public key $mpk = (pp, \widetilde{G}, \widetilde{q}, \widetilde{g}, \widetilde{n}, E, ek_{\mathsf{CH}}, (pk_i)_{i\in[n]})$, the master secret key $msk = (sk_i)_{i\in[n]}$ and the ciphertext $ct = (C, s, U, \pi, t_c)$ (which encrypts the message $x \in \{0,1\}^m$) into the circuit $\mathcal{G}$ (see Fig. 2), it indeed yields $y = f(x)$. Hence the correctness is guaranteed.

Theorem 4. *Assume the DDH assumption holds in both groups G and $\widetilde{G}$, CH is a chameleon hash function (see [30]), GC is a secure circuit garbling scheme, Ext is an average-case $(n \log q - \log \widetilde{q} - l_L, \epsilon_2)$-strong extractor, then the scheme FE constructed in Sect. 5.4 is l_L-LR-CCA secure if $l_L \leq n \log q - \log \widetilde{q} - m - \omega(\log \lambda)$ (i.e., $n \geq (l_L + \log \widetilde{q} + m + \omega(\log \lambda))/\log q$). In particular, the leakage rate in FE is the same as that in [30], i.e., $1/2 - o(1)$, and there exists PPT adversaries $\mathcal{A}_{ddh}$, $\mathcal{A}_{grl}$, $\mathcal{A}_{cr}$, and a PPT simulator Sim such that*

$$\mathsf{Adv}^{\mathsf{IND\text{-}LR\text{-}CCA}}_{\mathsf{FE},l_L,\mathcal{F},\mathcal{A}}(\lambda) \leq \mathsf{Adv}^{\mathsf{DDH}}_{G,\mathcal{A}_{ddh}}(\lambda) + 2\mathsf{Adv}^{\mathsf{gc}}_{\mathsf{GC},\mathsf{Sim},\mathcal{A}_{grl}}(\lambda)$$

$$+ q_d((2n+1)\mathsf{Adv}^{\mathsf{DDH}}_{\widetilde{G},\mathcal{A}_{ddh}}(\lambda) + \mathsf{Adv}^{\mathsf{cr}}_{\mathsf{CH},\mathcal{A}_{cr}}(\lambda))$$

$$+ q_d \cdot \widetilde{q} \cdot 2^{l_L + m}/(q^n - q_d) + 2\epsilon_2 \tag{4}$$

Proof. The Theorem can be proved directly by combining Theorems 2 and 3 in [30] and Theorem 1 in this paper.

Remark 2. *Note that if the parameters $\widetilde{q}$ and m are fixed, and n is increasing, then we have the same leakage rate as that of PKE in [30], i.e., $l_L/|sk_f| = (n \log q - \log \widetilde{q} - m - \omega(\lambda))/2n \log q = 1/2 - o(1)$, where $2n \log q$ is in fact the bit-length of the master secret key, i.e., $msk = sk = (x_{i,1}, x_{i,2})_{i \in [n]}$ which is implied in the private key sk_f.*

6   Efficiency Analysis

In this section, we give the performance analysis and comparison between our FE scheme and other related schemes, e.g., leakage-resilient (LR) attribute-based encryptions (ABE) [1,36] and leakage-resilient (LR) identity-based encryption (IBE) [1,16] in terms of private-key size, ciphertext size, leakage bound (see Table 1), leakage rate (denoted as δ), achievability of CCA security and realizability of general functionalities (see Table 2). Note that the LR secure ABEs (both ciphertext-policy ABE (CP-ABE) and key-policy ABE (KP-ABE)) in [36] are obtained by using a customized encoding mechanism. Zhang et al. [36] claim that their both schemes provide the tolerance of master secret key leakage and continual leakage and obtain short ciphertext in CP-ABE and short key in KP-ABE with the same leakage rate $1 - o(1)$. In fact, the desired leakage rates $1 - o(1)$, short ciphertext and short key in CP-ABE and KP-ABE directly arise from the variability of the parameter $\overline{n}$ (mainly decided by leakage bound l_L) in leakage rate equations $(\overline{n} - 1 - 2\tau)/(1 + \beta_1 + \beta_3)(\overline{n} + 2 + |\mathbb{S}|)$ and $(\overline{n} - 1 - 2\tau)/(1 + \beta_1 + \beta_3)(\overline{n} + 2\overline{m} + 1)$ (denoted via the leakage amount/the private key directly). So, for fixed $|\mathbb{S}|$, β_1, β_3 and smaller constants τ and $\overline{m}$, the two equations can be written as $1 - o(1)$. From Tables 1 and 2, we can see that the ABE and IBE in [1] have almost the same security level and properties as that of ABEs in [36]. For three IBEs in [16], their leakage rates only achieve $1/3 - o(1)$ and $1/9 - o(1)$ respectively, but all obtain about three group elements of ciphertext size and key size.

Table 1. Comparison in private-key size, ciphertext size and leakage bound.

Schemes	# of SK (# group)	# of CT (# group)	Leakage bound l_L (# bits)
CP-ABE [1]	$(\overline{n} + |\mathbb{S}| + 2)|\overline{G}|$	$(\overline{n} + 2n_1 + 1)|\overline{G}| + |\overline{G}_T|$	$2 + (\overline{n} - 1 - 2\tau)\log \overline{q}_2$
CP-ABE [36]	$(\overline{n} + |\mathbb{S}| + 2)|\overline{G}|$	$(\overline{n} + 2\overline{m} + 1)|\overline{G}| + |\overline{G}_T|$	$2 + (\overline{n} - 1 - 2\tau)\log \overline{q}_2$
KP-ABE [36]	$(\overline{n} + 2\overline{m} + 1)|\overline{G}|$	$(\overline{n} + |\mathbb{S}| + 2)|\overline{G}| + |\overline{G}_T|$	$2 + (\overline{n} - 1 - 2\tau)\log \overline{q}_2$
IBE [1]	$(\overline{n} + 2)|\overline{G}|$	$(\overline{n} + 2)|\overline{G}| + |\overline{G}_T|$	$2 + (\overline{n} - 1 - 2\tau)\log \overline{q}_2$
IBE(1) [16]	$3|\widetilde{G}|$	$|\widetilde{G}_T| + 2|\widetilde{G}| + o(1)$	$\log \widetilde{q}$
IBE(2) [16]	$3|\widetilde{G}|$	$|\widetilde{G}_T| + 2|\widetilde{G}| + o(1)$	$\log \widetilde{q}$
IBE(3) [16]	$3|\overline{G}|$	$|\overline{G}_T| + 2|\overline{G}| + o(1)$	$\log \overline{q}_1$
Our scheme	$2n|G|$	$(\widetilde{n} + 2)\widetilde{G}$	$n.\log q - \log \widetilde{q} - m - \omega(\log \lambda)$

Notations in Tables 1 and 2. $\overline{n}$, n, $\widetilde{n}$: leakage parameter; τ: allowable leakage probability parameter; δ: leakage rate, i.e., $\delta = l_L/|SK|$; $|G|$: size of an element in G of prime order q; $|\widetilde{G}|$: size of an element in $\widetilde{G}$ of prime order $\widetilde{q}$; $|\overline{G}|$: size of an element in $\overline{G}$ of prime order $\overline{q}$; $|\overline{G}_T|$: size of an element in $\overline{G}_T$ of prime order $\overline{q}$; $|\widetilde{G}_T|$: size of an element in $\widetilde{G}_T$ of prime order $\widetilde{q}$; $3|\overline{G}_{T_{\overline{q}_1}}|$: size of an element in $\overline{G}_{T_{\overline{q}_1}}$ of prime order $\overline{q}_1$; $\overline{q}_1$, $\overline{q}_2$, $\overline{q}_3$: prime order of $\overline{G}_{\overline{q}_1}$, $\overline{G}_{\overline{q}_2}$ and $\overline{G}_{\overline{q}_3}$; $\mathbb{S}$: attribute set; n_1: number of rows in LSSS matrix; m: the message length; $\overline{m}$: the number of set in minimal set method; β_1, β_3: value of $|\overline{G}_{\overline{q}_1}|/|\overline{G}|$ and $|\overline{G}_{\overline{q}_3}|/|\overline{G}|$.

Although these schemes in [1,16,36] achieve desired leakage or short ciphertext size and key size, all access structures are customized, e.g., in ABE schemes [1,36], access structures depend on specific encoding mechanism; while in IBEs [1,16], they are only identity function. In our work, we use generic functions to construct our scheme so that it can support a variety of access structures. Besides, the schemes in [1,16,36] only achieve LR-CPA security. As far as we know, realizing CCA security under standard model in IBE and ABE, especially for the security with leakage-resilience, is not easy. By using the technique of LF, our scheme does so. Furthermore, as our scheme is general, it can be also instantiated from other standard assumptions such as DCR by using the DCR-based HPS and OT-LF from [30]. Like analysis in [30], in a private key and ciphertext, we only consider the length of group elements, regardless of other non-group elements. We also assume that elements in Δ-order group can be encoded as bit strings of length $\log \Delta$. To reflect our goals clearly, we only focus on some core items such as leakage rate, achievability of CCA, etc., ignoring other ones e.g., the decryption cost. We begin by giving a comparison in the private key size, the ciphertext size and the leakage bound among the ABEs and IBEs in [1,16,36] and our scheme in Table 1. Then we give another comparison in the leakage rate, the achievability of CCA security and the realizability of general functionalities in Table 2. In addition, we also assume that the parameters $\overline{n}$, n and $\widetilde{n}$ and the prime orders $\overline{q}$, q, $\widetilde{q}$, etc. in these schemes have the same magnitude in bit length in the security parameter λ.

Table 2. Comparison in leakage rate, CCA and general functionalities.

Schemes	Leakage rate δ	CCA	General functionalities
CP-ABE [1]	$(\overline{n} - 1 - 2\tau)/(1 + \beta_1 + \beta_3)(\overline{n} + 2 + |\mathbb{S}|) = 1 - o(1)$	$\times$	$\times$
CP-ABE [36]	$(\overline{n} - 1 - 2\tau)/(1 + \beta_1 + \beta_3)(\overline{n} + 2 + |\mathbb{S}|) = 1 - o(1)$	$\times$	$\times$
KP-ABE [36]	$(\overline{n} - 1 - 2\tau)/(1 + \beta_1 + \beta_3)(\overline{n} + 2\overline{m} + 1) = 1 - o(1)$	$\times$	$\times$
IBE [1]	$(\overline{n} - 1 - 2\tau)/(1 + \beta_1 + \beta_3)(\overline{n} + 2) = 1 - o(1)$	$\times$	$\times$
IBE(1) [16]	$\log \widetilde{q}/(3\log \widetilde{q} + o(1)) = 1/3 - o(1)$	$\times$	$\times$
IBE(2) [16]	$\log \widetilde{q}/(3\log \widetilde{q} + o(1)) = 1/3 - o(1)$	$\times$	$\times$
IBE(3) [16]	$\log \overline{q}_1/3(\log \overline{q}_1 + \log \overline{q}_2 + \log \overline{q}_3 + o(1)) = 1/9 - o(1)$	$\checkmark$	$\times$
Our scheme	$(n.\log q - \log \widetilde{q} - m - \omega(\log \lambda))/2n\log q = 1/2 - o(1)$	$\checkmark$	$\checkmark$

7 Conclusions and Future Works

We propose a new generic construction of public-key functional encryption secure against leakage-resilient chosen-ciphertext attacks, from any ϵ-universal hash proof system, one-time lossy filter and garbled circuits. We explicitly employ garbled circuits to construct the scheme so that it can tolerate the master secret key-leakage from the private key. In our work, we use a universal function rather than a customized access structure to construct the private key which can support a variety of access structures. In addition, our results can be extended to the security of the master secret key leakage-resilient. Finally, the instantiation from DDH assumptions shows that our scheme is practical and achieves leakage rate $1/2 - o(1)$. Furthermore, our scheme can also be instantiated under the DCR assumption by using existing DCR-based HPS and OT-LF constructions. Our next work is to construct adaptive LR-CCA secure multi-key and multi-ciphertext FE.

Acknowledgements. The first author is supported by the National Natural Science Foundation of China (Grant Nos. NSFC61702007, NSFC61572318) and the National Key Research and Development Program of China (Grant No. 2017YFB0802000) and Other Foundations (Grant Nos. KJ2018A0533, ahnis20178002, KJ2017A519, 16ZB0140, LD14127X, ZRC2013380). The second author is supported by the National Key Research and Development Program of China (Grant No. 2017YFB0802000) and the National Natural Science Foundation of China (Grant Nos. NSFCU1705264, NSFC61133014, NSFC61472114).

References

1. Lewko, A., Rouselakis, Y., Waters, B.: Achieving leakage resilience through dual system encryption. In: Ishai, Y. (ed.) TCC 2011. LNCS, vol. 6597, pp. 70–88. Springer, Heidelberg (2011). https://doi.org/10.1007/978-3-642-19571-6_6
2. Agrawal, S., Agrawal, S., Badrinarayanan, S., Kumarasubramanian, A., Prabhakaran, M., Sahai, A.: On the practical security of inner product functional encryption. In: Katz, J. (ed.) PKC 2015. LNCS, vol. 9020, pp. 777–798. Springer, Heidelberg (2015). https://doi.org/10.1007/978-3-662-46447-2_35
3. Agrawal, S., Agrawal, S., Prabhakaran, M.: Cryptographic agents: towards a unified theory of computing on encrypted data. In: Oswald, E., Fischlin, M. (eds.) EUROCRYPT 2015. LNCS, vol. 9057, pp. 501–531. Springer, Heidelberg (2015). https://doi.org/10.1007/978-3-662-46803-6_17
4. Akavia, A., Goldwasser, S., Vaikuntanathan, V.: Simultaneous hardcore bits and cryptography against memory attacks. In: Reingold, O. (ed.) TCC 2009. LNCS, vol. 5444, pp. 474–495. Springer, Heidelberg (2009). https://doi.org/10.1007/978-3-642-00457-5_28
5. Alwen, J., et al.: On the relationship between functional encryption, obfuscation, and fully homomorphic encryption. In: IMA International Conference on Cryptography and Coding, pp. 65–84 (2013)
6. Alwen, J., Dodis, Y., Naor, M., Segev, G., Walfish, S., Wichs, D.: Public-key encryption in the bounded-retrieval model. In: Gilbert, H. (ed.) EUROCRYPT 2010. LNCS, vol. 6110, pp. 113–134. Springer, Heidelberg (2010). https://doi.org/10.1007/978-3-642-13190-5_6
7. Ananth, P., Brakerski, Z., Segev, G., Vaikuntanathan, V.: From selective to adaptive security in functional encryption. In: Gennaro, R., Robshaw, M. (eds.) CRYPTO 2015. LNCS, vol. 9216, pp. 657–677. Springer, Heidelberg (2015). https://doi.org/10.1007/978-3-662-48000-7_32
8. Ananth, P., Sahai, A.: Functional encryption for turing machines. In: Cryptology ePrint Archive, Report 2015/776 (2015). http://eprint.iacr.org/2015/776
9. Barbosa, M., Farshim, P.: On the semantic security of functional encryption schemes. In: Kurosawa, K., Hanaoka, G. (eds.) PKC 2013. LNCS, vol. 7778, pp. 143–161. Springer, Heidelberg (2013). https://doi.org/10.1007/978-3-642-36362-7_10
10. Bellare, M., O'Neill, A.: Semantically-secure functional encryption: possibility results, impossibility results and the quest for a general definition. In: Abdalla, M., Nita-Rotaru, C., Dahab, R. (eds.) CANS 2013. LNCS, vol. 8257, pp. 218–234. Springer, Cham (2013). https://doi.org/10.1007/978-3-319-02937-5_12
11. Bellare, M., Rogaway, P.: The security of triple encryption and a framework for code-based game-playing proofs. In: Vaudenay, S. (ed.) EUROCRYPT 2006. LNCS, vol. 4004, pp. 409–426. Springer, Heidelberg (2006). https://doi.org/10.1007/11761679_25
12. Boneh, D., Gentry, C., Hamburg, M.: Space-efficient identity based encryption without pairings. In: FOCS 2007, pp. 647–657 (2007)
13. Boneh, D., Sahai, A., Waters, B.: Functional encryption: definitions and challenges. In: Ishai, Y. (ed.) TCC 2011. LNCS, vol. 6597, pp. 253–273. Springer, Heidelberg (2011). https://doi.org/10.1007/978-3-642-19571-6_16
14. Boneh, D., Waters, B.: Conjunctive, subset, and range queries on encrypted data. In: Vadhan, S.P. (ed.) TCC 2007. LNCS, vol. 4392, pp. 535–554. Springer, Heidelberg (2007). https://doi.org/10.1007/978-3-540-70936-7_29

15. De Caro, A.D., Iovino, V., Jain, A., O'Neill, A., Paneth, O., Persiano, G.: On the achievability of simulation-based security for functional encryption. In: Canetti, R., Garay, J.A. (eds.) CRYPTO 2013. LNCS, vol. 8043, pp. 519–535. Springer, Heidelberg (2013). https://doi.org/10.1007/978-3-642-40084-1_29

16. Chow, S.S.M., Dodis, Y., Rouselakis, Y., Waters, B.: Practical leakage-resilient identity-based encryption from simple assumptions. In: Proceedings of the 17th ACM Conference on Computer and Communications Security, CCS 2010, pp. 152–161 (2010)

17. Cramer, R., Shoup, V.: Universal hash proofs and a paradigm for adaptive chosen ciphertext secure public-key encryption. In: Knudsen, L.R. (ed.) EUROCRYPT 2002. LNCS, vol. 2332, pp. 45–64. Springer, Heidelberg (2002). https://doi.org/10.1007/3-540-46035-7_4

18. Dodis, Y., Reyzin, L., Smith, A.: Fuzzy extractors: how to generate strong keys from biometrics and other noisy data. In: Cachin, C., Camenisch, J.L. (eds.) EUROCRYPT 2004. LNCS, vol. 3027, pp. 523–540. Springer, Heidelberg (2004). https://doi.org/10.1007/978-3-540-24676-3_31

19. Faonio, A., Venturi, D.: Efficient public-key cryptography with bounded leakage and tamper resilience. In: Cheon, J.H., Takagi, T. (eds.) ASIACRYPT 2016. LNCS, vol. 10031, pp. 877–907. Springer, Heidelberg (2016). https://doi.org/10.1007/978-3-662-53887-6_32

20. Garg, S., Gentry, C., Halevi, S., Raykova, M., Sahai, A., Waters, B.: Candidate indistinguishability obfuscation and functional encryption for all circuits. In: Advance in FOCS 2013, pp. 40–49. IEEE (2013)

21. Gentry, C.: Practical identity-based encryption without random oracles. In: Vaudenay, S. (ed.) EUROCRYPT 2006. LNCS, vol. 4004, pp. 445–464. Springer, Heidelberg (2006). https://doi.org/10.1007/11761679_27

22. Gentry, C., Peikert, C., Vaikuntanathan, V.: Trapdoors for hard lattices and new cryptographic constructions. In: STOC 2008, pp. 197–206 (2008)

23. Goldwasser, S., Kalai, Y., Popa, R.A., Vaikuntanathan, V., Zeldovich, N.: Reusable garbled circuits and succinct functional encryption. In: STOC 2013, pp. 555–564 (2013)

24. Gorbunov, S., Vaikuntanathan, V., Wee, H.: Attribute-based encryption for circuits. In: Advance in STOC 2013, pp. 545–554 (2013)

25. Goyal, V., Jain, A., Koppula, V., Sahai, A.: Functional encryption for randomized functionalities. In: Dodis, Y., Nielsen, J.B. (eds.) TCC 2015. LNCS, vol. 9015, pp. 325–351. Springer, Heidelberg (2015). https://doi.org/10.1007/978-3-662-46497-7_13

26. Goyal, V., Pandey, O., Sahai, A., Waters, B.: Attribute-based encryption for fine-grained access control of encrypted data. In: Advance in ACM CCS 2006, pp. 89–98 (2006)

27. Halderman, J.A., et al.: Lest we remember: cold boot attacks on encryption keys. In: van Oorschot, P.C. (ed.) USENIX Security Symposium, pp. 45–60. USENIX Association (2008)

28. Hofheinz, D.: Circular chosen-ciphertext security with compact ciphertexts. In: Johansson, T., Nguyen, P.Q. (eds.) EUROCRYPT 2013. LNCS, vol. 7881, pp. 520–536. Springer, Heidelberg (2013). https://doi.org/10.1007/978-3-642-38348-9_31

29. Katz, J., Sahai, A., Waters, B.: Predicate encryption supporting disjunctions, polynomial equations, and inner products. In: Smart, N. (ed.) EUROCRYPT 2008. LNCS, vol. 4965, pp. 146–162. Springer, Heidelberg (2008). https://doi.org/10.1007/978-3-540-78967-3_9

30. Qin, B., Liu, S.: Leakage-resilient chosen-ciphertext secure public-key encryption from hash proof system and one-time lossy filter. In: Sako, K., Sarkar, P. (eds.) ASIACRYPT 2013. LNCS, vol. 8270, pp. 381–400. Springer, Heidelberg (2013). https://doi.org/10.1007/978-3-642-42045-0_20

31. Qin, B., Liu, S.: Leakage-flexible CCA-secure public-key encryption: simple construction and free of pairing. In: Krawczyk, H. (ed.) PKC 2014. LNCS, vol. 8383, pp. 19–36. Springer, Heidelberg (2014). https://doi.org/10.1007/978-3-642-54631-0_2

32. Sahai, A., Waters, B.: Fuzzy identity-based encryption. In: Cramer, R. (ed.) EUROCRYPT 2005. LNCS, vol. 3494, pp. 457–473. Springer, Heidelberg (2005). https://doi.org/10.1007/11426639_27

33. Ristenpart, T., Shacham, H., Shrimpton, T.: Careful with composition: limitations of the indifferentiability framework. In: Paterson, K.G. (ed.) EUROCRYPT 2011. LNCS, vol. 6632, pp. 487–506. Springer, Heidelberg (2011). https://doi.org/10.1007/978-3-642-20465-4_27

34. Waters, B.: A punctured programming approach to adaptively secure functional encryption. In: Gennaro, R., Robshaw, M. (eds.) CRYPTO 2015. LNCS, vol. 9216, pp. 678–697. Springer, Heidelberg (2015). https://doi.org/10.1007/978-3-662-48000-7_33

35. Yao, A.C.: Protocols for secure computations. In: 23rd FOCS, pp. 160–164. IEEE Computer Society Press (1982)

36. Zhang, M., Shi, W., Wang, C., Chen, Z., Mu, Y.: Leakage-resilient attribute-based encryption with fast decryption: models, analysis and constructions. In: Deng, R.H., Feng, T. (eds.) ISPEC 2013. LNCS, vol. 7863, pp. 75–90. Springer, Heidelberg (2013). https://doi.org/10.1007/978-3-642-38033-4_6

Constrained (Verifiable) Pseudorandom Function from Functional Encryption

Pratish Datta[✉]

NTT Secure Platform Laboratories, 3-9-11 Midori-cho, Musashino-shi,
Tokyo 180-8585, Japan
pratish.datta.yg@hco.ntt.co.jp

Abstract. This paper presents a *constrained pseudorandom function* (CPRF) supporting constraints realizable by *polynomial-size circuits*, assuming the existence of (public key) *functional encryption* (FE) with standard *polynomial security* against arbitrary collusions. We further augment our CPRF construction with the *verifiability* feature under the same assumption. Earlier such constructions either work for very restricted settings or rely on highly powerful yet little-understood cryptographic objects such as multilinear maps or indistinguishability obfuscation (IO). Although, there are known transformations from FE to IO, the reductions suffer from an exponential security loss and hence cannot be directly employed to replace IO with FE in cryptographic constructions at the expense of only a polynomial loss. Thus, our results open up a new pathway towards realizing CPRF and its numerous extensions, which are interesting cryptographic primitives in their own right and, moreover, have already been shown instrumental in a staggering range of applications, both in classical as well as in cutting edge cryptography, based on progressively *weaker* and *well-studied* cryptographic building blocks. Besides, our work can also be interpreted as yet another stepping stone towards establishing FE as a substitute for IO in cryptographic applications, which is an active research direction of recent times. In order to achieve our results we build upon the *prefix puncturing* technique developed by Garg et al. [CRYPTO 2016, EUROCRYPT 2017].

Keywords: Constrained pseudorandom function
Constrained verifiable pseudorandom function · Functional encryption
Polynomial hardness

1 Introduction

Constrained pseudorandom functions (CPRF), concurrently introduced by Boneh and Waters [10], Boyle et al. [11], as well as Kiayias et al. [30], are promising extension of the notion of standard *pseudorandom functions* (PRF) [25] – a fundamental primitive in modern cryptography. A standard PRF is a deterministic keyed function with the following property: Given a key, the function can be computed in polynomial time at all points of its input domain. But, without the

© Springer Nature Switzerland AG 2018
C. Su and H. Kikuchi (Eds.): ISPEC 2018, LNCS 11125, pp. 141–159, 2018.
https://doi.org/10.1007/978-3-319-99807-7_9

key it is computationally hard to distinguish the PRF output at any arbitrary input from a uniformly random value, even after seeing the PRF evaluations on a polynomial number of inputs. A CPRF is an augmentation of a PRF with an additional *constrain algorithm* which enables a party holding a PRF key, also referred to as a master PRF key in this context, to derive constrained keys that allow the evaluation of the PRF over certain subsets of the input domain characterized by specific constraint predicates. However, given a set of constrained keys, the PRF evaluations still remain indistinguishable from random on all the inputs not covered by those constraint predicates.

Since their inception, CPRF's have found countless interesting applications in various branches of cryptography ranging from various sophisticated forms of encryption such as broadcast encryption, searchable encryption, and attribute-based encryption to policy-based key distribution as well as multi-party (identity-based) non-interactive key exchange. Even the simplest class of CPRF's, namely, the *puncturable pseudorandom functions* (PPRF) [10,33] have turned out to be a powerful tool in conjunction with indistinguishability obfuscation (IO) [21]. In fact, the combination of these two primitives have led to solutions of longstanding open problems including deniable encryption, full domain hash, universal samplers, adaptively secure functional encryption for general functionalities, and functional encryption for randomized functionalities through the classic punctured programming technique introduced By Sahai and Waters [33].

In view of its countless applications, over the last few years there has been a significant progress in the field of CPRF's. In terms of expressiveness of the constraint predicates, starting with very simple type of constraints such as prefix constraints [10,11,30] (which also encompass puncturing constraints) and bit fixing constraints [10,19], CPRF's have been constructed for highly rich constraint families such as circuit constraints [5,10,12,28] and even Turing machine constraints [1,2,16,17]. In terms of security, most of the existing CPRF constructions are only *selectively* secure. Selective security is a security notion for CPRF's where the adversary is bound to declare the challenge input, on which it wishes to distinguish the PRF output from random, before querying any constrained key or PRF value. The stronger and more realistic notion of *adaptive* security, which allows the adversary to specify the challenge input at any point in time during the security experiment, seems to be rather challenging to achieve without complexity leveraging. In fact, the best known results so far on adaptive security of CPRF's require super-polynomial security loss [19], or work for very restricted form of constraints such as the puncturing constraints [29], or attain the security in non-collusion mode [12], or accomplish security in the random oracle model [28]. Very recently, some progress has also been achieved towards providing security also for the constraints embedded within the constrained keys [7,13].

An interesting enhancement of the usual notion of CPRF is *verifiability*. A *verifiable constrained pseudorandom function* (CVPRF), independently introduced by Fuchsbauer [18] and Chandran et al. [14], is the unification of the notions of a *verifiable random function* (VRF) [31] and a standard CPRF. In a CVPRF system, just like a traditional VRF, a public verification key is set along with the master PRF key. Besides enabling the evaluation of the PRF, the master PRF key can be utilized to generate a non-interactive proof of the correctness of evaluation. This proof can be verified by any party using only the public verification key. On the other hand, as in the case of a CPRF, here also the master PRF key holder can give out constrained keys for specific constraint predicates. A constrained key corresponding to some constraint predicate allows the evaluation of the PRF together with the generation of a non-interactive proof of correct evaluation for only those inputs which are accepted by the associated constraint. In essence, CVPRF's resolve the issue of trust on a CPRF evaluator for the correctness of the received PRF output. CVPRF's have also been constructed for a wide variety of constraint families such as bit-fixing constraints [14,18], general circuits [14,18] and Turing machines [16].

While the current state-of-the-art CPRF and CVPRF constructions have been able to realize highly expressive families of constraints, the expressiveness has often been accomplished through the use of highly powerful yet poorly understood cryptographic primitives such as multilinear maps [15,20] or IO. Further, the known constructions of constraint-private CPRF for expressive constraint families either rely on IO [7] or work only in the non-collusion setting [13].

Unfortunately, all the existing multilinear map candidates have been subject to serious cryptanalytic attacks. On the other hand, majority of the currently available IO candidates also rely on multilinear maps and security flaws have recently been discovered in some of these constructions as well. This state of affairs has significantly reduced the confidence of the cryptographic community on multilinear maps and IO. Besides, there is another serious limitation that seems inherent to any IO construction is an exponential loss in the security reduction to the underlying computational assumption. Indeed, any reduction from IO to an underlying assumption would need to work for equivalent programs but should fail for inequivalent programs since IO only guarantees indistinguishability for equivalent programs. Thus, any reduction would seemingly need to decide whether two candidate programs actually compute equivalent functions. Assuming $P \neq NP$, this in general cannot be done in polynomial time. This exponential loss then carries over to any application of IO, even if the IO-to-application security reduction only incurs a polynomial loss. However, such an exponential loss may not be inherent to the application itself, as is the case for the specific problem of constructing CPRF or its variants with only selective security.

In view of the above, a recent research direction is to design cryptographic primitives, for which only multilinear-map or IO-based constructions were known so far, from relatively weaker and well-studied cryptographic tools. As a first attempt, researchers have considered (public key) *functional encryption* (FE). FE [9] supports "restricted" decryption keys, also known as "functional keys", which enable decrypters to learn specific functions of the encrypted data and nothing else. More precisely, in an FE scheme for certain function family $\mathbb{F}_{FE}$, it is possible to derive functional keys $SK_{FE}(\mathscr{F})$ for any function $\mathscr{F} \in \mathbb{F}_{FE}$ from a master secret key. Any party given such a functional key $\text{SK}_{\text{FE}}(\mathscr{F})$ and a ciphertext CT_{FE} encrypting some message μ under the corresponding master public key, should be able to learn $\mathscr{F}(\mu)$ and nothing beyond that about μ. FE, on the face of it, seems much less powerful compared to IO. In fact, unlike IO, polynomially-hard (public key) FE is already known to be a *polynomially falsifiable assumption* [32]. Moreover, in the past few years FE schemes supporting highly expressive function families as well as with different efficiency and security features were constructed from various computational assumptions [21, 26, 27, 34].

The confidence on using FE as a substitute for IO or multilinear maps in advanced applications is actually the outcome of a series of recent surprising results [3, 4, 6] which have demonstrated that selectively secure *weakly compact* FE, where the encryption time is polynomial in the message size and sublinear in the size of the functions for which functional keys are provided, is actually powerful enough to imply IO. However, the techniques presented in all of those FE-to-IO reductions also incur an exponential loss and hence cannot be directly employed to replace IO with FE in cryptographic applications if only a polynomial security loss is desired. Recently, Garg et al. [22] have developed new techniques to employ polynomially-hard weakly compact (public key) FE directly to resolve problems for which only IO-based solutions were known so far. Precisely, Garg et al. [22] have shown that PPAD-hardness can be based on polynomially-hard weakly compact public key FE. In a subsequent work, Garg et al. [23] have employed the technique of [22] to construct trapdoor permutations and universal samplers from weakly compact (public key) FE with polynomial loss. Weakly compact (public key) FE, as demonstrated by Bitansky and Vaikuntanathan [6] and Ananth et al. [4], can in turn be generically constructed from the standard collusion resistant FE [9] with *collusion-succinct ciphertexts*, i.e., where the encryption time is polynomial in the message and function sizes but sublinear in the number of functional keys issued. This latter form of FE has been designed from progressively simpler complexity assumptions with only a polynomial loss in a series of recent works.

Our Contributions: In this paper, we make further progress towards substituting IO or multilinear maps in advanced cryptographic applications with polynomially hard (public key) FE. As a specific goal, we consider the task of constructing CPRF and its verifiable variant. We precisely present the following results:

- We construct a selectively secure CPRF for constraints representable as *general polynomial-size circuits* directly from *polynomially-hard single-key weakly compact* (public key) FE.
- We further augment our CPRF construction to design a CVPRF, with the help of a standard *public key encryption* (PKE) scheme, which is again clearly implied by polynomially-hard single key weakly compact (public key) FE.

In fact, in our constructions we actually make use of *fully compact* (public key) FE, i.e., where the encryption time depends (polynomially) only on the message size, supporting multiple functional keys. We then invoke the generic polynomial reduction from single-key weakly compact public key FE to multi-key fully compact one presented by Garg and Srinivasan [24], and thereby obtain our end results. In order to achieve our results, we build upon the *prefix puncturing* technique presented in [22,23] which seems amenable to situations where the computation is altered on just a polynomial number of points, while for all other points, the exact same circuit is used to compute the output. Our work opens up a new pathway towards realizing CPRF's and their numerous extensions from progressively weaker and well-studied cryptographic building blocks. Our results can also be interpreted as unifying the study of CPRF and FE.

Technical Overview of Our CPRF Construction: We now provide a technical overview of our CPRF construction for general circuit constraints based on fully compact (public key) FE with polynomial loss. In order to ensure pseudorandomness of the function values, we consider a PRF having the same domain as that of the CPRF and simply define the CPRF value at some input to be the output of the PRF on that input. The master secret key of the CPRF would then include a key S for the underlying PRF. We now focus on designing the constrained keys. Clearly, a constrain key corresponding to some constraint circuit C should encode in its description the function $\mathscr{P}_{\mathrm{CPRF}}[C]$ which has the constraint circuit C hardwired in it. On input some domain point x, it checks whether $C(x) = 1$, or not, and outputs the proper CPRF value, namely, the PRF evaluation with key S on x, or a special empty string $\perp$ accordingly. Our goal is to produce an obfuscated or encrypted version of $\mathscr{P}_{\mathrm{CPRF}}[C]$ using FE.

In order to achieve the above target, similar to [22–24], we rely on the "binary-tree-based evaluation" idea utilized in the works of [3,6] for building IO from FE. Very roughly, the main idea of those works is as follows: The obfuscation of a circuit $\mathscr{C} : \{0,1\}^\sigma \to \{0,1\}^*$ consists of a sequence of $\sigma + 1$ functional keys $\mathrm{SK}_{\mathrm{FE},1}, \ldots, \mathrm{SK}_{\mathrm{FE},\sigma+1}$ generated using independently sampled master secret keys $\mathrm{MSK}_{\mathrm{FE},1}, \ldots, \mathrm{MSK}_{\mathrm{FE},\sigma+1}$ for the FE scheme, along with an FE ciphertext $\mathrm{CT}_{\mathrm{FE},1}^{(\perp)}$ encrypting the empty string $\perp$ under the FE master public key $\mathrm{MPK}_{\mathrm{FE},1}$ corresponding to $\mathrm{MSK}_{\mathrm{FE},1}$. For $\iota \in [\sigma]$, $\mathrm{SK}_{\mathrm{FE},\iota}$ implements the "bit-extension" functionality $\mathscr{G}_\iota$ that takes as input an $(\iota-1)$-length bit string $\vartheta \in \{0,1\}^{\iota-1}$, and outputs encryptions of $\vartheta\|0$ and $\vartheta\|1$ under the master public key $\mathrm{MPK}_{\mathrm{FE},\iota+1}$ corresponding to $\mathrm{MSK}_{\mathrm{FE},\iota+1}$. The functional key $\mathrm{SK}_{\mathrm{FE},\sigma+1}$ corresponds to the circuit $\mathscr{C}$.

To evaluate the obfuscated circuit on some input $z \in \{0,1\}^\sigma$, one proceeds as follows: First, it decrypts $\mathrm{CT}_{\mathrm{FE},1}^{(\perp)}$ using $\mathrm{SK}_{\mathrm{fe},1}$ to obtain encryptions of 0 and 1 under $\mathrm{MPK}_{\mathrm{FE},2}$. Depending on the first bit z_1 of z, it chooses either the encryption of 0 or 1, and further decrypts it using $\mathrm{SK}_{\mathrm{FE},2}$, and so on. Thus, in σ steps, one can obtain an encryption of z under $\mathrm{MPK}_{\mathrm{FE},\sigma+1}$, which can then be used to compute $\mathscr{C}(z)$ using $\mathrm{SK}_{\mathrm{FE},\sigma+1}$. This construction can be thought of as having a binary tree structure, where evaluating a circuit $\mathscr{C}$ on an input z corresponds to traversing along the path labeled z.

An intuitive reason why this construction incurs an exponential loss to achieve IO is that the behavior of the obfuscated circuit should be changed on all σ-bit inputs which are 2^σ in number. In contrast, as in the works of Garg et al. [22,23], our goal can be achieved by altering the behavior of the obfuscated circuits at only polynomially many inputs and thus seems to incur only a polynomial security loss. In view of this, to create an obfuscated version of our constrained key, we mimic the binary tree construction discussed above. Suppose the domain of our CPRF be $\{0,1\}^{\ell}$. A constrained key for some circuit C would consist of $\ell+1$ functional keys $\mathrm{SK}_{\mathrm{FE},1}, \ldots, \mathrm{SK}_{\mathrm{FE},\ell+1}$. For all $\iota \in [\ell]$, the functional key $\mathrm{SK}_{\mathrm{FE},\iota}$ would correspond to the bit-extension functionality $\mathscr{G}_{\iota}$. While evaluating the CPRF on some input $x \in \{0,1\}^{\ell}$, these ℓ functional keys would be used for eventually encrypting x under $\mathrm{MPK}_{\mathrm{FE},\ell+1}$ in the same way as outlined above. On the other hand, $\mathrm{SK}_{\mathrm{FE},\ell+1}$ corresponds to the function $\mathscr{P}_{\mathrm{CPRF}}[C]$ that checks whether the input x is accepted by the associated constraint circuit C or not, and outputs the value of the CPRF at x, i.e., the evaluation of the underlying PRF with key S on x, or $\perp$, accordingly.

However, observe that in order to output the CPRF value, $\mathscr{P}_{\mathrm{CPRF}}[C]$ must somehow have access to the PRF key S but this access should remain invisible to the outside world. Of course, the PRF key S cannot be hardwired directly within $\mathscr{P}_{\mathrm{CPRF}}$ as the notion of function-privacy which can be achieved in the context of public key FE is rather restricted [8]. One possible way to circumvent this problem is to "propagate" the PRF key S along the entire binary tree, i.e., we can encrypt the PRF key S within the ciphertext $\mathrm{CT}_{\mathrm{FE},1}^{(\perp)}$ (along with the empty string $\perp$) and modify the bit-extension functions $\mathscr{G}_{\iota}$ to take as input a key of the underlying PRF in addition to a $(\iota - 1)$-length bit string and include that key within the ciphertexts outputted by them. However, note that while reducing the selective pseudorandomness of the CPRF construction to the pseudorandomness of the underlying PRF, we must employ the punctured programming technique [33] in order to puncture the PRF key S at the challenge input $x^* \in \{0,1\}^{\ell}$. Considering the underlying PRF to be a puncturable one is a probable option. But, observe that we cannot alter the ciphertext $\mathrm{CT}_{\mathrm{FE},1}^{(\perp)}$ from encrypting the full PRF key S to encrypting the punctured key $S\{x^*\}$ punctured at x^*, relying on the security of FE since then the functional key $\mathrm{SK}_{\mathrm{FE},1}$, which corresponds to $\mathscr{G}_1$ would behave differently on the original and the modified ciphertexts.

To tackle the above problem, we rely on a more fine-grained puncturing technique. Precisely, we consider the underlying PRF to be a *prefix puncturable* one [22]. Intuitively, every string $\vartheta \in \bigcup_{j \in [\ell]} \{0,1\}^j$ has a natural association with a node in the binary tree of hight ℓ, where the root is associated with the empty string $\perp$. A prefix puncturable PRF is a PRF that has the property that a prefix punctured key $S_{\langle \vartheta \rangle}$ punctured at prefix ϑ can be further punctured to derive keys associated with all the nodes of the subtree rooted at the node corresponding to ϑ, but given $S_{\langle \vartheta \rangle}$, the function value at all the nodes which do not lie in the subtree rooted at ϑ still remain computationally indistinguishable from random. The first property is known as functionality under repeated puncturing, while the second property is termed as pseudorandomness at punctured prefix. Note that a PRF that inherits a natural binary tree structure and possesses all the properties of a prefix puncturable PRF is the classic PRF of Goldriech et al. [25]

constructed based solely on one way functions, which in turn can be instantiated by any FE scheme.

We use the repeated puncturing property of the underlying prefix puncturable PRF to propagate the prefix punctured keys through the ciphertexts outputted by the bit-extension functions. Specifically, we modify the bit-extension functions so that for all $\iota \in [\ell]$, the ιth bit-extension function $\mathscr{G}_\iota$ takes as input a string $\vartheta \in \{0,1\}^{\iota-1}$ along with the prefix punctured key $S_{\langle \vartheta \rangle}$ punctured at prefix ϑ, and outputs FE encryptions of $(\vartheta\|0, S_{\langle \vartheta\|0 \rangle})$ and $(\vartheta\|1, S_{\langle \vartheta\|1 \rangle})$. Consequently, while evaluating the CPRF on some input x using a constrained key, the iterative decryptions using the functional keys corresponding to the modified bit-extension functionalities along the path labeled x would eventually produce an FE encryption of $(x, S_{\langle x \rangle})$ under $\text{MPK}_{\text{FE},\ell+1}$. Hence, if $C(x) = 1$, the final decryption using the functional key $\text{SK}_{\text{FE},\ell+1}$ corresponding to $\mathscr{P}_{\text{CPRF}}[C]$ can readily output the CPRF value which is now the prefix punctured key $S_{\langle x \rangle}$ punctured at prefix x. At the same time, the pseudorandomness at punctured prefix property would enable us to surgically puncture the PRF key S along only the path of the challenge input x^* without affecting the distribution on rest of the inputs, which is crucial in proving the pseudorandomness of the CPRF.

Techniques Adapted in Our CVPRF Construction: Let us now sketch our technical ideas to extend our CPRF construction to incorporate the verifiability feature. The tool that we use for this enhancement is a public key encryption (PKE) scheme which is secure against chosen plaintext attack (CPA). Besides the prefix puncturable PRF key S used to generate the CVPRF output, we include within the master key another prefix puncturable PRF key $\widetilde{S}$ to generate randomness for the setup and encryption algorithms of PKE. As for the CPRF, the CVPRF output on some input x is $S_{\langle x \rangle}$, where $S_{\langle x \rangle}$ is the prefix punctured key punctured at prefix x. The non-interactive proof of correct evaluation consists of a PKE public key PK_{PKE} together with a pseudorandom string r_2. The randomness r_1 for setting up the PKE public key PK_{PKE} along with the pseudorandom string r_2 are formed as $r_1\|r_2 = \widetilde{S}_{\langle x \rangle}$.

The public verification key comprises of $\ell + 1$ functional keys. The first ℓ of the functional keys correspond to the same bit-extension functions $\mathscr{G}_\iota$ described above with the only modification that $\mathscr{G}_\iota$ now additionally takes as input the prefix punctured key $\widetilde{S}_{\langle \vartheta \rangle}$ (along with $(\iota - 1)$-length bit string ϑ and $S_{\langle \vartheta \rangle}$ as earlier) and includes it within the outputted ciphertexts. The $(\ell+1)^{\text{th}}$ functional key, on the other hand, corresponds to a function $\mathscr{V}_{\text{CVPRF}}$. The function $\mathscr{V}_{\text{CVPRF}}$ takes as input an ℓ-bit string ϑ, together with $S_{\langle \vartheta \rangle}$ and $\widetilde{S}_{\langle \vartheta \rangle}$. It first parses $\widetilde{S}_{\langle \vartheta \rangle}$ as $\widetilde{S}_{\langle \vartheta \rangle} = \widetilde{r}_1\|\widetilde{r}_2$. Next, it runs the PKE key generation algorithm using the generated randomness $\widetilde{r}_1$ and creates a PKE public key $\widetilde{\text{PK}}_{\text{PKE}}$. The function outputs $\widetilde{\text{PK}}_{\text{PKE}}$ together with the ciphertext $\widetilde{\text{CT}}_{\text{PKE}}$ encrypting $S_{\langle \vartheta \rangle}$ under $\widetilde{\text{PK}}_{\text{PKE}}$, utilizing the randomness $\widetilde{r}_2$.

To verify a purported CPRF value-proof pair $(y, \pi_{\text{CVPRF}} = (\text{PK}_{\text{PKE}}, r))$ for some input x using the public verification key, a verifier first performs the repeated FE decryption procedure using the first ℓ bit-extension functional keys along the path x, eventually obtaining an FE encryption of $(x, S_{\langle x \rangle}, \widetilde{S}_{\langle x \rangle})$. Next, it obtains a

PKE-public-key-ciphertext pair $(\widetilde{\mathrm{PK}}_{\mathrm{PKE}}, \widetilde{\mathrm{CT}}_{\mathrm{PKE}})$ by performing a final decryption using the $(\ell + 1)^{\mathrm{th}}$ functional key corresponding to the function $\mathscr{V}_{\mathrm{CVPRF}}$. The verifier accepts the proof if $\widetilde{\mathrm{PK}}_{\mathrm{PKE}}$ matches with $\mathrm{PK}_{\mathrm{PKE}}$, as well as $\widetilde{\mathrm{CT}}_{\mathrm{PKE}}$ matches with the ciphertext formed by encrypting the purported CVPRF value y under $\mathrm{PK}_{\mathrm{PKE}}$ using the string r included within the proof. Observe that the soundness of verification follows directly from the correctness of the underlying PKE scheme. Specifically, due to the correctness of PKE, it is guaranteed that two different values cannot map to the same ciphertext under the same public key.

Finally, to enable the generation of the proof along with the CVPRF value using a constrained key associated with some constraint circuit C, we modify the bit-extension functions corresponding to the first ℓ functional keys included within the constrained key the same way as mentioned above, as well as modify the function $\mathscr{P}_{\mathrm{CPRF}}[C]$, now denoted as $\mathscr{P}_{\mathrm{CVPRF}}$, associated with the $(\ell + 1)^{\mathrm{th}}$ functional key to take as input $\widetilde{S}_{\langle x \rangle}$ in addition to x and $S_{\langle x \rangle}$, and output the proof together with the CVPRF value in case $C(x) = 1$.

2   Preliminaries

2.1   Notations

Let $\lambda \in \mathbb{N}$ denotes the security parameter and 1^{λ} be its unary encoding. For $\nu \in \mathbb{N}$ and $\zeta \in \mathbb{N} \bigcup \{0\}$ (with $\zeta < \nu$), we let $[\nu] = \{1, \ldots, \nu\}$ and $[\zeta, \nu] = \{\zeta, \ldots, \nu\}$. For any set Υ, $\upsilon \xleftarrow{\$} \Upsilon$ represents the process of uniformly sampling an element υ from the set Υ. For a probabilistic algorithm $\mathcal{A}$, we denote by $\psi = \mathcal{A}(\tau; \rho)$ the output of $\mathcal{A}$ on input τ with the content of the random tape being ρ, while $\psi \xleftarrow{\$} \mathcal{A}(\tau)$ stands for the process of sampling ψ from the output distribution of $\mathcal{A}$ on input τ with a uniform random tape. Similarly, for any deterministic algorithm $\mathcal{A}$, $\psi = \mathcal{A}(\tau)$ denotes the output of $\mathcal{A}$ on input τ. We use the abbreviation PPT to mean probabilistic polynomial-time. We assume that all the algorithms are given the unary representation 1^{λ} of the security parameter λ as input and will not write 1^{λ} explicitly as input of the algorithms when it is clear from the context. For any binary string $s \in \{0, 1\}^{*}$, we let $|s|$ denote the bit-length of the string s and represent the string as $s = s_1 \ldots s_{|s|}$, where for $j \in [|s|]$, s_j denotes the jth bit of s with s_1 being the most significant or the highest order bit and $s_{|s|}$ the least significant or the lowest order bit. For any $j \in [|s|]$, the j-bit prefix $s_1 \ldots s_j \in \{0, 1\}^{j}$ of the binary string s is denoted by $s|_j$. The empty prefix of the string s is denoted as $s|_0 = \perp$, where $\perp$ represents a special empty string. For any two binary strings $s, t \in \{0, 1\}^{*}$, $s \| t$ represents the concatenation of s and t. For any $\nu \in \mathbb{N}$, and for any ν binary strings $s^{(1)}, \ldots, s^{(\nu)} \in \{0, 1\}^{*}$, we will use $\underset{j \in [\nu]}{\|} s^{(j)}$ to signify $s^{(1)} \| \ldots \| s^{(\nu)}$. For any $\nu \in \mathbb{N}$, $0^{\nu} \in \{0, 1\}^{\nu}$ represents the all zero string. A function $\mathsf{negl} : \mathbb{N} \to \mathbb{R}^{+}$ is said to be *negligible* if for every $c \in \mathbb{N}$, there exists $k \in \mathbb{N}$ such that for all $\lambda \in \mathbb{N}$ with $\lambda > k$, $|\mathsf{negl}(\lambda)| < 1/\lambda^{c}$.

2.2 Functional Encryption

We recall the notion of (public key) functional encryption (FE) with selective indistinguishability-based security from [9].

Definition 2.1 (Functional Encryption: FE): Let $\lambda \in \mathbb{N}$ be the security parameter. A functional encryption (FE) scheme for some message space $\mathbb{M}_{FE} \subset \{0,1\}^*$ and certain function family $\mathbb{F}_{FE}$ over $\mathbb{M}_{FE}$ consists of a tuple of PPT algorithms $\Pi_{FE} = (\text{FE.Setup}, \text{FE.Encrypt}, \text{FE.KeyGen}, \text{FE.Decrypt})$ with the following syntax:

FE.Setup($\mathbb{F}_{FE}$): The trusted authority takes as input the specifications of the associated function family $\mathbb{F}_{FE}$. It publishes a master public key MPK_{FE} while generates the corresponding master secret key MSK_{FE} for itself.

FE.Encrypt(MPK_{FE}, μ): On input the master public key MPK_{FE} together with a message $\mu \in \mathbb{M}_{FE}$, an encrypter outputs a ciphertext CT_{FE} encrypting the message μ under MPK_{FE}.

FE.KeyGen($\text{MSK}_{FE}, \mathscr{F}$): The trusted authority takes as input the master secret key MSK_{FE} along with a function $\mathscr{F} \in \mathbb{F}_{FE}$, and provides a functional key $\text{SK}_{FE}(\mathscr{F})$ to a legitimate decryptor.

FE.Decrypt($\text{SK}_{FE}(\mathscr{F}), \text{CT}_{FE}$): A decryptor takes as input a functional key $\text{SK}_{FE}(\mathscr{F})$ corresponding to some function $\mathscr{F} \in \mathbb{F}_{FE}$ and a ciphertext CT_{FE} encrypting some message $\mu \in \mathbb{M}_{FE}$. It outputs a string $\xi \in \{\bot\} \bigcup \{0.1\}^*$.

The algorithm FE.Decrypt is deterministic, while the others are probabilistic. An FE scheme satisfies the following correctness and security requirements:

▶ **Correctness:** An FE scheme for the function family $\mathbb{F}_{FE}$ is said to be correct if for any security parameter $\lambda \in \mathbb{N}$, any message $\mu \in \mathbb{M}_{FE}$ and any function $\mathscr{F} \in \mathbb{F}_{FE}$, we have

$$\Pr[\text{FE.Decrypt}(\text{SK}_{FE}(\mathscr{F}), \text{CT}_{FE}) = \mathscr{F}(\mu) : (\text{MPK}_{FE}, \text{MSK}_{FE}) \xleftarrow{\$} \text{FE.Setup}(\mathbb{F}_{FE});$$

$$\text{CT}_{FE} \xleftarrow{\$} \text{FE.Encrypt}(\text{MPK}_{FE}, \mu); \text{SK}_{FE}(\mathscr{F}) \xleftarrow{\$} \text{FE.KeyGen}(\text{MSK}_{FE}, \mathscr{F})] = 1.$$

▶ **Selective Security:** An FE scheme for the function family $\mathbb{F}_{FE}$ is said to be secure in the selective indistinguishability-based chosen plaintext attack (CPA) model if for any security parameter $\lambda \in \mathbb{N}$ and any PPT adversary $\mathcal{D}$, we have

$$\text{Adv}_{\mathcal{D}}^{\text{FE.SEL-IND}}(\lambda) = |\Pr[\text{Expt}_{\mathcal{D}}^{\text{FE.SEL-IND}}(0) = 1] - \Pr[\text{Expt}_{\mathcal{D}}^{\text{FE.SEL-IND}}(1) = 1]| \le \text{negl}(\lambda),$$

for some negligible function negl, where for $\beta \xleftarrow{\$} \{0,1\}$, $\text{Expt}_{\mathcal{D}}^{\text{FE.SEL-IND}}(\beta)$ is defined as the following experiment between the adversary $\mathcal{D}$ and a PPT challenger $\mathcal{C}$:

- $\mathcal{D}$ submits two messages $\mu_0, \mu_1 \in \mathbb{M}_{FE}$ such that $|\mu_0| = |\mu_1|$ to $\mathcal{C}$.
- $\mathcal{C}$ generates $(\text{MPK}_{FE}, \text{MSK}_{FE}) \xleftarrow{\$} \text{FE.Setup}(\mathbb{F}_{FE})$ and hands MPK_{FE} to $\mathcal{D}$.

- $\mathcal{C}$ also creates the challenge ciphertext $\mathrm{CT}^*_{\mathrm{FE}} \xleftarrow{\$} \mathsf{FE.Encrypt}(\mathrm{MPK}_{\mathrm{FE}}, \mu_\beta)$ and sends $\mathrm{CT}^*_{\mathrm{FE}}$ to $\mathcal{D}$.
- In response to a functional key query of $\mathcal{D}$ corresponding to some function $\mathscr{F} \in \mathbb{F}_{\mathrm{FE}}$ subject to the restriction that $\mathscr{F}(\mu_0) = \mathscr{F}(\mu_1)$, $\mathcal{C}$ provides $\mathcal{D}$ with the functional key $\mathrm{SK}_{\mathrm{FE}}(\mathscr{F}) \xleftarrow{\$} \mathsf{FE.KeyGen}(\mathrm{MSK}_{\mathrm{FE}}, \mathscr{F})$. $\mathcal{D}$ is allowed to adaptively request any polynomial number of such functional keys to $\mathcal{C}$.
- Eventually, $\mathcal{D}$ outputs a guess bit $\beta' \in \{0, 1\}$ which is the output of the experiment.

Remark 2.1: An FE scheme is said to be *q-key* selectively secure if the adversary $\mathcal{D}$ is allowed to query at most q functional keys to $\mathcal{C}$ in the above selective security experiment.

We now define the notion of compactness in the context of FE following [4, 6].

Definition 2.2 (Compactness in FE): An FE scheme is said to be fully compact (respectively weakly compact) if for any security parameter $\lambda \in \mathbb{N}$ and any message $\mu \in \mathbb{M}_{\mathrm{FE}}$, the running time of the encryption algorithm FE.Encrypt is $\mathsf{poly}(\lambda, |\mu|)$, for some polynomial poly (respectively $|\mathbb{F}_{\mathrm{FE}}|^{1-\epsilon}\mathsf{poly}(\lambda, |\mu|)$, for some $\epsilon > 0$ and some polynomial poly, where $|\mathbb{F}_{\mathrm{FE}}| = \max_{\mathscr{F} \in \mathbb{F}_{\mathrm{FE}}} |\mathscr{F}|$).

2.3   Prefix Puncturable Pseudorandom Function

We define the notion of prefix puncturable pseudorandom function (PPPRF) following [22].

Definition 2.3 (Prefix Puncturable Pseudorandom Function: PPPRF): Let $\lambda \in \mathbb{N}$ be the security parameter. A prefix puncturable pseudorandom function $\mathsf{PPPRF} : \mathbb{K}_{\mathrm{PPPRF}} \times \mathbb{D}_{\mathrm{PPPRF}} \rightarrow \mathbb{K}_{\mathrm{PPPRF}}$, where the key cum output space $\mathbb{K}_{\mathrm{PPPRF}} = \{0, 1\}^\varkappa$ and the domain space $\mathbb{D}_{\mathrm{PPPRF}} = \{\bot\} \bigcup (\bigcup_{\iota \in [\ell]} \{0, 1\}^\iota)$, for some polynomials $\varkappa$ and ℓ in λ, consists of a tuple of PPT algorithms $\Pi_{\mathrm{PPPRF}} = (\mathsf{PPPRF.KeyGen}, \mathsf{PPPRF.PrefixPuncture})$ with the following syntax:

$\mathsf{PPPRF.KeyGen}(\varkappa, \ell)$: This is a probabilistic algorithm that takes as input the dimensions $\varkappa$ and ℓ of the key and domain spaces, and outputs a uniformly sampled PPPRF key $K \xleftarrow{\$} \mathbb{K}_{\mathrm{PPPRF}}$.

$\mathsf{PPPRF.PrefixPuncture}(K, d)$: This is a deterministic algorithm that takes as input a PPPRF key $K \in \mathbb{K}_{\mathrm{PPPRF}}$ together with an input $d \in \mathbb{D}_{\mathrm{PPPRF}}$, and outputs a PPPRF key $K_{\langle d \rangle} \in \mathbb{K}_{\mathrm{PPPRF}}$ punctured at prefix d. For ease of notations, we will denote the output of this algorithm as $K_{\langle d \rangle} = \mathsf{PPPRF}(K, d)$. In the special case, when $d = \bot$, we have $K_{\langle \bot \rangle} = K$.

The algorithms satisfy the following properties:

▶ **Functionality under Repeated Puncturing:** A PPPRF is said to preserve functionality under repeated puncturing if for any security parameter $\lambda \in \mathbb{N}$, and any $u, v \in \mathbb{D}_{\text{PPPRF}}$ such that $u = v\|w$ for some $w \in \{0,1\}^*$, it holds that

$$\Pr[\text{PPPRF}(K_{\langle v \rangle}, w) = K_{\langle u \rangle} : K \xleftarrow{\$} \text{PPPRF.KeyGen}(\varkappa, \ell)] = 1.$$

▶ **Pseudorandomness at Selectively Punctured Prefix:** A PPPRF is said to be pseudorandom at selectively punctured prefix if for any security parameter $\lambda \in \mathbb{N}$ and any PPT adversary $\mathcal{D}$, we have

$$\text{Adv}_{\mathcal{D}}^{\text{PPPRF,SEL-PR}}(\lambda) = |\Pr[\text{Expt}_{\mathcal{D}}^{\text{PPPRF,SEL-PR}}(0) = 1] - \Pr[\text{Expt}_{\mathcal{D}}^{\text{PPPRF,SEL-PR}}(1) = 1]|$$
$$\leq \text{negl}(\lambda),$$

for some negligible function negl, where for $\beta \xleftarrow{\$} \{0,1\}$, $\text{Expt}_{\mathcal{D}}^{\text{PPPRF,SEL-PR}}(\beta)$ is defined as the following experiment between the adversary $\mathcal{D}$ and a PPT challenger $\mathcal{C}$:
  • $\mathcal{D}$ submits a challenge input $d^* \in \mathbb{D}_{\text{PPPRF}}$ to $\mathcal{C}$.
  • $\mathcal{C}$ generates a PPPRF key $K^* \xleftarrow{\$} \text{PPPRF.KeyGen}(\varkappa, \ell)$ and hands $(\Re_\beta^*, \{K^*_{\langle d^*|_{\iota-1}\|(1-d_\iota^*)\rangle}\}_{\iota \in [\ell]})$ to $\mathcal{D}$, where $\Re_0^* = K^*_{\langle d^* \rangle}$ and $\Re_1^* \xleftarrow{\$} \mathbb{K}_{\text{PPPRF}}$.
  • $\mathcal{D}$ outputs a guess bit $\beta' \in \{0,1\}$ which is the output of the experiment.

3   Our Constrained Pseudorandom Function

3.1   Notion

We start by presenting the formal notion of a constrained pseudorandom function (CPRF) following [10,11,30].

Definition 3.1 (Constrained Pseudorandom Function: CPRF): Let $\lambda \in \mathbb{N}$ be the underlying security parameter. A constrained pseudorandom function (CPRF) with key space $\mathbb{K}_{\text{CPRF}}$, input domain $\mathbb{D}_{\text{CPRF}} = \{0,1\}^\ell$, and output space $\mathbb{Y}_{\text{CPRF}} = \{0,1\}^m$ for a circuit family $\mathbb{C}_{\text{CPRF}}$, where ℓ and m are some polynomials in λ, consists of a constrained key space $\mathbb{K}_{\text{CPRF-CONST}}$ and a tuple of PPT algorithms $\Pi_{\text{CPRF}} = (\text{CPRF.Setup}, \text{CPRF.Eval}, \text{CPRF.Constrain}, \text{CPRF.Eval-Constrained})$ with the following syntax:

CPRF.Setup$(\ell, m, \mathbb{C}_{\text{CPRF}})$: The setup authority takes as input the dimension ℓ and m of the input domain and output space respectively, together with the specifications of the supported constraint circuit family $\mathbb{C}_{\text{CPRF}}$, and generates a master CPRF key $\text{MSK}_{\text{CPRF}} \in \mathbb{K}_{\text{CPRF}}$.

CPRF.Eval$(\text{MSK}_{\text{CPRF}}, x)$: On input the master CPRF key MSK_{CPRF} along with an input $x \in \mathbb{D}_{\text{CPRF}}$, the setup authority computes the value of the CPRF $y \in \mathbb{Y}_{\text{CPRF}}$. For simplicity of notation, we will use $y = \text{CPRF}(\text{MSK}_{\text{CPRF}}, x)$ to indicate the output of this algorithm.

CPRF.Constrain($\text{MSK}_{\text{CPRF}}, C$) : Taking as input the master CPRF key MSK_{CPRF} and a circuit $C \in \mathbb{C}_{\text{CPRF}}$, the setup authority provides a constrained key $\text{SK}_{\text{CPRF}}\{C\} \in \mathbb{K}_{\text{CPRF-CONST}}$ to a legitimate user.

CPRF.Eval-Constrained($\text{SK}_{\text{CPRF}}\{C\}, x$) : A user takes as input a constrained key $\text{SK}_{\text{CPRF}}\{C\} \in \mathbb{K}_{\text{CPRF-CONST}}$, corresponding to a legitimate constraint circuit $C \in \mathbb{C}_{\text{CPRF}}$, along with an input $x \in \mathbb{D}_{\text{CPRF}}$. It outputs either a value $y \in \mathbb{Y}_{\text{CPRF}}$ or the empty string $\perp$ indicating failure.

The algorithms CPRF.Setup and CPRF.Constrain are probabilistic, whereas, the other two are deterministic. A CPRF satisfies the following properties:

▶ **Correctness under Constraining:** A CPRF is said to be correct for a circuit class $\mathbb{C}_{\text{CPRF}}$ if for any security parameter $\lambda \in \mathbb{N}$, any circuit $C \in \mathbb{C}_{\text{CPRF}}$, and any input $x \in \mathbb{D}_{\text{CPRF}}$ such that $C(x) = 1$, the following holds:

$$\Pr[\text{CPRF.Eval-Constrained}(\text{SK}_{\text{CPRF}}\{C\}, x) = \text{CPRF}(\text{MSK}_{\text{CPRF}}, x) : \text{MSK}_{\text{CPRF}} \xleftarrow{\$}$$
$$\text{CPRF.Setup}(\ell, m, \mathbb{C}_{\text{CPRF}}); \text{SK}_{\text{CPRF}}\{C\} \xleftarrow{\$} \text{CPRF.Constrain}(\text{MSK}_{\text{CPRF}}, C)] = 1.$$

▶ **Selective Pseudorandomness:** A CPRF for the circuit family $\mathbb{C}_{\text{CPRF}}$ is said to be selectively pseudorandom if for any security parameter $\lambda \in \mathbb{N}$ and any PPT adversary $\mathcal{B}$, we have

$$\text{Adv}_{\mathcal{B}}^{\text{CPRF.SEL-PR}}(\lambda) = |\Pr[\text{Expt}_{\mathcal{B}}^{\text{CPRF.SEL-PR}}() = 1] - 1/2| \leq \text{negl}(\lambda),$$

for some negligible function negl, where $\text{Expt}_{\mathcal{B}}^{\text{CPRF.SEL-PR}}()$ is defined as the following experiment between the adversary $\mathcal{B}$ and a PPT challenger $\mathcal{D}$:

- $\mathcal{B}$ submits a challenge input $x^* \in \mathbb{D}_{\text{CPRF}}$ to $\mathcal{D}$.
- $\mathcal{D}$ generates a master CPRF key $\text{MSK}_{\text{CPRF}} \xleftarrow{\$} \text{CPRF.Setup}(\ell, m, \mathbb{C}_{\text{CPRF}})$. Next, it samples a random bit $b \xleftarrow{\$} \{0, 1\}$. If $b = 0$, it computes $y^* = \text{CPRF}(\text{MSK}_{\text{CPRF}}, x^*)$. Otherwise, it chooses a random $y^* \xleftarrow{\$} \mathbb{Y}_{\text{CPRF}}$. It returns y^* to $\mathcal{B}$.
- $\mathcal{B}$ may adaptively make any polynomial number of queries of the following kinds to $\mathcal{D}$:
  - *Evaluation query:* $\mathcal{B}$ queries the CPRF value at some input $x \in \mathbb{D}_{\text{CPRF}}$ such that $x \neq x^*$. $\mathcal{D}$ provides the CPRF value $\text{CPRF}(\text{MSK}_{\text{CPRF}}, x)$ to $\mathcal{B}$.
  - *Key query:* $\mathcal{B}$ queries a constrained key corresponding to some circuit $C \in \mathbb{C}_{\text{CPRF}}$ subject to the restriction that $C(x^*) = 0$. $\mathcal{D}$ gives the constrained key $\text{SK}_{\text{CPRF}}\{C\} \xleftarrow{\$} \text{CPRF.Constrain}(\text{MSK}_{\text{CPRF}}, C)$ to $\mathcal{B}$.
- $\mathcal{B}$ eventually outputs a guess bit $b' \in \{0, 1\}$. The output of the experiment is 1, if $b = b'$, and 0, otherwise.

Remark 3.1: As pointed out in [14,28], note that in the above selective pseudorandomness experiment, without loss of generality we may assume that the adversary $\mathcal{B}$ only makes constrained key queries and no evaluation query. This is because any evaluation query at input $x \in \mathbb{D}_{\text{CPRF}}$ can be replaced by constrained key query for a circuit $C[x] \in \mathbb{C}_{\text{CPRF}}$ which outputs 1 only at input x. Since, the restriction on the evaluation queries is that $x \neq x^*$, $C[x](x^*) = 0$, and thus $C[x]$ is a valid constrained key query. We will use this simplification in our security proof.

3.2   Construction

Let $\lambda \in \mathbb{N}$ be the underlying security parameter. We now present our CPRF construction for the constraint family $\mathbb{C}_{\mathrm{POLY}}$ of polynomial-size circuits, input domain $\mathbb{D}_{\mathrm{CPRF}} = \{0,1\}^{\ell}$, and output space $\mathbb{Y}_{\mathrm{CPRF}} = \{0,1\}^{m}$. In our CPRF construction, we use a selectively secure fully compact (public key) functional encryption (FE) scheme $\Pi_{\mathrm{FE}} = (\mathsf{FE.Setup}, \mathsf{FE.Encrypt}, \mathsf{FE.KeyGen}, \mathsf{FE.Decrypt})$ for function family $\mathbb{F}_{\mathrm{POLY}}$ consisting of all polynomial-size functions, a prefix-puncturable pseudorandom function (PPPRF) $\Pi_{\mathrm{PPPRF}} = (\mathsf{PPPRF.KeyGen}, \mathsf{PPPRF.PrefixPuncture})$ with domain $\mathbb{D}_{\mathrm{PPPRF}} = \{\bot\} \bigcup (\bigcup_{\iota \in [2\ell]} \{0,1\}^{\iota})$, and a secure symmetric key encryption (SKE) scheme $\Pi_{\mathrm{SKE}} = (\mathsf{SKE.KeyGen}, \mathsf{SKE.Encrypt}, \mathsf{SKE.Decrypt})$. Without loss of generality, we assume that the space of randomness used by the $\mathsf{FE.Encrypt}$ algorithm of Π_{FE} is $\{0,1\}^{m}$. Our CPRF construction follows:

$\mathsf{CPRF.Setup}(\ell, m, \mathbb{C}_{\mathrm{POLY}})$: The trusted authority takes as input the dimensions ℓ and m of the input domain and output space respectively, along with the specifications of the constraint family $\mathbb{C}_{\mathrm{POLY}}$. It proceeds as follows:

1. It samples Π_{PPPRF} keys $S \xleftarrow{\$} \mathsf{PPPRF.Setup}(m, 2\ell)$ and $\widehat{S} \xleftarrow{\$} \mathsf{PPPRF.Setup}(m, 2\ell)$.

2. Next, it generates $\ell + 1$ sets of Π_{FE} master public keys and the respective master secret keys $\{(\mathrm{MPK}_{\mathrm{FE},\iota}, \mathrm{MSK}_{\mathrm{FE},\iota}) \xleftarrow{\$} \mathsf{FE.Setup}(\mathbb{F}_{\mathrm{POLY}})\}_{\iota \in [\ell+1]}$.

3. Then, it generates a Π_{SKE} symmetric key $\mathrm{SK}_{\mathrm{SKE}} \xleftarrow{\$} \mathsf{SKE.KeyGen}()$ and creates ℓ Π_{SKE} ciphertexts $\{\mathrm{CT}_{\mathrm{SKE},\iota} \xleftarrow{\$} \mathsf{SKE.Encrypt}(\mathrm{SK}_{\mathrm{SKE}}, \omega_{\iota})\}_{\iota \in [\ell]}$, where $\omega_{\iota} = 0^{\wp_{\iota}}$ for all $\iota \in [\ell]$. Here, for $\iota \in [\ell]$, $\wp_{\iota}$ is an appropriate polynomial in λ that would be determined in the security proof.

4. Next, it forms ℓ Π_{FE} functional keys $\{\mathrm{SK}_{\mathrm{FE},\iota}(\mathscr{G}_{\mathrm{CPRF},\iota}[\iota, \mathrm{MPK}_{\mathrm{FE},\iota+1}, \mathrm{CT}_{\mathrm{SKE},\iota}]) \xleftarrow{\$} \mathsf{FE.KeyGen}(\mathrm{MSK}_{\mathrm{FE},\iota}, \mathscr{G}_{\mathrm{CPRF},\iota}[\iota, \mathrm{MPK}_{\mathrm{FE},\iota+1}, \mathrm{CT}_{\mathrm{SKE},\iota}])\}_{\iota \in [\ell]}$, where for $j \in \mathbb{N}$, $\mathscr{G}_{\mathrm{CPRF},j}$ is the function depicted in Fig. 1.

5. Then, it computes a Π_{FE} ciphertext $\mathrm{CT}_{\mathrm{FE},1}^{(\bot)} \xleftarrow{\$} \mathsf{FE.Encrypt}(\mathrm{MPK}_{\mathrm{FE},1}, (\bot, S, \widehat{S}, 0^{\kappa}, 0))$.

6. Finally, it sets the master CPRF key as $\mathrm{MSK}_{\mathrm{CPRF}} = (S, \mathrm{MSK}_{\mathrm{FE},\ell+1}, \{\mathrm{SK}_{\mathrm{FE},\iota}(\mathscr{G}_{\mathrm{CPRF},\iota}[\iota, \mathrm{MPK}_{\mathrm{FE},\iota+1}, \mathrm{CT}_{\mathrm{SKE},\iota}])\}_{\iota \in [\ell]}, \mathrm{CT}_{\mathrm{FE},1}^{(\bot)})$.

$\mathsf{CPRF.Eval}(\mathrm{MSK}_{\mathrm{CPRF}}, x)$: Taking as input the master CPRF key $\mathrm{MSK}_{\mathrm{CPRF}}$ together with an input $x \in \mathbb{D}_{\mathrm{CPRF}}$, the trusted authority outputs the CPRF value $y = S_{\langle x \rangle} = \mathsf{PPPRF}(S, x)$, where it extracts the PPPRF key S from $\mathrm{MSK}_{\mathrm{CPRF}}$.

$\mathsf{CPRF.Constrain}(\mathrm{MSK}_{\mathrm{CPRF}}, C)$: On input the master CPRF key $\mathrm{MSK}_{\mathrm{CPRF}}$ and a constraint circuit $C \in \mathbb{C}_{\mathrm{POLY}}$, the trusted authority executes the following steps:

1. It forms a Π_{FE} functional key $\mathrm{SK}_{\mathrm{FE},\ell+1}(\mathscr{P}_{\mathrm{CPRF}}[C]) \xleftarrow{\$} \mathsf{FE.KeyGen}(\mathrm{MSK}_{\mathrm{FE},\ell+1}, \mathscr{P}_{\mathrm{CPRF}}[C])$, where it extracts $\mathrm{MSK}_{\mathrm{FE},\ell+1}$ from $\mathrm{MSK}_{\mathrm{CPRF}}$. The function $\mathscr{P}_{\mathrm{CPRF}}$ is described in Fig. 2.

2. It provides the constrained key $\mathrm{SK}_{\mathrm{CPRF}}\{C\} = (\{\mathrm{SK}_{\mathrm{FE},\iota}(\mathscr{G}_{\mathrm{CPRF},\iota}[\iota, \mathrm{MPK}_{\mathrm{FE},\iota+1}, \mathrm{CT}_{\mathrm{SKE},\iota}])\}_{\iota \in [\ell]}, \mathrm{SK}_{\mathrm{FE},\ell+1}(\mathscr{P}_{\mathrm{CPRF}}[C]), \mathrm{CT}_{\mathrm{FE},1}^{(\bot)})$ to a legitimate user, where $\{\mathrm{SK}_{\mathrm{FE},\iota}(\mathscr{G}_{\mathrm{CPRF},\iota}[\iota, \mathrm{MPK}_{\mathrm{FE},\iota+1}, \mathrm{CT}_{\mathrm{SKE},\iota}])\}_{\iota \in [\ell]}$ and $\mathrm{CT}_{\mathrm{FE},1}^{(\bot)}$ are parts of $\mathrm{MSK}_{\mathrm{CPRF}}$.

CPRF.Eval-Constrained($\text{SK}_{\text{CPRF}}\{C\}, x$): A user takes as input a constrained key $\text{SK}_{\text{CPRF}}\{C\}$ corresponding to some legitimate constraint circuit $C \in \mathbb{C}_{\text{POLY}}$ along with an input $x \in \mathbb{D}_{\text{CPRF}}$. It performs the following:

1. For $\iota \in [\ell]$, it iteratively does the following
   (a) It computes $\Omega_\iota = \text{FE.Decrypt}(\text{SK}_{\text{FE},\iota}(\mathscr{G}_{\text{CPRF},\iota}[\iota, \text{MPK}_{\text{FE},\iota+1}, \text{CT}_{\text{SKE},\iota}]),$
       $\text{CT}_{\text{FE},\iota}^{(x|_{\iota-1})})$, where $\text{SK}_{\text{FE},\iota}(\mathscr{G}_{\text{CPRF},\iota}[\iota, \text{MPK}_{\text{FE},\iota+1}, \text{CT}_{\text{SKE},\iota}])$ is extracted from $\text{SK}_{\text{CPRF}}\{C\}$.
   (b) It parses Ω_ι as $\Omega_\iota = \text{CT}_{\text{FE},\iota+1}^{(x|_{\iota-1}\|0)} \| \text{CT}_{\text{FE},\iota+1}^{(x|_{\iota-1}\|1)}$.
2. Finally, it outputs $\Omega_{\ell+1} = \text{FE.Decrypt}(\text{SK}_{\text{FE},\ell+1}(\mathscr{P}_{\text{CPRF}}[C]), \text{CT}_{\text{FE},\ell+1}^{(x)})$, where it extracts $\text{SK}_{\text{FE},\ell+1}(\mathscr{P}_{\text{CPRF}}[C])$ from $\text{SK}_{\text{CPRF}}\{C\}$.

Constants: Index $j \in \mathbb{N}$, Π_{FE} master public key MPK_{FE}, Π_{SKE} ciphertext CT_{SKE}.
  Inputs: String $\vartheta \in \{0,1\}^{j-1}$, Π_{PPPRF} keys $K, \widehat{K} \in \mathbb{K}_{\text{PPPRF}}$, Π_{SKE} symmetric key SK_{SKE}, Mode $\gamma \in \{0,1\}$.
A) If Mode $\gamma = 0$, then output $\Omega = \text{CT}_{\text{FE}}^{(\vartheta\|0)} \| \text{CT}_{\text{FE}}^{(\vartheta\|1)}$, where for $\delta \in \{0,1\}$, $\text{CT}_{\text{FE}}^{(\vartheta\|\delta)} = \text{FE.Encrypt}(\text{MPK}_{\text{FE}}, (\vartheta\|\delta, K_{\langle\delta\rangle}, \widehat{K}_{\langle\delta\|0\rangle}, 0^\kappa, \gamma); \widehat{K}_{\langle\delta\|1\rangle})$, where κ, some polynomial in λ, is the length of the symmetric keys of Π_{SKE}.
B) Else, output $\Omega = \text{SKE.Decrypt}(\text{SK}_{\text{SKE}}, \text{CT}_{\text{SKE}})$.

Fig. 1. Function $\mathscr{G}_{\text{CPRF},j}$

Constants: Circuit $C \in \mathbb{C}_{\text{POLY}}$.
  Inputs: String $\vartheta \in \{0,1\}^\ell$, Π_{PPPRF} keys $K, \widehat{K} \in \mathbb{K}_{\text{PPPRF}}$, Π_{SKE} symmetric key SK_{SKE}, Mode $\gamma \in \{0,1\}$.
A) If $C(\vartheta) = 1$, output $\Omega = K$.
B) Else, output $\Omega = \bot$.

Fig. 2. Function $\mathscr{P}_{\text{CPRF}}$

Theorem 3.1 (Security of the Proposed CPRF): *Assuming Π_{FE} is a selectively secure FE scheme, Π_{PPPRF} satisfies all the properties of a PPPRF, and Π_{SKE} is a secure SKE scheme, our CPRF satisfies the correctness under constraining and selective pseudorandomness properties defined in Definition 3.1.*

The proof of Theorem 3.1 can be found in the full version of the paper.

4   Our Constrained Verifiable Pseudorandom Function

In this section, we will present our CVPRF construction. For the formal notion of CVPRF, please refer to [14,18]. Our CVPRF construction is extended from our CPRF construction of Sect. 3.2. Let $\lambda \in \mathbb{N}$ be the underlying security parameter. Like our CPRF, our CVPRF supports the constraint family $\mathbb{C}_{\text{POLY}}$

of polynomial-size circuits, has input domain $\mathbb{D}_{\text{CVPRF}} = \{0,1\}^{\ell}$, and output space $\mathbb{Y}_{\text{CVPRF}} = \{0,1\}^{m}$. In addition to the cryptographic tools employed in our CPRF construction, we will utilize a chosen-plaintext-attack (CPA)-secure public key encryption (PKE) scheme $\Pi_{\text{PKE}} = (\text{PKE.KeyGen}, \text{PKE.Encrypt}, \text{PKE.Decrypt})$ with $\{0,1\}^{\varphi_1}$ and $\{0,1\}^{\varphi_2}$, for some polynomials φ_1 and φ_2 in λ, being respectively the spaces of randomness used by the PKE.KeyGen and PKE.Encrypt algorithms. Without loss of generality, we will assume that $\varphi_1 + \varphi_2 = m$. Our CVPRF construction is presented below:

CVPRF.Setup($\ell, m, \mathbb{C}_{\text{POLY}}$): The trusted authority takes as input the dimension ℓ and m of the input domain and output space respectively, along with the specifications of the constraint family $\mathbb{C}_{\text{POLY}}$. It proceeds as follows:

1. It samples Π_{PPPRF} keys $S \xleftarrow{\$} \text{PPPRF.Setup}(m, \ell)$, $\widetilde{S} \xleftarrow{\$} \text{PPPRF.Setup}(m, \ell)$, and $\widehat{S} \xleftarrow{\$} \text{PPPRF.Setup}(m, \ell)$.

2. Next, it generates $\ell + 1$ sets of Π_{FE} master public keys and the respective master secret keys $\{(\text{MPK}_{\text{FE},\iota}, \text{MSK}_{\text{FE},\iota}) \xleftarrow{\$} \text{FE.Setup}(\mathbb{F}_{\text{POLY}})\}_{\iota \in [\ell+1]}$.

3. Then, it generates a Π_{SKE} symmetric key $\text{SK}_{\text{SKE}} \xleftarrow{\$} \text{SKE.KeyGen}()$ and creates $\ell + 1$ Π_{SKE} ciphertexts $\{\text{CT}_{\text{SKE},\iota} \xleftarrow{\$} \text{SKE.Encrypt}(\text{SK}_{\text{SKE}}, \omega_{\iota})\}_{\iota \in [\ell+1]}$, where $\omega_{\iota} = 0^{\wp_{\iota}}$ for all $\iota \in [\ell+1]$. Here, for $\iota \in [\ell+1]$, $\wp_{\iota}$ is an appropriate polynomial in λ that would be determined in the security proof.

4. After that, it generates ℓ Π_{FE} functional keys $\{\text{SK}_{\text{FE},\iota}(\mathscr{G}_{\text{CVPRF},\iota}[\iota, \text{MPK}_{\text{FE},\iota+1}, \text{CT}_{\text{SKE},\iota}]) \xleftarrow{\$} \text{FE.KeyGen}(\text{MSK}_{\text{FE},\iota}, \mathscr{G}_{\text{CVPRF},\iota}[\iota, \text{MPK}_{\text{FE},\iota+1}, \text{CT}_{\text{SKE},\iota}])\}_{\iota \in [\ell]}$, where for $j \in \mathbb{N}$, $\mathscr{G}_{\text{CVPRF},j}$ is the function depicted in Fig. 3.

5. Then, it creates another Π_{FE} functional key $\text{SK}_{\text{FE},\ell+1}(\mathscr{V}_{\text{CVPRF}}[\text{CT}_{\text{SKE},\ell+1}]) \xleftarrow{\$} \text{FE.KeyGen}(\text{MSK}_{\text{FE},\ell+1}, \mathscr{V}_{\text{CVPRF}}[\text{CT}_{\text{SKE},\ell+1}])$ for the function $\mathscr{V}_{\text{CVPRF}}$ is depicted in Fig. 4.

6. Next, it computes a Π_{FE} ciphertext $\text{CT}_{\text{FE},1}^{(\perp)} \xleftarrow{\$} \text{FE.Encrypt}(\text{MPK}_{\text{FE},1}, (\perp, S, \widetilde{S}, \widehat{S}, 0^{\kappa}, 0))$.

7. Finally, it sets the master CVPRF key as $\text{MSK}_{\text{CVPRF}} = (S, \widetilde{S}, \text{MPK}_{\text{FE},\ell+1}, \{\text{SK}_{\text{FE},\iota}(\mathscr{G}_{\text{CVPRF},\iota}[\iota, \text{MPK}_{\text{FE},\iota+1}, \text{CT}_{\text{SKE},\iota}])\}_{\iota \in [\ell]}, \text{CT}_{\text{FE},1}^{(\perp)})$ and publishes the public CVPRF verification key $\text{VK}_{\text{CVPRF}} = (\{\text{SK}_{\text{FE},\iota}(\mathscr{G}_{\text{CVPRF},\iota}[\iota, \text{MPK}_{\text{FE},\iota+1}, \text{CT}_{\text{SKE},\iota}])\}_{\iota \in [\ell]}, \text{SK}_{\text{FE},\ell+1}(\mathscr{V}_{\text{CVPRF}}[\text{CT}_{\text{SKE},\ell+1}]), \text{CT}_{\text{FE},1}^{(\perp)})$.

CVPRF.Eval($\text{MSK}_{\text{CVPRF}}, x$): Taking as input the master CVPRF key $\text{MSK}_{\text{CVPRF}}$ together with an input $x \in \mathbb{D}_{\text{CVPRF}}$, the trusted authority outputs the CVPRF value $y = S_{\langle x \rangle} = \text{PPPRF}(S, x)$, where it extracts the PPPRF key S from $\text{MSK}_{\text{CVPRF}}$.

CVPRF.Prove($\text{MSK}_{\text{CVPRF}}, x$): On input the master CVPRF key $\text{MSK}_{\text{CVPRF}}$ and an input $x \in \mathbb{D}_{\text{CVPRF}}$, the trusted authority performs the following steps:

1. It first computes the prefix-punctured Π_{PPPRF} keys $S_{\langle x \rangle} = \text{PPPRF}(S, x)$ and $\widetilde{S}_{\langle x \rangle} = \text{PPPRF}(\widetilde{S}, x)$, where S and $\widetilde{S}$ are extracted from $\text{MSK}_{\text{CVPRF}}$.

2. Next, it parses $\widetilde{S}_{\langle x \rangle}$ as $\widetilde{S}_{\langle x \rangle} = r_1 \| r_2$ such that $r_1 \in \{0,1\}^{\varphi_1}$ and $r_2 \in \{0,1\}^{\varphi_2}$.

3. Then, it forms the pair of Π_{PKE} public key and secret key $(\text{PK}_{\text{PKE}}, \text{SK}_{\text{PKE}}) = $ PKE.KeyGen$(\ ; r_1)$.
4. It outputs the proof $\pi_{\text{CVPRF}} = (\text{PK}_{\text{PKE}}, r_2)$.

CVPRF.Constrain$(\text{MSK}_{\text{CVPRF}}, C)$: On input the master CVPRF key $\text{MSK}_{\text{CVPRF}}$ and a constraint circuit $C \in \mathbb{C}_{\text{POLY}}$, the trusted authority executes the following steps:

1. It forms a Π_{FE} functional key $\text{SK}_{\text{FE},\ell+1}(\mathscr{P}_{\text{CVPRF}}[C]) \xleftarrow{\$} $ FE.KeyGen $(\text{MSK}_{\text{FE},\ell+1}, \mathscr{P}_{\text{CVPRF}}[C])$, where it extracts $\text{MSK}_{\text{FE},\ell+1}$ from $\text{MSK}_{\text{CVPRF}}$. The function $\mathscr{P}_{\text{CVPRF}}$ is described in Fig. 5.
2. It provides the constrained key $\text{SK}_{\text{CVPRF}}\{C\} = (\{\text{SK}_{\text{FE},\iota}(\mathscr{G}_{\text{CVPRF},\iota}$ $[\iota, \text{MPK}_{\text{FE},\iota+1}, \text{CT}_{\text{SKE},\iota}])\}_{\iota \in [\ell]}, \text{SK}_{\text{FE},\ell+1}(\mathscr{P}_{\text{CVPRF}}[C]), \text{CT}_{\text{FE},1}^{(\perp)})$ to a legitimate user.

CVPRF.Prove-Constrained$(\text{SK}_{\text{CVPRF}}(C), x)$: A user takes as input a constrained key $\text{SK}_{\text{CVPRF}}\{C\}$ corresponding to some legitimate constraint circuit $C \in \mathbb{C}_{\text{POLY}}$ along with an input $x \in \mathbb{D}_{\text{CVPRF}}$. It performs the following:

1. For $\iota \in [\ell]$, it iteratively does the following
   (a) It computes $\Omega_\iota = $ FE.Decrypt$(\text{SK}_{\text{FE},\iota}(\mathscr{G}_{\text{CVPRF},\iota}[\iota, \text{MPK}_{\text{FE},\iota+1}, \text{CT}_{\text{SKE},\iota}]),$ $\text{CT}_{\text{FE},\iota}^{(x|_{\iota-1})})$, where $\text{SK}_{\text{FE},\iota}(\mathscr{G}_{\text{CVPRF},\iota}[\iota, \text{MPK}_{\text{FE},\iota+1}, \text{CT}_{\text{SKE},\iota}])$ is extracted from $\text{SK}_{\text{CVPRF}}\{C\}$.
   (b) It parses Ω_ι as $\Omega_\iota = \text{CT}_{\text{FE},\iota+1}^{(x|_{\iota-1}\|0)} \| \text{CT}_{\text{FE},\iota+1}^{(x|_{\iota-1}\|1)}$.
2. Finally, it computes $\Omega_{\ell+1} = $ FE.Decrypt$(\text{SK}_{\text{FE},\ell+1}(\mathscr{P}_{\text{CVPRF}}[C]), \text{CT}_{\text{FE},\ell+1}^{(x)})$, where it extracts $\text{SK}_{\text{FE},\ell+1}(\mathscr{P}_{\text{CVPRF}}[C])$ from $\text{SK}_{\text{CVPRF}}\{C\}$.
3. If $\Omega_{\ell+1} = \perp$, it outputs $(\perp, \perp)$. Otherwise, it parses $\Omega_{\ell+1} = \Lambda_1 \| \Lambda_2 \| \Lambda_3$ and outputs $(y = \Lambda_1, \pi_{\text{CVPRF}} = (\Lambda_2, \Lambda_3))$.

CVPRF.Verify$(\text{VK}_{\text{CVPRF}}, x, y, \pi_{\text{CVPRF}})$: A verifier takes as input the public verification key VK_{CVPRF}, an input $x \in \mathbb{D}_{\text{CVPRF}}$, a value $y \in \mathbb{Y}_{\text{CVPRF}}$, and a proof $\pi_{\text{CVPRF}} = (\text{PK}_{\text{PKE}}, r) \in \mathbb{P}_{\text{CVPRF}}$. It executes the following steps:

1. For $\iota \in [\ell]$, it iteratively does the following
   (a) It computes $\Omega_\iota = $ FE.Decrypt$(\text{SK}_{\text{FE},\iota}(\mathscr{G}_{\text{CVPRF},\iota}[\iota, \text{MPK}_{\text{FE},\iota+1}, \text{CT}_{\text{SKE},\iota}]),$ $\text{CT}_{\text{FE},\iota}^{(x|_{\iota-1})})$, where $\text{SK}_{\text{FE},\iota}(\mathscr{G}_{\text{CVPRF},\iota}[\iota, \text{MPK}_{\text{FE},\iota+1}, \text{CT}_{\text{SKE},\iota}])$ is extracted from VK_{CVPRF}.
   (b) It parses Ω_ι as $\Omega_\iota = \text{CT}_{\text{FE},\iota+1}^{(x|_{\iota-1}\|0)} \| \text{CT}_{\text{FE},\iota+1}^{(x|_{\iota-1}\|1)}$.
2. Next, it computes $\widetilde{\Omega} = $ FE.Decrypt$(\text{SK}_{\text{FE},\ell+1}(\mathscr{V}_{\text{CVPRF}}[\text{CT}_{\text{SKE},\ell+1}]), \text{CT}_{\text{FE},\ell+1}^{(x)})$, where $\text{SK}_{\text{FE},\ell+1}(\mathscr{V}_{\text{CVPRF}}[\text{CT}_{\text{SKE},\ell+1}])$ is extracted VK_{CVPRF}, and parses $\widetilde{\Omega}$ as $\widetilde{\Omega} = \widetilde{\text{PK}}_{\text{PKE}} \| \widetilde{\text{CT}}_{\text{PKE}}$.
3. If it holds that $[\text{PK}_{\text{PKE}} = \widetilde{\text{PK}}_{\text{PKE}}] \wedge [\text{PKE.Encrypt}(\text{PK}_{\text{PKE}}, y; r) = \widetilde{\text{CT}}_{\text{PKE}}] = 1$, then it outputs 1. Otherwise, it outputs 0.

Theorem 4.1 (Security of the Proposed CVPRF): *Assuming Π_{FE} is a selectively secure FE scheme, Π_{PPPRF} satisfies all the properties of a PPPRF, Π_{SKE} is a secure SKE scheme, and Π_{PKE} satisfies the correctness and CPA security properties of a PKE scheme, our CVPRF satisfies the provability, uniqueness, constraint hiding, and selective pseudorandomness properties of a secure CVPRF as formulated in* [14,18].

The proof of Theorem 4.1 can be found in the full version of the paper.

Constants: Index $j \in \mathbb{N}$, Π_{FE} public key $\mathrm{MPK_{FE}}$, Π_{SKE} ciphertext $\mathrm{CT_{SKE}}$.

Inputs: String $\vartheta \in \{0,1\}^{j-1}$, Π_{PPPRF} keys $K, \widetilde{K}, \widehat{K} \in \mathbb{K}_{\mathrm{PPPRF}}$, Π_{SKE} symmetric key $\mathrm{SK_{SKE}}$, Mode $\gamma \in \{0,1\}$.

A) If Mode $\gamma = 0$, then output $\Omega = \mathrm{CT_{FE}^{(\vartheta\|0)}} \| \mathrm{CT_{FE}^{(\vartheta\|1)}}$, where for $\delta \in \{0,1\}$, $\mathrm{CT_{FE}^{(\vartheta\|\delta)}} =$ FE.Encrypt$(\mathrm{MPK_{FE}}, (\vartheta\|\delta, K_{\langle\delta\rangle}, \widetilde{K}_{\langle\delta\rangle}, \widehat{K}_{\langle\delta\|0\rangle}, 0^\kappa, \gamma); \widehat{K}_{\langle\delta\|1\rangle})$, where κ, some polynomial in λ, is the size of the symmetric keys of Π_{SKE}.

B) Else, output $\Omega = $ SKE.Decrypt$(\mathrm{SK_{SKE}}, \mathrm{CT_{SKE}})$.

Fig. 3. Function $\mathscr{G}_{\mathrm{CVPRF},j}$

Constants: Π_{SKE} ciphertext $\mathrm{CT_{SKE}}$.

Inputs: String $\vartheta \in \{0,1\}^\ell$, Π_{PPPRF} keys $K, \widetilde{K}, \widehat{K} \in \mathbb{K}_{\mathrm{PPPRF}}$, Π_{SKE} symmetric key $\mathrm{SK_{SKE}}$, Mode $\gamma \in \{0,1\}$.

A) If Mode $\gamma = 0$, then parse $\widetilde{K}$ as $\widetilde{K} = \widetilde{r}_1 \| \widetilde{r}_2$ such that $\widetilde{r}_1 \in \{0,1\}^{\varphi_1}$ and $\widetilde{r}_2 \in \{0,1\}^{\varphi_2}$, and output $\Omega = \widetilde{\mathrm{PK}}_{\mathrm{PKE}} \| \widetilde{\mathrm{CT}}_{\mathrm{PKE}}$ which are computed as $(\widetilde{\mathrm{PK}}_{\mathrm{PKE}}, \widetilde{\mathrm{SK}}_{\mathrm{PKE}}) = $ PKE.KeyGen$(\ ; \widetilde{r}_1)$ and $\widetilde{\mathrm{CT}}_{\mathrm{PKE}} = $ PKE.Encrypt$(\widetilde{\mathrm{PK}}_{\mathrm{PKE}}, K; \widetilde{r}_2)$.

B) Else, output $\Omega = $ SKE.Decrypt$(\mathrm{SK_{SKE}}, \mathrm{CT_{SKE}})$.

Fig. 4. Function $\mathscr{V}_{\mathrm{CVPRF}}$

Constants: Circuit $C \in \mathbb{C}_{\mathrm{POLY}}$

Inputs: String $\vartheta \in \{0,1\}^\ell$, Π_{PPPRF} keys $K, \widetilde{K}, \widehat{K} \in \mathbb{K}_{\mathrm{PPPRF}}$, Π_{SKE} symmetric key $\mathrm{SK_{SKE}}$, Mode $\gamma \in \{0,1\}$.

A) If $C(\vartheta) = 1$, parse $\widehat{K}$ as $\widehat{K} = r_1 \| r_2$ such that $r_1 \in \{0,1\}^{\varphi_1}$, $r_2 \in \{0,1\}^{\varphi_2}$, and output $\Omega = K \| \mathrm{PK_{PKE}} \| r_2$ where $\mathrm{PK_{PKE}}$ is computed as $(\mathrm{PK_{PKE}}, \mathrm{SK_{PKE}}) = $ PKE.KeyGen$(\ ; r_1)$.

B) Else, output $\Omega = \perp$.

Fig. 5. Function $\mathscr{P}_{\mathrm{CVPRF}}$

References

1. Abusalah, H., Fuchsbauer, G.: Constrained PRFs for unbounded inputs with short keys. In: Manulis, M., Sadeghi, A.-R., Schneider, S. (eds.) ACNS 2016. LNCS, vol. 9696, pp. 445–463. Springer, Cham (2016). https://doi.org/10.1007/978-3-319-39555-5_24

2. Abusalah, H., Fuchsbauer, G., Pietrzak, K.: Constrained PRFs for unbounded inputs. In: Sako, K. (ed.) CT-RSA 2016. LNCS, vol. 9610, pp. 413–428. Springer, Cham (2016). https://doi.org/10.1007/978-3-319-29485-8_24

3. Ananth, P., Jain, A.: Indistinguishability obfuscation from compact functional encryption. In: Gennaro, R., Robshaw, M. (eds.) CRYPTO 2015. LNCS, vol. 9215, pp. 308–326. Springer, Heidelberg (2015). https://doi.org/10.1007/978-3-662-47989-6_15

4. Ananth, P., Jain, A., Sahai, A.: Indistinguishability obfuscation from functional encryption for simple functions. Cryptology ePrint Archive, Report 2015/730

5. Banerjee, A., Fuchsbauer, G., Peikert, C., Pietrzak, K., Stevens, S.: Key-homomorphic constrained pseudorandom functions. In: Dodis, Y., Nielsen, J.B. (eds.) TCC 2015. LNCS, vol. 9015, pp. 31–60. Springer, Heidelberg (2015). https://doi.org/10.1007/978-3-662-46497-7_2

6. Bitansky, N., Vaikuntanathan, V.: Indistinguishability obfuscation from functional encryption. In: Foundations of Computer Science, FOCS 2015, pp. 171–190. IEEE (2015)
7. Boneh, D., Lewi, K., Wu, D.J.: Constraining pseudorandom functions privately. In: Fehr, S. (ed.) PKC 2017. LNCS, vol. 10175, pp. 494–524. Springer, Heidelberg (2017). https://doi.org/10.1007/978-3-662-54388-7_17
8. Boneh, D., Raghunathan, A., Segev, G.: Function-private identity-based encryption: hiding the function in functional encryption. In: Canetti, R., Garay, J.A. (eds.) CRYPTO 2013. LNCS, vol. 8043, pp. 461–478. Springer, Heidelberg (2013). https://doi.org/10.1007/978-3-642-40084-1_26
9. Boneh, D., Sahai, A., Waters, B.: Functional encryption: definitions and challenges. In: Ishai, Y. (ed.) TCC 2011. LNCS, vol. 6597, pp. 253–273. Springer, Heidelberg (2011). https://doi.org/10.1007/978-3-642-19571-6_16
10. Boneh, D., Waters, B.: Constrained pseudorandom functions and their applications. In: Sako, K., Sarkar, P. (eds.) ASIACRYPT 2013. LNCS, vol. 8270, pp. 280–300. Springer, Heidelberg (2013). https://doi.org/10.1007/978-3-642-42045-0_15
11. Boyle, E., Goldwasser, S., Ivan, I.: Functional signatures and pseudorandom functions. In: Krawczyk, H. (ed.) PKC 2014. LNCS, vol. 8383, pp. 501–519. Springer, Heidelberg (2014). https://doi.org/10.1007/978-3-642-54631-0_29
12. Brakerski, Z., Vaikuntanathan, V.: Constrained key-homomorphic PRFs from standard lattice assumptions. In: Dodis, Y., Nielsen, J.B. (eds.) TCC 2015. LNCS, vol. 9015, pp. 1–30. Springer, Heidelberg (2015). https://doi.org/10.1007/978-3-662-46497-7_1
13. Canetti, R., Chen, Y.: Constraint-hiding constrained PRFs for NC^1 from LWE. In: Coron, J.-S., Nielsen, J.B. (eds.) EUROCRYPT 2017. LNCS, vol. 10210, pp. 446–476. Springer, Cham (2017). https://doi.org/10.1007/978-3-319-56620-7_16
14. Chandran, N., Raghuraman, S., Vinayagamurthy, D.: Constrained pseudorandom functions: verifiable and delegatable. Cryptology ePrint Archive, Report 2014/522
15. Coron, J.-S., Lepoint, T., Tibouchi, M.: Practical multilinear maps over the integers. In: Canetti, R., Garay, J.A. (eds.) CRYPTO 2013. LNCS, vol. 8042, pp. 476–493. Springer, Heidelberg (2013). https://doi.org/10.1007/978-3-642-40041-4_26
16. Datta, P., Dutta, R., Mukhopadhyay, S.: Constrained pseudorandom functions for unconstrained inputs revisited: achieving verifiability and key delegation. In: Fehr, S. (ed.) PKC 2017. LNCS, vol. 10175, pp. 463–493. Springer, Heidelberg (2017). https://doi.org/10.1007/978-3-662-54388-7_16
17. Deshpande, A., Koppula, V., Waters, B.: Constrained pseudorandom functions for unconstrained inputs. In: Fischlin, M., Coron, J.-S. (eds.) EUROCRYPT 2016. LNCS, vol. 9666, pp. 124–153. Springer, Heidelberg (2016). https://doi.org/10.1007/978-3-662-49896-5_5
18. Fuchsbauer, G.: Constrained verifiable random functions. In: Abdalla, M., De Prisco, R. (eds.) SCN 2014. LNCS, vol. 8642, pp. 95–114. Springer, Cham (2014). https://doi.org/10.1007/978-3-319-10879-7_7
19. Fuchsbauer, G., Konstantinov, M., Pietrzak, K., Rao, V.: Adaptive security of constrained PRFs. In: Sarkar, P., Iwata, T. (eds.) ASIACRYPT 2014. LNCS, vol. 8874, pp. 82–101. Springer, Heidelberg (2014). https://doi.org/10.1007/978-3-662-45608-8_5
20. Garg, S., Gentry, C., Halevi, S.: Candidate multilinear maps from ideal lattices. In: Johansson, T., Nguyen, P.Q. (eds.) EUROCRYPT 2013. LNCS, vol. 7881, pp. 1–17. Springer, Heidelberg (2013). https://doi.org/10.1007/978-3-642-38348-9_1

21. Garg, S., Gentry, C., Halevi, S., Raykova, M., Sahai, A., Waters, B.: Candidate indistinguishability obfuscation and functional encryption for all circuits. SIAM J. Comput. **45**(3), 882–929 (2016)

22. Garg, S., Pandey, O., Srinivasan, A.: Revisiting the cryptographic hardness of finding a nash equilibrium. In: Robshaw, M., Katz, J. (eds.) CRYPTO 2016. LNCS, vol. 9815, pp. 579–604. Springer, Heidelberg (2016). https://doi.org/10.1007/978-3-662-53008-5_20

23. Garg, S., Pandey, O., Srinivasan, A., Zhandry, M.: Breaking the sub-exponential barrier in obfustopia. In: Coron, J.-S., Nielsen, J.B. (eds.) EUROCRYPT 2017. LNCS, vol. 10212, pp. 156–181. Springer, Cham (2017). https://doi.org/10.1007/978-3-319-56617-7_6

24. Garg, S., Srinivasan, A.: Single-key to multi-key functional encryption with polynomial loss. In: Hirt, M., Smith, A. (eds.) TCC 2016. LNCS, vol. 9986, pp. 419–442. Springer, Heidelberg (2016). https://doi.org/10.1007/978-3-662-53644-5_16

25. Goldreich, O., Goldwasser, S., Micali, S.: How to construct random functions. J. ACM (JACM) **33**(4), 792–807 (1986)

26. Gorbunov, S., Vaikuntanathan, V., Wee, H.: Functional encryption with bounded collusions via multi-party computation. In: Safavi-Naini, R., Canetti, R. (eds.) CRYPTO 2012. LNCS, vol. 7417, pp. 162–179. Springer, Heidelberg (2012). https://doi.org/10.1007/978-3-642-32009-5_11

27. Gorbunov, S., Vaikuntanathan, V., Wee, H.: Predicate encryption for circuits from LWE. In: Gennaro, R., Robshaw, M. (eds.) CRYPTO 2015. LNCS, vol. 9216, pp. 503–523. Springer, Heidelberg (2015). https://doi.org/10.1007/978-3-662-48000-7_25

28. Hofheinz, D., Kamath, A., Koppula, V., Waters, B.: Adaptively secure constrained pseudorandom functions. Cryptology ePrint Archive, Report 2014/720

29. Hohenberger, S., Koppula, V., Waters, B.: Adaptively secure puncturable pseudorandom functions in the standard model. In: Iwata, T., Cheon, J.H. (eds.) ASIACRYPT 2015. LNCS, vol. 9452, pp. 79–102. Springer, Heidelberg (2015). https://doi.org/10.1007/978-3-662-48797-6_4

30. Kiayias, A., Papadopoulos, S., Triandopoulos, N., Zacharias, T.: Delegatable pseudorandom functions and applications. In: Proceedings of the 2013 ACM SIGSAC Conference on Computer and Communications Security, pp. 669–684. ACM (2013)

31. Micali, S., Rabin, M., Vadhan, S.: Verifiable random functions. In: 40th Annual Symposium on Foundations of Computer Science, pp. 120–130. IEEE (1999)

32. Naor, M.: On cryptographic assumptions and challenges. In: Boneh, D. (ed.) CRYPTO 2003. LNCS, vol. 2729, pp. 96–109. Springer, Heidelberg (2003). https://doi.org/10.1007/978-3-540-45146-4_6

33. Sahai, A., Waters, B.: How to use indistinguishability obfuscation: deniable encryption, and more. In: Proceedings of the 46th Annual ACM Symposium on Theory of Computing-STOC 2014, pp. 475–484. ACM (2014)

34. Waters, B.: A punctured programming approach to adaptively secure functional encryption. In: Gennaro, R., Robshaw, M. (eds.) CRYPTO 2015. LNCS, vol. 9216, pp. 678–697. Springer, Heidelberg (2015). https://doi.org/10.1007/978-3-662-48000-7_33

Efficient Trapdoor Generation from Multiple Hashing in Searchable Symmetric Encryption

Takato Hirano[✉], Yutaka Kawai, and Yoshihiro Koseki

Mitsubishi Electric Corporation, Kamakura, Japan
Hirano.Takato@ay.MitsubishiElectric.co.jp,
Kawai.Yutaka@da.MitsubishiElectric.co.jp,
Koseki.Yoshihiro@ak.MitsubishiElectric.co.jp

Abstract. Searchable symmetric encryption (SSE) which can search encrypted data using encrypted keywords has been extremely studied. In Asiacrypt'10, Chase and Kamara formalized structured encryption which is a generalization of SSE, and its concrete schemes were proposed. An efficient SSE scheme (hereafter, Chase-Kamara scheme) which has a very simple encrypted index is obtained by simplifying the concrete schemes, and its adaptive security can be proved, easily. In the Chase-Kamara scheme, a search result for a keyword is represented as a bit string in which the i-th bit is 1 when the i-th document contains the keyword, and the encrypted index is built by directly masking the search result with each bit of the output of a pseudo-random function. Therefore, the Chase-Kamara scheme requires pseudo-random functions whose output lengths are longer than the number of documents that users would like to store. As a result, the trapdoor size of the Chase-Kamara scheme depends on the number of stored documents. In this paper, we propose a modified scheme whose trapdoor size does not depend on the number of stored documents. The modified scheme is constructed by using our multiple hashing technique which can transform a trapdoor of short length to that of long length without any secret information. We also show that the modified scheme achieves the same adaptive security as the Chase-Kamara scheme in the random oracle model.

Keywords: Searchable symmetric encryption
Chase-Kamara scheme · Trapdoor size · Multiple hashing

1 Introduction

1.1 Background

Nowadays, cloud services such as data storing on remote third-party providers give high data availability and reduce IT infrastructure costs of a company. From a viewpoint of security, company's sensitive data such as secret information or

C. Su and H. Kikuchi (Eds.): ISPEC 2018, LNCS 11125, pp. 160–175, 2018.
https://doi.org/10.1007/978-3-319-99807-7_10

privacy data of customers should be encrypted to be kept secret from people outside of the company when stored on the cloud. On the other hand, it is indispensable to search the stored data from a viewpoint of usability. However, data encrypting and keyword searching are incompatible in general, since keyword searching for encrypted data is intractable. Although there is a naive approach in which keyword searching is performed after decrypting encrypted data on the cloud, this is insufficient because malicious administrators or softwares on the cloud would steal the plain data or decryption keys when performed the decryption process. As a solution to these problems, searchable encryption has been proposed.

After the first searchable encryption scheme was proposed in [42], many concrete schemes have been constructed. Roughly speaking, searchable encryption schemes are typically classified into two types: symmetric-key type (e.g. [1,2,5,7–49]) and public-key type (e.g. [3,6]). This paper focuses on the former searchable encryption.

Searchable encryption of symmetric-key type is called *searchable symmetric encryption* or *SSE*. SSE consists of *document storing process* and *keyword searching process*, and these processes are performed by the same user since a unique secret key is used in typical SSE. In the document storing process, the user encrypts documents and generates an encrypted index from the secret key, and the server stores a pair of the encrypted documents and the encrypted index. In the keyword searching process, the user generates an encrypted query (called *trapdoor*) from the secret key and a keyword, and the server searches by applying the trapdoor to the encrypted index. Although the keyword searching cost in SSE is quite lower than that in public-key type, this cost becomes critical even in SSE as the number of stored documents increases. In order to reduce this cost, SSE schemes with useful indexes such as inverted index structure or Bloom filter have been constructed.

Security models for SSE also have been studied. Curtmola et al. [15,16] carefully extracted unavoidable information leaked from the document storing process and the keyword searching process of a typical SSE scheme, and formalized acceptable leakage information. Then, they defined that an SSE scheme is secure if information revealed from the processes of the SSE scheme is at most the acceptable leakage information. Their security model and its variants (e.g. [13]) are used in many SSE schemes. Especially, adaptive security definitions proposed in [13,15,16] is considered as one of the security goals in SSE literature.

1.2   Motivation

The SSE schemes (called SSE-1 and SSE-2) proposed by Curtmola et al. have search-friendly encrypted indexes such as inverted index structure [15,16]. Their schemes have had a big impact on constructing efficient SSE schemes. Especially, SSE-2 is constructed only from pseudo-random functions and achieves the adaptive security. Furthermore, the keyword searching process of SSE-2 is based on the binary searching operation, and therefore performed efficiently. However, there is a problem that the trapdoor size of SSE-2 depends on the number of stored documents.

Chase and Kamara formalized structured encryption which is a generalization of SSE, and its concrete schemes were proposed [13]. An efficient SSE scheme (hereafter, Chase-Kamara scheme) which has a very simple structure is obtained by simplifying the concrete schemes. It is very easy to show that the Chase-Kamara scheme achieves the adaptive security, thanks to simplicity of its encrypted index structure. In the Chase-Kamara scheme, a search result for a keyword is represented as a bit string in which the i-th bit is 1 when the i-th document contains the keyword, and the encrypted index is built by directly masking the search result with each bit of the output of a pseudo-random function. Therefore, the Chase-Kamara scheme requires pseudo-random functions whose output lengths are longer than the number of documents that the user would like to store. As a result, the trapdoor size of the Chase-Kamara scheme depends on the number of stored documents. This trapdoor size becomes critical as the number of stored documents increases. For example, the trapdoor size is about 120MB when the number of stored documents is one billion. Thus, the Chase-Kamara scheme has the same trapdoor size problem as SSE-2.

Recently, Miyoshi et al. proposed the SSE scheme with a small encrypted index [36]. Their scheme is constructed by hierarchical Bloom filters, and achieves the adaptive security. However, in their scheme, the trapdoor size also depends on the number of stored documents, and the number of communication rounds between the user and the server is two. Therefore, their keyword searching process is inefficient although the encrypted index size is reasonable.

1.3   Our Contributions

In this paper, we focus on the trapdoor size problem of the Chase-Kamara scheme, and propose a modified scheme whose trapdoor size does not depend on the number of stored documents. The modified scheme is constructed by using our multiple hashing technique which can transform a trapdoor of *short length* to that of *long length* without any secret information. With this technique, the trapdoor size of the modified scheme depends only on the output length of a used hash function (e.g. 512-bit if SHA-256 is used) even if the number of stored documents is one billion. We can show that the modified scheme is adaptively secure in the random oracle model.

A key point of our modified scheme is to securely divide the trapdoor generation process of the Chase-Kamara scheme by using our multiple hashing technique. According to this modification of the trapdoor generation process, the encrypted index of the Chase-Kamara scheme is also slightly modified. Informally, in the Chase-Kamara scheme, the user generates a trapdoor of long length and the server searches the encrypted index by directly using the trapdoor. On the other hand, in our modified scheme, the user generates a trapdoor of short length, and the server transforms the trapdoor to a meaningful value of long length, which consists of hash values and corresponds to the trapdoor of the Chase-Kamara scheme. This transformation uses only the trapdoor sent by the user, but not any secret information. After that, the server searches the encrypted index using the trapdoor and the meaningful value, similarly to the Chase-Kamara scheme.

We give a comparison result among the adaptively secure SSE schemes [13, 15, 36] and our modified scheme in Table 1, where ℓ and λ are the output lengths of a pseudo-random function and a hash function, respectively, n_D is the number of stored documents, n_w is the number of used keywords, $n_{\mathbf{D}(w)}$ is the number of documents containing the keyword w (i.e. the cardinality of the search result of w), $\Sigma_{\mathbf{D}(w)} = \sum_{i=1}^{n_w} n_{\mathbf{D}(w_i)}$, $m_{\mathbf{D}(w)} = \max_w(n_{\mathbf{D}(w)})$, and PRF and HF are the computation costs of a pseudo-random function and a hash function, respectively. Here, we assume that $\lambda < n_D$ and the binary complete-matching cost for N words is $\log N$. Note that these assumptions are reasonable in practical situations.

Table 1. Comparisons among related works [13, 15, 36] and our work.

Scheme	SSE-2 [15]	Chase-Kamara [13]	Miyoshi et al. [36]	Our work
Index size	$O(\ell n_w m_{\mathbf{D}(w)})$	$O(n_w n_D)$	$O(\ell(n_w \log n_w + \Sigma_{\mathbf{D}(w)}))$	$O(n_w n_D)$
Trapdoor size	$O(\ell m_{\mathbf{D}(w)})$	$O(n_D)$	$O(\ell n_{\mathbf{D}(w)})$	$O(\lambda)$
User's search cost	$O(m_{\mathbf{D}(w)}\mathrm{PRF})$	$O(\mathrm{PRF})$	$O(n_{\mathbf{D}(w)}\mathrm{PRF})$	$O(\mathrm{HF})$
Server's search cost	$O(m_{\mathbf{D}(w)} \log n_D)$	$O(\log n_D)$	$O(\mathrm{PRF} \log n_w + n_{\mathbf{D}(w)} \log m_{\mathbf{D}(w)})$	$O(\frac{n_D}{\lambda}\mathrm{HF} + \log n_w)$
Round	1	1	2	1

1.4   Related Works

Curtmola et al. proposed the SSE schemes (SSE-1 and SSE-2) whose encrypted indexes have search-friendly structures such as inverted index [15]. Their schemes have had a big impact on constructing efficient SSE schemes. Although SSE-2 achieves the adaptive security, the trapdoor size of SSE-2 depends on the number of stored documents.

The Chase-Kamara scheme [13] can build an encrypted index of a very simple structure, and therefore the keyword searching process is conducted efficiently. However, the trapdoor size depends on the number of stored documents.

The Miyoshi et al. scheme [36] can a construct small encrypted index by using hierarchical Bloom filters. However, the trapdoor size also depends on the number of stored documents, and the number of communication rounds between the user and the server is two.

While this paper focuses on constructing efficient SSE schemes, other useful functionalities for SSE have been studied, in addition to basic functionalities such as document storing and keyword searching: for example, document adding/deleting/updating functionalities (a.k.a. dynamic SSE) [9, 15,

20, 23, 26, 28, 29, 37, 38, 43, 45, 47–49], flexible search functionalities [5, 7, 10, 14, 18, 21, 27, 30, 31, 34, 35, 37, 41, 46], localities [2, 11, 17], forward security [8], UC-security [32, 33, 40], multi-user settings [1, 15, 16, 19, 24, 48], etc.

1.5   Organization

The rest of this paper is organized as follows. In Sect. 2, we recall cryptographic primitives and SSE definitions which are used throughout the paper. The Chase-Kamara scheme is given in Sect. 3, and its modified scheme is proposed in Sect. 4. We conclude in Sect. 5.

2   Preliminaries

In this section, we recall cryptographic primitives and SSE definitions which are used throughout the paper.

2.1   Notations and Basic Cryptographic Primitives

We denote the set of positive real numbers by $\mathbb{R}^+$. We say that a function $\mathtt{negl} : \mathbb{N} \to \mathbb{R}^+$ is negligible if for any (positive) polynomial p, there exists $n_0 \in \mathbb{N}$ such that for all $n \geq n_0$, it holds $\mathtt{negl}(n) < 1/p(n)$. If A is a probabilistic algorithm, $y \leftarrow A(x)$ denotes running A on input x with a uniformly-chosen random tape and assigning the output to y. $A^{\mathcal{O}}$ denotes an algorithm with oracle access to $\mathcal{O}$. If S is a finite set, $s \xleftarrow{u} S$ denotes that s is uniformly chosen from S. We denote the bit length of S by $|S|$, and the cardinality of S by $\#S$. For strings a and b, $a||b$ denotes the concatenation of a and b.

We recall the definition of pseudo-random functions. A function $f : \{0,1\}^\lambda \times \{0,1\}^k \to \{0,1\}^\ell$ is pseudo-random if f is polynomial-time computable in λ, and for any probabilistic polynomial-time (PPT) algorithm $\mathcal{A}$, it holds

$$|\Pr[1 \leftarrow \mathcal{A}^{f_K(\cdot)}(1^\lambda) \mid K \xleftarrow{u} \{0,1\}^\lambda] - \Pr[1 \leftarrow \mathcal{A}^{g(\cdot)}(1^\lambda) \mid g \xleftarrow{u} \mathsf{F}[k,\ell]]| \leq \mathtt{negl}(\lambda),$$

where $\mathsf{F}[k,\ell]$ is the set of functions mapping $\{0,1\}^k$ to $\{0,1\}^\ell$.

We recall the definition of *left-or-right indistinguishability against the chosen plaintext attack (LOR-CPA)* for symmetric-key encryption [4]. A symmetric-key encryption scheme is secure in the sense of LOR-CPA if for any PPT adversary $\mathcal{A}$, it holds

$$|\Pr[1 \leftarrow \mathcal{A}^{\mathtt{Enc}_K(\mathcal{LR}(\cdot,\cdot,1))}(1^\lambda) \mid K \leftarrow \mathtt{Gen}(1^\lambda)]$$
$$- \Pr[1 \leftarrow \mathcal{A}^{\mathtt{Enc}_K(\mathcal{LR}(\cdot,\cdot,0))}(1^\lambda) \mid K \leftarrow \mathtt{Gen}(1^\lambda)]| \leq \mathtt{negl}(\lambda),$$

where $\mathtt{Enc}_K(\mathcal{LR}(\cdot,\cdot,b))$ is the left-or-right oracle that takes an input (x_0, x_1) and outputs $C_0 \leftarrow \mathtt{Enc}_K(x_0)$ if $b = 0$ and $C_1 \leftarrow \mathtt{Enc}_K(x_1)$ if $b = 1$.

2.2 Definitions of SSE

We recall the definitions of SSE, formalized in [15]. Firstly, we give notions used in SSE literature.

- Let $D \in \{0,1\}^*$ be a document, and $\mathbf{D} = (D_1, \ldots, D_n)$ be a document collection. Let $\mathbf{C} = (C_1, \ldots, C_n)$ be a ciphertext collection of $\mathbf{D}$, where C_i is a ciphertext of D_i for $1 \leq i \leq n$. We assume that D_i and C_i contain the same unique identifier id_i.
- Let $w \in \{0,1\}^k$ be a keyword, and $\Delta \subseteq \{0,1\}^k$ be a set of possible keywords. Let $\Delta(\mathbf{D}) \subseteq \Delta$ be a set of keywords which are contained in some of $D_1, \ldots, D_n$. Throughout this paper, we assume that $\#\Delta$ is polynomially bounded in a security parameter λ.
- For $\mathbf{D} = (D_1, \ldots, D_n)$ and $w \in \Delta$, let $\mathbf{D}(w)$ be a set of identifiers of documents that contain w. Namely, $\mathbf{D}(w) = \{id_{i_1}, \ldots, id_{i_m}\}$ for $w \in \Delta(\mathbf{D})$ or $\emptyset$ for $w \notin \Delta(\mathbf{D})$. For a searching sequence $\mathbf{w} = (w_1, \ldots, w_q)$, let $\mathbf{D}(\mathbf{w}) = (\mathbf{D}(w_1), \ldots, \mathbf{D}(w_q))$.

An SSE scheme over Δ, $\mathtt{SSE} = (\mathtt{Gen}, \mathtt{Enc}, \mathtt{Trpdr}, \mathtt{Search}, \mathtt{Dec})$, is defined as follows.

- $K \leftarrow \mathtt{Gen}(1^\lambda)$: $\mathtt{Gen}$ is a probabilistic algorithm which takes a parameter 1^λ as an input and outputs a secret key K, where λ is a security parameter.
- $(\mathcal{I}, \mathbf{C}) \leftarrow \mathtt{Enc}(K, \mathbf{D})$: $\mathtt{Enc}$ is a probabilistic algorithm which takes a secret key K and a document collection $\mathbf{D}$ as input and outputs an encrypted index $\mathcal{I}$ and a ciphertext collection $\mathbf{C} = (C_1, \ldots, C_n)$.
- $T \leftarrow \mathtt{Trpdr}(K, w)$: $\mathtt{Trpdr}$ is a deterministic algorithm which takes a secret key K and a keyword w as input and outputs a trapdoor T.
- $S \leftarrow \mathtt{Search}(\mathcal{I}, T)$: $\mathtt{Search}$ is a deterministic algorithm which takes an encrypted index $\mathcal{I}$ and a trapdoor T as input and outputs an identifier set S.
- $D \leftarrow \mathtt{Dec}(K, C)$: $\mathtt{Dec}$ is a deterministic algorithm which takes a secret key K and a ciphertext C as input and outputs a plaintext D of C.

An SSE scheme is correct if for all $\lambda \in \mathbb{N}$, all $\mathbf{D}$, all $w \in \Delta(\mathbf{D})$, all K output by $\mathtt{Gen}(1^\lambda)$, and all $(\mathcal{I}, \mathbf{C})$ output by $\mathtt{Enc}(K, \mathbf{D})$, it holds $\mathtt{Search}(\mathcal{I}, \mathtt{Trpdr}(K, w)) = \mathbf{D}(w)$ and $\mathtt{Dec}(K, C_i) = D_i$ for $1 \leq i \leq n$.

We give security notions, *history*, *access pattern*, *search pattern*, *trace*, and *non-singular* [15].

- For a document collection $\mathbf{D} = (D_1, \ldots, D_n)$ and a searching sequence $\mathbf{w} = (w_1, \ldots, w_q)$, $H = (\mathbf{D}, \mathbf{w})$ is called *history*. This information is sensitive in SSE.
- $\alpha(H) = (\mathbf{D}(w_1), \ldots, \mathbf{D}(w_q))$ is called *access pattern* for a history $H = (\mathbf{D}, \mathbf{w})$. This information is appeared by performing the keyword searching processes.
- The following binary symmetric matrix $\sigma(H) = (\sigma_{i,j})$ is called *search pattern* for a history $H = (\mathbf{D}, \mathbf{w})$: for $1 \leq i \leq j \leq q$, $\sigma_{i,j} = 1$ if $w_i = w_j$, and $\sigma_{i,j} = 0$ otherwise. This information is appeared by performing the keyword searching processes because trapdoors are deterministically generated in SSE.

- $\tau(H) = (|D_1|, \ldots, |D_n|, \alpha(H), \sigma(H))$ is called *trace* for a history $H = (\mathbf{D}, \mathbf{w})$. This information is leaked while performing SSE protocols, and therefore considered as acceptable leakage information in SSE.
- H is called *non-singular* if (1) there exists a history $H' \neq H$ such that $\tau(H) = \tau(H')$, and (2) H' is computed from a given trace $\tau(H)$, efficiently. We assume that any history is non-singular throughout the paper.

Then, we give the adaptive security definition proposed in [15] (a.k.a. IND-CKA2), which is widely used in SSE literature.

Definition 1 ([15]). *Let* $\mathsf{SSE} = (\mathsf{Gen}, \mathsf{Enc}, \mathsf{Trpdr}, \mathsf{Search}, \mathsf{Dec})$, λ *be a security parameter,* $q \in \mathbb{N} \cup \{0\}$, *and* $\mathcal{A} = (\mathcal{A}_0, \ldots, \mathcal{A}_q)$ *and* $\mathcal{S} = (\mathcal{S}_0, \ldots, \mathcal{S}_q)$ *be probabilistic polynomial-time (PPT) algorithms. Here, we consider the following experiments* **Real** *and* **Sim**:

$\mathbf{Real}_{\mathcal{A}}(1^\lambda):$	$\mathbf{Sim}_{\mathcal{A}, \mathcal{S}}(1^\lambda):$
$K \leftarrow \mathsf{Gen}(1^\lambda)$	$(\mathbf{D}, st_{\mathcal{A}}) \leftarrow \mathcal{A}_0(1^\lambda)$
$(\mathbf{D}, st_{\mathcal{A}}) \leftarrow \mathcal{A}_0(1^\lambda)$	$(\mathcal{I}, \mathbf{C}, st_{\mathcal{S}}) \leftarrow \mathcal{S}_0(\tau(\mathbf{D}))$
$(\mathcal{I}, \mathbf{C}) \leftarrow \mathsf{Enc}(K, \mathbf{D})$	Let $\mathbf{w}_0 = \emptyset$ and $\mathbf{t}_0 = \emptyset$
Let $\mathbf{t}_0 = \emptyset$	For $1 \le i \le q:$
For $1 \le i \le q:$	$\quad (w_i, st_{\mathcal{A}}) \leftarrow \mathcal{A}_i(st_{\mathcal{A}}, \mathcal{I}, \mathbf{C}, \mathbf{t}_{i-1})$
$\quad (w_i, st_{\mathcal{A}}) \leftarrow \mathcal{A}_i(st_{\mathcal{A}}, \mathcal{I}, \mathbf{C}, \mathbf{t}_{i-1})$	$\quad$ Let $\mathbf{w}_i = \mathbf{w}_{i-1} \| w_i$
$\quad t_i \leftarrow \mathsf{Trpdr}(K, w_i)$	$\quad (t_i, st_{\mathcal{S}}) \leftarrow \mathcal{S}_i(st_{\mathcal{S}}, \tau(\mathbf{D}, \mathbf{w}_i))$
$\quad$ Let $\mathbf{t}_i = \mathbf{t}_{i-1} \| t_i$	$\quad$ Let $\mathbf{t}_i = \mathbf{t}_{i-1} \| t_i$
Output $(\mathcal{I}, \mathbf{C}, \mathbf{t}_q, st_{\mathcal{A}})$	Output $(\mathcal{I}, \mathbf{C}, \mathbf{t}_q, st_{\mathcal{A}})$

We define that SSE *is adaptively secure if for any* λ, *any* q *of polynomial size, and any* $\mathcal{A} = (\mathcal{A}_0, \ldots, \mathcal{A}_q)$, *there exists the following PPT algorithm* $\mathcal{S} = (\mathcal{S}_0, \ldots, \mathcal{S}_q):$ *For any PPT distinguisher* $\mathcal{D}$, *it holds*

$$| \Pr[\mathcal{D}(\mathcal{I}, \mathbf{C}, \mathbf{t}_q, st_{\mathcal{A}}) = 1 \mid (\mathcal{I}, \mathbf{C}, \mathbf{t}_q, st_{\mathcal{A}}) \leftarrow \mathbf{Real}_{\mathcal{A}}(1^\lambda)]$$
$$- \Pr[\mathcal{D}(\mathcal{I}, \mathbf{C}, \mathbf{t}_q, st_{\mathcal{A}}) = 1 \mid (\mathcal{I}, \mathbf{C}, \mathbf{t}_q, st_{\mathcal{A}}) \leftarrow \mathbf{Sim}_{\mathcal{A}, \mathcal{S}}(1^\lambda)]| \le \mathsf{negl}(\lambda).$$

3   The Chase-Kamara Scheme

In this section, we give the Chase-Kamara scheme which is directly obtained by simplifying the structured encryption schemes (especially, the associative structured encryption scheme for labeled data) proposed in [13].

Let $F : \{0, 1\}^\lambda \times \{0, 1\}^k \to \{0, 1\}^\ell$ be a pseudo-random function, and SKE be a symmetric-key encryption scheme. Let n be the number of stored documents, that is, $\mathbf{D} = \{D_1, \ldots, D_n\}$. In the Chase-Kamara scheme, we restrict that $\ell \ge n$. Here, we use the following bit string $b_1 \| \cdots \| b_n \| b_{n+1} \| \cdots \| b_\ell$ as another representation for $\mathbf{D}(w)$: $b_i = 1$ if $id_i \in \mathbf{D}(w)$, and $b_i = 0$ otherwise. For example, if $n = 3$, $\ell = 5$, and $\mathbf{D}(w) = \{id_1, id_3\}$, then we also regard $\mathbf{D}(w)$ as 10100. The encrypted index $\mathcal{I}$ built in the Chase-Kamara consists of $\{(key, val)\}$. Let the notation $\mathcal{I}[x]$ be y if there exists a pair (x, y) in $\mathcal{I}$, or $\perp$ otherwise. Then, the Chase-Kamara scheme is given as follows:

– Gen(1^λ):
1. Choose $K_1, K_2 \xleftarrow{u} \{0,1\}^\lambda$ and $K_3 \leftarrow$ SKE.Enc(1^λ).
2. Output $K = (K_1, K_2, K_3)$.
– Enc($K, \mathbf{D}$):
1. Let $\mathcal{I} = \emptyset$.
2. For $w \in \Delta$,
   (a) Compute $key = F(K_1, w)$ and $val = \mathbf{D}(w) \oplus F(K_2, w)$.
   (b) Append (key, val) to $\mathcal{I}$.
1. For $D \in \mathbf{D}$, compute $C \leftarrow$ SKE.Enc(K_3, D).
2. Output $\mathcal{I}$ and $\mathbf{C} = (C_1, \ldots, C_n)$.
– Trpdr(K, w):
1. Compute $T_1 = F(K_1, w)$ and $T_2 = F(K_2, w)$.
2. Output $T = (T_1, T_2)$.
– Search($\mathcal{I}, T$):
1. Parse $T = (T_1, T_2)$.
2. Let $S = \emptyset$.
3. If $\mathcal{I}[T_1] = \bot$ then output $\emptyset$.
4. Compute $v = \mathcal{I}[T_1] \oplus T_2$.
5. Parse $v = v_1 || \cdots || v_n || v_{n+1} || \cdots || v_\ell$, where $v_i \in \{0,1\}$ for $1 \leq i \leq \ell$.
6. For $1 \leq i \leq n$, append id_i to S if $v_i = 1$.
7. Output S.
– Dec(K, C):
1. Compute $D \leftarrow$ SKE.Dec(K_3, C).
2. Output D.

The Chase-Kamara scheme is adaptively secure if SKE is LOR-CPA secure and F is a pseudo-random function. This security proof is very simple and straightforward (see [13]).

We observe that the Chase-Kamara scheme can perform the keyword searching process, efficiently, thanks to very simple structures of the encrypted index $\mathcal{I}$ and the trapdoor T. On the other hand, the trapdoor size, especially $|T_2|$, depends on the number of stored documents (that is, n). The trapdoor size becomes critical as n is increased. For example, $|T_2|$ is of about one billion bits (approximately, 120MB) when n is one billion.

4   The Proposed Scheme

In this section, we tackle to the trapdoor size problem of the Chase-Kamara scheme, and propose its modified scheme by using our multiple hashing technique which can transform a trapdoor of short length to that of long length. Our modified scheme can break the restriction $\ell \geq n$, where n is the number of stored documents and ℓ is the output length of the used pseudo-random function F.

4.1   Our Strategy

A key point of our modified scheme is to securely divide the trapdoor generation process of the Chase-Kamara scheme by using our multiple hashing technique. According to this modification of the trapdoor generation process, the encrypted index of the Chase-Kamara scheme is also slightly modified. In the keyword searching process of the Chase-Kamara scheme, the user generates a trapdoor $T = (T_1, T_2)$ of long length (especially, $T_2 = F_2(K, w)$) and the server searches the encrypted index $\mathcal{I}$ by directly using the trapdoor T. In order to address the trapdoor size problem, we modify this process as follows. The user generates a trapdoor of *short length*, and the server transforms the trapdoor to a meaningful value of *long length*, which consist of multiple hash values and correspond to the trapdoor of the Chase-Kamara scheme. Then, the server searches the encrypted index using the trapdoor and the hash values. This process can be achieved by using our multiple hashing technique. This technical overview is as follows.

As shown in Sect. 3, the encrypted index $\mathcal{I}$ of the Chase-Kamara scheme is constructed by

$$\{(key, val)\}_w = \{(F(K_1, w), \mathbf{D}(w) \oplus F(K_2, w))\}_{w \in \Delta},$$

where w is a keyword, $F : \{0, 1\}^\lambda \times \{0, 1\}^k \to \{0, 1\}^\ell$ is a pseudo-random function, K_1 and K_2 are secret keys of F, and $\mathbf{D}(w)$ is a plain search result for a keyword w and represented as the special bit string form described in Sect. 3. A trapdoor T for a keyword w is computed by $T = (T_1, T_2) = (F(K_1, w), F(K_2, w))$, where $|T_2| = \ell \geq n$.

In order to address the above trapdoor size problem, we modify the encrypted index of the Chase-Kamara scheme by using the following multiple hashing technique. For a hash function $H : \{0, 1\}^* \to \{0, 1\}^\lambda$, we modify $\mathcal{I}$ as[1]

$$\{(key, val)\} = \{(F(K_1, w), \mathbf{D}(w) \oplus (h_{w,1} || \cdots || h_{w,N}))\}_{w \in \Delta},$$

where $N = \lceil n/\lambda \rceil$ and

$$h_{w,1} = H(H(K_2 || w) || 1), \ldots, h_{w,N} = H(H(K_2 || w) || N).$$

In addition to the above modification of the encrypted index, we further modify the trapdoor $T = (T_1, T_2)$ as $(F(K_1, w), H(K_2 || w))$.

Then, the keyword searching process in this modification is conducted as follows. For a trapdoor $T = (F(K_1, w), H(K_2 || w))$, the server computes hash values $h_{w,1}, \ldots, h_{w,N}$ from $T_2 = H(K_2 || w)$, and then checks its search result by $\mathcal{I}[T_1] \oplus (h_{w,1} || \cdots || h_{w,N})(= \mathbf{D}(w))$, similarly to the keyword searching process of the Chase-Kamara scheme. Thus, this modification dramatically reduce the trapdoor size from $O(n)$ to $O(\lambda)$. For example, the trapdoor size is of 512 bits when we use SHA-256. We also observe an advantage that the server can generate arbitrary long values corresponding to T_2 (i.e. the keyword w) with no secret

---

[1] Later, we also modify *key* and T_1 as $H(K_1 || w)$. Furthermore, we set $K_1 = K || 0$ and $K_2 = K || 1$ using a secret key K.

information. We believe that our multiple hashing technique would be applied to other SSE schemes which have the trapdoor size problem, due to its generality and simplicity. Our multiple hashing technique is summarized in Fig. 1.

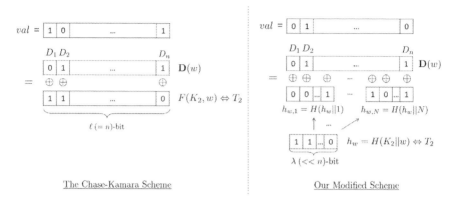

Fig. 1. Summary of our multiple hashing technique.

From a viewpoint of security, our multiple hashing technique leads that the server cannot infer not only hidden keywords from trapdoors, but also any information on relationships among elements of our encrypted index until received trapdoors, due to one-wayness of multiple hashing. As a result, we can also show its adaptive security from a similar strategy as the security proof of the Chase-Kamara scheme, but in the random oracle model since our proof strategy essentially requires randomness of hash functions.

4.2 Construction

Let $H : \{0,1\}^* \rightarrow \{0,1\}^\lambda$ be a hash function. Let $N = \lceil \frac{n}{\lambda} \rceil$ and $\mathbf{D}(w) = b_1 || \cdots || b_n || b_{n+1} || \cdots || b_{\lambda N}$, where $b_1, \ldots, b_n$ are represented as the special bit form described in Sect. 3 and $b_{n+1} = \cdots = b_{\lambda N} = 0$. The modified scheme is proposed as follows:

- Gen(1^λ):
    1. Choose $K_1 \xleftarrow{u} \{0,1\}^\lambda$ and $K_2 \leftarrow$ SKE.Enc(1^λ).
    2. Output $K = (K_1, K_2)$:
- Enc($K, \mathbf{D}$):
    1. Let $\mathcal{I} = \emptyset$.
    2. Compute $N = \lceil \frac{n}{\lambda} \rceil$.
    3. For $w \in \Delta$,
        (a) Compute $key = H(K_1 || 0 || w)$.
        (b) Compute $h_w = H(K_1 || 1 || w)$ and $h_{w,i} = H(h_w || i)$ for $1 \leq i \leq N$.
        (c) Compute $val = \mathbf{D}(w) \oplus (h_{w,1} || \cdots || h_{w,N})$.

      (d) Append (key, val) to $\mathcal{I}$.
   4. For $D \in \mathbf{D}$, compute $C \leftarrow \mathsf{SKE.Enc}(K_2, D)$.
   5. Output $\mathcal{I}$ and $\mathbf{C} = (C_1, \ldots, C_n)$.
- $\mathsf{Trpdr}(K, w)$:
   1. Compute $T_1 = H(K_1||0||w)$ and $T_2 = H(K_1||1||w)$.
   2. Output $T = (T_1, T_2)$.
- $\mathsf{Search}(\mathcal{I}, T)$:
   1. Parse $T = (T_1, T_2)$.
   2. Let $S = \emptyset$.
   3. If $\mathcal{I}[T_1] = \bot$ then output $\emptyset$.
   4. Compute $N = \lceil \frac{n}{\lambda} \rceil$.
   5. Compute $h'_1 = H(T_2||1), \ldots, h'_N = H(T_2||N)$.
   6. Compute $v = \mathcal{I}[T_1] \oplus (h'_1|| \cdots ||h'_N)$.
   7. Let $v = v_1|| \cdots ||v_n||v_{n+1}|| \cdots ||v_{\lambda N}$, where $v_i \in \{0,1\}$ for $1 \leq i \leq \lambda N$.
   8. For $1 \leq i \leq n$, add id_i into S if $v_i = 1$.
   9. Output S.
- $\mathsf{Dec}(K, C)$:
   1. Compute $D \leftarrow \mathsf{SKE.Dec}(K_2, C)$.
   2. Output D.

In the Chase-Kamara scheme, the user generates a trapdoor (T'_1, T'_2) for a keyword w', and the server searches the encrypted index $\mathcal{I}'$ by $\mathcal{I}'[T'_1] \oplus T'_2$. On the other hand, our modified scheme is that the user generates a trapdoor (T_1, T_2) for a keyword w, and the server transforms T_2 to the value $(h_{w,1}|| \cdots ||h_{w,N})$ and then searches the encrypted index $\mathcal{I}$ by $\mathcal{I}[T_1] \oplus (h_{w,1}|| \cdots ||h_{w,N})$.

Then, we can show the following security of the modified scheme.

Theorem 1. *The modified scheme is adaptively secure in the random oracle model if* SKE *is LOR-CPA secure.*

Before proving the security of our modified scheme, we give our proof strategy. Our security proof is straightforward, similarly to that of the Chase-Kamara scheme.

- **Simulation of $\mathcal{I}$:** From the leakage information $(|D_1|, \ldots, |D_n|)$ obtained by querying on $\mathbf{D}$, $\mathcal{S}$ chooses $k_i, r_{i,1}, \ldots, r_{i,N} \xleftarrow{u} \{0,1\}^\lambda$, and set $\mathcal{I} = \{(k_i, r_{i,1}|| \cdots ||r_{i,N})\}_{1 \leq i \leq \#\Delta}$. With this simulation, $\mathcal{S}$ cheats $\mathcal{A}$ as if $\mathcal{I} = \{(k_i, r_{i,1}|| \cdots ||r_{i,N})\}$ is generated in the real experiment.
- **Simulation of T:** If $\mathcal{A}$ queries on w_i, then for some j, $\mathcal{S}$ regards $r_{j,1}|| \cdots ||r_{j,N}$ as

$$r_{j,1}|| \cdots ||r_{j,N} = \mathbf{D}(w_i) \oplus (\quad r'_{j,1} \quad || \cdots || \quad r'_{j,N} \quad)$$
$$= \mathbf{D}(w_i) \oplus (\ H(r_j||1) \ || \cdots || \ H(r_j||N)\ )$$

by assigning some value $r_j \in \{0,1\}^\lambda$, and further regards r_j as $H(K_1||1||w_i)$. With this simulation, $\mathcal{S}$ cheats $\mathcal{A}$ as if r_j is obtained from $H(K_1||1||w_i)$ and $T = (k_j, r_j)$ is generated in the real experiment. In order to simulate the above completely, $\mathcal{S}$ computes $r'_{j,1}, \ldots, r'_{j,N}$ from $val_j = r_{j,1}|| \cdots ||r_{j,N}$ and the leakage information $\mathbf{D}(w_i)$ obtained by querying on w_i, chooses $r_j \xleftarrow{u} \{0,1\}^\lambda$, and appends

Input	Output
$r_j \| 1$	$r'_{j,1}$
$\vdots$	$\vdots$
$r_j \| N$	$r'_{j,N}$

into a random oracle hash table $\mathcal{H}$.

Our formal proof with the above simulation is given as follows.

Proof. Let $\mathcal{H} = \{(input, output)\}$ be a random oracle hash table which is set to $\emptyset$, initially. A PPT simulator $\mathcal{S} = (\mathcal{S}_0, \ldots, \mathcal{S}_q)$ is constructed as follows.

$\mathcal{S}_0$'s *simulation.* For the leakage information $(|D_1|, \ldots, |D_n|)$ obtained from $\mathcal{A}$'s output $\mathbf{D} = (D_1, \ldots, D_n)$, $\mathcal{S}_0$ computes $N = \lceil \frac{n}{\lambda} \rceil$, and chooses random numbers $r_{1,1}, \ldots, r_{1,N}, \ldots, r_{\delta,1}, \ldots, r_{\delta,N} \xleftarrow{u} \{0,1\}^\lambda$, where $\delta = \#\Delta$. Let

$$R_1 = r_{1,1} \| \cdots \| r_{1,N},$$

$$\vdots$$

$$R_\delta = r_{\delta,1} \| \cdots \| r_{\delta,N}.$$

$\mathcal{S}_0$ also chooses random numbers $k_1, \ldots, k_\delta \xleftarrow{u} \{0,1\}^\lambda$, and sets $\mathcal{I} = \{(k_i, R_i)\}_{1 < i \le \delta}$. Further, $\mathcal{S}_0$ runs $SK \leftarrow$ SKE.Gen(1^λ) and $C_i \leftarrow$ SKE.Enc$(SK, 0^{|D_i|})$ for $1 \le i \le n$. Then, $\mathcal{S}_0$ sends $\mathcal{I}$ and $\mathbf{C} = \{C_1, \ldots, C_n\}$ to $\mathcal{A}$.

$\mathcal{S}_i$'s *simulation* $(1 \le i \le q)$. For the leakage information $\alpha(\mathbf{D}, \mathbf{w}_i)$ and $\sigma(\mathbf{D}, \mathbf{w}_i)$ obtained from $\mathcal{A}$'s output w_i, $\mathcal{S}_i$ regards $\mathbf{D}(w_i)$ as $b_{i,1} \| \cdots \| b_{i,n} \| b_{i,n+1} (= 0) \| \cdots \| b_{i,\lambda N} (= 0)$, where $b_{i,j} = 1$ if $id_j \in \mathbf{D}(w_i)$ and $b_{i,j} = 0$ otherwise. After that, $\mathcal{S}_i$ checks whether $w_i \ne w_{i'}$ for any $w_{i'}$ $(1 \le i' < i)$. We note that this check can be efficiently done from the leakage information $\sigma(\mathbf{D}, \mathbf{w}_i)$.

If $w_i \ne w_{i'}$ for $1 \le i' < i$, $\mathcal{S}_i$ chooses $1 \le j \le \delta$ which has not been chosen yet, and computes $r'_{j,1} \| \cdots \| r'_{j,N} = \mathbf{D}(w_i) \oplus R_j$. Then, $\mathcal{S}_i$ chooses a random number $r_j \xleftarrow{u} \{0,1\}^\lambda$, appends

$$(r_j \| 1, r'_{j,1}), \ldots, (r_j \| N, r'_{j,N}),$$

into $\mathcal{H}$, and sends $T_i = (k_j, r_j)$ as a trapdoor of w_i to $\mathcal{A}$.

If there exists $i' < i$ such that $w_i = w_{i'}$, $\mathcal{S}_i$ merely re-sends $T_{i'} = (k_j, r_j)$, which has been already chosen in the i'-th simulation, to $\mathcal{A}$.

Analysis for $\mathcal{S}$'s simulation

- $\mathcal{I}$ and $(T_1, \ldots, T_q)$ output by $\mathcal{S}$ work correctly, similarly to **Real**.
- For any $1 \le i \le n$, $\mathcal{A}$ cannot distinguish C_i output by $\mathcal{S}_0$ from C_i output by **Real** since SKE is LOR-CPA secure.

– The probability that for any $1 \leq i \leq q$, $\mathcal{A}$ can query $K_1||0||w_i$ to the random oracle (i.e. $\mathcal{H}$) a priori (in other words, the probability that $\mathcal{A}$ can obtain its corresponding hash value k_j a priori), is negligible since $\mathcal{A}$ has no secret key and cannot infer it without querying on w_i.

– The probability that for any $1 \leq i \leq q$, $\mathcal{A}$ can query $K_1||1||w_i$ to $\mathcal{H}$ a priori (in other words, the probability that $\mathcal{A}$ can obtain its corresponding hash value r_j a priori), is negligible since $\mathcal{A}$ has no secret key and cannot infer it without querying on w_i.

– The probability that for any $1 \leq j \leq \delta$ and any $1 \leq i \leq N$, $\mathcal{A}$ can query $r_j||i$ to $\mathcal{H}$ a priori (in other words, the probability that $\mathcal{A}$ can obtain its corresponding hash value $r'_{j,i}$), is negligible since $\mathcal{A}$ cannot have r_j a priori for any $1 \leq j \leq \delta$ without querying on w_i.

– The probability that for any $1 \leq j \leq \delta$ and any $1 \leq i \leq N$, $\mathcal{A}$ can infer $r'_{j,i}$ from R_j, is negligible since $\mathcal{A}$ cannot have $\mathbf{D}(w_i)$ a priori for any $1 \leq i \leq q$ without querying on w_i.

From the above analysis, $\mathcal{A}$ and also any distinguisher $\mathcal{D}$ cannot distinguish (k_i, r_i) output by $\mathcal{S}$ from (key_i, val_i) output by **Real** for any $1 \leq i \leq \delta$. Thus, the modified scheme is adaptively secure in the random oracle model. $\square$

5   Conclusion

In this paper, we have shown the Chase-Kamara encryption scheme which is obtained by simplifying the structured encryption schemes [13]. We have focused on the trapdoor size problem of the Chase-Kamara scheme, and proposed the modified scheme whose trapdoor size does not depend on the number of stored documents. The modified scheme is based on our multiple hashing technique which can transform a trapdoor of short length to that of long length. We have shown that the modified scheme is adaptively secure in the random oracle model.

A future work is to show that our modified scheme is adaptively secure from standard assumptions. We note that our modified scheme satisfies non-adaptive security if employed pseudo-random functions instead of hash functions in our modified scheme.

Acknowledgments. The authors would like to thank anonymous reviewers of ISPEC 2018 for their valuable comments.

References

1. Alderman, J., Martin, K.M., Renwick, S.L.: Multi-level access in searchable symmetric encryption. In: Brenner, M. (ed.) FC 2017. LNCS, vol. 10323, pp. 35–52. Springer, Cham (2017). https://doi.org/10.1007/978-3-319-70278-0_3
2. Asharov, G., Naor, M., Segev, G., Shahaf, I.: Searchable symmetric encryption: optimal locality in linear space via two-dimensional balanced allocations. In: STOC 2016 (2016)

3. Bellare, M., Boldyreva, A., O'Neill, A.: Deterministic and efficiently searchable encryption. In: Menezes, A. (ed.) CRYPTO 2007. LNCS, vol. 4622, pp. 535–552. Springer, Heidelberg (2007). https://doi.org/10.1007/978-3-540-74143-5_30

4. Bellare, M., Desai, A., Jokipii, E., Rogaway, P.: A concrete security treatment of symmetric encryption. In: FOCS 1997, pp. 394–403 (1997)

5. Boldyreva, A., Chenette, N.: Efficient fuzzy search on encrypted data. In: Cid, C., Rechberger, C. (eds.) FSE 2014. LNCS, vol. 8540, pp. 613–633. Springer, Heidelberg (2015). https://doi.org/10.1007/978-3-662-46706-0_31

6. Boneh, D., Di Crescenzo, G., Ostrovsky, R., Persiano, G.: Public key encryption with keyword search. In: Cachin, C., Camenisch, J.L. (eds.) EUROCRYPT 2004. LNCS, vol. 3027, pp. 506–522. Springer, Heidelberg (2004). https://doi.org/10.1007/978-3-540-24676-3_30

7. Bösch, C., Brinkman, R., Hartel, P., Jonker, W.: Conjunctive wildcard search over encrypted data. In: Jonker, W., Petković, M. (eds.) SDM 2011. LNCS, vol. 6933, pp. 114–127. Springer, Heidelberg (2011). https://doi.org/10.1007/978-3-642-23556-6_8

8. Bost, R.: Σοφος - forward secure searchable encryption. In: ACM CCS 2016, pp. 1143–1154 (2016)

9. Cash, D., et al.: Dynamic searchable encryption in very-large databases: data structures and implementation. In: NDSS 2014 (2014)

10. Cash, D., Jarecki, S., Jutla, C., Krawczyk, H., Roşu, M.-C., Steiner, M.: Highly-scalable searchable symmetric encryption with support for boolean queries. In: Canetti, R., Garay, J.A. (eds.) CRYPTO 2013. LNCS, vol. 8042, pp. 353–373. Springer, Heidelberg (2013). https://doi.org/10.1007/978-3-642-40041-4_20

11. Cash, D., Tessaro, S.: The locality of searchable symmetric encryption. In: Nguyen, P.Q., Oswald, E. (eds.) EUROCRYPT 2014. LNCS, vol. 8441, pp. 351–368. Springer, Heidelberg (2014). https://doi.org/10.1007/978-3-642-55220-5_20

12. Chang, Y.-C., Mitzenmacher, M.: Privacy preserving keyword searches on remote encrypted data. In: Ioannidis, J., Keromytis, A., Yung, M. (eds.) ACNS 2005. LNCS, vol. 3531, pp. 442–455. Springer, Heidelberg (2005). https://doi.org/10.1007/11496137_30

13. Chase, M., Kamara, S.: Structured encryption and controlled disclosure. In: Abe, M. (ed.) ASIACRYPT 2010. LNCS, vol. 6477, pp. 577–594. Springer, Heidelberg (2010). https://doi.org/10.1007/978-3-642-17373-8_33

14. Chase, M., Shen, E.: Substring-searchable symmetric encryption. PETS 2015 **2015**(2), 263–281 (2015)

15. Curtmola, R., Garay, J., Kamara, S., Ostrovsky, R.: Searchable symmetric encryption: improved definitions and efficient constructions. In: ACM CCS 2006, pp. 79–88 (2006)

16. Curtmola, R., Garay, J., Kamara, S., Ostrovsky, R.: Searchable symmetric encryption: improved definitions and efficient constructions. J. Comput. Secur. **19**(5), 895–934 (2011)

17. Demertzis, I., Papamanthou, C.: Fast searchable encryption with tunable locality. In: ACM SIGMOD 2017, pp. 1053–1067 (2017)

18. Do, H.G., Ng, W.K.: Private boolean query processing on encrypted data. In: Lam, K.-Y., Chi, C.-H., Qing, S. (eds.) ICICS 2016. LNCS, vol. 9977, pp. 321–332. Springer, Cham (2016). https://doi.org/10.1007/978-3-319-50011-9_25

19. Dong, C., Russello, G., Dulay, N.: Shared and searchable encrypted data for untrusted servers. J. Comput. Secur. **19**(3), 367–397 (2011)

20. Etemad, M., Kupcu, A., Papamanthou, C.: Efficient dynamic searchable encryption with forward privacy. PETS 2018 **2018**(1), 5–20 (2018)

21. Faber, S., Jarecki, S., Krawczyk, H., Nguyen, Q., Rosu, M., Steiner, M.: Rich queries on encrypted data: beyond exact matches. In: Pernul, G., Ryan, P.Y.A., Weippl, E. (eds.) ESORICS 2015. LNCS, vol. 9327, pp. 123–145. Springer, Cham (2015). https://doi.org/10.1007/978-3-319-24177-7_7

22. Goh, E.-J.: Secure indexes. Cryptology ePrint Archive, Report 2003/216 (2003). http://eprint.iacr.org/2003/216

23. Hahn, F., Kerschbaum, F.: Searchable encryption with secure and efficient updates. In: ACM CCS 2014, pp. 310–320 (2014)

24. Hamlin, A., Shelat, A., Weiss, M., Wichs, D.: Multi-key searchable encryption, revisited. In: Abdalla, M., Dahab, R. (eds.) PKC 2018. LNCS, vol. 10769, pp. 95–124. Springer, Cham (2018). https://doi.org/10.1007/978-3-319-76578-5_4

25. Hayasaka, K., Kawai, Y., Koseki, Y., Hirano, T., Ohta, K., Iwamoto, M.: Probabilistic generation of trapdoors: reducing information leakage of searchable symmetric encryption. In: Foresti, S., Persiano, G. (eds.) CANS 2016. LNCS, vol. 10052, pp. 350–364. Springer, Cham (2016). https://doi.org/10.1007/978-3-319-48965-0_21

26. Hirano, T., et al.: Simple, secure, and efficient searchable symmetric encryption with multiple encrypted indexes. In: Ogawa, K., Yoshioka, K. (eds.) IWSEC 2016. LNCS, vol. 9836, pp. 91–110. Springer, Cham (2016). https://doi.org/10.1007/978-3-319-44524-3_6

27. Kamara, S., Moataz, T.: Boolean searchable symmetric encryption with worst-case sub-linear complexity. In: Coron, J.-S., Nielsen, J.B. (eds.) EUROCRYPT 2017. LNCS, vol. 10212, pp. 94–124. Springer, Cham (2017). https://doi.org/10.1007/978-3-319-56617-7_4

28. Kamara, S., Papamanthou, C., Roeder, T.: Dynamic searchable symmetric encryption. In: ACM CCS 2012, pp. 965–976 (2012)

29. Kamara, S., Papamanthou, C.: Parallel and dynamic searchable symmetric encryption. In: Sadeghi, A.-R. (ed.) FC 2013. LNCS, vol. 7859, pp. 258–274. Springer, Heidelberg (2013). https://doi.org/10.1007/978-3-642-39884-1_22

30. Kissel, Z.A., Wang, J.: Generic adaptively secure searchable phrase encryption. PETS 2017 **2017**(1), 4–20 (2017)

31. Kurosawa, K.: Garbled searchable symmetric encryption. In: Christin, N., Safavi-Naini, R. (eds.) FC 2014. LNCS, vol. 8437, pp. 234–251. Springer, Heidelberg (2014). https://doi.org/10.1007/978-3-662-45472-5_15

32. Kurosawa, K., Ohtaki, Y.: UC-secure searchable symmetric encryption. In: Keromytis, A.D. (ed.) FC 2012. LNCS, vol. 7397, pp. 285–298. Springer, Heidelberg (2012). https://doi.org/10.1007/978-3-642-32946-3_21

33. Kurosawa, K., Ohtaki, Y.: How to update documents *Verifiably* in searchable symmetric encryption. In: Abdalla, M., Nita-Rotaru, C., Dahab, R. (eds.) CANS 2013. LNCS, vol. 8257, pp. 309–328. Springer, Cham (2013). https://doi.org/10.1007/978-3-319-02937-5_17

34. Kuzu, M., Islam, M.S., Kantarcioglu, M.: Efficient similarity search over encrypted data. In: IEEE ICDE 2012, pp. 1156–1167 (2012)

35. Li, J., Wang, Q., Wang, C., Cao, N., Ren, K., Lou, W.: Fuzzy keyword search over encrypted data in cloud computing. In: IEEE INFOCOM 2010 (Mini-Conference), pp. 1–5 (2010)

36. Miyoshi, R., Yamamoto, H., Fujiwara, H., Miyazaki, T.: Practical and secure searchable symmetric encryption with a small index. In: Lipmaa, H., Mitrokotsa, A., Matulevicius, R. (eds.) NordSec 2017. LNCS, vol. 10674, pp. 53–69. Springer, Cham (2017). https://doi.org/10.1007/978-3-319-70290-2_4

37. Moataz, T., Shikfa, A.: Boolean symmetric searchable encryption. In: ASIACCS 2013, pp. 265–276 (2013)
38. Naveed, M., Prabhakaran, M., Gunter, C.A.: Dynamic searchable encryption via blind storage. In: IEEE S&P 2014, pp. 639–654 (2014)
39. Ogata, W., Koiwa, K., Kanaoka, A., Matsuo, S.: Toward practical searchable symmetric encryption. In: Sakiyama, K., Terada, M. (eds.) IWSEC 2013. LNCS, vol. 8231, pp. 151–167. Springer, Heidelberg (2013). https://doi.org/10.1007/978-3-642-41383-4_10
40. Ogata, W., Kurosawa, K.: Efficient no-dictionary verifiable searchable symmetric encryption. In: Kiayias, A. (ed.) FC 2017. LNCS, vol. 10322, pp. 498–516. Springer, Cham (2017). https://doi.org/10.1007/978-3-319-70972-7_28
41. Shen, Y., Zhang, P.: Ranked searchable symmetric encryption supporting conjunctive queries. In: Liu, J.K., Samarati, P. (eds.) ISPEC 2017. LNCS, vol. 10701, pp. 350–360. Springer, Cham (2017). https://doi.org/10.1007/978-3-319-72359-4_20
42. Song, D., Wagner, D., Perrig, A.: Practical techniques for searching on encrypted data. In: IEEE S&P 2000, pp. 44–55 (2000)
43. Stefanov, E., Papamanthou, C., Shi, E.: Practical dynamic searchable encryption with small leakage. In: NDSS 2014 (2014)
44. Taketani, S., Ogata, W.: Improvement of UC secure searchable symmetric encryption scheme. In: Tanaka, K., Suga, Y. (eds.) IWSEC 2015. LNCS, vol. 9241, pp. 135–152. Springer, Cham (2015). https://doi.org/10.1007/978-3-319-22425-1_9
45. van Liesdonk, P., Sedghi, S., Doumen, J., Hartel, P., Jonker, W.: Computationally efficient searchable symmetric encryption. In: Jonker, W., Petković, M. (eds.) SDM 2010. LNCS, vol. 6358, pp. 87–100. Springer, Heidelberg (2010). https://doi.org/10.1007/978-3-642-15546-8_7
46. Wang, C., Ren, K., Yu, S., Urs, K.M.R.: Achieving usable and privacy-assured similarity search over outsourced cloud data. In: IEEE INFOCOM 2012, pp. 451–459 (2012). https://doi.org/10.1109/INFCOM.2012.6195784
47. Xu, P., Liang, S., Wang, W., Susilo, W., Wu, Q., Jin, H.: Dynamic searchable symmetric encryption with physical deletion and small leakage. In: Pieprzyk, J., Suriadi, S. (eds.) ACISP 2017. LNCS, vol. 10342, pp. 207–226. Springer, Cham (2017). https://doi.org/10.1007/978-3-319-60055-0_11
48. Yang, Y.J., Ding, X.H., Deng, R.H., Bao, F.: Multi-user private queries over encrypted databases. Int. J. Appl. Crypt. 1(4), 309–319 (2009)
49. Yavuz, A.A., Guajardo, J.: Dynamic searchable symmetric encryption with minimal leakage and efficient updates on commodity hardware. In: Dunkelman, O., Keliher, L. (eds.) SAC 2015. LNCS, vol. 9566, pp. 241–259. Springer, Cham (2016). https://doi.org/10.1007/978-3-319-31301-6_15

(Post-quantum) Signature Schemes

Certificateless Public Key Signature Schemes from Standard Algorithms

Zhaohui Cheng[1]($\boxtimes$) and Liqun Chen[2]

[1] Olym Information Security Technology Ltd., Shenzhen, China
chengzh@myibc.net
[2] Surrey University, Guildford, England
liqun.chen@surrey.ac.uk

Abstract. Certificateless public key cryptography (CL-PKC) is designed to have succinct public key management without using certificates at the same time avoid the key-escrow attribute in the identity-based cryptography. Security mechanisms employing implicit certificates achieve same goals. In this work, we first unify the security notions of these two types of mechanisms with a modified CL-PKC formulation. We further present a general key-pair generation algorithm for CL-PKC schemes and use it to construct certificateless public key signature (CL-PKS) schemes from standard algorithms. The technique, which we apply, helps defeat known-attacks against existing constructions, and the resulting schemes could be quickly deployed based on the existing standard algorithm implementations.

1 Introduction

In a public key cryptography system, a security mechanism to unequivocally demonstrate the relationship between the public key and the identity of the key's owner is indispensable. In the public key infrastructure (PKI) system, the authority issues a certificate to bind a user's identity with his public key. While the solution is well-established and universal, the PKI system can be very complicated and faces many challenges in practice, such as the efficiency and scalability of the system. The identity-based cryptography (IBC) offers an attractive alternative. In an IBC system, a user treats his identity as his public key or more accurately everyone can derive a user's public key from his identity string through a pre-defined function with a set of system parameters. Hence, in such system, the public key authenticity problem becomes trivial, and certificates are no longer necessary. However, the key generation center (KGC) can generate the private key corresponding to any of identity in an IBC system. This key-escrow function sometimes causes concerns of users' privacy. Moreover, the compromise of the KGC resulting in leaking the master secret could be a disastrous event.

In 2003, Al-Riyami and Paterson introduced a new paradigm: the certificateless public key cryptography (CL-PKC) [1]. The CL-PKC is designed to have succinct public key management without certificates at the same time remove

© Springer Nature Switzerland AG 2018
C. Su and H. Kikuchi (Eds.): ISPEC 2018, LNCS 11125, pp. 179–197, 2018.
https://doi.org/10.1007/978-3-319-99807-7_11

the key-escrow property embedded in the IBC. In the CL-PKC, a user has a public key, and his private key is determined by two pieces of secrets: one secret associated with the user's identity is extracted from the KGC, and the other is generated by the user himself. Moreover, one secret is not computable from the other, so the KGC cannot compute the user's private key. Hence the CL-PKC is key-escrow free. The approach against the key replacement attack in the CL-PKC is not to directly prove the authenticity of a public key with a certificate. Instead, the CL-PKC guarantees that even if a malicious user successfully replaces a victim's public key with his own choice, he still cannot generate a valid signature or compute the agreed session key or decrypt a ciphertext generated with the false public key and the victim's identity. This effect will undoubtedly reduce the interest of launching the attack.

Interestingly, another line of work named "implicit certificate" [12,20] had been developed before the birth of CL-PKC. An implicit certificate is comprised of a user's identity and a public key reconstruction data, which is used to reconstruct user's public key together with KGC's public key. The validity of user's public key cannot be explicitly verified like a certificate with a CA's signature. Instead, like CL-PKC, a sound implicit-certificate-based security mechanism guarantees that the key replacement attack cannot compromise the intended security.

In 1998 Arazi submitted a paper [4] to IEEE P1363, which specifies a discrete logarithm (DL) based algorithm to generate a "certificate" from the modified Schnorr signature. Essentially, this scheme is an implicit certificate scheme. In 2000, Pintsov and Vanstone [35] proposed an implicit certificate scheme from the Schnorr signature, called the Optimal Mail Certificate (OMC) scheme. The scheme was then combined with the Pintsov-Vanstone signature forming a partial message recovery signature. As shown in [11], the OMC scheme cannot work directly with a standard signature such as ECDSA [28] to form a secure signature scheme. In 2001, Brown, Gallant and Vanston [12] described a modification of the OMC algorithm, which is essentially same as the Arazi's key generation algorithm. This scheme later becomes known as the elliptic curve Qu-Vanstone (ECQV) implicit certificate scheme [13]. However, as shown in [11], the composition of ECQV with ECDSA still suffers from the Kravitz's attack. Groves developed a certificateless signature named ECCSI [21] "by drawing on ideas set out by Arazi." But the scheme still maintains the key-escrow attribute.

In the literature, there are many publications of CL-PKC either presenting concrete constructions or researching the formal models of related security notions. A short and incomplete list includes [1,2,5,7,15,22–25,27,30–32,39,42,43]. In practice, many products have implemented standard cryptographic schemes. If the CL-PKC constructions can reuse these existing infrastructures, it will certainly help facilitate the adoption of CL-PKC-based security solutions. However, only some of the schemes such as [5,22–24,27,30,32,39,42] do not require pairing, which is a cumbersome operation, and none of the unbroken CL-PKC algorithms is constructed upon standard algorithms such as ECDSA, SM2 [18] and ECIES [29].

This type of occurrences happens because most of the work strictly follows the Al-Riyami-Paterson's formulation of CL-PKC, except a few such as [5] that made minor changes. The definition of key generation functions in the Al-Riyami-Paterson's CL-PKC formulation [1,2] excludes the use of implicit certificate schemes such as OMC and ECQV. And the formulation makes it difficult to construct secure CL-PKC schemes upon standard algorithms.

On the other hand, there lacks a systematic treatment of the security notions of an implicit certificate and the security mechanisms using it. In [12], Brown et al. presented an implicit certificate security model, which however does not address the impact of a malicious KGC. Moreover, a native composition of a sound implicit certificate scheme with a standard mechanism such as a provably-secure signature does not always result in a scheme to achieve the intended security properties. Hence, only a security definition of implicit certificate schemes is not enough, and it's important to formulate security notions for implicit-certificate-based security mechanisms and so to analyze the security of schemes.

The paper is organized as follows. In Sect. 2, we revisit the formulation of CL-PKC and define a unified model, which enables one to use implicit certificate schemes to generate public and private key to construct efficient CL-PKC schemes and allows one to systematically analyze the security of mechanisms using implicit certificates. Then, we present a concrete certificateless key generation algorithm (CL-KGA) and formally analyze its security in Sect. 3. We show how to apply a simple technique to combine the proposed CL-KGA with standard algorithms to securely form CL-PKS schemes in Sect. 4. The performance of the proposed schemes are compared with the related ones in the literature and an implementation on an ARM chip is reported in Sect. 5. Finally, we draw a conclusion.

2   CL-PKC Definition

In this section, we revisit the Al-Riyami-Paterson's definition of CL-PKC and redefine the formulations of CL-PKS and CL-PKE. Because this type of cryptographic schemes share a common key generation process (we call it CL-KGA), we define this process first and then describe signature and encryption functions.

Given a security parameter k, a CL-KGA uses following five functions to generate public and private key pairs. The first three functions are probabilistic and the others are deterministic. Function **CL.Setup** and **CL.Extract-Partial-Key** are typically executed by a KGC, which keeps $M_{\mathfrak{sk}}$ confidential.

- $(M_{\mathfrak{pk}}, M_{\mathfrak{sk}}) \leftarrow$ **CL.Setup**(1^k). The output is a master public/secret key pair.
- $(U_A, x_A) \leftarrow$ **CL.Set-User-Key**$(M_{\mathfrak{pk}}, \text{ID}_A)$. $\text{ID}_A \in \{0, 1\}^*$ refers to an identity string of entity A; the output is a pair of public/secret values.
- $(W_A, d_A) \leftarrow$ **CL.Extract-Partial-Key**$(M_{\mathfrak{pk}}, M_{\mathfrak{sk}}, \text{ID}_A, U_A)$. The output is a pair of partial public/private keys.
- $s_A \leftarrow$ **CL.Set-Private-Key**$(M_{\mathfrak{pk}}, \text{ID}_A, U_A, x_A, W_A, d_A)$. The output is the private key of entity A.
- $P_A \leftarrow$ **CL.Set-Public-Key**$(M_{\mathfrak{pk}}, \text{ID}_A, U_A, W_A)$. The output is the *claimed* public key of entity A.

The above key generation process is substantially different from the Al-Riyami-Paterson's definition [1,2], in which, two public key values U_A and W_A are not addressed. We replace their **CL.Set-Secret-Value** by **CL.Set-User-Key** to make U_A "visible". We also modify their **CL.Extract-Partial-Key** by specifically adding U_A as input and outputting W_A. Finally, in our definition, these two values are explicitly inputted to **CL.Set-Private-Key** and **CL.Set-Public-Key**, and x_A is excluded from the input to **CL.Set-Public-Key**.

Apparently, **CL.Set-User-Key** can compute any value, which needs x_A and is necessary to generate P_A, and include it in U_A. Hence, any key generation schemes following the Al-Riyami-Paterson's definition can be covered by our definition. On the other hand, some schemes such as the ones presented in this work achieve the same goals of CL-PKC but cannot fit with the Al-Riyami-Paterson's definition. Specifically, the schemes presented in this work require that **CL.Extract-Partial-Key** makes use of U_A. In [2], Al-Riyami and Paterson elaborated a method to construct Certificate-Based Encryption (CBE) [19] from CL-PKE. It requires to execute **CL.Set-Public-Key** immediately after **CL.Set-Private-Key** and uses P_A as part of ID_A to invoke **CL.Extract-Partial-Key**. This method essentially sets $U_A = P_A$ and calls **CL.Extract-Partial-Key**$(M_{\mathfrak{pk}}, M_{\mathfrak{sk}}, \text{ID}_A \| U_A, \varnothing)$ with an empty variable $\varnothing$ under our definition. We think this circumventive method, which forces inefficient constructions on many occasions, is unnatural. By removing x_A from the input to **CL.Set-Public-Key**, the KGC can compute P_A after executing **CL.Extract-Partial-Key**. This modification is important to facilitate the security definitions below.

Once having generated the key pair, the user should be able to execute **CL.Verify-Key** to check the correctness of it.

- {**valid** or **invalid**}$\leftarrow$ **CL.Verify-Key**$(M_{\mathfrak{pk}}, \text{ID}_A, P_A, s_A)$. The deterministic function outputs whether (ID_A, P_A, s_A) is valid with regard to $M_{\mathfrak{pk}}$.

In CL-PKC schemes, another value derived from the identity and the master public key together with P_A is used as the *real* public key. This derivation process is typically specified in the encryption or signature verification function. Here, we explicitly define this process as the **CL.Calculate-Public-Key** function which helps present a more distinct view of CL-PKC constructions.

- $O_A \leftarrow$ **CL.Calculate-Public-Key**$(M_{\mathfrak{pk}}, \text{ID}_A, P_A)$. The deterministic function outputs the *real* public key O_A of entity A.

So both P_A and O_A are treated as the public keys of entity ID_A. P_A is distributed in some way such as through an active directory or as part of a signature or message exchanged in a key establishment protocol, and O_A is computed from $M_{\mathfrak{pk}}$, ID_A, and P_A. O_A is the one used as the real public key of ID_A in the **CL.Encrypt** or **CL.Verify** or a session key computation function.

If **CL.Verify-Key**$(M_{\mathfrak{pk}}, \text{ID}_A, P_A, s_A)$ returns **valid**, the key pair (O_A, s_A), when used in cryptographic schemes such as encryption or signature, should satisfy the soundness requirement of those types of mechanisms.

Now we are ready to define the CL-PKS and CL-PKE. A CL-PKS scheme is specified by following two functions with the key generation scheme above.

- $\sigma \leftarrow$ **CL.Sign**$(M_{\mathfrak{p}\mathfrak{k}}, \text{ID}_A, P_A, s_A, m)$. The probabilistic function signs on a message m and outputs a signature σ.
- {**valid** or **invalid**}$\leftarrow$ **CL.Verify**$(M_{\mathfrak{p}\mathfrak{k}}, \text{ID}_A, P_A, m, \sigma)$. The deterministic function outputs whether σ is a valid signature of m with respect to $(M_{\mathfrak{p}\mathfrak{k}}, \text{ID}_A, P_A)$.

A CL-PKE scheme is specified by following two functions together with the key generation scheme above.

- $C \leftarrow$ **CL.Encrypt**$(M_{\mathfrak{p}\mathfrak{k}}, \text{ID}_A, P_A, m)$. The probabilistic function encrypts a message m with $(M_{\mathfrak{p}\mathfrak{k}}, \text{ID}_A, P_A)$ and outputs a ciphertext C.
- {m or $\perp$}$\leftarrow$ **CL.Decrypt**$(M_{\mathfrak{p}\mathfrak{k}}, \text{ID}_A, P_A, s_A, C)$. The deterministic function outputs a plaintext m or a failure symbol $\perp$.

As explained above, our CL-PKC formulation covers constructions following the Al-Riyami-Paterson's definition. As shown in the following sections, implicit-certificate-based mechanisms are also embraced by this definition. It has been demonstrated in [2] that Gentry's CBE can be constructed with the Al-Riyami-Paterson's CL-PKE. Our generalized definition obviously works for CBE as well.

Al-Riyami and Paterson defined the security notion of indistinguishability under adaptive chosen-ciphertext attack (IND-CCA) of CL-PKE [1]. A serial of work [25,43] refined the security notion of existential unforgeability against adaptive chosen-message attack (EUF-CMA) of CL-PKS. The formal security model of certificateless key agreement (CL-KA) can be found in such as [31]. All of these security notions are defined with two games. Game 1 is conducted between a challenger $\mathcal{C}$ and a Type-I adversary $\mathcal{A}_I$ who does not know the master secret key but can replace a user's public key with its choice. This type of adversary simulates those who may impersonate a party by providing others with a false public key. Game 2 is conducted between a challenger $\mathcal{C}$ and a Type-II adversary $\mathcal{A}_{II}$ who knows the master secret key (so every entity's partial private key). This type of adversary simulates a malicious KGC adversary who eavesdrops the communications between its subscribers or may even switch public keys among them. We refer to [1,31,43] for further details.

Here, we introduce a formal security model of CL-KGA which has not been defined in the literature and can also serve as a model for implicit certificate mechanisms.[1] In CL-PKC, a KGC and its users could be opponent to each other, but they work together to generate a key pair for an identity ID if both behave honestly. Hence, they are in a different security world from the classic signature. On the other hand, we show that one still can make use of the security definition of signature mechanism to address the security requirements of a CL-KGA.

Intuitively, a secure CL-PKE requires that an adversary knowing x_A but without d_A or knowing d_A without x_A for a valid key pair (ID_A, P_A, s_A) should not be able to decrypt a ciphertext encrypted with (ID_A, P_A). Following the two-game definition, a Type-I adversary $\mathcal{A}_I$ succeeds in Game 1, if it generates a valid

---

[1] In [12], a security model of the implicit certificate mechanism is defined. The model is more like for a key agreement and does not consider the Type-II adversary.

key pair $(\mathtt{ID}_*, P_*, s_*)$ from any $(\mathtt{ID}_*, U_*)$ and **CL.Extract-Partial-Key**$(M_{\mathtt{pf}},$ $M_{\mathtt{sf}}, \mathtt{ID}_*, U_*)$ has not been queried. A Type-II adversary $\mathcal{A}_{II}$ succeeds in Game 2 if it generates a valid key pair $(\mathtt{ID}_*, P_*, s_*)$ of which P_* is generated by the challenger through **CL.Set-Public-Key** and related functions and its related secret values x_* and s_* are not disclosed to the adversary. A secure CL-PKE requires that its CL-KGA is safe against these two types of adversaries. Game 1 is similar to the EUF-CMA notion of a signature scheme.

Similarly, a secure CL-PKS requires that an adversary knowing x_A but without d_A or knowing d_A without x_A should not be able to generate a valid signature with a key pair $(\mathtt{ID}_A, P_A, s_A)$. For non-repudiation, a secure CL-PKS further requires that an adversary should not be able to generate a signature on a message with a pair of keys different from the one obtained through a query with **CL.Extract-Partial-Key**. More formally, an adversary succeeds in Game 1 if it generates two valid key pairs $(\mathtt{ID}_*, P_*, s_*)$ and $(\mathtt{ID}_*, P'_*, s'_*)$ for any chosen $(\mathtt{ID}_*, U_*)$ and **CL.Extract-Partial-Key**$(M_{\mathtt{pf}}, M_{\mathtt{sf}}, \mathtt{ID}_*, U_*)$ has been queried *at most once*. A secure CL-PKS requires its CL-KGA is safe against this type of adversary. This requirement is similar to the strong EUF-CMA notion of a signature scheme [3]. As in a CL-PKE, a CL-PKS requires that its CL-KGA is also secure against Type-II adversaries.

The two games are depicted in Table 1. In these games, an adversary can access an oracle $\mathcal{O}_{\mathrm{CL}}$ to issue queries adaptively before outputting a key pair $(\mathtt{ID}_*, P_*, s_*)$ for test. In both games, query **CL.Get-Public-Key**, **CL.Get-Private-Key** and **CL.Get-User-Key** can be asked. And in Game 1, query **CL.Extract-Partial-Key** can also be asked.

- Query **CL.Extract-Partial-Key**$(M_{\mathtt{pf}}, M_{\mathtt{sf}}, \mathtt{ID}_A, U_A)$. The oracle follows the function definition to generate W_A and d_A and calls function **CL.Set-Public-Key**$(M_{\mathtt{pf}}, \mathtt{ID}_A, U_A, W_A)$ to get P_A. It returns W_A and d_A after recording $(\mathtt{ID}_A, P_A)$ in a set $\mathbb{Q}$. The oracle can build the set $\mathbb{Q}$ because **CL.Set-Public-Key** doesn't need x_A in our CL-KGA formulation.
- Query **CL.Get-Public-Key**$(\mathtt{ID}_A, bNewKey)$. If $bNewKey$ is true, the oracle follows function **CL.Set-User-Key**, **CL.Extract-Partial-Key**, **CL.Set-Private-Key**, and **CL.Set-Public-Key** sequentially to generate keys, and it returns P_A after recording all the internal keys as $(\mathtt{ID}_A, P_A, x_A, s_A)$ in a set $\mathbb{L}$ and putting P_A in a set $\mathbb{P}$. Otherwise, the oracle returns P_A from the latest record indexed by $\mathtt{ID}_A$ in $\mathbb{L}$.
- Query **CL.Get-Private-Key**$(\mathtt{ID}_A, P_A)$. The oracle returns s_A from the record indexed by $(\mathtt{ID}_A, P_A)$ in $\mathbb{L}$ after putting $(\mathtt{ID}_A, P_A)$ in a set $\mathbb{S}_1$.
- Query **CL.Get-User-Key**$(\mathtt{ID}_A, P_A)$. The oracle returns x_A from the record indexed by $(\mathtt{ID}_A, P_A)$ in $\mathbb{L}$ after putting $(\mathtt{ID}_A, P_A)$ in a set $\mathbb{S}_2$.

In these two games, if no record is found when searching $\mathbb{L}$, the oracle returns an error. To exclude the cases that the adversary can win trivially, **CL.Get-Private-Key**$(\mathtt{ID}_*, P_*)$ is disallowed in both games, i.e., $(\mathtt{ID}_*, P_*) \notin \mathbb{S}_1$. In Game 1, $(\mathtt{ID}_*, P_*)$ is not allowed in the final test if **CL.Extract-Partial-Key**$(M_{\mathtt{pf}},$ $M_{\mathtt{sf}}, \mathtt{ID}_*, U_*)$ has been queried for some U_*, and W_* from the query output satisfies $P_* = $ **CL.Set-Public-Key**$(M_{\mathtt{pf}}, \mathtt{ID}_*, U_*, W_*)$, i.e., $(\mathtt{ID}_*, P_*) \notin \mathbb{Q}$. In

Table 1. The CL-KGA games

Game 1: Type-I Adversary
1. $(M_{\mathrm{pk}}, M_{\mathrm{sk}}) \leftarrow$ **CL.Setup**(1^k).
2. $(\mathrm{ID}_*, P_*, s_*) \leftarrow \mathcal{A}_I^{\mathcal{O}^1_{\mathsf{CL}}}(M_{\mathrm{pk}})$.
3. succeed if $(\mathrm{ID}_*, P_*) \notin \mathbb{S}_1 \cup \mathbb{Q}$ and **valid**$\leftarrow$**CL.Verify-Key**$(M_{\mathrm{pk}}, \mathrm{ID}_*, P_*, s_*)$.

Game 2: Type-II Adversary
1. $(M_{\mathrm{pk}}, M_{\mathrm{sk}}) \leftarrow$ **CL.Setup**(1^k).
2. $(\mathrm{ID}_*, P_*, s_*) \leftarrow \mathcal{A}_{II}^{\mathcal{O}^2_{\mathsf{CL}}}(M_{\mathrm{pk}}, M_{\mathrm{sk}})$.
3. succeed if $P_* \in \mathbb{P}$, $(\mathrm{ID}_*, P_*) \notin \mathbb{S}_1 \cup \mathbb{S}_2$ and **valid**$\leftarrow$**CL.Verify-Key**$(M_{\mathrm{pk}}, \mathrm{ID}_*, P_*, s_*)$.

Game 2, **CL.Get-User-Key**(ID_*, P_*) is forbidden, i.e., $(\mathrm{ID}_*, P_*) \notin \mathbb{S}_2$, and P_* has to be a public key generated through a query **CL.Get-Public-Key**$(\mathrm{ID}_A,$ *true*$)$ for some ID_A, i.e., $P_* \in \mathbb{P}$.

Definition 1. *A CL-KGA is secure if the success probability of both $\mathcal{A}_I$ and $\mathcal{A}_{II}$ in the CL-KGA games is negligible.*

Table 2. The CL-PKS-EUF-CMA games

Game 1: Type-I Adversary
1. $(M_{\mathrm{pk}}, M_{\mathrm{sk}}) \leftarrow$ **CL.Setup**(1^k).
2. $(\mathrm{ID}_*, P_*, m_*, \sigma_*) \leftarrow \mathcal{A}_I^{\mathcal{O}^1_{\mathsf{CL}}}(M_{\mathrm{pk}})$.
3. succeed if $(\mathrm{ID}_*, P_*) \notin \mathbb{S}_1 \cup \mathbb{Q}$, $(\mathrm{ID}_*, P_*, m_*) \notin \mathbb{M}$ and **valid**$\leftarrow$**CL.Verify**$(M_{\mathrm{pk}}, \mathrm{ID}_*, P_*, m_*, \sigma_*)$.

Game 2: Type-II Adversary
1. $(M_{\mathrm{pk}}, M_{\mathrm{sk}}) \leftarrow$ **CL.Setup**(1^k).
2. $(\mathrm{ID}_*, P_*, m_*, \sigma_*) \leftarrow \mathcal{A}_{II}^{\mathcal{O}^2_{\mathsf{CL}}}(M_{\mathrm{pk}}, M_{\mathrm{sk}})$.
3. succeed if $P_* \in \mathbb{P}$, $(\mathrm{ID}_*, P_*) \notin \mathbb{S}_1 \cup \mathbb{S}_2$, $(\mathrm{ID}_*, P_*, m_*) \notin \mathbb{M}$ and **valid**$\leftarrow$**CL.Verify**$(M_{\mathrm{pk}}, \mathrm{ID}_*, P_*, m_*, \sigma_*)$.

For CL-PKS, we use the security model shown in Table 2 to define the security notion of EUF-CMA. As in the CL-KGA games, query **CL.Get-Public-Key**$(\mathrm{ID}_A, bNewKey)$, **CL.Get-Private-Key**(ID_A, P_A) and **CL.Get-User-Key**(ID_A, P_A) can be issued in both games, and in Game 1, query **CL.Extract-Partial-Key**$(M_{\mathrm{pk}}, M_{\mathrm{sk}}, \mathrm{ID}_A, U_A)$ can also be asked. To enable signature queries, the following extra query is allowed in both games.

– Query **CL.Get-Sign**(ID_A, P_A, m). The oracle uses the private key s_A from the record indexed by (ID_A, P_A) in $\mathbb{L}$ to sign the message m and returns the signature after recording (ID_A, P_A, m) in a set $\mathbb{M}$. If no private key is found corresponding to P_A belonging to ID_A, return an error.

In the security model of [25,43], the adversary in Game 1 is allowed to issue another query **CL.Replace-Public-Key**(ID_A, P_A), which replaces user ID_A's public with his choice P_A. This query simulates the attack to forge a signature for a targeted identity but with a faked public key. In this work, we don't use this query. Instead, we allow the adversary to provide a public key of his choice in **CL.Verify** in the final stage of both games. This arrangement implicitly empowers the adversary to cheat a signature verifier with a faked public key. Adversaries defined by this approach corresponds to the normal (instead of strong) adversaries in [25].

As in the CL-KGA games, same restrictions are applied to allowed queries to avoid trivial cases that the adversary can win. Moreover, **CL.Get-Sign**(ID_*, P_*, m_*) is disallowed in both games, which implies (ID_*, P_*, m_*) $\notin \mathbb{M}$, because the proposed schemes in this work are not strong EUF-CMA-secure.

Definition 2. *A CL-PKS is secure if the success probability of both $\mathcal{A}_I$ and $\mathcal{A}_{II}$ in the CL-PKS-EUF-CMA games is negligible.*

Similarly, the IND-CCA security notion of CL-PKE as in [1] can be defined. We skip it due to lack of space.

In [11], the authors interpreted the reason that "the composition of two 'provably secure' schemes, namely original OMC and ECDSA, results in an insecure scheme" as "This situation may be viewed as a specific limitation of the security definition for implicit certificates given in" [12], "or ... as a broader limitation of provable security, or ... as a need to formulate all security definitions according to the recently defined universal composability." Because both OMC and ECQV appear to be natural candidates to generate implicit certificates, we interpret this failure of universal composition as the limitation of implicit certificates in general. That is we should not purposely define a stronger security notion of implicit certificates, which maintains universal composability but excludes those natural constructions such as OMC and ECQV. Instead, we need to define proper security notion for signature schemes that employ implicit certificates. The CL-PKS definition above serves such purpose. Meanwhile, the Al-Riyami-Paterson's formulation in [1] does not allow to use implicit certificate schemes such as OMC and ECQV to generate private and public keys and makes it difficult to construct signature schemes upon widely used standard algorithms such as ECDSA and SM2. This is exactly what a good implicit certificate scheme intends to achieve. The new CL-PKC definition in this work overcomes this hurdle. The formulation above unifies the two types of security mechanisms, namely the one using implicit certificates and CL-PKC, under one umbrella, and brings forth the benefits of both realms, i.e., efficiency of implicit-certificate-based schemes and rigorous security analysis approach of CL-PKC.

3   Certificateless Key Generation

Here following the definition in Sect. 2, we present a certificateless key generation algorithm to generate private and public key pairs, which will be used in the CL-PKS schemes later. The algorithm can also be used to construct CL-PKE and CL-KA schemes. The scheme is built upon the standard elliptic curve Schnorr signature (specifically EC-FSDSA [28]). In the description, we use symbol $\in_R$ to denote the operation to randomly choose from a set, and x_G and y_G to signify the x-axle and y-axle of a point G respectively.

- **CL.Setup**(1^k)
  1. Select an elliptic curve $\mathbf{E} : Y^3 = X^2 + aX + b$ defined over a prime field $\mathbb{F}_p$. The curve has a cyclic point group $\mathbb{G}$ of prime order q.
  2. Pick a generator $G \in \mathbb{G}$.
  3. $s \in_R \mathbb{Z}_q^*$.
  4. $P_{KGC} = [s]G$.
  5. Pick two cryptographic hash functions: $H_1 : \{0,1\}^* \to \{0,1\}^n; H_2 : \{0,1\}^* \to \mathbb{Z}_q^*$ for some integer $n > 0$.
  6. Output $M_{p\mathfrak{k}} = (a, b, p, q, G, P_{KGC}, H_1, H_2)$ and $M_{s\mathfrak{k}} = s$.
- **CL.Set-User-Key**$(M_{p\mathfrak{k}}, \mathrm{ID}_A)$
  1. $x_A \in_R \mathbb{Z}_q^*$.
  2. $U_A = [x_A]G$.
  3. Output (U_A, x_A).
- **CL.Extract-Partial-Key**$(M_{p\mathfrak{k}}, M_{s\mathfrak{k}}, \mathrm{ID}_A, U_A)$
  1. $Z = H_1(a\|b\|x_G\|y_G\|x_{P_{KGC}}\|y_{P_{KGC}}\|\mathrm{ID}_A)$.
  2. $w \in_R \mathbb{Z}_q^*$.
  3. $X = [w]G$.
  4. $W = U_A + X$.
  5. $\lambda = H_2(x_W\|y_W\|Z)$.
  6. $t = (w + \lambda \cdot s) \mod q$.
  7. Output $(W_A = W, d_A = t)$.
- **CL.Set-Private-Key**$(M_{p\mathfrak{k}}, \mathrm{ID}_A, U_A, x_A, W_A, d_A)$
  1. Output $s_A = (x_A + d_A) \mod q$.
- **CL.Set-Public-Key**$(M_{p\mathfrak{k}}, \mathrm{ID}_A, U_A, W_A)$
  1. Output $P_A = W_A$.
- **CL.Calculate-Public-Key**$(M_{p\mathfrak{k}}, \mathrm{ID}_A, P_A)$
  1. $Z = H_1(a\|b\|x_G\|y_G\|x_{P_{KGC}}\|y_{P_{KGC}}\|\mathrm{ID}_A)$.
  2. $\lambda = H_2(x_{P_A}\|y_{P_A}\|Z)$.
  3. $O_A = P_A + [\lambda]P_{KGC}$.
- **CL.Verify-Key**$(M_{p\mathfrak{k}}, \mathrm{ID}_A, P_A, s_A)$
  1. $Z = H_1(a\|b\|x_G\|y_G\|x_{P_{KGC}}\|y_{P_{KGC}}\|\mathrm{ID}_A)$.
  2. $\lambda = H_2(x_{P_A}\|y_{P_A}\|Z)$.
  3. $P'_A = [s_A]G - [\lambda]P_{KGC}$.
  4. Output **valid** if $P_A = P'_A$, and **invalid** otherwise.

It is easy to check that $O_A = [s_A]G$ and everyone can compute it from public values. However, the **CL.Verify-Key** function makes use of s_A, so only the owner of the key pair can validate its correctness. It cannot be done by one just knowing O_A. The equations $P'_A = O_A - [\lambda]P_{KGC}$ and $P_A = P'_A$ do not mean a Schnorr signature. The hash-function H_1 in the description is unnecessary in theory, but useful for a neat implementation. The security of the CL-KGA can be summarised by following two theorems.

Definition 3. *Let $(\mathbb{G}, G, q)$ be a group of prime order q and G is a generator. The discrete logarithm problem is given a random $P \in \mathbb{G}$ to find α such that $P = [\alpha]G$.*

Theorem 1. *If there exists a Type-I adversary $\mathcal{A}_I$ that has a non-negligible probability of success in Game 1 against the CL-KGA, then the discrete logarithm in the group $\mathbb{G}$ can be solved in polynomial time in the random oracle model.*

Theorem 2. *If there exists a Type-II adversary $\mathcal{A}_{II}$ that has a non-negligible probability of success in Game 2 against the CL-KGA, then the discrete logarithm in the group $\mathbb{G}$ can be solved in polynomial time in the random oracle model.*

Due to lack of space, the reductions are presented in the full paper [14].

4   CL-PKS

4.1   Generic Approach to Construct CL-PKS

Using CL-KGA, a user with identity ID_A generates a pair of keys (P_A, s_A), and everyone can call function **CL.Calculate-Public-Key**$(M_{\mathfrak{pt}}, \text{ID}_A, P_A)$ to compute the real public key O_A. A standard signature scheme is defined by three functions $(\mathcal{G}, \Sigma, V)$ such that the key generation function $\mathcal{G}$ generates a key pair (O_A, s_A), the signing function Σ takes (O_A, s_A, m) as input and produces a signature σ, and the verification function V takes (O_A, m, σ) as input and tests whether σ is a valid signature of m with respect to O_A. An obvious way to construct a CL-PKS is to call a CL-KGA to generate keys and call Σ in **CL.Sign** and call **CL.Calculate-Public-Key** first to compute O_A and then call V to test a signature in **CL.Verify**. However, such crude construction with a CL-KGA that is secure by Definition 1 and a signature scheme that is EUF-CMA-secure even in the multi-user setting [34] does not always end up with a secure CL-PKS satisfying Definition 2.

Menezes and Smart investigated the security notions of digital signature in the multi-user setting [34]. They formulated two types of security notions for a signature scheme in this case. One security notion is formulated against weak-key substitution (WSK) attacks, which requires that an adversary, if outputs a pair of message and signature generated upon public key O_i that is also valid with respect to a different public key O_*, should know the private key corresponding to O_*. With this restriction, they proved that ECDSA is WSK-secure if users share the same domain parameters such as those in $M_{\mathfrak{pt}}$. In Sect. 3 we have proved that the CL-KGA, which bears high similarity with the OMC implicit certificate scheme, is secure by Definition 1. However, the simple combination of the CL-KGA with ECDSA following the suggested method does not produce a secure CL-PKS. In [11] Brown et al. detailed a security analysis which shows that the OMC with ECDSA is completely broken and the ECQV with ECDSA is not safe against an artificial forgery attack. These cases demonstrate that an EUF-CMA and WSK-secure DSA is not sufficient for universal composability. This happens because in the CL-PKS setting, an adversary may output a valid tuple $(\text{ID}_*, P_*, m_*, \sigma_*)$ without knowing the private key. Moreover, m_* may not have been signed by any entity in the system and P_* may not belong to any entity either. Hence, it is necessary that the used EUF-CMA-secure DSA is at least against the strong-key substitution (SKS) attacks [34], which does not require the adversary knows the private key corresponding to O_* after outputting $(\text{ID}_*, P_*, m_*, \sigma_*)$ for test, where $O_* \leftarrow$ **CL.Calculate-Public-Key**$(M_{\text{pf}}, \text{ID}_*, P_*)$ and **valid**$\leftarrow$**CL.Verify**$(M_{\text{pf}}, \text{ID}_*, P_*, m_*, \sigma_*)$.

Here, we show a simple technique to enhance the security of composed schemes. The intermediate value λ in the CL-KGA, which is generated in the Schnorr signing process, is called the *assignment* in the general framework defined in ISO/IEC 14888-3 [28] for signatures schemes based on discrete logarithm with randomized witness. If the signing function of the digital signature algorithm (DSA) is signing on $(\lambda\|m)$ instead of m, the two algorithms, the CL-KGA and DSA, are linked together to safeguard the security of resulting CL-PKS. Intuitively, with including λ as the prefix of the message to be signed, the signer is forced to commit to a public key P_A and hence the corresponding *real* public key O_A before generating a signature. This mechanism takes away the freedom of a forger to generate a signature before finding a public key P_A satisfying the verification equation. The security of a standard DSA such as ECDSA guarantees that without knowing the private key, it is unlikely to generate a valid signature with respect to a given public key O_A. Meanwhile, the security of the CL-KGA assures that without the help of the KGC, the adversary cannot compute the private key s_A corresponding to a given public key O_A.

This simple technique works like applying with the so-called "key prefixing" technique [8,34] by signing on a message together with the signer's public key and its identity indirectly. The technique has been used in [21] to construct ECCSI. We apply this technique to construct two CL-PKS schemes. We will show later that the technique indeed plays an essential role to defeat all the known attacks against the resulting CL-PKS.

4.2   CL-PKS1 from ECDSA

First, we present a scheme (CL-PKS1) using the CL-KGA and the standard ECDSA. The scheme uses another hash function $H_3 : \{0,1\}^* \rightarrow \{0,1\}^n$. In practice, both H_1 and H_3 are instantiated by a secure hash function like SHA256. H_2 is also constructed from the same hash function by excluding the zero output modulo q (Table 3).

Table 3. CL-PKS1

$\textbf{CL.Sign}(M_{\mathfrak{pk}}, \text{ID}_A, P_A, s_A, m)$	$\textbf{CL.Verify}(M_{\mathfrak{pk}}, \text{ID}_A, P_A, m, \sigma)$
1. $Z = H_1(a\|b\|x_G\|y_G\|$ $\quad x_{P_{KGC}}\|y_{P_{KGC}}\|\text{ID}_A)$. 2. $\lambda = H_2(x_{P_A}\|y_{P_A}\|Z)$. 3. $h = H_3(\lambda\|m)$. 4. $r \in_R \mathbb{Z}_q^*$. 5. $Q = [r]G$. 6. $u = x_Q \mod q$. 7. $v = r^{-1} \cdot (u \cdot s_A + h) \mod q$. 8. Output $\sigma = (u, v)$.	1. $Z = H_1(a\|b\|x_G\|y_G\|$ $\quad x_{P_{KGC}}\|y_{P_{KGC}}\|\text{ID}_A)$. 2. $\lambda = H_2(x_{P_A}\|y_{P_A}\|Z)$. 3. $O_A = P_A + [\lambda]P_{KGC}$. 4. $h = H_3(\lambda\|m)$. 5. $v_1 = v^{-1} \cdot h \mod q$. 6. $v_2 = v^{-1} \cdot u \mod q$. 7. $Q' = [v_1]G + [v_2]O_A$. 8. $u' = x_{Q'} \mod q$. 9. Output **valid** if $u = u'$, and **invalid** otherwise.

The presented **CL.Sign** function from step 3 exactly follows ECDSA to sign with private key s_A on message $(\lambda\|m)$. The first two steps can be treated as a message preparation process, which re-generates the *assignment* computed in the Schnorr signing process invoked by **CL.Extract-Partial-Key**. These two steps can further be saved if λ is pre-computed and stored. **CL.Verify** function invokes two functions sequentially. It first activates **CL.Calculate-Public-Key** to calculate the signer's supposed real public key O_A and then calls the verification function of ECDSA to verify signature σ on message $(\lambda\|m)$ with regard to O_A. We note that signing on $(\lambda\|m)$ instead of m does not require any modification to the implementation of ECDSA either in software or hardware.

In [11], it's been shown that both OMC and ECQV are insecure with ECDSA in direct composition. Our revisiting the analysis of [11] shows that after applying with the key prefixing technique of signing on $(\lambda\|m)$, both CL-PKS1 and ECQV with ECDSA are secure against the known attacks. Our analysis further shows that CL-PKS1 has the security equivalent to (in fact better than) the ECQV with the vanilla ECDSA scheme in the *combined* random oracle (for the hash function) and generic group model (for the elliptic curve group) [36]. Please refer to the full paper [14] for details.

4.3   CL-PKS2 from ECDSA-II

Because ECDSA lacks a security reduction based on a standard complexity assumption, several modifications to ECDSA such as [33] were proposed to address this issue. All modifications include u as an input to H_3. However the way to generate u is different in each proposal. We use a variant of ECDSA by setting $u = x_Q$ (called ECDSA-II in [33]). For most of the elliptic curves defined over prime fields used in practice, this modification will not change the size of the representation of u. On the other hand, this variant can be proved secure in the random oracle with the *Improved Forking Lemma* as in [33]. We use this modified ECDSA to construct CL-PKS2 (Table 4).

Table 4. CL-PKS2

CL.Sign(M_{pk}, ID_A, P_A, s_A, m)	**CL.Verify**(M_{pk}, ID_A, P_A, m, σ)
1. $Z = H_1(a\|b\|x_G\|y_G\|$ $x_{P_{KGC}}\|y_{P_{KGC}}\|\text{ID}_A)$.	1. $Z = H_1(a\|b\|x_G\|y_G\|$ $x_{P_{KGC}}\|y_{P_{KGC}}\|\text{ID}_A)$.
2. $\lambda = H_2(x_{P_A}\|y_{P_A}\|Z)$.	2. $\lambda = H_2(x_{P_A}\|y_{P_A}\|Z)$.
3. $r \in_R \mathbb{Z}_q^*$.	3. $O_A = P_A + [\lambda]P_{KGC}$.
4. $Q = [r]G$.	4. $h = H_3(u\|\lambda\|m)$.
5. $u = x_Q$.	5. $v_1 = v^{-1} \cdot h \mod q$.
6. $h = H_3(u\|\lambda\|m)$.	6. $v_2 = v^{-1} \cdot u \mod q$.
7. $v = r^{-1} \cdot (u \cdot s_A + h) \mod q$.	7. $Q' = [v_1]G + [v_2]O_A$.
8. Output $\sigma = (u,v)$.	8. $u' = x_{Q'}$.
	9. Output **valid** if $u = u'$, and **invalid** otherwise.

We note that without including λ, even with u as an input to H_3, such variant still suffers from the attacks as those in [11]. This again demonstrates the effectiveness of the key prefixing technique.

4.4   Security Analysis

Now, we analyze the security of the schemes. Apart from the analysis against the existing attacks as those in [11], we present two formal security results of CL-PKS1 for building confidence in the scheme. The analysis of CL-PKS1 with a few changes is also applicable to ECQV with ECDSA if the technique of signing on ($\lambda\|m$) is used. We fully analyze CL-PKS2's security.

Because the CL-PKS1 scheme is the composition of the CL-KGA and ECDSA, the security of the scheme won't be better than either of the components. For ECDSA, the known security result is either based on the collision resistance of the used hash function in the generic group model [9] or based on so-called the semi-logarithm problem in the random oracle model [10,17]. As we have already adopted the random oracle model to analyze the security of the CL-KGA, here we continue to analyze the security of the CL-PKS schemes in the same model.

To address the technique shortcoming of the proof, we put a restriction on the **CL.Get-Sign**(ID_A, P_A, m) query. If $\text{ID}_* = \text{ID}_A$ and $P_* = P_A$, then each message m can be queried *at most once*. This "one-per-message unforgeability" security notion [17] is weaker than the EUF-CMA. However, it is so far the provable one for ECDSA in the random oracle. We label these two types of adversaries as Type-I⁻ and Type-II⁻ adversary. We note that for CL-PKS2, this restriction is unnecessary because of including u in H_3.

Definition 4. *Let* $(\mathbb{G}, G, q)$ *be a group of prime order* q *and* G *is a generator. The semi-logarithm problem is given a random* $P \in \mathbb{G}$ *to find* (u, v) *such that* $u = \mathcal{F}([v^{-1}](G + [u]P))$, *where* $\mathcal{F}(X)$ *returns* x-*axle of point* X.

For Type-I adversaries, there are two possible attacking cases. Case 1: $\mathcal{A}_{Ia}$ generates a signature which is valid with a targeted $\texttt{ID}_*$ and $\texttt{ID}_*$'s public key. Case 2: $\mathcal{A}_{Ib}$ generates a signature which is valid with a targeted $\texttt{ID}_*$ but a public key different from $\texttt{ID}_*$'s. Note that in this case, $\texttt{ID}_*$ may have no public key yet. The security analysis results of these two CL-PKS schemes are as follows.

Lemma 1. *If there exists an adversary $\mathcal{A}_{Ia}^-$ that has a non-negligible probability of success in Game 1 against CL-PKS1 in the random oracle model, then the semi-logarithm problem in the group $\mathbb{G}$ can be solved in polynomial time.*

Theorem 3. *If there exists an adversary $\mathcal{A}_{II}^-$ that has a non-negligible probability of success in Game 1 against CL-PKS1 in the random oracle model, then the semi-logarithm problem in the group $\mathbb{G}$ can be solved in polynomial time.*

Lemma 2. *If there exists an adversary $\mathcal{A}_{Ia}$ that has a non-negligible probability of success in Game 1 against CL-PKS2 in the random oracle model, then the discrete logarithm problem in the group $\mathbb{G}$ can be solved in polynomial time.*

Lemma 3. *If there exists an adversary $\mathcal{A}_{Ib}$ that has a non-negligible probability of success in Game 1 against CL-PKS2 in the random oracle model, then the discrete logarithm problem in the group $\mathbb{G}$ can be solved in polynomial time.*

Theorem 4. *If there exists an adversary $\mathcal{A}_I$ that has a non-negligible probability of success in Game 1 against CL-PKS2 in the random oracle model, then the discrete logarithm problem in the group $\mathbb{G}$ can be solved in polynomial time.*

Theorem 5. *If there exists an adversary $\mathcal{A}_{II}$ that has a non-negligible probability of success in Game 2 against CL-PKS2 in the random oracle model, then the discrete logarithm problem in the group $\mathbb{G}$ can be solved in polynomial time.*

Due to lack of space, the reductions are presented in the full paper.

Overall, CL-PKS2 is a secure scheme with regard to Definition 2 in the random oracle model based on the DL assumption. With two results from Lemma 1 and Theorem 3, CL-PKS1 still lacks a formal security analysis against the $\mathcal{A}_{Ib}^-$ adversary without resorting to the generic group model or introducing new complexity assumption. On the other hand, it is shown that CL-PKS1 is more secure than ECQV+ECDSA (the detailed analysis is given in [14]).

5   Performance Evaluation and Application

We first compare the proposed CL-PKS schemes with the related schemes including existing CL-PKS schemes and standard signature schemes using implicit certificates. Many CL-PKS schemes with or without pairing are proposed in the literature. Pairing (denoted by P, which is a bilinear map: $\mathbb{G}_1 \times \mathbb{G}_2 \to \mathbb{G}_3$ such that $\mathbb{G}_1$ and $\mathbb{G}_2$ are two cyclic groups and $\mathbb{G}_3$ is a related extension field) is a much heavier computation operation than the point scalar (denoted by S) or exponentiation (denoted by E) in the field $\mathbb{G}_3$. We don't list all the existing

Table 5. Performance comparison

Scheme	Key size		Computation		Signature	Security	Upon
	Private	Public	Signing	Verification	Size	Status	Standard alg.
AP [1]	$\|\mathbb{G}_1\|$	$2\|\mathbb{G}_1\|$	$1P + 3S$	$4P + 1E$	$\|\mathbb{G}_1\| + \|q\|$	Broken [26]	No
CPHL [16]	$\|\mathbb{G}_1\|$	$\|\mathbb{G}_1\|$	$2S$	$2P + 2S$	$2\|\mathbb{G}_1\|$	Proof*	No
HMSWW [25]	$\|q\| + \|\mathbb{G}_1\|$	$\|\mathbb{G}_1\|$	$1S$	$3P$	$\|\mathbb{G}_1\|$	Proof*	No
ZWXF [43]	$\|q\| + \|\mathbb{G}_1\|$	$\|\mathbb{G}_1\|$	$3S$	$4P$	$2\|\mathbb{G}_1\|$	Proof*	No
ZZZ [44]	$\|q\| + \|\mathbb{G}_1\|$	$\|\mathbb{G}_2\|$	$1S + 2E$	$1P + 3E$	$\|\mathbb{G}_1\| + 2\|q\|$	Proof*	No
HRL [22]	$\|q\|$	$\|q\| + \|\mathbb{G}\|$	$1S$	$5S$	$2\|\mathbb{G}\|$	No proof*	No
HCZ [24]	$\|q\|$	$2\|\mathbb{G}\|$	$1S$	$3S$	$\|\mathbb{G}\| + \|q\|$	Broken [40]	No
JHLC [27]	$\|q\|$	$2\|\mathbb{G}\|$	$1S$	$3S$	$\|\mathbb{G}\| + \|q\|$	Proof*	No
LXWHH [32]	$2\|q\|$	$2\|\mathbb{G}\|$	$1S$	$3S$	$2\|q\|$	Proof*	No
YSCC [42]	$\|q\|$	$\|\mathbb{G}\|$	$1S$	$3S$	$\|\mathbb{G}\| + \|q\|$	Broken [27]	Schnorr
OMC+ ECDSA [11]	$\|q\|$	$\|\mathbb{G}\|$	$1S$	$3S$	$2\|q\|$	Broken [11]	ECDSA
ECQV+ ECDSA [11]	$\|q\|$	$\|\mathbb{G}\|$	$1S$	$3S$	$2\|q\|$	Known attack [11]	ECDSA
CL-PKS1	$\|q\|$	$\|\mathbb{G}\|$	$1S$	$3S$	$2\|q\|$	Partial proof	ECDSA
CL-PKS2	$\|q\|$	$\|\mathbb{G}\|$	$1S$	$3S$	$\|p\| + \|q\|$	Proof	Enhanced ECDSA

*We note that these schemes do not satisfy the CL-PKS security notion in Definition 2.

CL-PKS schemes. Instead, only some commonly referred pairing-based schemes and some most efficient pairing-free schemes are compared. $\|\mathbb{G}\|$ and $\|q\|$ denote the bit length of the size of a group $\mathbb{G}$ and an integer q respectively.

According to Table 5, it is known that our schemes are among the most efficient ones. Moreover, CL-PKS1 doesn't suffer from the Kravitz's attack that affects ECQV+ECDSA, and it can be realized by reusing the existing implementation of ECDSA. This is a particularly important advantage in practice because many security elements (SE) have ECDSA embedded and the private key is protected within the SE. Deploying CL-PKS1 doesn't need to modify existing hardware chips and won't cause extra security concerns because the signing process can use the private key stored in SE in the same way as ECDSA.

We have implemented CL-PKS1 on the 32-bit Cortex-M4 MCU STM32F4 to evaluate the performance. STMicroelectronics provides a crypto library [38], which has interfaces to access to the implementation of ECDSA and point scalar operation over the NIST p256 elliptic curve. The signing process of CL-PKS1 can directly call ECDSA signature generation function in the library by signing on $(\lambda\|m)$. The verification process first calls the scalar and addition operations to compute O_A and then calls the verification function of ECDSA in the library. We have also implemented CL-PKS1 from the scratch to evaluate the performance of a native implementation of the scheme. In the implementation, the Montgomery modular is applied to compute multiplication in $\mathbb{F}_p$. The addition and multiplication operations are implemented with the assembly language. The code is compiled with $-O3$ option and speed is measured with STM32F4 working at 168 MHz (Table 6).

Table 6. Implementation of CL-PKS1 on STM32F4

Implementation	Code size	Stack size	Signing time	Verification time
STM crypto lib	15K	0.5K	0.078 s	0.076 s (scalar) + 0.104 s (ECDSA ver.)
Our software	11K	0.7K	0.058 s	0.132 s

Our software implementation is even faster than the one using the library provided by STMicroelectronics. The speed of the implementation appears quick enough for most applications.

Systems employing CL-PKS will enjoy the benefit of lightweight key management. For example, inter-domain authentication in the Internet of Things such as V2V communication [41] requires PKC-based security solutions. Considering the constrained resource, diversity of devices and the scale of the IoT, an efficient CL-PKS scheme like CL-PKS1 offers clear advantages over the certificate-based, identity-based, and raw public key with out-of-band validation (RPK-OOBV) solutions. The certificate size and the complicated validation process could quickly drain available resources of a constrained device (see [37] for a detailed evaluation of the impact of a certificate on IoT devices). The RPK-OOBV has small public key data but requires other validation mechanisms such as DNSSEC. On the other hand, the proposed CL-PKS has small key size as RPK-OOBV and removes the necessity of public key validation. With only slightly larger communication overhead by including the public key P_A as part of a signature as suggested in [6], CL-PKS can work just like an IBS but is free of the key-escrow concern.

6   Conclusion

In this work, we redefine the formulation of CL-PKC to unify it with security mechanisms using implicit certificates. We then construct a CL-KGA from the Schnorr signature and prove its security in the random oracle model. Furthermore, we demonstrate that using the *assignment* computed in the **CL.Extract-Partial-Key** process as the *key prefixing* in the message signing process helps improve the security of a CL-PKS that is constructed by combining a secure CL-KGA with a standard signature algorithm. Two of such schemes are described. CL-PKS1 can be implemented based on existing security elements that support

ECDSA, and security analysis shows that it has stronger security than the composition of ECQV with ECDSA. CL-PKS2 has full security reductions based on the discrete logarithm assumption in the random oracle model. The results presented in the work may also shed light on the way of using of ECQV with ECDSA. With little cost, the security of the ECQV-based signature scheme can benefit from the key prefixing technique. However, whether using the assignment as the key prefixing allows universal composability of a secure CL-KGA with an EUF-CMA-secure DSA, which fits with the general framework defined in ISO/IEC 14888-3, remains an open problem.

References

1. Al-Riyami, S.S., Paterson, K.G.: Certificateless public key cryptography. In: Laih, C.-S. (ed.) ASIACRYPT 2003. LNCS, vol. 2894, pp. 452–473. Springer, Heidelberg (2003). https://doi.org/10.1007/978-3-540-40061-5_29
2. Al-Riyami, S.S., Paterson, K.G.: CBE from CL-PKE: a generic construction and efficient schemes. In: Vaudenay, S. (ed.) PKC 2005. LNCS, vol. 3386, pp. 398–415. Springer, Heidelberg (2005). https://doi.org/10.1007/978-3-540-30580-4_27
3. An, J.H., Dodis, Y., Rabin, T.: On the security of joint signature and encryption. In: Knudsen, L.R. (ed.) EUROCRYPT 2002. LNCS, vol. 2332, pp. 83–107. Springer, Heidelberg (2002). https://doi.org/10.1007/3-540-46035-7_6
4. Arazi, B.: Certification of DL/EC Keys. Submission to P1363 meeting (1998). http://grouper.ieee.org/groups/1363/StudyGroup/contributions/arazi.doc
5. Baek, J., Safavi-Naini, R., Susilo, W.: Certificateless public key encryption without pairing. In: Zhou, J., Lopez, J., Deng, R.H., Bao, F. (eds.) ISC 2005. LNCS, vol. 3650, pp. 134–148. Springer, Heidelberg (2005). https://doi.org/10.1007/11556992_10
6. Bellare, M., Namprempre, C., Neven, G.: Security proofs for identity-based identification and signature schemes. J. Cryptol. **22**, 1–61 (2009)
7. Bentahar, K., Farshim, P., Malone-Lee, J., Smart, N.P.: Generic constructions of identity-based and certificateless KEMs. J. Cryptol. **21**, 178–199 (2008)
8. Bernstein, D.J.: Multi-User Schnorr Security, Revisited. Cryptology ePrint Archive, Report 2015/996 (2015)
9. Brown, D.: Generic groups, collision resistance, and ECDSA. Des. Codes Cryptogr. **35**, 119–152 (2005)
10. Brown, D.: On the provable security of ECDSA. In: Advances in Elliptic Curve Cryptography, pp. 21–40. Cambridge University Press (2005)
11. Brown, D., Campagna, M., Vanstone, S.: Security of ECQV-certified ECDSA against passive adversaries. Cryptology ePrint Archive, Report 2009/620 (2009)
12. Brown, D.R.L., Gallant, R., Vanstone, S.A.: Provably secure implicit certificate schemes. In: Syverson, P. (ed.) FC 2001. LNCS, vol. 2339, pp. 156–165. Springer, Heidelberg (2002). https://doi.org/10.1007/3-540-46088-8_15
13. Certicom Research. SEC 4: Elliptic Curve Qu-Vanstone Implicit Certificate Scheme (ECQV). Version 1.0. (2013)
14. Cheng, Z., Chen, L.: Certificateless Public Key Signature Schemes from Standard Algorithms (Expanded Version). Cryptology ePrint Archive, Report 2018/386 (2018)

15. Cheng, Z., Chen, L., Ling, L., Comley, R.: General and efficient certificateless public key encryption constructions. In: Takagi, T., Okamoto, T., Okamoto, E., Okamoto, T. (eds.) Pairing 2007. LNCS, vol. 4575, pp. 83–107. Springer, Heidelberg (2007). https://doi.org/10.1007/978-3-540-73489-5_6

16. Choi, K.Y., Park, J.H., Hwang, J.Y., Lee, D.H.: Efficient certificateless signature schemes. In: Katz, J., Yung, M. (eds.) ACNS 2007. LNCS, vol. 4521, pp. 443–458. Springer, Heidelberg (2007). https://doi.org/10.1007/978-3-540-72738-5_29

17. Fersch, M., Kiltz, E., Poettering, B.: On the one-per-message unforgeability of (EC) DSA and its variants. In: Kalai, Y., Reyzin, L. (eds.) TCC 2017. LNCS, vol. 10678, pp. 519–534. Springer, Cham (2017). https://doi.org/10.1007/978-3-319-70503-3_17

18. GB/T 32918.2-2017. Public Key Cryptographic Algorithm SM2 Based on Elliptic Curves-Part 2: Digital Signature Algorithm (2017)

19. Gentry, C.: Certificate-based encryption and the certificate revocation problem. In: Biham, E. (ed.) EUROCRYPT 2003. LNCS, vol. 2656, pp. 272–293. Springer, Heidelberg (2003). https://doi.org/10.1007/3-540-39200-9_17

20. Girault, M.: Self-certified public keys. In: Davies, D.W. (ed.) EUROCRYPT 1991. LNCS, vol. 547, pp. 490–497. Springer, Heidelberg (1991). https://doi.org/10.1007/3-540-46416-6_42

21. Groves, M.: Elliptic Curve-Based Certificateless Signatures for Identity-Based Encryption (ECCSI). RFC 6507 (2012)

22. Harn, L., Ren, J., Lin, C.: Design of DL-based certificateless digital signatures. J. Syst. Softw. **82**(5), 789–793 (2009)

23. He, D., Chen, Y., Chen, J.: A new two-round certificateless authenticated key agreement protocol without bilinear pairings. Math. Comput. Model. **54**(11–12), 3143–3152 (2011)

24. He, D., Chen, J., Zhang, R.: An efficient and provably-secure certificateless signature scheme without bilinear pairings. Int. J. Commun. Syst. **25**(11), 1432–1442 (2012)

25. Huang, X., Mu, Y., Susilo, W., Wong, D.S., Wu, W.: Certificateless signature revisited. In: Pieprzyk, J., Ghodosi, H., Dawson, E. (eds.) ACISP 2007. LNCS, vol. 4586, pp. 308–322. Springer, Heidelberg (2007). https://doi.org/10.1007/978-3-540-73458-1_23

26. Huang, X., Susilo, W., Mu, Y., Zhang, F.: On the security of certificateless signature schemes from Asiacrypt 2003. Proc. CANS 2005, 13–25 (2005)

27. Jia, X., He, D., Liu, Q., Choo, K.-K.R.: An efficient provably-secure certificateless signature scheme for internet-of-things deployment. Ad Hoc Netw. (to appear)

28. ISO/IEC. Information Technology - Secruity Techniques - Digital Signatures with Appendix - Part 3: Discrete Logarithm Based Mechanisms. ISO/IEC 14888–3:2016 (2016)

29. ISO/IEC. Information Technology - Security Techniques - Encryption Algorithms - Part 2: Asymmetric Ciphers. ISO/IEC 18033–2:2006 (2006)

30. Lai, J., Kou, W.: Self-generated-certificate public key encryption without pairing. In: Okamoto, T., Wang, X. (eds.) PKC 2007. LNCS, vol. 4450, pp. 476–489. Springer, Heidelberg (2007). https://doi.org/10.1007/978-3-540-71677-8_31

31. Lippold, G., Boyd, C., Nieto, J.G.: Strongly secure certificateless key agreement. In: Shacham, H., Waters, B. (eds.) Pairing 2009. LNCS, vol. 5671, pp. 206–230. Springer, Heidelberg (2009). https://doi.org/10.1007/978-3-642-03298-1_14

32. Liu, W., Xie, Q., Wang, S., Han, L., Hu, B.: Pairing-free certificateless signature with security proof. J. Comput. Netw. Commun. **2014**, 6 p. (2014). https://doi.org/10.1155/2014/792063. Article no. 792063

33. Malone-Lee, J., Smart, N.P.: Modifications of ECDSA. In: Nyberg, K., Heys, H. (eds.) SAC 2002. LNCS, vol. 2595, pp. 1–12. Springer, Heidelberg (2003). https://doi.org/10.1007/3-540-36492-7_1

34. Menezes, A., Smart, N.P.: Security of signature schemes in a multi-user setting. Des. Codes Cryptogr. **33**, 261–274 (2004)

35. Pintsov, L.A., Vanstone, S.A.: Postal revenue collection in the digital age. In: Frankel, Y. (ed.) FC 2000. LNCS, vol. 1962, pp. 105–120. Springer, Heidelberg (2001). https://doi.org/10.1007/3-540-45472-1_8

36. Shoup, V.: Lower bounds for discrete logarithms and related problems. In: Fumy, W. (ed.) EUROCRYPT 1997. LNCS, vol. 1233, pp. 256–266. Springer, Heidelberg (1997). https://doi.org/10.1007/3-540-69053-0_18

37. Shafagh, H.: Leveraging public-key-based authentication for the Internet of Things. Master thesis. https://www.inf.ethz.ch/personal/mshafagh/master_thesis_Hossein_Shafagh_PKC_in_the_IoT.pdf

38. STMicroelectronics. UM1924: STM32 Crypto Library. http://www.st.com/resource/en/user_manual/dm00215061.pdf

39. Sun, Y., Zhang, F., Baek, J.: Strongly secure certificateless public key encryption without pairing. In: Bao, F., Ling, S., Okamoto, T., Wang, H., Xing, C. (eds.) CANS 2007. LNCS, vol. 4856, pp. 194–208. Springer, Heidelberg (2007). https://doi.org/10.1007/978-3-540-76969-9_13

40. Tian, M., Huang, L.: Cryptanalysis of a certificateless signature scheme without pairings. Int. J. Commun. Syst. **26**(11), 1375–1381 (2013)

41. Whyte, W., Weimerskircht, A., Kumar, V., Hehn, T.: A security credential management system for V2V communications. In: Proceedings of 2013 IEEE Vehicular Networking Conference, pp. 1–8 (2013)

42. Yeh, K.-H., Su, C.H., Choo, K.-K.R., Chiu, W.: A novel certificateless signature scheme for smart objects in the Internet-of-Things deployment. Sensors 2017, 17 (1001)

43. Zhang, Z., Wong, D.S., Xu, J., Feng, D.: Certificateless public-key signature: security model and efficient construction. In: Zhou, J., Yung, M., Bao, F. (eds.) ACNS 2006. LNCS, vol. 3989, pp. 293–308. Springer, Heidelberg (2006). https://doi.org/10.1007/11767480_20

44. Zhang, L., Zhang, F., Zhang, F.: New efficient certificateless signature scheme. In: Denko, M.K., Shih, C., Li, K.-C., Tsao, S.-L., Zeng, Q.-A., Park, S.H., Ko, Y.-B., Hung, S.-H., Park, J.H. (eds.) EUC 2007. LNCS, vol. 4809, pp. 692–703. Springer, Heidelberg (2007). https://doi.org/10.1007/978-3-540-77090-9_64

A New Design of Online/Offline Signatures Based on Lattice

Mingmei Zheng[1], Shao-Jun Yang[1(✉)], Wei Wu[1], Jun Shao[2], and Xinyi Huang[1]

[1] Fujian Provincial Key Laboratory of Network Security and Cryptology,
School of Mathematics and Informatics, Fujian Normal University, Fuzhou, China
mmingzheng@outlook.com, shao-junyang@outlook.com,
{weiwu,xyhuang}@fjnu.edu.cn
[2] School of Computer and Information Engineering,
Zhejiang Gongshang University, Hangzhou, China
chn.junshao@gmail.com

Abstract. With the rapid development of mobile internet, a large number of lightweight devices are widely used. Therefore, lightweight cryptographic primitives are urgently demanded. Among these primitives, online/offline signatures are one of the most promising one. Motivated by this situation, we propose a lattice-based online/offline signature scheme by using the hash-sign-switch paradigm, which was introduced by Shamir and Tauman in 2001. Our scheme not only has the advantages of online/offline signatures, but also can resist quantum computer attacks. The scheme we propose is built on several techniques, such as cover-free sets and programmable hash functions. Furthermore, we design a specific chameleon hash function, which plays an important role in the hash-sign-switch paradigm. Under the Inhomogeneous Small Integer Solution (ISIS) assumption, we prove that our proposed chameleon hash function is collision-resistant, which makes a direct application of this new design. In particular, our method satisfies existential unforgeability against adaptive chosen message attacks in the standard model.

Keywords: Online/offline signature · Lattice
Chameleon hash function
The Inhomogeneous Small Integer Solution (ISIS) assumption

1 Introduction

As one of fundamental cryptographic primitives, digital signatures are the essential inventions of modern cryptography. Informally, a signer Alice establishs a public key vk while keeping a secret key sk to herself. In addition, sk and pk satisfy a certain mathematical relation. The signer Alice signs a message M using sk and obtains a digital signature σ of M. Anyone, with pk, can verify the validity of the message-signature pair (M, σ). A digital signature scheme is said to be secure if it is existentially unforgettable against adaptive chosen message

© Springer Nature Switzerland AG 2018
C. Su and H. Kikuchi (Eds.): ISPEC 2018, LNCS 11125, pp. 198–212, 2018
https://doi.org/10.1007/978-3-319-99807-7_12

attacks [10]. Digital signatures are useful in e-contract signing, document nota-
rizing, authentication, and many other scenarios with the need of data integrity
check and undeniability guaranty (e.g., [3,10]). In addition, digital signatures
are the essential building blocks of more advanced cryptographic schemes, such
as fair exchange and authenticated data redaction (e.g., [5]).

Digital signature schemes are often built on mathematical operations, like
modular exponentiation, scalar multiplication and bilinear mapping, etc. However, these operations are much too heavy for smart cards, mobile devices, FRID
tags and other resource-constrained devices. For those devices with more power,
it would also be a critical issue when a large number of messages must be signed
within a short period of time.

As a result, a lot of approaches have been proposed to improve the efficiency of digital signatures, e.g., online/offline signatures. Online/Offline signatures speed up signature production by dividing the signing process into two
phases, offline and online. Most costly computations are completed in the offline
phase, when the messages to be signed are unknown and the device is idle. Such
pre-computation enables the online phase to quickly sign the messages with only
light computation. The notion of online/offline signatures was introduced by
Even, Goldreich and Micali [8] in 1989. Their design philosophy of online/offline
signatures is using the one-time signatures for the online phase, which are very
fast, and an ordinary signature scheme is used at the offline phase. Motivated
by the design in [8], Shamir and Tauman [16] use chameleon hash functions to
develop a new paradigm called hash-sign-switch, which can convert any signature scheme into a highly efficient online/offline signature scheme. From then
on, there are many results (e.g., [4,14,18]) adopting hash-sign-switch paradigm
to construct online/offline signature schemes.

The security of most existing online/offline signature schemes is based on traditional number-theoretic assumptions (e.g., [8,11,14]) and they are in danger
of being broken with the rapid development of quantum computing technology. Therefore, it is urgent to design online/offline signature schemes that can
resist quantum computer attacks. To the best of our knowledge, little attention
has been paid on anti-quantum online/offline signatures (e.g., [18,19]). In the
following section, we shall present a brief review of the related work.

1.1 Related Work

Even, Goldreich and Micali [8] proposed the notion of online/offline signatures
in 1989. They used a general method to convert any signature scheme into an
online/offline signature scheme. In their work, if the length of M is k, then the
length of σ is a quadratic polynomial in k. To further improve the efficiency,
Shamir and Tauman [16] proposed a hash-sign-switch paradigm. In [16], the
overhead of the signature is reduced to an additive factor of k.

Many online/offline signature schemes with different properties have been
proposed, such as threshold online/offline signature schemes (e.g., [4]) and
identity-based online/offline signature schemes (e.g., [14]). Nevertheless, almost

all of previous online/offline signature schemes are based on traditional number-theoretic assumptions, such as DLP and IF (e.g., [4,8,12,16]). There is a risk that these assumptions would be broken with the use of quantum computing technology. Therefore, it is necessary to design anti-quantum online/offline signature schemes. However, there are few results on anti-quantum online/offline signatures (e.g., [18,19]). Driven by the design philosophy raised by Xiang [18] and Zhang [20], we present a lattice-based online/offline signature scheme. Although the idea of [18] is enlightening, the chameleon hash function needs more rigorous proof and the correctness of some details in his scheme needs further discussion.

1.2 Our Contributions

Lightweight cryptographic primitives are widely demanded as the widespread use of lightweight devices. Online/offline signatures are one of the promising solutions for this dilemma. This makes it highly non-trivial to propose a lattice-based online/offline signature scheme, which not only has the advantages of online/offline signature schemes, but also can resist quantum computer attacks.

Compared to previous work [18], our proposed chameleon hash function includes rigorous proof and specific data. Furthermore, by applying our chameleon hash function to the original scheme [20], the new scheme is more efficient than the original one in the offline phase. The security of our scheme can be reduced to the Inhomogeneous Small Integer Solution (ISIS) assumption in the standard model.

1.3 Roadmap

After some preliminaries in Sect. 2, we give a specific chameleon hash function in Sect. 3.1, which is a core technical in our scheme. We propose a lattice-based online/offline signature scheme in Sect. 3.2, and a short conclusion is given in Sect. 4.

2 Preliminaries

In this section, we mainly describe the notion of lattice-based programmable hash functions [20] and online/offline signatures [4].

2.1 Notation

We denote the real numbers and the integers by $\mathbb{R}$ and $\mathbb{Z}$, respectively. For any positive integer N, we let $[N] = \{0, 1, \cdots, N - 1\}$. For positive integer n, let the standard notation O, ω classify the growth functions, and we say that $f(n) = \widetilde{O}(g(n))$ if $f(n) = O(g(n) \cdot \log^c n)$ for some fixed constant c. We use $poly(n)$ to denote the function $f(n) = O(n^c)$ for some constant c. A negligible function, denoted usually by $negl(n)$, is $f(n)$ such that $f(n) = o(n^{-c})$ for every fixed constant c. A probability is said to be overwhelming if it is $1 - negl(n)$.

The natural security parameter is κ throughout the paper, and all other quantities are implicitly functions of κ. The notation of $\leftarrow_r$ indicates randomly choosing elements from the distribution. Let $\mathbf{I}_n$ be the $n \times n$ identity matrix. Vectors are accustomed to being in column form and wrote by bold lower-case letters, e.g. $\mathbf{x}$. Matrices are used to be bold capital letters, e.g. $\mathbf{X}$. The notation of $(\mathbf{X}\|\mathbf{Y}) \in \mathbb{R}^{n \times (m+m')}$ means that the columns of $\mathbf{X} \in \mathbb{R}^{n \times m}$ are followed by the columns of $\mathbf{Y} \in \mathbb{R}^{n \times m'}$. The length of a matrix is denoted as the norm of its longest column, i.e., $\|\mathbf{X}\| = \max_i \|\mathbf{x}_i\|$. The largest singular value of matrix $\mathbf{X}$ is measured by $s_1(\mathbf{X}) = \max_{\mathbf{t}} \|\mathbf{X}\mathbf{t}\|$, where $\mathbf{t}$ is the unit vector. A hash function $H : \mathbb{Z}_q^n \to \mathbb{Z}_q^{n \times n}$ is an encoding with full-rank difference (FRD) [20] if it satisfies the following two conditions: (1) for any $\mathbf{u} \neq \mathbf{v}$, the matrix $H(\mathbf{u}) \pm H(\mathbf{v}) = H(\mathbf{u} \pm \mathbf{v}) \in \mathbb{Z}_q^{n \times n}$ is invertible; and (2) H is computable in polynomial time in $n \log q$. In particular, for any vector $\mathbf{v} = (v, 0, \cdots, 0)^\top$, we have that $H(\mathbf{v}) = v\mathbf{I}_n$.

2.2 Lattices

We now introduce the definition of lattice and its related parameters. Formally, given m linearly independent vectors $\mathbf{B} = (\mathbf{b}_1, \mathbf{b}_2, \cdots, \mathbf{b}_m) \in \mathbb{R}^{m \times m}$, the m-dimensional full-rank lattice generated by $\mathbf{B}$ is defined as $\Lambda = L(\mathbf{B}) = \{\sum_{i=1}^m x_i \mathbf{b}_i : x_i \in \mathbb{Z}\}$. For any $\mathbf{x} \in \mathbb{R}^m$, the Gaussian function $\rho_{s,\mathbf{c}}$ on $\mathbb{R}^m$ is defined as $\rho_{s,\mathbf{c}}(\mathbf{x}) = \exp(-\pi \|(\mathbf{x}-\mathbf{c})/s\|^2)$ with center $\mathbf{c} \in \mathbb{R}^m$ and $s > 0$. We have $\rho_{s,\mathbf{c}}(\Lambda) = \sum_{\mathbf{x} \in \Lambda} \rho_{s,\mathbf{c}}(\mathbf{x})$. For any $\mathbf{c} \in \mathbb{R}^m$, real $s > 0$ and $\mathbf{x} \in \Lambda$, the discrete Gaussian distribution $D_{\Lambda,s,\mathbf{c}}$ over Λ is denoted as $D_{\Lambda,s,\mathbf{c}}(\mathbf{x}) = \rho_{s,\mathbf{c}}(\mathbf{x})/\rho_{s,\mathbf{c}}(\Lambda)$. For some positive $m, n, q \in \mathbb{Z}$, let $\mathbf{A} \in \mathbb{Z}_q^{n \times m}$ be a matrix and considering the following two lattices: $\Lambda^\perp(\mathbf{A}) = \{\mathbf{z} \in \mathbb{Z}^m : \mathbf{A}\mathbf{z} = 0 \mod q\}$ and $\Lambda(\mathbf{A}) = \{\mathbf{z} \in \mathbb{Z}^m : \exists \mathbf{s} \in \mathbb{Z}_q^n \text{ s.t. } \mathbf{z} = \mathbf{A}^\top \mathbf{s} \mod q\}$. For any $\mathbf{u} \in \mathbb{Z}^n$ admitting an solution to $\mathbf{A}\mathbf{x} = \mathbf{u} \mod q$, we have the coset $\Lambda_{\mathbf{u}}^\perp(\mathbf{A}) = \{\mathbf{z} \in \mathbb{Z}^m : \mathbf{A}\mathbf{z} = \mathbf{u} \mod q\} = \Lambda^\perp(\mathbf{A}) + \mathbf{x}$.

The following result was quoted from [20], and it will be used in Sect. 3.

Lemma 1. *For any positive integer $m \in \mathbb{Z}$, vector $\mathbf{y} \in \mathbb{Z}^m$ and large enough $s \geq \omega(\sqrt{\log m})$, we have that*

$$\Pr_{\mathbf{x} \leftarrow_r D_{\mathbb{Z}^m, s}} [\|\mathbf{x}\| > s\sqrt{m}] \leq 2^{-m} \text{ and } \Pr_{\mathbf{x} \leftarrow_r D_{\mathbb{Z}^m, s}} [\mathbf{x} = \mathbf{y}] \leq 2^{1-m}.$$

Following [6,15], we say that a random variable $\mathbf{X}$ over $\mathbb{R}$ is subgaussian with parameter $s > 0$ if the moment-generating function satisfies $E[\exp(2\pi t \mathbf{X})] \leq \exp(\pi s^2 t^2)$ for all $t \in \mathbb{R}$,. If $\mathbf{X}$ is subgaussian, then its tails are dominated by a Gaussian with parameter s, i.e., $\Pr[|\mathbf{X}| \geq t] \leq 2\exp(-\pi t^2/s^2)$ for all $t \geq 0$. In addition, we get that a random matrix $\mathbf{X}$ is subgaussian with parameter s if all its one-dimensional marginals $\mathbf{u}^\top \mathbf{X}\mathbf{v}$ for unit vectors $\mathbf{u}, \mathbf{v}$ are subgaussian with parameter s. Moreover, we have that for any lattices $\Lambda \subset \mathbb{R}^m$ and $s > 0$, the distribution $D_{\Lambda,s}$ is subgaussian with parameter s.

We have the following results from the non-asymptotic theory of random matrices [17], and it gives the singular value of variable $\mathbf{X}$ exactly.

Lemma 2. *Let* $\boldsymbol{X} \in \mathbb{Z}_q^{m \times n}$ *be a subgaussian random matrix with parameter s. There exists an universal constant $C \approx 1/\sqrt{2\pi}$ such that for any $t \geq 0$, we have $s_1(\boldsymbol{X}) \leq C \cdot s \cdot (\sqrt{m} + \sqrt{n} + t)$ except with probability at most $2\exp(-\pi t^2)$.*

In 1999, Ajtai [2] proposed the first trapdoor generation algorithm to output an approximately uniform trapdoor matrix A that allows to efficiently sample short vectors in $\Lambda^\perp(A)$. Then this trapdoor generation algorithm has been improved in [15]. We now recall the publicly trapdoor matrix $\mathbf{G}$ in [15]. Formally, for any prime $q > 2$, integer $n \geq 1$, $k = \lceil \log_2 q \rceil$, and $\mathbf{g} = (1, 2, 4, \cdots, 2^{k-1})^\top \in \mathbb{Z}_q^k$, we have that the public trapdoor matrix $\mathbf{G} = \mathbf{I}_n \otimes \mathbf{g}^\top \in \mathbb{Z}_q^{n \times nk}$, where '$\otimes$' denotes the tensor product.

We show the formal definition of $\mathbf{G}$-trapdoor [15] in the following and it will be used in Sect. 3.

Definition 1. *Let* $\boldsymbol{A} \in \mathbb{Z}_q^{n \times \bar{m}}$ *and* $\boldsymbol{G} \in \mathbb{Z}_q^{n \times nk}$ *be matrices with $n, q, \bar{m} \in \mathbb{Z}$ and $k = \lceil \log_2 q \rceil$. A $\boldsymbol{G}$-Trapdoor for $\boldsymbol{A}$ is a martix $\boldsymbol{R} \in \mathbb{Z}_q^{(\bar{m}-nk) \times nk}$ such that $\boldsymbol{A} \begin{pmatrix} \boldsymbol{R} \\ \boldsymbol{I} \end{pmatrix} = \boldsymbol{SG}$ for some invertible matrix $\boldsymbol{S} \in \mathbb{Z}_q^{n \times n}$. The quality of the trapdoor is measured by its largest singular value $s_1(\boldsymbol{R})$.*

If $\mathbf{R}$ is a trapdoor for $\mathbf{A}$, then it can be made into an equally good trapdoor for any extension $(\mathbf{A}\|\mathbf{B})$ by padding $\mathbf{R}$ with zero rows. This leaves $s_1(\mathbf{R})$ unchanged.

Then we refer to [15] for a detailed description of the sampling algorithm, which plays an important role in our scheme in Sect. 3.

Theorem 1. *For any integer $n \geq 1$, $q > 0$, $k = \lceil \log_2 q \rceil$, sufficiently large $\bar{m} = O(n \log q)$ and some invertible tag $\boldsymbol{S} \in \mathbb{Z}_q^{n \times n}$, there is a polynomial time algorithm $\mathrm{TrapGen}(1^n, 1^{\bar{m}}, q, \boldsymbol{S})$ that outputs a matrix $\boldsymbol{A} \in \mathbb{Z}_q^{n \times \bar{m}}$ and a $\boldsymbol{G}$-trapdoor $\boldsymbol{R} \in \mathbb{Z}_q^{(\bar{m}-nk) \times nk}$ with quality $s_1(\boldsymbol{R}) \leq \sqrt{\bar{m}} \cdot \omega(\sqrt{\log n})$ such that the distribution of $\boldsymbol{A}$ is $\mathrm{negl}(\kappa)$-far from uniform. Moreover, given any $\boldsymbol{u} \in \mathbb{Z}_q^n$ and real $s > s_1(\boldsymbol{R}) \cdot \omega(\sqrt{\log n})$, there is an efficient algorithm $\mathrm{SampleD}(\boldsymbol{R}, \boldsymbol{A}, \boldsymbol{S}, \boldsymbol{u}, s)$ samples from a distribution within $\mathrm{negl}(\kappa)$ statistical distance of $D_{\Lambda_u^\perp(\boldsymbol{A}), s}$.*

The following lemma illustrates that the matrix we construct is statistically close to the uniform, which is applied to Theorem 4.

Lemma 3. *For any postive $n \geq 1$, $q > 2$, sufficiently large $\bar{m} = O(n \log q)$ and real $s \geq \omega(\sqrt{\log \bar{m}})$, we have that the distribution of $\boldsymbol{u} = \boldsymbol{A}\boldsymbol{e} \mod q$ is statistically close to uniform over $\mathbb{Z}_q^n$, where $\boldsymbol{e}$ is randomly sampled from $D_{\mathbb{Z}^{\bar{m}}, s}$ and $\boldsymbol{A}$ is a uniformly random matrix over $\mathbb{Z}_q^{n \times \bar{m}}$.*

The Inhomogeneous Small Integer Solution($ISIS_{q, \bar{m}, \bar{\beta}}$) problem was first raised by Ajtai [1]. The *ISIS* problem was an inhomogeneous variant of *SIS*, which is asked to find a short nonzero integer solution $\mathbf{e} \in \mathbb{Z}^{\bar{m}}$ to the homogeneous linear system $\mathbf{Ae} = \mathbf{0} \mod q$ for uniformly random $\mathbf{A} \in \mathbb{Z}_q^{n \times \bar{m}}$. If we set $n, q \in \mathbb{Z}$ be some polynomials in the security parameter κ, $\bar{m} = O(n \log q)$, then $\bar{\beta}$ in the $ISIS_{q, \bar{m}, \bar{\beta}}$ problem can be $\widetilde{O}(n^{5.5})$ according to [20]. Both hard problems on lattices are shown in detail in [9].

Definition 2. *The Inhomogeneous Small Integer Solution (ISIS) problem (in the ℓ_2 norm) is as follows: given an integer q, a matrix $\boldsymbol{A} \in \mathbb{Z}_q^{n \times m}$, a syndrone $\boldsymbol{u} \in \mathbb{Z}_q^n$ and a real $\bar{\beta}$, find a integer vector $\boldsymbol{e} \in \mathbb{Z}^{\bar{m}}$ such that $\boldsymbol{Ae} = \boldsymbol{u} \mod q$ and $\|\boldsymbol{e}\|_2 \leq \bar{\beta}$.*

2.3   Lattice-Based Programmable Hash Function

We use lattice-based PHFs to construct our signature and lattice-based PHFs was proposed by [20] in 2016. Formally, let $m, \bar{m}, n, \ell, q, u, v \in \mathbb{Z}$ be some polynomials in the security parameter κ. We denote $\mathcal{I}_n$ as the set of invertible matrices in $\mathbb{Z}_q^{n \times n}$. A hash function $\mathcal{H} : \chi \to \mathbb{Z}_q^{n \times m}$ consists of two algorithms $(\mathcal{H}.\text{Gen}, \mathcal{H}.\text{Eval})$, i.e., $K \leftarrow \mathcal{H}.\text{Gen}(1^\kappa)$ and $H_K(X) = \mathcal{H}.\text{Eval}(K, X)$ for any input $X \in \chi$. The following definition is referenced from [20].

Definition 3. (Lattice-Based Programmable Hash Function)
A hash function $\mathcal{H} : \chi \to \mathbb{Z}_q^{n \times m}$ is a $(u, v, \beta, \gamma, \delta)$-PHF if there exist a PPT trapdoor key generation algorithm $\mathcal{H}.\text{TrapGen}$ and an efficiently deterministic trapdoor evaluation algorithm $\mathcal{H}.\text{TrapEval}$ such that given a uniformly random $\boldsymbol{A} \in \mathbb{Z}_q^{n \times \bar{m}}$ and a public trapdoor matrix $\boldsymbol{B} \in \mathbb{Z}_q^{n \times m}$, the following properties hold:

Syntax: *The PPT algorithm $(K', td) \leftarrow \mathcal{H}.\text{TrapGen}(1^\kappa, \boldsymbol{A}, \boldsymbol{B})$ outputs a key K' with a trapdoor td. Besides, for any input $X \in \chi$, the deterministic algorithm $(\boldsymbol{R}_X, \boldsymbol{S}_X) \leftarrow \mathcal{H}.\text{TrapEval}(td, K', X)$ outputs $\boldsymbol{R}_X \in \mathbb{Z}_q^{m \times m}$ and $\boldsymbol{S}_X \in \mathbb{Z}_q^{n \times n}$ such that $s_1(\boldsymbol{R}_X) \leq \beta$ and $\boldsymbol{S}_X \in \mathcal{I}_n \cup \{\boldsymbol{0}\}$.*

Correctness: *For all possible $(K', td) \leftarrow \mathcal{H}.\text{TrapGen}(1^\kappa, \boldsymbol{A}, \boldsymbol{B})$, all $X \in \chi$ and its corresponding $(\boldsymbol{R}_X, \boldsymbol{S}_X) \leftarrow \mathcal{H}.\text{TrapEval}(td, K', X)$, we have $H_{K'}(X) = \mathcal{H}.\text{Eval}(K', X) = \boldsymbol{A}\boldsymbol{R}_X + \boldsymbol{S}_X \boldsymbol{B}$.*

Statistically close trapdoor keys: *For all $(K', td) \leftarrow \mathcal{H}.\text{TrapGen}(1^\kappa, \boldsymbol{A}, \boldsymbol{B})$ and $K \leftarrow \mathcal{H}.\text{Gen}(1^\kappa)$, the statistical distance between $(\boldsymbol{A}, K')$ and $(\boldsymbol{A}, K)$ is at most γ.*

Well-distributed hidden matrices: *Let all $(K', td) \leftarrow \mathcal{H}.\text{TrapGen}(1^\kappa, \boldsymbol{A}, \boldsymbol{B})$ and any inputs $X_1, \cdots, X_u, Y_1, \cdots, Y_v \in \chi$ enjoys $X_i \neq Y_j$ for any i, j. For $(\boldsymbol{R}_{X_i}, \boldsymbol{S}_{X_i}) \leftarrow \mathcal{H}.\text{TrapEval}(td, K', X_i)$ and $(\boldsymbol{R}_{Y_j}, \boldsymbol{S}_{Y_j}) \leftarrow \mathcal{H}.\text{TrapEval}(td, K', Y_j)$, we have that*

$$\Pr[\boldsymbol{S}_{X_1} = \cdots = \boldsymbol{S}_{X_u} = \{\boldsymbol{0}\} \wedge \boldsymbol{S}_{Y_1}, \cdots, \boldsymbol{S}_{Y_v} \in \mathcal{I}_n] \geq \delta.$$

If γ is negligible and $\delta > 0$ is noticeable, we simply say that $\mathcal{H}$ is a (u, v, β)-PHF.

A general trapdoor matrix $\mathbf{B}$ is used for utmost generality, but the publicly known trapdoor matrix $\mathbf{B} = \mathbf{G}$ in [15] is regarded for both efficiency and simplicity. In this paper, we apply two types of lattice-based programmable hash function constructions to our scheme. Then, we show their definitions and examples from [20].

Definition 4. [Type-1]

Let $\ell, n, m, q \in \mathbb{Z}$ be some polynomials in the security parameter κ. Let E be a deterministic encoding from χ to $(\mathbb{Z}_q^{n \times n})^\ell$. Then the hash function $\mathcal{H} = (\mathcal{H}.\mathsf{Gen}, \mathcal{H}.\mathsf{Eval})$ with key space $\mathcal{K} \subseteq (\mathbb{Z}_q^{n \times m})^{\ell+1}$ is defined as follows:

- $\mathcal{H}.\mathsf{Gen}(1^\kappa)$: Randomly choose $(\boldsymbol{A}_0, \cdots, \boldsymbol{A}_\ell) \leftarrow_r \mathcal{K}$, return $K = \{\boldsymbol{A}_i\}_{i \in \{0, \cdots, \ell\}}$.
- $\mathcal{H}.\mathsf{Eval}(K, X)$: Let $E(X) = (\boldsymbol{C}_1, \cdots, \boldsymbol{C}_\ell)$, return $\boldsymbol{Z} = \boldsymbol{A}_0 + \sum_{i=1}^{\ell} \boldsymbol{C}_i \boldsymbol{A}_i$.

In the following theorem, we show several examples of Type-1 PHF [20], which were implicated proved in [3,15].

Theorem 2. For large enough $\bar{m} = O(n \log q)$, the hash function $\mathcal{H}$ given in Definition 4 is a weak $(1, poly(v), \beta, \gamma, \delta)$-PHF with $\beta \le \sqrt{\ell \bar{m}} \cdot \omega(\sqrt{\log n})$, $\gamma = negl(\kappa)$, and $\delta = 1$ when instantiated as follows:

- Let $\mathcal{K} \subseteq (\mathbb{Z}_q^{n \times m})^2$ and $\chi = \mathbb{Z}_q^n$. Given an input $X \in \chi$, the encoding $E(X)$ returns $H(X)$ where $H : \mathbb{Z}_q^n \to \mathbb{Z}_q^{n \times n}$ is an FRD encoding.
- Let $\mathcal{K} \subseteq (\mathbb{Z}_q^{n \times m})^{\ell+1}$ and $\chi = \{0, 1\}^\ell$. Given an input $X \in (X_1, \cdots, X_\ell) \in \chi$, the encoding $E(X)$ returns $\boldsymbol{C}_i = X_i \cdot \boldsymbol{I}_n$ for all $i \in \{1, \cdots, \ell\}$.

The two instantiations in Theorem 2 are weak $(1, v, \beta)$-PHFs for some polynomials $v \in \mathbb{Z}$ and real $\beta \in \mathbb{R}$.

Definition 5. [Type-2]

Let $n, q \in \mathbb{Z}$ be some polynomials in the security parameter κ. For any $\ell, v \in \mathbb{Z}$ and $L = 2^\ell$, let $N \le 16v^2\ell$, $\eta \le 4v\ell$ and $CF = \{CF_X\}_{X \in [L]}$ be an η-uniform, v-cover-free set. Let $\tau = \lceil \log_2 N \rceil$ and $k = \lceil \log_2 q \rceil$. Then the hash function $\mathcal{H} = (\mathcal{H}.\mathsf{Gen}, \mathcal{H}.\mathsf{Eval})$ from $[L]$ to $\mathbb{Z}_q^{n \times nk}$ is defined as follows:

- $\mathcal{H}.\mathsf{Gen}(1^\kappa)$: Randomly choose $\hat{\boldsymbol{A}}, \boldsymbol{A}_i \leftarrow_r \mathbb{Z}_q^{n \times nk}$ for $i \in \{0, \cdots, \tau - 1\}$, return the key $K = (\hat{\boldsymbol{A}}, \{\boldsymbol{A}_i\}_{i \in \{0, \cdots, \tau\}})$.
- $\mathcal{H}.\mathsf{Eval}(K, X)$: Given $K = (\hat{\boldsymbol{A}}, \{\boldsymbol{A}_i\}_{i \in \{0, \cdots, \tau-1\}})$ and integer $X \in [L]$, the algorithm outputs $\boldsymbol{Z} = H_K(X)$.

Please refer to [20] for details of the algorithm in Definition 5. In the following, we show that the hash function $\mathcal{H}$ given in Definition 5 is a $(1, v, \beta)$-PHFs for some real $\beta \in \mathbb{R}$ and $v = poly(\kappa)$.

Theorem 3. Let $CF = \{CF_X\}_{X \in [L]}$ be an η-uniform, v-cover-free set. For any $n, q \in \mathbb{Z}$, $L = 2^\ell$, $N \le 16v^2\ell$, $\eta \le 4v\ell$ and $\bar{m} = O(n \log q)$, the hash function $\mathcal{H}$ given in Definition 5 is a $(1, poly(v), \beta, \gamma, \delta)$-PHF with $\beta \le \mu v \ell \bar{m}^{1.5} \cdot \omega(\sqrt{\log \bar{m}})$, $\gamma = negl(\kappa)$, and $\delta = 1/N$, where $\tau = \lceil \log_2 N \rceil$. In particular, if we set $\ell = n$ and $v = \omega(\log n)$, then $\beta = \tilde{O}(n^{2.5})$ and the key of $\mathcal{H}$ only consists of $\tau = O(\log n)$ matrices.

The detailed proof of this theorem has been shown in [20]. Let L, N be some polynomials in the security parameter κ and let $CF = \{CF_X\}_{X \in [L]}$ be a family of subsets of $[N]$. The family CF is said to be v-cover-free [7,13,20] over $[N]$ if for any subset $S \subseteq [L]$ of size at most v, then the union $\cup_{X \in S} CF_X$ does not cover CF_Y for all $Y \notin S$. In addition, we say that CF is η-uniform if every subset CF_X in the union family $CF = \{CF_X\}_{X \in L}$ have size $\eta \in \mathbb{Z}$. $CF = \{CF_X\}_{X \in [L]}$ is regarded as an η-uniform, v-cover-free set when mentioned in this paper. A hash function $\mathcal{H} : \chi \to \mathbb{Z}_q^{n \times m}$ can be a weak (u, v, β)-PHF, where the algorithm $\mathcal{H}.TrapGen$ additionally takes a list $X_1, \cdots, X_u \in \chi$ as inputs such that the well-distributed hidden matrices property holds.

2.4   Definition and Security Model of Online/Offline Signatures

First of all, we roughly introduce the notion of online/offline signatures defined in [16], and then introduce the security model of online/offline signatures. Shamir and Tauman use the hash-sign-switch paradigm to construct a highly efficient online/offline signature scheme, which combines any chameleon hash family (C, H) and any signature scheme (G, S, V) to get an online/offline signature scheme (G', S', V').

More specifically, let $(m_1, r_1) \in \mathcal{M} \times \mathcal{S}$ be randomly chosen. $\mathcal{M}$ is the message space, and $\mathcal{S}$ is some finite space. Generating a pair (sk, vk) of private key and public key, by applying G to the input 1^κ (where G is the key generation algorithm of the original scheme), and generating a pair (tk, hk) of private key and public key, by applying C to the input 1^κ (where C is the key generation algorithm of the chameleon hash family). $H = CH_{hk}$ is a family of randomized hash functions. In the offline phase, we run the signing algorithm S with the signing key sk to sign the message $CH_{hk}(m_1, r_1)$, and denote the output $S_{sk}(CH_{hk}(m_1, r_1))$ by σ^{off}. In the online phase, there exists a polynomial time algorithm that on inputs the pair (tk, hk), (m_1, r_1) and an actual message $m_2 \in \mathcal{M}$, then outputs a value $r_2 \in \mathcal{S}$ such that $CH_{hk}(m_1, r_1) = CH_{hk}(m_2, r_2)$. Denoting the output r_2 by σ^{on}, and sending $\sigma = (\sigma^{off}, \sigma^{on})$ as a signature of m_2. The verification algorithm V' verifies that $\sigma = (\sigma^{off}, \sigma^{on})$ is indeed a signature of the message m_2 with respect to the public key (vk, hk), and uses the algorithm V to check that σ^{off} is indeed a signature of the hash value $CH_{hk}(m_2, r_2)$ with vk.

The security notion for our online/offline signature scheme is existentially unforgeable under adaptative chosen message attacks (EUF-CMA), which says that any PPT attacker, after receiving valid signatures on a polynomial number of adaptively chosen messages, cannot produce a valid signature on a new message. Formally, the game between a challenger $\mathcal{C}$ and an attacker $\mathcal{A}$ is as follows.

KeyGen. The challenger $\mathcal{C}$ runs the key generation algorithm KeyGen(1^κ) and returns (sk, tk) as its private key, (vk, hk) as its public key. $\mathcal{C}$ gives the public key to the attacker $\mathcal{A}$, and keeps the private key.

Signing. The attacker $\mathcal{A}$ is allowed to ask for the signature of any fresh message $\mathbf{m}$. In the offline phase, the challenger $\mathcal{C}$ randomly chooses the information to compute a chameleon hash function, and then it uses sk to sign the chameleon hash function, which is regarded as offline signature message. Denote the result by σ^{off}. In the online phase, the challenger $\mathcal{C}$ uses tk and σ^{off} to sign the actual message $\mathbf{m}$, and return σ^{on} as its online signature. The challenger $\mathcal{C}$ sends the signature $\sigma = (\sigma^{off}, \sigma^{on})$ to the attacker $\mathcal{A}$. The attacker can repeat the query by any polynomial times.

Forge. The attacker $\mathcal{A}$ outputs a message-signature pair $(\mathbf{m}^*, \sigma^*)$. Let Q be the messages set required by $\mathcal{A}$ in the signing phase. If $\mathbf{m}^* \notin Q$ and $\mathsf{Verify}(vk, hk, \mathbf{m}^*, \sigma^*) = 1$, the game outputs 1, else outputs 0.

If the game outputs 1, $\mathcal{A}$ wins the game. The advantage of $\mathcal{A}$ in the above security game is defined as $\mathsf{Adv}_{\mathcal{A},\mathcal{SIG}}^{euf-cma}(1^k) = \Pr[\mathcal{C} \text{ outputs } 1]$.

Definition 6. *Let κ be the security parameter. A signature scheme $\mathcal{SIG}$ is said to be existentially unforgeable under adaptive chosen message attacks (EUF-CMA) if the advantage $\mathsf{Adv}_{\mathcal{A},\mathcal{SIG}}^{euf-cma}(1^k)$ is negligible in κ for any PPT attacker $\mathcal{A}$.*

3   Our Design of Online/Offline Signatures

We now introduce a specific chameleon hash function before proposing our online/offline signature scheme.

3.1   Our Chameleon Hash Function

A chameleon hash function is a special type of hash functions, whose collision resistance depends on the user's state of knowledge. It has three properties, i.e., efficiency, collision resistance and trapdoor collisions. Every chameleon hash function is connected with a pair of public key and private key. For further details, please refer to [16]. In particular, the chameleon hash function in [18] is defined in the ideal lattice. Inspired by this, we designed a chameleon hash function on the general lattice.

Definition 7. *Let $n, w, q \in \mathbb{Z}$ with $n = wq$, $\bar{m} = O(n \log q)$, $k = \lceil \log q \rceil$ and $(\mathbf{m}, \mathbf{r}) \in \{0,1\}^w \times \mathbb{Z}_q^{\bar{m}}$. Let $\mathbf{A}' \in \mathbb{Z}_q^{w \times \bar{m}}$, $\mathbf{B}' \in \mathbb{Z}_q^{w \times w}$ be randomly chosen. Then we have a function $CH(\mathbf{A}', \mathbf{B}', \mathbf{m}, \mathbf{r}) = (\mathbf{B}'\mathbf{m} + \mathbf{A}'\mathbf{r}) \mod q$.*

Lemma 4. *Let $n, w, q \in \mathbb{Z}$ with $n = wq$, $\bar{m} = O(n \log q)$, $k = \lceil \log_2 q \rceil$, $\mathbf{B}' \in \mathbb{Z}_q^{w \times w}$, $\mathbf{G}' \in \mathbb{Z}_q^{w \times wk}$ and $(\mathbf{m}, \mathbf{r}) \in \{0,1\}^w \times \mathbb{Z}_q^{\bar{m}}$. Let $\mathbf{R}' \in \mathbb{Z}_q^{(\bar{m}-wk) \times wk}$ be $\mathbf{G}'$-trapdoor of $\mathbf{A}' \in \mathbb{Z}_q^{w \times \bar{m}}$ such that $\mathbf{A}' \begin{pmatrix} \mathbf{R}' \\ \mathbf{I}_{wk} \end{pmatrix} = \mathbf{S}'\mathbf{G}'$ for some invertible matrix $\mathbf{S}' \in \mathbb{Z}_q^{w \times w}$ and $s > s_1(\mathbf{R}') \cdot \omega(\sqrt{\log n})$. Then we have that $CH(\mathbf{A}', \mathbf{B}', \mathbf{m}, \mathbf{r})$ in Definition 7 is a chameleon hash function.*

Proof. Let ue show the function $CH(\mathbf{A}', \mathbf{B}', \mathbf{m}, \mathbf{r})$ enjoys three properties of hash chameleon functions.

- **Efficiency.** The function $CH(\mathbf{A}', \mathbf{B}', \mathbf{m}, \mathbf{r}) = (\mathbf{B}'\mathbf{m} + \mathbf{A}'\mathbf{r}) \mod q$ is computable in polynomial time.
- **Collision Resistance.** Let $\mathbf{r}_1, \mathbf{r}_2 \in \mathbb{Z}_q^m$ and $\mathbf{m}_1, \mathbf{m}_2 \in \{0,1\}^w$ such that $\mathbf{m}_1 \neq \mathbf{m}_2$. We note that finding a pair of collision in $CH(\mathbf{A}', \mathbf{B}', \mathbf{m}, \mathbf{r})$ is at least as hard as solving the ISIS problem. Assuming that a collision of $CH(\mathbf{A}', \mathbf{B}', \mathbf{m}, \mathbf{r})$ is $(\mathbf{m}_1, \mathbf{r}_1)$ and $(\mathbf{m}_2, \mathbf{r}_2)$, then we get $CH(\mathbf{A}', \mathbf{B}', \mathbf{m}_1, \mathbf{r}_1) = CH(\mathbf{A}', \mathbf{B}', \mathbf{m}_2, \mathbf{r}_2)$. From this, we have

$$\mathbf{B}'(\mathbf{m}_1 - \mathbf{m}_2) + \mathbf{A}'(\mathbf{r}_1 - \mathbf{r}_2) = 0 \mod q. \tag{1}$$

We randomly choose $\bar{\mathbf{A}} \in \mathbb{Z}_q^{w \times (\bar{m} - wk)}$. Let $\mathbf{A}' = (\bar{\mathbf{A}} \| \mathbf{S}'\mathbf{G}' - \bar{\mathbf{A}}\mathbf{R}')$, $\mathbf{r}_{11}, \mathbf{r}_{21} \in \mathbb{Z}_q^{\bar{m}-wk}$, $\mathbf{r}_{12}, \mathbf{r}_{22} \in \mathbb{Z}_q^{wk}$, $\mathbf{r}_1 = \begin{pmatrix} \mathbf{r}_{11} \\ \mathbf{r}_{12} \end{pmatrix}$, $\mathbf{r}_2 = \begin{pmatrix} \mathbf{r}_{21} \\ \mathbf{r}_{22} \end{pmatrix}$ and $\mathbf{r}_1 - \mathbf{r}_2 = \begin{pmatrix} \mathbf{r}_{11} - \mathbf{r}_{21} \\ \mathbf{r}_{12} - \mathbf{r}_{22} \end{pmatrix}$.

Applying this variables into (1), then (1) can be rewritten as

$$\mathbf{B}'(\mathbf{m}_1 - \mathbf{m}_2) + (\bar{\mathbf{A}} \| \mathbf{S}'\mathbf{G}' - \bar{\mathbf{A}}\mathbf{R}') \begin{pmatrix} \mathbf{r}_{11} - \mathbf{r}_{21} \\ \mathbf{r}_{12} - \mathbf{r}_{22} \end{pmatrix} = 0 \mod q. \tag{2}$$

By (2), we get

$$\mathbf{B}'(\mathbf{m}_1 - \mathbf{m}_2) + \bar{\mathbf{A}}[(\mathbf{r}_{11} - \mathbf{r}_{21}) + \mathbf{R}'(\mathbf{r}_{22} - \mathbf{r}_{12})] = \mathbf{S}'\mathbf{G}'(\mathbf{r}_{22} - \mathbf{r}_{12}) \mod q. \tag{3}$$

Let $\mathbf{A} = (\bar{\mathbf{A}} \| \mathbf{B}')$, $\mathbf{z}_1 = (\mathbf{r}_{11} - \mathbf{r}_{21}) + \mathbf{R}'(\mathbf{r}_{22} - \mathbf{r}_{12})$, $\mathbf{z}_2 = \mathbf{m}_1 - \mathbf{m}_2$, $\mathbf{z} = \begin{pmatrix} \mathbf{z}_1 \\ \mathbf{z}_2 \end{pmatrix}$ and $\mathbf{u} = \mathbf{S}'\mathbf{G}'(\mathbf{r}_{22} - \mathbf{r}_{12})$. The formula (3) can be rewritten as $\mathbf{A}\mathbf{z} = \mathbf{u}$. Since $\mathbf{m}_1 \neq \mathbf{m}_2$, we have $\|\mathbf{z}\| \neq 0$. Moreover, we get

$$\|\mathbf{z}\| = \sqrt{\mathbf{z}_1^2 + \mathbf{z}_2^2} \leq |\mathbf{z}_1| + |\mathbf{z}_2| \leq (q + q^2 kw)\sqrt{\bar{m} - wk} + \sqrt{w} \leq \tilde{O}(n^{5.5}) = \bar{\beta}.$$

Therefore, $\mathbf{z}$ is a valid solution to the $ISIS_{q,\bar{m},\bar{\beta}}$ instance $(\mathbf{A}, \mathbf{u})$.
- **Trapdoor Collisions.** Let $\mathbf{r}_1 \in \mathbb{Z}_q^{\bar{m}}$ and $\mathbf{m}_1, \mathbf{m}_2 \in \{0,1\}^w$ such that $\mathbf{m}_1 \neq \mathbf{m}_2$. We can get $CH(\mathbf{A}', \mathbf{B}', \mathbf{m}_1, \mathbf{r}_1) = (\mathbf{B}'\mathbf{m}_1 + \mathbf{A}'\mathbf{r}_1) \mod q$ and let $\mathbf{U} = (\mathbf{B}'\mathbf{m}_1 + \mathbf{A}'\mathbf{r}_1) - \mathbf{B}'\mathbf{m}_2$. Then compute $\mathbf{r}_2 \leftarrow \text{SampleD}(\mathbf{R}', \mathbf{A}', \mathbf{S}', \mathbf{U}, s)$. Therefore, we have $\mathbf{A}'\mathbf{r}_2 = \mathbf{U}$ by Theorem 1. From this, we have that there exists an efficient algorithm TrapCol that inputs $(\mathbf{A}', \mathbf{B}', \mathbf{R}', \mathbf{m}_1, \mathbf{r}_1, \mathbf{m}_2)$ and outputs a vector $\mathbf{r}_2 \in \mathbb{Z}_q^{\bar{m}}$ such that $CH(\mathbf{A}', \mathbf{B}', \mathbf{m}_1, \mathbf{r}_1) = CH(\mathbf{A}', \mathbf{B}', \mathbf{m}_2, \mathbf{r}_2)$. By Theorem 1, we can easily get that $\mathbf{r}_2$ is computationally indistinguishable from uniform in $\mathbb{Z}_q^{\bar{m}}$.

Finally, we have proved that the function $CH(\mathbf{A}', \mathbf{B}', \mathbf{m}, \mathbf{r})$ in Definition 7 is a chameleon hash function. We denote $CH(\mathbf{A}', \mathbf{B}', \mathbf{m}, \mathbf{r})$ by $CH_{hk}(\mathbf{m}, \mathbf{r})$, where $hk = (\mathbf{A}', \mathbf{B}')$ is its public key and $tk = \mathbf{R}'$ is its private key. $\qquad \square$

3.2   Our Proposed Online/Offline Signature Scheme

Specifically, let $w, q \subset \mathbb{Z}$ be some polynomials in the security parameter κ, and let $n = wq$, $\ell < n$, $\bar{m} = O(n \log q)$, $k = \lceil \log_2 q \rceil$, $m = \bar{m} + nk$, $s = \tilde{O}(n^{2.5}) \in \mathbb{R}$,

$\mathcal{M} = \{0,1\}^w$ and $\mathcal{S} = \mathbb{Z}_q^{\bar{m}}$. The construction of the offline phase involves in the weak PHF $\mathcal{H}'$ and the $(1,v,\beta)$-PHF, which are the first instantiated Type-1 PHF $\mathcal{H}'$ given in Theorem 2 and the Type-2 PHF $\mathcal{H} = (\mathcal{H}.\text{Gen}, \mathcal{H}.\text{Eval})$ given in Definition 5 respectively. In particular, the weak PHF $\mathcal{H}'$ mapping from $\{0,1\}^\ell$ to $\mathbb{Z}_q^{n \times nk}$ has a form of $\mathcal{H}'_{K'}(\mathbf{t}) = \mathbf{A}_0 + H(\mathbf{t})\mathbf{G}$ where $K' = \mathbf{A}_0$. We are going to define our signature scheme $\mathcal{SIG} = (\textbf{KeyGen}, \textbf{Sign}, \textbf{Verify})$.

KeyGen(1^κ). Given a security parameter κ.

- Randomly choose $\mathbf{A}_0 \leftarrow_r \mathbb{Z}_q^{n \times nk}$, $\mathbf{u} \leftarrow_r \mathbb{Z}_q^n$, and let $\mathbf{S} \in \mathbb{Z}_q^{n \times n}$ be an invertible matrix. Then compute $(\mathbf{A}, \mathbf{R}) \leftarrow \text{TrapGen}(1^n, 1^{\bar{m}}, \mathbf{S}, q)$ such that $\mathbf{A} \in \mathbb{Z}_q^{n \times \bar{m}}$, $\mathbf{R} \in \mathbb{Z}_q^{(\bar{m}-nk) \times nk}$ and $K \leftarrow \mathcal{H}.\text{Gen}(1^\kappa)$. Return $(vk, sk) = ((\mathbf{A}, \mathbf{A}_0, K, \mathbf{u}), \mathbf{R})$.
- Randomly choose $\mathbf{B}' \leftarrow_r \mathbb{Z}_q^{w \times w}$, let $\mathbf{S}' \in \mathbb{Z}_q^{w \times w}$ be an invertible matrix. Then compute $(\mathbf{A}', \mathbf{R}') \leftarrow \text{TrapGen}(1^w, 1^{\bar{m}}, \mathbf{S}', q)$ such that $\mathbf{A}' \in \mathbb{Z}_q^{w \times \bar{m}}$, $\mathbf{R}' \in \mathbb{Z}_q^{(\bar{m}-wk) \times wk}$, and return $(hk, tk) = ((\mathbf{A}', \mathbf{B}'), \mathbf{R}')$.

The private key is (sk, tk) and the public key is (vk, hk).

Sign($sk, tk, \mathbf{m}$). Given a signing key (sk, tk), the signing algorithm operates as follows.

- Offline phase: Randomly choose $\mathbf{t} \leftarrow \{0,1\}^\ell$, $(\mathbf{m}_0, \mathbf{r}_0) \in \mathcal{M} \times \mathcal{S}$ and compute $CH_{hk}(\mathbf{m}_0, \mathbf{r}_0) = (\mathbf{B}'\mathbf{m}_0 + \mathbf{A}'\mathbf{r}_0) \mod q$. Each component in $CH_{hk}(\mathbf{m}_0, \mathbf{r}_0)$ is represented in binary, and the binary digits are arranged in the order of $CH_{hk}(\mathbf{m}_0, \mathbf{r}_0)$. Let $CH_{hk}(\mathbf{m}_0, \mathbf{r}_0)_{(2)} \in \{0,1\}^n$ and $\mathbf{A}_{CH_{hk}(\mathbf{m}_0, \mathbf{r}_0)_{(2)}, \mathbf{t}} = (\mathbf{A} \| \mathbf{A}_0 + H(\mathbf{t})\mathbf{G} + H_K(CH_{hk}(\mathbf{m}_0, \mathbf{r}_0)_{(2)})) \in \mathbb{Z}_q^{n \times m}$ such that $H_K(CH_{hk}(\mathbf{m}_0, \mathbf{r}_0)_{(2)})) = \mathcal{H}.\text{Eval}(K, CH_{hk}(\mathbf{m}_0, \mathbf{r}_0)_{(2)})) \in \mathbb{Z}_q^{n \times nk}$. Then compute $\mathbf{e} \leftarrow \text{SampleD}(\mathbf{R}, \mathbf{A}_{CH_{hk}(\mathbf{m}_0, \mathbf{r}_0)_{(2)}, \mathbf{t}}, \mathbf{S}, \mathbf{u}, s)$, store $CH_{hk}(\mathbf{m}_0, \mathbf{r}_0)$ and the output of offline phase is $\sigma^{off} = (\mathbf{e}, \mathbf{t})$.
- Online phase: Given the message $\mathbf{m} \in \{0,1\}^w$, $CH_{hk}(\mathbf{m}_0, \mathbf{r}_0)$ and σ^{off}, compute $\mathbf{r} = \text{TrapCol}(\mathbf{A}', \mathbf{B}', \mathbf{R}', \mathbf{m}_0, \mathbf{r}_0, \mathbf{m})$ and return $\sigma^{on} = \mathbf{r}$.

Finally, the signature of the message $\mathbf{m}$ is $\sigma = (\sigma^{off}, \sigma^{on})$.

Verify($vk, hk, \mathbf{m}, \sigma$). Given $vk, hk, \mathbf{m}$ and σ, compute $CH_{hk}(\mathbf{m}_0, \mathbf{r}_0) = CH_{hk}(\mathbf{m}, \mathbf{r})$. Return 1 if $\|\mathbf{e}\| \leq s\sqrt{m}$ and $\mathbf{A}_{CH_{hk}(\mathbf{m}, \mathbf{r})_{(2)}, \mathbf{t}} \cdot \mathbf{e} = \mathbf{u}$. Otherwise, return 0.

Correctness. From the third property of chameleon hash functions, we have $CH_{hk}(\mathbf{m}_0, \mathbf{r}_0) = CH_{hk}(\mathbf{m}, \mathbf{r})$. Since $\mathbf{R}$ is a $\mathbf{G}$-trapdoor of $\mathbf{A}$, it can be extended to a $\mathbf{G}$-trapdoor for $\mathbf{A}_{CH_{hk}(\mathbf{m}, \mathbf{r})_{(2)}, \mathbf{t}}$ by padding with zero rows with the same quality $s_1(\mathbf{R}) \leq \sqrt{m} \cdot \omega(\sqrt{\log n})$. Since $s = \tilde{O}(n^{2.5}) > s_1(\mathbf{R}) \cdot \omega(\sqrt{\log n})$, the vector $\mathbf{e}$ produced by SampleD follows the distribution $D_{\Lambda_{\mathbf{u}}^{\perp}(\mathbf{A}_{CH_{hk}(\mathbf{m}, \mathbf{r})_{(2)}, \mathbf{t}}), s}$ and has length at most $s\sqrt{m}$ with overwhelming probability by Lemma 1. In short, the signature σ is accepted by the verification algorithm.

Theorem 4. *Let $w, q, \bar{m} \in \mathbb{Z}$ be some polynomials in the security parameter κ, $n = wq$, $k = \lceil \log_2 q \rceil$, $\ell = O(\log n)$, $v = \omega(\log n)$ and $m = \bar{m} + nk$. If there exists a PPT attacker $\mathcal{A}$ against EUF-CMA security of $\mathcal{SIG}$ that makes at most*

$Q = poly(n)$ *signing queries and succeeds with probability* ϵ, *then there exists an* *algorithm* $\mathcal{B}$ *solving the* $ISIS_{q,\bar{m},\bar{\beta}}$ *problem for* $\bar{\beta} = \tilde{O}(n^{5.5})$ *with probability at* *least* $\epsilon' \geq \frac{\epsilon}{Q \cdot \tilde{O}(n)}$.

Proof. Assuming that there exists an attacker $\mathcal{A}$ forging the signature with probability ϵ, then we give the construction of the algorithm $\mathcal{B}$ solving $ISIS_{q,\bar{m},\bar{\beta}}$ problem with probability at least $\epsilon' \geq \frac{\epsilon}{Q \cdot \tilde{O}(n)}$. Formally, $\mathcal{B}$ randomly chooses a vector $\mathbf{t}' \leftarrow_r \{0,1\}^\ell$ and hopes that $\mathcal{A}$ will output a forgery signature with tag $\mathbf{t}^* = \mathbf{t}'$. Then, the algorithm $\mathcal{B}$ simulates the EUF-CMA game as follows:

KeyGen
- Given an $ISIS_{q,\bar{m},\bar{\beta}}$ challenge instance $(\mathbf{A}, \mathbf{u}) \in \mathbb{Z}_q^{n \times \bar{m}} \times \mathbb{Z}_q^n$, the algorithm $\mathcal{B}$ first randomly chooses $\mathbf{R}_0 \leftarrow_r (D_{\mathbb{Z}^{\bar{m}}, \omega(\sqrt{\log n})})^{nk}$ and computes $\mathbf{A}_0 = \mathbf{A}\mathbf{R}_0 - H(0\|\mathbf{t}')\mathbf{G}$. This is done by running $(K', td) \leftarrow \mathcal{H}.TrapGen(1^\kappa, \mathbf{A}, \mathbf{G})$ as in Definition 5. Therefore, the algorithm $\mathcal{B}$ returns $vk = (\mathbf{A}, \mathbf{A}_0, K', \mathbf{u})$ and $sk = (\mathbf{R}_0, td)$.
- The algorithm $\mathcal{B}$ randomly chooses $\mathbf{B}' \in \mathbb{Z}_q^{w \times w}$, an invertible matrix $\mathbf{S}' \in \mathbb{Z}_q^{w \times w}$ and computes $(\mathbf{A}', \mathbf{R}') \leftarrow TrapGen(1^w, 1^{\bar{m}}, \mathbf{S}', q)$. Then $\mathcal{B}$ returns $hk = (\mathbf{A}', \mathbf{B}')$ and $tk = \mathbf{R}'$.

Finally, the simulated public key is (vk, hk), and the simulated private key is (sk, tk). $(\mathbf{A}, \mathbf{u})$ is uniformly distributed over $\mathbb{Z}_q^{n \times \bar{m}} \times \mathbb{Z}_q^n$ by the definition of $ISIS$. Since $\mathbf{R}_0 \leftarrow_r (D_{\mathbb{Z}^{\bar{m}}, \omega(\sqrt{\log n})})^{nk}$, by Lemma 3 the matrix $\mathbf{A}_0$ is statistically close to uniform over $\mathbb{Z}_q^{n \times nk}$. Moreover, the simulated key K' is statistically close to the real key. $\mathbf{A}' \in \mathbb{Z}_q^{w \times \bar{m}}$ is $negl(\kappa)$-far from uniform by Theorem 1. Thus, the distribution of the simulated verification key is statistically close to that of the real one.

Signing. The algorithm $\mathcal{B}$ accepts signing queries from attacker $\mathcal{A}$.
- Offline phase: The algorithm $\mathcal{B}$ first randomly chooses $(\mathbf{m}_0, \mathbf{t}_0) \in \mathcal{M} \times \mathcal{S}$, and computes $\mu = CH_{hk}(\mathbf{m}_0, \mathbf{t}_0)_{(2)} \in \{0,1\}^n$. Then, $\mathcal{B}$ first randomly chooses $\mathbf{t} \leftarrow_r \{0,1\}^\ell$. If $\mathbf{t}$ has been chosen in answering the signature more than υ times, $\mathcal{B}$ aborts. Otherwise, compute $(\mathbf{R}_\mu, \mathbf{S}_\mu) \leftarrow \mathcal{H}.TrapEval(td, K', \mu)$ as in Definition 5. Then we have that $\mathbf{A}_{\mu,\mathbf{t}} = (\mathbf{A}\|(\mathbf{A}_0 + H(\mathbf{t})\mathbf{G}) + H_{K'}(\mu)) = (\mathbf{A}\|(\mathbf{A}(\mathbf{R}_0 + \mathbf{R}_\mu) + (H(0\|\mathbf{t}) - H(0\|\mathbf{t}') + \mathbf{S}_\mu)\mathbf{G})$. Since $\mathbf{S}_\mu = b\mathbf{I}_n = H(b\|0)$ for some $b \in \{-1,0,1\}$ by the proof of Theorem 3 (for details, please refer to [20]). Let $\hat{\mathbf{S}} = H(0\|\mathbf{t}) - H(0\|\mathbf{t}') + \mathbf{S}_\mu = H(b\|(\mathbf{t} - \mathbf{t}'))$ by the homomorphic property of the FRD in [20]. We split our analysis into two different cases:
  (1) If $\mathbf{t} \neq \mathbf{t}'$ or $\mathbf{t} = \mathbf{t}' \wedge b \neq 0$, we have that $\hat{\mathbf{S}}$ is invertible. Thus $\hat{\mathbf{R}} = -(\mathbf{R}_0 + \mathbf{R}_\mu)$ is a $\mathbf{G}$-trapdoor for $\mathbf{A}_{\mu,\mathbf{t}}$. Since $s_1(\mathbf{R}_0) \leq \sqrt{m} \cdot \omega(\sqrt{\log n})$ by Lemma 2 and $s_1(\mathbf{R}_\mu) \leq \tilde{O}(n^{2.5})$, we have $\hat{\mathbf{R}} \leq \tilde{O}(n^{2.5})$. Finally, compute $\mathbf{e} \leftarrow SampleD(\hat{\mathbf{R}}, \mathbf{A}_{\mu,\mathbf{t}}, \hat{\mathbf{S}}, \mathbf{u}, s)$ and return the signature $\sigma^{off} = (\mathbf{e}, \mathbf{t})$.
  (2) If $\mathbf{t} = \mathbf{t}' \wedge b = 0$, we have that $\hat{\mathbf{S}} = H(b\|(\mathbf{t} - \mathbf{t}')) = 0$. Thus $\mathcal{B}$ aborts.
- Online phase: Given the message $\mathbf{m} \in \{0,1\}^w$, $CH_{hk}(\mathbf{m}_0, \mathbf{t}_0)$ and σ^{off}, the algorithm $\mathcal{B}$ computes $\mathbf{r} - TrapCol(\mathbf{A}', \mathbf{B}', \mathbf{R}', \mathbf{m}_0, \mathbf{t}_0, \mathbf{m})$ and returns $\sigma^{on} = \mathbf{r}$.

Forge. After answering at most Q signature queries, the attacker $\mathcal{A}$ outputs a forgery $\sigma^* = ((\mathbf{e}^*, \mathbf{t}^*), \mathbf{r}^*)$ for some message $\mathbf{m}^* \in \{0,1\}^w$ satisfying $\|\mathbf{e}^*\| \leq s\sqrt{m}$ and $\mathbf{A}_{CH_{hk}(\mathbf{m}^*,\mathbf{t}^*)_{(2)},\mathbf{t}^*} \cdot \mathbf{e}^* = \mathbf{u}$, and we know that $\mathbf{A}_{CH_{hk}(\mathbf{m}^*,\mathbf{t}^*)_{(2)},\mathbf{t}^*} = (\mathbf{A}\|(\mathbf{A}_0 + H(0\|\mathbf{t}^*)\mathbf{G}) + H_K(CH_{hk}(\mathbf{m}^*,\mathbf{t}^*)_{(2)})) \in \mathbb{Z}_q^{n \times m}$. $\mathcal{B}$ computes that $(\mathbf{R}_{CH_{hk}(\mathbf{m}^*,\mathbf{r}^*)_{(2)}}, \mathbf{S}_{CH_{hk}(\mathbf{m}^*,\mathbf{r}^*)_{(2)}}) \leftarrow \mathcal{H}.TrapEval(td, K', CH_{hk}(\mathbf{m}^*,\mathbf{r}^*)_{(2)})$. Moreover, if $\mathbf{t}^* \neq \mathbf{t}'$ or $\mathbf{S}_{CH_{hk}}(\mathbf{m}^*, \mathbf{r}^*)_{(2)} \neq 0$, $\mathcal{B}$ aborts. Else, we have that $\mathbf{A}_{CH_{hk}(\mathbf{m}^*,\mathbf{r}^*)_{(2)},\mathbf{t}^*} = (\mathbf{A}\|(\mathbf{A}(\mathbf{R}_0 \| \mathbf{R}_{CH_{hk}(\mathbf{m}^*,\mathbf{r}^*)_{(2)}})) = \mathbf{A}(\mathbf{I}_{\bar{m}}\| - \hat{\mathbf{R}})$, where $\hat{\mathbf{R}} = \mathbf{R}_0 + \mathbf{R}_{CH_{hk}(\mathbf{m}^*,\mathbf{r}^*)_{(2)}}$. Let $\hat{\mathbf{e}}$ be $(\mathbf{I}_{\bar{m}}\| - \hat{\mathbf{R}})\mathbf{e}^*$. Since $s_1(\mathbf{R}_0) \leq \sqrt{m} \cdot \omega(\sqrt{\log n})$ by Lemma 2 and $s_1(\mathbf{R}_{CH_{hk}(\mathbf{m}^*,\mathbf{r}^*)_{(2)}}) \leq \beta = \tilde{O}(n^{2.5})$ by Theorem 3, we have $\|\hat{\mathbf{e}}\| \leq \tilde{O}(n^{2.5}) \cdot s\sqrt{m} = \tilde{O}(n^{5.5}) = \bar{\beta}$. Therefore, the algorithm $\mathcal{B}$ outputs $\hat{\mathbf{e}} = (\mathbf{I}_{\bar{m}}\| - \hat{\mathbf{R}})\mathbf{e}^*$ as the solution of $ISIS_{q,\bar{m},\bar{\beta}}$.

Since the algorithm $\mathcal{B}$ will receive at most $Q = poly(n)$ adaptive signing queries from the attacker $\mathcal{A}$. For each message, the algorithm $\mathcal{B}$ chooses a uniformly random tag $\mathbf{t}$. If some tag $\mathbf{t}$ is chosen for more than v times in the signing queries, $\mathcal{B}$ aborts. Let $\mathbf{m}_1, \cdots, \mathbf{m}_u$ be all the messages in the signing queries that $\mathcal{B}$ chooses the same tag $\mathbf{t} = \mathbf{t}'$ by accident. And corresponding to that, the algorithm $\mathcal{B}$ randomly selects $(\mathbf{a}_i, \mathbf{b}_i) \in \mathcal{M} \times \mathcal{S}$ for $i \in \{1, \cdots, u\}$. Let $(\mathbf{R}_{CH_{hk}(\mathbf{a}_i,\mathbf{b}_i)_{(2)}}, \mathbf{S}_{CH_{hk}(\mathbf{a}_i,\mathbf{b}_i)_{(2)}}) \leftarrow \mathcal{H}.TrapEval(td, K', CH_{hk}(\mathbf{a}_i,\mathbf{b}_i)_{(2)})$. If $\mathbf{S}_{CH_{hk}(\mathbf{a}_i,\mathbf{b}_i)_{(2)}}$ is not invertible, $\mathcal{B}$ aborts. Since $\ell = O(\log n)$, we have $\frac{Q}{2^\ell} \leq \frac{1}{2}$. Notice that the probability $\mathcal{B}$ uses any tag $\mathbf{t}$ in answering the signature queries over v times is less than $Q^2 \cdot (\frac{Q}{2^\ell})^v$ through a similar method in [11], which is negligible. Therefore, the possibility of using the same tag $\mathbf{t}$ in more than $u(\geq v)$ times signing queries is negligible. If $u < v$, the possibility that $\mathbf{S}_{CH_{hk}(\mathbf{a}_i,\mathbf{b}_i)_{(2)}}$ is invertible and $\mathbf{S}_{CH_{hk}(\mathbf{m}^*,\mathbf{r}^*)_{(2)}} = 0$ for all $i \in \{1, \cdots, u\}$ (using the fact that $CH_{hk}(\mathbf{m}^*,\mathbf{r}^*)_{(2)} \notin \{CH_{hk}(\mathbf{a}_i,\mathbf{b}_i)_{(2)}\}_{i \in \{1,\cdots,u\}}$) is at least $\delta = \frac{1}{16nv^2}$ - negl(κ) by Theorem 3. Then, we have $\Pr[\mathbf{t}^* = \mathbf{t}'] \geq \frac{1}{2^\ell}$. Therefore, the success probability of solving the $ISIS_{q,\bar{m},\bar{\beta}}$ instance is at least $\epsilon' = (\epsilon - Q^2 \cdot (\frac{Q}{2^\ell})^v) \cdot \delta \cdot (\frac{1}{2^\ell} - negl(\kappa)) = \frac{\epsilon}{Q \cdot \tilde{O}(n)}$. We conclude the proof. $\square$

3.3   Comparison

In Table 1, we give a (rough) comparison with existing schemes in the standard model. Let $w, q \in \mathbb{Z}$ be some polynomials in the security parameter and let $n = wq$ be the message length. Q presents the number of signature queries made by the attacker. Real $\bar{\beta}$ denotes the parameter for (I)SIS problem. The reducation loss is the ratio ϵ/ϵ' between the success probability ϵ of the attacker and the success probability ϵ' of the reduction.

Compared with the existing lattice-based signature schemes [6,18,20], the length of public key and signature (online) of our proposed scheme is the same as theirs. Our work is driven by the idea of Xiang [18] and Zhang [20]. Due to pre-computation in the offline phase, our scheme is more efficient than the original scheme [20] in signature production. The work [18] is motivated by [6]. As shown in Table 1, signature generation in our scheme is faster than [6] in the online phase. Compared to the work in [18], we have more rigorous proof and specific data in our proposed chameleon hash function. Furthermore, the parameters of Xiang's algorithm do not match those defined in [18].

Table 1. Comparison with existing schemes

Schemes	DM14 [6]	ZCZ16 [20]	Xiang17 [18]	Our $\mathcal{SIG}$
public key	$O(\log n)$	$O(\log n)$	$O(\log n)$	$O(\log n)$
Signature (online)	1	1	1	1
Reduction loss	$(Q^2/\epsilon)^2$	$Q \cdot \tilde{O}(n)$	$(Q^2/\epsilon)^2$	$Q \cdot \tilde{O}(n)$
param $\bar{\beta}$	$\tilde{O}(n^{3.5})$	$\tilde{O}(n^{5.5})$	$\tilde{O}(n^2)$	$\tilde{O}(n^{5.5})$
Calculation (online)	$O(\log^2 n)$	$O(\log^2 n)$	$\tilde{O}(w^2)$	$\tilde{O}(w^2)$

4 Conclusion

In this paper, we present a new chameleon hash function, the security of which can be reduced to the Inhomogeneous Small Integer Solution (ISIS) assumption. The main technical of our proposed online/offline signature scheme is our chameleon hash function and the construction of PHFs in [20]. Moreover, the online signature of our scheme consists of a single lattice vector and the public key includes a logarithmic number of matrices. In addition, our scheme is proved to be existentially unforgeable against adaptive chosen message attacks (EUF-CMA) in the standard model.

Acknowledgements. The authors would like to thank anonymous reviewers for their helpful comments. This work is supported by National Natural Science Foundation of China (61472083, 61771140, 11701089, 61472364), Distinguished Young Scholars Fund of Fujian (2016J06013), Fujian Normal University Innovative Research Team (NO. IRTL1207), Fujian Province Department of Education Project (JOPX 15066), and Zhejiang Provincial Natural Science Foundation (NO. LZ18F020003).

References

1. Ajtai, M.: Generating hard instances of lattice problems (extended abstract). In: Proceedings of the Twenty-Eighth Annual ACM Symposium on the Theory of Computing, Philadelphia, Pennsylvania, USA, 22–24 May 1996, pp. 99–108 (1996). https://doi.org/10.1145/237814.237838
2. Ajtai, M.: Generating hard instances of the short basis problem. In: Wiedermann, J., van Emde Boas, P., Nielsen, M. (eds.) ICALP 1999. LNCS, vol. 1644, pp. 1–9. Springer, Heidelberg (1999). https://doi.org/10.1007/3-540-48523-6_1
3. Boyen, X.: Lattice mixing and vanishing trapdoors: a framework for fully secure short signatures and more. In: Nguyen, P.Q., Pointcheval, D. (eds.) PKC 2010. LNCS, vol. 6056, pp. 499–517. Springer, Heidelberg (2010). https://doi.org/10.1007/978-3-642-13013-7_29

4. Crutchfield, C., Molnar, D., Turner, D., Wagner, D.: Generic on-line/off-line threshold signatures. In: Yung, M., Dodis, Y., Kiayias, A., Malkin, T. (eds.) PKC 2006. LNCS, vol. 3958, pp. 58–74. Springer, Heidelberg (2006). https://doi.org/10.1007/11745853_5
5. Deiseroth, B., Fehr, V., Fischlin, M., Maasz, M., Reimers, N.F., Stein, R.: Computing on authenticated data for adjustable predicates. In: Jacobson, M., Locasto, M., Mohassel, P., Safavi-Naini, R. (eds.) ACNS 2013. LNCS, vol. 7954, pp. 53–68. Springer, Heidelberg (2013). https://doi.org/10.1007/978-3-642-38980-1_4
6. Ducas, L., Micciancio, D.: Improved short lattice signatures in the standard model. In: Garay, J.A., Gennaro, R. (eds.) CRYPTO 2014. LNCS, vol. 8616, pp. 335–352. Springer, Heidelberg (2014). https://doi.org/10.1007/978-3-662-44371-2_19
7. Erdös, P., Frankl, P., Füredi, Z.: Families of finite sets in which no set is covered by the union of r others. Isr. J. Math. **51**(1–2), 79–89 (1985)
8. Even, S., Goldreich, O., Micali, S.: On-line/off-line digital signatures. J. Cryptol. **9**(1), 35–67 (1996). https://doi.org/10.1007/BF02254791
9. Gentry, C., Peikert, C., Vaikuntanathan, V.: Trapdoors for hard lattices and new cryptographic constructions. In: Proceedings of the 40th Annual ACM Symposium on Theory of Computing, Victoria, British Columbia, Canada, 17–20 May 2008, pp. 197–206 (2008). https://doi.org/10.1145/1374376.1374407
10. Goldwasser, S., Micali, S., Rivest, R.L.: A digital signature scheme secure against adaptive chosen-message attacks. SIAM J. Comput. **17**(2), 281–308 (1988). https://doi.org/10.1137/0217017
11. Hofheinz, D., Kiltz, E.: Programmable hash functions and their applications. In: Wagner, D. (ed.) CRYPTO 2008. LNCS, vol. 5157, pp. 21–38. Springer, Heidelberg (2008). https://doi.org/10.1007/978-3-540-85174-5_2
12. Krawczyk, H., Rabin, T.: Chameleon hashing and signatures. IACR Cryptology ePrint Archive 1998/10 (1998). http://eprint.iacr.org/1998/010
13. Kumar, R., Rajagopalan, S., Sahai, A.: Coding constructions for blacklisting problems without computational assumptions. In: Wiener, M. (ed.) CRYPTO 1999. LNCS, vol. 1666, pp. 609–623. Springer, Heidelberg (1999). https://doi.org/10.1007/3-540-48405-1_38
14. Liu, J.K., Baek, J., Zhou, J.Y., Yang, Y.J., Wong, J.W.: Efficient online/offline identity-based signature for wireless sensor network. Int. J. Inf. Sec. **9**(4), 287–296 (2010). https://doi.org/10.1007/s10207-010-0109-y
15. Micciancio, D., Peikert, C.: Trapdoors for lattices: simpler, tighter, faster, smaller. In: Pointcheval, D., Johansson, T. (eds.) EUROCRYPT 2012. LNCS, vol. 7237, pp. 700–718. Springer, Heidelberg (2012). https://doi.org/10.1007/978-3-642-29011-4_41
16. Shamir, A., Tauman, Y.: Improved online/offline signature schemes. In: Kilian, J. (ed.) CRYPTO 2001. LNCS, vol. 2139, pp. 355–367. Springer, Heidelberg (2001). https://doi.org/10.1007/3-540-44647-8_21
17. Vershynin, R.: Introduction to the non-asymptotic analysis of random matrices. CoRR abs/1011.3027 (2010). http://arxiv.org/abs/1011.3027
18. Xiang, X.Y.: Online/offline signature scheme based on ideal lattices (in Chinese). J. Cryptologic Res. **4**(3), 253–261 (2017)
19. Xiang, X.Y., Li, H.: Lattice-based online/offline signature scheme (in Chinese). J. Beijing Univ. Posts Telecommun. **38**(3), 117–120, 134 (2015)
20. Zhang, J., Chen, Y., Zhang, Z.: Programmable hash functions from lattices: short signatures and ibes with small key sizes. In: Robshaw, M., Katz, J. (eds.) CRYPTO 2016. LNCS, vol. 9816, pp. 303–332. Springer, Heidelberg (2016). https://doi.org/10.1007/978-3-662-53015-3_11

CHQS: Publicly Verifiable Homomorphic Signatures Beyond the Linear Case

Lucas Schabhüser[✉], Denis Butin, and Johannes Buchmann

Technische Universität Darmstadt, Darmstadt, Germany
{lschabhueser,dbutin,buchmann}@cdc.informatik.tu-darmstadt.de

Abstract. Sensitive data is often outsourced to cloud servers, with the server performing computation on the data. Computational correctness must be efficiently verifiable by a third party while the input data remains confidential. We introduce CHQS, a homomorphic signature scheme from bilinear groups fulfilling these requirements. CHQS is the first such scheme to be both context hiding and publicly verifiable for arithmetic circuits of degree 2. It also achieves amortized efficiency: after a precomputation, verification can be faster than the circuit evaluation itself.

1 Introduction

Today, it is common practice to outsource time-consuming computations to the cloud. In such a situation, it is desirable to be able to verify the outsourced computation. The verification must be *efficient*, by which we mean that the verification procedure is significantly faster than verified computation itself. Otherwise, the verifier could as well carry out the computation by himself, negating the advantage of outsourcing.

In addition, there are scenarios in which the verification is required to be *context hiding*, which refers to the verification not revealing anything about the input to the computation. For instance, consider a cloud service which collects signed health data of individuals and computes statistics on them. These statistical evaluations are then given to a third party: an insurance company, which does not trust the cloud service to provide correct statistics. As a consequence, the third party must be able to verify the statistical outcome. However, for privacy reasons, it must not be able to learn the individual health data. So the challenge arises to design efficient and context hiding verification procedures for outsourced computing.

Using a homomorphic signature scheme, the verification procedure for outsourced computations can be implemented as follows. The data owner uploads signed data to the cloud. The cloud server generates a signature on the computed function output from these signatures. The verifier uses this signature to check for correctness of the computation.

There are efficient and context hiding homomorphic signature schemes for linear functions (e.g. [8,25]). However, linear functions are insufficient for many

© Springer Nature Switzerland AG 2018
C. Su and H. Kikuchi (Eds.): ISPEC 2018, LNCS 11125, pp. 213–228, 2018.
https://doi.org/10.1007/978-3-319-99807-7_13

applications. For instance, statistics often require computing variance and covariance, which use quadratic functions. Still, beyond the linear case, no efficient and context hiding homomorphic signature schemes are known. For quadratic functions, efficient verification is possible as shown in [3]. However, this scheme is not context hiding. For a more detailed overview of related work, we refer to Sect. 6.

Contribution. In this paper, we solve the problem of providing efficient and context hiding verification for multivariate quadratic functions. The core component of our solution and our main contribution is the new homomorphic signature scheme CHQS (Context Hiding Quadratic Signatures). CHQS allows to generate a signature on the function value of a multivariate quadratic polynomial from signatures on the input values without knowledge of the signing key. CHQS is perfectly context hiding, i.e. the signature of the output value does not leak any information about the input values. Furthermore, verification time is linear (in an amortized sense). A trade-off of our approach is a signature size that grows during homomorphic evaluation, so our scheme is not succinct. Still, freshly generated signatures are of constant size. Like most solutions in this area, the CHQS construction is based on bilinear groups. However, CHQS showcases for the first time how to use such groups to simultaneously achieve both public verification and multiplicative depth.

Outline. We recall relevant definitions for homomorphic signature schemes in Sect. 2. In Sect. 3, we present CHQS, our homomorphic signature scheme for multivariate polynomials of degree 2. We address its properties, notably correctness and context hiding in Sect. 4 and give a security reduction in Sect. 5. Next, in Sect. 6, we compare our contribution to existing work. Finally, in Sect. 7, we summarize our results and give an outlook to future work and open problems.

2   Homomorphic Signatures

In this section, we formally define homomorphic signature schemes and their relevant properties. Intuitively, homomorphic signatures allow to generate new signatures from existing signatures without the knowledge of the secret signing key. It is necessary that the homomorphic property cannot be abused to create forgeries. In order to specify homomorphic signatures with strong security properties, the notions of labeled and multi-labeled programs (see e.g. [3]) are introduced. They enable security guarantees by restricting the signatures that may be homomorphically combined to new signatures.

A *labeled program* $\mathcal{P}$ consists of a tuple $(f, \tau_1, \ldots, \tau_n)$, where $f : \mathcal{M}^n \to \mathcal{M}$ is a function with n inputs and $\tau_i \in \mathsf{T}$ is a label for the i-th input of f from some set T. Given a set of labeled programs $\mathcal{P}_1, \ldots, \mathcal{P}_k$ and a function $g : \mathcal{M}^k \to \mathcal{M}$, they can be composed by evaluating g over the labeled programs, i.e. $\mathcal{P}^* = g(\mathcal{P}_1, \ldots, \mathcal{P}_k)$. The identity program with label τ is given by $\mathcal{I}_\tau = (f_{id}, \tau)$, where $f_{id} : \mathcal{M} \to \mathcal{M}$ is the identity function. The program $\mathcal{P} = (f, \tau_1, \ldots, \tau_n)$ can be expressed as the composition of n identity programs $\mathcal{P} = f(\mathcal{I}_{\tau_1}, \ldots, \mathcal{I}_{\tau_n})$.

A *multi-labeled program* $\mathcal{P}_\Delta$ is a pair $(\mathcal{P}, \Delta)$ of the labeled program $\mathcal{P}$ and a dataset identifier Δ. Given a set of k multi-labeled programs with the same dataset identifier Δ, i.e. $(\mathcal{P}_1, \Delta), \ldots, (\mathcal{P}_k, \Delta)$, and a function $g : \mathcal{M}^k \rightarrow \mathcal{M}$, a composed multi-labeled program $\mathcal{P}_\Delta^*$ can be computed, consisting of the pair $(\mathcal{P}^*, \Delta)$, where $\mathcal{P}^* = g(\mathcal{P}_1, \ldots, \mathcal{P}_k)$. Analogously to the identity program for labeled programs, we refer to a multi-labeled identity program by $\mathcal{I}_{(\Delta, \tau)} = ((f_{id}, \tau), \Delta)$.

Definition 1 (Homomorphic Signature Scheme). *A homomorphic signature scheme is a tuple of the following probabilistic polynomial time (PPT) algorithms:*

HKeyGen($1^\lambda, n$): *On input a security parameter λ and an integer n, the algorithm returns a key pair* (sk, pk), *where* sk *is the secret key kept private and* pk *is the public key which determines the message space $\mathcal{M}$, the signature space $\mathcal{Y}$, and the set $\mathcal{F}$ of admissible labeled programs $\mathcal{P} : \mathcal{M}^n \rightarrow \mathcal{M}$.*

HSign(sk, Δ, τ, m): *On input a secret key* sk, *a dataset identifier Δ, an input identifier τ, and a message $m \in \mathcal{M}$, the algorithm returns a signature $\sigma \in \mathcal{Y}$ which is the signature for the message labeled by τ in the dataset identified by Δ.*

HEval(pk, $\mathcal{P}_\Delta, \boldsymbol{\sigma}$): *On input a public key* pk, *a multi-labeled program $\mathcal{P}_\Delta$, and a set of signatures $\boldsymbol{\sigma} \in \mathcal{Y}^k$, the algorithm returns a signature $\sigma' \in \mathcal{Y}$ for the multi-labeled program $\mathcal{P}$ over the (tuple of) signatures $\boldsymbol{\sigma}$ identified by Δ.*

HVerify(pk, $\mathcal{P}_\Delta, m, \sigma$): *On input a public key* pk, *a multi-labeled program $\mathcal{P}_\Delta$, a message $m \in \mathcal{M}$, and a signature $\sigma \in \mathcal{Y}$, the algorithm either accepts the signature σ for the multi-labeled program $\mathcal{P}$ over the dataset identified by Δ, i.e. returns 1, or rejects the signature, i.e. returns 0.*

An obvious requirement of such a scheme is *correctness*: fresh signatures created using the secret key should be authenticated, and homomorphically derived signatures should be verified under the correct function.

Definition 2 (Correctness). *A homomorphic signature scheme* (HKeyGen, HSign, HEval, HVerify) *is called* correct *if, for any security parameter λ, any integer n, and any key pair* (sk, pk) $\leftarrow$ HKeyGen($1^\lambda, n$) *the following two conditions are satisfied:*

1. *For any dataset identifier Δ, input identifier τ, and message $m \in \mathcal{M}$,* HVerify(pk, $\mathcal{I}_{(\Delta, \tau)}, m,$ HSign(sk, Δ, τ, m)) $= 1$.
2. *For any multi-labeled program $\mathcal{P}_\Delta = (f, \tau_1, \ldots, \tau_n, \Delta)$ containing a valid function f, dataset identifier Δ, and set of messages $\boldsymbol{m} \in \mathcal{M}^n$ with $\boldsymbol{m} = (m_1, \ldots, m_n)$,* HVerify(pk, $\mathcal{P}_\Delta, f(m_1, \ldots, m_n),$ HEval(pk, $\mathcal{P}_\Delta, \boldsymbol{\sigma}$)) $= 1$ *where $\boldsymbol{\sigma} = (\sigma_{\tau_1}, \ldots, \sigma_{\tau_n}) \in \mathcal{Y}^n$ with $\sigma_{\tau_i} \leftarrow$ HSign(sk, Δ, τ, m_{τ_i}) for all $i \in [n]$.*

To formalise the security of a homomorphic signature scheme, we first provide a definition for *well defined programs*, which we need to define *forgeries* on these programs. Then, we introduce an experiment the attacker can run in order to make a successful forgery and present a definition for unforgeability based on this experiment. Due to their homomorphic properties, these schemes allow anyone to create signatures for messages not signed by the owner of the secret key. However, not only messages but also input- and dataset identifiers are used during signing. A verifier can thus always see whether a message has been signed by the owner of the secret key (by giving the identity function to HVerify), or whether a signature has been homomorphically derived. Based on this, there exists a meaningful definition of unforgeability for homomorphic signatures. In order to present this, we first define *well defined programs*.

Definition 3 (Well Defined Program). *A labeled program* $\mathcal{P} = (f, \tau_1, \ldots, \tau_n)$ *is well defined with respect to a list* $\mathcal{Q} \subset [n] \times \mathcal{M}$ *if one of the two following cases holds: First, there are messages* $m_1, \ldots, m_n$ *such that* $(\tau_i, m_i) \in \mathcal{Q}$ $\forall i \in [n]$. *Second, there is an* $i \in \{1, \ldots, n\}$ *such that* $(\tau_i, \cdot) \notin \mathcal{Q}$ *and* $f(\{m_j\}_{(\tau_j, m_j) \in \mathcal{Q}} \cup \{m'_l\}_{(\tau_l, \cdot) \notin \mathcal{Q}})$ *is constant over all possible choices of* $m'_l \in \mathcal{M}$.

Freeman pointed out [16] that it may generally not be possible to decide whether a multi-labeled program is well defined with regard to a list $\mathcal{Q}$. For this, we use this lemma:

Lemma 1 ([7]). *Let* $\lambda, n, d \in \mathbb{N}$ *and let* F *be the class of arithmetic circuits* $f : \mathbb{F}^n \to \mathbb{F}$ *over a finite field* $\mathbb{F}$ *of order* p, *such that the degree of* f *is at most* d, *for* $\frac{d}{p} \leq \frac{1}{2}$. *Then, there exists a PPT algorithm that for any given* $f \in F$, *decides if there exists* $y \in \mathbb{F}$, *such that* $f(u) = y$ *for all* $u \in \mathbb{F}$ *(i.e. if* f *is constant) and is correct with probability at least* $1 - 2^{-\lambda}$.

For the notion of unforgeability of a homomorphic signature scheme $\mathcal{H} =$ (HKeyGen, HSign, HEval, HVerify) we use the following experiment between an adversary $\mathcal{A}$ and a challenger $\mathcal{C}$ defined in [7]. During the experiment, the adversary $\mathcal{A}$ can adaptively query the challenger $\mathcal{C}$ for signatures on messages of his choice under identifiers of his choice.

Definition 4 (HomUF − CMA$_{\mathcal{A}, \mathcal{H}}(\lambda)$ [7])

> ***Key Generation*** $\mathcal{C}$ *calls* (sk, pk) $\xleftarrow{\$}$ HKeyGen($1^\lambda, k$) *and gives* pk *to* $\mathcal{A}$.
> ***Queries*** $\mathcal{A}$ *adaptively submits queries for* (Δ, τ, m) *where* Δ *is a dataset,* τ *is an input identifier, and* m *is a message.* $\mathcal{C}$ *proceeds as follows: if* (Δ, τ, m) *is the first query with dataset identifier* Δ, *it initializes an empty list* $\mathcal{Q} = \emptyset$ *for* Δ. *If* $\mathcal{Q}$ *does not contain a tuple* $(\tau, \cdot)$, *i.e.* $\mathcal{A}$ *never queried* $(\Delta, \tau, \cdot)$, $\mathcal{C}$ *calls* $\sigma \leftarrow$ HSign(sk, Δ, τ, m), *updates the list* $\mathcal{Q} = \mathcal{Q} \cup (\tau, m)$, *and gives* σ *to* $\mathcal{A}$. *If* $(\tau, m) \in \mathcal{Q}$, *then* $\mathcal{C}$ *returns the same signature* σ *as before. If* $\mathcal{Q}$ *already contains a tuple* (τ, m') *for* $m \neq m'$, $\mathcal{C}$ *returns* $\perp$.
> ***Forgery*** $\mathcal{A}$ *outputs a tuple* $(\mathcal{P}_\Delta, m, \sigma)$. *The experiment outputs* 1 *if* $(\mathcal{P}_\Delta, m, \sigma)$ *is a forgery in the following sense:*
> *A forgery is a tuple* $(\mathcal{P}^*_{\Delta^*}, m^*, \sigma^*)$ *such that* HVerify(pk, $\mathcal{P}^*_{\Delta^*}, m^*, \sigma^*$) = 1 *holds and exactly one of the following conditions is met:*
> **Type 1:** *The list* $\mathcal{Q}$ *was not initialized during the security experiment, i.e. no message was ever committed under the dataset identifier* Δ.

Type 2: $\mathcal{P}^*{}_{\Delta^*}$ *is well defined with respect to list* $\mathcal{Q}$ *and* m^* *is not the correct output of the computation, i.e.* $m^* \neq f(\{m_j\}_{(\tau_j, m_j) \in \mathcal{Q}})$

Type 3: $\mathcal{P}^*{}_{\Delta^*}$ *is not well defined with respect to* $\mathcal{Q}$ *(see Def. 3).*

Definition 5 (Unforgeability). *A homomorphic signature scheme* $\mathcal{H}$ *is* unforgeable *if for any PPT adversary* $\mathcal{A}$, $\Pr[\mathsf{HomUF} - \mathsf{CMA}_{\mathcal{A},\mathcal{H}}(\lambda) = 1] = \mathsf{negl}(\lambda)$, *where* $\mathsf{negl}(\lambda)$ *denotes any function negligible in the security parameter* λ.

We also require the following statement to deal with Type 3 forgeries:

Lemma 2 *([7, Proposition 2]). Let* $\lambda \in \mathbb{N}$, *and let* $\mathcal{F}$ *be the class of arithmetic circuits* $f : \mathbb{F}_p^n \to \mathbb{F}$ *such that the degree of* f *is at most* d *for* $\frac{d}{p} < \frac{1}{2}$. *Let* $\mathcal{H} = (\mathsf{HKeyGen}, \mathsf{HSign}, \mathsf{HEval}, \mathsf{HVerify})$ *be a homomorphic signature scheme with message space* $\mathbb{F}_p$. *Let* $\mathcal{E}_b$ *be the event that the adversary returns a Type b forgery (for* $b = 1, 2, 3$) *in experiment* $\mathsf{HomUF} - \mathsf{CMA}_{\mathcal{A},\mathcal{H}}(\lambda)$. *If for any adversary* $\mathcal{A}$ *we have* $\Pr[\mathsf{HomUF} - \mathsf{CMA}_{\mathcal{A},\mathcal{H}}(\lambda) = 1 \wedge \mathcal{E}_2] \leq \epsilon$, *then for any adversary* $\mathcal{A}'$ *producing a Type 3 forgery it holds that* $\Pr[\mathsf{HomUF} - \mathsf{CMA}_{\mathcal{A}',\mathcal{H}}(\lambda) = 1 \wedge \mathcal{E}_3] \leq \epsilon + 2^{-\lambda}$.

In order to use homomorphic signatures to improve bandwidth and computational effort further properties are desired, namely *succinctness* and *efficient verification*.

Definition 6 (Succinctness). *A homomorphic signature scheme* (HKeyGen, HSign, HEval, HVerify) *is called* succinct *if, for a fixed security parameter* λ, *the size of the signatures depends at most logarithmically on the dataset size* n.

Definition 7 (Efficient Verification *[8]). A homomorphic signature scheme for multi-labeled programs allows for* efficient verification *if there exist two additional algorithms* (HVerPrep, HEffVer) *such that:*

HVerPrep(pk, $\mathcal{P}$): *Given a public key* pk *and a labeled program* $\mathcal{P} = (f, \tau_1, \ldots, \tau_n)$, *generate a modified public key* $\mathsf{pk}_{\mathcal{P}}$. *This does not depend on a dataset identifier* Δ.

HEffVer($\mathsf{pk}_{\mathcal{P}}, m, \sigma, \Delta$): *Given a modified public key* $\mathsf{pk}_{\mathcal{P}}$, *a message* m, *a signature* σ *and a dataset* Δ, *output* 1 *or* 0.

The above algorithms are required to satisfy the following two properties:

Correctness: *Let* $(\mathsf{sk}, \mathsf{pk}) \leftarrow \mathsf{HKeyGen}(1^\lambda, n)$ *be honestly generated keys and* $(\mathcal{P}, m, \sigma)$ *be a tuple such that, for* $\mathcal{P}_\Delta = (\mathcal{P}, \Delta)$, $\mathsf{HVerify}(\mathsf{pk}, \mathcal{P}_\Delta, m, \sigma) = 1$. *Then, for every* $\mathsf{pk}_{\mathcal{P}} \xleftarrow{\$} \mathsf{HVerPrep}(\mathsf{pk}, \mathcal{P})$, $\mathsf{HEffVer}(\mathsf{pk}_{\mathcal{P}}, m, \sigma, \Delta) = 1$ *holds except with negligible probability.*

Amortized Efficiency: *Let* $\mathcal{P}$ *be a program, let* $m_1, \ldots, m_n$ *be valid input values and let* $t(n)$ *be the time required to compute* $\mathcal{P}(m_1, \ldots, m_n)$ *with output* m. *Then, for* $\mathsf{pk}_{\mathcal{P}} \xleftarrow{\$} \mathsf{HVerPrep}(\mathsf{pk}, \mathcal{P})$, *the time required to compute* $\mathsf{HEffVer}(\mathsf{pk}_{\mathcal{P}}, m, \sigma, \Delta)$ *is* $t' = o(t(n))$.

Here, *efficiency* is used in an amortized sense. There is a function-dependent pre-processing, so that the cost of verification amortizes over multiple datasets.

Finally, to derive additional privacy with regard to the verifier from using homomorphic signatures, we require a signature to the outcome of a computation not to leak information about the input values. Our definition is inspired by Gorbunov et al.'s definition [20]. However, in our case, the simulator is explicitly given the circuit for which the signature is supposed to verify. With respect to this difference, our definition is more general. We stress that the circuit is not hidden in either of the two context hiding notions.

Definition 8 (Context Hiding). *A homomorphic signature scheme for multi-labeled programs is called* context hiding *if there exist additional PPT procedures* $\tilde{\sigma} \leftarrow \mathsf{HHide}(\mathsf{pk}, m, \sigma)$ *and* $\mathsf{HHideVer}(\mathsf{pk}, \mathcal{P}_\Delta, m, \tilde{\sigma})$ *such that:*

Correctness: *For any* $(\mathsf{sk}, \mathsf{pk}) \leftarrow \mathsf{HKeyGen}(1^\lambda, n)$ *and any tuple* $(\mathcal{P}_\Delta, m, \sigma)$ *such that* $\mathsf{HVerify}(\mathsf{pk}, \mathcal{P}_\Delta, m, \sigma) = 1$ *and* $\tilde{\sigma} \leftarrow \mathsf{HHide}(\mathsf{pk}, m, \sigma)$, $\mathsf{HHideVer}(\mathsf{pk}, \mathcal{P}_\Delta, m, \tilde{\sigma}) = 1$.

Unforgeability: *The homomorphic signature scheme is unforgeable (see Definition 5) when replacing the algorithm* $\mathsf{HVerify}$ *with* $\mathsf{HHideVer}$ *in the security experiment.*

Context hiding security: *There is a simulator* Sim *such that, for any fixed (worst-case) choice of* $(\mathsf{sk}, \mathsf{pk}) \leftarrow \mathsf{HKeyGen}(1^\lambda, n)$, *any multi-labeled program* $\mathcal{P}_\Delta = (f, \tau_1, \ldots, \tau_n, \Delta)$, *messages* $m_1, \ldots, m_n$, *and distinguisher* $\mathcal{D}$ *there exists a function* $\epsilon(\lambda)$ *such that:*

$$|\Pr[\mathcal{D}(I, \mathsf{HHide}(\mathsf{pk}, m, \sigma)) = 1] - \Pr[\mathcal{D}(I, \mathsf{Sim}(\mathsf{sk}, \mathcal{P}_\Delta, m)) = 1]| = \epsilon(\lambda)$$

where $I = (\mathsf{sk}, \mathsf{pk}, \mathcal{P}_\Delta, \{m_i\}_{i=1}^n, m, \sigma)$ *for* $\sigma_i \leftarrow \mathsf{HSign}(\mathsf{sk}, \Delta, \tau_i, m_i)$, $m \leftarrow f(m_1, \ldots, m_n)$, $\sigma \leftarrow \mathsf{HEval}(\mathsf{pk}, \mathcal{P}_\Delta, \sigma_1, \ldots, \sigma_n)$, *and the probabilities are taken over the randomness of* $\mathsf{HSign}, \mathsf{HHide}$ *and* Sim. *If* $\epsilon(\lambda) = \mathsf{negl}(\lambda)$, *we call the homomorphic signature scheme* statistically context hiding, *if* $\epsilon(\lambda) = 0$, *we call it* perfectly context hiding.

3   Construction of CHQS

In this section, we present our novel homomorphic signature scheme CHQS. We first recall the hardness assumptions on which its security is based. Our construction is then described in detail. We now recall computational hardness assumptions on which CHQS is based.

Definition 9. *Let* $\mathcal{G}$ *be a generator of cyclic groups of order* p *and let* $\mathbb{G} \xleftarrow{\$} \mathcal{G}(1^\lambda)$. *We say the Discrete Logarithm assumption (DL) holds in* $\mathbb{G}$ *if there exists no PPT adversary* $\mathcal{A}$ *that, given* (g, g^a) *for a random generator* $g \in \mathbb{G}$ *and random* $a \in \mathbb{Z}_p$, *can output* a *with more than negligible probability, i.e. if* $\Pr[a \leftarrow \mathcal{A}(g, g^a) \mid g \xleftarrow{\$} \mathbb{G}, a \xleftarrow{\$} \mathbb{Z}_p] = \mathsf{negl}(\lambda)$.

Definition 10 (Asymmetric bilinear groups). *An asymmetric bilinear group is a tuple* $\mathsf{bgp} = (p, \mathbb{G}_1, \mathbb{G}_2, \mathbb{G}_T, g_1, g_2, e)$, *such that:*

- $\mathbb{G}_1, \mathbb{G}_2$, *and* $\mathbb{G}_T$ *are cyclic groups of prime order* p,
- $g_1 \in \mathbb{G}_1$ *and* $g_2 \in \mathbb{G}_2$ *are generators for their respective groups,*
- *the DL assumption holds in* $\mathbb{G}_1, \mathbb{G}_2$, *and* $\mathbb{G}_T$,
- $e : \mathbb{G}_1 \times \mathbb{G}_2 \to \mathbb{G}_T$ *is bilinear, i.e.* $e(g_1{}^a, g_2{}^b) = e(g_1, g_2)^{ab}$ *holds for all* $a, b \in \mathbb{Z}$,
- e *is non-degenerate, i.e.* $e(g_1, g_2) \neq 1_{\mathbb{G}_T}$, *and*
- e *is efficiently computable.*

We write $g_t = e(g_1, g_2)$.

Definition 11 *([8]). Let* $\mathcal{G}$ *be a generator of asymmetric bilinear groups and let* $\mathsf{bgp} = (p, \mathbb{G}_1, \mathbb{G}_2, \mathbb{G}_T, g_1, g_2, e) \xleftarrow{\$} \mathcal{G}(1^\lambda)$. *We say the Flexible Diffie–Hellman Inversion (FDHI) assumption holds in* bgp *if for every PPT adversary* $\mathcal{A}$,

$$\Pr[W \in \mathbb{G}_1 \backslash \{1_{\mathbb{G}_1}\} \wedge W' = W^{\frac{1}{z}} : (W, W') \leftarrow \mathcal{A}(g_1, g_2, g_2^z, g_2^v, g_1^{\frac{v}{z}}, g_1^r, g_1^{\frac{r}{v}})|$$

$$z, r, v \xleftarrow{\$} \mathbb{Z}_p] = \mathsf{negl}(\lambda).$$

We now present the algorithms making up CHQS. It is homomorphic with respect to arithmetic circuits $f : \mathbb{Z}_p^n \to \mathbb{Z}_p$ of degree 2, where $p \geq 5$ (see Lemma 1). CHQS is *graded*, i.e. there exist level-1 and level-2 signatures. Level-1 signatures are created by signing messages, whereas level-2 signatures occur during homomorphic evaluation over multiplication gates. Graded structures like this occur naturally in homomorphic schemes like the ones by Catalano and others [6, 10]. We use dedicated elements (which we will denote by T_τ) in our level-1 signatures to handle multiplication gates. Those elements no longer occur in the level-2 signatures.

$\mathsf{HKeyGen}(1^\lambda, n)$: On input a security parameter λ and an integer n, the algorithm runs $\mathcal{G}(1^\lambda)$ to obtain a bilinear group $\mathsf{bgp} = (p, \mathbb{G}_1, \mathbb{G}_2, \mathbb{G}_T, g_1, g_2, e)$. It chooses $x, y \leftarrow \mathbb{Z}_p$ uniformly at random. It sets $h_t = g_t^x$. It then samples t_{τ_i}, k_{τ_i} uniformly at random for all $i \in [n]$ and sets $F_{\tau_i} = g_2^{t_{\tau_i}}$, as well as $f_{\tau_i} = g_t^{y t_{\tau_i}}$, $f_{\tau_i, \tau_j} = g_t^{t_{\tau_i} k_{\tau_j}}$, for all $i, j \in [n]$.
Additionally, it uses a regular signature scheme $\mathsf{Sig}' = (\mathsf{KeyGen}', \mathsf{Sign}', \mathsf{Verify}')$ and a a pseudorandom function $\mathsf{PRF} : \mathcal{K} \times \{0, 1\}^* \to \mathbb{Z}_p$. For these it generates keys $(\mathsf{sk}', \mathsf{pk}') \leftarrow \mathsf{KeyGen}'(1^\lambda)$ and $K \xleftarrow{\$} \mathcal{K}$. It returns the key pair $(\mathsf{sk}, \mathsf{pk})$ with $\mathsf{sk} = (\mathsf{sk}', K, x, y, \{t_{\tau_i}\}_{i=1}^n)$ and $\mathsf{pk} = (\mathsf{pk}', \mathsf{bgp}, h_t, \{F_{\tau_i}, f_{\tau_i}\}_{i=1}^n, \{f_{\tau_i, \tau_j}\}_{i,j=1}^n)$.

$\mathsf{HSign}(\mathsf{sk}, \Delta, \tau, m)$: On input a secret key sk, a dataset identifier Δ, an input identifier $\tau \in \mathcal{T}$, and a message $m \in \mathbb{Z}_p$, the algorithm generates the parameters for the dataset identified by Δ, by running $z \leftarrow \mathsf{PRF}_K(\Delta)$ and computing $Z = g_2^{\frac{1}{z}}$. Z is bound to the dataset identifier Δ by using the regular signature scheme, i.e. it sets $\sigma_\Delta \leftarrow \mathsf{Sign}'(\mathsf{sk}', Z | \Delta)$.

It chooses $r, s \in \mathbb{Z}_p$ uniformly at random. Then it computes $\Lambda \leftarrow g_1^{z(xm+(y+s)t_\tau+r)}$, $R \leftarrow g_1^r$, $S_\tau \leftarrow g_1^s$, as well as $T_\tau \leftarrow g_1^{ym-k_\tau}$. It sets $\mathcal{T} = \{(\tau, S_\tau, T_\tau)\}$ and then returns the signature $\sigma = (m, \sigma_\Delta, Z, \Lambda, R, \mathcal{T})$. Following the convention of Backes et al. [3], our signature contains the message m.

HEval($\mathsf{pk}, \mathcal{P}_\Delta, \boldsymbol{\sigma}$): Inputs are a public key pk, a multi-labeled program $\mathcal{P}_\Delta$ containing an arithmetic circuit f of degree at most 2, and signatures $\boldsymbol{\sigma} = (\sigma_1, \ldots, \sigma_n)$, where $\sigma_i = (m_i, \sigma_{\Delta,i}, Z_i, \Lambda_i, R_i, \mathcal{T}_i)$. The algorithm checks if the signatures share the same public values, i.e. if $\sigma_{\Delta,1} = \sigma_{\Delta,i}$ and $Z_1 = Z_i$ for all $i = 2, \ldots, n$, and the signature for each set of public values is correct and matches the dataset identifier Δ, i.e. $\mathsf{Verify}'(\mathsf{pk}', Z_i|\Delta, \sigma_{\Delta,i}) = 1$ for any $i \in [n]$. If this is not the case, the algorithm rejects the signature. Otherwise, it proceeds as follows. We describe this algorithm in terms of six different procedures ($\mathsf{Add}_1, \mathsf{Mult}, \mathsf{Add}_2, \mathsf{cMult}_1, \mathsf{cMult}_2, \mathsf{Shift}$) allowing to evaluate the circuit gate by gate.

Add_1: On input two level-1 signatures $\sigma_i = (m_i, \sigma_\Delta, Z, \Lambda_i, R_i, \mathcal{T}_i)$ for $i = 1, 2$ it computes as follows: $m = m_1 + m_2$, $\Lambda = \Lambda_1 \cdot \Lambda_2$, $R = R_1 \cdot R_2$, and $\mathcal{T} = \mathcal{T}_1 \cup \mathcal{T}_2$. It outputs a level-1 signature $\sigma = (m, \sigma_\Delta, Z, \Lambda, R, \mathcal{T})$.

Mult: On input two level-1 signatures $\sigma_i = (m_i, \sigma_\Delta, Z, \Lambda_i, R_i, \mathcal{T}_i)$ for $i = 1, 2$ and the public key pk, it computes as follows: $m = m_1 m_2$, $\Lambda = \Lambda_1^{m_2}$, $R = R_1^{m_2}$, $S_\tau = S_{\tau_1}^{m_2} \cdot T_{\tau_2}$, for all $\tau \in \mathcal{T}_1$, and $\mathcal{L} = \{(\tau, S_\tau)\}$ for all $\tau \in \mathcal{T}_1$. It outputs a level-2 signature $\sigma = (m, \sigma_\Delta, Z, \Lambda, R, \mathcal{L})$.

Add_2: On input two level-2 signatures $\sigma_i = (m_i, \sigma_\Delta, Z, \Lambda_i, R_i, \mathcal{L}_i)$ for $i = 1, 2$, it computes as follows: $m = m_1 + m_2$, $\Lambda = \Lambda_1 \cdot \Lambda_2$, $R = R_1 \cdot R_2$, $S_\tau = S_{\tau,1} \cdot S_{\tau,2}$ for all $(\tau, \cdot) \in \mathcal{L}_1 \cap \mathcal{L}_2$, $S_\tau = S_{\tau,i}$ for all τ such that $(\tau, \cdot) \in \mathcal{L}_1 \Delta \mathcal{L}_2$, and $\mathcal{L} = \{(\tau, S_\tau)\}$ for all $(\tau, \cdot) \in \mathcal{L}_1 \cup \mathcal{L}_2$. It outputs a level-2 signature $\sigma = (m, \sigma_\Delta, Z, \Lambda, R, \mathcal{L})$.

cMult_1: On input a level-1 signature $\sigma' = (m', \sigma_\Delta, Z, \Lambda', R', \mathcal{T}')$ and a constant $c \in \mathbb{Z}_p$, it computes as follows: $m = cm'$, $\Lambda = \Lambda'^c$, $R = R'^c$, $S_\tau = S_\tau'^c$, $T_\tau = T_\tau'^c$ for all $\tau \in \mathcal{T}'$, and $\mathcal{T} = \{(\tau, S_\tau, T_\tau)\}_{\tau \in \mathcal{T}}$. It outputs a level-1 signature $\sigma = (m, \sigma_\Delta, Z, \Lambda, R, \mathcal{T})$.

cMult_2: On input a level-2 signature $\sigma = (m', \sigma_\Delta, Z, \Lambda', R', \mathcal{L}')$ and a constant $c \in \mathbb{Z}_p$, it computes as follows: $m = cm'$, $\Lambda = \Lambda'^c$, $R = R'^c$, $S_\tau = S_\tau'^c$ for all $(\tau, S_\tau') \in \mathcal{L}'$, and $\mathcal{L} = \{(\tau, S_\tau)\}$ for all $(\tau, S_\tau') \in \mathcal{L}'$. It outputs a level-2 signature $\sigma = (m, \sigma_\Delta, Z, \Lambda, R, \mathcal{L})$.

Shift: On input a level-1 signature $\sigma' = (m', \sigma_\Delta, Z, \Lambda', R', \mathcal{T}')$, it computes as follows: $m = m'$, $\Lambda = \Lambda'$, $R = R'$, and $\mathcal{L} = \{(\tau, S_\tau)\}_{\tau \in \mathcal{T}'}$. It outputs a level-2 signature $\sigma = (m, \sigma_\Delta, Z, \Lambda, R, \mathcal{L})$. Shift simply describes how to derive a level-2 signature from a level-1 signature.

HVerify($\mathsf{pk}, \mathcal{P}_\Delta, M, \sigma$): On input a public key pk, a message M, a (level-1 or -2) signature σ, a multi-labeled program $\mathcal{P}_\Delta$ containing an arithmetic circuit f of degree at most 2, the algorithm parses (without loss of generality) $\sigma = (m, \sigma_\Delta, Z, \Lambda, R, \mathcal{L})$.

It then checks whether the following three equations hold:

1. $M = m$
2. $\mathsf{Verify}'(\mathsf{pk}', Z|\Delta, \sigma_\Delta) = 1$

3.

$$e\left(\Lambda, Z\right) = e\left(R, g_2\right) \cdot h_t^m \cdot \prod_{i=1}^{n} f_i^{c_i} \cdot \prod_{(\tau,\cdot,\cdot) \in \mathcal{T}} e\left(S_\tau, F_\tau\right)$$

for level-1 signatures and

$$e\left(\Lambda, Z\right) = e\left(R, g_2\right) \cdot h_t^m \cdot \prod_{i,j=1}^{n} f_{i,j}^{c_{i,j}} \cdot \prod_{j=1}^{n} f_j^{c_j} \cdot \prod_{(\tau,\cdot) \in \mathcal{L}} e\left(S_\tau, F_\tau\right)$$

for level-2 signatures, respectively, where $c_{i,j}$ and c_j are the coefficients in $\mathcal{P}_\Delta$.

If all 3 equations hold respectively, it returns 1. Otherwise, it returns 0.

4 Correctness, Efficiency, and Context Hiding Property of CHQS

We now prove the essential properties of CHQS, in particular correctness, amortized efficiency, and context hiding.

Theorem 1. *CHQS is correct in the sense of Definition 2.*

Proof. We first show the correctness for freshly generated signatures. We then show the correctness of the six procedures ($\mathsf{Add}_1, \mathsf{Mult}, \mathsf{Add}_2, \mathsf{cMult}_1, \mathsf{cMult}_2, \mathsf{Shift}$).

Sign: Let $\sigma = (m, \sigma_\Delta, Z, \Lambda, R, \mathcal{T}) \leftarrow \mathsf{HSign}(\mathsf{sk}, \Delta, \tau, m)$. By construction, $\mathsf{Verify}'(\mathsf{pk}', Z|\Delta, \sigma_\Delta) = 1$. Also, $e\left(\Lambda, Z\right) = e\left(g_1^{z(xm+(y+s)t_\tau+r)}, g_2^{\frac{1}{z}}\right) = e\left(g_1^{xm+(y+s)t_\tau+r}, g_2\right) = g_t^{xm+(y+s)t_\tau+r} = h_t^m \cdot f_\tau \cdot e\left(R, g_2\right) \cdot e\left(S, F_\tau\right)$ and consequently σ is a correct signature.

Add_1: We have two valid signatures σ_1 and σ_2. Thus $Z_1 = Z_2$ and $\mathsf{Verify}'(\mathsf{pk}', Z_1|\Delta, \sigma_\Delta) = 1$. Furthermore, $e\left(\Lambda_i, Z_i\right) = e\left(R_i, g_2\right) \cdot h_t^{m_i} \cdot f_i \cdot e\left(S_i, F_i\right)$, by construction. After performing Add_1, $e\left(\Lambda, Z\right) = e\left(\Lambda_1 \cdot \Lambda_2, Z_1\right) = e\left(\Lambda_1, Z_1\right) \cdot e\left(\Lambda_2, Z_2\right)$

$$= e\left(R_1, g_2\right) \cdot h_t^{m_1} \cdot f_1 \cdot e\left(S_1, F_1\right) \cdot e\left(R_2, g_2\right) \cdot h_t^{m_2} \cdot f_2 \cdot e\left(S_2, F_2\right)$$
$$= e\left(R_1 \cdot R_2, g_2\right) \cdot h_t^{m_1+m_2} \cdot f_1 \cdot f_2 \cdot e\left(S_1, F_1\right) \cdot e\left(S_2, F_2\right)$$
$$= e\left(R, g_2\right) \cdot h_t^m \cdot f_1 \cdot f_2 \cdot e\left(S_1, F_1\right) \cdot e\left(S_2, F_2\right)$$

hence σ is a correct signature.

We also have $T = T_1 \cdot T_2 = g_1^{y(m_1+m_2)-(k_1+k_2)}$.

Mult: We have two valid signatures σ_1 and σ_2. Thus $Z_1 = Z_2$ and $\mathsf{Verify}'(\mathsf{pk}', Z_1|\Delta, \sigma_\Delta) = 1$. Furthermore, $e\left(\Lambda_i, Z_i\right) = e\left(R_i, g_2\right) \cdot h_t^{m_i} \cdot f_i \cdot$

$e\left(S_i, F_i\right)$, by construction. After performing Mult, $e\left(\Lambda, Z\right) = e\left(\Lambda_1^{m_2}, Z\right) = e(R_1^{m_2}, g_2) \cdot h_t^{m_1 m_2} \cdot f_1^{m_2} \cdot e\left(S_1, F_1\right)$

$$= e(R_1^{m_2}, g_2) \cdot h_t^{m_1 m_2} \cdot f_1^{m_2} \cdot e\left(S_1^{m_2}, F_1\right) \cdot g_t^{-y m_2 t_1} \cdot g_t^{-k_2 t_1} \cdot g_t^{y m_2 t_1 + k_2 t_1}$$

$$= e(R_1^{m_2}, g_2) \cdot h_t^{m_1 m_2} \cdot f_1^{m_2} \cdot g_t^{-y m_2 t_1} \cdot g_t^{k_2 t_1} \cdot e\left(g_1^{s_1 m_2 t_1} \cdot g_1^{y m_2 t_1 - k_2 t_1}, g_2\right)$$

$$= e(R_1^{m_2}, g_2) \cdot h_t^{m_1 m_2} \cdot f_1^{m_2} \cdot f_1^{-m_2} \cdot f_{1,2} \cdot e\left(g_1^{y m_2 - k_2 + s_1 m_2}, g_2^{t_1}\right)$$

$$= e(R, g_2) \cdot h_t^{m_1 m_2} \cdot f_{1,2} \cdot e\left(S_1^{m_2} \cdot T_1, F_1\right) \text{ so } \sigma \text{ is a correct signature.}$$

Add$_2$: We have two valid signatures σ_1 and σ_2. Thus $Z_1 = Z_2$ and Verify$'(\mathsf{pk}', Z_1 | \Delta, \sigma_\Delta) = 1$. Furthermore, $e\left(\Lambda_i, Z_i\right) = e\left(R_i, g_2\right) \cdot h_t^{m_i} \cdot f_i \cdot \prod_{(\tau, \cdot) \in \mathcal{L}_1} e\left(S_{\tau, i}, F_\tau\right)$, by construction. After performing Add$_2$,

$$e\left(\Lambda, Z\right) = e\left(\Lambda_1 \cdot \Lambda_2, Z_1\right) = (R_1, g_2) \cdot h_t^{m_1} \cdot f_1 \cdot \prod_{(\tau, \cdot) \in \mathcal{L}_1} e\left(S_{\tau, 1}, F_\tau\right)$$

$$\cdot e\left(R_2, g_2\right) \cdot h_t^{m_2} \cdot f_2 \cdot \prod_{(\tau, \cdot) \in \mathcal{L}_2} e\left(S_{\tau, 2}, F_\tau\right)$$

$$= e\left(R_1 \cdot R_2, g_2\right) \cdot h_t^{m_1 + m_2} \cdot f_1 \cdot f_2 \prod_{(\tau, \cdot) \in \mathcal{L}} e\left(S_\tau, F_\tau\right)$$

$$= e\left(R, g_2\right) \cdot h_t^m \cdot f_1 \cdot f_2 \prod_{(\tau, \cdot) \in \mathcal{L}} e\left(S_\tau, F_\tau\right) \text{ thus } \sigma \text{ is a correct signature.}$$

The correctness of cMult$_1$ and cMult$_2$ follows immediately from the correctness of Add$_1$ and Add$_2$ respectively. The correctness of Shift is trivial.

Theorem 2. *CHQS provides verification in time $\mathcal{O}(n)$ in an amortized sense.*

Proof. We describe the two algorithms (HVerPrep, HEffVer).

HVerPrep$(\mathsf{pk}, \mathcal{P})$: This algorithm parses $\mathcal{P} = (f, \tau_1, \ldots \tau_n)$ with $f(m_1, \ldots, m_n) = \sum_{i=1}^n c_i m_i + \sum_{i,j=1}^n c_{i,j} m_i m_j$ and takes the $f_i, f_{i,j}$ for $i, j \in [n]$ contained in the public key. It computes $F_{\mathcal{P}} \leftarrow \prod_{i,j=1}^n f_{i,j}^{c_{i,j}} \cdot \prod_{i=1}^n f_i^{c_i}$ and outputs $\mathsf{pk}_{\mathcal{P}} = (\mathsf{pk}', \mathsf{bgp}, h_t, \{F_i\}_{i=1}^n, F_{\mathcal{P}})$ where $\mathsf{pk}', \mathsf{bgp}, h_t, \{F_i\}_{i=1}^n$ are taken from pk.

HEffVer$(\mathsf{pk}_{\mathcal{P}}, m, \sigma, \Delta)$: This algorithm is analogous to HVerify, except that the value $\prod_{i,j=1}^n f_{i,j}^{c_{i,j}} \cdot \prod_{i=1}^n f_i^{c_i}$ has been precomputed as $F_{\mathcal{P}}$.

This satisfies correctness. During HEffVer, the verifier now computes

$$e\left(\Lambda, Z\right) = e\left(R, g_2\right) \cdot h_t^m \cdot F_{\mathcal{P}} \cdot \prod_{i=1}^n e\left(S_i, F_i\right)$$

The running time of HEffVer is thus $\mathcal{O}(n)$.

Thus, CHQS achieves amortized efficiency in the sense of Definition 7 for every arithmetic circuit f of multiplicative depth 2, that has *superlinear* runtime complexity.

Bandwidth: CHQS is *not succinct.* However, the output of HSign is of constant size and thus independent of n. Hence no extensive bandwidth is needed during the upload of the data. After a homomorphic evaluation a signature consists of up to $n + 2$ elements in $\mathbb{G}_1$, 1 element in $\mathbb{G}_2$, one conventional signature, the message and up to n input identifiers contained in a list. Using for instance 256 bit Barreto-Naehrig curves [19], we have an estimated security of 110 bits [23], elements of $\mathbb{G}_1$ can be represented by 256 bits, and elements of $\mathbb{G}_2$ require 512 bits.

Theorem 3. *CHQS is perfectly context hiding according to Definition 8 if* Sig$'$ *is a deterministic signature scheme.*

Proof. We show that our scheme is perfectly context hiding in the sense of Definition 8, by comparing the distributions of homomorphically derived signatures to that of simulated signatures. In our case, HHide is just the identity function, i.e. $\sigma \leftarrow$ HHide(pk, m, σ) for all pk, m, σ and HHideVer $=$ HVerify. We show how to construct a simulator Sim that outputs signatures perfectly indistinguishable from the ones obtained by running HEval. Parse the simulator's input as $\mathsf{sk} = (\mathsf{sk}', K)$, $\mathcal{P}_\Delta = (f, \tau_1, \ldots, \tau_n, \Delta)$. For each τ appearing in $\mathcal{P}_\Delta$, it chooses $s_\tau \in \mathbb{Z}_p$ uniformly at random as well as $r \in \mathbb{Z}_p$ uniformly at random. With this information, the simulator computes $m' = m$, $Z' = g_2^z$ where $z \leftarrow$ PRF$_K(\Delta)$, $\sigma'_\Delta \overset{\$}{\leftarrow}$ Sign$'(\mathsf{sk}', Z|\Delta)$, $\Lambda' = g_1^{z(xm' + y(\sum_{i,j=1}^n c_{ij}t_ik_j + \sum_{i=1}^n c_it_i) + \sum_{i=1}^n s_{\tau_i}t_i + r)}$, $R' = g_1^r$, $S'_\tau = g_1^{s_\tau}$ for all τ appearing in $\mathcal{P}_\Delta$, and $\mathcal{T}' = \{(\tau, S_\tau)\}_{\tau \in \mathcal{P}_\Delta}$. The simulator outputs the signature $\sigma' = (m', \sigma'_\Delta, Z', \Lambda', R', \mathcal{T}')$.

We now show that this simulator allows for perfectly context hiding security. We fix an arbitrary key pair $(\mathsf{sk}, \mathsf{pk})$, a multi-labeled program $(f, \tau_1, \ldots, \tau_n, \Delta)$, and messages $m_1, \ldots, m_n \in \mathbb{Z}_p$. Let $\sigma \leftarrow$ HEval$(\mathsf{pk}, \mathcal{P}_\Delta, \boldsymbol{\sigma})$ and parse it as $\sigma = (\sigma_\Delta, Z, \Lambda)$. We inspect each component of the signature. $Z = $ PRF$_K(\Delta)$ by definition and thus also $Z = Z'$. In particular, $z = z'$ where $Z = g_2^z$ and $Z' = g_2^{z'}$. We have $\sigma_\Delta = $ Sign$'(\mathsf{sk}', Z|\Delta)$ by definition, and since $Z = Z'$, also $\sigma_\Delta = \sigma'_\Delta$ since Sign$'$ is deterministic. We consider Λ as an exponentiation of g_1^z. Since $\Lambda = \prod_{i,j=1}^n \Lambda_i^{c_{ij}m_j}$ by construction, for the exponent we have:

$$xm + \sum_{i,j=1}^n c_{ij}m_j(s_it_i + yt_i + r_i) = xm' + \sum_{i,j=1}^n c_{ij}m_j(s_it_i + yt_i + r_i)$$

$$+ y(\sum_{i,j=1}^n c_{ij}t_ik_j + \sum_{i=1}^n c_it_i) - y(\sum_{i,j=1}^n c_{ij}t_ik_j + \sum_{i=1}^n c_it_i)$$

$$= xm' + \sum_{i=1}^n (\sum_{j=1}^n -yc_{ij}k_j - yc_i + c_{ij}m_jy + c_{ij}s_im_j)t_i$$

$$+ y(\sum_{i,j=1}^n c_{ij}t_ik_j + \sum_{i=1}^n c_it_i) + \sum_{i,j=1}^n c_{ij}m_jr_i$$

$$= xm' + y(\sum_{i,j=1}^n c_{ij}t_ik_j + \sum_{i=1}^n c_it_i) + \sum_{i=1}^n \tilde{s}_it_i + \tilde{r}$$

Thus the exponent corresponds to a different choice of $r, s_i \in \mathbb{Z}_p$. Analogously, $S_\tau = g_1^{\tilde{s}_{\tau_i}}$ and $R = g_1^{\tilde{r}}$, where $\tilde{r}, \tilde{s}_{\tau_i}$ are distributed uniformly at random as linear combinations of uniformly random field elements.

All elements are either identical, or have the exact same distribution. Thus even a computationally unbounded distinguisher has no advantage distinguishing the two cases.

5   Unforgeability of CHQS

This section deals with the security reduction of CHQS to the FDHI assumption (see Definition 11). We first present the hybrid games used in the proof, and then argue their indistinguishability for a PPT adversary $\mathcal{A}$.

Theorem 4. *If* Sig$'$ *is an unforgeable signature scheme,* PRF *is a pseudorandom function, and the FDHI assumption (see Definition 11) holds in* bgp, *then CHQS is an unforgeable homomorphic signature scheme in the sense of Definition 5.*

Proof. To prove Theorem 4, we define a series of games with the adversary $\mathcal{A}$ and we show that the adversary $\mathcal{A}$ wins, i.e. the game outputs 1 only with negligible probability. Following the notation of [8], we write $G_i(\mathcal{A})$ to denote that a run of game i with adversary $\mathcal{A}$ returns 1. We use flag values bad$_i$, initially set to false. If at the end of the game any of these flags is set to true, the game simply outputs 0. Let Bad$_i$ denote the event that bad$_i$ is set to true during game i. As shown in [10, Proposition 2], any adversary who outputs a Type 3 forgery (see Definition 4) can be converted into one that outputs a Type 2 forgery. Hence we only have to deal with Type 1 and Type 2 forgeries.

Game 1 is the security experiment HomUF $-$ CMA$_{\mathcal{A},\text{HSign}}$ between an adversary $\mathcal{A}$ and a challenger $\mathcal{C}$, where $\mathcal{A}$ only outputs Type 1 or Type 2 forgeries.

Game 2 is defined as Game 1, except for the following change. Whenever $\mathcal{A}$ returns a forgery $(\mathcal{P}^*_{\Delta^*}, \sigma*)$ with $\sigma* = (m^*, \mathcal{T}^*, \sigma^*_{\Delta^*}, Z^*, \Lambda^*, R^*, S^*)$ or $\sigma* = (m^*, \sigma^*_{\Delta^*}, Z^*, \Lambda^*, R^*, \mathcal{L}^*)$ and Z^* has not been generated by the challenger during the queries, then Game 2 sets bad$_2$ = true. After this change, the game never outputs 1 if $\mathcal{A}$ returns a Type 1 forgery.

Game 3 is defined as Game 2, except that the pseudorandom function F is replaced by a random function $\mathcal{R} : \{0,1\}^* \to \mathbb{Z}_p$.

Game 4 is defined as Game 3, except for the following change. At the beginning $\mathcal{C}$ chooses $\mu \in [Q]$ uniformly at random, where $Q = \text{poly}(\lambda)$ is the number of queries made by $\mathcal{A}$ during the game. Let $\Delta_1, \ldots, \Delta_Q$ be all the datasets queried by $\mathcal{A}$. Then if in the forgery $\Delta^* \neq \Delta_\mu$ set bad$_4$ = true.

Game 5 is defined as Game 4, except for the following change. At the very beginning $\mathcal{C}$ chooses $z_\mu \in \mathbb{Z}_p$ at random and computes $Z_\mu = g_2^{z_\mu}$. It will use Z_μ whenever queried for dataset Δ_μ. It chooses $a_i, b_i \in \mathbb{Z}_p$ uniformly at random for $i \in [n]$ and sets $f_{\tau_i} = g_t^{y(a_i + z_\mu b_i)}$, $F_{\tau_i} = g_2^{a_i + z_\mu b_i}$ as well as $f_{\tau_i, \tau_j} = g_t^{k_j y(a_i + z_\mu b_i)}$.

Game 6 is defined as Game 5, except for the following change. The challenger runs an additional check. If $\mathsf{HVerify}(\mathsf{pk}, \mathcal{P}_{\Delta}^*, m^*, \sigma^*) = 1$, the challenger computes $\hat{\sigma} \leftarrow \mathsf{HEval}(\mathsf{pk}, \mathcal{P}_{\Delta}^*, \boldsymbol{\sigma})$ over the signatures σ_i generated in dataset Δ^*. We have $\hat{\sigma} = (\hat{m}, \hat{\mathcal{T}}, \sigma_{\Delta}, Z, \hat{\Lambda}, \hat{R}, \hat{S})$ in case of a level-1 signature and $\hat{\sigma} = \sigma = (\hat{m}, \sigma_{\Delta}, Z, \hat{\Lambda}, \hat{R}, \hat{\mathcal{L}})$ in case of a level-2 signature. If $\Lambda^* \cdot \prod_{i=1}^{n} \hat{S}_i^{b_i} = \hat{\Lambda} \cdot \prod_{i=1}^{n} S_i^{*b_i}$, then $\mathcal{C}$ sets $\mathsf{bad}_6 = \mathsf{true}$.

Any noticeable difference between Games 1 and 2 can be reduced to producing a forgery for the signature scheme. If Bad_2 occurs, then $\mathcal{A}$ produced a valid signature $\sigma_{\Delta^*}^*$ for $(\Delta^*|Z^*)$ despite never having queried a signature on any $(\Delta^*|\cdot)$. This is obviously a forgery on the signature scheme.

Under the assumption that F is pseudorandom, Games 2 and 3 are computationally indistinguishable. We have, by definition, $\Pr[G_3(\mathcal{A})] = Q \cdot \Pr[G_4(\mathcal{A})]$. It is obvious that $\Pr[G_4(\mathcal{A})] = \Pr[G_5(\mathcal{A})]$, since the public keys are perfectly indistinguishable. It is easy to see that $|\Pr[G_5(\mathcal{A})] - \Pr[G_6(\mathcal{A})]| \leq \Pr[\mathsf{Bad}_6]$. This occurs only with negligible probability if the FDHI assumption holds. For a proof of this statement, we refer to the full version.

After these modifications, Game 6 can only output 1 if $\mathcal{A}$ produces a forgery $(\mathcal{P}^*_{\Delta^*}, m^*, \sigma^*)$ such that $\mathsf{HVerify}(\mathsf{pk}, \mathcal{P}_{\Delta}^*, m^*, \sigma^*) = 1$ and $m^* \neq \hat{m}$, $\Lambda^* \neq \hat{\Lambda}$. This only occurs with negligible probability if the FDHI assumption holds. For a corresponding proof, see the full version.

6   Related Work

Linearly homomorphic signature schemes were introduced by Desmedt [14] and later refined by Johnson et al. [21]. Freeman proposed stronger security definitions [16]. A first instantiation, based on the 2-out-of-3 Computational Diffie–Hellmann assumption, was proposed by Boneh et al [5]. It was followed by multiple schemes [1,2,4,8,9,18,25], based on various hardness assumptions. None of these schemes support quadratic functions.

Some constructions for homomorphic authenticators go beyond the linear case. Backes et al. presented a homomorphic MAC for arithmetic circuits of degree 2 constructed from bilinear maps [3]. However, this approach is not context hiding and only offers private verifiability, while we offer verifiability for arbitrary third parties and perfect context hiding. Catalano et al. showed how to construct homomorphic signatures for arithmetic circuits of fixed depth from graded encoding schemes, a special type of multilinear maps [10]. Existing graded encoding schemes [12,17] have, however, suffered strong cryptanalytic attacks in recent years [11,22,24]. In contrast, CHQS can be instantiated with elliptic curve-based bilinear groups, which have long been a reliable building block in cryptography.

Some lattice-based homomorphic signatures schemes [15,20] support boolean circuits of fixed degree. However, these schemes suffer the performance drawback of signing every single input bit, while our solution can sign entire finite field elements. Additionally [15] is also not shown to be context hiding.

More generally, verifiable computing can be used to achieve verifiability of delegated computations. Many different schemes have been proposed. For a detailed comparison we refer to [13]. A general feature of homomorphic-signature-based schemes is that they allow for incremental updates of data sets, i.e. additional data can be added after the first delegation of data. Other verifiable computing schemes require all data to be used during the computation to be known before outsourcing.

7   Conclusion

Our new homomorphic signature scheme CHQS can be instantiated from ordinary bilinear groups, but still allows public verifiability for polynomials of degree greater than 1. Previous proposals either were limited to private verifiability, or relied on advanced primitives like graded encoding schemes. Such alternatives have recently been threatened by substantial cryptanalytic progress. Bilinear groups, however, are well understood and have been a reliable cryptographic building block for years.

We have demonstrated a novel approach using pairings to obtain both public verifiability and the ability to homomorphically evaluate a multiplication at the same time. CHQS achieves several desirable properties, including context hiding and amortized efficiency. Furthermore, we reduced its security to the FDHI assumption in the standard model. This enables homomorphic signature schemes as a means of achieving verifiability for delegated computations over authenticated data, for example in the case of second-order statistics over health data in the cloud.

While CHQS is both context hiding and achieves efficient verification, the construction of a scheme also achieving succinctness and constant time verification is an open problem. Another question remains: can primitives supporting degrees higher than 2 still be constructed from bilinear maps?

Acknowledgment. This work has received funding from the European Union's Horizon 2020 research and innovation program under Grant Agreement No 644962.

References

1. Attrapadung, N., Libert, B., Peters, T.: Computing on authenticated data: new privacy definitions and constructions. In: Wang, X., Sako, K. (eds.) ASIACRYPT 2012. LNCS, vol. 7658, pp. 367–385. Springer, Heidelberg (2012). https://doi.org/10.1007/978-3-642-34961-4_23
2. Attrapadung, N., Libert, B., Peters, T.: Efficient completely context-hiding quotable and linearly homomorphic signatures. In: Kurosawa, K., Hanaoka, G. (eds.) PKC 2013. LNCS, vol. 7778, pp. 386–404. Springer, Heidelberg (2013). https://doi.org/10.1007/978-3-642-36362-7_24
3. Backes, M., Fiore, D., Reischuk, R.M.: Verifiable delegation of computation on outsourced data. In: ACM CCS 2013, pp. 863–874. ACM (2013)
4. Boneh, D., Freeman, D.M.: Linearly homomorphic signatures over binary fields and new tools for lattice-based signatures. In: Catalano, D., Fazio, N., Gennaro, R., Nicolosi, A. (eds.) PKC 2011. LNCS, vol. 6571, pp. 1–16. Springer, Heidelberg (2011). https://doi.org/10.1007/978-3-642-19379-8_1

5. Boneh, D., Freeman, D., Katz, J., Waters, B.: Signing a linear subspace: signature schemes for network coding. In: Jarecki, S., Tsudik, G. (eds.) PKC 2009. LNCS, vol. 5443, pp. 68–87. Springer, Heidelberg (2009). https://doi.org/10.1007/978-3-642-00468-1_5

6. Catalano, D., Fiore, D.: Using linearly-homomorphic encryption to evaluate degree-2 functions on encrypted data. In: ACM CCS 2015, pp. 1518–1529. ACM (2015)

7. Catalano, D., Fiore, D., Gennaro, R., Nizzardo, L.: Generalizing homomorphic MACs for arithmetic circuits. In: Krawczyk, H. (ed.) PKC 2014. LNCS, vol. 8383, pp. 538–555. Springer, Heidelberg (2014). https://doi.org/10.1007/978-3-642-54631-0_31

8. Catalano, D., Fiore, D., Nizzardo, L.: Programmable hash functions go private: constructions and applications to (homomorphic) signatures with shorter public keys. In: Gennaro, R., Robshaw, M. (eds.) CRYPTO 2015. LNCS, vol. 9216, pp. 254–274. Springer, Heidelberg (2015). https://doi.org/10.1007/978-3-662-48000-7_13

9. Catalano, D., Fiore, D., Warinschi, B.: Efficient network coding signatures in the standard model. In: Fischlin, M., Buchmann, J., Manulis, M. (eds.) PKC 2012. LNCS, vol. 7293, pp. 680–696. Springer, Heidelberg (2012). https://doi.org/10.1007/978-3-642-30057-8_40

10. Catalano, D., Fiore, D., Warinschi, B.: Homomorphic signatures with efficient verification for polynomial functions. In: Garay, J.A., Gennaro, R. (eds.) CRYPTO 2014. LNCS, vol. 8616, pp. 371–389. Springer, Heidelberg (2014). https://doi.org/10.1007/978-3-662-44371-2_21

11. Coron, J.-S., Lee, M.S., Lepoint, T., Tibouchi, M.: Cryptanalysis of GGH15 multilinear maps. In: Robshaw, M., Katz, J. (eds.) CRYPTO 2016. LNCS, vol. 9815, pp. 607–628. Springer, Heidelberg (2016). https://doi.org/10.1007/978-3-662-53008-5_21

12. Coron, J.-S., Lepoint, T., Tibouchi, M.: Practical multilinear maps over the integers. In: Canetti, R., Garay, J.A. (eds.) CRYPTO 2013. LNCS, vol. 8042, pp. 476–493. Springer, Heidelberg (2013). https://doi.org/10.1007/978-3-642-40041-4_26

13. Demirel, D., Schabhüser, L., Buchmann, J.A.: Privately and Publicly Verifiable Computing Techniques – A Survey. Springer Briefs in Computer Science. Springer, Heidelberg (2017). https://doi.org/10.1007/978-3-319-53798-6

14. Desmedt, Y.: Computer security by redefining what a computer is. In: NSPW, pp. 160–166. ACM (1993)

15. Fiore, D., Mitrokotsa, A., Nizzardo, L., Pagnin, E.: Multi-key homomorphic authenticators. In: Cheon, J.H., Takagi, T. (eds.) ASIACRYPT 2016. LNCS, vol. 10032, pp. 499–530. Springer, Heidelberg (2016). https://doi.org/10.1007/978-3-662-53890-6_17

16. Freeman, D.M.: Improved security for linearly homomorphic signatures: a generic framework. In: Fischlin, M., Buchmann, J., Manulis, M. (eds.) PKC 2012. LNCS, vol. 7293, pp. 697–714. Springer, Heidelberg (2012). https://doi.org/10.1007/978-3-642-30057-8_41

17. Garg, S., Gentry, C., Halevi, S.: Candidate multilinear maps from ideal lattices. In: Johansson, T., Nguyen, P.Q. (eds.) EUROCRYPT 2013. LNCS, vol. 7881, pp. 1–17. Springer, Heidelberg (2013). https://doi.org/10.1007/978-3-642-38348-9_1

18. Gennaro, R., Katz, J., Krawczyk, H., Rabin, T.: Secure network coding over the integers. In: Nguyen, P.Q., Pointcheval, D. (eds.) PKC 2010. LNCS, vol. 6056, pp. 142–160. Springer, Heidelberg (2010). https://doi.org/10.1007/978-3-642-13013-7_9

19. Geovandro, C.C.F.P., Simplício Jr., M.A., Naehrig, M., Barreto, P.S.L.M.: A family of implementation-friendly BN elliptic curves. J. Syst. Softw. **84**(8), 1319–1326 (2011)
20. Gorbunov, S., Vaikuntanathan, V., Wichs, D.: Leveled fully homomorphic signatures from standard lattices. In: STOC 2015, pp. 469–477. ACM (2015)
21. Johnson, R., Molnar, D., Song, D., Wagner, D.: Homomorphic signature schemes. In: Preneel, B. (ed.) CT-RSA 2002. LNCS, vol. 2271, pp. 244–262. Springer, Heidelberg (2002). https://doi.org/10.1007/3-540-45760-7_17
22. Lee, H.T., Seo, J.H.: Security analysis of multilinear maps over the integers. In: Garay, J.A., Gennaro, R. (eds.) CRYPTO 2014. LNCS, vol. 8616, pp. 224–240. Springer, Heidelberg (2014). https://doi.org/10.1007/978-3-662-44371-2_13
23. Menezes, A., Sarkar, P., Singh, S.: Challenges with assessing the impact of NFS advances on the security of pairing-based cryptography. In: Phan, R.C.-W., Yung, M. (eds.) Mycrypt 2016. LNCS, vol. 10311, pp. 83–108. Springer, Cham (2017). https://doi.org/10.1007/978-3-319-61273-7_5
24. Miles, E., Sahai, A., Zhandry, M.: Annihilation attacks for multilinear maps: cryptanalysis of indistinguishability obfuscation over GGH13. In: Robshaw, M., Katz, J. (eds.) CRYPTO 2016. LNCS, vol. 9815, pp. 629–658. Springer, Heidelberg (2016). https://doi.org/10.1007/978-3-662-53008-5_22
25. Schabhüser, L., Buchmann, J., Struck, P.: A linearly homomorphic signature scheme from weaker assumptions. In: O'Neill, M. (ed.) IMACC 2017. LNCS, vol. 10655, pp. 261–279. Springer, Cham (2017). https://doi.org/10.1007/978-3-319-71045-7_14

Achieving Almost-Full Security for Lattice-Based Fully Dynamic Group Signatures with Verifier-Local Revocation

Maharage Nisansala Sevwandi Perera[1(✉)] and Takeshi Koshiba[2]

[1] Graduate School of Science and Engineering, Saitama University, Saitama, Japan
perera.m.n.s.119@ms.saitama-u.ac.jp
[2] Faculty of Education and Integrated Arts and Sciences, Waseda University,
Tokyo, Japan
tkoshiba@waseda.jp

Abstract. This paper presents a lattice-based group signature scheme that provides both member registration and member revocation with verifier-local revocation. Verifier-local revocation (VLR) seems to be the most suitable revocation approach for any group since when a member is revoked VLR requires to update only verifiers. However, presenting a fully dynamic and fully secured lattice-based group signature scheme with verifier-local revocation is a significant challenge. Thus, we suggest a new security notion to prove the security of VLR schemes with member registration. As a result, we present a dynamical-almost-fully secured fully dynamic group signature scheme from lattices with VLR.

Keywords: Lattice-based group signatures · Verifier-local revocation
Almost-full anonymity · Dynamical-almost-full anonymity
Member registration

1 Introduction

In the setting of group signature scheme, each group member is capable of signing messages on behalf of the group anonymously (*anonymity*). On the other hand, the group manager should be able to identify the misbehaved members (*traceability*). Group signatures were initially introduced by Chaum and van Heyst [13] in 1991 and later made it scalable and collusion-resistance by Ateniese et al. [3]. The model proposed by Bellare et al. [4] (BMW03 model) gave the formal and strong security notions, "*full-anonymity*" and "*full-traceability*" for static group signatures. Then, Bellare et al. [5] presented a scheme which uses the BMW03 model to deliver a dynamic group signature scheme. However, their scheme supports only member registration. Recently, Bootel et al. [7] provided a security definition for fully dynamic group signatures.

Lattice-based cryptography has been an interesting research topic during the last decade since it provides security against the threat of quantum attacks. The

© Springer Nature Switzerland AG 2018
C. Su and H. Kikuchi (Eds.): ISPEC 2018, LNCS 11125, pp. 229–247, 2018.
https://doi.org/10.1007/978-3-319-99807-7_14

first lattice-based group signature scheme was proposed by Gordon et al. [16]. Then by achieving anonymity with a token system Camenisch et al. [12] extended the scheme proposed in [16]. Both of the schemes faced a problem of increasing the size of the signatures with the number of group members N. However, the scheme proposed by Laguillaumie et al. [18] was able to give a solution for the linear size problem. But, the scheme in [18] required relatively large parameters. Later, Ling et al. [22] provided a scheme with several prominent advantages such as simple construction and shorter size of keys and signatures. Moreover, their scheme has a strong security with the requirements of the BMW03 model. Nguyen et al. [26] also presented a simpler efficient scheme from lattices. However, none of the above schemes support dynamic groups.

The first lattice-based group signature that facilitates member revocation was proposed by Langlois et al. [19] in 2014. Their scheme manages the member revocation with *Verifier-local Revocation* (*VLR*) approach which requires updating only the verifiers with the latest information about revoked members. However, they were unable to maintain member registration. Moreover, the scheme in [19] relies on a weaker security notion called *selfless-anonymity*. The scheme proposed by Libert et al. [20] provides only member registration. However, full dynamicity is achieved by the scheme suggested by Ling et al. [23]. They have employed accumulators to update member information when a member is revoked or registered. Thus, the first lattice-based fully dynamic group signature scheme [23] uses Merkle tree accumulators. However, when a new member joins the group, the group manager has to update registration table, Merkle tree, and the user counter. Further, when a member is revoked, the group manager has to update both the registration table and the tree. When signing and verifying, the members and the verifiers have to download the respective information. Thus, it increases the workload of both the members and the verifiers. This yields constructing a group signature scheme based on lattices, which does not increase the workload of the current members, managers, and verifiers when achieving the full dynamicity.

1.1 Our Contribution

This paper presents a fully dynamic group signature scheme from lattices with verifier-local revocation and member registration.

However, gaining full anonymity (which was described in the BMW03 model [4] and which was used in [5]) for VLR scheme is a challenging problem. In case of the full-anonymity game between a challenger and an adversary, the challenger provides all the secret signing keys to the adversary. The previous VLR schemes constructed the revocation token by taking the part of the secret signing key of the relevant member. Thus, if we provide all the secret signing keys to the adversary, he can obtain the tokens of the members and check which member's index is used to generate the challenging signature. In our scheme, we separate the construction of the revocation tokens from the generation of the secret signing keys. Thus, we can provide all the secret signing keys to the adversary as in the full anonymity, without any issue.

Even though the full anonymity does not manage revocation queries, we allow the adversary to request revocation tokens. But, we will not provide challenged members' tokens to the adversary, or we will not generate challenged signatures for the member-indices whose tokens are already revealed by the adversary. This restricted version of the full-anonymity is known as *almost-full anonymity*. We adapt the almost-full anonymity suggested in [28] to cope with registration query to prove the security of our scheme. Thus, we propose a new security notion called *dynamical-almost-full anonymity* which is a restricted version of the full anonymity and extended version of the almost-full anonymity for fully dynamic group signatures with VLR and member registration.

Since the previous VLR schemes like the scheme in [19] have not considered member registration separately, they generated members' keys at the setup stage with the group public key. In our scheme, we separate member registration and allow new members to join the group with their secret keys as in [20]. Thus, in the member registration, we provide a simple method to generate keys for the members by using the group public key. First, we use trapdoors [15] to generate the group public key and the authority keys at the setup phase. Since the group manager needs to know the revoking member's revocation token, we allow new members to generate only their secret signing keys at the joining protocol. The group manager issues the revocation token with the member certification. When a member misbehaved, the group manager can revoke the misbehaved member by adding that member's token to the list called *revocation list* (*RL*) and updating the verifiers with the latest *RL* as any VLR scheme. When verifying a signature, verifiers have to check the validity of the signer using the latest *RL*.

Moreover, we provide an *explicit tracing algorithm* to trace signers. The *implicit tracing algorithm* presented in VLR requires executing Verify for each member until the relevant member is found. Since the time consumption is high in the implicit tracing algorithm, it is not convenient for large groups. Hence, if necessary the tracer can use the explicit tracing algorithm instead of using the implicit tracing algorithm for tracing signers.

2   Preliminaries

2.1   Notations

For any integer $k \geq 1$, we denote the set of integers $\{1, \ldots, k\}$ by $[k]$. We denote matrices by bold upper-case letters such as $\mathbf{A}$, and vectors by bold lower-case letters, such as $\mathbf{x}$. We assume that all vectors are in column form. The concatenation of matrices $\mathbf{A} \in \mathbb{R}^{n \times m}$ and $\mathbf{B} \in \mathbb{R}^{n \times k}$ is denoted by $[\mathbf{A}|\mathbf{B}] \in \mathbb{R}^{n \times (m+k)}$. The concatenation of vectors $\mathbf{x} \in \mathbb{R}^m$ and $\mathbf{y} \in \mathbb{R}^k$ is denoted by $(\mathbf{x}\|\mathbf{y}) \in \mathbb{R}^{m+k}$. If S is a finite set, $b \xleftarrow{\$} S$ means that b is chosen uniformly at random from S. If S is a probability distribution $b \xleftarrow{\$} S$ means that b is drawn according to S. The Euclidean norm of $\mathbf{x}$ is denoted by $\|\mathbf{x}\|$ and the infinity norm is denoted by $\|\mathbf{x}\|_\infty$. Let χ be a b-bounded distribution over $\mathbb{Z}$ (i.e., samples that output by χ is with norm at most b with overwhelming probability where $b = \sqrt{n}\omega(\log n)$).

2.2   Lattices

Let q be a prime and $\mathbf{B} = [\mathbf{b}_1 | \cdots | \mathbf{b}_m] \in \mathbb{Z}_q^{r \times m}$ be linearly independent vectors in $\mathbb{Z}_q^r$. The r-dimensional lattice $\Lambda(\mathbf{B})$ for $\mathbf{B}$ is defined as

$$\Lambda(\mathbf{B}) = \{\mathbf{y} \in \mathbb{Z}^r \mid \mathbf{y} \equiv \mathbf{Bx} \bmod q \text{ for some } \mathbf{x} \in \mathbb{Z}_q^m\},$$

which is the set of all linear combinations of columns of $\mathbf{B}$. The value m is the rank of $\mathbf{B}$.

We consider a discrete Gaussian distribution with respect to a lattice. The Gaussian function centered in a vector $\mathbf{c}$ with parameter $s > 0$ is defined as $\rho_{s,\mathbf{c}}(\mathbf{x}) = e^{-\pi \|(\mathbf{x}-\mathbf{c})/s\|^2}$ and the corresponding probability density function proportional to $\rho_{s,\mathbf{c}}$ is defined as $D_{s,\mathbf{c}}(\mathbf{x}) = \rho_{s,\mathbf{c}}(\mathbf{x})/s^n$ for all $\mathbf{x} \in \mathbb{R}^n$. With respect to a lattice Λ the discrete Gaussian distribution is defined as $D_{\Lambda,s,\mathbf{c}}(\mathbf{x}) = D_{s,\mathbf{c}}(\mathbf{x})/D_{s,\mathbf{c}}(\Lambda) = \rho_{s,\mathbf{c}}(\mathbf{x})/\rho_{s,\mathbf{c}}(\Lambda)$ for all $\mathbf{x} \in \Lambda$. Since $\mathbb{Z}^m$ is also a lattice, we can define a discrete Gaussian distribution for $\mathbb{Z}^m$. By $D_{\mathbb{Z}^m,\sigma}$, we denote the discrete Gaussian distribution for $\mathbb{Z}^m$ around the origin with the standard deviation σ.

2.3   Lattice-Related Computational Problems

The security of our scheme relies on the hardness of the two lattice-based problems defined below.

Learning with Errors (LWE)

Definition 1. *Learning With Errors (LWE) [27] is parametrized by integers $n, m \geq 1$, and $q \geq 2$. For a vector $\mathbf{s} \in \mathbb{Z}_q^n$ and χ, the distribution $\mathrm{A}_{s,\chi}$ is obtained by sampling $\mathbf{a} \in \mathbb{Z}_q^n$ uniformly at random and choosing $\mathrm{e} \leftarrow \chi$, and outputting the pair $(\mathbf{a}, \mathbf{a}^T \cdot \mathbf{s} + \mathrm{e})$.*

There are two LWE problems. They are Search-LWE and Decision-LWE. While Search-LWE is to find the secret $\mathbf{s}$ given LWE samples, Decision-LWE is to distinguish LWE samples and samples chosen according to the uniformly distribution. We use the hardness of Decision-LWE problem.

For a prime power q, $b \geq \sqrt{n}\omega(\log n)$, and distribution χ, solving $LWE_{n,q,\chi}$ problem is at least as hard as solving $SIVP_\gamma$ (*Shortest Independent Vector Problem*), where $\gamma = \tilde{\mathcal{O}}(nq/b)$ [15,29].

Short Integer Solution ($SIS_{n,m,q,\beta}$). SIS was first discussed in seminal work of Ajtai [2]. SIS problem asks to find a sufficiently short nontrivial integer combination of given uniformly random elements of a certain large finite additive group, which sums to zero [27].

Definition 2. *Short Integer Solution ($SIS_{n,m,q,\beta}$ [27,29]) is as follows. Given m uniformly random vectors $\boldsymbol{a}_i \in \mathbb{Z}_q^n$, forming the columns of a matrix $\boldsymbol{A} \in \mathbb{Z}_q^{n \times m}$, find a nonzero vector $\boldsymbol{x} \in \mathbb{Z}^m$ such that $\|\boldsymbol{x}\| \leq \beta$ and $\boldsymbol{Ax} = 0 \bmod q$.*

For any m, β, and for any $q > \sqrt{n}\beta$, solving $SIS_{n,m,q,\beta}$ problem with nonnegligible probability is at least as hard as solving $SIVP_\gamma$ problem, for some $\gamma = \beta \cdot \mathrm{O}(\sqrt{n})$ [15].

2.4 Lattice-Related Algorithms

We use a randomized nearest-plane algorithm SampleD, which is discussed in [15,24] in our scheme's construction. The algorithm SampleD samples from a discrete Gaussian $D_{\Lambda,s,\mathbf{c}}$ over any lattice Λ. The version given in [24] is defined below.

- SampleD($\mathbf{R}$, $\mathbf{A}$, $\mathbf{u}$, σ) takes as inputs a vector $\mathbf{u}$ in the image of $\mathbf{A}$, a trapdoor $\mathbf{R}$, and $\sigma = \omega(\sqrt{n \log q \log n})$, and outputs $\mathbf{x} \in \mathbb{Z}^m$ sampled from the distribution $D_{\mathbb{Z}^m,\sigma}$, where $\mathbf{x}$ should satisfy the condition $\mathbf{A} \cdot \mathbf{x} = \mathbf{u} \bmod q$.

Preimage sampleable trapdoor functions (PSTFs) [15] are defined by probabilistic polynomial-time algorithms. We use PSTFs discussed in [1,15,24].

- GenTrap(n, m, q) is an efficient randomized algorithm. For any given integers $n \geq 1, q \geq 2$, and sufficiently large $m = O(n \log q)$, GenTrap(n, m, q) outputs a matrix $\mathbf{A} \in \mathbb{Z}_q^{n \times m}$ and a trapdoor matrix $\mathbf{R}$. The distribution of the output $\mathbf{A}$ is negl(n)-far from the uniform distribution.

2.5 Other Tools

We denote the security parameter by n, and the maximum number of expected users in a group by $N = 2^\ell$. Depending on the security parameter n, other parameters we used are as in Table 1.

Table 1. Parameters of the scheme

Parameter	Value or asymptotic bound
Modulus q	$\omega(n^2 \log n)$
Dimension m	$\geq 2n \log q$
Gaussian parameter σ	$\omega(\sqrt{n \log q \log n})$
Integer norm bound β	$\lceil \sigma \cdot \log m \rceil$
Number of protocol repetitions t	$\omega(\log n)$

In the construction of our scheme, we use one-time signature scheme $\mathcal{OTS}$ = (OGen, OSign, OVer) [25]. $\mathcal{OTS}$ schemes are based on one-way functions, and they are simpler to implement and are computationally efficient than trapdoor functions. $\mathcal{OTS}$ schemes are digital signature schemes. Since $\mathcal{OTS}$ requires the signer to generate keys for each message to be signed newly, keys formed for each message are unique for the particular messages. OGen is the key generation algorithm, which takes as an input (1^n), and outputs a signing, verification key pair (**osk**, **ovk**). OSign is the signing algorithm, which uses the key **osk** and a message M as inputs, and outputs a signature Σ. OVer is the verification algorithm, which is a deterministic algorithm that takes as inputs the key **ovk**, the message M, and the signature Σ to validate the signature Σ. Depending on the validation of the signature, OVer outputs $\top$ or $\bot$ [14].

3   Achieving Security for VLR Schemes with Registration

This section first describes the security requirements of group signatures. Then we discuss VLR group signature schemes. Later, we explain the difficulties of achieving full-anonymity for VLR group signature schemes and put forward a new security notion called *dynamical-almost-full anonymity* that manages anonymity of VLR group signature schemes with member registration.

3.1   Security Requirements

The group signatures, which were introduced by Chaum and van Heyst [13] provided two main features called *anonymity* and *traceability*. *Anonymity* requires any adversary is not able to discover the signer. *Traceability* requires no one can create a signature that cannot be traced by the group manager. Nevertheless, in last decades, more security requirements have been presented. Bellare et al. [4] (BMW03 model) provided two appropriate security notions called *full-anonymity* and *full-traceability* that formalize the previous security requirements.

Full-anonymity requires no adversary can identify the signer same as in the anonymity suggested in [13]. But, in the full-anonymity, the adversary is stronger since he may corrupt all the members including the one issuing the signature. Moreover, he can view the outcome that group manager sees when tracing a signer.

Full-traceability also much stronger than the traceability in the past and it also acts as a strong version of collusion-resistance. Thus, a group of colluding group members who pool their secret keys cannot create a signature that belongs to none of them; even they know the secret key of the group manager. Thus, in the full traceability game, the adversary can query signatures for any message and index, and he can corrupt any member.

In the scheme in [5], non-frameability is separated from the traceability. In *traceability* game, the tracing manager's secret key is provided to the adversary but, the group manager's secret key is not provided. Thus, the adversary cannot create untraceable dummy members. But in *non-frameability*, the group manager's and the tracing manager's secret keys are given to the adversary.

3.2   VLR Group Signatures

The functionality of member revocation is a desirable requirement of any group signature since misbehaved members should be removed from the group and restricted them signing on behalf of the group. The simplest method is generating all the keys newly including public keys and secret keys (except for revoking member) when a member is revoked and broadcasting the new keys to existing members and verifiers. But this method is not appropriate for large groups. Bresson and Stern [8] suggested an approach that requires signers to prove that his member certification is not in the public revocation list at the time of signing. Since the signature size increases with the number of revoked members in this method, it is also not suitable for large groups. Later Camenisch et al. [11]

proposed an approach using dynamic accumulators, where the *accumulator* is an algorithm that allows hashing a large set of inputs to one shorter value, and the *dynamic accumulator* allows to add or delete inputs dynamically. However, this approach requires members to keep track of revoked user information, and needs to update their membership. Thus in this approach, workloads of the current group members increase. A different revocation method called *Verifier-local Revocation (VLR)* was proposed by Brickell [9] and formalized by Boneh et al. [6] in their group signature scheme. Other than the scheme in [6], schemes like [21, 28] use VLR to manage member revocation.

Verifier-local Revocation (VLR) uses a token system to manage the status of the members. Each member has a revocation token other than their secret signing keys. When a member is revoked, his revocation token is added to a list called *Revocation list (RL)* and passed to the verifiers. Thus, the verifiers can check the validity of the signer using the latest *RL*. Since VLR does not require to generate keys newly or keep track of information for the existing members, it is more convenient than any other approach. It simply asks to update the verifiers who are less than the members in number when a member is revoked. Thus, it is suitable for any size of groups.

In general, group signature schemes consist of four algorithms, KeyGen, Sign, Verify, and Open. VLR group signature schemes consist of former three algorithms, and VLR scheme has an *implicit tracing algorithm* for tracing signers instead of Open.

- KeyGen(n,N): This randomized PPT algorithm takes as inputs n and N. Then it outputs a group public key **gpk**, a vector of user secret keys **gsk** = (**gsk**[0], **gsk**[1], ..., **gsk**[$N-1$]), and a vector of user revocation tokens **grt** = (**grt**[0], **grt**[1], ..., **grt**[$N-1$]), where **gsk**[i] is the i-th user's secret key and **grt**[i] is his revocation token.
- Sign(**gpk**, **gsk**[d], M): This randomized algorithm takes as inputs the group public key **gpk**, a secret signing key **gsk**[d], and a message $M \in \{0,1\}^*$. Sign generates a group signature Σ on M.
- Verify(**gpk**, RL, Σ, M): This deterministic algorithm verifies whether the given signature Σ is a valid signature on given message M using the given group public key **gpk**. Moreover, Verify validates the signer is not being revoked using RL.

Implicit Tracing Algorithm: Any VLR group signature scheme has an *implicit tracing algorithm*. The implicit tracing algorithm uses **grt** as the tracing key. For a given valid message-signature pair (M, Σ), an authorized person can run Verify(**gpk**, RL=**grt**[i], Σ, M) for $i = 0, 1, \cdots, N-1$ until Verify returns *invalid*. The index of the signer is the first index $i^* \in \{0, 1, \cdots, N-1\}$ that Verify returns invalid. The implicit tracing algorithm fails if Verify verifies properly for all users on the given signature. Since the implicit tracing algorithm requires to run Verify linear times in N, it is inappropriate for large groups. In comparison to the algorithm Open, its time consumption is high.

Though VLR is the comparably convenient approach for any group signatures, the existing lattice-based group signature schemes with VLR such as

[19] relies on a weaker security notion called *selfless-anonymity*. Not like the full-anonymity, the selfless-anonymity has some limitations. According to the BMW03 model, in the full-anonymity game between a challenger and an adversary, all the secret keys of the group members including challenging keys are given to the adversary at the beginning of the game. But, in the selfless-anonymity game, the adversary is not given any secret keys. He can query secret keys at the query phase but not related to the challenging indices. However, the adversary is allowed for the queries; *Signing*, *Corruption*, and *Revocation*.

3.3   Achieving Stronger Security for VLR Schemes with Member Registration

Our scheme is for managing both member registration and revocation. Thus, the almost-full anonymity suggested in [28] is not sufficient for our scheme. We modify the almost-full anonymity by adding the registration query. Moreover, we add some restrictions to manage the attacks of the adversary. We concern how to secure our scheme (i) when the adversary joins the group as a legal user before the game starts and (ii) when he requests to join the group after the game begins. When any user joins the group, we provide revocation tokens to them. So the adversary can get the revocation tokens by adding new users. In concern (i), the adversary is getting the revocation tokens when joining the group before the game starts (he is a legal user) and he can use those indices in challenge phase after the game starts. Since the adversary has not queried those revocation tokens, this is not tracked by the almost-full anonymity. As a solution for the above concerns, we suggest a new security notion called *dynamical-almost-full anonymity*, which is an extended version of the almost-full anonymity for fully dynamic group signatures with VLR and member registration.

In the dynamical-almost-full anonymity, we allow the adversary to add new members to the group at the anonymity game as same as in previous group signature schemes like [5, 23] and we maintain a global list called **RU**. **RU** is used to track the details of the new members that the adversary adds via the registration query. **RU** only consists of indices of the members that the adversary added. Tracking the new user details is also done in the previous group signature schemes like in [5, 23]. However, we will not provide the revocation tokens of the new users at the registration query, but the adversary can request revocation tokens using the revocation query. At the challenge stage, we check **RU** and only generate the challenging signature for the indices in **RU**, but those are not used for the revocation queries. By creating challenging signature only for the indices in **RU** we give a solution to the concern (i) and not providing the revocation tokens for the members at the registration query we give a solution to the problem (ii). The dynamical-almost-full anonymity game between a challenger and an adversary is as follows.

– **Initial Phase:** The challenger C runs KeyGen to get a group public key **gpk**, authority secret keys (**ik**,**ok**). Then gives **gpk** and existing group members' secret signing keys **gsk** to the adversary A, and creates a new list **RU**.

- **Query Phase:** A can query any token (**grt**) of any user and can access the opening oracle, which results with $\mathsf{Open}(\mathbf{ok}, M, \Sigma)$. Moreover, A can add new users to the group using registration query. If the new user is valid and not already in the registration table *reg*, then C adds new user to the group. Then C generates token for the new user and updates both *reg* and **RU**. However, C does not return the token of the new user to A.
- **Challenge Phase:** A outputs a message M^* and two distinct identities i_0, i_1. If A already not queried the revocation tokens of i_0, i_1 and if i_0, i_1 are in **RU**, then C selects a bit $b \overset{\$}{\leftarrow} \{0,1\}$, generates $\Sigma^* = \mathsf{Sign}(\mathbf{gpk}, \mathbf{gsk}[i_b], M^*)$ and sends Σ^* to A. A still can query the opening oracle except the signature challenged and he is not allowed for revocation queries with challenging indices. A can add users to the group.
- **Guessing Phase:** Finally, A outputs a bit b', the guess of b. If $b' = b$, then A wins.

4 Our Scheme

In our scheme, there are two authorities, group manager and, tracing manager. The group manager interacts with new users who want to become group members and issues membership-certifications to the valid users. Moreover, he manages the member revocation. The tracing manager discovers the signers. Each manager has their public and privates keys. We assume the group manager and new users interact through a secure channel. The users generate their secret signing keys, and they can sign messages once the group manager accepted them as group members. The group manager creates group members' tokens. To track the details of the members, we maintain a registration table *reg*.

Every new user has to interact with the group manager by presenting a valid signature. The new user i, who has a personal public and private key pair $(upk[i], usk[i])$ (as in [5]), samples a short vector $\mathbf{x}_i \leftarrow D_{\mathbb{Z}^{4m}, \sigma}$ and computes $\mathbf{z}_i$ using $\mathbf{x}_i$ and $\mathbf{F}$, where $\mathbf{F}$ is a public parameter. Then the new user generates a signature Σ_{join} by signing $\mathbf{z}_i$ with his personal private key $usk[i]$. When the group manager receives the massage-signature pair $(\mathbf{z}_i, \Sigma_{join})$, first he checks whether $\mathbf{z}_i$ is used before. If $\mathbf{z}_i$ is not used before, then the group manager verifies Σ_{join} on $\mathbf{z}_i$ using the user's personal public key $upk[i]$. Then he samples the new user's revocation token and updates the registration table *reg* with the new user's details. Finally, the group manager sends revocation token to the user. Now the new user (group member) can sign messages on behalf of the group.

4.1 Supporting Zero-Knowledge Protocol

This section provides a general description of zero-knowledge argument system that we use in our scheme. Many other lattice-based schemes like [19,20,22] also use ZKAoK to prove the verifier that the signer is valid in zero-knowledge.

Let COM be the statistically hiding and computationally binding commitment scheme described in [17]. We use matrices $\mathbf{F}$, $\mathbf{A}$, $\mathbf{B}$, $\mathbf{V}$, $\mathbf{G}$, $\mathbf{H}$ and vectors $\mathbf{u}$, $\mathbf{v}$, $\mathbf{c}_1$, $\mathbf{c}_2$ as public parameters. The prover's witness consists of vectors

$\mathbf{x}$, $\mathrm{bin}(\mathbf{z})$, $\mathbf{r}$, $\mathbf{s}$, $\mathbf{e}_1$, and $\mathbf{e}_2$. The prover's goal is to convince the verifier that $\mathbf{F} \cdot \mathbf{x} = \mathbf{H}_{4n \times 2m} \cdot \mathrm{bin}(\mathbf{z})$ (as discussed in [20]), $\mathbf{V} \cdot (\mathbf{A} \cdot \mathbf{r}) + \mathbf{e}_1 = \mathbf{v} \mod q$ (as discussed in [19]), and $(\mathbf{c}_1 = \mathbf{B}^T \mathbf{s} + \mathbf{e}_1, \mathbf{c}_2 = \mathbf{G}^T \mathbf{s} + \mathbf{e}_2 + \lfloor q/2 \rfloor \mathrm{bin}(\mathbf{z}_i))$ (as discussed in [22]). Here $\mathbf{H}_{n \times n \lceil \log q \rceil} \in \mathbb{Z}^{n \times n \lceil \log q \rceil}$ is a "power-of-2" matrix and $\mathbf{z} = \mathbf{H}_{n \times n \lceil \log q \rceil} \cdot \mathrm{bin}(\mathbf{z})$ for any $\mathbf{z} \in \mathbb{Z}_q^n$.

4.2   Description of Our Scheme

This section describes the algorithms of our scheme. Our scheme consists of six algorithms namely, KeyGen, Join, Sign, Verify, Open, and Revoke. The former five algorithms follow the techniques given in [20]. We adapt algorithms presented in [20] to compatible with member revocation mechanism. We use algorithm Revoke to manage member revocation.

Setup: The randomized algorithm $\mathsf{KeyGen}(1^n, 1^N)$ works as follows.

1. Run PPT algorithm $\mathsf{GenTrap}(n, m, q)$ to get $\mathbf{A} \in \mathbb{Z}_q^{n \times m}$ and a trapdoor $\mathbf{T_A}$.
2. Sample vector $\mathbf{u} \xleftarrow{\$} \mathbb{Z}_q^n$.
3. Generate encryption and decryption keys by running $\mathsf{GenTrap}(n, m, q)$ to get $\mathbf{B} \in \mathbb{Z}_q^{n \times m}$ and a trapdoor $\mathbf{T_B}$.
4. Sample matrix $\mathbf{F} \xleftarrow{\$} \mathbb{Z}_q^{4n \times 4m}$.
5. Finally output, the group public key $\mathbf{gpk} := (\mathbf{A}, \mathbf{B}, \mathbf{F}, \mathbf{u})$, the group manager's (issuer's) secret key $\mathbf{ik} := \mathbf{T_A}$ and the opener's secret key $\mathbf{ok} := \mathbf{T_B}$.

Join: A new user i, who has a personal public key and private key pair $(\mathbf{upk}[i], \mathbf{usk}[i])$ can interact with the group manager (issuer) to join the group as follow.

1. User i samples a discrete Gaussian vector $\mathbf{x}_i \leftarrow D_{\mathbb{Z}^{4m}, \sigma}$, and computes $\mathbf{z}_i \leftarrow \mathbf{F} \cdot \mathbf{x}_i \in \mathbb{Z}_q^{4n}$. Then he generates a signature $\Sigma_{join} \leftarrow \mathsf{Sig}(\mathbf{usk}[i], \mathbf{z}_i)$ and sends both $\mathbf{z}_i$, and Σ_{join} to the group manager.
2. The group manager GM verifies that $\mathbf{z}_i$ was not used by any user previously, by checking the registration table reg. Then he verifies Σ_{join} is a valid signature on $\mathbf{z}_i$, using $\mathsf{Vf}(\mathbf{upk}[i], \mathbf{z}_i, \Sigma_{join})$. He aborts if any condition fails. Otherwise he will sign the user's index $d = \mathrm{bin}(\mathbf{z}_i)$, the binary representation of $\mathbf{z}_i$, using group manager's private key and generates the certificate for the index $cert\text{-}index_i = \mathsf{Sign}(\mathbf{ik}, \mathrm{bin}(\mathbf{z}_i))$.

   The group manager selects $\mathbf{R}_i \xleftarrow{\$} \mathbb{Z}_q^{n \times 4n}$ and computes $\mathbf{w}_i = \mathbf{R}_i \cdot \mathbf{z}_i$. Then he samples a vector $\mathbf{r}_i \in \mathbb{Z}^m \leftarrow \mathsf{SampleD}(\mathbf{T_A}, \mathbf{A}, \mathbf{u} - \mathbf{w}_i, \sigma)$, and generates the certificate for the token $cert\text{-}token_i = \mathsf{Sign}(\mathbf{ik}, (\mathbf{A} \cdot \mathbf{r}_i))$ $(\mathbf{ik} = \mathbf{T_A})$.

   Then he saves the details of the new member (user) i in the registration table $reg[i] \leftarrow (i, d, \mathbf{upk}[i], \mathbf{z}_i, \Sigma_{join}, \mathbf{R}_i, \mathbf{w}_i, \mathbf{r}_i, 1)$ and makes the record active (1). Finally, GM sends the $cert_i = (cert\text{-}index_i, cert\text{-}token_i, \mathbf{R}_i, (\mathbf{A} \cdot \mathbf{r}_i))$ as the new member's member-certificate.

Sign: $\mathsf{Sign}(\mathbf{gpk}, \mathbf{gsk}[i], cert_i, M)$ is a randomized algorithm, that generates a signature Σ on a given message M using $\mathbf{gsk}[i] = \mathbf{x}_i$ as follows.

1. Let $\mathcal{H}_1: \{0,1\}^* \to \mathbb{Z}_q^{n \times \ell}$, $\mathcal{H}_2: \{0,1\}^* \to \{1,2,3\}^t$ and $\mathcal{G}: \{0,1\}^* \to \mathbb{Z}_q^{n \times m}$ be hash functions, modeled as a random oracle.
2. Parse $\mathbf{gpk}$ as $(\mathbf{A}, \mathbf{B}, \mathbf{F}, \mathbf{u})$ and $cert_i$ as $(cert\text{-}index_i, cert\text{-}token_i, \mathbf{R}_i, (\mathbf{A} \cdot \mathbf{r}_i))$.
3. Run $\mathsf{OGen}(1^n) \to (\mathbf{ovk}, \mathbf{osk})$.
4. Encrypt the index $d = \mathsf{bin}(\mathbf{z}_i)$, where $\mathbf{z}_i = \mathbf{F} \cdot \mathbf{x}_i$.
   a) Let $\mathbf{G} = \mathcal{H}_1(\mathbf{ovk}) \in \mathbb{Z}_q^{n \times 2m}$.
   b) Sample $\mathbf{s} \leftarrow \chi^n$, $\mathbf{e}_1 \leftarrow \chi^m$ and $\mathbf{e}_2 \leftarrow \chi^\ell$.
   c) Compute the ciphertext $(\mathbf{c}_1, \mathbf{c}_2)$ pair
      $(\mathbf{c}_1 = \mathbf{B}^T \mathbf{s} + \mathbf{e}_1, \; \mathbf{c}_2 = \mathbf{G}^T \mathbf{s} + \mathbf{e}_2 + \lfloor q/2 \rfloor \mathsf{bin}(\mathbf{z}_i))$.
5. Sample $\rho \xleftarrow{\$} \{0,1\}^n$, let $\mathbf{V} = \mathcal{G}(\mathbf{A}, \mathbf{u}, M, \rho) \in \mathbb{Z}_q^{n \times m}$.
6. Compute $\mathbf{v} = \mathbf{V} \cdot (\mathbf{A} \cdot \mathbf{r}_i) + \mathbf{e}_1 \mod q$ ($\|\mathbf{e}_1\|_\infty \le \beta$ with overwhelming probability).
7. Execute $\mathsf{Verify}(\mathbf{A}, \mathsf{bin}(\mathbf{z}_i), cert\text{-}index_i)$ to prove $cert\text{-}index_i$ is generated on $\mathsf{bin}(\mathbf{z}_i)$ and $\mathsf{Verify}(\mathbf{A}, (\mathbf{A} \cdot \mathbf{r}_i), cert\text{-}token_i)$ to prove $cert\text{-}token_i$ is generated on $(\mathbf{A} \cdot \mathbf{r}_i)$. Then generate a proof as in Sect. 4.1, that the user is valid, honestly computed above $\mathbf{v}$, and index is correctly encrypted. By repeating the basic protocol of KTX commitment scheme in Sect. 4.1 $t = \omega(\log n)$ times to make the soundness error negligible. Then we make it non-interactive using the Fiat-Shamir heuristic as a triple, $\Pi = (\{CMT^{(k)}\}_{k=1}^t, CH, \{RSP^{(k)}\}_{k=1}^t)$, where $CH = (\{Ch^{(k)}\}_{k=1}^t) = \mathcal{H}_2(M, \{CMT^{(k)}\}_{k=1}^t, \mathbf{c}_1, \mathbf{c}_2)$.
8. Compute $\mathcal{OTS}; sig = \mathsf{OSig}(\mathbf{osk}, (\mathbf{c}_1, \mathbf{c}_2, \Pi))$.
9. Output signature $\Sigma = (\mathbf{ovk}, (\mathbf{c}_1, \mathbf{c}_2), \rho, \Pi, sig, \mathbf{v})$.

Verify: The deterministic algorithm $\mathsf{Verify}(\mathbf{gpk}, M, \Sigma, RL)$ works as follows, where $RL = \{\{\mathbf{u}_i\}_i\}$.

1. Parse the signature Σ as $(\mathbf{ovk}, (\mathbf{c}_1, \mathbf{c}_2), \rho, \Pi, sig, \mathbf{v})$.
2. Get $\mathbf{V} = \mathcal{G}(\mathbf{A}, \mathbf{u}, M, \rho) \in \mathbb{Z}_q^{n \times m}$.
3. If $\mathsf{OVer}(\mathbf{ovk}, ((\mathbf{c}_1, \mathbf{c}_2), \Pi), sig) = 0$ then return 0.
4. Parse Π as $(\{CMT^{(k)}\}_{k=1}^t, \{Ch^{(k)}\}_{k=1}^t, \{RSP^{(k)}\}_{k=1}^t)$.
5. If $(Ch^{(1)}, \ldots, Ch^{(t)}) \ne \mathcal{H}_2(M, \{CMT^{(k)}\}_{k=1}^t, \mathbf{c}_1, \mathbf{c}_2)$ return 0 else proceed.
6. For $k = 1$ to t run the verification steps of the commitment scheme to validate $RSP^{(k)}$ with respect to $CMT^{(k)}$ and $Ch^{(k)}$. If any of the conditions fails then output invalid.
7. For each $\mathbf{u}_i \in RL$ compute $\mathbf{e}'_i = \mathbf{v} - \mathbf{V} \cdot \mathbf{u}_i \mod q$ to check whether there exists an index i such that $\|\mathbf{e}'_i\|_\infty \le \beta$. If so return invalid.
8. Return valid.

Open: $\mathsf{Open}(\mathbf{gpk}, \mathbf{ok}, reg, M, \Sigma)$ functions as follows, where $\mathbf{ok} = \mathbf{T_B}$.

1. Let $\mathbf{G} = \mathcal{H}_1(\mathbf{ovk})$.
2. Then using $\mathbf{T_B}$ compute a small norm matrix $\mathbf{Y} \in \mathbb{Z}^{m \times 2m}$, where $\mathbf{B} \cdot \mathbf{Y} = \mathbf{G} \mod q$.

3. Compute $\mathsf{bin}(\mathbf{z}_i) = \lfloor (\mathbf{c}_2 - \mathbf{Y}^T \cdot \mathbf{c}_1)/(q/2) \rceil$, determine the signer using reg corresponds to $\mathsf{bin}(\mathbf{z}_i)$, and output the index.

Revoke: The algorithm $\mathsf{Revoke}(\mathbf{gpk}, \mathbf{ik}, i, reg, \mathrm{RL})$ functions as follows.

1. Query reg for i and obtain revoking member's revocation token $(\mathbf{A} \cdot \mathbf{r}_i)$.
2. Add $(\mathbf{A} \cdot \mathbf{r}_i)$ to RL and update $reg[i]$ to inactive (0).
3. Return RL.

5 Correctness and Security Analysis of the Scheme

To define correctness and the security requirements we use a set of experiments consisted of a set of oracles which can be executed by the adversary. We maintain a set of global lists, which are used by the oracles and performed by the challenger C. When the adversary A adds a new user to the group (registration query), and if the new user is excepted as a new member, his index is added to a list called **RU**. When A corrupts any user, then that user's index is added to **CUL**. **SL** contains the signatures that obtained from Sign oracle. When A requests a signature, the generated signature is added to **SL** with the index and the message. When A accesses Challenge oracle, the generated signature is added to **CL** with the message sent. When A reveals any user-revocation token, the challenger adds that user index to **TU**. When A reveals any user-secret signing key then that user index is added to **BU**. We use a set S to maintain a set of revoked users.

The oracles that we use in the experiments are as follows.

- AddU(i): The adversary A can add a user $i \in \mathbb{N}$ to the group as an honest user. The oracle adds i to **RU**. But the new user's revocation token is not returned to the adversary.
- CrptU(i, upk): A can corrupt user i by setting its personal public key $\mathbf{upk}[i]$ to upk. The oracle adds i to **CUL**, and initializes the issuer's state in *group-joining protocol*.
- SendToGM(i, M_{in}): A corrupts user i, and engages in *group-joining protocol* with Issue-executing issuer. The adversary provides i and M_{in} to the oracle. The oracle which maintains the Issue state, returns the outgoing message, and adds a record to reg.
- SendToUser(i, M_{in}): A corrupts the issuer and engages in *group-joining protocol* with Join-executing user. The adversary passes i and M_{in} to the oracle. The oracle which maintains the user i state, returns the outgoing message, and sets the private signing key of i to the final state of Join.
- RevealSk(i): A can retrieve the secret signing key of the user i. The oracle updates **BU** and returns $\mathbf{gsk}[i]$.
- RevealRt(i): A can retrieve the revocation token of user i, and the oracle returns revocation token and adds i to **TU**.
- ReadReg(i): A reads the information of i in reg.
- ModifyReg(i, val): A modifies $reg[i]$ by setting val.

– Sign(i, M): A obtains a signature Σ for a given message M and user i who is an honest user and has private signing key.
– Chal$_b$(i_0, i_1, M): This oracle is for defining anonymity and provides a group signature for the given message M under the private signing key of i_b, as long as both i_0, i_1 are active and honest users having private signing keys (in $\mathbf{RU}$). Moreover, those indices should not being used to reveal revocation tokens (not in $\mathbf{BU}$).
– Revoke(i): A can request to revoke user i. The oracle updates the record to 0 for i in reg and adds revocation token of i to the set S.
– Open(M, Σ): A can access the *opening* oracle with a message M and a signature Σ to obtain the identity of the user, who generated the signature Σ. If Σ is generated at Chal$_b$, then oracle will abort.

In addition, we use the following simple polynomial-time algorithm for ease.

– IsActive(i,reg): This algorithm determines whether the member i is active by querying the registration table reg and outputs either 0 or 1.

5.1 Correctness

$\mathbf{Exp}_{FDGS,A}^{corr}(\lambda)$

$(\mathbf{gpk}, \mathbf{ok}, \mathbf{ik}) \leftarrow \mathsf{GKg}(1^\lambda);$ $\mathbf{RU} \leftarrow \emptyset;$
$(i, M) \leftarrow A(\mathbf{gpk}; \mathsf{AddU}, \mathsf{ReadReg}, \mathsf{Revoke}, \mathsf{RevealRt});$
If $i \notin \mathbf{RU}$ or $\mathbf{gsk}[i] = \varepsilon$ or $cert_i = \varepsilon$ or $\mathsf{IsActive}(i, reg) = 0$ then return 0.
$\Sigma \leftarrow \mathsf{Sign}(\mathbf{gpk}, \mathbf{gsk}[i], cert_i, M);$
If $\mathsf{Verify}(\mathbf{gpk}, M, \Sigma, S) = 0$ then return 1.
$(i') \leftarrow \mathsf{Open}(\mathbf{gpk}, \mathbf{ok}, reg, M, \Sigma);$
If $i \neq i'$ then return 1.
Return 0.

First note Verify accepts signatures, which are only generated by active and honest users. If signer's revocation token is in RL, then his signature is not accepted. Steps 6 and 7 in both Sign and Verify guarantee this condition. Completeness of the underlying argument system guarantees that the valid signatures are always accepted and soundness of the underlying argument system guarantees that a revoked signer cannot pass the test. Open outputs the index of the signer with overwhelming probability. It computes $\mathsf{bin}(\mathbf{z}_i)$ and extracts the details of the signer from reg.

5.2 Anonymity

Theorem 1. *In the random oracle model, our scheme is dynamical-almost-full anonymous if $LWE_{n,q,\chi}$ problem is hard to solve.*

$\mathbf{Exp}_{FDGS,A}^{anon\text{-}b}(\lambda)$

$(\mathbf{gpk}, \mathbf{ok}, \mathbf{ik}) \leftarrow \mathsf{GKg}(1^\lambda);$ $\mathbf{RU}, \mathbf{CUL}, \mathbf{SL}, \mathbf{CL}, \mathbf{BU}, \mathbf{TU} \leftarrow \emptyset;$
$b^* \leftarrow A(\mathbf{gpk}, \mathbf{gsk};$

AddU, CrptU, SendToUser, RevealSk, RevealRt, Open, ModifyReg, Revoke, Chal$_b$);
Return b^*;

We prove that our scheme is dynamical-almost-full anonymous via a sequence of games.

Game 0: This is the above-defined experiment. The challenger C runs Key-Gen($1^n, 1^N$) to obtain group public keys and authority keys. Next, C gives the group public key **gpk** and all the existing group members' secret keys **gsk** to the adversary A. In the query phase, A can request for revocation tokens of any member, and A can access opening for any signature. Moreover, A can add new members to the group. C validates the new members and adds records to the registration table reg and **RU**. But C will not provide the revocation tokens of the new members without a request of A. Thus, the member certification will not be provided at the registration query and the challenger returns a success message only. When A corrupts the users, those users' indices are added to **CUL** and when he revokes users, those users' indices are added to S with tokens of them. Moreover, when A reveals any user token, C adds those users' indices to **TU** and returns the member certificate $cert$. In the challenge phase, A sends two indices (i_0, i_1) with a message M^*. If (i_0, i_1) are newly added as per **RU** and are not used for querying revocation tokens (not in **TU**), then C generates and sends back a signature $\Sigma^* = (\mathbf{ovk}^*, (\mathbf{c}_1^*, \mathbf{c}_2^*), \rho^*, \Pi^*, sig^*, \mathbf{v}^*)$ ← Sign($\mathbf{gpk}, \mathbf{gsk}[i_b]^*, cert_{i_b}, M^*$) for a random $b \leftarrow \{0, 1\}$. A returns $b' \in \{0, 1\}$ the guess of b. If $b' = b$ then returns 1 or 0 otherwise.

The following games are same as Game 0 with slight modifications. Thus, still A can access the oracles, and C maintains the global lists according to A's requests through the oracles. In any game, A's requests are almost the same up to some slight changes in inputs. Thus, C manages those queries as following games explained and updates the global lists according to A's requests.

Game 1: In this game, the challenger C makes a slight modification comparing to **Game** 0. C generates the one-time key pair $(\mathbf{ovk}^*, \mathbf{osk}^*)$ at the beginning of the game. If A accesses the opening oracle with a valid signature $\Sigma = (\mathbf{ovk}, (\mathbf{c}_1, \mathbf{c}_2), \rho, \Pi, sig, \mathbf{v})$, where $\mathbf{ovk}=\mathbf{ovk}^*$, C returns a random bit and aborts. However, $\mathbf{ovk}=\mathbf{ovk}^*$ contradicts the strong unforgeability of $\mathcal{OTS}$. Moreover, since the $\mathbf{ovk}^*$ is independent of the adversary's view, probability of $\mathbf{ovk}=\mathbf{ovk}^*$ is negligible. Besides, if A comes up with a valid signature Σ, where $\mathbf{ovk}=\mathbf{ovk}^*$, then sig is a forged signature. We assume that A does not request for opening of a valid signature with $\mathbf{ovk}^*$.

Game 2: In this game, C programs the random oracle $\mathcal{H}_1$. At the beginning of the game, C replaces the encrypting matrices $\mathbf{B}$ and $\mathbf{G}$. C chooses uniformly random $\mathbf{B}^* \in \mathbb{Z}_q^{n \times m}$ and $\mathbf{G}^* \in \mathbb{Z}_q^{n \times \ell}$. Then sets $\mathcal{H}_1(\mathbf{ovk}^*) = \mathbf{G}^*$. To answer the opening oracle requests with $\Sigma = (\mathbf{ovk}, (\mathbf{c}_1, \mathbf{c}_2), \rho, \Pi, sig, \mathbf{v})$, C samples $\mathbf{Y} \leftarrow (D_{z^m, \sigma})^{\ell}$, and computes $\mathbf{G} = \mathbf{B}^*\mathbf{Y} \in \mathbb{Z}_q^{n \times \ell}$. This $\mathbf{G}$ is used to answer the opening and keep track of $(\mathbf{ovk}, \mathbf{Y}, \mathbf{G})$ to be reused if A repeats the same requests for $\mathcal{H}_1(\mathbf{ovk})$. The distributions of $\mathbf{G}$ is statistically close to the uniform over $\mathbb{Z}_q^{n \times \ell}$ [15]. Thus, this game is indistinguishable from Game 1.

Game 3: In this game, instead of honestly generating the legitimate non-interactive proof Π, the challenger C simulates the proof without using the witness. This is done by invoking the simulator for each $k \in [t]$ and then program the random oracle $\mathcal{H}_1$ accordingly. The challenged signature Σ^* is statistically close to the signature in the previous games since the argument system is statistically zero-knowledge. Thus, Game 3 is indistinguishable from Game 2.

Game 4: In this game, the challenger C replaces the original revocation token. We have $\mathbf{v} = \mathbf{V} \cdot \mathbf{grt}[i_b] + \mathbf{e}_1 \mod q$. C samples $\mathbf{t} \xleftarrow{\$} \mathbb{Z}_q^n$ uniformly and computes $\mathbf{v} = \mathbf{V} \cdot \mathbf{t} + \mathbf{e}_1 \mod q$. $\mathbf{V}$ is uniformly random over $\mathbb{Z}_q^{m \times n}$, $\mathbf{e}_1$ is sampled from the error distribution χ, and C replaces only $\mathbf{grt}[i_b]$ with $\mathbf{t}$. The rest of the game is same as Game 3. Thus, the two games are statistically indistinguishable.

Game 5: In this game, the challenger C obtains $\mathbf{v}$ uniformly. Thus, C makes details of revocation token totally independent of the bit b. C samples $\mathbf{y} \xleftarrow{\$} \mathbb{Z}_q^m$ and sets $\mathbf{v} = \mathbf{y}$. In the previous game, the pair $(\mathbf{V}, \mathbf{v})$ is a proper $LWE_{n,q,\chi}$ instance and in this game C replaces $\mathbf{v}$ with truly uniformly sampled $\mathbf{y} \xleftarrow{\$} \mathbb{Z}_q^m$. Under the assumption of $LWE_{n,q,\chi}$ problem is hard, Game 4 and Game 5 are indistinguishable.

Game 6: In this game the challenger C modifies the generation of ciphertext $(\mathbf{c}_1^*, \mathbf{c}_2^*)$ uniformly. Let $\mathbf{c}_1^* = x_1$ and $\mathbf{c}_2^* = x_2 + \lfloor q/2 \rfloor d_b$, where $x_1 \in \mathbb{Z}^m$ and $x_2 \in \mathbb{Z}^\ell$ are uniformly random and d_b is the index of the challenger's bit. The rest of the game is same as Game 5. Game 5 and Game 6 are indistinguishable under the assumption of the hardness of $LWE_{n,q,\chi}$.

Game 7: Finally, we make Σ^* totally independent of the bit b. The challenger C samples $x_1' \in \mathbb{Z}_q^m$ and $x_2' \in \mathbb{Z}_q^\ell$ uniformly random and assigns $\mathbf{c}_1^* = x_1'$ and $\mathbf{c}_2^* = x_2'$. Thus, Game 6 and Game 7 are statistically indistinguishable. Since Game 7 is totally independent from the challenger's bit b, the advantage of the adversary in this game is 0.

Hence, these games prove that proposed scheme is secure with the dynamical-almost-full anonymity.

5.3   Traceability

Theorem 2. *In the random oracle model, our scheme is traceable if* **SIS** *problem is hard.*

$\underline{\mathbf{Exp}_{FDGS,A}^{trace}(\lambda)}$
$(\mathbf{gpk}, \mathbf{ok}) \leftarrow \mathsf{GKg}(1^\lambda); \mathbf{RU}, \mathbf{CUL}, \mathbf{SL}, \mathbf{BU}, \mathbf{TU} \leftarrow \emptyset;$
$(M, \Sigma) \leftarrow A(\mathbf{gpk}, \mathbf{ok};$
$\quad \mathsf{AddU}, \mathsf{CrptU}, \mathsf{SendToIssuer}, \mathsf{RevealSk}, \mathsf{RevealRt}, \mathsf{Sign}, \mathsf{Revoke});$
If $\mathsf{Verify}(\mathbf{gpk}, M, \Sigma, S) = 0$ then return 0.
$i \leftarrow \mathsf{Open}(\mathbf{gpk}, \mathbf{ok}, reg, M, \Sigma);$
If $i = 0$ or $\mathsf{IsActive}(i, reg) - 0$ then return 1 else return 0.

Suppose there is an algorithm B that solves SIS problem with non-negligible probability. The adversary A who has **gpk** and **ok** outputs (M, Σ) in the traceability game. He can add new users and replace members' personal public keys. Moreover, he can query for secret signing keys and revocation tokens of any member. For the queries of A, B answers as in [20,22] by using oracles.

Finally, A outputs forgery signature $\Sigma^* = (\mathbf{ovk}^*, (\mathbf{c}_1^*, \mathbf{c}_2^*), \rho^*, \Pi^*, sig^*, \mathbf{v}^*)$ on message M^*. B opens Σ^* and obtains the index. As same as in [20,22], the improved Forking Lemma [10] guarantees that, with probability at least $1/2$, B can obtain 3-fork involving tuple $(M, \{CMT^{(k)}\}_{k=1}^t, \mathbf{c}_1, \mathbf{c}_2)$ running A up to $32 \cdot Q_H / (\varepsilon - 3^{-t})$ times with the same tape. Rest of the proof flows as in [22] and [20] and finally we can say, if A has non-negligible success probability and runs in polynomial time, then so does B. This concludes our proof of traceability.

5.4   Non-frameability

Theorem 3. *In the random oracle model, our scheme is non-frameable if **SIS** problem is hard.*

We use the proof discussed in [20] to prove our scheme's non-frameability.

$\mathbf{Exp}_{FDGS,A}^{non\text{-}fram}(\lambda)$

$(\mathbf{gpk}, \mathbf{ok}, \mathbf{ik}) \leftarrow \mathsf{GKg}(1^\lambda); \mathbf{RU}, \mathbf{CUL}, \mathbf{SL}, \mathbf{BUTU} \leftarrow \emptyset;$

$(M, \Sigma, i) \leftarrow A(\mathbf{gpk}, \mathbf{ik}, \mathbf{ok};$
    $\mathsf{CrptU}, \mathsf{SendToUser}, \mathsf{RevealSk}, \mathsf{RevealRt}, \mathsf{Sign}, \mathsf{ModifyReg});$

If $\mathsf{Verify}(\mathbf{gpk}, M, \Sigma, S) = 0$ then return 0.

If $i \notin \mathbf{RU}$ or $i \in \mathbf{BU}$ or $(i, M, \Sigma) \in \mathbf{SL}$ then return 0 else 1.

Suppose there is a frameable adversary A with advantage ϵ. We construct a **PPT** algorithm B that solves *SIS* problem. B is given a matrix $\mathbf{F}$. B generates all the public keys and authority keys. Then B interacts with A by sending **gpk** and authority keys $(\mathbf{T_A}, \mathbf{T_B})$.

As discussed in [20], B responses to A's queries. A can act as a corrupted group manager and add a new user i to the group. When A requests user i to generate a signature on a message M, B generates and returns the signature $\Sigma = (\mathbf{ovk}, (\mathbf{c}_1, \mathbf{c}_2), \rho, \Pi, sig, \mathbf{v})$.

Finally, on a message M^*, A outputs $\Sigma^* = (\mathbf{ovk}^*, (\mathbf{c}_1^*, \mathbf{c}_2^*), \Pi^*, sig^*, \mathbf{v}^*)$, which opens to i^* who did not sign the message. Thus, (M^*, Σ^*) should frame user i^*. B has a short vector $\mathbf{z}_{i^*} = \mathbf{F} \cdot \mathbf{x}_{i^*} \mod q$. To solve SIS instance B should have another short vector $\mathbf{z}_{i\prime} = \mathbf{F} \cdot \mathbf{x}_{i\prime} \mod q$. To compute such a vector, B proceeds by replaying A sufficient times and applying Improved Forking Lemma [10].

As discussed in [20], B can extract a short vector $\mathbf{x}\prime$, where $\mathbf{z}_{i^*} = \mathbf{F} \cdot \mathbf{x}\prime \mod q$. According to Stern-like proof of knowledge, with overwhelming probability, we say $\mathbf{x}\prime \neq \mathbf{x}_{i^*}$. A nonzero vector $\mathbf{h} = \mathbf{x}_{i^*} - \mathbf{x}\prime$ is a solution for SIS problem.

This proves the non-frameability of our scheme.

6   Conclusion

This paper presented a simple lattice-based group signature scheme which satisfies both member registration and revocation with VLR. We have discussed VLR group signatures and difficulties of achieving full-anonymity for VLR group signatures. Moreover, we proved our scheme's security by suggesting a new security notion called dynamical-almost-full anonymity. However, achieving full-anonymity for VLR group signature schemes still remains as a problem.

Acknowledgments. This work is supported in part by JSPS Grant-in-Aids for Scientific Research (A) JP16H01705 and for Scientific Research (B) JP17H01695.

References

1. Agrawal, S., Boyen, X., Vaikuntanathan, V., Voulgaris, P., Wee, H.: Functional encryption for threshold functions (or Fuzzy IBE) from lattices. In: Fischlin, M., Buchmann, J., Manulis, M. (eds.) PKC 2012. LNCS, vol. 7293, pp. 280–297. Springer, Heidelberg (2012). https://doi.org/10.1007/978-3-642-30057-8_17

2. Ajtai, M.: Generating hard instances of lattice problems. In: Proceedings of the Twenty-eighth Annual ACM Symposium on Theory of Computing, pp. 99–108. ACM (1996)

3. Ateniese, G., Camenisch, J., Joye, M., Tsudik, G.: A practical and provably secure coalition-resistant group signature scheme. In: Bellare, M. (ed.) CRYPTO 2000. LNCS, vol. 1880, pp. 255–270. Springer, Heidelberg (2000). https://doi.org/10.1007/3-540-44598-6_16

4. Bellare, M., Micciancio, D., Warinschi, B.: Foundations of group signatures: formal definitions, simplified requirements, and a construction based on general assumptions. In: Biham, E. (ed.) EUROCRYPT 2003. LNCS, vol. 2656, pp. 614–629. Springer, Heidelberg (2003). https://doi.org/10.1007/3-540-39200-9_38

5. Bellare, M., Shi, H., Zhang, C.: Foundations of group signatures: the case of dynamic groups. In: Menezes, A. (ed.) CT-RSA 2005. LNCS, vol. 3376, pp. 136–153. Springer, Heidelberg (2005). https://doi.org/10.1007/978-3-540-30574-3_11

6. Boneh, D., Shacham, H.: Group signatures with verifier-local revocation. In: ACM-CCS 2004, pp. 168–177. ACM (2004)

7. Bootle, J., Cerulli, A., Chaidos, P., Ghadafi, E., Groth, J.: Foundations of fully dynamic group signatures. In: Manulis, M., Sadeghi, A.-R., Schneider, S. (eds.) ACNS 2016. LNCS, vol. 9696, pp. 117–136. Springer, Cham (2016). https://doi.org/10.1007/978-3-319-39555-5_7

8. Bresson, E., Stern, J.: Efficient revocation in group signatures. In: Kim, K. (ed.) PKC 2001. LNCS, vol. 1992, pp. 190–206. Springer, Heidelberg (2001). https://doi.org/10.1007/3-540-44586-2_15

9. Brickell, E.: An efficient protocol for anonymously providing assurance of the container of the private key. Submitted to the Trusted Computing Group, April 2003

10. Brickell, E., Pointcheval, D., Vaudenay, S., Yung, M.: Design validations for discrete logarithm based signature schemes. In: Imai, H., Zheng, Y. (eds.) PKC 2000. LNCS, vol. 1751, pp. 276–292. Springer, Heidelberg (2000). https://doi.org/10.1007/978-3-540-46588-1_19

11. Camenisch, J., Lysyanskaya, A.: Dynamic accumulators and application to efficient revocation of anonymous credentials. In: Yung, M. (ed.) CRYPTO 2002. LNCS, vol. 2442, pp. 61–76. Springer, Heidelberg (2002). https://doi.org/10.1007/3-540-45708-9_5

12. Camenisch, J., Neven, G., Rückert, M.: Fully anonymous attribute tokens from lattices. In: Visconti, I., De Prisco, R. (eds.) SCN 2012. LNCS, vol. 7485, pp. 57–75. Springer, Heidelberg (2012). https://doi.org/10.1007/978-3-642-32928-9_4

13. Chaum, D., van Heyst, E.: Group signatures. In: Davies, D.W. (ed.) EUROCRYPT 1991. LNCS, vol. 547, pp. 257–265. Springer, Heidelberg (1991). https://doi.org/10.1007/3-540-46416-6_22

14. Chow, S.S.M., Wong, D.S.: Anonymous identification and designated-verifiers signatures from insecure batch verification. In: Lopez, J., Samarati, P., Ferrer, J.L. (eds.) EuroPKI 2007. LNCS, vol. 4582, pp. 203–219. Springer, Heidelberg (2007). https://doi.org/10.1007/978-3-540-73408-6_15

15. Gentry, C., Peikert, C., Vaikuntanathan, V.: Trapdoors for hard lattices and new cryptographic constructions. In: ACM 2008, pp. 197–206. ACM (2008)

16. Gordon, S.D., Katz, J., Vaikuntanathan, V.: A group signature scheme from lattice assumptions. In: Abe, M. (ed.) ASIACRYPT 2010. LNCS, vol. 6477, pp. 395–412. Springer, Heidelberg (2010). https://doi.org/10.1007/978-3-642-17373-8_23

17. Kawachi, A., Tanaka, K., Xagawa, K.: Concurrently secure identification schemes based on the worst-case hardness of lattice problems. In: Pieprzyk, J. (ed.) ASIACRYPT 2008. LNCS, vol. 5350, pp. 372–389. Springer, Heidelberg (2008). https://doi.org/10.1007/978-3-540-89255-7_23

18. Laguillaumie, F., Langlois, A., Libert, B., Stehlé, D.: Lattice-based group signatures with logarithmic signature size. In: Sako, K., Sarkar, P. (eds.) ASIACRYPT 2013. LNCS, vol. 8270, pp. 41–61. Springer, Heidelberg (2013). https://doi.org/10.1007/978-3-642-42045-0_3

19. Langlois, A., Ling, S., Nguyen, K., Wang, H.: Lattice-based group signature scheme with verifier-local revocation. In: Krawczyk, H. (ed.) PKC 2014. LNCS, vol. 8383, pp. 345–361. Springer, Heidelberg (2014). https://doi.org/10.1007/978-3-642-54631-0_20

20. Libert, B., Ling, S., Mouhartem, F., Nguyen, K., Wang, H.: Signature schemes with efficient protocols and dynamic group signatures from lattice assumptions. In: Cheon, J.H., Takagi, T. (eds.) ASIACRYPT 2016. LNCS, vol. 10032, pp. 373–403. Springer, Heidelberg (2016). https://doi.org/10.1007/978-3-662-53890-6_13

21. Libert, B., Vergnaud, D.: Group signatures with verifier-local revocation and backward unlinkability in the standard model. In: Garay, J.A., Miyaji, A., Otsuka, A. (eds.) CANS 2009. LNCS, vol. 5888, pp. 498–517. Springer, Heidelberg (2009). https://doi.org/10.1007/978-3-642-10433-6_34

22. Ling, S., Nguyen, K., Wang, H.: Group signatures from lattices: simpler, tighter, shorter, ring-based. In: Katz, J. (ed.) PKC 2015. LNCS, vol. 9020, pp. 427–449. Springer, Heidelberg (2015). https://doi.org/10.1007/978-3-662-46447-2_19

23. Ling, S., Nguyen, K., Wang, H., Xu, Y.: Lattice-based group signatures: achieving full dynamicity with ease. In: Gollmann, D., Miyaji, A., Kikuchi, H. (eds.) ACNS 2017. LNCS, vol. 10355, pp. 293–312. Springer, Cham (2017). https://doi.org/10.1007/978-3-319-61204-1_15

24. Micciancio, D., Peikert, C.: Trapdoors for lattices: simpler, tighter, faster, smaller. In: Pointcheval, D., Johansson, T. (eds.) EUROCRYPT 2012. LNCS, vol. 7237, pp. 700–718. Springer, Heidelberg (2012). https://doi.org/10.1007/978-3-642-29011-4_41

25. Naor, D., Shenhav, A., Wool, A.: One-time signatures revisited: Have they become practical? IACR Cryptology ePrint Archive 2005/442 (2005)
26. Nguyen, P.Q., Zhang, J., Zhang, Z.: Simpler efficient group signatures from lattices. In: Katz, J. (ed.) PKC 2015. LNCS, vol. 9020, pp. 401–426. Springer, Heidelberg (2015). https://doi.org/10.1007/978-3-662-46447-2_18
27. Peikert, C.: A decade of lattice cryptography. Found. Trends Theor. Comput. Sci. **10**(4), 283–424 (2016). https://doi.org/10.1561/0400000074
28. Perera, M.N.S., Koshiba, T.: Fully dynamic group signature scheme with member registration and verifier-local revocation. In: ICMC 2018, Mathematics and Computing (to appear)
29. Regev, O.: On lattices, learning with errors, random linear codes, and cryptography. In: STOC, pp. 84–93. ACM Press (2005)

Entanglement Between Hash Encodings and Signatures from ID Schemes with Non-binary Challenges: A Case Study on Lightweight Code-Based Signatures

Bagus Santoso[(✉)], Taiyo Yamaguchi, and Tomoyuki Ohkubo

Department of Computer and Network Engineering,
University of Electro-Communications, Chofu, Japan
{santoso.bagus,t.yamaguchi}@uec.ac.jp, o1731027@edu.cc.uec.ac.jp

Abstract. We are interested in investigating the following issue which rises during the implementation of signature schemes derived from identification (ID) schemes via Fiat-Shamir (FS) transform. In FS transform, the "challenge" part of the ID scheme is substituted with the output of a hash function. However, the "challenge" part of several ID schemes, such as Stern's code-based ID scheme, is a ternary sequence ($\{0, 1, 2\}^*$), while all standard hash functions, e.g., SHA-256, outputs a binary sequence. Hence, we have to apply an encoding to transform the binary sequence of the hash functions' outputs into the ternary sequence. A naive encoding method is to store the whole outputs of the hash function in memory and then convert them into ternary afterwards. Although this naive encoding method seems sufficient, it is an interesting question whether we can have better encoding options with lower computing and storage costs, especially when we deal with implementation on lightweight devices with critical resources.

In this paper, we select two other simple hash encoding methods and plug them into the signature scheme generated from Stern's ID scheme. We summarize our results as follows.

– We discover an interesting phenomenon that the choice of the hash encoding method, which is widely considered as a mere implementation issue that is supposed to be independent to the stage of scheme design and the stage of the theoretical security proof construction, raises problems which make us redesign the scheme and reconstruct the security proof.
– Our machine experiment shows that our newly selected encoding methods combined with the redesigned signature schemes bring a significant performance improvement in practice. For the case of 128-bit security which is the standard for post-quantum security, in a single-board credit-card sized computer, i.e., Raspberry Pi, the first newly selected encoding method and the second one are shown to be around 53 times faster and 187 faster respectively with few kilobytes additional length in signature compared to the naive method above.

ⓒ Springer Nature Switzerland AG 2018
C. Su and H. Kikuchi (Eds.): ISPEC 2018, LNCS 11125, pp. 248–262, 2018.
https://doi.org/10.1007/978-3-319-99807-7_15

1   Introduction

Overview. When implementing cryptographic schemes in practice, sometimes there are implementation issues which occur exclusively only in the stage of implementation, and are not addressed at all in the stage of the scheme design. It is widely believed that implementation issues can be dealt independently without affecting the theoretical security of the scheme which have been evaluated in the design stage. However, there are special cases where how we deal with the implementation issue can affect the theoretical security of the scheme. In this paper, we try to address one example of such special cases we encounter during the implementation of a signature scheme built from identification (ID) schemes via Fiat-Shamir (FS) transform [5]. Especially, we are focusing on issues of implementation on lightweight devices.

Gap between Challenge in ID Scheme and Hash in Signatures. It is well-known that we can use Fiat-Shamir transform to construct a signature scheme from a canonical three-pass identification scheme with *commitment-challenge-response* procedures as described formally in [3]. As formally described by Bellare and Palacio [3], in a canonical three-pass identification scheme, the prover firstly sends a *"commitment"* to the verifier, and then verifier sends back a *"challenge"* to the prover, who responds with a "response" to the verifier. A typical signing procedure of a message m in such signature scheme substitutes the "challenge" part of the identification scheme with the hashing of "commitment" and m using a standard hash function h, e.g., SHA-256, etc. When the domain where the output of h belongs to and the domain of the "challenge" are same, there is no problem. However, in reality, they are not always be. For example, the code based identification scheme proposed by Stern [8] and multivariate polynomials based one proposed by Sakumoto [6] have the domain of the "challenge" to be the set $\{0, 1, 2\}$, while as widely known, all standard hash functions in reality have the domain of the outputs to be the binary set, i.e., $\{0, 1\}$.

Now, let us have a more detailed look on the construction of the signature schemes. First, as a common technique in Fiat-Shamir transform, note that rather than based on the original Stern's ID scheme, we construct the signature schemes based on the parallel version of Stern's ID scheme. Let $(, , \mathsf{chal}, \mathsf{resp})$ denote the communication transcript of the Stern's parallel ID scheme corresponding to the "commitment","challenge", and "response" respectively, where $\mathsf{chal} \in \{0, 1, 2\}^r$ and r is the parameter indicating the number of parallel instances required to guarantee the security level of the scheme against impersonation attack. Inside the signature scheme constructed from the identification scheme via Fiat-Shamir transform, during the process of creating the signature of message m, we compute $\mathsf{chal}' = h(, , m)$ to substitute chal which is originally chosen in random by the verifier of identification scheme. And, in order to produce the signature of m, we have to run the procedure used by the prover for computing resp. In the case of Stern's identification scheme, since this procedure takes the original chal as input, it can only works properly if the input is a sequence of values in $\{0, 1, 2\}^*$. However, since the output of h as a standard hash function is a sequence of values in $\{0,1\}$, the substitute for chal in the signature scheme, i.e., chal$'$, is taking value in the set $\{0,1\}^*$. Hence, we need to construct a procedure to encode the sequence of *binary* bits $\mathbf{b} \in \{0,1\}^*$ into sequence of *ternary* bits $\mathbf{t} \in \{0,1,2\}^*$, so that we can transform the output of h into a sequence of ternary bits and input it into the procedure for computing resp to produce the signature of m.

Motivation. One immediate way to convert the binary sequence into ternary sequence, which we call as *naive encoding method*, is by just taking the binary sequence as integer x in base 2, then compute the representation of x in base 3. However, our observation reveals that this naive method requires us to perform division operation multiple times and thus, it might not be suitable for implementation on lightweight devices.[1] Based on this observation, we pose the following question which is the initial motivation of this research.

"Can we do better than above *naive* encoding method? Do we have options other than naive methods which are better in the term of computational and/or storage costs ?"

Especially, we are interested only on encoding methods which are *simple, lightweight, and easy to implement* on any devices.

Our Results. Other than the above *naive* encoding method, we select two other methods of encoding sequence of binary bits into sequence of ternary bits which we denote as *Method 1* and *Method 2*. Our choice are based on our observation that the two methods are very simple, lightweight and easy to implement on any devices. We "plug" each selected encoding methods into the signature schemes and compare their performance.

In general, the newly selected encoding methods perform better compared to the naive encoding method. Our machine experiment shows that despite their simplicity, *Method 1* and *Method 2* can bring a significant performance difference in practice, compared to the naive method. For the case of 128-bit security which is the standard for post-quantum security, for implementation on a single-board credit-card sized computer, i.e., Raspberry Pi, *Method 1* and *Method 2* are shown to be around 53 times faster and 187 faster respectively compared to the naive encoding method.

The initialization procedure of *Method 1* and *Method 2* are same, i.e., given sequence of binary bits $\mathbf{b}$, we divide $\mathbf{b}$ into blocks of two bits. An i-th two-bits-block of $\mathbf{b}$ is denoted by $\mathbf{b}_i = b_{i,0}b_{i,1}$, where $b_{i,0}, b_{i,1} \in \{0,1\}$. For simplicity, let us assume that the length of the output of the hash function 2ℓ, and thus we obtain a total of ℓ two-bits-block of $\mathbf{b}$. After executing the corresponding procedure shown below, an encoding method will output a sequence of ternary bits ($\{0,1,2\}^*$).

---

[1] As we show later in this paper, when generating ternary bits for 128-bit security level, in practice, this naive encoding method can require more than 53 times of the time required by other selected encoding methods.

- *Method 1: Encoding with droppings.* For each i-th two-bits-block $\mathbf{b}_i$, this encoding basically firstly coverts the value of $\mathbf{b}_i$ into its decimal value, and then outputs the converted value if and only if the converted value is in the set $\{0, 1, 2\}$. The important properties of this encoding are as follows: (1) all blocks from input with binary value "11" are dropped, and (2) there is one-to-one corresponding between the ternary bits at the output and the two-bits-block of binary bits at the input. One can see this method as variant of the classical rejection sampling algorithm [9], and therefore this method produces uniformly random ternary bits assuming that the binary random bits are also uniformly random. Note that we can not guarantee how many ternary bits we can obtain in deterministic way. However, but as shown later, we can estimate the number of necessary binary random bits in order to obtain a certain number of ternary bits with probability larger than half.
- *Method 2: Encoding without dropping.* For each i-th two-bits-block $\mathbf{b}_i$, this encoding maps the value of $\mathbf{b}_i$ into its Hamming's weight, i.e., the number of non-zero value. The most important property of this encoding is that blocks with value "01" and "10" are mapped into the same ternary bit "1". This method guarantees that we can always get ℓ ternary bits from 2ℓ binary bits. However, in contrast to *Method 1*, this method does not produce ternary bits in uniform distribution. As shown later, this actually affect the security of the signature scheme which is constructed based on this method.

Constructed Signature Schemes and Their Properties. For each method, we construct a signature scheme based on it. We use the proof technique developed in [1] to construct the security proof for each scheme. In a nutshell, at the heart of the security proof is the relation between three values $(\varepsilon_\mathcal{A}, \varepsilon_D, \gamma)$, where $\varepsilon_\mathcal{A}$ denotes the success probability of an adversary $\mathcal{A}$ breaking the signature scheme, ε_D denotes the success probability of breaking the underlying decisional version of the hard problem, and γ denotes the success cheating probability of dishonest prover in the underlying identification scheme. The relation can be informally written as follows: $\varepsilon_\mathcal{A} \approx \varepsilon_D + \gamma^r$. Based on the fact that *the distribution of the ternary bits resulted from the encoding can be translated into the distribution of "challenge"s* in the underlying identification scheme, we derive another fact that the distribution of the ternary bits resulted from the encoding affects the success cheating probability of dishonest prover in the underlying identification scheme, i.e., γ, and thus also affects the success probability of adversary breaking the unforgeability of the signature scheme, i.e., $\varepsilon_\mathcal{A}$. Our first signature scheme Sig1 is constructed based on *Method 1* and our second signature scheme Sig2 is constructed based on *Method 2*.

We show the trade-off of performance between the naive encoding methods and our proposed encoding methods in Table 1. In general, the faster the encoding method, the larger the signature size is. However, it should be noted that our proposed encoding methods achieve a huge speed improvement with only a little payoff on the signature size compared to the naive method.

Related Works and Generalization. The signature scheme derived from Stern's ID scheme via FS transform has been mentioned in Stern's original paper [8],

Table 1. Performance comparison of encoding methods

Encoding methods	Computational cost [μs]	Signature size [MB]
Naive Method	326.738	1.57
Method 1	6.146	1.58
Method 2	1.740	2.42

but it does not give any explanation on concrete construction of the signature scheme. Alamélou et al. introduced a code-based group signature scheme based on Stern's ID scheme [2] with security proof based on the search version of Syndrome Decoding problem. It should be noted that the basic signature scheme mentioned in [2] does not have tight security proof, while our security proofs for signatures in this paper offer tight security proof based on the decisional version of Syndrome Decoding problem. We are sure that this works can be generalized to other ID schemes with non-binary challenges, such as the 3-pass ID scheme based on multivariate quadratic polynomials (MQ) problem proposed by Sakumoto [6]. The only requirement is that since our security proof is based on the decisional problem, the decisional version of the underlying computationally hard problem corresponding to the ID scheme must also be hard.

2   Preliminaries

Notations. The empty string is denoted by λ. If x is a string, then $x \in \{0,1\}^n$ denotes that x is the n-bit binary string and if A is a matrix, then $A \in \{0,1\}^{m \times n}$ denotes that A is the binary matrix of m rows and n columns. Hamming weight of a string x, denoted by $w_H(x)$ is the number of 1s it includes and $\mathbb{S}_p^n$ is the set of n-bit binary strings of hamming weight p. Π_n denotes the set of permutations order n. The symbol $\|$ denotes concatenation. Also we define complexity related notations. A function μ is called negligible iff $\forall c > 0 \ \exists n_0 \in \mathbb{N}$ such that $\forall n \geq n_0$, $\mu(n) < n^{-c}$ holds. And a function μ is called non-negligible iff $\exists c > 0 \ \forall n_0 \in \mathbb{N}$ such that $\exists n \geq n_0$, $\mu(n) \geq n^{-c}$ holds. We say that any problem $\mathbb{P}$ is *hard* if there is no algorithm solves it within polynomial time with non-negligible probability. Unless noted otherwise, any algorithm is probabilistic polynomial time algorithm.

Definition 1 (Decisional Syndrome Decoding (DSD) Problem). *A Decisional Syndrome Decoding (DSD) problem parameterized with $(n, k, p) \in \mathbb{N}^3$ is associated with the following sets: $S_{n,k,p} := \{(H, s, p) | H \in \{0,1\}^{(n-k) \times n}, s \in \{0,1\}^{n-k}\}$, $T_{n,k,p} := \{(H, s, p) | (H, s, p) \in S_{n,k,p}, \exists e \ s.t. H \cdot e^{\mathrm{T}} = s, w_H(e) = p\}$, $\tilde{T}_{n,k,p} := S_{n,k,p} \backslash T_{n,k,p}$. A DSD adversary $\mathcal{D}$ is given inputs $(H, s, p) \in S_{n,k,p}$, and outputs one bit $d \in \{0,1\}$ within polynomial time. The advantage of DSD adversary $\mathcal{D}$ is defined as follows.*

$$\left| \Pr\Big[\mathcal{D}((H, s, p) \in T_{n,k,p}) = 1 \Big] - \Pr\Big[\mathcal{D}((H, s, p) \in \tilde{T}_{n,k,p}) = 1 \Big] \right|$$

The DSD problem parameterized with (n, k, p) is ε_{DSD}-hard if there is no DSD adversary $\mathcal{D}$ with advantage larger than equal to ε_{DSD}.

DSD problem is shown to be NP-complete by Berlekamp et al. [4]. Therefore, DSD problem is *hard* in the worst-case even for quantum computers. If we assume that ε_{DSD} in the above definition to be negligible, then it means that we assume that DSD problem is also hard in the average-case even for quantum computers.

Definition 2 (String Commitment Scheme [6]). *The string commitment scheme Com is a two-stage interactive protocol between a sender and a receiver using a string commitment function Com. In the first stage, the sender computes a commitment value $c \leftarrow Com(s; \rho)$ and sends c to the receiver, where s is a string and ρ is a random string. In the second stage, the sender gives (s, ρ) to the receiver and the receiver verifies $c = Com(s; \rho)$. Informally, the string commitment scheme Com is called statistically hiding iff no receiver can distinguish two commitment values generated from two different strings even if the receiver is computationally unbounded. And the string commitment scheme Com is called computationally binding iff no polynomial time sender can change the committed string after the first phase.*

Definition 3 (Collision Resistant Hash Function). *A collision resistant hash function is a function $\{h : \{0,1\}^* \to \{0,1\}^k\}$ (for some integer k) such that any polynomial time algorithm can only succeed in finding two different strings $x \neq y$ such that $h(x) = h(y)$ with negligible probability.*

2.1 Signature Schemes

Definition 4. *A   signature   scheme   Sig   consists   three   algorithms* (KeyGen, Sign, Verify) *such that:*

- KeyGen *is the key generation algorithm that outputs a pair of the public key* pk *and secret key* sk *from the security parameter κ.*
- Sign *is the signing algorithm that outputs a signature σ from a message m and the secret key* sk.
- Verify *is the verification algorithm that outputs 1 if the signature is correct and 0 otherwise from a message m, a signature σ and the public key* pk.

The standard security notion for signature scheme is existential unforgeability against adaptive chosen-message attacks which informally means that any adversary cannot produce a valid signature for a new message with a non-negligible probability after obtaining signatures on polynomially many arbitrary messages of his choice.

Definition 5 (Unforgeability in Random Oracle Model). *Let* Sig = (KeyGen, Sign, Verify) *be a signature scheme and let RO be a random oracle.*

We say that Sig *is* (q_S, q_H, ε)-*existentially unforgeable against adaptive chosen-message attacks, if there is no algorithm* $\mathcal{A}$ *that runs while making at most* q_h *hash queries and at most* q_S *signing queries, such that*

$$\Pr[(\mathsf{pk}, \mathsf{sk}) \leftarrow \mathsf{KeyGen}(\kappa); (m, \sigma) \leftarrow \mathcal{A}^{\mathsf{Sign}(\mathsf{sk}, \cdot), RO(\cdot)}(\mathsf{pk}) : m \notin \{m_1, \cdots, m_{q_S}\}$$
$$\wedge \, \mathsf{Verify}(m, \sigma, \mathsf{pk}) = 1] \geq \varepsilon,$$

where $\{m_1, \cdots, m_{q_S}\}$ *is the set of messages queried to the signing oracle.*

3   Signature Schemes

We establish the signature schemes based on the Stern's protocol [8] via the Fiat-Shamir transform [5]. In our signature, we use a hash function outputs a ternary string. However, general hash function outputs a binary string. Therefore, it must be converted from a binary string to a ternary string. Hence, as described in the Introduction, we propose two different signature schemes according to the difference in binary to ternary conversion method.

3.1   Scheme 1

We describe our first signature scheme Sig1 = (KeyGen, Sign, Verify) in Fig. 1. In Sig1, if two adjacent bits of $\mathbf{b}$, $(b_j || b_{j+1})$ is 00, it is regarded as 0 in Stern's protocol. Similarly, if $b_j || b_{j+1}$ is 01, it is regarded as 1, and if $b_j || b_{j+1}$ is 10, it is regarded as 2. But if $b_j || b_{j+1}$ is 11, we do nothing and go on to the next 2-bits. By doing so, we can regard the output of the hash function as a ternary string. However, if $k < r$ when converting $\mathbf{b} \in \{0, 1\}^{r'}$ to the $\mathbf{t} \in \{0, 1, 2\}^k$, it is necessary to call the hash function again with a different input to obtain a new $\mathbf{b}$. So, we introduce α to change the input with minimal processing. It is easy to see that any signature produced by the Sign algorithm of Sig1 will be accepted by Verify algorithm of Sig1. We will show the security proof of Sig1 in Sect. 4.

3.2   Scheme 2

Sig2 = (KeyGen, Sign, Verify) is the signature scheme based on another conversion procedure. The detailed is described in Fig. 2. In Sig2, if two adjacent bits of $\mathbf{b}$ $(b_{2i-1} || b_{2i})$ is 00, it is regarded as 0 in Stern's protocol. Similarly, if $b_{2i-1} || b_{2i}$ is 01 or 10, it is regarded as 1, and if $b_{2i-1} || b_{2i}$ is 11, it is regarded as 2. Thus, we can regard the output of the hash function as a ternary string as in Sig1. The difference from Sig1 is that $\mathbf{b}$ can always be converted to the n-bit ternary string in Sig2. It is easy to see that any signature produced by the Sign algorithm of Sig2 will be accepted by Verify algorithm of Sig2. We will show the security proof of Sig2 in Sect. 4.2.

Remark 1. Sig1 and Sig2 are actually always implicitly parameterized with $(n, k, p) \in \mathbb{N}^3$. For simplicity, throughout this paper we omit the mentioning of parameter (n, k, p) and unless otherwise noted, Sig1 and Sig2 are parameterized with the same $(n, k, p) \in \mathbb{N}^3$.

KeyGen($\kappa = \{\,n,k,p,r,r'\,\}$) :	Sign(sk, m) :	Verify(pk, m, σ) :
1. $H \xleftarrow{\$} \{0,1\}^{(n-k)\times n}$	1. $i \leftarrow 0$	1. $\mathbf{b}' = \{b_1', \cdots, b_{r'}'\}$
2. $s_U \xleftarrow{\$} \mathbb{S}_p^n$	2. **while** $i < r$ **do**	$\quad \leftarrow h(\{c_1^i||c_2^i||c_3^i\}_{i=1}^r ||\alpha||m)$
3. $i_U \leftarrow H \cdot s_U$	3. $\quad i \leftarrow i+1$	2. $i \leftarrow 1, j \leftarrow 1$
4. choose a collision resistant	4. $\quad y_i \xleftarrow{\$} \{0,1\}^n, \pi_i \xleftarrow{\$} \Pi_n$	3. **while** $i < r$ and $j < r'-1$ **do**
$\quad$ hash function	5. $\quad c_1^i \leftarrow Com(\pi_i||H \cdot y_i^{\mathrm{T}})$	4. $\quad$ **if** $b_{j-1}'||b_j' = 00$
$\quad h : \{0,1\}^* \to \{0,1\}^{r'}$	$\qquad c_2^i \leftarrow Com(y_i \cdot \pi_i)$	5. $\qquad$ **if** $c_1^i \neq Com(z_2^i||H \cdot z_1^{iT})$
5. choose a commitment	$\qquad c_3^i \leftarrow Com((y_i \oplus s_U) \cdot \pi_i)$	$\qquad\qquad \vee c_2^i \neq Com(z_1^i \cdot z_2^i)$
$\quad$ function	6. **end while**	$\qquad\quad$ **then return** 0
$\qquad Com(\cdot)$	7. $\alpha \xleftarrow{\$} \{0,1\}^\beta$	6. $\qquad$ **else** $i \leftarrow i+1$
6. **return**	8. $\mathbf{b} = \{b_1, \cdots, b_{r'}\}$	7. $\quad$ **else if** $b_{j-1}'||b_j' = 01$
$\quad$ pk $= (H, i_U, h, Com, p, r, r')$	$\quad \leftarrow h(\{c_1^i||c_2^i||c_3^i\}_{i=1}^r ||\alpha||m)$	8. $\qquad$ **if** $c_1^i \neq Com(z_2^i||H \cdot z_1^{iT} \oplus i_U)$
$\quad$ and sk $= s_U$	9. $i \leftarrow 1, j \leftarrow 1$	$\qquad\qquad \vee c_3^i \neq Com(z_1^i \cdot z_2^i)$
	10. **while** $i \leq r$ and $j < r'$ **do**	$\qquad\quad$ **then return** 0
	11. $\quad$ **if** $b_j||b_{j+1} = 00$, **then**	9. $\qquad$ **else** $i \leftarrow i+1$
	$\qquad t_i \leftarrow 0, i \leftarrow i+1$	10. $\quad$ **else if** $b_{j-1}'||b_j' = 10$
	12. $\quad$ **else if** $b_j||b_{j+1} = 01$, **then**	11. $\qquad$ **if** $w_H(z_2^i) \neq p \vee c_2^i \neq Com(z_1^i)$
	$\qquad t_i \leftarrow 1, i \leftarrow i+1$	$\qquad\qquad \vee c_3^i \neq Com(z_1^i \oplus z_2^i)$
	13. $\quad$ **else if** $b_j||b_{j+1} = 10$, **then**	$\qquad\quad$ **then return** 0
	$\qquad t_i \leftarrow 2, i \leftarrow i+1$	12. $\qquad$ **else** $i \leftarrow i+1$
	14. $\quad j \leftarrow j+2$	13. $\quad j \leftarrow j+2$
	15. **end while**	14. **end while**
	16. **if** $j \geq r'$, **then goto** Step 7	15. **if** $i < r$ **then return** 0
	17. $i \leftarrow 1$	16. **return** 1
	18. **while** $i \leq r$ **do**	
	19. $\quad$ **if** $t_i = 0$ **then** $z_1^i \leftarrow y_i, z_2^i \leftarrow \pi_i$	
	20. $\quad$ **else if** $t_i = 1$ **then**	
	$\qquad z_1^i \leftarrow y_i \oplus s_U, z_2^i \leftarrow \pi_i$	
	21. $\quad$ **else if** $t_i = 2$ **then**	
	$\qquad z_1^i \leftarrow y_i \cdot \pi_i, z_2^i \leftarrow s_U \cdot \pi_i$	
	22. $\quad i \leftarrow i+1$	
	23. **end while**	
	24. **return**	
	$\quad \sigma = \{\{c_1^i, c_2^i, c_3^i, z_1^i, z_2^i\}_{i=1}^r, \alpha\}$	

Fig. 1. Signature scheme Sig1

4   Security Proof

To analyze the security of Sig1 and Sig2, we use a random oracle model. And with that, we define adversary to perform existential forgery by adaptive chosen message attack as follows.

Definition 6. *If the adversary produces a valid signature forgery with probability greater than ε while making at most q_H hash queries and q_S sign queries, we call it (ε, q_H, q_S)-adversary.*

Remark 2. For simplicity, in this paper, we omit the explicit statement on running time of the adversary. We assume that q_H and q_S are the polynomials and (ε, q_H, q_S)-adversary is probabilistic polynomial time algorithm.

4.1   Scheme 1

Theorem 1. *If DSD problem is ε_{DSD}-hard, then Sig1 is $(q_H, q_S, \varepsilon_1)$-existentially unforgeable against adaptive chosen-message attacks in the random*

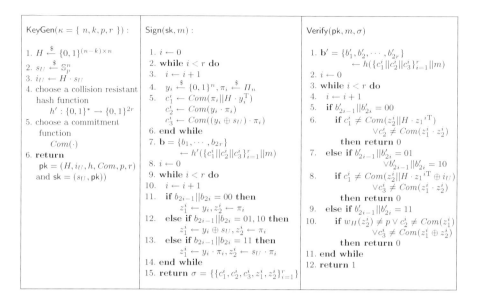

Fig. 2. Signature scheme 2

oracle model for:

$$\varepsilon_1 = \varepsilon_{DSD} + \frac{(q_H + 1)}{\varepsilon_{GOOD}} \left(\frac{2}{3}\right)^r + \frac{q_S(q_S + q_H + 1)}{2^{3rN+\beta}}. \tag{4.1}$$

(where r is the number of rounds, ε_{DSD} is the hardness of DSD-problem, ε_{GOOD} is the probability that $k = r$ when converting $\mathbf{b} \in \{0,1\}^{r'}$ to the k-bit ternary string and N is the output length of commitment value.)

Proof Overview. In order to prove the security of Sig1, the main idea is to construct the algorithm $\mathcal{B}$ that outputs a bit indicating whether $(\varepsilon_1, q_H, q_S)$-adversary $\mathcal{A}$ has succeeded in producing a valid signature forgery of Sig1. Let pk be the public key generated from honest key generator KeyGen, pk$'$ be the public key generated from dishonest key generator KeyGen$'$, where honest key generator KeyGen means that KeyGen generates the correct public key pk $= (H \in \{0,1\}^{(n-k)\times n)}, i_U \in \{0,1\}^{n-k}, p \in \mathbb{N})$ such that $\exists s : H \cdot s = i_U, w_H(s) = p$, and dishonest key generator KeyGen$'$ means that KeyGen$'$ generates pk$' = (H' \in \{0,1\}^{(n-k)\times n)}, i'_U \in \{0,1\}^{n-k}, p' \in \mathbb{N})$ such that $\nexists s : H' \cdot s = i'_U, w_H(s) = p'$. We denote $\Pr[\mathcal{B}(\mathsf{pk}) = 1]$ is the probability that $\mathcal{B}$ outputs 1 with pk, $\Pr[\mathcal{B}(\mathsf{pk}') = 1]$ is the probability that $\mathcal{B}$ outputs 1 with pk$'$.

Notice that the difference between $\Pr[\mathcal{B}(\mathsf{pk}) = 1]$ and $\Pr[\mathcal{B}(\mathsf{pk}') = 1]$ is less than ε_{DSD} due to the complexity of DSD-problem. By the way, to answer a query m to the signing oracle Σ from $\mathcal{A}$, we need to program the random oracle to set $h(\{c_1^k || c_2^k || c_3^k\}_{k=1}^r || \alpha || m) = \mathbf{b}$ so that $(\{c_1^k, c_2^k, c_3^k, z_1^k, z_2^k\}_{k=1}^r, \alpha)$ is a valid signature for m. Unfortunately, this programming may conflict with previous values output by the random oracle. The probability that such collisions happen

pk : commitment function $Com(\cdot), H \in \{0,1\}^{(n-k) \times n}, i_U \in \{0,1\}^{n-k}, p \in \mathbb{N}$
sk : $s_U \in \{0,1\}^n$ such that $H \cdot s_U{}^{\mathrm{T}} = i_U, w_H(s_U) = p$ holds

1. Prover computes commitments as follows:

$y_i \xleftarrow{\$} \{0,1\}^n;\ \pi_i \xleftarrow{\$} \Pi_n$
$c_1^i \leftarrow Com(\pi_i \| H \cdot y_i{}^{\mathrm{T}}),$
$c_2^i \leftarrow Com(y_i \cdot \pi_i),$
$c_3^i \leftarrow Com((y_i \oplus i_U) \cdot \pi_i)$

2. Prover sends $\{c_1^i, c_2^i, c_3^i\}_{i=1}^r$

3. Verifier sends $\mathbf{b} = (b_1, \cdots, b_{r'}) \xleftarrow{\$} \{0,1\}^{r'}$

4. Prover converts $\mathbf{b}$ to $\mathbf{t} = (t_1, \cdots, t_k) \in \{0,1,2\}^k$ as follows:

$i \leftarrow 1, j \leftarrow 1$
while $i \leq r$ and $j < r'$ **do**
  if $b_j \| b_j + 1 = 00$, **then** $t_i \leftarrow 0, i \leftarrow i + 1$
  if $b_j \| b_j + 1 = 01$, **then** $t_i \leftarrow 1, i \leftarrow i + 1$
  if $b_j \| b_j + 1 = 10$, **then** $t_i \leftarrow 2, i \leftarrow i + 1$
  $j \leftarrow j + 2$
end while

5. For $1 \leq i \leq r$, Prover sends (z_1^i, z_2^i) as follows:
if $k < r$, **then** $z_1^i \leftarrow \lambda, z_2^i \leftarrow \lambda$
if $t_i = 0$, **then** $z_1^i \leftarrow y_i, z_2^i \leftarrow \pi_i$
if $t_i = 1$, **then** $z_1^i \leftarrow y_i \oplus s_U, z_2^i \leftarrow \pi_i$
if $t_i = 2$, **then** $z_1^i \leftarrow y_i \cdot \pi_i, z_2^i \leftarrow s_U \cdot \pi_i$

6. If $z_1^i = \lambda, z_2^i = \lambda$, go to Step 3

7. Else, Verifier converts $\mathbf{b}$ to $\mathbf{t}$ as in Step 4 and does the operation as follows:
if $t_i = 0$, **then** Verifier checks
$c_1^i = Com(z_2^i \| H \cdot z_1^i{}^{\mathrm{T}}), c_2^i = Com(z_1^i \cdot z_2^i)$
if $t_i = 1$, **then** Verifier checks
$c_1^i = Com(z_2^i \| H \cdot z_1^i{}^{\mathrm{T}} \oplus i_U), c_3^i = Com(z_1^i \cdot z_2^i)$
if $t_i = 2$, **then** Verifier checks
$c_2^i = Com(z_1^i), c_3^i = Com(z_1^i \oplus z_2^i)$
and $w_H(z_2^i) = p$

8. Verifier outputs *Accept* if all checks passed
Reject otherwise

Fig. 3. Parallel protocol 1

is at most $q_S(q_S + q_H + 1)/2^{3rN+\beta}$. Therefore, $\Pr[\mathcal{B}(\mathsf{pk}) = 1] \approx \varepsilon_1 - q_S(q_S + q_H + 1)/2^{3rN+\beta}$ and $\Pr[\mathcal{B}(\mathsf{pk}') = 1] \approx \varepsilon_1' - q_S(q_S + q_H + 1)/2^{3rN+\beta}$, where ε_1' is the probability that $\mathcal{A}$ succeeds in producing a valid signature forgery of Sig1 with pk'. Hence, ε_1 is approximately bounded as follows:

$$\varepsilon_1 - q_S(q_S + q_H + 1)/2^{3rN+\beta} - (\varepsilon_1' - q_S(q_S + q_H + 1)/2^{3rN+\beta}) < \varepsilon_{DSD}$$
$$\therefore \quad \varepsilon_1 < \varepsilon_1' + \varepsilon_{DSD} \tag{4.2}$$

However, ε_1' is unknown. To find ε_1', we construct the algorithm P' that successfully impersonates the prover in the parallel protocol 1 (Fig. 3) using $\mathcal{A}$ with KeyGen' to find the upper bound of the ε_1'.

The following Lemma 1 holds for the parallel protocol 1 shown in Fig. 3.

Lemma 1. *If the public key* pk' *of parallel protocol 1 is generated from dishonest key generator* KeyGen', *the probability that any adversary succeeds in impersonating the prover in the parallel protocol 1 with* pk' *is at most* $(2/3)^r$.

From Lemma 1, we know that the probability that P' succeeds in impersonating the prover in the parallel protocol 1 is bounded above by $(2/3)^r$. However, to succeed in impersonating the prover, we need to guess the hash query which will be used in the forgery and to be able to impersonate the prover. Also it is necessary that we get r-bit ternary string converted from $\mathbf{b} \in \{0,1\}^{r'}$ sent from the verifier in parallel protocol 1. The probability that P' succeeds in impersonating the prover is the product of $\Pr[\mathcal{B}(\mathsf{pk}') = 1]$ and the probability that we meet these two conditions. Therefore, we lose a factor $(q_h + 1)/\varepsilon_{GOOD}$ in the reduction, resulting in the term $\frac{(q_H+1)}{\varepsilon_{GOOD}} \left(\frac{2}{3}\right)^r$ in the theorem. As a result,

ε_1' is bounded above by $q_S(q_S + q_H + 1)/2^{3rN+\beta} + \frac{(q_H+1)}{\varepsilon_{GOOD}} \left(\frac{2}{3}\right)^r$ and ε_1 is bounded above by $\varepsilon_{DSD} + \frac{(q_H+1)}{\varepsilon_{GOOD}} \left(\frac{2}{3}\right)^r + \frac{q_S(q_S+q_H+1)}{2^{3rN+\beta}}$.   □

The full proof of Theorem 1 and Lemma 1 will be shown in our full paper.

4.2   Scheme 2

Theorem 2. *If DSD problem is ε_{DSD}-hard, then* Sig2 *is* $(q_H, q_S, \varepsilon_2)$-*existentially unforgeable against adaptive chosen-message attacks in the random oracle model for*:

$$\varepsilon_2 = \varepsilon_{DSD} + (q_H + 1) \left(\frac{3}{4}\right)^r + \frac{q_S(q_S + q_H + 1)}{2^{3rN}}. \tag{4.3}$$

Proof Overview. In order to prove the security of Sig2, the main idea is to construct the algorithm $\mathcal{B}$ that outputs a bit indicating whether $(\varepsilon_2, q_H, q_S)$-adversary $\mathcal{A}$ has succeeded in producing a valid signature forgery of Sig2. Let pk be the public key generated from honest key generator KeyGen, pk$'$ be the public key generated from dishonest key generator KeyGen$'$, where honest key generator KeyGen means that KeyGen generates the correct public key pk $= (H \in \{0,1\}^{(n-k) \times n}, i_U \in \{0,1\}^{n-k}, p \in \mathbb{N})$ such that $\exists s : H \cdot s = i_U, w_H(s) = p$, and dishonest key generator KeyGen$'$ means that KeyGen$'$ generates pk$' = (H' \in \{0,1\}^{(n-k) \times n}, i_U' \in \{0,1\}^{n-k}, p' \in \mathbb{N})$ such that $\nexists s : H' \cdot s = i_U', w_H(s) = p'$. We denote $\Pr[\mathcal{B}(\mathsf{pk}) = 1]$ is the probability that $\mathcal{B}$ outputs 1 with pk, $\Pr[\mathcal{B}(\mathsf{pk}') = 1]$ is the probability that $\mathcal{B}$ outputs 1 with pk$'$.

Notice that the difference between $\Pr[\mathcal{B}(\mathsf{pk}) = 1]$ and $\Pr[\mathcal{B}(\mathsf{pk}') = 1]$ is less than ε_{DSD} due to the complexity of DSD-problem. By the way, to answer a query m to the signing oracle Σ from $\mathcal{A}$, we need to program the random oracle to set $h(\{c_1^k || c_2^k || c_3^k\}_{k=1}^r || m) = \mathbf{b}$ so that $(\{c_1^k, c_2^k, c_3^k, z_1^k, z_2^k\}_{k=1}^r)$ is a valid signature for m. Unfortunately, this programming may conflict with previous values output by the random oracle. The probability that such collisions happen is at most $q_S(q_S + q_H + 1)/2^{3rN}$. Therefore, $\Pr[\mathcal{B}(\mathsf{pk}) = 1] \approx \varepsilon_2 - q_S(q_S + q_H + 1)/2^{3rN}$ and $\Pr[\mathcal{B}(\mathsf{pk}') = 1] \approx \varepsilon_2' - q_S(q_S + q_H + 1)/2^{3rN}$, where ε_2' is the probability that $\mathcal{A}$ succeeds in producing a valid signature forgery of Sig2 with pk$'$. Hence, ε_2 is bounded as follows:

$$\varepsilon_2 - q_S(q_S + q_H + 1)/2^{3rN} - (\varepsilon_2' - q_S(q_S + q_H + 1)/2^{3rN}) < \varepsilon_{DSD}.$$
$$\therefore \quad \varepsilon_2 < \varepsilon_2' + \varepsilon_{DSD} \tag{4.4}$$

However, ε_2' is unknown. Then, we construct the algorithm P' that successfully impersonates the prover in the parallel protocol 2 (Fig. 4) using $\mathcal{A}$ with KeyGen$'$ to find the upper bound of ε_2'.

The difference of parallel protocol 2 (Fig. 4 from parallel protocol 1 3 is that re-transmission of $\mathbf{b}$ is unnecessary and the probability that $t_i = 1$ is $1/2$ and the probability that $t_i = 0$ or $t_i = 2$ is $1/4$. Similar to Lemma 1, Lemma 2 holds for parallel protocol 2.

pk : $Com(\cdot)$. $H \in \{0,1\}^{(n-k)\times n}$. $i_U \in \{0,1\}^{n-k}$. $p \in \mathbb{N}$

sk : $s_U \in \{0,1\}^n$ such that $H \cdot s_U^{\mathrm{T}} = i_U$, $w_H(s_U) = p$ holds

1. Prover computes commitments as follows:

$y_i \xleftarrow{\$} \{0,1\}^n$, $\pi_i \xleftarrow{\$} \Pi_n$

$c_1^i \leftarrow Com(\pi_i||H \cdot y_i^{\mathrm{T}})$.

$c_2^i \leftarrow Com(y_i \cdot \pi_i)$.

$c_3^i \leftarrow Com((y_i \oplus i_U) \cdot \pi_i)$

2. Prover sends $\{c_1^i, c_2^i, c_3^i\}_{i=1}^r$

3. Verifier sends $\mathbf{b} = (b_1, \cdots, b_r) \xleftarrow{\$} \{0,1\}^{2r}$

4. For $1 \le i \le r$. Prover sends (z_1^i, z_2^i) as follows:

if $b_{2i-1}||b_{2i} = 00$. then $z_1^i \leftarrow y_i$, $z_2^i \leftarrow \pi_i$

if $b_{2i-1}||b_{2i} = 01, 10$. then $z_1^i \leftarrow y_i \oplus s_U$, $z_2^i \leftarrow \pi_i$

if $b_{2i-1}||b_{2i} = 11$. then $z_1^i \leftarrow y_i \cdot \pi_i$, $z_2^i \leftarrow s_U \cdot \pi_i$

5. Verifier does the operation as follows:

if $b_{2i-1}||b_{2i} = 00$. then Verifier checks

$c_1^i = Com(z_2^i||H \cdot z_1^{i\,\mathrm{T}})$, $c_2^i = Com(z_1^i \cdot z_2^i)$

if $b_{2i-1}||b_{2i} = 01, 10$. then Verifier checks

$c_1^i = Com(z_2^i||H \cdot z_1^{i\,\mathrm{T}} \oplus i_U)$, $c_3^i = Com(z_1^i \cdot z_2^i)$

if $b_{2i-1}||b_{2i} = 11$. then Verifier checks

$c_2^i = Com(z_1^i)$, $c_3^i = Com(z_1^i \oplus z_2^i)$

and $w_H(z_2^i) = p$

6. Verifier outputs $Accept$ if all checks passed

$Reject$ otherwise

Fig. 4. Parallel protocol 2

Lemma 2. *If the public key* pk$'$ *of parallel protocol 2 is generated from dishonest key generator* KeyGen$'$, *the probability that any adversary succeeds in impersonating the prover in the parallel protocol 2 with* pk$'$ *is at most* $(3/4)^r$.

To succeed in impersonating the prover, we need to guess the hash query which will be used in the forgery and to be able to impersonate the prover. From Lemma 2, the probability P' succeeds in impersonating the prover in the parallel protocol 2 is bounded above by $(3/4)^r$. As a result, ε_2' is bounded above, and the upper bound of ε_2 is found.   □

The full proof of Theorem 2 and Lemma 2 will be shown in our full paper.

5   Discussion

5.1   Security Comparison

In Table 2 we summarize the complexity of the our two signature schemes with some properties under 128-bit security and 192-bit security. However, as the machine environment, we assume that the CPU is 4-core, 3.50 GHz processor. And we assume that the hash function and the commitment function are SHA-256.

Table 2. Comparison Sig1 and Sig2 with $(n, k, p) = (4096, 3424, 60)$ under 128-bit security $((n, k, p) = (6144, 5024, 96)$ under 192-bit security)

Schemes	r	The length of hash value $|\mathbf{b}|$ [bits]	Calculation time to commitment [ms]	Calculation time to challenge [µs]	The size of sign $|\sigma|$ [MB]
Sig1 (128-bit)	324	864	1.57	41.7	1.58
Sig2 (128-bit)	453	906	2.20	29.1	2.42
Sig1 (192-bit)	433	1154	3.29	55.7	3.28
Sig2 (192-bit)	608	1216	4.62	39.1	5.05

5.2   Machine Experiment

We perform a machine experiment on each of the proposed encoding method and the naive encoding method. We measure the time required by each encoding method to produce sufficient ternary bits to guarantee 128-bit (192-bit) security of the corresponding signature scheme, assuming that the input is a random binary bits.

Recall the description of each encoding method as follows.

– *Method 0: Naive encoding.* Interpreting the binary string as integer, and then just converting it to a base 3 representation.
– *Method 1: Encoding with droppings.* Let $\mathbf{b}$ denote the inputted sequence of binary bits. We divide $\mathbf{b}$ into blocks of two bits. An i-th two-bits-block of $\mathbf{b}$ is denoted by $\mathbf{b}_i = b_{i,0} b_{i,1}$, where $b_{i,0}, b_{i,1} \in \{0,1\}$. For each i-th two-bits-block $\mathbf{b}_i$, this encoding basically firstly coverts the value of $\mathbf{b}_i$ into its decimal value, and then outputs the converted value if and only if the converted value is in the set $\{0,1,2\}$. The important properties of this encoding are as follows: (1) all blocks from input with binary value "11" are dropped, and (2) there is one-to-one corresponding between the ternary bits at the output and the two-bits-block of binary bits at the input.
– *Method 2: Encoding without dropping.* We use the same notation as *Method 1.* For each i-th two-bits-block $\mathbf{b}_i$, this encoding maps the value of $\mathbf{b}_i$ into its Hamming's weight, i.e., the number of non-zero value. The most important property of this encoding is that blocks with value "01" and "10" are mapped into the same ternary bit "1".

As shown above, in order that the signature scheme corresponding to each encoding method satisfies 128-bit or 192-bit safety, the ternary string must be r bits or more. For each method, we measured average the length of time required to convert from a $|\mathbf{b}|$ bits binary string to a r bits ternary string. For *Method 1*, we set $|\mathbf{b}| = 864$ (1154) and $r = 324$ (433), and for *Method 2*, we set $|\mathbf{b}| = 906$ (1216) and $r = 453$ (608) as computed in subsection 5.1. For *Naive Method*, we estimate that the security of signature scheme based on this method will be same to that of Sig1, but with $\varepsilon_{GOOD} = 1$, since it always produce uniformly distributed ternary bits without fail. Thus, for *Naive Method* we can set $r = 323$ (432), and accordingly $|\mathbf{b}| = 514$ (687), since $2^{514} - 1 > 3^{324} - 1 > 2^{513} - 1$ ($2^{687} - 1 > 3^{433} - 1 > 2^{686} - 1$). Also, for implementation of *Naive Method*, we use the code provided in [7] which efficiently removes the requirement for explicit division operation and big number library.

Our experiment environment is as follows and the results are shown in Tables 3 and 4.

– Machine: Raspberry Pi 2 Model B, OS: Raspbian NOOBS v2.3.0, Kernel: Linux ver.4.4
– CPU: A 900MHz quad-core ARM Cortex-A7 CPU, Memory: 1 GB
– Language: C, Compiler: GCC v4.9.2 (Raspbian 4.9.2-10)

Table 3. Comparison of conversion time under 128-bit security

	With optimization [μs]	Without optimization [μs]
Naive method	326.738	7207.075
Method 1 (Encoding with dropping, Sig1)	6.146	45.469
Method 2 (Encoding without dropping, Sig2)	1.740	20.857

Table 4. Comparison of conversion time under 192-bit security

	With optimization [μs]	Without optimization [μs]
Naive method	448.572	13040.845
Method 1 (Encoding with dropping, Sig1)	6.442	65.052
Method 2 (Encoding without dropping, Sig2)	1.704	26.293

6   Conclusion

We have proposed two methods to encode sequence of binary bits into ternary bits and constructed two signature schemes based on them. We have evaluated the security of the signature schemes against unforgeability under chosen message attacks and shown that the encoding methods influence the performance and the security of the signature schemes constructed based on them. We have also compared the performance of the proposed encoding methods against naive encoding method when implemented in a lightweight device, and shown that the encoding methods are significantly faster compared to the naive method.

Acknowledgement. This work was supported by JSPS Grants-in-Aid for Scientific Research (KAKENHI) Grant Number JP18K11292.

References

1. Abdalla, M., Fouque, P.-A., Lyubashevsky, V., Tibouchi, M.: Tightly-secure signatures from lossy identification schemes. In: Pointcheval, D., Johansson, T. (eds.) EUROCRYPT 2012. LNCS, vol. 7237, pp. 572–590. Springer, Heidelberg (2012). https://doi.org/10.1007/978-3-642-29011-4_34
2. Alamélou, Q., Blazy, O., Cauchie, S., Gaborit, P.: A code-based group signature scheme. Des. Codes Crypt. **82**(1), 469–493 (2017)
3. Bellare, M., Palacio, A.: GQ and Schnorr identification schemes: proofs of security against impersonation under active and concurrent attacks. In: Yung, M. (ed.) CRYPTO 2002. LNCS, vol. 2442, pp. 162–177. Springer, Heidelberg (2002). https://doi.org/10.1007/3-540-45708-9_11

4. Berlekamp, E., McEliece, R., van Tilborg, H.: On the inherent intractability of certain coding problems (corresp.). IEEE Trans. Inf. Theor. **24**(3), 384–386 (1978)

5. Fiat, A., Shamir, A.: How to prove yourself: practical solutions to identification and signature problems. In: Odlyzko, A.M. (ed.) CRYPTO 1986. LNCS, vol. 263, pp. 186–194. Springer, Heidelberg (1987). https://doi.org/10.1007/3-540-47721-7_12

6. Sakumoto, K., Shirai, T., Hiwatari, H.: Public-key identification schemes based on multivariate quadratic polynomials. In: Rogaway, P. (ed.) CRYPTO 2011. LNCS, vol. 6841, pp. 706–723. Springer, Heidelberg (2011). https://doi.org/10.1007/978-3-642-22792-9_40

7. Stackoverflow: Conversion of binary bitstream to and from ternary bitstream? August 2012. https://stackoverflow.com/questions/12015752/conversion-of-binary-bitstream-to-and-from-ternary-bitstream. Code is from answer provided by Stephen Ressler (http://stephenjressler.com) under pseudonym Gene

8. Stern, J.: A new paradigm for public key identification. IEEE Trans. Inf. Theor. **42**(6), 1757–1768 (1996)

9. von Neumann, J.: Various techniques used in connection with random digits. Monte Carlo methods. Nat. Bur. Stand. **12**, 36–38 (1951)

Security Protocols

Efficient Evaluation of Low Degree Multivariate Polynomials in Ring-LWE Homomorphic Encryption Schemes

Sergiu Carpov[✉] and Oana Stan

CEA, LIST, Point Courrier 172, 91191 Gif-sur-Yvette Cedex, France
sergiu.carpov@cea.fr

Abstract. Homomorphic encryption schemes allow to perform computations over encrypted data. In schemes based on RLWE assumption the plaintext data is a ring polynomial. In many use cases of homomorphic encryption only the degree-0 coefficient of this polynomial is used to encrypt data. In this context any computation on encrypted data can be performed. It is trickier to perform generic computations when more than one coefficient per ciphertext is used.

In this paper we introduce a method to efficiently evaluate low-degree multivariate polynomials over encrypted data. The main idea is to encode several messages in the coefficients of a plaintext space polynomial. Using ring homomorphism operations and multiplications between ciphertexts, we compute multivariate monomials up to a given degree. Afterwards, using ciphertext additions we evaluate the input multivariate polynomial. We perform extensive experimentations of the proposed evaluation method. As example, evaluating an *arbitrary* multivariate degree-3 polynomial with 100 variables over Boolean space takes under 13 s.

1 Introduction

The widespread of cloud storage and computing services has conducted to a massive shift towards data and computation outsourcing both for particular users and businesses. Between the incontestable advantages of using cloud computing, one can cite the cost reduction in the development and in the maintenance of data centers, the scalability and elasticity of cloud resources, improved accessibility (via only an Internet connection) and a guaranteed reliability (with redundancy and back-up mechanisms).

However, one of the main barriers in the large-scale adoption of cloud based services for data processing and storage concerns the data privacy, since the data owners have little or no control on the cloud provider security policies and practices. One immediate and recommended solution is to encrypt the highly

This work has been supported in part by the French's FUI project CRYPTOCOMP and by the European Union's H2020 research and innovation programme under grant agreement No. 727528 (project KONFIDO).

C. Su and H. Kikuchi (Eds.): ISPEC 2018, LNCS 11125, pp. 265–281, 2018.
https://doi.org/10.1007/978-3-319-99807-7_16

sensitive data before sending and migrating it to a cloud environment. In this context one can use Homomorphic Encryption (HE) schemes, which allow to perform computations directly over encrypted data.

Homomorphic encryption schemes have been known for a long time, with the first partial constructions dating back to the seventies [23]. In his seminal work [13], Gentry proposed the first Fully Homomorphic Encryption (FHE) scheme capable to evaluate an arbitrary number of additions and multiplications over encrypted data (allowing, in theory, to execute any computation). From this major theoretical breakthrough, there was an increased research interest for homomorphic encryption. Many fully and somewhat homomorphic encryption schemes (SHE) have been proposed in literature [5,10,12,20,26] based on different security assumptions. Compared to FHE schemes, SHE schemes allow to perform only a limited number of homomorphic operations and are used as a basis to construct FHE schemes. In one of the latest surveys on homomorphic encryption [1], FHE schemes are classified into four main families:

- Ideal Lattice based [13]
- Schemes over integers [26]
- Schemes based on the Learning With Error (LWE) or the ring version (RLWE) problem [5,6]
- NTRU-like schemes [20]

Using both addition and multiplication over ciphertexts, one can execute arbitrary arithmetic circuits, evaluate multivariate polynomials, etc. A typical use of FHE is to express the function to be computed on encrypted data as a static control-flow program and execute homomorphically the associated Boolean circuit [8]. Despite their recent and successive improvements, the main issue about FHE schemes is the performance (in terms of execution time and memory requirements) and, consequently, the practical applicability.

Contribution

In this work, we focus on the third category of schemes, the ones based on the RLWE assumption, and we propose a new method for the efficient evaluation of multivariate polynomials in the homomorphic domain. For this type of schemes the plaintext and, respectively, the ciphertext space are polynomial ring elements with coefficients of different size (i.e. being defined over different integer modulus). In many applications using RLWE schemes only the zero degree coefficient is used to encode useful data.

Several researches were conducted in order to improve the evaluation performance of polynomials over encrypted data and take advantage of the plaintext space polynomial structure. The coefficient packing method, introduced in [22], allows to pack several messages into a single ciphertext. In a series of papers [27,28] the authors describe how to evaluate multivariate linear polynomials over coefficient packed messages. In this work, we further generalize their method to allow evaluation of low-degree multivariate polynomials. The coefficients of the evaluated multivariate polynomial can be either in clear or encrypted forms. The proposed packing and computation methods allow not only to reduce ciphertext expansion ratio[1] but also to perform computations using messages encoded in the same ciphertext. As shown later, our method reduces the complexity of basic operations performed in homomorphic space, and thus ameliorates the performances for different types of computations manipulating private data. As example of applications in which using our polynomial evaluation method can be useful are the machine learning algorithms.

Related Works

Several research works found in the literature propose solutions on how to ameliorate the efficiency of homomorphic encryption schemes in the context of practical applications.

In [22] it is introduced the coefficient packing technique for homomorphic ciphertexts. Besides decreasing ciphertext size this method allows to accelerate multi-bit additions/multiplications. Roughly speaking, the main idea is to encode a bit-wise representation of integers into plaintext polynomial coefficients. Under certain conditions, adding and multiplying such encrypted plaintexts allows to perform binary addition and respectively binary multiplication of initial integers. As such, this method is appropriate in computations using a small number of multiplications (i.e. computing standard deviation). The authors used this technique to efficiently compute means, variances and inner products (i.e. degree-1 polynomials). The inner product is used in a protocol for making logistic model predictions over homomorphically encrypted data.

In [28] the authors propose an extension of the data packing technique introduced in [22] and use it to homomorphically compute inner products and Hamming distances. Hamming distance computation is equivalent to evaluating a particular degree-2 polynomial or a degree-1 polynomial with encrypted coefficients. As explained earlier, our work is an extension of the approach from [28] for general polynomials of degree larger than one.

In [9] the authors introduce an "unpacking" technique for coefficient packed ciphertexts, thus they describe how to obtain several ciphertexts from a single one in the encrypted domain. No computation methods over packed ciphertext is proposed.

One of the first approaches aiming to efficiently encode the messages for HE schemes is the packing method proposed by Smart and Vercauteren in [14,24]. By using CRT (Chinese Remainder Theorem) on polynomials, one can perform SIMD (Single Instructions Multiple Data) operations on encrypted data. Roughly speaking, the plaintext space is split into several independent "slots" if the cyclotomic polynomial defining the polynomial ring can be factored. The multivariate polynomial evaluation method we introduce is complementary to the batching and can be applied on top of it (i.e. do a polynomial evaluation in each slot).

For a view on the different applications of these optimization methods for RLWE-based schemes, we refer to paper [15] where the authors discuss which machine learning algorithms can be expressed in polynomial form. As said earlier only polynomials can be evaluated using homomorphic encryption. Several

---

[1] The ratio between ciphertext and plaintext message sizes.

homomorphic implementations of classification algorithms are proposed in [3]. In particular, the authors describe how to perform hyperplane decision (linear classifier), Naive Bayes and decision trees classification algorithms on HE encrypted data. In a series of papers [27,29] the authors discuss different applications (pattern matching and biometric authentication) of secure inner-product computation. Different encoding methods for representing fixed-point numbers, designed for Ring-based SHE schemes, were presented in [2,11] along with their applications to a homomorphic forecasting algorithm and respectively to an image processing algorithm.

This paper is organized as follows. After a brief introduction of generic operations supported by a RLWE based homomorphic scheme (Sect. 2), we describe the proposed evaluation method for multivariate polynomials in Sect. 3. Later on we provide some experimental results in Sect. 4 followed by an example of a practical application of our method. Finally, Sect. 5 concludes the paper and provides some perspectives on the future work.

2   Homomorphic Encryption

2.1   Preliminiaries

Let us first give the basic notation and introduce the RLWE problem. Let $\mathbb{A} = \mathbb{Z}[X]/f(x)$ be the ring of polynomials modulo a monic irreducible polynomial $f(x)$. Usually, one would typically restrict $f(x)$ to be the cyclotomic polynomial $\Phi_m(X)$, i.e. the minimal polynomial of the primitive m-th root of unity. Let $\mathbb{A}_q = \mathbb{A} \mod q$ be the set of polynomials modulo $\Phi_m(X)$ with coefficients modulo q. Thus an element in $\mathbb{A}$ is a polynomial of degree d over $\mathbb{Z}_q$, with $d = \varphi(m)$ (Euler's totient function) in the case of a cyclotomic polynomial modulus.

Using these above notations, we recall a simple definition of the RLWE problem, first introduced by Lyubashevsky, Peikert and Regev [21].

RLWE Problem. For security parameter λ, $f(x)$ is the cyclotomic polynomial depending on λ, the ring $\mathbb{A}$ is defined as before and q is an integer. Let $\chi(\lambda)$ be an error distribution over $\mathbb{A}$. The decision-RLWE problem is to distinguish between two distributions: a first distribution obtained by sampling (a_i, b_i) uniformly from $\mathbb{A}_q^2$ and a second distribution made of a polynomial number of samples of the form $(a_i, b_i = a_i * s + e_i) \in \mathbb{A}_q^2$, where a_i is uniformly random in $\mathbb{A}_q$, $e_i \leftarrow \chi$ and $s \leftarrow \mathbb{A}_q$ is a uniformly random element. The $\text{RLWE}_{d,q,\lambda}$ assumption is that the RLWE problem is infeasible.

This problem can be reduced using a quantum algorithm to the shortest vector problem over ideal lattices and its hardness is independent of q (usually either prime or power of 2). The above RLWE problem easily leads to several homomorphic encryption schemes, such as BGV [5] or FV [12].

In RLWE based homomorphic encryption scheme ciphertexts and secret keys are elements from the ring $\mathbb{A}_q$. The plaintext space is the ring of polynomials $\mathbb{A}_t$ $(t \ll q)$.

Leveled SHE schemes [5] use a series of integer modulus $q_0, q_1, \ldots$ for ciphertexts at different moments of an homomorphic evaluation. A modulus switching technique is used (switch ciphertext from modulus q_i to modulus $q_{i+1}, q_i > q_{i+1}$) to deal with the noise increase. In [4] a notion of scale-invariance for leveled SHE schemes is introduced. In scale-invariant schemes a single modulus, q, is used for ciphertexts during the whole homomorphic evaluation.

Usually, the plaintext space is chosen for $t = 2$ and a single binary message is encrypted per ciphertext, in the zero-degree coefficient of the polynomial from $\mathbb{A}_2$, allowing to homomorphically evaluate arbitrary Boolean circuits. By using a larger modulus ($t > 2$) for the plaintext space it is possible to execute operations on integers modulo t homomorphically or even on elements from the polynomial ring $\mathbb{A}_t$ (see next section).

In the so-called batched schemes [14], the plaintext space ring $\mathbb{A}_t$ can be factored into sub-rings (defined by the factorization of the polynomial $\Phi_m(X)$ modulo t) such that homomorphic operations apply to each sub-ring independently. Batching several messages into ciphertext slots allows to execute homomorphic operations on all messages in parallel at the same time.

To summarize, RLWE based HE schemes allow to execute homomorphic operations (batched or not) over polynomial ring $\mathbb{A}_t$ elements (includes the integer modulo ring and finite field cases). In the next section, we will present more formally the basic operations a SHE can execute.

2.2 Homomorphic Operations

Beside the typical key generation, encryption and decryption, a homomorphic encryption scheme is also defined by a set of plaintext operations which can execute in the encrypted domain. Below, we give a generic list of operations supported by any public-key RLWE SHE scheme ignoring implementation details. We limit our description to the non-batched schemes, the results presented in this paper being also valid for the batched ones.

KeyGen $\left(1^\lambda\right)$ – generate the set of keys: a secret key sk used for encrypting and decrypting messages, a public key pk used for encrypting messages and an additional set of evaluation keys evk (for key-switching in homomorphic multiplications and ring homomorphism operations).

$\text{Enc}_{pk}(m)$ – encrypts a plaintext message $m \in \mathbb{A}_t$ using the public key pk.

$\text{Dec}_{sk}(\text{ct})$ – decrypts a ciphertext ct using the secret key sk.

$\text{Add}(\text{ct}_1, \text{ct}_2)$ – outputs a ciphertext which represents the addition of plaintext messages encrypted by ct_1 and ct_2:
$$\text{Dec}_{sk}(\text{Add}(\text{ct}_1, \text{ct}_2)) \equiv \text{Dec}_{sk}(\text{ct}_1) + \text{Dec}_{sk}(\text{ct}_2)$$

$\text{Mult}(\text{ct}_1, \text{ct}_2, evk)$ – outputs a ciphertext which represents the multiplication of plaintext messages encrypted by ct_1 and ct_2:
$$\text{Dec}_{sk}(\text{Mult}(\text{ct}_1, \text{ct}_2, evk)) \equiv \text{Dec}_{sk}(\text{ct}_1) \cdot \text{Dec}_{sk}(\text{ct}_2)$$

$\text{Hom}(\text{ct}, k, evk)$ – outputs a ciphertext which represents the application of the ring homomorphism $X \mapsto X^k$ over the plaintext message polynomial encrypted by ct:

$\text{Dec}_{sk}\left(\text{Hom}\left(\text{ct}, k, evk\right)\right) \equiv p\left(X \mapsto X^k\right)$ where $p\left(X\right) = \text{Dec}_{sk}\left(\text{ct}\right)$
For some homomorphic encryption scheme instantiations, this homomorphism operation can be performed with only a small noise increase.

For simplicity sake, we use addition and multiplication operators for homomorphic addition and multiplication of ciphertexts: $\text{ct}_1 + \text{ct}_2 = \text{Add}\left(\text{ct}_1, \text{ct}_2\right)$ and respectively $\text{ct}_1 \cdot \text{ct}_2 = \text{Mult}\left(\text{ct}_1, \text{ct}_2, evk\right)$. The ring homomorphism operation $\text{Hom}\left(\text{ct}, k, evk\right)$ is denoted using $\phi^k\left(\text{ct}\right)$. Evaluation key evk use is implicit in operator notation. We recall that all the arithmetic operations are performed over the plaintext space ring $\mathbb{A}_t$.

Homomorphic addition and multiplication can be applied to a plaintext and a ciphertext, e.g. $\text{ct}_1 + m_2$ means an addition between the ciphertext ct_1 and the plaintext message m_2. Such an homomorphic operation shall be denoted as a plaintext-ciphertext homomorphic operation. The noise increase of a plaintext-ciphertext operation is lower when compared to the noise increase of this operation applied onto ciphertexts.

3   Homomorphic Evaluation of Multivariate Polynomials

Let $\mathcal{P}^n$ be the space of all the polynomials with n variables, $x_0, \ldots, x_{n-1}$. Without loss of generality we suppose that the constant term is zero. The subspace of polynomials of maximal degree d, $1 \leq d \leq n$, is denoted by $\mathcal{P}_d^n$ and composed by polynomials defined as:

$$P\left(x_0, \ldots, x_{n-1}\right) = \sum_{1 \leq k \leq d} \sum_{0 \leq e_1 \leq \ldots \leq e_k < n} c_{e_1, \ldots, e_k} \cdot x_{e_1} \cdot \ldots \cdot x_{e_k} \qquad (1)$$

In this formulation the monomial terms $x_{e_1} \cdot \ldots \cdot x_{e_k}$ are grouped by their degree k. The inner sum adds up all the combinations with repetition of k variables. Variables $x_0, \ldots, x_{n-1}$ and coefficients $c_{e_1, \ldots, e_k}$ belong to a ring. In this work the plaintext space for homomorphic encryption is used, namely the ring of integers modulo t.

In what follows we describe some naive methods for multivariate polynomial evaluation over homomorphically encrypted data and afterwards we introduce an optimized method for multivariate polynomial evaluation.

Let $P\left(x_0, \ldots, x_{n-1}\right)$ be a polynomial from $\mathcal{P}_d^n$ which has to be evaluated at an encrypted point $a_0, \ldots, a_{n-1}$. The polynomial is evaluated over the integer ring $\mathbb{Z}_t$, with $t \geq 2$. In this work we focus on efficient evaluation of polynomials over homomorphic domain using the lowest possible parameters for the configuration of the HE scheme.

3.1   Naive Methods

A straightforward method is to encrypt each value $a_0, \ldots, a_{n-1}$ into separate homomorphic ciphertexts. Using homomorphic multiplications/additions one can compute polynomial representation (1). As mentioned in Sect. 2, the parameters of HE schemes depend mainly on the degree of monomials and less on their number (noise increase due to homomorphic additions is much smaller than for homomorphic multiplications). The lowest HE scheme parameters are obtained when a tree-like structure is used to compute the monomials of P. Homomorphic polynomial evaluation time mainly depends on the number of homomorphic multiplications. Note that $P(x_0, \ldots, x_{n-1})$ can have as many as $\frac{(n+d)!}{n! \cdot d!}$ monomials[2]. So, in the general case, the number of homomorphic multiplications is not polynomial, but potentially factorial.

As different monomials share common parts we can minimize the number of homomorphic multiplications by evaluating them once and reusing them when needed. Finding the optimal way to do so is a difficult optimization problem and has been studied from multiple standpoints: common subexpression elimination, arithmetic circuit optimization, etc. [7,18,19]. Larger HE scheme parameters should be used for the aforementioned methods as the multiplicative depth of computation increases when compared to direct homomorphic computation of polynomial terms. In return, the number of homomorphic operations needed for polynomial evaluation is lower.

Let us now present our method to be applied when the degree of the polynomials to be evaluated homomorphically respects certain condition with regard to the ciphertext space.

3.2   Optimized Method for $n^d \leq \deg(\Phi(X))$

In the naive methods presented earlier only a single coefficient (the degree zero one) of the polynomial ($\in \mathbb{A}_t$) to be encrypted in a homomorphic ciphertext is used. Other coefficients are set to zero and are not used. A better solution will be to use more than one coefficient of the polynomial. In this section we introduce an optimized method for polynomial evaluation in which the values $a_0, \ldots, a_{n-1}$ are packed in the coefficients of a homomorphic plaintext polynomial (2). The polynomial is further encrypted into the ciphertext $\mathtt{ct}$. This packing technique was introduced by the authors of [22]. The proposed evaluation method is restricted to cases where relation $n^d \leq \deg(\Phi(X))$ is verified (we explain later why).

$$Q(X) = \sum_{0 \leq i < n} a_i \cdot X^i \qquad (2)$$

$$\mathtt{ct} = \mathtt{Enc}_{pk}(Q(X))$$

First, we describe the proposed polynomial evaluation method applied on plain data. Afterwards we explain how to perform this evaluation over homomorphic encrypted data, i.e. having ciphertext $\mathtt{ct}$ as input.

---

[2] The number of combinations with repetitions for k degree monomials is $\frac{(n+k-1)!}{(n-1)! \cdot k!}$. Polynomial P has monomials of degree up to d (inclusive). By summing up the number of degree-k monomials one can obtain the expression $\frac{(n+d)!}{n! \cdot d!}$.

Polynomial $P(x_0, \ldots, x_{n-1})$ **evaluation.** Let $R^{(k)}(X)$ be a polynomial defined as follows:

$$R^{(k)}(X) = Q(X) \cdot \ldots \cdot Q\left(X^{n^{k-1}}\right), \ k \geq 1 \tag{3}$$

Polynomial $R^{(1)}(X)$ has n non-zero coefficients and $R^{(1)}(X) \equiv Q(X)$. Polynomial $R^{(2)}(X)$ has n^2 non-zero coefficients and is given by expression:

$$
\begin{aligned}
R^{(2)}(X) &= Q(X) \cdot Q(X^n) \\
&= \left(\sum_{0 \leq i < n} a_i \cdot X^i\right) \cdot \left(\sum_{0 \leq j < n} a_j \cdot X^{n \cdot j}\right) \\
&= \sum_{0 \leq i,j < n} a_i \cdot a_j \cdot X^{i+n \cdot j}
\end{aligned}
$$

Namely, $R^{(2)}(X)$ coefficients are evaluations of degree-2 monomials $x_i \cdot x_j$ with $0 \leq i, j < n$, at point $a_0, \ldots, a_{n-1}$. Equivalently we can see that polynomial $R^{(k)}(X)$ has n^k non-zero coefficients which are evaluations of degree-k monomials:

$$R^{(k)}(X) = \sum_{0 \leq e_1, \ldots, e_k < n} a_{e_1} \cdot \ldots \cdot a_{e_k} \cdot X^{\sum_{1 \leq i \leq k} e_i \cdot n^{k-i}} \tag{4}$$

The l-th degree coefficient of $R^{(k)}(X)$ is $a_{e_1} \cdot \ldots \cdot a_{e_k}$ where $(e_1, \ldots, e_k)$ is the base-n decomposition of l. The polynomial $R^{(k)}(X)$ contains the products of all k-element permutations with repetition from the set $\{a_0, \ldots, a_{n-1}\}$. As the multiplication is a commutative operation, the same monomial is found several times in different coefficients of $R^{(k)}(X)$. The number of "useless" coefficients (coefficients representing the same monomial) is equal to $(n^k - \frac{(n+k-1)!}{k!(n-1)!})$, i.e. the difference between the number of $R^{(k)}(X)$ coefficients (permutations with repetitions) and the number of possible monomials of degree k (combinations with repetitions).

When $R^{(k)}(X)$ computation is performed in the ring $\mathbb{A}$ relation (5) must be verified, otherwise monomials will mix (due to modular reduction by $\Phi(X)$). So, instead of a single monomial per $R^{(k)}(X)$ coefficient we will obtain a sum of monomials.

$$n^d \leq \deg(\Phi(X)) \tag{5}$$

Having a way to compute monomial values up to degree d, lets now focus on how to multiply them by the corresponding coefficients of polynomial $P(x_0, \ldots, x_{n-1})$ and compute the inner sum from relation (1).

Let $C^{(k)}(X)$ be a polynomial which packs degree-k monomial coefficients $c_{e_1, \ldots, e_k}$ of polynomial $P(x_0, \ldots, x_{n-1})$:

$$C^{(k)}(X) = \sum_{0 \leq e_1 \leq \ldots \leq e_k < n} c_{e_1, \ldots, e_k} \cdot X^{N - \sum_{1 \leq i \leq k} e_i \cdot n^{k-i}} \tag{6}$$

where $N = \deg(\Phi(X))$. When polynomials $C^{(k)}(X)$ and $R^{(k)}(X)$ are multiplied together, the N-th degree coefficient of the resulting polynomial[3] is exactly the inner sum of Eq. (1). The product $C^{(k)}(X) \cdot R^{(k)}(X)$ is thus equal to:

$$\left(X^N \cdot \sum_{0 \le e_1 \le \ldots \le e_k < n} c_{e_1,\ldots,e_k} \cdot a_{e_1} \cdot \ldots \cdot a_{e_k} \right) + \ldots \tag{7}$$

Other coefficients are also sum of monomial evaluations except that they are multiplied by "wrong" coefficients of multivariate polynomial $P(x_0, \ldots, x_{n-1})$.

Summing up these polynomial products for $k = 1, \ldots, d$ we obtain, in the highest degree coefficient, the evaluation of polynomial $P(x_0, \ldots, x_{n-1})$ at point $a_0, \ldots, a_{n-1}$:

$$\sum_{1 \le k \le d} C^{(k)}(X) \cdot R^{(k)}(X) =$$

$$\left(X^N \cdot \underbrace{\sum_{1 \le k \le d} \sum_{0 \le e_1 \le \ldots \le e_k < n} c_{e_1,\ldots,e_k} \cdot a_{e_1} \cdot \ldots \cdot a_{e_k}}_{P(a_0,\ldots,a_{n-1})} \right) + \ldots \tag{8}$$

Polynomial $P(x_0, \ldots, x_n - 1)$ Evaluation over Binary Plaintext Space. Formulation of $\mathcal{P}_d^n$ polynomials is simpler when evaluated over the binary ring $\mathbb{Z}_2$ because, for any $a \in \mathbb{Z}_2$ and $p \ge 1$, we have $a^p \equiv a$. Any monomial $x_{e_1}^{l_0} \cdot \ldots \cdot x_{e_k}^{l_k}$ of degree $(l_0 + \ldots + l_k)$ is equivalent to monomial $x_{e_1} \cdot \ldots \cdot x_{e_k}$ of degree k. It is easy to see in this case, that polynomial $R^{(k)}(X)$ contains all the monomials of degree up to k (not only monomials of degree exactly k as previously). Employing relation (8) is not necessary for binary plaintext space. Polynomial evaluation can be performed using only $R^{(d)}(X)$ as it contains all the needed monomial evaluations. On the other hand, a new coefficient packing polynomial should be used:

$$C(X) = \sum_{1 \le k \le d} \sum_{0 \le e_1 < \ldots < e_k < n} c_{e_1,\ldots,e_k} \cdot X^{p_k} \tag{9}$$

where

$$p_k = N - \sum_{1 \le i \le k} e_i \cdot n^{k-i} - e_1 \cdot \sum_{k \le i \le d-1} n^i.$$

The final evaluation is performed by multiplying the newly introduced coefficient packing polynomial with $R^{(d)}(X)$. As previously, the N-th degree coefficient of the result is the evaluation $P(a_0, \ldots, a_{n-1})$.

Polynomial $P(x_0, \ldots, x_n - 1)$ Homomorphic Evaluation. Ciphertext ct encrypts the polynomial $Q(X)$ in which the values $a_0, \ldots, a_{n-1}$ are coefficient

---

[3] Observe that the term $\sum_{1 \le i \le k} e_i \cdot n^{k-i}$ from the X-th power cancels out when $e_1, \ldots, e_k$ are equal in (4) and (6).

packed. Polynomial $R^{(k)}(X)$ can be homomorphically computed using multiplication and ring homomorphism operations applied on the packed ciphertext $\mathtt{ct}$:

$$\mathtt{Enc}_{pk}\left(R^{(k)}(X)\right) \equiv \mathtt{ct} \cdot \ldots \cdot \phi^{n^{k-1}}(\mathtt{ct}), \, 1 \le k \le d$$

With homomorphic encryption schemes defined in Sect. 2 the best way to compute this expression is to use a tree-shaped structure to perform the multiplications. The homomorphic cryptosystem should support a logarithmic (in the degree d of the polynomial) multiplicative depth. As $R^{(k)}(X)$ computations for different k share common parts we can further decrease the number of employed homomorphic multiplications by a logarithmic factor.

Homomorphic multiplication with a plaintext input is used to compute monomials multiplied by respective polynomial P coefficients (i.e. terms $C^{(k)}(X) \cdot R^{(k)}(X)$) and homomorphic additions for the final sum. The decryption of the obtained ciphertext gives (in the highest degree coefficient) the polynomial $P(x_0, \ldots, x_{n-1})$ evaluated at point $a_0, \ldots, a_{n-1}$.

For binary plaintext space evaluating polynomial is simpler as only a single $R^{(d)}(X)$ must be computed. This saves several homomorphic operations. The multiplicative depth of the HE scheme remains the same.

In Table 1 are shown the complexity values in terms of homomorphic operations of polynomial evaluations for different kind of operations.

Table 1. Polynomial evaluation complexity in case of binary ($\mathbb{Z}_2$) and general ($\mathbb{Z}_t$) plaintext spaces.

Operations\plaintext space	$\mathbb{Z}_t$	$\mathbb{Z}_2$
Hom	$d-1$	$d-1$
Add	$d-1$	0
Mult	$\frac{d \log_2 d}{2}$	$d-1$
Mult with plaintext	d	1

Polynomial Evaluation Example. Suppose we want to evaluate a polynomial $P(x_0, x_1, x_2)$ of degree $d = 2$ with $n = 3$ variables at a point a_0, a_1, a_2. The generic formulation of this polynomial is:

$$\begin{aligned} P(x_0, x_1, x_2) = c_0 x_0 \quad &+ c_1 x_1 \quad\quad + c_2 x_2 \\ &+ c_{0,0} x_0^2 + c_{0,1} x_0 x_1 + c_{0,2} x_0 x_2 \\ &+ c_{1,1} x_1^2 + c_{1,2} x_1 x_2 + c_{2,2} x_2^2 \end{aligned}$$

Let $Q(X) = a_0 + a_1 \cdot X + a_2 \cdot X^2$ be the polynomial packing values a_0, a_1, a_2. Polynomials $R^{(k)}(X)$, $1 \le k \le 2$, computed using relation (3) are:

$$\begin{aligned} R^{(1)}(X) = a_0 \quad &+ \quad a_1 X \quad + \quad a_2 X^2 \\ R^{(2)}(X) = a_0^2 \quad &+ \quad a_0 a_1 X \quad + a_0 a_2 X^2 \\ + a_0 a_1 X^3 + \quad &a_1^2 X^4 \quad + a_1 a_2 X^5 \\ + a_0 a_2 X^6 + \quad &a_1 a_2 X^7 + \quad a_2^2 X^8 \end{aligned}$$

The coefficients of $R^{(1)}(X)$ and $R^{(2)}(X)$ are evaluations at point a_0, a_1, a_2 of degree-1 and respectively degree-2 monomials. Polynomials $C^{(1)}(X)$ and $C^{(2)}(X)$ (relation (6)) pack the coefficients of polynomial $P(x_0, x_1, x_2)$:

$$C^{(1)}(X) = c_0 X^N \quad + c_1 X^{N-1} \quad + c_2 X^{N-2}$$
$$\begin{aligned}C^{(2)}(X) = c_{0,0} X^N &+ c_{0,1} X^{N-1} + c_{0,2} X^{N-2} \\ &+ c_{1,1} X^{N-4} + c_{1,2} X^{N-5} \\ &+ c_{2,2} X^{N-8}\end{aligned}$$

Multiplying together $R^{(k)}(X)$ and $C^{(k)}(X)$, $1 \le k \le 2$, and summing up the results we obtain in the degree-N coefficient the polynomial P evaluated at point a_0, a_1, a_2. We note that only 6 out of 9 coefficients of $R^{(2)}(X)$ participate in the final computation. The other 3 (X^3, X^6 and X^7 coefficients) are the "useless" coefficients we talked about earlier.

In the case of binary plaintext space polynomial $P(x_0, x_1, x_2)$ formulation is simpler because the square terms disappear:

$$\begin{aligned}P(x_0, x_1, x_2) = c_0 x_0 \quad &+ c_1 x_1 \quad + c_2 x_2 \\ &+ c_{0,1} x_0 x_1 + c_{0,2} x_0 x_2 + c_{1,2} x_1 x_2\end{aligned}$$

$R^{(2)}(X)$ and $C(X)$ polynomials found using relations (4) and (9) are:

$$\begin{aligned}R^{(2)}(X) = a_0 \quad &+ a_0 a_1 X \quad + a_0 a_2 X^2 \\ &+ a_0 a_1 X^3 + a_1 X^4 \quad + a_1 a_2 X^5 \\ &+ a_0 a_2 X^6 + a_1 a_2 X^7 + a_2 X^8\end{aligned}$$

$$\begin{aligned}C(X) = c_0 X^N &+ c_{0,1} X^{N-1} + c_{0,2} X^{N-2} \\ &+ c_1 X^{N-4} \quad + c_{1,2} X^{N-5} \\ &+ c_2 X^{N-8}\end{aligned}$$

$R^{(2)}(X)$ contains all the degree-1 monomial evaluations in addition to degree-2 ones. The coefficient packing polynomial $C(X)$ has all polynomial $P(x_0, x_1, x_2)$ coefficients in the right place. Multiplying these polynomials gives in the N-th degree coefficient the evaluation $P(a_0, a_1, a_2)$.

4   Experimentations

We have implemented the optimized polynomial evaluation method using the HELib library [16,17]. HELib is an open-source library implementing BGV scheme introduced in [5] together with some utility functions. Cyclotomic polynomials are used in HELib as the irreducible modulus of the plaintext and respectively the ciphertext rings. A workstation with an Intel Xeon E3-1240 (3.50GHz) processor and 16 GB of RAM was used to execute test applications.

Let $\Phi_m(X)$ be the m-th cyclotomic polynomial. The degree of $\Phi_m(X)$ is given by Euler's totient function $\varphi(m)$. HELib implements a BGV variant in which the polynomial rings are of the form $\mathbb{A} = \mathbb{Z}[X]/\Phi_m(X)$. The native plaintext space is defined by elements over $\mathbb{A}_2$ but other plaintext spaces in the form $\mathbb{A}_{p'}$ with p an arbitrary, small prime (not dividing m and r) are also possible. The ciphertext space consists of polynomials over $\mathbb{A}_q$ where q is an odd modulus evolving with the homomorphic evaluation. More specifically, there are L modulus $q_1 < q_2 < \cdots < q_L$ where freshly encrypted ciphertexts are defined over q_L.

As such, the maximal ciphertext coefficient size is chosen automatically as a function of the multiplication levels L to support. The security of the obtained homomorphic encryption scheme (security of the RLWE instance) depends on the cyclotomic polynomial degree and on the ciphertext coefficient size. Many other parameters allow to fine tune HELib execution performance. In our experiments we limit ourselves to the selection of the following parameters: plaintext modulo t, number of multiplication levels L and cyclotomic polynomial order m.

Under certain conditions, polynomial $\Phi_m(X)$ can be factored modulo t (the modulo for the plaintext coefficients), i.e.

$$\Phi_m(X) = F_1(X) \cdot F_2(X) \cdot \ldots \cdot F_w(X) \quad \mod t.$$

Each factor $F_i(X)$ have the same degree $\frac{\varphi(m)}{w}$, where w is the number of factors. The polynomial evaluation method we propose can be implemented either using the full polynomial or the polynomials of each slot independently (i.e. in batching mode). In the later case our method is able to evaluate w different multivariate polynomials in parallel. The points over which polynomials are evaluated are also different. The drawback of using batching is that the polynomials which can be evaluated are smaller, due to relation (5) which should stay valid. In our experiments we test only the first case, thus the largest possible polynomials are evaluated.

Table 2 shows the results of our evaluation methods when varying the plaintext modulo t and the cyclotomic polynomial order m for multivariate polynomials with degree d, $1 \leq d \leq 4$, in the form defined by relation (1). All the experiments have been performed with at least 128 bits of security. Column "m" gives the cyclotomic polynomial order defining the ciphertext space, "deg" is the degree d of the multivariate polynomial $P(x_0, \ldots, x_{n-1})$, "#vars" is the number of variables n, "L" is the number of multiplication levels the HELib is configured with, "ct. size" is the ciphertext size in MB and "time" is the evaluation time of multivariate polynomial in seconds (i.e. computing expression $\sum_{1 \leq k \leq d} C^{(k)}(X) \cdot R^{(k)}(X)$). Obtained evaluation time is an average over 10 executions. Ciphertext ring homomorphism ($X \rightarrow X^t$) and ciphertext multiplication are the predominant part of the computation. As expected, the execution times for the polynomial evaluation increases with its degree but also with the parameter m defining the ciphertext space and parameter t, the plaintext modulus.

Quadratic Classifier

Let us now present a possible application of the polynomial evaluation method we propose here and compare the results with those obtained in [25].

Table 2. Results of polynomial evaluation method using HELib.

m	deg	#vars	Plaintext space size								
			2			2^8			2^{16}		
			L	ct. size	Time	L	ct. size	Time	L	ct. size	Time
10007	1	10006	1	0.025	0.002	3	0.077	0.006	3	0.077	0.006
	2	100	3	0.077	0.034	5	0.129	0.069	5	0.129	0.069
	3	21	3	0.077	0.079	5	0.129	0.143	7	0.181	0.223
	4	10	4	0.077	0.158	5	0.129	0.260	7	0.181	0.403
100003	1	100002	1	0.262	0.019	3	0.783	0.056	3	0.783	0.056
	2	316	3	0.783	0.440	5	1.303	0.695	5	1.303	0.699
	3	46	3	0.783	1.054	5	1.303	1.444	7	1.822	1.883
	4	17	4	0.783	2.097	5	1.303	2.627	7	1.822	3.323
1000003	1	1000002	1	2.984	0.197	3	8.188	0.787	3	8.188	0.784
	2	1000	3	8.188	5.157	5	13.354	11.024	5	13.354	10.412
	3	100	3	8.188	12.439	5	13.354	22.449	7	18.515	29.281
	4	31	4	8.188	24.965	5	13.354	40.858	7	18.515	51.578

We investigate the performances of our method in the context of a classification algorithm used by a remote service to label the residentials buildings in a small district based on their energy consumption. A basic Gaussian classifier can be adapted such that the prediction step is executed on homomorphically encrypted data. As such, given an encrypted attribute vector x, the purpose is to predict its class label based on the learning model acquired during the training step. We focus here only on the labeling step using private data and we suppose that the model building was realized previously in the clear domain.

In the case of a Gaussian Classifier, each class C_j from the m classes defined during the training phase is assumed characterized by a Gaussian distribution with a mean μ_j and a covariance matrix Σ_j. The mean of a class C_j is the vector $\mu_j \in \mathbb{R}^n$: $\mu_j^{\mathsf{T}} = \{\mu_{j_i}\}$ with μ_{j_i} the mean for the components i of the examples vectors x belonging to class C_j (i.e. $\mu_{j_i} = \frac{\sum_i^n x(i)}{n}$). For vectors with n features, the covariance matrix of a class C_j is a positive semi-definite matrix of size $n \times n$ computed as: $\Sigma_j = \{c(a,b)\}$ with $a, b \in \{1, \ldots, n\}$ and $c(a,b)$ the covariance between the features a and b, measuring their tendency to vary together.

A feature vector x from the testing set is thus classified by measuring a Mahalanobis distance from x to each of the classes and by selecting the minimal norm. The main steps of the prediction phase of the Gaussian classification algorithm are Steps 4–6 from Algorithm 1. The training phase realized on T_0, the set of training vectors x_0, has been realized before, resulting in a model with m classes. After computing the mean and the covariance of each class C_j (Steps 1–3), a class label is predicted for each testing vector $x \in T$.

Algorithm 1. Gaussian classifier - prediction step

Require: $T_0 = \{x_0 \in \mathbb{R}^n\}$; $T = \{x \in \mathbb{R}^n\}$; m classes C_j
1: **for** $\forall C_j$, $j \in \{1, \ldots, m\}$ **do**
2:      compute μ_j and Σ_j using x_0
3: **end for**
4: **for** $x \in T$ **do**
5:      compute $d_M(x, C_j)$, $\forall j \in \{1, \ldots, m\}$
6:      $C(x) \leftarrow argmin(d_M(x, C_j))$
7: **end for**
Ensure: $C(x)$, $\forall x \in T$

It seems then that the most important step to be performed on homomorphic encrypted data is the computation of distances between the attribute vector x and the classes. The Mahanalobis distance from an encrypted vector x to a class c_j is defined as:

$$d_M^2(x, C_j) = (x - \mu_j)^\mathsf{T} \Sigma_j^{-1}(x - \mu_j).$$

Note that in the particular case where the features are uncorrelated or of a unidimensional feature vector the Mahalanobis distance is equivalent to the Euclidean distance.

For their experiments, the authors from [25] consider an additive Paillier cryptosystem as well as BGV cryptosystem as implemented in HELib library to classify 40 residential profiles using a feature vector size of 6. For the HELib-based prototype, they use the batching technique in two different ways. In a first solution, for a given attribute vector x with n elements, each of the attributes x_i, $i = 1, \ldots, n$, is embedded in a different plaintext slot in the form of an integer modulo 2^8. This allows to encrypt all the attributes of x in the same ciphertext. The references, i.e. the means of the classes, are represented as m vectors of dimension n. As such, for one instance to label, they obtain m ciphertexts corresponding to the encrypted distances to each class. When such a ciphertext is decrypted, the sum on the slots for the obtained plaintext gives the clear distance to the associated class.

In the second solution, they exploit the free plaintexts slots by remarking that usually the number of slots is much larger than the number of attributes and, for a single instance x of dimension n to label with regards to m classes, they replicate it m times and embedded into the slots of a plaintext, by padding with 0 the remaining space. In this configuration, the means are expressed as a single array of dimension $m \times n$ and all the distances are computed in the same time using a single ciphertext. Once received and decrypted, one can obtain the clear distances by making the sum on sub-sets of successive slots. The necessary condition for the second approach is that the number of slots has to be higher or equal to $m \times n$.

Even if the number of operations to be executed on homomorphic domain is reduced through batching (more specifically, for the second approach, one ciphertext-ciphertext multiplication, two multiplications between a ciphertext and a plaintext, a sum between two ciphertext and a sum between a ciphertext and a plaintext), at the end, they have to perform a quite costly operation i.e. a running sum to recuperate the actual distances by bunches of m slots.

With our approach using multivariate polynomials combined with the batching, it is possible to ameliorate even more the evaluation times of the distances. All we need is to evaluate a degree-2 multivariate polynomial with $n = 6$ variables (i.e. the degree of the slot defining plaintext space polynomial should be at least n^2), embedded in a number of slots equal to the number of vectors we want to classify in parallel (in the example, 40 residential energy consumption therefore at least 40 slots).

Table 3 resumes the results we obtained for two configurations of parameters in HELib with a security level (column λ) similar to the one determined by the tests in [25] (and at least 80 bits). The plaintext module 2^8 is used in the experiments. As before, m stands for the cyclotomic polynomial order and L is the number multiplication levels. The overall polynomial which will be encrypted as a single ciphertext can be dived into "#fact" polynomials, each one of degree "deg_fact". The total execution time (column "time") is expressed in seconds and the ciphertext size in MB (column "ct. size"). The execution times and ciphertext sizes are a lot smaller than the ones obtained by the authors of [25]. This is partly due to a smaller number of homomorphic operations (no need to add slots together) and to a smaller multiplications level.

Table 3. Results for quadratic classifier with HELib.

m	deg_fact	#fact	L	λ	Time	ct. size
2113	44	48	2	173	0.004	0.340
3191	55	58	2	315	0.005	0.514

5   Conclusion

This paper presents a new method to efficiently evaluate low-degree multivariate polynomial over homomorphic encrypted data. With this new technique applicable to RLWE based homomorphic schemes, one can perform all types of computation, with the condition to express it using polynomial (of relatively low-degree) operations. Since all the coefficients of the plaintext space polynomial are used to encode the messages, this method is more efficient than the usual case in which only the lowest degree of the polynomial is used. Moreover, as shown by the experiments we conducted, our method is compatible with the batching technique allowing to perform operations in a SIMD manner.

We have implemented and executed the proposed polynomial evaluation method using the HELib library. Besides measuring the performance of the evaluation method within diverse settings, we have tested its performance for a machine learning application (namely a quadratic classification algorithm).

In future works, we plan to investigate the case when $n^d > \deg(\Phi(X))$, which will permit to evaluate higher degree multivariate polynomials. Another research line, more applicative, is to use the evaluation method on homomorphically encrypted data for more complex classes of machine learning algorithms.

References

1. Acar, A., Aksu, H., Uluagac, A.S., Conti, M.: A survey on homomorphic encryption schemes: theory and implementation. arXiv preprint arXiv:1704.03578 (2017)
2. Bonte, C., Bootland, C., Bos, J.W., Castryck, W., Iliashenko, I., Vercauteren, F.: Faster homomorphic function evaluation using non-integral base encoding. IACR Cryptology ePrint Archive, 2017:333 (2017)
3. Bost, R., Popa, R.A., Tu, S., Goldwasser, S.: Machine learning classification over encrypted data. In: NDSS. The Internet Society (2015)
4. Brakerski, Z.: Fully homomorphic encryption without modulus switching from classical GapSVP. In: Safavi-Naini, R., Canetti, R. (eds.) CRYPTO 2012. LNCS, vol. 7417, pp. 868–886. Springer, Heidelberg (2012). https://doi.org/10.1007/978-3-642-32009-5_50
5. Brakerski, Z., Gentry, C., Vaikuntanathan, V.: (Leveled) fully homomorphic encryption without bootstrapping. In: Proceedings of the 3rd Innovations in Theoretical Computer Science Conference, ITCS 2012, pp. 309–325 (2012)
6. Brakerski, Z., Vaikuntanathan, V.: Fully Homomorphic Encryption from Ring-LWE and Security for Key Dependent Messages. In: Rogaway, P. (ed.) CRYPTO 2011. LNCS, vol. 6841, pp. 505–524. Springer, Heidelberg (2011). https://doi.org/10.1007/978-3-642-22792-9_29
7. Breuer, M.A.: Generation of optimal code for expressions via factorization. Commun. ACM **12**(6), 333–340 (1969)
8. Carpov, S., Dubrulle, P., Sirdey, R.: Armadillo: a compilation chain for privacy preserving applications. In: SCC@ASIACCS, pp. 13–19. ACM (2015)
9. Carpov, S., Sirdey, R.: Another compression method for homomorphic ciphertexts. In: SCC@AsiaCCS, pp. 44–50. ACM (2016)
10. Chillotti, I., Gama, N., Georgieva, M., Izabachène, M.: Faster fully homomorphic encryption: bootstrapping in less than 0.1 seconds. In: Cheon, J.H., Takagi, T. (eds.) ASIACRYPT 2016. LNCS, vol. 10031, pp. 3–33. Springer, Heidelberg (2016). https://doi.org/10.1007/978-3-662-53887-6_1
11. Costache, A., Smart, N.P., Vivek, S., Waller, A.: Fixed point arithmetic in she scheme. IACR Cryptology ePrint Archive 2016:250 (2016)
12. Fan, J., Vercauteren, F.: Somewhat practical fully homomorphic encryption. IACR Cryptology ePrint Archive 2012:144 (2012)
13. Gentry, C., et al.: Fully homomorphic encryption using ideal lattices. In: STOC, vol. 9, pp. 169–178 (2009)
14. Gentry, C., Halevi, S., Smart, N.P.: Fully homomorphic encryption with polylog overhead. In: Pointcheval, D., Johansson, T. (eds.) EUROCRYPT 2012. LNCS, vol. 7237, pp. 465–482. Springer, Heidelberg (2012). https://doi.org/10.1007/978-3-642-29011-4_28
15. Graepel, T., Lauter, K., Naehrig, M.: ML confidential: machine learning on encrypted data. In: Kwon, T., Lee, M.-K., Kwon, D. (eds.) ICISC 2012. LNCS, vol. 7839, pp. 1–21. Springer, Heidelberg (2013). https://doi.org/10.1007/978-3-642-37682-5_1
16. Halevi, S., Shoup, V.: Algorithms in HElib. In: Garay, J.A., Gennaro, R. (eds.) CRYPTO 2014. LNCS, vol. 8616, pp. 554–571. Springer, Heidelberg (2014). https://doi.org/10.1007/978-3-662-44371-2_31

17. Halevi, S., Shoup, V.: Bootstrapping for `HElib`. In: Oswald, E., Fischlin, M. (eds.) EUROCRYPT 2015. LNCS, vol. 9056, pp. 641–670. Springer, Heidelberg (2015). https://doi.org/10.1007/978-3-662-46800-5_25

18. Hosangadi, A., Fallah, F., Kastner, R.: Optimizing polynomial expressions by algebraic factorization and common subexpression elimination. IEEE Trans. CAD Integr. Circ. Syst. **25**, 2012–2022 (2006)

19. Leiserson, C.E., Li, L., Maza, M.M., Xie, Y.: Efficient evaluation of large polynomials. In: Fukuda, K., Hoeven, J., Joswig, M., Takayama, N. (eds.) ICMS 2010. LNCS, vol. 6327, pp. 342–353. Springer, Heidelberg (2010). https://doi.org/10.1007/978-3-642-15582-6_55

20. López-Alt, A., Tromer, E., Vaikuntanathan, V.: On-the-fly multiparty computation on the cloud via multikey fully homomorphic encryption. In: Proceedings of the Forty-Fourth Annual ACM Symposium on Theory of Computing, pp. 1219–1234. ACM (2012)

21. Lyubashevsky, V., Peikert, C., Regev, O.: On ideal lattices and learning with errors over rings. In: Gilbert, H. (ed.) EUROCRYPT 2010. LNCS, vol. 6110, pp. 1–23. Springer, Heidelberg (2010). https://doi.org/10.1007/978-3-642-13190-5_1

22. Naehrig, M., Lauter, K., Vaikuntanathan, V.: Can homomorphic encryption be practical? In: Proceedings of the 3rd ACM Workshop on Cloud Computing Security Workshop, CCSW 2011, pp. 113–124 (2011)

23. Rivest, R.L., Adleman, L., Dertouzos, M.L.: On data banks and privacy homomorphisms. Found. Secure Comput. **4**(11), 169–180 (1978)

24. Smart, N.P., Vercauteren, F.: Fully homomorphic SIMD operations. Des. Codes Cryptogr. **71**, 1–25 (2014)

25. Stan, O., Zayani, M.-H., Sirdey, R., Hamida, A.B., Leite, A.F., Mziou-Sallami, M.: A new crypto-classifier service for energy efficiency in smart cities. IACR Cryptology ePrint Archive, 2017:1212 (2017)

26. van Dijk, M., Gentry, C., Halevi, S., Vaikuntanathan, V.: Fully homomorphic encryption over the integers. In: Gilbert, H. (ed.) EUROCRYPT 2010. LNCS, vol. 6110, pp. 24–43. Springer, Heidelberg (2010). https://doi.org/10.1007/978-3-642-13190-5_2

27. Yasuda, M., Shimoyama, T., Kogure, J., Yokoyama, K., Koshiba, T.: Packed homomorphic encryption based on ideal lattices and its application to biometrics. In: Cuzzocrea, A., Kittl, C., Simos, D.E., Weippl, E., Xu, L. (eds.) CD-ARES 2013. LNCS, vol. 8128, pp. 55–74. Springer, Heidelberg (2013). https://doi.org/10.1007/978-3-642-40588-4_5

28. Yasuda, M., Shimoyama, T., Kogure, J., Yokoyama, K., Koshiba, T.: Practical packing method in somewhat homomorphic encryption. In: Garcia-Alfaro, J., Lioudakis, G., Cuppens-Boulahia, N., Foley, S., Fitzgerald, W.M. (eds.) DPM/SETOP -2013. LNCS, vol. 8247, pp. 34–50. Springer, Heidelberg (2014). https://doi.org/10.1007/978-3-642-54568-9_3

29. Yasuda, M., Shimoyama, T., Kogure, J., Yokoyama, K., Koshiba, T.: Secure pattern matching using somewhat homomorphic encryption. In: CCSW, pp. 65–76. ACM (2013)

Keyword-Based Delegable Proofs
of Storage

Binanda Sengupta$^{(\boxtimes)}$ and Sushmita Ruj

Indian Statistical Institute, Kolkata, India
{binanda_r,sush}@isical.ac.in, binandas@smu.edu.sg

Abstract. Cloud users (clients) with limited storage capacity at their end can outsource bulk data to the cloud storage server. A client can later access her data by downloading the required data files. However, a large fraction of the data files the client outsources to the server is often archival in nature that the client uses for backup purposes and accesses less frequently. An untrusted server can thus delete some of these archival data files in order to save some space (and allocate the same to other clients) without being detected by the client (data owner). *Proofs of storage* enable the client to audit her data files uploaded to the server in order to ensure the integrity of those files. In this work, we introduce a type of (selective) proofs of storage that we call *keyword-based delegable proofs of storage*, where the client wants to audit all her data files containing a specific keyword (e.g., "important"). Moreover, it satisfies the notion of *public verifiability* where the client can delegate the auditing task to a third-party auditor who audits the set of files corresponding to the keyword on behalf of the client. We formally define the security of a keyword-based delegable proof-of-storage protocol. We construct such a protocol based on an existing proof-of-storage scheme and analyze the security of our protocol. We argue that the techniques we use can be applied atop *any* existing publicly verifiable proof-of-storage scheme for static data. Finally, we discuss the efficiency of our construction.

Keywords: Cryptographic protocols · Proofs of storage
Cloud computing · Keyword-based audits · Public verifiability

1 Introduction

Cloud computing platform provides a robust infrastructure to the cloud users (clients) in order to enable them storing large amount of data on cloud servers. The clients can access their data as often as needed by downloading them from the cloud servers. Several storage service providers like Amazon Simple Storage Service (S3), Microsoft OneDrive, Dropbox and Google Drive offer storage outsourcing facility to their clients (data owners). The clients pay these providers for the service and expect that their (untampered) data can be retrieved at any point of time. However, a client's data can be lost due to the failure of some of the

© Springer Nature Switzerland AG 2018
C. Su and H. Kikuchi (Eds.): ISPEC 2018, LNCS 11125, pp. 282–298, 2018.
https://doi.org/10.1007/978-3-319-99807-7_17

storage nodes or due to a malicious activity of the cloud server (an untrusted server can delete some part of the client's data in order to save some space). Therefore, the client needs an assurance that her data files are stored by the server intact. A possible cryptographic solution of the above problem is that the client computes an authenticator (tag) on a data file. Then, she uploads the file and the tag to the server. To check the integrity of the data file, the client downloads the file and the tag, and she checks if the file has been modified. However, this solution is inefficient in practice due to the large communication bandwidth required between the client and the cloud server.

Proofs of storage provide an efficient mechanism to check the availability of the client's data outsourced to a remote storage server. In a proof-of-storage protocol, the client can *audit* her data file stored on the server without accessing the whole file, and still, be able to detect an unwanted modification of the file done by the (possibly malicious) server. Proof-of-storage protocols can be typically classified as: *provable data possession* (PDP) protocols [2,12,30] and *proof-of-retrievability* (POR) protocols [8,15,26]. In these schemes, the client computes an authentication tag for each segment of her data file and uploads the file along with these authentication tags. Later, the client audits the data file via *spot-checking*, where the client, based on *proofs* computed by the cloud server, verifies the integrity of some randomly sampled segments of the file. We note that PDP schemes provide the guarantee of retrievability of *almost all* segments of the data file. On the other hand, *all* segments of the file can be retrieved in POR schemes. These schemes are designed for dynamic or static data depending on whether the client can change the content of her data file after the initial outsourcing. Some of these schemes are *publicly verifiable* where anyone with an access to the public parameters can perform audits. In case of *privately verifiable* schemes, only the client (data owner) with some secret information can perform audits. In a publicly verifiable proof-of-storage scheme, the client can *delegate* the auditing task to a third-party auditor (TPA) who performs audits on the client's data and lets the client know if she finds any discrepancies.

The client often has a large repository of data files (documents), and she classifies these documents for performing different types of analyses on them later. Document-clustering is a popular technique where the data owner groups her data files depending on some attributes of the files. Keyword-based document-clustering is one of the examples of document-clustering where the clusters are formed based on the distinct keywords present in the data files [9,16]. It has various applications in data mining and information retrieval such as designing an efficient scheme for searching over these data files [27,28]. Similarly, in a proof-of-storage protocol for such a clustered file repository, the client (data owner) might need different degrees of availability-assurance for different outsourced files based on the keywords they contain. Obviously, the client can check integrity of all the data files she has uploaded to the cloud server. However, the cloud server can charge the client for the associated (computational and bandwidth) cost involved in an audit (this cost is wasted in case the server is storing the client's data properly). Typically, the more files are audited by the client, the higher is this associated cost. Thus, the client might want to run audits only on important files having some specific keywords. For example, the guarantee of availability for the files containing the keyword "important" might be of higher priority rather than that for the files containing the keyword "movie". In this scenario, there must be some mechanism such that the client can efficiently check the integrity of all of her data files (uploaded to the server) that contain a particular keyword.

We note that there exist many searchable encryption schemes [7,10] in the literature that address efficient keyword-search over *encrypted* data files stored on a remote server. These schemes can be potentially integrated with existing proof-of-storage schemes to audit the set of data files matching a particular keyword. However, these searchable encryption schemes aim to minimize the information regarding the encrypted files that is leaked to the (typically) semi-honest remote server (that follows the protocol honestly but tries to learn some information regarding the content of the files or the keywords being searched). On the other hand, the untrusted server in proof-of-storage schemes is considered to be malicious (i.e., it can corrupt the client's data in an arbitrary fashion). Moreover, the definition of a proof-of-storage scheme does not demand encrypting the data files or hiding the search (or access) patterns during a keyword-search (which involves storage and computational overhead).

Our Contribution. We summarize our contributions in this paper as follows.

- We introduce the notion of keyword-based delegable proofs of storage, where the client can audit all her outsourced data files that contain a specific keyword (keyword-based audits). Moreover, any third-party auditor with the knowledge of some public parameters can perform audits on the set of files corresponding to the keyword on behalf of the client.
- We formalize the security model for a keyword-based delegable proof-of-storage protocol and define the security for such a protocol.
- We construct a secure keyword-based delegable proof-of-storage (KDPoS) protocol based on an existing publicly verifiable proof-of-storage scheme. We describe a non-interactive challenge-generation method for keyword-based audits in our construction, where the verifier does not know a priori the set of files matching a particular keyword. Our techniques can be used with any existing publicly verifiable proof-of-storage scheme for static data (that is based on spot-checking random locations of a file) in order to enable keyword-based audits.
- We describe the efficiency of our KDPoS protocol.

The rest of the paper is organized as follows. Section 2 describes some preliminaries and background related to our work. In Sect. 4, we introduce the notion of keyword-based delegable proofs of storage (KDPoS) and discuss some possible constructions of a keyword-based delegable proof-of-storage protocol. In Sect. 5, we propose a concrete KDPoS construction. In Sect. 6, we define the security of a keyword-based delegable proof-of-storage protocol. Section 7 describes the efficiency of our KDPoS scheme. In the concluding Sect. 8, we summarize the work done in this paper.

2 Preliminaries and Background

2.1 Notation

We take λ to be the security parameter. An algorithm $\mathcal{A}(1^\lambda)$ is a probabilistic polynomial-time algorithm when its running time is polynomial in λ and its output is a random variable that depends on the internal coin tosses of $\mathcal{A}$. An element a chosen from a set S uniformly at random is denoted as $a \xleftarrow{R} S$. A function $f : \mathbb{N} \to \mathbb{R}$ is called negligible in λ if for all positive integers c and for all sufficiently large λ, we have $f(\lambda) < \frac{1}{\lambda^c}$. The notation '$\cdot || \cdots || \cdot$' denotes the concatenation of multiple strings. For two integers a and b (where $a \leq b$), the set $\{a, a+1, \ldots, b\}$ is denoted by $[a, b]$ as well.

2.2 Bilinear Maps

Let G_1, G_2 and G_T be multiplicative cyclic groups of prime order $p = \Theta(2^{2\lambda})$. Let g_1 and g_2 be generators of the groups G_1 and G_2, respectively. A bilinear map (or pairing) [13,17] is a function $e : G_1 \times G_2 \to G_T$ such that: (1) for all $u \in G_1, v \in G_2, a, b \in \mathbb{Z}_p$, we have $e(u^a, v^b) = e(u, v)^{ab}$ (bilinear property), (2) e is non-degenerate, that is, $e(g_1, g_2) \neq 1$. Furthermore, properties (1) and (2) imply that: (3) for all $u_1, u_2 \in G_1, v \in G_2$, we have $e(u_1 \cdot u_2, v) = e(u_1, v) \cdot e(u_2, v)$. If $G_1 = G_2 = G$, the bilinear map is known as a symmetric bilinear map; otherwise, it is asymmetric. Unless otherwise mentioned, we consider bilinear maps which are symmetric and efficiently computable. Let $\text{BLSetup}(1^\lambda)$ be an algorithm which outputs (p, g, G, G_T, e) as the parameters of a bilinear map, where g is a generator of G (i.e., $G = \langle g \rangle$).

2.3 Computational Diffie-Hellman Assumption

The computational Diffie-Hellman problem over a multiplicative group $G = \langle g \rangle$ of prime order $p = \Theta(2^{2\lambda})$ and generated by g is defined as follows.

Definition 1 (Computational Diffie-Hellman Problem). *Given $g, g^a, h = g^b \in G$ for some $a, b \in \mathbb{Z}_p$, the computational Diffie-Hellman problem over G is to compute $h^a \in G$.*

We say that the computational Diffie-Hellman assumption holds in the group G if, for any probabilistic polynomial-time adversary $\mathcal{A}(1^\lambda)$, the probability

$$\Pr_{a,b \xleftarrow{R} \mathbb{Z}_p} [h^a \leftarrow \mathcal{A}(g, g^a, h = g^b)]$$

is negligible in λ, where the probability is taken over the internal coin tosses of $\mathcal{A}$ and the random choices of a and b.

3   Bitcoin

Nakamoto introduces a peer-to-peer cryptocurrency known as Bitcoin [20] that does not rely on any trusted server. The users in the Bitcoin network make payments by digitally signing transactions with their secret keys. The network maintains a blockchain (a public ledger containing valid transactions) in a distributed fashion. A new block is appended to the Bitcoin blockchain roughly in every 10 min (an epoch). These blocks are generated by the miners (users trying to mine Bitcoins) in the network who provide a cryptographic proof-of-work to show, in order to claim a mining reward, that they have indeed expended a large amount of computational power. Presently, Bitcoin uses Back's Hashcash [3] as the proof-of-work. The mining scheme in Bitcoin involves solving a cryptographic mining puzzle that is not precomputable. Finding a solution of the puzzle works in the following way: Let $T_1, T_2, \ldots, T_z$ be some of the valid transactions for a certain epoch which are not included in any previous block. The miners try to find a nonce η such that SHA-256 $(BH\|root_{MHT}\|\eta) \leq Z$, where Z is a predefined target value (the difficulty level), BH is the hash of the latest block appended to the Bitcoin blockchain and $root_{MHT}$ is the root-digest of the Merkle hash tree [18] built over $T_1, T_2, \ldots, T_z$. Due to the preimage-resistance property of SHA-256, the only way to compute such a nonce η is to search over all possible values of the nonce in a brute-force manner.

3.1   Proofs of Storage

Proofs of storage provide a client (data owner) with an efficient mechanism to verify the integrity of her data outsourced to a remote cloud server. Ateniese et al. [2] introduce the notion of *provable data possession* (PDP) where the client computes an authentication tag for each segment of her data file and uploads the file along with these tags. During an audit, the client verifies the integrity of the data file via *spot-checking*, where she samples $l = O(\lambda)$ random segment-indices (challenge) and sends them to the server. The server generates a proof based on the challenged segments (and their corresponding tags) and sends the proof (response) to the client who verifies the proof. This scheme also introduces the notion of "public verifiability" where the client can delegate the auditing task to a third-party auditor (TPA) who performs audits on the client's behalf. For a "privately verifiable" scheme, only the client with some secret information can perform an audit. Other schemes achieving PDP include [12,14,23,29,30].

Juels and Kaliski [15] introduce the notion of *proofs of retrievability* (POR) for static data. The underlying idea of a proof-of-retrievability scheme is to encode the original file with an erasure code [21], authenticate the segments of the encoded file, and then upload them on the cloud storage server [25]. Due to the encoding, the server has to delete a large number of segments to actually delete a file-segment, and this can be detected by the client with high probability. This ensures that all segments of the file are retrievable from the responses of the server which passes audits with some non-negligible probability. Other POR schemes include [6,8,11,24,26].

4   Keyword-Based Delegable Proofs of Storage

In this section, we introduce the notion of keyword-based delegable proofs of storage (KDPoS) and describe some possible constructions. We define a keyword-based delegable proof-of-storage protocol as follows.

Definition 2 (Keyword-Based Delegable Proofs of Storage).   *A keyword-based delegable proof-of-storage (KDPoS) protocol consists of the following procedures.*

- Setup(1^λ): *The client runs this algorithm which sets the parameters of the protocol and generates a secret key-public key pair $K = (sk, pk)$ for the client.*
- Outsource($\bar{F}, sk, \overline{\mathtt{fid}}$): *Given a set of data files $\bar{F}$ associated with a set of random file-identifiers $\overline{\mathtt{fid}}$, the client processes $\bar{F}$ to form another set of files $\bar{F}'$ (including respective authentication information computed using sk) and uploads $\bar{F}'$ to the server. The client stores some metadata $\bar{d}$ corresponding to $\bar{F}'$ at her end.*
- AuthRead($j, \bar{F}', \bar{d}, pk, \mathtt{fid}$): *When the client wants to read the j-th block of the file F' identified by $\mathtt{fid}$, the server sends to the client $F'[j]$, the j-th block of the file, along with the corresponding proof of storage $\Pi(j)$.*
- VerifyRead($j, \bar{d}, pk, sk, F'[j], \Pi(j), \mathtt{fid}$): *After receiving $(F'[j], \Pi(j))$ from the server, the client checks the validity of $\Pi(j)$. The client outputs 1 if $\Pi(j)$ is a valid proof for $F'[j]$; she outputs 0, otherwise.*
- SChallenge($pk, l, \bar{d}, \widetilde{\mathtt{fid}}$): *During an audit on a set of files identified by $\widetilde{\mathtt{fid}} \subseteq \overline{\mathtt{fid}}$, the verifier[1] sends the set $\widetilde{\mathtt{fid}}$ and a random challenge set Q of cardinality $l = O(\lambda)$ to the server.*
- SProve($Q, pk, l, \bar{F}', \widetilde{\mathtt{fid}}$): *Given the challenge set Q and a set of files identified by $\widetilde{\mathtt{fid}}$, the server computes a proof of storage T corresponding to the challenge set Q and sends T to the verifier.*
- SVerify($Q, T, pk, l, \bar{d}, \widetilde{\mathtt{fid}}$): *The verifier checks if T is a valid proof of storage corresponding to the challenge set Q. The verifier outputs 1 if the proof passes the verification; she outputs 0, otherwise.*
- KChallenge($pk, l, w, \bar{d}$): *During a keyword-based audit on the files containing a given keyword w, the verifier sends a token t_w (for w) and a random challenge set Q to the server.*
- KProve($Q, pk, l, \bar{F}', t_w$): *Upon receiving t_w and Q, the server computes a proof of storage T corresponding to all the data files containing the keyword w and sends T to the verifier.*
- KVerify($Q, T, pk, l, t_w, \bar{d}$): *The verifier checks if T is a valid proof of storage corresponding to the challenge set Q. The verifier outputs 1 if the proof passes the verification; she outputs 0, otherwise.*

We note that we have added two extra functionalities over a basic publicly verifiable proof-of-storage protocol for static data: *file-identifier-based audits* (audits on a set of files) and *keyword-based audits*. Definition 2 implicitly includes

---

[1] The verifier can be a third-party auditor (TPA) or the client (data owner) herself. In case the verifier is a TPA, the client shares the metadata $\bar{d}$ with the TPA.

a "regular" audit on a single data file associated with an identifier fid, where $\widetilde{\text{fid}}$ contains only the file-identifier fid. A file-identifier-based audit consists of the procedures SChallenge, SProve and SVerify; a keyword-based audit consists of the procedures KChallenge, KProve and KVerify. An authenticated read comprises the procedures AuthRead and VerifyRead.

In order to perform a keyword-based audit for a particular keyword w, there are two options that the client can adopt. First, the client identifies the set (say, F_w) of files containing w correctly and runs a proof-of-storage protocol on these files. Second, the client sends to the server the keyword w so that the server can identify the corresponding files itself and generate responses during an audit properly. From the security point of view, the client must be assured of the following guarantees.

1. The integrity of the files outsourced to the (possibly malicious) server should be maintained, be it verified via file-identifier-based audits or via keyword-based audits.
2. For keyword-based audits, audits must be performed on *all* the files containing the challenged keyword w (e.g., the server cannot cheat by sending proofs of storage for a set $F'_w \subsetneq F_w$ or by sending proofs of storage for a set $F'_w \not\subset F_w$).

Towards providing a framework of a keyword-based delegable proof-of-storage protocol, we describe briefly a series of possible constructions and highlight some issues regarding each of these constructions.

4.1 A Naive Approach

The client builds an inverted index $\mathcal{I}$ on the set of files $\bar{F}$. A simple inverted index $\mathcal{I}$ stores, for each keyword, a list of identifiers of all the files containing the keyword. The client splits each (possibly encoded) file $F \in \bar{F}$ into segments and generates authentication tags on these segments using her secret key. She stores the inverted index $\mathcal{I}$ at her end and uploads the files (along with the authentication tags) to the cloud server. During an audit for a keyword w, she consults $\mathcal{I}$ in order to get the identifiers of all files that contain w. Given these file-identifiers, the client (or a TPA) can perform audits on the corresponding files and check their integrity. However, this solution is not suitable for clients having low storage capacity (e.g., clients using low end mobile devices) as the inverted index can be large (of the order of tens/hundreds of Gigabytes [7]) compared to the storage available at the client's side.

4.2 Outsourcing Inverted Index to Storage Server

To overcome the shortcomings of the naive solution, one possibility is to outsource the inverted index $\mathcal{I}$ itself to the untrusted (malicious) storage server. This enables the storage server to compute the responses given a keyword w. Now, for a keyword-based audit, the verifier (the client herself or a TPA) sends the keyword w along with a random challenge set Q to the server. The server searches in $\mathcal{I}$ for the identifiers of all files containing the specific keyword w, computes a proof of storage for these files using Q and sends the proof to the verifier (client or TPA). However, the storage server in our security model (and in most of the existing proof-of-storage protocols) is considered to be malicious, and it can delete a client's data in order to utilize the space thus gained to store other clients' data (e.g., the server can actually store only 1,000 out of 10,000 files containing a particular keyword). To be precise, there must be some mechanism for the verifier to check that: (1) the server is actually storing *all* files containing the specific keyword and (2) the corresponding proofs of storage are computed *only* on these files (during an audit).

4.3   Our Approach

To achieve the guarantees mentioned above, we let the server store the inverted index (in the form of a lookup table) in an authenticated fashion which makes the exact set of file-identifiers (matching a particular keyword) returned by the server *verifiable*. Moreover, for each file outsourced to the server, the client embeds its file-identifier fid in the authenticator tags computed on the segments of the file. This ensures that the server responds with the proofs of storage computed on *exactly* those files that contain the particular keyword.

During an audit in a KDPoS scheme (see Definition 2), the verifier can perform either a file-identifier-based audit (on a set of files) or a keyword-based audit (on the set of all files containing a particular keyword). For a *file-identifier-based audit*, the verifier selects a set of file-identifiers $\widetilde{\text{fid}}$ and generates a random challenge set Q for $\widetilde{\text{fid}}$. Then, she sends $\widetilde{\text{fid}}$ and Q to the server, and the server computes proofs of storage based on these inputs. The verifier verifies the proofs with respect to $\widetilde{\text{fid}}$ and Q.

On the other hand, for a *keyword-based audit*, the verifier cannot generate the random challenge set Q for a keyword w as she does not know a priori the set of file-identifiers $\widetilde{\text{fid}}$ matching w. One trivial way to resolve this issue is the following. The verifier sends the keyword w to the server, and the server sends the corresponding $\widetilde{\text{fid}}$ (with an authentication proof) to the verifier. Then, the verifier generates Q (using the procedure SChallenge) and sends it to the server. However, this solution increases the number of communication rounds between the verifier and the server. Another probable solution is to generate Q in a non-interactive fashion such that both the server and the verifier, given some randomness $\mathfrak{r}$, can produce the same challenge set Q. However, this randomness $\mathfrak{r}$ used to generate Q must be non-precomputable by the server (and also verifiable by the verifier); otherwise, a malicious server might manipulate $\mathfrak{r}$ to get Q of its choice in order to pass a keyword-based audit. We describe a non-interactive challenge-generation method used in our construction as follows.

Non-interactive Challenge Generation for Keyword-Based Audits. In a prior work, Armknecht et al. [1] use a time-dependent pseudo-randomness generator GetRandomness $: \mathcal{T} \rightarrow \{0,1\}^{l_{\text{seed}}}$ with an access to a secure time-dependent source, where $\mathcal{T}$ denotes a set of discrete timestamps and $l_{\text{seed}} = O(\lambda)$. Let cur denote the current timestamp. Given a timestamp $t \in \mathcal{T}$, the generator GetRandomness outputs a uniform random string in $\{0,1\}^{l_{\text{seed}}}$ if $t \leq$ cur; otherwise, it outputs $\bot$. Armknecht et al. instantiate GetRandomness by using Bitcoin (see Sect. 3) as a secure time-dependent source to achieve unpredictability of the output string. For a timestamp $t \in \mathcal{T}$, GetRandomness outputs the hash of the first block appended to the Bitcoin blockchain after t. Given t, this pseudorandom output string can be generated (and verified) by anyone. Although the original scheme [1] uses this method in order to protect an honest party (among the client, the cloud server and the third-party auditor) in case the other parties collude, this method works well for non-interactive challenge generation in our KDPoS scheme also (during keyword-based audits). Given the pseudorandom string output by GetRandomness, the challenge set Q can be generated in a similar way as described in [19,22].

To sum up, the underlying idea is that the client sends to the server the current timestamp t as a part of a challenge. The server generates Q based on t and sends proofs of storage to the client. The client follows the same procedure to generate Q from t and verifies the proofs sent by the server. We describe the method in details for keyword-based audits (comprising the procedures KChallenge, KProve and KVerify) in our scheme.

5   Our KDPoS Construction

We use the publicly verifiable POR scheme for static data proposed by Shacham and Waters [25] as the underlying proof-of-storage scheme, and modify the same in order to support keyword-based audits. Our keyword-based delegable proof-of-storage (KDPoS) protocol consists of the following procedures. We recall that the authenticated read sub-protocol comprises the procedures AuthRead and VerifyRead; the file-identifier-based audit sub-protocol consists of the procedures SChallenge, SProve and SVerify; the keyword-based audit sub-protocol consists of the procedures KChallenge, KProve and KVerify (see Definition 2).

– **Setup**(1^λ): Let the algorithm BLSetup(1^λ) output (p, g, G, G_T, e) as the parameters of a bilinear map (or pairing), where G and G_T are multiplicative cyclic groups of prime order $p = \Theta(2^{2\lambda})$, g is a generator of G (i.e., $G = \langle g \rangle$) and $e : G \times G \to G_T$ (see Sect. 2.2). The client chooses a random element $x \xleftarrow{R} \mathbb{Z}_p$ and sets $v = g^x$. Let $\alpha \xleftarrow{R} G$ be another generator of G and $H : \{0,1\}^* \to G$ be the BLS hash [5] modeled as a random oracle [4]. Let $H_1 : \{0,1\}^* \to \{0,1\}^{\lceil \log_2 p \rceil}$ be a (public) cryptographic hash function. Let $\mathcal{F}$ be the space of file-identifiers. Let GetRandomness be a time-dependent pseudo-randomness generator as described in Sect. 4.3. For a given timestamp $t \in \mathcal{T}$, GetRandomness outputs the hash of the first block appended to the Bitcoin blockchain after t. Let (ssk, psk) be the pair of signing and verification keys for a digital signature scheme $\mathcal{S} = (\text{KeyGen}, \text{Sign}, \text{Verify})$. The secret key of the client is $sk = (x, ssk)$, the public key is $pk = (v, psk, \alpha)$.

– **Outsource**$(\bar{F}, sk, \overline{\mathtt{fid}})$: Let the set of $\bar{n}_f$ data files the client wants to outsource to the server be $\bar{F} = \{F_1, F_2, \ldots, F_{\bar{n}_f}\}$. Let the file-identifiers corresponding to these files form the set $\overline{\mathtt{fid}} = \{\mathtt{fid}_1, \mathtt{fid}_2, \ldots, \mathtt{fid}_{\bar{n}_f}\}$, where each of these file-identifiers is drawn from the space $\mathcal{F}$ uniformly at random. The space $\mathcal{F}$ must be large enough (e.g., $\mathbb{Z}_p$) such that each file is associated with a distinct file-identifier except with a negligible probability.

For each file $F \in \bar{F}$, the client extracts the keywords present in F. Let W be the set of all *distinct* keywords present in any of these files. The client builds a lookup table T_L such that, for each keyword $w \in W$, the row indexed by the keyword w contains an ordered list L_w of file-identifiers matching w. For each row indexed by $w \in W$, the client computes a signature

$$\gamma_w = \mathcal{S}.\mathrm{Sign}(ssk, w\|L_w) \tag{1}$$

and appends this signature γ_w to L_w present in that row. Let n_w be the number of file-identifiers present in L_w. Then, the row indexed by w is of the form

$$\boxed{\mathtt{fid}_{i_1}\|\mathtt{fid}_{i_2}\|\cdots\|\mathtt{fid}_{i_{n_w}}\|\gamma_w}$$

for some $i_1, i_2, \ldots, i_{n_w} \in [1, \bar{n}_f]$. We note that each signature γ_w authenticates the binding between the *exact* list (L_w) of file-identifiers matching w and the corresponding keyword w.

For each $i \in [1, \bar{n}_f]$, the client performs the following.
- The client encodes F_i with an erasure code to form another file F_i' with n_i segments, where $m_{ij} = F_i'[j] \in \mathbb{Z}_p$ for all $1 \le j \le n_i$.
- For all $1 \le j \le n_i$, the client computes an authentication tag on the j-th segment as

$$\sigma_{ij} = (H(\mathtt{fid}_i\|j) \cdot \alpha^{m_{ij}})^x \in G. \tag{2}$$

Let $\Gamma_i = \{\sigma_{i1}, \sigma_{i2}, \ldots, \sigma_{in_i}\}$ be the ordered list of tags for F_i'.

Finally, the client uploads $\bar{F}' = (\{(F_i', \Gamma_i, \mathtt{fid}_i, n_i)\}_{1 \le i \le \bar{n}_f}, T_L)$ to the cloud server. The client stores $\bar{d} = \{(\mathtt{fid}_i, n_i)\}_{1 \le i \le \bar{n}_f}$ at her end in order to check the integrity of some of these files later.

– **AuthRead**$(j, \bar{F}', \bar{d}, pk, \mathtt{fid})$: When the client wants to read the j-th block of a file F' identified by $\mathtt{fid}$, the server sends to the client $F'[j]$, the j-th block of the file, along with its tag σ.

– **VerifyRead**$(j, \bar{d}, pk, sk, F'[j], \sigma, \mathtt{fid})$: After receiving the pair $(F'[j], \sigma)$, the client checks whether $\sigma \stackrel{?}{=} (H(\mathtt{fid}\|j) \cdot \alpha^{F'[j]})^x \in G$. The client outputs 1 if the equality holds; she outputs 0, otherwise.

– **SChallenge**$(pk, l, \bar{d})$: During a file-identifier-based audit, the verifier selects an ordered list of file-identifiers $\widetilde{\mathtt{fid}}$ to be challenged. For each $\mathtt{fid}_i$ present in $\widetilde{\mathtt{fid}}$, the verifier generates a random challenge set $Q_i = \{(r_j, \nu_j)\}_i$ of cardinality $l = \lambda$, where each $r_j \stackrel{R}{\leftarrow} [1, n_i]$ and each $\nu_j \stackrel{R}{\leftarrow} \mathbb{Z}_p$. The verifier sends $\widetilde{\mathtt{fid}}$ and $Q = \{\{(r_j, \nu_j)\}_i\}_{\mathtt{fid}_i \in \widetilde{\mathtt{fid}}}$ to the server.

- **SProve**$(Q, pk, l, \bar{F}', \widetilde{\text{fid}})$: For each $\text{fid}_i \in \widetilde{\text{fid}}$, the server computes a pair $(\sigma_i, \mu_i) \in G \times \mathbb{Z}_p$, where

$$\sigma_i = \prod_{(r_j, \nu_j) \in Q_i} \sigma_{ir_j}{}^{\nu_j}, \qquad \mu_i = \sum_{(r_j, \nu_j) \in Q_i} \nu_j m_{ir_j} \bmod p. \tag{3}$$

The server sends $T = \{(\sigma_i, \mu_i)\}_{\text{fid}_i \in \widetilde{\text{fid}}}$ to the verifier.
- **SVerify**$(Q, T, pk, l, \bar{d})$: For each $\text{fid}_i \in \widetilde{\text{fid}}$, the verifier checks whether the equality

$$e(\sigma_i, g) \overset{?}{=} e\left(\prod_{(r_j, \nu_j) \in Q_i} H(\text{fid}_i || r_j)^{\nu_j} \cdot \alpha^{\mu_i}, v \right) \tag{4}$$

holds or not. The verifier outputs 1 if all the equalities hold; otherwise, she outputs 0.
- **KChallenge**$(pk, l, w, \bar{d})$: During a keyword-based audit for a given keyword w, the verifier chooses two random strings s_0 and s_1 each of size λ bits. She also chooses the current timestamp t. Finally, she constructs a token $t_w = w || s_0 || s_1 || t$ and sends it to the server. The challenge set Q is null.
- **KProve**$(Q, pk, l, \bar{F}', t_w)$: Initially, the challenge set Q is null. The server parses the token t_w as $w || s_0 || s_1 || t$. Given the keyword w, the server fetches $T_L[w]$ containing the ordered list L_w of matching file-identifiers and the corresponding signature $\gamma_w = \mathcal{S}.\text{Sign}(ssk, w || L_w)$. Given t, the server computes the pseudorandom string $\text{str}_t = \text{GetRandomness}(t)$. Let $\widetilde{\text{fid}} = L_w$. For each $\text{fid}_i \in \widetilde{\text{fid}}$, the challenge set $Q_i = \{(r_j, \nu_j)\}_i$ of cardinality $l = \lambda$ is generated as

$$\forall j \in \mathbb{Z}_l : \quad r_j = H_1(\text{str}_t || \text{fid}_i || j || s_0) \bmod n_i + 1, \tag{5}$$
$$\nu_j = H_1(\text{str}_t || \text{fid}_i || j || s_1) \bmod p.$$

For each $\text{fid}_i \in \widetilde{\text{fid}}$, the server computes a pair $(\sigma_i, \mu_i) \in G \times \mathbb{Z}_p$, where

$$\sigma_i = \prod_{(r_j, \nu_j) \in Q_i} \sigma_{ir_j}{}^{\nu_j}, \qquad \mu_i = \sum_{(r_j, \nu_j) \in Q_i} \nu_j m_{ir_j} \bmod p. \tag{6}$$

The server sends $T = (T_L[w], \{(\sigma_i, \mu_i)\}_{\text{fid}_i \in \widetilde{\text{fid}}})$ to the verifier.
- **KVerify**$(Q, T, pk, l, t_w, \bar{d})$: Initially, the set Q is null. The verifier parses t_w as $w || s_0 || s_1 || t$ and T as $(T_L[w], \{(\sigma_i, \mu_i)\}_{\text{fid}_i \in L_w})$. She verifies the validity of the signature γ_w by checking whether

$$\mathcal{S}.\text{Verify}(psk, w || L_w, \gamma_w) \overset{?}{=} \text{accept}. \tag{7}$$

If the verification outputs reject, the verifier outputs 0. Otherwise, the verifier proceeds as follows.

Given the timestamp t, the verifier computes $\text{str}_t = \text{GetRandomness}(t)$. Let $\widetilde{\text{fid}} = L_w$. For each $\text{fid}_i \in \widetilde{\text{fid}}$, the challenge set $Q_i = \{(r_j, \nu_j)\}_i$ of cardinality $l = \lambda$ is generated using Eq. 5. For each $\text{fid}_i \in \widetilde{\text{fid}}$, the verifier checks whether the equality

$$e(\sigma_i, g) \overset{?}{=} e\left(\prod_{(r_j, \nu_j) \in Q_i} H(\texttt{fid}_i || r_j)^{\nu_j} \cdot \alpha^{\mu_i}, v\right) \tag{8}$$

holds or not. Finally, the verifier outputs 1 if all the equalities hold; otherwise, she outputs 0.

Observations. We make the following observations regarding our KDPoS construction.

- The random challenge set Q used in file-identifier-based audits (involving the procedures SChallenge, SProve and SVerify) can also be generated in a non-interactive fashion similar to that used in keyword-based audits. This non-interactive (and verifiable) generation of Q reduces the overall communication between the verifier and the server (as the verifier need not send Q to the server).
- We have used techniques (such as building an authenticated lookup table T_L over keywords present in data files, and generating the random challenge set Q with the help of the Bitcoin blockchain) on top of a particular POR scheme [25] in order to construct a KDPoS scheme. We note that these techniques are independent of the underlying POR scheme and do not modify the same. Thus, *we can integrate our techniques with any existing publicly verifiable POR/PDP scheme for static data (which is based on spot-checking random locations of a file) to obtain such a KDPoS construction.*

6   Security

A keyword-based delegable proof-of-storage (KDPoS) protocol must satisfy the following properties. The security model of a KDPoS scheme is described later in this section. The untrusted cloud server acts as the adversary in this security model. We assume that the untrusted server is malicious that can corrupt the client's data in an arbitrary fashion.

1. **Authenticity.** The authenticity requirements are twofold. First, the cloud server must produce proofs of storage computed *exactly* on the challenged files for file-identifier-based audits (and proofs of storage computed *exactly* on the files matching the challenged keyword in case of keyword-based audits). Second, the cloud server cannot produce valid proofs during audits without correctly storing the challenged segments of those files and their respective authentication information.

2. **Retrievability.** Retrievability of data requires that, given a probabilistic polynomial-time adversary $\mathcal{A}$ that can respond correctly to a challenge Q with some non-negligible probability, there exists a polynomial-time extractor algorithm $\mathcal{E}$ that can extract (at least) the challenged segments of the challenged files (or the challenged segments of the files containing the challenged keyword) by performing file-identifier-based audits (or keyword-based

audits) with $\mathcal{A}$ for a polynomial (in λ) number of times. The algorithm $\mathcal{E}$ has a rewinding access to $\mathcal{A}$. *The authenticity property restricts the adversary $\mathcal{A}$ to produce, during these interactions, valid responses (without storing these segments of the challenged files) only with some probability negligible in λ.*

Security Model. We describe the following security game between the challenger (acting as the client) and the adversary (acting as the cloud server).

– The challenger generates a secret key-public key pair and gives the public key to the adversary. The adversary selects a set of files $\bar{F}$ associated with a set of file-identifiers $\overline{\mathtt{fid}}$ to store. The challenger processes $\bar{F}$ to form another set of files $\bar{F}'$ and returns $\bar{F}'$ to the adversary. The adversary stores $\bar{F}'$ at its end. The challenger stores only some metadata $\bar{d}$ for verification purpose.
– The adversary adaptively chooses and sends to the challenger a sequence of operations defined by $\{\mathtt{op}_i\}_{1 \leq i \leq q}$ (q is a polynomial in the security parameter λ), where $\mathtt{op}_i$ is an authenticated read (comprising AuthRead and VerifyRead) or a file-identifier-based audit (comprising SChallenge, SProve and SVerify) or a keyword-based audit (comprising KChallenge, KProve and KVerify). For each file-identifier-based audit (or a keyword-based audit), the set of files $\widetilde{\mathtt{fid}} \subseteq \overline{\mathtt{fid}}$ (or the keyword) is chosen by the adversary, and the challenger executes an audit on the designated files stored by the adversary. The challenger lets the adversary know the result of each verification (i.e., the output of VerifyRead or the output of SVerify or the output of KVerify).
– Let $\bar{F}^*$ be the final state of the set of files initially outsourced to the adversary after q operations. Finally, the challenger executes an audit protocol (file-identifier-based or keyword-based) with the adversary as follows. The challenger chooses a set of file-identifiers (or a token for a keyword chosen by the challenger) and sends them along with a random challenge set Q to the adversary, and the adversary returns a cryptographic proof to the challenger. The adversary wins the game if it passes the verification.

Definition 3 (Security of a KDPoS Scheme). *A keyword-based delegable proof-of-storage protocol is secure if, given any probabilistic polynomial-time adversary $\mathcal{A}$ who can win the security game mentioned above with some non-negligible probability, there exists a polynomial-time extractor algorithm $\mathcal{E}$ that can extract, except with some probability negligible in λ, (at least) the challenged segments of the files (that are challenged via file-identifier-based/keyword-based audits) by interacting with $\mathcal{A}$ polynomially many times.*

According to Definition 3, our KDPoS construction is secure in the random oracle model [4] under the computational Diffie-Hellman assumption over $G = \langle g \rangle$ (see Sect. 2.3). The full security proof will appear in the extended version of this paper.

7   Efficiency of Our KDPoS Scheme

The efficiency of our KDPoS scheme depends on the underlying POR scheme [25]. For each file challenged by the verifier, the proof consists of a pair of the form

(σ, μ) that is of size $2 \cdot \log_2 p$ bits, where $\sigma \in G$, $\mu \in \mathbb{Z}_p$ and $p = \Theta(2^{2\lambda})$. For example, such a pair is 64 bytes long for 128-bit security (i.e., $\lambda = 128$). On the other hand, for each challenged file, the verifier needs to compute 2 pairings along with other operations ($l + 1$ exponentiations and one multiplication in G). However, we later describe a method in order to make both of these parameters independent of the number of files being audited (see Sect. 7.4).

7.1   Storage Overhead

We have described our KDPoS scheme assuming that an authentication tag (an element of G) is generated for each segment (an element of $\mathbb{Z}_p$) of a file. Therefore, the storage overhead (for the tags) is same as the storage itself. This can be mitigated by grouping s segments as a single chunk and computing an authentication tag for each of these chunks [25]. Thus, the storage overhead is $1/s$-fraction of the storage. However, during an audit, the size of the aggregated segment (μ) sent by the server as a proof is now $s \cdot \log_2 p$ bits. In addition, we have introduced an authenticated lookup table T_L in order to enable keyword-based audits. Let W be the set of all distinct keywords present in any file $F \in \bar{F}$ and n_w be the number of files containing a keyword $w \in W$. Let $b_\mathcal{S}$ be the size (in bits) of a signature in $\mathcal{S}$ and $b_\mathcal{F}$ be the number of bits required to represent the space of file-identifiers $\mathcal{F}$. Then, the storage overhead incurred for storing T_L is $\sum_{w \in W} (n_w \cdot b_\mathcal{F} + b_\mathcal{S})$ bits.

7.2   Efficient Search over Lookup Table

In order to enable the server to search over the lookup table T_L efficiently, the client builds a dictionary data structure (e.g., trie, hash table, self-balancing binary search tree) over all distinct keywords in W (during the procedure Outsource). The node in this data structure corresponding to a keyword w contains $L_w \| \gamma_w$, where L_w is the ordered list of file-identifiers matching w and $\gamma_w = \mathcal{S}.\mathrm{Sign}(ssk, w \| L_w)$. The client uploads this data structure along with the processed files to the server. During a keyword-based audit, the server makes an efficient search to find the exact node corresponding to the challenged keyword.

7.3   Communication Complexity

In case of a keyword-based audit, the server sends to the verifier the row of T_L indexed by w (containing the list of file-identifiers matching w) along with the corresponding proofs of storage (during the procedure KProve). We note that for a file-identifier-based audit as well, the verifier sends a list of file-identifiers along with the challenge set (during the procedure SChallenge). Therefore, the overall communication complexity is of the same order for both types of audits. Moreover, the challenge set Q can be generated in a non-interactive way (for both types of audits) eliminating the need for communicating the same.

7.4   Proof Generation and Verification in a Batch

We observe that given a list of file-identifiers $\widetilde{\texttt{fid}}$ and a challenge set $Q = \{\{(r_j, \nu_j)\}_i\}_{\texttt{fid}_i \in \widetilde{\texttt{fid}}}$, the server computes a pair (σ_i, μ_i) for each $\texttt{fid}_i \in \widetilde{\texttt{fid}}$ (see Eqs. 3 and 6). Therefore, the corresponding proof T consists of $|\widetilde{\texttt{fid}}|$ pairs of the form (σ, μ), where $\sigma \in G$ and $\mu \in \mathbb{Z}_p$. Hence, the proof size is $|T| = 2 \cdot |\widetilde{\texttt{fid}}| \cdot \log_2 p$ bits. On the other hand, for each $\texttt{fid}_i \in \widetilde{\texttt{fid}}$, the verifier checks whether the following equality

$$e(\sigma_i, g) \overset{?}{=} e\left(\prod_{(r_j, \nu_j) \in Q_i} H(\texttt{fid}_i || r_j)^{\nu_j} \cdot \alpha^{\mu_i}, v \right) \tag{9}$$

holds or not (see Eqs. 4 and 8). Therefore, the verifier needs to perform expensive pairing operations for $2 \cdot |\widetilde{\texttt{fid}}|$ times.

   To reduce both the size of the proof and the number of pairing operations required to verify a proof, we adopt an idea similar to that of aggregating the challenged segments and their corresponding tags for a single file. We observe that, for each challenged file identified by $\texttt{fid}_i$ in our KDPoS scheme, the server aggregates all the challenged segments into a single segment μ_i and all the corresponding tags into a single tag σ_i (see Eqs. 3 and 6), and the verifier runs the verification procedure on the aggregated segment and the aggregated tag (see Eq. 9). We extend this simple idea for multiple files (that are present in $\widetilde{\texttt{fid}}$) as follows. The server computes the proof $(\sigma, \mu) \in G \times \mathbb{Z}_p$, where

$$\sigma = \prod_{\texttt{fid}_i \in \widetilde{\texttt{fid}}} \prod_{(r_j, \nu_j) \in Q_i} \sigma_{ir_j}{}^{\nu_j} = \prod_{\texttt{fid}_i \in \widetilde{\texttt{fid}}} \sigma_i,$$

$$\mu = \sum_{\texttt{fid}_i \in \widetilde{\texttt{fid}}} \sum_{(r_j, \nu_j) \in Q_i} \nu_j m_{ir_j} \bmod p = \sum_{\texttt{fid}_i \in \widetilde{\texttt{fid}}} \mu_i \bmod p.$$

Given the aggregated segment μ and the aggregated tag σ, the verifier checks if

$$e(\sigma, g) \overset{?}{=} e\left(\prod_{\texttt{fid}_i \in \widetilde{\texttt{fid}}} \prod_{(r_j, \nu_j) \in Q_i} H(\texttt{fid}_i || r_j)^{\nu_j} \cdot \alpha^{\mu}, v \right). \tag{10}$$

   In this case, the reduced proof size is $|T| = 2 \cdot \log_2 p$ bits, and the verifier needs to perform only 2 pairing operations. It is important to note that both of these parameters are now constant, irrespective of the number of files involved in either a file-identifier-based audit or a keyword-based audit.

8   Conclusion

In this work, we have introduced keyword-based delegable proofs of storage, where the data owner (or a third-party auditor) can selectively check the integrity of all her data files containing a particular keyword. We have formally defined the security of a keyword-based delegable proof-of-storage protocol. We have provided an efficient construction of a secure keyword-based delegable proof-of-storage protocol. Any existing publicly verifiable proof-of-storage scheme (based on spot-checking techniques) can be extended in a similar fashion as described in this work. We have also discussed the efficiency of our construction and some possible ways to enhance this efficiency.

Acknowledgments. This work is partially supported by Cisco University Research Program Fund, CyberGrants ID: #698039 and Silicon Valley Community Foundation. The authors would like to thank Chris Shenefiel and Samir Saklikar for their comments and suggestions.

References

1. Armknecht, F., Bohli, J., Karame, G.O., Liu, Z., Reuter, C.A.: Outsourced proofs of retrievability. In: ACM Conference on Computer and Communications Security, CCS, pp. 831–843 (2014)
2. Ateniese, G., et al.: Provable data possession at untrusted stores. In: ACM Conference on Computer and Communications Security, CCS, pp. 598–609 (2007)
3. Back, A.: Hashcash - a denial of service counter-measure, August 2002. http://www.hashcash.org/papers/hashcash.pdf
4. Bellare, M., Rogaway, P.: Random oracles are practical: a paradigm for designing efficient protocols. In: ACM Conference on Computer and Communications Security, CCS, pp. 62–73 (1993)
5. Boneh, D., Lynn, B., Shacham, H.: Short signatures from the Weil pairing. J. Cryptol. **17**(4), 297–319 (2004)
6. Bowers, K.D., Juels, A., Oprea, A.: Proofs of retrievability: theory and implementation. In: ACM Cloud Computing Security Workshop, CCSW, pp. 43–54 (2009)
7. Cash, D., et al.: Dynamic searchable encryption in very-large databases: data structures and implementation. In: Network and Distributed System Security Symposium, NDSS (2014). http://www.internetsociety.org/doc/dynamic-searchable-encryption-very-large-databases-data-structures-and-implementation
8. Cash, D., Küpçü, A., Wichs, D.: Dynamic proofs of retrievability via oblivious RAM. In: Johansson, T., Nguyen, P.Q. (eds.) EUROCRYPT 2013. LNCS, vol. 7881, pp. 279–295. Springer, Heidelberg (2013). https://doi.org/10.1007/978-3-642-38348-9_17
9. Chang, H., Hsu, C.: Using topic keyword clusters for automatic document clustering. IEICE Trans. **88-D**(8), 1852–1860 (2005)
10. Curtmola, R., Garay, J.A., Kamara, S., Ostrovsky, R.: Searchable symmetric encryption: improved definitions and efficient constructions. In: ACM Conference on Computer and Communications Security, CCS, pp. 79–88 (2006)
11. Dodis, Y., Vadhan, S.P., Wichs, D.: Proofs of retrievability via hardness amplification. In: Theory of Cryptography Conference, TCC, pp. 109–127 (2009)
12. Erway, C.C., Küpçü, A., Papamanthou, C., Tamassia, R.: Dynamic provable data possession. In: ACM Conference on Computer and Communications Security, CCS, pp. 213–222 (2009)
13. Galbraith, S.D., Paterson, K.G., Smart, N.P.: Pairings for cryptographers. Discret. Appl. Math. **156**(16), 3113–3121 (2008)

14. Gritti, C., Chen, R., Susilo, W., Plantard, T.: Dynamic provable data possession protocols with public verifiability and data privacy. In: International Conference on Information Security Practice and Experience, ISPEC, pp. 485–505 (2017)
15. Juels, A., Kaliski, B.S.: PORs: Proofs of retrievability for large files. In: ACM Conference on Computer and Communications Security, CCS, pp. 584–597 (2007)
16. Kang, S.: Keyword-based document clustering. In: International Workshop on Information Retrieval with Asian Languages, IRAL, pp. 132–137 (2003)
17. Koblitz, N., Menezes, A.: Pairing-based cryptography at high security levels. In: Smart, N.P. (ed.) Cryptography and Coding 2005. LNCS, vol. 3796, pp. 13–36. Springer, Heidelberg (2005). https://doi.org/10.1007/11586821_2
18. Merkle, R.C.: A digital signature based on a conventional encryption function. In: Pomerance, C. (ed.) CRYPTO 1987. LNCS, vol. 293, pp. 369–378. Springer, Heidelberg (1988). https://doi.org/10.1007/3-540-48184-2_32
19. Miller, A., Juels, A., Shi, E., Parno, B., Katz, J.: Permacoin: repurposing bitcoin work for data preservation. In: IEEE Symposium on Security and Privacy, S&P, pp. 475–490 (2014)
20. Nakamoto, S.: Bitcoin: a peer-to-peer electronic cash system (2008). http://bitcoin.org/bitcoin.pdf
21. Reed, I.S., Solomon, G.: Polynomial codes over certain finite fields. J. Soc. Ind. Appl. Math. **8**(2), 300–304 (1960)
22. Sengupta, B., Bag, S., Ruj, S., Sakurai, K.: Retricoin: bitcoin based on compact proofs of retrievability. In: International Conference on Distributed Computing and Networking, ICDCN, pp. 14:1–14:10 (2016)
23. Sengupta, B., Ruj, S.: Publicly verifiable secure cloud storage for dynamic data using secure network coding. In: ACM Asia Conference on Computer and Communications Security, ASIACCS, pp. 107–118 (2016)
24. Sengupta, B., Ruj, S.: Efficient proofs of retrievability with public verifiability for dynamic cloud storage. IEEE Trans. Cloud Comput. **PP**(99) (2017). https://doi.org/10.1109/TCC.2017.2767584
25. Shacham, H., Waters, B.: Compact proofs of retrievability. J. Cryptol. **26**(3), 442–483 (2013)
26. Shi, E., Stefanov, E., Papamanthou, C.: Practical dynamic proofs of retrievability. In: ACM Conference on Computer and Communications Security, CCS, pp. 325–336 (2013)
27. Tao, J.J.: Hybrid and iterative keyword and category search technique. US Patent 8667007 B2, March 2014. https://www.google.com/patents/US8667007
28. Tao, J.J.: Semantic context based keyword search techniques. US Patent 9589050 B2, March 2017. https://www.google.com/patents/US9589050
29. Wang, C., Chow, S.S.M., Wang, Q., Ren, K., Lou, W.: Privacy-preserving public auditing for secure cloud storage. IEEE Trans. Comput. **62**(2), 362–375 (2013)
30. Wang, Q., Wang, C., Ren, K., Lou, W., Li, J.: Enabling public auditability and data dynamics for storage security in cloud computing. IEEE Trans. Parallel Distrib. Syst. **22**(5), 847–859 (2011)

A Generic Framework for Accountable Optimistic Fair Exchange Protocol

Jia-Ch'ng Loh$^{(\boxtimes)}$, Swee-Huay Heng, and Syh-Yuan Tan

Faculty of Information Science and Technology, Multimedia University,
Melaka, Malaysia
jasonlohjc@gmail.com, {shheng,sytan}@mmu.edu.my

Abstract. Optimistic Fair Exchange protocol was designed for two parties to exchange in a fair way where an arbitrator always remains offline and will be referred only if any dispute happens. There are various optimistic fair exchange protocols with different security properties in the literature. Most of the optimistic fair exchange protocols satisfy resolution ambiguity where a signature signed by the signer is computational indistinguishable from the one resolved by the arbitrator. Huang et al. proposed the first generic framework for accountable optimistic fair exchange protocol in the random oracle model where it possesses resolution ambiguity and is able to reveal the actual signer when needed. Ganjavi et al. later proposed the first generic framework in the standard model. In this paper, we propose another generic framework for accountable optimistic fair exchange protocol in the standard model using ordinary signature, convertible undeniable signature, and ring signature as the underlying building blocks.

Keywords: Accountability · Convertible undeniable signature
Optimistic fair exchange · Ring signature

1 Introduction

A fair exchange protocol was first designed to overcome the issue of fairness during an exchange between two parties. The first optimistic fair exchange (OFE) protocol with offline arbitrator was proposed by Asokan et al. [1] in 1997. It was later broken and repaired by Dodis and Reyzin [7] and they also formally redefined its security model in 2003. An OFE protocol consists of three parties, a signer, a verifier, and an arbitrator. The arbitrator always remains offline and will be referred only if any dispute happens. At the beginning of the protocol, the signer first generates a partial signature as an offer to the verifier. The verifier then returns a full signature as a confirmation. If everything goes well, the signer replies a full signature, and the protocol ends. However, if a dispute happens, the verifier can then contact the arbitrator by sending an evidence for resolving the issue.

© Springer Nature Switzerland AG 2018
C. Su and H. Kikuchi (Eds.): ISPEC 2018, LNCS 11125, pp. 299–309, 2018.
https://doi.org/10.1007/978-3-319-99807-7_18

The security model of OFE protocol is setup-driven if the initial key registration needs to be done between the signer and the arbitrator, and the model is setup-free if that is not required. Most of the existing exchange protocols consider more than one signer in the system. An OFE protocol should be applicable to multi-user setting, but items are exchanged between one signer and one verifier. A multi-user setting consists of many signers and many verifiers along with only one arbitrator [6]. Huang et al. claimed that the property of the strong resolution ambiguity in the single-user setting OFE protocol is preserved in the multi-user setting [16], where a strong resolution ambiguity requires that one can convert a partial signature into a full signature using either the signer's private key or the arbitrator's private key, and no one knows which key is used. As previous works only considered in the certified-key model, Huang et al. [15] then proposed a secure OFE protocol in the multi-user setting and chosen-key model. In contrast to the certified-key model, the adversary in chosen-key model is able to make queries with respect to the public key even without showing the knowledge of the private key.

Motivation. Most of the OFE protocols possess resolution ambiguity where the full signature generated by the signer (actual signature) should be computational indistinguishable with the full signature resolved by the arbitrator (resolved signature) [6,15]. In some scenarios, this property can actually compromise the fairness, i.e. there is a dishonest arbitrator colludes with a verifier such that the dishonest arbitrator resolves the partial signature without validating the evidence. Due to the resolution ambiguity, others will not know whether the full signature is generated by the original signer or the arbitrator. In order to overcome the above issue, the notion of accountable OFE protocol was formalised by Huang et al. [17] in 2011. A generic framework for accountable OFE was proposed where the partial signature is an ordinary signature, and the full signature consists of a partial signature, a random salt, and an undeniable signature along with an OR-signature.

It possesses resolution ambiguity due to the anonymity of undeniable signature and the OR-signature. Undeniable signature is a special featured signature which cannot be verified without the help of the signer [4]. In order to construct the OR-signature in their framework, one must use the private key of undeniable signature to generate a signature based on proofs of knowledge (SPK) [2]. Due to the ability of SPK, one can generate a proof to either claim or deny an undeniable signature during the stage of revealing the original signer in an accountable OFE protocol. An SPK can be constructed by applying the Fiat-Shamir heuristic [8] to a proof of knowledge where it is a zero-knowledge protocol that allows the signer to convince the verifier that he knows a secret without leaking it [5]. It is known that an SPK that transformed by applying Fiat-Shamir heuristic is secure in the random oracle model [8].

Ganjavi et al. [11] then proposed the first generic framework for accountable OFE protocol which is secure in the standard model. In their framework, the partial signature is also an ordinary signature, and the full signature consists of a partial signature and a traceable ring signature [10]. Traceable ring signature is a variant of ring signature [19] having the additional ability to restrict the anonymity of the signer. It consists of two additional security properties, namely, traceability and exculpability. Traceability ensures that the identity of the signer can be traced as long as the signer signs two different messages with respect to the same tag, whereas exculpability ensures that the signer cannot be accused of signing twice with respect to the same tag. Although Ganjavi et al.'s framework is proven secure in the standard model, to the best of our knowledge, there are very few traceable ring signature schemes provably secure in the standard model [9,13] and random oracle model [10,14] respectively. Hence it limits the application to accountable OFE protocol.

Table 1. A Comparison of the frameworks for accountable OFE protocol

Framework	Partial Signature σ_p	Full Signature σ	Proof π	Standard Model
Huang et al. [17]	OS	σ_p,US, r,OR-Signature	SPK	$\times$
Ganjavi et al. [11]	OS	σ_p,TRS	TRS	$\checkmark$
Proposed	OS	σ_p,CUS,RS	token	$\checkmark$

r: Random salt   OS: Ordinary signature
US: Undeniable signature   RS: Ring signature
CUS: Convertible undeniable signature   TRS: Traceable ring signature
SPK: Signature based on proofs of knowledge

Contribution. In this paper, we propose another generic framework for accountable OFE protocol. As shown in Table 1, the partial signature in our framework is also an ordinary signature, and the full signature is an intermediate solution between Huang et al. and Ganjavi et al.'s protocol, where it consists of a partial signature, a convertible undeniable signature, and a ring signature. There are two types of convertible undeniable signature, namely, selectively convertible and universally convertible. Our generic framework requires a selectively convertible one which allows the signer to convert only a specific undeniable signature into universally verifiable one. We show that the proposed framework is secure in the standard model under multi-user setting and chosen-key model as long as the underlying schemes satisfy certain security properties.

2 Accountable OFE Protocol

An accountable OFE protocol consists of the following algorithms:

- **PMGen**: On input a security parameter 1^k, it outputs a system parameter PM.

- **$Setup^A$**: On input PM, it generates an arbitrator's public and private key pair (APK, ASK).
- **$Setup^U$**: On input PM, it generates a user's public and private key pair (UPK_i, USK_i).
- **$PSign$**: On input a message m and (USK_i, APK), it generates a partial signature σ_p.
- **$PVer$**: On input $(m, \sigma_p, UPK_i, APK)$, it validates (m, σ_p) under (UPK_i, APK) and outputs "1" if σ_p is valid or "0" otherwise.
- **$Sign$**: On input $(m, \sigma_p, USK_i, APK)$, it generates a full signature σ.
- **Ver**: On input (m, σ, UPK_i, APK), it validates (m, σ) under (UPK_i, APK) and outputs "1" if σ is valid or "0" otherwise.
- **Res**: On input $(m, \sigma_p, ASK, UPK_i)$, it resolves σ_p by checking its validity first. If σ_p is valid on UPK_i, it generates a full signature σ or outputs "$\perp$" otherwise.
- **$Prove^A$**: On input $(m, \sigma, UPK_i, APK, ASK)$, it generates an arbitrator proof π^A that can claim or deny whether σ was generated by APK.
- **$Prove^U$**: On input $(m, \sigma, UPK_i, APK, USK_i)$, it generates a user proof π^U that can claim or deny whether σ was generated by UPK_i.
- **$Open$**: On input $(m, \sigma, UPK_i, APK, \pi)$, it first validates (m, σ) under (UPK_i, APK). It then outputs "UPK_i" if π can prove σ is generated by the algorithm $Sign$ or "APK" if σ is generated by the algorithm Res. Otherwise, it outputs "$\perp$" which indicates π is invalid and it cannot be opened.

Correctness: The following algorithms will always output "1" if σ is generated correctly. If σ is a valid on (UPK_i, APK) and π is generated correctly, the algorithm $Open$ will always output either "UPK_i" or "APK".

$-PVer(m, \boldsymbol{PSign}(m, USK_i, APK), UPK_i, APK) = $ "1"

$-Ver(m, \boldsymbol{Sign}(m, \boldsymbol{PSign}(m, USK_i, APK), USK_i, APK), UPK_i, APK) = $ "1"

$-Ver(m, \boldsymbol{Res}(m, PSign(m, USK_i, APK), UPK_i, ASK), UPK_i, APK) = $ "1"

$-Open(m, \sigma, UPK_i, APK, \boldsymbol{Prove}^A(m, \sigma, UPK_i, APK, ASK)) = $ "UPK_i"or"APK"

$-Open(m, \sigma, UPK_i, APK, \boldsymbol{Prove}^U(m, \sigma, UPK_i, APK, USK_i)) = $ "UPK_i"or"APK"

2.1   Security Properties

An accountable OFE protocol possesses resolution ambiguity, accountability, security against signer(s), security against verifier(s), and security against arbitrator. Its security models in the multi-user setting and chosen-key model are defined as the game between a probabilistic polynomial time (PPT) adversary $\mathcal{A}$ and a challenger $\mathcal{C}$. In this paper, we only recall their definitions, the full details can be referred from [11, 17].

Resolution Ambiguity: A full signature σ generated by the signer and resolved by the arbitrator should be computationally indistinguishable.

Definition 1. *An OFE is (t, q, ϵ)-resolution ambiguous if there is no (t, q)-adversary that can have success probability more than $\epsilon + \frac{1}{2}$ in its game with at most q queries to its accessible oracles in time t.*

Accountability: An OFE protocol has accountability if it satisfies three types of accountability as follows.

- **Type I:** It is impossible for a dishonest signer to produce a full signature that can be proven as an output of APK with algorithm Res.
- **Type II:** It is impossible for a dishonest arbitrator to resolve a full signature that can be proven as an output of UPK_i with algorithm $Sign$.
- **Type III:** It is impossible for the signer and the arbitrator to both claim or deny a valid full signature σ.

Definition 2. *An OFE has accountability if it satisfies the three types of accountability.*

Security against Signer(s): It is impossible for a dishonest signer to produce a valid σ_p, but cannot be resolved by the arbitrator using Res.

Definition 3. *An OFE is (t, q_{res}, ϵ)-secure against signers if there is no (t, q_{res})-adversary that can have success probability more than ϵ in its game with at most q_{res} queries to res oracle in time t.*

Security Against Verifier(s): It is impossible for a dishonest verifier to produce a valid σ without the assistance from the signer or the arbitrator. Its security model is adopted from Ganjavi et al. [11], and we allow $\mathcal{A}$ to access sign oracle $\mathcal{O}_{Sig}$ as we want to simulate that a dishonest verifier can forge a full signature on either the signer or the arbitrator.

Definition 4. *An OFE is $(t, q_{psig}, q_{sig}, q_{res}, \epsilon)$-secure against verifiers if there is no $(t, q_{psig}, q_{sig}, q_{res})$-adversary that can have success probability more than ϵ in its game with at most q_{psig} queries to psign oracle, q_{sig} queries to sign oracle, and q_{res} queries to res oracle in time t.*

Security Against Arbitrator: It is impossible for a dishonest arbitrator to produce a valid σ without having the corresponding σ_p from the signer.

Definition 5. *An OFE is (t, q_{psig}, ϵ)-secure against arbitrator if there is no (t, q_{psig})-adversary that can have success probability more than ϵ in its game with at most q_{psig} queries to psign oracle in time t.*

Definition 6. *An accountable OFE is secure in the multi-user setting and chosen-key model if it is accountable, secure against signer(s), secure against verifier(s), and secure against arbitrator.*

3   Building Blocks

3.1   Ordinary Signature [12]

An ordinary signature consists of the following three algorithms. ***KeyGen*** that on input a security parameter 1^k, it outputs a public and private key pair (pk, sk). ***Sign*** that on input a message and private key pair (m, sk), it outputs an ordinary signature σ^{os}. ***Verify*** that on input (m, σ^{os}, pk), it outputs "1" if σ^{os} is valid and outputs "0" otherwise. Its *Correctness* requires that every ordinary signature generated in a correct way can always be accepted.

Unforgeability: This security property ensures that there is no computational way to forge a signature with only the knowledge of the public key pk.

Definition 7. *An ordinary signature scheme is (t, q_s, ϵ)-existential unforgeable against chosen message attack (EUF-CMA) if there is no (t, q_s)-adversary can have success probability more than ϵ in its game with at most q_s queries to sign oracle in time t.*

3.2   Convertible Undeniable Signature [18]

Convertible undeniable signature consists of the following four algorithms and an interactive protocol. ***KeyGen*** that on input a security parameter 1^k, it outputs a public and private key pair (pk, sk). ***Sign*** that on input a message and a private key (m, sk), it outputs an undeniable signature χ. ***SConvert***[1] that on input (m, χ, sk), it computes a selective token π^s which can be used to publicly verify (m, χ). ***SVerify*** that on input (m, χ, pk, π^s), it outputs "$\perp$" if π is an invalid token on pk. Else, it outputs "1" if (m, χ, pk) is valid and outputs "0" otherwise. ***Confirmation/Disavowal Protocol*** that run between the signer and the verifier on input (m, χ, pk, sk), the output is a non-transferable proof ("*Accept*"/"*Deny*") that shows χ is valid/invalid on (m, pk). Its *Completeness* and *Soundness* requires that every valid (invalid) signature can always be proven valid (invalid), and every valid (invalid) signature cannot be proven as invalid (valid).

Unforgeability: This security property ensures that there is no computational way to forge a convertible undeniable signature with only the knowledge of public key pk.

Definition 8. *A convertible undeniable signature scheme is $(t, q_s, q_{cd}, q_{sc}, \epsilon)$-EUF-CMA, if there is no (t, q_s, q_{cd}, q_{sc})-adversary can have success probability more than ϵ in its game with at most q_s queries to sign oracle, q_{cd} queries to confirmation/disavowal oracle, and q_{sc} queries to sconvert oracle in time t.*

---

[1] We require the signer to be able to convert a selective token of a signature that was not generated by his private key, and the selective token can be used to publicly deny the signature.

Anonymity: This security property requires that given a valid (m, χ) and two possible signers' public keys (pk_0, pk_1), there is no computational way to decide who the real signer is.

Definition 9. *A convertible undeniable signature scheme is $(t, q_s, q_{cd}, q_{sc}, \epsilon)$-anonymous against chosen message attack, if there is no (t, q_s, q_{cd}, q_{sc})-adversary can have success probability more than ϵ in its game in time t.*

3.3 Ring Signature

Ring signature consists of the following three algorithms. ***KeyGen*** that on input 1^k, it outputs a public and private key pair (pk, sk). ***Sign*** that on input a message, a private key, and a list of public keys (m, sk, PK_L) where $PK_L = (pk_1, \ldots, pk_n)$ with n members, it outputs a ring signature η. ***Verify*** that on input (m, η, PK_L), it outputs "1" if η is valid and output "0" otherwise. Its *Correctness* requires that every ring signature generated in a correct way can always be accepted.

Unforgeability: This security property ensures there is no computational way to forge a ring signature with only the knowledge of a list of public keys $PK_L = (pk_i, \ldots, pk_n)$ of n members.

Definition 10. *A ring signature scheme is (t, q_s, ϵ)-unforgeable against chosen-subring attack, if there is no (t, q_s)-adversary can have success probability more than ϵ in its game with at most q_s queries to sign oracle in time t.*

Anonymity:[2] This security property requires that given a valid (m, η) and two possible signers' public keys (pk_0, pk_1), there is no computational way to decide who the real signer is.

Definition 11. *A ring signature scheme is (t, q_s, ϵ)-anonymous with respect to adversarially-chosen keys, if there is no (t, q_s)-adversary can have success probability negligibly close to $\frac{1}{2}$ in its game with at most q_s queries to sign oracle in time t.*

4 Generic Transformation

4.1 Generic Framework

We propose a generic framework for accountable OFE protocol using ordinary signature, convertible undeniable signature, and ring signature as our building blocks. The partial signature is an ordinary signature, $\sigma_p = \sigma^{os}$, and the full signature consists of a partial signature, a convertible undeniable signature, and a

---

[2] The definition of anonymity for ring signature scheme can be phrased in either a computational or an unconditional sense [3]. In this paper, the requirement we need can be either one.

ring signature, $\sigma = (\sigma_p, \chi, \eta)$. Let OS $= (KeyGen, Sign, Verify)$ be an ordinary signature scheme, CUS $= (KeyGen, Sign, SConvert, SVerify)$ be a convertible undeniable signature scheme, and RS $= (KeyGen, Sign, Verify)$ be a ring signature scheme. We need a hash function $H : \{0,1\}^* \rightarrow \mathcal{M}$, where $\mathcal{M}$ is the message space.

- **$PMGen$**: On input the security parameter 1^k, it generates the system parameters PM needed for the OS, CUS, and RS.
- **$Setup^A$**: On input PM, it runs CUS.$KeyGen(1^k) \rightarrow (apk^{cus}, ask^{cus})$ and RS.$KeyGen(1^k) \rightarrow (apk^{rs}, ask^{rs})$ to compute an arbitrator public and private key pair $(APK, ASK) = ((apk^{cus}, apk^{rs}), (ask^{cus}, ask^{rs}))$.
- **$Setup^U$**: On input PM, it runs OS.$KeyGen(1^k) \rightarrow (pk_i^{os}, sk_i^{os})$, CUS.$KeyGen(1^k) \rightarrow (pk_i^{cus}, sk_i^{cus})$, and RS.$KeyGen(1^k) \rightarrow (pk_i^{rs}, sk_i^{rs})$ to compute a user public and private key pair $(UPK_i, USK_i) = ((pk_i^{os}, pk_i^{cus}, pk_i^{rs}), (sk_i^{os}, sk_i^{cus}, sk_i^{rs}))$.
- **$PSign$**: On input a message and a signer private key (m, USK_i), it runs OS.$Sign(m, sk_i^{os}) \rightarrow \sigma^{os}$ and outputs a partial signature $\sigma_p = \sigma^{os}$.
- **$PVer$**: On input (m, σ_p, UPK_i), it can validate σ_p by running OS.$Ver(m, \sigma^{os}, pk_i^{os})$. It outputs "1" if σ_p is valid and outputs "0" otherwise.
- **$Sign$**: On input $(m, \sigma_p, USK_i, APK, UPK_i)$. Let $m' = H(m, \sigma_p, UPK_i)$. It runs CUS.$Sign(m', sk_i^{cus}) \rightarrow \chi$ and RS.$Sign(\chi, sk_i^{rs}, PK_L) \rightarrow \eta$, where $PK_L = (pk_i^{rs}, apk^{rs})$ and outputs a full signature $\sigma = (\sigma_p, \chi, \eta)$.
- **Ver**: On input (m, σ, UPK_i, APK), it can verify $\sigma = (\sigma_p = \sigma^{os}, \chi, \eta)$ by running OS.$Verify(m, \sigma^{os}, pk_i^{os})$ and RS.$Verify(\chi, \eta, PK_L)$, where $PK_L = (pk_i^{rs}, apk^{rs})$. Therefore, if σ_p and η are valid, this algorithms outputs "1" and "0" otherwise.
- **Res**: On input $(m, \sigma_p, ASK, APK, UPK_i)$, it first checks the validity of σ_p by running OS.$Verify(m, \sigma^{os}, pk_i^{os})$. It outputs "$\bot$" if σ_p is invalid. Otherwise, it continues to compute $m' = H(m, \sigma_p, UPK_i)$. It then runs CUS.$Sign(m', ask^{cus}) \rightarrow \chi$ and RS.$Sign(\chi, ask_i^{rs}, PK_L) \rightarrow \eta$, where $PK_L = (pk_i^{rs}, apk^{rs})$ and outputs a full signature $\sigma = (\sigma_p, \chi, \eta)$
- **$Prove^A$**: On input $(m, \sigma, ASK, APK, UPK_i)$, it first runs $Ver(m, \sigma, UPK_i, APK)$ to check its validity and continue if and only if it is valid. Then it computes $m' = H(m, \sigma_p, UPK_i)$ and runs CUS.$SConvert(m', \chi, ask^{cus}) \rightarrow \pi^A$ and outputs a proof $\pi = \pi^A$. Otherwise, it outputs "$\bot$".
- **$Prove^U$**: On input $(m, \sigma, USK_i, APK, UPK_i)$, it first runs $Ver(m, \sigma, UPK_i, APK)$ to check its validity and continue if and only if it is valid. Then it computes $m' = H(m, \sigma_p, UPK_i)$ and runs CUS.$SConvert(m', \chi, sk_i^{cus}) \rightarrow \pi^U$ and outputs a proof $\pi = \pi^U$. Otherwise, it outputs "$\bot$".
- **$Open$**: On input $(m, \sigma, UPK_i, APK, \pi)$, it first runs $Ver(m, \sigma, UPK_i, APK)$ to check its validity and continue if and only if it is valid. Otherwise, it outputs "$\bot$". It computes $m' = H(m, \sigma_p, UPK_i)$ and parses π in the following cases:

- If $\pi = \pi^A$, it runs CUS.$Verify(m', \chi, \pi^A, apk^{cus}) \rightarrow b \in \{0,1\}$. If $b = 1$, it outputs "APK" which indicates χ is originally generated by apk. Otherwise, it outputs "UPK_i". If the output is $\perp$", it means π is invalid.
- Else if $\pi = \pi^U$, it runs CUS.$Verify(m', \chi, \pi^U, pk_i^{cus}) \rightarrow b \in \{0,1\}$. If $b = 1$, it outputs "UPK_i" which indicates χ is originally generated by pk_i^{cus}. Otherwise, it outputs "APK". If the output is "$\perp$", it means π is invalid.

Correctness: The correctness of our generic framework follows the underlying OS, CUS, and RS.

4.2   Security Analysis

The proof approach for resolution ambiguity and accountability are inspired by Huang et al.'s framework [17], and the proof approach for security against signer(s), security against verifier(s), and security against arbitrator are inspired by Ganjavi et al.'s framework [11]. Due to page limit, we only briefly describe the proof. It follows that we assume there exists a PPT adversary $\mathcal{A}$ who breaks the proposed accountable OFE framework, we then construct a PPT algorithm $\mathcal{D}$ which runs $\mathcal{A}$ as subroutine to break the security of the underlying building blocks. This contradicts to the claim of the security, hence the proposed accountable OFE framework is secure.

Theorem 1. *Our generic framework is secure in the multi-user setting and chosen-key model if it satisfies Lemma 1–7 below:*

Lemma 1. *Our generic framework is resolution ambiguity if the underlying CUS and RS satisfy anonymity.*

Lemma 2. *Our generic framework is $(t, q_{res}, q_{pa}, \epsilon)$-type I accountable if the underlying CUS is $(t, q_{res}, q_{pa}, \epsilon)$-EUF-CMA and complete and sound.*

Lemma 3. *Our generic framework is $(t, q_{psig}, q_{sig}, q_{pu}, \epsilon)$-type II accountable if the underlying CUS is $(t, q_{psig}, q_{sig}, q_{pu}, \epsilon)$-EUF-CMA and complete and sound.*

Lemma 4. *Our generic framework is (t, ϵ)-type III accountable if the underlying CUS is (t, ϵ)-complete and sound.*

Lemma 5. *Our generic framework is unconditionally secure against signers.*

Lemma 6. *Our generic framework is $(t, q_{psig}, q_{sig}, q_{res}, \epsilon)$-secure against verifiers if the underlying CUS and RS are $(t + t_1 q_{psig}, q_{sig}, q_{res}, \epsilon)$-existentially unforgeable.*

Lemma 7. *Our generic framework is (t, q_{psig}, ϵ)-secure against the arbitrator if the underlying OS is (t, q_{psig}, ϵ)-existentially unforgeable.*

5   Conclusion

We proposed a generic framework to construct accountable OFE protocol in the multi-user setting and chosen-key model which can be proven secure in the standard model by using the ordinary signature, convertible undeniable signature and ring signature as the underlying building blocks.

Acknowledgement. The authors would like to acknowledge the Malaysia government's Fundamental Research Grant Scheme (FRGS/1/2015/ICT04/MMU/03/5) for supporting this work.

References

1. Asokan, N., Shoup, V., Waidner, M.: Optimistic fair exchange of digital signatures. In: Nyberg, K. (ed.) EUROCRYPT 1998. LNCS, vol. 1403, pp. 591–606. Springer, Heidelberg (1998). https://doi.org/10.1007/BFb0054156
2. Bellare, M., Goldreich, O.: On defining proofs of knowledge. In: Brickell, E.F. (ed.) CRYPTO 1992. LNCS, vol. 740, pp. 390–420. Springer, Heidelberg (1993). https://doi.org/10.1007/3-540-48071-4_28
3. Bender, A., Katz, J., Morselli, R.: Ring signatures: stronger definitions, and constructions without random oracles. J. Cryptol. **22**(1), 114–138 (2009). https://doi.org/10.1007/s00145-007-9011-9
4. Chaum, D., van Antwerpen, H.: Undeniable signatures. In: Brassard, G. (ed.) CRYPTO 1989. LNCS, vol. 435, pp. 212–216. Springer, New York (1990). https://doi.org/10.1007/0-387-34805-0_20
5. Cramer, R., Damgård, I., Schoenmakers, B.: Proofs of partial knowledge and simplified design of witness hiding protocols. In: Desmedt, Y.G. (ed.) CRYPTO 1994. LNCS, vol. 839, pp. 174–187. Springer, Heidelberg (1994). https://doi.org/10.1007/3-540-48658-5_19
6. Dodis, Y., Lee, P.J., Yum, D.H.: Optimistic fair exchange in a multi-user setting. In: Okamoto, T., Wang, X. (eds.) PKC 2007. LNCS, vol. 4450, pp. 118–133. Springer, Heidelberg (2007). https://doi.org/10.1007/978-3-540-71677-8_9
7. Dodis, Y., Reyzin, L.: Breaking and repairing optimistic fair exchange from PODC 2003. In: Proceedings of the 3rd ACM Workshop on Digital Rights Management, DRM 2003, pp. 47–54. ACM, New York (2003). https://doi.org/10.1145/947380.947387
8. Fiat, A., Shamir, A.: How to prove yourself: practical solutions to identification and signature problems. In: Odlyzko, A.M. (ed.) CRYPTO 1986. LNCS, vol. 263, pp. 186–194. Springer, Heidelberg (1987). https://doi.org/10.1007/3-540-47721-7_12
9. Fujisaki, E.: Sub-linear size traceable ring signatures without random oracles. In: Kiayias, A. (ed.) CT-RSA 2011. LNCS, vol. 6558, pp. 393–415. Springer, Heidelberg (2011). https://doi.org/10.1007/978-3-642-19074-2_25
10. Fujisaki, E., Suzuki, K.: Traceable ring signature. In: Okamoto, T., Wang, X. (eds.) PKC 2007. LNCS, vol. 4450, pp. 181–200. Springer, Heidelberg (2007). https://doi.org/10.1007/978-3-540-71677-8_13
11. Ganjavi, R., Asaar, M.R., Salmasizadeh, M.: A traceable optimistic fair exchange protocol. In: 2014 11th International ISC Conference on Information Security and Cryptology, pp. 161–166, September 2014. https://doi.org/10.1109/ISCISC.2014.6994041

12. Goldwasser, S., Micali, S., Rivest, R.: A digital signature scheme secure against adaptive chosen-message attacks. SIAM J. Comput. **17**(2), 281–308 (1988). https://doi.org/10.1137/0217017
13. Gu, K., Wu, N.: Constant size traceable ring signature scheme without random oracles. Cryptology ePrint Archive, Report 2018/288 (2018). https://eprint.iacr.org/2018/288
14. Hu, C., Li, D.: Forward-secure traceable ring signature. In: Eighth ACIS International Conference on Software Engineering, Artificial Intelligence, Networking, and Parallel/Distributed Computing (SNPD 2007), vol. 3, pp. 200–204, July 2007
15. Huang, Q., Yang, G., Wong, D.S., Susilo, W.: Efficient optimistic fair exchange secure in the multi-user setting and chosen-key model without random oracles. In: Malkin, T. (ed.) CT-RSA 2008. LNCS, vol. 4964, pp. 106–120. Springer, Heidelberg (2008). https://doi.org/10.1007/978-3-540-79263-5_7
16. Huang, X., Mu, Y., Susilo, W., Wu, W., Xiang, Y.: Optimistic fair exchange with strong resolution-ambiguity. IEEE J. Sel. Areas Commun. **29**(7), 1491–1502 (2011). https://doi.org/10.1109/JSAC.2011.110814
17. Huang, X., Mu, Y., Susilo, W., Wu, W., Zhou, J., Deng, R.H.: Preserving transparency and accountability in optimistic fair exchange of digital signatures. IEEE Trans. Inf. Forensics Secur. **6**(2), 498–512 (2011). https://doi.org/10.1109/TIFS.2011.2109952
18. Phong, L.T., Kurosawa, K., Ogata, W.: Provably secure convertible undeniable signatures with unambiguity. In: Garay, J.A., De Prisco, R. (eds.) SCN 2010. LNCS, vol. 6280, pp. 291–308. Springer, Heidelberg (2010). https://doi.org/10.1007/978-3-642-15317-4_19
19. Rivest, R.L., Shamir, A., Tauman, Y.: How to leak a secret: theory and applications of ring signatures. In: Goldreich, O., Rosenberg, A.L., Selman, A.L. (eds.) Theoretical Computer Science. LNCS, vol. 3895, pp. 164–186. Springer, Heidelberg (2006). https://doi.org/10.1007/11685654_7

Network Security

Towards Securing Challenge-Based Collaborative Intrusion Detection Networks via Message Verification

Wenjuan Li[1,2], Weizhi Meng[2(✉)], Yu Wang[3], Jinguang Han[4], and Jin Li[3]

[1] Department of Computer Science, City University of Hong Kong,
Kowloon Tong, Hong Kong
[2] Department of Applied Mathematics and Computer Science,
Technical University of Denmark, Kongens Lyngby, Denmark
weme@dtu.dk
[3] School of Computer Science, Guangzhou University, Guangzhou, China
[4] Department of Computer Science, University of Surrey, Guildford, UK

Abstract. With the increasing number of Internet-of-Things (IoT) devices, intrusion detection systems (IDSs) have been widely deployed in a distributed or collaborative setting, in which a collaborative intrusion detection network (CIDN) improves the detection accuracy of a single IDS by enabling IDS nodes to exchange useful information with each other. To protect CIDNs against insider attacks, challenge-based trust mechanisms are one promising solution to detect malicious nodes through sending challenges. However, several studies have revealed that this kind of mechanism is still vulnerable to some advanced insider attacks like *passive message fingerprint attack (PMFA)*. Motivated by this observation, in this work, we focus on enhancing the security of challenge-based CIDNs and propose a compact but efficient message verification approach to defeat such insider attack by inserting a verifying alarm into each normal request. In the evaluation, we investigate the attack performance under both simulated and real network environments. Experimental results demonstrate that our approach can identify malicious nodes under PMFA and decrease their trust values in a quick manner.

Keywords: Intrusion detection · Collaborative network
Insider attack · Passive message fingerprint attack
Challenge-based trust mechanism

1 Introduction

Intrusion detection systems (IDSs) are an essential and widely deployed security mechanism, with the purpose of protecting various resources and assets [31,34]. Based on the locations, an IDS can be classified as host-based IDS (HIDS) and

---

W. Meng—Who was previously known as Yuxin Meng.

C. Su and H. Kikuchi (Eds.): ISPEC 2018, LNCS 11125, pp. 313–328, 2018.
https://doi.org/10.1007/978-3-319-99807-7_19

network-based IDS (NIDS). Further, an IDS can be classified into two categories according to detection approaches: *signature-based NIDS* and *anomaly-
based NIDS*. The former like [33,39] (also known as *rule-based NIDS*) detects
a suspicious event by comparing its available signatures with current system
events or packets. The latter like [8,38] identifies an anomaly by discovering a
significant deviation between the normal profile and the observed system or network events. An alarm will be triggered if an accurate match is identified or the
suspicious value is above a threshold [9].

With the increasing capability of network intrusions, a traditional IDS could
be bypassed very easily and are hard to identify some complex attacks like
Denial-of-Service (DoS) attacks. The detection failure can cause potential damage and financial loss, i.e., causing paralysis of the entire network without timely
detection and response [40]. To enhance the detection capability of an IDS, collaborative (or distributed) intrusion detection networks (CIDNs) are developed
allowing different IDS nodes to exchange information with each other by sending
a normal request [6]. Due to the distributed architecture, a CIDN is often vulnerable to insider attacks, where an attacker can perform an adversarial action
after the control of an insider node.

To mitigate this problem, challenge-based trust mechanisms (shortly *challenge mechanisms*) are one of the promising solutions to safeguard CIDNs against
insider attacks. This kind of mechanisms aims to evaluate the trustworthiness of
other nodes by sending challenges in a periodic way. In particular, a challenge
usually contains a set of alarms requesting for alarm severity [6]. As the testing
node knows the actual severity of requested alarms, it can utilize the received
feedback to derive a trust value (e.g., satisfaction level) for the tested node. Former studies have demonstrated that such mechanism can prevent insider attacks
like betrayal attacks and collusion attacks, where malicious nodes may collaborate to give false information of alarm rankings to reduce the effectiveness of
alarm aggregation in CIDNs.

Motivations. However, it is identified that challenge mechanisms are depending
heavily on two assumptions: (a) challenges are sent out in a way that makes
them difficult to be distinguished from normal messages; and (b) malicious nodes
always send feedback opposite to its truthful judgment. In real-world scenarios,
malicious nodes may behave much more dynamic and complex, i.e., a malicious
node can choose whether to send untruthful feedback or not. As a result, the
adopted assumptions may leave challenge-based CIDNs vulnerable to advanced
insider attacks in real scenarios. Recently, Li *et al.* [17] developed an advanced
collusion attack, called *passive message fingerprint attack (PMFA)*, which can
compromise the challenge mechanism through passively collecting messages and
distinguishing normal requests. Then, malicious nodes can maintain their trust
values by giving false information to only normal request while providing truthful
feedback to other messages.

Contributions. In this work, we focus on PMFA and propose a message verification approach to improve the security of current challenge-based CIDNs.
The main idea is to insert a verification alarm into each normal request among

different nodes, and then check its labelling in the feedback. The contributions can be summarized as below:

- PMFA enables a malicious node to distinguish normal requests from challenges and behave untruthfully to only normal requests. In this work, we develop a compact but efficient message verification approach by inserting a verification alarm into each normal request, aiming to improve the security of challenge-based CIDNs against advanced insider attacks. In this way, a malicious node is expected to be detected by discovering any malicious response to the verification alarm.
- In the evaluation, we investigate the performance of our approach under both simulated and real CIDN environments by collaborating with an IT company. Experimental results demonstrate that our approach can defend against advanced insider attacks like PMFA by decreasing the trust values of malicious nodes in a quick manner.

The remaining parts are organized as follows. Section 2 introduces the background of challenge-based CIDNs. In Sect. 3, we analyze the original challenge mechanisms and introduce how *passive message fingerprint attack (PMFA)* works. Section 4 details our proposed message verification approach in enhancing challenge-based CIDNs. Section 5 evaluates the performance of our approach and discusses the results. Section 6 reviews relevant studies on distributed and collaborative intrusion detection. Finally, we conclude the work in Sect. 7.

2   Background on Challenge-Based CIDNs

Challenge-based mechanisms are one promising solution to defend collaborative networks against insider threats. Figure 1 depicts the high-level architecture of a typical challenge-based CIDN. In addition to an IDS module, a CIDN node often contains three major components: *trust management component, collaboration component* and *P2P communication* [17].

- *Trust management component* is responsible for evaluating the trustworthiness of another node. Challenge-based mechanism computes the trust values through comparing the received feedback with the expected answers. Each node can send out either normal requests or challenges for alert ranking (consultation). To further protect challenges, the original work [6] assumed that challenges should be sent out in a random manner and in a way that makes them difficult to be distinguished from a normal alarm ranking request.
- *Collaboration component* is mainly responsible for assisting a node to calculate the trust values of another node by sending out *normal requests* or *challenges*, and receiving the relevant *feedback*. This component can help a tested node deliver its feedback when receiving a request or challenge. For instance, Fig. 1 shows that when node *A* sends a *request* or *challenge* to node *B*, it can receive relevant feedback.

– *P2P communication.* This component is responsible for connecting with other IDS nodes and providing network organization, management and communication among IDS nodes.

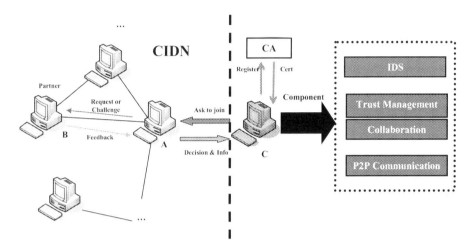

Fig. 1. The high-level architecture of a typical challenge-based CIDN with its major components.

Network Interactions. Generally, each node can choose its partners based on its own policies and experience, and maintain a list of collaborated nodes, called *partner list.* This list is customizable and stores the information of other nodes like the existing trust values. Before a node asks for joining the network, A node has to obtain its unique proof of identity (e.g., a public key and a private key) by registering to a trusted certificate authority (*CA*). As depicted in Fig. 1, if node *C* asks for joining the network, it has to send a request to a CIDN node, say node *A*. Then, node *A* makes a decision and sends back an initial *partner list*, if node *C* is accepted. A CIDN node can typically send two types of messages: challenge and normal request.

– A *challenge* mainly contains a set of IDS alarms, where a testing node can send these alarms to the tested nodes for labeling alarm severity. Because the testing node knows the severity of these alarms in advance, it can compute the trustworthiness or satisfaction level for the tested node, based on the received feedback.
– A *normal request* is sent by a node for alarm aggregation, which is an important feature of collaborative networks in improving the detection performance of a single detector. The aggregation process usually only considers the feedback from highly trusted nodes. As a response, an IDS node should send back alarm ranking information as their feedback.

3   Passive Message Fingerprint Attack

Challenge-based CIDNs may be still vulnerable to advanced insider attacks like *passive message fingerprint attack (PMFA)* [17], which is a kind of collusion attack, where malicious nodes are able to maintain their trust through passively exchanging received messages and distinguishing normal requests.

Basic Idea. The challenge-based mechanism assumes that an IDS node is hard to distinguish challenges from messages. However, previous work found a way to distinguish normal requests from messages [17]. It is worth noting that normal requests are responsible for alarm aggregation through sending one or several alarms to other nodes for alarm ranking. In this case, a set of (trusted) IDS nodes could receive this request and give feedback, whereas such kind of request should include the same alarms for alarm aggregation. This causes a request to become distinguishable through comparing the received messages among several nodes. If several nodes receive the message consisting of the same alarms, the corresponding message should be a normal request rather than a challenge. Taking advantage of this, malicious nodes can employ a strategy by only sending untruthful feedback to the identified normal requests, while giving truthful responses to other messages.

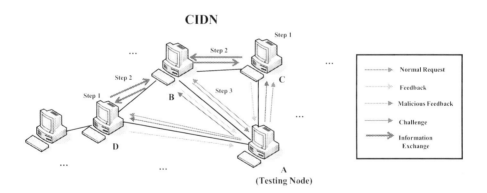

Fig. 2. Passive message fingerprint attack (PMFA) on challenge-based CIDNs.

Figure 2 details the steps of PMFA. Suppose node A is a testing node that sends out messages including normal requests and challenges to its partner nodes. Then, all tested nodes should give feedback accordingly. If nodes B, C and D are malicious, then the steps of *PMFA* can be summarized as below [17]:

- **Step 1.** Malicious node should collect and store all received messages from the testing node. This attack accepts that a challenge is sent in a random manner and cannot be distinguished from normal messages, so that all malicious nodes are not able to identify a challenge directly.

- **Step 2.** Meanwhile, malicious nodes has to exchange the stored messages with each other. In real deployment, normal requests will be sent out to all trusted nodes for alarm ranking; thus, it is possible to compare the received messages and check whether it is a normal request. For instance, nodes B compares the received messages from nodes C and D. If a match is identified, then the relevant message should be a normal request.
- **Step 3.** Once identifying a normal request, node B can send back a malicious response (e.g., false alarm ranking) to affect the alarm aggregation of node A. For other received messages, node B still sends back its truthful answers.

Overall, PMFA enables malicious nodes to work collaboratively and distinguish normal requests from the received messages. This attack employs an advanced strategy, in which a malicious node provides untruthful feedback to only the identified requests while truthfully responding to other messages. Thus, malicious nodes have a good chance to make a negative impact on alarm aggregation of testing node without decreasing their trust values.

4   Our Approach

On the whole, we found that the basic structure between a normal request and a challenge is the same, but the contained alarm items are a bit different, leaving malicious nodes under PMFA a chance to distinguish a normal request from the received messages. Figure 3 shows the alarm content for normal requests and challenges, and how challenge mechanism works in a practical environment. In particular, Fig. 3(a) presents that a normal request contains the same alarm items for alarm ranking by trusted nodes, while Fig. 3(b) presents that a challenge usually consists of different alarm items due to a random selection process. Under an advanced collusion attack like PMFA, several malicious nodes can exchange the received messages and identify a normal request. As a result, there is a need to improve the security of existing challenge mechanism.

In this work, we propose a compact but efficient message verification approach by adding one more verification alarm(s) to each normal request. The inserting place relies on a random selection process in order to protect the verification alarm. Figure 4 shows how our approach works: suppose there are three normal requests (e.g., #1, #2, #3), then we randomly insert one verification alarm to each normal request (e.g., Alarm #2, Alarm #3, Alarm #10). By receiving the feedback from the tested nodes, our verification module checks the labelling for each verification alarm. If all alarms are labelled correctly, then the received feedback is considered to be normal; otherwise, the received feedback is regarded as malicious. In this case, if malicious nodes under PMFA identify and respond maliciously to normal requests, their untruthful behavior can be detected, resulting in a rapid decease of trust values. It is worth noting that the inserted verification alarm should be extracted from the challenge database.

Formally, let $NR = (A_1, A_2, ..., A_i), i = 1, 2, 3, ..., N$ denote a normal request and A_i denote the ith alarm item. In our approach, running a pseudo

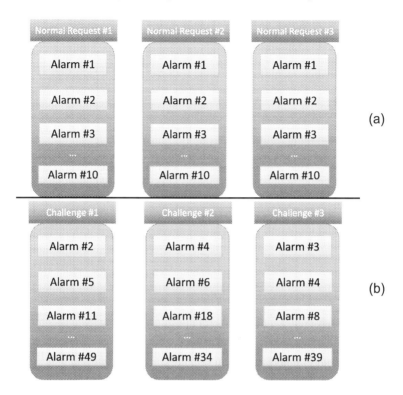

Fig. 3. The content difference for (a) normal requests and (b) challenges in a practical challenge-based CIDN.

random number generator to get a number $n \in [1, N]$. Then, inserting a verification alarm A_n into NR and obtain an improved normal request $NR' = (A_1, A_2, ..., A_n, ...A_i), i = 1, 2, 3, ..., N$. In the end, checking the label of A_n to decide whether a received feedback is malicious or not.

- If A_n is verified successfully, then the received feedback is considered as normal.
- If A_n is unable to be verified properly, then the received feedback is regarded as a malicious one.

It is worth noting that a malicious feedback could cause a rapid decrease of reputation levels. Thus, our proposed message verification approach is compact but would be efficient in identifying advanced insider attacks like PMFA.

5 Evaluation

In this section, we evaluate the performance of our approach against PMFA under a simulated and a real network environment, respectively. We mainly conduct two experiments as follows.

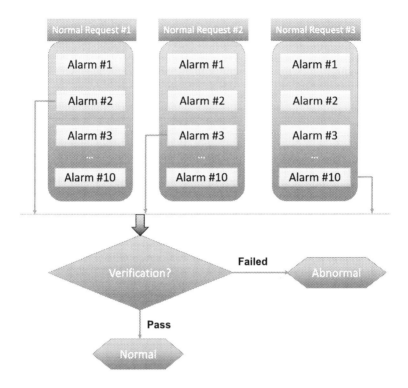

Fig. 4. An example of our message verification approach.

- *Experiment-1.* In this experiment, we aimed to explore the feasibility of our approach against PMFA in a simulated CIDN.
- *Experiment-2.* In this experiment, we cooperated with an IT company and investigated the practical performance of our approach against PMFA in a real CIDN environment.

In the remaining parts, we introduce how to setup a CIDN, how to compute trust values (satisfaction levels), and discuss experimental results.

5.1   CIDN Settings

The simulated CIDN environment was composed of 40 nodes, which were randomly distributed in a 10×10 grid region. Each IDS node adopted Snort [36] as IDS plugin. All nodes can communicate with each other and build an initial *partner list*. The trust values of all nodes in the *partner list* were initialized as $T_s = 0.5$ based on the results in [6]. According to [16], we set the number of alarms to 40 in either a normal request or a challenge.

To evaluate the trustworthiness of partner nodes, each node can send out challenges randomly to its partners with an average rate of ε. There are two levels of request frequency: ε_l and ε_h. The request frequency is low for a highly trusted or highly untrusted node, as it should be very confident about their feedback. On the other hand, the request frequency should be high for other nodes whose trust values are close to the threshold. To facilitate comparisons, all the settings can be referred to similar studies [6,14]. The detailed parameters are shown in Table 1.

Table 1. Simulation parameters in the experiment.

Parameters	Value	Description
λ	0.9	Forgetting factor
ε_l	10/day	Low request frequency
ε_h	20/day	High request frequency
r	0.8	Trust threshold
T_s	0.5	Trust value for newcomers
m	10	Lower limit of received feedback
d	0.3	Severity of punishment

Node Expertise. This work adopted three expertise levels for an IDS node as: low (0.1), medium (0.5) and high (0.95). A beta function was utilized to model the expertise of an IDS:

$$f(p'|\alpha, \beta) = \frac{1}{B(\alpha, \beta)} p'^{\alpha-1}(1 - p')^{\beta-1}$$
$$B(\alpha, \beta) = \int_0^1 t^{\alpha-1}(1 - t)^{\beta-1}dt \tag{1}$$

where $p'(\in [0,1])$ is the probability of intrusion examined by the IDS. $f(p'|\alpha, \beta)$ means the probability that a node with expertise level l responses with a value of p' to an intrusion examination of difficulty level $d(\in [0,1])$. A higher value of l means a higher probability of correctly identifying an intrusion, while a higher value of d means that an intrusion is more difficult to detect. In particular, α and β can be defined as below [7]:

$$\alpha = 1 + \frac{l(1-d)}{d(1-l)}r$$
$$\beta = 1 + \frac{l(1-d)}{d(1-l)}(1-r) \tag{2}$$

where $r \in \{0,1\}$ is the desirable detection result. For a fixed difficulty level, the node with higher level of expertise can achieve higher probability of correctly detecting an intrusion. As an example, a node with expertise level of 1 can accurately identify an intrusion with guarantee if the difficulty level is 0.

Trust Evaluation at Nodes. To calculate the trust value of a CIDN node, a testing node can send a *challenge* to the target node via a random generation process, and then compute its satisfaction level by comparing the received feedback

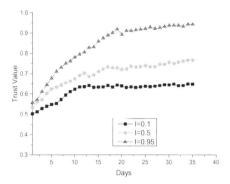
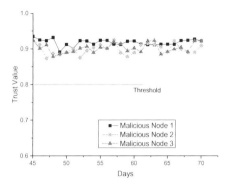

Fig. 5. Convergence of trust values of IDS nodes regarding three expertise levels.

Fig. 6. Trust values of malicious nodes under PMFA.

with the expected response. Based on [6], we can evaluate the trustworthiness of a node i according to node j as follows:

$$T_i^j = (w_s \frac{\sum_{k=0}^{n} F_k^{j,i} \lambda^{tk}}{\sum_{k=0}^{n} \lambda^{tk}} - T_s)(1 - x)^d + T_s \tag{3}$$

where $F_k^{j,i} \in [0,1]$ is the score of the received feedback k and n is the total number of feedback. λ is a *forgetting factor* that assigns less weight to older feedback. w_s is a *significant weight* depending on the total number of received feedback, if there is only a few feedback under a certain minimum m, then $w_s = \frac{\sum_{k=0}^{n} \lambda^{tk}}{m}$, otherwise $w_s = 1$. x is the percentage of "don't know" answers during a period (e.g., from $t0$ to tn). d is a positive incentive parameter to control the severity of punishment to "don't know" replies.

Satisfaction Evaluation. Suppose there are two factors: an expected feedback ($e \in [0,1]$) and an actual received feedback ($r \in [0,1]$). Then, a function F ($\in [0,1]$) can be used to reflect the satisfaction by measuring the difference between the received answer and the expected answer as follows [7].

$$F = 1 - (\frac{e - r}{max(c_1 e, 1 - e)})^{c_2} \quad e > r \tag{4}$$

$$F = 1 - (\frac{c_1(r - e)}{max(c_1 e, 1 - e)})^{c_2} \quad e \leq r \tag{5}$$

where c_1 controls the degree of penalty for wrong estimates and c_2 controls satisfaction sensitivity. Based on the work [7], we set $c_1 = 1.5$ and $c_2 = 1$.

5.2   Experiment-1

In this experiment, we conducted an experiment to investigate the initial performance of our approach against PMFA in a simulated CIDN. Figure 5 illustrates

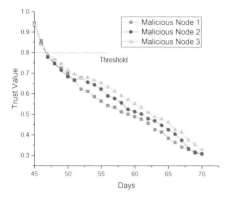 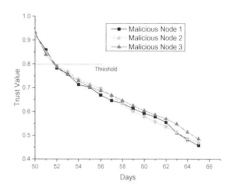

Fig. 7. The performance of our approach against PMFA in the simulated CIDN.

Fig. 8. The performance of our approach in a real CIDN environment.

the convergence of trust values regarding different expert nodes with three expertise levels: low ($I = 0.1$), medium ($I = 0.5$) and high ($I = 0.95$). The obtained results are in line with the results in [6,7], in which the nodes with higher expertise can achieve higher reputation levels. In this simulated environment, the trust values of all nodes become stable after around 20 days, because challenge-based CIDNs ask for a long time for building a high reputation level.

The Impact of PMFA. We randomly selected three expert nodes (called *malicious node 1*, *malicious node 2* and *malicious node 3*) to launch PMFA. Figure 6 depicts the trust values of malicious nodes, and indicates that all malicious nodes could maintain their reputation levels over the threshold without being detected. This validates that malicious nodes under PMFA can distinguish normal requests from the received messages and greatly degrade the security of challenge mechanisms. By maintaining the reputation, malicious nodes have a good chance to make an impact on alarm aggregation.

The Performance of Our Approach. For the same CIDN environment, we deployed our message verification approach and run the experiment again. The trust values of malicious nodes are shown in Fig. 7. It is found that the reputation levels of *malicious node 1*, *malicious node 2* and *malicious node 3* decreased rapidly below the threshold of 0.8 within only one day. The results demonstrated that our proposed approach was able to detect PMFA nodes by decreasing their reputation levels in a quick manner.

5.3   Experiment-2

In this experiment, we collaborated with an IT company to validate the practical performance of our approach in a wired CIDN environment including a total of 35 nodes. Similar to the above experiment, we adopted the same network settings and monitored the whole network to become stable. We then deployed our approach with the help of IT administrators and randomly selected three expert nodes as malicious to launch PMFA.

Figure 8 depicts the trust values of malicious nodes. It is noticeable that the trust values could drop quickly to below the threshold within one day, which was in line with the observations in the first experiment. The results validated that our approach is effective to defend against PMFA in a practical CIDN environment, by quickly decreasing the trust values of malicious nodes. The security administrator from the participating company also confirmed the observations and considered our approach to be effective for practical usage.

5.4   Discussion

In this work, our major goal is to enhance challenge-based CIDNs against advanced insider attacks like PMFA, by means of a compact but efficient message verification approach. Our obtained results demonstrated the effectiveness of our approach, whereas we still leave some issues for future investigation.

– *Increased resource consumption.* Our approach needs to insert one verification alarm into each normal request, which may increase the resource consumption. In our practical evaluation, we initially explored this issue and found an average workload increase of 1.1%. The IT administrator from the participating organization considered it is acceptable. It is one of our future topics to analyze the resource consumption in a practical scenario.
– *Scalability.* In this work, we explored the performance of our approach under both simulated and real CIDN environments, whereas we did not perform a particular experiment to investigate the scalability issue. In our future work, we plan to investigate this issue with a systematic evaluation.
– *Advanced insider attacks.* In this work, we mainly focus on the detection of PMFA, an advanced collusion attack for challenge-based CIDNs. In the literature, there are several other advanced insider attacks like Special On-Off Attacks (SOOA) [18]. To explore the performance of our approach against other advanced attacks is one of our future directions.

6   Related Work

In a real-world application, a single IDS usually has no information about the protected environment where it was deployed, hence the detector is very easy to be bypassed under some advanced attacks [40]. To mitigate this issue, there is a need to construct a distributed or collaborative network. Several related distributed systems can be classified as below. (1) *Centralized/Hierarchical systems*: Emerald [32] and DIDS [35]; (2) *Publish/subscribe systems*: COSSACK [30] and DOMINO [41]; and (3) *P2P Querying-based systems*: Netbait [1] and PIER [11].

Generally, collaborative or distributed intrusion detection networks enable an IDS node to achieve more accurate detection by collecting and communicating information from/with other IDS nodes. However, it is well-recognized by the literature that such collaborative networks are vulnerable to insider attacks [2]. The previous work [12] figured out that most distributed intrusion detection systems (DIDS) relied on centralized fusion, or distributed fusion with unscalable communication mechanisms. They then proposed a distributed detection system based on the decentralized location and routing infrastructure for this issue. However, their system is vulnerable to insider attacks, as they assumes that all peers are trusted.

To protect distributed systems against insider attacks, building appropriate trust models is one of the promising solutions. For instance, Duma *et al.* [3] proposed a P2P-based overlay IDS to examine traffic by using a trust-aware engine for correlating alerts and an adaptive scheme for managing trust. The trust-aware correlation engine is capable of filtering out warnings sent by untrusted or low quality peers, while the adaptive trust management scheme uses past experiences of peers to predict their trustworthiness. Tuan [37] then utilized game theory to model and analyze the processes of reporting and exclusion in a P2P network. They identified that if a reputation system was not incentive compatible, the more numbers of peers in the system, the less likely that anyone will report about a malicious peer.

Later, Fung *et al.* initialized a type of challenge-based CIDNs, in which the reputation level of a node depends on the received answers to the challenges. In the beginning, they focus on host-based detection and proposed a host-based collaboration framework that enables each node to evaluate the trustworthiness of others based on its own experience and a forgetting factor [6]. The forgetting factor is used to highlight the recent experience of peers. To enhance challenge mechanisms, Li *et al.* [13,16] identified that different IDS nodes may have different levels of sensitivity in detecting particular intrusions. Then, they introduced a notion of *intrusion sensitivity* that measures the detection sensitivity of an IDS in detecting different kinds of intrusions. As an example, if a signature-based detector deploys more signatures (or rules) in detecting DoS attacks, then it should be considered to be more powerful in detecting such specific attacks as compared to other nodes, which have relatively fewer signatures.

Based on the notion, they further developed a trust management model for CIDNs through allocating *intrusion sensitivity* via machine learning techniques in an automatic way [14]. They also studied how to apply *intrusion sensitivity* for aggregating alarms and defending against pollution attacks, in which a group of malicious peers collaborate together by providing false alarm rankings [15]. Some other related work about how to enhance the performance of IDSs can be referred to [4,5,10,19–29].

7   Conclusion

Challenge-based trust mechanisms are one promising solution to protect CIDNs against insider threats, which can identify malicious nodes by evaluating the satisfaction levels between challenges and responses. However, in real-world deployment, it is found that such mechanisms rely heavily on two major assumptions, which may result in a weak threat model and would be still vulnerable to advanced insider attacks like PMFA. This attack enables malicious nodes maintaining their trust values, by giving untruthful feedback to only normal requests, while providing truthful response to other messages.

In this work, we focus on PMFA and proposed a compact but efficient message verification approach by inserting a verification alarm into each normal request. In the evaluation, we performed experiments under both simulated and practical CIDN environments, and found that our approach could help identify malicious nodes under PMFA by decreasing their trust values in a fast manner. Our work attempts to stimulate more research in designing secure CIDN architectures in real-world scenarios. There are many feasible future directions, i.e., investigating our approach in identifying other advanced insider attacks like Special On-Off Attacks (SOOA) [18].

Acknowledgments. The authors would like to thank security administrators and managers from the participating organization for their help and support in deploying our mechanism.

References

1. Chun, B., Lee, J., Weatherspoon, H., Chun, B.N.: Netbait: a distributed worm detection service. Technical report IRB-TR-03-033, Intel Research Berkeley (2003)
2. Douceur, J.R.: The sybil attack. In: Druschel, P., Kaashoek, F., Rowstron, A. (eds.) IPTPS 2002. LNCS, vol. 2429, pp. 251–260. Springer, Heidelberg (2002). https://doi.org/10.1007/3-540-45748-8_24
3. Duma, C., Karresand, M., Shahmehri, N., Caronni, G.: A trust-aware, P2P-based overlay for intrusion detection. In: DEXA Workshop, pp. 692–697 (2006)
4. Fadlullah, Z.M., Taleb, T., Vasilakos, A.V., Guizani, M., Kato, N.: DTRAB: combating against attacks on encrypted protocols through traffic-feature analysis. IEEE/ACM Trans. Netw. **18**(4), 1234–1247 (2010)
5. Friedberg, I., Skopik, F., Settanni, G., Fiedler, R.: Combating advanced persistent threats: from network event correlation to incident detection. Comput. Secur. **48**, 35–47 (2015)
6. Fung, C.J., Baysal, O., Zhang, J., Aib, I., Boutaba, R.: Trust management for host-based collaborative intrusion detection. In: De Turck, F., Kellerer, W., Kormentzas, G. (eds.) DSOM 2008. LNCS, vol. 5273, pp. 109–122. Springer, Heidelberg (2008). https://doi.org/10.1007/978-3-540-87353-2_9
7. Fung, C.J., Zhang, J., Aib, I., Boutaba, R.: Robust and scalable trust management for collaborative intrusion detection. In: Proceedings of the 11th IFIP/IEEE International Conference on Symposium on Integrated Network Management (IM), pp. 33–40 (2009)
8. Ghosh, A.K., Wanken, J., Charron, F.: Detecting anomalous and unknown intrusions against programs. In: Proceedings of Annual Computer Security Applications Conference (ACSAC), pp. 259–267 (1998)
9. Gong, F.: Next Generation Intrusion Detection Systems (IDS). McAfee Network Security Technologies Group (2003)
10. Gou, Z., Ahmadon, M.A.B., Yamaguchi, S., Gupta, B.B.: A petri net-based framework of intrusion detection systems. In: Proceedings of the 4th IEEE Global Conference on Consumer Electronics, pp. 579–583 (2015)

11. Huebsch, R., et al.: The architecture of PIER: an internet-scale query processor. In: Proceedings of the 2005 Conference on Innovative Data Systems Research (CIDR), pp. 28–43 (2005)
12. Li, Z., Chen, Y., Beach, A.: Towards scalable and robust distributed intrusion alert fusion with good load balancing. In: Proceedings of the 2006 SIGCOMM Workshop on Large-Scale Attack Defense (LSAD), pp. 115–122 (2006)
13. Li, W., Meng, Y., Kwok, L.-F.: Enhancing trust evaluation using intrusion sensitivity in collaborative intrusion detection networks: feasibility and challenges. In: Proceedings of the 9th International Conference on Computational Intelligence and Security (CIS), pp. 518–522. IEEE (2013)
14. Li, W., Meng, W., Kwok, L.-F.: Design of intrusion sensitivity-based trust management model for collaborative intrusion detection networks. In: Zhou, J., Gal-Oz, N., Zhang, J., Gudes, E. (eds.) IFIPTM 2014. IAICT, vol. 430, pp. 61–76. Springer, Heidelberg (2014). https://doi.org/10.1007/978-3-662-43813-8_5
15. Li, W., Meng, W.: Enhancing collaborative intrusion detection networks using intrusion sensitivity in detecting pollution attacks. Inf. Comput. Secur. **24**(3), 265–276 (2016)
16. Li, W., Meng, W., Kwok, L.-F., Ip, H.H.S.: Enhancing collaborative intrusion detection networks against insider attacks using supervised intrusion sensitivity-based trust management model. J. Netw. Comput. Appl. **77**, 135–145 (2017)
17. Li, W., Meng, W., Kwok, L.-F., Ip, H.H.S.: PMFA: Toward passive message fingerprint attacks on challenge-based collaborative intrusion detection networks. In: Chen, J., Piuri, V., Su, C., Yung, M. (eds.) NSS 2016. LNCS, vol. 9955, pp. 433–449. Springer, Cham (2016). https://doi.org/10.1007/978-3-319-46298-1_28
18. Li, W., Meng, W., Kwok, L.-F.: SOOA: exploring special on-off attacks on challenge-based collaborative intrusion detection networks. In: Au, M.H.A., Castiglione, A., Choo, K.-K.R., Palmieri, F., Li, K.-C. (eds.) GPC 2017. LNCS, vol. 10232, pp. 402–415. Springer, Cham (2017). https://doi.org/10.1007/978-3-319-57186-7_30
19. Meng, Y., Kwok, L.F.: Enhancing false alarm reduction using voted ensemble selection in intrusion detection. Int. J. Comput. Intell. Syst. **6**(4), 626–638 (2013)
20. Meng, Y., Li, W., Kwok, L.F.: Towards adaptive character frequency-based exclusive signature matching scheme and its applications in distributed intrusion detection. Comput. Netw. **57**(17), 3630–3640 (2013)
21. Meng, W., Li, W., Kwok, L.-F.: An evaluation of single character frequency-based exclusive signature matching in distinct IDS environments. In: Chow, S.S.M., Camenisch, J., Hui, L.C.K., Yiu, S.M. (eds.) ISC 2014. LNCS, vol. 8783, pp. 465–476. Springer, Cham (2014). https://doi.org/10.1007/978-3-319-13257-0_29
22. Meng, W., Li, W., Kwok, L.-F.: EFM: enhancing the performance of signature-based network intrusion detection systems using enhanced filter mechanism. Comput. Secur. **43**, 189–204 (2014)
23. Meng, W., Li, W., Kwok, L.-F.: Design of intelligent KNN-based alarm filter using knowledge-based alert verification in intrusion detection. Secur. Commun. Netw. **8**(18), 3883–3895 (2015)
24. Meng, W., Au, M.H.: Towards statistical trust computation for medical smartphone networks based on behavioral profiling. In: Steghöfer, J.-P., Esfandiari, B. (eds.) IFIPTM 2017. IAICT, vol. 505, pp. 152–159. Springer, Cham (2017). https://doi.org/10.1007/978-3-319-59171-1_12
25. Meng, W., Li, W., Xiang, Y., Choo, K.K.R.: A Bayesian inference-based detection mechanism to defend medical smartphone networks against insider attacks. J. Netw. Comput. Appl. **78**, 162–169 (2017)

26. Meng, W., Li, W., Kwok, L.-F.: Towards effective trust-based packet filtering in collaborative network environments. IEEE Trans. Netw. Serv. Manage. **14**(1), 233–245 (2017)

27. Meng, W., Wang, Y., Li, W., Liu, Z., Li, J., Probst, C.W.: Enhancing intelligent alarm reduction for distributed intrusion detection systems via edge computing. In: Susilo, W., Yang, G. (eds.) ACISP 2018. LNCS, vol. 10946, pp. 759–767. Springer, Cham (2018). https://doi.org/10.1007/978-3-319-93638-3_44

28. Meng, W., Li, W., Wang, Y., Au, M.H.: Detecting insider attacks in medical cyber-physical networks based on behavioral profiling. Future Gener. Comput. Syst. (2018). https://doi.org/10.1016/j.future.2018.06.007

29. Mishra, A., Gupta, B.B., Joshi, R.C.: A comparative study of distributed denial of service attacks, intrusion tolerance and mitigation techniques. In: Proceedings of the 2011 European Intelligence and Security Informatics Conference, pp. 286–289 (2011)

30. Papadopoulos, C., Lindell, R., Mehringer, J., Hussain, A., Govindan, R.: COS-SACK: coordinated suppression of simultaneous attacks. In: Proceedings of the 2003 DARPA Information Survivability Conference and Exposition (DISCEX), pp. 94–96 (2003)

31. Paxson, V.: Bro: a system for detecting network intruders in real-time. Comput. Netw. **31**(23–24), 2435–2463 (1999)

32. Porras, P.A., Neumann, P.G.: EMERALD: event monitoring enabling responses to anomalous live disturbances. In: Proceedings of the 20th National Information Systems Security Conference, pp. 353–365 (1997)

33. Roesch, M.: Snort: Lightweight intrusion detection for networks. In: Proceedings of Usenix Lisa Conference, pp. 229–238 (1999)

34. Scarfone, K., Mell, P.: Guide to Intrusion Detection and Prevention Systems (IDPS), vol. 800, no. 94. NIST Special Publication (2007)

35. Snapp, S.R., et al.: DIDS (distributed intrusion detection system) - motivation, architecture, and an early prototype. In: Proceedings of the 14th National Computer Security Conference, pp. 167–176 (1991)

36. Snort: An an open source network intrusion prevention and detection system (IDS/IPS). http://www.snort.org/

37. Tuan, T.A.: A game-theoretic analysis of trust management in P2P systems. In: Proceedings of ICCE, pp. 130–134 (2006)

38. Valdes, A., Anderson, D.: Statistical methods for computer usage anomaly detection using NIDES. Technical report, SRI International, January 1995

39. Vigna, G., Kemmerer, R.A.: NetSTAT: a network-based intrusion detection approach. In: Proceedings of Annual Computer Security Applications Conference (ACSAC), pp. 25–34 (1998)

40. Wu, Y.-S., Foo, B., Mei, Y., Bagchi, S.: Collaborative intrusion detection system (CIDS): a framework for accurate and efficient IDS. In: Proceedings of the 2003 Annual Computer Security Applications Conference (ACSAC), pp. 234–244 (2003)

41. Yegneswaran, V., Barford, P., Jha, S.: Global intrusion detection in the DOMINO overlay system. In: Proceedings of the 2004 Network and Distributed System Security Symposium (NDSS), pp. 1–17 (2004)

A Two-Stage Classifier Approach
for Network Intrusion Detection

Wei Zong, Yang-Wai Chow[✉], and Willy Susilo

Institute of Cybersecurity and Cryptology, School of Computing and Information
Technology, University of Wollongong, Wollongong, NSW, Australia
wz630@uowmail.edu.au, {caseyc,wsusilo}@uow.edu.au

Abstract. Network Intrusion Detection Systems (NIDS) are essential to
combat security threats in network environments. These systems monitor
and detect malicious behavior to provide automated methods of identifying and dealing with attacks or security breaches in a network. Machine
learning is a promising approach in the development of effective NIDS.
One of the problems faced in the development of such systems is that the
datasets used in the construction of classifiers are typically imbalanced.
This is because the classification categories do not have relatively equal
representation in the datasets. This study investigates a two-stage classifier approach to NIDS based on imbalanced intrusion detection datasets
by separating the training and detection of minority and majority intrusion classes. The purpose of this is to allow flexibility in the classification
process, for example, two different classifiers can be used for detecting
minority and majority classes respectively. In this paper, we performed
experiments using the random forests classifier and the contemporary
UNSW-NB15 dataset was used to evaluate the effectiveness of the proposed approach.

Keywords: Machine learning · Network intrusion detection
Random forests

1 Introduction

For many people, the Internet has become a ubiquitous part of daily life and
numerous online services and applications are used everyday. At the same time,
the threat of cyber attacks is increasing and cyber security experts have under-
taken extensive studies on methods of combating such security threats. Network
Intrusion Detection Systems (NIDS) are potential automated solutions for protecting online environments [17]. While the most effective method for the development of NIDS remains a challenging and open question, machine learning is
seen as a very promising approach as these techniques can perform real-time
automated detection of potential threats [2,17].

Misuse detection and anomaly detection are two major approaches adopted
in NIDS. Misuse detection focuses on identifying the signatures or patterns of

© Springer Nature Switzerland AG 2018
C. Su and H. Kikuchi (Eds.): ISPEC 2018, LNCS 11125, pp. 329–340, 2018.
https://doi.org/10.1007/978-3-319 99807-7_20

malicious records. When a new record is received, a misuse detection system compares it with existing signatures to classify it as normal or malicious activity. One of the major problems of misuse detection is that it performs poorly against novel attacks, since the system cannot match it with signatures that have previously been classified as malicious activity [7,17]. On the other hand, anomaly detection attempts to identify behaviors that differ significantly from regular network activity. Thus, accurate behavior profiles of normal behavior are important in such systems [7]. While anomaly detection systems outperform misuse detection systems when it comes to detecting novel attacks, they typically produce high false alarm rates, which is undesirable and researchers often attempt to reduce the number of false alarms [6].

Another problem faced in the development of NIDS based on machine learning, is that the datasets used in the construction of classifiers are typically extremely imbalanced. A dataset in which the classification categories are not approximately equally represented is considered to be imbalanced [3,4]. The characteristic representation of malicious activity in datasets that are used for intrusion detection is usually extremely imbalanced, as certain attacks occur more often than others. The problem that this creates is that some machine learning intrusion detection approaches may perform well at the task of detecting frequent attacks, but are much less effective when it comes to the detection of infrequent attacks, due to the lack of sufficient training data for infrequent attacks [12].

This paper investigates the use of a two-stage approach to the development of NIDS based on imbalanced intrusion detection datasets. The underlying notion behind this approach is to filter the dataset into majority and minority malicious activity classes, and to apply classification algorithm on them separately to produce different models for detection. The purpose of this is to improve the overall detection rate of minority classes and to reduce the error rate. The proposed approach is flexible in that a different classifier can be used for each stage of the NIDS. This study examines the two-stage approach using the random forests classifier and also evaluates the effectiveness of the proposed approach on the contemporary UNSW-NB15 dataset.

Our Contributions. In this study we examine an innovative two-stage classifier approach to NIDS. The main purpose of this approach is to be able to handle imbalanced intrusion detection datasets, by separating the intrusion detection data into majority and minority classes, and training two separate classifiers for each category respectively. In this manner, different classifiers can be used to detect the majority and minority classes, with the overall aim of improving the detection rate, especially of minority classes and to reduce the error rate. While this paper examines the two-stage classifier approach using the random forests classifier, note that different classifiers can be used for each of the two-stages.

2   Background

This section introduces related work on machine learning and the various techniques for dealing with imbalanced intrusion detection datasets. In addition, it also provides a background description of different datasets that are typically used for the development of NIDS.

2.1   Related Work

Over the years, researchers have proposed a variety of different machine learning approaches for intrusion detection, including artificial neural networks, Bayesian networks, support vector machines, etc. [2]. The random forests classifier is an approach that combines decision trees and ensemble learning into an ensemble classifier that consists of multiple decision trees, where each tree grows to the largest possible extent without pruning [1]. The advantages of using random forests include its resistance to over-fitting, and its low number of control and model parameters [2].

Zhang et al. [22] proposed a random forests based NIDS for both misuse detection and anomaly detection. For misuse detection, their approach applies sampling techniques and feature selection algorithms to improve the overall detection performance. Conversely for anomaly detection, an unsupervised outlier detection approach was adopted by first building patterns of network services, then using this to determine anomalies in network traffic.

Intrusion detection datasets are typically imbalanced, as some attacks occur at higher frequencies compared with others. The random forests algorithm attempts to minimize the overall classification errors by lowering the error rate on majority classes while increasing the error rate on minority classes [1,22]. Therefore, imbalanced datasets will adversely affect the overall performance of accurately classifying minority classes. One of the approaches for dealing with imbalance datasets and to improve the detection rate of minority intrusions, is to over-sample minority intrusions or to down-sample majority intrusions, or to implement both methods [4].

Chawla et al. [3] proposed a method for over-sampling the minority classes by creating synthetic minority classes to achieve better classifier performance in imbalanced datasets. They named this method the Synthetic Minority Oversampling Technique (SMOTE) and showed its improved performance when used in conjunction with down-sampled majority classes using C4.5, Ripper and a Naïve Bayes classifier. The SMOTE method has also been used in other work on machine learning classification models for intrusion detection [12,13,19].

Feature selection is an important step in building NIDS, as only certain features may be essential to distinguish intrusions from normal activity. Unessential features may increase the computation cost and error rate [22]. While in many NIDS methods the features are designed by security experts, it would be ideal to have an automated approach to selecting important features. Information gain can be used as a criterion for feature selection, where features with low information gain can be eliminated because they have relatively small relevance on classification [15].

The following is a formal definition of information gain [15]:

Definition 1. *Let* X *and* Y *be discrete variables representing sample attributes* $(x_1, x_2, \ldots, x_m)$ *and class attributes* $(y_1, y_2, \ldots, y_n)$, *respectively. Then, the information gain,* IG, *of a given attribute* X *regarding a class attribute* Y *is calculated as:*

$IG(Y, X) = Entrophy(Y) - Entrophy(Y|X)$

where

- $Entrophy(Y) = -\sum_{i=1}^{n} P(Y = y_i) log_2 P(Y = y_i)$, *where* $P(Y = y_i)$ *is the probability that* y_i *occurs, and*
- $Entrophy(Y|X) = -\sum_{i=1}^{m} P(X = x_j) Entrophy(Y|X = x_j)$.

2.2   Network Intrusion Detection Datasets

Network intrusion detection datasets are vital for evaluating the effectiveness of NIDS. It has been contended that the commonly used KDD98, KDD_CUP99 and NSL_KDD benchmark datasets for intrusion detection were generated more than a decade ago, and many studies have highlighted flaws in these datasets [8,18]. Furthermore, it has been argued that these datasets no longer reflect the current network threat environment. The UNSW-NB15 dataset was created as a hybrid of real modern normal and contemporary synthesized attack activities of network traffic [10]. As such, this modern dataset was used in this study for evaluating the effectiveness of the proposed approach.

Table 1 shows the characteristics of a part of the UNSW-NB15 data set, where the training and testing sets have been divided into an approximately 60% to 40% ratio. There were no redundant records among the training and testing set [11]. It can clearly be seen that the different categories are unequally represented in the dataset. For example, the analysis, backdoor, shellcode and worms categories are minority classes that collectively only make up <3% of the sets. This imbalance creates problems for classifiers and results in poor detection performance of these minority classes.

3   Proposed Approach

The method proposed in this study adopts a two-stage classification approach for majority and minority classes. From Table 1, it can be seen that majority classes like normal, exploits, generic, etc. occur frequently and there is an abundance of such training samples. On the other hand, minority classes like analysis, backdoor, shellcode and worms only make up less than 3% of the overall dataset. This imbalance typically adversely affects classifier performance, and the purpose of the proposed approach is to increase the performance of minority class detection.

Table 1. Categories and their distribution in part of the UNSW-NB15 dataset [11].

Category	Training set	Testing set
Normal	56,000	37,000
Analysis	2,000	677
Backdoor	1,746	583
DoS	12,264	4,089
Exploits	33,393	11,132
Fuzzers	18,184	6,062
Generic	40,000	18,871
Reconnaissance	10,491	3,496
Shellcode	1,133	378
Worms	130	44
Total records	175,341	82,332

An overview of dividing the dataset into majority and minority classes for the two stages is depicted in Fig. 1. During the first stage, majority classes, which occupy a major proportion of a training set, are classified as "others" and a model is trained to identify the minority classes using a classifier, the random forests approach was used in this study. In the second stage, the minority classes are removed and another model is trained to identify the majority classes. This results in two different intrusion detection models for identifying the minority and majority classes respectively. While this study uses the random forests classifier for both stages, other classifiers can also be used. In fact, it is possible to use different classifiers for each of the stages.

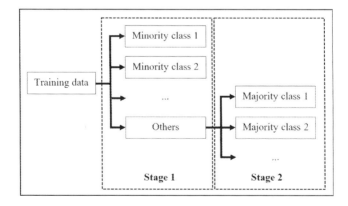

Fig. 1. Overview of the two-stage classification approach.

Figure 2 shows a more detailed depiction of the processes involved in the proposed approach. The processes are divided into a training phase and a detection phase. It can be seen that the training phases is divided into two stages for the majority and minority classes respectively. Stage 1 involves the training of all the minority classes that are extracted from the full training set, while the majority classes are grouped together into another category for training in the second stage.

3.1 Training Phase

In stage 1, after extracting the minority classes, feature selection is performed using the information gain method that was previously defined in Definition 1,

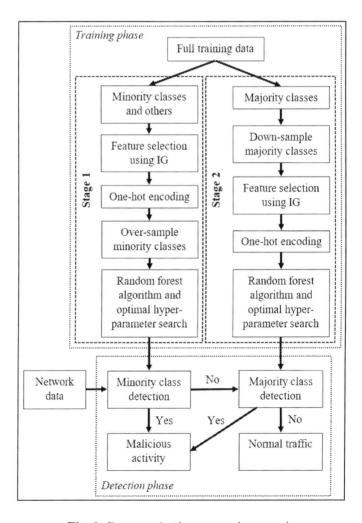

Fig. 2. Processes in the proposed approach.

and all categorical features are then converted into binary features using one-hot encoding to produce a set of numeric values. The SMOTE method is then used to over-sample the minority classes. The purpose of over-sampling the minority classes is to alleviate the imbalance in the minority classes. From Table 1, it can be seen that even though classes like analysis, backdoor, shellcode and worms are grouped into minority classes, samples for the worms category are extremely under represented. Hence, over-sampling attempts to bring this closer to the other categories.

The resulting set is then used for the training, in which optimal hyper-parameters are found for the random forests algorithm. Three hyper-parameters are considered for fine tuning the model, namely, the maximum depth of a tree in the forest, the number of trees and the number of features considered when looking for the best split. During the training phase, the random forests algorithm calculates the out-of-bag (oob) error. Since the oob error rate can be taken as an indication of whether the model is well trained, a random search is performed to find the lowest oob error rate, and the corresponding hyper-parameters are obtained from this.

Stage 2 undergoes a relatively similar process to obtain a trained model for identifying the majority classes. Only the majority classes are used in the training set, the minority classes are removed, since this was handled in stage 1. Down-sampling is performed to balance the majority classes using a random selection method. This is done for the same reason as over-sampling the minority classes. The distribution of network traffic within the majority classes in itself is unbalances, hence, down-sampling is performed to balance certain categories. Information gain is again used for feature selection, followed by one-hot encoding. This is subsequently used for training, and the optimal hyper-parameters search is performed for stage 2 random forest optimization.

It should be noted that while the random forests approach was used for both stages in this study, the proposed approach is flexible in that other classifiers can also be used for each stage respectively. For example, other classifiers like decision tree approach, logistic regression, artificial neural network, etc. can also be used and may potentially result in better performance.

3.2   Detection Phase

During the next phase of the proposed approach, which is the detection phase, network data is input into the system. When used for intrusion detection, the model for identifying minority classes is used first to determine whether an activity is malicious. If it is not identified as one of the minority classes, the second model is then applied to identify whether the activity is a majority intrusion. Otherwise, it is determined to be normal network traffic.

4   Results and Discussion

To evaluate the effectiveness of the proposed approach, an experiment was performed on the UNSW-NB15 dataset. The UNSW-NB15 training dataset was used to train the two intrusion detection models, and the full testing dataset was used to evaluate the performance of the proposed approach.

Table 2 shows results of the minimum oob error (MoE) rates and their corresponding hyper-parameters for the respective stages. In the table, the hyper-parameters are the maximum depth (MD), which refers to the maximum depth of a tree in the forest, the number of trees (NoT), and the number of features (NoF) for best split after one-hot encoding. The total number of features (TNoF) refers to the number of features remaining after one-hot encoding and feature selection.

Table 2. Minimum oob error rates and the corresponding hyper-parameters.

	MoE	MD	NoT	NoF	TNoF
Stage 1	0.119	29	179	109	138
Stage 2	0.167	23	248	80	170

A comparison of the proposed approach with the five different techniques (i.e. Decision Tree (DT), Logistic Regression (LR), Naïve Bayes (NB), Artificial Neural Network (ANN) and Expectation-Maximization (EM) clustering) as presented in Moustafa and Slay [11] is shown in Table 3. From the table, it can be seen that the resulting accuracy of the proposed approach is higher than the other techniques, while the False Alarm Rate (FAR) is lower. This suggests that the overall performance of the proposed approach is better than most of the other techniques and comparable with the DT technique. Figure 3 shows the confusion matrix depicting the performance results of the proposed approach for the individual categories.

Table 3. Comparison with the different techniques from [11].

Technique	Accuracy (%)	FAR (%)
DT [20]	85.56	15.78
LR [21]	83.15	18.48
NB [16]	82.07	18.56
ANN [21]	81.34	21.13
EM clustering [14]	78.47	23.79
Proposed approach	85.78	15.64

While the attacks represented in the minority classes are typically infrequent, they are nevertheless potentially dangerous. However, most of these attacks (i.e. analysis, shellcode and worms) could not be detected using the NB and EM clustering approaches as reported in Moustafa and Slay [9]. Only backdoor attacks could be detected by the NB approach with a low accuracy of 20%.

					Predicted						
		Normal	Fuzzers	Reconnaissance	DoS	Exploits	Generic	Analysis	Backdoor	Shellcode	Worms	Recall (%)
Actual	Normal	26024	8602	10	144	344	3	1271	23	565	14	70.3
	Fuzzers	541	3680	12	1026	299	1	171	139	183	10	60.7
	Reconnaissance	11	21	2927	267	154	2	14	57	42	1	83.7
	DoS	36	72	36	2834	540	5	159	348	56	3	69.3
	Exploits	119	219	408	2743	6756	10	306	464	80	27	60.7
	Generic	10	61	2	149	399	18205	1	15	25	4	96.5
	Analysis	13	1	0	462	13	0	118	70	0	0	17.4
	Backdoor	0	4	1	384	13	0	88	93	0	0	16.0
	Shellcode	3	44	6	25	34	0	0	4	262	0	69.3
	Worms	0	0	0	0	3	1	0	0	0	40	90.9
	Precision (%)	97.3	29.0	86.0	35.3	79.0	99.9	5.5	7.7	21.6	40.4	

Fig. 3. Confusion matrix.

In other recent work, these attacks could be detected at low rates using a random forests with stratified cross-validation method [5]. Figures 4 and 5 provide a comparison of the recall and precision performances, respectively, between the results reported in Janarthanan and Zargari [5] and the proposed approach. It can be seen from Fig. 4 that the recall results of the proposed two-stage approach performs better in comparison. However, the precision performance in Fig. 5 is lower. Nevertheless, for minority classes a higher recall rate is more important than precision, because these attacks are potentially more dangerous than other attacks. Therefore, higher recall values prevent these attacks from escaping detection.

Upon closer inspection of the overall results, it was found that most of the misclassification was to do with fuzzing activity. Table 4 provides the rate of normal traffic that was misclassified as malicious activity. It can be seen from the table at a large portion of the misclassification are for fuzzers. Fuzzers are attacks where the attacker attempts to discover security loopholes in a program, operating system or network [11]. They are not necessarily dangerous in themselves when compared with other attacks. Fuzzing activity has to do with inputting lots of random data. As such, they do not have a fixed pattern and are more difficult to distinguish from normal network traffic. Nevertheless, as future work

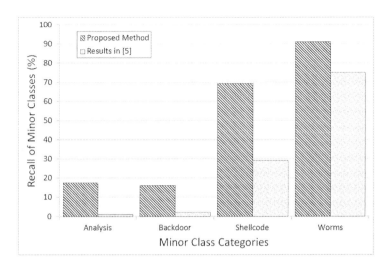

Fig. 4. Comparison of minority classes recall performance.

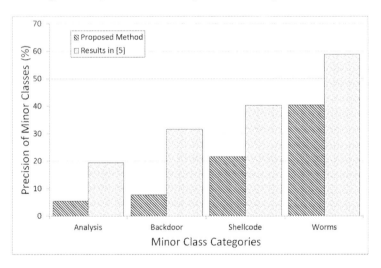

Fig. 5. Comparison of minority classes precision performance.

it would be ideal to be able to reduce the misclassification rate of this category of activity.

It should be noted that even though this study uses the random forests approach for both stages of the proposed approach, each stage can potentially use a different classification technique. For example, for the minority classifier, other techniques like a decision tree approach, logistic regression, or artificial neural network can be used to potentially increase the detection precision. As such, this will the subject of future work.

Table 4. Normal activity misclassified as malicious.

Categories	Misclassification (%)
Analysis	3.4
Backdoor	0.1
DoS	0.4
Exploits	0.9
Fuzzers	23.2
Generic	0.0
Reconnaissance	0.0
Shellcode	1.5
Worms	0.0

5   Conclusion

This study has demonstrated a two-stage classifier approach to NIDS based on imbalanced intrusion detection datasets. The purpose is to address the problem faced in the development of NIDS, which is that the datasets used in the construction of classifiers are typically imbalanced. The primary notion is to separate the training and detection of minority and majority intrusion classes to improve the overall detection rate of minority classes and to reduce the error rate. The effectiveness of the proposed approach was evaluated using the contemporary UNSW-NB15 dataset and was shown to produce favorable results when compared with other approaches. Future work will focus on examining the proposed approach with other classifiers in the two-stages.

References

1. Breiman, L.: Random forests. Mach. Learn. **45**(1), 5–32 (2001)
2. Buczak, A.L., Guven, E.: A survey of data mining and machine learning methods for cyber security intrusion detection. IEEE Commun. Surv. Tutor. **18**(2), 1153–1176 (2016)
3. Chawla, N.V., Bowyer, K.W., Hall, L.O., Kegelmeyer, W.P.: SMOTE: synthetic minority over-sampling technique. J. Artif. Intell. Res. **16**, 321–357 (2002)
4. Chen, C., Liaw, A., Breiman, L.: Using random forest to learn imbalanced data. Technical report, University of California, Berkeley (2004)
5. Janarthanan, T., Zargari, S.: Feature selection in UNSW-NB15 and KDDCUP'99 datasets. In: 2017 IEEE 26th International Symposium on Industrial Electronics (ISIE), pp. 1881–1886, June 2017
6. Ji, S., Jeong, B., Choi, S., Jeong, D.H.: A multi-level intrusion detection method for abnormal network behaviors. J. Netw. Comput. Appl. **62**, 9–17 (2016)
7. Kevric, J., Jukic, S., Subasi, A.: An effective combining classifier approach using tree algorithms for network intrusion detection. Neural Comput. Appl. **28**(S–1), 1051–1058 (2017)

8. McHugh, J.: Testing intrusion detection systems: a critique of the 1998 and 1999 DARPA intrusion detection system evaluations as performed by lincoln laboratory. ACM Trans. Inf. Syst. Secur. **3**(4), 262–294 (2000)

9. Moustafa, N., Slay, J.: The significant features of the UNSW-NB15 and the KDD99 data sets for network intrusion detection systems. In: 2015 4th International Workshop on Building Analysis Datasets and Gathering Experience Returns for Security (BADGERS), pp. 25–31, November 2015

10. Moustafa, N., Slay, J.: UNSW-NB15: a comprehensive data set for network intrusion detection systems (UNSW-NB15 network data set). In: 2015 Military Communications and Information Systems Conference, MilCIS 2015, Canberra, Australia, 10–12 November 2015, pp. 1–6. IEEE (2015)

11. Moustafa, N., Slay, J.: The evaluation of network anomaly detection systems: statistical analysis of the UNSW-NB15 data set and the comparison with the KDD99 data set. Inf. Secur. J.: Glob. Persp. **25**(1–3), 18–31 (2016)

12. Pajouh, H.H., Dastghaibyfard, G., Hashemi, S.: Two-tier network anomaly detection model: a machine learning approach. J. Intell. Inf. Syst. **48**(1), 61–74 (2017)

13. Parsaei, M.R., Rostami, S.M., Javidan, R.: A hybrid data mining approach for intrusion detection on imbalanced NSL-KDD dataset. Int. J. Adv. Comput. Sci. Appl. **7**(6), 20–25 (2016)

14. Salem, M., Buehler, U.: Mining techniques in network security to enhance intrusion detection systems. Int. J. Netw. Secur. Appl. **4**(6) (2012)

15. Sangkatsanee, P., Wattanapongsakorn, N., Charnsripinyo, C.: Practical real-time intrusion detection using machine learning approaches. Comput. Commun. **34**(18), 2227–2235 (2011)

16. Shyu, M., Sarinnapakorn, K., Kuruppu-Appuhamilage, I., Chen, S., Chang, L., Goldring, T.: Handling nominal features in anomaly intrusion detection problems. In: 15th International Workshop on Research Issues in Data Engineering (RIDE-SDMA 2005), Stream Data Mining and Applications, Tokyo, Japan, 3–7 April 2005, pp. 55–62. IEEE Computer Society (2005)

17. Sommer, R., Paxson, V.: Outside the closed world: on using machine learning for network intrusion detection. In: 31st IEEE Symposium on Security and Privacy, S&P 2010, Berleley/Oakland, California, USA, 16–19 May 2010, pp. 305–316. IEEE Computer Society (2010)

18. Tavallaee, M., Bagheri, E., Lu, W., Ghorbani, A.A.: A detailed analysis of the KDD CUP 99 data set. In: 2009 IEEE Symposium on Computational Intelligence for Security and Defense Applications, CISDA 2009, Ottawa, Canada, 8–10 July 2009, pp. 1–6. IEEE (2009)

19. Tesfahun, A., Bhaskari, D.L.: Intrusion detection using random forests classifier with smote and feature reduction. In: 2013 International Conference on Cloud Ubiquitous Computing Emerging Technologies, pp. 127–132, November 2013

20. The Bro Project. The Bro Network Security Monitor (2014). https://www.bro.org/

21. Witten, I.H., Frank, E., Hall, M.A.: Data Mining: Practical Machine Learning Tools and Techniques, 3rd edn. Morgan Kaufmann Publishers Inc., San Francisco (2011)

22. Zhang, J., Zulkernine, M., Haque, A.: Random-forests-based network intrusion detection systems. IEEE Trans. Syst. Man Cybern. Part C **38**(5), 649–659 (2008)

DSH: Deniable Secret Handshake Framework

Yangguang Tian[1(✉)], Yingjiu Li[1], Yinghui Zhang[1], Nan Li[2], Guomin Yang[3], and Yong Yu[4]

[1] School of Information System,
Singapore Management University, Singapore, Singapore
{ygtian,yjli,yinghuizhang}@smu.edu.sg
[2] School of Electrical Engineering and Computing, University of Newcastle,
Callaghan, NSW, Australia
nan.li@newcastle.edu.au
[3] School of Computing and Information Technology, University of Wollongong,
Wollongong, NSW, Australia
gyang@uow.edu.au
[4] School of Computer Science, Shaanxi Normal University, Xi'an, China
yuyong@snnu.edu.cn

Abstract. Secret handshake is a useful primitive that allows a group of authorized users to establish a shared secret key and authenticate each other anonymously. It naturally provides a certain degree of user privacy and deniability which are also desirable for some private conversations that require secure key establishment. The inherent user privacy enables a private conversation between authorized users without revealing their real identities. While deniability allows authorized users to later deny their participating in conversations. However, deniability of secret handshakes lacks a comprehensive treatment in the literature. In this paper, we investigate the deniability of existing secret handshakes. We propose the first generic framework that converts any secret handshake protocols into fully deniable ones. In particular, we define two formal security models, including session key security and deniability for our proposed framework.

Keywords: Secret handshake · Deniability · Generic framework

1 Introduction

The notion of secret handshake (SH) was firstly introduced by Balfanz et al. [1], and has been extensively studied afterwards. Specifically, it allows authorized users of the same organization to establish a shared secret key in an anonymous manner. To ensure a successful handshake, authorized users need to prove his/her membership to its peer. The only information they need to know is the peer belongs to the same organization.

© Springer Nature Switzerland AG 2018
C. Su and H. Kikuchi (Eds.): ISPEC 2018, LNCS 11125, pp. 341–353, 2018.
https://doi.org/10.1007/978-3-319-99807-7_21

While anonymity implicitly holds in the secret handshakes setting, other properties are also desirable, such as affiliation-hiding [9], unlinkability [11] and user untraceability [16]. The affiliation-hiding secret handshake is a stronger privacy guarantee than conventional SH, which means non-authorized users cannot identify the membership of authorized users from their handshake sessions or computed session keys. Unlinkable secret handshakes are intuitively more desirable than linkable ones, which means multiple sessions with the same user cannot be linked together. However, it is a challenging task to construct an unlinkable secret handshakes with efficient and practical revocation mechanism (e.g., linear computation complexity in the number of revoked users at [11]). We stress that linkable constructions can easily provide efficient revocation mechanism using pseudonym/certificate revocation list. As for user untraceability, it allows authorized users to remain untraceable during private conversations with respect to the untrusted issuing authority.

Motivation. In addition to aforementioned privacy properties, the secret handshakes can further be explored in the context of "off the record" (OTR). We allow session participants to later deny participating in a private conversation, while anonymous authentication between handshake users is still held. We stress that such deniable communications are particularly important to private conversations in practice. For example, private conversations among handshake users may under mass surveillance by intelligence services, and personal or business communications may be revealed or leaked.

The existing deniable key exchanges allow session participants to plausibly deny their participating in conversations, even if the security of communications is later compromised [5,21]. In particular, deniability is the most important property in secure messaging protocols such as Off-the-Record Messaging protocol [2]. In other words, deniability is particularly useful to some applications that require secure and private channels without producing cryptographic evidence of communication. Therefore, the main *goal* of this work is to design secret handshakes with maximal range of deniability while the existing privacy guarantees are preserved.

Deniable secret handshake cannot be simply constructed by implementing the existing *fully* deniable authenticated key exchange (AKE) protocols. Full deniability means that anyone can produce protocol transcripts and session keys that look valid to a trusted party (judge). In particular, the fully deniable AKE requires the resulting shared key is merely generated from Diffie-Hellman (DH) exponents [23,24]. With regard to secret handshakes, authorized users may use their given secret certificate to derive a shared secret key. The fully deniable secret handshakes allow any authorized users (even issuing authority) of the same organization to produce those protocol transcripts and session keys. Therefore, the maximal range of deniable secret handshakes limits to a group of authorized users in the same organization.

In this work, we introduce the notion of deniable secret handshake (DSH in short), and we briefly summarize our main *contributions* as follows: (1) The proposed generic framework can convert any secret handshakes into fully deniable ones; (2) The handshake users can plausibly deny their participating in secure and private conversations, even if the security of their conversations are completely compromised later; (3) We provide two security models for our proposed generic framework, which is used to capture the security and privacy requirements of deniable secret handshakes.

1.1   Related Work

Secret Handshakes. The secret handshake protocol proposed by Balfanz et al. [1] allows any users in the same group to generate a shared value secretly using the reusable (i.e., long-term) certificate approach. Afterwards, Castelluccia et al. [4] constructed a more efficient scheme than [1] under the standard assumptions. However, their schemes [1,4] did not provide the "unlinkability" property. In [22], Xu and Yung provided an unlinkable scheme with a new notion, namely, k-unlinkability. That is, an adversary can infer that a session participant is one out of certain k users in the worst case.

As for achieving full unlinkability, Jarecki et al. [9] proposed two group secret handshake protocols using the Burmester and Desmedt (BD) group key exchange protocol [3]. In particular, their second construction can achieve full unlinkability using unlimited one-time certificate. Meanwhile, another research line was formed in the literature [7,8]. Their solutions can also achieve full unlinkability using long-time certificate. However, their proposed solutions [7,8] lack revocation mechanism, which is necessary and imperative in the secret handshake setting. Recently, Tian et al. [20] proposed a k-time unlinkable secret handshake protocol. Specifically, the proposed solution achieves full unlinkability based on a k-size one-time certificates set, but the central authority (CA, also known as group authority GA) is fully trusted.

To relax the strong assumption on CA, Kawai et al. [14] split the CA into (non-colluding) authorities: one is responsible for registration and issuing certificates, while the other is responsible for tracing users based on protocol transcript. Meanwhile, Manulis et al. [16] considered user's traceability against untrusted CA. Their solution is based on the construction in [10], and uses blinded RSA signature schemes at Add stage for tackling untrusted CA. Similarly, Manulis et al. [17] also proposed a Discrete-Logarithm based secret handshake, and used blinded Schnorr signature to tackle untrusted CA.

Deniable Key Exchange. Deniable authentication was formally introduced by Dwork et al. [6] using the simulation-based paradigm. It requires that the transmitted messages are authenticated, and the simulator's view can be simulated using adversary's knowledge only. Later, Di Raimondo et al. [5] considered deniability of key exchange protocols, and formally presented two definitions: *strong* deniability and *partial* deniability. In particular, they used novel techniques to analyze strong deniability of SKEME and partial deniability of SIGMA respectively. More precisely, they prove strong deniability of SKEME based on the plaintext awareness of the underlying encryption scheme, and prove *partial* deniability of SIGMA based on a special "oracle" since non-repudiable digital signature schemes are *explicitly* used for authentication.

Jiang and Safavi-Naini [12] proposed an efficient key exchange protocol with *full* deniability, such that anyone can prove to a judge that the communication between two participants happened. Their deniable key exchange protocol is formally proven secure in the public random oracle (pRO)[1]. A similar deniable work was proposed by Yao and Zhao [24]. They proposed the first provably secure internet key exchange protocol that provides strong deniability for protocol participants simultaneously. In particular, their deniability analysis relies on the restricted random oracle model[2] and (concurrent) knowledge of exponent assumption (KEA).

Also, *implicitly* AKE protocols [15,19,23] formed another important research direction in the literature. They not only enjoy high performance, but also ensure strong deniability. The *strong* sense of deniability (e.g., [19,21]) means that adversary acts as one of protocol participants (see Definition 2 for detailed comparison between *strong* and *full* deniability).

2   Security Model

In this section, we present the security models for secret handshakes. Note that the secret handshake protocol in this work should (at least) achieve session key security and deniability. The linkable affiliation-hiding (LAH) and untraceability models are directly from [10,16] respectively.

States. We define a system user set $\mathcal{U}$ with n users, i.e. $|\mathcal{U}| = n$. We say an oracle Π_U^i may be *used* or *unused*. The oracle is considered as unused if it has never been initialized. Each unused oracle Π_U^i can be initialized with a secret key x. The oracle is initialized as soon as it becomes part of a group. After the initialization the oracle is marked as used and turns into the *stand-by* state where it waits for an invocation to execute a protocol operation. Upon receiving such invocation the oracle Π_U^i learns its partner identifier pid_U^i and turns into a *processing* state where it sends, receives and processes messages according to the description of the protocol. During that stage, the internal state information $state_U^i$ is maintained by the oracle. The oracle Π_U^i remains in the processing state until it collects enough information to compute the session key K_U^i. As soon as K_U^i is computed Π_U^i *accepts* and *terminates* the protocol execution meaning that it would not send or receive further messages. If the protocol execution fails then Π_U^i terminates without having accepted.

Partnering. We denote the i-th session established by a user U by Π_U^i, and pseudonyms of all the users recognized by Π_U^i during the execution of that session by pid_U^i. We define sid_U^i as the unique session identifier belonging to the session i established by the user U. Specifically, $\mathsf{sid}_U^i = \{m_j\}_{j=1}^n$, where $m_j \in \{0,1\}^*$ is the message transcript among users. We say two instance oracles Π_U^i and $\Pi_{U'}^j$ are *partners* if and only if $\mathsf{pid}_U^i = \mathsf{pid}_{U'}^j$ and $\mathsf{sid}_U^i = \mathsf{sid}_{U'}^j$.

---

[1] pRO is introduced by Pass [18], and it is a weaker assumption compared to random oracle model.

[2] It analogous to Pass's non-programmable random oracle methodology pRO, see detailed comparison in [25].

2.1   System Model

A deniable secret handshake (DSH) protocol consists of the following algorithms:

- Setup: The algorithm takes security parameter λ as input, outputs public parameters params.
- KeyGen: CA takes public parameter param as input, outputs public/secret key pair (mpk, msk) of group $\mathbb{G}$, and an empty pseudonym revocation list L.
- Add: This is an interactive algorithm between a user and CA. It takes group secret key msk as input, outputs a pseudonym/certificate pair (pk, cert), where pk denotes public pseudonym and cert denotes secret certificate. The user will become a registered user after interaction with CA. Note that the interaction between CA and users is assumed to be authentic, and CA maintains a group pseudonym list L by adding public pseudonym pk.
- Revoke: This algorithm is executed by CA of group $\mathbb{G}$ and results in the update of the pseudonym revocation list L.
- Handshake: This is an interactive algorithm among registered users. Each user takes his/her certificate (pk, cert), mpk and L as input, outputs a shared secret key SK if and only if his/her counterparts are non-revoked and registered users.

2.2   Session Key Security

We define the session key security model for DSH protocols, in which each user obtains secret certificate from group CA, and establishes a session key using the given secret certificate. The model is defined via a game between a probabilistic polynomial time (PPT) adversary $\mathcal{A}$ and a simulator $\mathcal{S}$ (i.e., challenger). $\mathcal{A}$ is an active attacker with full control of the communications channel among all the users.

- Setup: $\mathcal{S}$ first generates group public/secret key pair $(\mathrm{mpk}_j, \mathrm{msk}_j)$ $(j \in [1, \cdots m])$ for m groups in the system. In addition, $\mathcal{S}$ generates the public pseudonym and secret certificate $(\mathrm{pk}_i/\mathrm{cert}_i^j)$ $(i \in [1, \cdots n])$ for n users in a group $\mathbb{G}_j$ by running the corresponding Add algorithm, and returns $\{\mathrm{mpk}_j, \mathrm{pk}_i\}$ to $\mathcal{A}$. $\mathcal{S}$ also tosses a random coin b which will be used later in the game. Let $\mathcal{U}$ denote all the registered and non-revoked users in group $\mathbb{G}_j$.
- Training: $\mathcal{A}$ can make the following queries in arbitrary sequence to $\mathcal{S}$.
  - establish: $\mathcal{A}$ is allowed to register a user U' with public pseudonym $\mathrm{pk} \in \mathbb{G}_j$. If a user is registered by $\mathcal{A}$, then we call this user *dishonest*; Otherwise, it is *honest*.
  - send: If $\mathcal{A}$ issues send query in the form of $(U_i, \mathbb{G}_j, s, m)$ to simulate a network message for the s-th session of user U_i in group $\mathbb{G}_j$, then $\mathcal{S}$ would simulate the reaction of instance oracle $\Pi_{U_i}^s$ upon receiving message m, and returns to $\mathcal{A}$ the response that $\Pi_{U_i}^s$ would generate; If $\mathcal{A}$ issues send query in the form of $(U_i, \mathbb{G}_j, s, \text{'}start\text{'})$, then $\mathcal{S}$ creates a new instance oracle $\Pi_{U_i}^s$ and returns to $\mathcal{A}$ the first protocol message.

- ephemeral secret key reveal: If $\mathcal{A}$ issues an ephemeral secret key reveal query to (possibly unaccepted) instance oracle $\Pi^s_{U_i}$, then $\mathcal{S}$ will return all ephemeral secret values contained in $\Pi^s_{U_i}$ at the moment the query is asked.
- long-term secret key reveal: If $\mathcal{A}$ issues a long-term secret key reveal (or corrupt, for short) query to user i, then $\mathcal{S}$ will return the secret certificate cert^j_i to $\mathcal{A}$.
- group secret key reveal: If $\mathcal{A}$ issues a group secret key reveal query w.r.t. $\mathbb{G}_j$, then $\mathcal{S}$ will return the group secret key msk_j to $\mathcal{A}$.
- session key reveal: $\mathcal{A}$ can issue reveal query to an accepted instance oracle $\Pi^s_{U_i}$. If the session is accepted, then $\mathcal{S}$ will return the session key to $\mathcal{A}$; Otherwise, a special symbol '$\perp$' is returned to $\mathcal{A}$.
- test: This query can only be made to an accepted and *fresh* (as defined below) session i of a user U ($U \in \mathcal{U}$) in group $\mathbb{G}_j$. Then $\mathcal{S}$ does the following:
  * If the coin $b = 1$, $\mathcal{S}$ returns the real session key to $\mathcal{A}$;
  * Otherwise, a random session key is drawn from the session key space and returns to $\mathcal{A}$.

  It is also worth noting that $\mathcal{A}$ can continue to issue other queries after the test query. However, the test session must maintain fresh throughout the entire game.

Finally, $\mathcal{A}$ outputs b' as its guess for b. If $b' = b$, then $\mathcal{S}$ outputs 1; Otherwise, $\mathcal{S}$ outputs 0.

Freshness. We say an *accepted* instance oracle Π^i_U in group $\mathbb{G}_j$ is fresh if $\mathcal{A}$ does not perform any of the following actions during the game:

- $\mathcal{A}$ issues establish query, where the new user $U' \in \mathsf{pid}^i_U$;
- $\mathcal{A}$ issues session key reveal query to Π^i_U or its accepted partnered instance oracle $\Pi^j_{U'}$;
- $\mathcal{A}$ issues both long-term secret key reveal query to U' s.t. $U' \in \mathsf{pid}^i_U$ and ephemeral secret key reveal query for an instance $\Pi^j_{U'}$ partnered with Π^i_U;
- $\mathcal{A}$ issues long-term secret key reveal query to user U' s.t. $U' \in \mathsf{pid}^i_U$ prior to the acceptance of instance Π^i_U and there exists no instance oracle $\Pi^j_{U'}$ partnered with Π^i_U.

Note that group secret key reveal query to CA is equivalent to the long-term secret key reveal to all registered users in group $\mathbb{G}_j$. We define the advantage of $\mathcal{A}$ in the above game as

$$\mathsf{Adv}_{\mathcal{A}}(\lambda, n, m) = |\Pr[\mathcal{S} \to 1] - 1/2|. \tag{1}$$

Definition 1. *We say a DSH protocol has* session key security *if for any PPT $\mathcal{A}$, $\mathsf{Adv}_{\mathcal{A}}(\lambda, n, m)$ is a* negligible *function of the security parameter λ.*

2.3   Deniability

Informally, an adversary aims to present a "proof" to a third party judge, claim that any non-revoked and authorized users of the same organization were participated in a conversation. We formally define the deniability model for secret handshake protocols as follows.

Definition 2. *Let Σ be a secret handshake protocol defined by a key generation algorithm* KeyGen *and interactive machines Σ_I, Σ_R specifying the role of the initiator and responder respectively. We say that* (KeyGen, Σ_I, Σ_R) *is a concurrently deniable SH protocol w.r.t the class* Aux[3] *of auxiliary inputs if for any PPT $\mathcal{A}$, for any input of public pseudonym* pk $= (pk_1, \cdots, pk_n)$*, group public keys* mpk $= (mpk_1, \cdots, mpk_n)$ *and any auxiliary input $aux \in Aux$, there exists a simulator $\mathcal{S}$ who runs the same inputs as $\mathcal{A}$[4], aims to produce a simulated view which is indistinguishable from the real view of $\mathcal{A}$. That is, considering the following two probability distributions where* pk $= (pk_1, \cdots, pk_n)$ *is the set of public pseudonym of honest users and* mpk $= (mpk_1, \cdots, mpk_n)$ *is the set of honest group public keys:*

$$\mathsf{Real}(\lambda, aux) = [(\mathsf{cert}_i, \mathsf{pk}_i, \mathsf{msk}_j, \mathsf{mpk}_j)$$
$$\leftarrow \mathsf{KeyGen}(\lambda, n, m); (aux, \mathsf{pk}, \mathsf{mpk}, \mathsf{View}(aux, \mathsf{pk}, \mathsf{mpk}))]$$
$$\mathsf{Sim}(\lambda, aux) = [(\mathsf{cert}_i, \mathsf{pk}_i, \mathsf{msk}_j, \mathsf{mpk}_j)$$
$$\leftarrow \mathsf{KeyGen}(\lambda, n, m); (aux, \mathsf{pk}, \mathsf{mpk}, \ \mathcal{S} \ (aux, \mathsf{pk}, \mathsf{mpk}))]$$

then for all PPT distinguishers Dist *and all $aux \in$ Aux, we have*

$$|\mathrm{Pr}_{x \in \mathsf{Real}(\lambda, aux)}[\mathsf{Dist}(x)] = 1 - \mathrm{Pr}_{x \in \mathsf{Sim}(\lambda, aux)}[\mathsf{Dist}(x)] = 1| \leq \epsilon(\lambda) \qquad (2)$$

where ϵ is a negligible function of the security parameter λ. In particular, the actions of distinguisher Dist *after protocol executions are described as follows:*

- *The* Dist *is given the full protocol transcripts and accepted session keys in which $\mathcal{A}$ participated.*
- *The* Dist *is allowed to obtain the secret certificates of all participants and the corresponding master secret key in specific group $\mathbb{G}$.*

Remark. In the sense of *full* deniability, the View$(aux, \mathsf{pk}, \mathsf{mpk})$ means that $\mathcal{A}$'s view when honest users are faithfully performing secret handshake protocols in group $\mathbb{G}$, while $\mathcal{S}(aux, \mathsf{pk}, \mathsf{mpk})$ means that the simulator $\mathcal{S}$ produces an indistinguishable view to $\mathcal{A}$ *without* honest user's certificates and CA's master secret key. As for the *strong* sense of deniability, where $\mathcal{A}$ acts as one of protocol participants in group $\mathbb{G}$. The View$(aux, \mathsf{pk}, \mathsf{mpk})$ means that $\mathcal{A}$ maliciously performs

---

[3] Aux may consist of legal transcripts of protocol runs.
[4] $\mathcal{A}$ is not allowed to reveal honest user's secret certificates $\{\mathsf{cert}_i^j\}$ and group secret keys $\{\mathsf{msk}_j\}$.

secret handshakes with other honest users in a real view. While $\mathcal{S}(aux, \mathsf{pk}, \mathsf{mpk})$ means that the simulator $\mathcal{S}$, who is running on the same inputs as $\mathcal{A}$ (including $\mathcal{A}$'s secret certificates and randomness), simulates an indistinguishable view from a real view to a judge.

3 Our Construction

In this section, we firstly review some complexity assumptions and the building blocks that will be used in our proposed generic framework. We then present our construction afterwards.

3.1 Preliminaries

Secret Handshake (SH). A *forward-secure* secret handshake protocol consists of the following algorithms: $\mathsf{SH} = (\mathsf{Setup}, \mathsf{KeyGen}, \mathsf{Add}, \mathsf{Revoke}, \mathsf{Handshake})$.

- Setup: The algorithm takes security parameter λ as input, outputs public parameters params.
- KeyGen: CA takes security parameter param as input, outputs public/secret key pair $(\mathsf{mpk}_l, \mathsf{msk}_l)$ of group $\mathbb{G}_l$, and an empty certificate revocation list L_l.
- Add: CA takes secret key msk_l and user $U_i \in \mathcal{U}$ as input, outputs a certificate cert_i for user U_i.
- Revoke: CA takes user U_i as input, retrieves the corresponding cert_i, and updates the group revocation list L_l by adding this certificate cert_i.
- Handshake: This is an interactive algorithm between two users, e.g. U_i and U_j. The input of user U_i (resp., U_j) is a tuple $(\mathsf{cert}_i, \mathsf{mpk}_l, \mathsf{L}_l, \mathsf{role}_i)$, where cert_i is U_i's certificate in that group, mpk_l is the public key of the group with which U_i wants to establish an authenticated connection, L_l is U_i's current L_l for this group and $\mathsf{role}_i \in \{\mathsf{init}, \mathsf{resp}\}$ (resp., $(\mathsf{cert}_j, \mathsf{mpk}_j, \mathsf{L}_j, \mathsf{role}_j)$). Each party either outputs a shared key K or reject otherwise. Note that the interactive Handshake algorithm generally consists of the following sub-algorithms.

  - Handshake.Ephemeral: User i outputs an ephemeral secret/public key pair $(\mathsf{esk}_i, \mathsf{epk}_i)$;
  - Handshake.KE: Users exchange their ephemeral public keys, i.e., epk_i and epk_j;
  - Handshake.KDF: User i executes a key derivation function and obtains $K = \mathsf{KDF} : (\mathsf{esk}_i, \mathsf{epk}_j, \mathsf{cert}_i, \mathsf{mpk}_l, \mathsf{L}_i, \mathsf{role}_i)$ $(j \neq i)$.

We discover that many existing secret handshake protocols (either RSA based or Discrete-Logarithm based constructions [7–10,16,17]) can support strong deniability, then we have the following Lemma.

Lemma 1. *Forward-secure SH protocols have inherent strong deniability.*

Proof. For simplicity, we assume a SH protocol executed between Alice and Bob where Alice sends ephemeral public key epk_A to Bob, and vice versa for Bob. We assume that Alice and Bob aim to establish a shared key $K \leftarrow (\mathsf{esk}_A, \mathsf{epk}_B, \mathsf{cert}_A, \mathsf{mpk}, \mathsf{L}, \mathsf{role})$ in a real view. Note that two simulated values are presented to a distinguisher: the exchanged ephemeral public keys and the resulting shared keys.

The exchanged ephemeral public key pair $(\mathsf{epk}_A, \mathsf{epk}_B)$ derives from either the ephemeral secret key pair $(\mathsf{esk}_A, \mathsf{esk}_B)$ or the function $f(\mathsf{esk}_A, \mathsf{cert}_A)$, $f(\mathsf{esk}_B, \mathsf{cert}_B)$ (f denotes a randomized function, such as hash function or pseudorandom function). Simulator $\mathcal{S}$ (i.e., adversary Bob) is simply choosing a random value epk_A from ephemeral public space to simulate transmitted ephemeral public key on behalf of Alice, while the judge cannot *statistically* distinguish it since the real/simulated value is uniformly distributed in either ephemeral public key space or the output of function f (except collisions with a negligible probability);

The resulting shared key K, can be easily simulated by simulator $\mathcal{S}$. Specifically, $\mathcal{S}$ (i.e., adversary Bob) randomly chooses ephemeral public key epk_B and computes $K \leftarrow (\mathsf{epk}_A, \mathsf{esk}_B, \mathsf{cert}_B, \mathsf{mpk}, \mathsf{L}, \mathsf{role})$, where ephemeral secret key esk_B and secret certificate cert_B are known to $\mathcal{S}$. Note that the correctness of resulting shared keys require Alice and Bob also exchange their public pseudonyms $(\mathsf{pk}_A, \mathsf{pk}_B)$ which is deriving from respective secret certificates $(\mathsf{cert}_A, \mathsf{cert}_B)$. $\qquad\square$

Definition 3 (Generic Concurrent Knowledge Extraction Assumption (GCKEA)). *We define a domain* $\{\mathsf{Dom}_\lambda\}_{\lambda \in \mathbb{N}}$, *where* $\mathbb{N}$ *is the set of natural numbers, and define a set* $\mathcal{D} \xleftarrow{R} \mathsf{Dom}_\lambda$. *We denote* $p(\lambda), q(\lambda)$ *are two polynomials in the security parameter* λ, *and define a predicate algorithm* $\mathcal{O}_\mathcal{C}$ *w.r.t the random challenge set* $\mathcal{C} = \{C_1, \cdots, C_{p(\lambda)}\}$. *On a query of the form* (X, Y, Z), *for arbitrary* $(X, Y) \xleftarrow{R} \mathcal{D}$ *outputs 1 if* $X \xleftarrow{R} \mathcal{C}$ *and* $Z = \mathsf{PKDF}(X, Y)$[5]. *We define an algorithm* $\mathcal{A}$ *with predicate oracle* $\mathcal{O}_\mathcal{C}$, *denote* $\mathcal{A}^{\mathcal{O}_\mathcal{C}}$, *which takes* $\mathcal{C}$ *as input, outputs a set of triples* $\{(X_1, Y_1, Z_1), \cdots, (X_{q(\lambda)}, Y_{q(\lambda)}, Z_{q(\lambda)})\}$. *We say* $\mathcal{A}^{\mathcal{O}_\mathcal{C}}$ *is a GCKEA extractor if, with overwhelming probability,* $\mathcal{A}^{\mathcal{O}_\mathcal{C}}(\mathcal{C})$ *outputs* $\{(X_1, Y_1, Z_1), \cdots, (X_{q(\lambda)}, Y_{q(\lambda)}, Z_{q(\lambda)})\}$ *satisfying* $X_i \in \mathcal{C}$ *and* $Z_i = \mathsf{PKDF}(X_i, Y_i)$ *for all* $i, 1 \leq i \leq q(\lambda)$.

We say that the GCKEA holds if for every PPT algorithm $\mathcal{A}$, *there exists another PPT algorithm* $\mathcal{A}'$ *that given the same inputs, random coins, oracle answers, and additionally outputs* y_i *such that* $Y_i \leftarrow G(y_i)$ *for all* $i, 1 \leq i \leq q(\lambda)$, *where* G *denotes an efficient computable function which takes* y_i *as input and outputs* Y_i.

Remark. GCKEA is a *generalized* version of Concurrent KEA (CKEA) [24] and Knowledge of Pairing Pre-Image Assumption (KPA) [19]. Specifically, the extracted value y_i by extractor $\mathcal{A}'$ is either exponent w.r.t. CKEA assumption [24] or group element w.r.t. KPA assumption [19]. For example, the concrete

---

[5] The PKDF algorithm means that a key derivation function in the public-key setting.

CKEA assumption [24] is used to extract the DH exponent for their proposed *interactive* protocol, while running against the *concurrent* man-in-the-middle adversaries.

3.2   Proposed Framework

Our proposed generic framework (GF) consists of the following building blocks.

- A forward-secure secret handshake protocol SH = (Setup, KeyGen, Add, Revoke, Handshake); Note that SH protocol may have LAH property.
- A blind digital signature scheme BS = (KeyGen, Signer and User, Verify); Note that if SH has untracebility property, then this building block is removed.
- A public key based key derivation function PKDF;
- A proof of knowledge PoK;
- A collision-resistant hash function H.

Now we present our proposed generic framework below (for simplicity, we use user $\widehat{A}$ and user $\widehat{B}$ in the two-party setting here, and we can extend it to a multi-party setting using BD protocol [3]):

- Setup: This algorithm takes security parameter λ as input, outputs public parameters params ← SH.Setup which are published to all users and groups.
- KeyGen: The group CA runs the SH.KeyGen algorithm to obtain the group public/secret key pair (mpk, msk) and an empty pseudonym revocation list L.
- Add: The group CA and user $\widehat{A}$ run the BS.Signer and User(msk) interactive algorithm[6] to obtain a pseudonym/certificate pair $(\mathsf{pk}_a, \mathsf{cert}_a)$ of user $\widehat{A}$. Note that user $\widehat{A}$ takes pk_a as public pseudonym.
- Revoke: The group CA runs the SH.Revoke(pk_a) algorithm to update the group pseudonym revocation list L. Note that public pseudonym pk_a is added to revocation list L.
- Handshake:
  - User $\widehat{A}$ runs the SH.Handshake.Ephemeral algorithm to obtain ephemeral secret/public key pair $(\mathsf{esk}_a, \mathsf{epk}_a)$ and sends $(\mathsf{epk}_a, \mathsf{pk}_a)$ to user $\widehat{B}$;
  - Upon receiving $(\mathsf{epk}_a, \mathsf{pk}_a)$ from user $\widehat{A}$, user $\widehat{B}$ performs the following steps.
    1. Run the SH.Handshake.Ephemeral algorithm to obtain ephemeral secret and public key pair $(\mathsf{esk}_b, \mathsf{epk}_b)$;
    2. Compute the proof of knowledge PoK$\{(\mathsf{esk}_b) : \mathsf{H}(\mathsf{PKDF}(\mathsf{epk}_b, \mathsf{epk}_a))\}$;
    3. Send $(\mathsf{epk}_b, \mathsf{pk}_b, \mathsf{PoK}(\mathsf{esk}_b))$ to user $\widehat{A}$.
  - Upon receiving $(\mathsf{epk}_b, \mathsf{pk}_b, \mathsf{PoK}(\mathsf{esk}_b))$ from user $\widehat{B}$, user $\widehat{A}$ computes the proof of knowledge (i.e., non-malleable zero-knowledge) PoK$\{(\mathsf{esk}_a, \mathsf{cert}_a) : \mathsf{H}(\mathsf{PKDF}(\mathsf{epk}_a, \mathsf{epk}_b)\|\mathsf{PKDF}(\mathsf{pk}_a, \mathsf{epk}_b))\}$ and sends it to user $\widehat{B}$. Meanwhile, $\widehat{A}$ computes the final session key $SK_a = \mathsf{H}(K_a\|\mathsf{sid})$, where $K_a = \mathsf{SH.Handshake.KDF}(\mathsf{esk}_a, \mathsf{epk}_b, \mathsf{cert}_a, \mathsf{mpk}, \mathsf{L}, \mathsf{init})$ and the session identifier is sid = $(\mathsf{epk}_a\|\mathsf{epk}_b)$.

---

[6] Refer to [13] for detailed Signer and User algorithm of BS scheme.

- Upon receiving $\mathsf{PoK}(\mathsf{esk}_a, \mathsf{cert}_a)$ from user $\widehat{A}$, user $\widehat{B}$ computes the proof of knowledge $\mathsf{PoK}\{(\mathsf{esk}_b, \mathsf{cert}_b) : \mathsf{H}(\mathsf{PKDF}(\mathsf{epk}_b, \mathsf{epk}_a) \| \mathsf{PKDF}(\mathsf{pk}_b, \mathsf{epk}_a))\}$ and sends it to user $\widehat{A}$. Meanwhile, $\widehat{B}$ computes the final session key $SK_b = \mathsf{H}(K_b \| \mathsf{sid})$, where $K_b = \mathsf{SH.Handshake.KDF}(\mathsf{esk}_b, \mathsf{epk}_a, \mathsf{cert}_b, \mathsf{mpk}, \mathsf{L}, \mathsf{resp})$. Note that the equation $K_a = K_b$ holds due to the correctness of $\mathsf{SH.Handshake}$ algorithm.

3.3 Security Analysis

Theorem 1. *The proposed generic framework achieves session key security (Definition 1) in the random oracle model if the underlying* SH *is session key secure.*

Proof Sketch. Due to page limitation, the detailed security proof and the subsequent proof are deferred to the full version of this work. We here only present the proof sketch. We define a sequence of games G_i, $i = 0, \cdots, 4$ for session key security and analyze the advantage of the adversary in game G_i.

The first game G_0 is original game for session key security. The second game G_1 is used to capture replay attacks, such that no PPT adversary can find the collision of hash function H if users follow the framework execution honestly. In game G_2, we assume that the adversary must choose the specific session for test query, which is specified by the simulator. In game G_3, we assume that if adversary can distinguish game G_2 and G_3 (the real SH session key is replaced by a random value), then we can built an attacker to break the session key security of underlying SH protocol. In the last game G_4, the final session key in the test session is replaced by a random value. No PPT adversary can distinguish this change since we model H as a random oracle. Therefore, the advantage of adversary in this game is zero.

Theorem 2. *The proposed generic framework achieves* full deniability *in the sense of* Definition 2.

The full deniability proof is similar to the proof of deniability described in [24].

4 Conclusion

In this paper, we proposed a generic framework for deniable secret handshake protocols. We defined the formal security models for session key security and deniability of secret handshake protocols, and proved the security of the proposed generic framework is secure under standard assumptions. We leave the construction of an efficient and fully deniable instantiation as our future work.

Acknowledgements. This work is supported by the Singapore National Research Foundation under NCR Award Number NRF2014NCR-NCR001-012, the NSFC Research Fund for International Young Scientists (61750110528), National Cryptography Development Fund during the 13th Five-year Plan Period (MMJJ20170216), the Fundamental Research Funds for the Central Universities (GK201702004).

References

1. Balfanz, D., Durfee, G., Shankar, N., Smetters, D.K., Staddon, J., Wong, H.: Secret handshakes from pairing-based key agreements. In: IEEE (S&P 2003), pp. 180–196 (2003)
2. Borisov, N., Goldberg, I., Brewer, E.: Off-the-record communication, or, why not to use PGP. In: Proceedings of the 2004 ACM Workshop on Privacy in the Electronic Society, pp. 77–84 (2004)
3. Burmester, M., Desmedt, Y.G.: Efficient and secure conference-key distribution. In: Lomas, M. (ed.) Security Protocols 1996. LNCS, vol. 1189, pp. 119–129. Springer, Heidelberg (1997). https://doi.org/10.1007/3-540-62494-5_12
4. Castelluccia, C., Jarecki, S., Tsudik, G.: Secret handshakes from CA-oblivious encryption. In: Lee, P.J. (ed.) ASIACRYPT 2004. LNCS, vol. 3329, pp. 293–307. Springer, Heidelberg (2004). https://doi.org/10.1007/978-3-540-30539-2_21
5. Di Raimondo, M., Gennaro, R., Krawczyk, H.: Deniable authentication and key exchange. In: CCS, pp. 400–409. ACM (2006)
6. Dwork, C., Naor, M., Sahai, A.: Concurrent zero-knowledge. J. ACM (JACM) **51**(6), 851–898 (2004)
7. Gu, J., Xue, Z.: An improved efficient secret handshakes scheme with unlinkability. IEEE Commun. Lett. **15**(2), 259–261 (2011)
8. Huang, H., Cao, Z.: A novel and efficient unlinkable secret handshakes scheme. IEEE Commun. Lett. **13**(5), 363–365 (2009)
9. Jarecki, S., Kim, J., Tsudik, G.: Group secret handshakes or affiliation-hiding authenticated group key agreement. In: Abe, M. (ed.) CT-RSA 2007. LNCS, vol. 4377, pp. 287–308. Springer, Heidelberg (2006). https://doi.org/10.1007/11967668_19
10. Jarecki, S., Kim, J., Tsudik, G.: Beyond secret handshakes: affiliation-hiding authenticated key exchange. In: Malkin, T. (ed.) CT-RSA 2008. LNCS, vol. 4964, pp. 352–369. Springer, Heidelberg (2008). https://doi.org/10.1007/978-3-540-79263-5_23
11. Jarecki, S., Liu, X.: Private mutual authentication and conditional oblivious transfer. In: Halevi, S. (ed.) CRYPTO 2009. LNCS, vol. 5677, pp. 90–107. Springer, Heidelberg (2009). https://doi.org/10.1007/978-3-642-03356-8_6
12. Jiang, S., Safavi-Naini, R.: An efficient deniable key exchange protocol (extended abstract). In: Tsudik, G. (ed.) FC 2008. LNCS, vol. 5143, pp. 47–52. Springer, Heidelberg (2008). https://doi.org/10.1007/978-3-540-85230-8_4
13. Juels, A., Luby, M., Ostrovsky, R.: Security of blind digital signatures. In: Kaliski, B.S. (ed.) CRYPTO 1997. LNCS, vol. 1294, pp. 150–164. Springer, Heidelberg (1997). https://doi.org/10.1007/BFb0052233
14. Kawai, Y., Yoneyama, K., Ohta, K.: Secret handshake: strong anonymity definition and construction. In: Bao, F., Li, H., Wang, G. (eds.) ISPEC 2009. LNCS, vol. 5451, pp. 219–229. Springer, Heidelberg (2009). https://doi.org/10.1007/978-3-642-00843-6_20
15. Krawczyk, H.: HMQV: a high-performance secure Diffie-Hellman protocol. In: Shoup, V. (ed.) CRYPTO 2005. LNCS, vol. 3621, pp. 546–566. Springer, Heidelberg (2005). https://doi.org/10.1007/11535218_33
16. Manulis, M., Poettering, B., Tsudik, G.: Affiliation-hiding key exchange with untrusted group authorities. In: Zhou, J., Yung, M. (eds.) ACNS 2010. LNCS, vol. 6123, pp. 402–419. Springer, Heidelberg (2010). https://doi.org/10.1007/978-3-642-13708-2_24

17. Manulis, M., Poettering, B., Tsudik, G.: Taming big brother ambitions: more privacy for secret handshakes. In: Atallah, M.J., Hopper, N.J. (eds.) PETS 2010. LNCS, vol. 6205, pp. 149–165. Springer, Heidelberg (2010). https://doi.org/10.1007/978-3-642-14527-8_9

18. Pass, R.: On deniability in the common reference string and random oracle model. In: Boneh, D. (ed.) CRYPTO 2003. LNCS, vol. 2729, pp. 316–337. Springer, Heidelberg (2003). https://doi.org/10.1007/978-3-540-45146-4_19

19. Schäge, S.: TOPAS: 2-pass key exchange with full perfect forward secrecy and optimal communication complexity. In: CCS, pp. 1224–1235. ACM (2015)

20. Tian, Y., Zhang, S., Yang, G., Mu, Y., Yu, Y.: Privacy-preserving k-time authenticated secret handshakes. In: Pieprzyk, J., Suriadi, S. (eds.) ACISP 2017. LNCS, vol. 10343, pp. 281–300. Springer, Cham (2017). https://doi.org/10.1007/978-3-319-59870-3_16

21. Unger, N., Goldberg, I.: Deniable key exchanges for secure messaging. In: CCS, pp. 1211–1223. ACM (2015)

22. Xu, S., Yung, M.: K-anonymous secret handshakes with reusable credentials. In: CCS 2004, pp. 158–167. ACM (2004)

23. Yao, A.C.-C., Zhao, Y.: OAKE: a new family of implicitly authenticated Diffie-Hellman protocols. In: CCS, pp. 1113–1128. ACM (2013)

24. Yao, A.C.-C., Zhao, Y.: Privacy-preserving authenticated key-exchange over internet. IEEE TIFS **9**(1), 125–140 (2014)

25. Yung, M., Zhao, Y.: Interactive zero-knowledge with restricted random oracles. In: Halevi, S., Rabin, T. (eds.) TCC 2006. LNCS, vol. 3876, pp. 21–40. Springer, Heidelberg (2006). https://doi.org/10.1007/11681878_2

Authentication

Non-adaptive Group-Testing Aggregate MAC Scheme

Shoichi Hirose[1(✉)] and Junji Shikata[2]

[1] Faculty of Engineering, University of Fukui, Fukui, Japan
hrs_shch@u-fukui.ac.jp
[2] Graduate School of Environment and Information Sciences,
Yokohama National University, Yokohama, Japan
shikata@ynu.ac.jp

Abstract. This paper applies non-adaptive group testing to aggregate message authentication code (MAC) and introduces non-adaptive group-testing aggregate MAC. After formalization of its syntax and security requirements, simple and generic construction is presented, which can be applied to any aggregate MAC scheme formalized by Katz and Lindell in 2008. Then, two instantiations of the construction is presented. One is based on the aggregate MAC scheme by Katz and Lindell and uses addition for tag aggregate. The other uses cryptographic hashing for tag aggregate. Provable security of the generic construction and two instantiations are also discussed.

Keywords: Message authentication · Aggregate · Group testing
Provable security

1 Introduction

Background. A message authentication code (MAC) is a tag attached to a message to detect tampering of the message. The tag is computed with a cryptographic symmetric-key primitive called a MAC function such as HMAC [1,5] and CMAC [8,13].

An aggregate MAC scheme allows one to aggregate multiple tags to multiple messages into a shorter tag. It is possible to verify the validity of the multiple messages only with the single tag. It is impossible in general, however, to identify invalid messages once the multiple messages are judged invalid with respect to the single tag.

It is expected that the problem above can be solved with group testing [3]. Group testing is a method to be able to verify whether each sample is negative or positive with a smaller number of tests than a naive method to test each sample individually on the assumption that the number of positive samples is at most a constant. In group testing, each test involves a subset of the given samples. The result of a test is negative if and only if all the involved samples are negative. The group testing is called adaptive if one can choose samples to be tested after one sees the result of the previous test and is called non-adaptive otherwise.

© Springer Nature Switzerland AG 2018
C. Su and H. Kikuchi (Eds.): ISPEC 2018, LNCS 11125, pp. 357–372, 2018.
https://doi.org/10.1007/978-3-319-99807-7_22

Contribution. This paper applies non-adaptive group testing to aggregate MAC and introduces non-adaptive group-testing aggregate MAC (GTA MAC).

First, GTA MAC and its security requirements are formalized. The security requirements are unforgeability and identifiability. Unforgeability means that a message is judged invalid by the group testing if the tag to the message is not generated by a legitimate user. Identifiability is composed of completeness and soundness. Completeness captures the notion that group testing for pairs of a message and a tag should judge a pair valid if it is valid. Soundness captures the notion that group testing should judge a pair invalid if it is invalid. In the formalization of identifiability, an adversary is allowed to obtain correct tags even for invalid pairs given to the group testing by the adversary. It does matter for soundness, and we introduce weak soundness which does not allow an adversary to obtain a correct tag for any invalid pair given to the group testing and show that weak soundness is actually implied by unforgeability. Weak soundness is still a practical notion since it excludes message tampering.

Second, simple and generic construction of a GTA MAC scheme is presented. It can be applied to any aggregate MAC scheme formalized by Katz and Lindell [9]. The generic construction produces a GTA MAC scheme satisfying unforgeability and completeness from any unforgeable aggregate MAC scheme.

Finally, two instantiations of the generic construction are presented: One is from the Katz-Lindell aggregate MAC scheme [9] and the other is from an aggregate MAC scheme using hashing for aggregate. In particular, the latter is shown to satisfy soundness if the underlying hash function is a random oracle.

Related Work. Aggregate MAC and its security requirement were first formalized by Katz and Lindell [9]. They also proposed an aggregate MAC scheme and proved its unforgeability on the assumption that the underlying MAC function is unforgeable. Their scheme aggregates tags by their addition. The formalization of GTA MAC in the paper is based on that of aggregate MAC by Katz and Lindell.

Sequential aggregate MAC and its security requirement were formalized by Eikemeier et al. [4]. They also presented a provably secure sequential aggregate MAC scheme. Forward-secure sequential aggregate MAC was introduced by Ma and Tsudik [10]. It was also discussed by Ma and Tsudik [11] and Hirose and Kuwakado [7]. A typical application of the forward-secure sequential aggregate MAC is secure audit log.

The group testing was already applied to MAC schemes by Goodrich et al. [6] and Minematsu [12]. The major difference between their approach and ours is that their schemes do not, precisely speaking, aggregate tags for messages. Their schemes compute a tag of a subset of messages for each test in group testing. Minematsu [12] proposed a scheme based on PMAC [2,14] aiming at reduction of amount of computation required to compute tags for group testing.

Organization. This paper is organized as follows. Section 2 gives notations and introduces MAC functions and non-adaptive group testing. Section 3 introduces the syntax and security requirement of aggregate MAC. It also describes the aggregate MAC scheme proposed by Katz and Lindell. Section 4 formalizes the syntax and security requirements of GTA MAC. Section 5 gives a method for generic construction of GTA MAC schemes. It also describes provable security for the generic construction. Section 6 presents a GTA MAC scheme based on the Katz-Lindell aggregate MAC scheme. Section 7 presents another GTA MAC scheme using a cryptographic hash function for aggregate. Section 8 gives a brief concluding remark.

2 Preliminaries

2.1 Notations

Selecting an element s uniformly at random from a set S is denoted by $s \leftarrow S$.

For $\{0,1\}$-sequences x and y, $x\|y$ represents their concatenation.

Let $\boldsymbol{v} = (v_1, v_2, \ldots, v_n)$ and $\boldsymbol{w} = (w_1, w_2, \ldots, w_n)$ be vectors such that $v_i \in \{0,1\}$ and $w_i \in \{0,1\}^l$ for $1 \leq i \leq n$. Let $\boldsymbol{x} = (x_1, x_2, \ldots, x_n) \in X^n$ for some set X. $\langle \boldsymbol{v}, \boldsymbol{w} \rangle$ represents inner product of $\boldsymbol{v}$ and $\boldsymbol{w}$, that is, $\langle \boldsymbol{v}, \boldsymbol{w} \rangle = \bigoplus_{i=1}^n v_i w_i$. Let $\langle\!\langle \boldsymbol{v}, \boldsymbol{w} \rangle\!\rangle = w_{i_1} \| w_{i_2} \| \cdots \| w_{i_d}$, and $\boldsymbol{v} \boxdot \boldsymbol{x} = (x_{i_1}, x_{i_2}, \ldots, x_{i_d})$, where $1 \leq i_1 < i_2 < \cdots < i_d \leq n$, and $v_i = 1$ if $i \in \{i_1, i_2, \ldots, i_d\}$ and $v_i = 0$ otherwise.

For vectors $\boldsymbol{v} = (v_1, v_2, \ldots, v_n)$ and $\boldsymbol{v}' = (v_1', v_2', \ldots, v_n')$ in $\{0,1\}^n$, $\boldsymbol{v} \preceq \boldsymbol{v}'$ if $v_i \leq v_i'$ for $1 \leq i \leq n$.

2.2 MAC Functions

A MAC function is defined to be a keyed function $f : \mathcal{K} \times \mathcal{M} \to \mathcal{T}$, where $\mathcal{K}$ is its key space, $\mathcal{M}$ is its message space, and $\mathcal{T}$ is its tag space. $f(K, \cdot)$ is often denoted by $f_K(\cdot)$. The security requirement for a MAC function is unforgeability. Let $\mathbf{A}$ be an adversary against f. $\mathbf{A}$ is given access to the tagging oracle f_K and the corresponding verification oracle V_K, where $K \leftarrow \mathcal{K}$. The tagging oracle f_K returns $f_K(M)$ in reply to a query $M \in \mathcal{M}$. The verification oracle V_K, in reply to a query $(M, T) \in \mathcal{M} \times \mathcal{T}$, returns $\top$ if $f_K(M) = T$ and $\bot$ otherwise. It is assumed that $\mathbf{A}$ does not make a query on $(M, T) \in \mathcal{M} \times \mathcal{T}$ once it gets T from f_K as a reply to its query M. Let $\mathsf{Forge}(\mathbf{A})$ represent an event that $\mathbf{A}$ succeeds in making a query to which V_K returns $\top$. The advantage of $\mathbf{A}$ against f is defined as

$$\mathrm{Adv}_f^{\mathrm{mac}}(\mathbf{A}) \triangleq \Pr\left[\mathsf{Forge}(\mathbf{A})\right].$$

2.3 Non-adaptive Group Testing

A non-adaptive group-testing algorithm with n samples and u tests can be represented by a $u \times n$ $\{0,1\}$-matrix, which is called a group-testing matrix. For $1 \leq i \leq u$ and $1 \leq j \leq n$, the i-th test involves the j-th sample if and only if the (i, j) element of the corresponding group-testing matrix equals 1. Each sample is either positive or negative. It is assumed that the result of a test is negative if all the samples involved in the test are negative, and positive otherwise. All of the positive samples can be detected by the following simple procedure:

1. $J \leftarrow \{1, 2, \ldots, n\}$, where $j \in \{1, 2, \ldots, n\}$ represents the j-th sample.
2. For $1 \leq i \leq u$, if the result of the i-th test is negative, then $J \leftarrow J \backslash \{j_{i,1}, j_{i,2}, \ldots, j_{i,w_i}\}$, where $\{j_{i,1}, j_{i,2}, \ldots, j_{i,w_i}\}$ are all of the samples involved in the i-th test.
3. Output J.

The output J of the procedure presented above includes all the positive samples. It may also include (some of) the negative samples in general.

Definition 1 (d-disjunct). *A $\{0, 1\}$-matrix G is said to be d-disjunct if, any d columns of G do not cover any other column of G. Here, d columns $\boldsymbol{g}_{j_1}^{\mathrm{c}}, \boldsymbol{g}_{j_2}^{\mathrm{c}}, \ldots, \boldsymbol{g}_{j_d}^{\mathrm{c}}$ are said to cover a column $\boldsymbol{g}^{\mathrm{c}}$ if $\boldsymbol{g}^{\mathrm{c}} \preceq \boldsymbol{g}_{j_1}^{\mathrm{c}} \vee \boldsymbol{g}_{j_2}^{\mathrm{c}} \vee \cdots \vee \boldsymbol{g}_{j_d}^{\mathrm{c}}$, where $\vee$ is the component-wise disjunction.*

d-disjunct matrices are useful for group testing. If the group-testing matrix is d-disjunct and at most d of n samples are positive, then the set J computed by the procedure above does not contain any negative samples.

3   Aggregate MAC

3.1   Syntax

An aggregate MAC scheme is composed of the following algorithms:

Key generation $k \leftarrow \mathsf{KG}(1^p)$.
This algorithm takes as input a security parameter p and produces a secret key k.

Tagging $t \leftarrow \mathsf{Tag}(k_{id}, id, m)$.
This algorithm takes as input a pair of an ID and a message (id, m) and a secret key k_{id} corresponding to id, and produces as output a tag t.

Aggregate $T \leftarrow \mathsf{Agg}((id_1, m_1, t_1), \ldots, (id_n, m_n, t_n))$.
This algorithm takes tuples of an ID, a message and a tag (id_i, m_i, t_i)'s as input and produces an aggregate tag T as output. Notice that it is not given secret keys used by the tagging algorithm Tag.

Verification $d \leftarrow \mathsf{Ver}((k_1, \ldots, k_n), ((id_1, m_1), \ldots, (id_n, m_n)), T)$.
This algorithm takes pairs of an ID and a message (id_i, m_i)'s and an aggregate tag T as input and checks their validity with respect to the keys corresponding to the given IDs. Here, k_i is a key corresponding to id_i for $1 \leq i \leq n$. The decision d is either $\top$ or $\bot$. If $d = \top$, the pair $((id_1, m_1), \ldots, (id_n, m_n))$ and T are judged as valid with respect to $(k_1, \ldots, k_n)$. Otherwise, they are judged invalid.

For $(id_1, m_1), \ldots, (id_n, m_n)$ and T, if $t_j = \mathsf{Tag}(k_j, id_j, m_j)$ for $1 \leq j \leq n$ and $T = \mathsf{Agg}((id_1, m_1, t_1), \ldots, (id_n, m_n, t_n))$, then $\mathsf{Ver}((k_1, \ldots, k_n), ((id_1, m_1), \ldots, (id_n, m_n)), T) = \top$.

3.2   Security Requirement

The security requirement of an aggregate MAC scheme $\mathsf{AM} \triangleq (\mathsf{KG}, \mathsf{Tag}, \mathsf{Agg}, \mathsf{Ver})$ is unforgeability. An adversary against AM is given access to the oracles listed below:

Tagging. The tagging oracle $\mathcal{TG}$ receives a pair of ID and a message (id, m) as a query and returns a tag t, where $t \leftarrow \mathsf{Tag}(k_{id}, id, m)$.

Key disclosure. The key-disclosure oracle $\mathcal{KD}$ receives an ID id as a query and returns the corresponding key k_{id}.

Verification. The verification oracle $\mathcal{VR}$ receives $(((id_1, m_1), \ldots, (id_n, m_n)), T)$ as a query and returns d, where

$$d \leftarrow \mathsf{Ver}((k_1, \ldots, k_n), ((id_1, m_1), \ldots, (id_n, m_n)), T).$$

Definition 2 (Unforgeability). *Let* $\mathbf{A}$ *be an adversary against an aggregate MAC scheme* AM. $\mathbf{A}$ *is given access to* $\mathcal{TG}, \mathcal{KD}$ *and* $\mathcal{VR}$, *and is allowed to make multiple queries adaptively to each of them. Let* $\mathsf{Forge}(\mathbf{A})$ *be an event that* $\mathbf{A}$ *succeeds in asking* $\mathcal{VR}$ *a query* $(((id_1, m_1), \ldots, (id_n, m_n)), T)$ *satisfying the following conditions:*

- $\mathsf{Ver}((k_1, \ldots, k_n), ((id_1, m_1), \ldots, (id_n, m_n)), T) = \top$.
- *Before asking* $(((id_1, m_1), \ldots, (id_n, m_n)), T)$, *for some* $1 \leq j \leq n$, $\mathbf{A}$ *asks neither* (id_j, m_j) *to* $\mathcal{TG}$ *nor* id_j *to* $\mathcal{KD}$.

Then, the advantage of $\mathbf{A}$ *against* AM *with respect to unforgeability is defined as*

$$\mathrm{Adv}_{\mathsf{AM}}^{\mathrm{uf}}(\mathbf{A}) \triangleq \Pr[\mathsf{Forge}(\mathbf{A})].$$

An aggregate MAC scheme AM is informally said to satisfy unforgeability if $\mathrm{Adv}_{\mathsf{AM}}^{\mathrm{uf}}(\mathbf{A})$ is negligibly small for any adversary $\mathbf{A}$ with realistic computational resources.

3.3   Katz-Lindell Aggregate MAC Scheme

An aggregate MAC scheme proposed by Katz and Lindell [9] is described in this section. Here, their scheme is called KL-AM.

Scheme. Let $F : \mathcal{K} \times \mathcal{M} \rightarrow \mathcal{T}$ be a MAC function.

- The key generation algorithm just picks up a secret key uniformly at random from $\mathcal{K}$ for each user.
- For an input (id, m), the tagging algorithm returns $t \triangleq F(k_{id}, m)$.
- For an input $((id_1, m_1, t_1), \ldots, (id_n, m_n, t_n))$, the aggregate algorithm returns $T = t_1 \oplus t_2 \oplus \cdots \oplus t_n$.
- For an input $(((id_1, m_1), \ldots, (id_n, m_n)), T)$, the verification algorithm returns d such that

$$d = \begin{cases} \top & \text{if } T = F(k_1, m_1) \oplus \cdots \oplus F(k_n, m_n), \\ \bot & \text{otherwise.} \end{cases}$$

Security. Katz and Lindell [9] showed that their aggregate MAC scheme satisfies unforgeability assuming a single query to the verification oracle. We show for later use that their scheme satisfies unforgeability assuming multiple queries to the verification oracle.

Proposition 1 (Unforgeability). *For the Katz-Lindell aggregate MAC scheme* KL-AM, *let ℓ be the number of the users. For any adversary* **A** *against* KL-AM *running in time at most s and making at most q_t queries to its tagging oracle and at most q_v queries to its verification oracle, there exists some adversary* **B** *against F such that*

$$\mathrm{Adv}_{\mathsf{KL\text{-}AM}}^{\mathrm{uf}}(\mathbf{A}) \leq \ell \cdot \mathrm{Adv}_F^{\mathrm{mac}}(\mathbf{B}),$$

where **B** *runs in time at most $s + S_F(q_t + \ell q_v)$, making at most q_t queries to its tagging oracle, and making at most q_v queries to its verification oracle. S_F is time required to compute F.*

Proof. The adversary **B** attacks F by making use of an adversary **A** against KL-AM. **B** has oracle access to the tagging oracle F_K and the verification oracle V_K, where $K \leftarrow \mathcal{K}$.

B first picks up a user id_r uniformly at random among ℓ users. **B** also selects a secret key uniformly at random from $\mathcal{K}$ for each of the other $(\ell - 1)$ users. Then, **B** runs **A**.

For a tagging query made by **A** on the user id_r, **B** transfers it to F_K and returns the reply from F_K to **A**. For a tagging query made by **A** on a user other than id_r, **B** computes the tag using the corresponding secret key chosen by itself and returns it to **A**. If **A** makes a key-disclosure query on a user other than id_r, then **B** simply returns the corresponding secret key to **A**. If **A** makes a key-disclosure query on id_r, then **B** aborts.

Suppose that **A** succeeds in forgery. Then, **A** makes a verification query such that the verification oracle returns $\top$ in reply to it and, for some (id', m') included in it, **A** asks neither (id', m') to the tagging oracle nor id' to the key-disclosure oracle prior to it. Let Hit be the event such that $id' = id_r$. The conditional probability that Hit occurs when **A** succeeds in forgery is at least $1/\ell$.

Suppose that **A** succeeds in forgery and that Hit occurs. For a verification query from **A** not related to id_r, **B** verifies it by itself and returns the result. For a verification query from **A** including (id_r, m_r), **B** computes a tag t_r for (id_r, m_r) from the query and the secret keys of the other users and asks (m_r, t_r) to its verification query. Then, **B** makes at most q_v queries to its verification oracle, which returns $\top$ for at least one of them. Thus,

$$\begin{aligned}
\Pr[\mathsf{Forge}(\mathbf{B})] &= \Pr[\mathsf{Forge}(\mathbf{A}) \cap \mathsf{Hit}] \\
&= \Pr[\mathsf{Hit} \,|\, \mathsf{Forge}(\mathbf{A})] \Pr[\mathsf{Forge}(\mathbf{A})] \\
&\geq \frac{1}{\ell} \Pr[\mathsf{Forge}(\mathbf{A})]
\end{aligned}$$

and $\mathrm{Adv}_{\mathsf{KL\text{-}AM}}^{\mathrm{uf}}(\mathbf{A}) \leq \ell \cdot \mathrm{Adv}_F^{\mathrm{mac}}(\mathbf{B})$. □

4   Group-Testing Aggregate MAC

4.1   Syntax

A group-testing aggregate MAC (GTA MAC) scheme using a $u \times n$ group-testing matrix consists of the following algorithms:

Key generation $k \leftarrow \mathsf{KG}(1^p)$. This algorithm takes as input a security parameter p and produces a secret key k.

Tagging $t \leftarrow \mathsf{Tag}(k_{id}, id, m)$. This algorithm takes as input a pair of an ID and a message (id, m) and a secret key k_{id} corresponding to id, and produces as output a tag t.

Group-testing aggregate. This algorithm GTA takes tuples of an ID, a message and a tag (id_j, m_j, t_j)'s as input and produces a tuple of aggregate tags $(T_1, \ldots, T_u)$ as output:

$$(T_1, \ldots, T_u) \leftarrow \mathsf{GTA}((id_1, m_1, t_1), \ldots, (id_n, m_n, t_n)).$$

Notice that it is not given secret keys used by the tagging algorithm.

Group-testing verification. This algorithm GTV takes pairs of an ID and a message (id_j, m_j)'s and a tuple of aggregate tags T_i's as input and tries to identify invalid pairs of an ID and a message using the corresponding keys:

$$J \leftarrow \mathsf{GTV}((k_1, \ldots, k_n), ((id_1, m_1), \ldots, (id_n, m_n)), (T_1, \ldots, T_u)).$$

The output J of this algorithm is a set of $(id_{j'}, m_{j'})$'s which are judged invalid.

For $((id_1, m_1), \ldots, (id_n, m_n))$ and $(T_1, \ldots, T_u)$, if $t_j = \mathsf{Tag}(k_j, id_j, m_j)$ for $1 \leq j \leq n$ and $(T_1, \ldots, T_u) = \mathsf{GTA}((id_1, m_1, t_1), \ldots, (id_n, m_n, t_n))$, then $\mathsf{GTV}((k_1, \ldots, k_n), ((id_1, m_1), \ldots, (id_n, m_n)), (T_1, \ldots, T_u)) = \emptyset$.

4.2   Security Requirement

The security requirements of a GTA MAC scheme $\mathsf{GTAM} \triangleq (\mathsf{KG}, \mathsf{Tag}, \mathsf{GTA}, \mathsf{GTV})$ are unforgeability and identifiability. An adversary against GTAM is given access to the oracles listed below:

Tagging. This oracle $\mathcal{TG}$ receives a pair of ID and a message (id, m) as a query and returns a tag $t \leftarrow \mathsf{Tag}(k_{id}, id, m)$, where k_{id} is the secret key of the user id.

Key disclosure. This oracle $\mathcal{KD}$ receives an ID id as a query and returns the corresponding secret key k_{id}.

Group-testing verification. Given $(((id_1, m_1), \ldots, (id_n, m_n)), (T_1, \ldots, T_u))$ as a query, this oracle $\mathcal{GTV}$ returns

$$J \leftarrow \mathsf{GTV}((k_1, \ldots, k_n), ((id_1, m_1), \ldots, (id_n, m_n)), (T_1, \ldots, T_u)).$$

Unforgeability. Let $\mathbf{A}$ be an adversary against a GTA MAC scheme GTAM. $\mathbf{A}$ is given access to the oracles $\mathcal{TG}$, $\mathcal{KD}$ and $\mathcal{GTV}$, and is allowed to make multiple queries adaptively to each of them. Let GTForge($\mathbf{A}$) be an event that $\mathbf{A}$ succeeds in asking $\mathcal{GTV}$ a query $(((id_1, m_1), \ldots, (id_n, m_n)), (T_1, \ldots, T_u))$ satisfying the following conditions: There exists some $1 \leq j \leq n$ such that

- $(id_j, m_j) \notin \mathsf{GTV}((k_1, \ldots, k_n), ((id_1, m_1), \ldots, (id_n, m_n)), (T_1, \ldots, T_u))$, and
- before asking $(((id_1, m_1), \ldots, (id_n, m_n)), (T_1, \ldots, T_u))$, $\mathbf{A}$ asks neither (id_j, m_j) to $\mathcal{TG}$ nor id_j to $\mathcal{KD}$.

Then, the advantage of $\mathbf{A}$ against GTAM with respect to unforgeability is defined as

$$\mathrm{Adv}_{\mathsf{GTAM}}^{\mathrm{uf}}(\mathbf{A}) \triangleq \Pr[\mathsf{GTForge}(\mathbf{A})].$$

GTAM is informally said to satisfy unforgeability if $\mathrm{Adv}_{\mathsf{GTAM}}^{\mathrm{uf}}(\mathbf{A})$ is negligibly small for any adversary $\mathbf{A}$ with realistic computational resources.

Identifiability. For identifiability, completeness and soundness are introduced. Completeness requires that any valid tuple (id, m, t) is judged valid by the group testing. On the other hand, soundness requires that any invalid tuple is judged invalid. Let $\mathbf{A}$ be an adversary for identifiability. $\mathbf{A}$ is given access to the tagging oracle $\mathcal{TG}$ and the key-disclosure oracle $\mathcal{KD}$. $\mathbf{A}$ is also given access to a group-testing oracle: $\mathcal{GT}_{\mathrm{c}}$ for completeness and $\mathcal{GT}_{\mathrm{s}}$ for soundness. $\mathbf{A}$ is allowed to make multiple queries adaptively to each of them. Both of the group-testing oracles $\mathcal{GT}_{\mathrm{c}}$ and $\mathcal{GT}_{\mathrm{s}}$ accept $((id_1, m_1, t_1), \ldots, (id_n, m_n, t_n))$ as a query, and apply the group testing to it. Namely, they compute

1. $(T_1, \ldots, T_u) \leftarrow \mathsf{GTA}((id_1, m_1, t_1), \ldots, (id_n, m_n, t_n))$,
2. $J \leftarrow \mathsf{GTV}((k_1, \ldots, k_n), ((id_1, m_1), \ldots, (id_n, m_n)), (T_1, \ldots, T_u))$.

Then, $\mathcal{GT}_{\mathrm{c}}$ returns

$$\begin{cases} 1 & \text{if } J \cap \{(id_j, m_j) \mid t_j = \mathsf{Tag}(k_j, id_j, m_j)\} \neq \emptyset, \\ 0 & \text{otherwise.} \end{cases}$$

On the other hand, $\mathcal{GT}_{\mathrm{s}}$ returns

$$\begin{cases} 1 & \text{if } \{(id_j, m_j) \mid t_j \neq \mathsf{Tag}(k_j, id_j, m_j)\} \setminus J \neq \emptyset, \\ 0 & \text{otherwise.} \end{cases}$$

The advantage of $\mathbf{A}$ against GTAM with respect to completeness or soundness is defined as

$$\mathrm{Adv}_{\mathsf{GTAM}}^{\mathrm{id}\text{-}x}(\mathbf{A}) \triangleq \Pr\left[\mathcal{GT}_x \text{ returns 1 during interaction with } \mathbf{A}\right],$$

where $x \in \{\mathrm{c}, \mathrm{s}\}$.

In the game of identifiability described above, prior to a query to the group-testing oracle, an adversary is allowed to obtain a correct tag for any pair (id, m)

involved in the query by asking (id, m) to $\mathcal{TG}$ or id to $\mathcal{KD}$. It does not matter for completeness. On the other hand, it does matter for soundness as will be seen in the following sections. The correct tag for (id, m) can be useful to make the group-testing verification algorithm judge the invalid tuple (id, m, t') valid.

According to the observation above, we introduce weak soundness. In the game of weak soundness, an adversary $\mathbf{A}$ is not allowed to get a correct tag for (id, m) prior to a group-testing query involving a invalid tuple (id, m, t'). $\mathbf{A}$ is given access to $\mathcal{TG}$, $\mathcal{KD}$ and a group-testing oracle $\mathcal{GT}_{\mathrm{ws}}$. $\mathcal{GT}_{\mathrm{ws}}$ accepts $((id_1, m_1, t_1), \ldots, (id_n, m_n, t_n))$ as a query, and apply the group testing to it. Then, it returns 1 if there exists some $(id_j, m_j) \notin J$ such that $t_j \neq \mathsf{Tag}(k_j, id_j, m_j)$, and $\mathbf{A}$ asks neither (id_j, m_j) to $\mathcal{TG}$ nor id_j to $\mathcal{KD}$ before the group-testing query. Otherwise, it returns 0. The advantage of $\mathbf{A}$ against GTAM with respect to weak soundness is defined as

$$\mathrm{Adv}_{\mathsf{GTAM}}^{\mathrm{id\text{-}ws}}(\mathbf{A}) \triangleq \Pr\big[\mathcal{GT}_{\mathrm{ws}} \text{ returns 1 during interaction with } \mathbf{A}\big].$$

Weak soundness is still useful since it covers message tampering.

It is not difficult to see from the descriptions of weak soundness and unforgeability that a GTA MAC scheme satisfies weak soundness if it satisfies unforgeability:

Proposition 2. *For any adversary $\mathbf{A}$ against weak soundness of* GTAM *running in time at most s and making at most q_{t} queries to its tagging oracle, at most q_{k} queries to its key-disclosure oracle and at most q_{g} queries to its group-testing oracle, there exists some adversary $\mathbf{B}$ against unforgeability of* GTAM *such that*

$$\mathrm{Adv}_{\mathsf{GTAM}}^{\mathrm{id\text{-}ws}}(\mathbf{A}) \leq \mathrm{Adv}_{\mathsf{GTAM}}^{\mathrm{uf}}(\mathbf{B}),$$

where $\mathbf{B}$ runs in time at most $s + q_{\mathrm{g}} S_{\mathsf{GTA}}$ and makes at most $q_{\mathrm{t}} + n q_{\mathrm{g}}$ queries to its tagging oracle, at most q_{k} queries to its key-disclosure oracle and at most q_{g} queries to its group-testing verification oracle. S_{GTA} is time required to run GTA.

Proof. The adversary $\mathbf{B}$ is constructed by making use of $\mathbf{A}$. $\mathbf{B}$ runs $\mathbf{A}$. For a tagging query made by $\mathbf{A}$, $\mathbf{B}$ transfers it to its tagging oracle and returns the reply to $\mathbf{A}$. For a key-disclosure query made by $\mathbf{A}$, $\mathbf{B}$ also transfers it to its key-disclosure oracle and returns the reply to $\mathbf{A}$. For a group-testing query made by $\mathbf{A}$, $\mathbf{B}$ simulates the group-testing oracle as follows. Let $((id_1, m_1, t_1), \ldots, (id_n, m_n, t_n))$ be the query made by $\mathbf{A}$. $\mathbf{B}$ computes $(T_1, \ldots, T_u) \leftarrow \mathsf{GTA}((id_1, m_1, t_1), \ldots, (id_n, m_n, t_n))$, ask $(((id_1, m_1), \ldots, (id_n, m_n)), (T_1, \ldots, T_u))$ to its group-testing verification oracle, and receives J. Then, $\mathbf{B}$ returns 1 if there exists some $(id_j, m_j) \notin J$ such that $t_j \neq \mathsf{Tag}(k_j, id_j, m_j)$, and $\mathbf{A}$ asks neither (id_j, m_j) to its tagging oracle nor id_j to its key-disclosure oracle before the group-testing query. Otherwise, it returns 0. $\mathbf{B}$ makes at most n queries to its tagging oracle. If $\mathbf{B}$ returns 1, then $\mathbf{B}$ succeeds in forgery. $\qquad\square$

5   Generic Construction of GTA MAC Scheme

This section first presents generic construction of a GTA MAC scheme from an aggregate MAC scheme and a group-testing matrix. Then, it discusses the security of the GTA MAC scheme.

5.1   Generic Construction

Let $\mathsf{AM} = (\mathsf{KG}, \mathsf{Tag}, \mathsf{Agg}, \mathsf{Ver})$ be an aggregate MAC scheme. Let $\boldsymbol{G}$ be a $u \times n$ group-testing matrix, where $\boldsymbol{G} = (g_{i,j})$ for $1 \le i \le u$ and $1 \le j \le n$ and $\boldsymbol{g}_i = (g_{i,1}, \ldots, g_{i,n}) \in \{0,1\}^n$ is the i-th row of $\boldsymbol{G}$ for $1 \le i \le u$. A GTA MAC scheme $\mathsf{GTAM}_{\mathrm{g}} = (\mathsf{KG}_{\mathrm{g}}, \mathsf{Tag}_{\mathrm{g}}, \mathsf{GTA}_{\mathrm{g}}, \mathsf{GTV}_{\mathrm{g}})$ is constructed from AM and $\boldsymbol{G}$ as follows:

- $\mathsf{KG}_{\mathrm{g}} \triangleq \mathsf{KG}$.
- $\mathsf{Tag}_{\mathrm{g}} \triangleq \mathsf{Tag}$.
- $(T_1, \ldots, T_u) \leftarrow \mathsf{GTA}_{\mathrm{g}}((id_1, m_1, t_1), \ldots, (id_n, m_n, t_n))$, where, for $1 \le i \le u$, $T_i \leftarrow \mathsf{Agg}(\boldsymbol{g}_i \boxdot ((id_1, m_1, t_1), \ldots, (id_n, m_n, t_n)))$.
- $J \leftarrow \mathsf{GTV}_{\mathrm{g}}((k_1, \ldots, k_n), ((id_1, m_1), \ldots, (id_n, m_n)), (T_1, \ldots, T_u))$, where
  1. $J \leftarrow \{(id_1, m_1), \ldots, (id_n, m_n)\}$.
  2. For $1 \le i \le u$, if

$$\mathsf{Ver}(\boldsymbol{g}_i \boxdot (k_1, \ldots, k_n), \boldsymbol{g}_i \boxdot ((id_1, m_1, t_1), \ldots, (id_n, m_n, t_n)), T_i) = \top,$$

  then
$$J \leftarrow J \backslash \{(id_j, m_j) \mid 1 \le j \le n \wedge g_{i,j} = 1\}.$$

5.2   Unforgeability

The following theorem says that generic construction produces an unforgeable GTA MAC scheme from any unforgeable aggregate MAC scheme.

Theorem 1. *For the GTA MAC scheme* $\mathsf{GTAM}_{\mathrm{g}}$, *let ℓ be the number of the users. For any adversary $\mathbf{A}$ against* $\mathsf{GTAM}_{\mathrm{g}}$ *running in time at most s and making at most q_{t} queries to its tagging oracle, at most q_{k} queries to its key-disclosure oracle and at most q_{v} queries to its group-testing verification oracle, there exists some adversary $\mathbf{B}$ against* AM *with ℓ users such that*

$$\mathrm{Adv}^{\mathrm{uf}}_{\mathsf{GTAM}_{\mathrm{g}}}(\mathbf{A}) \le \mathrm{Adv}^{\mathrm{uf}}_{\mathsf{AM}}(\mathbf{B}),$$

where $\mathbf{B}$ runs in time at most s and makes at most q_{t} queries to its tagging oracle, at most q_{k} queries to its key-disclosure oracle and at most $u q_{\mathrm{v}}$ queries to its verification oracle.

Proof. The adversary $\mathbf{B}$ against AM tries forgery by making use of the adversary $\mathbf{A}$ against $\mathsf{GTAM}_{\mathrm{g}}$. $\mathbf{B}$ has oracle access to the tagging oracle, the key-disclosure oracle, and the verification oracle.

B simply runs **A**. For a tagging query made by **A**, **B** transfers it to its tagging oracle and returns the reply to **A**. For a key-disclosure query made by **A**, **B** also transfers it to its key-disclosure oracle and returns the reply to **A**. For a group-testing verification query made by **A**, **B** executes GTV_g using its verification oracle u times.

Suppose that **A** succeeds in forgery and $(((id_1, m_1), \ldots, (id_n, m_n)), (T_1, \ldots, T_u))$ is a successful forgery. Then, there exists some $1 \leq j \leq n$ such that

- $(id_j, m_j) \notin \mathsf{GTV}_g((k_1, \ldots, k_n), ((id_1, m_1), \ldots, (id_n, m_n)), (T_1, \ldots, T_u))$, and
- before asking $((id_1, m_1), \ldots, (id_n, m_n)), (T_1, \ldots, T_u))$, **A** asks neither (id_j, m_j) to its tagging oracle nor id_j to its key-disclosure oracle.

It implies that there exists some $1 \leq i \leq u$ such that the i-th test involves (id_j, m_j) and passes the verification. Thus, the i-th test is a successful query made by **B** to its verification oracle. $\qquad \square$

5.3 Identifiability

An adversary **A** is said to be d-dishonest if, for any group-testing query $((id_1, m_1, t_1), \ldots, (id_n, m_n, t_n))$ made by **A**, $|\{(id_j, m_j) \mid t_j \neq \mathsf{Tag}_g(k_j, id_j, m_j)\}| \leq d$.

Completeness. The theorem below says that the GTA MAC scheme GTAM_g satisfies completeness against any d-dishonest adversary if the group-testing matrix is d-disjunct.

Theorem 2 (Completeness). *For the GTA MAC scheme* GTAM_g, *suppose that the group-testing matrix* **G** *is d-disjunct. Then, for any d-dishonest adversary* **A**,

$$\mathrm{Adv}^{\mathrm{id\text{-}c}}_{\mathsf{GTAM}_g}(\mathbf{A}) = 0.$$

Proof. Let **A** be any d-dishonest adversary. Suppose that **A** makes a query $((id_1, m_1, t_1), \ldots, (id_n, m_n, t_n))$ to $\mathcal{GT}_c$ and let $V = \{(id_j, m_j) \mid t_j = \mathsf{Tag}_g(k_j, id_j, m_j)\}$. Since the group-testing matrix **G** is d-disjunct and **A** is d-dishonest, for any $(id, m) \in V$, there exists some test in **G** involving (id, m) and no invalid pairs. Thus, (id, m) is judged valid. $\qquad \square$

Soundness. Notice that Theorem 1 implies that GTAM_g satisfies weak soundness if AM satisfies unforgeability. On the other hand, the GTA MAC scheme GTAM_g may not satisfy soundness. It depends on how to aggregate tags.

Let us consider the following adversary $\tilde{\mathbf{A}}$. $\tilde{\mathbf{A}}$ first obtains valid (id_j, m_j, t_j) such that $t_j = \mathsf{Tag}_g(k_j, id_j, m_j)$ using its tagging oracle for $1 \leq j \leq n$. Let $T_i = \mathsf{Agg}(\boldsymbol{g}_i \boxdot ((id_1, m_1, t_1), \ldots, (id_n, m_n, t_n)))$ for $1 \leq i \leq u$. Suppose that $\tilde{\mathbf{A}}$ succeeds in finding $((id_1, m_1, \tilde{t}_1), \ldots, (id_n, m_n, \tilde{t}_n)))$ such that, for some i^*, $\boldsymbol{g}_{i^*} \boxdot ((id_1, m_1, \tilde{t}_1), \ldots, (id_n, m_n, \tilde{t}_n)) \neq \boldsymbol{g}_{i^*} \boxdot ((id_1, m_1, t_1), \ldots, (id_n, m_n, t_n))$ and $T_{i^*} = \mathsf{Agg}(\boldsymbol{g}_{i^*} \boxdot ((id_1, m_1, \tilde{t}_1), \ldots, (id_n, m_n, \tilde{t}_n)))$. Then, the result of the i^*-th test $\boldsymbol{g}_{i^*}$ is valid, and there exists some j^* such that $\tilde{t}_{j^*} \neq \mathsf{Tag}(k_{j^*}, id_{j^*}, m_{j^*})$ and (id_{j^*}, m_{j^*}) is judged valid.

6 GTA MAC Scheme Based on Katz-Lindell Aggregate MAC

From the generic construction, it is straightforward to obtain a GTA MAC scheme based on the Katz-Lindell aggregate MAC scheme. Let us call it $\mathsf{GTAM_X}$.

$\mathsf{GTAM_X}$ is unforgeable if the underlying MAC function is unforgeable. For identifiability, $\mathsf{GTAM_X}$ satisfies completeness. It also satisfies weak soundness if the underlying MAC function is unforgeable, while it does not satisfy soundness.

6.1 Scheme

Let $F : \mathcal{K} \times \mathcal{M} \to \{0,1\}^\tau$ be a MAC function. The key generation and tagging algorithms of $\mathsf{GTAM_X}$ are identical to those of the Katz-Lindell scheme. It is assumed that the group-testing aggregate algorithm of $\mathsf{GTAM_X}$ is based on a $u \times n$ group-testing matrix $\boldsymbol{G} = (g_{i,j})$.

– The key generation algorithm just picks up a secret key uniformly at random from $\mathcal{K}$ for each user.
– For an input (id, m), the tagging algorithm returns $t \triangleq F(k_{id}, m)$.
– For an input $((id_1, m_1, t_1), \ldots, (id_n, m_n, t_n))$, the group-testing aggregate algorithm returns $(T_1, \ldots, T_u)$, where $T_i \triangleq \langle \boldsymbol{g}_i, (t_1, t_2, \ldots, t_n) \rangle$ for $1 \le i \le u$.
– For an input $(((id_1, m_1), \ldots, (id_n, m_n)), (T_1, \ldots, T_u))$, the verification algorithm returns J computed in the following way:
  1. $J \leftarrow \{(id_1, m_1), \ldots, (id_n, m_n)\}$.
  2. For $1 \le i \le u$, if $T_i = \langle \boldsymbol{g}_i, (F(k_1, m_1), \ldots, F(k_n, m_n)) \rangle$, then

$$J \leftarrow J \backslash \{(id_j, m_j) \mid 1 \le j \le n \wedge g_{i,j} = 1\}.$$

6.2 Unforgeability

The following theorem says that $\mathsf{GTAM_X}$ is unforgeable if the underlying MAC function is unforgeable. It directly follows from Proposition 1 and Theorem 1, and the proof is omitted.

Theorem 3 (Unforgeability). *For* $\mathsf{GTAM_X}$, *let* ℓ *be the number of the users. For any adversary* $\mathbf{A}$ *against* $\mathsf{GTAM_X}$ *running in time at most* s *and making at most* q_t *queries to its tagging oracle, at most* q_k *queries to its key-disclosure oracle and at most* q_v *queries to its group-testing verification oracle, there exists some adversary* $\mathbf{B}$ *against* F *such that*

$$\mathrm{Adv}^{\mathrm{uf}}_{\mathsf{GTAM_X}}(\mathbf{A}) \le \ell \cdot \mathrm{Adv}^{\mathrm{mac}}_F(\mathbf{B}),$$

where $\mathbf{B}$ *runs in time at most* $s + S_F(q_t + nq_v)$ *and makes at most* q_t *queries to its tagging oracle and at most* uq_v *queries to its verification oracle.* S_F *is time required to compute* F.

6.3 Identifiability

Completeness. Theorem 2 applies to $\mathsf{GTAM_X}$. It satisfies completeness against any d-dishonest adversary if $\boldsymbol{G}$ is d-disjunct.

Soundness. From Theorem 3, $\mathsf{GTAM_X}$ satisfies weak soundness if the underlying MAC function is unforgeable. On the other hand, $\mathsf{GTAM_X}$ does not satisfy soundness.

Let us consider an adversary $\tilde{\mathbf{A}}$ behaving in the following way. $\tilde{\mathbf{A}}$ obtains valid $(id_1, m_1, t_1), \ldots, (id_n, m_n, t_n)$ using its tagging oracle, that is, $t_j = F(k_j, m_j)$ for $1 \leq j \leq n$. Then, $\tilde{\mathbf{A}}$ can easily compute $(\tilde{t}_1, \ldots, \tilde{t}_n)$ such that $\langle \boldsymbol{g}_{i^*}, (\tilde{t}_1, \ldots, \tilde{t}_n) \rangle = \langle \boldsymbol{g}_{i^*}, (t_1, \ldots, t_n) \rangle$ and $\boldsymbol{g}_{i^*} \boxdot (\tilde{t}_1, \ldots, \tilde{t}_n) \neq \boldsymbol{g}_{i^*} \boxdot (t_1, \ldots, t_n)$ for some i^*. Then, there exists some j^* such that $\tilde{t}_{j^*} \neq F(k_{j^*}, m_{j^*})$ and (id_{j^*}, m_{j^*}) is judged valid.

7   GTA MAC Scheme Using Hashing for Aggregate

7.1   Scheme

Let $F : \mathcal{K} \times \mathcal{M} \to \{0,1\}^\tau$ be a MAC function. Let $H : \{0,1\}^* \to \{0,1\}^\tau$ be a cryptographic hash function. The proposed GTA MAC scheme $\mathsf{GTAM_H}$ uses the hash function H for aggregate. The key generation and tagging algorithms of $\mathsf{GTAM_H}$ are identical to those of $\mathsf{GTAM_X}$. The group-testing aggregate algorithm of $\mathsf{GTAM_H}$ is also assumed to be based on a $u \times n$ group-testing matrix $\boldsymbol{G} = (g_{i,j})$.

- The key generation algorithm just picks up a secret key uniformly at random from $\mathcal{K}$ for each user.
- For an input (id, m), the tagging algorithm returns $t \triangleq F(k_{id}, m)$.
- For an input $((id_1, m_1, t_1), \ldots, (id_n, m_n, t_n))$, the group-testing aggregate algorithm returns $(T_1, \ldots, T_u)$, where $T_i \triangleq H(\langle\!\langle \boldsymbol{g}_i, (t_1, t_2, \cdots, t_n) \rangle\!\rangle)$. To make each aggregate tag unique, it is assumed that $((id_1, m_1, t_1), \ldots, (id_n, m_n, t_n))$ is ordered in a lexicographic order.
- For an input $(((id_1, m_1), \ldots, (id_n, m_n)), (T_1, \ldots, T_u))$, the verification algorithm returns J computed in the following way:
    1. $J \leftarrow \{(id_1, m_1), \ldots, (id_n, m_n)\}$.
    2. For $1 \leq i \leq u$, if $T_i = H(\langle\!\langle \boldsymbol{g}_i, (F(k_1, m_1), \ldots, F(k_n, m_n)) \rangle\!\rangle)$, then

$$J \leftarrow J \setminus \{(id_j, m_j) \mid 1 \leq j \leq n \wedge g_{i,j} = 1\}.$$

7.2   Unforgeability

The following theorem says that $\mathsf{GTAM_H}$ is unforgeable if the underlying MAC function F is unforgeable and the underlying hash function H is a random oracle.

Theorem 4 (Unforgeability). *For the GTA MAC scheme* $\mathsf{GTAM_H}$*, let ℓ be the number of the users. For any adversary* $\mathbf{A}$ *against* $\mathsf{GTAM_H}$ *running in time at most s and making at most q_h queries to H, at most q_t queries to its tagging oracle, at most q_k queries to its key-disclosure oracle and at most q_v queries* to its group-testing verification oracle, there exists some adversary $\mathbf{B}$ against F such that

$$\mathrm{Adv}^{\mathrm{uf}}_{\mathsf{GTAM_H}}(\mathbf{A}) \leq \ell \cdot \mathrm{Adv}^{\mathrm{mac}}_F(\mathbf{B}) + \frac{uq_{\mathrm{v}}}{2^\tau} + \frac{(q_{\mathrm{h}} + uq_{\mathrm{v}})^2}{2^{\tau+1}},$$

where $\mathbf{B}$ runs in time at most $s + S_F(q_{\mathrm{t}} + nq_{\mathrm{v}})$ and makes at most $q_{\mathrm{h}} + uq_{\mathrm{v}}$ queries to H, at most q_{t} queries to its tagging oracle and at most uq_{v} queries to its verification oracle. S_F is time required to compute F.

Proof. Let $\mathsf{Coll}(H)$ be the event that a collision is found for H. Then,

$$\begin{aligned}
\mathrm{Adv}^{\mathrm{uf}}_{\mathsf{GTAM_H}}(\mathbf{A}) &= \Pr[\mathsf{GTForge}(\mathbf{A})] \\
&\leq \Pr[\mathsf{GTForge}(\mathbf{A}) \cap \overline{\mathsf{Coll}(H)}] + \Pr[\mathsf{Coll}(H)] \\
&\leq \Pr[\mathsf{GTForge}(\mathbf{A}) \cap \overline{\mathsf{Coll}(H)}] + (q_{\mathrm{h}} + uq_{\mathrm{v}})^2/2^{\tau+1}.
\end{aligned}$$

Let $\mathsf{GTF}(\mathbf{A}) \subseteq \mathsf{GTForge}(\mathbf{A}) \cap \overline{\mathsf{Coll}(H)}$ be the event that there exists some successful group-testing verification query without a query of correct tags to H. Then,

$$\Pr[\mathsf{GTF}(\mathbf{A})] \leq uq_{\mathrm{v}}/2^\tau,$$

Similarly to the proof of Theorem 3, it can be shown that there exists some adversary $\mathbf{B}$ against F such that

$$\Pr\left[\left(\mathsf{GTForge}(\mathbf{A}) \cap \overline{\mathsf{Coll}(H)}\right) \cap \overline{\mathsf{GTF}(\mathbf{A})}\right] \leq \ell \cdot \mathrm{Adv}^{\mathrm{mac}}_F(\mathbf{B}).$$

$\square$

7.3   Identifiability

Completeness. Theorem 2 also applies to $\mathsf{GTAM_H}$, and it satisfies completeness against any d-dishonest adversary if $\boldsymbol{G}$ is d-disjunct.

Soundness. The following theorem says that $\mathsf{GTAM_H}$ satisfies soundness for any d-dishonest adversary if $\boldsymbol{G}$ is d-disjunct on the assumption that H is a random oracle.

Theorem 5 (Soundness). *For the GTA MAC scheme* $\mathsf{GTAM_H}$, *suppose that the hash function* H *is a random oracle and that the group-testing matrix* $\boldsymbol{G}$ *is d-disjunct. Then, for any d-dishonest adversary* $\mathbf{A}$ *making at most q_{h} queries to H and at most q_{g} queries to its group-testing oracle,*

$$\mathrm{Adv}^{\mathrm{id\text{-}s}}_{\mathsf{GTAM_H}}(\mathbf{A}) \leq \frac{(q_{\mathrm{h}} + 2uq_{\mathrm{g}})^2}{2^{\tau+1}}.$$

Proof. Let $((id_1, m_1, \tilde{t}_1), \ldots, (id_n, m_n, \tilde{t}_n))$ be a query made by $\mathbf{A}$ to $\mathcal{GT}_{\mathrm{s}}$ and let $t_j = F_{k_j}(m_j)$ for $1 \leq j \leq n$. $\mathcal{GT}_{\mathrm{s}}$ returns 1 in response to the query only if there exists some i^* such that $\boldsymbol{g}_{i^*} \boxdot (\tilde{t}_1, \ldots, \tilde{t}_n) \neq \boldsymbol{g}_{i^*} \boxdot (t_1, \ldots, t_n)$ and $H(\langle\!\langle\!\langle \boldsymbol{g}, (\tilde{t}_1, \ldots, \tilde{t}_n) \rangle\!\rangle\!\rangle) = H(\langle\!\langle\!\langle \boldsymbol{g}, (t_1, \ldots, t_n) \rangle\!\rangle\!\rangle)$, which implies a collision for H. H is called $(q_{\mathrm{h}} + 2uq_{\mathrm{g}})$ times in total. $\square$

8 Conclusion

The paper has formalized the syntax and security requirements of GTA MAC schemes and presented their generic construction. Then, it has also presented two instantiations with distinct aggregate methods. One is based on the Katz-Lindell aggregate MAC scheme and aggregates tags with addition for group testing. The other aggregates tags with hashing. The paper has analyzed the provable security of the proposed schemes. Future work includes design of an efficient algorithm to verify whether a given group-testing matrix is d-disjunct or not.

Acknowledgements. This research was conducted under a contract of Research and Development for Expansion of Radio Wave Resources funded by the Ministry of Internal Affairs and Communications, Japan.

References

1. Bellare, M., Canetti, R., Krawczyk, H.: Keying hash functions for message authentication. In: Koblitz, N. (ed.) CRYPTO 1996. LNCS, vol. 1109, pp. 1–15. Springer, Heidelberg (1996). https://doi.org/10.1007/3-540-68697-5_1
2. Black, J., Rogaway, P.: A block-cipher mode of operation for parallelizable message authentication. In: Knudsen, L.R. (ed.) EUROCRYPT 2002. LNCS, vol. 2332, pp. 384–397. Springer, Heidelberg (2002). https://doi.org/10.1007/3-540-46035-7_25
3. Du, D.Z., Hwang, F.K.: Combinatorial Group Testing and Its Applications. Series on Applied Mathematics, vol. 12, 2nd edn. World Scientific, Singapore (2000)
4. Eikemeier, O., et al.: History-free aggregate message authentication codes. In: Garay, J.A., De Prisco, R. (eds.) SCN 2010. LNCS, vol. 6280, pp. 309–328. Springer, Heidelberg (2010). https://doi.org/10.1007/978-3-642-15317-4_20
5. FIPS PUB 198-1: The keyed-hash message authentication code (HMAC) (2008)
6. Goodrich, M.T., Atallah, M.J., Tamassia, R.: Indexing information for data forensics. In: Ioannidis, J., Keromytis, A., Yung, M. (eds.) ACNS 2005. LNCS, vol. 3531, pp. 206–221. Springer, Heidelberg (2005). https://doi.org/10.1007/11496137_15
7. Hirose, S., Kuwakado, H.: Forward-secure sequential aggregate message authentication revisited. In: Chow, S.S.M., Liu, J.K., Hui, L.C.K., Yiu, S.M. (eds.) ProvSec 2014. LNCS, vol. 8782, pp. 87–102. Springer, Cham (2014). https://doi.org/10.1007/978-3-319-12475-9_7
8. Iwata, T., Kurosawa, K.: OMAC: one-key CBC MAC. In: Johansson, T. (ed.) FSE 2003. LNCS, vol. 2887, pp. 129–153. Springer, Heidelberg (2003). https://doi.org/10.1007/978-3-540-39887-5_11
9. Katz, J., Lindell, A.Y.: Aggregate message authentication codes. In: Malkin, T. (ed.) CT-RSA 2008. LNCS, vol. 4964, pp. 155–169. Springer, Heidelberg (2008). https://doi.org/10.1007/978-3-540-79263-5_10
10. Ma, D., Tsudik, G.: Extended abstract: forward-secure sequential aggregate authentication. In: IEEE Symposium on Security and Privacy, pp. 86–91. IEEE Computer Society (2007). Also published as IACR Cryptology ePrint Archive: Report 2007/052, http://eprint.iacr.org/
11. Ma, D., Tsudik, G.: A new approach to secure logging. ACM Trans. Storage **5**(1), 2:1–2:21 (2009)

12. Minematsu, K.: Efficient message authentication codes with combinatorial group testing. In: Pernul, G., Ryan, P.Y.A., Weippl, E. (eds.) ESORICS 2015. LNCS, vol. 9326, pp. 185–202. Springer, Cham (2015). https://doi.org/10.1007/978-3-319-24174-6_10
13. NIST Special Publication 800-38B: Recommendation for block cipher modes of operation: the CMAC mode for authentication (2005)
14. Rogaway, P.: Efficient instantiations of tweakable blockciphers and refinements to modes OCB and PMAC. In: Lee, P.J. (ed.) ASIACRYPT 2004. LNCS, vol. 3329, pp. 16–31. Springer, Heidelberg (2004). https://doi.org/10.1007/978-3-540-30539-2_2

TMGMap: Designing Touch Movement-Based Geographical Password Authentication on Smartphones

Weizhi Meng[1] and Zhe Liu[2,3(✉)]

[1] Department of Applied Mathematics and Computer Science,
Technical University of Denmark, Copenhagen, Denmark
[2] Nanjing University of Aeronautics and Astronautics, Nanjing, China
zhe.liu@nuaa.edu.cn
[3] Interdisciplinary Centre for Security, Reliability and Trust,
University of Luxembourg, Esch-sur-Alzette, Luxembourg

Abstract. Although textual passwords are the most widely adopted authentication method, they are vulnerable to many known limitations. Graphical password is considered as one alternative to complement the existing authentication systems, based on the observation that humans can remember images better than textual information. In order to obtain a large password space, geographical passwords have received much attention, which enable users to select one or more places on a map for authentication. For example, PassMap requires users to choose two places on a world map as their credentials, and GeoPass enables users to click only one place for authentication. However, we identify that users are able to perform more particular gestures like touch movement on mobile devices as compared to a common computer. Motivated by the observation, in this work, we develop TMGMap, a touch movement-based geographical password scheme on smartphones, which allows users to draw their secrets on a world map via touch movement events. We conducted a user study with a total of 60 participants, and found that users could achieve better results with our scheme in the aspects of both security and usability, as compared to similar schemes.

Keywords: Graphical password · Smartphone security
User authentication · Touch dynamics · Biometric authentication

1 Introduction

With the increasing capability, smartphones have become a personal assistant for individuals. Many people are willing to save their personal data on phones (e.g., credit card numbers, personal photos) and use the phone for sensitive transactions (e.g., trade credentials) [12,36]. However, smartphones are easily lost and

---

W. Meng and Z. Liu are co-first authors.

© Springer Nature Switzerland AG 2018
C. Su and H. Kikuchi (Eds.): ISPEC 2018, LNCS 11125, pp. 373–390, 2018.
https://doi.org/10.1007/978-3-319-99807-7_23

an attractive target for hackers [31]. The personal data stored on phones could be explored by attackers for malicious use. As a result, designing an appropriate user authentication mechanism becomes very essential and important.

Currently, textual passwords are the most widely implemented user authentication mechanism for various systems and network platforms; however, this kind of passwords has well-known limitations in the aspects of both security and usability [39]. A strong textual password is usually hard for a human to remember, making most users tend to create weak passwords. Intuitively, a weak password can be easily guessed and cracked by hackers, which would greatly degrade the security of authentication. In real-world scenarios, the security of textual passwords would be even worse than people believed before, i.e., most created passwords by users only achieved a password space lower than 10 bits of security against online trawling attacks [1,38].

Many early psychological research studies have revealed that users can generally remember images better than textual passwords [26,28]. Based on this observation, graphical passwords (GPs) are proposed as a potential alternative to complement existing textual password authentication, which require users to create their passwords by means of one or more images. In order to obtain a large password space, geographical password (or called map-based password) schemes have recently received much attention that allow users to create passwords by meas of a world map, which is expected to offer more potential places for users. PassMap [33] and GeoPass [35] are two typical examples: PassMap asks users to choose two places in a sequence at any zoom-level on a world map, while GeoPass only requires users to select one location at zoom level of 16.

Regarding PassMap and GeoPass, Meng *et al.* [24] figured out that selecting one location is more vulnerable to shoulder surfing attacks, while increasing the security (e.g., selecting two places) may cause more burden on users, i.e., consuming more authentication time. For smartphones, we are aware that touchscreen has become the leading input method, which allows users to perform more actions like touch movement than on a desktop computer. This shows that the design of graphical passwords like geographical password schemes should consider the different input methods and platforms.

Contributions. To our knowledge, there is only a modified version of GeoPass, called SmartPass, was implemented and evaluated in a mobile device [30], whereas fewer studies focusing on the design of geographical passwords particularly on smartphones. Motivated by this observation, in this work, we design TMGMap, a touch movement-based geographical password scheme for smartphones, and conduct a user study including 60 participants. The contributions of this work can be summarized as below.

– To enhance the authentication security of mobile platforms, we develop a touch movement-based geographical password scheme (TMGMap) on smartphones, which requires users to firstly select one place on a world map and then draw a pattern on a linked image via touch movement. The associated image will be partitioned into a 16×16 table with 256 valid squares.

- In this work, we focus on three issues: (1) theoretical password space, (2) success rate and time consumption, and (3) the number of selected squares on the image. To test the performance, we conducted a user study with a total of 60 participants and compared our scheme with SmartPass and a mobile version of DAS. Experimental results show that TMGMap can enhance the authentication security as compared to SmartPass and mobile DAS without degrading the usability.

Road Map. The remaining parts of this paper are organized as follows. In Sect. 2, we review some relevant studies regarding graphical password schemes, especially map-based (geographical) password schemes. Section 3 describes our proposed TMGMap and analyzes the potential password space. Section 4 discusses the results and feedback obtained from a user study with a total of 60 participants. Section 5 makes a discussion and points out limitations with open challenges. Finally, we conclude our work in Sect. 6.

2   Related Work

In the literature, an appropriate textual password is believed to be at least eight random characters including upper-case, lower-case and special characters. In practice, this kind of password is usually difficult for users to remember. As an alternative solution, research has been moved to graphical passwords.

2.1   Graphical Password

Generally, there are three major types of graphical password (GP) schemes [3, 32]: recognition-based scheme (i.e., remembering and recognizing images), pure recall-based scheme (i.e., generating a pattern without a hint) and cued recall-based scheme (i.e., making a pattern with hints).

- *Recognition-based scheme.* This kind of choice-based scheme needs users to select several images from a pool of candidates. As a typical example, *Pass-Faces* [27] enables users to select several face images in the phase of password creation and re-select these images from several decoys in the phase of password login. Davis *et al.* [5] then utilized the basic idea from *PassFaces* and introduced a scheme called *Story*, which encourages users to select daily images in an ordered sequence and made a story to help improve the recall capability, i.e., better remembering the images and the order.
- *Pure recall-based scheme.* This type of drawing-based scheme requires users to create a pattern on an image as their credentials. In the year of 1999, Jermyn *et al.* [11] proposed *DAS* ('draw-a-secret'), allowing users to create a pattern on a grid and redraw it for authentication. For better recall capability, a *Backgroud DAS* was then designed by adding a background image to the original DAS scheme [7]. Tao *et al.* [34] introduced *Pass-Go* that demands users to create a password by selecting intersections on a grid. Following

the idea of *Pass-Go*, current Android phones often deploy the application of unlock patterns, which allows users to unlock the phone if they can input a correct pattern.[1]

– *Cued recall-based scheme*. This kind of click-based GP enables users to select a sequence of points on an image as their passwords. Wiedenbeck *et al.* [37] developed *PassPoints*, in which users have to make their credentials by clicking on any place on an image. To improve the security, Chiasson *et al.* [2] then introduced Cued Click Points (CCP), in which the next image displayed can be varied with the previous click-point and users have to select five points in a sequence of images.

By considering both security and usability, some combined graphical password schemes have been studies, like click-draw based graphical password scheme (CD-GPS) [15], which combined the major inputting types of creating a graphical password, including clicking, selecting and drawing. Several related research studies on graphical passwords can be referred to but not limited to [4,6,10,13,16–18,20–22,25,40].

2.2 Geographical Password Schemes

In the year of 2010, Fox [8] showed an idea of creating a password by using a digital map. At the same time, Spitzer *et al.* [29] presented an authentication scheme through combining the concept of graphical passwords with user's familiarity with navigating on Google maps. For implementation, they designed a prototype by using an image of the United States that allowed users simply clicking several key destinations. They further involved 50 participants in a study and found that most users could remember their scheme in an easier way than traditional textual passwords.

Geographical password (or map-based graphical password) schemes received much more attention from the year of 2012, by using a world map to achieve large password space. Georgakakis *et al.* [9] introduced a geographical scheme of *NAVI*, which allowed users drawing a route on a pre-loaded map image. A major limitation is no real performance was given. Sun *et al.* [33] developed *PassMap*, a geographical password scheme that requires users to choose two sequenced places on a world map. In the evaluation, users found that they could more easily remember *PassMap* passwords than textual passwords. Then, Thorpe *et al.* [35] introduced *GeoPass*, a digital geographical password scheme, allowing users to select only one place on a world map to reduce the time consumption. The major difference between *PassMap* and *GeoPass* is the number of locations allowed by the system, i.e., selecting one or two locations on a world map. Similarly, MacRae *et al.* [14] proposed GeoPassNotes as an improved version of GeoPass, which require users to further select a note associated with their chosen location in the second step. Focused on this issue, Meng *et al.* [24] conducted a study with 60 participants and found that users achieved a similar performance under

---

[1] https://www.berkeleychurchill.com/software/android-pwgen/pwgen.php.

both schemes. That is, there is no significant difference by choosing either one or two locations. Regarding mobile platforms, Shin *et al.* [30] revised the scheme of *GeoPass* and performed a study on smartphones.

Further, some studies started investigating the impact of using a map on multi-password interference. For instance, Meng [19] proposed *RouteMap*, which requires users to create a path on a world map for authentication. Their user study with 60 participants indicated that users could better remember multi-passwords under *RouteMap* than other similar schemes. Then, Meng *et al.* [23] explored the recall of multiple passwords between textual passwords and geographical passwords using six different accounts. Participants in the geographical password condition were found to do better than those in the textual password condition, for both short-term (one-hour session) and long term (after two weeks).

To our knowledge, there have been fewer studies focusing on the design of geographical passwords on mobile devices. Although most geographical password schemes can be implemented in both common computers and mobile platforms, we notice that users actually can perform much more gestures like touch movement on smartphones as compared to a common computer. This observation motivates our work in designing a particular geographical password scheme by leveraging touch movement gestures on smartphones.

3   Design of TMGMap on Smartphones

In the literature, the use of map has demonstrated its effectiveness like PassMap and GeoPass. However, it is identified that GeoPass is vulnerable to offline guessing attacks due to the selection of only one location, while selecting two locations would greatly increase the authentication time, or may result in weak password creation. As a result, there is a balance should be made in the aspects of both security and usability.

3.1   Basic Design

Basically, adding one more step is a promising solution for the above balance issue. For example, MacRae *et al.* [14] introduced GeoPassNotes in order to improve the performance of GeoPass, allowing users to firstly select a location and then choose a note associated with their chosen location in the second step. Their major goal is to combine the geographical password scheme with a note, where users could be verified by correctly inputting both a place and an annotation on a map. However, it would be time-consuming and inconvenient to write a note on some mobile devices with a small touchscreen.

In this work, we notice that users can perform much more gestures like touch movement to interact with a touchscreen compared to a common computer. We particularly develop TMGMap, a touch movement-based geographical password scheme on smartphones. Similar to GeoPassNotes, TMGMap adopts a two-step

Fig. 1. The first step of TMGMap: selecting a location on a world map.

method, requiring users to select a location at first and then draw a pattern on a linked image using one or more touch movement events.

Step 1: Location Selection. The first step of TMGMap is to locate a place on a world map. Figure 1 shows an example of selecting a map location. Users can utilize the search bar to navigate in a quick manner, i.e., users can find a place by easily inputting a nation name like Denmark. We took advantage of the Google Maps API drop-down menu to recommend the locations. When the searched term appears, users can choose a specific item from the drop-down menu.

In addition, users can use zooming function to find a particular location. For example, users can identify a place by double-clicking to zoom in, or just using the zoom bar (with '+' and '−' buttons and a 'drag-zoom' option). Similar to GeoPass and previous work [19,24], our scheme requires users to locate a place at zoom level of 16. Users can adjust the zoom level and the system can check whether the minimum zoom level is reached. If users failed to reach the zoom level, the system will show a box to remind.

Step 2: Draw a Pattern. The second step requires users to draw a pattern using one or several touch movement events on an associated image with the pre-selected location. This step is similar to previous work [15]. Figure 2 gives an example of associated image by selecting a location named 'Tivoli' (corresponding to Fig. 1). Our scheme partitions the image into a 16×16 table with 256 effective squares, which are identified by coordinate numbers, e.g., (2, 5), (3, 6), (1, 2). The coordinate numbers are expected to help users easily recall and create their passwords with hints (i.e., users can remember the beginning and end coordinates of their created patterns).

Figure 3 gives two examples of patterns drawn by users with touch movement events. In particular, Fig. 3(a) shows a pattern drawn on 'Tivoli' image like '+' including the coordinates (9, 8), (9, 9), (9, 10), (9, 11), (9, 12), (9, 13), (8, 10), (10, 10), (11, 10), (12, 10) and (13, 10), shortly {(9, (8–13)), ((8–13), 10)}.

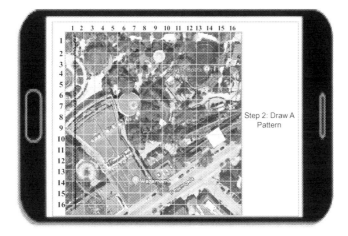

Fig. 2. The second step of TMGMap: drawing a pattern on an associated image with the selected location.

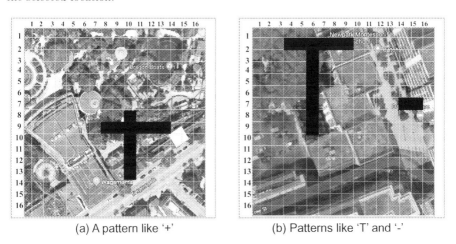

(a) A pattern like '+'   (b) Patterns like 'T' and '-'

Fig. 3. Two examples of patterns created by users in the second step.

Figure 3(b) shows patterns drawn on an image near 'London', including 'T' and '-' patterns, shortly $\{(2, (4\text{--}9)), ((2\text{--}9), 6), (7, (14\text{--}15))\}$.

For a successful login, users need to select the same map location within a reasonable error tolerance and then draw the pattern(s) in the correct ordered sequence. As compared to PassMap and GeoPass, our scheme is believed to offer the following merits between the security and the usability.

– Our scheme allows users to choose only one location on a world map, which can reduce the time consumption in zooming out or zooming in on the map to locate another place, as compared to PassMap. Finding an appropriate location on a world map is believed to be a very time-consuming task for password creation and login [14].

– Our scheme consists of two steps, where the second step needs users to draw a pattern on an associated image with the pre-selected map location, by means of touch movement events. Similar to [14], two-step graphical password schemes are expected to provide a better password space and can increase the cracking difficulty of attackers.

– For most geographical password authentication schemes like [14,24,35], users are encouraged to select a familiar location where they have travelled or visited before, in order to achieve a better recall. In this case, users can easily remember the map location, and the image in the second step has a reasonable probability to become a hint or memorable place for users. All these can facilitate users to remember their created credentials.

3.2   Password Space

In the study, we adopted a Google/HTC Nexus One Android phone (with resolution 480×800 px and CPU 1 GHz) to implement the above schemes. The main merit of using this particular phone is that we could easily modify the customized OS version. The modification mainly focused on the application framework layer like recording touch movement events and corresponding touchscreen coordinates. According to the results from several studies, we set the error tolerance to a 21×21 pixel box around the selected location. As a comparison, it is worth noting that *GeoPass* and *PassMap* each has an error tolerance of 21×21 pixel and 20×20 pixel. The recorded passwords will be hashed stored to defend against plaintext attack.

For our scheme, the password space consists of two steps. The first step is the same as GeoPass, thus the password space is $2^{36.9}$. The derivation details can refer to [35]. In the second step, the feasible password space can be calculated as $\frac{N_c!}{(N_c - K_i)!}$ ($i = 1, 2, 3, \ldots$) where $N_c = 256$ and K_i means there are totally i *selected squares* on the associated image. For instance, the feasible password space is $\frac{256!}{(256-12)!} = 6.10 \times 10^{28}$ for the pattern in Fig. 3(a), which contains a total of 11 selected squares with one square selected twice. As our scheme considers the drawing sequence, double-selected squares should be counted twice. Similarly, the password space for the pattern in Fig. 3(b) is $\frac{256!}{(256-16)!} = 2.11 \times 10^{38}$ with totally 15 selected squares with one square selected twice.

In this case, by combining the password space from two steps, the overall password space can be calculated as below:

$$2^{36.9} \times \frac{256!}{(256 - K_i)!} (i = 1, 2, 3, \ldots)$$

K_i means there are totally i *selected squares* on the associated image.

4   User Study

To investigate the scheme performance, we conducted a user study with up to 60 common Android phone users, including 33 females and 27 males with an average age of 29.3. All participants have no background in security and are volunteers. The participants' background is summarized in Table 1.

Table 1. Detailed information of participants in the user study.

Age range	Male	Female	Occupation	Male	Female
18–30	12	21	Business people	5	4
31–40	8	6	Students	15	23
41–50	5	4	Researchers	5	4
Above 50	2	2	Senior people	2	2

4.1   Study Design

In this study, our major purpose is to evaluate the performance of our scheme and compare it with the schemes of SmartPass [30] and DAS [11], based on both study results and users' feedback. SmartPass is a web-based mobile interface as an improved version of GeoPass and thus can be used in a mobile device. The implementation of SmartPass can refer to previous work [30]. Actually, the basic implementation is very similar to GeoPass. On the other hand, DAS needs users to draw something on a 2D grid as the password via a pen and re-draw the pattern for authentication. For comparison in this work, we implemented it on a smartphones (called *mobile DAS*), which needs users to draw a secret by means of a touch pen. An example of mobile DAS password is shown in Fig. 4. In order to avoid any bias on the collected feedback, we did not reveal the name of the tested two schemes and encouraged users to give feedback based on the actual scheme performance.

For evaluation, we randomly divided the participants into two groups with 30 individuates each, denoted as *Group1* and *Group2*. More specifically, *Group1* focuses on a comparison between TMGMap and SmartPass, while *Group2* evaluates the performance between TMGMap and mobile DAS. To avoid any bias, we followed the same steps to train all participants, i.e., how to use these example systems. Before they started, we introduced the study's goals and specific tasks to each participant and required them to sign a consent form. In addition, every participant has 3 trials to get familiar with the relevant prototypes, and could ask any questions to make sure that they indeed understood the steps and the use of prototype systems.

In the user study, each participant needed to make 5 passwords for each scheme based on their group, and had to finish password creation and login in the same day. In this case, a total of 300 trials were collected from each group during the study. The detailed steps in each group are summarized as follows:

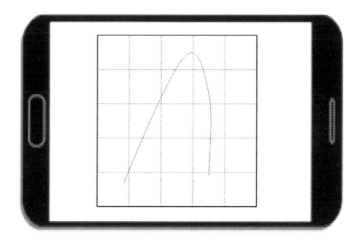

Fig. 4. The scheme of DAS (Draw A Secret).

Table 2. Success rate and average completion time for the step of creation, confirmation and login for two groups in the user study.

	Creation	Confirmation	Login
Group1: TMGMap			
Success rate (the first time)	116/150 (77.3%)	131/150 (87.3%)	124/150 (82.7%)
Completion time (average in seconds)	30.2	16.6	16.8
Standard deviation (SD in seconds)	6.9	5.3	7.4
Group1: SmartPass			
Success rate (the first time)	117/150 (78.0%)	127/150 (84.7%)	121/150 (80.7%)
Completion time (average in seconds)	29.3	14.3	16.2
Standard deviation (SD in seconds)	7.8	6.9	8.1
Group2: TMGMap			
Success rate (the first time)	117/150 (78.0%)	133/150 (88.7%)	129/150 (86.0%)
Completion time (average in seconds)	29.6	15.2	15.1
Standard deviation (SD in seconds)	7.1	6.3	6.8
Group2: Mobile DAS			
Success rate (the first time)	121/150 (80.7%)	92/150 (61.3%)	95/150 (63.3%)
Completion time (average in seconds)	27.3	28.3	25.5
Standard deviation (SD in seconds)	10.1	9.7	10.5

- *Group1*. Participants in this group needed to make 5 passwords for TMGMap, and 5 passwords for SmartPass after a half hour rest. The start from which scheme was selected by random.
- *Group2*. Participants in this group needed to make 5 passwords for TMGMap, and 5 passwords for mobile DAS after a half hour rest. The start from which scheme was selected by random.

Participants from both groups should follow the same steps as shown below:

- Step 1. Creation phase: participants should create a password based on the rules.
- Step 2. Confirmation phase: participants should confirm the password by inputting the correct secrets. If users are failed to confirm the password, they can try to confirm again or just return to Step 1.
- Step 3. Distributed memory: participants were provided two paper-based finding tasks to distract them for 15 min. Then participants could take a 5-min rest.
- Step 4. Login phase: participants should use all created passwords to enter the example system. They can repeal an attempt if they found a mistake or anomaly.
- Step 5. Feedback form: participants should complete a *feedback form* regarding password creation, confirmation and login.

The feedback form contains a set of questions regarding scheme usage for different group participants. Each question employs ten-point Likert scales: namely, 1-score indicates strong disagreement and 10-score indicates strong agreement.

4.2 Result Analysis

Success Rate and Time Consumption. Table 2 shows the success rate and average time consumption regarding creation, confirmation and login for two groups. We discuss the observations as below.

- For Group1, it is found that participants in TMGMap could have similar performance of password generation as those in SmartPass in the aspect of success rate. For example, participants achieved a success rate of 77.3% and 78.0% for each scheme. With regard to the confirmation, participants in TMGMap achieved a slightly higher rate than those in SmartPass, i.e., 87.3% versus 84.7%. Regarding login, it is similar that participants in TMGMap could do better than those in SmartPass, i.e., 82.7% versus 80.7%. In the aspect of time consumption, participants mostly spent similar time creating both schemes. For instance, participants in TMGMap and SmartPass should spend 16.8 s and 16.2 s for login on average.
- For Group2, it is found that participants in Mobile DAS could achieve better performance in password creation, as they could easily draw some lines on the 2D grid. However, participants in TMGMap could achieve greatly better results than those in Mobile DAS regarding confirmation and login, i.e., 88.7% versus 61.3% for password confirmation, and 86.0% versus 63.3% for password login. In the aspect of time consumption, both schemes require around 30 s for creation on average, but TMGMap requires less time regarding password confirmation and login, i.e., participants spent averagely 15 s and 28 s for confirming TMGMap and Mobile DAS, respectively.

Table 3. Major questions and relevant scores collected from the user study.

Questions (Group1)	TMGMap	SmartPass
1. I could easily create a password	8.9	9.1
2. The time consumption of password creation is acceptable	8.8	9.0
3. I could easily login to the system	9.1	8.9
Questions (Group2)	TMGMap	Mobile DAS
1. I could easily create a password	8.7	8.5
2. The time consumption of password creation is acceptable	8.6	6.2
3. I could easily login to the system	8.5	5.3

To better make a comparison, we apply Chi-squared (χ^2) tests to evaluate non-ordered categorical or nominal data, and regard a value of $\rho < 0.05$ as showing that the results from groups being tested are statistically significant. For Group1, based on the Chi-squared (χ^2) tests, there is no significant difference between TMGMap and SmartPass in the aspects of success rate and time consumption regarding password creation, confirmation and login. By contrast, for Group2, although the results are not significantly different between TMGMap and Mobile DAS regarding password creation, there are significant differences regarding password confirmation $(\chi^2 \approx 9.2, \rho < 0.01)$ and login $(\chi^2 \approx 8.9, \rho < 0.01)$.

User Feedback. Although users' feedback is a kind of subjective evaluation on a password scheme, it provides valuable comments on the designed schemes. Table 3 summarizes the major questions and relevant scores (feedback) collected from this study. For Group1, both schemes received similar average scores regarding password creation, login and time consumption. It is worth noting that our scheme had increase an additional step as compared to SmartPass, but this didn't degrade the usability on the users' side, at least based on their feedback. For Group2, unexpectedly, both schemes achieved a similar score regarding password creation; however, TMGMap got a much better score than mobile DAS regarding password login and time consumption. We informally interviewed most participants and they indicated that it would be difficult to re-draw an accurate pattern on a smartphone. As compared our scheme with SmartPass, most participants considered our scheme was more secure since it involves two-step creation method.

The Number of Selected Squares. Intuitively, more selected squares can help increase password space, but would add more burden on users' side. In this work, how many squares users would like to choose in creating their passwords via touch movement is an interesting and important question. To explore this issue, Table 4 analyzes the number of selected squares.

For Group1, most participants preferred to select 7, 10 and 12 squares with a percentage of 13.2%, 10.3% and 15.2%, respectively. There are around 4.6% participants selected 14 squares, but still 5.1% participants selected more than 14 squares. For Group2, most participants would like to choose 7, 8, 10, 11, 12 squares to construct their passwords, with 12.5%, 10.5%, 13.2%, 10.3%, and

10.1%, respectively. There are still 9.2% participants choosing above 13 squares. According to the equation for computing password space, our scheme can further increase the security of GeoPass (or SmartPass).

Table 4. The number of selected squares in Group1 and Group2, respectively.

# of selected squares	Group1	Group2
5 squares	7.2%	8.5%
6 squares	8.5%	9.2%
7 squares	13.2%	12.5%
8 squares	8.5%	10.5%
9 squares	8.5%	8.3%
10 squares	10.3%	13.2%
11 squares	9.1%	10.3%
12 squares	15.2%	10.1%
13 squares	9.8%	8.2%
14 squares	4.6%	5.2%
Above 14 squares	5.1%	4.0%

5   Discussion and Limitations

5.1   Discussion

In this part, we firstly discuss the aspects of security and usability of TMGMap, i.e., defending against some common attacks.

– *Security aspect.* As our scheme is a two-step GP scheme, intuitively, it provides another layer of protection on user authentication. For authentication, users have to input both right map location and correct pattern(s) with touch movement events. For theoretical password space, our scheme can enhance the security of GeoPass or SmartPass, which only requires users to select one location. Based on the feedback collected in the study, most participants believed that TMGMap can be more secure than SmartPass.

– *Usability aspect.* It is found that participants spent similar time creating both TMGMap and SmartPass, but our scheme can provide an additional layer of protection. As compared with mobile DAS, our scheme requires much less time consumption regarding password confirmation and login. Based on the users' feedback, most participants considered the usability of our scheme is similar to SmartPass, but much better than mobile DAS.

Brute-Force Attack. This type of attack means that an attacker checks all possible values to crack an authentication system. Cyber-criminals often try such attack when it is impossible or very hard to use any vulnerabilities in an encryption system. For our scheme of TMGMap, the theoretical password space can be computed as $2^{36.9} \times \frac{256!}{(256-K_i)!}$ ($i = 1, 2, 3, \ldots$). For a 7-square pattern, the password space reaches $2^{36.9} \times \frac{256!}{(256-7)!}$, which is very hard to be cracked by simple brute-force attack. According to Table 4, there are many participants would select more squares as their passwords and thus further enhance the password space in practice.

Dictionary Attack. To reduce the time consumption in finding correct values, an attacker can use advanced adversarial techniques to crack a graphical password, i.e., they can construct a dictionary by collecting 'hot-spots' on an image to identify a right pattern in an efficient way. The main purpose of a dictionary attack is to try those values that are most likely to be successful.

For clicking and selection-based graphical password systems, 'hot-spots' can be regarded as some particular image locations, where many users may choose as part of their credentials. An attacker can thus build a password dictionary by combining these hotspots, which can help reduce the potential locations and narrow down the password space. Our scheme actually reduces the success rate of this attack through increasing the difficulty of guesses, as attackers have to select a right location in the first step and guess how many squares are selected in the second step. Further, attackers have to guess the right beginning and ending coordinate of the pattern(s), which increase the difficulty of cracking, i.e., increasing the cost of a successful intrusion. This is one of our future work for investigation.

5.2 Limitations

In this work, we have demonstrated the effectiveness of TMGMap according to the results in success rate, time consumption, users' feedback and the pattern analysis (e.g., the number of selected squares). Due to the nature of graphical passwords, there are still many open challenges in this direction.

– *Advanced attacks.* In this work, our major objective is to investigate the performance of our scheme as compared to SmartPass and DAS. We initially analyzed the security of our scheme but didn't implement any advanced attacks. In this field, this is often a particular direction requiring a systematic evaluation. We leave the investigation of our scheme under several advanced attacks in our future work, i.e., identifying the hotspot and exploring the scheme performance under dictionary attack.
– *Comparison with other schemes.* In the field of graphical passwords, it is an open challenge to evaluate the performance among different schemes in a direct manner for the sake of distinct design ideas and scheme implementations. In our future work, it is an interesting topic to compare our scheme with more schemes like GeoPassNotes, where users have to select a note associated with their chosen location in the second step [14].
– *More participants.* In our study, we have involved a total of 60 participants, which are similar to most studies. However, it is always an open challenge to invite more participants with more diverse backgrounds. For example, it

is an interesting topic to investigate the difference between right handed and left handed participants to validate the results obtained in our study.

- *The effect of selected squares.* In literature, PassPoints used the technique of "Robust Discretization" to determine the tolerance squares. In comparison, our scheme divides an image into 256 valid squares using a 16×16 table. The previous work has shown that the use of either a $N \times N$ table or "Robust Discretization" could provide a similar function, while the table partition is more easier to implemented [15]. One of our future work is to explore the impact of setting different square numbers.
- *Consideration of other touch gestures.* In this work, we mainly designed a geographical password on smartphones by means of touch movement events. In practice, there are many touch gestures available on smartphones, e.g., various multi-touch gestures. It is an interesting topic for our future work to explore the performance by adding other touch gestures.
- *Finger size and usability.* During our informal interview, most participants indicated that it is easier to utilize a touch movement event to select more squares in creating a pattern in the second step. For example, performing two touch movement events may result in nearly 6–7 selected squares based on the finger size. To investigate such relationship would be an interesting issue for our future work.

6   Conclusion

Graphical password authentication is considered as an alternative to complement existing textual password mechanisms, which needs users to generate their passwords on a (world) map. The use of a world map aims to provide a large password space. In this work, we notice that users can have more touch gestures like touch movement on a smartphone than a common computer, and thus develop a touch movement-based geographical password authentication scheme (TMGMap) on smartphones. Our scheme enables users to firstly locate a place on a world map and then draw their secrets via one or more touch movement events. In the evaluation, we conducted a user study including up to 60 participants, and found that TMGMap can improve the security without degrading the usability as compared to SmartPass and mobile DAS.

Acknowledgments. We would like to thank all participants for their hard work in the user study.

References

1. Bonneau, J.: The science of guessing: analyzing an anonymized corpus of 70 million passwords. In: Proceedings of the 2012 IEEE Symposium on Security and Privacy, pp. 538–552 (2012)
2. Chiasson, S., van Oorschot, P.C., Biddle, R.: Graphical password authentication using cued click points. In: Biskup, J., López, J. (eds.) ESORICS 2007. LNCS, vol. 4734, pp. 359–374. Springer, Heidelberg (2007). https://doi.org/10.1007/978-3-540-74835-9_24

3. Chiasson, S., Biddle, R., van Oorschot, P.C.: A second look at the usability of click-based graphical passwords. In: Proceedings of the 3rd Symposium on Usable Privacy and Security, SOUPS, pp. 1–12. ACM, New York (2007)

4. Chiasson, S., Stobert, E., Forget, A., Biddle, R.: Persuasive cued click-points: design, implementation, and evaluation of a knowledge-based authentication mechanism. IEEE Trans. Dependable Secur. Comput. **9**(2), 222–235 (2012)

5. Davis, D., Monrose, F., Reiter, M.K.: On user choice in graphical password schemes. In: Proceedings of the 13th Conference on USENIX Security Symposium, SSYM, pp. 151–164. USENIX Association, Berkeley (2004)

6. Dirik, A.E., Memon, N., Birget, J.C.: Modeling user choice in the PassPoints graphical password scheme. In: Proceedings of the 3rd Symposium on Usable Privacy and Security, SOUPS, pp. 20–28. ACM, New York (2007)

7. Dunphy, P., Yan, J.: Do background images improve "draw a secret" graphical passwords? In: Proceedings of the 14th ACM Conference on Computer and Communications Security, CCS, pp. 36–47 (2007)

8. Fox, S.: Future Online Password Could be a Map (2010). http://www.livescience. com/8622-future-online-password-map.html

9. Georgakakis, E., Komninos, N., Douligeris, C.: NAVI: novel authentication with visual information. In: Proceedings of the 2012 IEEE Symposium on Computers and Communications, ISCC, pp. 588–595 (2012)

10. Gołofit, K.: Click passwords under investigation. In: Biskup, J., López, J. (eds.) ESORICS 2007. LNCS, vol. 4734, pp. 343–358. Springer, Heidelberg (2007). https://doi.org/10.1007/978-3-540-74835-9_23

11. Jermyn, I., Mayer, A., Monrose, F., Reiter, M.K., Rubin, A.D.: The design and analysis of graphical passwords. In: Proceedings of the 8th Conference on USENIX Security Symposium, pp. 1–14. USENIX Association, Berkeley (1999)

12. Karlson, A.K., Brush, A.B., Schechter, S.: Can I borrow your phone?: Understanding concerns when sharing mobile phones. In: Proceedings of the 27th International Conference on Human Factors in Computing Systems, CHI, pp. 1647–1650. ACM, New York (2009)

13. Lin, D., Dunphy, P., Olivier, P., Yan, J.: Graphical passwords & qualitative spatial relations. In: Proceedings of the 3rd Symposium on Usable Privacy and Security, SOUPS, pp. 161–162 (2007)

14. MacRae, B., Salehi-Abari, A., Thorpe, J.: An exploration of geographic authentication schemes. IEEE Trans. Inf. Forensics Secur. **11**(9), 1997–2012 (2016)

15. Meng, Y.: Designing click-draw based graphical password scheme for better authentication. In: Proceedings of the 7th IEEE International Conference on Networking, Architecture, and Storage, NAS, pp. 39–48 (2012)

16. Meng, Y., Li, W.: Evaluating the effect of tolerance on click-draw based graphical password scheme. In: Chim, T.W., Yuen, T.H. (eds.) ICICS 2012. LNCS, vol. 7618, pp. 349–356. Springer, Heidelberg (2012). https://doi.org/10.1007/978-3-642-34129-8_32

17. Meng, Y., Li, W.: Evaluating the effect of user guidelines on creating click-draw based graphical passwords. In: Proceedings of the 2012 ACM Research in Applied Computation Symposium, RACS, pp. 322–327 (2012)

18. Meng, Y., Li, W., Kwok, L.-F.: Enhancing click-draw based graphical passwords using multi-touch on mobile phones. In: Janczewski, L.J., Wolfe, H.B., Shenoi, S. (eds.) SEC 2013. IAICT, vol. 405, pp. 55–68. Springer, Heidelberg (2013). https://doi.org/10.1007/978-3-642-39218-4_5

19. Meng, W.: RouteMap: a route and map based graphical password scheme for better multiple password memory. Network and System Security. LNCS, vol. 9408, pp. 147–161. Springer, Cham (2015). https://doi.org/10.1007/978-3-319-25645-0_10

20. Meng, W.: Evaluating the effect of multi-touch behaviours on android unlock patterns. Inf. Comput. Secur. **24**(3), 277–287 (2016)

21. Meng, W., Li, W., Wong, D.S., Zhou, J.: TMGuard: a touch movement-based security mechanism for screen unlock patterns on smartphones. In: Manulis, M., Sadeghi, A.-R., Schneider, S. (eds.) ACNS 2016. LNCS, vol. 9696, pp. 629–647. Springer, Cham (2016). https://doi.org/10.1007/978-3-319-39555-5_34

22. Meng, W., Li, W., Kwok, L.-F., Choo, K.-K.R.: Towards enhancing click-draw based graphical passwords using multi-touch behaviours on smartphones. Comput. Secur. **65**, 213–229 (2017)

23. Meng, W., Li, W., Lee, W.H., Jiang, L., Zhou, J.: A pilot study of multiple password interference between text and map-based passwords. In: Gollmann, D., Miyaji, A., Kikuchi, H. (eds.) ACNS 2017. LNCS, vol. 10355, pp. 145–162. Springer, Cham (2017). https://doi.org/10.1007/978-3-319-61204-1_8

24. Meng, W., Lee, W.H., Au, M.H., Liu, Z.: Exploring effect of location number on map-based graphical password authentication. In: Pieprzyk, J., Suriadi, S. (eds.) ACISP 2017. LNCS, vol. 10343, pp. 301–313. Springer, Cham (2017). https://doi.org/10.1007/978-3-319-59870-3_17

25. Meng, W., Wang, Y., Wong, D.S., Wen, S., Xiang, Y.: TouchWB: touch behavioral user authentication based on web browsing on smartphones. J. Netw. Comput. Appl. **117**, 1–9 (2018)

26. Nelson, D.L., Reed, V.S., Walling, J.R.: Pictorial superiority effect. J. Exp. Psychol.: Hum. Learn. Mem. **2**(5), 523–528 (1976)

27. Passfaces. http://www.realuser.com/

28. Shepard, R.N.: Recognition memory for words, sentences, and pictures. J. Verbal Learn. Verbal Behav. **6**(1), 156–163 (1967)

29. Spitzer, J., Singh, C., Schweitzer, D.: A security class project in graphical passwords. J. Comput. Sci. Coll. **26**(2), 7–13 (2010)

30. Shin, J., Kancharlapalli, S., Farcasin, M., Chan-Tin, E.: SmartPass: a smarter geolocation-based authentication scheme. Secur. Commun. Netw. **8**, 3927–3938 (2015)

31. Shabtai, A., Fledel, Y., Kanonov, U., Elovici, Y., Dolev, S., Glezer, C.: Google Android: a comprehensive security assessment. IEEE Secur. Priv. **8**(2), 35–44 (2010)

32. Suo, X., Zhu, Y., Owen, G.S.: Graphical passwords: a survey. In: Proceedings of the 21st Annual Computer Security Applications Conference, ACSAC, pp. 463–472. IEEE Computer Society, USA (2005)

33. Sun, H., Chen, Y., Fang, C., Chang, S.: PassMap: a map based graphical-password authentication system. In: Proceedings of ASIACCS, pp. 99–100 (2012)

34. Tao, H., Adams, C.: Pass-Go: a proposal to improve the usability of graphical passwords. Int. J. Netw. Secur. **2**(7), 273–292 (2008)

35. Thorpe, J., MacRae, B., Salehi-Abari, A.: Usability and security evaluation of GeoPass: a geographic location-password scheme. In: Proceedings of the 9th Symposium on Usable Privacy and Security, SOUPS, pp. 1–14 (2013)

36. Van Thanh, D.: Security issues in mobile eCommerce. In: Proceedings of the 11th International Workshop on Database and Expert Systems Applications, DEXA, pp. 412–425. IEEE, USA (2000)

37. Wiedenbeck, S., Waters, J., Birget, J.-C., Brodskiy, A., Memon, N.: PassPoints: design and longitudinal evaluation of a graphical password system. Int. J. Hum.-Comput. Stud. **63**(1–2), 102–127 (2005)
38. Weir, M., Aggarwal, S., Collins, M., Stern, H.: Testing metrics for password creation policies by attacking large sets of revealed passwords. In: Proceedings of CCS, pp. 162–175 (2010)
39. Yan, J., Blackwell, A., Anderson, R., Grant, A.: Password memorability and security: empirical results. IEEE Secur. Priv. **2**, 25–31 (2004)
40. Yu, X., Wang, Z., Li, Y., Li, L., Zhu, W.T., Song, L.: EvoPass: evolvable graphical password against shoulder-surfing attacks. Comput. Secur. **70**, 179–198 (2017)

Seeing Is Believing: Authenticating Users with What They See and Remember

Wayne Chiu[1] , Kuo-Hui Yeh[1(✉)] , and Akihito Nakamura[2]

[1] National Dong Hwa University, Hualien 97401, Taiwan
{410235014,khyeh}@gms.ndhu.edu.tw
[2] The University of Aizu, Aizuwakamatsu, Fukushima 965-8580, Japan
nakamura@u-aizu.ac.jp

Abstract. Brainwaves, as external signals of a functioning brain, provide a possible glimpse into how we think and react. However, seen another way, we could reasonably expect that a given action or event could be linked back to its corresponding brainwave reaction. Recently, commercial products in the form of commercial brainwave headsets have flooded into the market, opening up the possibility of exploiting brainwaves for various purposes and making this more feasible. In this paper, we build an authentication system based on brainwave reactions to a chain of events. We use a commercially available brainwave headset to collect brainwave data of participants for use in the proposed authentication system. After the brainwave data collection process, we apply a machine learning-based approach to extract features from brainwaves to serve as authentication tokens in the system and to support the authentication system itself.

Keywords: Authentication · Brainwave · Wearable · Machine learning

1 Introduction

IoT stands for the Internet of Things—a concept that has become one of the most oft-mentioned topics in the computer domain. The prospect of an IoT-based economic system has brought small, embeddable devices with Internet connectivity and data collection capabilities to the market and they are becoming increasingly commonplace in our daily life. These devices are mostly resource-limited, and in many cases, the devices are implemented with microcontrollers and equipped with little usable memory. Modern society is both fast-paced and competitive, and most companies focus more on device functionality than on the underlying security framework and mechanism. This leaves the door open to security breaches as vulnerabilities are maliciously exploited.

The work was supported in part by the Academia Sinica, in part by the Taiwan Information Security Center, and in part by the Ministry of Science and Technology, Taiwan under Grants MOST 105-2221-E-259-014-MY3, MOST 105-2221-E-011-070-MY3, MOST 105-2923-E-182-001-MY3, and MOST 106-3114-E-011-003.

© Springer Nature Switzerland AG 2018
C. Su and H. Kikuchi (Eds.): ISPEC 2018, LNCS 11125, pp. 391–403, 2018.
https://doi.org/10.1007/978-3-319-99807-7_24

Most IoT devices lack a fully functional user interaction interface, and this limitation makes the implementation of traditional authentication schemes in the IoT impractical. In traditional authentication schemes, a user is authenticated at the very moment of login, which is not suitable for most IoT devices, as they operate continuously for a long time following authentication. The entire duration of a device's operation, from the moment of login onward, should be guaranteed and protected. Continuous authentication is the best candidate for guaranteeing the whole session, meaning authentication and auditing in the IoT network must be ongoing at every moment.

Some implementations of continuous authentication for the IoT and smart devices have been developed, such as Google SmartLock and Microsoft Dynamic Lock. Google SmartLock is a combination of environmental-based, behavior-based, and biometric-based Continuous authentication schemes [1], while Microsoft Dynamic Lock is environmental-based [2]. In this research, we focus on the Biometric-based continuous authentication model. In this early stage of biometric-based continuous authentication, the model is generally considered impractical because of the costly and non-portable apparatus required [6]. The lack of computing power is another unsolvable situation. With the advancement of information technology, however, the infrastructure has become more functional and practical for continuous authentication, and chipsets are larger-sized, more energy efficient, and offer better performance than before. Wearables operate with biometric sensors and a variety of communicating interfaces are attainable. Biometric information can be easily collected and exchanged. For these reasons, biometric-based continuous authentication has become practical.

1.1 Why Brainwaves?

The brain, as the most sophisticated organ, serves as the command center of the human body. Basically, it might be said to be the origin of every action we take. Brainwaves are the external signals of a functioning brain, and thus provide a glimpse into what we are thinking and doing [7]. A good example is that, when an individual closes their eyes, we can observe a slightly shivering alpha wave embedded in the brainwaves [3]. This sparks our curiosity and leads us to the assumption that any action or recognition will have a distinct type of brainwave waveform. Recently, more brainwave wearable sensing devices have entered the market, lower the entry level barrier to collecting brainwave data and performing research on brainwaves. As this trend continues, further such usage of brainwave data can be anticipated.

1.2 Recognition Pattern as Your Token

Every person has his/her own experiences navigating the environment he/she lives in or has contact with. A simple example of this can be found in talking with many people about the same topic. Although there might be some similarities between individuals, most of the time, we can expect that answers will vary along a continuum being from totally different to being slightly different. If we tried to discuss a series of topics with many people, the possibility of any two individuals having exactly the same point of view about all of them is nearly impossible. The reactions to different things create a unique identity for each individual, much the same as a password. A password 5 characters long with only lower case letters allowed can result in 26^5 combinations of possible passwords, which can be contrasted with a chain of events 5 events long where the brainwave reaction to each is X^5, where X is the total number of possible reactions. We want to evaluate the possibility of extracting unique tokens of each individual from their brainwave data while they are facing a chain of events.

2 The Proposed Method

In this research, we focus mainly on the brainwaves corresponding to reactions between human memories and events that they have encountered, and we use a classifier to extract tokens of each individual from their brainwaves. In this way, we use the extracted tokens to create a brainwave-based authentication system. In the previous section, we mentioned that every individual has his/her own experiences of the environment. Although it is a dauntingly complex task to describe or quantize personal experience, there still is a possible way to do it. A person might have numerous divergent reactions or feelings toward different events. Although the reactions or feelings can vary, they still can be roughly categorized as "Familiar", "Deja-vu" and "Unfamiliar" [4]. If we collect images that include familiar ones to two individuals, respectively and mix them with other unrelated images, we expect the two individuals' reactions would be as shown in Table 1.

Table 1. The recognition table of two individuals. A stands for images that P1 is familiar with, while B stands for images that P2 is familiar with. C stands for Unrelated images for both.

Ind.\img.	A1	A2	B1	B2	C1	C2
P1	Familiar	Familiar	Unfamiliar	Familiar	Deja-vu	Unfamiliar
P2	Unfamiliar	Deja-vu	Familiar	Familiar	Unfamiliar	Deja-vu

If the above assumption is correct, we can expect that everyone has his/her own distinct familiarity pattern regarding a chain of images, based on his/her recognition pattern toward the environment. The more images we provide, the lower the probability of two individuals sharing the same familiarity pattern.

What can we expect from the familiarity patterns of individuals? Brainwaves are signals; external manifestations of an active brain and how it is functioning. Any action originating in the human brain has a corresponding brainwave from the very portion of the brain that is in charge of the specific action being signaled. For example, when you close your eyes, we can observe a slightly shivering alpha wave embedded in the brainwave [1]. Based on this result, we extended the theory to encompass familiarity. Specifically, we posit that an individual's familiarity with images might have different corresponding brainwave. Based on the assumptions we have outlined, we designed our experiment as shown in Fig. 1.

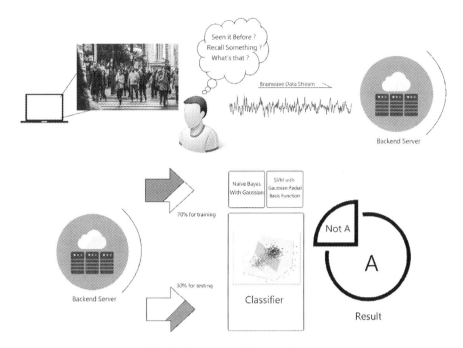

Fig. 1. Overview of the experiment.

For the experiment, we prepared three different sets of images for the participants. The first set are images that participants are respectively familiar with. To collect these images, we asked each participant to provide their own familiar image set. The researchers did not collect this set of images by ourselves since we could not know what each participant was familiar with. We also stipulated to participants that the images they provided to us should not be exchanged with or otherwise sent to other participants. These image sets were labeled with a code that corresponded with each participant. The second set of images is what we call the deja-vu images. We collected deja-vu images by randomly taking photos either on campus or in the immediate area around campus. We collected the images in this way since all participants attend school at the same campus. The last set of images are the unfamiliar ones. We collected these by randomly searching for images of unpopular topics on the Internet, since there is a chance images of more popular topics might have already been seen by some of the participants.

With all the image sets collected, we scheduled times for the participants to take part in the experiment. The participants were asked to wear the brainwave headset (BR8) as they observed a series of images on the computer screen (See Fig. 2). While the images were displayed on the screen, the computer sent the brainwave data it received to the backend server for further analysis. The program used to display the images does not require any interaction with participants, and all unnecessary elements on screen (i.e. icons, notifications) were turned off or eliminated, in order to lower the possible extraneous influences (See Fig. 3). Furthermore, to be sure no participants saw the images beforehand, participants who were waiting for their turn to do the experiment were asked to wait in a different room from participants who were engaged in doing the experiment. Moreover, it was ensured that participants who finished the experiment left without returning to the waiting room.

Fig. 2. Actual view of experimental set-up

Fig. 3. Actual view of experimental setting

After the experiment, data was retrieved from the backend server for analysis. We took 70% of the data to train the classification model and left 30% of the data to test the trained data model. The following hardware and software were used to construct the experimental environment. (See Table 2 for software, Table 3 for hardware.)

Table 2. Software used for the experiment

Item	Illustration
Microsoft Windows 10	Computer operating system
Oracle Java 8	Programming language and executing environment of the interface for participants
libSVM	SVM classifier
nb_classify	Naïve Bayes classifier
BRI	Brainwave signal data collecting program for BR8
Eltima virtual serial Port	Data communication interface for BRI software and Java platform

Table 3. Hardware used for the experiment

Item	Illustration
Asus MD570 PC	Computer used for the experiment
BR8	Brainwave headset

We designed the participant interface to display images in the following pattern:

1. Calm down blank screen (15 s of blank screen for participants to calm down)
2. 5 Unfamiliar images (Each image displayed for 3 s with a 3 s blank screen gap between images)
3. 5 Deja-vu images (Same display pattern as previous)
4. 5 Familiar images (Same display pattern as previous).

Between every change of the displayed image, the program sends a signal to the BRI program. The BRI program, at the same time, makes a marker every time the participant interface signals.

The 15 s of calm down time at the start is not only vital for ensuring participants have stable brainwaves, but is also necessary for the BR8 headset itself. Based on our observation, the headset also needs time to adapt. We provide brainwave graphs corresponding to two different time intervals for a person who is doing nothing but sitting still for comparison. In the graphs of the first 15 s (See Fig. 4), we observe a huge spike, which is completely out of character compared with the graphs from 15 to 30 s (See Fig. 5).

We carefully considered the time duration for displaying the images to ensure both enough time to measure brainwave reaction and enough time for the participant to remain clear-headed in order to prevent fatigue. A single round of the experiment took

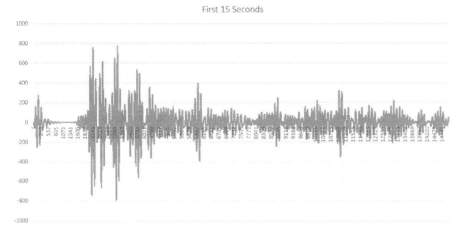

Fig. 4. Graph of first 15 s

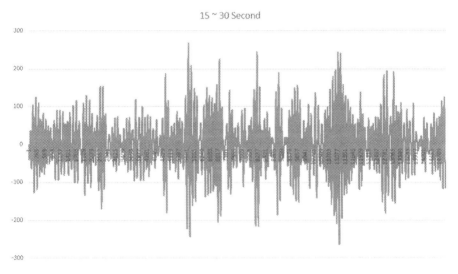

Fig. 5. Graph of 15 to 30 s

around 2 min, with 15 images displayed. The hardware capability of the BR8 head-set allows it to sample brainwave signals at 1000 Hz. Therefore 15 images with a duration of 3 s each can create 45000 records of brainwave data.

BRI saves the brainwave data in CSV format with event markers placed at the end of the specific data records. These markers can assist us to pull brainwave data that corresponds only to the duration an image was displayed. We illustrate this in Fig. 6.

After the brainwave data collection process, we proceeded to the data preprocessing process. The brain has many different sections, each with different functionality. In this research, we focused on familiarity as an authentication token. To this end, the

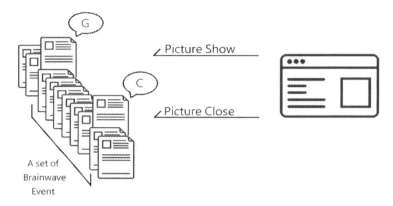

Fig. 6. Illustration of how markers assist in pulling a brainwave event data set

brainwaves originating from the parietal lobe are most likely target data for us to analyze. If we take a look at the sensor placement of the BR8 headset, we can pinpoint brainwave data received by sensor Pz as the most interesting to us (See Fig. 7) since this sensor is closest to the parietal lobe.

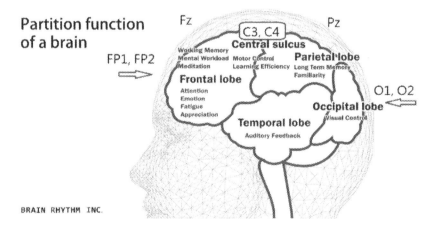

Fig. 7. The sensor's locations and their corresponding sections of the brain [5]

Currently commercialized brainwave headsets are all non-invasive, relying on sensors being kept properly in contact to the participant's skin. Environmental issues can therefore influence the data the sensors obtain. For example, the skin condition of the participant (i.e. conductivity) or other electronic appliances in the immediate area (e.g. a high-power-consumption apparatus) can interfere with the headset's detection of brainwave signal data. Although the BRI software provides a notch filter to filter out the 50 Hz/60 Hz noise caused by the alternating current running through the power cable, however, this is not enough. We applied Eq. (1) to all the data in order to partially solve the issue and keep the behavior data. For comparison, we provide a graph of brainwave data without applying Eq. (1) alongside a graph of brainwave data with Eq. (1) applied below (See Figs. 8 and 9).

$$\Delta R_i = R_i - R_{i-1} \tag{1}$$

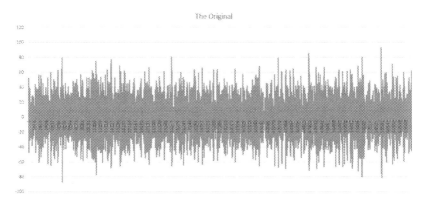

Fig. 8. Graph of brainwave without applying Eq. (1)

Fig. 9. Graph of brainwave with Eq. (1) applied

After the data preprocessing process was completed, we started to filter out the similarities between profiles. We separated each participant's brainwave data into data for model training and data for model testing, according to a ratio of 7:3. Then we appended all the data for model training from each participant to a single file and trained it into another model for similarity removal. We then likewise fed each participant's data to be used for model training into the model for similarity removal. This ensured any correctly classified records in the data would be kept, while wrongly classified data would be discarded. If the amount of any participant's data to be used for model training reached 30%, the whole data set of that particular participant would be eliminated and recollected. After removal of similarities, we trained the cleaned-up model training data into the model. We tested our model with the following procedure:

1. Choose a participant's data as a target.
2. Set the SVM label other participants' data into the target participant in order to impersonate the target, in order to evaluate whether or not the classifier could correctly classify the testing data as others but not the target participant.
3. Feed the testing data, respectively, into the trained model.

In brief, we expected the results illustrated in Table 4.

Table 4. Brief test procedure illustration and expected result

Test set	Real label	Faking as	Expected result
1	A	A	Is A
2	B	A	Not A
3	C	A	Not A

In this research, 20 participants took part in the experiment. That means there were 400 test cases.

Similarity removal improved the results significantly. For comparison, we provide both the results of the model data without similarities removed (Table 5) and the results of the model data with similarities removal (Table 6) below.

Table 5. Results without similarities removed

Profile	Err. count	Profile	Err. count	Profile	Err. count
CBH	1	HJK	2	SUT	1
CTY	3	HKU	3	TAC	1
CYX	1	HSY	1	WJH	3
DCZ	3	HYL	3	XCY	3
DYH	3	LBY	2	YXU	2
GJY	2	LRW	0	ZYT	2
HCH	3	LZZ	5		

In Table 5, we see that 50 out of 400 cases were wrongly classified. In contrast, with similarities removed, we see from Table 6 that only 15 out of 400 cases were wrongly classified.

Table 6. Result with similarities removed

Profile	Err. count	Profile	Err. count	Profile	Err. count
CBH	1	HJK	1	SUT	0
CTY	2	HKU	1	TAC	1
CYX	1	HSY	2	WJH	0
DCZ	0	HYL	0	XCY	0
DYH	0	LBY	3	YXU	1
GJY	0	LRW	0	ZYT	0
HCH	0	LZZ	2		

3   Experiment Results

We extracted the tokens from brainwaves successfully after one round of data pre-processing and two rounds of similarity removal. If we took 20 participants' brainwave data into the system, it was capable of reaching 100% accuracy, as shown in Table 7.

Table 7. The final results with the authentication system

Profile	Cor. count	Err. count	Profile	Cor. count	Err. count
CBH	20	0	HYL	20	0
CTY	20	0	LBY	20	0
CYX	20	0	LRW	20	0
DCZ	20	0	LZZ	20	0
DYH	20	0	SUT	20	0
GJY	20	0	TAC	20	0
HCH	20	0	WJH	20	0
HJK	20	0	XCY	20	0
HKU	20	0	YXU	20	0
HSY	20	0	ZYT	20	0

During data preprocessing, we observed an interesting phenomenon in the results of the SVM and Naïve Bayes classifiers. Without any kind of data preprocessing of brainwave data, SVM performed shockingly poorly in terms of classification, with 19 errors out of 20 in all cases. Basically, the trained model cannot tell which test data belongs to which participant's model, as shown in Table 8. The Naïve Bayes classifier, however, performed classification of brainwave data without any preprocessing at an acceptable rate of correctness, as shown in Table 9.

The SVM classifier achieved a result of 380 out of 400 cases wrongly classified, while the Naïve Bayes classifier achieved a result of 55 out of 400 cases wrongly classified. With a round of data preprocessing, however, SVM achieved a result similar to the result attained by the Naïve Bayes classifier when handling brainwave data without data preprocessing, with 47 out of 400 cases wrongly classified (See Table 9). The performance of SVM sharply increased, while that of Naïve Bayes slightly

Table 8. The result of SVM classification of brainwave data without data preprocessing.

Profile	Err. count	Profile	Err. count	Profile	Err. count
CBH	19	HJK	19	SUT	19
CTY	19	HKU	19	TAC	19
CYX	19	HSY	19	WJH	19
DCZ	19	HYL	19	XCY	19
DYH	19	LBY	19	YXU	19
GJY	19	LRW	19	ZYT	19
HCH	19	LZZ	19		

Table 9. The result of Naïve Bayes classification of brainwave data without data preprocessing

Profile	Err. count	Profile	Err. count	Profile	Err. count
CBH	0	HJK	2	SUT	4
CTY	1	HKU	3	TAC	1
CYX	1	HSY	2	WJH	6
DCZ	4	HYL	3	XCY	5
DYH	2	LBY	1	YXU	1
GJY	9	LRW	0	ZYT	4
HCH	2	LZZ	3		

increased, with 30 out of 400 cases wrongly classified (See Table 10). Without the similarity removal process, it is possible that the Naïve Bayes classifier performs better in terms of handling brainwave data.

Table 10. The result of SVM classification of the preprocessed brainwave data

Profile	Err. count	Profile	Err. count	Profile	Err. count
CBH	5	HJK	2	SUT	0
CTY	2	HKU	2	TAC	1
CYX	1	HSY	2	WJH	8
DCZ	1	HYL	1	XCY	4
DYH	5	LBY	2	YXU	3
GJY	2	LRW	1	ZYT	2
HCH	0	LZZ	3		

4   Conclusion

In this research, we explore the link between experienced events and brainwave reaction in a specific area of the brain. Understanding the link between the encountered event and the area of the brain most likely to react to it, we can limit our focus to brainwave data from this specific part of the brain, eliminating potential unwanted data tuples in both the model and test data. Using a wearable headset with brainwave retrieval functionality built in and machine-learning classifiers, we successfully retrieved tokens from brainwave data and built an authentication system based on the tokens. The data pre-processing step affects the classification results of the SVM classifier dramatically. Without the pre-processing, the SVM classifier cannot correctly classify the data. The Naïve Bayes classifier, on the other hand, does a better job of handling raw brainwave data. After a similarity removal process, the results provided by the SVM classifier becomes more acceptable. In the future, linking events and reactions in specific sections of the brain can provide us with a better view of the small parameters hidden in brainwaves. Uncovering those links could allow us to exploit a wider range of possible uses of brainwaves.

References

1. Google SmartLock. https://get.google.com/smartlock/. Accessed 12 Apr 2018
2. How to take advantage of the Dynamic Lock feature in Windows 10. https://www.techrepublic.com/article/how-to-take-advantage-of-.the-dynamic-lock-feature-in-windows-10/. Accessed 12 Apr 2018
3. Eye Closed Brainwave Dataset. http://www.bri.com.tw/data/sample_data/BR8_sample%20data_eyeclosed20141205.rar. Accessed 12 Apr 2018
4. Zhou, L.: You think, therefore you are: transparent authentication system with brainwave-oriented bio-features for IoT networks. IEEE Trans. Emerg. Top. Comput. (Early Access)
5. Brain Partition. http://www.bri.com.tw/. Accessed 12 Apr 2018
6. Yeh, K.H.: I walk, therefore i am: continuous user authentication with plantar biometrics. IEEE Commun. Mag. **56**, 150–157 (2018)
7. Matsuyama, Y.: Brain signal's low-frequency fits the continuous authentication. Neurocomputing **164**, 137–143 (2015)

Side-Channel Attacks

T_SM: Elliptic Curve Scalar Multiplication Algorithm Secure Against Single-Trace Attacks

Bo-Yeon Sim[1], Kyu Young Choi[2], Dukjae Moon[2], Hyo Jin Yoon[2],
Jihoon Cho[2], and Dong-Guk Han[1(✉)]

[1] Department of Mathematics, Kookmin University, Seoul, South Korea
{qjdusls,christa}@kookmin.ac.kr
[2] Security Research Team, Samsung SDS, Inc., Seoul, South Korea
{ky12.choi,dukjae.moon,hj1230.yoon,jihoon1.cho}@samsung.com

Abstract. At present, Elliptic Curve Digital Signature Algorithm (ECD-SA) is extensively used because its implementation can be achieved more efficiently with the same security level compared to RSA and Digital Signature Algorithm (DSA). In particular, blockchain and Fast IDentity Online (FIDO), which are attracting attention as key infrastructure technologies to lead the fourth industrial revolution, use ECDSA. However, scalar multiplication, which is the main operation of ECDSA, has been reported to be vulnerable to side-channel attacks that use only a single-trace. Notably, there is no perfectly secure countermeasure against Collision Attack (CA), which is the main form of attack using a single-trace. As the attacks become more and more sophisticated and powerful, such as CA, taking countermeasures against them is required. Thus, in this paper, we propose a new scalar multiplication algorithm called the T_SM method. It is secure against Simple Power Analysis (SPA) and Key Bit-dependent Attack (KBA). In particular, the T_SM method can fully cope with CA. To the best of our knowledge, the T_SM method is the first countermeasure against SPA, CA, and KBA. Although it requires memory for pre-computation tables, it has a computational advantage when we apply it to cryptosystems, such as ECDSA, which use ordinary scalar multiplication based on a fixed point P and random scalar k. The main operation consists of the smallest number of operations compared with existing scalar multiplication algorithms in which P is fixed.

Keywords: ECC · Scalar multiplication · Side-channel attacks
Single-trace attacks · Countermeasures

1 Introduction

A digital signature is a mathematical scheme to guarantee the authenticity of digital messages or documents. This scheme provides authentication, non-repudiation, and content integrity. Three types of algorithms are used for this

© Springer Nature Switzerland AG 2018
C. Su and H. Kikuchi (Eds.): ISPEC 2018, LNCS 11125, pp. 407–423, 2018.
https://doi.org/10.1007/978-3-319-99807-7_25

signature: RSA [32], Digital Signature Algorithm (DSA) [8] and Elliptic Curve DSA (ECDSA) [21,25]. RSA and DSA have been used widely in various applications, such as online shopping, banking, and billing, as well as VPN and anti-cloning and Firmware Over the Air (FOTA) applications.

However, with changing security and performance requirements nowadays, more mobile devices and web services are pointing toward the need for smaller and faster signatures. A small key size and a more efficient implementation with the same security level compared to the RSA and DSA make the ECDSA scheme a viable alternative.

This scheme has been used in web-based TLS, various browsers and OSs (e.g., Firefox, Safari, IE, Chrome, Opera, Android, iOS, and Blackberry), and crypto libraries (e.g., OpenSSL, Boring SSL, GnuTLS, Bouncy Castle, and Botan). In particular, there are many popular ECDSA implementations related to the blockchain and Fast IDentity Online (FIDO) running on various mobile devices [18,24]. However, many key-extraction side-channel attacks (SCAs) against ECDSA implementation on small devices (e.g., smartcards, RFID tags, FPGA, and microcontrollers), mobile devices, and PCs have been presented from the end of 1990 [1,6,10,19,31].

SCAs using physical vulnerabilities that occur when algorithms are performed on an embedded system were primally presented by Kocher in 1996 [22]. Subsequently, various attacks against elliptic curve cryptography (ECC) have been studied to verify physical vulnerabilities. In particular, SCAs that must be considered for ECDSA, which uses a fixed point P and a random scalar k, are Simple Power Analysis (SPA) [23], Collision Attack (CA) [2,4,5,9,12–15,29,30,33–35,37], and Key Bit-dependent Attack (KBA) [36].

Various countermeasures against SPA have been proposed, but there is no countermeasure which is perfectly secure against CA. The proposed countermeasures to increase CA complexity have a significant performance penalty, and these measures cannot perfectly counteract CA [16]. KBA, which has been recently proposed at [36], is a potent attack because it can defeat any combination of existing countermeasures. It does not require sophisticated pre-processing to eliminate noise. Besides, it is possible to recover a secret scalar using a single-trace in hardware and software implementation with respectively success rate at 100% and 96.13%.

ECDSA is used in various application environments to ensure its safety, and following the advent of the fourth industrial revolution and increasing attention toward the blockchain and FIDO, the demand for a secure scalar multiplication algorithm against single-trace attacks has been growing.

Our Contributions. In this paper, we propose a secure scalar multiplication algorithm against single-trace attacks; this algorithm is called T_SM (Sequence Subset-based Scalar Multiplication) method. If some memory is available and the point P is fixed like ECDSA, the proposed algorithm can be accelerated by pre-computing some data that depend on P. Moreover, to the best of our knowledge, the T_SM method is the first countermeasure of elliptic curve scalar multiplication algorithm to secure against all SPA, CA, and KBA, as shown in Table 1.

There was no theoretically perfect secure algorithm against CA. However, our newest T_SM method can fully cope with CA, since it uses pre-computation tables which consist of distinct random values. Besides, the T_SM method does not scan the secret scalar bit by bit and does not base its calculation on the scanned bit value. These are the main differences between our method and the other proposed countermeasures. These differences also ensure safety against KBA as well as SPA.

Table 1. Security evaluation

Algorithm	SPA	CA	KBA
Montgomery Ladder [17]	Secure	Insecure	Insecure
Möller window method [26]	Secure	Insecure	Insecure
width-w NAF method [28]	Secure	Insecure	Insecure
mLSB-set comb method [7]	Secure	Insecure	Insecure
Our T_SM method	Secure	Secure	Secure

*See details in Table 3 in Sect. 4

The remainder of this paper is organized as follows. In Sect. 2, we briefly describe single-trace attacks on ECC. In Sect. 3, we describe our proposed algorithm, and we show security and performance evaluation in Sect. 4. Conclusions are presented in Sect. 5.

2 Preliminaries

In this section, we describe ECC that we discuss in this paper. Then, we explain what single-trace attacks are. Prior to this, we define notations which are used in this paper in Table 2.

2.1 Elliptic Curve Cryptography

Scalar multiplication, which is the main operation of ECC, is supposed to be implemented securely against SCA. Since the most efficient and primary implementation method is Algorithm 1, countermeasures that are based on modifications of this algorithm have been proposed. Thus, until now, the proposed scalar multiplication algorithms have comprised iterative operations such as Algorithm 1, which scans the secret scalar bit by bit and whose calculations are based on the scanned bit value.

Nowadays, ECDSA, which is shown in Algorithm 2, is used in various application environments such as web-based TLS, various browsers and OSs, and crypto libraries. In particular, ECDSA implementations related to blockchain and FIDO running on various mobile devices are very popular. However, scalar multiplication is vulnerable to SCA, so we need to consider countermeasures. In particular, in environments in which the secret scalar changes randomly every execution, such as ECDSA, we must consider security against single-trace attacks.

Table 2. Notations

Notation	Description
q	The field order
$\mathbb{F}_q$	The finite field of order q
$E(\mathbb{F}_q)$	The elliptic curve over $\mathbb{F}_q$
FR	The field representation used for the elements of $\mathbb{F}_q$
S	The seed selected to randomly generate the coefficients of $E(\mathbb{F}_q)$
a, b	The coefficients that define the equation of $E(\mathbb{F}_q)$
P	The base point $(x_P, y_P) \in E(\mathbb{F}_q)$ and $x_P, y_P \in \mathbb{F}_q$
q_t	The order of the base point P
h	The cofactor $h = \#E(\mathbb{F}_q)/n$
∞	The point at infinity
$\mathcal{H}$	A hash function
k	A λ-bit secret scalar $k = (k_{\lambda-1}, k_{\lambda-2}, \cdots, k_0)_2$
k_i	An i-th bit of secret scalar k where $0 \leq i \leq \lambda - 1$
$\in_R (\leftarrow_R)$	random selection
$\{0,1\}^\lambda$	A set of λ-bit strings

Algorithm 1. Scalar Multiplication : Left to Right Binary Method

Input : $P = (x, y)$ a point on $E(\mathbb{F}_q)$, a λ-bit scalar $k = (k_{\lambda-1}, k_{\lambda-2}, \cdots, k_0)_2$
Output : $Q = k \cdot P$

1: $Q \leftarrow \infty$
2: **for** $i = \lambda - 1$ down to 0 **do**
3:    $Q \leftarrow 2Q$
4:    **if** $k_i = 1$ **then**
5:       $Q \leftarrow Q + P$
6:    **end if**
7: **end for**
8: **Return** Q

Algorithm 2. ECDSA signature generation [11]

Input : Domain parameter $D = (q, FR, S, a, b, P, q_t, h)$, secret key d, message m
Output : Signature (r, s)

1: Compute random integer k with $0 < k < q_t$
2: Compute $k \cdot P = (x_R, y_R)$
3: Compute $r = x_R \bmod q_t$; If $r = 0$ then go to step 1
4: Compute $k' = k^{-1} \bmod q_t$
5: Compute $h = \mathcal{H}(m)$
6: Compute $s = k'(h + dr) \bmod q_t$. If $s = 0$ then go to step 1
7: Signature of m is (r, s)

2.2   Single-Trace Attacks on Scalar Multiplication

Our proposed scalar multiplication algorithm is intended for application in environments in which the secret scalar changes randomly with every execution, as seen in the execution of ECDSA. Thus, we need not consider Differential Power Analysis (DPA) [23] as a risk. Therefore, in this section, we describe single-trace attacks, which are differentiated into SPA, CA, and KBA.

Simple Power Analysis exploits the patterns of secret scalar bit-dependent conditional branches from a single-trace [23]. For instance, Algorithm 1 can be broken by distinguishing the differences between point doubling and point addition operations, as shown in Fig. 1. Mainly, to extract the secret scalar, these attacks are based on a vulnerability in which the algorithm behaves irregularly according to the secret scalar bit k_i. That is, there is an irregularity that a point doubling operation always occurs, but a point addition operation only occurs when the value of k_i is one.

Theorem 1. *If the point doubling operation is different from the point addition operation and an algorithm behaves irregularly according to the secret scalar bit k_i, then the algorithm is vulnerable to SPA.*

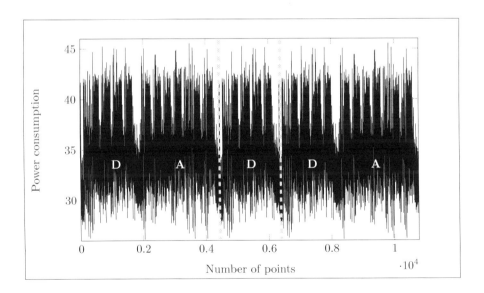

Fig. 1. Partial power trace of scalar multiplication

Algorithm 3. Scalar Multiplication : Doubling and Addition Always [3]

Input : $P = (x, y)$ a point on $E(\mathbb{F}_q)$, a λ-bit scalar $k = (k_{\lambda-1}, k_{\lambda-2}, \cdots, k_0)_2$
Output : $Q_0 = k \cdot P$

1: $Q_0 \leftarrow \infty,\ Q_1 \leftarrow \infty$
2: **for** $i = \lambda - 1$ down to 0 **do**
3:   $Q_0 \leftarrow 2Q_0$
4:   $Q_{1-k_i} \leftarrow Q_0 + P$
5: **end for**
6: **Return** Q_0

Collision Attack is a kind of higher-order DPA based on the interrelationships between data. It is also known as a horizontal attack which can extract secret scalar bits from a single-trace [37]. For example, collision attack on Algorithm 3, when the $k_i = 0$, collision of input data $(k_{\lambda-1}, k_{\lambda-2}, \cdots, k_{i+1}, 0)_2 \cdot P$ occurs between the point addition operation of i iteration and the point doubling operation of $(i - 1)$ iteration as follows:

- point doubling of i iteration $= 2((k_{\lambda-1}, k_{\lambda-2}, \cdots, k_{i+1})_2 \cdot P)$

- point addition of i iteration $= (k_{\lambda-1}, k_{\lambda-2}, \cdots, k_{i+1}, 0)_2 \cdot P + P$

- point doubling of $(i-1)$ iteration $= \begin{cases} 2((k_{\lambda-1}, k_{\lambda-2}, \cdots, k_{i+1}, 0)_2 \cdot P), \text{ if } k_i = 0 \\ 2((k_{\lambda-1}, k_{\lambda-2}, \cdots, k_{i+1}, 1)_2 \cdot P), \text{ if } k_i = 1 \end{cases}$

but when $k_i = 1$, input data collision does not occur. Thus, depending on the occurrence of the collision, the secret scalar bits can be extracted. We can classify CA into five types, which are experimentally proven, as follows.

Theorem 2. *If information collision is determined according to the secret scalar bit k_i, then the algorithm is vulnerable to CA.*

(i) *When the collision of input data of two same operations is determined according to the secret scalar bit k_i [9, 12, 15, 35, 37].*
(ii) *When the collision of input data of two different operations is determined according to the secret scalar bit k_i [12].*
(iii) *When the collision of two operations, using the same input data, is determined according to the secret scalar bit k_i [15].*
(iv) *When the use of register for data saving (or loading) is determined according to the secret scalar bit k_i [13, 14, 29, 30, 33].*
(v) *When the collision between saved and loaded data, at the data saving and loading step, is determined according to the secret scalar bit k_i [12].*

Additionally, for algorithms with operations that refer to a pre-computation table, there exists a vulnerability to CA when repeating the reference to the same position of the table. This vulnerability comes about because, if the algorithm refers to the same position, register and input data value can collide when loading data from the pre-computation table [20, 27].

Theorem 3. *If the algorithm repeats the reference to the same position of the pre-computation table, then the algorithm is vulnerable to CA.*

Key Bit-Dependent Attack uses the leakage which occurs in a secret scalar bit check phase [36]. This phase involves extracting the scalar bit value from an λ-bit scalar string $k = (k_{\lambda-1}, k_{\lambda-2}, \cdots, k_0)_2$ and storing this value in a k_i variable. For example, at the beginning of each iteration of Algorithm 1, that is, before starting Step 3, there is a phase which involves checking of the secret scalar bit k_i value to operate according to the k_i value. This phase exists in various countermeasures because most of these measures are based on the structure of Algorithm 1. In this phase, the secret scalar bits are directly loaded, thus affecting power consumption, as shown in Fig. 2.

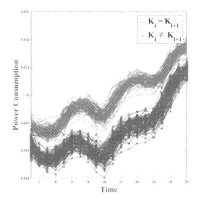
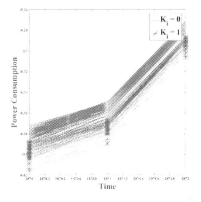

(a) Classification according to hamming distance between k_i and k_{i+1} (in case of hardware implementation)

(b) Classification according to hamming weight of k_i (in case of software implementation)

Fig. 2. Key Bit-dependent attack [36]

For this reason, power consumption is related to the hamming distance between k_{i+1} and k_i $(0 \leq i < \lambda - 1)$ in hardware implementation. Thus, the attacker can extract the secret scalar by classifying power consumption traces into two groups: one group represents information $k_{i+1} = k_i$ and the other $k_{i+1} \neq k_i$. A large difference between the two groups appears at the beginning of each sub-trace since the scalar bit check operation is performed at the starting point of the iteration. Moreover, in [36], Sim et al. showed that it is possible to distinguish two groups through SPA precisely when the attacker classifies using this point, as shown in Fig. 2(a). That is to say, the success rate of extracting the secret scalar bits is 100%. A similar vulnerability also exists in software implementation, as shown in Fig. 2(b). In case of software implementation, the success rate is 96.13%. KBA does not require any knowledge about the input values; it only needs a single-trace.

Theorem 4. *If a secret scalar bit check phase to operate according to a secret scalar bit k_i value exists, then the algorithm is vulnerable to KBA.*

3   Our Proposal

In this section, we propose a Sequence Subset-based Scalar Multiplication algorithm, called T_SM, which is a new method to counteract the three kinds (SPA, CA, and KBA) of single-trace attacks. This method can be applied to cryptosystems, such as ECDSA, which use an ordinary scalar multiplication based on a fixed generator of a group.

3.1   T_SM Method

Our proposed method, T_SM, requires two pre-computation tables comprising the following values: one is a set of random scalar values, and the other is a set of scalar multiplication values of each random scalar value. The method consists of the following two algorithms: Setup and Calculation.

Setup(λ, P). Given a security parameter $\lambda \in \mathbb{Z}^+$ and an (additional) group element P, the setup algorithm runs as follows:
1. Pick two integers $m, n \in \mathbb{Z}^+$ such that $mn = \lambda$. Choose $2^m \times n$ distinct random scalar values $x_{(i,j)} \in_R \{0,1\}^\lambda$ where $0 \le i < 2^m$ and $1 \le j \le n$.
2. Construct a table $\mathcal{T}_s$ with 2^m rows and n columns. Set $x_{(i,j)}$ to be the (i,j)-entry of $\mathcal{T}_s$.
3. Construct 2^m by n table $\mathcal{T}_P$ corresponding to the table $\mathcal{T}_s$. Compute $Q_{(i,j)} = x_{(i,j)} \cdot P$ and set $Q_{(i,j)}$ to be the (i,j)-entry of $\mathcal{T}_P$. (To easily explain of our calculation algorithm, we set the row index starts at 0 and the column is 1.)
4. Output two tables $\mathcal{T}_s$ and $\mathcal{T}_P$ (see Algorithm 4).

Algorithm 4. Setup

Input : a security parameter $\lambda \in \mathbb{Z}^+$, an additional group element $P \in E$
Output : $m, n, \mathcal{T}_s, \mathcal{T}_P$

1: Pick two integers $m, n \in \mathbb{Z}^+$ $(m \times n = \lambda)$
2: **for** $i := 0$ up to $2^m - 1$ **do**
3:     **for** $j := 1$ up to n **do**
4:         $x_{(i,j)} \leftarrow_R \{0,1\}^\lambda$
5:         $Q_{(i,j)} \leftarrow x_{(i,j)} \cdot P$
6:     **end for**
7: **end for**
8: **Return** $m, n, \mathcal{T}_s = \{x_{(i,j)}\}, \mathcal{T}_P = \{Q_{(i,j)}\}$

Algorithm 5. Calculation

Input : a security parameter $\lambda \in \mathbb{Z}^+$, m, n, q_t, pre-computation tables $\mathcal{T}_s$ and $\mathcal{T}_P$
Output : k, $Q = k \cdot P$

1: Choose a random string $r \in_R \{0,1\}^\lambda$
2: $k \leftarrow 0$, $Q \leftarrow \infty$
3: $mask \leftarrow m$-bit string with 1's for all bits
4: **for** $j := n$ down to 1 **do**
5:     $t_j \leftarrow (r \gg (\lambda - m \times j))$ & $mask$
6:     $k \leftarrow k + x_{(t_j,j)}$
7:     $Q \leftarrow Q + Q_{(t_j,j)}$
8: **end for**
9: $k \leftarrow k \bmod q_t$
10: **Return** k, Q

Calculation$(\lambda, m, n, q_t, \mathcal{T}_s, \mathcal{T}_P)$. To calculate scalar multiplication, the algorithm does the following:

1. Choose a random string $r \in_R \{0,1\}^\lambda$.
2. Split the random string r into m-bit substring blocks as $r = (r_{\lambda-1}, r_{\lambda-2}, \cdots, r_0)_2 = t_1||t_2||\cdots||t_n$ where $t_j = (r_{\lambda-m(j-1)-1}, \cdots, r_{\lambda-mj})_2$ is an m-bit substring, i.e., the j-th block of r.
3. For each substring t_j where $1 \leq j \leq n$, pick the (t_j, j)-th entries $x_{(t_j,j)}$ and $Q_{(t_j,j)}$ from the tables $\mathcal{T}_s$ and $\mathcal{T}_P$, respectively.
4. Generate a scalar k and compute its scalar (point) multiplication $k \cdot P$ to be

$$k = \sum_{j=1}^n x_{(t_j,j)} \bmod q_t, \quad k \cdot P = \sum_{j=1}^n Q_{(t_j,j)}$$

   where q_t is the order of the group.
5. Output the two values k and $k \cdot P$ (see Algorithm 5).

Note that the proposed method can be used to compute modular exponentiation $g^k \bmod N$ for secret exponent k by multiplying $\{Q_{(t_j,j)}\} = \{g^{x_{(t_j,j)}}\}$ values, where N is the modulus, $g \in \mathbb{Z}^+$ $(0 < g < N)$, and $k = \sum_{j=1}^n x_{(t_j,j)} \bmod N$. The value k in our method is unpredictable. Therefore, the method does not compute scalar multiplication for a given value k.

3.2   Example

In this section, we describe the T_SM method with $\lambda = 256$, $m = 8$, and $n = 32$ (see Fig. 3).

Setup$(256, P)$. Choose $2^8 \times 32$ distinct random scalar values $x_{(i,j)} \in_R \{0,1\}^\lambda$ where $0 \leq i < 2^8$ and $1 \leq j \leq 32$. Construct two tables $\mathcal{T}_s$ and $\mathcal{T}_P$ by computing $Q_{(i,j)} = x_{(i,j)} \cdot P$.

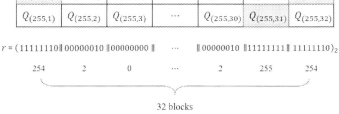

$\mathcal{T}_s$

$x_{(0,1)}$	$x_{(0,2)}$	$x_{(0,3)}$	$\cdots$	$x_{(0,30)}$	$x_{(0,31)}$	$x_{(0,32)}$
$x_{(1,1)}$	$x_{(1,2)}$	$x_{(1,3)}$	$\cdots$	$x_{(1,30)}$	$x_{(1,31)}$	$x_{(1,32)}$
$x_{(2,1)}$	$x_{(2,2)}$	$x_{(2,3)}$	$\cdots$	$x_{(2,30)}$	$x_{(2,31)}$	$x_{(2,32)}$
$\vdots$	$\vdots$	$\vdots$	$\vdots$	$\vdots$	$\vdots$	$\vdots$
$x_{(254,1)}$	$x_{(254,2)}$	$x_{(254,3)}$	$\cdots$	$x_{(254,30)}$	$x_{(254,31)}$	$x_{(254,32)}$
$x_{(255,1)}$	$x_{(255,2)}$	$x_{(255,3)}$	$\cdots$	$x_{(255,30)}$	$x_{(255,31)}$	$x_{(255,32)}$

$r = (\underset{254}{11111110} \| \underset{2}{00000010} \| \underset{0}{00000000} \| \quad \cdots \quad \| \underset{2}{00000010} \| \underset{255}{11111111} \| \underset{254}{11111110})_2$

32 blocks

(a) secret scalar

$\mathcal{T}_P$

$Q_{(0,1)}$	$Q_{(0,2)}$	$Q_{(0,3)}$	$\cdots$	$Q_{(0,30)}$	$Q_{(0,31)}$	$Q_{(0,32)}$
$Q_{(1,1)}$	$Q_{(1,2)}$	$Q_{(1,3)}$	$\cdots$	$Q_{(1,30)}$	$Q_{(1,31)}$	$Q_{(1,32)}$
$Q_{(2,1)}$	$Q_{(2,2)}$	$Q_{(2,3)}$	$\cdots$	$Q_{(2,30)}$	$Q_{(2,31)}$	$Q_{(2,32)}$
$\vdots$	$\vdots$	$\vdots$	$\vdots$	$\vdots$	$\vdots$	$\vdots$
$Q_{(254,1)}$	$Q_{(254,2)}$	$Q_{(254,3)}$	$\cdots$	$Q_{(254,30)}$	$Q_{(254,31)}$	$Q_{(254,32)}$
$Q_{(255,1)}$	$Q_{(255,2)}$	$Q_{(255,3)}$	$\cdots$	$Q_{(255,30)}$	$Q_{(255,31)}$	$Q_{(255,32)}$

$r = (\underset{254}{11111110} \| \underset{2}{00000010} \| \underset{0}{00000000} \| \quad \cdots \quad \| \underset{2}{00000010} \| \underset{255}{11111111} \| \underset{254}{11111110})_2$

32 blocks

(b) scalar multiplication

Fig. 3. Calculate using 256-bit random scalar sequence ($m = 8, n = 32$)

Calculation($256, 8, 32, q_t, \mathcal{T}_s, \mathcal{T}_P$). Suppose a random string r is as follows.

$$r = 11111110||00000010||00000000|| \cdots ||00000010||11111111||1111110$$

Set $t_1 = (11111110)_2 = 254$, $t_2 = (00000010)_2 = 2, \ldots$, and $t_{32} = (11111110)_2 = 254$. Then, as shown in Fig. 3, k is calculated as $(x_{(254,1)} + x_{(2,2)} + x_{(0,3)} + \cdots + x_{(2,30)} + x_{(255,31)} + x_{(254,32)})$ mod q_t and $k \cdot P$ is computed as $Q_{(254,1)} + Q_{(2,2)} + Q_{(0,3)} + \cdots + Q_{(2,30)} + Q_{(255,31)} + Q_{(254,32)} = (x_{(254,1)} + x_{(2,2)} + \cdots + x_{(255,31)} + x_{(254,32)}) \cdot P = k \cdot P$, where q_t is the order of the group.

4   Security Evaluation Against Single-Trace Attacks and Performance Evaluation

4.1   Security Evaluation Against Single-Trace Attacks

We prove the security of the proposed T_SM method against single-trace attacks.

Simple Power Analysis Resistant. The proposed T_SM method consists of only point addition operations, $Q \leftarrow Q + Q_{(t_j,j)}$. Moreover, there is no phase in which the secret scalar k is scanned bit by bit and where calculations are made according to the scanned scalar bit k_i. The T_SM method operates regardless of the secret scalar bit k_i, and it only depends on the random string r, which is not associated with the secret scalar k, as shown in Algorithm 5 Steps 6 and 7. Accordingly, it does not satisfiy the assumption of the proposed SPA so far, that is, the assumption of Theorem 1. Therefore, the attacker cannot obtain any information about the secret scalar bits from SPA, so the T_SM method guarantees safety against SPA.

Collision Attack Resistant. The proposed T_SM method uses a pre-computation table $\mathcal{T}_s$ which consists of $2^m \times n$ distinct random scalar values $x_{(i,j)}$, where $0 \leq i < 2^m$ and $1 \leq j \leq n$. Thus, the input data $x_{(t_j,j)}$ of Step 6, $k \leftarrow k + x_{(t_j,j)}$, of Algorithm 5 are always different. Therefore, the collision of the input data is impossible. Moreover, the input data are loaded from a pre-computation table regardless of the secret scalar bit k_i. When performing Step 7, $Q \leftarrow Q + Q_{(t_j,j)}$ of Algorithm 5, the collision of the input data $Q_{(t_j,j)}$ is also impossible. Accordingly, it does not satisfy the attack assumption of Theorem 2(i), so it guarantees safety for Theorem 2(i). It is also impossible to have CA using Theorem 2(i), when performing Step 7, $Q \leftarrow Q + Q_{(t_j,j)}$, of Algorithm 5.

The following confirms that it does not satisfy the proposed CA assumptions, as shown in Theorem 2(ii–v).

(i) The T_SM method uses pre-computation tables $\mathcal{T}_s$ and $\mathcal{T}_P$ which consist of $2^m \times n$ distinct random values, where $0 \leq i < 2^m$ and $1 \leq j \leq n$.

(ii) The T_SM method always performs regular operations regardless of the secret scalar bit k_i, and its input data differ from each other.

(iii) The T_SM method saves the results of its operations to the same registers k and Q during Steps 6 and 7 of Algorithm 5. Besides, it does not refer to the same position of the array during Steps 6 and 7 of Algorithm 5 for each iteration because i increases in every iteration.

(iv) The saved and loaded data k (or Q) at the data saving and loading step during Step 6 (or 7) of Algorithm 5 is always the same.

As we explained above, because i increases in every iteration, the T_SM method refers to another position of the array when executing Steps 6 and 7 of Algorithm 5 for each iteration. Thus, the proposed CA assumptions shown in Theorem 3 are not satisfied. Consequently, the attacker cannot obtain useful information about the secret scalar through CA, so the proposed T_SM method guarantees safety against CA.

Key Bit-Dependent Attack Resistant. In the proposed T_SM method, the data-dependent branch does not exist. That is, there is no operation dependent on the secret scalar bit value. Besides, there is no secret scalar bit check phase and power consumption which is affected by the secret scalar bit value. There is only a phase which involves checking the random r value not associated with the secret scalar k. Thus, it is impossible to acquire the secret scalar by applying KBA. Hence, it is impossible to acquire the secret scalar by applying KBA because it does not satisfy KBA assumption of Theorem 4. As a result, the proposed method guarantees safety against KBA.

4.2   Performance Evaluation

The proposed T_SM method can execute efficiently by calling pre-computed values. As shown in Table 3, it only needs to perform n point addition operations. Figure 4 shows that the T_SM method is faster than other algorithms, such as the fixed-base method, when λ is 256 and $\mathcal{A}$ is $1.5\mathcal{D}$ (in the case of a prime field and projective coordinates) [11]. That is, it has an advantage when applied to public key cryptosystems, such as ECDSA, which use a fixed P and a random secret scalar k. Besides, our T_SM method does not require scalar recoding. When we construct the matrix of size $2^m \times n$, m, and n satisfying $m \times n = \lambda$, memory is required to store the pre-computation tables, as shown in Table 3. Thus, this proposed algorithm consumes much memory to store the pre-computation tables. However, since ECDSA is an algorithm widely used in general environments, for instance, laptops, mobile devices, and hardware appliances, the table size of T_SM method can be practical.

Table 3 shows the security and performance evaluation results. We compare whether there is resistance to single-trace attacks, whether scalar recoding is necessary, the pre-computation table size, and main operation amount. The proposed T_SM method can counter single-trace attacks and has a small main operation amount compared with other algorithms based on the fixed-base method. Moreover, to the best of our knowledge, the T_SM method is the first countermeasure secure against SPA, CA, and KBA. Thus, though it needs memory for pre-computation tables, applying our proposed algorithm is essential.

Table 3. Security and performance evaluation

Algorithm	SPA	CA	KBA	Recoding	Pre-computation Table size	Main operation
Montgomery ladder [17]	O	X	X	Y	0	$(\lambda - 1) \cdot \mathcal{A}$ $+(\lambda - 1) \cdot \mathcal{D}$
$\lambda = 256$					0	$255\mathcal{A} + 255\mathcal{D}$
Möller window method [26]	O	X	X	N	$(2^w \cdot 2\lambda)$-bit	$d \cdot \mathcal{A} + d \cdot w \cdot \mathcal{D}$ (where $d' = d + 1$)
$\lambda = 256, w = 2$					256 B	$128\mathcal{A} + 256\mathcal{D}$
$\lambda = 256, w = 4$					1 KB	$64\mathcal{A} + 256\mathcal{D}$
$\lambda = 256, w = 8$					16 KB	$32\mathcal{A} + 256\mathcal{D}$
$\lambda = 256, w = 16$					4 MB	$16\mathcal{A} + 256\mathcal{D}$
Möller window method [26]	O	X	X	N	$(2^w \cdot 2\lambda)$-bit	$d \cdot \mathcal{A} + d \cdot w \cdot \mathcal{D}$ (where $d' = d + 1$)
$\lambda = 256, w = 2$					256 B	$128\mathcal{A} + 256\mathcal{D}$
$\lambda = 256, w = 4$					1 KB	$64\mathcal{A} + 256\mathcal{D}$
$\lambda = 256, w = 8$					16 KB	$32\mathcal{A} + 256\mathcal{D}$
$\lambda = 256, w = 16$					4 MB	$16\mathcal{A} + 256\mathcal{D}$
width-w NAF method [28]	O	X	X	N	$(2^{w-1} \cdot 2\lambda)$-bit	$d \cdot \mathcal{A} + d \cdot w \cdot \mathcal{D}$ (where $d' = d + 1$)
$\lambda = 256, w = 2$					128 B	$128\mathcal{A} + 256\mathcal{D}$
$\lambda = 256, w = 4$					512 B	$64\mathcal{A} + 256\mathcal{D}$
$\lambda = 256, w = 8$					8 KB	$32\mathcal{A} + 256\mathcal{D}$
$\lambda = 256, w = 16$					2 MB	$16\mathcal{A} + 256\mathcal{D}$
mLSB-set comb method [7]	O	X	X	N	$((v \cdot 2^{w-1}) \cdot 2\lambda)$-bit	$(ev - 1) \cdot \mathcal{A}$ $+(e - 1) \cdot \mathcal{D}$
$\lambda = 256, w = 2, v = 2$					256 B	$127\mathcal{A} + 63\mathcal{D}$
$\lambda = 256, w = 4, v = 2$					1 KB	$63\mathcal{A} + 31\mathcal{D}$
$\lambda = 256, w = 8, v = 2$					16 KB	$31\mathcal{A} + 15\mathcal{D}$
$\lambda = 256, w = 16, v = 2$					4 MB	$15\mathcal{A} + 7\mathcal{D}$
Our T_SM method	O	O	O	Y	$((2^m \times n) \cdot 3\lambda)$-bit	$n \cdot \mathcal{A}$
$\lambda = 256, m = 2, n = 128$					48 KB	$128\mathcal{A}$
$\lambda = 256, m = 4, n = 64$					96 KB	$64\mathcal{A}$
$\lambda = 256, m = 8, n = 32$					768 KB	$32\mathcal{A}$
$\lambda = 256, m = 16, n = 16$					96 MB	$16\mathcal{A}$

* $\mathcal{D}$ is a point doubling operation
* $\mathcal{A}$ is a point addition oeration
* λ is the bitlength of the secret scalar k
* w is window width, $d = \lceil \lambda/w \rceil$
* d' is the length of the recorded scalar, which is either d or $d + 1$
* v is a table parameter $v \geq 1$, $e = \lceil \lambda/wv \rceil$
* m and n are satisfying $m \times n = \lambda$
* O: algorithm is an effective countermeasure against an attack
* X: algorithm is attacked by an attack
* N: scalar recoding is needed before Main operation
* Y: scalar recoding is not needed before Main operation

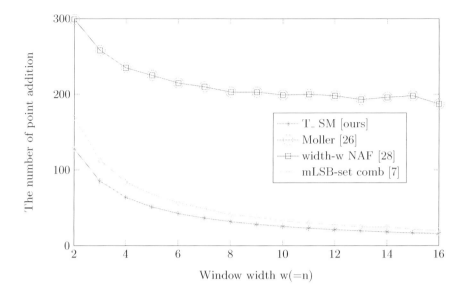

Fig. 4. The number of point addition in main operation ($\lambda = 256, \mathcal{A} = 1.5 \cdot \mathcal{D}$)

5   Conclusion

In this paper, we proposed the T_SM method which can counter single-trace attacks. In particular, our proposed algorithm is a state-of-the-art scalar multiplication algorithm that can fully resist CA. No existing countermeasure is theoretically perfect to counter CA. Besides, the T_SM method can counter SPA and KBA because it does not scan the secret scalar bit by bit and its calculation is not based on the scanned bit value. Even though the proposed algorithm requires much memory to store pre-computation tables, there is a benefit concerning speed since the main operation consists solely of n point addition operations. Moreover, environments which use ECDSA usually have sufficient memory, so the table size is practical, and it has advantages when applied to cryptosystems, such as ECDSA, which use a fixed P and random secret scalar k.

Acknowledgments. This work was supported by Institute for Information & communications Technology Promotion (IITP) grant funded by the Korea government (MSIT) (No.2017-0-00520, Development of SCR-Friendly Symmetric Key Cryptosystem and Its Application Modes).

References

1. Belgarric, P., Fouque, P.-A., Macario-Rat, G., Tibouchi, M.: Side-channel analysis of Weierstrass and Koblitz curve ECDSA on Android smartphones. In: CT-RSA 2016 (2016)

2. Clavier, C., Feix, B., Gagnerot, G., Roussellet, M., Verneuil, V.: Horizontal correlation analysis on exponentiation. In: Soriano, M., Qing, S., López, J. (eds.) ICICS 2010. LNCS, vol. 6476, pp. 46–61. Springer, Heidelberg (2010). https://doi.org/10.1007/978-3-642-17650-0_5

3. Coron, J.-S.: Resistance against differential power analysis for elliptic curve cryptosystems. In: Koç, Ç.K., Paar, C. (eds.) CHES 1999. LNCS, vol. 1717, pp. 292–302. Springer, Heidelberg (1999). https://doi.org/10.1007/3-540-48059-5_25

4. Diop, I., Liardet, P.Y., Maurine, P.: Collision based attacks in practice. In: DSD 2015, pp. 367–374 (2015)

5. Diop, I., Carbone, M., Ordas, S., Linge, Y., Liardet, P.Y., Maurine, P.: Collision for estimating SCA measurement quality and related applications. In: Homma, N., Medwed, M. (eds.) CARDIS 2015. LNCS, vol. 9514, pp. 143–157. Springer, Cham (2016). https://doi.org/10.1007/978-3-319-31271-2_9

6. Fan, J., Verbauwhede, I.: An updated survey on secure ECC implementations: attacks, countermeasures and cost. In: Naccache, D. (ed.) Cryptography and Security: From Theory to Applications. LNCS, vol. 6805, pp. 265–282. Springer, Heidelberg (2012). https://doi.org/10.1007/978-3-642-28368-0_18

7. Faz-Hernández, A., Longa, P., Sánchez, A.H.: Efficient and secure algorithms for GLV-Based scalar multiplication and their implementation on GLV-GLS curves. In: Benaloh, J. (ed.) CT-RSA 2014. LNCS, vol. 8366, pp. 1–27. Springer, Cham (2014). https://doi.org/10.1007/978-3-319-04852-9_1

8. FIPS 186: Digital signature standard. In: Federal Information Processing Standards Publication 186, U.S. Department of commerce (1994)

9. Fouque, P.-A., Valette, F.: The doubling attack – *why upwards is better than downwards*. In: Walter, C.D., Koç, Ç.K., Paar, C. (eds.) CHES 2003. LNCS, vol. 2779, pp. 269–280. Springer, Heidelberg (2003). https://doi.org/10.1007/978-3-540-45238-6_22

10. Genkin, D., Pachmanov, L., Pipman, I., Tromer, E., Yarom, Y.: ECDSA key extraction from mobile devices via nonintrusive physical side channels. In: ACM-CCS 2016 (2016). ISBN 978-1-4503-4139-4/16/10

11. Hankerson, D., Menezes, A., Vanstone, S.: Guide to Elliptic Curve Cryptography. Springer, New York (2003). https://doi.org/10.1007/b97644. ISBN 0-387-95273-X

12. Hanley, N., Kim, H.S., Tunstall, M.: Exploiting collisions in addition chain-based exponentiation algorithms using a single trace. In: Nyberg, K. (ed.) CT-RSA 2015. LNCS, vol. 9048, pp. 431–448. Springer, Cham (2015). https://doi.org/10.1007/978-3-319-16715-2_23

13. Heyszl, J., Mangard, S., Heinz, B., Stumpf, F., Sigl, G.: Localized electromagnetic analysis of cryptographic implementations. In: Dunkelman, O. (ed.) CT-RSA 2012. LNCS, vol. 7178, pp. 231–244. Springer, Heidelberg (2012). https://doi.org/10.1007/978-3-642-27954-6_15

14. Heyszl, J., Ibing, A., Mangard, S., De Santis, F., Sigl, G.: Clustering algorithms for non-profiled single-execution attacks on exponentiations. In: Francillon, A., Rohatgi, P. (eds.) CARDIS 2013. LNCS, vol. 8419, pp. 79–93. Springer, Cham (2014). https://doi.org/10.1007/978-3-319-08302-5_6

15. Homma, N., Miyamoto, A., Aoki, T., Satoh, A.: Comparative power analysis of modular exponentiation algorithms. IEEE Trans. Comput. **59**(6), 795–807 (2010)
16. Järvinen, K., Balasch, J.: Single-trace side-channel attacks on scalar multiplications with precomputations. In: Lemke-Rust, K., Tunstall, M. (eds.) CARDIS 2016. LNCS, vol. 10146, pp. 137–155. Springer, Cham (2017). https://doi.org/10.1007/978-3-319-54669-8_9
17. Joye, M., Yen, S.-M.: The montgomery powering ladder. In: Kaliski, B.S., Koç, K., Paar, C. (eds.) CHES 2002. LNCS, vol. 2523, pp. 291–302. Springer, Heidelberg (2003). https://doi.org/10.1007/3-540-36400-5_22
18. Karame, G., Androulaki, E.: Bitcoin and Blockchain Security. Artech House, Norwood (2016)
19. Kenworthy, G., Rohatgi, P.: Mobile device security: the case for side channel resistance. In: Cryptography Research Inc. (2012)
20. Kim, H.-S., Kim, T.-H., Yoon, J.-C., Hong, S.-H.: Practical second-order correlation power analysis on the message blinding method and its novel countermeasure for RSA. ETRI J. **32**(1), 102–111 (2010)
21. Koblitz, N.: Elliptic curve cryptosystems. Math. Comput. **48**(177), 203–209 (1987)
22. Kocher, P.C.: Timing attacks on implementations of Diffie-Hellman, RSA, DSS, and other systems. In: Koblitz, N. (ed.) CRYPTO 1996. LNCS, vol. 1109, pp. 104–113. Springer, Heidelberg (1996). https://doi.org/10.1007/3-540-68697-5_9
23. Kocher, P., Jaffe, J., Jun, B.: Differential power analysis. In: Wiener, M. (ed.) CRYPTO 1999. LNCS, vol. 1666, pp. 388–397. Springer, Heidelberg (1999). https://doi.org/10.1007/3-540-48405-1_25
24. Lindemann, R.: FIDO ECDAA Algorithm. In: FIDO Alliance Implementation Draft 2 (2017). https://fidoalliance.org/specs/fido-uaf-v1.1-id-20170202/fido-ecdaa-algorithm-v1.1-id-20170202.html
25. Miller, V.S.: Use of elliptic curves in cryptography. In: Williams, H.C. (ed.) CRYPTO 1985. LNCS, vol. 218, pp. 417–426. Springer, Heidelberg (1986). https://doi.org/10.1007/3-540-39799-X_31
26. Möller, B.: Securing elliptic curve point multiplication against side-channel attacks. In: Davida, G.I., Frankel, Y. (eds.) ISC 2001. LNCS, vol. 2200, pp. 324–334. Springer, Heidelberg (2001). https://doi.org/10.1007/3-540-45439-X_22
27. Okeya, K., Sakurai, K.: A second-order DPA attack breaks a window-method based countermeasure against side channel attacks. In: Chan, A.H., Gligor, V. (eds.) ISC 2002. LNCS, vol. 2433, pp. 389–401. Springer, Heidelberg (2002). https://doi.org/10.1007/3-540-45811-5_30
28. Okeya, K., Takagi, T.: The width-w NAF method provides small memory and fast elliptic scalar multiplications secure against side channel attacks. In: Joye, M. (ed.) CT-RSA 2003. LNCS, vol. 2612, pp. 328–343. Springer, Heidelberg (2003). https://doi.org/10.1007/3-540-36563-X_23
29. Perin, G., Imbert, L., Torres, L., Maurine, P.: Attacking randomized exponentiations using unsupervised learning. In: Prouff, E. (ed.) COSADE 2014. LNCS, vol. 8622, pp. 144–160. Springer, Cham (2014). https://doi.org/10.1007/978-3-319-10175-0_11
30. Perin, G., Chmielewski, Ł.: A semi-parametric approach for side-channel attacks on protected RSA implementations. In: Homma, N., Medwed, M. (eds.) CARDIS 2015. LNCS, vol. 9514, pp. 34–53. Springer, Cham (2016). https://doi.org/10.1007/978-3-319-31271-2_3
31. van de Pol, J., Smart, N.P., Yarom, Y.: Just a little bit more. In: Nyberg, K. (ed.) CT-RSA 2015. LNCS, vol. 9048, pp. 3–21. Springer, Cham (2015). https://doi.org/10.1007/978-3-319-16715-2_1

32. Rivest, R., Shamir, A., Adelman, L.: A method for obtaining digital signatures and public-key cryptosystems. Commun. ACM **21**(2), 120–126 (1978)

33. Specht, R., Heyszl, J., Kleinsteuber, M., Sigl, G.: Improving non-profiled attacks on exponentiations based on clustering and extracting leakage from multi-channel high-resolution EM measurements. In: Mangard, S., Poschmann, A.Y. (eds.) COSADE 2014. LNCS, vol. 9064, pp. 3–19. Springer, Cham (2015). https://doi.org/10.1007/978-3-319-21476-4_1

34. Sugawara, T., Suzuki, D., Saeki, M.: Internal collision attack on RSA under closed EM measurement. In: SCIS 2014 (2014)

35. Sugawara, T., Suzuki, D., Saeki, M.: Two operands of multipliers in side-channel attack. In: Mangard, S., Poschmann, A.Y. (eds.) COSADE 2014. LNCS, vol. 9064, pp. 64–78. Springer, Cham (2015). https://doi.org/10.1007/978-3-319-21476-4_5

36. Sim, B.-Y., Han, D.-G.: Key bit-dependent attack on protected PKC using a single trace. In: Liu, J.K., Samarati, P. (eds.) ISPEC 2017. LNCS, vol. 10701, pp. 168–185. Springer, Cham (2017). https://doi.org/10.1007/978-3-319-72359-4_10

37. Walter, C.D.: Sliding windows succumbs to big Mac attack. In: Koç, Ç.K., Naccache, D., Paar, C. (eds.) CHES 2001. LNCS, vol. 2162, pp. 286–299. Springer, Heidelberg (2001). https://doi.org/10.1007/3-540-44709-1_24

Recovering Memory Access Sequence with Differential Flush+Reload Attack

Zhiwei Yuan[1], Yang Li[2(✉)], Kazuo Sakiyama[2], Takeshi Sugawara[2], and Jian Wang[1]

[1] Nanjing University of Aeronautics and Astronautics, Nanjing, Jiangsu, China
{yuanzw,wangjian}@nuaa.edu.cn
[2] The University of Electro-Communications, Tokyo, Japan
{liyang,sakiyama,sugawara}@uec.ac.jp

Abstract. Side-channel attacks are effective attacks against modern cryptographic schemes, which exploit the leaking information besides input and output to the algorithm. As one of the cache-based side-channel attacks, Flush+Reload features high resolution, low noise, and virtual machine compatibility. However, a state-of-the-art Flush+Reload attack only reveals whether the memory address is accessed or not. This paper presents differential Flush+Reload attack that can recover the access sequence of memory addresses, which could lead to new vulnerabilities. The idea is to analyze statistical difference among multiple Flush+Reload results. Specifically, we add controlled delay between the start of victim calculation and the memory flush. Multiple Flush+Reload results with different delays are measured to determine the memory access sequence. Under this concept, we demonstrate the details of a successful recovery of T-table access sequences for an AES implementation from MatrixSSL version 3.9.3 on an Intel CPU.

Keywords: Side-channel · Cache attack · Differential Flush+Reload
Access sequence

1 Introduction

Cryptographic schemes prevent confidential information from being accessed by unauthorized entities and have been adopted in wide range of applications. Most cryptographic schemes have been thoroughly reviewed to avoid potential weakness. However, a theoretically secure scheme will not guarantee its security in its practical application. An unconsidered implementation will weaken the scheme, even make it exploitable to attackers.

The side-channel attack is an important part of the modern cryptographic analysis, and is recognized as the most practical approach to break a strong cryptographic algorithm. In addition to the input and output to the algorithm, side-channel attacks exploit extra leaked information, such as power consumption, electromagnetic emission, timing information, etc. [11] to extract the secret key.

C. Su and H. Kikuchi (Eds.): ISPEC 2018, LNCS 11125, pp. 424–439, 2018.
https://doi.org/10.1007/978-3-319-99807-7_26

Cache-based side-channel attacks have received more attention in recent years. These attacks exploit the difference of data access latency between CPU cache and main memory. Measuring cache-based leakage does not require additional equipment, the attack can be mounted without special privileges. Therefore, cache-based side-channel attacks are the threat for software cryptographic implementation, especially in cloud environments.

In 1992, Hu [7] demonstrated the possibility of extracting data from a cache channel for the first time. Kocher [10] and Kelsey et al. [9] mentioned that cache could threaten the security of cryptographic algorithms. The first formal studies of such attacks were given by Page [14,15]. The first practical cache-attack against DES cryptographic algorithm was proposed by Tsunoo et al. [16].

Aciiçmez et al. [1] were the first to exploit the instruction cache as well as the data cache, targeting OpenSSL's RSA implementation. Brumley and Boneh [3] carried out a practical remote timing attack. Chen et al. [4] improved the instruction cache-based trace-driven timing attack on RSA. Meanwhile, AES implementation is one of the most popular targets for cache-based side-channel attacks. Based on time-driven attacks, Bernstein [2] demonstrated the first cache-based side-channel attack on AES. Osvik et al. [13] presented Evict+Prime and Prime+Probe attacks for a spy process to monitor cache usage in the victim process, both of them recovered the AES encryption key.

This paper focuses on the cache-attack categories as Flush+Reload. The Flush+Reload attack can reveal whether a piece of memory has been accessed between the flush and reload operation. The attack was first proposed by Gullasch et al. [5], in which the victim was slowed down by abusing Completely Fair Scheduler. Yarom et al. [18] proposed a Flush+Reload attack to recover RSA private keys using instruction cache. Yarom et al. [17] also showed Flush+Reload attack could be used to recover secret keys from Elliptic Curve Digital Signature Algorithm (ECDSA). Irazoqui et al. [8] presented the first cross-VM attack on AES. Gülmezoğlu et al. [6] proposed an improvement to [8] that flushed in between the encryption rounds to achieve lower noise and better efficiency. Zhang et al. [19] proposed an automation-driven framework to attack web applications in PaaS environments with Flush+Reload.

The time resolution for Flush+Reload is the time span between the flush and reload operation, which is usually the duration of entire encryption. Improving time resolution generally yields better results. For example, Gülmezoğlu et al. [6] proposed an improvement to [8], the number of traces to recover the key reduces from $100,000$ to $3,000$ in spy-processes based attacks, and from $400,000$ to $10,000$ in cross-VM attacks.

Compared with other cache-based attacks, Flush+Reload attacks have a relatively lower resolution in time. In [12], by utilizing CPU interrupts, a Prime+Probe attack was applied to obtain every access to T-tables and recovers the key with 30 traces. Also, Flush+Reload attacks will not leak any information if the entire T-tables are accessed during the encryption.

We further improve the time resolution of Flush+Reload attack. By statically analyzing the difference between Flush+Reload results, we not only reduce the noise but achieve better time resolution than the general Flush+Reload. Specifically, our contribution is summarized as follows: we present a new cache-based side-channel attack named differential Flush+Reload, which is capable of retrieving memory address access sequence, rather than whether the memory is accessed or not, during the encryption. We start from a straightforward approach that could theoretically recover the memory access sequence by sorting their timestamps. Then we propose the differential Flush+Reload that compares cache line status with different delays to determine their access sequence. Furthermore, we validate our proposal and determine the memory address access sequence with AES implementation from MatrixSSL version 3.9.3.

The rest of paper organizes as follows. Section 2 presents the background on CPU cache and general Flush+Reload attacks. Section 3 presents both approaches to retrieve memory access sequence. Section 4 reports results of validation. Section 5 discusses the pros and cons as well as future works.

2   Background

2.1   CPU Cache and Memory

The CPU, or Central Processing Unit, is one of the key components in computer systems, whose main task is executing instructions. The CPU reads instructions from the memory and performs computation with data on register or on main memory. While most operations can be done in a few clock cycles, accessing main memory costs hundreds of cycles, and becomes the bottleneck. Cache is introduced to improve performance, which is a piece of small but fast storage inside the CPU. When accessing data from memory, the CPU first checks if the cache contains the data. If so, the data will be read from cache, saving the time to access from the main memory, which is called a cache hit. If not, the data will be read from the main memory and saved to cache for future use, which is called a cache miss.

CPU cache breaks into several levels. Level one cache is the smallest and the fastest, and usually dedicated to one physical CPU core. Last Level Cache (LLC) is the largest and the slowest, and usually shared among all cores on the same CPU socket. CPU cache is exchanged with main memory in the granularity of cache lines, which is the minimum size of data to be cached. For most x86 CPUs, each cache line is 64 bytes.

2.2   Cache-Based Side-Channel Attack

With mechanics of cache and memory described in the previous subsection, CPU cache might leak information from one process to another process even though there is no data exchange between them. Assuming that a *spy process* S and a *victim process* V run on the same multi-tasking operation system, if S and V have shared physical memory, S can monitor victim's memory access with Flush+Reload, which consists of following steps:

- **Flush Stage:** S flushes the chosen memory address out of CPU cache with `clflush` instruction, to make sure that the next access to the address will be fetched from memory.
- **Victim Access Stage:** S waits for V to execute, which may possibly access the memory flushed by S.
- **Reloading Stage:** S performs a timed reload on the chosen memory address. If V accessed the flushed memory address, the data would be loaded into not only the level one cache but also the last level shared cache, S would have a lower reload latency since the data would be retrieved from the shared cache. If V did not access the flushed memory address, the data would not be loaded into cache, and S would have a high reload latency, because the data had to be retrieved from the main memory.

2.3   Flush During Encryption

Figure 1 shows the scheme of general Flush+Reload without accurate synchronization. The attacker flushes out memory address before encryption and reloads the memory address after encryption completes, to infer whether the memory address is accessed by the victim during the encryption. However, given that the attacker is usually interested in the memory address accessed in the last round of the encryption, there might be a lot of noise for the memory address access in previous rounds.

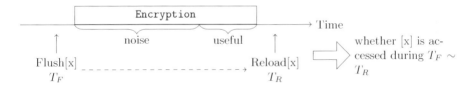

Fig. 1. The scheme of general Flush+Reload

To reduce noise, [6] proposes an improvement that flushes during the encryption. The attacker is required to detect the execution of encryption function from the victim process, which can be implemented as detecting whether the code for encryption function is cached in CPU. The memory address is flushed afterward. As shown in Fig. 2, memory address accesses before T_{DF} will be flushed and will not affect reload results. Only memory address accesses occurring after T_{DF} will affect reloads. Compared with original Flush+Reload, the improved method reduces noise, thus contributes to a better key recovery. However, this method is still unable to recover the access sequence of each memory address, with which the key recovery efficiency might be further improved.

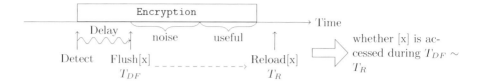

Fig. 2. The scheme of improved Flush+Reload proposed by [6]

3   Recover Access Sequence with Flush+Reload

Existing Flush+Reload attacks can only reveal whether a piece of memory has been accessed between the flush and reload operation, which contains more noise than the information interested by attackers. They cannot reveal the memory address sequence, that might contains more information for efficient key recover.

We present an approach to determine the access sequence of multiple memory addresses. The first point is to flush multiple memory addresses simultaneously during encryption and reload them afterward. Thus we can split the memory addresses into two groups by whether they are reloaded by the victim after the flush, and determine the access sequence between two groups. The second point is to compare the group of cached memory addresses from different delays to determine the access sequence among the addresses.

In this section, we first analyze the necessary capabilities for attackers to mount the attack. Then we present a straightforward approach to recover the access sequence by comparing the timestamp when the memory is accessed. Later we present a practical method to recover the access sequence with differential Flush+Reload technique.

3.1   Attacker Capabilities

Similar to [6], we assume that attacker can run an unprivileged *spy process* S on the same physical CPU as the *victim process* V, so that S shares the last level cache with V. Besides, S should have access to the shared tables from V, which can be achieved via memory map mechanism provided by the operating system, or via memory deduplication by Virtual Machine Manager (VMM). In other words, S has access to the same cache corresponding to the memory, enabling S to monitor the memory access activity from V. Besides the memory address for the tables used in encryption, S also needs the memory address which contains the beginning of encryption code, in order to detect the start of encryption using the Flush+Reload method.

S should also be able to trigger an encryption with fixed input. Apart from [6], S should be able to delay its execution by a fraction of time, ranging from a few to hundreds of cycles, in order to observe the memory access starting from a different time of the encryption progress.

3.2   Naïve Approach: By Timestamp

Method. To determine the access sequence of given memory addresses by V, a straightforward solution is to find out all absolute timestamps when each memory address is accessed by V, and sort the timestamps to get the memory access sequence. However attackers cannot record the timestamp from the *victim process*, since it requires modifying the *victim program*, which goes beyond attacker's ability.

A workaround for attackers is to find the access timestamp with Flush+Reload. Assuming memory address M is accessed during the encryption, M's access timestamp can be determined with following steps:

- **Flush:** S flushes all possible shared memory with V to slow down the encryption.
- **Request:** S triggers encryption in V with fixed input.
- **Synchronize:** S performs Flush+Reload with the memory address containing the code of encryption. If the reload time is lower than the average time to load data from memory, S can conclude that V has been running the encryption function, and should continue on the next step; otherwise V is not running the encryption, and S should try to **synchronize** again.
- **Delay:** S delays its execution for a controlled duration immediately after synchronization.
- **Flush+Reload:** S performs Flush+Reload on one of the tables' memory address. More specifically, S first **flushes** the memory address out of cache. Then **waits** for encryption to finish, either via network communication or just waiting for a fixed time. Finally S **reloads** the memory address to determine whether V accessed the memory M after S flushed it.

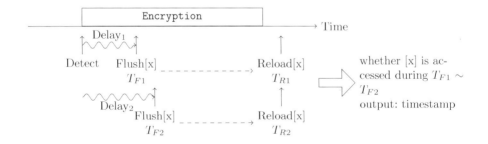

Fig. 3. The scheme of Naïve Flush+Reload

Analysis. Assuming that the synchronization is accurate, S forwards into **delay** immediately after V starts encryption. If S does not delay at all, it will flush M at the beginning of victim's encryption. Afterward, V will access M during the encryption, and S will have a fast reload time, since the cache contains M.

We still assume that M is accessed during the encryption and the synchronization is accurate. If S delays for a time longer than encryption, S will flush after encryption finishes. Since the encryption is finished and V will not access M anymore, S will always have a slow reload time, because the cache does not contain M.

Based on the accurate synchronization assumption and the analysis above, we can infer that by increasing delay time, spy's observation for M changes from cache hit to cache miss. If the attacker can delay the flush accurately, the exact delay time when attacker's observations change is also the exact time when V accesses M. By repeating the procedure for each memory address, we can determine the access sequence among them.

Limitation. If M is accessed multiple times during the encryption, only the timestamp of the last access can be retrieved, because the Flush+Reload works by checking the existence of cache, the latter access will overwrite the cache status, thus only the last access time can be recovered.

Meanwhile, this approach only allows one memory address to be probed at one time, since flushing cache will slow down the victim process, and delay any consequent memory access to make the latter timestamp not accurate at all.

Another limitation for this approach is the requirement for accurate synchronization and delay. The memory accesses in last round are usually cache hits and their access latencies are small, even smaller than the timing jitter from synchronization and delay. Picking up the signal from access sequence requires a large number of samples, rendering it impractical for attackers to extract information.

3.3   Differential Approach

To workaround with the limitation of the native approach, especially the requirement for accurate synchronization and delay, we propose another approach that requires neither of them. Instead of determining access sequence by timestamp, we compare the set of cached memory addresses during a general Flush+Reload attack from arbitrary delays, and recover the access sequence from their difference.

Method. Assuming memory address $M_1, M_2 \ldots M_n$ are accessed during encryption, S can determine their access sequence by:

- **Request:** S triggers encryption operation in V with fixed input.
- **Synchronize:** S tries to synchronize with the beginning of encryption in V, and this step is the same as the previous approach.
- **Delay:** S delays its execution for a roughly controlled time immediately after synchronization.
- **Flush+Reload:** S performs Flush+Reload on $M_1, M_2 \ldots M_n$ in batch, and determines which memory addresses are reloaded during the encryption. More

specifically, S first **flushes** $M_1, M_2 \ldots M_n$ out of cache, then **waits** for encryption to finish, finally S **reloads** $M_1, M_2 \ldots M_n$ to determine whether V has accessed these memory addresses after S flushed them.

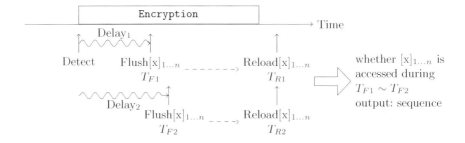

Fig. 4. The scheme of differential Flush+Reload

Recover Sequence. If both memory addresses M_1 and M_2 are accessed by the victim during the encryption, but in one trace retrieved by attacker, M_1 has a long reload time, while M_2 has a short reload time, the attacker can conclude that M_2 is accessed by the victim after the flush stage, but M_1 is not. Given that M_1 is accessed during the encryption, it must have been accessed before the flush stage, thus M_1 is accessed before M_2.

With this method, the attacker can divide memory addresses into two sets from any single trace: a *reloaded* set of memory addresses which are accessed after flush stage, so they have short reload latencies; and an *unloaded* set of memory addresses which are not accessed after flush stage, so they have long reload latencies. The *reloaded* set is always accessed after the *unloaded* set, no matter how long the delay stage is taken.

To determine the access order for memory address M, a possible method is to find two *reloaded* sets GR_1, GR_2, such that $GR_1 \setminus GR_2 = \{M\}$, we can conclude that the M is accessed just before any other memory addresses in GR_2, thus M's access sequence can be determined. By repeating this process for all memory addresses, the attacker can learn the whole access sequence.

However, determining access order by difference of two *reloaded* sets is not fault tolerant, the *reloaded* sets should be all correct for a successful recovery, which is not realistic for side-channel attacks.

To make the recovery fault tolerant, a common approach is to repeat the attack and use statistical results. For a group of memory addresses flushed at the same time, the later the memory address is accessed, the more likely that it will be reloaded after the flush, ending up with a cache hit from the S. By accumulating the cache hit count, the access sequence can be recovered with error tolerance: the more cache hit count a memory address gets, the later the memory address is accessed during the encryption.

Noise. This approach is insensitive to the delay. However, it is sensitive to the flushing sequence.

When flushing multiple memory addresses, the attacker is expected to flush all addresses at the same time, but it is not practical since each `clflush` instruction takes a few clock cycles. As the result, the last memory address is flushed some time after the first memory address, and it might interfere cache status in reload stage.

To minimize the delay among flushing memory addresses, the number of memory addresses to be flushed at one time is limited in our approach. Less memory addresses results fewer delay and more stable output. But the attacker has to split interested memory addresses into groups, recover the access sequence in each group, and merge the results to get the whole access sequence.

Another approach is randomizing flush sequence every time, so all addresses get the equal chance to be flushed at every position.

Flush+Reload also introduces noise, even it features low noise. It might report false positives or false negatives. This noise can be reduced by repeating the attack, as long as most of the results are correct.

Merging. Given that the number of memory addresses to be flushed at one time is limited, the attacker has to get access sequence of small groups of memory addresses, and merge them to get the entire memory access sequence. The memory access sequence's correctness inside the small groups might be wrong.

The merge problem could be described as: given set

$$S = \{[a_{i,1}, a_{i,2}, \ldots, a_{i,n_i}] | i = 1, 2 \ldots m\}$$

set S contains m ordered lists $a_1, a_2, \ldots a_m$. For each list a_i, it contains n_i elements, representing the access sequence $a_{i,1}, a_{i,2}, \ldots a_{i,n_i}$ recovered from the i-th group. $(a_{i,j}, a_{i,j+1})$ means memory address $a_{i,j}$ is accessed before $a_{i,j+1}$. Some elements in the set S might be erroneous. The goal is to find the entire access sequence that contradicts to as less a_i as possible, in the assumption that most of the partial sequence retrieved from differential Flush+Reload is correct.

A straightforward solution is to enumerate all possible erroneous $E \subseteq S$, in the order of increasing $\|E\|$, until $(S - E)$ has possible access sequences. This solution guarantees to find the best solution, i.e., the access sequence that contradicts minimum $\|E\|$, but its time complexity is $\mathcal{O}(2^n)$, so it can only handle small inputs.

Another solution is random based, which takes the following steps: (1) randomly choose small subset $S' \subseteq S$; (2) find a possible access sequence Q satisfying S'; (3) test how many $a_i \in S$ the Q violates; (4) repeat previous steps, and outputs the Q with the minimum violation. This solution is faster than the straightforward one, but it cannot always find the best solution.

Limitation. As the nature of Flush+Reload attack, this approach can only detect the sequence of last memory access. This might affect some attacks which focus on the first round of encryption, because the cache state will be overwritten by memory access afterward. However attackers can utilize the access sequence from the last encryption rounds to recover the secret key. There are no memory accesses after encryption, so that the cache state for the last round can be preserved to recover the access sequence.

4   Experiment

In this section, we perform experiments to verify that the differential Flush+ Reload can recover the memory access sequence. The experiment is conducted on an Intel Core 3632QM CPU. The CPU has four physical cores, which share one common timestamp counter running at a fixed frequency of 2.2 GHz. Although the property of common time source is not used for attacks, it simplifies our analysis across different cores.

Running on its top speed, the CPU takes about 40 cycles to read data from last level cache, and 170 cycles from main memory. Flushing data from cache requires about 25 cycles, and reading timestamp takes 25 cycles on average as well.

The experiment targets an AES implementation from `MatrixSSL` version 3.9.3, compiled with `GCC` version 7.3.1. The secret key used by the victim is `972ea36b3d5728a5d49d86d74df0ecea`, and the plaintext chosen by attacker is `2d0c9efc567a0ea70f34394e6566b593`, both of them are chosen randomly.

4.1   Synchronization

Before experimenting on recovering access sequence, we perform preliminary experiment to determine the synchronization accuracy on detecting encryption. The synchronization utilizes repeated Flush+Reload on the binary code of AES encryption to detect its execution. there is a fixed delay of executing 10 `rdtscp` instructions between the flush and reload operation.

The victim reads the timestamp before invoking AES encryption. After the detection of AES execution, the spy also reads the timestamp. The two timestamps are compared to determine the synchronization delta. If the synchronization is accurate, both spy and victim process will read the timestamp at the same time, resulting the difference between two timestamps to be zero. The synchronization is repeated for $2^{18} = 262144$ times.

As Fig. 5 shows, the x-axis shows the synchronization delta between the spy and the victim, the blue bars show the occurrences of the given synchronization delta, and the red curve shows the cumulative distribution function. Near 60% of the synchronization delta falls within 60 clocks, and 75% within 175 clocks. Given that the memory access latency on this system is about 170 cycles, attackers can easily slow down the encryption by flushing out the const tables, which will enable attackers to observe the most memory activities of encryption process after the encryption begins.

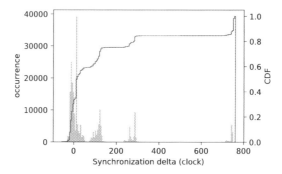

Fig. 5. Synchronization delta distribution, a larger delta means the spy process is slower than the victim process after synchronization.

4.2   Naïve Approach

To evaluate the naïve approach, we use the similar spy-process setup as [8]. The *victim process* encrypts incoming requests with a secret key. The attacker tries to determine the access sequence to the T-table by the victim with shared cache.

Four memory addresses are chosen for attacker to determine their access sequence: `Te'2[b]` is accessed during the first round of AES, marking the beginning of the encryption; `Te0[0]` `Te1[3]` `Te0[a]` are accessed during the last round of AES. Unknown to attackers, the ground truth access sequence of the four memory addresses is `Te'2[b]` `Te0[0]` `Te1[3]` `Te0[a]`.

To recover the access sequence, we independently synchronize with encryption and perform Flush+Reload for each memory address, repeating 1000 times for each delay. The result is shown in Fig. 6. The clock on x-axis shows the controlled delay before Flush+Reload stage, the cache hit count on y-axis shows the number of occurrence when the memory is reloaded by V after flush stage from S. The four traces represent the four chosen memory addresses.

The trace for `Te'2[b]` drops around 900 cycles, and has the least total cache hit among the four memory addresses, thus the attacker can infer that `Te'2[b]` is accessed at 900 cycles after synchronization, and is the first accessed memory address among the four, which consists with the ground truth. However, the other three traces drop around 1300 cycles simultaneously, they are almost overlapped, and suffer from noises, so the access sequence of their respective memory addresses cannot be determined from the traces.

One of the causes is inaccurate timing from synchronization and delay. By inspecting the time span from the access in the first round to that in the last round, the Fig. 6 reveals that the main part of the encryption between first round and last round takes about 400 cycles. Given the AES encryption accesses the memory 160 times, each memory access takes about $400 \div 160 = 2.5$ cycles on average, which is much smaller than the synchronization accuracy shown in Fig. 5. Theoretically the noise from synchronization inaccuracy could be canceled with a larger number of samples, but the required number of samples is too large for a practical attack.

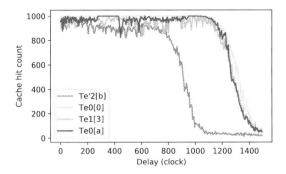

Fig. 6. Cache hit count for four memory addresses. The ground truth access sequence is `Te'2[b] Te0[0] Te1[3] Te0[a]`.

4.3   Differential Approach

Validation. To evaluate the differential approach, we use the same setup as the naïve approach, except the chosen memory addresses. The four chosen memory addresses `Te3[9] Te2[c] Te1[3] Te0[a]`, are the last four memory address accessed during AES encryption. These memory addresses are usually prefetched into CPU cache by the previous AES encryption rounds, thus the time between two memory accesses is short, making their access sequence more difficult to distinguish by their absolute timestamps. However, the differential technique slows down all accesses to the flushed memory sequentially, so the access sequence can still be extracted from the traces.

As shown in Fig. 7, the clock on x-axis shows the delay time that the attacker applies. The occurrence on y-axis shows the attacker's observation that the trace's corresponding memory is cached. It can be told that the `Te3[9]` is the memory address with least cache hit count, thus `Te3[9]` is the first memory address accessed among the four, followed by `Te2[c] Te1[3] Te0[a]`, which is the correct access sequence by the victim.

The crucial difference between Figs. 6 and 7 is the number of memory addresses flushed at one time. In Fig. 6 one memory address is flushed per synchronization and the four traces are combined from different synchronizations, thus the gap between neighboring traces is expected to be the latency of cache access, which is too small for accurate measurement. In Fig. 7 four memory addresses are flushed per synchronization and the four traces come from the same synchronization, thus the gap between neighboring traces is expected to be the latency of main memory access, which can be measured with practical timing resolution.

Flush Sequence vs Access Sequence. Since the ground truth memory access sequence in the target process is unknown to attacker, if the attacker flushes the memory in the same order as they are accessed by the victim, i.e. `Te3[9] Te2[c]`

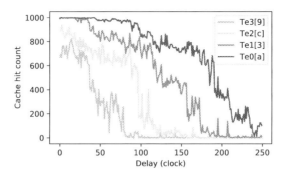

Fig. 7. The spy flushes the memory in the reverted order that the victim accesses, resulting distinguishable traces

Te1[3] Te0[a], it will end up with four overlapped traces that cannot reveal any information about their access sequence by the victim, as shown in Fig. 8.

Take Te3[9] for example, the prerequisite for memory address Te3[9] to have less cache hit count than other traces is: Te3[9] should be flushed after victim's access, and others should be flushed before victim's access. This is unlikely to happen, because the time gap between V's access to Te3[9] and Te2[c] is too short for flushing three memory addresses. As the result, Te3[9] will not have less cache hit count. On the other hand, the Te3[9] will not have more cache hit count than others because of the access sequence determined by victim. So the Te3[9] can only have the same cache hit count as others, if the attacker flushes in the same sequence as the victim accesses.

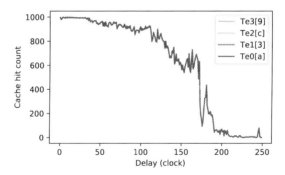

Fig. 8. The spy flushes the memory in the same order that the victim accesses, resulting in overlapped and indistinguishable traces

To avoid this worst case, attackers should change the flush order every time, which can result in relatively stable output and the memory access can be distinguished, as shown in Fig. 9.

Improving Efficiency. While it takes at least $1000 \times 250 = 250,000$ encryptions to plot the Fig. 9, the access sequence can be still determined with a much lower resolution. With reduced sample rate, taking 6 timeslot (50 cycle interval) and each repeated for 20 times, the traces in Fig. 10 require only $6 \times 20 = 120$ successful synchronization and encryption, and it can still reveal the same access sequence.

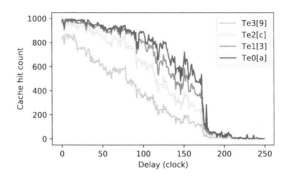

Fig. 9. The spy flushes the memory in random order to avoid overlapped traces.

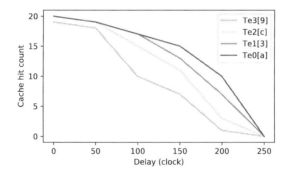

Fig. 10. The spy can still distinguish access sequence with reduced resolution

5   Conclusion

In this paper we propose the differential Flush+Reload attack, which successfully retrieved the memory address access sequence of a software AES implementation from MatrixSSL. Differential Flush+Reload attack inserts random delays before flush operations and compares cache status from different delays in order to deduce the memory access sequence. Our proposal leverages the general Flush+Reload attacks to obtain additional leakage information, while keeping the features such as low noise and cross-VM compatibility. The experiment validates the effectiveness of the proposed attack by distinguishing two continuous memory accesses, even when both of them are cached on the CPU. As an variant of Flush+Reload attack, the proposed attack naturally requires physically shared memory, and only can recover the access sequence for the last access of the same memory address. Additionally, the attacker should be able to repeat the same encryption on the victim process.

As for the future work, we will test the differential Flush+Reload technique for other environments, such as AES implementation from OpenSSL, or cross-VM scenarios. Furthermore, appropriate algorithm will be developed to combine the access sequences for a small group of memory addresses into that for a large group of memory addresses.

Acknowledgement. This work was supported by National Natural Science Foundation of China 61602239, Jiangsu Province Natural Science Foundation BK20160808 and JSPS KAKENHI Grant Number JP18H05289.

References

1. Aciiçmez, O.: Yet another microarchitectural attack: exploiting I-cache. In: Proceedings of the 2007 ACM Workshop on Computer Security Architecture, pp. 11–18. ACM (2007)
2. Bernstein, D.J.: Cache-timing attacks on AES. Vlsi Des. IEEE Comput. Soc. **51**(2), 218–221 (2005)
3. Brumley, D., Boneh, D.: Remote timing attacks are practical. Comput. Netw. **48**(5), 701–716 (2005). https://doi.org/10.1016/j.comnet.2005.01.010
4. Chen, C., Wang, T., Kou, Y., Chen, X., Li, X.: Improvement of trace-driven I-cache timing attack on the RSA algorithm. J. Syst. Softw. **86**(1), 100–107 (2013). https://doi.org/10.1016/j.jss.2012.07.020
5. Gullasch, D., Bangerter, E., Krenn, S.: Cache games - bringing access-based cache attacks on AES to practice. In: Security and Privacy (SP), IEEE Symposium on 2011, pp. 490–505. IEEE (2011)
6. Gülmezoğlu, B., İnci, M.S., Irazoqui, G., Eisenbarth, T., Sunar, B.: A faster and more realistic flush+reload attack on AES. In: Mangard, S., Poschmann, A.Y. (eds.) COSADE 2014. LNCS, vol. 9064, pp. 111–126. Springer, Cham (2015). https://doi.org/10.1007/978-3-319-21476-4_8
7. Hu, W.M.: Lattice scheduling and covert channels. In: Proceedings Research in Security and Privacy, 1992 IEEE Computer Society Symposium on 1992. pp. 52–61. IEEE (1992). DOI: https://doi.org/10.1109/RISP.1992.213271
8. Irazoqui, G., Inci, M.S., Eisenbarth, T., Sunar, B.: Wait a minute! A fast, cross-VM attack on AES. In: Stavrou, A., Bos, H., Portokalidis, G. (eds.) RAID 2014. LNCS, vol. 8688, pp. 299–319. Springer, Cham (2014). https://doi.org/10.1007/978-3-319-11379-1_15
9. Kelsey, J., Schneier, B., Wagner, D., Hall, C.: Side channel cryptanalysis of product ciphers. In: Quisquater, J.-J., Deswarte, Y., Meadows, C., Gollmann, D. (eds.) ESORICS 1998. LNCS, vol. 1485, pp. 97–110. Springer, Heidelberg (1998). https://doi.org/10.1007/BFb0055858
10. Kocher, P.C.: Timing attacks on implementations of diffie-hellman, RSA, DSS, and other systems. In: Koblitz, N. (ed.) CRYPTO 1996. LNCS, vol. 1109, pp. 104–113. Springer, Heidelberg (1996). https://doi.org/10.1007/3-540-68697-5_9

11. Koeune, F., Standaert, F.-X.: A tutorial on physical security and side-channel attacks. In: Aldini, A., Gorrieri, R., Martinelli, F. (eds.) FOSAD 2004-2005. LNCS, vol. 3655, pp. 78–108. Springer, Heidelberg (2005). https://doi.org/10.1007/11554578_3

12. Moghimi, A., Irazoqui, G., Eisenbarth, T.: CacheZoom: how SGX amplifies the power of cache attacks. In: Fischer, W., Homma, N. (eds.) CHES 2017. LNCS, vol. 10529, pp. 69–90. Springer, Cham (2017). https://doi.org/10.1007/978-3-319-66787-4_4

13. Osvik, D.A., Shamir, A., Tromer, E.: Cache attacks and countermeasures: the case of AES. In: Pointcheval, D. (ed.) CT-RSA 2006. LNCS, vol. 3860, pp. 1–20. Springer, Heidelberg (2006). https://doi.org/10.1007/11605805_1

14. Page, D.: Theoretical use of cache memory as a cryptanalytic side-channel. IACR Cryptol. Eprint Arch. **2002**, 169 (2002)

15. Page, D.: Defending against cache-based side-channel attacks. Inf. Secur. Tech. Rep. **8**(1), 30–44 (2003)

16. Tsunoo, Y., Saito, T., Suzaki, T., Shigeri, M., Miyauchi, H.: Cryptanalysis of DES implemented on computers with cache. In: Walter, C.D., Koç, Ç.K., Paar, C. (eds.) CHES 2003. LNCS, vol. 2779, pp. 62–76. Springer, Heidelberg (2003). https://doi.org/10.1007/978-3-540-45238-6_6

17. Yarom, Y., Benger, N.: Recovering OpenSSL ecdsa nonces using the flush+reload cache side-channel attack. IACR Cryptol. Eprint Arch. **2014**, 140 (2014)

18. Yarom, Y., Falkner, K.: Flush+reload: a high resolution, low noise, l3 cache side-channel attack. In: Usenix Conference on Security Symposium, pp. 719–732 (2014)

19. Zhou, Z., Reiter, M.K., Zhang, Y.: A software approach to defeating side channels in last-level caches. In: Proceedings of the 2016 ACM SIGSAC Conference on Computer and Communications Security, pp. 871–882. ACM (2016)

Revisiting the Sparsification Technique in Kannan's Embedding Attack on LWE

Yuntao Wang[1,2(✉)] and Thomas Wunderer[3]

[1] Kyushu University, Fukuoka, Japan
[2] The University of Tokyo, Tokyo, Japan
y-wang@math.kyushu-u.ac.jp
[3] Technische Universität Darmstadt, Darmstadt, Germany
twunderer@cdc.informatik.tu-darmstadt.de

Abstract. The Learning with Errors (LWE) problem is one of the most important computational problems in modern lattice-based cryptography. It can be viewed as a Bounded Distance Decoding (BDD) problem, which can be reduced to the unique Shortest Vector Problem (uSVP). The standard way to reduce BDD to uSVP is via Kannan's embedding. At ICALP 2016, Bai, Stehlé, and Wen presented an improved theoretical reduction from BDD to uSVP which uses sparsification techniques. So far, the implications of this improved reduction and the use of sparsification to the hardness of LWE have not been studied. In this work, we consider a sparsified embedding attack on LWE which is deduced from the Bai–Stehlé–Wen reduction. In particular, we analyze its performance under the so-called 2016 estimate introduced at USENIX 2016 by Alkim, Ducas, Pöppelmann, and Schwabe and analyzed at ASIACRYPT 2017 by Albrecht, Göpfert, Virdia, and Wunderer. Our results suggest that in general the sparsified embedding attack does not yield a better attack on LWE in practice than Kannan's embedding. However, for certain parameter sets and scenarios with a reasonable amount of computing clusters, the use of sparsification may be beneficial.

Keywords: Lattice-based cryptography · Sparsification
Cryptanalysis · BDD · SVP · LWE

1 Introduction

The hardness of the Learning with Errors (LWE) problem [Reg09] is the foundation of many modern lattice-based cryptographic constructions, e.g., [Reg09, LP11, ADPS16, BG14, GSW13]. Informally, the LWE problem is the problem of solving a set of noisy linear equations $\mathbf{As} + \mathbf{e} = \mathbf{b} \bmod q$, where the matrix $\mathbf{A}$ and the vector $\mathbf{b}$ are known, while the (short) vectors $\mathbf{s}$ and $\mathbf{e}$ are secret. LWE can be seen as a Bounded Distance Decoding (BDD_α) problem [Var97, LLM06]. BDD_α is the problem of finding the closest vector in a lattice Λ to some target point $\mathbf{t}$ in space, given the promise that the distance between $\mathbf{t}$ and Λ is at

© Springer Nature Switzerland AG 2018
C. Su and H. Kikuchi (Eds.): ISPEC 2018, LNCS 11125, pp. 440–452, 2018.
https://doi.org/10.1007/978-3-319-99807-7_27

most $\alpha\lambda_1(\Lambda)$, where $\lambda_1(\Lambda)$ is the length of the shortest non-zero vector in Λ. BDD_α in turn can be reduced to the unique shortest vector problem (uSVP_γ). The uSVP_γ is the problem of finding a shortest non-zero vector $\mathbf{v}$ in a lattice Λ, given the promise that the shortest vector in Λ which is not a scalar multiple of $\mathbf{v}$ has length at least $\gamma\lambda_1(\Lambda)$. In this case, γ is called the gap. There is a *deterministic* reduction from BDD_α to uSVP_γ with $\gamma = \frac{1}{2\alpha}$, or more refined, with $\alpha = (2\lfloor\gamma\rfloor)/(2\gamma^2 + \lfloor\gamma\rfloor\lfloor\gamma+1\rfloor)$, see [BSW16, LM09, LWXZ14]. Ideally, one would like to have the relation $\gamma \geq \frac{1}{\alpha}$ between the factor α and the gap γ. The techniques used in this reduction naturally translate to the so-called embedding attack on LWE (also called Kannan's embedding) [Kan87], one of the most common approaches to solve LWE. The steps of the embedding attack on LWE can briefly be described as follows: (1) view LWE as a BDD problem (2) embed the BDD problem into a uSVP problem (3) use lattice basis reduction (e.g., BKZ 2.0 [CN11] or progressive BKZ [AWHT16]) to solve the uSVP problem. In 2016, Bai et al. [BSW16] presented a *probabilistic* reduction from BDD_α to uSVP_γ with $\gamma = \frac{1}{\sqrt{2}\alpha}$, improving the relation between α and γ. To achieve this improvement, the so-called sparsification technique is used prior to the embedding. The sparsification technique was first introduced by Khot [Kho03, Kho04], and specified in [DK13, DRS14, SD16]. Informally, sparsification chooses a random sublattice of the BDD lattice. With a certain probability, the BDD solution is contained in this sublattice, and in this case, BDD in the sublattice is potentially easier to solve than in the original one. Again, the techniques used in the reduction can be translated into an attack on LWE, which we call the sparsified embedding attack. In both of the attacks described above, the embedding attack and the sparsified embedding attack, the final step is to solve the corresponding uSVP instance, e.g., by using BKZ 2.0 or progressive BKZ. In order to evaluate the effort of solving this uSVP instance, the so-called 2016 estimate provided by [ADPS16] and analyzed by Albrecht et al. [AGVW17] can be used to determine the required block size. So far, an analysis of the practical behavior of the sparsified embedding attack on LWE is missing in the literature, so the natural question weather the use of sparsification leads to a better attack on LWE remains open.

In this work, we provide a detailed theoretical performance analysis of the sparsified embedding attack on LWE in practice and compare it to Kannan's embedding approach. Our analysis is based on the 2016 estimate. Our results show that, in general, using the sparsified embedding approach does not lead to a better attack on LWE compared to Kannan's embedding approach. This is due to the fact that the decrease in success probability introduced by sparsification in general is not compensated for or exceeded by the obtained speedup in the success case. However, the use of sparsification may be beneficial for certain instances and scenarios. In particular, running the attack with different sparsifications in parallel may amplify the success probability of the sparsified embedding attack sufficiently for certain parameters.

Outline. This work is structured as follows. After providing the mathematical background for this work in Sect. 2 we provide a description of Kannan's embedding and the sparsified embedding attack on LWE in Sect. 3. Their behavior in practice under some common heuristics and the 2016 estimate is analyzed in Sect. 4. We conclude this work in Sect. 5.

2   Preliminaries

Lattices and Lattice Problems. An n-dimensional *lattice* is a discrete additive subgroup of $\mathbb{R}^n$. Each lattice $\Lambda \subset \mathbb{R}^n$ can be represented by a *basis*, i.e., a set of linearly independent vectors $\mathbf{B} = \{\mathbf{b}_1, \ldots, \mathbf{b}_m\} \subset \mathbb{R}^n$ such that $\Lambda = \mathbb{Z}\mathbf{b}_1 + \cdots + \mathbb{Z}\mathbf{b}_m$. For a basis $\mathbf{B} = \{\mathbf{b}_1, \ldots, \mathbf{b}_m\} \subset \mathbb{R}^n$ we write $\Lambda(\mathbf{B}) = \mathbb{Z}\mathbf{b}_1 + \cdots + \mathbb{Z}\mathbf{b}_m$ for the lattice generated by $\mathbf{B}$. We identify bases with column vectors of matrices and vice versa. The cardinality of a basis of a lattice Λ, which is uniquely determined by the lattice, is called the *rank* of Λ. A lattice $\Lambda \subset \mathbb{R}^n$ of rank n is called a *full-rank* lattice. The *(co-)volume* (also called the *determinant*) of a lattice $\Lambda \subset \mathbb{R}^n$ is defined as $\det(\Lambda) = \sqrt{|\det(\mathbf{B}^t\mathbf{B})|}$, where $\mathbf{B}$ is any basis of Λ. In the case that Λ is a full-rank lattice, this can be simplified to $\det(\Lambda) = |\det(\mathbf{B})|$. Let Λ be a lattice of rank m. Then for $i \in \{1, \ldots, m\}$ the *i-th successive minimum* $\lambda_i(\Lambda)$ of Λ is defined as the smallest radius $r \geq 0$ such that the lattice Λ contains i linearly independent vectors of norm at most r. In particular, the length of the shortest non-zero vector in Λ is given by $\lambda_1(\Lambda)$. For a "random" lattice $\Lambda \subset \mathbb{R}^n$, the *Gaussian Heuristic* estimates the length of the shortest non-zero vector to be

$$\lambda_1(\Lambda) \approx \sqrt{\frac{n}{2\pi e}} \det(\Lambda)^{1/n}.$$

One of the most important lattice problems in modern lattice-based cryptography is the *learning with errors (LWE)* problem.

Definition 1 *(LWE). For a vector $\mathbf{s} \in \mathbb{Z}_q^n$ and a distribution χ over $\mathbb{Z}_q$, the LWE distribution $L_{\mathbf{s},\chi}$ over $\mathbb{Z}_q^n \times \mathbb{Z}_q$ is sampled by choosing $\mathbf{a} \in \mathbb{Z}_q^n$ uniformly at random, choosing $e \leftarrow \chi$, and outputting $(\mathbf{a}, b = \langle \mathbf{a}, \mathbf{s} \rangle + e \mod q)$.*
The search version of the LWE problem is defined as follows. Given positive integers $n \in \mathbb{N}$ and $q \geq 2$, a probability distribution χ on $\mathbb{Z}_q$, and m independent samples from the distribution $L_{\mathbf{s},\chi}$ for some fixed secret $\mathbf{s}$ that was chosen uniformly at random, find $\mathbf{s}$.

We also write LWE instances in matrix form $(\mathbf{A}, \mathbf{b} = \mathbf{A}\mathbf{s} + \mathbf{e} \mod q)$, where $\mathbf{A} \in \mathbb{Z}_q^{m \times n}$, $\mathbf{b} \in \mathbb{Z}_q^m$ and rows correspond to samples $(\mathbf{a}_i, b_i)$ for some number of samples m. LWE can be seen as a *bounded distance decoding (BDD)* problem, which is a variant of the *closest vector problem (CVP)*.

Definition 2 *(BDD_α). Given $0 < \alpha \leq 1/2$, a full-rank lattice $\Lambda \subset \mathcal{R}^n$, and a target point $\mathbf{t} \in \mathcal{R}^n$ with $\mathsf{dist}(\mathbf{t}, \Lambda) < \alpha\lambda_1(\Lambda)$, find the unique lattice vector $\mathbf{v} \in \Lambda$ such that $\|\mathbf{t} - \mathbf{v}\| < \alpha\lambda_1(\Lambda)$.*

The bounded distance decoding problem can be embedded into a version of the *shortest vector problem (SVP)* called the *unique shortest vector problem (uSVP)*.

Definition 3 (*uSVP$_\gamma$*). *Given $\gamma \geq 1$ and a lattice Λ with $\lambda_2(\Lambda) \geq \gamma\lambda_1(\Lambda)$, find a shortest nonzero lattice vector in Λ.*

Basis Reduction. Basis reduction algorithms aim at improving the quality of a lattice basis $\mathbf{B}$, which can be measured by its root Hermite factor δ defined via $\|\mathbf{b}_1\| = \delta^d \cdot \det(\Lambda(\mathbf{B}))^{1/d}$, where d is the lattice dimension. Basis reduction algorithms can be used to find short(est) vectors in lattices, where a smaller Hermite factor results in shorter vectors. The BKZ basis reduction algorithm [SE94] and its variants such as BKZ 2.0 [CN11] or progressive BKZ [AWHT16] proceed by finding shortest vectors in projected lattices of smaller dimension. This smaller dimension is called the block size, which specifies the BKZ algorithm. For more details on BKZ and its variants, we refer to the respective works. For BKZ, the used block size β can be related to the achieved Hermite factor δ of the output basis by the asymptotic formula

$$\delta = \left(\left(\left(\pi\beta\right)^{1/\beta}\beta\right)/(2\pi e)\right)^{1/(2(\beta-1))},$$

see [Che13, APS15]. Throughout this work we will assume this relation between δ and β whenever they appear. The 2016 estimate [ADPS16, AGVW17] provides an estimate for the block size required to solve uSVP. It states that the unique shortest vector in a d-dimensional lattice Λ can be found if the block size β satisfies

$$\sqrt{\beta/d}\lambda_1(\Lambda) \leq \delta^{2\beta-d}\det(\Lambda)^{1/d}.$$

3 Kannan's and the Sparsified Embedding Attack

In this section we describe Kannan's embedding and the sparsified embedding attack, which can be deduced from the reduction provided in [BSW16]. For the rest of this section, let $(\mathbf{A}, \mathbf{b} = \mathbf{As} + \mathbf{e} \bmod q) \in \mathbb{Z}_q^{m \times n}, \mathbb{Z}_q^m$ be an LWE instance. We focus on recovering $\mathbf{e}$, since if $\mathbf{e}$ is known, $\mathbf{s}$ can be found by Gaussian elimination. Note that the number of samples m can be chosen by the attacker to obtain an optimal attack.

3.1 Kannan's Embedding Technique

Kannan's Embedding approach [Kan87] to solve LWE can be described as follows. Consider the lattice

$$\Lambda_{(\mathbf{A},q)} = \{\mathbf{v} \in \mathbb{Z}_q^m \mid \mathbf{v} \equiv \mathbf{Ax} \pmod q \text{ for some } \mathbf{x} \in \mathbb{Z}^n\}$$

and let $\mathbf{B}$ be some basis of $\Lambda_{(\mathbf{A},q)}$. Then it holds that $\mathbf{b} \in \Lambda_{(\mathbf{A},q)} + \mathbf{e}$, since $\mathbf{b} = \mathbf{As} + \mathbf{e} \bmod q$. Hence $\mathbf{e}$ can be recovered by solving a BDD problem in $\Lambda_{(\mathbf{A},q)}$ with target vector $\mathbf{b}$. In order to solve this BDD problem, it is embedded into a uSVP instance

$$\begin{pmatrix} \mathbf{e} \\ M \end{pmatrix} \in \Lambda(\mathbf{B}') \text{ with } \mathbf{B}' = \begin{pmatrix} \mathbf{B} & \mathbf{b} \\ \mathbf{0} & M \end{pmatrix} \in \mathbb{Z}^{(m+1)\times(m+1)},$$

Algorithm 1. Kannan's embedding approach

Input   : An LWE instance $(\mathbf{A}, \mathbf{b} = \mathbf{A}\mathbf{s} + \mathbf{e} \mod q) \in \mathbb{Z}_q^{m \times n} \times \mathbb{Z}_q^m$, embedding factor M

Output : The error vector $\mathbf{e}$

1 Construct a lattice basis $\mathbf{B} \in \mathbb{Z}^{m \times m}$ of the lattice
$\Lambda_{(\mathbf{A},q)} = \{\mathbf{v} \in \mathbb{Z}_q^m \mid \mathbf{v} \equiv \mathbf{A}\mathbf{x} \pmod{q} \text{ for some } \mathbf{x} \in \mathbb{Z}^n\}$;

2 Set $\mathbf{B}' = \begin{pmatrix} \mathbf{B} & \mathbf{b} \\ \mathbf{0} & M \end{pmatrix} \in \mathbb{Z}^{(m+1) \times (m+1)}$;

3 Recover $\pm \begin{pmatrix} \mathbf{e}^T \\ M \end{pmatrix}$ by solving uSVP in $\Lambda(\mathbf{B}')$ using basis reduction;

4 **return** $\mathbf{e}$;

---

where M is the so-called embedding factor. Typical choices of M are discussed in, e.g., [LM09, AFG14, APS15], and include $M = 1$ or $M = \|\mathbf{e}\|$. As pointed out in [APS15, WAT18], $M = 1$ is typically more efficient and therefore often used in practice, including this work. This uSVP instance is then solved by running lattice reduction on the basis $\mathbf{B}'$. A simplified pseudocode of Kannan's embedding approach is given in Algorithm 1.

3.2   Sparsifying Kannan's Embedding Technique

In the following we describe a sparsified embedding attack on LWE which can be deduced from [BSW16]. The sparsified embedding approach is similar to Kannan's embedding. The main difference is that the BDD lattice $\Lambda_{(\mathbf{A},q)} = \{\mathbf{v} \in \mathbb{Z}_q^m \mid \mathbf{v} \equiv \mathbf{A}\mathbf{x} \pmod{q} \text{ for some } \mathbf{x} \in \mathbb{Z}^n\}$ is sparsified prior to the procedure of embedding it into a uSVP lattice. Roughly speaking, sparsifying a lattice means choosing a random sublattice of some index p. In more detail, let p be the desired index and $\mathbf{B}$ be a basis of $\Lambda_{(\mathbf{A},q)}$. Sample $\mathbf{z}$ and $\mathbf{u}$ uniformly and independently from $\mathbb{Z}_p^m$ and set $\mathbf{w} = \mathbf{B}\mathbf{u}$. If $\|\mathbf{b} + \mathbf{w}\| < (m+1)l_0/\sqrt{2}$, where the parameter l_0 is chosen as described in [BSW16], resample $\mathbf{u}$ until $\|\mathbf{b} + \mathbf{w}\| \geq (m+1)l_0/\sqrt{2}$. The vector $\mathbf{z}$ is used to sparsify the lattice $\Lambda_{(\mathbf{A},q)}$ and $\mathbf{w}$ is used to offset the target vector $\mathbf{b}$. The sparsified lattice $\Lambda_{p,\mathbf{z}}$ of Λ is now defined as

$$\Lambda_{p,\mathbf{z}} = \{\mathbf{v} \in \Lambda(\mathbf{B}) \mid \langle \mathbf{z}, \mathbf{B}^{-1}\mathbf{v} \rangle = 0 \mod p\}.$$

If $\mathbf{z} \neq \mathbf{0}$ then $\Lambda_{p,\mathbf{z}}$ is a sublattice of $\Lambda_{(\mathbf{A},q)}$ of index p as shown in the following lemma.

Lemma 1. *Let Λ be a d-dimensional full-rank lattice, $\mathbf{B}$ be a basis of Λ, p be some prime, $\mathbf{z} \in \mathbb{Z}_p^n \setminus \{\mathbf{0}\}$ and $\Lambda_{p,\mathbf{z}} = \{\mathbf{v} \in \Lambda(\mathbf{B}) \mid \langle \mathbf{z}, \mathbf{B}^{-1}\mathbf{v} \rangle = 0 \mod p\}$. Then it holds that $[\Lambda : \Lambda_{p,\mathbf{z}}] = p$.*

Proof. Consider the homomorphism

$$\varphi : \Lambda \to (\mathbb{Z}_p, +), \quad \mathbf{v} \mapsto \langle \mathbf{z}, \mathbf{B}^{-1}\mathbf{v} \rangle \mod p.$$

We first show that φ is surjective. Let j be an index with $z_j \neq 0$. Let a be some arbitrary element in $\mathbb{Z}_p$. Then for $\mathbf{v} = \mathbf{Bx}$, where $\mathbf{x} \in \mathbb{Z}^n$ with $x_i = 0$ for $i \neq j$ and $x_j = (z_j^{-1} \bmod p)a$, it holds that $\varphi(\mathbf{v}) = a$. Hence φ is surjective and by the isomorphism theorem we have

$$\Lambda/\Lambda_{p,\mathbf{z}} = \Lambda/\ker(\varphi) \simeq \text{im}(\varphi) = \mathbb{Z}_p \quad \text{and} \quad [\Lambda : \Lambda_{p,\mathbf{z}}] = p.$$

A basis $\mathbf{B}_{p,\mathbf{z}}$ of $\Lambda_{p,\mathbf{z}}$ is constructed (as described in Lemma 9 of [BSW16]) and then embedded into

$$\mathbf{B}' = \begin{pmatrix} \mathbf{B}_{p,\mathbf{z}} & \mathbf{b} + \mathbf{w} \\ \mathbf{0} & M \end{pmatrix} \in \mathbb{Z}^{(m+1)\times(m+1)}$$

using the vector $\mathbf{b}+\mathbf{w}$. How to choose the embedding factor M for the proof of the reduction is described in [BSW16]. However, as typical for Kannan's embedding approach, we choose $M = 1$ in our analysis. Finally, a shortest non-zero vector $\mathbf{v}$ of $\Lambda(\mathbf{B}')$ is recovered by basis reduction and the vector consisting of its first m components is returned. Note that the output is not necessarily given by $\pm\mathbf{e}$, hence the attack is not always successful. This is the case because the attack can only succeed in recovering $\mathbf{e}$ if the vector closest to $\mathbf{b} + \mathbf{w}$ is in $\Lambda_{(\mathbf{A},q)}$, $\mathbf{b}+\mathbf{w}-\mathbf{e}$ namely is also contained in $\Lambda_{p,\mathbf{z}}$. If the sparsified lattice $\Lambda_{p,\mathbf{z}}$ is chosen randomly as described above, the success probability of the attack is roughly $\frac{1}{p}$, see Corollary 2.17 in [SD16] and Lemma 13 in [BSW16]. We experimentally verified this success probability as can be seen in Fig. 1. For more details on sparsification, we refer to [BSW16]. The pseudocode for a simple version of the sparsified embedding attack on LWE is given in Algorithm 2.

Algorithm 2. The sparsified embedding approach

Input : An LWE instance $(\mathbf{A}, \mathbf{b} = \mathbf{As} + \mathbf{e} \bmod q) \in \mathbb{Z}_q^{m\times n} \times \mathbb{Z}_q^m$, a prime p, and $l_0 > 0$, embedding factor M

Output : A potential solution $\mathbf{x}$ s.t. $\mathbf{x} = \pm\mathbf{e}$ with probability roughly $\frac{1}{p}$

1 Construct a lattice basis $\mathbf{B} \in \mathbb{Z}^{m\times m}$ of the lattice
$\Lambda_{(\mathbf{A},q)} = \{\mathbf{v} \in \mathbb{Z}_q^m \mid \mathbf{v} \equiv \mathbf{Ax} \pmod{q} \text{ for some } \mathbf{x} \in \mathbb{Z}^n\}$;

2 Sample $\mathbf{z}$ and $\mathbf{u}$ uniformly and independently from $\mathbb{Z}_p^m$ and set $\mathbf{w} = \mathbf{Bu}$ until $\|\mathbf{b} + \mathbf{w}\| \geq (m+1)l_0/\sqrt{2}$;

3 Construct a lattice basis $\mathbf{B}_{p,\mathbf{z}}$ of the sparsified lattice
$\Lambda_{p,\mathbf{z}} = \{\mathbf{v} \in \Lambda(\mathbf{B}) \mid \langle\mathbf{z}, \mathbf{B}^{-1}\mathbf{v}\rangle = 0 \bmod p\}$;

4 Set $\mathbf{B}' = \begin{pmatrix} \mathbf{B}_{p,\mathbf{z}} & \mathbf{b} + \mathbf{w} \\ \mathbf{0} & M \end{pmatrix} \in \mathbb{Z}^{(m+1)\times(m+1)}$;

5 Recover $\mathbf{v} = \begin{pmatrix} \mathbf{x} \\ y \end{pmatrix}$ by solving (u)SVP in $\Lambda(\mathbf{B}')$ using basis reduction;

6 **return x**;

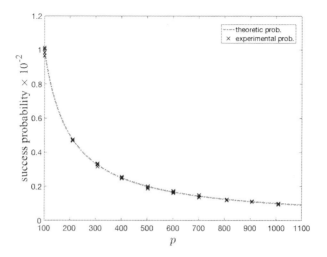

Fig. 1. Success probability of the sparsified embedding approach for the instances in [LP10] with $(n, m, q, \sigma) \in \{(128, 320, 2053, 6.77), (192, 480, 4093, 8.87), (256, 640, 4093, 8.35), (320, 800, 4093, 8.00)\}$ for each $p \in \{101, 211, 307, 401, 503, 601, 701, 809, 907, 1009\}$. We used one million samples for each instance.

4   Analysis

In [BSW16], it is shown that the sparsified embedding yields an improved reduction from BDD_α to $uSVP_\gamma$ compared to Kannan's embedding in the sense that it gives better gaps ($\gamma = \frac{1}{\sqrt{2}\alpha}$ instead of $\gamma = \frac{1}{2\alpha}$). This improvement, however, comes at the cost of a probabilistic reduction instead of a deterministic one. In this section we theoretically analyze and compare the practical behavior of both embedding approaches under common heuristics used in lattice-based cryptography. Note that the practical behavior substantially differs from the provable reductions, since in those reductions "worst cases" that can occur need to be taken into account while the practical behavior is determined by the average case. Let Λ_s be the embedded sparsified lattice of dimension d. From the 2016 estimate [ADPS16, AGVW17], it can be deduced that the sparsified embedding attack succeeds if the unique shortest non-zero vector is contained in Λ_s and the block size β satisfies

$$\sqrt{\beta/d}\lambda_1(\Lambda_s) \leq \delta^{2\beta-d}\det(\Lambda_s)^{1/d}.$$

In the following, we elaborate on this assumption by analyzing how to solve BDD using the two embedding approaches (the results carry over to LWE if viewed as an instance of BDD as described in Sect. 3).

4.1   Heuristics for Kannan's Embedding

For Kannan's embedding, most works considered with the practicality of the attack implicitly assume that there is no reduction loss in practice, i.e., that

$\gamma = \frac{1}{\alpha}$ instead of $\gamma = \frac{1}{2\alpha}$ (see for example [APS15, AGVW17]). In the following, we elaborate on this assumption. Let Λ be the m-dimensional BDD lattice, Λ' be the d-dimensional uSVP lattice obtained by using Kannan's embedding technique for the BDD lattice Λ and the BDD target vector $\mathbf{t}$ as described in Sect. 3. Let $\alpha = \mathsf{dist}(\mathbf{t}, \Lambda)/\lambda_1(\Lambda)$ be the approximation factor of the BDD instance and $\gamma = \lambda_2(\Lambda')/\lambda_1(\Lambda')$ be the approximation factor of the resulting uSVP instance. In practice, it is common (see for example [APS15, AGVW17]) to make the following heuristic assumptions.

1. Under the assumption that Λ is a random lattice, $\lambda_1(\Lambda)$ corresponds to the Gaussian heuristic for Λ.
2. As Kannan's embedding adds the uniquely distance short vector from $\mathbf{t}$ to the nearest lattice point to the lattice, we can assume that $\lambda_1(\Lambda')$ corresponds to $\mathsf{dist}(\mathbf{t}, \Lambda) = \alpha\lambda_1(\Lambda)$, i.e., $\lambda_1(\Lambda') = \alpha\lambda_1(\Lambda)$.
3. Under the assumption that except for this uniquely short vector Λ' behaves as a random lattice, we can assume that $\lambda_2(\Lambda')$ corresponds to the Gaussian heuristic for Λ', which is the same as the Gaussian heuristic for Λ, i.e., $\lambda_2(\Lambda') = \lambda_1(\Lambda)$.
4. In conclusion, we obtain $\frac{1}{\alpha} = \frac{\lambda_1(\Lambda)}{\lambda_1(\Lambda')} = \frac{\lambda_2(\Lambda')}{\lambda_1(\Lambda')} = \gamma$.

This shows that heuristically, Kannan's embedding approach performs much better in practice than guaranteed by the theoretical reduction, which only guarantees the gap $\frac{1}{2\alpha}$.

It remains to determine the necessary block size for BKZ to solve such an instance. According to the 2016 estimate [ADPS16, AGVW17], the Gaussian heuristic, and $\gamma = \frac{1}{\alpha}$, we get that the required block size β is the minimal β that satisfies

$$\alpha = \frac{1}{\gamma} \leq \sqrt{\frac{2\pi e}{\beta}}\delta^{2\beta-d} = \sqrt{\frac{2\pi e}{\beta}}\left((((\pi\beta)^{1/\beta}\beta)/(2\pi e))^{1/(2(\beta-1))}\right)^{2\beta-d}.$$

In the LWE case, parameterized by the secret dimension n, the number of samples m, the modulus q, and the standard deviation σ of the error distribution, we may instead use the condition

$$\sqrt{\beta}\sigma \leq \delta^{2\beta-(m+1)}(q^{m-n})^{1/(m+1)},$$

since according to the Gaussian heuristic the gap can be estimated as

$$\alpha = \frac{\lambda_1(\Lambda)}{\lambda_2(\Lambda)} = \frac{\sigma\sqrt{d}}{\sqrt{d/(2\pi e)}\det(\Lambda)^{1/d}} = \frac{\sigma\sqrt{2\pi e}}{(q^{m-n})^{1/d}}.$$

This condition takes the extra dimension introduced by the embedding into account (i.e., $d = m + 1$) and corresponds to the 2016 estimate for LWE [AGVW17].

4.2   Heuristics for the Sparsified Embedding

In this subsection, we analyze how the sparsified embedding performs in practice, assuming that the heuristics presented in Subsect. 4.1 are reasonable. Let Λ, Λ', d, α, $\mathbf{t}$, and γ be as in Subsect. 4.1. Let p be the prime number used for the sparsification of Λ and $\Lambda_s \subset \Lambda$ be some sparsified sublattice of Λ with $[\Lambda : \Lambda_s] = p$, due to Lemma 1. Then it holds that $\det(\Lambda_s) = p \cdot \det(\Lambda)$. If the sparsification is random (as described in the reduction), then the probability to keep the closest vector in Λ to the target $\mathbf{t}$ in the sparsified lattice Λ_s is roughly $\frac{1}{p}$. So the probability that one can solve the BDD problem at all in the sparsified lattice is close to $\frac{1}{p}$. This assertion is verified experimentally in Sect. 3.2. Assume that we are in the success case, i.e., the closest lattice vector in Λ to the target $\mathbf{t}$ is kept in the sparsified lattice Λ_s. Let Λ'_s be the d-dimensional embedded lattice of Λ_s. Then we can apply the following heuristics.

1. $\lambda_1(\Lambda_s)$ corresponds to the Gaussian heuristic for Λ_s which yields $\lambda_1(\Lambda_s) = p^{1/d}\lambda_1(\Lambda)$.
2. $\lambda_1(\Lambda'_s)$ corresponds to $\mathsf{dist}(\mathbf{t}, \Lambda_s) = \mathsf{dist}(\mathbf{t}, \Lambda) = \alpha\lambda_1(\Lambda)$, i.e., $\lambda_1(\Lambda'_s) = \alpha\lambda_1(\Lambda) = \lambda_1(\Lambda')$.
3. $\lambda_2(\Lambda'_s)$ corresponds to the Gaussian heuristic for Λ'_s, which is the same as the Gaussian heuristic for Λ_s, i.e., $\lambda_2(\Lambda'_s) = \lambda_1(\Lambda_s) = p^{1/d}\lambda_1(\Lambda) = p^{1/d}\lambda_2(\Lambda')$.
4. Let γ_s be the uSVP gap in Λ'_s. Then we get $\gamma_s = \frac{\lambda_2(\Lambda'_s)}{\lambda_1(\Lambda'_s)} = \frac{p^{1/d}\lambda_2(\Lambda')}{\lambda_1(\Lambda')} = p^{1/d}\gamma = p^{1/d}\frac{1}{\alpha}$.

In conclusion, heuristically the gap of the sparsified embedding technique $\gamma_s = p^{1/d}\frac{1}{\alpha}$ improves by a factor of $p^{1/d}$ compared to Kannan's embedding, and of course it improves the gap $\frac{1}{\sqrt{2}\alpha}$ guaranteed by the theoretical reduction. Note however, that this improvement comes at the cost of a success probability of (roughly) $\frac{1}{p}$.

It remains to determine the necessary block size for BKZ to solve such an instance. Similar as above, for the success case with $\gamma_s = p^{1/d}\frac{1}{\alpha}$, we get that the required block size β is the minimal β that satisfies

$$\alpha = \frac{1}{\gamma} \le p^{1/d}\sqrt{\frac{2\pi e}{\beta}}\delta^{2\beta - d} = p^{1/d}\sqrt{\frac{2\pi e}{\beta}}\left(\left(((\pi\beta)^{1/\beta}\beta)/(2\pi e)\right)^{1/(2(\beta-1))}\right)^{2\beta - d}.$$

In the LWE case parameterized by n, m, q, and σ as above we may instead use the condition

$$\sqrt{\beta}\sigma \le \delta^{2\beta - (m+1)}(pq^{m-n})^{1/(m+1)}.$$

4.3   Comparison

As shown in the previous subsections, the heuristic improvement of using sparsification in the embedding approach is a factor of $p^{1/d}$ in the uSVP gap which results in a smaller necessary block size for BKZ to solve the resulting uSVP problem. In the following, we further analyze this improvement. First, note that if $p = p(d)$ is chosen to be polynomial in d, the improvement factor $p^{1/d}$ tends to 1 as d increases, i.e., asymptotically, the improvement vanishes. On the other hand, if $p = p(d)$ is chosen to be exponential in d, the success probability of roughly $\frac{1}{p}$ is negligible. Therefore, to achieve an overall improvement in practice, taking the success probability into account, if at all possible, p must be chosen carefully for the specific instance. The choice of p also depends on the use case. For instance, if one has access to a parallel computing architecture, different sparsifications can be run in parallel, then the success probability might not be relevant. However, if this is not the case, the low success probability seems to render the attack less efficient than Kannan's embedding. Therefore, we emphasize that this must be taken into account when comparing the two approaches. In Table 1 we show the predicted minimal block sizes for BKZ according to the

Table 1. Minimal block sizes β according to the 2016 estimate for various dimensions d, approximation factors α, and primes p. The exception $p = 1$ indicates that no sparsification is used.

$d = 256, \alpha = 1/2$			$d = 256, \alpha = 1/4$		
$1 \le p \le 3$	$5 \le p \le 59$	$61 \le p \le 751$	$1 \le p \le 31$	$37 \le p \le 1899$	$1901 \le p \le 119563$
$\beta = 157$	$\beta = 156$	$\beta = 155$	$\beta = 101$	$\beta = 100$	$\beta = 99$
$d = 512, \alpha = 1/2$			$d = 512, \alpha = 1/4$		
$1 \le p \le 5$	$7 \le p \le 127$	$131 \le p \le 2447$	$1 \le p \le 3$	$5 \le p \le 409$	$419 \le p \le 42257$
$\beta = 350$	$\beta = 349$	$\beta = 348$	$\beta = 253$	$\beta = 252$	$\beta = 251$
$d = 1024, \alpha = 1/2$			$d = 1024, \alpha = 1/4$		
$1 \le p \le 11$	$13 \le p \le 349$	$353 \le p \le 9661$	$1 \le p \le 47$	$53 \le p \le 7309$	$7321 \le p \le 1063399$
$\beta = 748$	$\beta = 747$	$\beta = 746$	$\beta = 572$	$\beta = 571$	$\beta = 570$

Table 2. Minimal block sizes β according to the 2016 estimate for various LWE instances parameterized by the secret dimension n, the number of samples m, the modulus q, and the standard deviation σ of the error distribution and for various primes p. The exception $p = 1$ indicates that no sparsification is used.

$n = 65, m = 182, q = 521, \sigma = 8/\sqrt{2\pi}$		
$1 \le p \le 23$	$29 \le p \le 887$	$907 \le p \le 27953$
$\beta = 56$	$\beta = 55$	$\beta = 54$
$n = 80, m = 204, q = 1031, \sigma = 8/\sqrt{2\pi}$		
$1 \le p \le 43$	$47 \le p \le 2593$	$2609 \le p \le 157393$
$\beta = 59$	$\beta = 58$	$\beta = 57$
$n = 100, m = 243, q = 2053, \sigma = 8/\sqrt{2\pi}$		
$1 \le p \le 113$	$127 \le p \le 21859$	$21863 \le p \le 4141603$
$\beta = 67$	$\beta = 66$	$\beta = 65$
$n = 108, m = 261, q = 2053, \sigma = 8/\sqrt{2\pi}$		
$1 \le p \le 3$	$5 \le p \le 59$	$61 \le p \le 751$
$\beta = 77$	$\beta = 76$	$\beta = 75$
$n = 110, m = 272, q = 2053, \sigma = 8/\sqrt{2\pi}$		
$1 \le p \le 263$	$269 \le p \le 77689$	$77699 \le p \le 24198547$
$\beta = 79$	$\beta = 78$	$\beta = 77$

2016 estimate required by Kannan's embedding and the sparsified embedding approach for BDD instances of various parameter sets. As indicated by these examples, the benefit of using sparsification (in the success case) depends on different parameters. Taking the success probability into account, these examples suggest that in general sparsification does not yield a better attack in practice, as one needs to use huge sparification primes p (hence tiny success probabilities of roughly $\frac{1}{p}$) to obtain a noticeable decrease in the block size. In Table 2 we show the same for the LWE instances analyzed in [AGVW17]. Note that we could not reproduce the exact block sizes for Kannan's embedding for the instances with $n = 80$ (block size 59 instead of 60) and $n = 110$ (block size 79 instead of 78), as they seem to be chosen incorrectly in [AGVW17]. The examples presented in Table 2 imply the same conclusions as can be drawn from the examples presented in Table 1.

5   Conclusion

While applying sparsification yields an improved theoretical reduction from BDD to uSVP, our analysis suggests that the corresponding sparsified embedding attack does not necessarily perform better than Kannan's embedding approach. The main reason for this is that in order to obtain a noticeable improvement in the runtime of the success cases, one needs to use a very large prime p for sparsifying the lattice. This however comes at the cost of a very low success probability of roughly $\frac{1}{p}$ of the attack and in general the trade-off does not seem to be in favor of using sparsification. Nevertheless, there may be instances where it is better to use the sparsified embedding attack with small or medium sized primes. In particular, running the sparsified embedding attack in parallel with different sparsifications may compensate for not too small success probabilities.

Acknowledgments. This work has been supported by JSPS KAKENHI Grant Number JP17J01987 and by the DFG as part of project P1 within the CRC 1119 CROSS-ING.

References

[ADPS16] Alkim, E., Ducas, L., Pöppelmann, T., Schwabe, P.: Post-quantum key exchange - a new hope. In: Holz, T., Savage, S. (eds.) 25th USENIX Security Symposium, USENIX Security 16, pp. 327–343. USENIX Association (2016)

[AFG14] Albrecht, M.R., Fitzpatrick, R., Göpfert, F.: On the efficacy of solving LWE by reduction to unique-SVP. In: Lee, H.-S., Han, D.-G. (eds.) ICISC 2013. LNCS, vol. 8565, pp. 293–310. Springer, Cham (2014). https://doi.org/10.1007/978-3-319-12160-4_18

[AGVW17] Albrecht, M.R., Göpfert, F., Virdia, F., Wunderer, T.: Revisiting the expected cost of solving uSVP and applications to LWE. In: Takagi, T., Peyrin, T. (eds.) ASIACRYPT 2017. LNCS, vol. 10624, pp. 297–322. Springer, Cham (2017). https://doi.org/10.1007/978-3-319-70694-8_11

[APS15]   Albrecht, M.R., Player, R., Scott, S.: On the concrete hardness of Learning with Errors. J. Math. Cryptol. **9**(3), 169–203 (2015)

[AWHT16] Aono, Y., Wang, Y., Hayashi, T., Takagi, T.: Improved progressive BKZ algorithms and their precise cost estimation by sharp simulator. In: Fischlin, M., Coron, J.-S. (eds.) EUROCRYPT 2016. LNCS, vol. 9665, pp. 789–819. Springer, Heidelberg (2016). https://doi.org/10.1007/978-3-662-49890-3_30

[BG14]   Bai, S., Galbraith, S.D.: An improved compression technique for signatures based on learning with errors. In: Benaloh, J. (ed.) CT-RSA 2014. LNCS, vol. 8366, pp. 28–47. Springer, Cham (2014). https://doi.org/10.1007/978-3-319-04852-9_2

[BSW16]   Bai, S., Stehlé, D., Wen, W.: Improved reduction from the bounded distance decoding problem to the unique shortest vector problem in lattices. In: Chatzigiannakis, I., Mitzenmacher, M., Rabani, Y., Sangiorgi, D. (eds.) ICALP 2016, Volume 55 of LIPIcs, pp. 76:1–76:12. Schloss Dagstuhl, July 2016

[Che13]   Chen, Y.: Réduction de réseau et sécurité concrete du chiffrement completement homomorphe. Ph.D. thesis, ENS-Lyon, France (2013)

[CN11]   Chen, Y., Nguyen, P.Q.: BKZ 2.0: better lattice security estimates. In: Lee, D.H., Wang, X. (eds.) ASIACRYPT 2011. LNCS, vol. 7073, pp. 1–20. Springer, Heidelberg (2011). https://doi.org/10.1007/978-3-642-25385-0_1

[DK13]   Dadush, D., Kun, G.: Lattice sparsification and the approximate closest vector problem. In: Khanna, S. (ed.) 24th SODA, pp. 1088–1102. ACM-SIAM, January 2013

[DRS14]   Dadush, D., Regev, O., Stephens-Davidowitz, N.: On the closest vector problem with a distance guarantee. In: IEEE 29th Conference on Computational Complexity, CCC 2014, Vancouver, BC, Canada, June 11–13, 2014, pp. 98–109. IEEE Computer Society (2014)

[GSW13]   Gentry, C., Sahai, A., Waters, B.: homomorphic encryption from learning with errors: conceptually-simpler, asymptotically-faster, attribute-based. In: Canetti, R., Garay, J.A. (eds.) CRYPTO 2013. LNCS, vol. 8042, pp. 75–92. Springer, Heidelberg (2013). https://doi.org/10.1007/978-3-642-40041-4_5

[Kan87]   Kannan, R.: Minkowski's convex body theorem and integer programming. Math. Oper. Res. **12**(3), 415–440 (1987)

[Kho03]   Khot, S.: Hardness of approximating the shortest vector problem in high Lp norms. In: 44th FOCS, pp. 290–297. IEEE Computer Society Press, October 2003

[Kho04]   Khot, S.: Hardness of approximating the shortest vector problem in lattices. In: 45th FOCS, pp. 126–135. IEEE Computer Society Press, October 2004

[LLM06]   Liu, Y.-K., Lyubashevsky, V., Micciancio, D.: On bounded distance decoding for general lattices. In: Díaz, J., Jansen, K., Rolim, J.D.P., Zwick, U. (eds.) APPROX/RANDOM-2006. LNCS, vol. 4110, pp. 450–461. Springer, Heidelberg (2006). https://doi.org/10.1007/11830924_41

[LM09]   Lyubashevsky, V., Micciancio, D.: On bounded distance decoding, unique shortest vectors, and the minimum distance problem. In: Halevi, S. (ed.) CRYPTO 2009. LNCS, vol. 5677, pp. 577–594. Springer, Heidelberg (2009). https://doi.org/10.1007/978-3-642-03356-8_34

[LP10] Lindner, R., Peikert, C.: Better key sizes (and attacks) for LWE-based encryption. Cryptology ePrint Archive, Report 2010/613 (2010). http://eprint.iacr.org/2010/613

[LP11] Lindner, R., Peikert, C.: Better key sizes (and attacks) for LWE-based encryption. In: Kiayias, A. (ed.) CT-RSA 2011. LNCS, vol. 6558, pp. 319–339. Springer, Heidelberg (2011). https://doi.org/10.1007/978-3-642-19074-2_21

[LWXZ14] Liu, M., Wang, X., Guangwu, X., Zheng, X.: A note on BDD problems with λ_2-gap. Inf. Process. Lett. **114**(1–2), 9–12 (2014)

[Reg09] Regev, O.: On lattices, learning with errors, random linear codes, and cryptography. J. ACM **56**(6), 140 (2009)

[SD16] Stephens-Davidowitz, N.: Discrete Gaussian sampling reduces to CVP and SVP. In: Krauthgamer, R. (ed.) 27th SODA, pp. 1748–1764. ACM-SIAM, January 2016

[SE94] Schnorr, C.-P., Euchner, M.: Lattice basis reduction: improved practical algorithms and solving subset sum problems. Math. Program. **66**, 181–199 (1994)

[Var97] Vardy, A.: Algorithmic complexity in coding theory and the minimum distance problem (invited session). In: 29th ACM STOC, pp. 92–109. ACM Press, May 1997

[WAT18] Wang, Y., Aono, Y., Takagi, T.: An experimental study of kannan's embedding technique for the search LWE problem. In: Qing, S., Mitchell, C., Chen, L., Liu, D. (eds.) ICICS 2017. LNCS, vol. 10631, pp. 541–553. Springer, Cham (2018). https://doi.org/10.1007/978-3-319-89500-0_47

Security for Cyber-physical Systems

Efficient and Secure Firmware Update/Rollback Method for Vehicular Devices

Yuichi Komano[(✉)], Zhengfan Xia, Takeshi Kawabata, and Hideo Shimizu

Toshiba Corporation, Kawasaki, Japan
{yuichi1.komano,takeshi3.kawabata,hideo.shimizu}@toshiba.co.jp

Abstract. Updating a firmware of a vehicular device is inevitable in order to improve not only the functionality but also the security. The vehicle consists of devices which are resource-constrained and produced by different vendors. Therefore, a lightweight update method, which ensure the correctness of the update as a vehicular system, is required. Moreover, since the update is a critical task, it is mandatory to ensure the security of the update. Recently, on the other hand, the vehicular system becomes complicated, sometimes with a non-genuine device attached by car owner; and hence, we should consider the case where a vehicular system becomes inconsistent even though a patch has been correctly applied. In such case, a rollback of the firmware should be required. In this paper, we propose a secure and efficient firmware update/rollback method to solve above issues. We also demonstrate it with our experiments.

1 Introduction

Recently, a vehicle consists of electronic devices, called electronic control units (ECUs), connected to an in-vehicle network. These ECUs communicate with each other to execute complicated operations, such as a self-driving. On the vehicles, lots of cyber attacks and countermeasures have been reported [1–3].

There are plenty of discussions to improve the security of in-vehicle network, especially, the controller area network (CAN, [4]). Since there is no security mechanism in the CAN specification, some extension should be required for a secure CAN communication. The most popular solution is to use a message authentication code (MAC, [5,6]). However, since the code (e.g., 128-bit) is longer than the CAN message payload (64-bit), the code should be either truncated by degrading its security (e.g., 8-bit) or transmitted with multiple CAN messages by decreasing the communication rate (e.g., two additional messages). Another solution is to use an Anonymized-ID (A-ID, [7–9]). The A-ID is a random string generated with a seed shared between legitimate ECUs in secret. It is embedded in the extended ID area (up to 18-bit) and a receiver ECU discards illegitimate

---

Z. Xia—Presently, the author is with the University of Toronto.

C. Su and H. Kikuchi (Eds.): ISPEC 2018, LNCS 11125, pp. 455–467, 2018.
https://doi.org/10.1007/978-3-319-99807-7_28

messages with invalid A-IDs by a lightweight ID filter. With the A-ID, although the consistency of payload is not ensured, the DoS attack from the illegitimate devices can be invalidated.

As for the ECU, threats of physical and logical attacks have been discussed. On the physical attacks, side channel attacks, including the power analysis attacks [10,11] and its extensions [12–16], can be serious threats; however, careful designs with well-known countermeasures [17] can protect the ECU from such attacks. Compared to the physical attacks, the logical attacks are easy to implement and many researchers report vulnerabilities in vehicular devices' firmwares (softwares). A popular countermeasure against such logical attacks is an (on-line[1]) firmware update. Let us discuss the firmware update below.

1.1 Firmware Update

Firmware update is a popular solution to improve the functionality and security of electronic devices. It is widely used for PCs, network equipments, and mobile devices. In the vehicular system, firmwares of the *resourceful* devices, such as the gateway and telematics equipments, can be updated in the similar way. However, it should be difficult to apply the similar way to the *resource-constrained ECUs*, via the in-vehicle narrow-band network.

For the resource-constrained ECUs, Teraoka et al. [18,19] proposed *an incremental update method*, which decreases the sizes both of transmitted patch files and of working memory required for the ECU. They modified the BSDiff [20] to update the firmware block by block, where the block is a (e.g., 4 KB) segment of the flash memory in the ECU. They also changed both the data structure of the patch file in order to be incrementally applicable, and the compression method from bzip2 to LZMA [21] in order to decrease the size of working memory in the decompression.

1.2 Our Contribution

As we reviewed, the firmware update plays an important role to ensure the security of the vehicle system. However, once the firmware is updated with a malicious code, it leads a serious problem. Hence, the firmware update itself should be well-protected. Generally speaking, using a message authentication code (MAC) or digital signature is a promising solution. From the resource constraint of ECU, the MAC is supposed to be used.

On the other hand, the vehicle consists of devices produced by different vendors. It leads another issue with the MAC. Let us assume that the ECU vendor provides a patch file and sends it (from a cloud server) to the ECU via the gateway. Also assume that the gateway controls the vehicular state; it changes the state to be unmovable during the update. Though the MAC can ensure the end-to-end security between the ECU vendor and ECU (when the

---

[1] Firmwares can be updated off-line via. e.g., a device connected to the OBD-II or USB port. In this paper, we omit it and focus on the on-line update.

predetermined key is implemented in the ECU before the shipment), it does not help the gateway to check the correctness of the update. In other word, only with the MAC, the gateway cannot control the vehicular state correctly. We propose a systematic method, *a verifiable end-to-end firmware update* with a hash chain, realizing a correct and secure update.

In addition to the update, let us discuss a rollback of the firmware. Recently, the vehicle system becomes complicated, and it may further include an (illegal) device attached by a car owner. Hence, ensuring the consistency of (updated) firmware becomes a hard task. If the system is inconsistent after a firmware is updated, a rollback of the firmware should be required. The rollback can executed with another patch file; however, it may increase the data size in the update/rollback. We also present an efficient method, *two-way patch for update/rollback*, which realizes the update/rollback with only one patch file.

The remainder of this paper is organized as follows. Section 2 reviews the related works. In Sect. 3, we discuss the problems to be solved and propose our method. We show our experiments in Sect. 4, and then, we discuss the pros and cons in Sect. 5. Finally, Sect. 6 concludes this paper.

2   Related Works on Firmware Update Methods

As stated in Sect. 1.1, the firmware update is widely used for recent electronic systems. As for the vehicle system, several reports [22–24] proposed the methods to accelerate the update by using high-speed in-vehicle network other than CAN, and by paralleling updates of firmwares in multiple ECUs.

With a restricted environment, Teraoka et al. [18,19] proposed *an incremental update method* to update a firmware of single resource-constrained ECU over the low-speed CAN, based on the BSDiff/BSPatch [20].

Let us briefly review the BSDiff/BSPatch. Assume that a software vendor will release a patch file to enable devices to update a software. To do so, the vendor generates a patch file including a difference between the old and new softwares with the BSDiff, and sends the patch file to a device. The size of the patch file is supposed to be smaller than the (compressed) new software, because the new software should be close to the old software and the difference can be small to be compressible. The device, receiving the patch file, updates the old software to the new one by adding the difference with BSPatch. The BSDiff/BSPatch has been used to update softwares for FreeBSD and so on. However, since it is designed to update a software for resourceful PCs, especially, with lots of working memory, it is unsuitable for the resource-constrained devices. Teraoka et al. made three modifications to the BSDiff/BSPatch as follows.

Block Delta Encoding: The firmware is stored in the flash memory within each ECU. In general, when we modify data in the flash memory, we first erase the data block by block, where the block consists of e.g., 64-pages, and then, we write new data into the erased block. In order to decrease working memory required for a firmware update, the incremental update method divides the program code of the firmware into above blocks, and updates the firmware block by block. The patch file is generated as in Fig. 1; for each block from the bottom to the top in the new firmware, the block delta encoding looks for a block of the old firmware which gives a minimum patch file.

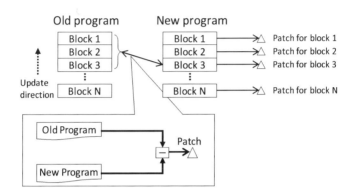

Fig. 1. Block delta encoding

Two-Stage Compression: The BSDiff compresses a difference between the softwares with the bzip2, which is a combination of the Burrows-Wheeler transform [25] and the Huffman coding [26]. However, this compression algorithm requires lots of working memory in its decompression (in the BSPatch). Teraoka et al. changed the algorithm from the bzip2 to the LZMA. The LZMA is a combination of the LZ77 encoding [27] and the binary range encoding [28], as in Fig. 2, which requires less working memory than the bzip2 does.

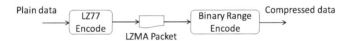

Fig. 2. Two-stage compression

Data-Format Serialization: The original BSDiff generates a patch file which consists of control commands for each block, differences for each block, and extra data for each block. Since the control command, difference, and extra data for each block is not in serial, the BSPatch requires the whole patch file in the update. Namely, it requires lots of working memory to extend the whole patch file. In the incremental update method, on the other hand, a patch file consists of three-tuples, for each block in serial, of control command, difference, and extra data, as in Fig. 3. The resulting patch file might be less compressible than the original one. However, in the execution of (modified) BSPatch, only a part of the patch file to update the block is required. Therefore, there is no need to extend the whole patch file and their method can save the working memory.

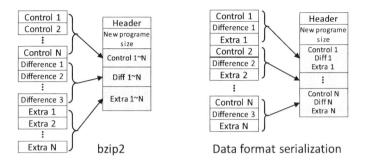

Fig. 3. Data format serialization

3   Our Efficient Firmware Update/Rollback Method

We explain issues to be solved and propose our firmware update/rollback method.

3.1   Our Issues

We aim to solve two issues; (a) a verifiable update for hierarchical and multi-vendor system, and (b) an efficient rollback mechanism.

(a) Verifiable Update for Hierarchical and Multi-vendor System: Let us model the firmware update with a cloud server storage, ECU vendors and vehicles, as in Fig. 4. We assume the

- Cloud storage server
  - It stores a patch file for an update and a corresponding MAC for the updated firmware.
    - * It also stores an auxiliary data, such as the release date of the patch file. For simplicity, we omit it in this paper.
  - It sends a patch file and a corresponding MAC to ECU via the gateway (Step 2 in Fig. 4). We assume that transmitted data between the server and gateway are encrypted and authenticated with their digital signatures.
- ECU vendor
  - It provides an ECU and its firmware.
  - It also provides a patch file and a corresponding MAC for the firmware update and registers them to the cloud storage server (Step 1).
- Vehicle
  - It consists of the gateway and ECUs provided by different vendors.
  - Gateway
    - * It is supposed to be resourceful, different from ECUs, to communicate with the cloud storage server via secure channel with encryptions and digital signatures.

    * It controls the vehicle. Namely, upon receiving a patch file and a
      MAC, it first changes the vehicle's mode to be unmovable (Step 3)
      and then passes the patch file and MAC to a corresponding ECU via
      in-vehicle network (Step 4).
    * It changes the vehicle's mode to be movable if the firmware update is
      over (Step 7).
  • ECU
    * It, upon receiving the patch file and MAC, updates its firmware by
      checking the MAC (Step 5). It returns a reply to report the result of
      the update (Step 6).

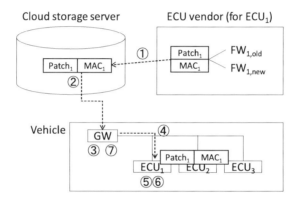

Fig. 4. Firmware update model

The MAC ensures the end-to-end security. It may be replaced by the digital signature. However, the digital signature is unsuitable for the resource-
constrained ECU.

At Step 7 in Fig. 4, the gateway changes the vehicle's mode depending on
the reply from the ECU at Step 6. However, the reply is untrusted without any
cryptographic assurance function. Moreover, even if some assurance function is
used, it may be problematic that the overhead enlarges when multiple ECUs in
the same vehicle updates their firmware at the same time. Our issues on these
topics are:

(A1) How does the gateway trust the ECU's reply to control the vehicle
correctly?
(A2) How are updates of multiple ECUs' firmwares executed efficiently?

(b) Efficient Rollback Mechanism: As discussed in Sect. 1.1, in this paper,
we discuss a functionality of software rollback. The straightforward way is to
apply a patch file, which downgrades the new firmware to the old one, to the new
firmware. Note that, in the original BSDiff, the patch file for rollback ($patch_{rb}$) is
different from that for update ($patch_{ud}$). Therefore, the gateway needs to receive

both patch files from the cloud storage server and pass them to ECU; moreover, the gateway needs to verify two signatures for both patch files.

On the roll back, we have a question to be solved:

(B1) Is there any efficient mechanism for the rollback?

3.2 Our Solutions

In this section, we give our solution against the above issues.

(a) Verifiable End-to-End Firmware Update: On the (A1) in the previous subsection, we extend the model of Fig. 4 to one with a "firmware check code (FCC)" as in Fig. 5.

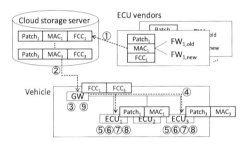

Fig. 5. Model of verifiable end-to-end firmware update

Each ECU vendor provides an FCC based on a new firmware. An examples of FCC is a chained hash value of the firmware, $FCC_1 = \mathsf{hash}(\mathsf{hash}(FW_{1,new}))$. In order to avoid an attack, which reuses an FCC used for another vehicle, the input of inner hash function hash can include some unique information of ECU such as its serial number. The procedure of firmware update is as follows.

1. The ECU vendor generates a patch file, an MAC, and an FCC. It registers them to the cloud storage server (Step 1 in Fig. 5).
2. The cloud storage server sends a three-tuple, of the patch file, the MAC, and the FCC, to the gateway (Step 2), with its signature on the tuple.
3. The gateway receives the three-tuple (Step 3) and signatures on it. Then the gateway verifies the signature; if it is invalid, then the gateway discards the tuple and signature.
4. The gateway changes the mode of vehicle to be unmovable. The gateway sends, to the corresponding ECU, a pair of the patch file and the MAC of the three-tuple (Step 4).
5. The ECU receives the pair of patch file and MAC (Step 5), and checks the MAC (Step 6). If the MAC is valid, then it updates its firmware; otherwise, it discards the pair (Step 7). The ECU sends a report (REP) back to the gateway (Step 8).

6. The gateway checks whether the ECU completes the firmware update with FCC and REP. If it confirms the update, then it changes the mode of vehicle to be movable; otherwise, it outputs an error signal (Step 9).

An example of REP is a hash value of the firmware, $REP = \mathsf{hash}(FW_{1,new})$. With this REP and $FCC_1 = \mathsf{hash}(\mathsf{hash}(FW_{1,new}))$ above, Step 9 checks whether $FCC_1 = \mathsf{hash}(REP)$ holds or not.

(b) Two-way Patch for Update/Rollback: In order to achieve an efficient update/rollback, we slightly change the block delta encoding. In the block delta encoding, the difference is calculated with an arithmetic subtraction as in Fig. 1. We replace the arithmetic subtraction by an XOR operation.

The XOR operation has a property where, if $n = o \oplus p$, $n \oplus p = o$ holds. Namely, a patch file for an update can be used for the corresponding rollback. With this change, we can reuse a patch file for both an update and a rollback, in other word, only one patch file is sufficient for both ways.

Changing an operation in the BSDiff may degrades the compression rate, depending on the data structure etc. However, our modification to a single two-way patch file shall save the transmission time of the patch file for the rollback and the storage for it.

In considering the use of rollback, we should use adequate FCC and REP. Let us assume that a firmware for ECU_1 is updated incrementally as $FW_{1,1}$, $FW_{1,2}$, $FW_{1,3}$, $\cdots$, that FCC and REP are set with $FCC_{1,i} = \mathsf{hash}(\mathsf{hash}(FW_{1,i}))$ and $REP = \mathsf{hash}(FCC_{1,i})$ as above, and that the transmission over the CAN is not encrypted. When the firmware is updated from $FW_{1,1}$ to $FW_{1,2}$, the $REP_{1,2} = \mathsf{hash}(\mathsf{hash}(FW_{1,2}))$ is transmitted from an ECU to the gateway over the CAN. Let us consider the case where a rollback is required after the firmware is updated from $FW_{1,2}$ to $FW_{1,3}$. The rollback downgrades the firmware from $FW_{1,3}$ to $FW_{1,2}$. However, $REP_{1,2}$ cannot be used to verify the rollback because it has already revealed over the CAN at the previous update and may be reused as a replay attack.

The use of hash chain, with length more than two, can solve the replay attack by reusing an REP. Let us assume that ECU vendor prepares a chain with length 10 in advance: $\mathsf{hash}^{(10)}(FW_{1,2}) = \mathsf{hash}(\mathsf{hash}(\cdots(\mathsf{hash}(FW_{1,2}))\cdots))$. The initial FCC, for the first update from $FW_{1,1}$ to $FW_{1,2}$, is set with $\mathsf{hash}^{(10)}(FW_{1,2})$ and the corresponding REP is set with $\mathsf{hash}^{(9)}(FW_{1,2})$. The FCC, for the first rollback, is set with $\mathsf{hash}^{(9)}(FW_{1,2})$ and the corresponding REP is set with $\mathsf{hash}^{(8)}(FW_{1,2})$. Similarly, with the chain, at most five times of update and rollback can be verified.

4   Experiments

We have an experiment to test the feasibility of our proposal, especially, on the two-way patch file for the update/rollback.

4.1   Settings

Figure 6 depicts our system model. We emulate an in-vehicle network by connecting a PC and a TMPM369FDFG board with Lawicel's CANUSB. In this model, we regard the PC and the board as a gateway and an ECU, respectively. Their specifications are summarized in Table 1.

Fig. 6. Our experimental system

Table 1. Settings for our experiments

PC	OS	Windows 7 professional
	CPU	Xeon(R) W3690 @ 3.47 GHz
	RAM	24 GB
Evaluation board	Model	Toshiba TMPM369FDFG
	ROM (Flash)	512 KB
	RAM	128 KB
	512 KB Flash erase	0.4 s
	512 KB Flash write	1.28 s
CAN tool	CANUSB by LAWICEL	500 kbps

Table 2 summarizes the profile of our software implementing the BSPatch with the block XOR encoding with 4 KB table.

Table 2. Software for TMPM369FDFG in our experiment

Progam size (byte)	Code	30592
	RO-data	688
	RW-data	20
Memory (byte)	stack size	>31232
	.text size	944
	.data size	5140
	.bss size	188

4.2   Experimental Results

By using the above settings, we estimate (i) the size of patch file and (ii) the execution time.

(i) Size of Patch File: We compare the sizes of patch files using the block delta encoding and the block XOR encoding. To estimate these sizes, we generate 32 KB random data as an old firmware, modify bits by 10% to 60% of the data (change ratio), and compress each encoded data to generate two patch files. In the modification of 32 KB data, we prepare two datasets: data1: flip bytes randomly chosen from the data, e.g., if the ration is 10%, we randomly choose 3.2 KB by byte and flip them; and data2: one-bit shift bytes randomly chosen from the data, e.g., if the ration is 10%, we randomly choose 3.2 KB by byte and circularly shift each byte by one-bit to the right.

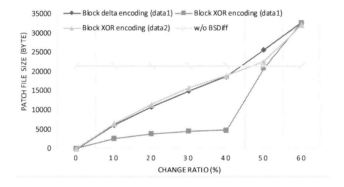

Fig. 7. Sizes of patch files for each change ratio

Figure 7 depicts the sizes of patch files. In this figure, "w/o BSDiff" shows sizes of compressed new firmware with the LZMA, without applying the block delta encoding nor the block XOR one. From this figure, there is an advantage to use the block delta encoding or the block XOR one, compared to "w/o BSDiff" if the change ratio is smaller than about 50%. Moreover, with data1, the block XOR encoding saves the sizes of patch files, compared to the block delta encoding. The result depends on the data as we discuss in Sect. 5 later.

(ii) Execution Time: We then evaluate the execution time on the data transmission, the decoding with decompression, the flash erase and flash write, and the MAC verification. We evaluate each 50 times and regard the minimum one for each execution time.

Table 3 shows the execution times of the block delta encoding and block XOR one. In this experiment, we compare the block delta encoding and the block XOR

Table 3. Execution time in our experiments

	Block delta encoding		Block XOR encoding	
Patch + MAC	6100 B	10592 B	6580 B	11528 B
Transmission	1.521 s	2.643 s	1.640 s	2.877 s
Decoding	0.122 s	0.278 s	0.124 s	0.288 s
Flash erase	0.102 s			
Flash write	0.083 s			
MAC check	0.115 s			

encoding by preparing data whose sizes (including 32 B MAC) are almost same: the block delta encoding (data1) and the block XOR encoding (data2), for the change ratios 10% and 20%, in Fig. 7.

5   Discussion

Our method provides the verifiable end-to-end (vendor-to-ECU) security for the vehicular firmware update. Moreover, from the property of block XOR encoding, even though a rollback is required, a single two-way patch file is sufficient.

Experiments in Sect. 4.2 showed that our method, specifically, the block XOR encoding, is feasible. As for the size of patch file, if the difference is made by bit-flips (data1) in our experiment, the block XOR encoding leads small (namely, more compressed) patch files compared to the block delta encoding. The sizes of patch files, from both the block delta encoding and block XOR one, are smaller than the compression of the new firmware, w/o BSDiff, if the change ratio is smaller than 50%. In both encodings, the seizes of patch files are almost the same as the size of firmware when the change ratio is 60%. It seems because the table size is too small (4 KB) in our settings. Checking the relation between the table size and the size of patch file remains as our future work.

On the other hand, let us discuss the execution time. The difference between the block delta encoding and the block XOR one is only one operation; the arithmetic subtraction and the XOR. Since the difference is small, their execution times for decoding are almost same.

6   Conclusion and Future Works

In this paper, we proposed a firmware update method suitable for a vehicular system with efficient rollback function. We also demonstrated that our method was feasible with experiments. Feasibility tests with a firmware for real ECU is one of our future work.

References

1. Koscher, K., et al.: Experimental security analysis of a modern automobile (2010)
2. Miller, C., Valasek, C.: Adventures in automotive networks and control units. DEF-CON **21**, 260–264 (2013)
3. Miller, C., Valasek, C.: Remote exploitation of an unaltered passenger vehicle. Black Hat 2015 (2015)
4. International Organization for Standardization (ISO): ISO11898:2015–1, road vehicles - controller area network (CAN) (2015)
5. National Institute of Standards and Technology (NIST): The keyed-hash message authentication code (HMAC) (2008)
6. National Institute of Standards and Technology (NIST): Recommendation for block cipher modes of operation: the CMAC mode for authentication (2016)
7. Han, K., Weimerskirch, A., Shin, K.G.: A practical solution to achieve real-time performance in the automotive network by randomizing frame identifier. In: 13th escar Europe 2015 (2015)
8. Xia, Z., Kawabata, T., Komano, Y.: A secure design for practical identity-anonymized CAN application. In: 14th escar Europe 2016 (2016)
9. Xia, Z., Komano, Y., Kawabata, T., Shimizu, H.: A centrally managed identity-anonymized CAN communication system. SAE Int. J. Transp. Cybersecur. Priv. **1**(1), 19–37 (2018)
10. Kocher, P.C.: Timing attacks on implementations of Diffie-Hellman, RSA, DSS, and other systems. In: Koblitz, N. (ed.) CRYPTO 1996. LNCS, vol. 1109, pp. 104–113. Springer, Heidelberg (1996). https://doi.org/10.1007/3-540-68697-5_9
11. Kocher, P., Jaffe, J., Jun, B.: Differential power analysis. In: Wiener, M. (ed.) CRYPTO 1999. LNCS, vol. 1666, pp. 388–397. Springer, Heidelberg (1999). https://doi.org/10.1007/3-540-48405-1_25
12. Chari, S., Jutla, C.S., Rao, J.R., Rohatgi, P.: Towards sound approaches to counteract power-analysis attacks. In: Wiener, M. (ed.) CRYPTO 1999. LNCS, vol. 1666, pp. 398–412. Springer, Heidelberg (1999). https://doi.org/10.1007/3-540-48405-1_26
13. Chari, S., Rao, J.R., Rohatgi, P.: Template attacks. In: Kaliski, B.S., Koç, K., Paar, C. (eds.) CHES 2002. LNCS, vol. 2523, pp. 13–28. Springer, Heidelberg (2003). https://doi.org/10.1007/3-540-36400-5_3
14. Quisquater, J.-J., Samyde, D.: ElectroMagnetic Analysis (EMA): measures and counter-measures for smart cards. In: Attali, I., Jensen, T. (eds.) E-smart 2001. LNCS, vol. 2140, pp. 200–210. Springer, Heidelberg (2001). https://doi.org/10.1007/3-540-45418-7_17
15. Agrawal, D., Archambeault, B., Rao, J.R., Rohatgi, P.: The EM side—channel(s). In: Kaliski, B.S., Koç, K., Paar, C. (eds.) CHES 2002. LNCS, vol. 2523, pp. 29–45. Springer, Heidelberg (2003). https://doi.org/10.1007/3-540-36400-5_4
16. Komano, Y., Shimizu, H., Kawamura, S.: BS-CPA: built-in determined sub-key correlation power analysis. IEICE Trans. **93-A**(9), 1632–1638 (2010)
17. Coron, J.-S., Goubin, L.: On Boolean and arithmetic masking against differential power analysis. In: Koç, Ç.K., Paar, C. (eds.) CHES 2000. LNCS, vol. 1965, pp. 231–237. Springer, Heidelberg (2000). https://doi.org/10.1007/3-540-44499-8_18
18. Teraoka, H., Nakahara, F., Kurosawa, K.: Incremental update method for resource-constrained in-vehicle ECUs. In: IEEE 5th Global Conference on Consumer Electronics, pp. 1–2 (2016)

19. Teraoka, H., Nakahara, F., Kurosawa, K.: Incremental update method for in-vehicle ECUs. IPSJ Trans. Consum. Devices Syst. **7**(2), 41–50 (2017)
20. http://www.daemonology.net/bsdiff/. Accessed 26 Feb 2018
21. http://www.7-zip.org/sdk.html. Accessed 26 Feb 2018
22. Lee, Y.S., Kim, J.H., Hung, H.V., Jeon, J.W.: A parallel re-programming method for in-vehicle gateway to save software update time. In: IEEE International Conference on Information and Automation, pp. 1497–1502. IEEE (2015)
23. Jang, S.J., Jeon, J.W.: Software reprogramming performance analysis of CAN FD and FLEXRAY protocols. In: IEEE International Conference on Information and Automation, pp. 2535–2540. IEEE (2015)
24. Lee, Y.S., Kim, J., Jang, S.J., Jeon, J.W.: Automotive ECU software reprogramming method based on ethernet backbone network to save time. In: 10th International Conference on Ubiquitous Information Management and Communication, IMCOM 2016, pp. 39:1–39:8. ACM (2016)
25. Burrows, M., Wheeler, D.: Incremental update method for in-vehicle ECUs. Digital SRC Research report, SRC-RR-124, 1–18 (1994)
26. Huffman, D.A.: A method for the construction of minimum redundancy codes. Proc. IRE **40**(9), 1098–1101 (1952)
27. Ziv, J., Lempel, A.: A universal algorithm for sequential data compression. IEEE Trans. Inf. Theory **23**(3), 337–343 (1977)
28. Martin, G.N.N.: Range encoding: an algorithm for removing redundancy from a digitized message. In: Video & Data Recording Conference (1979)

Regulating IoT Messages

Alban Gabillon[1]([⊠]) [iD] and Emmanuel Bruno[2]

[1] Université de la Polynésie Française, BP 6570,
98702 Punaauia, Faa'a, French Polynesia
alban.gabillon@upf.pf
[2] Université de Toulon, CNRS, LIS, UMR 7020, 83957 La Garde, France
emmanuel.bruno@univ-tln.fr

Abstract. The MQTT (Message Queuing Telemetry Transport) protocol is becoming the main protocol for the Internet of Things (IoT). In this paper, we define a highly expressive ABAC (Attribute-Based Access Control) security model for the MQTT protocol. Our model allows us to regulate not only publications and subscriptions but also distribution of messages to subscribers. We can express various types of contextual security rules, (temporal security rules, content-based security rules, rules based on the frequency of events etc.).

Keywords: Security policy · MQTT · ABAC · IoT · First-order logic

1 Introduction

The MQTT (Message Queuing Telemetry Transport) protocol is becoming the main protocol behind pub-sub networks for the Internet of Things, that is, in networks implementing the publication-subscription paradigm. The MQTT protocol is an ISO standard (ISO/IEC PRF 20922) [1] and the 3.1 version became an OASIS specification in 2013 [2]. Basically, the MQTT protocol works as follows: publishers post messages to logical channels called topics; subscribers receive messages published to the topics to which they subscribed; the MQTT broker routes messages from publishers to subscribers.

The MQTT protocol supports very few security features. It includes a MQTT client identification mechanism and supports the basic login/password authentication scheme. Consequently, there have been several papers aiming at defining security solutions for the MQTT protocol or more generally for the pub-sub pattern. These papers address various issues like how to implement a security policy regulating publications and subscriptions [3–5], how to distribute the evaluation and the enforcement of the security policy at the edge of the IoT network [6, 7], how to distribute and synchronize the security policy between different pub-sub architectures [8] or how to protect the confidentiality of the messages from the broker or the pub-sub architecture itself [9, 10]. Although these issues are all very important, we noticed that none of these papers fully addressed the definition of a security model allowing to express security policies for regulating IoT messages. Some of the papers [4, 5] mention that they are using the ABAC (Attribute-Based Access Control) model [11] for expressing the security policy controlling publications and subscriptions. However, they do not go much into details

© Springer Nature Switzerland AG 2018
C. Su and H. Kikuchi (Eds.): ISPEC 2018, LNCS 11125, pp. 468–480, 2018.
https://doi.org/10.1007/978-3-319-99807-7_29

and do not elaborate on the expressive power of the security policy. In this paper, we define a highly expressive ABAC model for regulating IoT messages in a MQTT network. We believe that the definition of such a security model (which does not contradict the solutions proposed by the aforementioned papers) has been missing in the literature related to security solutions for pub-sub architectures. Our model allows us to regulate not only publications or subscriptions but also *distribution* of messages by the broker to subscribers. Our model supports positive and negative authorizations and allows us to express various types of context-based policies, including policies based on the *frequency* of events.

The remainder of this paper is organized as follows: In Sect. 2, we define our model. In Sect. 3, we sketch our secure MQTT broker prototype based on our model. In Sect. 4, we conclude this paper.

2   ABAC Model

Some papers [4, 5] mention that they are using the ABAC (Attribute-Based Access Control) model [11] for expressing the security policy controlling publications and subscriptions in a pub-sub network. However, these papers do not go much into details and do not elaborate on the expressive power of the security policy. Moreover, none of these papers address the security administration issue. Our aim in this paper is to define a security model which can be seen as a *profile* of the ABAC model for pub-sub networks based on MQTT. We first identify some requirements specific to IoT security policies. Then we make some assumptions on the IoT network and on some security aspects that we shall not cover. Finally, we devise our model starting from the requirements we identified.

2.1   Requirements

- Our model should offer the possibility to regulate not only publications and sub-scriptions but also *distribution* of messages by the broker to subscribers. Controlling distribution of messages is essential to regulate the various flows of messages coming from the broker. Solely controlling subscriptions is too coarse grained to achieve that task.
- Our model should allow for various types of dynamic and contextual authorization rules i.e. authorization rules whose outcome (permit ort deny) depend on some contextual conditions applying to the nodes, the messages (including the content of the messages) or the environment. In particular, *authorization rules based on the frequency of events* should be supported since controlling the rate at which a node may send or receive messages is important in many IoT applications.

2.2   Assumptions

- For the sake of simplicity, we assume a pub-sub architecture with only one MQTT broker. Since we focus on the expressive power of the security policy, we do not investigate issues like distributing and synchronizing the security policy between different bridged brokers or evaluating the security policy at the edge of the network [6–8].

- We assume the broker to be trusted i.e. we do not investigate solutions to protect the confidentiality of the messages from the broker [9, 10].
- We do not investigate authentication techniques. We believe that standard authentication techniques can be used to authenticate both nodes and attributes.
- Finally, we assume TLS/SSL is used at the transport layer between all nodes of the IoT network. Most existing MQTT servers support the use of TLS/SSL.

2.3   Language

We use first-order logic with equality to define our model, i.e. we define a logical language allowing us to represent nodes, attributes, events (like publications, subscriptions, messages distribution) and authorization rules. Note, however, that the reader who is not familiar with logic should be able to understand the main principles of our model since we translate in plain English each logical formula.

Although, we define our own logical language, we wish to make it clear that this paper is *not* about a new logic-based policy language. To specify our model, we could use XACML [12] (but it would be unreadable by a human), or an existing logical language like SecPAL [13]. However, we prefer defining our own language so that we can restrict ourselves to Horn clauses which can easily be read by a human and for which there exists efficient resolution methods.

Constants
Constants of our language are string expressions. They are node identifiers such as *sensor1, user1* etc. or the special string *broker* referring to the MQTT broker.

Topics are defined by path expressions (written as strings) such as *temperatures/ sensor1*. Several topics can be referenced by using wildcards # and +. For examples, *temperatures/#* addresses any topic having *temperature* as path root and *home/+/ temperatures* addresses topics such as *home/room1/temperature*, *home/room2/ temperature* etc. See [2] for more details about the use of wildcards in MQTT topics.

Note that, to lighten the notations, we omit the quotation marks for the strings.

Variables
Variables are written in capitalized letters like in Prolog. Our language includes the anonymous variable _ which means *anything*. If variable S contains a string value, then we assume this value can be referred to in a path expression. For example, if S contains the string *sensor1* then *temperatures/S* represents the topic *temperatures/sensor1*.

In this paper, to distinguish variables from constants, we constrain ourselves to consider only constants written as strings of lowercase characters.

Predicates
Authorizations can be derived from a set of facts $\mathcal{F}$ and from a set of logical rules $\mathcal{R}$. Set $\mathcal{F}$ keeps track of registered nodes and events (publications, subscriptions and distributions) whereas set $\mathcal{R}$ records the nodes hierarchy.

Set $\mathcal{F}$ includes instances from the following node predicates (Table 1):

Table 1. Node predicates

Predicate	Meaning
$node(N)$	N is an IoT node
$broker(N)$	N is the broker
$sensor(N)$	N is a sensor
$client(N)$	N is a client

Registering a node creates an instance of one of these node predicates. Set $\mathcal{R}$ includes the following rules:

$$node(N) \leftarrow broker(N) \tag{1}$$

$$node(N) \leftarrow sensor(N) \tag{2}$$

$$node(N) \leftarrow client(N) \tag{3}$$

These three rules can be used to derivate that the broker or a sensor or a client is also a node. These rules define a roles hierarchy that could be expanded according to the needs of the application.

Set $\mathcal{F}$ also includes instances from the following event predicates:

Table 2. Event predicates

Predicate	Meaning
$hasPublished(N, T, D)$	At time D, node N has published a message in topic T
$hasSubscribed(N, T, D)$	At time D, node N has subscribed to topic T
$hasDelivered(T, N, D)$	At time D, the broker has delivered a message from topic T to node N

Publishing a message creates an instance of the *hasPublished/3* predicate. Subscribing to a topic creates an instance of the *hasSubscribed/3* predicate. Delivering a message creates an instance of the *hasDelivered/3* predicate. As we shall see in Sect. 2.3, recording these events allows us to express security rules controlling the frequency of publishing/delivering messages.

Since topics are path expressions possibly written with wildcards, set $\mathcal{F}$ also includes instances from the following predicate (Table 3):

Table 3. Matching predicate

Predicate	Meaning
$addresses(T, T')$	Topic T addresses topic T'

For example, fact *addresses*(*temperature*/∗, *temperature*/*sensor*1) belongs to $\mathcal{F}$. For the sake of simplicity, we do not give the logical rules allowing us to derive instances of the *addresses/2* predicate.

Functions

Functions of our language represent attributes. They are either,

- Functions applying to messages or
- Functions for evaluating temporal conditions or any other contextual conditions.

Table 4. Message attribute functions

Function	Purpose
length(M)	Returns the length of the message M
retained(M)	Returns true if the message M is retained, false else
value(M)	Returns the content of the message M
encoding(M)	Returns the character encoding of the message M
ciphered(M)	Returns true if the message M is encrypted[a], false else

[a]Encrypting a message means encrypting the payload of the MQTT packet transporting the message. This should not be confused with encrypting the whole communication between nodes at the transport layer by means of TLS/SSL.

Table 5. Contextual functions

Function	Purpose
time()	Returns the current time
date()	Returns the current date
latency()	Returns the network's latency
bandwidth()	Returns the network's bandwidth

Lists of functions in Tables 4 and 5 are not exhaustive and can be extended depending on the needs.

2.4 Security Policy

Actions

We define the three *compound terms* to represent the following three actions:

Table 6. Actions

Term	Action
publish(M, T, Q)	Publishing message M in topic T at QoS Q
subscribe(T, Q)	Subscribing to topic T at QoS Q
deliver(M, T, N)	Delivering message M from topic T to node N

Variables represent action parameters. Note that there is no QoS parameter for the deliver operation. This is because the QoS used by the broker to deliver a message to node N is the QoS chosen by node N when it subscribed to topic T. This means that if, in our security policy, we need to restrict the QoS used by the broker to deliver messages, then it should be done during the subscription step.

Contextual Authorization Rules

We consider positive authorizations and negative authorizations represented by the two following predicates (Table 7):

Table 7. Authorizations

Predicate	Meaning
$allow(N, A)$	Node N is allowed to perform action A
$deny(N, A)$	Node N is denied to perform action A

Variable A contains any of the three compound terms of Table 6. Note that if A is a *deliver* action then we assume that N cannot be different from *broker*.

The security policy $\mathcal{P}$ regulates publish, subscribe and deliver operations. It consists of a set of authorization rules. Any authorization rule is an instance of one of the following rule templates:

$$allow(N, A) \leftarrow conditions \tag{4}$$

$$deny(N, A) \leftarrow conditions \tag{5}$$

Symbol *conditions* stands for a possibly empty conjunction of *contextual conditions* on nodes, topics, QoS, messages and the environment. Here are a few examples of authorization rules:

$$deny(sensor1, publish(\_, alarms/sensor1, \_)) \\ \leftarrow time() > 8 \wedge time() < 20 \tag{6}$$

Rule 6 denies *sensor1* to publish messages (whichever the QoS is), in topic *alarms/sensor1* during day time.

$$allow(N, subscribe(alarms/\#, \_)) \\ \leftarrow guest(N) \tag{7}$$

Rule 7 allows guest nodes to subscribe to the alarms hierarchy of topics. Here we assume *guest/1* is a role predicate expanding the hierarchy defined in Sect. 2.2.

Regarding the delivering operation, we should first note that the normal MQTT behavior is to deliver messages from topic T to the nodes which subscribed to topic T.

This can be expressed by the following *default policy rule*:

$$allow(broker, deliver(\_, T, N)) \qquad\qquad (8)$$
$$\leftarrow hasSubscribed(N, T, \_)$$

Rule 8 allows the broker to deliver any messages from topic T to the nodes which subscribed to topic T. However, this default policy can be *overridden* in some specific cases (see Sect. 2.4 for conflicts resolution between rules):

$$deny(broker, deliver(M, alarms/\#, N)) \qquad\qquad (9)$$
$$\leftarrow guest(N) \wedge value(M) = \ 'failure'$$

Rule 9 overrides rule 8 and denies the broker to deliver failure messages from the alarms hierarchy of topics to guest nodes. Rule 9 is an example of a *content-based* authorization rule.

In rules 7 and 9, there is a path expression referring to the set of topics alarms/#. Therefore, we need to include in set $\mathcal{P}$ some rules to derive instances of predicates *allow/2* and *deny/2* addressing any subset of a set of topics expressed by means of wildcards:

$$allow/deny(N, publish(M, T', Q)) \qquad\qquad (10)$$
$$\leftarrow allow/deny(N, publish(M, T, Q)) \wedge addresses(T, T')$$

Rule 10 says that if publication is allowed/denied for a set of topics T then publication is also allowed/denied for each subset T' of T. We could write similar rules for the *subscribe/3* and *deliver/3* predicates.

For example, since *addresses(alarms/#,alarms/sensor1)* is true, then *allow(subscribe(user1,alarms/sensor1,1))* can be derived from *allow(subscribe(user1, alarms/#,1))*.

Controlling the Frequency of Events

Our experience has shown us that in some applications being able to control the frequency of publications, subscriptions and messages distribution is important. Consider for example an online trading broker. An online trading broker is a pub-sub service where clients may send trade orders and receive various tips and hints related to the stock market. Assume that the online broker sells standard accounts and premium accounts. Premium account holders receive more hints and tips per day than standard account holders. Moreover, premium account holders can send more trading orders per day than standard account holders. In such a scenario, we would need to express authorization rules controlling the frequency of publications (e.g. trade orders) and the frequency of messages (e.g. hints and tips) delivered by the broker. Another obvious use of having authorization rules based on the frequency of publications would be to mitigate the effects of compromised sensors involved in DDOS attacks against the pub-sub architecture.

To define authorization rules allowing us to express conditions on the frequency of events, we define the following high-order predicate (Table 8):

Frequencies are always evaluated at the time the policy is evaluated. This explains why instances of the *freq/3* predicates represent *instant* frequencies.

Table 8. Frequency predicate

Predicate	Meaning
$freq(E, F, I)$	F is the instant frequency of repeating event E per unit of time I

Variable E refers to any formula instance of the three event predicates *hasPublished/3*, *hasSubscribed/3* and *hasDelivered/3* defined in Sect. 2.2, with the last variable referring to the timestamp of the event always equal to the anonymous variable _.

Here are two examples of frequencies:

$$freq(hasPublished(sensor1, alarms/sensor1, \_), 5, 24) \tag{11}$$

Formula 11 says that the instant frequency of publications made by *sensor1* in topic *alarms/sensor1* is 5 in the last 24 h.

$$freq(hasPublished(\_, alarms/\#, \_), 152, 24) \tag{12}$$

Formula 12 says that the instant frequency of publications (made by all sensors) in topics hierarchy *alarms/#* is 152 in the last 24 h.

Note that, by defining the high-order predicate *freq/3*, we are no longer in strict first-order logic. However, computing instances of the *freq/3* predicate can easily be done by using some aggregate predicate which would be implemented in many inference engines. For example, the rule below is the SWI Prolog [14] definition of the *freq/3* predicate for the *hasPublished/3* predicate. It uses the Prolog built-in *aggregate_all/3* predicate:

$$\begin{array}{c} freq(hasPublished(N, T, \_), F, I)) \\ \leftarrow aggregate\_all(count, (hasPublished(N, T, D) \wedge (time() - D) < I)), F) \end{array} \tag{13}$$

Basically, Prolog rule 13 counts the number of instances of the *hasPublished/3* predicate referring to node N and topic T with a timestamp not older than I hours.

The following rules are examples of authorization rules regulating the frequency of publications and messages distribution:

$$\begin{array}{c} allow(sensor1, publish(\_, alarms/sensor1, \_)) \\ \leftarrow freq(hasPublished(sensor1, alarms/sensor1, \_), F, 24) \wedge F < 5 \end{array} \tag{14}$$

Rule 14 allows *sensor1* to publish messages in topic *alarms/sensor1* as long as it does not post more than 5 alert messages per 24 h.

$$\begin{array}{c} deny(broker, deliver(\_, alarms/sensor1, N)) \leftarrow guest(N) \\ \wedge freq(hasDelivered(alarms/sensor1, N, \_), F, 24) \wedge F > 1 \end{array} \tag{15}$$

Rule 15 denies the broker to deliver to guest nodes more than one alert message per 24 h from topic *alarms/sensor1*.

2.5   Conflict Resolution Policy

Since our authorization model allows for positive and negative authorizations, conflicts between rules may arise. For example, consider the following two rules:

$$deny(N, subscribe(\_, \_)) \leftarrow sensor(N) \tag{16}$$

$$allow(N, subscribe(N/\#, \_)) \leftarrow sensor(N) \tag{17}$$

Rule 16 says that subscriptions are forbidden for sensors while rule 17 says that sensors can subscribe (at any QoS) to topic for which the path root corresponds to their identifier. Clearly these two rules conflict whenever a sensor subscribes to a topic for which the path root corresponds to the sensor identifier.

There are many possible solutions to solve conflicts between authorization rules. The XACML standard [12] enumerates several *combining algorithms* to solve conflicts between rules (deny overrides, permit overrides, first applicable overrides, permit unless deny, deny unless permit etc.). We can use any of these algorithms depending on our needs. Regarding the small example above, the *permit overrides* algorithm would allow a node subscribing to a topic for which the path root corresponds to the node identifier.

2.6   Security Administration Model

Definition of a security model must include the definition of a model for administering the security policy. To introduce our model, let us first consider the scheme depicted in Fig. 1.

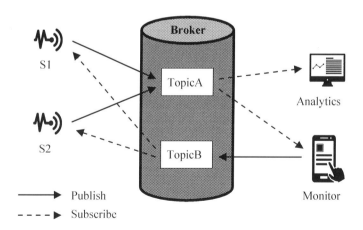

Fig. 1. IoT network

Sensors (*S1* and *S2*) sends messages to *Analytics* through topic *A*. *Monitor* sends commands to sensors through topic *B*. Monitor *owns* sensors *S1* and *S2* and created topics *A* and *B*. This scenario suggests us that *Monitor* could be the administrator defining the security policy regulating messages going through channels *A* and *B*. Of course, this is not the only possible scenario. The IoT network could be more centralized; topics *A* and *B* could also be shared by other applications and sensors etc. Nevertheless, decentralizing the security administration should be possible even if the network contains only one broker. Moreover, to give flexibility, delegation of rights should also be supported.

In our model, security administration is *topic-based*. We state that there is *at least* one security administrator for each topic. A security administrator for a given topic *T* is responsible for defining the security policy regulating publications/subscriptions to topic *T* and distribution of messages from topic *T*. There is also one *Root Administrator* (*RA*) who can administrate the security policy for all topics. However, due to space limitations, we cannot present the security administration model in detail.

3 Prototype

3.1 Architecture

This paper is more about the model than the implementation. Nevertheless, we have implemented a proof-of-concept prototype depicted in Fig. 2. Our prototype is built according to the XACML architecture [12]. We use the EMQ[1] MQTT broker written in Erlang/OTP for which we have developed the MQTTsec plugin acting as a Policy Enforcement Point (PEP). The Policy Information Point (PIP) contains OWL2 ontologies representing nodes, topics and events. The Policy Administration Point (PAP) contains a set of SWRL [15] rules representing the security policy. The MQTTsec manager, written as a Java Web Application, acts as a Policy Decision Point (PDP).

First, the PEP intercepts an event (publication, subscription or distribution of a message). It then submits the event to the PDP. The PDP loads the security policy from the PAP and queries the PIP to retrieve the necessary attribute values. Then it runs an OWL2 [16] inference engine which applies the conflict resolution policy and eventually issues a decision (allow/deny). Whether the request is authorized or not, it is always recorded in the PIP as a new instance of the *event* class of our ontology model. If the request has been authorized then the corresponding instance is tagged as *allowed*, *denied* otherwise. It should be noted that instances of the event predicates defined in Table 2 correspond to the *allowed* events recorded in the PIP. In our prototype, we also keep track of the denied requests for traceability purpose.

3.2 Proof Graphs

We should also mention that the inference engine can show the logical reasoning that led to the decision producing a proof graph of the decision. This feature can be very useful for debugging security policies, auditing, or devising new conflict resolution algorithms. Basically, it works as follows:

---

[1] http://emqtt.io/.

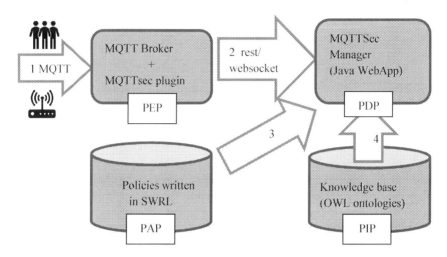

Fig. 2. MQTTsec broker prototype

- Policy rules and captured events (publication, subscription or message distribution) are represented in the OWL language.
- The inference engine computes a list of possible authorization values and shows the derivation steps for each value.
- If the list is empty, then the default policy is applied.
- If there are conflicting values in the list (at least one permit and one deny) then the conflict solver computes the final decision according to the predefined conflict resolution algorithm and shows the derivation steps.
- Whether rejected or accepted, the event is timestamped and added to the PIP.

4   Conclusion

In this paper, we have defined a model to express security policies for a pub-sub architecture consisting of a single MQTT broker. The most important contributions of our paper are the followings:

- Our model allows us to regulate not only publications and subscriptions but also distribution of messages. To our knowledge, this feature has not been addressed in any other paper related to IoT security.
- Our model is an interpretation of the ABAC model for the pub-sub architecture with some unique features like the possibility to control the frequency of events.
- We have developed a prototype based on OWL2 and SWRL showing the feasibility of our approach.

Regarding future works, we are planning to investigate the following issues:

- We will extend our model to the case of a pub-sub architecture consisting of several *bridged* brokers. In such a scenario, we might need to apply the solution presented in [8] to synchronize the security policy at every node of the pub-sub architecture.
- We will also consider an IoT network consisting of a TCP/IP network hosting the pub-sub architecture coupled with a Low Power Wide Area Network (LPWAN) hosting the sensors. In such a scenario, we might also need to implement solutions proposed by others [6, 7] to move, for scaling purposes, the security controls at the various gateways between the TCP/IP network and the LPWAN network.
- We are also planning to include the possibility to declare obligations in the security policy.
- Finally, we will update and improve our prototype to turn it into a scalable secure broker engine.

References

1. ISO/IEC 20922:2016: Information Technology – Message Queuing Telemetry Transport (MQTT) v3.1.1. [En ligne]. Disponible sur: https://www.iso.org/standard/69466.html. Consulté le: 12 janv 2018
2. Banks, A., Gupta, R.: MQTT version 3.1.1. OASIS Standard, vol. 29 (2014)
3. Neisse, R., Steri, G., Fovino, I.N., Baldini, G.: SecKit: a model-based security toolkit for the internet of things. Comput. Secur. **54**, 60–76 (2015)
4. Rizzardi, A., Sicari, S., Miorandi, D., Coen-Porisini, A.: AUPS: an open source AUthenticated publish/subscribe system for the internet of things. Inf. Syst. **62**, 29–41 (2016)
5. Sciancalepore, S., et al.: Attribute-based access control scheme in federated IoT platforms. In: Podnar Žarko, I., Broering, A., Soursos, S., Serrano, M. (eds.) InterOSS-IoT 2016. LNCS, vol. 10218, pp. 123–138. Springer, Cham (2017). https://doi.org/10.1007/978-3-319-56877-5_8
6. Sicari, S., Rizzardi, A., Miorandi, D., Coen-Porisini, A.: Security towards the edge: sticky policy enforcement for networked smart objects. Inf. Syst. **71**, 78–89 (2017)
7. Phung, P.H., Truong, H.-L., Yasoju, D.T.: P4SINC-an execution policy framework for IoT services in the edge. In: 2017 IEEE International Congress on Internet of Things (ICIOT), pp. 137–142 (2017)
8. Sicari, S., Rizzardi, A., Miorandi, D., Coen-Porisini, A.: Dynamic policies in internet of things: enforcement and synchronization. IEEE Internet Things J. **4**(6), 2228–2238 (2017)
9. Wang, C., Carzaniga, A., Evans, D., Wolf, A.L.: Security issues and requirements for internet-scale publish-subscribe systems. In: Proceedings of the 35th Annual Hawaii International Conference on System Sciences, HICSS 2002, pp. 3940–3947 (2002)
10. Choi, S., Ghinita, G., Bertino, E.: A privacy-enhancing content-based publish/subscribe system using scalar product preserving transformations. In: Bringas, P.G., Hameurlain, A., Quirchmayr, G. (eds.) DEXA 2010. LNCS, vol. 6261, pp. 368–384. Springer, Heidelberg (2010). https://doi.org/10.1007/978-3-642-15364-8_32
11. Yuan, E., Tong, J.: Attributed based access control (ABAC) for web services. In: 2005 Proceedings of the IEEE International Conference on Web Services, ICWS 2005 (2005)
12. Moses, T., et al.: Extensible access control markup language (XACML) version 2.0. OASIS Standard, vol. 02 (2005)

13. Becker, M.Y., Fournet, C., Gordon, A.D.: SecPAL: design and semantics of a decentralized authorization language. J. Comput. Secur. **18**(4), 619–665 (2010)
14. Wielemaker, J., Ss, S., Ii, I.: SWI-Prolog 2.7-Reference Manual (1996)
15. Horrocks, I., et al.: SWRL: a semantic web rule language combining OWL and RuleML. W3C Member Submiss. **21**, 79 (2004)
16. W3C OWL Working Group, et al.: OWL 2 Web Ontology Language Document Overview (2009)

A Security Cycle Clock Synchronization Method Based on Mobile Reference Nodes in Wireless Sensor Networks

Jing Xu[1(✉)], Yuqiang Zhang[2], Fei Xu[3], Lei Zhou[4], and Shuanglin Jiang[4]

[1] Department of Automation, Tsinghua University, Beijing 100084,
People's Republic of China
xujing2016@mail.tsinghua.edu.cn
[2] Beijing Institute of Aerospace Control Devices, Beijing 100854,
People's Republic of China
tourist215512@163.com
[3] Institute of Information Engineering, Chinese Academy of Sciences,
Beijing 100093, People's Republic of China
xufei@iie.ac.cn
[4] Shenzhen Andisec Technology Co. Ltd., Beijing 100191,
People's Republic of China
{zhoulei,jiangsl}@andisec.com

Abstract. The wireless sensor network is a typical distributed system where a standard reference time is prerequisite for all nodes to cooperate with each other. This paper proposes a security cycle clock synchronization method based on mobile reference nodes. First, a periodic synchronization model is established, where nodes are directly synchronized through the periodic movement of mobile reference nodes. Second, we proposed a key management method based on random number authentication to defense various attacks in the network. Through experimental analysis, we can see that this security strategy improves the network security and improves the synchronization accuracy of the whole network.

Keywords: Security clock synchronization · Mobile reference nodes
Wireless sensor networks

1 Introduction

In wireless sensor networks in many practical applications and key technologies are required to achieve security sensor nodes clock synchronization, such as forest fire monitoring of environmental monitoring and earthquake early warning [1]. In wireless sensor networks based on data fusion applications, only under

Supported by the project of the National Natural Science Foundation of China under Grant U1736116.

C. Su and H. Kikuchi (Eds.): ISPEC 2018, LNCS 11125, pp. 481–492, 2018.
https://doi.org/10.1007/978-3-319-99807-7_30

the premise of the network to achieve clock synchronization, all this application is meaningful [2]. Over the past few decades, a large number of researchers have proposed a number of clock synchronization protocol. However, because of the wireless sensor network has a large scale, node energy is limited, insufficient bandwidth, processing power is poor, network topology is not unique characteristics, there are a lot of clock synchronization protocol application is greatly limited [3–5]. Therefore, the study of clock synchronization technology in wireless sensor network, there are still many challenging issues, for instance synchronization accuracy and security relations, the balance between synchronization accuracy and energy efficiency, security cycle clock synchronization algorithm designed and other issues [6,7].

2   Reviews of the Existing Clock Synchronization Method

Wireless sensor nodes clock crystal generally consists of hardware and software counter [8]. Crystal oscillator is the local clock source of the node. The counter divides the clock waveform generated by crystal oscillator into frequency division and so on, to get the clock. The clock pulse generated by crystal oscillator is the basis of node clock [9]. Synchronous information transmission in the network is susceptible to all kinds of interference. The synchronization information is transmitted from the sending node to the receiving node, and there is time delay in each link of the synchronization. The greater the uncertainty of the sending time, the access time, and the receiving and processing time, the longer the delay [10], and the delay of information transmission is also determined by other factors, such as hardware platform [11].

Boukerche et al. proposed that the LTS-MB algorithm would synchronize the clock synchronization as another latitude of the node location information, namely the positioning problem of the 4 dimensions. In this method, the mobile reference node moves along a specific curve in the network and covers the nodes 3 times [12]. When the reference node moves to the specific location of the network, it communicates directly with the node, and uses packet delay measurement technology or data packet round trip time technology (RTT) to achieve node synchronization. In the LTS-MB algorithm, the moving path of the reference node is sinusoidal, and the path of the LTS-MB algorithm reference node moves like Fig. 1.

This method does not explain whether the mobile reference node moves periodically. Assuming that the mobile reference node moves at the starting point of coordinates (0, 45), it moves along the sine curve, and the mobile counters broadcast time 0.5 s, when the counter is 0, the mobile reference node arrives at the synchronization point and stops moving. Using the RTT clock synchronization algorithm, broadcast synchronization information contains a time stamp T1, the ordinary node receives and records the current time T2, waiting for a very small random time (in order to avoid collision), sends a RTT request packet containing the local time T3. The mobile reference node records the receiving time T4, then sends the response packet (above all the time) and the current

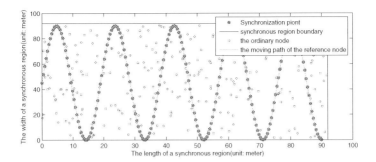

Fig. 1. LTS-MB algorithm reference node movement trajectory

timestamp T5. After receiving the response packet, the ordinary node records the local time T6. The entire communication process is shown in Fig. 2. According to the calculation formula of RTT, we can see:

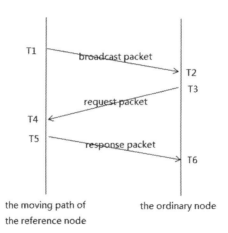

Fig. 2. By using the synchronous process of RTT

$$d_1 = \frac{(T_4 - T_1) - (T_3 - T_2)}{2} \tag{1}$$

$$d_2 = \frac{(T_6 - T_3) - (T_5 - T_4)}{2} \tag{2}$$

$$d = \frac{d_1 + d_2}{2} \tag{3}$$

According to the formula RTT seen under the same conditions as LTS-MB algorithm does not move at the same speed to shorten the cycle of moving, it failed to reach inside to improve the accuracy of the effect cycle [13].

LTS-MB algorithms on two-way communication using the traditional mode of communication, fall short of reduce node energy consumption target [14].

3   The Scheme Description of Security Cycle Clock Synchronization

Aiming at the clock synchronization model for mobile reference node security problem, we propose a method of security cycle clock synchronization based on mobile reference nodes, short for MRN-CS.

First, a periodic synchronization method based on mobile reference nodes is proposed, which adopts the seamless coverage method of synchronous point area, and designs an efficient reference node mobility model. Then, the synchronization of security mechanisms is proposed.

3.1   Reference Node Mobility Model

The security synchronization scheme has the following characteristics:

1. The synchronization information is sent directly from a trusted mobile reference node to a common node via a unicast mode. It eliminates the communication energy consumption of common nodes acting as "reference nodes" after synchronization, and eliminates the accumulation of synchronous errors caused by multi hop transmission, and also improves the security and defense ability in the process of clock synchronization.
2. The synchronization point selection method can quickly calculate all the synchronization points in the network. Then, according to the path planning model, determines the optimal mobile path, shortens the synchronization period, accelerates the synchronization speed, and improves the synchronization accuracy.
3. Unicast communication mode balances the energy consumption of the network, and achieves the purpose of preventing the common nodes close to the reference node to consume their own energy because of multi hop transmission.
4. The proposed security mechanism defends the internal and external threats and attacks in the synchronization process, and improves the security and accuracy of synchronization.

The MRN-CS model is suitable for such application scenario that lacks of reference nodes or only a small number of reference nodes in the field, and requires higher synchronization accuracy, faster synchronization speed and lower node energy consumption.

This method provides clock synchronization information to the common node by moving the reference node, and its basic process includes the following three steps:

Step 1: Mobile reference node periodically to move in a certain route, and every other period of time at set intervals to reach a synchronization point, the reference node in the synchronization point broadcast time synchronization information, the ordinary node receives the synchronization information to adjust their own time, and then realize the synchronization with the reference node clock.

Step 2: When the reference node completes the clock synchronization of its neighbor common nodes at a synchronization point, it moves to the next synchronization point and to repeat step 1.

Step 3: Mobile reference node performs unicast direct communication with all nodes in the process of periodic migration, achieving network synchronization and then performing periodic synchronization.

3.2 Synchronization Security Scheme

The MRN-CS model is based on the following premise and assumption: a common reference node and each node has a pre-assigned shared key k_i; mobile reference node is a special node, may have a special energy supply, can through the GPS to carry out their own positioning and can communicate directly with the central server. This section will consider the security strategy from the requirements of the above location model.

The Clock Synchronization Attack. The clock synchronization attack in this paper is the synchronization information sent by malicious nodes, which enables ordinary nodes to receive and believe as a reference clock, and synchronize with them, resulting in asynchronous node time in the network.

At present, the attack on time is derived from the internal and external of the network, namely, network internal attack and network external attack [15]. Network external attack means that the enemy does not get the communication key in the network. The internal attack of the network means that the enemy has attacked and captured the reference node, or has the identity of the reference node, and obtains the communication key of the network [16,17].

Forged attack [18,19]: also known as deception attack. When the malicious node attacks in common node form, malicious nodes eavesdrop the data which is sending by mobile reference node, and disguise as a moving reference node transmits forgery synchronization information, so that ordinary nodes believe this synchronization information for the reference time, and then complete synchronization, ordinary nodes which in the communication range of the malicious nodes eventually asynchronous with the network time

Replay attack [20]: malicious nodes constantly replay the synchronization information sent by the reference node. The common node that receives the synchronization information continues to synchronize to a clock, causing the common node to be in high-energy consumption state.

In this paper, a key management method based on random number authentication is proposed, which deal with network external attacks and network internal attacks, respectively.

The Key Management Method Based on Random Numbers. Before the common node is deployed, the node stores a master key corresponding to its own ID in advance. The normal node initiates the authentication request to the reference node by using the pre-made master key. After the authentication

Table 1. Analysis of attack style

Attack style	Aggressive behavior
Forge attack	Falsifying the identity or information of a reference node to cause the network asynchronous or consumption of node energy, etc.
Replay attack	Replay the synchronization information of the reference nodes, causing the network asynchrony or the energy consumption of the node etc.

is passed, the reference node sends the encrypted shared key separately. That is, there is a shared key between the reference node and the common node at each synchronization point, and the keys at each synchronization point are different.

Table 2. Node ID and master key mapping table

Node ID	Master key	Generated the random number
ID_i	K_i	$rand_i$

The specific implementation steps are as follows:

1. Master key deployment phase
   - Before a common node is deployed, a random number is generated to do XOR operation with each node ID number, and hash XOR value. The random number corresponds to the node ID for the unique master key, the formula is as follows:

$$K_i = hash(rand_i \oplus ID_I)\ i = 1 \cdots n \tag{4}$$

Rand is a random number, and ID is the only identity of the node, and there are n common nodes in the network. Therefore, the master key generated is random and does not have correlation with each other.
   - The parameters and packet format stored in the common node. Parameters: Node identity; Master key; Reference node identifier ID. Packet format:

$$ID||ID_i||K_i(ID||Authentication information||rand_i)$$

The mapping of the master key and the node ID stored by the mobile reference node is as follows (Table 2):
2. Shared key establishment phase
   - When the mobile reference node moves to the synchronization point, the common node in the broadcast domain is required to be authenticated.

- After receiving the authentication request, the common node generates a random number $rand_1$ and saves it, and then initiates the authentication request message.
The format is:

$$ID||ID_i||K_i(ID||Requst||rand_1)$$

- The mobile reference node collects the authentication request packets of all the ordinary nodes in the broadcast domain, according to the ID_i in the message, look up the mapping relation Table 1 and get K_i corresponding to it. Compare the obtained by decrypting the packet with the of the packet header to prevent the node from disguising. If the two are equal, the node identity is correct.
- According to the location ID of the current synchronization point and the generated random number rand2, the reference node generates the shared key for communication at this synchronization point using formula 5 as follow:

$$K_j = hash(rand_j \oplus ID_j)\ j = 1 \cdots m \tag{5}$$

Where ID_j is the unique identifier of the synchronization point in the area, $rand_j$ is a random number generated by the reference node, and there are m synchronization points in the area.
- The mobile reference node ID set up the packet for the common node.
The message format is as follow:

$$ID||ID_i||K_i(ID||ID_i||K_i||rand_2||rand_1)$$

- After receiving the packet sent by the mobile reference node, the common node decrypts the packet using the master key K_i, and obtains the reference node ID as compared with the header ID to prevent the camouflage attack. If the ID are equal, the obtained random number rand1 is compared with the previously stored random number, and if the two random numbers are equal, the shared secret key is accepted.

3. key confirmation phase
   - The common node uses the shared key obtained to generate a random number $rand_3$, sets up a key confirmation message and sends it.
   The message format is as follows:

$$ID||ID_i||K_i(ID||ID_i||K_i||rand_3||rand_2)$$

   - After receiving the message of each node, the mobile reference node uses the shared key to decrypt the key confirmation message and compares the decrypted ID_i with the ID_i of the message header to prevent the camouflage attack. Then compare the random number $rand_2$ and the previously saved random number $rand_2$.
   If all are equal, the shared key is established successfully.

4. Key update stage
   In order to ensure the security of cycle clock synchronization, after the clock synchronization period is executed m times, the key update is performed in two ways:

– First, re-run the above shared key establishment and key confirmation phase.
– Second, the reference node moves to the synchronization point, encrypts the new key with the old shared key, and then broadcasts it. The message format is as follows:

$$ID||K_j(ID||(K_j)'||rand_4)$$

Figure 3 shows the data flow in the key management method based on random number authentication:

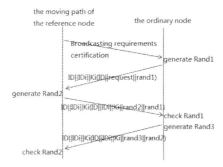

Fig. 3. Data flow diagram of the security method

4   Simulation and Analysis

4.1   Experiment and Analysis of Synchronization Performance

In the simulation experiment, we used the hardware platformd for the wireless network development suite developed by SmeshLink company, and used the Contiki Studio operating system [21].

First, in the ideal security network environment, comparing the MRN-CS algorithm with other synchronization algorithms to analyze the synchronization performance; Then, the security performance of the MRN-CS algorithm is tested and analyzed in the network environment with security threat.

Compare Synchronization Error. MRN-CS algorithm, TPSN algorithm, FTSP algorithm unified set of reference nodes in the same position, that synchronization point coordinates $(52, 45)$, TPSN algorithm, FTSP algorithm requires 5 to jump to cover the synchronization area all common nodes. Location LTS-MB algorithm reference node disposed at the coordinates $(45, 0)$.

As can be seen from the trend of the synchronization error in Fig. 4, as the hop count increases, the synchronization error between the FTSP algorithm and the TPSN algorithm gradually increases, However, the synchronization errors

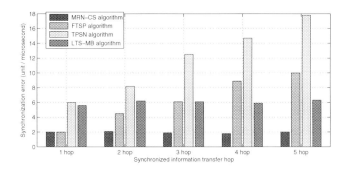

Fig. 4. Comparison of the synchronization error

between MRN-CS and LTS-MB do not change with the increase of synchronization information transfer hops, and the synchronization error remains basically unchanged. With the increase of the number of hops, the synchronization error between MRN-CS and LTS-MB is far less than that of the other two algorithms, and FTSP is better than TPSN.

From the value of the synchronization error in Figure 4, the synchronization error of FTSP algorithm in first hop is the same as that of MRN-CS algorithm is 2 μs. The average synchronization error at fifth jump is 10 μs. From first hop to fifth hop, the average increase of 2 μs per hop. The synchronization error of TPSN algorithm in first hop is 6 μs, and in the fifth hop is almost 18 μs, from first to fifth, with an average increase of 3 μs per hop. However, the synchronization error of MRN-CS and LTS-MB algorithms are not affected by the number of hops, which are better than the above two algorithms. The error range of MRN-CS algorithm is basically at a jump average of 2 μs. The clock synchronization error range of LTS-MB algorithm is also about 6 μs. Because LTS-MB algorithm uses RTT synchronization method in unicast communication, it can not overcome the transmission time, access time and receiving processing time delay. From the results of this experiment, the present MRN-CS algorithm is superior to the LTS-MB algorithm, and it is the optimal algorithm in the four algorithms.

Probability Cumulative Comparison of Synchronization Errors. If we have the same synchronization error, we will carry out probability statistics for 256 nodes in the synchronization area, and the probability cumulative distribution function curves of the 4 synchronization algorithms are shown in Fig. 5.

From Fig. 5, we can see that the MRN-CS algorithm and LTS-MB algorithm have a steep rising edge, while the TPSN algorithm and FTSP algorithm are slower. The steepness of the curve reflects the number of nodes under the same synchronization error, and the more steepen, the more nodes have the smaller synchronization error. In the MRN-CS algorithm, 90% of the node errors are less than 2 μs, and almost all nodes' errors are within 3 μs, which is much better than TPSN and FTSP algorithms.

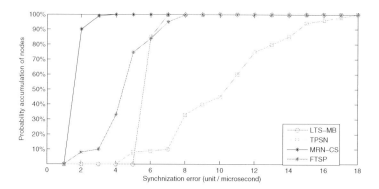

Fig. 5. Probability cumulative distribution function curve of synchronization error

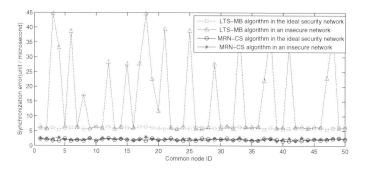

Fig. 6. Comparison of Synchronization errors

4.2   Experiment and Analysis of Security Performance

Comprehensively consider the internal and external attacks of the network, compare the synchronization errors of the nodes, and compare the MRN-CS algorithm and the LTS-MB algorithm in the ideal security network and the insecure network.

Fifty nodes were randomly deployed in a rectangular area of 92 meters by 92 meters for clock synchronization experiments. The communication radius between the reference node and the normal node was set to 15 meters. Then, randomly deploy six malicious nodes, their attacks include both internal and external attacks. During the experiment, the synchronization errors of 50 common nodes and reference nodes were collected, the synchronization errors of the nodes just after clock synchronization were collected, and each synchronization period was collected once. Each algorithm collected 50 synchronization periods, then take the average of the collected data. The two algorithms are tested in different environments. Finally, we get the synchronization error diagram of LTS-MB algorithm and MRN-CS algorithm in ideal secure network and unsafe network as shown in Fig. 6.

5   Conclusion

In this paper, we propose a security cycle synchronization method in WSN based on mobile reference node, short for MRN-CS algorithm. The mobile reference node in the sensor network periodically move along the planned path, synchronize the nodes through single-hop communication. And a security policy based on random number authentication for key management is proposed to deal with malicious attacks in the network.

We can evaluate the key management method based on random numbers from two aspects. First, trusted identity. In the key establishment and confirmation phase, three major messages need to be transmitted. Each message transmission needs to send the ID of the reference node and the ordinary node, after the information is passed through the encryption, the correct reference can be decrypted before the reference nodes and common nodes can be clearly identified, ensuring the credibility of the identification. Second, attack analysis. External attacks cannot attack common nodes because they are unable to obtain shared keys at the synchronization point. Even if a common key is acquired by attacking ordinary nodes, that is, ordinary nodes are captured. The key of common node and the shared key of this synchronization point may be leaked, but the shared key is only valid in the first synchronization process, so it will not affect the clock synchronization.

In the experiment, the simulation results show that the proposed security synchronization method based on mobile reference node, compared with traditional clock synchronization method, has higher node synchronization accuracy, and more effectively protected network from threats.

References

1. Lamonaca, F., Gasparri, A., Garone, E., Grimaldi, D.: Clock synchronization in wireless sensor network with selective convergence rate for event driven measurement applications. IEEE Trans. Instrum. Meas. **63**(9), 2279–2287 (2014)
2. Moreira, P., Alvarez, P., Serrano, J., Darwazeh, I.: Sub-nanosecond digital phase shifter for clock synchronization applications. In: 2012 IEEE International Conference on Frequency Control Symposium (FCS), pp. 1–6 (2012)
3. Bizagwira, H., Toussaint, J., Misson, M.: Synchronization protocol for dynamic environment: design and prototype experiments. In: IEEE 23rd International Conference on Telecommunications (ICT), pp. 1–7 (2016)
4. Lenzen, C., Sommer, P., Wattenhofer, R.: PulseSync: an efficient and scalable clock synchronization protocol. IEEE/ACM Trans. Netw. **23**(3), 717–727 (2015)
5. Nayyar, E.R.K.A.: Analytical study of time synchronization protocols for wireless sensor networks. Int. J. Comput. Trends Technol. **4**(3), 323–332 (2013)
6. Rahamatkar, S., Agarwal, A., Kumar, N.: Analysis and comparative study of clock synchronization schemes in wireless sensor networks. Int. J. Comput. Sci. Eng. **2**(3), 536–541 (2010)
7. Wu, J.: A survey of energy-efficient task synchronization for real-time embedded systems. In: 2017 IEEE 23rd International Conference Embedded and Real-Time Computing Systems and Applications (RTCSA), pp. 1–6 (2017)

8. Kumar, S., Lee, S.R.: A voltage compensated approach for clock drift compensation in wireless sensor networks. Inf. Jpn. **17**(11), 5891–5896 (2014)

9. Er-Peng, L.I., Wen, K.Z., Wang, Y.: Design of high precision digital clock based on crystal oscillator compensation. Mod. Electron. Tech. (2014)

10. Li, C.S., Zhang, H.: Research on wireless power and information synchronous transmission method based on magnetic resonance for fuzes. Acta Armamentarii **32**(5), 537–542 (2011)

11. Wang, Q., Zhang, H., Chen, G.: Effect of the heterogeneous neuron and information transmission delay on stochastic resonance of neuronal networks. Chaos Interdiscip. J. Nonlinear Sci. **22**(4), 043123 (2012)

12. Boukerche, et al.: A new solution for the time-space localization problem in wireless sensor network using UAV. In: The Third ACM International Symposium on Design and Analysis of Intelligent Vehicular Networks and Applications, pp. 153–160. ACM (2013)

13. Gura, N., Patel, A., Wander, A., Eberle, H., Shantz, S.C.: Comparing elliptic curve cryptography and RSA on 8-bit CPUs. In: Joye, M., Quisquater, J.-J. (eds.) CHES 2004. LNCS, vol. 3156, pp. 119–132. Springer, Heidelberg (2004). https://doi.org/10.1007/978-3-540-28632-5_9

14. Roman, R., Alcaraz, C., Lopez, J., Sklavos, N.: Key management systems for sensor networks in the context of the Internet of Things. Comput. Electr. Eng. **37**(2), 147–159 (2011)

15. Kanavalli, A., Shenoy, P.D., Venugopal, K.R., Patnaik, L.M.: Recovery based time synchronization for wireless networks. Int. J. Comput. Sci. Eng. **3**(11), 3596 (2011)

16. Tao, L., Gan, H., Yi-Dong, G.: Key agreement with authenticated between trusted nodes based on self-issued certificate in WSN. In: 2014 IEEE International Conference on Computing, Communication and Networking Technologies (ICCCNT), pp. 1–3 (2014)

17. Zhang, L., Zhang, H., Conti, M., Di Pietro, R., Jajodia, S., Mancini, L.V.: Preserving privacy against external and internal threats in WSN data aggregation. Telecommun. Syst. **52**(4), 2163–2176 (2013)

18. Jinwala, D., Patel, D., Dasgupta, K.: FlexiSec: a configurable link layer security architecture for wireless sensor networks. arXiv preprint arXiv:1203-4697 (2012)

19. Dhanalakshmi, T.G., Bharathi, N., Monisha, M.: Safety concerns of Sybil attack in WSN. In: 2014 IEEE International Conference Science Engineering and Management Research (ICSEMR), pp. 1–4 (2014)

20. Sharma, V., Hussain, M.: Mitigating replay attack in wireless sensor network through assortment of packets. In: Satapathy, S.C., Prasad, V.K., Rani, B.P., Udgata, S.K., Raju, K.S. (eds.) Proceedings of the First International Conference on Computational Intelligence and Informatics. AISC, vol. 507, pp. 221–230. Springer, Singapore (2017). https://doi.org/10.1007/978-981-10-2471-9_22

21. Xu-Jun, W.U., Wang, W.: Research on new features of IPv6 unicast routing protocol and application. Comput. Technol. Dev. (2013)

Security in Mobile Environment

Attribute-Based Traceable Anonymous Proxy Signature Strategy for Mobile Healthcare

Entao Luo[1] , Guojun Wang[2(✉)] , Kun Tang[1] , Quanyou Zhao[1], Chen He[1], and Liyong Guo[1]

[1] School of Electronics and Information Engineering,
Hunan University of Science and Engineering, Yongzhou 425199, China
cs_entaoluo@csu.edu.cn
[2] School of Computer Science and Technology, Guangzhou University,
Guangzhou 510006, China
csgjwang@163.com
http://trust.gzhu.edu.cn/faculty/~csgjwang/

Abstract. To solve doctor's service bottlenecks under the peak condition of mobile medical, the paper proposes utilizing authorized agents to provide service, so as to reduce the burden of doctors and enhance the flexibility of service as well. We use attribute encryption technology to encrypt medical data, the ciphertext can be decrypted correctly when the proxy attribute satisfies the policy set by the authorized user, so as to obtain proxy signature to provide medical service for medical users. The scheme not only can alleviate the burden on the mobile medical service providers in the peak of the bottleneck, but also can solve the authorization problem during the absence of doctors. At the same time, we can achieve proxy traceback to preform the agency accountability and to avoid unauthorized agency audit. This scheme can be used to reduce the computing cost of authorized doctors by using trusted authorization center. The simulation results reveal that the performance can be improved significantly than other scheme.

Keywords: Mobile health-care · Digital signature
Anonymous agent · Attribute-based encryption · Traceable

This work is supported in part by the National Natural Science Foundation of China under Grant Numbers 61632009 and 61472451, in part by the Guangdong Provincial Natural Science Foundation under Grant 2017A030308006 and High-Level Talents Program of Higher Education in Guangdong Province under Grant 2016ZJ01; The Hunan Provincial Natural Science Foundation of China (2015JJ3046, 2018JJ2147); The Hunan Provincal Science and Technology Key Development Project 2017NK2390. Key Construction of Computer Application Technology, Hunan University of Science and Engineering (128030219-001).

C. Su and H. Kikuchi (Eds.): ISPEC 2018, LNCS 11125, pp. 495–505, 2018.
https://doi.org/10.1007/978-3-319-99807-7_31

1   Introduction

With the rapid development of the Internet and mobile health-care system, mobile health-care (MHC) has gradually become a hot area of research [1–4]. By using the MHC, doctors can use mobile medical terminals (wearable devices, etc.) to directly make electronic prescriptions and medical diagnostic records for medical users remotely. Users can check the health of the body according to the electronic inspection reports. Therefore, the MHC system can effectively alleviate the patients' medical difficulties and improve the efficiency of doctors and medical staffs.

In the process of mobile medical diagnosis, doctors' electronic prescriptions, electronic medical records, etc., which usually contain some sensitive data referring the privacy of medical users, if the data is illegally obtained, it will have unpredictable consequences for the privacy of medical users. For example, the personal medical health information and treatment process of the tour DE France cyclist is regarded as the absolute secret of his medical team. Therefore, in order to protect the privacy of medical users, the medical data of users should only be viewed and processed by a few doctors who have access to treatment. Meanwhile, in order to ensure that the patients' privacy is not disclosed, doctors need to digitally sign the treatment plan in the course of treatment to ensure the accountability of medical accidents and the traceability of the treatment plan.

However, in some special scenarios, doctors are not able to provide medical services to medical users at any time. For example, the doctor is attending an important meeting or is undergoing a key operation, thus the doctors require a trustable agent (legally authorized doctor) to help they dealing with the issues within the scope of authorization [5]. In order to avoid the illegal behavior of the surrogate doctors, the doctors can set up access authority to the privacy data of medical users. At the same time, medical users can verify the validity of the scheme through their electronic signature.

2   Related Work

In the studies of privacy protection in mobile medical treatment, many researchers have put forward their own research results. Waters proposed an identity-based encryption scheme [6], and Kim et al. proposed a self-proxy signature scheme [7]. Although proxy signature can be combined with other signature technologies to produce a digital signature scheme that adapted to various application scenarios, this signature scheme lacked effective protection for the agents' privacy. Subsequently, Yu et al. proposed an anonymous proxy signature scheme that can be proved safe [8], where the scheme is a combination of proxy signature and ring signature to realize the anonymity of the proxy signer and protect the privacy of the proxy signer. On this basis, a standard model based on identity signature scheme is proposed [9], but this kind of signature is relatively simple, which cannot adapt to a variety of environmental signatures. At the same time, the above mentioned schemes only considered the signature of the data, and did not consider the access control of the permission and how to find a matching legal signer effectively.

3   Our Focus and Contribution

3.1   Our Focus

Therefore, this paper proposes a fine-grained digital proxy signature scheme based on attribute, which focuses on the research on the properties of proxy authorization, proxy anonymous and signature tracking. The scheme not only solves the problem of anonymous privacy protection of the acting doctor, but also proposes a method to trace the signature of the anonymous proxy doctor. Under the condition of anonymity, when dispute is appeared, the trusted authorization center and the original signer can together reveal the identity of the agents to ensure the traceability for an acting doctor.

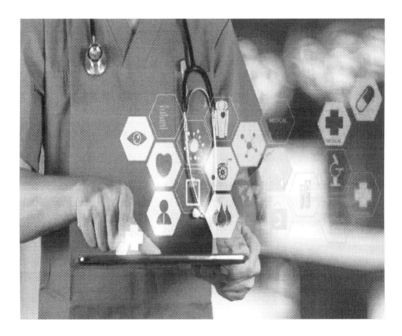

Fig. 1. Information sharing process in mobile health-care networks

3.2   Our Contributions

The main contributions of this paper are shown as follows:

(1) We propose a method that combines users' identities with users' attribute characteristics, where only an agent doctor who satisfies the specific attributes of the licensed physician or the specified control strategy can be authorized and signed;

(2) The method of anonymizing the agent through the authorization center is proposed, in which the privacy of the agent is guaranteed not to be leaked, and the user cannot distinguish the difference between the authorized doctors and the acting doctors.

(3) A signature method that can track anonymous proxy doctors is proposed. If the signature is disputed, the trusted authorization center and the original signer can verify the identity of the agent and jointly ensure the traceability of the agent.

Figures 1 and 2 are an overview of the mobile health-care network.

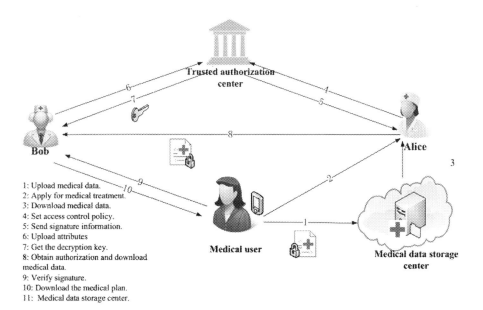

1: Upload medical data.
2: Apply for medical treatment.
3: Download medical data.
4: Set access control policy.
5: Send signature information.
6: Upload attributes
7: Get the decryption key.
8: Obtain authorization and download medical data.
9: Verify signature.
10: Download the medical plan.
11: Medical data storage center.

Fig. 2. Attribute-based traceable anonymous proxy signature strategy processing.

4   Preliminaries

In this section, some preliminaries related to bilinear maps, complexity assumptions are presented.

4.1   Mathematical Basis

Let $\mathbb{G}_1$ and $\mathbb{G}_2$ be two multiplicative cyclic groups with big prime order p. Let e be a bilinear map $e : \mathbb{G}_1 \times \mathbb{G}_2 \to \mathbb{G}_T$ with the following properties[10]:

- **Bilinearity.** $e(P^a, Q^b) = e(P, Q)^{ab}, \forall P \in \mathbb{G}_1, Q \in \mathbb{G}_2$ and $a, b \in \mathcal{Z}_p$.
- **Non-degeneracy.** There exists $\forall g \in \mathbb{G}_1, h \in \mathbb{G}_2$ such that $e(g, h) \neq 1$, which means the mapping will not map all pairs in $\mathbb{G}_1 \times \mathbb{G}_2$ to the identity in $\mathbb{G}_T$.
- **Computability.** There exists an efficient algorithm to calculate bilinear map $e : \mathbb{G}_1 \times \mathbb{G}_2 \to \mathbb{G}_T$.

4.2   Decisional Bilinear Diffie-Hellman (DBDH) Problem

Given multiplicative groups $\mathbb{G}_1$ and $\mathbb{G}_2$ with an order of a prime number p, given (g, g^a, g^b, g^c, T), where $T = e(g, g)^\theta$ and $a, b, c, \theta \in \mathcal{Z}_p$. Randomly choose the generator $g \in \mathbb{G}_1$. Send the elements $g, g^a, g^b, g^c \in \mathbb{G}_1$ and $T \in \mathbb{G}_2$ to $\mathcal{A}$. $\mathcal{A}$ will check whether T is equal to $e(g, g)^{abc}$.

We define the advantage obtained by solving the problem above using $\mathcal{A}$ as follows:

$$
\begin{aligned}
Adv_{DBDH} = {} & \Pr[A(g, g^a, g^b, g^c, e(g, g)^{abc}) = 1] \\
& - \Pr[A(g, g^a, g^b, g^c, T) = 1] \geq \varepsilon
\end{aligned}
\tag{1}
$$

If there is no polynomial time algorithm that can address the DBDH hypothesis with non-negligible advantage ε, we regard the DBDH hypothesis valid in groups $\mathbb{G}_1$ and $\mathbb{G}_2$.

5   System Definition and Model

The proposed scheme consists of data center (**DC**), trusted authority (**TA**), data owner doctor (**DO**), data proxy doctor (**DP**), and medical user (**MU**).

DC: Responsible for storing electronic case histories and health records of users.

TA: Responsible for initializing the system, generating and distributing keys.

DO: Responsible for encrypting the user's medical data and formulating the access control strategies. The decryption keys cannot be obtained to decrypt the private document of **MU** unless the features of **DP** satisfy the access control strategy of **DO**. In this paper, let Alice denote the authorized doctor and the original signer of the treatment plan.

DP: Obtain authorization from **DO** and match his or her own features with the features in the **DO**-defined access control strategies. If the match succeeds, **DP** is granted the key to decrypt the user's medical data and formulate the treatment plan. Meanwhile, digital signature should be put to the treatment plan he or she formulates in order to ensure traceability in the case of medical accident. In this paper, let Bob denote **DP** and the proxy signer of the treatment plan.

MU: Responsible for providing doctor **DO** with his or her own medical data and verifying authenticity of the treatment plan's signature. Let Cindy denote the user who requests to make friends.

In this paper, assume that **TA** and **DO** are completely reliable. It is also assumed that **DC** is curious and honest [10–12,15,16], but **DP** is completely unreliable [13,14], i.e. the proxy users may collude to access the data without authorization. In other words, while fulfilling his or her duties based on the agreement, **DC** may attempt to obtain private information of the user by technical means out of curiosity. Therefore, it is necessary for the medical user to decrypt his or her own data before importing it.

6   Proposed Scheme

Operation of the proposed scheme during each stage is described as follows. Its safety is based on the CP-ABE scheme and the dual system encryption framework [17–20]. Let $\mu = \{\mu_1, \mu_2, ..., \mu_n\}$ denote the attribute set of proxy signer and $Agent_i(1 \leq i \leq n)$ denote an individual proxy signer.

6.1   System Initialization

TA randomly chooses the groups G_0 and G_1 with an order of a prime number p, generating the element $g, p \in G_0$, where $e : G_0 \times G_0 \rightarrow G_1$.

The security parameter k is also randomly selected to control the size of group. Also, the Lagrange coefficient $\Delta_{i,s}, i \in Z_p$ is defined and let S denote the element of set Z_p, where $\Delta_{i,s}(x) = \prod_{j \in S, j \neq i} \frac{x-j}{i-j}$.

The Hash function $H : \{0,1\}^* \rightarrow G_0$ is able to map any attribute which can be represented with a binary string into random elements of the group. Similarly, we have encrypted Hash functions $H_0 : \{0,1\}^* \times G_0 \rightarrow Z_q^*$ and $H_1 : \{0,1\}^* \rightarrow \{0,1\}^k$.

We randomly choose $\alpha, \beta \in Z_p$ to generate the system's public key PK, and let $MK = \beta, g^\alpha$ denote the system's master cryptography key.

$$PK = \{G_0, g, h = g^\beta, e(g,g)^\alpha\} \tag{2}$$

$$MK = \beta, g^\alpha \tag{3}$$

6.2   Key Generation

Doctor $Alice$ chooses a random number $x_0 \in Z_q^*$ as his or her private key, and the public key is computed as $Y_0 = x_0 g$. Similarly, each of the proxy doctors chooses $x_i \in Z_p^*$ as his or her private key and the public key is computed as $Y_i = x_i g$.

6.3   Data Encryption

Prior to this stage, Alice needs to encrypt the user's medical data using his or her own access strategy and upload the access strategy tree to the trusted authority for storage. The proxy right must be awarded at **TA** by matching the attributes of Alice. In other words, unless the proxy doctor's attributes satisfy the access control strategy of Alice, Alice will not grant the proxy right to the proxy doctor to access medical records and formulate treatment plans of users.

(1) The doctor creates the signature authorization certificate: Alice generates the authorization delegation certificate as the original signer, which contains the valid time of proxy signature authorization, the identity of original signer and all proxy signers, as well as the range of signed messages. A random number $r \in Z_p^*$ is generated to compute $\{R, \lambda\}$, and $\{m_w, R, \lambda\}$ is sent to the trusted authority.

$$R = rp \tag{4}$$

$$\lambda = r + x_0 H_0(m_w, R) \bmod p \tag{5}$$

(2) The doctor encrypts the user's medical data: In order to guarantee user privacy, Alice needs to encrypt the user's medical data m_w using the encryption algorithm under the access structure τ. Details of this process are described as follows.

First, the encryption algorithm $Encrypt(PK, m_w, \tau)$ is used to choose a polynomial q_x for each node of τ (including the child node). The polynomials are selected in a top-down manner, with root $\widehat{R}$ as the starting point. The degree d_x of the polynomial of node x is smaller than the node's threshold k_x by 1, i.e. $d_x = k_x - 1$.

Next, the algorithm begins to choose the random number $s \in Z_p$, with root R as the starting point, and sets $q_R(0) - s$. Next, the algorithm proceeds to completely define q_R by choosing d_R points from polynomial q_R. For other vertex x, let $q_x(0) = q_{parent(x)}(index(x))$. Other d_x vertexes are selected randomly to completely define q_x. Let Y denote the set of all children in τ. Therefore, given the access control tree τ, the cipher text of the medical data is obtained as:

$$CT = \{\tau, \tilde{C} = m_w \cdot e(g,g)^{\alpha s}, C = h^s\} \tag{6}$$

6.4   Data Decryption

(1) Proxy doctor Bob generates the access authorization key: the proxy doctor runs the key generation algorithm $KeyGen(MK, S)$, where S denotes the attribute set. The algorithm begins with choosing a random number $r \in Z_p$ and then proceeds to choose a random number $r_j \in Z_p$ for each $j \in S$. Finally, it computes the decryption key SK.

$$SK = \{D = g^{(\alpha+r)/\beta}, \forall j \in S : D_j = g^r \cdot H(j)^{r_j}, D'_j = g^{r_j}\} \tag{7}$$

(2) Proxy doctor Bob decrypts the medical data. The decryption algorithm $Decrypt(PK, CT, SK)$ is recursive. To facilitate discussion, we propose the simplest form of the decryption algorithm. Consider the recursive algorithm $Decrypt(PK, CT, x)$, where cipher text CT is correlated with attribute set S, and x is a node in τ.
If x is a child, let $i = att(x)$. If $i \in S$, then we have.
If $i \notin S$, then $DecryptNode(CT, SK, x) = \perp$.

Consider recursion when x is not a child. Operation of $Decrypt(CT, SK, x)$ is as follow. For all children z of x, compute $F_z = DecryptNode(CT, SK, z)$. Let S_x denote the set z of which has a size of k_x and satisfies $F_z \neq \perp$. If this set does not exist, then this node does not satisfy the condition and the function returns $\perp$. Otherwise, compute F_x.

$$F_x = \prod_{z \in S(x)} F_z^{\Delta_{i,s'_x}(0)} \tag{8}$$

where $i = index(z)$, $S'_x = \{index(z) : z \in S_x\}$.

After defining the function $DecryptNode$, the algorithm calls $DecryptNode$ $(CT, SK, \widehat{R})$, where $\widehat{R}$ denotes the root of tree τ. If the tree satisfies S, then we define.

$$A = DecryptNode(CT, SK, \widehat{R}) = e(g,g)^{rq_{\widehat{R}}(0)} = e(g,g)^{rs} \tag{9}$$

The plain text m_w of the medical data can be recovered via decryption using the decryption algorithm.

$$\tilde{C} \Big/ \frac{e(C, D)}{A} = \tilde{C} \Big/ \frac{e(h^s, g^{(\alpha+r)/\beta})}{e(g,g)^{rs}} = m_w \tag{10}$$

Table 1. Safety comparison

Scheme	Anonymity	Infrangibility	Traceability
Yu's scheme	$\checkmark$	$\times$	$\times$
Our's scheme	$\checkmark$	$\checkmark$	$\checkmark$

Table 2. Performance comparison

Scheme	Key generation	Agent authorization	Signature generation	Signature verification
Yu's scheme	1	P_a	$(3n-2)P_a + (n+1)P_b$	$(n+1)e + nP_a + 2nP_a$
Our's scheme	1	$ke + P_a$	$3P_a + (n-1)P_b$	$3e + 2P_a + 2nP_a$

6.5 Signature

The signature is authorized at TA. As we know, several proxy doctors $Agent_i (1 \leq i \leq n)$ can provide medical proxy service. Consider proxy doctor Bob whose attributes satisfy the access strategy tree. Bob is thus able to recover the plain text m_w by decrypting the cipher text $\tilde{C}$.

At this time, TA will choose a random number k'_i and compute $PID_i = H_1(k'_i, ID_i)$ as the signature identity of the proxy signer μ_i, where ID_i denotes the real identity of proxy doctor μ_i.

In addition, (R, λ, PID_i), $R = rp, r \in Z_q$, is sent to the proxy doctor via the safe channel. On reception of (R, λ, PID_i), the proxy doctor will check whether $\lambda P = R + H_0(m_w, R)Y_0, Y_0 = x_0 p, x_0 \in Z_q$ holds on behalf of μ_i. Proxy authorization is accepted if the equation holds and rejected otherwise.

After being granted the access authorization certificate, the proxy doctor are able to compute his or her proxy private key, formulate treatment plan for medical users and sign the documents on behalf of original signer *Alice*.

(1) Generation of private key for signature: after obtaining m_w, the signer randomly chooses $k \in Z_p^*$ and computes the private key for signature $psk_s = k(\lambda + x_s H_0(m_w, R))$.

(2) Signature: the signature process is as simple as computing four signature components.

$$V = k \cdot H_0(m_w, R), \widehat{Y} = k \sum_{i=1, i \neq s}^{n} (Y_0 + Y_i) \tag{11}$$

$$\sigma_s = psk_s^{-1} \cdot H(m_w || m), R' = kR \tag{12}$$

The signature of the treatment plan can be derived from the calculation of the four components above.

6.6 Signature Verification

After receiving the treatment plan of the proxy doctor, the medical user needs to first check the signature's validity. Given the public keys of the proxy signer and the anonymous proxy signature σ, the verifier checks whether the following equation holds.

The verifier accepts the treatment plan if the equation holds and rejects the plan otherwise.

6.7 Correctness Verification

The proposed scheme is described in detail in the previous section. The proxy doctor can sign the document after being granted the proxy authority. The correctness of the signature in the proposed scheme can be verified directly using the following equations.

(1) **Verifiability**

The signature $\sigma = \{\sigma_s, m, m_w, R', R, V, \widehat{Y}, PID_s\}$ contains the proxy authorization m_w, and the verification process involves the public key of the original signer. Therefore, if the verifier confirms that the anonymous proxy signature is authorized by the original signer, verifiability is satisfied.

(2) **Traceability**

In the case of disagreement, the verifier sends the proxy signature to the authorization server, which can reveal the anonymous proxy signer's identity. After receiving proxy signature, the authorization server extracts PID_i from the signature, and retrieves ID_i corresponding to PID_i from the locally stored information, determining the proxy signer's identity. Therefore, the proposed scheme is traceable.

$$\begin{aligned} t_i P &= (x_i h_0(m_w, K_i) + k_i) P \\ &= h_0(m_w, K_i) x_i P + k_i P \\ &= Y_i h_0(m_w, K_i) + K_i; \end{aligned} \tag{13}$$

$$\lambda P = (r + x_0 H_0(m_w, R))P$$
$$= rP + H_0(m_w, R)x_0 P \qquad (14)$$
$$= R + H_0(m_w, R)Y_0;$$

7   Performance Analysis

In this subsection, the proposed scheme is compared with the scheme of Yu et al. in terms of security and computational complexity. The comparison results are presented in Tables 1 and 2, where e denotes bilinear mapping, P_a and P_b denote group multiplication and addition, n denotes the number of proxy signers, and k denotes the number of attributes.

Comparison in security and computational complexity is presented in Tables 1 and 2, respectively. It can be learned from the tables that the two schemes are equally efficient during key generation. In the process of proxy authorization, the proposed scheme is inferior to that of Yu in efficiency. But the authorization process of the proposed scheme is performed in TA, without consumption of any computational resources of signer and proxy. In the stage of signature generation and verification, the proposed scheme is more efficient than that of Yu when $n > 2$. And the larger the value of n, the larger the superiority. The number of proxy signers should be much larger than 2 to ensure the scheme's anonymity. Therefore, the proposed scheme is more efficient than the anonymous signature scheme of Yu et al.

8   Conclusion

The focus of this paper is to authorize signature proxy using the attribute encryption-based access control method for the mobile medical care system. Privacy of user and proxy is protected via attribute encryption and anonymity of proxy identity. Malicious users can be traced in the case of disagreement. Unlike the previous methods, the proposed scheme is able to implement identity traceability and attribute matching-based proxy authorization simultaneously.

References

1. Lu, Z., Chen, X., Dong, Z.: A prototype of reflection pulse oximeter designed for mobile healthcare. IEEE J. Biomed. Health Inform. **20**(5), 1 (2015)
2. Zhang, K., Yang, K., Liang, X.: Security and privacy for mobile healthcare networks: from a quality of protection perspective. IEEE Wirel. Commun. **22**(4), 104–112 (2015)
3. Ren, Y., Chen, Y., Chuah, M.C.: User verification leveraging gait recognition for smartphone enabled mobile healthcare systems. IEEE Trans. Mob. Comput. **14**(9), 1961–1974 (2015)
4. Jiang, S., Zhu, X., Hao, R., et al.: Lightweight and privacy-preserving agent data transmission for mobile healthcare. In: IEEE International Conference on Communications, pp. 7322–7327. IEEE (2015)

5. Santos-Pereira, C., Augusto, A.B., Cruz-Correia, R., et al.: A secure RBAC mobile agent access control model for healthcare institutions. In: Proceedings of the 26th IEEE International Symposium on Computer-Based Medical Systems, pp. 349–354 IEEE (2013)

6. Waters, B.: Efficient identity-based encryption without random oracles. In: Cramer, R. (ed.) EUROCRYPT 2005. LNCS, vol. 3494, pp. 114–127. Springer, Heidelberg (2005). https://doi.org/10.1007/11426639_7

7. Kim, Y.S., Chang, J.H.: Self proxy signature scheme. IJCSNS Int. J. Comput. Sci. Netw. Secur. **7**(2), 335–338 (2007)

8. Yu, Y., Xu, C., Huang, X.: An efficient anonymous proxy signature scheme with provable security. Comput. Stand. Interfaces **31**(2), 348–353 (2009)

9. Li, F., Zhong, D., Takagi, T.: Practical identity-based signature for wireless sensor networks. IEEE Wirel. Commun. Lett. **1**(6), 637–640 (2012)

10. Jung, T., Li, X., Wan, Z.: Control cloud data access privilege and anonymity with fully anonymous attribute-based encryption. IEEE Trans. Inf. Forensics Secur. **10**(1), 190–199 (2015)

11. Guo, L., Zhu, X., Zhang, C., et al.: Privacy-preserving attribute-based friend search in geosocial networks with untrusted servers. In: Global Communications Conference on 2013, pp. 629–634. IEEE (2013)

12. Liu, Z., Cao, Z., Wong, D.S.: Traceable CP-ABE: How to Trace Decryption Devices Found in the Wild. IEEE Trans. Inf. Forensics Secur. **10**(1), 55–68 (2015)

13. Fugkeaw S, Sato H. An Extended CP-ABE Based Access Control Model for Data Outsourced in the Cloud. In: Computer Software and Applications Conference IEEE, pp. 73–78. IEEE Computer Society (2015)

14. Zhu, H., Du, S., Li, M., Gao, Z.: Fairness-aware and privacy-preserving friend matching protocol in mobile social networks. IEEE Trans. Emerging Topics in Comput. **1**(1), 192–200 (2013)

15. Chen, Y., Zhang, L., Weng, Y.: A data encryption algorithm based on dual chaotic system. In: International Conference on Computer Application and System Modeling, vol. 4, pp. V431–435. IEEE (2010)

16. Hazay, C., Toft, T.: Computationally secure pattern matching in the presence of malicious adversaries. J. Cryptol. **27**, 358–395 (2014)

17. Lindell, Y., Pinkas, B., Smart, N.P.: Implementing two-party computation efficiently with security against malicious adversaries. In: Ostrovsky, R., De Prisco, R., Visconti, I. (eds.) SCN 2008. LNCS, vol. 5229, pp. 2–20. Springer, Heidelberg (2008). https://doi.org/10.1007/978-3-540-85855-3_2

18. Chang, W., Wu, J.: Progressive or conservative: rationally allocate cooperative work in mobile social networks. IEEE Trans. Parallel Distrib. Syst. **26**(7), 2020–2035 (2015)

19. Tang, K., Shi, R.H., Dong J.: Throughput Analysis of Cognitive Wireless Acoustic Sensor Networks with Energy Harvesting. Futur. Gener. Comput. Syst. (2017). https://doi.org/10.1016/j.future.2017.07.032

20. Xie, K., Cao, J., Wang, X., Wen, J.: Optimal resource allocation for reliable and energy efficient cooperative communications. IEEE Trans. Wireless Commun. **12**(10), 4994–5007 (2013)

Privacy-Preserving Data Collection for Mobile Phone Sensing Tasks

Yi-Ning Liu[1]([▷◁]), Yan-Ping Wang[1], Xiao-Fen Wang[2], Zhe Xia[3], and Jingfang Xu[4]

[1] Guangxi Key Laboratory of Trusted Software,
Guilin University of Electronic Technology, Guilin, China
ynliu@guet.edu.cn
[2] School of Computer Science and Engineering,
University of Electronics Science and Technology of China, Chengdu, China
[3] School of Computer Science, Wuhan University of Technology, Wuhan, China
[4] School of Computer, Central China Normal University, Wuhan, China

Abstract. Lack of reliable data is a major obstacle in some research works because users are unwilling to provide their own private data to any third parties directly. Since statistical inference is aimed to analyze the overall data of a well-defined group rather than a specific individual, the paradigm of privacy-preserving data collection scheme is proposed recently, which can motivate users to contribute their data to research works. In this paper, two probable properties that promote the success of sensing tasks are analyzed, and a fog-assisted data collection scheme for mobile phone sensing tasks is proposed. Sensitive measurements are particularly protected by obfuscating them with the group values, which not only provides anonymity for participants but also enables accurate data for the task provider. Especially, the dynamic change of participants is also considered. Theoretical analysis shows that this method achieves the desired security goals, and experiments are performed to demonstrate the efficiency and feasibility.

Keywords: Privacy-preservation · Sensing tasks · Anonymity

1 Introduce

Nowadays, the sensors, which can sense, process, and disseminate information, are deployed into areas to monitor and track various objects, such as animals, vehicles, physical phenomena. Since mobile devices (e.g. smart phones) have proliferation and ever-increasing capabilities, a plethora of phone sensing applications (camera, GPS etc.) has been deployed [1–3]. Compared with the traditional sensor networks, mobile phone sensors have the advantages of efficiency, flexibility and functionality. Therefore, these kinds of sensors have been applied in an extensive sensing scenario. In data collection tasks, participants can use mobile phones or portable devices embedded with sensors to collect their own data and report them to the laboratory or medical organizations for further analyses. These analyzed data provide opportunities to make sophisticated inference about people, which can make people's life more convenient.

© Springer Nature Switzerland AG 2018
C. Su and H. Kikuchi (Eds.): ISPEC 2018, LNCS 11125, pp. 506–518, 2018.
https://doi.org/10.1007/978-3-319-99807-7_32

The existing sensing works can be divided into three categories [4, 5]: public, personal and social centric sensing. The public sensing tasks are mainly designed for monitoring physical phenomena such as traffic [1], noise [6], air pollution [7]. Personal sensing tasks are based on the single individual activities, such as personal health related activities [8] and sports experiences monitoring [9]. In social sensing tasks, participants collect and report the sensing data collectively in specific conditions related to each field of studies [3, 10–12]. These kinds of sensing tasks can be implemented only when users are willing to participate in the sensing activity. However, the sensing data often contains various kinds of sensitive information that may reveal the fine-grained details about participants. What's more disturbing is that the current network architecture makes internet packets to be eavesdropped and traceable. The security of these data has become an important concern due to the open and hostile network environment [13–16]. Assuming a data center, who recruits a group of participants to perform a time series sensing task [3, 11, 17], the data from the individual user is privacy-sensitive, and users do not trust any third-party to obtain the relationship between their identity and their sensing data. In this case, users may refuse the sensing task, and this can directly cause the failure of the task.

Since the protection of participants' privacy can motivate users to attend sensing campaigns, efficiency privacy-preserving data collection schemes are proposed in [10–12, 18–22] and some are intend to protect participants' privacy while implement a specific function e.g. sum [12, 18, 19], max/min [10, 11, 18], median [22] etc. However, a certain aggregation function cannot completely satisfy the complicated statistic analysis in many cases. For example, a medical organization conducts a sensing campaign to collect the body temperature of a group of users in order to predict the totally number of people infected by flu, which requires the exact temperature value rather than a single aggregation sum.

Additionally, providing incentives can highly motivate users to participate these sensing tasks. On the basis of previous articles [4, 17, 23], an efficiency anonymous data collection protocol which considers the motivation of participants and designs for a practical scale group has been proposed in this paper. Assuming a task provider, who conducts a sensing campaign which contains several rounds data collection. The provider is required to collect accurate data without knowing which data belongs to which participant. The incentive factors for participants are also considered. When the campaign is over, participants can get incentives from the provider. For an overview in mobile participatory sensing works, the readers are referred to the paper [24]. The main contributions of this paper are as follows:

(1) This paper provides a strong network structure that leverages the intermediate fog nodes, the cipher is replayed by the fog node rather than being transmitted directly to the cloud.
(2) This paper proposed a novel session key agreement scheme which is suitable for the real mobile phone data collection environment.
(3) The theoretical analysis is performed from the aspect of security. In addition, experiments have been conducted to prove that the protocol can be implemented effectively.

The rest of this paper is organized as follows: Sect. 2 discusses the related work. The system architecture and threat model are formulated in Sect. 3. Section 4 describes the proposed scheme. Efficiency evaluation is performed in Sect. 5. Finally, we conclude in Sect. 6.

Table 1. The characteristics comparison

	[3]	[4]	[17]	[23]	The proposed
Anonymity	Yes	Yes	Yes	Yes	Yes
Shared key in each pair of participants	No	Yes	No	Yes	No
Trust third-parties	No	No	Yes	No	No
The resistance of neighbors collusion attack	No	Yes	No	Yes	Yes
Incentive mechanism	No	No	No	Yes	Yes

2 Related Work

Cryptographic privacy-preserving methods provide good privacy for participants and accurate values for sensing task providers. In [25], a data collection scheme which uses ElGamal cryptosystem has been proposed, their work allows the data to be collected anonymously. To obtain the data, their scheme has t leaders, all participants encrypt their data with the t leaders' public keys. According to the analysis of Brickell and Shmatikov [26], the scheme in [25] cannot resist the collusion attack and they proposed a complement scheme, in which each participant has two public/private key pairs, the plaintext is encrypted under the data collector's public key and each participant's two public keys, all participants decrypt layers of the cipher collectively, the output is sent to the data collector who finally decrypts the cipher using all participants' secondary private keys. Their scheme needs extra interactions between the final destination and all users in every task period. Wang and Ku [27] proposed an anonymous data collection scheme for mobile participatory sensing, their method utilizes peer-to-peer network to achieve anonymous data transmission, however, their scheme requires an extra maintenance of the peer-to-peer network and the data collection is confronted a long time delay.

In recent years, an efficient and excellent idea for anonymous data collection is n-source anonymity scheme [3, 4, 17, 23]. Zhang et al. [17] designed an anonymous data collection scheme, in which the aggregator can obtain the accurate data of each participant. However, in their scheme, the participant $i-1$ and $i+1$ owns half part of i's secret keys respectively, if $i-1$ and $i+1$ collude with each other then the participant i's data would be disclosed. Thus their scheme cannot resist the neighbor collusion attack. Additionally, there is a trust authority in their scheme, it is nontrivial to find such an institute and make sure it is worthy to trust. Inspired by their works, Shen et al. [3] analyzed two categories of mobile sensing task according to the actual demands, they proposed two privacy-preserving schemes without the trust authority. Since the anonymity of their protocol is based on the group key which is known to all participants, their scheme needs all participants to be honest. Slot reservation scheme is proposed in [4], it solved the problem of unique number assignment, and achieved the goal that data be submitted anonymously, this scheme strongly resists the collusion attack. The [23] proposed an efficiency anonymity data submission scheme with incentive mechanism based on Yao et al.'s [4] scheme. In Li et al.'s [23] scheme, there is a credit authority who firstly distributes a unique token for each of the participant in each data submission round, then all participants submit the token with their sensing data to the final destination, which means extra communication and computation. In both Yao et al.'s [4] and Li et al.'s [23] protocol, each pair of participants need to share a session key, which may not applicable to the practice sensing task environment.

Based on these works, this paper has proposed a fog-assisted data collection scheme for mobile sensing tasks which balanced the communication cost and anonymity property. Table 1 shows the characteristics of this protocol in contrast to the above data collection schemes.

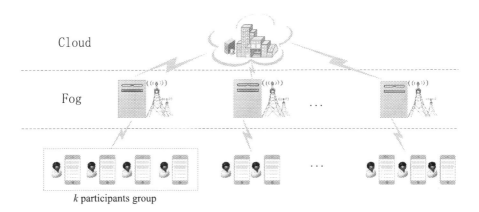

Fig. 1. The network framework

3   System Model

3.1   Communication Model

Assuming there is a sensing task which contains several rounds data collections, a provider recruits a set of mobile phone participants $\{p_1, p_2, \ldots, p_n\}$ to complete this sensing task and they can be rewarded after the task completed. And a three levels architecture for mobile sensing campaign is showed in Fig. 1. The system mainly comprises three entities: the participants $(p_i, i \in [1, n])$, a series parallel fog nodes (FNs) and a cloud server (CS).

The Participant. $(p_i, i \in [1, n])$ collects and processes the real-time data, then p_i sends the processed data to FN and will obtain a reward from FN when the sensing task ended.

***The Fog Node* (FN).** FN can implement fog computing services bases on a set of rules [28] and the detail illustration can be read in [29]. In this model, FNs are located in different geographical locations of the Internet and can provide service for both the phone participants and CS. Specifically, FNs can communicate with participants, package and forward their real-time responses to CS, they also play the role of the parties that help participants to get their rewards and assist the dynamic change of participants.

***The Cloud Server* (CS).** The sensing data that FNs received will be eventually sent to CS which can central manage and store sensing data for commercial or for-profit uses. And CS can decide when the task starts and the reward channel launches.

Table 2. Summary of symbols

Symbols	Meaning
$p_i(i \in 1, 2, \ldots, n)$	The mobile sensing task participant i
FN	Fog node which can play the role of the intermediary server
CS	Cloud server
$h(\cdot)$	Hash function $\{0, 1\}^* \rightarrow \{0, 1\}^l$
(x, y)	The key pair of CS
(x_i, y_i)	The key pair of p_i
(x_{cs}, y_{cs})	The one-time sign/verify key pair which is generated by CS
$E_y(\cdot)$	Encryption under the public key y
$D_x(\cdot)$	Decryption under the private key x
$Sig_x(\cdot)$	Digital signature under the private key x
m_i	The sensing data of p_i
C_i	The cipher of p_i in the slot negotiation and incentive phase
$\bar{C_i}$	The cipher of p_i in the data collection and reword phase

3.2   Threat Model

The adversary includes external attackers and internal attackers.

External Attacker. Supposing there are external attackers who are trying to gain some information about participants' data.

Internal Attacker. Supposing it is possible that all parties may break privacy but they would faithfully follow the protocol.

(1) Participants: mobile phone participants sense and transmit their data. However, they attempt to passively breach other participants' privacy.
(2) FN: FN is considered as an entity which can be bribed, but it does not modify the received data and it will obey the protocol.
(3) CS: CS stores the data, but it attempts to derive the connection between each piece of data and its contributor, which the participant does not want to be leaked.

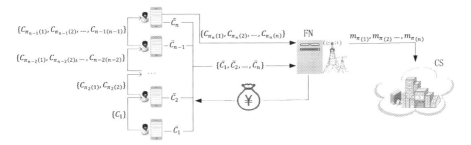

Fig. 2. Overview of the proposed protocol

4 The Fog-Assisted Privacy-Preserving Data Collection Protocol

In this section, a fog-assisted privacy-preserving data collection scheme is proposed, which mainly comprises three phases: the setup phase, the slot negotiation and incentive phase, the data collection and reward phase. In the second phase, the blind signature scheme is referred in the literature [30]. The mobile sensor senses data and transmits it to FN, then FN processes and replays these data to CS. Some notions are listed in Table 2 and the overview of the proposed scheme is showed in Fig. 2.

4.1 Setup Phase

The Global Key Generation. This protocol uses the standard ElGamal encryption. CS selects the **params** $= \{G, g, p\}$ and a key pair $(x, y)\left(x \in Z_p^*, y \in G\right)$ such that $y = g^x$. CS publishes $\{G, g, p, y\}$. Every $p_i(i \in [1, n])$ generates (x_i, y_i) based on **params** and $y_i = g^{x_i}$, then p_i broadcasts y_i as public key. When CS prepares to start a sensing task, CS selects a random $x_{cs} \in Z_p^*$ and generates $y_{cs} = g^{x_{cs}}$, a formulated message $\{TIMESTAMP, y_{cs}\}$, $Sig_x\{TIMESTAMP, y_{cs}\}$ from CS is sent to FN. Let FN broadcasts the start message.

Setup for Slot Negotiation and Incentive Phase. Prior to the slot agreement and incentive phase, there is a transmission order list which is known to all participants. Each p_i has a predecessor and a successor, the data is flowed from the predecessor and flowed to the successor. Participant $p_i(i \in [1, n-1])$ selects the public keys $\{y_{i+1}, y_{i+2}, \ldots, y_n\}$ and computes $Y_i = y_{i+1} \cdot y_{i+2}, \ldots, y_n$, then p_i stores Y_i.

Setup for Data Collection and Reward Phase. In [4, 23], each pair of members shares a session key. In this protocol, $p_i(i \in [1, n])$ selects $\beta(1 \leq \beta \leq n-1)$ participants (e.g. his/her friends) in the group, shares a session key $k_{ij}(i, j \in [1, n], i \neq j)$ with the selected p_j (Fig. 3), which is more applicable to the reality mobile sensing environment. p_i stores all the session keys $\{k_{i1}, k_{i2}, \ldots, k_{i\beta}\}$ $(1 \leq \beta \leq n-1)$ which contains the session keys he/she communicates with others passively or actively.

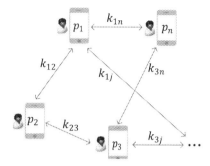

Fig. 3. The session key distribution

4.2   Slot Agreement and Incentive Phase

In this phase, the unique slot for participants' data is negotiated and the incentive device for participants is prepared without any third-parties. p_i chooses a random number $\lambda_i (\lambda_i \in G)$ which is called blind signature coefficient and computes a slot data $SN_i = id_i \cdot \lambda_i \, modp$, then p_i performs:

Slot Data Encrypt. Each p_i encrypts SN_i using ElGamal *PKE* as follows:

(1) p_i firstly selects a random number $r_i \in \{1, 2, \ldots, p-1\}$ and calculates:

$$C_{i1} = g^{r_i} modp. \tag{1}$$

(2) p_i encrypts SN_i with the key Y_i by calculating:

$$C_{i2} = SN_i \cdot (Y_i)^{r_i} modp. \tag{2}$$

$C_i = E_{Y_i}(SN_i) = (C_{i1}, C_{i2})$ is the cipher of p_i.

Shuffle. When p_i received the cipher list $CL_{\pi_{i-1}} = \left\{ C_{\pi_{i-1}(1)}, C_{\pi_{i-1}(2)}, \ldots, C_{\pi_{i-1}(i-1)} \right\}$ from his/her predecessor p_{i-1}, p_i performs:

(1) p_i strips off one layer of each $C_{\pi_{i-1}(j)} (j \in [1, i-1])$ by computing $\sum_{j=1}^{j=i-1} D_{x_i}$ $\left(C_{\pi_{i-1}(j)} \right)$.
(2) p_i shuffles the cipher list using a random permutation π and Y_i^μ (μ is a random number and $\mu \in Z_p^*$).
(3) p_i adds C_i into the cipher list and outputs a new cipher list $CL_{\pi_i} = \left\{ C_{\pi_i(1)}, C_{\pi_i(2)}, \ldots, C_{\pi_i(i)} \right\}$.
(4) p_i sends the list CL_{π_i} to p_{i+1}.

This process continues until p_n who has the last transmission order. p_n strips off the last layer of each $C_{\pi_{n-1}(j)} (j \in \{1, 2, \ldots, n-1\})$, and gets the slot number list $SNL_{\pi_{n-1}} = \left\{ SN_{\pi_{n-1}(1)}, SN_{\pi_{n-1}(2)}, \ldots, SN_{\pi_{n-1}(n-1)} \right\}, p_n$ adds SN_n into $SNL_{\pi_{n-1}}$, permutes it and sends $SNL_{\pi_n} = \left\{ SN_{\pi_n(1)}, SN_{\pi_n(2)}, \ldots, SN_{\pi_n(n)} \right\}$ to FN.

Slot and Signature Obtains. This operation begin with FN received the list *SNL*. And the details are as follows:

(1) FN forwards the slot list $SNL = \{SN_{\pi_n(1)}, SN_{\pi_n(2)}, \ldots, SN_{\pi_n(n)}\}$ to CS.
(2) CS signs each SN_i by $sig_{x_{cs}}\{SN_i\}(i \in [1, n])$ and returns the signature list to FN.
(3) FN publishes *SNL* and $sig_{x_{cs}}\{SNL\}$.

The position of SN_i is p_i's sensing data slot (denoted by $slot(i)$ in the subsequent data collection phase). p_i gets the $sig_{x_{cs}}\{SN_i\}$ which is placed in the same slot corresponding to SN_i, removes the signature factor λ_i, and gets the $sig_{x_{cs}}\{ID_i\}$.

4.3 Data Collection and Reward Phase

After the slot agreement phase, every p_i has a $slot(i)$ which is oblivious to other parties. Note that the data collection phase can be executed several rounds using the same slot. Only when the participant complete all the data sensing collections, can he/she get the rewards, therefore, we don't allow the dynamic change during the task.

Sensing Data Encrypt. Assuming that when the setup phase ended, p_i possesses β session key. Once p_i received the starting message, p_i performs:

(1) $p_i(j \in [1, n])$ constructs $e_i^j(j \in [1, n])$ with time t (assuming in every time period each participant uses the same t) such as:

$$
\begin{aligned}
e_i^1 &= h(k_{i1}|t|1) \oplus h(k_{i2}|t|1)\ldots, h(k_{i\beta}|t|1) \\
e_i^2 &= h(k_{i1}|t|2) \oplus h(k_{i2}|t|2)\ldots, h(k_{i\beta}|t|2) \\
& \ldots \\
e_i^n &= h(k_{i1}|t|n) \oplus h(k_{i2}|t|n)\ldots, h(k_{i\beta}|t|n)
\end{aligned}
\tag{3}
$$

(2) p_i adds m_i to the $slot(i)$-th slot, $\bar{C}_i$ is constructed as follows:

$$
\bar{C}_i = e_i^1|e_i^2|\ldots|e_i^{slot(i)} \oplus m_i|\ldots|e_i^n.
\tag{4}
$$

FN Aggregates and Forwards. FN eventually receives n $\bar{C}_i(i = 1, 2\ldots, n)$ from the n participants. FN performs:

(1) FN XOR all the $\bar{C}_i(i = 1, 2, \ldots, n)$ and obtains a plaintext list $ML = \{m_{\pi_n(1)}, m_{\pi_n(2)}\ldots, m_{\pi_n(n)}\}$.
(2) FN replays the list *ML* to CS.

CS Stores and Rewards. CS obtains a random permutation of plaintext $m_i(i = 1, 2\ldots, n)$ and stores it. when all data collection rounds are completed, then CS informs FN that the reward channel can be launched. Each p_i who possesses $sig_{x_{cs}}\{ID_i\}$ can obtain a payment from FN in a specific time period. Surely, FN would records the participant who has already rewarded to prevent the participant from receives reward repeatedly.

5 System Analysis

In this section, the theoretical analysis is firstly presented, followed by experiments, which are aimed to demonstrate the feasibility and evaluate the efficiency of the proposed scheme.

5.1 Anonymity

Theorem 1. *Since at least two participants faithfully perform the slot agreement and incentive phase, anyone (expect the owner) cannot link the data to its contributor.*

Proof: Since each $SN_i(i \in [1, n])$ is encrypted using ElGamal cryptosystem which can achieve the IND-CCA (*indistinguishable chosen ciphertext attack*), it is computation intractable for the attacker to gain any information about SN_i. In the slot negotiation phase, we construct a simulator S_1 from the views of semi-honest participants and FN. Let $f_n(X) = \{f(x_1), f(x_2) \ldots, f(x_n)\}$ for a set $\{x_1, x_2 \ldots, x_n\}$ where $f \in \{E, D\}$. Given v semi-honest participants $J = \{j_1, j_2 \ldots, j_v\}(v < n)$, and their inputs $\{m_1, m_2 \ldots, m_v\}$. S_1 proceed as follows:

(1) Let $I := [n] \backslash J$, for each, $p_{i \in I}$ chooses a key pair (x_i, y_i) such that $y_i = g^{x_i}$, and chooses a permutation $\pi(i)$.

(2) All the user choose their new random input.

(3) For $i \in I$ and $i = 1$, p_i, computes $E_{Y_1}(m_i)$ and outputs c_1. If $j \neq 1$ and $j \neq J$, for each pair $(i, j) \in I \times J$ such that $j = i + 1$ and $0 < i < n$, p_j computes $C'_i = D_{x_j}(C_i)$ where $C_i = \{c_{v \in I, v \in [1, i]} \cup c_{k \in J, k \in [1, j-1]}\}$ and $c_j = E_{Y_j}$. p_j adds c_j in the list C'_i and shuffles C_j, then p_j outputs C_j. For each $(i, i'), i = i' + 1$, and $0 < i' < n$, p_j computes C_i using the x_i, m_i and $\pi(i)$.

(4) If $j = n$ and $j \in J$, p_j outputs $\tilde{Z} = \{m_{i \in I} \cup m_{j \in J}\}$. If $i = n$ and $i \in I$, p_i outputs $\tilde{Z} = \{m_{i \in I} \cup m_{j \in J}\}$ and sends $\tilde{Z}$ to FN.

Absolutely, the output can be executed by S as a polynomial function of $\tilde{Z}$. Every participant $(p_i, p_j)(i, j) \in I \times J$ sees only the encrypted and permuted list. For $0 < i < n, C_i$ and C_{i+1} is computationally indistinguishable, we can prove it by prove $Q = \{G, g, p, g^a, g^b, g^{ab}\}$ is indistinguishable to $Q' = \{G, g, p, g^a, g^b, E_{Y_i}(r)(E_{Y_i}(r) \in G)\}$, since the DDH assumption is hold, the conclusions is established. In step 3, even if the neighbors p_{i-1} and p_{i+1} is corrupted, they cannot derive which data is belong to i. We claim that the simulator's in J and FN's view cannot get the information of which data is belong to its contributor. Thus, we can conclude that the simulator S_1 cannot link any piece of data with its contributor.

Theorem 2. *In the data collection and reward phase, assuming p_i has shared β session keys with group crews, FN and CS cannot link the data with its source if there is at least one honest participants in the β participants.*

Proof: For the data collection phase, we can construct a simulator S_2. Given a set of semi-honest participants $J = \{j_1, j_2 \ldots, j_v\}(v < n)$, their inputs $M_J = \{m_{j_1}, m_{j_2} \ldots, m_{j_v}\}$, a fog node, and an output list Z of data collection phase. S_2 proceed as follows:

(1) Let $I := [n] \backslash J$, for each $p_{j \in J}$ chooses arbitrary β_j participants belong to $I \times J$ to share a session key. For each $p_{i \in I}$ chooses one participant $p_{h \in I}$ and another $\beta_i - 1$ participants arbitrarily to share a session key.

(2) For each $(p_i, p_j)(i \times j \in I \times J)$, constructs C_i and C_j with the input m_i and m_j as Eq. (3) that showed in Sect. 4.3.

(3) For each $(p_i, p_j)(i \times j \in I \times J)$, submits C_i and C_j to FN respectively.

FN receives all $C_{i \in I} \cup C_{j \in J}$, performs the XOR operation, then FN can obtain $M = \{m_{i \in I} \cup m_{j \in J}\}$. If FN wants to link $C_{i \in I}$ with its contributor p_i, there are two strategies that FN may take: (1) decrypts $C_{i \in I}$ directly. For this case, FN must know all the β_i session keys that $p_{i \in I}$ shared with others. However, FN cannot decrypt $C_{i \in I}$ for that p_i shared session key with at least one participant $p_{h \in I}$, FN cannot obtain all the session keys, thus, FN cannot decrypt $C_{i \in I}$. (2) FN knows the slot of participant p_i, when FN aggregates all the cipher $C = \{C_{i \in I} \cup C_{j \in J}\}$, it obtains a random permutation of $M = \{m_{i \in I} \cup m_{i \in J}\}$, and can infer $m_{i \in I}$ is belonged to participants p_i. However, according to **Theorem 1**, we know that FN cannot get the slot of $p_i (i \in I)$, namely, FN cannot link any piece of data with its source. Absolutely, we can conclude that the S_2 cannot link any piece of data with its source.

5.2   Efficiency

According to [31], communication is more energy-hungry than computation. In this protocol, we don't assume each pair of participants share a session key, which can reduce some communication burdens compared to [4, 23]. The slots negotiation phase is based on ElGamal encryption, the total computational complexity is $O(nlogp)$. Since the data collection phase is mainly based on hash function and the total computational complexity is $O(n)$. In our protocol, especially, the slot negotiation phase only executes once while the data collection phase may execute several rounds in a sensing task.

For the slot negotiation phase, participants encrypt their slot data, shuffle the cipher and send the new cipher to their successor. The main time impacts in participants side are the encryption key length and the transmit order in the group. The participant is simulated by a mobile phone of Hornor V9 with 6 GB run memory, we measured the encryption time of the slot negotiation phase varies with participants' location in the group and the result is showed in Fig. 4a, in our experiment, the computation time corresponding to different data length is different when $|p|$ is given. The encryption time of data collection scheme (Fig. 4b) is mainly based on the group size and data length, and we evaluated the efficiency which varies with the different group size and the different data length, what's more, the hash function is completed using SHA-512.

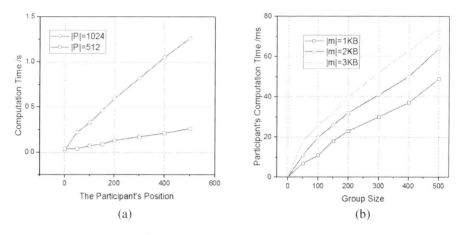

Fig. 4. Execution time of participants

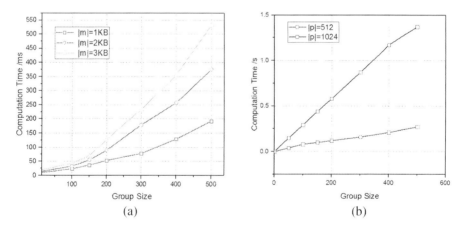

Fig. 5. Execution time of servers

The main computation of FN is XOR operation, and blind signature is the main computation for CS. The XOR and blind signature are supposed to operated by a desktop computer with Intel(R) Core(TM) i5-6500M CPU @3.20 GHz and 8.00 GB memory, based on the eclipse 4.8.0. The determine factor of computation efficiency to these operations are the total number of participants. The participant number is assumed to be from 50 to 500, $|p| = 512$ and $|m| = 1024$ to test the proposed scheme and the measurement is showed in Fig. 5a and b respectively.

6   Conclusion

In this paper, a practical method for mobile phone sensing tasks was proposed. This scheme achieved anonymity data collection without the assumption that the third parties existed. It also provided sufficient incentives for participants in order to motivate people to intend or adopt the sensing campaign. Even based on the assumption that the data center and a fraction of participants were unreliable, they still could not link any piece of relevant value to its contributors. All the time series data could be collected in parallel, which could drastically reduce the time delay. Theoretical analysis and experiments were performed to demonstrate the feasibility and efficiency of the proposed scheme.

Acknowledgment. This work was partly supported by National Natural Science Foundation of China under grant Nos. 61662016 and 61772224, GUET Excellent Graduate Thesis Program No. 16YJPYSS17, and Innovation Project of Guangxi Graduate Education No. YCSW2017139.

References

1. Mohan, P., Padmanabhan, V.N., Ramjee, R.: Nericell: rich monitoring of road and traffic conditions using mobile smartphones. In: Proceedings of the 6th ACM Conference on Embedded Network Sensor Systems, pp. 323–336. ACM, Raleigh (2008)
2. Dai, J., Bai, X., Yang, Z., et al.: Mobile phone-based pervasive fall detection. Pers. Ubiquit. Comput. **14**(7), 633–643 (2010)
3. Shen, W., Yin, B., Cheng, Y., et al.: Privacy-preserving mobile crowd sensing for big data applications. In: 2017 IEEE International Conference on Communications (ICC), pp. 1–6. IEEE, Paris (2017)
4. Yao, Y., Yang, L.T., Xiong, N.N.: Anonymity-based privacy-preserving data reporting for participatory sensing. IEEE IoT J. **2**(5), 381–390 (2015)
5. Khan, W.Z., Xiang, Y., Aalsalem, M.Y., et al.: Mobile phone sensing systems: a survey. IEEE Commun. Surv. Tutor. **15**(1), 402–427 (2013)
6. Kanjo, E.: NoiseSPY: a real-time mobile phone platform for urban noise monitoring and mapping. Mob. Netw. Appl. **15**(4), 562–574 (2010)
7. Devarakonda, S., Sevusu, P., Liu, H., et al.: Real-time air quality monitoring through mobile sensing in metropolitan areas. In: Proceedings of the 2nd ACM SIGKDD International Workshop on Urban Computing, pp. 1–8. ACM, Chicago (2013)
8. Denning, T., Andrew, A., Chaudhri, R., et al.: BALANCE: towards a usable pervasive wellness application with accurate activity inference. In: Proceedings of the 10th Workshop on Mobile Computing Systems and Applications, pp. 1–6. ACM, Santa Cruz (2009)
9. Eisenman, S.B., Miluzzo, E., Lane, N.D., et al.: BikeNet: a mobile sensing system for cyclist experience mapping. ACM Trans. Sens. Netw. (TOSN) **6**(1), 1–39 (2009)
10. Groat, M.M., He, W., Forrest, S.: KIPDA: k-indistinguishable privacy-preserving data aggregation in wireless sensor networks. In: 2011 Proceedings IEEE, INFOCOM, pp. 2024–2032. IEEE, Shanghai (2011)
11. Zhang, Y., Chen, Q., Zhong, S.: Efficient and privacy-preserving min and k-th min computations in mobile sensing systems. IEEE Trans. Dependable Secur. Comput. **14**(1), 9–21 (2017)
12. Badra, M., Zeadally, S.: Lightweight and efficient privacy-preserving data aggregation approach for the smart grid. Ad Hoc Netw. **64**, 32–40 (2017)

13. Hu, L., Evans, D.: Secure aggregation for wireless networks. In: Proceedings 2003 Symposium on Applications and the Internet Workshops, pp. 384–391. IEEE, Orlando (2003)
14. Castelluccia, C., Mykletun, E., Tsudik, G.: Efficient aggregation of encrypted data in wireless sensor networks. In: International Conference on Mobile and Ubiquitous Systems: Networking and Services, pp. 109–117. IEEE Computer Society/IEEE, San Diego (2005)
15. Madden, S., Franklin, M.J., Hellerstein, J.M., et al.: TAG: a Tiny AGgregation service for ad-hoc sensor networks. ACM Sigops Oper. Syst. Rev. **36**(1), 131–146 (2002)
16. Jadia, P., Mathuria, A.: Efficient secure aggregation in sensor networks. In: Bougé, L., Prasanna, V.K. (eds.) HiPC 2004. LNCS, vol. 3296, pp. 40–49. Springer, Heidelberg (2004). https://doi.org/10.1007/978-3-540-30474-6_10
17. Zhang, Y., Chen, Q., Zhong, S.: Privacy-preserving data aggregation in mobile phone sensing. IEEE Trans. Inf. Forensics Secur. **11**(5), 980–992 (2016)
18. Li, Q., Cao, G.: Efficient and privacy-preserving data aggregation in mobile sensing. In: 2012 20th IEEE International Conference on Network Protocols (ICNP), pp. 1–10. IEEE, Austin (2012)
19. Shi, E., Chan, H.T.H., Rieffel, E., et al.: Privacy-preserving aggregation of time-series data. In: Proceedings of the Network and Distributed System Security Symposium, pp. 1–17. DBLP, San Diego (2011)
20. Sweeney, L.: K-anonymity: a model for protecting privacy. Int. J. Uncertain. Fuzziness Knowl.-Based Syst. **10**(5), 557–570 (2002)
21. Qiu, F., Wu, F., Chen, G.: Privacy and quality preserving multimedia data aggregation for participatory sensing systems. IEEE Trans. Mob. Comput. **14**(6), 1287–1300 (2015)
22. Shrivastava, N., Buragohain, C., Agrawal, D., et al.: Medians and beyond: new aggregation techniques for sensor networks. In: Proceedings of the 2nd International Conference on Embedded Networked Sensor Systems, pp. 239–249. ACM, Baltimore (2004)
23. Li, Y., Zhao, Y., Ishak, S., et al.: An anonymous data reporting strategy with ensuring incentives for mobile crowd-sensing. J. Ambient. Intell. Hum. Comput. 1–15 (2017)
24. Christin, D.: Privacy in mobile participatory sensing: current trends and future challenges. J. Syst. Softw. **116**, 57–68 (2015)
25. Yang, Z., Zhong, S., Wright, R.N.: Anonymity-preserving data collection. In: Proceedings of the Eleventh ACM SIGKDD International Conference on Knowledge Discovery in Data Mining, pp. 334–343. ACM, Chicago (2005)
26. Brickell, J., Shmatikov, V.: Efficient anonymity-preserving data collection. In: Proceedings of the 12th ACM SIGKDD International Conference on Knowledge Discovery and Data Mining, pp. 76–85. ACM, Philadelphia (2006)
27. Wang, C.J., Ku, W.S.: Anonymous sensory data collection approach for mobile participatory sensing. In: 2012 IEEE 28th International Conference on Data Engineering Workshops, pp. 220–227. IEEE, Arlington (2012)
28. Lin, Y., Shen, H.: Cloud fog: towards high quality of experience in cloud gaming. In: 2015 44th International Conference on Parallel Processing, pp. 500–509. IEEE, Beijing (2015)
29. Lyu, L., Nandakumar, K., Rubinstein, B., et al.: PPFA: privacy preserving fog-enabled aggregation in smart grid. IEEE Trans. Ind. Inform. 1–15 (2018)
30. Boldyreva, A.: Threshold signatures, multisignatures and blind signatures based on the gap-diffie-hellman-group signature scheme. In: Desmedt, Y.G. (ed.) PKC 2003. LNCS, vol. 2567, pp. 31–46. Springer, Heidelberg (2003). https://doi.org/10.1007/3-540-36288-6_3
31. Balasubramanian, N., Balasubramanian, A., Venkataramani, A.: Energy consumption in mobile phones: a measurement study and implications for network applications. In: ACM SIGCOMM Conference on Internet Measurement, pp. 280–293. ACM, Chicago (2009)

Secure Computation and Data Privacy

M-ORAM Revisited: Security and Construction Updates

Karin Sumongkayothin[✉]

Faculty of Information and Communication Technology,
Mahidol University Nakhon Pathom, Phutthamonthon, Thailand
karin.sum@mahidol.ac.th

Abstract. Oblivious Random Access Machine (ORAM) [4] was introduced in regard to secure the access patterns seen by a server when the data have been retrieved. Matrix based ORAM (M-ORAM) [5] is one of ORAM constructions. It has been introduced in the matrix data structure format and can achieve $O(1)$ for both bandwidth overhead and computation complexity. With the impressive performance results; however, the given security proof is not well defined. We therefore revisit the paper to give a new proper proof method to construct the access sequence which is statically indistinguishable from random accesses. In addition according to our new security proof, M-ORAM has a security weakness in a specific circumstance. Hence, the improved M-ORAM construction which can solve the problem is also introduced.

1 Introduction

ORAM is widely known as one of the methods to secure the access pattern generated during read/write operations. Since uploading data, downloading data and performing operations on the server may reveal valuable information to server although the data are encrypted [6,7], the role of ORAM is to generate the similar access pattern regardless of the types of operation. Generally, the ORAM system consists of *ORAM server*: the ORAM logical structure, and *ORAM client*: an application which generates the oblivious access patterns. To kindly note, from now on *"client"*, *"ORAM"*, and *"ORAM construction"* are used to represent ORAM client, ORAM server, and ORAM system, respectively for more readability. To create an oblivious access pattern, it requires three major approaches:

Equivalent Number of Accesses: is generating a same number of reads and writes for an access operation. Both read and write must be performed whether the client wants to read or write; otherwise, the server can distinct the differentiation. In addition to an access request, accessing multiple blocks of data on the server is required to hide a data of interest.

Random Relocation: is a writing data which has been read to a random location on ORAM in order not to let the server do statistical analysis.

© Springer Nature Switzerland AG 2018
C. Su and H. Kikuchi (Eds.): ISPEC 2018, LNCS 11125, pp. 521–532, 2018.
https://doi.org/10.1007/978-3-319-99807-7_33

Random Re-encryption: is a re-encrypting data with the new secret key before writing to the server. In order to prevent the server recognizes the non-updated data.

With these three approaches, the result is that all been requested is indistinguishable from the server's perspective. There have many ORAM constructions been proposed [5,9,11–13] in various data structure formats. The ORAM construction is generally categorized into without position map [4,8,11,14] and vice versa [2,3,10,12,13]. Position map is the client's buffer which contains the location of data stored on the ORAM. Despite having less operation complexity and bandwidth cost, ORAM construction with a position map has to sacrifice some spaces from client's storage as a trade-off.

This paper proposes the new proof method to show that the proposed M-ORAM construction has a security weakness when some data are more often accessed than others. We therefore propose the improved version of M-ORAM to fix the problem. Our contributions are:

1. Propose the new security proof method for M-ORAM construction.
2. Detailed the new design of M-ORAM construction focusing on the client.
3. Security analysis of the new M-ORAM model.

The rest of the paper is organized as follows. Section 2 overviews an original M-ORAM construction and its security weakness. Then the new M-ORAM with detailed design of the storage and operations are given in Sect. 3. The techniques used in new design to achieve the ORAM security requirements are given in Sect. 4. In Sect. 5, the security game between client and server is introduced to construct the indistinguishable access pattern. In Sect. 6, we show that the performance of new construction still remains the same as its original version. Section 7 shows the experimental results of data movement characteristic which is seen by the server. Finally, we give a conclusion in Sect. 8.

2   Recall the M-ORAM

Matrix based ORAM (M-ORAM) is a position map ORAM where the design aims to achieve ORAM functionality by requiring only simple operation under constant bandwidth usage. Besides M-ORAM, most of the simple operation ORAMs(e.g. Path ORAM) [12], randomly relocating the data relies on the ORAM data structure. The major disadvantage of those proposed constructions is that the bandwidth varies with the size of the ORAM. M-ORAM was designed with the different concept. Instead of relying the relocation on the logical data structure, M-ORAM does so by using the client's operation. Since M-ORAM's data relocation is independent of the data structure; it can operate over any data structure formats while keeps the bandwidth constant for any size of ORAM. Even though M-ORAM data structure does not necessarily be arranged in the matrix format, Steven et al. [5] described the M-ORAM's functionality based on matrix data structure for better understanding.

2.1   Construction and Operation

Original M-ORAM construction is arranged in a matrix format containing N blocks of data. The client has buffers consisting *stash, position map,* and *previous access list.* Stash is used to temporarily store the data which have been accessed. The position map is used to store the logical address of all data kept on the ORAM, and previous access list is used to keep the list of block locations which have been accessed during a previous access operation. Once the client wants to access a data either read or write, it generates series of reads then writes on multiple blocks of the ORAM. The height of matrix represents the number of data blocks that are being accessed per access operation. Once the request starts, client randomly read (i.e. download) a block from each row, except the row that contains a data of interest. To kindly note that, the choosing is not uniformly random. It is actually a random with a condition which some (not all) of chosen blocks must be accessed in the last access operation. Each of reading data is randomly stored in a different stash, then the value within a position map is updated according to the new data location then the write operation will start. To write (i.e. upload) the data, client randomly selects a data from each stash then write it to the corresponding matrix column at the location which was read.

2.2   Security Weakness

The current version of M-ORAM has the security problem in a specific circumstance. If the one data has been frequently requested than others, the curious server can distinguish the data of interest from other data with high probability. Suppose an access sequence consists of 3 accesses and each access desires to retrieve a different data of interest. The square of Fig. 1 represents the sample space of blocks in the ORAM that could be accessed by the client. The light blue circle represents a set of blocks which was accessed of an access operation. The security problem of current M-ORAM reveals when an access sequence contains 3 or more accesses. According to the access sequence shown in Fig. 1a and b, they are obviously distinguishable by the statistical test. Suppose ORAM contains N blocks and H blocks are accessed per access request, the probability of the blocks beside the data of interest of 3rd access will be chosen from the 1st access is pretty low when $H \ll N$. On the other hand, if the data of interest of 3rd access is one among the blocks accessed by 1st request, the probability of there exists a block accessed by the 1st access in the 3rd access is equal to 1. Therefore, if there is a block accessed in both 1st and 3rd access, that block is most likely to contain a data of interest of 3rd access.

3   New M-ORAM

To solve the problem which has been discussed in Sect. 2.2, the new design of M-ORAM is introduced along with some additional operations.

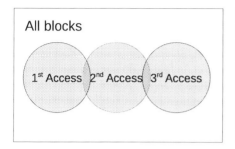

(a) No block from 1st access

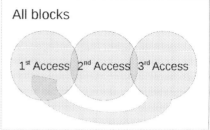

(b) Some blocks from 1st access

Fig. 1. Two possible access patterns of three consecutive requests

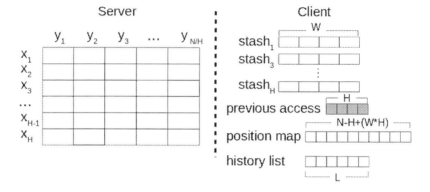

Fig. 2. New M-ORAM construction

3.1   Construction

The new buffer, *history list*, is added to the client as shown in Fig. 2. The idea
behind having this buffer is to equalize the probability of choosing the non-
interesting data and interesting data after 2 or more consecutive access operations. The history list is a fixed size buffer where its size depends on the highest
number of accessing the same interested data repeatedly by a client. Therefore
this construction, the client must not have access to any data beyond the maximum number of accesses that have been designed.

3.2   Operation

Slightly different from the original construction, new M-ORAM needs an operation called *warm-up* to randomly preset the value within the history list buffer.
This operation is required only once when the new client joins the system. By
the fact that the list of accessed blocks will end up with the size of ORAM if the
new list continually added, the oldest set of accessed blocks must be replaced by
the new set of recent blocks to keep the history list size fixed.

An operation consists of reads and writes same as the original M-ORAM; however, their details are slightly changed according to the changing structure. Algorithms 1 and 2 illustrate the steps of read and write when an access operation is activated. The access operation starts with reading an address of an interesting data from the position map (line 2) by using its *ID*. If the address locates in stash (line 3), a client does a local access to a data of interest. Otherwise, the client downloads it from the ORAM. To download data, the client does so by randomly selecting $H-1$ IDs which consists of o from previous access buffer, l from history list buffer, and n from uncategorized (see. Algorithm 3) then read their address from the position map (line 9). H data are downloaded from ORAM then randomly stored in different stashes (lines 10–13). Finally, the position map is updated according to the new addresses (line 15).

To write the data, a data is selected from each stash uniformly at random (line 2 of Algorithm 2). The IDs of chosen data are updated to history list and previous access buffer then the position map will be updated conforming to the new data location (lines 3–4). At the end of the operation, all selected data are written to the ORAM. A data from stash$_1$ is written to the column 1 of matrix ORAM, and so on (line 5).

Algorithm 1. Read Operation

1: **Input:** $ID, d^*, \{ID_{prev}\}$
2: $(x, y)_d \leftarrow$ ReadPositionMap(ID)
3: **if** $(x, y)_d$ in stash **then**
4:    **if** updata **then**
5:        Stash$((x, y)_d) \leftarrow d^*$
6:    **end if**
7:    $d \leftarrow$ Stash$((x, y)_d)$
8: **else**
9:    $\{(x, y)_{old}\}, \{(x, y)_{hist}\}, \{(x, y)_{un}\} \leftarrow$ SelectBlocks($ID, \{ID_{prev}\}$)
10:   $d, \{d_{other}\} \leftarrow$ ReadORAM$((x, y)_d, \{(x, y)_{old}\}, \{(x, y)_{hist}\}, \{(x, y)_{un}\})$
11:   **if** updata **then**
12:       $d \leftarrow d^*$
13:   **end if**
14:   $\{(x, y)_{update}\} \leftarrow$ RndPutStash$(d, \{d_{other}\})$
15:   UpdatePositionMap$(\{(x, y)_{update}\})$
16: **end if**
17: **return** d

Algorithm 2. Write Operation

1: **Input:** none
2: $\{ID_{prev}\}, \{x, y\}_{wr}, \{d_{wr}\} \leftarrow$ RndFromStash()
3: ReplaceHist($\{ID_{prev}\}$)
4: UpdatePosionMap($\{x, y\}_{wr}$)
5: WriteORAM$(\{\{x, y\}_{upload}, \{d_{wr}\})$
6: **return** $\{ID_{prev}\}$

Algorithm 3. SelectBlocks()

1: **Input:** $ID, \{ID_{prev}\}$
2: **if** $ID \in \{ID_{prev}\}$ **then**
3:     $\{ID_{old}\}, \{(x_{old}, y_{old})\} \leftarrow \text{RndSelect}(\{ID_{prev}\} \setminus ID, o-1)$
4: **else**
5:     $\{ID_{old}\} \leftarrow \text{RndSelect}(\{ID_{prev}\}, o)$
6: **end if**
7: **if** $ID \in \{\{ID_{hist\_list}\} \setminus \{ID_{:prev}\}\}$ **then**
8:     $\{ID_{hist}\} \leftarrow \text{RndSelect}(\{ID_{hist\_list}\} \setminus \{\{ID_{prev}\} \uplus ID\}, l-1)$
9: **else**
10:     $\{ID_{hist}\} \leftarrow \text{RndSelect}(\{ID_{hist\_list}\} \setminus \{ID_{prev}\}, l)$
11: **end if**
12: **if** $ID \in \{\{ID_{all}\} \setminus \{\{ID_{hist\_list}\} \uplus \{ID_{prev}\}\}\}$ **then**
13:     $\{ID_{un}\} \leftarrow \text{RndSelect}(\{ID_{all}\} \setminus \{\{ID_{prev}\} \uplus \{ID_{hist\_list}\} \uplus ID\}, h-o-l-1)$
14: **else**
15:     $\{ID_{un}\} \leftarrow \text{RndSelect}(\{ID_{all}\} \setminus \{\{ID_{prev}\} \uplus \{ID_{hist\_list}\}\}, h-o-l)$
16: **end if**
17: $\{(x,y)_{old}\}, \{(x,y)_{hist}\}, \{(x,y)_{un}\} \leftarrow \text{PositionMap}(\{ID_{old}\} \uplus \{ID_{hist}\} \uplus \{ID_{un}\})$
18: **return** $\{(x,y)_{old}\}, \{(x,y)_{hist}\}, \{(x,y)_{un}\}$

---

4   Security over New Construction

Generally, to achieve the security as an ORAM construction, several properties are required as follows:

1. The relationship between a data and its address cannot be observed
2. The updated and non-updated data are indistinguishable
3. The data of interest of the client and other downloaded data are indistinguishable
4. The difference of two access sequences with the same length are statistical and computational indistinguishable

In ORAM the indistinguishability can be considered as the term of statistic and computation. The client handles the indistinguishability in term of a statistical test by randomly storing to and retrieving from stash as described in Sect. 3.2. It courses the data shuffled on the ORAM while being accessed. The computational indistinguishability, on the other hands, we rely on the security of encryption algorithm. In M-ORAM, the symmetric key algorithm is used since the only client can decrypt the ciphertext. Therefore, the underlying security mechanisms depend upon generating the different ciphertext for any write operation. Figure 3 illustrates the position map block structure and data block structure. Data block has two parts consisting *data* and *integrity checking value (ICV)* which are encrypted before written to the ORAM. Position map blocks consist of three parts: *address, counter, and common secret number*. The address is a location of data on the ORAM. Counter and common secret number are used for the secret key generation which both are a random number at the first stage.

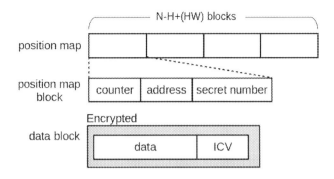

Fig. 3. New M-ORAM construction

The differences between a counter and common secret number are that the common secret number is a secret value shared among every data while the counter belongs to each data. To generate the secret key, a strong *pseudo-random function (PRF)* is used which takes data ID, counter and common random number as the inputs. Every time a data is accessed, the counter is increased by one. The data ID is used to ensure that the different secret keys will be applied for encrypting the different data blocks with high probability. Furthermore, the counter is used to guarantee that the same secret key is not applied twice in a row. Since the data ID is fixed and the counter has a constant size, the secret key will be eventually reused once the counter is rolled back to its beginning value. The common secret number's role is to change the pattern of key generator as the 3rd input parameter.

To calculate the time period (number of uploads) for changing the common secret number, a size of counter and the probability of choosing data to be uploaded are taken into consideration. Let the size of counter be c bits and a client repeatedly requests one specific data without changing the content. The probability which the same secret key will be applied to the same data is according to Theorem 1.

Theorem 1. *Let T denotes the time period (number of uploads) to change a common secret number. Suppose a counter has size c bits and stash width is equal to W blocks. $P(X = t)$ is the probability that client spends t trails until first success to retrieve data of interest from stash with the probability of success p. Therefore, the expected period of time to change a common secret number is:*

$$T = c \cdot (W - 1) \tag{1}$$

Proof. Since *PRF* is a deterministic function, the same input value must be used to generate the same output. The c bits counter must take c uploads before the same value of counter will be reused. In addition, the probability of successful picking a specific data from stash to be uploaded is $\frac{1}{W}$. Therefore, the expected value of number of uploads can be determined by using geometric distribution as follows:

$$T = c \cdot \sum_{t=1}^{\infty} \frac{t}{W}(1 - \frac{1}{W})^{t-1}$$
$$= c \cdot (W - 1) \tag{2}$$

5   Constructing the Indistinguishable Access Sequence

The security game between the curious server and the client is used to construct the indistinguishable access sequences. To set up the game, suppose H block locations has been accessed per access request. The history list and the previous access list have size L and H tuples, respectively. Let one access operation contains three data sets consisting: o from previous access list($\mathbb{O}$), l from history list($\mathbb{L}$), and $n = H - l - o$ from the locations which are not included in those lists. A client generates two same length access sequences which one of two is a choosing the data uniformly at random from those three sets, another is a normal access sequence which one among those chosen locations is of data of interest ($pos(ID)$). The server wins the game if the random sequence can be distinguished from a normal sequence with the probability greater than $\frac{1}{2} + \epsilon$.

To start the game, the client chooses the size of history list(L) and the stash(W) and keeps as a secret. Suppose $\mathbb{A}$ is a sequence of accesses, and each access is represented as a_i where $i \in \{1, 2, \dots, k\}$. The access sequence can be arranged as an Eq. 3:

$$\mathbb{A} = a_1 + a_2 + a_3 + \cdots + a_{k-1} + a_k \tag{3}$$

Suppose set of block locations in ORAM is represented as $\mathbb{N}$. One access is therefore composed of as follows:

$$a = \begin{cases} \bar{l} + \bar{o} + \bar{n} + pos(ID), & \text{if } a \text{ is a normal access.} \\ l + o + n, & \text{if } a \text{ is a random access.} \end{cases}$$

where $\tag{4}$

$$\bar{o} = \begin{cases} o - 1, & \text{if } pos(ID) \in \mathbb{O} \\ o, & \text{otherwise.} \end{cases} \quad \bar{l} = \begin{cases} l - 1, & \text{if } pos(ID) \in \mathbb{L} \setminus \{\mathbb{O}\} \\ l, & \text{otherwise.} \end{cases}$$

$$\bar{n} = \begin{cases} n - 1, & \text{if } pos(ID) \in \mathbb{N} \setminus \{\mathbb{O}, \mathbb{L}\} \\ n, & \text{otherwise.} \end{cases}$$

Let $\mathbb{A}_r$ and $\mathbb{A}_n$ be a random and normal access sequence, respectively. As independently selecting the block locations from $\mathbb{O}$ and $\mathbb{N} \setminus \{\mathbb{O}, \mathbb{L}\}$ for each access, only choosing l from $\mathbb{L}$ can reveal the differentiate between $\mathbb{A}_r$ and $\mathbb{A}_n$. In $\mathbb{A}_r$, l locations from $\mathbb{L}$ are chosen with probability $\frac{l}{L}$. Therefore to emulate $\mathbb{A}_n$ as $\mathbb{A}_r$, if $pos(ID)$ is not in $\mathbb{O}$, it must be reaccessed after passing more than $\frac{L}{l}$ accesses. Furthermore, the period of accessing the addresses contained in $\mathbb{O}$ and $\mathbb{L}$ must be inconsistent so that $\mathbb{A}_n$ does not differ from $\mathbb{A}_r$.

Since the only difference between $\mathbb{A}_n$ and $\mathbb{A}_r$ is every access request of $\mathbb{A}_n$ must include a location of data interested by client, as long as $pos(ID)$ is accessed with probability $\frac{l}{L}$ or less, $\mathbb{A}_n$ and $\mathbb{A}_r$ are indistinguishable by the probability $\frac{1}{2} + \epsilon$. Besides the size of $\mathbb{L}$ can be secretly changed on the fly by the client, the statistical analysis is more complicated.

6   Performance Analysis

New M-ORA has the same performance of its previous design in term of asymptotic performance. The performance of ORAM can be analyzed in three aspects: bandwidth consumption used to conduct the oblivious access, storage usage on the client to store the necessary data for the operations, and the computation complexity (i.e. time complexity) is required for completing the operation.

6.1   Bandwidth Consumption

By the fact that the warm-up access increases the bandwidth used by the system; however, it is required only when the history list is empty. Since data transfer is the long-term operation, the bandwidth caused by warm-up access is very small and can be neglected when compared to the total bandwidth consumption. New M-ORAM requires constant bandwidth for access operation since the number of blocks to be downloaded and uploaded is unchanged from the original construction. Therefore, new M-ORAM requires $O(1)$ bandwidth cost for the operation.

6.2   Storage Space Requirement

Storage space requirement on M-ORAM system can be categorized into space requirement on the server (ORAM), and the client. Same as the original design, new M-ORAM does not require dummy information for oblivious access operation, since other uninterested real data are used instead. Hence, new M-ORAM can achieve 100 percents of storage used for containing the client's information. Regarding the client storage usage, same as its original design, the previous access list has a constant size while the position map has $N + W \cdot H$ tuples to contain the data address. The only difference is the history list which has been added aiming to improve the oblivious access ability. As the size of history list is independent of ORAM size and reserved as a fixed size buffer, the asymptotic cost of storage used by new M-ORAm is therefore equal to $O(N)$.

6.3   Computational Complexity

In term of computational complexity, we measure in the terms of time complexity of the operation. The major operations and their complexity to be performed the oblivious access are categorized as follows:

Pseudo Random Number Generator: We suppose that the PRNG which is used in our construction is efficient which has $O(1)$ complexity. Therefore, the operations based on this PRNG such as a secret key generator or random number generator also has cost $O(1)$ complexity.

Searching for Particular Information: Searching information from sorted elements and finite set of elements costs $O(1)$. Since position map is a fixed size buffer which stores the ordered data addresses, searching and updating the address by data *ID* is therefore cost $O(1)$.

Randomly Choosing Data to Be Accessed: Randomly choosing data to be accessed of new M-ORAM is performed under constant value o, l, and $H - o - l$. The o, l, and $H - o - l$ addresses are randomly chosen form $\mathbb{O}, \mathbb{L}$, and $\mathbb{N} \setminus \{\mathbb{O}, \mathbb{L}\}$, respectively. Since the complexity of random number generator is $O(1)$, with the naive solution, the cost to generate the unique k random numbers is $O(k^2)$[1]. As k is o, l, and $H - o - l$; also it is a constant for any size of ORAM; the cost to generate k can be implied to be $O(1)$. Therefore, the computational complexity of randomly choosing data of new M-ORAM construction is $O(1)$.

From the computational complexity of operations which have been mentioned, the overall computational complexity of new M-ORAM construction is therefore $O(1)$.

7   Experimental Analysis on Random-Relocation

One security evidence was not mentioned in the original M-ORAM manuscript is the behavior of data relocation when it has been retrieved by a client. Once the data of interest has been retrieved, the random location within ORAM will be assigned when it is written back to the ORAM. To protect the identity of data from the curious server, it must be safe from the statistical and computational analysis. An encryption algorithm is used to prevent the identity of data from the computational analysis, while random relocation is used in term of statistical test prevention. The random relocation is based on random read and write operation on stash. According to the details described in Sect. 3.2, the probability of writing the data to the same location which it has been read is $\frac{1}{H \cdot W}$. However, it is difficult to see how the location is changed from a server's perspective. This section shows the experiment conducted on reading and writing one particular data for 4 million accesses. The chi-square (χ^2) test is used for measuring a random relocation characteristic. Figure 4 illustrates the result, *p-value* of the experiment conducted on three different sizes of ORAM: 1200, 2400, and 3000 blocks, with $H = 4$. According to NIST, the significant level (α) greater than 0.01 means the sequence of samples are random. It shows that when the width of stash is greater than 7 blocks, changing the location of data seen by a server is random.

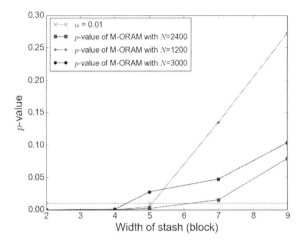

Fig. 4. *p-value* from χ^2 test over $H = 4$

8   Conclusion

New M-ORAM is an improved version of M-ORAM to remove the probability
that the server can benefit from doing a statistical analysis on the client's access
pattern. The new buffer, history list, is added to the client for this purpose. The
history list is a fixed size buffer which contains the list of addresses which have
been accessed by the client for the past L accesses. This results in same amortize
cost of storage space requirement on original M-ORAM. In addition, the cost of
computation and bandwidth still remain the same as the original construction.
This paper also shows the experimental results that the characteristic of data
relocation under new construction with proper H and W is seen as random by
the server.

Acknowledgement. This research project was partially supported by Faculty of
Information and Communication Technology, Mahidol University.

References

1. How can we generate k unique random integers in the range [1...n] with equal proba-
   blity?. https://www.quora.com/How-can-we-generate-k-unique-random-integers-
   in-the-range-1-n-with-equal-probablity. Accessed 30 May 2018
2. Boneh, D., Mazieres, D., Popa, R.A.: Remote oblivious storage: Making oblivious
   RAM practical. Technical report, MIT-CSAIL-TR-2011-018, Massachusetts Institute of Technology, March 2011. http://hdl.handle.net/1721.1/62006
3. Dautrich, J., Stefanov, E., Shi, E.: Burst ORAM: minimizing ORAM response
   times for bursty access patterns. In: Proceedings 23rd USENIX Security Symposium, San Diego, CA, pp. 749–764, August 2014
4. Goldreich, O., Ostrovsky, R.: Software protection and simulation on oblivious
   RAMs. J. ACM **43**(3), 431–473 (1996)

5. Gordon, S., Miyaji, A., Su, C., Sumongkayothin, K.: A matrix based ORAM: design, implementation and experimental analysis. IEICE Trans. Inf. Syst. **E99-D**(8), 2044–2055 (2016)

6. Islam, M.S., Kuzu, M., Kantarcioglu, M.: Access pattern disclosure on searchable encryption: ramification, attack and mitigation. In: Proceedings of 19th Annual Network and Distributed System Security Symposium, San Diego, CA, February 2012

7. Liu, C., Zhu, L., Wang, M., Tan, Y.: Search pattern leakage in searchable encryption: attacks and new construction. Inf. Sci.: Int. J. **265**, 176–188 (2014)

8. Moataz, T., Mayberry, T., Blass, E.-O., Chan, A.H.: Resizable tree-based oblivious RAM. In: Böhme, R., Okamoto, T. (eds.) FC 2015. LNCS, vol. 8975, pp. 147–167. Springer, Heidelberg (2015). https://doi.org/10.1007/978-3-662-47854-7_9

9. Pinkas, B., Reinman, T.: Oblivious RAM revisited. In: Rabin, T. (ed.) CRYPTO 2010. LNCS, vol. 6223, pp. 502–519. Springer, Heidelberg (2010). https://doi.org/10.1007/978-3-642-14623-7_27

10. Ren, L., Fletcher, C.W., Yu, X., Kwon, A., van Dijk, M., Devadas, S.: Unified oblivious-RAM: improving recursive ORAM with locality and pseudorandomness. Proceeding of IACR Cryptology ePrint Archive 2014/205 (2014)

11. Shi, E., Chan, T.H., Stefanov, E., Li, M.: Oblivious RAM with $O(log^3 N)$ worst-case cost. In: Proceedings of 17th International Conference on the Theory and Application of Cryptology and Information Security, Seol, South Korea, pp. 197–214, December 2011

12. Stefanov, E., et al.: Path ORAM: an extremely simple oblivious RAM protocol. In: Proceedings ACM SIGSAC Conference on Computer and Communications Security, Berlin, Germany, pp. 299–310, November 2013

13. Stefanov, E., Shi, E., Song, D.X.: Towards practical oblivious RAM. In: Proceedings of the 19th Annual Network Distributed System Security Symposium, The Internet Society, San Diego, CA, USA, February 2012

14. Zhang, J., Ma, Q., Zhang, W., Qiao, D.: KT-ORAM: a bandwidth-efficient ORAM built on K-ary tree of PIR nodes. Proceedings of IACR Cryptology ePrint Archive 2014/624 (2014)

Secure Computation of Inner Product of Vectors with Distributed Entries and Its Applications to SVM

Sabyasachi Dutta[1(✉)], Nishant Nikam[2], and Sushmita Ruj[2]

[1] R. C. Bose Centre for Cryptology and Security, Indian Statistical Institute,
Kolkata, India
saby.math@gmail.com
[2] Cryptology and Security Research Unit,
Computer and Communication Sciences Division, Indian Statistical Institute,
Kolkata, India
nikam_nishant@outlook.com, sush@isical.ac.in

Abstract. Nowadays organizations and individuals outsource computation and storage to cloud. This poses a threat to the privacy of users. Different users encrypt their private data with (possibly) different keys to prevent any kind of outside attack on their privacy. In this outsourced model of computation where the data owners have already encrypted and uploaded private data, to enable the users for collaborative data mining a scheme is needed that can process encrypted data under multiple keys. Privacy preserving inner product computation is an essential tool on which many data mining algorithms are based. Several papers address the problem of outsourced privacy preserving inner product computation but none of them deals with the scenario when the entire database is arbitrarily partitioned among the users. We propose two outsourced privacy preserving protocols for computation of inner product of vectors when the underlying database is arbitrarily partitioned. We provide an SVM training model that preserves the privacy of the user's data-vectors. Our scheme is based on an integer vector encryption scheme.

Keywords: Privacy preserving · Support vector machine
Inner product · Homomorphic encryption

1 Introduction

A *support vector machine* (SVM) [4] is one of the most commonly used classifiers that divides its input space into two regions, separated by a hyperplane. To build

---

S. Dutta—Grateful to the NICT, Japan for granting a financial support under the NICT International Exchange Program.
S. Ruj—This work is partially supported by Cisco University Research Program Fund, CyberGrants ID: 698039 and Silicon Valley Community Foundation.

C. Su and H. Kikuchi (Eds.): ISPEC 2018, LNCS 11125, pp. 533–543, 2018.
https://doi.org/10.1007/978-3-319-99807-7_34

an SVM, the basic building block is the computation of inner products (a.k.a dot products) of the data vectors (i.e. input vectors). These inner products of the available data vectors help to construct *kernel matrix*. Based on this kernel matrix, an optimization problem is solved to obtain the required hyperplane.

In certain areas e.g. medical records, data points contain sensitive information owned by different entities or organizations and thus can not be revealed. Two pioneering works [2,7] paved the path for reasearch in data mining without the disclosure of private data.

In the present day the outsourced model of computation is very relevant as organizations are finding it extremely difficult to store huge amount of personal data. More and more organizations are becoming motivated to outsource data to a cloud system. However, while enjoying the benefits of outsourced storage and management, organizations face the risk of private information disclosure. This motivates the problem of how the cloud executes data mining process on encrypted data if need be.

As mentioned earlier, the main building block for SVM is the computation of the inner products of the available data vectors. If the inner products can be computed in a privacy preserving manner then an SVM can be modeled securely based on that.

Some private inner product protocols were proposed in the literature of distributed computation model [5,6,14]. Vaidya et al. [15] and Yu et al. [18,19] provided privacy preserving inner product computation protocols and constructed SVM for horizontally and vertically partitioned data sets.

In the outsourced model of computation, Liu et al. [8] first proposed the construction using BGN cryptosystem [3]. Cloud computation supporting multiple secret keys were developed in [13,16]. However, they assumed the existence of non colluding servers and are applicable to construct linear mean classifier.

Recently, Zhang et al. [20] proposed outsourced secure inner product protocol and its application to SVM for horizontally and vertically partitioned data. They used an Integer Vector encryption scheme proposed by Zhou and Wornell [22]. Zheng et al.'s construction supports outsourced model of computation with multiple keys and does not require existence of two non colluding servers. However, they have given constructions of SVM for horizontally and vertically partitioned database.

A recent work [12] considered privacy preserving analytics on arbitrarily partitioned data. But, they have built their scheme on secure gradient descent method and left open the problem of privacy preserving SVM classifier.

1.1   Our Contribution

We propose a method for secure inner product computation of vectors whose entries are arbitrarily distributed between the parties. We propose a solution on the basis of Integer Vector Encryption. We first build a secure protocol based on Zhang et al.'s construction and later propose a modified algorithm for SVM training for arbitrarily partitioned database. The modification in the algorithm reduces the communication rounds between the parties and the cloud. There is only one round of key-agreement between the parties. Our protocol is very efficient and supports outsourced model of computation. We achieve sufficient security when there is only one server and our scheme is fully secure if the existence of non-colluding servers is assumed.

2   Preliminaries

To start with we recall some basic terminologies and building blocks and give a short overview of system model and the threat model.

System Model. We consider the outsourced model of computation where there are multiple users and one cloud. Different users encrypt their private data using different keys and then upload the encrypted data to the cloud. The cloud stores and manages the data. It runs data mining algorithms on the encrypted data when requested by the users and computes the encrypted classifier.

Threat Model. We assume that the cloud and the users are honest but curious. They will follow the protocol honestly but will try to infer sensitive information. We further assume that there is no collusion between the parties and the cloud. More detailed discussion can be found in Sect. 4.

Integer Vector Encryption. Our protocols rely on the integer vector (homomorphic) encryption scheme of Zhou and Wornell [22]. For the sake of completeness we give a brief description of the scheme and its useful properties. Integer vector encryption encrypts a vector as a whole with a single key, rather than encrypting every element of the vector one by one.

- **Encryption:** Let $x \in \mathbb{Z}_N^m$ be a plaintext vector, where N denotes the alphabet size, m denotes the vector-length. Let $S \in \mathbb{Z}^{m \times n}$ be the secret-key. Let t be a large integer and $e \in \mathbb{Z}^m$ be an *error* vector such that $||e||_\infty < \frac{t}{2}$. The ciphertext is a vector $\mathcal{E}(x) = c \in \mathbb{Z}^n$ which satisfies: $Sc = tx + e$.
- **Decryption:** With the help of secret key S, given a ciphertext vector c the decryption algorithm works as $\mathcal{D}(c) = \lceil \frac{Sc}{t} \rfloor$.

Most important properties of the cryptosystem are:

- **Key-switching:** From a ciphertext vector c under the private-key S it is possible to convert it to another ciphertext $c_1 \in \mathbb{Z}^{n'}$ under a *different* key $S_1 \in \mathbb{Z}^{m \times n'}$ such that $Sc = S_1 c_1$.
- **Addition:** Given two ciphertext vectors c_1 and c_2 corresponding to two plaintext vectors x_1 and x_2 under the same key S, the addition $c_1 + c_2$ corresponds to the plaintext vector $x_1 + x_2$. It is to be noted that if the two plaintext vectors are encrypted using two different keys S_1 and S_2 then using the *key-switching* technique the ciphertext vectors can be converted to ciphertexts under a common key S. Now they can be added.

$$S(c_1 + c_2) = t(x_1 + x_2) + (e_1 + e_2) \tag{1}$$

– **Inner Product:** Given a pair $(\boldsymbol{x}_1, \boldsymbol{c}_1)$ under key S_1 and another pair $(\boldsymbol{x}_2, \boldsymbol{c}_2)$ under S_2,

$$S_1 \boldsymbol{c}_1 = t\boldsymbol{x}_1 + \boldsymbol{e}_1; S_2 \boldsymbol{c}_2 = t\boldsymbol{x}_2 + \boldsymbol{e}_2 \tag{2}$$

the encrypted inner product of plaintext vectors can be obtained as $\mathcal{E}(\boldsymbol{x}_1^T.\boldsymbol{x}_2) = \lceil \frac{vec(\boldsymbol{c}_1 \boldsymbol{c}_2^T)}{t} \rfloor$. The secret key which decrypts this cipertext is $vec(S_1^T S_2)^T$.

3   Protocol for Secure Inner Product Computation on Outsourced Vectors

We consider the model where the encrypted data is stored in the Cloud by both the parties and the cloud is responsible for majority part of the storage and computation.

Suppose there are two m-dimensional vectors $\boldsymbol{x} = (x_1, x_2, \ldots, x_m)$ and $\boldsymbol{y} = (y_1, y_2, \ldots, y_m)$. Target is to find the scalar product $\boldsymbol{x}.\boldsymbol{y} = \sum\limits_{i=1}^{m} x_i y_i$ when the vectors are arbitrarily partitioned between the parties. Suppose party A owns the entries $(x_i)_{i \in I}$ and $(y_j)_{j \in J}$ where $I, J \subset [1, m]$. Party B owns the rest namely, $(x_i)_{i \in I'}$ and $(y_j)_{j \in J'}$ where I' and J' are complements of I and J respectively. We will denote a missing entry by $*$. More specifically, if the ith entry is missing then we will denote it by $*_i$. In this scenario, both the parties replace their missing entries $*$ by 0, encrypt these modified vectors and upload to the cloud. We denote these modified vectors by $\boldsymbol{x}_A^*, \boldsymbol{y}_A^*, \boldsymbol{x}_B^*, \boldsymbol{y}_B^*$.

Now we give a privacy preserving protocol for the secure dot product computation. We assume that the original data vectors consist of non-zero entries so that when a party downloads some data vectors from the cloud and decrypt it to see some zero entries, he can readily conclude that the corresponding entries were missing. This assumption although restrictive, is quite realistic. For example, in medical domain most test results have non zero values.

Party A randomly chooses a secret key $S_1 = [I||T_1]$, the concatenation of the identity matrix of size $m \times m$ and a "*thin*" (possibly a column) matrix T_1. A encrypts his vectors $\boldsymbol{x}_A^*$ and $\boldsymbol{y}_A^*$ with the help of the secret matrix S_1 to output ciphertext vectors $\boldsymbol{c}_{x,A}$ and $\boldsymbol{c}_{y,A}$ and uploads to the *cloud*. Similarly, B chooses a secret matrix $S_2 = [I||T_2]$, outputs ciphertext vectors $\boldsymbol{c}_{x,B}$ and $\boldsymbol{c}_{y,B}$ and uploads to the cloud.

Recall that the cloud needs to compute $\boldsymbol{x}_A^*.\boldsymbol{y}_A^* + \boldsymbol{x}_A^*.\boldsymbol{y}_B^* + \boldsymbol{y}_A^*.\boldsymbol{x}_B^* + \boldsymbol{x}_B^*.\boldsymbol{y}_B^*$ in order to get the inner product of $\boldsymbol{x}$ and $\boldsymbol{y}$. So there are inner product of vectors from the same user as well as inner product of vectors from different users. To compute the inner products of the plaintext vectors from the ciphertext vectors the cloud requires corresponding secret keys. For example, the encryption of $\boldsymbol{x}_A^*.\boldsymbol{y}_A^*$ is obtained from $\lceil \frac{vec(\boldsymbol{c}_{x,A} \, \boldsymbol{c}_{y,A}^T)}{t} \rfloor$ and the corresponding secret key is $vec(S_1^T S_1)^T$. Similarly, the other secret keys are $vec(S_1^T S_2)^T$ (for encrypted inner products of vectors from both users A and B) and $vec(S_2^T S_2)^T$ (for encrypted inner product of vectors from B).

In order to transform the encryption of $\boldsymbol{x}_A^* \cdot \boldsymbol{y}_A^*$ from $vec(S_1^T S_1)^T$ to secret key $[I||T_s]$ of the cloud, A computes the *key-switching* matrix M_1 as follows:

$$\left[\begin{array}{c} (vec(S_1^T S_1)^T)^* - T_s A_a + E_a \\ A_a \end{array} \right],$$

where A_a is a random matrix and E_a is a random noise matrix chosen by A.

Similarly, for computing the encrypted inner product $\boldsymbol{x}_B^* \cdot \boldsymbol{y}_B^*$, B computes the *key-switching* matrix M_2 as

$$\left[\begin{array}{c} (vec(S_2^T S_2)^T)^* - T_s A_b + E_b \\ A_b \end{array} \right],$$

where A_b is a random matrix and E_b is a random noise matrix chosen by B.

However, the secret key corresponding to the encrypted inner products of the vectors from the users A and B is given by $vec(S_1^T S_2)^T$ and hence it requires a joint computation. From the form of S_1 and S_2 it follows that:

$$S_1^T S_2 = \left[\begin{array}{cc} I & T_2 \\ T_1^T & T_1^T T_2 \end{array} \right] = \left[\begin{array}{cc} I & \mathbf{0} \\ T_1^T & \mathbf{0} \end{array} \right] + \left[\begin{array}{cc} \mathbf{0} & T_2 \\ \mathbf{0} & \mathbf{0} \end{array} \right] + \left[\begin{array}{cc} \mathbf{0} & \mathbf{0} \\ \mathbf{0} & T_1^T T_2 \end{array} \right].$$

A now generates a random invertible matrix P_1, computes $P_1 T_1^T$ and sends it to B. B then generates a random invertible matrix P_2 and sends $P_1 T_1^T T_2 P_2$ to S. A and B separately send P_1^{-1} and P_2^{-1} to S who then recovers $T_1^T T_2$. Therefore at this point of time A, B and S separately hold $\left[\begin{array}{cc} I & \mathbf{0} \\ T_1^T & \mathbf{0} \end{array} \right]$, $\left[\begin{array}{cc} \mathbf{0} & T_2 \\ \mathbf{0} & \mathbf{0} \end{array} \right]$ and $\left[\begin{array}{cc} \mathbf{0} & \mathbf{0} \\ \mathbf{0} & T_1^T T_2 \end{array} \right]$. They can now compute corresponding key-switching matrices M_A, M_B and M_S separately. Notice that the ultimate key-switching matrices will be the sum $M_A + M_B + M_S = M_{final}$, say. Once these three final key-switching matrices viz. M_1, M_2 and M_{final} are obtained, S can transform the encrypted inner product $\boldsymbol{x}_A^* \cdot \boldsymbol{y}_A^* + \boldsymbol{x}_A^* \cdot \boldsymbol{y}_B^* + \boldsymbol{y}_A^* \cdot \boldsymbol{x}_B^* + \boldsymbol{x}_B^* \cdot \boldsymbol{y}_B^*$ into an encryption with respect to his private key $[I||T_s]$. With the help of his secret key S can now construct the Kernel matrix and run the SVM algorithm.

We now describe an SVM training algorithm and classification protocol in the following Algorithms 1 and 2.

4 Security Analysis

We first describe our *adversarial* model.

Adversarial Model: We assume that A, B and the *cloud* all are semi-honest (also known as honest-but-curious). Each of them follows the protocols correctly but tries to gather or infer extra information than they are supposed to know. We also assume that none of the parties and the cloud collude with each other.

In order to carry out the security analysis, first we prove that the "key-switching" technique is secure. That is, the *cloud* cannot deduce the private

---

Algorithm 1. SVM Training

1: **procedure** KEY-AGREEMENT
2: A, B secretly agree on an internal private key $S_{int} = [I||T_{int}]$ completely hidden from the cloud.
3: **procedure** KEY-SWITCHING
4: A uploads key-switching matrix $M_1 = \begin{bmatrix} (vec(S_1^T S_1)^T)^* - T_s A_a + E_a \\ A_a \end{bmatrix}$.
5: B uploads key-switching matrix $M_2 = \begin{bmatrix} (vec(S_2^T S_2)^T)^* - T_s A_b + E_b \\ A_b \end{bmatrix}$.
6: $A, B, Cloud$ jointly compute $M_{final} = \begin{bmatrix} (vec(S_1^T S_2)^T)^* - T_s A_{ab} + E_{ab} \\ A_{ab} \end{bmatrix}$.
7: **procedure** COMPUTATION OF ENCRYPTED DOT PRODUCT BY THE CLOUD
8: Using M_1, the *cloud* transforms the encryption of $\boldsymbol{x}_A^* . \boldsymbol{y}_A^*$ to an encryption with underlying secret key $S_c = [I||T_s]$.
9: Using M_2, the *cloud* transforms the encryption of $\boldsymbol{x}_B^* . \boldsymbol{y}_B^*$ to an encryption with underlying secret key $S_c = [I||T_s]$.
10: Using M_{final}, the *cloud* transforms encryptions of $\boldsymbol{x}_A^* . \boldsymbol{y}_B^*$ and $\boldsymbol{x}_B^* . \boldsymbol{y}_A^*$ to encryptions with underlying secret key $S_c = [I||T_s]$.
11: Adding these the *cloud* gets the encryption of $\boldsymbol{x}.\boldsymbol{y}$ under the secret key S_c.
12: **procedure** COMPUTATION OF GRAM MATRIX BY THE CLOUD
13: Repeating steps $6 - 9$ the *cloud* can compute the encrypted Gram matrix $\mathcal{E}_{S_c}(K)$ which can be decrypted by using S_c.
14: Using K, the *cloud* can now run the SVM algorithm to obtain α_is which are greater than zero. Suppose, without loss of generality, first k coefficients $\alpha_1, \ldots, \alpha_k > 0$.
15: **procedure** COMPUTATION OF ENCRYPTED WEIGHT-VECTOR BY THE CLOUD
16: Cloud computes $y_1\alpha_1 \boldsymbol{c}_{1,A}^* + \cdots + y_k\alpha_k \boldsymbol{c}_{k,A}^* = \mathcal{E}_{S_1}(\boldsymbol{w}_A)$.
17: Cloud computes $y_1\alpha_1 \boldsymbol{c}_{1,B}^* + \cdots + y_k\alpha_k \boldsymbol{c}_{k,B}^* = \mathcal{E}_{S_2}(\boldsymbol{w}_B)$.
18: A and B generate key-switching matrices separately to transform the secret keys of $\mathcal{E}_{S_1}(\boldsymbol{w}_A)$ and $\mathcal{E}_{S_2}(\boldsymbol{w}_B)$ to S_{int}. Uploading the key-switching matrices to the *cloud* will enable it to find $\mathcal{E}_{S_{int}}(\boldsymbol{w}) = \mathcal{E}_{S_{int}}(\boldsymbol{w}_A) + \mathcal{E}_{S_{int}}(\boldsymbol{w}_B)$, where S_{int} is completely hidden from the *cloud*.
19: **procedure** COMPUTATION OF THE BIAS ITEM b
20: Cloud takes an $\alpha_i > 0$ and selects the corresponding $\boldsymbol{c}_{i,A}^*$ and $\boldsymbol{c}_{i,B}^*$.
21: Cloud computes the dot products $\mathcal{E}_{S_{int}}(\boldsymbol{w})^T \boldsymbol{c}_{i,A}^*$ and $\mathcal{E}_{S_{int}}(\boldsymbol{w})^T \boldsymbol{c}_{i,B}^*$ and sends them to A and B respectively.
22: A uses $vec(S_1^T S_{int})^T$ and B uses $vec(S_2^T S_{int})^T$ for decryption to find $\boldsymbol{w}^T \boldsymbol{x}_{i,A}^*$ and $\boldsymbol{w}^T \boldsymbol{x}_{i,B}^*$ respectively.
23: Using the symmetric key encryption A and B send each other these scalars and they individually compute $b = \boldsymbol{w}^T \boldsymbol{x}_{i,A}^* + \boldsymbol{w}^T \boldsymbol{x}_{i,B}^* - y_i$

---

keys of the parties from the key-switching matrices. To prove the result we need the following hardness assumption of *learning with errors* (LWE) problem.

Learning with Errors Problem: Given arbitrary many samples $(\boldsymbol{a}_i, b_i) \in \mathbb{Z}_q^m \times \mathbb{Z}_q$, it is infeasible to recover (with non-negligible probability) $\boldsymbol{v} \in \mathbb{Z}_q^m$ from $b_i = \boldsymbol{v}.\boldsymbol{a}_i + \epsilon_i$, where ϵ_i denotes random noise chosen suitably from a distribution over $\mathbb{Z}_q$.

Algorithm 2. SVM Classification

1: **procedure** PRIVATE-INPUTS
2: A, B possess secret-key $S_{int} = [I||T_{int}]$, bias b and z_A, z_B which are arbitrary partitions of a vector z.
3: Cloud possesses $\mathcal{E}_{S_{int}}(w)$.

4: **procedure** PRE-PROCESSING THE DATA VECTOR
5: A fills the missing entries in z_A by 0 to prepare z_A^*.
6: B fills the missing entries in z_B by 0 to prepare z_B^*.
7: A and B separately compute $\mathcal{E}_{S_{int}}(z_A^*)$ and $\mathcal{E}_{S_{int}}(z_B^*)$ and send them to the *cloud*.

8: **procedure** COMPUTATION OF ENCRYPTED DOT PRODUCT BY THE CLOUD
9: Cloud first adds $\mathcal{E}_{S_{int}}(z_A^*)$ and $\mathcal{E}_{S_{int}}(z_A^*)$ to get $\mathcal{E}_{S_{int}}(z)$.
10: Cloud finds the encrypted dot product of $\mathcal{E}_{S_{int}}(w)$ with $\mathcal{E}_{S_{int}}(z)$ and sends to both A and B.

11: **procedure** CLASSIFICATION
12: A and B decrypt the encrypted dot product $\mathcal{E}_{S_{int}}(w^T z)$ and compare the value with b to output the class label.

Theorem 1. *Let S denote the private-key (matrix), S^* its intermediate representation, M the key-switching matrix from S to S'. Thus, $S'M = S^* + E$ where E is a random noise matrix.*

It is infeasible for the cloud to recover, with non-negligible probability, S^* although it has access to both S' and M.

Proof. Choose a prime modulus $q >> max.\{||S||_\infty, ||M||_\infty, ||S'||_\infty, ||E||_\infty\}$ so that every element in $\mathbb{Z}$ for the protocol can be treated as elements in $\mathbb{Z}_q$. When the cloud knows S' and M, it can compute the ith row of $S'M$. Let b_i denote the ith row vector of $S'M$. Then $b_i = v + \epsilon_i$, where v, ϵ_i respectively denote the ith rows of S^*, E. Hence, the cloud has a set of approximate linear equations $b_{ij} = v_j + \epsilon_{ij}$ modulo the prime modulus q. It is now not very hard to see that if the cloud can solve this set of approximate linear equations then it essentially solves the LWE problem. ☐

The security of the protocols can be proved using real world/ideal world based paradigm. Due to space constraint we only state them without proof.

Theorem 2. *Computation and uploading the key-switching matrices in Algorithm 1 (lines 4,5,6 & 18) do not reveal any private information of parties A and B.*

Theorem 3. *With the assumption that the integer vector encryption is semantically secure, it is infeasible for the cloud to infer about the original data vectors of the parties with non-negligible probability during the SVM training phase given in Algorithm 1.*

Theorem 4. *The SVM classification phase given in Algorithm 2 is secure in the sense that the cloud cannot deduce the class label of the testing sample, given the semantic security of the integer vector encryption.*

4.1   Modified Protocol

In order to reduce the communication rounds of the parties we now give a protocol for SVM training. We note that with this modification the cloud has no partial information about the secret keys of the parties (in Algorithm 1 the cloud knows the product $T_1^T T_2$ with no randomization). Moreover, there is only one round of communication between the parties during the training period. The computational cost is also reduced for the parties as they do not have to jointly collaborate to compute the key-switching matrix. The *classification* protocol remains the same as *Algorithm 2*.

Algorithm 3. Modified Protocol for SVM Training

1: **procedure** KEY-AGREEMENT
2: A, B secretly agree on an internal private key $S_{int} = [I||T_{int}]$ completely hidden from the cloud.
3: **procedure** KEY-SWITCHING
4: A uploads key-switching matrix $M_{S_1 \rightarrow S_{int}} = \begin{bmatrix} (vec(S_1)^T)^* - T_{int} A_a + E_a \\ A_a \end{bmatrix}$.
5: B uploads key-switching matrix $M_{S_2 \rightarrow S_{int}} = \begin{bmatrix} (vec(S_2)^T)^* - T_{int} A_b + E_b \\ A_b \end{bmatrix}$.
6: A or B uploads $M_{S_{int}^T S_{int} \rightarrow S_c} = \begin{bmatrix} (vec(S_{int}^T S_{int})^* - T_s A_{ab} + E_{ab} \\ A_{ab} \end{bmatrix}$.
7: **procedure** COMPUTATION OF ENCRYPTED DOT PRODUCT BY THE CLOUD
8: Using $M_{S_1 \rightarrow S_{int}}$, the *cloud* transforms the encryption of $\boldsymbol{x}_A^*$ and $\boldsymbol{y}_A^*$ to encryptions with underlying secret key $S_{int} = [I||T_{int}]$.
9: Using $M_{S_2 \rightarrow S_{int}}$, the *cloud* transforms the encryption of $\boldsymbol{x}_B^*$ and $\boldsymbol{y}_B^*$ to an encryption with underlying secret key $S_{int} = [I||T_{int}]$.
10: Cloud adds $\mathcal{E}_{S_{int}}(\boldsymbol{x}_A^*) + \mathcal{E}_{S_{int}}(\boldsymbol{x}_B^*)$ to output $\mathcal{E}_{S_{int}}(\boldsymbol{x})$.
11: Cloud adds $\mathcal{E}_{S_{int}}(\boldsymbol{y}_A^*) + \mathcal{E}_{S_{int}}(\boldsymbol{y}_B^*)$ to output $\mathcal{E}_{S_{int}}(\boldsymbol{y})$.
12: *Cloud* gets the encryption of the dot product $\mathcal{E}(\boldsymbol{x}^T \boldsymbol{y})$ with underlying secret key $S_{int}^T S_{int}$ of which the cloud is completely unaware.
13: Using the uploaded matrix $M_{S_{int}^T S_{int} \rightarrow S_c}$, *cloud* then transforms $\mathcal{E}(\boldsymbol{x}^T \boldsymbol{y})$ into $\mathcal{E}_{S_c}(\boldsymbol{x}^T \boldsymbol{y})$ and then decrypt to find $\boldsymbol{x}.\boldsymbol{y}$.
14: **procedure** COMPUTATION OF GRAM MATRIX BY THE CLOUD
15: Same as Algorithm 1.
16: **procedure** COMPUTATION OF ENCRYPTED WEIGHT-VECTOR BY THE CLOUD
17: Same as Algorithm 1.
18: **procedure** COMPUTATION OF THE BIAS ITEM b
19: Same as Algorithm 1.

Discussions on the Security of the Modified Protocol. The main difference between the modified protocol and the original protocol is in the key-switching procedure. Parties A and B upload the key-switching matrices to convert their ciphertexts (under their personal keys) to ciphertexts under a common agreed key S_{int}. Once the *cloud* makes these transformations, it then performs addition on the ciphertexts and dot products which can be proved to be secure.

Theorem 5. *Under the assumption that the integer vector encryption is semantically secure, it is infeasible for the cloud to infer about the original data vectors of the parties with non-negligible probability during the SVM training phase given in Algorithm 3.*

5   Experimental Results and Comparison

We use Number Theory Library (NTL) [1] for our implementation. The configuration of our PC is Ubuntu 16.04 64 bit operating system with Intel Core(TM) $i5$ $CPU(2\ cores)$, 3.60 GHz and 8 GB memory. Party A and Party B are two parties who own training samples such that if A owns some entries of a sample, then other entries are owned by B. In Fig. 1a, we show running time for encryption, key-switching matrix generation, dot product computation and decryption using Algorithm 1. In Fig. 1b, we show the running times of the same operations when we use Algorithm 3. We take 100 many samples of data vectors with dimensions varying from 10 to 50.

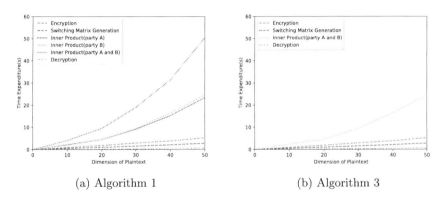

(a) Algorithm 1   (b) Algorithm 3

Fig. 1. Performance of our scheme

Encryption and decryption for both the parties are very efficient as can be seen from Fig. 1. Using Algorithm 1, for n samples, number of products to be computed by the cloud will be $2n^2$. However, in Algorithm 3, the cloud needs to compute $\frac{n(n+1)}{2}$ many products.

The works [8,10] give asymptotic analysis of complexity and no concrete results. We compare our scheme with [9] and [20]. We encrypt 3.6×10^5 samples of dimension 10. The time required for encryption is 158 s, whereas [20] needs 69 s and [9] needs 360 s. Experimental Platform for [9] (8x Intel Xeon CPU, 3.6 GHz) and [20] (Intel Core(TM) i7 CPU(2 cores), 2.2 GHz) is better than us. So, integer vector encryption performs better than FHE, which is consistent with the test results of [21].

The communication overhead is mainly due to transmission of key-switching matrices. The overhead depends on dimension of sample (m) and dimension of the secret key (T). In Fig. 2a, we fix $T = 10$ and vary m of samples from 50 to 400. The size of key-switching matrix M changes from MB to $\approx$1 GB. We observe that, if T is fixed, overhead is $O(m^2)$ which is consistent with [20]. In Fig. 2b, we fix the dimension of m at 100 and vary the dimension of T from 10 to 50. We observe that the size of M varies from 50 MB to $\approx$ 500 MB.

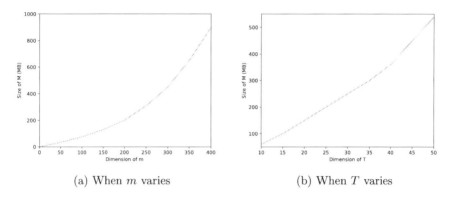

(a) When m varies   (b) When T varies

Fig. 2. Communication overhead

6   Conclusion

We have discussed two outsourced privacy preserving protocols for inner product of vectors when their entries are distributed among parties. It finds natural application in private SVM when the underlying database is arbitrarily partitioned. Allowing some minimal leakage about the inner products our scheme provides an efficient algorithm for SVM training. Fully secure computation is possible with our methodology if existence of two non-colluding servers is assumed. Our protocol for SVM classification is fully secure. Estimating the trade off between efficiency and privacy can be an interesting problem for further study.

References

1. NTL: A Library for doing Number Theory. http://www.shoup.net/ntl/
2. Agrawal, R., Srikant, R.: Privacy-preserving data mining. In: ACM SIGMOD Conference on Management of Data 2000, pp. 439–450 (2000)
3. Boneh, D., Goh, E.-J., Nissim, K.: Evaluating 2-DNF Formulas on ciphertexts. In: Kilian, J. (ed.) TCC 2005. LNCS, vol. 3378, pp. 325–341. Springer, Heidelberg (2005). https://doi.org/10.1007/978-3-540-30576-7_18

4. Cortes, C., Vapnik, V.: Support-vector networks. Mach. Learn. **20**(3), 273–297 (1995)
5. Du, W., Atallah, M.J.: Privacy-preserving cooperative statistical analysis. In: ACSAC 2001, pp. 102–110 (2001)
6. Goethals, B., Laur, S., Lipmaa, H., Mielikäinen, T.: On private scalar product computation for privacy-preserving data mining. In: Park, C., Chee, S. (eds.) ICISC 2004. LNCS, vol. 3506, pp. 104–120. Springer, Heidelberg (2005). https://doi.org/10.1007/11496618_9
7. Lindell, Y., Pinkas, B.: Privacy preserving data mining. J. Cryptol. **15**(3), 177–206 (2002)
8. Liu, F., Ng, W.K., Zhang, W.: Encrypted scalar product protocol for outsourced data mining. In: IEEE CLOUD 2014, pp. 336–343 (2014)
9. Liu, F., Ng, W.K., Zhang, W.: Encrypted SVM for outsourced data mining. IEEE CLOUD 2015, pp. 1085–1092 (2015)
10. Liu, F., Ng, W.K., Zhang, W.: Secure scalar product for big-data in MapReduce. In: IEEE Big Data Service 2015, pp. 120–129 (2015)
11. Lopez-Alt, A., Tromer, E., Vaikuntanathan, V.: On-the-fly multiparty computation on the cloud via multikey fully homomorphic encryption. In: STOC 2012, pp. 1219–1234 (2012)
12. Mehnaz, S., Bertino, E.: Privacy-preserving multi-party analytics over arbitrarily partitioned data. In: CLOUD 2017, pp. 342–349 (2017)
13. Peter, A., Tews, E., Katzenbeisser, S.: Efficiently outsourcing multiparty computation under multiple keys. IEEE Trans. Inf. Forensics Secur. **8**(12), 2046–2058 (2013)
14. Vaidya, J., Clifton, C.: Privacy preserving association rule mining in vertically partitioned data. In: KDD 2002, pp. 639–644 (2002)
15. Vaidya, J., Yu, H., Jiang, X.: Privacy-preserving SVM classification. Knowl. Inf. Syst. **14**(2), 161–178 (2008)
16. Wang, B., Li, M., Chow, S.S., Li, H.: Computing encrypted cloud data efficiently under multiple keys. In: IEEE CNS 2013, pp. 504–513 (2013)
17. Wang, B., Li, M., Chow, S.S., Li, H.: A tale of two clouds: computing on data encrypted under multiple keys. In: IEEE CNS 2014, pp. 337–345 (2014)
18. Yu, H., Vaidya, J., Jiang, X.: Privacy-preserving SVM classification on vertically partitioned data. In: Ng, W.-K., Kitsuregawa, M., Li, J., Chang, K. (eds.) PAKDD 2006. LNCS (LNAI), vol. 3918, pp. 647–656. Springer, Heidelberg (2006). https://doi.org/10.1007/11731139_74
19. Yu, H., Jiang, X., Vaidya, J.: Privacy-preserving SVM using nonlinear kernels on horizontally partitioned data. In: SAC 2006, pp. 603–610 (2006)
20. Zhang, J., Wang, X., Yiu, S.M., Jiang, Z.L., Li, J.: Secure dot product of outsourced encrypted vectors and its application to SVM. In: SCC@AsiaCCS 2017, pp. 75–82 (2017)
21. Yu, A., Lai, W.L., Payor, J.: Efficient integer vector homomorphic encryption (2015). https://courses.csail.mit.edu/6.857/2015/files/yu-lai-payor.pdf
22. Zhou, H., Wornell, G.W.: Efficient homomorphic encryption on integer vectors and its applications. In: ITA 2014, pp. 1–9 (2014)

(k, l)-Clustering for Transactional Data Streams Anonymization

Jimmy Tekli[1,3]([⊠]), Bechara Al Bouna[2]([⊠]), Youssef Bou Issa[2]([⊠]),
Marc Kamradt[1], and Ramzi Haraty[4]

[1] BMW Group, Munich, Germany
jimmy.tekli@bmw.de
[2] TICKET Lab., Antonine University, Baabda, Lebanon
{bechara.albouna,youssef.bouissa}@ua.edu.lb
[3] Université de Franche Comté, Belfort, France
[4] Department of Computer Science and Mathematics,
Lebanese American Univesity, Beirut, Lebanon

Abstract. In this paper, we address the correlation problem in the anonymization of transactional data streams. We propose a bucketization-based technique, entitled *(k, l)*-clustering to prevent such privacy breaches by ensuring that the same k individuals remain grouped together over the entire anonymized stream. We evaluate our algorithm in terms of utility by considering two different *(k, l)*-clustering approaches.

Keywords: Data privacy · Data stream · Correlation · Anonymization

1 Introduction

We live in an era where the world is more connected than ever before, and everything is digitized from smartphones, smart vehicles to smart homes and smart cities, continually generating a tremendous amount of information. With this information at hand, many concerns may arise, one in particular, is the critical exposure of individuals' privacy, putting their anonymity at risk [1,2]. Several anonymization techniques are developed in the literature to preserve privacy. Whether they are *generalization-based* techniques [3–5] that alter the original values or *bucketization-based* techniques [6–10] that preserve privacy by splitting the dataset into sensitive and non-sensitive tables to hide the link between their values, they all assume that there is a trade-off between good privacy and utility. It is a trade-off that is highly required to keep the dataset suitable for analysis while preserving the individuals' anonymity. However, it keeps anonymization vulnerable and unable to cope with all sort of attacks [11–14]. It is indeed difficult to provide a completely anonymous dataset without losing utility. There are many reasons for this to happen, notably, is the ability to presume knowledge of the adversary's prior belief and her/his ability to gain

C. Su and H. Kikuchi (Eds.): ISPEC 2018, LNCS 11125, pp. 544–556, 2018.
https://doi.org/10.1007/978-3-319-99807-7_35

insights after looking at the anonymized dataset. Besides, a dataset in which several tuples relate to the same individual may expose significant correlations between identifying and sensitive values. An adversary can use his/her knowledge of such correlations [11,13], or use these correlations as foreground knowledge [15] to breach individuals' privacy. To cope with this particular problem, safe grouping is proposed in [16,17] to ensure that the individuals' tuples are grouped in one and only one quasi-identifying group (QI-group) that is at the same time *l*-diverse, respects a minimum diversity for identifying attribute values, and all individuals in the same QI-group have an equal number of tuples. The *(k,l)*-diversity [18] is another technique that uses generalization to associate *k* distinct individuals to *l*-diverse QI-groups. While these techniques are useful in dealing with the correlation problem on bulk datasets, they provide no proof of effectiveness in anonymizing data streams where data must be protected on the fly before being stored in an anonymized dataset. The anonymization technique has a partial view of the dataset, limited to the batch of tuples undergoing the anonymization.

Let us consider a car rental example scenario where each smart vehicle triggers an event between two piers in the form of a transaction to be stored in a dataset for analysis. Transactions are generated continuously as long as customers are driving their vehicles to form a data stream. In this scenario, we assume that the anonymization must be performed on the stream of tuples generated by the data source to output an anonymized dataset in the form shown in Fig. 1.

User ID	VIN Number	TS	Location
Allen_U1	abfb32fd10ad2*	1	10,31;17,32
Betty_U2	00983503e35d*	2	30,29;24,12
Cathy_U3	0f550377353d*	3	23,45;11,23
Allen_U1	abfb32fd10ad2*	4	10 32;15,32
David_U4	936e2c77b9du*	5	22,25;11,33
Allen_U1	abfb32fd10ad2*	6	13.32;15,32
Betty_U2	00983503e35d*	7	42,45;11,23
Cathy_U3	0f550377353d*	8	23,45;11,24
Carol_U5	1qwfq2fd10ad2*	9	40,42;14,31
Cathy_U3	0f550377353d*	10	30,30;24,12
...	...	...	...

User ID	VIN Number	GID		GID	Location	TS
Allen_U1	abfb32fd10ad2*	1		1	10.31;17,32	1
Betty_U2	00983503e35d*	1		1	30.29;24,12	2
Cathy_U3	0f550377353d*	2		2	23,45;11,23	3
Allen_U1	abfb32fd10ad2*	2		2	10.32;15,32	4
David_U4	936e2c77b9du*	3		3	22,25;11,33	5
Allen_U1	abfb32fd10ad2*	3		3	13.32;15,32	6
Betty_U2	00983503e35d*	4		4	42,45;11,23	7
Cathy_U3	0f550377353d*	4		4	23,45;11,24	8
Carol_U5	1qwfq2fd10a*	5		5	40,42;14,31	9
Cathy_U3	0f550377353d*	5		5	30,30;24,12	10
...	...	...		...	...	...

(a) Incoming Stream S   (b) Anonymized Stream S*

Fig. 1. Rental data stream anonymized

The released 2-diverse dataset is divided into two separate tables to hide the link between the identifying and sensitive values as in [6,7,19]. In a QI-group an identifying value cannot be associated with a sensitive value with a probability higher than 1/2. The problem arises when the identifying and sensitive values correlate across the QI-groups [16,18,20] (e.g., first two QI-groups in Fig. 1(b)). This leads to an implication that the values belong to the same individual.

In this paper, we extend the work in [16,17] to address the correlation problem in the anonymization of transactional data streams where data dynamically changes and its distribution is imbalanced. We propose (k, l)-clustering that continuously groups k distinct individuals into l-diverse QI-groups and ensures that these individuals remain grouped together in future releases of QI-groups. (k, l)-clustering keeps track of incoming identifying values to safely release them across the QI-groups. It is a bucketization technique that prevents attribute disclosure, releasing trustful information. Our contributions in this paper include:

- defining privacy properties that are required to bind the correlations in a data stream.
- proposing a novel clustering approach to enforce the aforementioned privacy properties.

The remainder of this paper is organized as follows. In Sect. 2, we investigate works related to the anonymization of data streams. In Sect. 3, we define the basic concepts and definitions. We present our privacy model in Sect. 4 and describe the (k, l)-clustering approaches. Section 5 evaluates the performance of our algorithm by adopting two clustering techniques to data streams.

2   Related Work

In [21], Cao et al. extend the definition of k-anonymity to apply it on data streams and propose CASTLE, a clustering-based algorithm, that publishes k-anonymized clusters in an acceptable delay. An extension of CASTLE is presented in [22] to reduce the number of tuples in the clusters and to maximize the utility of the anonymized dataset. In another work [23], FAANST is proposed to anonymize numerical data streams. FADS is an anonymization algorithm proposed in [24,25] that has convenient time and space scale with additional constraints on the size of the clusters size and their reuse strategy. While these techniques extend privacy solutions based on k-anonmyity and l-diversity on transactional data streams, they do not take into account the correlation of the identifying and sensitive values across the QI-groups. Moreover, several studies [11,13,18,20] have shown that correlations attacks can be launched not only on bucketization techniques but on generalization-based techniques as well.

A similar work to ours is defined in [26] where the authors include background knowledge in their anonymization algorithm to deal with strong adversaries. They propose a hierarchical agglomerative algorithm to prevent attribute and identity disclosure. However, the authors only address correlations known to the adversary. Here, we consider that the correlations can be mined from the dataset and used as foreground knowledge to link individuals to their sensitive values. Alternatively, in [20], the authors present a sequential bottom-up anonymization algorithm, KSAA, that uses generalization to protect against background knowledge attacks on different anonymized views of the same original dataset. KSAA clusters tuples and generates QI-groups satisfying the privacy model in the current view. It checks, in a second step, if the privacy constraint is satisfied when several views are joined together. Here, our clustering algorithm is applied on a stream of tuples on the fly where three requirements must be met including low retention of tuples, balanced memory usage and runtime. In [27], the authors propose a generalization-based microaggregation algorithm for stream *k*-anonymity that meets a maximum delay constraint, without preserving the order of incoming tuples in the published stream such as in [21]. Then, they improve the preservation of the original order of the tuples by using steered microaggregation while adding the timestamp as an artificial attribute. Similar to [21], we do not publish the time stamp attribute due to privacy constraints however we use it for experimental purposes.

On the other side, several notable works [29–31] have been done for differential privacy [32] for streaming data. In this work, we choose to work with bucketization technique that publishes trustworthy information. We particularly extend previous works [16,17] to address correlations in the data stream in data sharing scenarios.

3   Preliminary Definitions

In this section, we present the basic concepts and definitions to be used in the remainder of this paper.

Definition 1 (Tuple - t). *In a relational dataset, a tuple t is a finite ordered list of values $\{v_1, v_2, ..., v_b\}$ where, given a set of attributes $\{A_1, ..., A_b\}$, $\forall i (1 \leq i \leq b) \, v_i = t[A_i]$ refers to the value of attribute A_i in t. We categorize attributes as follows:*

- *Identifier (A^{id}) is an attribute whose value is linked to an individual in a given dataset. For example, a social security number anonymized in a way to represent uniquely an individual but cannot explicitly identify her/him.*
- *Sensitive attribute (A^s) reveals critical and sensitive information about a certain individual and must not be directly linked to individuals' identifying values in data sharing, publishing or releasing scenarios.*
- *Time-stamp (A^{ts}) indicates the arrival time of the tuple, its position in the stream. The time-stamp is considered identifying, which can be used to expose individuals' privacy in a transactional data stream. Here, we do not publish the time-stamp, we use it instead for evaluating the utility of our anonymization technique.*

Definition 2 (Data Stream - S). *A data stream $S = t_1, t_2...$, is a continuously growing dataset composed of infinite series of tuples received at each instance. Let U be the set of individuals of a specific population, $\forall \, u \in U$ we denote by S_u the set of tuples in S related to the individual u, where $\forall \, t \in S_u, t[A^{id}] = v_{id}$.*

Definition 3 (Cluster - C). *Let $S' \subset S$ be a set of tuples in S. A cluster C over S' is defined as a set of tuples $\{t_1, ..., t_n\}$ and a centroid V_{id} consisting of a set of identifying values such that, $\forall t \in C, t[A^{id}] \in V_{id}$. We use the notation $V_{id}(C)$ to denote the centroid V_{id} of C.*

Table 1. Notations

S	Incoming stream
t_p	Tuple in S arriving at instance p
u	Individual described in S
S_u	Set of tuples related to individual u
A	Attribute of S
A^{id}	Identifying attribute of S
A^{sv}	Sensitive attribute of S
A^{ts}	Time-stamp attribute of S
v_{id}	Identifying value of a tuple in S
v_s	Sensitive value of a tuple in S
QI	Quasi-identifier group
$|U|$	Number of distinct individuals in S
$|S|$	Total number of tuples in S
C	Cluster over S
$V_{id}(C)$	Centroid of a cluster C
S^*	Anonymized version of S

Definition 4 (Equivalence class/QI-group) [1]. *A quasi-identifier group (QI-group) is defined as a subset $QI_j, j = 1, 2, \ldots$ of released tuples in $S^* = \bigcup_{j=1}^{\infty} QI_j$ such that, for any $j_1 \neq j_2$, $QI_{j1} \cap QI_{j2} = \emptyset$.*

We stick with the QI-group terminology for compatibility with the broader anonymization literature, which can include identifying as well as quasi-identifying attributes (Table 1).

4   Privacy Preservation

We work under the assumption that the anonymization of the data stream will continuously release l-diverse QI-groups, and these QI-groups, if joined together, will not expose unsafe correlations between identifying and sensitive values. We define two types of adversaries, passive and active.

Passive adversary has no prior knowledge concerning the individuals and the correlations of their identifying and sensitive values in the dataset. She/He is able, however, to extract foreground knowledge from the anonymized dataset that can be used to breach privacy. For example knowing renting patterns of individuals, which might lead to link their identifying values to their identity and track them in the anonymized dataset.

Active adversary is equipped with certain knowledge about the individuals and the correlations of their identifying and sensitive values in the dataset before having access to its anonymized version. She/he can use that background knowledge to provoke a privacy breach. In our renting example, knowing the true identity, in plain text, of an individual (e.g. Full Name) alongside her/his location patterns might lead to link her/his identity to her/his identifying value in the stream thus exposing him in the anonymized dataset.

4.1 Privacy Model

Given a stream S and two user-defined constants $l \geq 2$ and $k \geq 2$, we say that an anonymization technique safely anonymizes S if it produces a stream S^* that satisfies the following properties:

Property 1 (Safe release of QI-groups). *Provides safe correlation of identifying and sensitive values across the released QI-groups such that the intersection of any QI-groups in S^* on their identifying attribute A^{id} yields either k identifying values or none. Formally,*

$\forall v_{id} \in \mathcal{D}(A^{id})$, *if* $v_{id} \in \pi_{A^{id}}QI_1 \cap \ldots \cap \pi_{A^{id}}QI_j$, *then there exists a set of identifying values* $V_{id} \subseteq \mathcal{D}(A^{id})$, *such that* $V_{id} = \{v_{id}, v_{id_1}, \ldots, v_{id_{k-1}}\}$ *and* $V_{id} = \pi_{A^{id}}QI_1 \cap \ldots \cap \pi_{A^{id}}QI_j$. *In other words,*

$$\pi_{A^{id}}QI_1 \cap \ldots \cap \pi_{A^{id}}QI_j = \begin{cases} V_{id} & if \ \exists v_{id} \in \pi_{A^{id}}QI_1 \\ & \cap \ldots \cap \pi_{A^{id}}QI_j \\ \emptyset & otherwise \end{cases} \quad (1)$$

In a less formal definition, the identifying values that are grouped together in a QI-group must always remain grouped together throughout the entire anonymized stream.

Property 2 (*l*-diverse QI-groups). *Ensures that all the anonymized and released QI-groups are l-diverse. Formally,*
$\forall v_{id} \in \mathcal{D}(A^{id}), \forall QI \in S^*, Pr(v_{id}, v_s | QI) \leq 1/l.$

Property 3 (Safe correlation of identifying values). *Prohibits linking correlated identifying values in the same QI-group to their corresponding sensitive values, which result in an inherent violation of l-diversity [16–18]. Formally,*

$\forall v_{id_1}, v_{id_2}, f(v_{id_1}, QI_j) = f(v_{id_2}, QI_j)$ *where* $f(v_{id_i}, QI_j)$ *is a function that returns the number of occurrences of* v_{id_i} *in* QI_j.

Property 3 hides frequent correlations of identifying values in the same QI-groups. It handles cases arising when an adversary may be able to link an individual to his/her sensitive value or to narrow the possibilities for other individuals.

4.2 (*k, l*)-Clustering for Privacy Preservation

To preserve our privacy properties, we propose a (k, l)-clustering technique that groups tuples into clusters of disjoint centroids and releases, from these clusters, *l*-diverse QI-groups containing k distinct identifying values. In brief, our clustering technique works as follows:

- It creates centroids containing k distinct identifying values: $\forall QI_i, QI_j$ two QI-groups released from C, $\pi_{A^{id}} QI_i = \pi_{A^{id}} QI_j = V_{id}(C)$ where $|V_{id}(C)| = k$.
- It ensures that an identifying value exists in one and only centroid: $\forall C_1, C_2$ $V_{id}(C_1) \cap V_{id}(C_2) = \emptyset$.
- It releases a QI-group from a cluster C such that: $\forall QI$, a QI-group created from a subset of tuples in the cluster C, and $\forall t \in QI$, $t[A^{id}] \in V_{id}(C)$.

(k, l)-clustering is a bucketization technique that releases l-diverse QI-groups created from a subset of clusters having disjoint centroids. It ensures safe correlation of identifying and sensitive values across the QI-groups, i.e., once k identifying values are grouped in a QI-group, they will remain grouped together in future releases of QI-groups throughout the anonymized stream. We assume that the clustering can be done in two ways, *unsupervised* and *supervised* as defined below.

Unsupervised (k, l)-clustering has no prior knowledge about the distribution of identifying values in the original dataset. The clustering is done on first-come, first-serve basis inspired by "bottom-up" agglomerative clustering algorithms [26]. Unsupervised (k, l)-clustering creates cluster centroids and groups tuples accordingly, in reference to their identifying values and privacy constants k and l.

Supervised (k, l)-clustering has a partial or full view over the distribution of identifying values in the original dataset, thus and unlike the unsupervised clustering, clusters are created based on a predefined set of centroids $\mathcal{V} = \{V_{id}^1, ..., V_{id}^m\}$ that are fed to the clustering technique prior the anonymization. Hence, the identifying and sensitive values that are highly correlated are grouped together in the same cluster to reduce the chances of having these values anonymized/suppressed to meet the privacy properties.

As shown in Fig. 2(c), 'Allen_U1' and 'Cathy_U3' are grouped together in 3 QI-groups because they occur the most in the incoming stream. However in Fig. 2(b), 'Allen_U1' is grouped alongside 'Betty_U2' and 'Cathy_U3' alongside 'David_U4' due to the order of their tuples in the data stream.

User ID	VIN Number	TS	Location
Allen_U1	abfb32fd10ad2*	1	10.31;17,32
Betty_U2	00983503e35d*	2	30.29;24,12
Cathy_U3	0f550377353d*	3	23,45;11,23
Allen_U1	abfb32fd10ad2*	4	10.32;15,32
David_u4	936e2c77b9du*	5	22,25;11,33
Allen_U1	abfb32fd10ad2*	6	13.32;15,32
Betty_U2	00983503e35d*	7	42.45;11,23
Cathy_U3	0f550377353d*	8	23.45;11,24
Carol_U5	1qwfq2fd10ad2*	9	40,42;14,51
Cathy_U3	0f550377353d*	10	30,30;24,12
...	...	...	...

(a) Incoming Stream S

User ID	VIN Number	GID		GID	Location	TS
Allen_U1	abfb32fd10ad2*	1		1	10.31;17,32	1
Betty_U2	00983503e35d*	1		1	30.29;24,12	2
Cathy_U3	0f550377353d*	2		2	23,45;11,23	3
David_u4	936e2c77b9du*	2		2	22,25;11,33	5
Betty_U2	00983503e35d*	3		3	10.32;15,32	4
...	...	...		3	42,45;11,23	7
				...	...	...

(b) Anonymization using Unsupervised (k,l)-Clustering

User ID	VIN Number	GID		GID	Location	TS
Allen_U1	abfb32fd10ad2*	1		1	10.31;17,32	1
Cathy_U3	0f550377353d*	1		1	23,45;11,23	3
Allen_U1	abfb32fd10ad2*	2		2	10.32;15,32	4
Cathy_U3	0f550377353d*	2		2	23,45;11,24	8
Allen_U1	abfb32fd10ad2*	3		3	13.32;15,32	6
Cathy_U3	0f550377353d*	3		3	30.30;24,12	10
Betty_U2	00983503e35d*	4		4	30.29;24,12	2
David_U4	936e2c77b9du*	4		4	22,25;11,33	5
...	...	...		...	...	...

(c) Anonymization using Supervised (k,l)-Clustering with $\mathcal{V} = \{\{U1,U3\},\{U2,U4\},\{U5\}\}$

Fig. 2. Applying unsupervised and supervised (k, l)-clustering on a data stream with $k, l = (2, 2)$

Lemma 1. *Given a transactional stream S, safe clustering ensures the safe release of QI-groups in the published version S^*.*

Proof. Since (k, l)-clustering is applied, $\forall QI_i, QI_j$ two QI-groups released from C, $\pi_{A^{id}} QI_i = \pi_{A^{id}} QI_j = V_{id}(C)$ where $|V_{id}(C)| = k$. Alternatively, since (k, l)-clustering ensures that an identifying value exists in one and only centroid, $\forall C_1, C_2$, two distinct clusters over S^*, $V_{id}(C_1) \cap V_{id}(C_2) = \emptyset$ can be written as $\pi_{A^{id}} QI_1 \cap \pi_{A^{id}} QI_2 = \emptyset$ where, QI_1, QI_2 are two QI-groups released respectively from C_1 and C_2. Hence, the intersection of any QI-groups in S^* on the identifying values yields either k identifying values or none.

4.3 (k, l)-Clustering Algorithm

In this section, we present our *(k, l)*-clustering algorithm applied on a transactional data stream. The main idea behind it is to process incoming tuples on the fly while guarantying safe release of l-diverse QI-groups. It requires two privacy constants k and l, the stream S, and a set of centroids $\mathcal{V}$. *(k, l)*-clustering outputs an anonymized data stream. The algorithm is composed of two main steps; safe clustering and tuple assignment.

4.4 Safe Clustering

The function assigns tuples to their corresponding clusters based on their identifying values.

$$t_p \text{ is assigned to } \begin{cases} C_e & \text{if } \exists V_{id}(C_e) \subset \mathcal{V} \text{ where} \\ & t_p[A_{id}] \in V_{id}(C_e) \\ C_q \text{ where } |V_{id}(C_q)| < k & \text{otherwise} \end{cases}$$

```
 1: function SAFE_CLUSTERING(t_p, 𝒱)
 2:     selected_cluster:={};
 3:     if (t_p[A_id] ∉ 𝒱) then
 4:         C_q:= Find C_q in C where |V_id(C_q)| < k;
 5:         if C_q = null then
 6:             V_id(C_q):={};
 7:             V_id(C_q) ← t_p[A_id];   /**Adds t_p[A_id] to the empty centroid V_id(C_q)*/;
 8:             selected_cluster:= C_q;
 9:         else
10:             V_id(C_q) ← t_p[A_id]; /**Adds t_p[A_id] to the non-empty centroid V_id(C_q) */;
11:             selected_cluster:= C_q;
12:         end if
13:     else
14:         Find C_e in C where t_p[A_id] ∈ V_id(C_e);
15:         selected_cluster:= C_e;
16:     end if
           return selected_cluster;
17: end function
```

4.5   Tuple Assignment

It assigns a tuple t_p to the selected cluster C_{sel} as follow: In a given cluster, all tuples are distributed over multiple *sub-groups*. *sub-groups* must contain at least k distinct identifying values before verifying their *l*-diversity.

After processing the entire stream, the algorithm will publish all *sub-groups* which are not *l*-diverse nor reached size k (i.e., stored in the *temp* structure), by suppressing the identifying values. This guarantees the privacy constraints but impacts the utility of the dataset.

5   Experiments

In this section, we evaluate the efficiency of our unsupervised and supervised *(k, l)*-clustering techniques by conducting a set of experiments detailed here-inafter. The algorithm is implemented in JAVA and tested on a PC with 2.20 GHz Intel Core i7 CPU, 8.0 GB RAM.

```
 1: procedure TUPLE_ASSIGNMENT(t_p,C_sel)
 2:     sub-group:={};
 3:     sub-group:=Find largest sub-group in C_sel.subgroups[] where t_p[A_id] ∉ π_{A_id} sub-group;
 4:     if sub-group ≠ null then
 5:         sub-group ← t_p; /**Add t_p to sub-group*/
 6:         if (sub-group.size = k) then
 7:             if (sub-group is l-diverse) then
 8:                 Publish sub-group as QItable and SVtable linked by GID
 9:                 Delete sub-group
10:             else
11:                 temp := temp ∪ sub-group
12:                 if (temp.size > k and temp is l-diverse) then
13:                     Publish temp as QItable and SVtable linked by GID
14:                     Delete temp
15:                 end if
16:             end if
17:         end if
18:     else
19:         sub-group ← t_p;
20:         subgroups[] ← sub-group; /**Add sub-group to the rest of the non-published subgroups
        in the cluster*/
21:     end if
22: end procedure
```

To simulate a data stream scenario, we used a rental transaction dataset[1] composed of 109763 tuples where each tuple is associated with a timestamp used only for evaluation purposes. We assume that at each time instant exactly one tuple arrives. As a result, timestamps range from 1 to $|S|$. The dataset contains 2374 distinct identifying values.

We designed two sets of experiments to examine the effectiveness of our approach in terms of utility:

– Evaluating the percentage of suppressed identifying values.
– Evaluating the delay-retention of tuples in the queue before being released in QI-groups.

---

[1] https://github.com/JMTCoder/test12/blob/master/sourcedata.txt

5.1   Percentage of Suppressed Identifying Values

As previously stated, after processing the stream over a specified interval of time, our algorithm suppresses the identifying values in the QI-groups that are not l-diverse nor of size k.

Using the unsupervised (k, l)-clustering, we vary the value of k from 3 to 8, and examine the percentage of suppressed values. The parameter l is set to 3. For high values of k, the percentage of suppressed values increases. It reaches almost 60% for $k = 8$ as shown in Fig. 3. Here, we cluster identifying values based on their order of arrival. Each k individuals clustered together might not have the same distribution over the stream. Therefore, when k increases, it becomes more difficult to form QI-groups leading to an increase in the amount of suppressed values. Hence, we did not evaluate the unsupervised approach for k values higher than 8.

Using the supervised (k, l)-clustering, we ensure that the most frequent identifying values are clustered then grouped together in the QI-groups. Consequently, we suppress fewer identifying values and thus, obtain better utility, as shown in Fig. 3, where the percentage of suppressed values reaches 1% for $k = 20$.

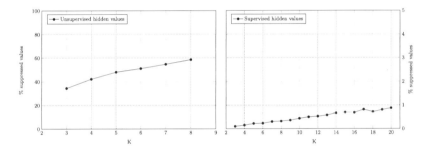

Fig. 3. Percentage of suppressed values for $l = 3$ while varying k for both Unsupervised and Supervised (k, l)-clustering approaches

5.2   Retention of Tuples

A tuple is retained in the queue if it remains (a) in a *sub-group* that did not reach size k or (b) in the *temporary sub-group* of the corresponding cluster.

For each set of $\{k, l\}$ values, we measure the retention delay of each tuple in memory. Then we compute the average delay time of all the tuples. This value is chosen as the delay constraint δ defined in [28].

We consider a tuple that remains more than the specified delay δ in memory a "delayed or outdated tuple". δ slightly varies with k. We applied our algorithm to the same rental dataset we used before, while adopting both approaches, as shown in Fig. 4. The delay constraint can be chosen depending on the data stream application requirement regarding availability of the anonymized tuples as stated in [28].

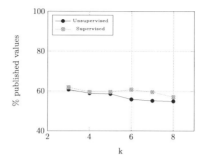

Fig. 4. Percentage of published tuples for both approaches before δ

6   Conclusion

In this paper, we have defined new privacy properties to address the correlation problem in the anonymization of transactional data streams. A bucketization based technique, entitled (k, l)-clustering, is proposed to enforce these privacy properties. (k, l)-clustering processes incoming tuples on the fly. It continuously groups k distinct individuals into l-diverse QI-groups and ensures that these individuals remain grouped together in future releases of QI-groups. We evaluated our algorithm in terms of utility by considering two approaches: *supervised* and *unsupervised*. We showed, by conducting a set of experiments, that both approaches cope well with the streaming nature of the data while respecting the privacy constraints. The *supervised* approach yielded better results because it has a partial or full view over the distribution of identifying values in the dataset.

References

1. Samarati, P.: Protecting respondents' identities in microdata release. IEEE Trans. Knowl. Data Eng. **13**(6), 1010–1027 (2001)
2. Sweeney, L.: k-anonymity: a model for protecting privacy. Int. J. Uncertain. Fuzziness Knowl.-Based Syst. **10**(5), 557–570 (2002)
3. Campan, A., Cooper, N., Truta, T.M.: On-the-fly generalization hierarchies for numerical attributes revisited. In: Jonker, W., Petković, M. (eds.) SDM 2011. LNCS, vol. 6933, pp. 18–32. Springer, Heidelberg (2011). https://doi.org/10.1007/978-3-642-23556-6_2
4. He, Y., Naughton, J.F.: Anonymization of set-valued data via top-down, local generalization. Proc. VLDB Endow. **2**(1), 934–945 (2009)
5. Anjum, A., Raschia, G.: BangA: an efficient and flexible generalization-based algorithm for privacy preserving data publication. Computers **6**(1), 1 (2017)
6. Xiao, X., Tao. Y.: Anatomy: simple and effective privacy preservation. In: Proceedings of 32nd International Conference on Very Large Data Bases (VLDB 2006), Seoul, Korea (2006)
7. Li, T., Li, N., Zhang, J., Molloy, I.: Slicing: a new approach for privacy preserving data publishing. IEEE Trans. Knowl. Data Eng. **24**(3), 561–574 (2012)

8. Ciriani, V., De Capitani Di Vimercati, S., Foresti, S., Jajodia, S., Paraboschi, S., Samarati, P.: Combining fragmentation and encryption to protect privacy in data storage. ACM Trans. Inf. Syst. Secur. **13**, 22:1–22:33 (2010)

9. Manolis, T., Nikos, M., John, L., Spiros, S.: Privacy preservation by disassociation. Proc. VLDB Endow. **5**(10), 944–955 (2012)

10. Wang, K., Wang, P., Fu, A.W., Wong, R.C.: Generalized bucketization scheme for flexible privacy settings. Inf. Sci. **348**, 377–393 (2016)

11. Wong, R.C., Fu, A.W., Wang, K., Yu, P., Jian, P.: Can the utility of anonymized data be used for privacy breaches? ACM Trans. Knowl. Discov. Data **5**(3), 16:1–16:24 (2011)

12. Cormode, G., Li, N., Li, T., Srivastava, D.: Minimizing minimality and maximizing utility: analyzing method-based attacks on anonymized data. Proc. VLDB Endow. **3**, 1045–1056 (2010)

13. Kifer, D., Attacks on privacy and deFinetti's theorem. In: SIGMOD Conference, pp. 127–138 (2009)

14. Al Bouna, B., Clifton, C., Malluhi, Q.M.: Efficient sanitization of unsafe data correlations. In: Proceedings of the Workshops of the EDBT/ICDT 2015 Joint Conference (EDBT/ICDT), Brussels, Belgium, pp. 278–285 (2015)

15. Li, T., Li, N.: Injector: mining background knowledge for data anonymization. In: ICDE, pp. 446–455 (2008)

16. Al Bouna, B., Clifton, C., Malluhi, Q.: Using Safety constraint for transactional dataset anonymization. In: Wang, L., Shafiq, B. (eds.) DBSec 2013. LNCS, vol. 7964, pp. 164–178. Springer, Heidelberg (2013). https://doi.org/10.1007/978-3-642-39256-6_11

17. Al Bouna, B., Clifton, C., Malluhi, Q.M.: Anonymizing transactional datasets. J. Comput. Secur. **23**(1), 89–106 (2015)

18. Gong, Q., Luo, J., Yang, M., Ni, W., Li, X.I.: Anonymizing 1: M microdata with high utility. Knowl.-Based Syst. **115**(Suppl. C), 15–26 (2017)

19. Lu, J., Wang, P., Zhao, L., Yang, J.: Sanatomy: privacy preserving publishing of data streams via anatomy. In: 2010 Third International Symposium on Information Processing (ISIP). IEEE (2010)

20. Yazdani, N., Amiri, F., Shakery, A.: Bottom-up sequential anonymization in the presence of adversary knowledge. Inf. Sci. **405**, 316–335 (2018)

21. Cao, J., Carminati, B., Ferrari, E., Tan, K.: Castle: continuously anonymizing data streams. IEEE Trans. Dependable Secur. Comput. **8**(3), 337–352 (2011)

22. Zhao, L., Wang, P., Lu, J., Yang, J.: B-castle: an efficient publishing algorithm for k-anonymizing data streams. In: 2010 Second WRI Global Congress on Intelligent Systems (GCIS), pp. 2155–6083. IEEE (2011)

23. Zakerzadeh, H., Osborn, S.L.: FAANST: fast anonymizing algorithm for numerical streaming DaTa. In: Garcia-Alfaro, J., Navarro-Arribas, G., Cavalli, A., Leneutre, J. (eds.) DPM/SETOP -2010. LNCS, vol. 6514, pp. 36–50. Springer, Heidelberg (2011). https://doi.org/10.1007/978-3-642-19348-4_4

24. Guo, K., Zhang, Q.: Fast clustering-based anonymization approaches with time constraints for data streams. Knowl.-Based Syst. **46**, 95–108 (2013)

25. Noferesti, M., Mohammadian, E., Jalili, R.: Fast: Fast anonymization of big data streams. In: Proceeding BigDataScience, 14 Proceedings of the 2014 International Conference on Big Data Science and Computing. ACM (2014)

26. Shakery, A., Amiri, F., Yazdani, N., Chinaei, A.H.: Hierarchical anonymization algorithms against background knowledge attack in data releasing. Knowl.-Based Syst. **101**, 71–89 (2016)

27. Domingo-Ferrer, J., Soria-Comas, J.: Steered microaggregation: a unified primitive for anonymization of data sets and data streams. In: 2017 IEEE International Conference on Data Mining Workshops (ICDMW). IEEE (2017)

28. Ghafoor, A., Pervaiz, Z., Aref, W.G.: Precision-bounded access control using sliding-window query views for privacy-preserving data streams. IEEE Trans. Knowl. Data Eng. **27**, 1992–2004 (2015)

29. Bonomi, L., Xiong, L.: On differentially private longest increasing subsequence computation in data stream. Trans. Data Priv. **9**, 73–100 (2016)

30. Nie, Y., et al.: Geospatial streams publish with differential privacy. In: Wang, S., Zhou, A. (eds.) CollaborateCom 2016. LNICST, vol. 201, pp. 152–164. Springer, Cham (2017). https://doi.org/10.1007/978-3-319-59288-6_14

31. Liu, X., et al.: On efficient and robust anonymization for privacy protection on massive streaming categorical information. IEEE Trans. Dependable Secur. Comput. **14**, 507–520 (2017)

32. Dwork, C., McSherry, F., Nissim, K., Smith, A.: Calibrating noise to sensitivity in private data analysis. In: Halevi, S., Rabin, T. (eds.) TCC 2006. LNCS, vol. 3876, pp. 265–284. Springer, Heidelberg (2006). https://doi.org/10.1007/11681878_14

Cryptographic Protocols

A New Insight—Proxy Re-encryption Under LWE with Strong Anti-collusion

Wei Yin, Qiaoyan Wen, Wenmin Li, Hua Zhang$^{(\boxtimes)}$, and Zhengping Jin

Beijing University of Posts and Telecommunications, Beijing, China
zhanghua_288@bupt.edu.cn

Abstract. Proxy re-encryption is a special type of public key encryption that allows an intermediate proxy to transform a ciphertext from one public key to another without learning any information about the original message. Therefore, it can be regarded as a consignation of decryption right. In this paper, we put forward two novel definitions of anti-collusion called strong anti-collusion and weak anti-collusion, and propose an improved strong anti-collusion lattice based proxy re-encryption scheme. Moreover, our scheme based on the hardness of standard Learning With Error (LWE) problem is the CPA secure in the standard model, which can be reduced to the worst-case lattice hard problems. In addition, we give a detailed analysis of key privacy and proof of security.

1 Introduction

In 1998, Blaze, Bleumer and Strauss [4] proposed a new cryptographic primitives called proxy re-encryption. Its prominent feature is that a third party intermediate agent could be allowed to convert the ciphertext of one (often called Alice) into the ciphertext of another (often called Bob). In this process such a few parties involved:

1. Delegator: This role gives his decryption right to the delegatee through proxy, for this he would generate a re-encryption key and sent it to the proxy. We usually call this character Alice.
2. Proxy: This role transfers the ciphertext under one public key to another with the re-encryption key. And the proxy would not learn any additional information in this process.
3. Delegatee: This role is endowed the right of decryption, although the ciphertext is not originally aimed at him. We usually call this character Bob.

The proxy re-encryption scheme can be applied in many scenarios due to the special property that the ciphertext is convertible. Including key escrow, distributed file system, secure mail system, DRM (Digital Rights Management, interoperable architecture of DRM), access control system, privacy transmission, etc. The prominent feature of proxy re-encryption is that the proxy is unable to get any information about the original message in the whole process. Furthermore, the proxy also could not obtain the private key information of the

C. Su and H. Kikuchi (Eds.): ISPEC 2018, LNCS 11125, pp. 559–577, 2018.
https://doi.org/10.1007/978-3-319-99807-7_36

delegator and delegatee on the premise of the honest execution protocol of the proxy. However, it is dangerous if the delegator's private key S_A (or the delegatee's private key S_B) could be derived from the re-encryption key $rk_{A \to B}$ and the delegatee's private key S_B (or the delegator's private key S_A). So anti-collusion attack is an important security property in proxy re-encryption scheme, this property conveys the safeness of the participant's private key against collusion attacks. Through our analysis, the anti-collusion property in proxy re-encryption could be divided into strong anti-collusion and weak anti-collusion, respectively (The concept of weak and strong anti-collusion is explained in further detail below). If a proxy re-encryption scheme is not anti-collusion, it is not necessary that we consider the scheme is strong or weak anti-collusion. That is to say, we only consider whether one scheme is strong or weak anti-collusion under the conditions of anti-collusion.

The first proxy re-encryption scheme was presented by Blaze, Bleumer and Strauss [4] in 1998, which based on Elgamal public encryption. Their scheme plays a very important role in the enlightenment, and has a great impact on the subsequent work. Unfortunately, their scheme is not able to resist collusion attack: Alice with the proxy can obtain the Bob's private key, and vice versa. Since the first scheme was proposed, many different types proxy re-encryption schemes have been proposed recently. Ateniese et al. [22] proposed a first unidirectional proxy re-encryption scheme in 2006, which is based on bilinear pairings. In their paper, the idea of two-level ciphertext was proposed for the first time. And their scheme achieves the CPA security in the standard model. Green and Ateniese [10] presented the first identity-based proxy re-encryption scheme (IB-PRE) in 2007. So called identity-based means that the identity of user can be used as public key in their scheme. Their scheme is unidirectional, multi-hop, and CPA security in random oracle model. However, their scheme can not resist collusion attack, the delegatee can obtain the private key of delegator with the proxy. Canetti and Hohenberger [12] presented the first CCA security bidirectional proxy re-encryption scheme in the standard model in 2007. In order to achieve CCA security, they utilized a one-time signature scheme into the ciphertext. Bur their scheme can not resist collusion attack. The same year, Chu et al. [8] proposed two identity-based proxy re-encryption schemes based on the identity-based encryption of Waters [30]. Their schemes' security could be reduced to the security of Waters' scheme, and to the DBDH hypothesis problem in the end. Their first scheme achieves the CPA security in the standard model, and their second scheme achieves RCCA security, but these two schemes can not resist collusion attack. In 2008, Libert and Vergnaud [24] presented a few RCCA security unidirectional proxy re-encryption schemes in the standard model. Weng et al. [31] presented a bidirectional proxy re-encryption scheme without bilinear pairings in 2010, which is CCA security in random model. And their scheme is more efficient based on CDH hard problem, rather than bilinear pairings. In 2013, Singh et al. [6] proposed a lattice based identity based proxy re-encryption scheme in the random oracle model for the single bit as well as for the multi-bit. Both of their schemes are anonymous, bidirectional and multi-hop.

In 2014, Kirshanova [7] presented a CCA1 secure scheme, which is based on the public key encryption (PKE) scheme that is CCA1 secure in [2]. Singh presented a unidirectional proxy re-encryption scheme in 2014, the delegatee published his private key by LWE form in advance so that their scheme is non-interactive, but their scheme only achieves weak anti-collusion rather than strong anti-collusion. Kim et al. presented a lattice based proxy re-encryption scheme in 2016 [36], which enjoys anti-collusion property, however the public and private key space size are double in their scheme.

Lattice based cryptography has been developed rapidly in recent years [1–3,13–15], and utilized the hard problems on lattices in $\mathbb{R}^n$ as a foundation for secure cryptographic scheme construction. The attractive features of lattice based cryptography are as follows:

- **Lattice based cryptography can resist quantum attacks**
  At present, most traditional cryptography based on number theory, such as Diffie-Hellman protocol [25] and RSA encryption algorithm [26] based on integer factorization and discrete logarithm problem. However, Shor [27] proposed an efficient quantum algorithm to solve these problem, this leads cryptography based on number theory no longer secure under the quantum computing environment in the future. On the contrary, there is no effective quantum algorithm to solve the hard problem in lattice so far.
- **High algorithmic efficiency and parallelism**
  Lattice based cryptography are algorithmic simplicity and high parallelism [32], including mainly some linear operations on vectors and matrices modulo relatively small integers. Furthermore, the lattice can also be combined with some particular algebraic structure, such as a ring lattice, this system performs better than the traditional system in some scenarios.
- **Worst-case hardness guarantees strong security**
  In the pioneering work of [18], Ajtai gave a extraordinary connection between the worst case and the average case in lattice. He proved that the problems are hard in the average-case could be reduced to the related problems are hard in the worst-case. Applying this conclusion, a designed lattice based cryptographic construction could be proved that it is impossible to break, unless all instances of this type problems are easy to resolved.

Up to now, there are several lattice based proxy re-encryption scheme to the best of our knowledge: Xagawa et al. [16] presented the first lattice based proxy re-encryption scheme. Their scheme is bidirectional, interactive, transitive, but not resistant to collusions attack. Aono et al. [9] proposed the lattice based key-private proxy re-encryption scheme based on the Learning With Error (LWE) hard problem, which is CPA security in the standard model. Their scheme is unidirectional, interactive and non-transitive, and limited number of hops. Unfortunately, their scheme can not resist collusion attack. (Our main work in this paper is that how to improve their scheme and make it resist to collusions from the proxy and the delegatee. Detailed analysis will be given later.) Kirshanova et al. [7] presented a CCA1-secure proxy re-encryption scheme which is based on strong trapdoors from [2]. Nunez et al. [33] presented a bidirectional, multi-use, interactive scheme, which is based on the NTRU system. But their scheme is not anti-collusion attack.

1.1 Our Contribution

For the problem that the lattice based proxy re-encryption scheme in [9] can not resist collusion attack, we design an improved PRE scheme that can resist the strong collusion attack (The definition would be given later). In other words, the proxy and the delegator (or the delegatee) could not be collusion to obtain any information on private key of the delegatee (or the delegator). Moreover, we reinforce the property of key-privacy in our scheme. We can note that the scheme in original paper could hide the identity of delegator, but the identity of delegatee is exposure, because the public key of delegatee is exposed in proxy re-encryption key explicitly. Specifically, the proxy has the re-encryption key

$$rk_{A \to B} = (P_B, Q)$$
$$= (P_B, \begin{pmatrix} X & -XS_B + E + \mathsf{PowerOf2}(S_A) \\ 0 & I \end{pmatrix})$$

where the $(X, -XS_B + E)$ is generated by Bob, so he and the proxy conspire to obtain $\mathsf{PowerOf2}(S_A)$ that is the variant of Alice's private key by $-XS_B + E + \mathsf{PowerOf2}(S_A) - (-XS_B + E)$, then they could obtain S_A from the first row of $\mathsf{PowerOf2}(S_A)$ based on the property of this algorithm $\mathsf{PowerOf2}()$. Alice's private key is compromised in this case.

Maybe someone would suggest that the private key of Alice could be added the interference noise vectors so that the proxy conspired with Bob could only get the offset of S_A instead of S_A itself. More specifically, Alice makes use of $\mathsf{PowerOf2}(S_A) + E_2$ instead of $\mathsf{PowerOf2}(S_A)$ after Bob sent $(X, -XS_B + E_1)$ to him, generates the re-encryption key

$$rk_{A \to B} = (P_B, Q)$$
$$= (P_B, \begin{pmatrix} X & -XS_B + E' + \mathsf{PowerOf2}(S_A) \\ 0 & I \end{pmatrix})$$

where $E' = E_1 + E_2$. In this case, even if the proxy and Bob conspire to get $\mathsf{PowerOf2}(S_A) + E_2$, it seems to cover up the private key of Alice successfully, but in fact it is not feasible. Although Bob does not have direct access to the private key S_A, it is equivalent to Bob acquires the decryption right of Alice:

$$(\mathsf{BitD}(C_1)|C_2) \begin{pmatrix} \mathsf{PowerOf2}(S_A) + E_2 \\ I \end{pmatrix}$$
$$= \underbrace{\mathsf{BitD}(C_1)E_2}_{noise} + C_1 S_A + C_2$$

So the proxy and Bob would chalk up the decryption right of Alice instead of private key itself (i.e. the approximate value about the private key).

Since the problem can not be solved easily by adding noise as above, we need to find a better way to protect the private key of Alice (the re-encryption key $rk_{A \to B}$ contains Bob's secret information on S_B: $((A, P_B = R_B - AS_B)$ and $(X, -XS_B + E)$, which could be written in LWE form, so we do not consider leakage problem of Bob's private key). In this paper, we adopt the form of LWE hard problem to hide S_A. Namely, we put the private key of Alice S_A in the re-encryption key with the shape of $(Y, \mathsf{PowersOf2}(S_A)Y + \varpi), Y \in \psi_s$ (This thesis will explain later the reason why a new parameter Y is introduced). More concretely, the main construction of this paper is a novel proxy re-encryption key:

$$\Omega = \begin{pmatrix} X & -XS_B + \varpi_1 + \mathsf{PowersOf2}(S_A)Y + \varpi_2 \\ 0 & I \end{pmatrix}$$

Thus Ω is pseudo-random if the S_A is kept secret. In this case, even if the proxy, in collusion with Bob, could only get the pseudo-random vector, and its security is guaranteed by the LWE difficult problem. However, this is not a straight-forward construction due to the increased noise after we have adopted the above method (More details in Sect. 3). We design a two-level ciphertext in our scheme: $\mathbb{C}_1$ and $\mathbb{C}_2$. The $\mathbb{C}_1 = (c_1, c_2) = (\omega_1 A + \omega_2, \omega_1 P + \omega_3 + m \lfloor \frac{q}{2} \rfloor)$ is a standard ciphertext, whose decryption method is normal decryption operation. The function of $\mathbb{C}_2 = (\mathsf{BitD}(c_1), c_2 Y + m \lfloor \frac{q}{2} \rfloor)$ is for re-encryption, and we introduce a new parameter $Y \in \psi_s^{l \times l}$ for this reason. The noise term consists of two parts after Re-encryption algorithm: $noise_1$ and $noise_2$, where $noise_2 = c_1 S_A Y + \mathsf{BitD}(c_1)\varpi_1 + \mathsf{BitD}(c_1)\varpi_2 + c_2 Y = (\omega_1 R + \omega_2 S + \omega_3 + m \lfloor \frac{q}{2} \rfloor)Y + \mathsf{BitD}(c_1)\varpi_1 + \mathsf{BitD}(c_1)\varpi_2$. The main contribution of this paper is a unidirectional proxy re-encryption scheme based on the hardness of lattice problem. Our scheme is lattice based construction that achieves strong anti-collusion and interactivity. (Table 1 shows the comparison of our scheme with previous schemes that all based on lattice.)

Table 1. Comparison with the previous schemes

Authors	Based on	Unidirectional	Non-interactivity	Anti-collusion	Multi-use
XT10 [16]	LWE	×	×	×	✓
ABW13 [9]	LWE	✓	×	×	✓
Kir14 [7]	LWE	✓	✓	✓	×
NAL15 [33]	NTRU	×	×	×	✓
Ours	LWE	✓	×	✓	✓

1.2 Paper Outline

The rest of our paper is organized as follows. In Sect. 2, we give some basic definitions, hard problems, some conclusions in lattice, and PRE security model.

In Sect. 3, we present a CPA-secure anti-collusion proxy re-encryption scheme in the standard model, and prove the security of our scheme. In Sect. 4, we conclude the summary of this paper.

2   Preliminaries

2.1   Definitions for Unidrectional Proxy Re-encryption Scheme (uPRE)

Definition 1 (Unidrectional Proxy Re-encryption Scheme). *An unidirectional proxy re-encryption scheme is a tuple of algorithms-(PRE-KeyGen, PRE-Encrypt, PRE-ReKeyGen, PRE-ReEnc, PRE-Decrypt):*

– PRE-Setup(λ): On input a security λ, outputs public parameters pp, a public key pk and a secret key sk.
– PRE-Encrypt(pk, M): On input a public key pk, and a message M, this algorithm outputs ciphertext C.
– PRE-ReKeyGen(pk_i, pk_j, sk_i, sk_j): On input a secret key pk_i, sk_i and pk_j, sk_j in some way, the algorithm outputs a re-encryption key $rk_{i,j}$. (The scheme is non-interactive if the secret key of the delegatee sk_j is not needed, otherwise, the scheme is interactive)
– PRE-ReEnc($C_i, rk_{i,j}$): On input a ciphertext C_i and a re-encryption key $rk_{i,j}$, the algorithm outputs a re-encrypted ciphertext C_j.
– PRE-Decrypt(C, sk): On input public parameters, a private key sk and a ciphertext C, this algorithm outputs message M.

Correctness. Unidrectional Proxy Re-encryption Scheme is correct if:

– For all sk output by PRE-Setup and for all M in plaintext space, it holds that $PRE - Decrypt(sk, PRE - Encrpt(pk, M)) = M$
– For re-encryption key $rk_{i,j}$ output by ReKeyGen and for any C_i output by Encrypt(pk_i, M), and for all M in plaintext space, it holds that $PRE - Decrypt(sk_j, PRE - ReEnc(rk_{i,j}, C_i)) = M$

Definition 2. *A proxy re-encryption system is called multi-hop if a proxy can re-encrypt the encrypted ciphertext repeatedly. By comparison in a single-hop system setting a ciphertext can be re-encrypted only once.*

Regardless of the encryption system is single-hop or multi-hop, that the requirements of correctness for decryption algorithms are the same. That is to say, the plaintext message can be obtained from the resulting ciphertext by decryption algorithm. No matter how the ciphertext is just produced or re-encrypted.

Security Game [8,10,11]. We define CPA security of uPRE using a series of games which are played between the challenger and adversary. This security includes semantic security and recipient anonymity. The games play as follows.

Before introducing the game model we first divide all users into two categories: honest user (HU) and corrupted user (CU). HU represents honest user, that adversary only knows their public key, and CU represents corrupted user, that adversary not only knows their public key, but also knows their private key. We denote the message space by $\mathcal{M}$ and the ciphertext space by $\mathcal{C}$.

Setup. The challenger runs $Setup(1^n)$ and gives the public parameters pp to adversary. HU and CU defined as above.

Phase 1. The adversary can make the following queries:

- The adversary can ask a private key queries on user i except challenge identity i^*, challenger responds by running PRE-Setup algorithm to generate a private key sk_i for user i and sent it to the adversary. The adversary can repeat polynomial times for different identities.
- The adversary can ask a re-encryption key query $rk_{i,j}$ from user i to user j, challenger responds by running PRE-ReKeyGen algorithm to generate a re-encryption key $rk_{i,j}$ from user i to user j and sent it to the adversay, all queries where $i = j$ or $i \in HU, j \in CU$ are ignored. The adversary can repeat polynomial times for different couple of identities.
- The adversary can ask re-encryption query C_j from (id_i, id_j, C_i), challenger responds by running PRE-ReKeyGen algorithm to generate a re-encryption key $rk_{i,j}$ from user i to user j and then challenger generates ciphertext C_j by running PRE-ReEnc algorithm, and return the C_j to the adversary. All queries where $i = j$ or where $i \in HU, j \in CU$ are ignored. The adversary can repeat polynomial times for different couple of identities.

Challenge. Once adversary considers that Phase 1 could be over then it outputs $(m_0, m_1) \in \mathcal{M}$ which it wishes to challenge on, submits user i^* and (m_0, m_1), i^* should be in HU. The challenger picks a random bit $r \in \{0, 1\}$, and then return $C_{i^*} = Encrypt(PP, pk_{i^*}, m_r)$. Afterwards it sends C_{i^*} as a challenge ciphertext to the adversary.

Phase 2. The adversary could ask extra queries that for private key query, re-encryption key query and re-encryption query on the user $i \neq i^*$, the challenger responds as in Phase 1.

Guess. Finally, the adversary outputs a guess $r' \in \{0, 1\}$ and wins if $r = r'$.

We refer to the adversary $\mathcal{A}$ in above game as an CPA adversary. We define the advantage of the adversary $\mathcal{A}$ in attacking an uPRE scheme ϵ as

$$Adv_{\epsilon, \mathcal{A}} = |Pr[r = r'] - \frac{1}{2}|$$

Definition 3. *We say that an uPRE scheme is CPA if for all probabilistic polynomial time algorithm $\mathcal{A}$ and negligible function ε, we always have that $Adv_{\epsilon, \mathcal{A}}$ is a negligible function, that is, $Adv_{\epsilon, \mathcal{A}} \leqslant \varepsilon$.*

Security Game of Key Privacy. We give a series of games between the challenger and the adversary to define the property of key privacy. Considering the following interactions:

- The phase 1 is same as above in the Definition 2.
- Re-encryption key query(i, j). The adversary asks re-encryption key query about users (i, j), where $i \neq j, i \in HU, j \in HU \cup CU$. Then the challenger returns $rk_{i \rightarrow j}$ for answer. We do not need to think about the situation that $i \in CU$, since the adversary would know sk_i if $i \in CU$. In order to give the adversary the ability to verify the returned re-encryption key $rk_{i \rightarrow j}$, we need to consider the case $j \in CU$.
- Re-encryption query(i, j, C_i). The adversary asks re-encryption query about users (i, j) and ciphertext C_i. The challenger returns re-encrypted ciphertext $C_j = ReEnc(C_i, rk_{i \rightarrow j}, pp)$, and the $rk_{i \rightarrow j}$ would be generated by the challenger if it does not already exist.
- Challenge(i^*, j^*). The adversary asks re-encryption key query about the challenge users (i^*, j^*), we should pay attention to the followings: 1. $rk_{i^* \rightarrow j^*}$ should not have been queried before. 2. There is no chain from j^* to any $k \in CU$. 3. Setting $i^* \neq j^*, j^* \in HU, j^* \notin CU$. There are no limits to i^*, namely $i^* \in CU \bigcup HU$. And the third point means that the adversary could not verify the $rk_{i^* \rightarrow j^*}$ in the process of challenge, but it is allowed in the query phase. Finally the challenger takes a bit b by the toss of a coin. He would returned $rk_{i^* \rightarrow j^*} = ReKeyGen(sk_{i^*}, pk_{j^*})$ as the answer if $b = 1$, and returned random rk^* as the answer if $b = 0$.

In the end, the adversary conjectures a bit b' and outputs it. That the advantage probability of adversary wins the games above is defined as: $P = |Pr[b' = b] - \frac{1}{2}|$. We say the proxy re-encryption scheme is key-privacy if the advantage probability is negligible for a polynomial time adversary.

2.2   Strong and Weak Anti-collusion

Here we propose two novel security definitions of the anti-collusion, which called strong anti-collusion and weak anti-collusion, respectively. And these schemes are divided into two types: interactive and non-interactive.

Definition 4 (Strong anti-collusion of PRE). *In the proxy re-encryption scheme, if the proxy and a participant conspire neither get the private key of another participant (if scheme is non-interactive, the proxy and delegatee conspire against the delegator), nor obtain the value of approximate value about the private key of another participant.*

Definition 5 (Weak anti-collusion of PRE). *In the proxy re-encryption scheme, if the proxy and a participant conspire cannot get the private key of another participant (if scheme is non-interactive, the proxy and delegatee conspire against the delegator), but it could obtain the approximate value about the private key of another participant.*

In the above, the approximate value about the private key is that the private key vector adds noise vectors to form an offset of private key. An example is given to illustrate this concept here: The proxy re-encryption key in [35] is

$$Q = \begin{pmatrix} e_1 X \ e_1 P_2 + e_2 + \mathsf{PowerOf2}(S_A) \\ 0 & I \end{pmatrix}, \text{ where } e_1 \in \psi_s^{nk \times nk}, e_2 \in \psi_s^{nk \times l}, \psi_s \text{ is a}$$

gaussian distribution. If the proxy conspires with delegatee to compute:

$$\begin{pmatrix} e_1 X \ e_1 P_2 + e_2 + \mathsf{PowerOf2}(S_A) \\ 0 & I \end{pmatrix} \begin{pmatrix} S_B \\ I \end{pmatrix} = \begin{pmatrix} e_1 E + e_2 + \mathsf{PowerOf2}(S_A) \\ I \end{pmatrix}$$

where $E \in \psi_s^{nk \times l}$. Although they cannot get the private key S_A of delegator from the calculation results above, could obtain the first n rows of
$e_1 E + e_2 + Power2(S_A)$ that are approximate to S_A, which becomes the potential threaten to proxy re-encryption scheme. So their scheme enjoys weak anti-
collusion property, and our construction satisfies the strong anti-collusion property in this paper.

2.3   Lattice Definiton

Definition 6 (Integer Lattice [13,15]). *Let $B = [b_1 | \dots | b_m] \in \mathbb{R}^{m \times m}$ be an
$m \times m$ matrix whose columns are linearly independent vectors $b_1, \dots, b_m \in \mathbb{R}^m$.
The m-dimensional full-rank lattice Λ generated by B is the set,*

$$\Lambda = \mathcal{L}(B) = \{y \in \mathbb{R}^m \quad s.t. \quad \exists s \in \mathbb{Z}^m, y = Bs = \sum_{i=1}^{m} s_i b_i\}$$

*Here, we are interested in integer lattices, i.e., when $\mathcal{L}$ is contained in $\mathbb{Z}^m$. We
let $det(\Lambda)$ denote the determinant of Λ.*

Definition 7 (q-ary lattice). *For prime q, $A \in \mathbb{Z}_q^{n \times m}$ and $u \in \mathbb{Z}_q^n$, define:*

$$\Lambda(A)_q := \{e \in \mathbb{Z}^m \quad s.t. \quad \exists s \in \mathbb{Z}_q^n \quad where \quad A^\top s = e(mod q)\}$$

$$\Lambda_q^\perp(A) := \{e \in \mathbb{Z}^m \quad s.t. \quad Ae = 0(mod q)\}$$

$$\Lambda_q^u(A) := \{e \in \mathbb{Z}^m \quad s.t. \quad Ae = u(mod q)\}$$

*We can observe that if $t \in \Lambda_q^u(A)$ then $\Lambda_q^u(A) = \Lambda_q^\perp(A) + t$ and hence $\Lambda_q^u(A)$ is
a shift of $\Lambda_q^\perp(A)$.*

Theorem 1. *Let $q \geqslant 3$ be odd and $m := \lceil 6n log q \rceil$. There is a probabilistic
polynomial -time algorithm $\mathsf{TrapGen}(q,n)$ that outputs a pair $(A \in \mathbb{Z}_q^{n \times m}, S \in
\mathbb{Z}^{n \times m})$ such that A is statistically close to a uniform matrix in $\mathbb{Z}_q^{n \times m}$ and S is
a basis for $\Lambda_q^\perp(A)$ satisfying*

$$\|\tilde{S}\| \leqslant O(\sqrt{nlogq}) \quad and \quad \|S\| \leqslant O(nlogq)$$

with all but negligible probability in n.

2.4   The LWE Problems

Construction of this paper reduces to the **Learning with Errors** problem, which may be seen as average case problem related to the family of lattices described above.

Definition 8 (Learning with Errors ([9])). *Succinctly, the assumption LWE(m, n, α, q) asserts that*

$$(A, Ax + e) \overset{c}{\approx} (A, r)$$

where

- $\overset{c}{\approx}$ *is used for computational indistinguishability.*
- $A \in \mathbb{Z}_q^{m \times n}$ *and* $r \in \mathbb{Z}_q^{m \times 1}$ *are randomly chosen.*
- $x \in \psi_{\alpha q}^{n \times 1}, e \in \psi_{\alpha q}^{m \times 1}$, *and* $Ax + e$ *is computed over* $\mathbb{Z}_q$. *Moreover* $\psi_{\alpha q}$ *is the Gaussian distribution over the integers* $\mathbb{Z}$, *with mean 0 and deviation* αq *for real number* $0 < \alpha < 1$.

By a standard hybrid argument over columns of $X \in \psi_{\alpha q}^{n \times l}$, we have under the LWE assumption

$$(A, AX + E) \overset{c}{\approx} (A, R)$$

for random $R \in \mathbb{Z}_q^{m \times l}$ and Gaussian noise $E \in \psi_{\alpha q}^{m \times l}$. This fact is used in our security proofs.

We give a outline of Gaussian distributions over lattice. For any $s > 0$ and dimension $m \geq 1$, the Gaussian function $\rho_s : \mathbb{R}^m \to (0, 1]$ is defined as $\rho_s(\mathbf{x}) = exp(-\pi \|\mathbf{x}\|^2/s^2)$. For any coset $\Lambda_{\mathbf{y}}^{\perp}(A)$, and probability zero elsewhere. We summarize several facts from the literature about discrete Gaussian over lattices, again specialized to our family of interest.

Lemma 1 ([21], Lemma 4.4). *For any n-dimensional lattice* Λ, *vector* $\mathbf{c} \in \mathbb{R}^n$, *and reals* $0 < \epsilon < 1$, $s \geqslant \eta_\epsilon(\Lambda)$, *we have*

$$\Pr_{\mathbf{x} \sim \mathcal{D}_{\Lambda, s, \mathbf{c}}} \{\|\mathbf{x} - \mathbf{c}\| > s\sqrt{n}\} \leqslant \frac{1+\epsilon}{1-\epsilon} \cdot 2^{-n}$$

Lemma 2 ([13]). *There are two PPT algorithms* $SampeGaussia(A, T_A, \sigma, \mathbf{c})$ *and a PPT algorithm* $SamplePre(A, T_A, \sigma, u)$, *the former returns* $x \in \Lambda_q^{\perp}(A)$ *drawn from a distribution statistically close to* $\mathcal{D}_{\Lambda, s, \mathbf{c}}$, *and the latter returns* $x \in \Lambda_q^u(A)$ *sampled from a distribution statistically close to* $\mathcal{D}_{\Lambda_q^u(A), \sigma}$, *whenever* $\Lambda_q^u(A)$ *is not empty, where* T_A *be a basis for* $\Lambda_q^{\perp}(A)$ *and* $\sigma \geqslant \|\widetilde{T_A}\|\omega(\sqrt{logm})$, *for* $\mathbf{c} \in \mathbb{R}^m$ *and* $u \in \mathbb{Z}_q^n$.

There are two lemmas below, their proof can be found in the literature [28, 29], where $|\cdot|$ denotes Euler norm, $< \cdot >$ denotes inner product.

Lemma 3. *Let* $c \geqslant 1$ *and* $C = c \cdot exp(\frac{1-c^2}{2})$. *Then for any real* $s > 0$ *and any integer* $n \geqslant 1$, *we have* $Pr[|\psi_s^n| \geqslant \frac{c \cdot s\sqrt{n}}{\sqrt{2\pi}}] \leqslant C^n$.

Lemma 4. *For any real* $s > 0$ *and* $T > 0$, *and any* $x \in \mathbb{R}^n$, *we have*

$$Pr[| < x, \psi_s^n > | \geqslant Ts|x|] < 2exp(-\pi T^2).$$

2.5   Vector Decomposition

We show how to decompose vectors in a way that preserves inner product.

Vector Decomposition. We decompose vectors into bit representations as defined below [34]:

- BitD($\mathbf{x}$): For $\mathbf{x} \in \mathbb{Z}^n$, let $\mathbf{x}_i \in \{0,1\}^n$ be such that $\mathbf{x} = \sum_{i=0}^{k-1} 2^i \cdot \mathbf{x}_i (mod q)$. Output the vector

$$\mathsf{BitD}(\mathbf{x}) = (\mathbf{x}_0, \cdots, \mathbf{x}_{k-1}) \in \{0,1\}^{1 \times nk} (k = \lceil \lg q \rceil)$$

- PowersOf2($\mathbf{y}$): For $\mathbf{y} = (\mathbf{y}_1 | \cdots | \mathbf{y}_l) \in \mathbb{Z}^{n \times l}$ where $\mathbf{y}_i$ are column vectors, output

$$\mathsf{PowersOf2}(\mathbf{y}) = \begin{pmatrix} \mathbf{y}_1 & \cdots & \mathbf{y}_l \\ 2\mathbf{y}_1 & \cdots & 2\mathbf{y}_l \\ \vdots & & \vdots \\ 2^{k-1}\mathbf{y}_1 & \cdots & 2^{k-1}\mathbf{y}_l \end{pmatrix} \in \mathbb{Z}_q^{nk \times l}$$

It is easy to check that for all $q \in \mathbb{Z}$, it holds that

$$<\mathsf{BitD}(\mathbf{x}), \mathsf{PowersOf2}(\mathbf{y})> = <\mathbf{x}, \mathbf{y}> \in \mathbb{Z}_q^{1 \times l}$$

3   The Basic Construction

Our improvement proxy re-encryption scheme is as follows:

Parameters Generation(λ): On input a security parameter λ, and choose positive integers q, n, take matrix $A \in \mathbb{Z}_q^{n \times n}$ randomly.

Key Generation(pk, sk): Let $s = \alpha q$ for $0 < \alpha < 1$. Take Gaussian noise matrices $R, S \in \psi_s^{n \times l}$. The public key is $pk = P = R - AS \in \mathbb{Z}_q^{n \times l}$, and the secret key is $sk = S$. Here, l is the message length in bits, while n is the key dimension.

Encryption(pk, sk, m): To encrypt $m \in \{0,1\}^l$, take Gaussian noise vectors $\omega_1, \omega_2 \in \psi_s^{1 \times n}$ and $\omega_3 \in \psi_s^{1 \times l}$, and return ciphertext $c = (c_1, c_2) \in \mathbb{Z}_q^{1 \times (n+l)}$ in which

$$\mathbb{C}_1 = (c_1, c_2) = (\omega_1 A + \omega_2, \omega_1 P + \omega_3 + m \lfloor \frac{q}{2} \rfloor) \in \mathbb{Z}_q^{1 \times (n+l)}$$

$$\mathbb{C}_2 = (\mathsf{BitD}(c_1), c_2 Y_1 + m \lfloor \frac{q}{2} \rfloor), Y_1 \in \psi_s^{l \times l}$$

Proxy Key Generation(P_A, S_A, P_B, S_B): Alice with keys (A, P_A, S_A) and Bob with keys (A, P_B, S_B) want to set up proxy key $rk_{A \to B} = (P_B, \Omega)$ in which

$$\Omega = \begin{pmatrix} X & -XS_B + \varpi_1 + \mathsf{PowersOf2}(S_A)Y_2 + \varpi_2 \\ 0 & I \end{pmatrix}$$

where matrices $X \in \mathbb{Z}_q^{nk \times n} (k = \lceil \lg q \rceil), Y_2 \in \psi_s^{l \times l}$ are chosen randomly. Noise matrix ϖ_1, ϖ_2 are chosen from $\psi_s^{nk \times l}$. Therefore, one way to generate Ω is as follows.

1. Bob creates X, ϖ_1, and securely sends $(X, -XS_B + \varpi_1)$ to Alice. The completion of this step does not need interaction by encrypting the tuple under the A's public key which Alice has the corresponding private key. And this transmission way of tuple is security.
2. Alice could set up the proxy re-encryption key with the above information from Bob.

Re-encryption$(\mathbb{C}_2, P_A, S_A, rk_{A \to B})$: Let $\mathbb{C}_2 = (\mathsf{BitD}(c_1), c_2 Y_1 + m \lfloor \frac{q}{2} \rfloor), Y_1 \in \psi_s^{l \times l}$ and $rk_{A \to B} = (P_B, \Omega)$. To transform the ciphertext (c_1, c_2) of Alice into the ciphertext of Bob, return

$$\eta_1 [A | P_B] + [\eta_2 | \eta_3] + \mathbb{C}_2 \cdot \Omega$$

where $\eta_1, \eta_2 \in \psi_s^{1 \times n}$, and $\eta_3 \in \psi_s^{1 \times l}$ are chosen by the proxy.

Decryption$(sk, \mathbb{C}_1)$: We decrypt the $\mathbb{C}_1$ by secret key sk, and the ciphertext $\mathbb{C}_2$ is used to re-encrypt. Compute $\widetilde{m} = \mathbb{C}_1 \begin{pmatrix} S \\ I \end{pmatrix} = c_1 S + c_2 \in \mathbb{Z}_q^l$. Let $\widetilde{m} = (\widetilde{m}_1, \cdots, \widetilde{m}_l)$. If $\widetilde{m}_i \in (-\lfloor \frac{q}{4} \rfloor, \lfloor \frac{q}{4} \rfloor)$, let $m_i = 0$; otherwise $m_i = 1$.

Correctness: The decryption algorithm is divided into two levels, the first level is the normal standard ciphertext $\mathbb{C}_1 = (\omega_1 A + \omega_2, \omega_1 P + \omega_3 + m \lfloor \frac{q}{2} \rfloor)$ can be decrypted by the operation $\mathbb{C}_1 \begin{pmatrix} S \\ I \end{pmatrix}$ to obtain the plaintext message M, specifically,

$$\mathbb{C}_1 \begin{pmatrix} S \\ I \end{pmatrix} = \omega_1 R + \omega_2 S + \omega_3 + m \lfloor \frac{q}{2} \rfloor$$

we would get the correct message M when the error term $\omega_1 R + \omega_2 S + \omega_3$ is small enough.

For the second level is re-encryption ciphertext $\eta_1 [A | P_B] + [\eta_2 | \eta_3] + \mathbb{C}_2 \cdot \Omega$ can be decrypted by the private key of Bob S_B. This process is approximately same as the decryption process of Alice, specifically:

$$(\eta_1 [A | P_B] + [\eta_2 | \eta_3] + \mathbb{C}_2 \cdot \Omega) \begin{pmatrix} S_B \\ I \end{pmatrix}$$

$$= \underbrace{\eta_1 (A S_B + P_B) + \eta_2 S_B + \eta_3}_{noise_1} + \mathbb{C}_2 \cdot \Omega \cdot \begin{pmatrix} S_B \\ I \end{pmatrix} \quad (1)$$

where

$$\mathbb{C}_2 \cdot \Omega \cdot \begin{pmatrix} S_B \\ I \end{pmatrix}$$

$$= (\mathsf{BitD}(c_1), c_2 Y_1$$

$$+ m \lfloor \frac{q}{2} \rfloor) \begin{pmatrix} \mathsf{PowersOf2}(S_A) Y_2 + \varpi_1 + \varpi_2 \\ I \end{pmatrix} \quad (2)$$

$$= \underbrace{c_1 S_A Y_2 + \mathsf{BitD}(c_1) \varpi_1 + \mathsf{BitD}(c_1) \varpi_2 + c_2 Y_1}_{noise_2}$$

$$+ m \lfloor \frac{q}{2} \rfloor \quad (3)$$

so we get formula below from (1)

$$(\eta_1[A|P_B] + [\eta_2|\eta_3] + \mathbb{C}_2 \cdot \Omega)\begin{pmatrix} S_B \\ I \end{pmatrix}$$

$$= (noise_1) + (noise_2) + m\left\lfloor \frac{q}{2} \right\rfloor \tag{4}$$

Theorem 2 *(Correctness). Let q, n, s be as in the scheme, and ρ be the error of decryption per message symbol. For correctness of our proxy re-encryption scheme, we need $s \leqslant \dfrac{\sqrt{2}q\pi}{4\sqrt{\ln(\frac{2}{\rho})}(c \cdot s\sqrt{4n} + \sqrt{4\pi nk + 2\pi l + 4\pi})}.$*

Proof. It suffices to check correctness of the transformed ciphertexts, since the $noise_1 + noise_2$ is bigger than that in original ones. Continuing the main re-encryption scheme, let us now check the decryption of transformed ciphertexts of $\mathbb{C}_2$, which is

$$\underbrace{\eta_1(AS_B + P_B) + \eta_2 S_B + \eta_3}_{noise_1}$$

$$+ \underbrace{c_1 S_A Y_2 + \mathsf{BitD}(c_1)\varpi_1 + \mathsf{BitD}(c_1)\varpi_2 + c_2 Y_1}_{noise_2} + m\left\lfloor \frac{q}{2} \right\rfloor$$

$$= \underbrace{\eta_1 R_B + \eta_2 S_B + \eta_3}_{\tilde{noise_1}} + noise_2 + m\left\lfloor \frac{q}{2} \right\rfloor$$

where

$$noise_2 = (\omega_1 R + \omega_2 S + \omega_3 + m\left\lfloor \frac{q}{2} \right\rfloor)Y + \mathsf{BitD}(c_1)\varpi_1$$

$$+ \mathsf{BitD}(c_1)\varpi_2,$$

$$|Y| = max\{|Y_1|, |Y_2|\}.$$

The $noise_1 + noise_2$ can be written as the inner product of two vectors

$$e = (\eta_1, \eta_2, \eta_3, \omega_1, \omega_2, \omega_3 Y, \left\lfloor \frac{q}{2} \right\rfloor Y, \varpi_{1,1},$$

$$\cdots, \varpi_{1,nk}\varpi_{2,1}, \cdots, \varpi_{2,nk})$$

and

$$x = (r_B, s_B, 010_{1\times l}, r_A Y, s_A Y, 010_{1\times l},$$

$$1_{1\times l}, 1_{1\times nk}, 1_{1\times nk})$$

in which $010_{1\times l}$ stands for a vector of length l with all 0's except one 1; $1_{1\times l}$ for a vector of length l with all 1's (Suppose $\mathsf{BitD}(c_1)$ and m contains all 1's). We have $e \in \psi_s^{1\times(4n+2nk+3l)}$ and $|x| \leqslant |(r_B, s_B, r_A Y, s_A Y)| + \sqrt{2nk + 2 + l}$ in which $(r_B, s_B, r_A Y, s_A Y) \in \psi_s^{1\times 4n}$. Applying Lemma 1, we have $|x| \leqslant \frac{c \cdot s\sqrt{4n}}{\sqrt{2\pi}} + \sqrt{2nk + l + 2}$ with high probability.

We now use Lemma 2 with x and $e \in \psi_s^{1 \times (4n + 2nk + 3l)}$. Let ρ be the error per message symbol in decryption, we set $2 \cdot e^{-\pi T^2} = \rho$, so $T = \frac{\sqrt{ln(\frac{2}{\rho})}}{\sqrt{\pi}}$. For correctness, we need $Ts|x| \leqslant \frac{q}{4}$, which holds true provide that

$$\frac{\sqrt{ln(\frac{2}{\rho})}}{\sqrt{\pi}} \cdot s \cdot (\frac{c \cdot s\sqrt{4n}}{\sqrt{2\pi}} + \sqrt{2nk + l + 2}) \leqslant \frac{q}{4}$$

then we have

$$s \leqslant \frac{\sqrt{2}q\pi}{4\sqrt{ln(\frac{2}{\rho})}(c \cdot s\sqrt{4n} + \sqrt{4\pi nk + 2\pi l + 4\pi})}$$

as claimed.

Theorem 3 (*CPA security*). *Our PRE scheme is CPA-secure under the $LWE(n+ql, n, \alpha, q)$ assumption. Here q is the maximum number of re-encryption key queries that the adversary $\mathcal{A}$ can make.*

Proof. We consider that an adversary attack our PRE scheme. Then our scheme could be reduced to the LWE hard problem through a series of games. Let $Game_0$ be the interactions which in accordance with the Definition 1 between the adversary $\mathcal{A}$ and the challenger. In the original game, $PP = (q, n, A)$ and we mark the notation that HU is Honest User, CU is Corrupted User. Challenger makes the key pair of user P_i, S_i, where $P_i = R_i - AS_i$, R_i, S_i is Gaussian noise matrix. The re-encryption key from user i to user j $rk_{i \to j}$ is $(P_i, \Omega_{i \to j})$, where

$$\Omega_{i \to j} = \begin{bmatrix} X_{ij} & -X_{ij} + \varpi_1 + \mathsf{PowersOf2}(S_i)Y + \varpi_2 \\ 0 & I \end{bmatrix}$$

the X_{ij}, ϖ_1 are generated by user j, the Y, ϖ_2 are generated by user i. Therefore the challenge ciphertext of user i^* is $\mathbb{C}_1^* = (c_1^*, c_1^*) = (\omega_1^* A + \omega_2^*, \omega_1^* P^* + \omega_3^* + m_b \cdot \lfloor \frac{q}{2} \rfloor)$, where $\omega_1^*, \omega_2^*, \omega_3^*$ are Gaussian noise vectors, and P^* is challenge public key.

We mark Honest User with symbol $\Upsilon_H = 1, \cdots, N$ in order to express convenience. We design a series of games, each of which has small modifications compared to the previous game. The $Game_k$ and $Game_k - 1$ are equal for honest participant $k \in \Upsilon_H$ in $Game_{1 \leqslant K \leqslant N}$ except for the following

- $P_K = R_K - AS_K$ in $Game_{k-1}$ would be changed into P_K' in $Game_k$ which is random matrix from user i to user k.
- The re-encryption key $rk_{i \to k} = (P_k', \Omega_{ik} = \begin{pmatrix} X_{ik} & -X_{ik}S_k + \varpi_1 + \mathsf{PowersOf2}(S_i)Y + \varpi_2 \\ 0 & I \end{pmatrix})$ in $Game_{k-1}$ would be changed into $rk_{i \to k} = (P_k', \Omega_{ik}' = \begin{pmatrix} X_{ik} & R_{ik} + R_i' \\ 0 & I \end{pmatrix})$, where $X_{ik}, R_{ik} + R_i'$ are uniformly random matrix.

- When the adversary $\mathcal{A}$ makes a re-encryption query, the challenger returns a random vector $\delta \in \mathbb{Z}_q^{1 \times (n+l)}$ to the adversary $\mathcal{A}$.
- The challenge ciphertext in $Game_{final}$ would be changed into

$$\begin{cases} c_1^* = r_1^* \\ c_2^* = r_2^* + m_b \left\lfloor \dfrac{q}{2} \right\rfloor \end{cases}$$

which is the difference in the $Game_N$.

The challenger hides the information of bit b from the adversary $\mathcal{A}$ through this manner basically. So the probability of $b' = b$ is $\frac{1}{2}$, where b' is the adversary 's guess. Therefore the advantage of the adversary $\mathcal{A}$ in $Game_{final}$ is 0.

Now we need to show that there is no distinction between the above games provided by the challenger from the view of the adversary.

First, the change from $Game_{k-1}$ to $Game_k$ is that

$$\begin{cases} P_k = R_k - AS_k \rightarrow P_k' \\ R_{ik} = -X_{ik}S_k + E_{ik} \rightarrow R_{ik}' \end{cases} \quad P_k', R_{ik}' \text{ are random matrix.}$$

The indistinguishability of the two games is guaranteed by the LWE hard problem, since the S_k is privacy. In this from

$$\begin{pmatrix} A \\ \vdots \\ X_{ik} \\ \vdots \end{pmatrix}, -\begin{pmatrix} A \\ \vdots \\ X_{ik} \\ \vdots \end{pmatrix} S_k + \begin{pmatrix} R_k \\ \vdots \\ E_{ik} \\ \vdots \end{pmatrix}$$

All re-encryption key queries are correspond to serial number i. Here we depend on the $LWE(n, n, \alpha, q)$ hard problem. The change of $f_1[A|P_k'] + [f_2|f_3]$ is also random when the adversary ask the re-encryption query under the LWE hypothesis. The change of last step from $Game_N$ to $Game_{final}$ involving the conversion of $\begin{pmatrix} c_1^* = \omega_1^* A + \omega_2^* \\ c_2^* = \omega_1^* p^* + \omega_3^* \end{pmatrix}$ to random vectors. The confidentiality is also depend on the LWE hypothesis where the private key e_1^* is privacy.

$$[(A|P^*) \, (\omega_1^*[A|P^*] + [\omega_2^*|\omega_3^*])]$$

where p^* is pseudorandom, and parameters in above LWE hypothesis is $LWE(n + l, n, \alpha, q)$ as the statement in the above theorem.

Theorem 4 *(Key Privacy). We state that the above scheme is key-privacy under the LWE assumption. That is to say, the proxy re-encryption key would not disclose the information of identity of the delegators and delegatees.*

Proof. Here we adopt the heuristic method to prove the key-privacy of the above scheme. To begin with the proxy re-encryption key includes the following privacy information: the private key $sk_B = S_B$ of Bob stores in form of $-XS_B + \varpi_1$, and the private key $sk_A = S_A$ of Bob stores in form of $-S_A Y + \varpi_2$.

The re-encryption key is pseudorandom if the sk_B or sk_A is privacy. In other words, both Alice and Bob do not need to be honest simultaneously.

The randomness of $rk_{A \to B}$ would not be affected even if one of them is corrupted, as long as the two parties are not corrupted at the same time (there is no significance for the two parties are corrupted). So the above scheme enjoys the property that anonymizes the delegators and delegatees, since the P_B is pseudorandom and is not related with the identity of Bob. (In addition, even if the P_B concerns the identity of Bob, we just need to get rid of P_B from $rk_{A \to B}$. Because the role of P_B is to act as a random value in the $Re - encryption$ algorithm. We definitely use a set of noise vectors $(f_1|f_2)$ which conforms to the requirement for error to substitute for $\eta_1[A|P_B] + [\eta_2|\eta_3]$.)

Intuition on Interactivity and Recipient-Anonymous. The generation process of re-encryption key $rk_{id_i \to id_j}$ depends upon secret key SK_{id_j} of user F_{id_j}, which means the process requires the participation of id_j, that is interactivity. Error term in re-encryption ciphertext stem from raw ciphertext which is random and unrelated to Bob, which is the recipient anonymous property.

Undirectionality. Essentially, this property is mainly to ensure that user id_i and proxy cannot through collusion to decrypt user id_j's ciphertexts. Intuitively, the information id_j provided is $(X, -XS_j + \varpi_1)$, where X, ϖ_1 are chosen by himself. Alice and proxy can only obtain this tuple, which is pseudo random based on the LWE hard problem, so the information is useless. Actually, neither $rk_{id_i \to id_j}$ is impossible to reverse, nor get it through the calculation method expect making use of d_j's secret information. So the information would not contribute to the directionality.

Strong Anti-collusion of PRE. Now we elaborate that why our scheme achieve strong anti-collusion rather than weak anti-collusion. The proxy has the re-encryption key $\begin{pmatrix} X & -XS_B + \varpi_1 + \mathsf{PowersOf2}(S_A)Y_2 + \varpi_2 \\ 0 & I \end{pmatrix}$ and the delegatee has his private key, then they conspire to compute

$$\begin{pmatrix} X & -XS_B + \varpi_1 + \mathsf{PowersOf2}(S_A)Y_2 + \varpi_2 \\ 0 & I \end{pmatrix} \begin{pmatrix} S_B \\ I \end{pmatrix}$$

$$= \begin{pmatrix} \mathsf{PowersOf2}(S_A)Y_2 + \varpi_1 + \varpi_2 \\ I \end{pmatrix}$$

where $Y_2 \in \psi_x^{l \times l}, \varpi_1, \varpi_2 \in \psi_s^{nk \times l}$. Using the formula given above, it can be seen that the proxy and delegatee could not obtain the approximate value about the private key S_A because of the presence of Y_2.

4   Conclusion

In this paper we have improved the proxy re-encryption scheme in Aono [9], enabled it to resist collusion attack which is very important in the network protocol. And we maintain the good properties of key privacy, unidirectionality etc. Our new PRE scheme is CPA security in the standard model, and its security could be reduced to LWE hard problem in lattices.

Acknowledgments. This work is supported by NSFC (Grant No. 61502044).

References

1. Agrawal, S., Boyen, X.: Identity-based encryption from lattices in the standard model. Manuscript, July 2009
2. Micciancio, D., Peikert, C.: Trapdoors for lattices: simpler, tighter, faster, smaller. In: Pointcheval, D., Johansson, T. (eds.) EUROCRYPT 2012. LNCS, vol. 7237, pp. 700–718. Springer, Heidelberg (2012). https://doi.org/10.1007/978-3-642-29011-4_41
3. Agrawal, S., Boneh, D., Boyen, X.: Efficient lattice (H)IBE in the standard model. In: Gilbert, H. (ed.) EUROCRYPT 2010. LNCS, vol. 6110, pp. 553–572. Springer, Heidelberg (2010). https://doi.org/10.1007/978-3-642-13190-5_28
4. Blaze, M., Bleumer, G., Strauss, M.: Divertible protocols and atomic proxy cryptography. In: Nyberg, K. (ed.) EUROCRYPT 1998. LNCS, vol. 1403, pp. 127–144. Springer, Heidelberg (1998). https://doi.org/10.1007/BFb0054122
5. Shamir, A.: How to share a secret. Commun. ACM **22**, 612–613 (1979)
6. Singh, K., Rangan, C.P., Banerjee, A.K.: Lattice based identity based proxy re-encryption scheme. J. Internet Serv. Inf. Secur. **3**(3/4), 38–51 (2013)
7. Kirshanova, E.: Proxy re-encryption from lattices. In: Krawczyk, H. (ed.) PKC 2014. LNCS, vol. 8383, pp. 77–94. Springer, Heidelberg (2014). https://doi.org/10.1007/978-3-642-54631-0_5
8. Chu, C.-K., Tzeng, W.-G.: Identity-based proxy re-encryption without random oracles. In: Garay, J.A., Lenstra, A.K., Mambo, M., Peralta, R. (eds.) ISC 2007. LNCS, vol. 4779, pp. 189–202. Springer, Heidelberg (2007). https://doi.org/10.1007/978-3-540-75496-1_13
9. Aono, Y., Boyen, X., Phong, L.T., Wang, L.: Key-private proxy re-encryption under LWE. In: Paul, G., Vaudenay, S. (eds.) INDOCRYPT 2013. LNCS, vol. 8250, pp. 1–18. Springer, Cham (2013). https://doi.org/10.1007/978-3-319-03515-4_1
10. Green, M., Ateniese, G.: Identity-based proxy re-encryption. In: Katz, J., Yung, M. (eds.) ACNS 2007. LNCS, vol. 4521, pp. 288–306. Springer, Heidelberg (2007). https://doi.org/10.1007/978-3-540-72738-5_19
11. Jiang, Z., Zhenfeng, Z., Chen, Y.: PRE: stronger security notions and efficient construction with non-interactive opening. Theor. Comput. Sci. **542**, 1–16 (2014)
12. Canetti, R., Hohenberger, S.: Chosen-ciphertext secure proxy re-encryption. In: Proceedings of the 14th ACM Conference on Computer and Communications Security, pp. 185–194 (2007)
13. Gentry, C., Peikert, C., Vaikuntanathan, V.: Trapdoors for hard lattices and new cryptographic constructions. In: Proceedings of the 40th Annual ACM Symposium on Theory of Computing, pp. 197–206 (2008)
14. Cash, D., Hofheinz, D., Kiltz, E.: How to delegate a lattice basis. IACR Cryptology ePrint Archive, p. 351 (2009)
15. Micciancio, D., Regev, O.: Lattice-based cryptography. In: Bernstein, D.J., Buchmann, J., Dahmen, E. (eds.) Post-Quantum Cryptography, pp. 147–191. Springer, Heidelberg (2009). https://doi.org/10.1007/978-3-540-88702-7_5

16. Xagawa, D.K.: Cryptography with lattices (2010)
17. Daniele, M., Goldwasser, S.: Complexity of Lattice Problems: A Cryptographic Perspective. Springer, Boston (2002). https://doi.org/10.1007/978-1-4615-0897-7
18. Ajtai, M.: Generating hard instances of lattice problems. In: Proceedings of the Twenty-Eighth Annual ACM Symposium on Theory of Computing, pp. 99–108 (1996)
19. Regev, O.: On lattices, learning with errors, random linear codes, and cryptography. J. ACM (JACM) **56**(6), 34 (2009)
20. Cramer, R., Damgård, I.: On the amortized complexity of zero-knowledge protocols. In: Halevi, S. (ed.) CRYPTO 2009. LNCS, vol. 5677, pp. 177–191. Springer, Heidelberg (2009). https://doi.org/10.1007/978-3-642-03356-8_11
21. Micciancio, D., Regev, O.: Worst-case to average-case reductions based on Gaussian measures. In: Proceedings - Annual IEEE Symposium on Foundations of Computer Science, pp. 372–381 (2004)
22. Ateniese Giuseppe, F., Kevin, G.M., Susan, H.: Improved proxy re-encryption schemes with applications to secure distributed storage. ACM Trans. Inf. Syst. Secur. (TISSEC) **9**(1), 1–30 (2006)
23. Ateniese, G., Benson, K., Hohenberger, S.: Key-private proxy re-encryption. In: Fischlin, M. (ed.) CT-RSA 2009. LNCS, vol. 5473, pp. 279–294. Springer, Heidelberg (2009). https://doi.org/10.1007/978-3-642-00862-7_19
24. Libert, B., Vergnaud, D.: Unidirectional chosen-ciphertext secure proxy re-encryption. In: Cramer, R. (ed.) PKC 2008. LNCS, vol. 4939, pp. 360–379. Springer, Heidelberg (2008). https://doi.org/10.1007/978-3-540-78440-1_21
25. Diffie, W., Hellman, M.: New directions in cryptography. IEEE Trans. Inf. Theory **22**(6), 644–654 (1976)
26. Rivest, R.L., Shamir, A., Adleman, L.: A method for obtaining digital signatures and public-key cryptosystems. Commun. ACM **21**(2), 120–126 (1978)
27. Shor, P.W.: Polynomial-time algorithms for prime factorization and discrete logarithms on a quantum computer. SIAM Rev. **41**(2), 303–332 (1999)
28. Wojciech, B.: New bounds in some transference theorems in the geometry of numbers. Mathematische Annalen **296**(1), 625–635 (1993)
29. Wojciech, B.: Inequalities for convex bodies and polar reciprocal lattices in R^n. Discret. Comput. Geom. **13**(1), 217–231 (1995)
30. Waters, B.: Efficient identity-based encryption without random oracles. In: Cramer, R. (ed.) EUROCRYPT 2005. LNCS, vol. 3494, pp. 114–127. Springer, Heidelberg (2005). https://doi.org/10.1007/11426639_7
31. Weng, J., Deng, R.H., Liu, S., Chen, K.: Chosen-ciphertext secure bidirectional proxy re-encryption schemes without pairings. Inf. Sci. **180**(24), 5077–5089 (2010)
32. Xagawa, K., Tanaka, K.: Proxy re-encryption based on learning with errors. In: Proceedings of the 2010 Symposium on Cryptography and Information Security, pp. 29–35 (2010)
33. Nunez, D., Agudo, I., Lopez, J.: NTRUReEncrypt: an efficient proxy re-encryption scheme based on NTRU. In: Proceedings of the 10th ACM Symposium on Information, Computer and Communications Security, pp. 179–189 (2015)
34. Brakerski, Z., Gentry, C., Vaikuntanathan, V.: (Leveled) fully homomorphic encryption without bootstrapping. ACM Trans. Comput. Theory (TOCT) **6**(3), 13 (2014)
35. Singh, K., Rangan, C.P., Banerjee, A.K.: Cryptanalysis of unidirectional proxy re-encryption scheme. In: Linawati, M.M.S., Neuhold, E.J., Tjoa, A.M., You, I. (eds.) ICT-EurAsia 2014. LNCS, vol. 8407, pp. 564–575. Springer, Heidelberg (2014). https://doi.org/10.1007/978-3-642-55032-4_58

36. Kim, K.S., Jeong, I.R.: Collusion-resistant unidirectional proxy re-encryption scheme from lattices. J. Commun. Netw. **18**(1), 1–7 (2016)
37. Nuñez, D., et al.: Proxy re-encryption: analysis of constructions and its application to secure access delegation. J. Netw. Comput. Appl. **87**, 193–209 (2017)
38. Shao, J.: SCCR: a generic approach to simultaneously achieve CCA security and collusion resistance in proxy re encryption. Secur. Commun. Netw. **4**(2), 122–135 (2011)
39. Zhang, L., Ma, H., Liu, Z., Dong, E.: Security analysis and improvement of a collusion-resistant identity-based proxy re-encryption scheme. In: Barolli, L., Xhafa, F., Yim, K. (eds.) BWCCA 2016. LNDECT, vol. 2, pp. 839–846. Springer, Cham (2017). https://doi.org/10.1007/978-3-319-49106-6_86
40. Lu, Y., Li, J.: A pairing-free certificate-based proxy re-encryption scheme for secure data sharing in public clouds. Future Gener. Comput. Syst. **62**, 140–147 (2016)
41. Ge, C.: Identity-based conditional proxy re-encryption with fine grain policy. Comput. Stand. Interfaces **52**, 1–9 (2017)

Hierarchical Secret Sharing Schemes Secure Against Rushing Adversary: Cheater Identification and Robustness

Partha Sarathi Roy[1](✉), Sabyasachi Dutta[2], Kirill Morozov[3],
Avishek Adhikari[4], Kazuhide Fukushima[1], Shinsaku Kiyomoto[1],
and Kouichi Sakurai[5]

[1] Information Security Laboratory, KDDI Research, Inc., Fujimino, Japan
{pa-roy,ka-fukushima,kiyomoto}@kddi-research.jp
[2] R. C. Bose Centre for Cryptology and Security, Indian Statistical Institute,
Kolkata, India
saby.math@gmail.com
[3] Department of Computer Science and Engineering, University of North Texas,
Denton, USA
Kirill.Morozov@unt.edu
[4] Department of Pure Mathematics, University of Calcutta, Kolkata, India
avishek.adh@gmail.com
[5] Faculty of Information Science and Electrical Engineering, Kyushu University,
Fukuoka, Japan
sakurai@inf.kyushu-u.ac.jp

Abstract. Threshold access structures of secret sharing schemes capture a scenario in which all the participants have the same weight (or power) and their contributions are equal. However, in some situations such as gradation among officials in an organization, the participants have different weights. Hierarchical access structures capture those natural scenarios, where different levels of hierarchy are present and a participant belongs precisely to one of them. Although an extensive research addressing the issues of cheater identifiability and robustness have been done for threshold secret sharing, no such research has been carried out for hierarchical secret sharing (HSS). This paper resolves this long-standing open issue by presenting definitions and constructions of both cheater identifiable and robust HSS schemes secure against *rushing* adversary, in the information-theoretic setting.

Keywords: Hierarchical secret sharing · Cheater identification
Robustness · Rushing adversary · Multi-receiver authentication code
Universal hash function

The second author is grateful to the NICT, Japan for granting a financial support under the NICT International Exchange Program.

© Springer Nature Switzerland AG 2018
C. Su and H. Kikuchi (Eds.): ISPEC 2018, LNCS 11125, pp. 578–594, 2018.
https://doi.org/10.1007/978-3-319-99807-7_37

1   Introduction

Secret sharing is a process that allows to store secret information in a distributed manner among several "participants" (e.g., humans, clouds, computers). Traditional threshold secret sharing schemes do not address the problem of sharing a secret when there is a gradation among the participants. Hierarchical secret sharing (HSS) realize access structures where different levels of hierarchy are present and a participant belongs precisely to one of the levels. Two initial solutions for HSS were proposed by Shamir [17] and Kothari [10]. In Shamir's approach, the participants, who belong to higher level in the hierarchy, possess more shares. In Kothari's solution, participants are grouped in different sets that require to multiple instantiations of secret sharing schemes. Disjunctive HSS as introduced by Simmons in [18], is the first approach that used only one instantiation of a secret sharing scheme. However, his scheme is not *ideal*, where ideal means that the size of shares and secret are the same. Brickell [4] provided two ideal schemes for disjunctive HSS, however both of them are inefficient. One of the schemes suffers from the same problem as that of Simmons', while the other scheme requires to find an algebraic number satisfying an irreducible polynomial over a finite field. Later, Ghodosi et al. [9] presented efficient constructions. Finally, in [19] Tassa further advanced this line of research by providing an efficient disjunctive secret sharing scheme based on the Birkoff interpolation. The main difference between the works of [9,19] is that in the former one, the secret recovery is deterministic whereas for the latter the secret is recovered except with small probability. Authors in [3,20] also considered secret sharing for disjunctive hierarchical access structure.

In its basic form, a secret sharing scheme deals with *semi-honest* adversaries who do not deviate from the protocol but are interested in gathering more information than they are supposed to. In order to encompass more realistic scenarios, it is required to consider *malicious* adversaries who can deviate from the protocol in an arbitrary way. Moreover, most schemes known so far implicitly assume existence of *synchronous network*, and they do not deal with cheating by *rushing* cheaters who may submit their shares *after* observing shares of honest users. In presence of malicious participants—also called *cheaters*—it is *not guaranteed* that all the shares submitted in the reconstruction phase are correct. At the end of the reconstruction phase, several issues may occur, in particular: an incorrect secret may be reconstructed or the secret may not be reconstructed at all. Therefore, it is an important issue to safeguard the interest of honest participants in presence of malicious participants. Many cheater identifiable schemes for threshold access structure are proposed, e.g., [2,7,11,12,15,23]. *However, none of these approaches provides cheater identification for hierarchical access structure.* Note that cheater identifiable schemes do not guarantee recovery of the secret, focusing—as the name suggests—on exposure of malicious participants. On the contrary, robust secret sharing schemes do guarantee reconstruction of the secret. During the last three decades, many results on robust secret sharing have been published, e.g., [1,6,8,12–14] in case of threshold access structure. *None of these approaches deals with robustness for hierarchical access structure.*

Recently, Traverso et al. [21] proposed verifiable HSS scheme. However, their construction is not information-theoretic.

Our Contribution: In this paper, for the first time, we propose definition as well as *constructions* of *cheater identifiable* and *robust* secret sharing schemes realizing disjunctive hierarchical access structure secure against *rushing* adversary. In order to construct our definition, we first propose a realistic model encompassing rushing adversaries. Our methodology is generic in the sense that it does not depend upon the underlying hierarchical secret sharing scheme. We provide two constructions for cheater identifiable HSS. Second construction significantly reduces the share size. We provide an estimation of the share sizes of the proposed schemes. Our constructions make use *universal hash functions* and *multi-receiver authentication codes*.

Organization of the Paper: In Sect. 2, the necessary prerequisites for the proposed construction are provided. In Sect. 3, we propose the definition and constructions of cheater identifiable HSS along with the cheating model. In Sect. 4, definition and construction of Robust HSS are proposed and finally we conclude in Sect. 5.

2   Preliminaries

To start with, let us first describe some basic terminologies and building blocks.

2.1   Hierarchical Secret Sharing

We begin with the definition of disjunctive hierarchical access structure [19] on a set $\mathcal{P} = \{P_1, P_2, \ldots, P_n\}$ of n participants.

Definition 1. *Let a set of participants $\mathcal{P} = \{P_1, \ldots, P_n\}$ be composed of l disjoint levels $\mathcal{L}_1, \mathcal{L}_2, \ldots, \mathcal{L}_l$ such that $\mathcal{P} = \cup_{i=1}^{l} \mathcal{L}_i$, where $\mathcal{L}_i \cap \mathcal{L}_j = \emptyset$ for all $1 \leq i \neq j \leq l$. With each level $\mathcal{L}_i$ a positive integer (threshold) t_i is associated such that $t_1 < t_2 < \cdots < t_l$ and $|\mathcal{L}_i| = n_i \geq t_i + 1$. A disjunctive hierarchical access structure, denoted by $\bigsqcup_{i=1}^{l} (t_i, n_i)_{\mathcal{P}}$ is completely defined by the collection of minimal qualified sets $\mathcal{Q}_{min} \subset 2^{\mathcal{P}}$ where $U \in \mathcal{Q}_{min}$ means either*

- *U contains exactly $t_j + 1$ members from $\mathcal{L}_j$ for some $1 \leq j \leq l$ or*
- *if $j = max\{i : U \cap \mathcal{L}_i \neq \emptyset\}$ then U contains precisely $t_j + 1$ many members from $\cup_{i=1}^{j} \mathcal{L}_i$ such that for every k, $1 \leq k \leq j - 1$, $|U \cap (\cup_{i=1}^{k} \mathcal{L}_i)| \leq t_k$.*

Any subset of participants that contains at least one minimal qualified set is a qualified set. Collection of qualified sets will be denoted with Γ.

Note: We call a level $\mathcal{L}_i$ *higher* than another level $\mathcal{L}_j$ if and only if $i < j$. Another point we want to mention here is that by (t, n)-threshold secret sharing scheme we mean that any $t + 1$ many parties are able to recover the secret but t many can not.

Next we define maximal forbidden sets for disjunctive hierarchical access structures which are important to carry out the security analysis. We keep the same notations as above for the rest of the paper.

Definition 2. *A subset $F \subset \mathcal{P}$ is called maximal forbidden set if the following conditions hold*

1. if l is the maximum of levels then $|F| = t_l$ and also
2. $|F \cap \mathcal{L}_i| \leq t_i$ for all $1 \leq i \leq l$.

We will denote the cardinality of maximal forbidden set by t_{max}.

We are now in a position to define secret sharing for a disjunctive hierarchical access structure $\bigsqcup_{i=1}^{l}(t_i, n_i)_{\mathcal{P}}$ on a set $\mathcal{P} = \{P_1, \ldots, P_n\}$ of n participants.

Definition 3. *A perfectly secure disjunctive HSS scheme for $\bigsqcup_{i=1}^{l}(t_i, n_i)_{\mathcal{P}}$ consists of two algorithms, viz., sharing algorithm $\overline{\mathsf{ShareGen}}$ and reconstruction algorithm $\overline{\mathsf{Reconst}}$. The share generation algorithm $\overline{\mathsf{ShareGen}}$ takes a secret $s \in \mathcal{S}$ as input and outputs a list $(v_1, v_2, \ldots, v_n)$. Each $v_i \in \mathcal{V}_i$ is called a share and is given to a party P_i. In a usual setting, $\overline{\mathsf{ShareGen}}$ is invoked by the dealer. The secret reconstruction algorithm $\overline{\mathsf{Reconst}}$ takes a list of shares and outputs a secret $s \in \mathcal{S}$. A hierarchical secret sharing scheme $\mathbf{HSS} = (\overline{\mathsf{ShareGen}}, \overline{\mathsf{Reconst}})$ is called perfect if the following two conditions are satisfied for the output $(v_1, \ldots, v_n)$ of $\mathsf{ShareGen}(\hat{s})$ where the probabilities are taken over the random tape of $\mathsf{ShareGen}$.*

1. if $\{P_{i_1}, \ldots, P_{i_t}\} \in \mathcal{Q}_{min}$ then $\Pr[\overline{\mathsf{Reconst}}(v_{i_1}, \ldots, v_{i_t}) = \hat{s}] = 1$,
2. if $\{P_{i_1}, \ldots, P_{i_k}\}$ is a forbidden set then $\Pr[\hat{s} = s \mid \mathcal{V}_{i_1} = v_{i_1}, \ldots, \mathcal{V}_{i_k} = v_{i_k}] = \Pr[\hat{s} = s]$ for any $s \in \mathcal{S}$.

2.2 Strongly Universal Family of Hash Function

Here, we will review the definitions and constructions of strongly universal families of hash function [5,22].

Definition 4. *A family of hash functions $H : A \rightarrow B$ is called ϵ almost strongly universal family of hash functions (ϵ-ASU_2 for short) if it satisfies following two conditions:*

1. $|\{h \mid h \in H, h(a) = b\}| = |H|/|B|$ holds for any $a \in A$ and for any $b \in B$.
2. For any distinct $a, a' \in A$ and for any $b, b' \in B$, the following equality holds:

$$\frac{|\{h \mid h \in H, h(a) = b, h(a') = b'\}|}{|\{h \mid h \in H, h(a) = b\}|} \leq \epsilon.$$

*H is called **strongly** universal family of hash functions (SU_2 for short) if $\epsilon = 1/|B|$.*

We specify an element of a hash family H by associating it with a key e and use a notation h_e to denote an element of H specified by the key e. It is obvious that the number of keys is equal to the size of hash family $|H|$.

Let $GF(q)$ denote the finite field with q elements.

Proposition 1. *The keyed hash family[1] $\mathcal{H} : GF(q)^n \rightarrow GF(q)^n$ defined by $\mathcal{H} = \{h_{(e_0,e_1,\ldots,e_n)} \mid e_0, e_i \in GF(q), 1 \leq i \leq n$ and $h_{(e_0,e_1,\ldots,e_n)}(s_1, s_2, \ldots, s_n) = (e_0.s_1 + e_1, e_0.s_2 + e_2, \ldots, e_0.s_n + e_n)\}$ is $1/q$-ASU$_2$. Furthermore, the family $\mathcal{H}$ can be used to authenticate n messages $s_1, s_2, \ldots, s_n \in GF(q)$.*

Proof. We present a simplified proof of the fact, give an upper bound and show how the bound can be achieved. First we observe that $|\mathcal{H}| = q^{n+1}$ as the keys $(e_0, e_1, \ldots, e_n)$ can be chosen in q^{n+1} ways. Now for any $c, d \in GF(q)^n$, $|\{h \in \mathcal{H} \mid h(c) = d\}| =$ number of keys $(e_0, \ldots, e_n)$ such that $(e_0.c_1 + e_1, e_0.c_2 + e_2, \ldots, e_0.c_n + e_n) = (d_1, \ldots, d_n)$. There are q choices for e_0 and for each choice there are unique choices for e_i's. Thus, $|\{h \in \mathcal{H} \mid h(c) = d\}| = q$ and hence the first condition of Definition 4 is satisfied. Now we observe that either there is a unique tuple of keys (equivalently, unique hash function) that takes c to d as well as c' to d' or there is none. In either case the second condition is satisfied with $\epsilon = \frac{1}{q}$. This proves the first part of our claim.

It remains to show that the family can be used to authenticate n messages $s_1, s_2, \ldots, s_n$.

The situation can be described as a game between a challenger $\mathcal{C}$ and an adversary $\mathcal{A}$ who is possibly computationally unbounded.

- **Set up:** $\mathcal{C}$ secretly chooses (randomly) $e_i \in_R GF(q)$ for $0 \leq i \leq n$ and computes $h_{(e_0,e_1,\ldots,e_n)}(s_1, s_2, \ldots, s_n) = (e_0.s_1 + e_1, e_0.s_2 + e_2, \ldots, e_0.s_n + e_n) = (a_1, a_2, \ldots, a_n)$.
- **Challenge Phase:** $\mathcal{C}$ gives the set of valid pairs $\{(s_1, a_1), (s_2, a_2), \ldots, (s_n, a_n)\}$ to $\mathcal{A}$.
- **Output Phase:** $\mathcal{A}$ outputs a set of message-tag pairs $\{(s'_1, a'_1), \ldots, (s'_n, a'_n)\}$ where $s'_i \neq s_i$ for all i. $\mathcal{A}$ wins if at least one of the pairs is a valid pair with respect to the keys chosen by $\mathcal{C}$ in the Set-up phase.

In the game described above the adversary wishes to substitute at least one "original" valid (*message, tag*) pair by a forged pair that passes the validity test. The substitution probability is $Pr[E_1|E_2]$ where the probability is computed over the randomness of the keys $e_0, e_1, \ldots, e_n$ and by E_1 we mean the event that "at least one forged message-tag pairs in $\{(s'_1, a'_1), \ldots, (s'_n, a'_n)\}$ is valid", and by E_2 the event that "$\{(s_1, a_1), \ldots, (s_n, a_n)\}$ are valid".

The adversary $\mathcal{A}$ views the following system of equations with unknowns $x, y_1, \ldots, y_n$.

$$x.s_1 + y_1 = a_1 \tag{1}$$

$$x.s_2 + y_2 = a_2 \tag{2}$$

$$\cdots = \cdots \tag{3}$$

$$x.s_n + y_n = a_n \tag{4}$$

---

[1] Family of hash function is adopted from [22]. But, the proof has been done independently to make compatible with the argument of the security proof of the proposed constructions.

Now for any fixed value of x, there exists one and only one solution for this system of equations. Thus, there are in total q solutions to the above system of equations as there are q many choices for x. More importantly, each possible value of the key x appears with equal probability in the view of the adversary $\mathcal{A}$.

If $\mathcal{A}$ outputs a pair (s_i', a_i') then a unique value of x (hence also for y_i) is determined from the equations $x.s_i + y_i = a_i$ and $x.s_i' + y_i = a_i'$. If this value matches with e_0 then $\mathcal{A}$ has successfully cheated the challenger $\mathcal{C}$ for the pair (s_i, a_i). But this happens with probability at most $\frac{1}{q}$, from the second condition of Definition 4. Now the above argument is true for all $i = 1, \ldots, n$ and thus from the **union bound** we see that for the entire game, $Pr[\mathcal{A}\ wins] \leq \frac{n}{q}$.

We now give a strategy for $\mathcal{A}$ such that the successful cheating probability achieves the upper bound. The strategy is to output a list $\mathcal{L} = \{r_1, r_2, \ldots, r_n : r_i \in \mathbb{F}_q\ and\ r_i \neq r_j\ \forall i \neq j\}$. Now the adversary outputs (s_i', a_i') assuming $x = r_i$ for $i = 1, 2, \ldots, n$. In this case, the probability of successful cheating is

$$Pr[\mathcal{A}\ wins] = 1 - \frac{\binom{q-1}{n}n!}{\binom{q}{n}n!} = \frac{n}{q}.$$ Hence, the proposition. $\square$

Remark 1. Following the above proposition we can see that given n many valid message-tag pairs the adversary can produce t many forged pairs with success probability at most $\frac{t}{q}$.

2.3   Unconditionally Secure Multi-Receiver Authentication Code

A Multi-Receiver Authentication (MRA) code involves one transmitter, one opponent and n receivers. When authenticating a source/message, the transmitter broadcasts a message to n receivers and each receiver verifies the authenticity of the message based on their own keys. If an MRA code ensures that neither the outside opponent nor the coalition of t receivers can deceive any other honest player, it is called a (t, n) MRA code. Safavi-Naini and Wang [16] gave construction of (t, n) MRA code to allow multiple messages to be authenticated with the same key. We briefly describe Safavi-Naini and Wang's construction [16] in Algorithm 1 and its property in Proposition 2.

– **Algorithm 1 ((t, n) MRA with w messages)**
  Assume that $q \geq w$, where w is the number of possible messages, and that $q \geq n$. The system consists of the following steps:
    1. **Key distribution:** The key distribution center (KDC) randomly generates $w + 1$ polynomials $g_0(x), g_1(x), \ldots, g_w(x)$ from $GF(q)[x]$ each of degree at most t and chooses n distinct elements $x_1, x_2, \ldots, x_n$ of $GF(q)$. KDC makes all x_i public and sends privately $(g_0(x), \ldots, g_w(x))$ to the sender T as her authentication key, and $e_i = (g_0(x_i), \ldots, g_w(x_i))$ to the receiver R_i as her verification key.
    2. **Broadcast:** For a message s, T computes $A_s(x) = g_0(x) + sg_1(x) + \cdots + s^w g_w(x)$ and broadcasts $(s, A_s(x))$.
    3. **Verification:** R_i accepts $(s, A_s(x))$ as authentic if $A_s(x_i) = g_0(x_i) + sg_1(x_i) + \cdots + s^w g_w(x_i)$.

Proposition 2. *Let $L = \{i_1, \ldots, i_t\}$ be the list of indices of the corrupt receivers, and let $e_L = \{e_{i_1}, \ldots, e_{i_t}\}$ be the verification keys for the corrupt receivers. The maximal probability that t corrupt receivers and/or the outside opponent succeed in deceiving any receiver R_j is*

$$\max_{e_L} \max_{(s_{w+1}, As_{w+1}(x))} \Pr[R_j accepts(s_{w+1}, As_{w+1}(x)) | e_L, A_{s_1}(x), \ldots, A_{s_w}(x)] = 1/q,$$

for any choice of $(s_i, A_{s_i}(x))$ $(i = 1, \ldots, w)$ with $s_{w+1} \neq s_i$ for $i = 1, \ldots, w$; for any choice of $g_0(x), \ldots, g_w(x)$ from $GF(q)[x]$ each of degree at most t, and for any choice of $L = \{i_1, \ldots, i_t\} \subseteq [n] \setminus \{j\}$.

3   Hierarchical Secret Sharing: Cheater Identification

In this section we first fix the model and definitions of cheater identification in the hierarchical setting. We then give two constructions of cheater identifiable hierarchical secret sharing schemes.

3.1   Hierarchical Secret Sharing with Cheater Identification Against Rushing Cheater (HSSCI)

In order to define the cheating model, we first formally describe maximal cheating sets against which cheating identification is possible.

Definition 5. *We recursively define maximal cheating sets as follows:*

- *Maximal cheating set for Level 1: The collection of all possible cheating sets is defined as $\mathcal{C}_1 = \{C_1 \subset \mathcal{P}_1 : |C_1| \leq \frac{t_1}{2}\}$. A maximal element C_1^{max} of this collection is called a maximal cheating set for level 1.*
- *Maximal cheating set for Level i: For level $2 \leq i \leq l$, the collection of all possible cheating sets is defined as $\mathcal{C}_i = \{F_1 \cup \ldots \cup F_{i-1} \cup C_i : F_j \subset \mathcal{P}_j \forall 1 \leq j \leq i-1, |F_j| \leq t_j, C_i \subset \mathcal{P}_i$ and $|F_1 \cup \ldots \cup F_{i-1} \cup C_i| \leq \frac{t_i}{2}\}$. A maximal element C_i^{max} of this collection is called a maximal cheating set for level i. That is, $C_i^{max} \in \mathcal{C}_i$ and $C_i^{max} = \frac{t_i}{2}$.*

Note that, $F_1, F_2, \ldots, F_{i-1}$ can be empty so that C_i^{max} can contain exactly $\frac{t_i}{2}$ members of level i only.

Remark 2. We note that since l is the maximum of all levels then a maximal cheating set C_l^{max} for level l is a maximal cheating set over all the levels. We will denote the cardinality of maximal cheating set by k_{max}.

Remark 3. For l levels viz. $\mathcal{L}_1, \ldots, \mathcal{L}_l$ we observe that $k_{max} = \frac{t_l}{2}$ which denotes the maximum number of cheaters that can be tolerated. Let us consider a qualified subset of m participants come together to reconstruct the secret and $\mathcal{L}_{high}$ is the highest level in which a qualified set is formed by some or all of the m available participants. It is not hard to see that k_{max} can be even greater than m theoretically. So for correct reconstruction, we will consider only $\bar{k}_{max} = \frac{t_{high}}{2}$ cheaters where t_{high} denotes the threshold value corresponding to level $\mathcal{L}_{high}$ (see Construction 3.2).

The model of HSSCI consists of a share generation algorithm ShareGen and a secret reconstruction algorithm Reconst. ShareGen takes a secret as input and outputs a list of shares $(v_1, \ldots, v_n)$ and Reconst is modeled as interactive Turing machine, which interacts with users multiple times and they release a part of their shares to Reconst in each round. Therefore, Reconst takes round identifier rid, user identifier P_i, and part of share $v_i^{(rid)}$ and state information state_R as input and outputs (s, L), where L is a list of cheaters ($L = \emptyset$ if no cheater is identified), if Reconst detects cheating and honest participants do not form a qualified set, it outputs $(\perp, L)$, where "$\perp$" is a special symbol indicating failure of secret reconstruction.

Figure 1 models the interaction between participants and the reconstruction algorithm Reconst. Here, a pair of Turing machine $\mathcal{A} = (\mathcal{A}_1, \mathcal{A}_2)$ represents rushing cheaters $P_{i_1}, \ldots, P_{i_{\overline{k}_{max}}}$ who try to cheat honest participants $P_{i_{\overline{k}_{max}+1}}, \ldots, P_{i_m}$. In the $\mathsf{Game}^{\mathsf{Rushing}}(\mathbf{HSS}, \mathcal{A})$, $\mathcal{A}_1$ first chooses rushing cheaters $P_{i_1}, \ldots, P_{i_{\overline{k}_{max}}}$ to attack the participants $P_{i_{\overline{k}_{max}+1}}, \ldots, P_{i_m}$. Next, in each round, $\mathcal{A}_2$ determines the forged share, denoted by $(v_{i_1}'^{(rid)}, \ldots, v_{i_{\overline{k}_{max}}}'^{(rid)})$, to be submitted by rushing cheaters. Note that $\mathcal{A}_2$ takes shares $(v_{i_{\overline{k}_{max}+1}}^{(rid)}, \ldots, v_{i_m}^{(rid)})$ as input in determining forged shares, which captures the rushing capability of cheaters.

The cheater P_{i_j} submitting an invalid share succeeds, if Reconst fails to identify P_{i_j} as a cheater. The successful cheating probability of P_{i_j} against $\mathbf{HSS} = (\mathsf{ShareGen}, \mathsf{Reconst})$ is denoted as $\epsilon(\mathbf{HSS}, \mathcal{A}, P_{i_j})$ where the probability $\epsilon(\mathbf{HSS}, \mathcal{A}, P_{i_j})$ is defined by

$$\epsilon(\mathbf{HSS}, \mathcal{A}, P_{i_j}) = \Pr[(s', L) \leftarrow \mathsf{Reconst}(\cdot, \cdot, \mathsf{state}_R) : i_j \notin L].$$

Based on the above definition, we define the security of hierarchical secret sharing schemes capable of identifying cheaters, who submit forged shares as follows:

Definition 6. A $\bigsqcup_{i=1}^{l}(t_i, n_i)_{\mathcal{P}}$ $\mathbf{HSS} = (\mathsf{ShareGen}, \mathsf{Reconst})$ *is called a* $(\overline{k}_{max}, \epsilon)$ *cheater identifiable HSS scheme, if:*

(1) $\epsilon(\mathbf{HSS}, \mathcal{A}, P_j) \leq \epsilon$ *for any* $\mathcal{A}$ *representing a set of* $\overline{k}_{max}$ *or less cheaters* L, *and for any cheater* $P_j \in L$ *who submits forged share* $v_j' \neq v_j$,
(2) $P_i \notin L$ *for any party* P_i *who does not forge its share.*

Now, we are in the right place to propose constructions for cheater identifiable HSS. To authenticate the shares, we have used the universal hash function of Proposition 1 and MRA code. Towards the constructions, we first fix the communication model.

Communication Model: We assume that the dealer and the participants are pairwise connected by a private and authenticated channel. We further assume that a common broadcast channel is available to every participant and the dealer. We can replace common broadcast channel by assuming the reconstructor $\mathcal{R}$ to be honest.

$\mathsf{Game}^{\mathsf{Rushing}}(\mathbf{HSS}, \mathcal{A})$

$s \leftarrow \mathcal{S}$ (according to the probability distribution over $\mathcal{S}$)

$(v_1, \ldots, v_n) \leftarrow \mathsf{ShareGen}(s)$

$((i_1, \ldots, i_{\overline{k}_{max}}), (i_{\overline{k}_{max}+1}, \ldots, i_m), \mathsf{state}_C) \leftarrow \mathcal{A}_1()$

$\mathsf{state}_R \leftarrow \emptyset$

for $rid = 1$ **to** RidMax* **do**

    for $\ell = \overline{k}_{max} + 1$ **to** m **do**

        $\mathsf{state}_R \leftarrow \mathsf{Reconst}(rid, P_{i_\ell}, v_{i_\ell}^{(rid)}, \mathsf{state}_R)$

    done

    $((v_{i_1}'^{(rid)}, \ldots, v_{i_{\overline{k}_{max}}}'^{(rid)}), \mathsf{state}_C) \leftarrow \mathcal{A}_2(rid, (v_{i_{\overline{k}_{max}+1}}^{(rid)}, \ldots, v_{i_m}^{(rid)}), (v_{i_1}, \ldots, v_{i_{\overline{k}_{max}}}), \mathsf{state}_C)$

    for $\ell = 1$ **to** $\overline{k}_{max}$ **do**

        $\mathsf{state}_R \leftarrow \mathsf{Reconst}(rid, P_{i_\ell}, v_{i_\ell}'^{(rid)}, \mathsf{state}_R)$

    done

done

$\mathsf{output} \leftarrow \mathsf{Reconst}(\cdot, \cdot, \mathsf{state}_R)$

* RidMax denotes the maximum number of rounds in the reconstruction phase.

Fig. 1. Game between Reconst and Rushing Adversary for HSSCI.

3.2   HSSCI Using Universal Hash Function

High Level Idea: To identify the cheaters, *dealer* (honest) will produce authentication information, using universal hash function, during the share generation phase. At reconstruction phase, participants will broadcast their shares and compute t_{high} (see Remark 3) to execute the process of identification of cheaters. As the access structure is public, participants can compute t_{high} using the knowledge of the public information. Due to the existence of rushing adversary, participants will have to broadcast their shares in two different rounds.

Share Generation: Suppose $(\overline{\mathsf{ShareGen}}, \overline{\mathsf{Reconst}})$ be an ideal secret sharing scheme realizing our access structure (HSS). On input a secret $s \in GF(q)$, the share generation algorithm $ShareGen$ outputs a list of shares $(v_1, \ldots, v_n)$, where $n = n_1 + \cdots + n_l$, as follows:

1. The dealer D first runs the protocol
   $\overline{\mathsf{ShareGen}}(s) \rightarrow (s_1, \ldots, s_n) \in GF(q)^n$.
2. Generate a random $e_{0,i} \in_R GF(q)$ and a random polynomial of degree at most t_l with free coefficient 0, $a_i(x) = a_{i,1}x + a_{i,2}x^2 + \cdots + a_{i,t_l}x^{t_l}$ from $GF(q)[x]$. This is done for each $i = 1, \ldots, n$.
3. Compute $a_{ij} = a_i(j)$ and $e_{1,i,j} = a_j(i) - e_{0,i} \cdot s_j$ for $j \in [n] \setminus i$.
4. Compute $v_i = (s_i, a_i(x), e_{0,i}, e_{1,i,1}, \ldots, e_{1,i,i-1}, e_{1,i,i+1}, \ldots, e_{1,i,n})$.

Secret Reconstruction: On input a list of m shares, the secret reconstruction algorithm Reconst outputs "a secret and a list of identities of cheaters" or "$\perp$ and a list of identities of cheaters" as follows.

1. [Round 1] Broadcast $s_i, a_{i,1}', \ldots, a_{i,t_l}'$ by each $P_i \in core$, where "*core*" denotes the set of available participants during reconstruction.

2. [Round 2] Broadcast $e'_{0,i}, e'_{1,i,1}, \ldots, e'_{1,i,n}$ by each $P_i \in core$.
3. **Local Computation:** Every party in $core$
   - computes $high = max\{i : |core \cap \mathcal{L}_i| \geq t_i + 1\}$
   - sets $\overline{k}_{max} = \frac{t_{high}}{2}$.

   For each $P_i \in core$, every party in $core$ computes $support_i = \{P_j : e'_{0,j} \cdot s'_i + e'_{1,j,i} = a'_{i,1}j + a'_{i,2}j^2 + \cdots + a'_{i,t_l}j^{t_l}\} \cup \{P_i\}$.

   If $|support_i| < \overline{k}_{max} + 1$, then put P_i in L, where L is the list of the cheaters.
4.   - If $core \backslash L$ **is a qualified set:** Using s'_i for all $P_i \in core \backslash L$, run $\overline{\text{Reconst}}\{s'_i : P_i \in core \backslash L\}$ to output (s', L).
   - If $core \backslash L$ **is a forbidden set:** Output $(\bot, L)$.

Lemma 1. *The above scheme provides perfect secrecy. That is, any adversary $\mathcal{A}$ controlling any forbidden set of parties during the sharing phase, will get no information about the secret s.*

Proof. Possible highest cardinality of a forbidden set of participants is t_l. Without loss of generality, we may assume that the participants $P_1, \ldots, P_{t_l}$ (they may be all from l-th level or from all levels) are under the control of the adversary $\mathcal{A}$. The available information to the adversary is :

$$
\begin{array}{ccccccccccc}
s_1 & a_{1,1} & a_{1,2} & \cdots & a_{1,t_l} & e_{0,1} & \bot & e_{1,1,2} & \cdots & e_{1,1,n} \\
s_2 & a_{2,1} & a_{2,2} & \cdots & a_{2,t_l} & e_{0,2} & e_{1,2,1} & \bot & \cdots & e_{1,2,n} \\
\cdots & \cdots & \cdots & \cdots & \cdots & \cdots & \cdots & \cdots & \cdots & \cdots \\
s_{t_l} & a_{t_l,1} & a_{t_l,2} & \cdots & a_{t_l,t_l} & e_{0,t_l} & e_{1,t_l,1} & e_{1,t_l,l} & \cdots & e_{1,t_l,n}
\end{array}
$$

Now, t_l such values provide no information on s, according to the perfect privacy property of the underlying HSS. Thus, the adversary needs to choose one more s_k, where $k \in \{1, 2, \ldots, n\} \backslash I$ and $I = \{1, 2, \ldots, t_l\}$. Without loss of generality, we may assume that the adversary tries to learn s_k with the information at hand. Note that each player P_i ($i \in I$) has the information $(e_{0,i}, e_{1,i,k})$ regarding s_k. Now,

$$
e_{0,1}s_k + e_{1,1,k} = a_{k,1}1 + a_{k,2}1^2 + \cdots + a_{k,t_l}1^{t_l}
$$
$$
e_{0,2}s_k + e_{1,2,k} = a_{k,1}2 + a_{k,2}2^2 + \cdots + a_{k,t_l}2^{t_l}
$$
$$
\cdots = \cdots
$$
$$
e_{0,t_l}s_k + e_{1,t_l,k} = a_{k,1}t_l + a_{k,2}t_l^2 + \cdots + a_{k,t_l}t_l^{t_l}
$$

Suppose, the adversary $\mathcal{A}$ tries to find out s_k. Now, as the matrix

$$
\begin{bmatrix}
1 & 1^2 & \ldots & 1^{t_l} \\
2 & 2^2 & \ldots & 2^{t_l} \\
\cdots & \cdots & \cdots & \cdots \\
t_l & t_l^2 & \ldots & t_l^{t_l}
\end{bmatrix}
$$

is non-singular, the above system of linear equations is consistent for all possible values of s_k. So, the best probability for $\mathcal{A}$ to guess s_k is $1/q$. So that the adversary has no information regarding the secret s. Hence, the lemma. $\qquad\square$

Lemma 2. *The proposed scheme satisfies correctness condition. In other words, during the reconstruction phase, if any $P_i \in core$ is under the control of rushing $\mathcal{A}$ and produces $v_i' \neq v_i$, then except with error probability $\epsilon = (m - \overline{k}_{max})/q$, P_i will be identified as a cheater and will be included in the list L.*

Proof. Without loss of generality, let *core* be formed by a qualified set of m parties, namely $P_1, \ldots, P_m$ (participants may come from any level). Moreover, let $P_1, \ldots, P_{\overline{k}_{max}}$ be under the control of $\mathcal{A}$. Now suppose that P_1 submits $s_1' \neq s_1$ and P_1 is not identified as a cheater. This implies that $|support_1| \geq \overline{k}_{max} + 1$. In the worst case, $P_1, \ldots, P_{\overline{k}_{max}}$ may be present in $support_1$, as all of them are under the control of $\mathcal{A}$. But $|support_1| \geq \overline{k}_{max} + 1$ implies that there exists at least one honest party in *core*, say P_j, such that $P_j \in support_1$. This is possible only if $e_{0,j}s_1' + e_{1,j,1} = ja_{1,1}' + j^2 a_{1,2}' + \cdots + j^{t_l} a_{1,t_l}'$. Now in *Round* 1 of reconstruction phase each player P_i broadcasts $s_i, a_{i,1}, \ldots, a_{i,t_l}$ and in *Round* 2 of reconstruction phase P_i broadcasts $e_{0,i}, e_{1,i,1}, \ldots, e_{1,i,i-1}, e_{1,i,i+1}, \ldots, e_{1,i,n}$.

After round 1 of the reconstruction phase, the cheating adversary can see the share of underlying ideal HSS and authentication tags of each player. And $\mathcal{A}$ also knows the authentication keys of player $P_1, P_2, \ldots, P_{\overline{k}_{max}}$. But he does not know the authentication keys of players $P_{\overline{k}_{max}+1}, \ldots, P_m$.

Now we evaluate the probability that P_1 succeeds in deceiving at least one honest player to accept her fake share and fake tag. This probability is given by $\Pr[E_1|E_2]$, where E_1 and E_2 respectively denote the events "at least one player in $[P_{\overline{k}_{max}+1}, \ldots, P_m]$ accepts $(s_1', a_1'(x))$", and "$[P_{\overline{k}_{max}+1}, \ldots, P_m]$ accept $(s_1, a_1(x)), \ldots, (s_n, a_n(x))$".

Now, using the Proposition 1, we can conclude that $\Pr[E_1|E_2] < (m - \overline{k}_{max})/q$. So we get ϵ-correctness for $\epsilon = (m - \overline{k}_{max})/q$. Hence, the lemma. $\qquad\square$

Theorem 1. *The proposed construction gives a cheating identifiable HSS scheme, secure against rushing adversary, over the space of secrets $GF(q)$ with error probability $\epsilon = \frac{m - \overline{k}_{max}}{q}$ and share size $|v_i| = |s|q^{t_l+n}$.*

Proof. Perfect secrecy follows from Lemma 1 and correctness follows from Lemma 2. $\qquad\square$

3.3   HSSCI Using MRA Code

High Level Idea: Following construction is in the same spirit of the construction of Sect. 3.2. But, here *dealer* uses MRA code instead of universal hash function to generate authentication information during sharing phase. It will help to reduce the share size significantly.

Share Generation: On input a secret $s \in GF(q)$, the share generation algorithm *ShareGen* outputs a list of shares $(v_1, \ldots, v_n)$, where $n = n_1 + \cdots + n_l$, as follows:

1. The dealer D first runs the protocol
   $\overline{ShareGen}(s) \rightarrow (s_1, \ldots, s_n) \in GF(q)^n$.

2. Generate random $g_0(x), g_1(x), \ldots, g_n(x)$ from $GF(q)[x]$ each of degree at most k_{max} for a (k_{max}, n) MRA code with n messages, where $k_{max} = \frac{t_l}{2}$.
3. Compute $a_i(x) = g_0(x) + s_i g_1(x) + \ldots + s_i^n g_n(x)$ for $i \in [n]$ as the authentication tag for s_i.
4. Compute $v_i = (s_i, a_i(x), e_i)$ where $e_i = (g_0(i), \cdots, g_n(i))$ is verification key of the i-th participants.

Secret Reconstruction: On input a list of m shares, the secret reconstruction algorithm Reconst outputs "a secret and a list of identities of cheaters" or "$\perp$ and a list of identities of cheaters" as follows.

1. [Round 1] Broadcast $s_i, a_i'(x)$ by each $P_i \in core$.
2. [Round 2] Broadcast e_i' by each $P_i \in core$.
3. **Local Computation:** Every party in $core$
   - computes $high = max\{i : |core \cap \mathcal{L}_i| \geq t_i + 1\}$
   - sets $\overline{k}_{max} = \frac{t_{high}}{2}$.

   For each $P_i \in core$, every party in $core$ computes
   $support_i = \{P_j : a_i'(j) = g_0(j) + s_i g_1(j) + \ldots + s_i^n g_n(j)\} \cup \{P_i\}$.
   If $|support_i| < \overline{k}_{max} + 1$, then put P_i in L, where L is the list of the cheaters.
4. Output (s', L) or $(\perp, L)$ as in HSSCI using universal hash function of Sect. 3.2.

Theorem 2. *The proposed construction gives a cheating identifiable HSS scheme, secure against rushing adversary, over the space of secrets $GF(q)$ with error probability $\epsilon = \frac{m - \overline{k}_{max}}{q}$ and share size $|v_i| = |s|q^{n + \frac{t_l}{2} + 2}$.*

Proof. – **Perfect Secrecy:** As keys of MRA are independent of shares, the perfect secrecy follows from the perfect secrecy of the underlying scheme (ShareGen, Reconst).
- **Correctness:** Without loss of generality, let $core$ be formed by a qualified set of m parties, namely $P_1, \ldots, P_m$ (participants may come from any level). Moreover, let $P_1, \ldots, P_{\overline{k}_{max}}$ be under the control of $\mathcal{A}$. Now suppose that P_1 submits $s_1' \neq s_1$ and P_1 is not identified as a cheater. As in the argument of Lemma 2, it is required to evaluate the probability that P_1 succeeds in deceiving at least one honest player to accept her fake share and fake tag. This probability is given by $\Pr[E_1|E_2]$, where E_1 and E_2 respectively denote the events "at least one player in $[P_{\overline{k}_{max}+1}, \ldots, P_m]$ accepts $(s_1', a_1'(x))$", and "$[P_{\overline{k}_{max}+1}, \ldots, P_m]$ accept $(s_1, a_1(x)), \ldots, (s_n, a_n(x))$".
  Now, using the Proposition 2, we can conclude that $\Pr[E_1|E_2] < (m - \overline{k}_{max})/q$. So we get ϵ-correctness for $\epsilon = (m - \overline{k}_{max})/q$. $\square$

Remark 4. In Table 1, we have provided comparison between two proposed HSSCI schemes. It is evident from Table 1 that the use of MRA code reduce the share size of HSSCI. But, to reduce the share size, we tradeoff the *flexibility*. We call the scheme flexible, when the security level (i.e. a success probability of the cheater(s)) can be set independently of the secret size. Use of authentication technique of Proposition 1 makes the first scheme flexible.

Table 1. Comparison between two proposed HSSCI.

Scheme	#Cheaters	Share Size	Efficiency*	Rushing	Flexible
HSSCI using universal hash function	k_{max}	$|s|q^{n+t_l}$	Yes	Yes	Yes
HSSCI using MRA	k_{max}	$|s|q^{n+\frac{t_l}{2}+2}$	Yes	Yes	No

*This column indicates, whether computational complexity of the reconstruction phase is polynomial in the number of participants n or not.

4   Hierarchical Secret Sharing: Robustness

In this section we first fix the model and definitions of robustness of hierarchical secret sharing and then give a construction to realize the robustness.

4.1   Robust Hierarchical Secret Sharing Against Rushing Cheater

As in the ordinary $\bigsqcup_{i=1}^{l}(t_i, n_i)_{\mathcal{P}}$ **HSS** = ($\overline{\mathsf{ShareGen}}$, $\overline{\mathsf{Reconst}}$) hierarchical secret sharing schemes, the model of robust secret sharing scheme against rushing adversary consists of two algorithms. Share generation algorithm $\mathsf{ShareGen}$ is same as that in the ordinary secret sharing schemes. The secret reconstruction algorithm $\mathsf{Reconst}$ is changed: the reconstruction algorithm is modeled as an interactive Turing machine, which interacts with participants multiple times, and they release a part of their shares to $\mathsf{Reconst}$ in each round. Therefore, $\mathsf{Reconst}$ takes round identifier rid, user identifier P_i, and part of share $v_i^{(rid)}$ and state information state_R as input and outputs updated state information. When interactions with users are finished, $\mathsf{Reconst}$ outputs the secret.

Figure 2 below models the interaction between participants and the reconstruction algorithm $\mathsf{Reconst}$. Here, a pair of Turing machine $\mathcal{A} = (\mathcal{A}_1, \mathcal{A}_2)$ representing rushing adversary $P_{i_1}, \ldots, P_{i_{t_{max}}}$ who try to cheat honest users $P_{i_{t_{max}+1}}$, $\ldots, P_{i_n}$. In the $\mathsf{Game}^{\mathsf{Rushing}}(\mathbf{HSS}, \mathcal{A})$, $\mathcal{A}_1$ first chooses rushing cheater $P_{i_1}, \ldots$, $P_{i_{t_{max}}}$ and users $P_{i_{t_{max}+1}}, \ldots, P_{i_n}$ to cheat. Next, in each round, $\mathcal{A}_2$ determines forged share $(v_{i_1}^{\prime (rid)}, \ldots, v_{i_{t_{max}}}^{\prime (rid)})$ to be submitted by rushing cheaters. Note that $\mathcal{A}_2$ takes shares $(v_{i_{t_{max}+1}}^{(rid)}, \ldots, v_{i_n}^{(rid)})$ as input in determining forged shares, which captures the rushing capability of cheaters.

The successful cheating probability $\delta(\mathbf{HSS}, \mathcal{A})$ of the cheaters $\mathcal{A}$ against **HSS** = ($\mathsf{ShareGen}$, $\mathsf{Reconst}$) is defined by

$$\delta(\mathbf{HSS}, \mathcal{A}) = \Pr[s' \leftarrow \mathsf{Reconst}(\cdot, \cdot, \mathsf{state}_R) : s' \in \mathcal{S} \wedge s' \neq s],$$

where the probability is taken over the distribution of $\mathcal{S}$, and the random tapes of $\mathsf{ShareGen}$ and $\mathcal{A}$. The security of robust secret sharing schemes against t_{max} rushing cheaters is formalized in Definition 7.

Definition 7. A $\bigsqcup_{i=1}^{l}(t_i, n_i)_{\mathcal{P}}$ *hierarchical secret sharing* **HSS** = ($\mathsf{ShareGen}$, $\mathsf{Reconst}$) *is called* δ *robust against rushing cheaters if* $\delta(\mathbf{HSS}, \mathcal{A}) \leq \delta$ *for any adversary* $\mathcal{A}$.

$$
\begin{array}{l}
\mathsf{Game}^{\mathsf{Rushing}}(\mathbf{HSS}, \mathcal{A}) \\
\hline
s \leftarrow \mathcal{S} \qquad (\textit{according to the probability distribution over } \mathcal{S}) \\
(v_1, \ldots, v_n) \leftarrow \mathsf{ShareGen}(s) \\
((i_1, \ldots, i_{t_{max}}, (i_{t_{max}+1}, \ldots, i_n), \mathsf{state}_C) \leftarrow \mathcal{A}_1() \\
\mathsf{state}_R \leftarrow \emptyset \\
\mathbf{for}\ rid = 1\ \mathbf{to}\ \mathtt{RidMax}\ \mathbf{do} \\
\quad \mathbf{for}\ \ell = t_{max} + 1\ \mathbf{to}\ n\ \mathbf{do} \\
\qquad \mathsf{state}_R \leftarrow \mathsf{Reconst}(rid, P_{i_\ell}, v_{i_\ell}^{(rid)}, \mathsf{state}_R) \\
\quad \mathbf{done} \\
\quad ((v_{i_1}'^{(rid)}, \ldots, v_{i_{t_{max}}}'^{(rid)}), \mathsf{state}_C) \\
\qquad\qquad \leftarrow \mathcal{A}_2(rid, (v_{i_{t_{max}+1}}^{(rid)}, \ldots, v_{i_n}^{(rid)}), (v_{i_1}, \ldots, v_{i_{t_{max}}}), \mathsf{state}_C) \\
\quad \mathbf{for}\ \ell = 1\ \mathbf{to}\ t_{max}\ \mathbf{do} \\
\qquad \mathsf{state}_R \leftarrow \mathsf{Reconst}(rid, P_{i_\ell}, v_{i_\ell}'^{(rid)}, \mathsf{state}_R) \\
\quad \mathbf{done} \\
\mathbf{done} \\
\mathsf{output} \leftarrow \mathsf{Reconst}(\cdot, \cdot, \mathsf{state}_R)
\end{array}
$$

* `RidMax` denotes the maximum number of rounds in the reconstruction phase.

Fig. 2. Game between Reconst and Rushing Adversary for RSS.

4.2 (t_{max}, δ) Robust HSS

We now give construction for robust HSS. To authenticate the shares, we have used the universal hash function of Proposition 1 and communication model is same as in Sect. 3.

High Level Idea: Dealer will produce authentication information, using universal hash function, during the share generation phase. At reconstruction phase, participants will broadcast their shares and find out a qualified set of participants with correct shares to reconstruct the shared secret correctly.

To start with the construction, first we recapitulate the definition of t_{max}. Suppose, there are l levels viz. $\mathcal{L}_1, \ldots, \mathcal{L}_l$. Here, we assume that $n = n_1 + \cdots + n_l > 2t_{max}$ and from Definition 2, it follows that $t_{max} = t_l$. Moreover, among these t_{max} corrupt parties, at most $t_1, \ldots, t_{l-1}$ can be from Level $1, \ldots, l-1$ respectively.

Share Generation: On input a secret $s \in GF(q)$, the share generation algorithm *ShareGen* outputs a list of shares $(v_1, \ldots, v_n)$ as the Share Generation phase of Sect. 3.2.

Secret Reconstruction: On input a list of n shares, the secret reconstruction algorithm *Recon* outputs a secret or $\perp$ as follows.

1. [Round 1] Receive $s_i, a_{i,1}', \ldots, a_{i,t_{max}}'$ from each P_i.
2. [Round 2] Receive $e_{0,i}', e_{1,i,1}', \ldots, e_{1,i,n}'$ from each P_i.

3. **Local Computation:**
   - Set z_{ij}, $i,j \in \{1,2,\ldots,n\}$, to be 1 if P_i's authentication tag is accepted by P_j, i.e., if $e'_{0,j} \cdot s_i + e'_{1,j,i} = a'_{i,1}j + a'_{i,2}j^2 + \cdots + a'_{i,t_{max}}j^{t_{max}}$ otherwise set z_{ij} to 0.
   - compute the largest set $\mathcal{I} \subseteq \{1,2,\ldots,n\}$ with the property that $\forall i \in [n]$: $|\{j \in \mathcal{I}|z_{ij} = 1\}| = \Sigma_{j \in [n]}z_{ij} \geq t_{max} + 1$.
     Clearly, $\mathcal{I}$ contains all honest participants, i.e., a qualified set of participants with correct shares.
4. Run $\mathsf{Reconst}\{s'_i : P_i \in \mathcal{I}\}$ and output the secret. If no such secret exists, output $\perp$.

Lemma 3. *Any corrupted participant P_i who submits $v'_i \neq v_i$ in Round 1 of the reconstruction phase will be accepted by an honest participant with probability at most $\delta' = \frac{1}{q}$.*

Proof. Without loss of generality, we assume that the corrupted participant is P_1 who submits $v'_1 \neq v_1$ in Round 1 of the reconstruction phase. P_1 will be accepted by honest P_j if $e'_{0,j} \cdot s_1 + e'_{1,j,1} = a'_{1,1}j + a'_{1,2}j^2 + \cdots + a'_{1,t_{max}}j^{t_{max}}$. Now using the Proposition 1, we can conclude that $\delta' = \frac{1}{q}$. □

Theorem 3. *The proposed construction forms (t_{max}, δ)-robust secret sharing scheme for n participants with the space of secrets $GF(q)$, $\delta = \frac{t_{max}}{q}$ and share size $|S|(t_{max}/\delta)^{t_{max}+n}$.*

Proof. – **Perfect Secrecy:** As in Lemma 1.
   – **Reconstructability:** In round 1 of reconstruction phase, adversary will corrupt t_{max} number of participants. Optimal strategy of the adversary is to make acceptance of at least one corrupted participant in round 2. From Lemma 3 and Remark 1, it is only possible with probability δ. Apart from the corrupted participants, there exists a qualified set of honest participants. So, the rest of the proof follows from the correctness property of HSS. □

Remark 5. (An alternative construction) It is possible to construct (t_{max}, δ) Robust HSS using MRA code. The *share generation* phase is same as the Share-Gen of Sect. 3.3 with the modification that k_{max} is replaced by t_{max}. The *reconstruction* phase is identical to the protocol given in Sect. 3.3. However, share size of Robust HSS using MRA is $|S|(t_{max}/\delta)^{t_{max}+n+1}$ which is little higher than the construction of Sect. 4.2.

5   Conclusion

We provided definitions for cheater identifiable and robust secret sharing schemes on hierarchical access structure and constructed schemes which are information theoretically secure against *rushing* adversary. Studying the lower bounds of share sizes is an interesting problem. In general, secret sharing schemes assume that the access structure is a public information. An interesting problem can be to consider the scenario where each participant is unaware of the levels where other participants belong. Only the dealer has the knowledge of the access structure to distribute the secret.

References

1. Adhikari, A., Morozov, K., Obana, S., Roy, P.S., Sakurai, K., Xu, R.: Efficient threshold secret sharing schemes secure against rushing cheaters. IACR Cryptology ePrint Archive 2015/23 (2015)

2. Adhikari, A., Morozov, K., Obana, S., Roy, P.S., Sakurai, K., Xu, R.: Efficient threshold secret sharing schemes secure against rushing cheaters. In: Nascimento, A.C.A., Barreto, P. (eds.) ICITS 2016. LNCS, vol. 10015, pp. 3–23. Springer, Cham (2016). https://doi.org/10.1007/978-3-319-49175-2_1

3. Belenkiy, M.: Disjunctive multi-level secret sharing. IACR Cryptology ePrint Archive 2008/18 (2008)

4. Brickell, E.F.: Some ideal secret sharing schemes. In: Quisquater, J.-J., Vandewalle, J. (eds.) EUROCRYPT 1989. LNCS, vol. 434, pp. 468–475. Springer, Heidelberg (1990). https://doi.org/10.1007/3-540-46885-4_45

5. Carter, J.L., Wegman, M.N.: Universal classes of hash functions. J. Comput. Syst. Sci. **18**(2), 143–154 (1979)

6. Cevallos, A., Fehr, S., Ostrovsky, R., Rabani, Y.: Unconditionally-secure robust secret sharing with compact shares. In: Pointcheval, D., Johansson, T. (eds.) EUROCRYPT 2012. LNCS, vol. 7237, pp. 195–208. Springer, Heidelberg (2012). https://doi.org/10.1007/978-3-642-29011-4_13

7. Choudhury, A.: Brief announcement: optimal amortized secret sharing with cheater identification. In: Proceedings of the 2012 ACM Symposium on Principles of Distributed Computing, pp. 101–102. ACM (2012)

8. Cramer, R., Damgård, I., Fehr, S.: On the cost of reconstructing a secret, or VSS with optimal reconstruction phase. In: Kilian, J. (ed.) CRYPTO 2001. LNCS, vol. 2139, pp. 503–523. Springer, Heidelberg (2001). https://doi.org/10.1007/3-540-44647-8_30

9. Ghodosi, H., Pieprzyk, J., Safavi-Naini, R.: Secret sharing in multilevel and compartmented groups. In: Boyd, C., Dawson, E. (eds.) ACISP 1998. LNCS, vol. 1438, pp. 367–378. Springer, Heidelberg (1998). https://doi.org/10.1007/BFb0053748

10. Kothari, S.C.: Generalized linear threshold scheme. In: Blakley, G.R., Chaum, D. (eds.) CRYPTO 1984. LNCS, vol. 196, pp. 231–241. Springer, Heidelberg (1985). https://doi.org/10.1007/3-540-39568-7_19

11. Kurosawa, K., Obana, S., Ogata, W.: t-Cheater identifiable (k, n) threshold secret sharing schemes. In: Coppersmith, D. (ed.) CRYPTO 1995. LNCS, vol. 963, pp. 410–423. Springer, Heidelberg (1995). https://doi.org/10.1007/3-540-44750-4_33

12. McEliece, R.J., Sarwate, D.V.: On sharing secrets and reed-solomon codes. Commun. ACM **24**(9), 583–584 (1981)

13. Rabin, T., Ben-Or, M.: Verifiable secret sharing and multiparty protocols with honest majority. In: Proceedings of the Twenty-First Annual ACM Symposium on Theory of Computing, pp. 73–85. ACM (1989)

14. Roy, P.S., Adhikari, A., Xu, R., Morozov, K., Sakurai, K.: An efficient robust secret sharing scheme with optimal cheater resiliency. In: Chakraborty, R.S., Matyas, V., Schaumont, P. (eds.) SPACE 2014. LNCS, vol. 8804, pp. 47–58. Springer, Cham (2014). https://doi.org/10.1007/978-3-319-12060-7_4

15. Roy, P.S., Adhikari, A., Xu, R., Morozov, K., Sakurai, K.: An efficient t-cheater identifiable secret sharing scheme with optimal cheater resiliency. IACR Cryptology ePrint Archive 2014/628 (2014)

16. Safavi-Naini, R., Wang, H.: New results on multi-receiver authentication codes. In: Nyberg, K. (ed.) EUROCRYPT 1998. LNCS, vol. 1403, pp. 527–541. Springer, Heidelberg (1998). https://doi.org/10.1007/BFb0054151

17. Shamir, A.: How to share a secret. Commun. ACM **22**(11), 612–613 (1979)
18. Simmons, G.J.: How to (really) share a secret. In: Goldwasser, S. (ed.) CRYPTO 1988. LNCS, vol. 403, pp. 390–448. Springer, New York (1990). https://doi.org/10.1007/0-387-34799-2_30
19. Tassa, T.: Hierarchical threshold secret sharing. J. Cryptol. **20**(2), 237–264 (2007)
20. Tentu, A.N., Paul, P., Vadlamudi, C.V.: Conjunctive hierarchical secret sharing scheme based on MDS codes. In: Lecroq, T., Mouchard, L. (eds.) IWOCA 2013. LNCS, vol. 8288, pp. 463–467. Springer, Heidelberg (2013). https://doi.org/10.1007/978-3-642-45278-9_44
21. Traverso, G., Demirel, D., Buchmann, J.: Dynamic and verifiable hierarchical secret sharing. In: Nascimento, A.C.A., Barreto, P. (eds.) ICITS 2016. LNCS, vol. 10015, pp. 24–43. Springer, Cham (2016). https://doi.org/10.1007/978-3-319-49175-2_2
22. Wegman, M.N., Carter, J.L.: New classes and applications of hash functions. In: 20th Annual Symposium on Foundations of Computer Science, pp. 175–182. IEEE (1979)
23. Xu, R., Morozov, K., Takagi, T.: Cheater identifiable secret sharing schemes via multi-receiver authentication. In: Yoshida, M., Mouri, K. (eds.) IWSEC 2014. LNCS, vol. 8639, pp. 72–87. Springer, Cham (2014). https://doi.org/10.1007/978-3-319-09843-2_6

An Efficient and Provably Secure Private Polynomial Evaluation Scheme

Zhe Xia[1], Bo Yang[2(✉)], Mingwu Zhang[3], and Yi Mu[4]

[1] School of Computer Science, Wuhan University of Technology,
Wuhan 430070, China
xiazhe@whut.edu.cn
[2] School of Computer Science, Shaanxi Normal University,
Xi'an 710062, China
byang@snnu.edu.cn
[3] School of Computers, Hubei University of Technology,
Wuhan 430068, China
csmwzhang@gmail.com
[4] School of Computing and Information Technology,
University of Wollongong, Wollongong 2522, Australia
ymu@uow.edu.au

Abstract. Private Polynomial Evaluation (PPE) allows the service provider to outsource the computation of a polynomial to some third party (e.g. the Cloud) in a verifiable way. And meanwhile, the polynomial remains hidden to the clients who are able to query the service. In ProvSec 2017, Bultel et al. have presented the formal security definitions for PPE, including *polynomial protection* (PP), *proof unforgeability* (UNF) and *indistinguishability against chosen function attack* (IND-CFA). They have introduced a PPE scheme that satisfies all these properties, and they have also shown that a polynomial commitment scheme in Asiacrypt 2010, called PolyCommit_Ped, enjoys these properties as well. In this paper, we introduce another provably secure PPE scheme, which not only has computational advantages over these two existing ones, but also relies on a much weaker security assumption. Moreover, we further explore how our PPE scheme can be implemented in the distributed fashion, so that a number of third parties jointly respond to the query but none of them could learn the polynomial unless they all collude.

1 Introduction

Mathematical models have various applications in our everyday life. For example, a patient collects her medical data such as blood pressure, body temperature and heart rate by sensors, and the expert system can use some pre-defined mathematical model to evaluate her health status. A farmer collects the data of the soil, such as humidity, acidity and thermal parameters, and the agricultural consultant can use some well analysed mathematical model to predict the state

© Springer Nature Switzerland AG 2018
C. Su and H. Kikuchi (Eds.): ISPEC 2018, LNCS 11125, pp. 595–609, 2018.
https://doi.org/10.1007/978-3-319-99807-7_38

of the soil for the next year. The benefits for these examples are obvious: the patient gets better medical treatments, and the farmer obtains precise information regarding how much seeds to buy and when to plant them in the coming year. As the development of computer and communication technologies, things could get even better. The service provider can outsource the computation of the mathematical model to some third party, e.g. the Cloud. In this way, the service provider reduces its operation cost, because it does not need to maintain the resources of computation, storage and communication. And meanwhile, the client could access the service more conveniently, e.g. the patient can be monitored continuously in real-time.

However, the above attractive features and economical initiatives cannot succeed unless the following issues have been well addressed. On one hand, to protect its intellectual property, the service provider may not be willing to reveal the mathematical model to the clients. On the other hand, the clients may not trust the third party, and would like to verify that the mathematical model has been computed correctly. To harmonise these two contradicting requirements, several cryptographic solutions have been proposed recently in the literature. One subclass of these solutions focusing on the case where the mathematical model can be expressed as univariable polynomials are called private polynomial evaluation (PPE) schemes [6].

In a PPE scheme, as illustrated in Fig. 1, the service provider outsources the evaluation of the polynomial $f(\cdot)$ to a third party and it broadcasts some public information vk. The paid client can query the service by submitting the input data x to the third party. After evaluating the polynomial, the third party returns $f(x)$ as well as a proof π to the client. Finally, the client is able to verify whether the polynomial has been evaluated correctly using the public information vk and the proof π. Note that during this process, the client should not learn any information of the polynomial $f(\cdot)$. This not only requires that the client cannot derive the entire polynomial $f(\cdot)$, but also requires that even if the client has some prior knowledge of two polynomials $f_0(\cdot)$ and $f_1(\cdot)$, she cannot distinguish which one has been used to evaluate her input data.

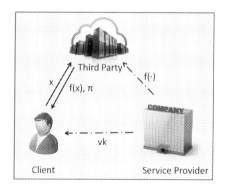

Fig. 1. An illustration of the PPE scheme

1.1 Related Works

Verifiable computation, first introduced by Gennaro et al. in [13], requires that the party who performs the computation to prove the correctness of output. Hence, it allows the service provider who has limited resources to delegate expensive computations to some untrusted parties. Furthermore, if the correctness of output can be checked by anyone who is interested, it is called publicly verifiable computation [19]. The formal security model and definitions of verifiable computation have been presented by Canetti et al. in [8]. Afterwards, this technique has been further extended in various aspects. For example, Choi et al. [9] have extended verifiable computation to the multi-client setting. Papamanthou et al. [17] have introduced the concept of signatures of correct computation, which uses multivariate polynomials for verification. Fiore and Gennaro [11] have proposed a verifiable computation scheme for polynomial evaluation and matrix computation. Parno et al. [18] have demonstrated, using a concrete prototype called Pinocchio, that some of the verifiable computations are practical in the real use. The research focus of the above works is that the verification of the proof should require less computational costs than computing the function from scratch, but they have not considered protecting the function against the client which is required in PPE.

Another related work was introduced by Naor and Pinkas [16], called oblivious polynomial evaluation (OPE), in which the service provider has some polynomial $f(\cdot)$, and the client has some input x. After the execution of the protocol, the client should obtain $f(x)$ but not the original polynomial $f(\cdot)$, and the service provider should not learn x. Although OPE and PPE shares some similarities, they still differ in several aspects: OPE does not consider verifying the correctness of polynomial evaluation, and PPE does not consider protection of x from the service provider.

Recently, several works have tried to address these two contradicting requirements simultaneously, so that the client can verify that the function has been correctly computed, and meanwhile, the function is not revealed to the client. To simplify the design, most of these works have restricted the function as univariate polynomials. In ProvSec 2017, Bultel et al. [6] called this type of schemes as private polynomial evaluation (PPE), and they presented the formal security definitions for PPE. Informally, a PPE scheme should satisfy the following three properties: (1) *polynomial protection* (PP) requires that the client cannot evaluate the polynomial by herself on any new input that she has not queried before; (2) *proof unforgeability* (UNF) requires that the third party cannot cheat the client using incorrect result; (3) *indistinguishability against chosen function attack* (IND-CFA) requires that the client cannot distinguish which polynomial has been evaluated even if she has some prior knowledge of the polynomials. In the same paper, Bultel et al. also showed that one of the polynomial commitment schemes in [15], called PolyCommit$_{Ped}$, satisfies these properties as well, although PolyCommit$_{Ped}$ is originally designed as a verifiable secret sharing (VSS) scheme with constant size commitments. Note that a few other works [12,14] have introduced verifiable and privacy-preserving solutions for various applications and they have claimed implicitly to achieve similar properties. But it was shown later that in these works, a malicious client can retrieve the entire polynomial in a single query. To the best of our knowledge, Bultel's scheme in [6] and PolyCommit$_{Ped}$ in [15] are the existing ones that can achieve all the above three properties, and we will compare our proposed scheme with these two schemes.

1.2   Our Contributions

The contributions of this paper are summarised as follows:

- We introduce a new PPE scheme and we formally prove that it achieves PP, UNF and IND-CFA properties. Our proposed scheme not only has computational advantages over the two existing ones, but also relies on a much weaker security assumption. Regarding the computational costs, in one aspect, our scheme uses Pedersen's VSS [20] to replace Feldman's VSS [10] as used in [6], and the benefit is that we no longer need to use any CPA encryption scheme and zero-knowledge proof in order to achieve the IND-CFA property. In the other aspect, although Pedersen's VSS has been used as the main building block both in our scheme and in PolyCommit$_{Ped}$, the client's verification of polynomial evaluation in our scheme does not need any expensive pairing computation. Regarding the security assumptions, our scheme only relies on the discrete logarithm (DL) assumption, while Bultel's scheme needs the decisional Diffie-Hellman (DDH) assumption and PolyCommit$_{Ped}$ needs the t-strong Diffie-Hellman (t-SDH) assumption [4]. It is well known that DL is a much weaker assumption than DDH and t-SDH. Moreover, the t-SDH assumption is not as well analysed by researchers in computational number theory as the other two, and the DDH assumption may fail in some special groups, e.g. the bilinear map [5].
- We further explore how our proposed scheme can be implemented in the distributed fashion. A number of third parties jointly evaluate the polynomial, but none of them can learn the secret polynomial unless they all collude. In the client's view, the polynomial appears to have been evaluated by a single third party. Note that this extension could better reflect the demands in real world applications, since the service provider may wish to keep the polynomial private from the third party as well.

1.3   Organisation of the Paper

The rest of the paper is organised as follows: In Sect. 2, we outline some preliminaries. The model and definitions of PPE are described in Sect. 3. Our proposed PPE scheme as well as its security proofs are presented in Sect. 4. We further extend the PPE scheme into a distributed version and briefly sketch its security in Sect. 5. Finally, we conclude in Sect. 6.

2   Preliminaries

2.1   Notations

In the paper, all participants are assumed to be probabilistic polynomial time (PPT) algorithms with respect to the security parameter λ, unless stated otherwise. We use standard notions for expressing probabilistic algorithms and experiments. If A is a probabilistic algorithm, then $A(x_1, x_2, \ldots; r)$ is the result of running A on inputs $x_1, x_2, \ldots$ and a random coin r. We denote $y \leftarrow A(x_1, x_2, \ldots; r)$ as the experiment of picking r at random and assigning y as $A(x_1, x_2, \ldots; r)$. If S is a finite set, then $x \xleftarrow{R} S$ denotes the operation of picking an element uniformly from S. $\Pr[x \leftarrow S; y \leftarrow T; \ldots : p(x, y, \ldots)]$ is denoted as the probability that the predicate $p(x, y, \ldots)$ will be true after the ordered execution of the algorithms $x \leftarrow S, y \leftarrow T$, etc. A function $\epsilon(\cdot) : \mathbb{N} \to \mathbb{R}^+$ is called negligible if for all $c > 0$, there exists a k_0 such that $\epsilon(k) < 1/k^c$ for all $k > k_0$. Moreover, let p, q be large primes such that $q | p - 1$, and G is a subgroup of $\mathbb{Z}_p^*$ with order q. Both g and h are generators of G, but it is required that nobody knows $\log_g h$. We assume that all computations are modulo p unless stated otherwise.

2.2   Building Blocks

Pedersen's Verifiable Secret Shairng [20]. Secret sharing is a useful technique to ensure secrecy and availability of sensitive information. The dealer can share the secret among a number of participants, so that a quorum of these participants work together can recover the secret, but less participants cannot learn any information of the secret. However, in traditional secret sharing schemes, the dealer may cheat by distributing inconsistent shares, and the participants may cheat by revealing fake shares when reconstructing the secret. Using verifiable secret sharing (VSS), these dishonest behaviours can be detected. Pedersen's VSS is based on Shamir secret sharing, and it works as follows:

- The dealer first generates two polynomials $f(\cdot)$ and $f'(\cdot)$ over $\mathbb{Z}_q$ with degree k as:

$$f(z) = a_0 + a_1 z + \ldots + a_k z^k \qquad f'(z) = b_0 + b_1 z + \ldots + b_k z^k$$

  where the secret $s = a_0$.
- Then dealer publishes the commitments $C_i = g^{a_i} h^{b_i}$ for $i = 0, 1, \ldots, k$.
- The x_i values for $i = 1, 2, \ldots, n$ are public parameters associate with each participant such that $x_i \neq x_j$ if $i \neq j$. For each participant, the dealer computes the share $s_i = f(x_i)$ and $s'_i = f'(x_i)$.
- Once receiving the share s_i and s'_i, each participant verifies its validity by:

$$g^{s_i} h^{s'_i} = \prod_{j=0}^{k} (C_i)^{x_i{}^j}$$

If the above verification fails, a participant can make an accusation against the dealer. Note that the same verification also can be used to prevent the participants from revealing fake shares when reconstructing the secret.

Homomorphic Secret Sharing [3]: Denote $(s_1, s_2, \ldots, s_n)$ as a set of shares encoding the secret s, and $(s'_1, s'_2, \ldots, s'_n)$ as another set of shares encoding the secret s'. Moreover, $\oplus$ and $\otimes$ are denoted as the operation of shares and the operation of the secret, respectively. Secret sharing is said to have the homomorphic property if the set $(s_1 \oplus s'_1, s_2 \oplus s'_2, \ldots s_n \oplus s'_n)$ encodes the secret $s \otimes s'$. It is obvious that Pedersen's VSS enjoys the $(+, +)$-homomorphic property, where the symbol $+$ denotes the addition operation in the group $\mathbb{Z}_q$. We will use this property to extend our PPE scheme into the distributed version.

3   Model and Definitions

3.1   Private Polynomial Evaluation (PPE)

A PPE scheme [6] is specified by the following four randomised algorithms: Setup, Init, Compute, Verif:

- Setup: takes as input the security parameter λ, and returns the system parameters params.
- Init: takes as input params, and returns some public information vk associated with the secret polynomial $f(\cdot) \in \mathbb{Z}_q[X]$.
- Compute: takes as inputs params, vk, the polynomial $f(\cdot)$ and the client's input x, and returns $y = f(x)$ as well as some proof π.
- Verif: takes as inputs params, vk, x, y and π, and returns 1 if accepting the evaluation of $f(\cdot)$ on x, and returns 0 otherwise.

3.2   Security Properties and Assumptions

Definition 1 (k-polynomial protection (k-PP)): *A PPE scheme is said to be k-PP secure if there exists a negligible function $\epsilon(\cdot)$ such that for all PPT adversaries $\mathcal{A}_{PP}$, we have:*

$$\Pr\Big[\text{params} \leftarrow \text{Setup}(\lambda); f(\cdot) \leftarrow \mathbb{Z}_q[X]_k; \text{vk} \leftarrow \text{Init}(\text{params}, f(\cdot));$$

$$\Sigma \leftarrow \emptyset; (x^*, y^*) \leftarrow \mathcal{A}_{PP}{}^{\mathcal{O}_{PP}(\cdot)}(\text{params}, \text{vk}):$$

$$f(x^*) = y^* \wedge (x^*, y^*) \notin \Sigma \Big] < \epsilon(\lambda)$$

In the above expression, $f(\cdot)$ is a polynomial over $\mathbb{Z}_q$ with degree k, and $\mathcal{O}_{PP}$ is an oracle that takes as input x and returns $f(x)$ as well as some proof π. The adversary $\mathcal{A}_{PP}$ is restricted to query $\mathcal{O}_{PP}$ at most k times. The set Σ records all pairs $(x, f(x))$ that have been queried.

Definition 2 (Proof unforgeability (UNF)): *A PPE scheme is said to be UNF secure if there exists a negligible function $\epsilon(\cdot)$ such that for all PPT adversaries $\mathcal{A}_{UNF}$, we have:*

$$\Pr\Big[\mathsf{params} \leftarrow \mathsf{Setup}(\lambda); f(\cdot) \leftarrow \mathcal{A}_{UNF}(\mathbb{Z}_q[X]_k); \mathsf{vk} \leftarrow \mathsf{Init}(\mathsf{params}, f(\cdot));$$
$$(x^*, y^*, \pi^*) \leftarrow \mathcal{A}_{UNF}(\mathsf{params}, \mathsf{vk}, f(\cdot)):$$
$$f(x^*) \neq y^* \wedge \mathsf{Verif}(\mathsf{params}, \mathsf{vk}, x^*, y^*, \pi^*) = 1\Big] < \epsilon(\lambda)$$

Definition 3 (Indistinguishability against chosen function attack (IND-CFA)): *A PPE scheme is said to be IND-CFA secure if there exists a negligible function $\epsilon(\cdot)$ such that for all PPT adversaries $\mathcal{A}_{CFA}$, we have:*

$$\Pr\Big[\mathsf{params} \leftarrow \mathsf{Setup}(\lambda); (f_0(\cdot), f_1(\cdot)) \leftarrow \mathcal{A}_{CFA}(\mathbb{Z}_q[X]_k); b \xleftarrow{R} \{0,1\};$$
$$\mathsf{vk} \leftarrow \mathsf{Init}(\mathsf{params}, f_b(\cdot)), b^* \leftarrow \mathcal{A}_{CFA}{}^{\mathcal{O}_{CFA}(\cdot)}(\mathsf{params}, \mathsf{vk}):$$
$$b^* = b\Big] < 1/2 + \epsilon(\lambda)$$

In the above expression, both $f_0(\cdot)$ and $f_1(\cdot)$ are polynomials over $\mathbb{Z}_q$ with degree k. Moreover, $f_0(\cdot)$ and $f_1(\cdot)$ agree at most k points (x_i, y_i) for $i = 1, 2, \ldots, k$. When the adversary $\mathcal{A}_{CFA}$ queries the oracle $\mathcal{O}_{CFA}(\cdot)$ using some of these x_i values, it will output the corresponding y_i as well as a proof π. Otherwise, the oracle $\mathcal{O}_{CFA}(\cdot)$ outputs the symbol $\bot$.

Definition 4 (Discrete logarithm (DL) assumption): *Given the description of the group G and $x \xleftarrow{R} \mathbb{Z}_q$, the discrete logarithm assumption implies that there exits a negligible function $\epsilon(\cdot)$ such that for all PPT adversaries $\mathcal{A}_{DL}$, we have $\Pr[x^* \leftarrow \mathcal{A}_{DL}(g, g^x) : x^* = x] < \epsilon(\lambda)$.*

4   Our Proposed PPE Scheme

4.1   Our Scheme

Our proposed PPE scheme contains four algorithms Setup, Init, Compute, Verif, and it works as follows:

– Setup: Given a security parameter λ, this algorithm first generates two primes p and q such that $q|p-1$. It then generates the group G which is a subgroup of $\mathbb{Z}_p^*$ with order q, and two generators g, h of G such that $\log_g h$ is unknown[1]. Finally, all these parameters are made public as params.

---

[1] Note that such a value h can be generated by a distributed coin flipping protocol that outputs a random value $r \in \mathbb{Z}_p^*$, followed by computing $h = r^{(p-1)/q}$ satisfying that $h \neq 1$.

- Init: Before outsourcing the polynomial $f(z) = a_0 + a_1 z + \ldots + a_k z^k$ over $\mathbb{Z}_q$ with degree k to the third party, the service provider randomly selects another polynomial $f'(z) = b_0 + b_1 z + \ldots + b_k z^k$ over $\mathbb{Z}_q$ with degree k, and computes the commitments $C_i = g^{a_i} h^{b_i}$ for $i = 0, 1, \ldots, k$. Then, the service provider sends both these polynomials $f(z)$ and $f'(z)$ to the third party using a private channel, and broadcasts the commitments as the public information vk.
- Compute: Once receiving the client's input x, the third party computes two values $y = f(x)$ and $y' = f'(x)$, and then sends back y and y' to the client. Note that in our proposed PPE scheme, the proof π is an empty string.
- Verif: The client checks the correctness of polynomial evaluation by verifying the following equation:

$$g^y h^{y'} = \prod_{i=0}^{k} (C_i)^{x^i}$$

4.2   Security Analysis

We first show that the proposed PPE scheme is correct. In other words, if the third party has correctly evaluated the polynomial $f(\cdot)$ on x, then the client's verification will always be successful. Considering the case that the third party is honest, then we have $y = f(x) = \sum_{i=0}^{k} a_i x^i$ and $y' = f'(x) = \sum_{i=0}^{k} b_i x^i$. Therefore, the following equation will always hold:

$$g^y h^{y'} = g^{\sum_{i=0}^{k} a_i x^i} h^{\sum_{i=0}^{k} b_i x^i} = \prod_{i=0}^{k} (g^{a_i} h^{b_i})^{x^i} = \prod_{i=0}^{k} (C_i)^{x^i}$$

Theorem 1. *The proposed PPE scheme achieves the k-PP property.*

Proof. Because the adversary $\mathcal{A}_{PP}$ can query the oracle $\mathcal{O}_{PP}$ at most k times, $\mathcal{A}_{PP}$ can obtains at most k points $(x_i, f(x_i))$ for $i = 1, 2, \ldots, k$. Without loss of generality, we assume that $\mathcal{A}_{PP}$ aims to compute $f(x_{x+1})$ for some value x_{x+1} that she has not queried, and we prove that $\mathcal{A}_{PP}$ can succeed only with negligible probability.

Since the secret polynomial $f(\cdot)$ is with degree k, there are $k + 1$ unknown coefficients. Obtaining k points $(x_i, f(x_i))$ for $i = 1, 2, \ldots, k$ only gives k equations, hence none of these coefficients can be derived. In particular, the constant coefficient $a_0 = f(0)$ is uniformly distributed within $\mathbb{Z}_q$. Using the Lagrange interpolation, the value $f(x_{k+1})$ can be expressed as:

$$f(x_{k+1}) = f(0) \prod_{j=1}^{k} \frac{x_{k+1}}{x_j} + \sum_{i=1}^{k} f(x_i) \prod_{j=1, j \neq i}^{k} \frac{x_{k+1} - x_i}{x_j - x_i}$$

Because both $\prod_{j=1}^{k} \frac{x_{k+1}}{x_j}$ and $\sum_{i=1}^{k} f(x_i) \prod_{j=1, j \neq i}^{k} \frac{x_{k+1} - x_i}{x_j - x_i}$ are constant values, we denote them as a and b respectively. Then, the above equation can be rewritten as $f(x_{k+1}) = f(0)a + b$, which is an affine cipher. Moreover, because q is a prime and all these values $x_i \in \mathbb{Z}_q$, we have $\gcd(a, q) = 1$. This further implies that the value $f(x_{k+1})$ will be randomly distributed within $\mathbb{Z}_q$. Therefore, the probability that $\mathcal{A}_{PP}$ correctly computes the value $f(x_{x+1})$ is exactly $1/q$, which is negligible with respect to the security parameter λ.

Theorem 2. *The proposed scheme achieves the* **UNF** *property under the discrete logarithm assumption.*

Proof. Suppose there exists an adversary $\mathcal{A}_{UNF}$ who violates the **UNF** property with non-negligible probability, then we demonstrate that $\mathcal{A}_{UNF}$ can be used to construct an algorithm that computes $\log_g h$.

Based on the definition of **UNF** property, the adversary $\mathcal{A}_{UNF}$ has the knowledge of the two polynomials $f(\cdot)$ and $f'(\cdot)$. Her purpose is to output a triple (x^*, y^*, y'^*) such that within the following two inequalities $y^* \neq f(x^*)$ and $y'^* \neq f'(x^*)$, at least one of them is true, and meanwhile the verification of the equation $g^{y^*} h^{y'^*} = \prod_{i=0}^{k}(C_i)^{x^{*i}}$ is satisfied.

Firstly, we prove by contradiction that if $y^* \neq f(x^*)$, then we also have $y'^* \neq f'(x^*)$. Suppose we have $y^* \neq f(x^*)$ but $y'^* = f'(x^*)$, then $g^{y^*} h^{y'^*} = \prod_{i=0}^{k}(C_i)^{x^{*i}}$ implies that $g^{y^*} h^{y'^*} = g^{f(x^*)} h^{f'(x^*)}$, which further implies that $g^{y^*} = g^{f(x^*)}$. But this contradicts the pre-condition that $y^* \neq f(x^*)$. Hence the case $y^* \neq f(x^*)$ but $y'^* = f'(x^*)$ cannot happen. For similar reasons, the case $y'^* \neq f'(x^*)$ but $y^* = f(x^*)$ cannot happen neither. Therefore, it must be the case that both inequalities $y^* \neq f(x^*)$ and $y'^* \neq f'(x^*)$ are true.

Next, we prove that such an adversary $\mathcal{A}_{UNF}$ allows us to compute $\log_g h$. Since the verification of the equation $g^{y^*} h^{y'^*} = \prod_{i=0}^{k}(C_i)^{x^{*i}}$ is satisfied, this implies that $g^{y^*} h^{y'^*} = g^{f^*} h^{f'(x^*)}$. Hence, we have $\log_g h = \frac{y^* - f(x^*)}{f'(x^*) - y'^*}$. And because we have already proved that $f'(x^*) \neq y'^*$, the discrete logarithm $\log_g h$ can be computed with the same probability as $\mathcal{A}_{UNF}$ violates the **UNF** property. Therefore, based on the discrete logarithm assumption, there cannot exist an adversary $\mathcal{A}_{UNF}$ who violates the **UNF** property with non-negligible probability.

Theorem 3. *The proposed scheme achieves the* **IND-CFA** *property.*

Proof. We prove this theorem using the following strategy: suppose there are two games, Game_0 and Game_1. In Game_i for $i \in \{0, 1\}$, the polynomial $f_i(\cdot)$ is selected. We then show that the adversary $\mathcal{A}_{CFA}$'s view is perfectly indistinguishable between these two games. Hence, $\mathcal{A}_{CFA}$ will output the same b^* in both games with equal probability, and this proves that $\mathcal{A}_{CFA}$ guesses b correctly with probability exactly $1/2$.

In Game_0, $\mathcal{A}_{CFA}$ will be provided with the params in the first step. Then, in the second step, $\mathcal{A}_{CFA}$ chooses a polynomial $f_0(z) = a_{0,0} + a_{0,1}z + \ldots + a_{0,k}z^k$ over $\mathbb{Z}_q$ with degree k. In the third step, the challenger selects another random polynomial $f'_0(z) = b_{0,0} + b_{0,1}z + \ldots + b_{0,k}z^k$ over $\mathbb{Z}_q$ with degree k, and compute the commitments $C_{0,i} = g^{a_{0,i}} h^{b_{0,i}}$ for $i = 0, 1, \ldots, k$. Then, the challenger publishes vk which contains all these commitments.

In Game$_1$, $\mathcal{A}_{CFA}$ will be provided with exactly the same params in the first step. Then, in the second step, $\mathcal{A}_{CFA}$ chooses an independent polynomial $f_1(z) = a_{1,0} + a_{1,1}z + \ldots + a_{1,k}z^k$ over $\mathbb{Z}_q$ with degree k. In the third step, the challenger selects a random polynomial $f_1'(z) = b_{1,0} + b_{1,1}z + \ldots + b_{1,k}z^k$ over $\mathbb{Z}_q$ with degree k, and compute the commitments $C_{1,i} = g^{a_{1,i}} h^{b_{1,i}}$ for $i = 0, 1, \ldots, k$. $\mathcal{A}_{CFA}$ receives the public information vk which contains all the commitments in this step.

In the first step, $\mathcal{A}_{CFA}$'s view of the two games is exactly the same because the same params is output by the challenger. In the second step, $\mathcal{A}_{CFA}$ selects a random polynomial in both games. Hence, her view is exactly the same in this step as well. In the third step, $\mathcal{A}_{CFA}$ sees $C_{0,i} = g^{a_{0,i}} h^{b_{0,i}}$ for $i = 0, 1, \ldots, k$ in Game$_0$, and she sees $C_{1,i} = g^{a_{1,i}} h^{b_{1,i}}$ for $i = 0, 1, \ldots, k$ in Game$_1$. But all these commitments are randomly distributed in $\mathbb{Z}_p^*$. Therefore, $\mathcal{A}_{CFA}$'s view in the third step is also exactly the same. Moreover, although $\mathcal{A}_{CFA}$ can query the oracle $\mathcal{O}_{CFA}$, the oracle only responses to the query when the points lie both on $f_0(\cdot)$ and $f_1(\cdot)$. Hence, the oracle $\mathcal{O}_{CFA}$ does not give $\mathcal{A}_{CFA}$ any additional power. Therefore, $\mathcal{O}_{CFA}$ cannot distinguish these two games, and she guesses b correctly with probability exactly $1/2$.

4.3 Some Comparisons

The comparison of our proposed scheme with Bultel's PPE scheme in [6] and PolyCommit$_{Ped}$ in [15] is summarised as in Table 1. The description of Bultel's PPE scheme and PolyCommit$_{Ped}$ can be found in the appendix.

Table 1. Comparison of the three schemes

	params size	vk size	Verif	Assumption	Model	Trusted party
Bultel's PPE	$\mathcal{O}(1)$	$\mathcal{O}(k)$	Pairing free	DDH	RO	No
PolyCommit$_{Ped}$	$\mathcal{O}(k)$	$\mathcal{O}(1)$	Pairing based	t-SDH	Standard	Yes
Our PPE	$\mathcal{O}(1)$	$\mathcal{O}(k)$	Pairing free	DL	Standard	No

The main advantage of PolyCommit$_{Ped}$ is that the size of vk is constant, which is much smaller than the other two schemes. However, its size of params is much larger, and this offsets the previous advantage. Recall that the client needs to know both params and vk, all these three schemes have similar communication costs. To verify the correctness of polynomial evaluation, the client in PolyCommit$_{Ped}$ needs to perform pairing computations, and the client in Bultel's scheme needs to verify some additional zero-knowledge proofs. Our proposed scheme has some computational advantages over these two existing PPE schemes, because it is pairing free and the client only needs to perform some standard VSS verification.

In Bultel's scheme, the IND-CFA property relies on the DDH assumption, and the UNF property is proved in the Random Oracle (RO) model [2]. Although the RO model is of some value, it only provides heuristic proofs. In particular, it does not rule out the possibility of breaking the scheme without finding the weakness in the hash function [7]. Therefore, when the other parameters are equal, a proof in the standard model is still preferred. The security of PolyCommit$_{\text{Ped}}$ is proved in the standard model, but it needs a trusted party to initialise the params and its UNF property relies on a less standard t-SDH assumption. Our proposed scheme also has some security advantages over these two existing PPE schemes, because it does not need any trusted party, it can be proved in the standard model, and it relies on a much weaker assumption[2].

5 A Distributed PPE Scheme

In many applications, it may require that the PPE scheme also keeps the polynomial private from the third party. In this section, we introduce a natural extension of our propose PPE scheme in order to satisfy this requirement. In this distributed PPE scheme, the secret polynomial is outsourced to a number of third parties instead of a single one. These parties jointly evaluate the polynomial for the client in a verifiable way, but none of them could learn the polynomial unless they all collude.

The distributed PPE scheme is composed of the following four algorithms Setup, Init, Compute, Verif:

- Setup: Given a security parameter λ, two primes p and q are generated such that $q|p-1$. Then a group G is generated which is a subgroup of $\mathbb{Z}_p^*$ with order q. Moreover, g and h are denoted as two generators of G such that $\log_g h$ is unknown. Finally, all these parameters are made public as params.
- Init: Suppose the service provider wants to outsource the k degree polynomial $f(z) = a_0 + a_1 z + \ldots + a_k z^k$ over $\mathbb{Z}_q$ among t independent third parties. It first randomly selects another polynomial $f'(z) = b_0 + b_1 z + \ldots + b_k z^k$ over $\mathbb{Z}_q$ with the same degree, and then computes the commitments $C_i = g^{a_i} h^{b_i}$ for $i = 0, 1, \ldots, k$. Next, the service provider randomly generates two groups of t polynomials $f_j(z) = a_{j,0} + a_{j,1} z + \ldots + a_{j,k} z^k$ and $f'_j(z) = b_{j,0} + b_{j,1} z + \ldots + b_{j,k} z^k$ over $\mathbb{Z}_q$ with degree k, for $j = 1, 2, \ldots, t$, such that $f(z) = \sum_{j=1}^t f_j(z)$ and $f'(z) = \sum_{j=1}^t f'_j(z)$, and it computes the commitments $C_{j,i} = g^{a_{j,i}} h^{b_{j,i}}$ for $j = 1, 2, \ldots, t$ and $i = 1, 2, \ldots, k$. The service provider sends a pair of polynomials $f_j(z)$ and $f'_j(z)$ to each of the third party using a private channel. Finally, it broadcasts all the commitments generated in this step as the public information vk.
- Compute: Once receiving the client's input x, each of the third party computes two values $y_j = f_j(x)$ and $y'_j = f'_j(x)$, and sends these two values back to the client.
- Verif: The client first checks whether $C_i = \prod_{j=1}^t C_{ji}$ for $i = 1, 2, \ldots, k$. This verification ensures that $f(z) = \sum_{j=1}^t f_j(z)$ and $f'(z) = \sum_{j=1}^t f'_j(z)$. Note

---

[2] If there exists an adversary who can break the DL assumption with non-negligible probability, then an algorithm can be designed that uses this adversary as a subroutine and breaks both DDH and t-SDH assumptions with non-negligible probability.

that such a check only needs to be performed once, even if the client may query the polynomial several times. Then, for each of the third party, the client verifies whether it has correctly evaluated its assigned polynomials by checking the following equation:

$$g^{y_j} h^{y'_j} = \prod_{i=0}^{k} (C_{j,i})^{x^i}$$

If all the above checks are satisfied, the client computes $y = f(x) = \sum_{j=1}^{t} y_j$.

Note that if batch techniques [1] were used in the Verif algorithm, the client can verify all the equations at once instead of verifying t equations individually. Here, we only briefly sketch the security of the above scheme, since it is very similar as in the standard PPE scheme. Firstly, each third party evaluates a random polynomial, hence none of them learns the secret polynomial unless they all collude. The client is allowed to query the polynomial $f(\cdot)$ at most k times, and $f(\cdot)$ is with degree k. Hence, the client cannot learn any information of the polynomial and she only has negligible probability to violate the PP property. Furthermore, unless one can break the discrete logarithm assumption, the client can use the VSS equation to detect any incorrect evaluation of the polynomial, and this implies the UNF property. Finally, because all the commitments are in the Pedersen format which is information theoretically hiding, the IND-CFA property also holds in the above scheme.

6   Conclusion

As the wide deployment of Cloud platforms, PPE is a useful primitive to delegate the evaluation of secret polynomials in a verifiable way. In this paper, we introduce a new PPE scheme that satisfies all the PP, UNF and IND-CFA properties as advocated recently. And we show that compared with the existing PPE schemes with similar properties, our scheme not only has computational advantages but also relies on a much weaker assumption. Moreover, we explore how the PPE scheme can be implemented in a distributed way so that the polynomial is also kept private from the third party. We extend our proposed PPE scheme as an example, but the same method also can be used to extend the existing PPE schemes into the distributed version.

Acknowledgement. This work was partially supported by the National Natural Science Foundation of China (Grant No. 61572303, 61772326, 61672010, 61672398), and Natural Science Foundation of Hubei Province (Grant No. 2017CFB303, 2017CFA012). We are also grateful to the anonymous reviewers for their valuable comments on the paper.

Appendix A – PolyCommit$_{Ped}$

The PolyCommit$_{Ped}$ scheme [15] contains four algorithms (Setup, Init, Compute, Verif), and it works as follows:

- Setup: This algorithm is operated by a trusted party. Given the security parameter λ, it generates two cyclic groups G and G_T with prime order p such that there exists a symmetric bilinear pairing $\hat{e} : G \times G \to G_T$. It also chooses two generators g and h of G such that $\log_g h$ is unknown. Moreover, it selects $\alpha \xleftarrow{R} \mathbb{Z}_p^*$ and sets params $= (G, G_T, p, \hat{e}, g, h, (g^\alpha, \ldots, g^{\alpha^k}), (h^\alpha, \ldots, h^{\alpha^k}))$.
- Init: For the secret polynomial $f(z) = a_0 + a_1 z + \ldots + a_k z^k$, the service provider chooses a random polynomial $f'(z) = b_0 + b_1 z + \ldots + b_k z^k$ over $\mathbb{Z}_p^*$ with degree k. It computes the commitment $C = \prod_{i=0}^{k} (g^{\alpha^i})^{a_i} (h^{\alpha^i})^{b_i} = g^{f(\alpha)} h^{f'(\alpha)}$ and sets vk $= C$.
- Compute: Once receiving the client's input x. The third party computes $y = f(x)$ and $y' = f'(x)$. Moreover, it computes $\phi(z) = \frac{f(z) - f(x)}{z - x} = \sum_{i=0}^{k} \delta_i z^i$ and $\phi'(z) = \frac{f'(z) - f'(x)}{z - x} = \sum_{i=0}^{k} \sigma_i z^i$. It further computes $w = \prod_{j=0}^{k} (g^{\alpha^j})^{\delta_j} (h^{\alpha^j})^{\sigma_j} = g^{\phi(\alpha)} h^{\phi'(\alpha)}$. It sets the proof as $\pi = (x, y', w)$ and returns (y, π) to the client.
- Verif: The client verifies whether $\hat{e}(C, g) = \hat{e}(w, g^{\alpha - x}) \hat{e}(g^{f(x)} h^{g'(x)}, g)$. If this equation holds, the client outputs 1, and outputs 0 otherwise.

Appendix B – Bultel's PPE Scheme

The Bultel's PPE scheme [6] also contains four algorithms (Setup, Init, Compute, Verif) as follows:

- Setup: Given the security parameter λ, the service provider generates a group G with prime order p and a generator g for the group. It chooses a hash function $H : \{0, 1\}^* \to \mathbb{Z}_p^*$, and it sets params $= (G, p, g, H)$. Note that the hash function is only used to generate non-interactive zero-knowledge proofs.
- Init: For the secret polynomial $f(z) = a_0 + a_1 z + \ldots + a_k z^k$, the service provider picks sk $\xleftarrow{R} \mathbb{Z}_p^*$ and computes pk $= g^{sk}$. For $i = 0, 1, \ldots, k$, it picks $r_i \xleftarrow{R} \mathbb{Z}_p^*$ and computes $c_i = g^{r_i}$ and $d_i = pk^{r_i} g^{a_i}$. Note that (c_i, d_i) is an ElGamal ciphertext encrypting the commitment g^{a_i}. Finally, it sets vk $= (\{c_i, d_i\}_{0 \le i \le k}, pk)$.
- Compute: Once receiving the client's input x, the third party computes $y = f(x)$. It also computes $c = \prod_{i=0}^{k} (c_i)^{x^i} = \prod_{i=0}^{k} g^{r_i \cdot x^i} = g^{r(x)}$ and $d = \prod_{i=0}^{k} (d_i)^{x^i} = (\prod_{i=0}^{k} h^{r_i \cdot x^i}) \cdot (\prod_{i=0}^{k} g^{a_i \cdot x^i}) = h^{r(x)} g^{f(x)}$ for some polynomial $r(x) = \sum_{i=0}^{k} r_i \cdot x^i$. Moreover, it generates a non-interactive zero-knowledge proof π that (c, d) is an ElGamal ciphertext encrypting $g^{f(x)}$. Finally, it return (y, π) to the client.
- Verif: Using params and vk, the client can also compute (c, d). Then, she can verify whether π is a valid non-interactive zero-knowledge proof such that (c, d) encrypts g^y. If the verification satisfies, the client outputs 1, and outputs 0 otherwise.

References

1. Bellare, M., Garay, J.A., Rabin, T.: Batch verification with applications to cryptography and checking. In: Lucchesi, C.L., Moura, A.V. (eds.) LATIN 1998. LNCS, vol. 1380, pp. 170–191. Springer, Heidelberg (1998). https://doi.org/10.1007/BFb0054320

2. Bellare, M., Rogaway, P.: Random oracles are practical: a paradigm for designing efficient protocols. In: Proceedings of the 1st ACM Conference on Computer and Communications Security, pp. 62–73. ACM (1993)

3. Benaloh, J.C.: Secret sharing homomorphisms: keeping shares of a secret secret (extended abstract). In: Odlyzko, A.M. (ed.) CRYPTO 1986. LNCS, vol. 263, pp. 251–260. Springer, Heidelberg (1987). https://doi.org/10.1007/3-540-47721-7_19

4. Boneh, D., Boyen, X.: Short signatures without random oracles and the SDH assumption in bilinear groups. J. Cryptol. **21**(2), 149–177 (2008)

5. Boneh, D., Franklin, M.: Identity-based encryption from the Weil pairing. In: Kilian, J. (ed.) CRYPTO 2001. LNCS, vol. 2139, pp. 213–229. Springer, Heidelberg (2001). https://doi.org/10.1007/3-540-44647-8_13

6. Bultel, X., Das, M.L., Gajera, H., Gérault, D., Giraud, M., Lafourcade, P.: Verifiable private polynomial evaluation. In: Okamoto, T., Yu, Y., Au, M.H., Li, Y. (eds.) ProvSec 2017. LNCS, vol. 10592, pp. 487–506. Springer, Cham (2017). https://doi.org/10.1007/978-3-319-68637-0_29

7. Canetti, R., Goldreich, O., Halevi, S.: The random oracle methodology, revisited. J. ACM (JACM) **51**(4), 557–594 (2004)

8. Canetti, R., Riva, B., Rothblum, G.N.: Two protocols for delegation of computation. In: Smith, A. (ed.) ICITS 2012. LNCS, vol. 7412, pp. 37–61. Springer, Heidelberg (2012). https://doi.org/10.1007/978-3-642-32284-6_3

9. Choi, S.G., Katz, J., Kumaresan, R., Cid, C.: Multi-client non-interactive verifiable computation. In: Sahai, A. (ed.) TCC 2013. LNCS, vol. 7785, pp. 499–518. Springer, Heidelberg (2013). https://doi.org/10.1007/978-3-642-36594-2_28

10. Feldman, P.: A practical scheme for non-interactive verifiable secret sharing. In: 1987 28th Annual Symposium on Foundations of Computer Science, pp. 427–438. IEEE (1987)

11. Fiore, D., Gennaro, R.: Publicly verifiable delegation of large polynomials and matrix computations, with applications. In: Proceedings of the 2012 ACM Conference on Computer and Communications Security, pp. 501–512. ACM (2012)

12. Gajera, H., Naik, S., Das, M.L.: On the security of "verifiable privacy-preserving monitoring for cloud-assisted mHealth systems". In: Ray, I., Gaur, M.S., Conti, M., Sanghi, D., Kamakoti, V. (eds.) ICISS 2016. LNCS, vol. 10063, pp. 324–335. Springer, Cham (2016). https://doi.org/10.1007/978-3-319-49806-5_17

13. Gennaro, R., Gentry, C., Parno, B.: Non-interactive verifiable computing: outsourcing computation to untrusted workers. In: Rabin, T. (ed.) CRYPTO 2010. LNCS, vol. 6223, pp. 465–482. Springer, Heidelberg (2010). https://doi.org/10.1007/978-3-642-14623-7_25

14. Guo, L., Fang, Y., Li, M., Li, P.: Verifiable privacy-preserving monitoring for cloud-assisted mHealth systems. In: 2015 IEEE Conference on Computer Communications, INFOCOM, pp. 1026–1034. IEEE (2015)

15. Kate, A., Zaverucha, G.M., Goldberg, I.: Constant-size commitments to polynomials and their applications. In: Abe, M. (ed.) ASIACRYPT 2010. LNCS, vol. 6477, pp. 177–194. Springer, Heidelberg (2010). https://doi.org/10.1007/978-3-642-17373-8_11

16. Naor, M., Pinkas, B.: Oblivious transfer and polynomial evaluation. In: Proceedings of the Thirty-First Annual ACM Symposium on Theory of Computing, pp. 245–254. ACM (1999)

17. Papamanthou, C., Shi, E., Tamassia, R.: Signatures of correct computation. In: Sahai, A. (ed.) TCC 2013. LNCS, vol. 7785, pp. 222–242. Springer, Heidelberg (2013). https://doi.org/10.1007/978-3-642-36594-2_13

18. Parno, B., Howell, J., Gentry, C., Raykova, M.: Pinocchio: nearly practical verifiable computation. In: 2013 IEEE Symposium on Security and Privacy, SP, pp. 238–252. IEEE (2013)

19. Parno, B., Raykova, M., Vaikuntanathan, V.: How to delegate and verify in public: verifiable computation from attribute-based encryption. In: Cramer, R. (ed.) TCC 2012. LNCS, vol. 7194, pp. 422–439. Springer, Heidelberg (2012). https://doi.org/10.1007/978-3-642-28914-9_24

20. Pedersen, T.P.: Non-interactive and information-theoretic secure verifiable secret sharing. In: Feigenbaum, J. (ed.) CRYPTO 1991. LNCS, vol. 576, pp. 129–140. Springer, Heidelberg (1992). https://doi.org/10.1007/3-540-46766-1_9

Efficient Traceable Oblivious Transfer and Its Applications

Weiwei Liu[1,4], Yinghui Zhang[2,3(✉)], Yi Mu[4], Guomin Yang[4], and Yangguang Tian[5]

[1] School of Mathematics and Statistics,
North China University of Water Resources and Electric Power, Zhengzhou, China
liuweiwei@ncwu.edu.cn
[2] National Engineering Laboratory for Wireless Security,
Xi'an University of Posts and Telecommunications, Xi'an 710121, China
yhzhaang@163.com
[3] Westone Cryptologic Research Center, Beijing 100070, China
[4] Institute of Cybersecurity and Cryptology,
School of Computing and Information Technology, University of Wollongong,
Wollongong, NSW 2522, Australia
{ymu,gyang}@uow.edu.au
[5] School of Information Systems, Singapore Management University,
Singapore, Singapore
ygtian@smu.edu.sg

Abstract. Oblivious transfer (OT) has been applied widely in privacy-sensitive systems such as on-line transactions and electronic commerce to protect users' private information. Traceability is an interesting feature of such systems that the privacy of the dishonest users could be traced by the service provider or a trusted third party (TTP). However, previous research on OT mainly focused on designing protocols with unconditional receiver's privacy. Thus, traditional OT schemes cannot fulfill the traceability requirements in the aforementioned applications. In this paper, we address this problem by presenting a novel traceable oblivious transfer (TOT) without involvement of any TTP. In the new system, an honest receiver is able to make a fixed number of choices with perfect receiver privacy. If the receiver misbehaves and tries to request more than a pre-fixed number of choices, then all his previous choices could be traced by the sender. We first give the formal definition and security model of TOT, then propose an efficient TOT scheme, which is proven secure under the proposed security model.

Keywords: Oblivious transfer · Secret sharing · Privacy · Traceability

1 Introduction

Oblivious Transfer is one of the fundamental cryptographic primitives that has been used widely in various security applications such as exchange of secrets

© Springer Nature Switzerland AG 2018
C. Su and H. Kikuchi (Eds.): ISPEC 2018, LNCS 11125, pp. 610–621, 2018.
https://doi.org/10.1007/978-3-319-99807-7_39

[22,25], contract signing [3,12], secure multiparty computation [24] and Internet of Things (IoT) [2]. Roughly speaking, an oblivious transfer scheme is an interactive protocol running between a sender with a set of messages $\{m_1, m_2, \ldots, m_n\}$ and a receiver with a set of choices $\{\sigma_1, \sigma_2, \ldots, \sigma_k\}$. After running the protocol, the receiver learns the intended messages $m_{\sigma_1}, m_{\sigma_2}, \ldots, m_{\sigma_k}$ but cannot learn anything about m_i for $i \notin \{\sigma_1, \sigma_2, \ldots, \sigma_k\}$. Meanwhile, the receiver's choices $\{\sigma_1, \sigma_2, \ldots, \sigma_k\}$ are completely hidden from the sender. The concept of oblivious transfer was first introduced by Rabin in 1981 [22]. In their original construction, the sender sends a single bit 0 or 1 to the receiver in such a way that with $1/2$ probability the receiver will receive the same bit and with $1/2$ probability that the receiver will receive nothing. At the same time, the sender has no idea whether the receiver receives the message or not. Since then, oblivious transfer has attracted a lot of attentions, and a number of work [5,8,10,12,20] have been done to improve the original OT scheme in different aspects.

Even et al. [12] proposed a 1-out-of-2 OT (OT_2^1) scheme, in which the sender obliviously sends a message m_i, $i \in \{0, 1\}$, to the receiver. Shortly after that, Brassard et al. [5] extended the OT_2^1 [12] to a more general k-out-of-n (OT_n^k) setting, where the receiver is able to make multiple choices $m_{\sigma_1}, m_{\sigma_2}, \ldots, m_{\sigma_k}$ ($\sigma_i \in \{1, 2, \ldots, n\}$, $1 \leq i \leq k$) from a set of n messages $\{m_1, m_2, \ldots, m_n\}$ held by the sender, meanwhile the receiver's choices remain oblivious to the sender. Since then, many subsequent work [10,19] aimed to design more efficient OT_n^k schemes. Different from normal OT_n^k, another important research direction on OT is adaptive OT_n^k [20]. In adaptive OT_n^k, the receiver can choose the messages adaptively, namely, the ith value chosen by the receiver depends on the first $i-1$ values.

In the early OT schemes reviewed above, there is no condition on restricting the receiver's ability. Any user in the system can act as a receiver and run the OT protocol to choose messages held by the sender obliviously. To address this problem, Coull et al. [11] proposed an OT scheme supporting access control using state graphs, where for every transaction, the state of the receiver shifts from one to another. The receiver can access the protected services only if some of his states are not used. Camenisch et al. [6] proposed another approach to enforce access control. In their system, the receiver first authenticates himself to a trusted third party to obtain some credentials. Later, the receiver proves to the sender that he possesses a valid credential from the third party using zero-knowledge proof. However, in this construction, the access policy is publicly known.

To address this problem, Camenisch et al. [7] proposed another oblivious transfer with access control (AC-OT) in which only the receivers whose attributes satisfy a predicate can access the services. In order to reduce the computation and communication cost, Han et al. [14] proposed two efficient oblivious transfer schemes without using zero-knowledge proof. In addition, different form previous schemes, the receivers could obtain credentials from a trusted third party but do not have to authenticate themselves. Thus, the communication and computation cost is lower than previous schemes supporting access control.

Later on, Han et al. [13] proposed accountable oblivious transfer with access control, such that authorized users are allowed to access sensitive records with accountable times. They claim that it is the first AC-OT scheme where both the timely revocation and the prevention of overusing records are addressed simultaneously. In particular, if a dishonest user misuse the given credential, then his public identity will be revealed due to the k-time anonymous authentication technique [23] is used.

There have been a lot of research works [8,15,21] on defining OT security, which can be classified into honest-but-curious model, half-simulation model [21], full-simulation model [6–8] and Universally Composable (UC) model [13,15], according to whether the OT scheme can provide simulatable security for the sender and/or receiver. In the honest-but-curious model, all participants in the protocol are assumed to be honest, which makes this model too idealistic for practical use. Naor and Pinkas [21] introduced the half-simulation model that allows malicious senders and receivers. However, in this model, the security of the sender and receiver are considered separately. Half-simulation model achieves simulatable security for sender privacy and computationally indistinguishability for receiver privacy.

In order to capture the selective-failure attacks that may be performed by the cheating sender, the full simulatability is introduced. In the full-simulation model [8,15], it achieves simulatable security for both the receiver and sender together. As for the UC-related model, the security of sender and receiver is defined by the indistinguishability between a real world and an ideal world as described in the UC framework [9]. We then compare our proposed TOT with typical works in Table 1 to highlight our distinction: it shows that our proposed TOT enjoys traceability[1] to the receiver's choice if the user misbehaves, and secures in the half simulation model under dynamic assumptions. In Table 1, adaptive means that the receiver chooses the k records one after the other. † denotes the various security models, which includes the honest but curious model, the half/full simulation model and the UC model. Dynamic means that the assumptions are depending on the number of n, such as strong Diffie-Hellman assumptions [4].

1.1   Our Motivation

All the previous research on OT aimed to design OT schemes with perfect receiver and sender privacy. In real-world applications [1,16], it is desirable for the sender to trace the choices of the receiver if they misbehave. Thus, the previous OT schemes are not suitable in these scenarios. To the best of our knowledge, there is only one work [18] aiming to construct OT schemes with traceable receiver's privacy. However, this OT scheme involves a trusted time

---

[1] Note that the traceability means that the previously *choices* of the cheating receiver are revealed, which is the major distinction between our proposed TOT and the construction in [13]. In the table, we use the symbol traceability* to distinguish our work with that one in [13].

Table 1. A comparative summary for OT protocols.

Function/algorithm	NP [21]	CT [10]	CGS [8]	KN [15]	HSM* [13]	Ours
Adaptive	✓	✓	✓	✓	✓	✓
†-simulation	Half	Half	Full	UC	UC	Half
Standard model	✓	×	✓	✓	✓	×
Dynamic assumptions	×	×	✓	×	✓	✓
Access control	×	×	×	×	✓	✓
Traceability	×	×	×	×	✓	×
Traceability*	×	×	×	×	×	✓

server that publishes trapdoors on a time basis. After releasing the trapdoor, the privacy of all the receivers, including the honest ones, will be lost. The motivation of this work is to propose a new OT with traceable receiver's privacy such that the privacy of an honest receiver is protected unconditionally while all the previous *choices* of a misbehaving receiver can be revealed by the sender if the receiver makes more than the pre-determined number of choices in the OT protocol. It is worth noting that in some real-life applications, the service provider (i.e., database provider) may not only need to detect the identity of dishonest users, but also want to reveal their choices that was made previously in the system. By doing so, the service provider may revoke the operations on the corresponding sensitive data which was anonymously and obliviously made by that cheating user.

Our Contribution. In this paper, we present a novel traceable oblivious transfer that allows a sender to trace the dishonest receivers' choices without the help of any trusted third party. Our contributions can be summarized as follows:

- We present the *first* traceable adaptive OT_n^k scheme and analysed its security under the half-simulation model [21];
- The *traceable* OT_n^k scheme allows the receiver to obtain a fixed number of messages $m_{\sigma_1}, m_{\sigma_2}, \ldots, m_{\sigma_k}$ from the message set $\{m_1, m_2, \ldots, m_n\}$ held by the sender where $\sigma_i \in \{1, 2, \ldots, n\}$ for $1 \leq i \leq k$, while receiver's choice is hidden from the sender;
- The *traceable* OT_n^k scheme allows the receiver cannot learn anything on message m_i such that $i \notin \{\sigma_1, \sigma_2, \ldots, \sigma_k\}$ for $1 \leq i \leq n$. In particular, if the receiver makes more than k requests, then all his previous *choices* $(m_{\sigma_1}, m_{\sigma_2}, \ldots, m_{\sigma_k})$ could be traced by the sender.

Paper Organization. The rest of the paper is organized as follows. We introduce the formal definition and the security model of TOT in Sect. 2. Some preliminaries are presented in Sect. 3 and a concrete scheme TOT scheme is presented in Sect. 4. We prove its security in Sect. 5 and the paper is concluded in Sect. 6.

2   Formal Definition and Security Model

We present the formal definition and security model for TOT in this section. There are two participants in a TOT system, namely, a sender S and a receiver R. S possesses a set of messages $\{m_1, m_2, \ldots, m_n\}$ and R makes a set of choices $\{\sigma_1, \sigma_2, \ldots, \sigma_k\}$ such that $\sigma_i \in \{1, 2, \ldots, n\}$ for $1 \leq i \leq k$.

2.1   Definitions of Traceable Oblivious Transfer

A TOT scheme is essentially an interactive protocol consisting of a tuple of PPT algorithms (*Setup, Commitment, Request, Response, Extract, Tracing*).

1. *Setup*: Taking as input of a security parameter κ, the setup algorithm outputs the system public parameters.

$$params \leftarrow Setup(1^\kappa)$$

2. *KeyGen*: Taking as input of the public parameter *params*, the key generation algorithm outputs a retrievable key pair[2] (rpk, rsk) for the receiver and a one-time key pair for the sender.

$$(rpk, rsk) \leftarrow KeyGen(params)$$
$$(opk, osk) \leftarrow KeyGen(params)$$

3. *Commitment*: Taking as input of the system parameters *params*, the retrievable public key rpk of the receiver, the messages $m_1, m_2, \ldots, m_n$ and one-time secret key osk of the sender, the commitment algorithm outputs a set of ciphertext $c_1, c_2, \ldots, c_n$.

$$c_1, c_2, \ldots, c_n \leftarrow Commitment(rpk, m_1, m_2, \ldots, m_n, osk, params)$$

4. *Request*: Taking as input of the intended indexes σ, the retrievable private key rsk and *params*, this algorithms outputs the commitment of the user's choice.

$$A_\sigma \leftarrow Request(\sigma; rsk; params)$$

5. *Response*: Taking as input of the commitment A_σ from the receiver, the secret of the sender, the output of the algorithm is response of the sender.

$$D_\sigma \leftarrow Response(A_\sigma, osk, params)$$

6. *Extract*: Taking as input of the response D_σ from the sender, the cipertext c_α and the system parameters *params*, output the message of the receiver's choice.

$$m_\sigma \leftarrow Extract(D_\sigma, c_\sigma, params)$$

---

[2] We assume there exists a public key infrastructure (PKI) issuing certificates on the users' public keys in our system.

7. *Tracing*: The *Tracing* algorithm is performed by the sender, taking as input of the $k + 1$ transcripts $A_{\sigma_1}, A_{\sigma_2}, \ldots, A_{\sigma_{k+1}}$ from a receiver, the retrievable public key rpk and $params$, outputs the receiver's choice $\sigma_1, \sigma_2, \ldots, \sigma_k$.

$$\sigma_1, \sigma_2, \ldots, \sigma_k \leftarrow Tracing(A_{\sigma_1}, A_{\sigma_2}, \ldots, A_{\sigma_{k+1}}; rpk; params)$$

Correctness: We require that for any security parameter $\kappa \in \mathbb{N}$, if $params \leftarrow ParamGen(1^\kappa)$, $(rpk, rsk) \leftarrow KeyGen(params)$, $(opk, osk) \leftarrow KeyGen(params)$, $c_1, c_2, \ldots, c_n \leftarrow Commitment(rpk, m_1, m_2, \ldots, m_n, osk, params)$, $A_\sigma \leftarrow Request(\sigma; rsk, params)$, $D_\sigma \leftarrow Response(A_\sigma, osk; parmas)$, then

- The receiver can extract the correct message.

$$\Pr(m_\sigma \leftarrow Extract(D_\sigma, rsk, params)) = 1.$$

- If the receiver makes less than $k + 1$ requests, then the sender cannot obtain any information about the receiver's choice.

$$\Pr('\perp' \leftarrow Tracing(A_{\sigma_1}, A_{\sigma_2}, \ldots, A_{\sigma_\delta}; rpk; params | \delta \leq k)) = 1.$$

- If the receiver makes more than k requests, then the sender can trace the previous choice of the receiver.

$$\Pr(\sigma_1, \sigma_2, \ldots, \sigma_\delta \leftarrow Tracing(A_{\sigma_1}, A_{\sigma_2}, \ldots, A_{\sigma_\delta}; rpk; params | \delta > k)) = 1.$$

2.2   Security Model for Traceable Oblivious Transfer

In this paper, we review the half-simulation model proposed in [21] to evaluate the security of TOT schemes. Besides the sender and receiver's privacy, we define a new property named traceability to capture the additional feature of TOT. In the half-simulation model, the security of the sender and receiver is considered separately. A secure TOT scheme should meet the following security requirements:

1. *Receiver's Privacy*:
   - If R makes less than $k+1$ requests, then S cannot obtain any information about R's choice.
   - For any two different choice sets $\mathcal{C} = \{\sigma_1, \sigma_2, \ldots, \sigma_k\}$ and $\mathcal{C}' = \{\sigma'_1, \sigma'_2, \ldots, \sigma'_k\}$, the transcripts $\mathcal{A} = \{A_{\sigma_1}, A_{\sigma_2}, \ldots, A_{\sigma_k}\}$ and $\mathcal{A}' = \{A'_{\sigma_1}, A'_{\sigma_2}, \ldots, A'_{\sigma_k}\}$ received by S corresponding to $\mathcal{M} = \{m_{\sigma_1}, m_{\sigma_2}, \ldots, m_{\sigma_k}\}$ and $\mathcal{M}' = \{m'_{\sigma_1}, m'_{\sigma_2}, \ldots, m'_{\sigma_k}\}$ are indistinguishable if the received messages $\mathcal{M} = \{m_{\sigma_1}, m_{\sigma_2}, \ldots, m_{\sigma_k}\}$ and $\mathcal{M}' = \{m'_{\sigma_1}, m'_{\sigma_2}, \ldots, m'_{\sigma_k}\}$ are identically distributed.
2. *Sender's Privacy*:
   - R cannot obtain any information on $m_i, i \notin \{\sigma_1, \sigma_2, \ldots, \sigma_k\}$ for $1 \leq i \leq n$.
   - In the half-simulation model, the security of R is defined by the real-world/ideal-world paradigm. In the real world, R and S execute the

protocol. In the ideal world, the protocol is implemented with the help a trusted third party (TTP). S sends all the messages $m_1, m_2, \ldots, m_n$ to the TTP. While R sends his choices $\{\sigma_1, \sigma_2, \ldots, \sigma_k\}$ adaptively to the TTP. If $\{\sigma_1, \sigma_2, \ldots, \sigma_k\} \in \{1, 2, \ldots, n\}$ the TTP sends messages $\{m_{\sigma_1}, m_{\sigma_2}, \ldots, m_{\sigma_k}\}$ to the receiver. A TOT scheme is said to provide the privacy of the sender if for any receiver R in real world, there exists an probabilistic polynomial-time (PPT) R' in the ideal world such that the output of R and R' are indistinguishable.

3. *Traceability*:
Traceability is not a necessary requirement for traditional OT schemes, we consider traceability as a special property of our TOT schemes. If a dishonest receiver R makes $k + 1$ choices $\{\sigma_1, \sigma_2, \ldots, \sigma_k, \sigma_{k+1}\}$ from S, suppose $\mathcal{A} = \{A_{\sigma_1}, A_{\sigma_2}, \ldots, A_{\sigma_k}, A_{\sigma_{k+1}}\}$ is the transcript set of the $k + 1$ choices, then S is able to trace R's choices through an efficient PPT algorithm *Tracing*.

3   Preliminaries

In this section, we introduce some preliminaries that will be used throughout this paper.

Definition 1. *Decisional Diffie-Hellman (DDH) Assumption:* *Given a cyclic group G_q of prime order q, the DDH problem states that, given $g, g^a, g^b, Z \in G_q$ for some random $a, b \in \mathbb{Z}_q$ and a random generator g, decide $Z = g^{ab}$. Define the success probability of a polynomial algorithm $\mathcal{A}$ in solving the DDH problem as:*

$$Succ_{\mathcal{A}, \mathbb{G}_q}^{DDH}(\kappa) = |\Pr[\mathcal{A}(G_q, g, g^a, g^b, g^{ab}) = 1] - \Pr[\mathcal{A}(G_q, g, g^a, g^b, Z) = 1]|$$

where $\kappa = \log(q)$ is the security parameter. The DDH assumption states that for any probabilistic polynomial algorithm time $\mathcal{A}$, $Succ_{\mathcal{A}, \mathbb{G}_q}^{DDH}(\kappa)$ is negligible in κ.

Definition 2. *One More Diffie-Hellman (OMDH) Assumption* [21]: *Given a cyclic group G_q of prime order q and g is a generator of G, let $DH(\cdot)$ be the Diffie-Hellman oracle that takes $X = g^x, Y = g^y \in G_q$ for some $x, y \in \mathbb{Z}_q$ and returns the Diffie-Hellman value $Z = g^{xy}$. Let $C(\cdot)$ be a challenge oracle that takes no input and returns a random element in G_q. Let $Y_1, Y_2, \ldots, Y_t$ denote the challenges returned by $C(\cdot)$, we say an OMDH adversary $\mathcal{A}$ wins if $\mathcal{A}$ can output the sequence of Diffie-Hellman values $Z_1, Z_2, \ldots, Z_t$ of all DHP instances with input X, Y_i, $i = 1, 2, \ldots, t$ and the number of queries q_{dh} made by $\mathcal{A}$ to the Diffie-Hellman oracle $DH(\cdot)$ is less than t. Define the success probability of a polynomial algorithm $\mathcal{A}$ in solving the OMDH problem as:*

$$Succ_{\mathcal{A}, G_q}^{OMDH}(\kappa) = \Pr[Z_1, Z_2, \ldots, Z_t \leftarrow \mathcal{A}_{DH(\cdot), q_{dh} < t}(X, (Y_1, Y_2, \ldots, Y_t \leftarrow C(\cdot)))]$$

the OMDH assumption states that, for any polynomial algorithm $\mathcal{A}$, $Succ_{\mathcal{A}, G_q}^{OMDH}(\kappa)$ is negligible in κ.

4   One Construction of Efficient Traceable Oblivious Transfer Schemes

The proposed scheme consists of a tuple of PPT algorithms as follows.

1. **Setup:** Let G_q denote a subgroup of $\mathbb{Z}_p$ with prime order q and $g, h_1, h_2, \ldots,$ h_n be generators of G_q, where $p = 2q + 1$ is also prime. Choose two collision resistant hash functions H, H_1 such that $H : \mathbb{N} \to Z_q^*$ and $H_1 : G_q \to G_q$. The system parameters $params = (G_q, p, q, g, h_1, h_2, \ldots, h_n, H, H_1)$.
2. **KeyGen:** The receiver R chooses a random number $s \in \mathbb{Z}_q^*$ and generates a retrievable key pair $(rpk, rsk) = (g^s, s)$. R chooses k random numbers $s_1, s_2, \ldots, s_k \in_R \mathbb{Z}_q$ and computes $S_1 = g^{s_1}, S_2 = g^{s_2}, \ldots, S_k = g^{s_k}$. S chooses a random number $z \in_R \mathbb{Z}_q^*$ and generates a one-time key pair $(opk, osk) = (g^z, z)$. R publishes rpk and $S_1, S_2, \ldots, S_k$ and S publishes opk.
3. **Commitment Phase:** S computes the ciphertext of $m_1, m_2, \ldots, m_n$ as $c_i = H_1((rpk \cdot h_i^{H(i)})^z) \cdot m_i$, $1 \le i \le n$, S sends $c_1, c_2, \ldots, c_n$ to R.
4. **Request:** In the i-th round,
   - R chooses $r_i \in_R \mathbb{Z}_q^*$, and computes $B_i = g^{r_i}, B_i' = h_{\alpha_i}^{r_i}$ and $A_i = (g^{r_i})^s (h_{\alpha_i}^{r_i})^{H(\alpha_i)}$, where $\alpha_i \in_R \{1, 2, \ldots, n\}$ is the receiver's choice and $f(B_i) = s + s_1 B_i + \ldots s_k B_i^k$.
   - R sends $(B_i, B_i', f(B_i), A_i)$ to S, and simultaneously does the following proof of knowledge. $PoK\{(H(\alpha_i), s) : A = B_i^s B_i'^{H(\alpha_i)} \wedge rpk = g^s\}$.
5. **Response:** S first verifies B_i, the secret share $f(B_i)$ and the PoK by checking:
   - S checks whether B_i appears in previous session.
   - $g^{f(B_i)} \stackrel{?}{=} rpk \cdot S_1^{B_i} \cdot S_2^{B_i^2} \cdot \ldots \cdot S_k^{B_i^k}$. If this equation holds,
   - S verifies $PoK\{(H(\alpha_i), s) : A_i = B_i^s B_i'^{H(\alpha_i)} \wedge rpk = g^s\}$.
   If either of the verification fails, S aborts; Otherwise, S stores $(B_i, B_i', f(B_i), A_i)$ and S generates $D_i = A_i^z$ and sends D_i to R.
6. **Extract:** Upon receiving D_i from S, R computes $K_{\alpha_i} = D_i^{\frac{1}{r_i}}$ and extracts the intended message $m_{\alpha_i} = c_{\alpha_i} / H_1(K_{\alpha_i})$.
7. **Tracing:** Once R and S execute the OT for $k+1$ times, S obtains $k+1$ shares of the secret. S is able to recover s from secret sharing. Once s is calculated, for the previous commitments $A_i = B_i^s B_i'^{H(\alpha_i)}$, given B_i, B_i' for $1 \le i \le k$. S is able to retrieve α_i for $1 \le i \le k$.

The proof of knowledge $PoK\{(H(\alpha_i), s) : A_i = B_i^s B_i'^{H(\alpha_i)} \wedge rpk = g^s\}$ can be implemented as follows:

1. R randomly chooses two random numbers $t_1, t_2 \in \mathbb{Z}_p$, computes $T_1 = B_i^{t_1} B_i'^{t_2}, T_2 = g^{t_1}$, $c = H(f(B_i), B_i, B_i', T_1, T_2)$, $v_1 = t_1 - cs$ and $v_2 = t_2 - cH(\alpha_i)$. R sends v_1, v_2, T_1, T_2 to S.
2. S accepts if both $A_i^c B_i^{v_1} B_i'^{v_2} = T_1$ and $rpk^c g^{v_1} = T_2$ hold.

5   Security Analysis

Theorem 1. *The proposed TOT scheme is correct.*

Proof. The correctness of the proposed scheme is shown as follows:

1. **Correctness of PoK:** If R is honest, then R has knowledge of $H(\alpha_i)$ and s, R computes $v_1 = t_1 - cs$ and $v_2 = t_2 - cH(\alpha_i)$. S can verify correctly that:

$$A^c B_i^{v_1} B_i'^{v_2} = B_i^{sc} B_i'^{H(\alpha_i)c} B_i^{t_1-cs} B_i'^{t_2-cH(\alpha_i)} = B_i^{t_1} B_i'^{t_2} = T_1.$$
$$rpk^c g^{v_1} = g^{sc} g^{t_1-cs} = g^{t_1} = T_2.$$

2. **Correctness of extracting the message:**

$$m_{\alpha_i} = \frac{c_{\alpha_i}}{H_1(K_{\alpha_i})} = \frac{m_{\alpha_i} H_1(rpk \cdot h_{\alpha_i}^{H(\alpha_i)})^z)}{H_1((g^{r_i sz} h_{\alpha_i}^{r_i H(\alpha_i)z})^{\frac{1}{r_i}})} = \frac{m_{\alpha_i} H_1(g^{sz} h_{\alpha_i}^{H(\alpha_i)z})}{H_1(g^{sz} h_{\alpha_i}^{H(\alpha_i)z})} = m_{\alpha_i}$$

Theorem 2. *The proposed TOT scheme provides receiver's privacy for honest receivers.*

Proof. We followed the methods described in [17] to analyse the security of the proposed TOT scheme. Suppose a honest receiver runs the OT protocol with the sender for k times. The sender could obtain k pairs of transcripts $\{(A_1, B_1, B_1'), (A_2, B_2, B_2'), \ldots, (A_k, B_k, B_k')\}$ such that $A_1 = (g^{r_1})^s (h_{\alpha_1}^{r_1})^{H(\alpha_1)}$, $A_2 = (g^{r_2})^s (h_{\alpha_2}^{r_2})^{H(\alpha_2)}, \ldots, A_k = (g^{r_k})^s (h_{\alpha_k}^{r_k})^{H(\alpha_k)}$, where $\alpha_1, \alpha_2, \ldots, \alpha_k \in \{1, 2, \ldots, n\}$ are the user's choice and $r_1, r_2, \ldots, r_k \in_R \mathbb{Z}_q^*$. Given $B_j = g^{r_j}, rpk = g^s$ for some random $r_j \in \mathbb{Z}_q^*$, it is computation-infeasible to decide the masked value equals $g^{r_j s}$ or a random value Z in G_q, thus for any two transcripts A_j and A_i such that $1 \leq i \neq j \leq k$ from the user, they are computationally indistinguishable to the service provider as long as the DDH problem is hard in G_q.

Theorem 3. *The proposed TOT scheme provides sender's privacy.*

Proof. Suppose a honest receiver runs the OT protocol with the sender k times. For any probabilistic polynomial-time malicious receiver $\hat{R}$ in the real-world model, we are able to construct a probabilistic polynomial-time malicious receiver $\hat{R}^*$ in the ideal model such that the outputs of $\hat{R}$ and $\hat{R}^*$ are indistinguishable.

Briefly, the ideal-world cheating receiver $\hat{R}^*$ can extract α from the proof of knowledge. This enables him to obtain the message m_α form the TTP. $\hat{R}^*$ simulates the honest sender S in the real-world and interacts with $\hat{R}$ as follows:

1. S sends $m_1, m_2, \ldots, m_n$ to the trusted third party TTP.
2. $\hat{R}^*$ sends $c_1^*, c_2^*, \ldots, c_n^*$ to TTP such that $c_i^* \in_R G_q$ for $i = 1, 2, \ldots, n$.
3. $\hat{R}^*$ monitors the outputs $A_{\alpha_1}, A_{\alpha_2}, \ldots, A_{\alpha_k}$ of $\hat{R}$, $\hat{R}^*$ chooses $A_{\alpha_1}^*, A_{\alpha_2}^*, \ldots, A_{\alpha_k}^* \in_R G_q$.

4. After $\hat{R}$ runs *Request* protocol, if the verification of *PoK* fails, $\hat{R}^*$ sends a value $\alpha_i \notin \{1, 2, \ldots, n\}$ to TTP.
5. If the verification of *PoK* successes, $\hat{R}^*$ extracts $\hat{R}$'s choice α_i from the *PoK* and gets back $D_{\sigma_1}^*, D_{\sigma_2}^*, \ldots, D_{\sigma_k}^*$ such that $D_{\sigma_i}^* = A_{\alpha_i}^{z^*}$ for $i = 1, 2, \ldots, k$.
6. If $\hat{R}$ can compute $K_{\alpha_i} = g^{sz} h_{\alpha_i}^{H(\alpha_i)z}$, $\hat{R}^*$ sends α_i to TTP, TTP returns $\frac{c_{\alpha_i}^*}{m_{\alpha_i}}$.
7. $\hat{R}^*$ outputs $(A_{\alpha_1}^*, A_{\alpha_2}^*, \ldots, A_{\alpha_k}^*, D_{\sigma_1}^*, D_{\sigma_2}^*, \ldots, D_{\sigma_k}^*, c_1^*, c_2^*, \ldots, c_n^*)$.

We can see from Theorem 2 and Claim (see proof below) that $\{A_{\alpha_1}, A_{\alpha_2}, \ldots, A_{\alpha_k}\}$ and $\{c_1, c_2, \ldots, c_n\}$ are indistinguishable from random elements in G_q. In addition, the sets of $\{D_{\sigma_1}, D_{\sigma_2}, \ldots, D_{\sigma_k}\}$ and $\{D_{\sigma_1}^*, D_{\sigma_2}^*, \ldots, D_{\sigma_k}^*\}$ are identically distributed. Therefore, no distinguishers can distinguish the outputs of $\hat{R}$ and $\hat{R}'$ with a non-negligible probability.

Claim. The proposed encryption scheme is semantic secure.

Proof. The security proof is performed using random oracle. Suppose the simulator $\mathcal{B}$ maintains a table T_1 for the hash queries. $\mathcal{B}$ obtains $n + 1$ values $Z, Y_1, Y_2, \ldots, Y_n$ from the challenge oracle $C(\cdot)$. $\mathcal{B}$ sets the one-time public key of the sender $opk = Z$ and sends $Z, Y_1, Y_2, \ldots, Y_n$ to a PPT adversary $\mathcal{A}$. Assume $\mathcal{A}$ queries on a message m_i for $1 \leq i \leq n - 1$. $\mathcal{B}$ first obtain the diffie-hellman value of (Z, Y_i) with help of $DH(\cdot)$ oracle. Then $\mathcal{A}$ checks if $DH(Z, Y_i)$ has existed in T_1. If not, $\mathcal{B}$ chooses a new random $Z_i \in G_q$ and stores $(DH(Z, Y_i), Z_i)$ to T_1. Otherwise, assume $H_1(DH(Z, Y_i)) = Z_i$, $\mathcal{B}$ returns $c_i = Z_i \cdot m_i$ as the ciphertext on m_i. After $n - 1$ queries, $\mathcal{A}$ sends two challenge messages m_0^*, m_1^*, $\mathcal{B}$ chooses $b \in \{0, 1\}$ and a random number $Z_n \in G_q$. $\mathcal{A}$ sets the ciphertext c_b^* on m_b^* as $c_b^* = Z_n \cdot m_b^*$. If $\mathcal{A}$ has a non-negligible probability ϵ in distinguishing c_b^* than random guess. Then with an overwhelming probability that $DH(Z, Y_n)$ has been submitted in the hash queries. Thus $\mathcal{B}$ breaks the OMDH assumption, we reach a contradiction. Therefore the proposed encryption scheme is semantic secure.

Theorem 4. *The proposed TOT scheme provides traceability to the receiver.*

Proof. After running the protocol $k + 1$ times with the receiver, the sender obtains $k + 1$ shares of the retrievable private key s with respect to the unknown integers $s_1, s_2, \ldots, s_k$ such that

$$f(B_i) = s + s_1 B_i + s_2 B_i^2 \ldots + s_k B_i^k, 1 \leq i \leq k + 1.$$

The corresponding linear equations in a matrix form are as follows:

$$\begin{pmatrix} 1 & B_1 & B_1^2 & \cdots & B_1^k \\ 1 & B_2 & B_2^2 & \cdots & B_2^k \\ \vdots & \vdots & \vdots & \vdots & \vdots \\ 1 & B_{k+1} & B_{k+1}^2 & \cdots & B_{k+1}^k \end{pmatrix} * \begin{pmatrix} s \\ s_1 \\ \vdots \\ s_k \end{pmatrix} = \begin{pmatrix} f(B_1) \\ f(B_2) \\ \vdots \\ f(B_{k+1}) \end{pmatrix}$$

As we can see the coefficient matrix is a Vandermonde matrix or a non-singular matrix. The determinant of such a matrix is not equal to zero. Thus the equations have a unique solution to $s, s_1, s_2, \ldots, s_k$.

Once the sender obtains the value of the retrievable private key rsk. For previous commitments on receiver's choice $A_i = B_i^{rsk} B_i'^{H(\alpha_i)}$ for $1 \leq i \leq k$. Since S has store the values of B_i and B_i' in the i-th round. Thus, the sender could trace the receiver choice $\alpha_i = j$ in the i-th round by checking that $A_i = B_i^{rsk} B_i'^{H(\alpha_i)} = B_i^{rsk} B_i'^{H(j)}$ for $1 \leq j \leq n$.

6   Conclusion

In this paper, we proposed a novel oblivious transfer scheme that can achieve retrievable receiver's privacy without the help of a trusted third party. The misbehaving receivers' choices could be traced while the honest receivers' privacy is well protected. We proved the security of the scheme under the proposed security model. We leave the construction of an adaptive traceable OT scheme that is proven secure under non-dynamic assumptions in the full-simulation model or UC model as our future work.

Acknowledgements. This work is supported by the National Key R&D Program of China (2017YFB0802000), the National Natural Science Foundation of China (Nos. 61772418, 61402366). Yinghui Zhang is supported by New Star Team of Xi'an University of Posts & Telecommunications (2016-02).

References

1. Aiello, B., Ishai, Y., Reingold, O.: Priced oblivious transfer: how to sell digital goods. In: Pfitzmann, B. (ed.) EUROCRYPT 2001. LNCS, vol. 2045, pp. 119–135. Springer, Heidelberg (2001). https://doi.org/10.1007/3-540-44987-6_8
2. Ashton, K.: That internet of things? Thing (1999)
3. Ben-Or, M., Goldreich, O., Micali, S., Rivest, R.L.: A fair protocol for signing contracts. IEEE Trans. Inf. Theory **36**(1), 40–46 (1990)
4. Boneh, D., Boyen, X.: Short signatures without random oracles. In: Cachin, C., Camenisch, J.L. (eds.) EUROCRYPT 2004. LNCS, vol. 3027, pp. 56–73. Springer, Heidelberg (2004). https://doi.org/10.1007/978-3-540-24676-3_4
5. Brassard, G., Crépeau, C., Robert, J.-M.: All-or-nothing disclosure of secrets. In: Odlyzko, A.M. (ed.) CRYPTO 1986. LNCS, vol. 263, pp. 234–238. Springer, Heidelberg (1987). https://doi.org/10.1007/3-540-47721-7_17
6. Camenisch, J., Dubovitskaya, M., Neven, G.: Oblivious transfer with access control. In: Proceedings of the 2009 ACM Conference on Computer and Communications Security, CCS 2009, Chicago, Illinois, USA, 9–13 November 2009, pp. 131–140 (2009)
7. Camenisch, J., Dubovitskaya, M., Neven, G., Zaverucha, G.M.: Oblivious transfer with hidden access control policies. In: Catalano, D., Fazio, N., Gennaro, R., Nicolosi, A. (eds.) PKC 2011. LNCS, vol. 6571, pp. 192–209. Springer, Heidelberg (2011). https://doi.org/10.1007/978-3-642-19379-8_12
8. Camenisch, J., Neven, G., Shelat, A.: Simulatable adaptive oblivious transfer. In: Naor, M. (ed.) EUROCRYPT 2007. LNCS, vol. 4515, pp. 573–590. Springer, Heidelberg (2007). https://doi.org/10.1007/978-3-540-72540-4_33

9. Canetti, R.: Universally composable security: a new paradigm for cryptographic protocols. In: IEEE Symposium on Foundations of Computer Science, p. 136 (2001)

10. Chu, C.-K., Tzeng, W.-G.: Efficient k-out-of-n oblivious transfer schemes with adaptive and non-adaptive queries. In: Vaudenay, S. (ed.) PKC 2005. LNCS, vol. 3386, pp. 172–183. Springer, Heidelberg (2005). https://doi.org/10.1007/978-3-540-30580-4_12

11. Coull, S., Green, M., Hohenberger, S.: Controlling access to an oblivious database using stateful anonymous credentials. In: Jarecki, S., Tsudik, G. (eds.) PKC 2009. LNCS, vol. 5443, pp. 501–520. Springer, Heidelberg (2009). https://doi.org/10.1007/978-3-642-00468-1_28

12. Even, S., Goldreich, O., Lempel, A.: A randomized protocol for signing contracts. Commun. ACM **28**(6), 637–647 (1985)

13. Han, J., Susilo, W., Mu, Y., Au, M.H., Cao, J.: AAC-OT: accountable oblivious transfer with access control. IEEE Trans. Inf. Forensics Secur. **10**(12), 2502–2514 (2015)

14. Han, J., Susilo, W., Mu, Y., Yan, J.: Efficient oblivious transfers with access control. Comput. Math. Appl. **63**(4), 827–837 (2012)

15. Kurosawa, K., Nojima, R.: Simple adaptive oblivious transfer without random oracle. In: Matsui, M. (ed.) ASIACRYPT 2009. LNCS, vol. 5912, pp. 334–346. Springer, Heidelberg (2009). https://doi.org/10.1007/978-3-642-10366-7_20

16. Liu, W., Mu, Y., Yang, G.: An efficient privacy-preserving e-coupon system. In: Lin, D., Yung, M., Zhou, J. (eds.) Inscrypt 2014. LNCS, vol. 8957, pp. 3–15. Springer, Cham (2015). https://doi.org/10.1007/978-3-319-16745-9_1

17. Liu, W., Mu, Y., Yang, G., Yu, Y.: Efficient e-coupon systems with strong user privacy. Telecommun. Syst. **64**(4), 695–708 (2017)

18. Ma, X., Xu, L., Zhang, F.: Oblivious transfer with timed-release receiver's privacy. J. Syst. Softw. **84**(3), 460–464 (2011)

19. Mu, Y., Zhang, J., Varadharajan, V.: m out of n oblivious transfer. In: Batten, L., Seberry, J. (eds.) ACISP 2002. LNCS, vol. 2384, pp. 395–405. Springer, Heidelberg (2002). https://doi.org/10.1007/3-540-45450-0_30

20. Naor, M., Pinkas, B.: Oblivious transfer with adaptive queries. In: Wiener, M. (ed.) CRYPTO 1999. LNCS, vol. 1666, pp. 573–590. Springer, Heidelberg (1999). https://doi.org/10.1007/3-540-48405-1_36

21. Naor, M., Pinkas, B.: Computationally secure oblivious transfer. J. Cryptol. **18**(1), 1–35 (2005)

22. Rabin, M.O.: How to exchange secrets by oblivious transfer (1981)

23. Teranishi, I., Furukawa, J., Sako, K.: k-times anonymous authentication. IEICE Trans. **92-A**(1), 147–165 (2009)

24. Yao, A.C.: Protocols for secure computations (extended abstract). In: 23rd Annual Symposium on Foundations of Computer Science, Chicago, Illinois, USA, 3–5 November 1982, pp. 160–164 (1982)

25. Yao, A.C.: How to generate and exchange secrets (extended abstract). In: 27th Annual Symposium on Foundations of Computer Science, Toronto, Canada, 27–29 October 1986, pp. 162–167 (1986)

Author Index

Printed in the United States
By Bookmasters